BRYAN'S DICTIONARY

OF

PAINTERS AND ENGRAVERS

IN FIVE VOLUMES

CAMBRIDGE: DEIGHTON, BELL & CO.
NEW YORK: THE MACMILLAN CO.
BOMBAY: A. H. WHEELER & CO.

The Magnificat

From the painting by Botticelli, in the Uffizi Gallery, Florence.

Bryan's Dictionary

of

Painters and Engravers

NEW EDITION REVISED AND ENLARGED

UNDER THE SUPERVISION OF

GEORGE C. WILLIAMSON, Litt.D.

WITH NUMEROUS ILLUSTRATIONS

VOLUME II. D-G

New York
THE MACMILLAN COMPANY
LONDON: GEORGE BELL AND SONS
1903

NOTE TO VOL. II

AMONGST English artists who have died since the issue of the last edition, and whose lives appear in this volume, should be mentioned those of Du Maurier, written by Mr. F. W. Whyte; Kate Greenaway, by Mr. G. Somes Layard; Charles Green, by Mr. Clifford Smith; A. D. Fripp, G. A. Fripp, George D. Davidson, Sir W. Fettes Douglas and Walter Goodall, all by Dr. Laing; Sir John Gilbert, Birket Foster, Louis Fagan, Thomas Faed, W. H. Deverell, E. U. Eddis and others. Of Old Masters whose lives have been re-written in the light of modern research, we would direct special attention to the long biography of Giorgione, the work of Julia Cartwright (Mrs. H. Ady); the important article on Foppa, written by Miss Constance Jocelyn Ffoulkes, and those of Downman, Engleheart, Fragonard, Etienne, De Caylus, R. and N. Delaunay and others.

Many of the existing biographies have been carefully examined and corrected by the leading experts of the day, so as to embody in them the latest information without violating the settled plan of the work. In this way Mr. Campbell Dodgson has corrected the life of Dürer; Professor Langton Douglas those of Benozzo Gozzoli and Fra Angelico; Mr. Weale those of Gheeraert David, Hubert, Jan, Lambert and Margaret Van Eyck; also Daret and Gossart; Mr. L. Binyon those of Claude and Girtin; Miss Streeter that of Filipepi (Botticelli); Mr. C. Holroyd those of Duccio and Finiguerra, almost re-writing the last; and Mr. Lionel Cust that of Sir Anthony Van Dyck.

In addition to this there are in this volume new biographies of the following artists—Richard Dadd, Eduard Daege, Michael Dahl, J. E. Dantan, E. Dardoize, M. Darby, William Daniell, E. T. Daniell, J. M. Donald, W. C. T. Dobson, Thomas Doughty, V. Deroche, Thomas Danby, J. B. E. Detaille, Sophie Desaux, M. G. Desboutin, N. Dixon, George T. Doo, Thomas Dove, L. De Deyster, Richard Doyle, A. Dedreux, Amaury Duval, Jean Duvet, F. De Braekeleer, J. L. Demarne, J. A. Duvaux, J. L. Dyckmans, Jules Dupré, F. J. and N. B. Dequevauviller, Mark Dessurne, G. Den Duyts, Karl Ebert, C. D. Eisen, Charles Escot, Edwin Ellis, Henri Evenepoel, Otto Faber du Faur, John Faed, James Fahey, E. F. Feron, Eugène Fichel, W. H. Fisk, J. P. Flandrin, Lucien Falize, J. A. J. Falquière, Léon Faure, J. E. Freeman, C. T. Frere, P. E. Frere, E. Feyen-Perrin, Giacomo Favretto, C. F. Felou, F. Ferramola, Luis Falero, E. J. Forster, F. L. Français, A. Fraser, Otto Fröhlicher, G. Fouace, G. F. Gaillard, P. T. and C. Galle, and the younger members of that

family, P. V. Galland, A. Gastaldi, E. Gaujean, Karl Gehrts, W. H. L. Grüner, Noel
Garnier, B. Galofré, Wilhelm Gentz, A. Geyer, T. Gide, J. Gigoux, A. Gill, E. Gill,
Margaret Gillies, David Des Granges, E. G. Giran, P. Girardet, R. Gleichauf, James
W. Glass, B. Goddard, N. Goeneutte, William Gosling, Charles Gosselin, — Gouge,
T. R. Gould, J. A. Goupil, H. P. Gray, N. E. Green, J. B. Greuze, J. E. Gridel, W.
H. L. Grimes, H. C. Guérard, O. E. Gunther, L. Gurlitt, J. P. Gulich, and P. L. N.
Grolleron.

There are thus some 130 new biographies, 17 have been corrected, added to,
and amended, and about 500 separate corrections have been made throughout the
volume.

LIST OF ILLUSTRATIONS

A

BIOGRAPHICAL DICTIONARY

OF

PAINTERS AND ENGRAVERS

DA, ABRAHAM, an engraver, was probably a native of Germany, as he appears to have imitated the style of Theodor De Bry. There is a plate by him of 'The Last Supper,' executed with the graver in a neat but stiff style, and inscribed *Abraham Da fecit*; from which it may be presumed that it is from his own design.

DA ANNUNCIAÇÃO, THOMAS JOSÉ, who was born at Ajuda near Lisbon, in 1821, learned his art in the Academy of that city, and afterwards travelled through Spain and France. He was principally an animal painter, and was considered the best artist in that branch of art in the Peninsula; but he occasionally executed genre pictures. He was Director of the Academy of Fine Arts at Lisbon, where he died in 1879. The following are some of his most noteworthy works:

Lisbon. *Galeria Nacional.* View of Amora.
,, ,, Two Women at a Fountain.
,, ,, View of the Penha de França.
,, ,, Oxen treading out Corn at Ribatejo.
,, ,, After Pasture—View on the Tagus.
,, ,, The Shepherd's Rest. 1852.

DABOS, LAURENT, a painter of portraits and of historical and genre subjects, who was born at Toulouse in 1761, was instructed by François André Vincent, and first exhibited at the Exposition de la Jeunesse in 1788. Among his works may be mentioned: 'Mary of England, Queen of France, lamenting the death of her husband, Louis XII.,' 'The Return of the Grande Armée,' and 'Louis XVI. writing his Will,' a picture painted in the Temple during the captivity of the royal family. Besides these he painted from life the portrait of the Dauphin (Louis XVII.). He died in Paris in 1835. His wife, JEANNE BERNARD, who was a pupil of Madame Guyard, also painted genre subjects. She was born at Luneville in 1763, and died in 1842.

DACH, JEAN. See AACHEN, JOHANN VON.

DACHBRETT, PETER. See TAGPRET.

DA CUNHA TABORDA, JOSÉ, a Portuguese painter and architect, was born at Fundão, in the diocese of Guarda, in 1766. After studying painting under Joaquim Manoel da Rocha, he went in 1788 to Rome, where he placed himself under the tuition of Antonio Cavallucci, and gained reputation by a picture of 'The Summoning of Cincinnatus to the Dictatorship.' After his return to Portugal he was in 1799 appointed professor at the Lisbon Academy, and in 1803 court painter, in which capacity he painted in the royal palace of Ajuda and the hall of the Cortes. There is no mention of the date of his death.

DADD, RICHARD, the son of a chemist at Chatham, was born in that town in 1817. On the removal of his father to London to take over the business of a dealer in art objects, Dadd joined the schools of the Royal Academy, and started as a painter of genre pictures. In 1838 he contributed for the first time to the Royal Academy, exhibiting a picture entitled 'Angling.' Then followed 'Study of a Head' (1839), 'Alfred the Great in Disguise of a Peasant' (1840), and in 1841 a successful work, 'Titania Sleeping,' which attracted some attention. At the exhibitions of the Society of British Artists he exhibited, among other pictures, the following in oils and water-colours— 'Head of a Man' (1837), 'Scene in Whitsand Bay' and 'Coast Scene, Hastings' (1838), 'Don Quixote' and 'Boy Reading' (1839), 'Scene from "As you like it"' (1840), and 'When I speak, let no Dog bark' (1841). His most important work was a series of upwards of a hundred pictures with subjects chosen from Byron's 'Manfred' and Tasso's 'Jerusalem Delivered,' which he painted for Lord Foley. In 1842, for Hall's 'Book of British Ballads,' he illustrated the ballad 'Robin Goodfellow.' In the summer of the same year, in company with Sir Thomas Philips, to whom he had been introduced by his friend David Roberts, he left London on a journey to Egypt, travelling through Italy, Greece, and Asia Minor. Dadd, who had already showed signs of weakness of the brain, appears to have suffered from sunstroke in Egypt, and on his way home suddenly left his friend, and returned to London in the spring of 1843. During the journey and the months succeeding his return he produced some excellent work in water-colours, including 'Tombs of the Khalifs, Cairo,' 'Entrance to an Egyptian Tomb,' and 'Eastern Scene, Rocky Landscape,' and contributed to a Liverpool exhibition a scene entitled 'Arabs.' The cartoon, however, which he sent to the Westminster Hall competition proved the unsound condition of his mind. Towards the autumn of the same year his mind became seriously unhinged, and he was constantly watched by his father. On the 28th of October he accompanied his father to Cobham Park, Surrey, and there murdered him, and fled to France. Near Fontainebleau his attack upon a fellow-traveller led to his capture and identification. He was acquitted on the plea of insanity, and sentenced to imprisonment for life in Bethlehem Hospital. During his confinement he was allowed to follow his profession, and produced several highly-finished but eccentric works in water-colours, of which 'Christ rescuing St. Peter from the Waves' (1852), 'Sketch to illustrate the Passions—Patriotism' (1857), and 'Leonidas with the Wood-cutters' (1873), are in the Victoria and Albert Museum, South Kensington. He died in 1887.

DADDI, BERNARDO, a Florentine painter, was the contemporary and colleague of Jacopo Landini di Casentino in the formation of the Academy of St. Luke at Florence in 1349. He was born towards the close of the 13th century, and was one of the most able of the pupils of Giotto. He painted in fresco the histories of St. Lawrence and St. Stephen in the Berardi chapel in Santa Croce, and also the gates of the old city of Florence; but the only frescoes which remain are those representing the Martyrdoms of St. Stephen and St. Lawrence. In 1346-7 he painted his best work, the miracle-working picture of the Virgin, which is still in Or San Michele at Florence. His death took place in 1350.

Besides the above-mentioned, the following works by Daddi are extant:

England.		The Crucifixion (*formerly in the church of St. George at Ruballa*). 1348.
Florence.	*Accademia.*	Virgin enthroned, with two Saints (*central portion of a small triptych, erroneously ascribed in the catalogue to Bernardo Orcagna*). 1332?
„	*Ognissanti.*	Virgin and Child, with St. Matthew and St. Nicholas. 1328.
Pisa.	*Campo Santo.*	Frescoes of the Triumph of Death, the Last Judgment, and the Inferno.
Siena.	*Istituto di Belle Arti.*	Virgin and Child, with Saints (*a small triptych*). 1336.
„	„	Virgin and Child, with a corona of Saints in adoration (*central portion of a triptych*).

DADDI, COSIMO, was a native of Florence, who flourished about the year 1614. He was a scholar of Battista Naldini, and painted historical subjects with much skill; but he is better known as having been the master of Volterrano. Several of his works are noticed by Baldinucci, particularly a picture of the 'Visitation of the Virgin to St. Elizabeth,' and some subjects from the Life of the Virgin, at the monastery of San Lino, at Florence. In the church of Or San Michele is an altar-piece, representing the Archangel discomfiting the rebel Angels. Daddi died of the plague in 1630. Zani says that his name was Dati, and that he painted in 1588.

DADURE, MARIE MICHEL ALPHONSE, a French portrait and historical painter, who was a pupil of Ingres, was born in Paris in 1804, and died there in 1868. His best work is the 'Pilgrimage of St. Helena, Queen of Sweden.'

DAEGE, EDUARD. This artist was born in Berlin

in 1805, and was a pupil of Niedlich and Wach. He became a member of the Academy of Berlin and eventually Professor of the same school, where as a lad he had taken many prizes. He went to Italy in 1832, and this journey and the long time which he spent in the country had a marked effect upon his painting. At the National Gallery of Berlin there are two of his best works, 'The Old Sacristan,' and 'The Invention of Painting.' He died in 1883.

DAEHLING, HEINRICH ANTON, a historical and genre painter, was born at Hanover in 1773. In 1794 he went to Berlin, where he was engaged in miniature painting and as a teacher of drawing. In 1802 he visited Paris, and the study of the galleries there first induced him to attempt painting in oil. From 1811 until his death he was a member of the Berlin Academy, and professor at the same from 1814 onwards. He died at Potsdam in 1850. One of his most famous pictures is 'The Descent from the Cross,' the altar-piece at the Garrison Church in Potsdam. In the Berlin Gallery is a 'State Entry,' painted by him.

DAEL, JAN FRANS VAN, an excellent painter of fruit and flowers, was born at Antwerp in 1764, but went early to Paris and settled there. He was self-instructed in art, but made such progress that he soon distinguished himself at the exhibitions, on one occasion obtaining the prize of 4000 francs, and on two others, the large gold medal. His style is in the manner of Van Huysum and Van Spaendonck, although he did not confine himself strictly to fruit and flowers, but painted other subjects, in which such objects might with propriety be introduced. Two of his pictures, which he painted for the Empress Joséphine, represent 'An Offering to Flora,' and 'The Tomb of Julia'; the latter is now in the Louvre. His master-piece, known as 'La Croisée,' the fruit of three years' labour, was likewise purchased by the Empress Joséphine, and is now in a private collection at Liége. He was also patronized by the Empress Marie Louise, who took one of his pictures with her to Parma. He died in Paris in 1840, and was buried in the cemetery of Père Lachaise by the side of his friend Van Spaendonck. The Louvre has also by him three pictures of 'Flowers' and one of 'Fruit.'

DAELE, JAN VAN, a Flemish landscape painter, who was born at Antwerp in 1530, and died in 1601, excelled in representing mountainous and rocky scenery. Balkema erroneously names him Cornelis.

DAELENS, DIRK VAN. See DEELEN.

DAERINGER, JOHANN GEORG, an Austrian historical painter, was born at Ried in 1759. He painted many altar pictures, and held the post of corrector of the Academy at Vienna, where he died in 1809.

DAFFINGER, MORIZ MICHAEL, a distinguished miniature painter, who has been called the Austrian Isabey, was born at Vienna in 1790. While studying at the Academy under Füger he showed considerable talent for portrait painting, which he improved at a later period by a study of the manner of Lawrence, who visited Vienna during the Congress of 1814. Daffinger painted portraits of the Duke of Reichstadt and many of the nobility of the court of Vienna, and etched four plates, one of which was his own portrait. He died at Vienna in 1849.

DA' FRUTTI, IL GOBBO. See BONZI.

DAGIÙ, FRANCESCO, called IL CAPELLA, who

MADONNA AND CHILD WITH ST. ANNE

was born at Venice in 1714, was a scholar of Giovanni Battista Piazzetta. He painted history, and was chiefly employed for the churches at Bergamo, and by the state. One of his best pictures is 'St. George and the Dragon,' in the church of San Bonate. He died in 1784.

DAGLEY, RICHARD, an English subject painter, was born in the latter half of the 18th century. He was brought up at Christ's Hospital, and at first made designs for jewellery. From 1784 to 1806 he exhibited domestic subjects at the Royal Academy. He then turned his attention to teaching drawing, but again appeared at the Academy from 1815 to 1833. As a medallist he obtained some success, and he published works on Gems in 1804 and 1822. His life was a continued struggle against poverty. He died in London in 1841.

DAGLI OCCHIALI, GABRIELE. See FERRANTINI.

DAGLI OCCHIALI, GASPARO. See WITTEL.

DAGNAN, ISIDORE, a French landscape painter, was born at Marseilles in 1794, and died in Paris in 1873. Among his pictures, which consist chiefly of views in Southern France, Italy, and Switzerland, are the following:

Fontainebleau.	*Palace.*	View of Lausanne. 1822.
"	"	View in Dauphiné. 1827.
Versailles.	*Trianon.*	Lake of Geneva. 1822.
"	"	View of Paris from the Quai de la Cité, 1831 (*one of his best works*).
"	"	Banks of the Vigne near Vaucluse.
"	"	Valley of the Lauterbrunnen. 1841.
"	"	Petrarch's House.
"	"	Old Beeches in the Forest of Fontainebleau.

D'AGOTY, GAUTHIER. See GAUTHIER D'AGOTY.

DAGUERRE, LOUIS JACQUES MANDÉ, a French scene-painter, was born at Cormeilles-en-Parisis in Normandy in 1787. He studied under Degoti, and very soon surpassed all other masters in the art of theatrical decoration. In 1822, in conjunction with Bouton, he founded at Paris the Diorama, which enjoyed great popularity until its destruction by fire in 1839. But the great event of Daguerre's life was his discovery of the art of photography, or, as it was named after him, the Daguerreotype. His first experiments were made in 1826, and in 1829 he associated himself with Niepce, who had since the year 1814 been endeavouring to solve the problem of fixing the image formed in the camera obscura. The discovery was ceded to the public in 1839, when Daguerre received a pension of 6000 francs. He died suddenly at Petit-Bry-sur-Marne, near Paris, in 1851.

DAHL, JOHAN CHRISTIAN CLAUSEN, a Norwegian landscape painter, was born at Bergen in 1788. His parents wished him to enter the Church, but he speedily followed his own inclination for art. In 1811 he attended the Academy of Copenhagen, and in 1818 went to Dresden. Later on, he travelled in the Tyrol and Germany, and repeatedly visited his native country, whose coasts and fiords, lakes and towns, he painted with loving exactitude, but with a singular dryness. He likewise etched four plates. Dahl died at Dresden in 1857. His 'Storm at Sea,' in the Berlin Gallery, and his 'Winter Landscape,' in the Munich Pinakothek, are paintings worthy of mention.

DAHL, MICHAEL, a Swedish portrait painter, was born at Stockholm in 1656, and received some instruction from Ehrenstral, an esteemed Swedish artist. At the age of twenty-two he came to England, but did not at that time remain longer than a year; he continued his travels in search of improvement through France to Italy, where he studied for some years, and whilst at Rome painted the portrait of the celebrated Queen Christina of Sweden. In 1688 he returned to England, where he found Sir Godfrey Kneller rising to the head of his profession; but Dahl possessed sufficient merit to distinguish himself as no mean competitor. Queen Anne and Prince George of Denmark both sat to him. He died in London in 1743. Amongst his more notable portraits should be mentioned:

Equestrian portrait of Charles XI. of Sweden (*Windsor*). Full-length portrait of Queen Anne and her son (*National Portrait Gallery*). Portraits of Lady Anne Harvey, Barbara Lady Longueville, Rachel Duchess of Devonshire, the Duchess of Ormond, Anne Countess of Carlisle, Margaret Countess of Pembroke, Juliana Lady Howe, and Jane Countess of Portland (*all at Petworth Park*). Mr. Arthur Vansittart and Anne Lady Coleraine (*North Cray Park, Kent*).

DAHLEN, REINER, who was born at Cologne in 1836, was originally brought up as a saddler, but chose to devote himself to art, and studied at the Academy of Düsseldorf. He visited England, North America, and Paris. His works mostly represent horses, carriages, hunting parties, and so forth. Although there is a study of nature exhibited in his paintings, his peculiarly original style did not meet with much approbation. He died at Düsseldorf in 1874.

DAHLSTEIN, AUGUSTIN, a German painter who flourished in the middle of the 18th century, was a native of Cassel. He visited Sweden and Russia, and etched a series of 50 plates of the 'Cries of St. Petersburg and Moscow.'

DAIGREMONT, M., was a French engraver, who flourished from about 1670 to about 1700. He engraved some of the plates for Berain's 'Ornemens,' and several views of Versailles.

DAI LIBRI, FRANCESCO, the elder, born at Verona in 1452, was the son of Stefano dai Libri, an illuminator of books. He was the father of Girolamo dai Libri, and is known as an illuminator of choir books for the churches of his native city.

DAI LIBRI, FRANCESCO, the younger, the grandson of the above and son of Girolamo dai Libri, was born in 1500, and lived chiefly at Venice and at Padua. He was at first a painter of miniatures, but afterwards a painter in oil and an architect.

DAI LIBRI, GIROLAMO, the son of Francesco dai Libri, was born at Verona in 1474. He was brought up by his father to his own profession of a miniature painter and illuminator of books, but he soon abandoned its pursuit. His earlier style inclines to that of Andrea Mantegna. His first picture, painted when he was only sixteen, is in the church of Malcesine, on the Lake of Garda, and represents the 'Deposition from the Cross, with the Virgin and Saints.' In the Museum of Verona is a painting representing 'The Virgin, St. Joseph, St. John the Baptist, and St. Jerome, adoring the Infant Christ'; and at Sant' Anastasia in the same city, is a 'Madonna and Child with Saints,' which is one of his earliest productions. In 1515 he and Francesco Morone painted the organ shutters of Santa Maria in Organo, which are now at Malcesine. In 1526 he finished his masterpiece, the 'Virgin and Child enthroned, between Lorenzo Giustiniani and St. Zeno,' at San Giorgio Maggiore in Verona; and of about the same period is the 'Virgin and Child, with SS. Anne and Joachim and two donors,' in the church of San Paolo in the same city. In 1530 were executed the 'Virgin and Saints,' for the church of the Vittoria Nuova, and the 'Virgin in Glory, with SS. Andrew and Peter,' for Sant Andrea; both pictures are now in the Gallery of Verona. Girolamo died at Verona in 1556. Guilio Clovio and his son, Francesco dai Libri, were his pupils. He never painted in fresco, and his works are rare out of his native city. Pictures by him are in the followng collections:

Berlin.	Gallery.	Virgin and Child, between SS. Bartholomew and Zeno.
London.	Nat. Gallery.	Madonna and Child, with Saint Anne.
Paris.	Louvre.	Virgin and Child.

DAIWAILLE, JEAN AUGUSTIN, a Dutch portrait painter, was born at Cologne in 1786, and went when young to Amsterdam where he studied under A. De Lelie, and was director of the Academy from 1820 to 1826. After that time he resided at Rotterdam, where he was very successful in painting portraits, and where he died in 1850. There is by him one etching, which is scarce.

DAL COLLE, RAFFAELLO, or RAFFAELLINO, called also RAFFAELLINO DAL BORGO SAN SEPOLCRO, was born at Borgo San Sepolcro, about the year 1490. He was first a disciple of Raphael, but after the death of that master he became the scholar of Giulio Romano, whom he assisted in his principal works at Rome, and in the Palazzo del Te, at Mantua. Of his own compositions, the principal are two pictures at Borgo San Sepolcro, one of which, representing the 'Resurrection,' in the choir of the cathedral, exhibits a grandeur not unworthy of the great school in which he had been educated. The figure of Christ is dignified and majestic, and the terror of the guards of the sepulchre is admirably expressed. The other is in the church of the Conventuali, and represents the 'Assumption of the Virgin.' It is a graceful and impressive composition; and being placed near one of the best pictures of Giorgio Vasari, establishes its merit by its decided superiority. Raffaellino dal Colle was one of the artists employed by Raphael in the decorations of the Loggie of the Vatican, and painted one of the small cupolas in the roof with a portion of the history of Moses. In Città di Castello is an 'Annunciation' by him, which is a very graceful composition. An 'Entombment,' in the Servi, is another beautiful picture. A picture of 'The Virgin attended by St. Sebastian and St. Roch,' was in the church of San Francesco at Cagli, the figures and landscape of which much resembled the manner of Raphael. In one of the chapels of the Olivet monks at Gubbio there are pictures by him, in one of which he has introduced a figure of Virtue, who seems to be a sister to Raphael's Sibyls. He assisted Bronzino and Vasari in their decorations and cartoons—the latter upon the occasion of the visit of Charles V. to Florence. He had many scholars who proved able artists, but few equalled him in grace and high finish; Cristofano Gherardi and Giovanni de' Vecchi are noticeable amongst them.

DALEN, CORNELIS VAN, a Flemish engraver, was born at Antwerp about the year 1620. He was called 'the younger,' to distinguish him from his father, who was likewise an engraver, and whose works it is not easy to distinguish from those of his son. He was instructed in engraving by his father, and also by Cornelis Visscher, whose style he followed for some time. His prints occasionally resemble those of A. Blooteling, and at other times those of Pontius and Bolswert. He worked entirely with the graver, which he handled in a bold and free manner, and with considerable taste. He usually marked his plates with the initials *C. D.* We have by him several portraits, and a few historical subjects.

PORTRAITS.

Catharine de' Medici; in the back-ground the City of Amsterdam.
Charles II., King of England; *after P. Nason.*
James, Duke of York; *after S. Luttichuys.*
Henry, Duke of Gloucester; *after the same.*
William III.
Mary II., his Queen.
Algernon Percy, Earl of Northumberland.
John Maurice, Prince of Nassau; *after G. Flink.*
Pietro Aretino, with a book; *after Titian.*
Giovanni Boccaccio; *after the same.*
Giorgio Barbarelli, called Giorgione; *after the same.*
Sebastiano del Piombo; *after Tintoretto.* (The four last are thought by Kramm to be the work of Cornelis van Dalen, the elder.)
Anna Maria Schurman, painter; *after C. Janssens.*
Old Parr, aged 152 years.

SUBJECTS AFTER VARIOUS MASTERS.

The Adoration of the Shepherds.
The Virgin, with the Infant Jesus.
The Four Fathers of the Church; *after Rubens;* in the style of Pontius.
Nature adorned by the Graces; *after the same;* in the manner of Bolswert.
A Shepherd and Shepherdess; *after Casteleyn.*
The Virgin suckling the Infant Saviour; *after G. Flink.*
Venus and Cupid; *after the same.*
The Four Elements, represented by Children; *after A. Diepenbeck.*
The Concert; *after Giorgione;* for the 'Cabinet de Reynst.'
The Monument of Admiral Cornelis Tromp.

DALENS, DIRK, a Dutch landscape painter, was born at Amsterdam in 1659. He was the son of Willem Dalens, an artist of little celebrity, who taught him the first lessons in the art. The principal works of Dalens are large landscapes, painted with a free and firm touch, and very agreeably coloured, which decorate the saloons of some of the principal houses in Amsterdam. He also painted some cabinet pictures of landscapes, with figures, which are deemed worthy of being placed in the best collections in Holland. He died in 1688.

DALENS, DIRK, called 'the younger,' the posthumous son of the preceding, was born at Amsterdam in 1688. He was instructed by Theodoor van Pee, and became a painter of landscapes with cattle and figures, enriched with ruins, in the manner of Pynacker, which are executed with great ability. He died in 1753.

DA' LIBRI. See DAI LIBRI.

DALIPHARD, EDOUARD, a French landscape painter, was born at Rouen in 1833. He studied under Gustave Morin, the Director of the Rouen Museum, and spent a considerable time in the East, where he made a good collection of water-colour sketches. His works appeared at the Salon from 1864 to 1876, and he also contributed to the French journal, 'L'Art.' He died at Rouen after a long and painful illness in 1877. Amongst his best productions are:

The Sun appearing after a Storm. 1866.
Souvenir of the Forest of Eu. 1873.
The flooded Farm, Poissy. 1873.
Melancholy. 1875.

DALL, NICHOLAS THOMAS, was a native of Denmark, who settled in London as a landscape painter, about the year 1760. He painted some excellent scenes for Covent Garden Theatre, and his engagements in that branch of art prevented him from painting many pictures. In 1768 he obtained the first premium given by the Society for the Encouragement of Arts for the best landscape. He was chosen an Associate of the Royal Academy in 1771, and died in London in 1777.

DALL' ACQUA, CRISTOFORO, who was born at Vicenza in 1734, engraved, principally for the booksellers, plates of various subjects, portraits, history, genre, landscapes, and architecture. Among his works may be noticed a portrait of Frederick the Great, King of Prussia, and an allegory of 'Merit crowned by Apollo,' after Andrea Sacchi, as well as numerous plates after the works of Cipriani, Houel, Joseph Vernet, and others. He died at Vicenza in 1787.

DALLAMANO, GIUSEPPE, born at Modena in 1679, is a remarkable instance of the progress that untutored genius has sometimes made in the art without the help of a master. Dallamano is stated by Lanzi to have been hardly removed from an idiot; ignorant even of the alphabet, and unaided by professional instruction, he nevertheless reached an excellence in painting architectural views which surprised the most intelligent judges. His best works are in the royal palace at Turin. He died in 1758.

DALL' AQUILA, POMPEO, is stated in the 'Abecedario Pittorico' of Orlandi, to have been a good historical painter, both in oil and in fresco. He flourished in the latter part of the 16th century. There is a fine picture by him in the church of Santo Spirito in Sassia at Rome, representing the 'Descent from the Cross,' which was engraved by Orazio de Santis in 1572. Several considerable works by him in fresco are to be seen at Aquila, where he was born.

DALL' ARGENTO, ANTONIO. See ALEOTTI.

DALL' ARZERE, STEFANO, who, according to Ridolfi and others, was a native of Padua, painted numerous altar-pieces for the churches and convents of that city. In the Chiesa degli Eremitani, he painted some subjects from the Old Testament, and two pictures of 'St. Peter' and 'St. Paul,' and in the church of the Servite monastery the principal altar-piece is by him. He flourished in the 16th century.

DALLE FACCIATE, BERNARDINO. See BARBATELLI.

DALLE GROTTESCHE, BERNARDINO. See BARBATELLI.

DALLE MADONNE, LIPPO. See SCANNABECCHI.

DALLEMAGNE, VIRGINIE POLYXÈNE AUGUSTINE PHILIPPE, a French miniature painter, whose maiden name was Decagny, was a native of Beauvais. She was a pupil of Madame de Mirbel, and showed much talent in the execution of portraits in miniature and in crayons. She married Adolphe Dallemagne, a landscape painter, and died at Corbeil in 1875.

DALLE MUSE, BERNARDINO. See BARBATELLI.

DALLE NINFE, CESARE, who flourished from about 1590 to 1600, was a Venetian, whom we find mentioned by Zanetti among the imitators of Tintoretto. He possessed the readiness of invention, and the facility of hand, for which that painter was remarkable, and was an excellent colourist, though deficient in drawing.

DALLE NOTTI, GERARDO. See HONTHORST.

DALLE PROSPETTIVE, AGOSTINO. See AGOSTINO.

DALLE PROSPETTIVE, MIRANDOLESE. See PALTRONIERI.

DALLE TESTE, IL BORGOGNONE. See GIACCHINETTI GONZALEZ.

DALLEVIA, A., was an Italian engraver, who resided at Venice about the year 1686. Among other prints, he engraved a set of plates representing triumphal processions, entitled, 'Giuochi Festivi e Militari,' and published at Venice in 1686. They are executed in a coarse, indifferent style.

DALLIKER, JOHANN RUDOLPH, a Swiss portrait painter, was born at Zurich in 1694. He visited successively Magdeburg, Brunswick, Cassel, Leipsic, Berne, and Paris, where he made the acquaintance of Largillière and Rigaud. He resided at St. Gall, but died at Schaffhausen in 1769. Most of the celebrated persons of his country sat to him.

DALLINGER, FRANZ THEODOR, an Austrian painter of landscapes, fruit, and animals, was born at Linz in 1710, and died at Prague in 1771.

DALLINGER VON DALLING, ALEXANDER JOHANN, a son of Johann Dallinger von Dalling, the elder, was born at Vienna in 1783. He studied under his father, and became a landscape and animal painter, as well as an engraver and a restorer of old pictures. In the Belvedere, at Vienna, there is a picture by him representing 'A Herdsman driving Cows across a Brook.' He died at Vienna in 1844.

DALLINGER VON DALLING, JOHANN, an Austrian painter, was born at Vienna in 1741, and distinguished himself as director of the Liechtenstein Gallery. He painted animals, historical subjects, and large altar-pieces, most of which are in Russia and Poland. He died in 1806.

DALLINGER VON DALLING, JOHANN, a son of the preceding, was born in Vienna in 1782, and painted landscapes and animals in the old Dutch style, as well as portraits and conversation-pieces. Some of his works are in the Belvedere and Liechtenstein Galleries. He died at Vienna in 1868.

DALLWIG, HEINRICH, a landscape painter, was born at Cassel in 1811, and died at Munich in 1857. He had been settled in the latter city since 1839, but undertook frequent tours in search of scenery for his brush.

DALMASIO, LIPPO DI. See SCANNABECCHI.

DALMATIA, IL FEDERIGHETTO DI. See BENCOVICH.

DALMAU, LODOVICO. A 'Virgin and Child' by this artist is in the church of San Miguel at Barcelona; it is painted in the style of Van Eyck, and dated 1445.

DAL PERON, SIMONE. See CUSIGHE.

DAL POZZO, ISABELLA. In the 'Nuova Guida di Torino,' this lady is mentioned as having painted a picture in the church of San Francesco at Turin, representing the 'Virgin and Child, with St. Blaise and other Saints,' which is signed, and dated 1666. According to Lanzi, few of her contemporaries in that city could have produced a more creditable performance.

DAL SOLE, GIOVANNI ANTONIO MARIA, was born at Bologna in 1606, and was brought up in the school of Francesco Albani. He excelled in painting landscapes, which he decorated with groups of figures, gracefully designed in the style of Albani. He always worked with his left hand, and thus

5

acquired the appellation of 'Il Monchino dai Paesi.' He died in 1684.

DAL SOLE, GIOVANNI GIUSEPPE, the son of Antonio dal Sole, was born at Bologna in 1654, and was instructed in the first principles of design by his father, but he afterwards became a disciple of Domenico Maria Canuti, and ultimately studied under Lorenzo Pasinelli. Following the example of his last instructor, he based his system of colouring upon the study of the works of the best masters of the Venetian School. He imitated the agreeable style of Pasinelli with great success, and his compositions are embellished with landscape and architecture, which he introduced with admirable taste. In many particulars, as in the hair and plumes of the angels, and in the accessories, such as veils, bracelets, crowns, and armour, he displays exquisite grace. He seems to have been inclined to treat lofty themes, and was more observant of costume, more methodical in composition, and better informed in architecture and landscape, than his master, Pasinelli. In these, indeed, he is almost unique. The most beautiful specimens, perhaps, are to be seen at the Casa Zappi in Imola, representing Evening, Night, and Morning, all harmonized with the sober tints belonging to the subjects. There are several of the works of this eminent artist in the public edifices at Bologna. Among the most esteemed are 'The Incredulity of St. Thomas,' in the church of La Madonna di Galiera; 'The Annunciation,' in San Gabrielle; and some frescoes in San Biagio, which are accounted his finest works. For the Giusti family at Verona he executed several Scriptural and mythological subjects, truly beautiful. One, of 'Bacchus and Ariadne,' which occupied but a week of his time, was pronounced by artists excellent; yet he cancelled almost the whole, to remodel it according to his own idea, declaring that it was enough to have shown his rapidity of hand to satisfy others, but that it became his duty, by additional accuracy, to satisfy himself also. For executing his altar-pieces, which are few and valuable, as well as his pictures for private collections, which are very numerous, he demanded high remuneration, persevering in his determination to paint only with care. In his works two manners are observable; the second partakes of that of Guido. A large portion of his pictures nearly approach the style of that master; so that the surname of 'The Modern Guido,' conferred on him by so many, has not been granted as a favour, but as his desert. Bartsch describes three etchings by him; an allegorical representation of Envy, a Group of Angels, after a design for a ceiling by Pasinelli, and another of Olympus, after the same. Gori mentions one of St. Francis Xavier confuting, or rather confounding, by his holy doctrine, the satraps of Japan, also after Pasinelli. Several portraits were etched by him in 1674, which were intended for the 'Felsina Pittrice,' but are not found in that work. He died at Bologna in 1719.

DALTON, RICHARD, an engraver and draughtsman, was born in Cumberland about 1720. After passing some time in Italy and Greece, he became librarian to the Prince of Wales, then keeper of the royal drawings and medals, and finally, in 1778, surveyor of the royal pictures. He made some engravings from the Holbein drawings, and after antique statues. He also published 'Manners and Customs of the Present Inhabitants of Egypt,' 1781. His name is to be found in connection with

some of the art societies which preceded the Royal Academy. He died at St. James's Palace in 1791.

DAM, ANTHONY VAN, born at Middelburg, painted marine subjects of large dimensions. He flourished in the latter half of the last century.

DAM, WOUTER, born at Dort in 1726, was a scholar of Aart Schouman, whose manner he followed for some time, but ultimately became an imitator and copyist of Cuyp and Bakhuisen. He died at Dort in 1785 or 1786.

DAMAME DEMARTRAIS, MICHEL FRANÇOIS, a French painter and engraver, was born in Paris in 1763. After having studied in the school of David, he went to Russia, where he resided for some years. On his return to France he engraved and published 'Vues des principales villes de Russie, costumes et usages des habitants de cet empire,' 1813-14; 'Collection de Costumes du royaume de Naples,' 1818; 'Paris et ses alentours,' 1819. His most important picture was 'The Great Sanhedrim of the Jews of France and Italy,' exhibited at the Salon of 1810. He died in Paris in 1827.

DAMBRUN, JEAN. a French line-engraver, was born in Paris in 1741. He was one of the small band of artists to whom are due the vignettes which adorn many of the books issued towards the close of the last century which have of late become of such fabulous value. His best works are 'La Partie de Wisch,' after Moreau, for the 'Monument de Costume,' and 'Le Calendrier des Vieillards,' after Fragonard, for the 'Contes' of La Fontaine. He also engraved with much delicacy Quéverdo's illustrations to the remarkable series of Almanacs which appeared in Paris just before the outbreak of the French Revolution. There is no record of Dambrun after 1808.

DAME, GILES LA. See LA DAME.

DAMERY, JACOB, the brother of Walter Damery, was a good painter of flowers, of fruit, and especially of vases. He was born at Liége in 1619, but went to Rome when young, and remained there until his death, which occurred in 1685. He executed some etchings, among them a series of twelve vases, dated 1657.

DAMERY, SIMON, a Flemish historical painter, was born at Liége in 1604. He was a pupil of Jean Taulier, who married his sister, but while yet very young he ran away from his master and went to Italy. He afterwards settled at Milan, where he died of the plague in 1640.

DAMERY, WALTER, the brother of Jacob Damery, was born at Liége in 1614. He learned the rudiments of art in his native city, but in 1636 he came to England, and remained here several years, during which he painted a large number of portraits. He afterwards went to France and then to Italy, where he became a scholar of Pietro da Cortona. Subsequently he returned to Paris, where he painted for the Carmelite church his masterpiece, 'The Ascension of Elijah.' His productions are distinguished for their beautiful backgrounds and also for the nude figures of the children, in the depicting of which he exhibited great skill. He died at Liége in 1678.

DAMIANI, FELICE, was a native of Gubbio, who flourished from the year 1584 until 1606. He is by some supposed to have been educated in the Venetian school, and his picture of the 'Circumcision,' in San Domenico, partakes of that style: but in general his works evince more of the Roman taste, which he probably acquired under Benedetto

6

Nucci. One of his best works is 'The Decollation of St. Paul,' at the Castel Nuovo in Recanati; the expression in the head of the martyr is admirable, the drawing correct, and the colouring brilliant and harmonious. It is dated 1584. About twelve years afterwards he decorated two chapels in the church of La Madonna de' Lumi, at San Severino, with pictures representing the Life of the Virgin and the Infancy of Christ. But his most admired production is the 'Baptism of St. Augustine,' painted in 1594 for the church dedicated to that saint at Gubbio; a grand composition of many figures, finely grouped, with an admirable expression of piety in the heads, and enriched with noble architecture. He was still living in 1616.

DAMINI, GIORGIO, a brother of Pietro Damini, was an excellent painter of portraits, and of historical subjects of a small size. Like his brother, he was carried off by the plague at Venice in 1631.

DAMINI, PIETRO, was born at Castelfranco in 1592, and, according to Ridolfi, was a scholar of Giovanni Battista Novelli, who had been educated in the school of Palma. Such was the extraordinary expectation occasioned by the early display of his talents, that some writers have not hesitated to affirm that he would have equalled Titian if he had not died young, an assertion, which, as Lanzi observes, may be regarded as a hyperbole. There are many of his works at Castelfranco, Vicenza, Crema, and particularly at Padua, where, in the church of San Clemente, is his picture of 'Christ giving the Keys to St. Peter,' and in the church of Il Santo, his most celebrated work, 'The Crucifixion, with the Virgin Mary and St. John,' a picture of extraordinary beauty, and of the most harmonious colour. In the cloister of the Padri Serviti, at Vicenza, he painted several pictures of the Life of St. Philip, the founder of their order. The style of Damini is vague and elegant, but he is by no means uniform. He appears to have frequently changed his manner, in search of greater perfection; and his last works are evidently his best. He had acquired a distinguished reputation when he fell a victim to the plague in Venice in 1631.

DAMINI, VINCENZO, was an excellent portrait painter who resided in London from 1720 to 1730. He is said to have been a native of Venice and a pupil of Pellegrini.

DAMIS, AMÉDÉE GUSTAVE FRANÇOIS, a Belgian painter of flowers and fruit, was born at Bruges in 1811. While still young he went to Paris and became a pupil of Redouté. He was likewise a sculptor, and he decorated many of the ecclesiastical edifices of Paris. In 1848 he returned to Bruges, and died there in 1851.

DAMISSEN, LUCAS. See DE HOEY.

DAMOPHILOS, a Greek painter and modeller in terra-cotta, worked in conjunction with Gorgasos in the Temple of Ceres at Rome in B.C. 493. Zeuxis is said to have been his pupil.

DANBY, FRANCIS, who was born near Wexford, Ireland, in 1793, learned the first principles of his art under a landscape painter named O'Connor, in Dublin, where his first picture, a landscape view called 'Evening,' was exhibited in 1812. In the following year, master and pupil, accompanied by George Petrie, set off together to seek their fortunes in London, but their funds becoming exhausted before they reached the metropolis, they stopped at Bristol. Here Danby managed to sell some drawings, and with the proceeds paid O'Connor's

expenses to Dublin, but he himself remained in Bristol, and for a few years supported himself by giving lessons in water-colour painting, now and then sending a picture to the Royal Academy. In 1825 his 'Delivery of Israel out of Egypt' gained him the Associateship of the Academy, and he then went to live in London. In 1830, a quarrel with that body drove him from England, and for the next eleven years he lived in Switzerland, giving up his time to boat-building, yachting, and the painting of unimportant pictures on commission. Two works only appeared at the annual London Exhibitions during this long interval, the 'Golden Age' and 'Rich and Rare were the Gems she wore.' In 1841 he returned to England, took up his residence at Lewisham, and began painting large subjects for exhibition at the British Institution and the Royal Academy with all his old enthusiasm. He died in 1861 at Exmouth, where he had resided since 1847. The following are some of his best works:

The Upas, or Poison-tree of Java (at South Kensington). Disappointed Love. Sunset at Sea after a Storm. The Delivery of Israel out of Egypt (Stafford House). The Opening of the Sixth Seal. The Golden Age. Rich and Rare were the Gems she wore. The Fisherman's Home, Sunrise, 1846 (National Gallery). The Evening Gun.

DANBY, JAMES FRANCIS, an English landscape painter, the son of Francis Danby, A.R.A., was born at Bristol in 1816. His works appeared at the Royal Academy, and at the Society of British Artists, of which latter he was a member. He died of apoplexy in London in 1875. He excelled in depicting sunrise and sunset. Amongst his best works are:

Loch Lomond. Dover, from the Canterbury Road, 1849. Dumbarton Rock, 1854. Morning on the Thames, 1860. Wreck on Exmouth Bar, 1861. Carrickfergus Castle, 1867. North Shields: Sunrise, 1869.

DANBY, THOMAS, marine painter, was the son of Francis Danby, A.R.A., and was born in Ireland, but spent his early youth chiefly at Bristol, where his father practised and taught drawing. He first exhibited in London in 1841, when he sent a small oil picture, 'The Wreck,' to the British Institution, and in 1843 he appeared at the Royal Academy with an illustration of one of Wordsworth's poems. He was elected an Associate of the Society of Painters in Water-Colours in 1867, and became a full member in 1870. He died March 25, 1886.

DANCE, NATHANIEL. See HOLLAND.

DANCKERTS, DANCKERT, the son of Cornelis Danckerts de Ry, was born at Antwerp about the year 1600. He succeeded his father in his business as a printseller, and surpassed him in his talent as an engraver. His plates are sometimes only etched, but more frequently finished with the graver. We have by him a considerable number of plates after Berchem, Wouwerman, and other painters. He also engraved some portraits and other subjects from various masters, among which are:

Charles II.; Departure of Charles II. for England; Venus and Cupid, with a Satyr; after Titian. Hawking, called Het Vinkebaantje. A Stag Hunt, called De Hartenjagt. Four Landscapes and Figures; all after Berchem. Four plates, of Landscapes and Figures. Six plates, the title having a Shepherd riding on an Ox and playing on the Flute, and a

7

Shepherdess dancing. Four Landscapes; on the title print is inscribed, *Danckert Danckerts fec. et exc.* Etchings; *after Wouwerman.*

DANCKERTS, HENDRIK, a son of Justus Danckerts, was born at the Hague about the year 1630. He was brought up as an engraver, and made copies of the works of Titian and Palma, but afterwards was recommended to study painting, and went to Italy for improvement. On his return to Holland he acquired some reputation as a landscape painter, and was invited to England by Charles II., who employed him in painting views of the royal palaces, and of the sea-ports of England and Wales. In the collection of James II. there were twenty-eight landscapes and views by this master. He died at Amsterdam about 1678. He engraved a few plates, as follow:

Charles II.; *after A. Hanneman.* View of Amsterdam and the Y, with Shipping; in three sheets. Views of Palaces and Sea-ports in England.

DANCKERTS, JOHANNES, a son of Justus Danckerts, resided at Amsterdam about the year 1660. He painted historical subjects with some skill, and etched a few plates, among which is one after Titian, representing 'Venus reclining on a Couch.'

DANCKERTS, JUSTUS, was a Dutch engraver who worked at Amsterdam. We have the following plates by him:

William III., Prince of Orange, afterwards King of England.
Casimir, King of Poland.
Seven plates of the Gates of Amsterdam.

DANCKERTS DE RY, CORNELIS, a Dutch architect and engraver, was born at Amsterdam in 1561. He established himself at Antwerp as a printseller, where he engraved several plates of portraits and other subjects, which are not without considerable merit. He was still living in 1634. Among others, we have the following by him:

Gustavus Adolphus, King of Sweden.
Jacob Wassenaer, Lord of Obsdam.
Cornelis de Wit, with a battle in the background.
Jean Calvin; oval.
John Casimir, Count of Nassau.
Four Figures on Horseback, called the Monarchies; representing Ninus, Cyrus, Aléxander, and Cæsar, with emblematical ornaments.
Seven, of the Planets, with Emblems.
The Seven Wonders of the World, with the same.
Twelve, of the Sibyls; full-length.
Twelve, of Animals and Birds.
Sixteen Views in Holland.
One hundred Subjects from the Old Testament; four on each plate.
A set of Views of the Ruins of Rome.
Meleager and Atalanta; an etching; *after R. Picou.*

DANCKERTS DE RY, PIETER, a celebrated portrait and genre painter, who is supposed to have been the son of Cornelis Danckerts de Ry, was born at Amsterdam in 1605. Several of his paintings have been engraved by W. Hondius. He went to Sweden, and died at Stockholm in 1659. There are by him in the Brussels Gallery portraits of Cornelis Danckerts de Ry and his wife.

DANDINI, CESARE, was born at Florence about the year 1595. He was first a scholar of Francesco Curradi, but afterwards studied under Domenico Cresti, called Passignano, and Cristofano Allori. Under these masters he acquired a tolerable correctness of design, and an agreeable tone of colouring. One of his best works is a picture of St.

Charles, with other Saints, in one of the churches at Ancona. He also painted easel and cabinet pictures, which were admired for their neatness and finish. He died in 1658.

DANDINI, OTTAVIANO, was the son of Pietro Dandini, and painted history in the style of his father. Some fresco paintings in the cloister of San Spirito, a picture of several Saints in San Lorenzo, and his works in the church of the Magdalene at Pescia, evince the respectability of his talent. He afterwards entered the Society of Jesus, and died about 1750.

DANDINI, PIETRO, the nephew of Vincenzo Dandini, was born about 1646. Having lost his father when he was only four years of age, he was taken under the protection of his uncle, who instructed him in the principles he had himself adopted of the style of Cortona. He afterwards travelled through great part of Italy, and improved himself by studying the great masters of the Venetian and Lombard schools. On his return to Florence he was patronized by the Grand Duke Cosmo III., for whom he painted many works in oil and in fresco. It is to be lamented that the avarice of this artist led him into a slight and negligent manner of finishing his works; a habit to which he was the more easily tempted by the possession of uncommon facility of execution. Lanzi mentions, as one of his most important works, the cupola of Santa Maria Maddalena, at Florence. In the church of Santa Maria Maggiore is a picture of St. Francis; and in the church of the Servites is an altar-piece representing a saint of that order officiating at the altar. He died in 1712.

DANDINI, VINCENZO, the brother of Cesare Dandini, was born at Florence in 1607. After receiving some instruction from his brother, he went to Rome, where he studied some time under Pietro da Cortona, whose style he followed. He was an eminent painter of history, and, according to Orlandi, was made principal of the Academy at Rome, on succeeding to which appointment he painted a large picture which gained him great reputation. He returned to Florence, where he executed several works for the churches. In the church of Ognissanti is an admired picture of 'The Conception.' He was employed in the palaces of the Grand-Duke; in one of which he painted a ceiling, representing 'Aurora with the Hours,' much in the style of Pietro da Cortona. He died at Florence in 1675.

DANDRÉ - BARDON, MICHEL FRANÇOIS. See ANDRÉ-BARDON.

DANDRIDGE, BARTHOLOMEW, a portrait painter, was born in the early part of the 18th century. He obtained a considerable practice in the reign of George II., but died young, soon after the middle of the century. His portrait of Hook, the historian, is in the National Portrait Gallery.

DANDRILLON, PIERRE CHARLES, a French landscape painter, was born in Paris in 1757. He was a pupil of De Machy, and in 1807 became professor of perspective in the École des Beaux-Arts. He died in Paris in 1812.

DANEDI, GIOSEFFO, or GIUSEPPE, called MONTALTO, was the younger brother of Stefano Danedi, and was born at Treviglio in 1618. When young he went to Bologna, where he entered the school of Guido Reni. On leaving that master he settled at Turin, where he executed some works for the public edifices. Towards the latter part of his life he joined his brother at Milan, where he was much employed. In the church of San Sebastiano is a

8

fine picture by this master of 'The Massacre of the Innocents,' and in the Dresden Gallery is one of 'St. Anthony of Padua caressing the Infant Jesus.' He died in 1688.

DANEDI, STEFANO, called MONTALTO, was born at Treviglio, in the Milanese, in 1608, and was a scholar of Cavaliere Morazzone. During a long residence at Milan, he painted a great number of pictures for the churches of that city, and in the State. One of his best works is 'The Martyrdom of St. Justina,' in Santa Maria in Pedone. He died at Milan 1689.

DANET, JEAN. See DUVET.

DANHAUER, —, (or DONAUER,) a German miniature painter, was a native of Swabia. He was the son of a watchmaker, and was brought up to his father's trade; he afterwards went to Italy and studied painting under S. Bombelli, but this art he in turn abandoned for that of sculpture. He resided for many years in Russia, and died at St. Petersburg in 1733.

DANHAUSER, JOSEPH, born at Vienna in 1805, followed the principles of Peter Krafft. He visited Venice, and after his return painted genre pieces, which he executed in a pleasing and popular manner. From 1838 to 1844 he was corrector at the Academy at Vienna, where he died in 1845. Among his works the following are worthy of mention:

The Rioter.
Franz Liszt at the Piano.
The Little Virtuoso.
The Oculist.
The Reasoner in the Public-house.

DANIELE, BATTISTA DA SAN. See SAN DANIELE.
DANIELE, IL CAVALIERE. See SYDER.
DANIELE, PELLEGRINO DA SAN. See SAN DANIELE.

DANIELL, ABRAHAM, a miniature painter, was a native of Bath. He possessed considerable ability, and died in 1803.

DANIELL, EDWARD THOMAS, was born in London in 1804, but was bred at Norwich, learned drawing at the Grammar School there under Crome, and became one of the most original and interesting artists of the so-called Norwich school. In 1823 he entered Balliol College, Oxford, and after leaving the University spent some years in travelling. His etchings of English landscape executed during this period are full of the true etching spirit, with fine qualities of light and shadow, among the best being his 'Burough Bridge.' With Crome and Cotman, Wilkie and Geddes, he may claim the honour of anticipating the modern revival of etching—associated with the names of Whistler and Seymour Haden. In London he was on terms of intimate friendship with Linnell, Turner, David Roberts, Dyce, and Stanfield. In 1840–41, fired by Roberts' sketches, Daniell travelled in Greece, Egypt, and Syria. At Smyrna he joined the expedition sent by the Government to bring home the antiquities discovered by Sir Charles Fellowes at Xanthus. Remaining with two other members of the party, he made a thorough survey of Asia Minor, and brought home a series of sixty-four water-colour drawings, now in the British Museum. Two of his landscapes in oil are in the gallery of the Norwich Museum. In 1842 he rashly undertook a solitary expedition into Pisidia at the hottest season of the year, and falling ill at Adalia, died there on Sept. 23, at the age of thirty-eight. M. H.

DANIELL, JAMES, a mezzotint engraver, flourished in England towards the close of the 18th and the beginning of the 19th century. The following works are by him:

Nelson at the Battle of Cape St. Vincent; after Singleton.
The Death of Captain Alexander Hood; after Singleton.
The Capture of Admiral Winter; after Singleton.
Samuel and Eli; after Copley.

DANIELL, SAMUEL, a landscape painter, the brother of William, and the nephew of Thomas Daniell, was born in 1775. He studied under Medland, and first exhibited at the Royal Academy in 1792. He passed several years in Africa, returning to England in 1804. About a year after, he went to Ceylon, where he died in 1811. He made numerous drawings of tropical scenery, and published works on 'African Scenery and Animals,' 1804-5, and 'The Scenery, Animals, and Native Inhabitants of Ceylon,' 1808. At the South Kensington Museum is a water-colour drawing by him: 'Deer and Birds in a Tropical Landscape.'

DANIELL, THOMAS, was born at Kingston-upon-Thames in 1749, and commenced his artistic career as a painter of English landscape scenery, with some attempts at poetical composition. In 1784 he went to India with his nephew, William Daniell; they were absent about ten years, gathering materials for their great work on 'Oriental Scenery,' which was published between the years 1795 and 1815, in six volumes, the whole of which, with the exception of the volume of 'Excavations,' was executed by William. He seldom painted any but Indian subjects. In 1796 he was elected an Associate of the Royal Academy, and in 1799 an Academician. He died in London in 1840. The works of William Daniell are so blended with those of his uncle Thomas, that they may be considered, artistically, as one, though some give the preference to the latter.

DANIELL, WILLIAM, a landscape painter, was born in 1769. In 1784 he went to India with his uncle, Thomas Daniell, and assisted him in his drawings and sketches; he also engraved the views for the greater part of their 'Oriental Scenery.' He first exhibited at the Royal Academy in 1795, and entered the Academy Schools in 1799. He was elected an Associate in 1807, and an Academician in 1822. The British Institution awarded him a prize of £100 in 1826 for his 'Battle of Trafalgar.' In his later years he painted several panoramic views of India. He died in London in 1837. Amongst the works which he published are:

A Picturesque Voyage to India. 1810.
Animated Nature. 1809.
Views of London. 1812.
Views of Windsor Castle, Eton, and Virginia Water.
A Voyage round Great Britain. 1814-25.
Illustrations of the Island of Staffa. 1818.
The Oriental Annual. 1834-39.

Mention should also be made of the following pictures by him:

View of the Long Walk, Windsor (Royal Collection).
Castel Nuovo (South Kensington Museum).
Durham Cathedral. 1805. (South Kensington Museum.)
Benares (South Kensington Museum).

DANIELS, WILLIAM, painter, born about 1812, was the son of a brickmaker at Liverpool. He studied drawing at the Liverpool Institution, and was then apprenticed to an engraver on wood. At the close of his apprenticeship he set up as a painter in his native town, and might have risen to eminence in his art but for his fondness for drink and for jovial company. He died in

9

Liverpool, October 13, 1880. There are five portraits by him at South Kensington, among them those of George Stephenson, and Charles Kean as Hamlet. See 'Magazine of Art,' June 1882.

DANIELSKI, JAN NEPOMUCEN, a Polish painter of portraits in oil and in miniature, was a native of Cracow. He was a pupil of Dominik Estreicher, and also painted some frescoes. He died at Cracow in 1844.

DANKERTS. See DANCKERTS.

DANKS, FRANS, surnamed 'the Tortoise,' was born about 1650 at Amsterdam, where he died in 1703. He painted historical subjects and portraits, and showed considerable talent in modelling and sculpture.

DANLOUX, HENRI PIERRE, a French painter, born in Paris in 1753, was a pupil of J. B. Lépicié and of Vien. On the outbreak of the French Revolution he came to England and remained here for ten years, gaining a high reputation for his portraits, many of which were in chalk. The Fitzwilliam Museum at Cambridge has by him the portrait of Louis XVIII. After his return to France, he exhibited at the Salon of 1802 'Le Supplice d'une Vestale,' a picture which met with much praise. His best work is a full-length portrait of the Abbé Delille, now at Versailles. Danloux died in Paris in 1809.

DANNECKER (or DANNEKER). See DE NECKER.

DANNOOT, PIETER, was a Flemish engraver, who flourished about the year 1690. He engraved a plate representing the 'Head of Christ crowned with Thorns,' after Rubens, and a 'Portrait of Père Mastrille.'

DANTAN, JOSEPH EDWARD, French painter, son of the sculptor Jean Pierre Dantan, and nephew of the sculptor Antoine Laurent Dantan, born in Paris, August 20, 1848. Became pupil of Pilo for historical, and of Henri Lehmann for portrait painting. His first picture exhibited at the Salon of 1869 was entitled 'An Episode in the Destruction of Pompeii.' He executed a great picture of 'The Holy Trinity' for the Bezin chapel at Marnes. He was decorated with the Legion of Honour in 1880, and was killed in a carriage accident near Trouville in 1897.

DANTE, GIROLAMO, called GIROLAMO DI TIZIANO (from having been a scholar of Titian and an assistant to him in some of his less important works), flourished at Venice from 1550 to 1580. It is said that in copying the originals of his master, he attained so high a degree of excellence, that such of his pieces as were retouched by Titian bid defiance often to the judgment of the most expert connoisseurs. He also produced works of his own design; the altar-piece attributed to him at San Giovanni Nuovo, representing 'SS. Cosmo and Damianus,' reflects credit on the school to which he belonged.

DANTI, GIROLAMO, the younger brother of Vincenzio and Ignazio Danti, was born at Perugia in 1547. He painted frescoes in the style of Vasari, and gave promise of becoming a great painter when his career was prematurely terminated by his death at Perugia in 1580.

DANTI, IGNAZIO, Bishop of Alatri, whose secular name was PELLEGRINO, a Dominican monk and cosmographer, was born at Perugia in 1536. He was a brother of Vincenzio Danti, the sculptor, and was instructed by his father, Giulio Danti, a goldsmith, and his aunt Teodora. At Florence he painted the 'Tables of Ptolemy,' in 57 oil-pictures, and also produced a number of maps. Subsequently he was employed by Pope Gregory XIII. to decorate the walls of the Vatican with geographical delineations of ancient and modern Italy. The Pope having determined to complete the continuation of the Gallery of Raphael in conformity with the original plan, and to paint four subjects in every arcade of the gallery, all from the New Testament, Danti was employed by him to superintend the work; the entire abandonment of a design to the direction of practical artists being found by experience to be injurious to its execution, owing to the choice of their inferior assistants being liable to be governed by influence, avarice, or jealousy. The selection, therefore, was reserved to Danti, who, to an excellent practical knowledge of the art of design, united moral qualities that ensured success; and under his direction the whole work was regulated and conducted in such a manner that the spirit of Raphael seemed to be resuscitated in the precincts of the Vatican. He was consecrated Bishop of Alatri in 1583, and died at Rome in 1586.

DANTI, TEODORA, the aunt of Vincenzio and Ignazio Danti, is mentioned in the 'Vite de' Pittori Perugini,' by Lione Pascoli, who states that she was born at Perugia in 1498. She painted small pictures, in imitation of the style of Pietro Perugino, and died in 1573.

DANTI, VINCENZIO, an Italian sculptor, architect, and poet, was born at Perugia in 1530. In 1555 he cast in bronze the statue of Pope Julius III., which is still to be seen at Perugia, and is considered to be his masterpiece. He afterwards went to Florence, where he was employed by the Grand-Duke Cosmo, and made many designs for the Escorial which were sent to Spain. He also painted historical subjects, which are but seldom mentioned, and died in 1576.

DANUS, MIGUEL, a Spanish historical painter, who flourished about 1700, was a native of Majorca. He studied first at Valencia, and afterwards in Italy in the school of Carlo Maratti. After an absence of several years he returned to his own country, where he painted, in the manner of his master, the pictures in the cloisters of the convent of the Socorro at Palma; and others which are to be found in private collections in the island of Majorca.

DANVIN, VICTOR MARIE FÉLIX, a French landscape painter, was born in Paris in 1802. He studied successively under Lethière, Guérin, Watelet, and Rémond, and died in Paris in 1842. His wife, whose maiden name was CONSTANCE AMÉLIE LAMBERT, was born at Lille in 1810, and also painted landscapes.

DANZEL, JACQUES CLAUDE, a French engraver, was born at Abbeville in 1735. He was a pupil of Beauvarlet, and engraved several plates in a firm, neat style. He died at Abbeville in 1809. We have by him the following prints:

An old Man, half-length ; *after Rembrandt.*
Coresus sacrificing himself for love of Callirrhoe ; *after Fragonard ;* his chef-d'œuvre.
Le Roi boit, Le Gateau des Rois ; two plates ; *after Tilborgh.*
Venus and Adonis ; *after J. Bethon.*
Venus and Æneas ; *after A. Boizot.*
Alexander giving Campaspe to Apelles ; *after Lagrenée.*
Socrates pronouncing his Discourse on the Immortality of the Soul ; *after Sané.*
Roman Charity ; *after N. N. Coypel.*

10

Vulcan presenting to Venus the arms of Æneas; *after Boucher.*
Neptune and Amymone; *after the same.*
The Washerwoman; *after Greuze.*
The Rape of Proserpine; *after Vien.*

DANZICA, SALOMONE DI, is known by works which are finely and laboriously executed, and generally represent jocose subjects. His portrait by C. Gregori is in the Museo Fiorentino. He is said to have been brought up in Dantzic, from whence in 1695 he went to Italy. He died at Milan.

DAPPER. See TAMM, FRANZ WERNER.

DARBY, MATTHEW, engraver and caricaturist, practised in London and at Bath in the second half of the 18th century. He kept a shop in the Strand for the sale of artists' materials, and advertised himself as a teacher of engraving. Anthony Pasquin was one of his pupils. He also published comic drawings, among them some of H. W. Bunbury's early works, and a series of 'Caricatures' by various hands. He himself is said to have produced about three hundred caricatures.

DARCIS, J. LOUIS, was a French engraver, who died in Paris in 1801. His best works are:

Les Incroyables; *after Carle Vernet.*
Les Merveilleuses; *after the same.*
L'Anglomane; *after the same.*
La Course de Chevaux; *after the same.*
Marius at Minturnæ; *after Drouais the younger.*
La Brouille; *after Guérin.*
Le Raccommodement; *after the same.*

DARDANI, ANTONIO, an Italian historical painter, was born at Bologna in 1677, and was a pupil of M. A. Toni and of J. Viani. He died in 1735.

DARDEL, ROBERT GUILLAUME, a French sculptor, and pupil of Pajou, was born in Paris in 1749, and died there in 1821. He engraved a 'Diana' and an 'Endymion.' His wife engraved after him 'La Danse' and 'La Musique.'

DARDOIZE, EMILE, French landscape painter of note, born in Paris in 1826. Though it was his boast that he was a pupil of no master, he kept pretty closely to French traditions, and deserves to be ranked with Harpignies or Pelouse. His interpretation of Nature was perhaps wanting in breadth, but his work had the merit of sincerity, his colour being most fresh and agreeable. Among his best-known works we may mention 'Solitude' (in the Salon of 1869), 'Soleil Couchant' (1874), 'Nuit Verte' (1880), 'La Source' (1882), 'Le Bois des Rossignols,' 'Le Bois Pierre' (1894), 'Les Tourterelles' (1895). He also contributed frequently to some of the Paris illustrated publications such as 'L'Illustration,' 'Le Tour du Monde,' &c. His death occurred in Paris on October 30, 1901.

P. P.

DARET, DANIEL, pupil of his brother James, was admitted free master into the Guild of Saint Luke at Tournay, February 10, 1440. In 1449 he was appointed court painter by Philip Duke of Burgundy, in succession to John van Eyck, since whose death the office had remained vacant.

DARET, JAMES, native of Tournay, member of a family of artists, learned his art under Robert Campin, to whom he was apprenticed on April 12, 1427; he was admitted free master into the Guild of Saint Luke on October 18, 1432, seven weeks after his fellow-apprentice, Roger De la Pasture. On the same day he was elected provost of the confraternity of Saint Luke. In 1441 he moved to Arras, where he resided until 1448; there he was chiefly employed in making designs for metal-work and tapestry. Amongst others he painted a cartoon in distemper of the Resurrection, which occupied thirty-six yards of canvas. In 1454 he worked during nineteen days on the decorations for the festival held at Lille, known as the *Vœu du Faisan;* he received as wage 8s. a day. In October 1459 he was back at Tournay. In 1468 he was called to Bruges to design decorations of the palace for the marriage of Charles the Bold and Margaret of York; on this occasion he received the high wage of 27s. a day. He returned again to Tournay and died shortly after. A large number of paintings, formerly attributed to Roger De la Pasture, are now supposed to be by Daret. The chief of these are some life-size figures in the Staedel Institute, Frankfort, of the Most Holy Trinity, the Blessed Virgin, Saint Veronica (the original design of this is in the Fitzwilliam Museum, Cambridge), and one wing of a Calvary triptych formerly in the priory church of Flémalle. An early copy of the triptych, with the added portrait of a donor, and figures in grisaille on the exterior, of SS. John Baptist and Julian, formerly in the Hospice of Saint Julian at Bruges, is now in the museum at Liverpool.

Bibliography: De la Grange and Cloquet, 'Etudes sur l'Art à Tournai.' 1888.

W. H. J. W.

DARET, JEAN, a Flemish painter, was born at Brussels in 1613. He went to Italy, whence he returned in 1638, and settled at Aix in Provence, where he painted many Scriptural subjects for the churches and convents of that city. He also painted portraits, and engraved a set of plates representing the Virtues. He died at Aix in 1668. There is an excellent portrait of a Magistrate by him in the Museum of Marseilles. His sons, MICHEL and JEAN BAPTISTE, were painters who worked together.

DARET DE CAZENEUVE, PIERRE, a French portrait painter and engraver, was born in Paris in 1604. After receiving some instruction in engraving, he went to Rome in search of improvement, and there passed a considerable time. He was received into the Academy of Painting in 1663, and died at the château of La Luque, near Dax (Landes) in 1678. Mariette says that this artist began and finished his career with painting. He engraved upwards of four hundred plates, not without merit, but very deficient in taste and correctness of drawing. They are frequently marked **D** and among them are the following:

PORTRAITS.

Bust of Alexander the Great.
Pope Alexander VII.
Charles I., King of Great Britain.
Henri de Bourbon, Prince of Condé.
Charlotte Marguerite de Montmorency, Princess of Condé.
Marguerite Gaston, Duchess of Orleans.
Vladislas IV., King of Poland.

SUBJECTS AFTER VARIOUS MASTERS.

St. John sitting in the Desert with his Lamb; *after Guido.*
The Virgin suckling the Infant; *after A. Carracci.*
St. Peter delivered from Prison; *after Domenichino.*
The Entombment of Christ; *after Barocci.*
A Holy Family, with Angel presenting fruit to the Infant Jesus; *after S. Vouet.*
The Dead Christ, with the Marys; *after the same.*
St. Jerome; half-length; *after Blanchard.*

11

Thetis ordering Vulcan to forge arms for Achilles
  after the same.
A Charity with five Children ; after the same.
The Visitation of the Virgin to St. Elizabeth ; after
  Corneille.
The Virgin and Infant ; after Sarazin.

He also engraved one hundred small plates for a work entitled, 'La Doctrine des Mœurs,' after the designs of Otto van Veen, 1646 ; and a great number of portraits for a publication entitled, 'Tableaux historiques, où sont gravés les illustres François et Etrangers de l'un et l'autre sexe ; par Pierre Daret, Louis Boissevin, et B. Moncornet,' published in 1652 and 1656.

There was also a PIERRE DARET, a painter upon vellum and in water-colours, who was living in 1664.

DARGENT, MICHEL, a Flemish miniature painter, was born at Liége in 1751, and died in 1824. He possessed talent which was still more remarkable in his son, who was born at Liége in 1794, and died in the flower of youth in 1812. His daughter, MARIE JOSÈPHE, who was born at Liége in 1789 and died in 1863, likewise painted miniatures.

D'ARGENVILLE, ANTOINE JOSEPH DESALLIER. See DESALLIER D'ARGENVILLE.

DARIO DA TREVIGI. See TREVIGI.

DARJOU, HENRI ALFRED, a French painter and draughtsman, born in Paris in 1832, was the son of Victor Darjou, a portrait painter of some ability. He studied under his father and under Léon Cogniet, and exhibited first at the Salon of 1853, from which time onwards he almost every year sent pictures which were for the most part of genre subjects. The paintings of Darjou have, however, done less for his reputation than the numerous designs which he made for the 'Illustration' and the 'Monde illustré.' He died in Paris in 1874.

DARLY, JEAN BAPTISTE, was a French portrait painter, who flourished at Tours about 1530. He had a great reputation, and many persons came from distant parts in order to have their portraits painted by him.

DARNSTÄDT, JOHANN ADOLF, a German line-engraver, who was born at Auma, near Dippoldiswalda in Saxony, in 1768, was a scholar of Schulze and of Zingg. Amongst his works are an engraving of Dresden after Hammer and Thurmayer, and some book illustrations. For his plates of 'The Magi' and 'The Magi among the Shepherds,' after Dietrich, he obtained the gold medal at Milan. He resided at Dresden, and died there in 1844.

DASSONNEVILLE, JACQUES, a French engraver, was born in the harbour of St. Ouen near Rouen, in 1619. We have by this artist about fifty etchings, in the style of A. van Ostade, which, although by no means equal to the playful point of that master, are not without considerable merit.

DASSY, JEAN JOSEPH, a French historical and portrait painter, and lithographer, was born at Marseilles in 1796. He studied under Goubaud and Girodet-Trioson, and commenced exhibiting at the Paris Salon in 1819. There are several pictures by him at Versailles, among which are 'The Battle of Saucourt' and 'Charibert.' He died at Marseilles in 1865.

DASVELT, JAN, a Dutch landscape painter, was born at Amsterdam in 1770. He was a pupil of Hendrik Stokvisch, and, although at first only an amateur, he soon acquired the reputation of being a good artist. He excelled especially in the manner in which he painted the dogs which he

12

introduced into his pictures. He died at Amsterdam in 1855.

DATHAN, GEORG, was born at Mannheim in 1703. He excelled in painting portraits and historical subjects. One of his best works, an 'Allegory upon the marriage of the Dauphin, son of Louis XV., with the Princess Marie Joséphine of Poland,' is in the Dresden Gallery.

DATI, COSIMO. See DADDI.

DATTI, NATALIS, was an Italian engraver, who flourished at Ravenna in the early part of the 16th century, to whom Zani, without giving any proof, assigns the very few plates which bear the signature *NA. DAT*. and the device of a rat-trap, on account of which the artist is often called, THE MASTER OF THE RAT-TRAP. The prints thus marked are small and executed entirely with the graver. From the resemblance of the style of Dati to that afterwards adopted by Theodor De Bry, it is probable that the latter was his pupil. Bartsch and Passavant mention the following prints by him :

The Virgin and Child, with St. Anne ; in an arch to
  the right is the Angel appearing to St. Joseph, and
  to the left an Angel appearing to St. Joachim.
The Battle of Ravenna. 1512.
Two Monstrous Children joined back to back.

DAUBIGNY, CHARLES FRANÇOIS, one of the most distinguished French landscape painters and etchers of recent years, was born in Paris in 1817. He was the son of Edme François Daubigny, under whose tuition he painted boxes, clock-cases, and other articles of commerce. At the age of eighteen he visited Italy, and on his return to France in the following year he entered the studio of Paul Delaroche. He first exhibited at the Salon of 1838, and obtained medals in 1848 and 1853, besides medals at the Paris Universal Exhibitions of 1855 and 1867. His etchings are characterized by their purity and effect. Several of them appeared in Curmer's 'Jardin des Plantes' and 'Beaux Arts,' and in the 'Artiste ;' but the best are 'Le Buisson' and 'Le Coup de Soleil,' after the pictures of Ruisdael in the Louvre. Daubigny died in Paris in 1878. He excelled in river scenes, which he often painted from a barge fitted up as a floating studio. Amongst his best works are :

The Seine at Bezons. 1840.
The Harvest. 1852.
Sunrise. (In the Lille Museum.)
The Pool of Gylien. 1853.
Sluice in the Valley of Optevoz. 1855. (In the Luxem-
  bourg Gallery.)
The Banks of the Oise. 1861.
The Vintage. 1863. (In the Luxembourg Gallery.)
Windmills at Dordrecht. 1872.
Moonrise. 1877.

Fuller details respecting this artist may be found in Henriet's 'C. Daubigny et son œuvre gravé,' Paris, 1875, 8vo.

DAUBIGNY, EDME FRANÇOIS, a French landscape painter, was a pupil of Victor Bertin. He was born in Paris in 1789, and died there in 1843. His favourite subjects were views in Italy and in the environs of Paris.

DAUBIGNY, KARL PIERRE, the son of the famous landscape painter, was a pupil and imitator of his father, and painted the same class of subjects. Born in Paris in 1846, he gained medals in 1868 and 1874, and died in May 1886.

DAUBIGNY, PIERRE, a French miniature painter, was the brother of Edme François Daubigny, and a pupil of Aubry. He was born in Paris in 1793,

C. F. DAUBIGNY

THE GRAPE-GATHERERS OF BURGUNDY, OR THE VINTAGE

C. F. DAUBIGNY

Neurdein photo]

SPRING

[*The Luxembourg, Paris*

and died there in 1858. His wife, AMÉLIE DAUTEL, was likewise a miniature painter, and a pupil of Aubry and of Granger. She was born in 1796 in Paris, where she died in 1861.

DAUDET, ROBERT, a French engraver of landscapes in line, was born at Lyons in 1737. He was the son of Robert Daudet, an engraver and printseller, who in 1766 sent him to Paris, where he studied under Baléchou, and afterwards became the favourite pupil of J. G. Wille. He died in 1824. His best works are as follow:

Two Landscapes, with Figures and Cattle; *after Berchem*.
An Italian Landscape, with Figures and Cattle; *after Both and Berchem*.
Going out to the Chase; *after A. van Ostade and Hackert*.
A Stag-Hunt; *after Wouverman*.
Italian Ruins; *after C. Poelemburg*.
Ruins of Palmyra; *after Cassas*.
Combat of Horsemen; *after Van der Meulen*.
The Corsican Fishermen; *after Joseph Vernet*.
The Young Washerwomen; *after the same*.
Roman Ruins; two plates, *after Dietrich*.
Evening; *after the same*.
Two Views of Pirna, in Saxony.

DAULLÉ, JEAN, a French engraver, was born at Abbeville in 1703. He received his first lessons in engraving from Dom Robart, a monk of the priory of St. Peter at Abbeville, and afterwards went to Paris, where his fellow-citizen, Robert Hecquet, taught him what little he himself knew. His merit did not remain long unnoticed, and he was received into the Academy in 1742. He died in Paris in 1763. After his death some of his engravings were published by his widow as his 'Œuvre.' He engraved several portraits and plates of historical and other subjects, which are chiefly executed with the graver in a clear and firm style, which entitles him to rank with the ablest artists of his time. He marked his works *J. D.* The following are his principal plates:

PORTRAITS.

Catherine, Countess of Feuquières, daughter of Pierre Mignard; *after Mignard*.
Hyacinthe Rigaud, painter; *after Rigaud*; engraved for his reception at the Academy in 1742.
Marguerite de Valois, Countess of Caylus; *after the same*.
Charles Edward Stuart, son of the Pretender.
Clementina, Princess of Poland, his consort; *after David*.
Madame Favart, in the part of 'Bastienne;' *after Carle van Loo*.
Claude Deshayes Gendron, oculist; *after Rigaud*.
Jean Baptiste Rousseau; *after Aved*.
Jean Mariette, engraver; *after Pesne*.

SUBJECTS AFTER VARIOUS MASTERS.

The Magdalen; *after Correggio*; for the Dresden Gallery.
Diogenes with his Lantern; *after Spagnoletto*; for the same.
Quos Ego; *after Rubens*.
The Two Sons of Rubens; *after the same*; for the Dresden Gallery.
Neptune appeasing the Tempest; *after the same*.
Charity with Three Children; *after Albani*.
The Triumph of Venus; *after Boucher*.
Latona; *after J. Jouvenet*.
Four Marine subjects; *after Joseph Vernet*.
The Bath of Venus; *after Raoux*.
Two subjects; *after G. Metsu*.
Jupiter and Calisto; *after N. Poussin*.
St. Margaret; *after Correggio*.
Child playing with Cupid; *after Van Dyck*.

A detailed account of this artist's works is contained in Delignière's 'Catalogue raisonné de l'Œuvre gravé de Jean Daullé d'Abbeville,' 1872, 8vo.

DAUMIER, HONORÉ, a French caricaturist and painter, was born at Marseilles in 1808. His most celebrated work was the series of 'Robert Macaire,' published in the 'Charivari.' No one ever represented with greater truth the varied types of Parisian character. He became blind in 1877, and died in 1879 at Valmondois (Seine-et-Oise) in a house given him by Corot, the landscape painter.

DAUPHIN, CHARLES CLAUDE, (or DOFIN,) called in Italian DELFINO, a French painter of historical subjects and portraits, was the son of Olivier Dauphin. He went to Turin about the year 1664, and worked there for the Prince of Carignano. He was also employed for the churches, but his works are in no great estimation, abounding as they do with the most ridiculous absurdities. In the church of San Carlo is an altar-piece by him, described by Lanzi as a most ludicrous composition. He died in 1677.

DAUPHIN, FRANÇOIS GUSTAVE, a French historical painter, was born at Belfort in 1804. He was a pupil of Hersent, and executed Scriptural subjects, and occasionally portraits. He died in Paris in 1859.

DAUPHIN, OLIVIER, (or DOFIN,) called in Italian DELFINO, a French painter and engraver, was born in Lorraine in the early part of the 17th century. He was instructed by Simon Vouet, and worked, in particular, at the court of Modena. He etched several plates after the Carracci and other masters, but nothing is known of his works as a painter. He died at Bologna in 1693.

DAUPHIN DE BEAUVAIS, CHARLES NICOLAS, the son of Nicolas Dauphin de Beauvais, was born in Paris in 1730, and was instructed in the art of engraving by his father. He died in 1783. Amongst other plates he engraved the following:

Portrait of Just Aurèle Meissonnier, architect.
Le Sommeil interrompu; *after F. Boucher*.
Map of the Empire of Alexander.

DAUPHIN DE BEAUVAIS, JACQUES PHILIPPE, the eldest son of Nicolas Dauphin de Beauvais, was a sculptor, who engraved three 'Livres de Vases' and some views of Venice. He was born in 1738, and died in Paris in 1781.

DAUPHIN DE BEAUVAIS, NICOLAS, was born in Paris in 1687. He learned the art of engraving under Jean Audran, and his works are held in considerable estimation. It is probable that he passed some time in England, as he engraved a part of the frescoes of the dome of St. Paul's, after Sir James Thornhill. He died in Paris in 1753. We have also by him:

The Descent of the Holy Ghost; *after J. André*.
All Saints; *after the same*.
The Resurrection; *after P. J. Cazes*.
The Four Seasons; *after the same*; four plates, engraved conjointly with *Desplaces*.
The Madonna of St. George; *after Correggio*; for the Dresden Gallery.
St. Jerome; *after Van Dyck*; for the same.
The Burning of Æneas's Ships, and their Metamorphosis into Nymphs; *after Coypel*.
The Companion, a subject from the Life of Æneas; *after the same*.
Monument of William, Earl Cowper.
Cupid stealing Jupiter's Thunderbolts; *after Le Sueur*.
St. Mary Magdalen in the Desert; *after B. Luti*; for the Crozat Collection.
The Triumph of Bacchus and Ariadne; *after N. Poussin*.

DAUTEL, AMÉLIE. See DAUBIGNY.

13

DAUZATS, ADRIEN, a French landscape and genre painter, was born at Bordeaux in 1804. He became a pupil of Gué, and afterwards travelled in France, Spain, Egypt, and Palestine, for the purpose of making illustrations for Baron Taylor's 'Voyages pittoresques et romantiques de l'ancienne France,' 1820-63; 'Voyage pittoresque en Espagne, en Portugal, et sur la côte d'Afrique, de Tanger à Tétouan,' 1826-32; 'La Syrie, l'Égypte, la Palestine et la Judée,' 1835-39, and other books. He was a frequent exhibitor at the Salon of genre subjects and interiors of churches, and was also a lithographer. He died in Paris in 1868.

DAVENPORT, SAMUEL, an English engraver, was born at Bedford in 1783. He was articled to Charles Warren, and worked much at book illustration, after Shenton, Corbould, and others. He also engraved many portraits, and was one of the first to practise engraving on steel. He died in 1867.

DAVENT, LEONARD. See THIRY.

DAVID, CHARLES, a French engraver, was born in Paris about 1600. It is not ascertained by whom he was instructed, but he ranks as an estimable artist among the engravers of his time. The exact date of his death is not known, but it was neither earlier than 1636, nor later than 1638. His plates are executed with the graver in a clear, firm manner, and his drawing is tolerably correct. His prints are held in considerable estimation. He usually marked his plates *C. D.* or *C. D. F.* The following are by him:

Ecce Homo, or Christ shown to the People by Pilate.
The Virgin and Infant with Angels; *after J. B. de Champaigne.*
The Virgin with St. Bernard; *after P. de Champaigne.*
Wisdom awaking a Man sleeping; *after the same.*
A Nurse carrying a Child; with six verses.
The Roman Charity.
Twelve plates of the Labours of Hercules; *after Frans Floris.*
Sixteen plates of the Cries of Rome; *after Villamena;* copied with such exactness that they may easily be mistaken for the originals.
A set of Landscapes; *after M. and P. Bril.*
A Man with a Snail on his Finger, with a Goat wearing a Crown of Snails on its Head; *after Callot.*

DAVID, CHARLES, a French miniature painter, was born at Avignon in 1798. He was the brother of the eminent composer Félicien David, and was also a musician. He died at Avignon in 1869.

DAVID, CLAUDE, a French sculptor and engraver, was a native of Franche-Comté. He was in England in 1720, and is noticed by Vertue as having engraved a plate from a model of a fountain intended to have been erected at the conduit in Cheapside, and comprising statues of Queen Anne and the Duke of Marlborough on horseback, with River Gods.

DAVID, FRANÇOIS ANNE, a French line-engraver, was born in Paris in 1741, and died in the same city in 1824. He was a pupil of Le Bas, and engraved several portraits and other subjects in a neat, finished style; among them are the following:

PORTRAITS.

Louis Stanislas Xavier, Monsieur, afterwards Louis XVIII.; *after Drouais.*
Louis XVIII.; full-length, in his robes; *after himself.*
Denis Diderot; *after L. M. van Loo.*
César Gabriel de Choiseul, Duc de Praslin; *after Roslin.*
Catharine II., Empress of Russia; *after Mlle. Durameau.*
Gaspard Netscher, painter, his Wife and Son; *after Netscher.*
Charles I. of England with his Family; *after Van Dyck.*

14

SUBJECTS AFTER VARIOUS MASTERS.

Adam and Eve in Paradise; *after Santerre.*
Christ crowned with thorns; *after Titian.*
St. Cecilia; *after Raphael.*
The Dutch Sportsman; *after G. Metsu.*
The Green-Market at Amsterdam; *after the same.*
The Quack Doctor; *after Karel Du Jardin.*
The Bull; *after Paul Potter.*
Two Views of the Gulf of Venice; *after Joseph Vernet.*
Two Views near Dunkirk; *after the same.*

DAVID, GHEERAERT. Although the name of this painter appears to have been known to Guicciardini, Sanderus, and other early writers, it was completely lost in later times until 1860. Researches in the archives of Bruges proved that this 'Gerard, son of John, son of David,' was a native of Oudewater in South Holland; that he settled in Bruges in 1483, and on the 14th of January, 1484, was admitted as master-painter into the Guild of Saint Luke, and paid the usual entrance fee of £6. David soon acquired a good position in Bruges, for in 1488 we find him fourth 'vinder' of his guild, in 1495 and 1498 first 'vinder,' and in 1501 'dean,' a proof that he then stood at the top of his profession in Bruges. In 1496, or very shortly after, he married Cornelia, daughter of James Cnoop, dean of the Guild of Goldsmiths. David was also a miniaturist, and as such a member of the Booksellers' Guild. He was also a member of the confraternity of 'Our Lady of the Dry Tree.' He was a pious and charitable man, and attained a great reputation both as painter and miniaturist. He was in good circumstances, for besides the house in which he lived, he rented three others as workshops. In 1509 he completed the picture now in the Museum of Rouen, and presented it as a gift to the convent of the Carmelites of Sion at Bruges. This beautiful altar-piece represents the Virgin and Child seated in the midst of angels and a company of virgin saints. In the background to the right the painter has introduced his own figure, while his wife stands similarly placed on the left. The convent was suppressed by the Emperor Joseph in 1783, and the altar-piece sold; it afterwards passed into the Rouen Museum. David died on the 13th of August, 1523, as certified by the register of his burial in Notre-Dame at Bruges, where he was laid to rest beneath the tower, his gravestone bearing escutcheons charged with his own and his wife's arms.

It is not known where Gerard learned his art, but most probably at Haarlem, or under Dirk Bouts, but the composition and colouring of his earliest known pictures show that before settling in Bruges he had travelled in Italy and come under the influence of the Venetian school, probably of Carpaccio. Certain details such as the amorini, the garlands of fruit and flowers, and the Medicean cameos reproduced in these prove him to have visited Florence. His works were formerly often attributed to Memlinc, with whose style they have a certain affinity. David lived in Bruges for forty years, and received many commissions not only from the magistrates and citizens of that city, but also from France, Italy, Spain, and Portugal. He is reckoned among the most esteemed Netherlandish painters, remarkable among other qualities for his careful and truthful painting of landscape. Some critics suppose indeed that his landscape backgrounds were executed by Joachim Patenir. His best authenticated works are as follow:

A CANON AND HIS PATRON SAINTS

The Judgment of Cambyses, and the Punishment of Sisamnes; commissioned by the Magistrates of Bruges in 1488 and completed in 1498 (*now in the Museum of Bruges*).

The Blessed Virgin and Child, SS. Barbara, Mary Magdalene, and Katherine, and Richard De Visch Van der Capelle, cantor of the collegiate church of S. Donatian. It was painted in 1501 for the altar of S. Katherine in that church.

A Canon protected by three Saints (*now in the National Gallery*). This painting was formerly the right wing of an altar-piece in the church of S. Donatian at Bruges. It was completed in 1501–2 for a certain Bernardin de Salviatis, the illegitimate son of a rich Florentine merchant, who held the office of Canon in the church, and is represented with three patron saints—SS. Donatian, Bernardine of Siena, and Martin of Tours. The landscape background in this picture is a good example of his treatment; indeed, the picture altogether affords English students an excellent opportunity of judging this master, for it is a characteristic work, and well preserved.

The Baptism of Christ; a fine triptych, containing portraits of the donor's family. 1501–8 (*in the Museum of Bruges*).

The Assumption of the Blessed Virgin, S. Andrew, and S. Katherine (*at Grancey le Château; Côte d'Or*).

The Virgin and Child, with Saints (*altar-piece, in the Rouen Museum*).

S. Michael expelling the fallen angels from heaven; SS. Jerome, Anthony of Padua, Sebastian, Julitta, and Cyriacus (*Imperial Gallery, Vienna*).

Six panels representing three scenes in the life of S. Nicholas, and three in that of S. Anthony of Padua; formerly in the possession of Cardinal Despuig, at Palma, in Majorca (*now in the possession of Lady Wantage*).

The Blessed Virgin and Child enthroned; S. Jerome and S. Benedict (*Municipal Palace, Genoa*).

The Carriage of the Cross and the Resurrection; on the reverse, the Annunciation, in grisaille (*in the possession of M. R. Kann, Paris*).

The Deposition from the Cross; a triptych in the church of S. Basil at Bruges (*authenticity contested*).

These are about the only paintings that can with certainty be attributed to David, although many others are now assigned to him by critics.

Bibliography: Weale: 'Le Beffroi,' vols. i., ii., and iii.; 'Gazette des Beaux Arts,' vols. xx. and xxi.; 'Gerard David, Painter and Illuminator,' London, 1895.   W. H. J. W.

DAVID, JACQUES LOUIS, an eminent French historical painter, was born at Paris in 1748. His father lost his life in a duel, and the care of his early years devolved on his mother, who intended that he should follow the profession of an architect. By the advice, however, of his uncle Boucher, from whom he received his first instruction, he became a pupil of Vien at the age of twenty-one. His master does not appear to have behaved altogether well to him, for, owing to pique, he prevented his obtaining the 'prix de Rome' in 1771. In the two following years he competed unsuccessfully, and it was not till 1774 that he obtained the blue ribbon of French art. In the next year he set out for Rome, accompanying Vien, who had just been appointed director of the French Academy in that city. While in Italy he painted but few pictures, directing his attention sedulously to drawing from the antique. He returned to France in 1780, and his 'Belisarius' procured his election at the Academy, for his admission into which, in 1783, he painted the 'Death of Hector.' Shortly afterwards he married, and again visited Italy, and also Flanders. It was during this period that he painted 'The Oath of the Horatii,' 'Brutus,' and other works of a similar character, which were the first steps in the classic movement of which he was the prophet, and which

exercised an influence, not only on the politics, but even on the furniture and passing fashions of the day. Elected in 1792 a representative of Paris in the Convention, he sided with the extreme party of Robespierre, after whose fall he was twice thrown into prison, and narrowly escaped with his life. On his release, in 1795, he considered it prudent to abandon politics, and to devote himself to art. He was one of the original members of the Institute, in connection with which he became acquainted with the first Napoleon, who ever proved himself his warm friend and patron. He made David his first painter, and gave him many important commissions, such as the pictures of his 'Coronation,' the 'Distribution of the Eagles,' &c. This friendship effected a strange metamorphosis in the politics of the painter, for from an ardent republican he became an equally stanch imperialist, so that, on the restoration of the Bourbons, he sought refuge at Brussels. In this city he remained, notwithstanding an offer from the King of Prussia of the directorship of Fine Arts at Berlin, until his death in 1825. The influence of David on the French school was very great. He rescued it from the littleness and trivialities to which it had been reduced by the followers of the Watteau school; but, on the other hand, he established a despotism, which in several respects was baneful to the progress of art. For many years he reigned with an absolute supremacy, and amongst his pupils and disciples were Girodet, Gros, Gérard, the elder Isabey, Léopold Robert, Abel de Pujol, and Ingres. It was not until the rise of the Romantic school, under the leadership of Géricault and Delacroix, that any real opposition was offered to the all-prevalent classicism. David's chief excellence is in the correctness of his drawing, which, however, it must be said, frequently becomes hard and statuesque, whilst his weakness is most apparent in his treatment of light and in his colouring, which is monotonous and frequently unpleasant. The following is a list of his chief works:

Avignon, *Museum*, Death of Joseph Barra. Cherbourg, *Museum*, Philoctetes in the Island of Lemnos. Dublin, *National Gallery*, Death of Milo. Lille, *Museum*, Belisarius asking alms, 1780. Montpellier, *Museum*, Portrait of Alphonse Leroy; Portrait of M. de Joubert (*sketch*); Three studies. Nantes, *Museum*, Death of Cleonice (*sketch*). Paris, *Louvre*, Leonidas at Thermopylæ, 1814; The Sabine Women, 1799; The Oath of the Horatii, 1784; Brutus, 1789; Belisarius asking alms, 1784; Combat of Minerva and Mars, 1711; The Loves of Paris and Helen, 1788; Academic figure, 1779; Portrait of himself when young (*sketch*); Portrait of M. Pécoul, 1783; Portrait of Madame Pécoul; Portrait of Pope Pius VII., 1805; Portrait of Madame Récamier (*sketch*); Portrait of Bailly (*sketch*); *Comédie Française*, Portrait of Mademoiselle Joly. Rouen, *Museum*, Portrait of Mme. Vigée Le Brun. Valence, *Museum*, Ugolino. Versailles, *Museum*, Bonaparte crossing Mount St. Bernard, 1805; The Coronation of Napoleon I. and the Empress Joséphine, 1808; The Oath of the Army at the Champ de Mars, 1810; Portrait of Barère (*unfinished*), 1790; Portrait of Pius VII. (*a replica of the Louvre picture*). Warwick, *Castle*, Portrait of Napoleon I.   O. J. D.

DAVID, JEAN LOUIS, a French painter in water-colours, was born in Paris in 1791. He executed chiefly military subjects and landscapes, and died in Paris in 1868.

DAVID, JÉRÔME, a French engraver, brother to Charles David, was born in Paris about the year 1638, and died at Rome about 1670. He engraved a considerable number of plates in the same style as his brother, many of them being portraits. The work of the two brothers consists of about two hundred and twenty prints. Jérôme marked his plates either with the letters *H. D. F.*, or with the cipher [cipher] or [cipher]. We have by him:

Charles I., King of England, on horseback. Henrietta Maria, his Queen, on horseback. Anne, Queen of France. Gaston, Duke of Orleans. Cardinal Richelieu. Giovanni Battista Montano, sculptor, 1621. The Heads of the Philosophers, thirty-six plates from his own designs. Adam and Eve driven from Paradise; *after himself.* Christ bearing the Cross; *after Ercole Ferrata,* 1630. Ecce Homo; *after Guercino.* The Virgin of the Rosary; *after Guido,* 1633. The Assumption of the Virgin; *after Camillo Procaccino.* St. Francis of Paolo; *after Robert Picou.*

DAVID, LODOVICO ANTONIO, was born at Lugano in 1648. After studying for some time at Milan, under the Cavaliere Cairo and Ercole Procaccini, he went to Bologna, where he entered the school of Carlo Cignani. In the church of San Silvestro, in Venice, is a picture by him of the Nativity.

DAVID, LOUIS, a French engraver, was a native of Avignon, who worked there and at Rome from 1665 to 1706. We have by him an upright plate of the 'Descent from the Cross,' marked with the cipher [cipher],

DAVID, MAXIME, a French miniature painter, was born at Châlons-sur-Marne in 1798. He was a pupil of Madame de Mirbel, and died at Passy in 1870. Three portraits of Abd-el-Kader by him are in the Luxembourg.

DAVIDSON, GEORGE DUTCH, the only child of Dundee parents, was born in 1879. A severe illness in his seventeenth year left him an invalid, and for amusement he attended drawing classes. Enthusiastic in his new interest, he worked as hard as strength permitted, drawing from the antique and from life, and, in 1898, completed in water-colour his first symbolical design, 'Envy.' He studied Celtic ornament, and its spirit appears in several designs. In 1899 he visited London, where the early Italian masters and the Greek vases most impressed him. After a short residence in Antwerp he went to Italy and remained some months, chiefly in Florence. Cimabue, Gaddi, Memmi, Giotto, and Angelico were his constant study. On his return he took a studio in Dundee, and worked happily for a few months until, quite suddenly, he died, early in January 1901. His character was one of great sweetness, and his work corresponds. Refined and delicate pen drawings, a few lovely water-colours instinct with the early Italian spirit, and designs for embroidery make up a life-work of rare accomplishment and yet rarer promise. Ancient stories and beliefs, Omar Khayyám, and Celtic romance furnished his chief subjects. A memorial volume with collotype reproductions of his works was published in Dundee in 1902.   J. H. W. L.

DAVIDSON, JEREMIAH, a Scottish portrait painter, was born in England, of Scotch parentage, about 1695. He had a large practice both in Edinburgh and in London, and died in 1745. A portrait of Richard Cooper, the engraver, by him, is in the National Gallery of Scotland, and a portrait of Admiral Byng is in Greenwich Hospital. Roubiliac's statue of President Forbes in the Parliament House, Edinburgh, is after a portrait by him.

DAVIN, CÉSARINE HENRIETTE FLORE, a French painter of portraits and miniatures, whose maiden name was Mirvault, was born in Paris in 1773. She studied under Suvée, David, and Augustin, and afterwards established a school of drawing and painting, in which she had many pupils. Madame Davin died in Paris in 1844.

DAVIS, EDWARD LE. See LE DAVIS.

DAVIS, J. P., a portrait and subject painter, first exhibited at the Royal Academy in 1811. In 1824 he went to Rome, and painted 'The Talbot Family receiving the Papal Benediction:' whence his cognomen of 'Pope Davis.' He next year received a prize of £50 from the British Institution. With his friend Haydon, he was a great opponent of the Academy, where he did not exhibit after 1843. He died in 1862, and after his death was published his 'Thoughts on Great Painters.' His best-known work is 'The Love-Letter,' exhibited at the British Institution in 1826.

DAVIS, JOHN SCARLETT, a subject painter, was born at Hereford in the beginning of the 19th century. He studied and spent much time abroad. He first exhibited at the Royal Academy in 1825 with 'My Den,' and his views of the interiors of public buildings had considerable success; but he fell into dissipated habits, and died soon after 1841. At the South Kensington Museum is a water-colour drawing by him of the 'Porte St. Martin, Paris.'

DAVIS, RICHARD BARRETT, an animal and landscape painter, was born at Watford in 1782. He studied under Evans of Eton, under Beechey, and in the schools of the Royal Academy, where he first exhibited in 1802. He joined the Society of British Artists in 1829, and was appointed animal painter to William IV. in 1831. He died in 1854. Amongst his works are:

Mares and Foals from the Royal Stud, 1806. Going to Market, 1814. Horse Fair, 1821. Travellers attacked by Wolves, 1831. Near Virginia Water (*South Kensington*).

DAVIS, WILLIAM, a landscape painter, was born at Dublin in 1812. Having studied at the Dublin Academy of Arts, he afterwards came to Liverpool, where he at first practised as a portrait-painter. After some time he was elected a member of the Liverpool Academy, in which institution he was appointed Professor of Painting, having by this date almost entirely devoted himself to landscape. He exhibited at the Royal Academy in 1851, and was from that time an occasional contributor. A picture by him called 'Harrowing' was also in the International Exhibition of 1862. His landscapes show a truthful feeling for nature, and are highly finished, though somewhat varying in merit. He died in London in 1873.

DAWE, GEORGE, a portrait painter, was born in London in 1781. He was the son of Philip Dawe, the mezzotint-engraver, by whom he was brought up to his own branch of art, but he abandoned it for painting, after having executed a few plates of great merit. In 1819 he went to Russia, where he painted for the Emperor about 400 portraits of the chiefs of the Russian army, who had, with the assistance of the snow, vanquished Napoleon. He became an Associate of the Royal Academy in 1809, and an Academician in 1814. He made much money by his expedition to Russia, but did not live to enjoy it; for he died six weeks after his return to England in 1829, and was buried in St. Paul's Cathedral. His portraits are reckoned good likenesses of the persons, but not expressive of character.

WILLIAM DAVIS

VIEW NEAR HALE

[Collection of W. Coltart, Esq

HENRY DAWSON

ST. PAUL'S FROM THE RIVER

DAWE, HENRY, an engraver and subject painter, was born at Kentish Town, near London, in 1790. He was taught by his father, Philip Dawe, the engraver, and he also studied in the schools of the Royal Academy. He assisted Turner in the 'Liber Studiorum,' and mezzotinted many of his brother's portraits. As a painter, he exhibited at the Society of British Artists, of which he was elected a member in 1830. He died at Windsor in 1848.

DAWE, PHILIP, an engraver in mezzotint, worked under Hogarth about 1760, and must have died about the end of the century. He engraved several subjects after George Henry Morland, and among other portraits by him we have those of Mrs. Yates, in the character of Electra, after Cotes, and Admiral Sir Charles Hardy, after Hudson.

DAWSON, HENRY, a landscape painter, was born in Hull in 1811, but came with his parents to Nottingham when an infant, so that he always regarded the latter as his native town. His parents were poor, and he began life in a Nottingham lace factory. But even while engaged in lace-making he continued to find time for art, and used to paint small pictures, which he sold at first for about half-a-crown each. In 1835 he gave up the lace trade and set up as an artist, his earliest patron being a hairdresser in Nottingham, who possessed a taste for art. In 1844 he removed to Liverpool, where after a time he got into greater repute, and received higher prices for his works. In 1849 he came with his family to London, and settled at Croydon, where some of his best pictures were painted. Among these may be reckoned 'The Wooden Walls of Old England,' exhibited at the British Institution in 1853, 'The Rainbow,' 'The Rainbow at Sea,' 'London Bridge,' and 'London at Sunrise.' With the exception of six lessons from Pyne received in 1838, Henry Dawson was entirely a self-taught artist, and his art shows much originality and careful realism. He studied nature for himself, but he seems in later life to have been moved by Turner's influence to try more brilliant effects than he had before dared. Many of his works indeed are very Turneresque in treatment, though he can scarcely be called an imitator of Turner, for he had a distinct style of his own. Henry Dawson, though painting much, and selling his pictures for high prices in his later life, remained, strange to say, very little known except to artists and connoisseurs until the large and very interesting collection of his works that was made for the Nottingham Exhibition in 1878 brought him wider fame. This exhibition showed him to be a genuine English landscape painter, of no great imaginative or intellectual power, but who delighted in nature, and represented her faithfully to the best of his ability. He died in December, 1878, at Chiswick, where he had for some time resided. M.M.H.

DAX, PAUL, was born in 1503, in the Tyrol. He led a very unsteady life, and after having gained reputation as a painter, he gave up art, and entered the army, engaging in several campaigns and the sieges of Naples, Florence, and Vienna. In 1530 he devoted himself to glass-painting, and his works, which are of considerable merit, are now in the court-house of Innsbruck, and in the town-hall at Ensisheim, Alsace. He also published several maps of his country. His death occurred in 1561.

DAY, ALEXANDER, a miniature painter, was born in 1772. He resided for several years in Rome, whence he brought with him on his return to England in 1800 many fine works by the old masters, which passed into the Angerstein and other collections. Among these were Titian's 'Rape of Ganymede' and 'Venus and Adonis,' Raphael's 'St. Catharine' and 'Madonna, Infant Christ, and St. John' (the Garvagh Raphael), Leonardo da Vinci's 'Christ disputing with the Doctors,' Domenichino's 'St. Jerome and the Angel,' Annibale Carracci's 'Christ appearing to Simon Peter after his Resurrection,' and Gaspard Poussin's 'Landscape with Abraham and Isaac,' which are now in the National Gallery. His miniatures of ladies are particularly graceful. He died at Chelsea in 1841.

DAY, THOMAS, a miniature painter, exhibited at the Royal Academy between the years 1772 and 1778. He also painted water-colour landscapes and drew crayon portraits.

DAYES, EDWARD, a water-colour painter, was born in 1763. He studied under W. Pether, and first exhibited at the Royal Academy in 1786. His works are topographical, drawn in Indian ink, and tinted, with figures introduced. He also painted miniatures, and engraved in mezzotint. He died by his own hand in 1804. Amongst his works are:

> The Royal Procession to St. Paul's in 1789. The Trial of Warren Hastings. Buckingham House, 1790. Ely Cathedral, 1792. Windermere. Keswick Lake. View of Bath (all at South Kensington).

His wife, who exhibited repeatedly at the Royal Academy, was also a painter of miniatures.

DEAN, HUGH PRIMROSE, a landscape painter, was born in Ireland towards the middle of the 18th century, and was known as the 'Irish Claude.' Assisted by Lord Palmerston, he spent several years in Italy, returning in 1779. He was of unprincipled character, and in his latter years his art failed him. He died about 1784. Amongst the works he exhibited at the Spring Gardens Exhibition and at the Royal Academy were:

> View of the Danube, 1768. View of Naples, 1775. Morning, 1778. Evening, 1778. Eruption of Mount Vesuvius, 1779. The Banks of the Tiber, 1780.

DEAN, JOHN, an engraver in mezzotint, was a pupil of Valentine Green. He scraped several plates of portraits and other subjects in a very respectable style, and died in London in 1798. The following are among his best works:

> James, Earl of Abercorn; George, Lord Vernon; after Gainsborough. James Caulfield, Earl of Charlemont; after Livesy. The son of Sir Watkin Williams Wynne, when a child, as St. John; Lady Elizabeth Herbert, afterwards Countess of Carnarvon, with her son; Lady Gertrude Fitzpatrick; after Sir Joshua Reynolds. Elizabeth Hamilton, Countess of Derby; after Romney. The Four Evangelists; after Rubens and Jordaens. St. Anthony of Padua; after Murillo.

DEANE, WILLIAM WOOD, an architectural water-colour painter, was born at Islington in 1825. He entered the schools of the Royal Academy in 1844, where he gained the silver medal of that year. He was at the same time a member of the Institute of British Architects, from which association he received two premiums. Having travelled in Italy, he exhibited at the Royal Academy in 1853 a view of 'St. Peter's, Rome,' and continued for many years an occasional contributor of architectural subjects treated in a pictorial manner. In 1863 he relinquished the profession of an architect, which he had pursued, not very successfully, and became an Associate of the Institute of Painters in Water-Colours, of which in 1867 he was made a member. Here he exhibited until 1870, when he resigned, and in the following year became an

Associate of the old 'Society of Painters in Water-Colours.' He died in 1873. His pictures display individuality and sympathetic blending of colours.

DEARMAN, THOMAS, a landscape and cattle painter, exhibited at the Royal Academy between 1842 and 1856. He lived at Shere, near Guildford, and died young about 1857.

DE BAAN. See DE BAEN.

DE BACKER, FRANS, was a painter of historical subjects and portraits, who practised in Italy and Germany as a portrait painter and engraver from about 1704 to 1752, but it is uncertain whether he belonged to the Dutch or Flemish families of this name. There are a 'Death of Abel,' after Schoonjans, and a portrait of William V., Prince of Orange, after A. Rotterdam, engraved by him. His own Portrait, painted by himself at Rome in 1721, is in the Uffizi at Florence.

DE BACKER, JAQUES, a Flemish historical painter, who was born at Antwerp in 1530, was the son of an artist of no great celebrity, from whom he received his instruction in art. His father dying when he was young, he was taken into the employment of a dealer in pictures, named Palermo; on which account he was sometimes called Jacopo Palermo. Whilst in the employment of this person, he gained a great facility of handling, and, from the practice of copying the works of the great masters, became an excellent colourist. He, however, painted several historical pictures from his own designs, which are highly praised by Van Mander, who states him to have been one of the most promising young painters of his time. Three works, which he particularly commends, represent 'Adam and Eve,' a 'Charity,' and the 'Crucifixion.' The altar-piece of the chapel of the Plantin family, in the cathedral at Antwerp, was painted by this artist: it represents the 'Last Judgment,' and is a grand composition, correctly drawn, and finely coloured. He died at Antwerp in 1560.

DE BACKER, NICOLAAS, who was born at Antwerp in 1648, came to England, and was employed by Kneller as an assistant. He also painted perspective views of English churches. He died in London in 1689.

DEBACQ, CHARLES ALEXANDRE, a French historical and portrait painter, was born in Paris in 1804. He became a pupil of Gros, and was greatly appreciated in his own country. There are several pictures by him at Versailles. He died in Paris in 1853.

DE BAEN, JACOBUS, the son and scholar of Jan De Baen, was born at the Hague in 1673. When he was twenty years of age he came to England, amongst the attendants of King William. The celebrity of his father, and the favour of the court, procured him immediate employment, and he painted the portraits of the Duke of Gloucester and several of the nobility. Notwithstanding this flattering encouragement, his desire of seeing Italy induced him to leave England; and on his way to Rome he visited Florence, and was favoured with the patronage of the grand-duke. On his arrival at Rome he applied himself with much diligence to the study of the works of the great masters, and painted some portraits and conversation pieces, which were much esteemed. He gave promise of surpassing his father in the art, but died at Vienna at the early age of twenty-seven, in 1700. From his gigantic build he was called by his comrades 'Gladiator.'

DE BAEN, JAN, a Dutch portrait painter, was

18

born at Haarlem in 1633. After receiving some instruction from an uncle named Piemans, he was sent to Amsterdam, and placed under the care of Jacob Backer, with whom he remained until he was eighteen years of age. His success in portrait painting was so great that he paid but little attention to the other branches of the art. King Charles II., who had become acquainted with his talents during his residence on the Continent, invited him to England, where he had the honour of painting that monarch, and several of the nobility. He died at the Hague in 1702. Jan De Baen was a great admirer of the works of Van Dyck, whose style he imitated in his pictures. He painted many portraits of distinguished persons of the time, some of which are not inferior to those of Van Dyck. One of his best is that of John Maurice, Prince of Nassau, in the Gallery of the Hague. Louis XIV., after conquering part of Holland, was desirous of having his portrait painted by De Baen, and sent for him to Utrecht for that purpose; but the painter excused himself by observing, that while his country was in mourning, he could not think it proper for him to trace the features of her conqueror.

DE BAETS, ENGEL, a Belgian painter of portraits and architectural subjects, was born at Everghem in 1794. He executed a great number of pictures, most of them views in Ghent and its environs, which are much esteemed. He died at Ghent in 1855.

DE BAILLIU, BAREND, a Flemish engraver, was born at Antwerp about the year 1625. He spent some time in Rome, but returned to Flanders, where he died, although the place and the date are not recorded. His plates, which consist chiefly of portraits, with some historical subjects, are entirely executed with the graver. He engraved four of the plates for the collection of portraits of Cardinals created by Innocent XI. (1676-1689), entitled 'Effigies Cardinalium nunc viventium,' published at Rome; as well as the following prints, on which his name occurs spelled in various ways:

The Saviour between St. Peter of Alcantara and St. Mary Magdalen of Pazzi; *after Lazzaro Baldi.*
St. Peter of Alcantara visited in his cell by the Virgin and Child; *after the same.*
St. Mary Magdalen of Pazzi, with the Virgin raising her Veil; *after the same.*
St. Louis Bertrand; *after G. B. Gaulli.*
Pope Clement X.
The Five Saints canonized by Clement X. in 1671; *after Ciro Ferri.*

DE BAILLIU, PIETER, a Flemish engraver, was born at Antwerp in 1613. After having learned the first principles of engraving in his own country, he visited Italy for improvement, and there engraved some plates. He returned to Antwerp after 1637, and from 1640 to 1660 engraved several of the works of the most celebrated of the Flemish masters, particularly Rubens and Van Dyck. Although by no means equal to Vorsterman, Bolswert, or Pontius, his prints are held in considerable estimation. Meyer's 'Künstler-Lexikon' gives a list of 103 of his engravings, on which his name is found spelled in a variety of ways. The following are his principal works:

PORTRAITS.

Lodovico Pereira de Castro, Envoy at the Peace of Münster.
Claude de Chabot, Envoy to Münster.

Johann Leuber, Envoy to Münster.

Pope Urban VIII.

Jacob Backer, Dutch painter; *after Backer.*

Jan Bylert, painter, of Utrecht; *after Bylert.*

Albert, Prince of Arenberg; *after Van Dyck.*

Lucy, Countess of Carlisle; *after the same.*

Antoine de Bourbon, Comte de Morel, *after the same.*

Honoré d'Urfé, Comte de Châteauneuf; *after the same.*

SUBJECTS AFTER VARIOUS MASTERS.

Heliodorus driven from the Temple; *from a drawing by P. van Lint, after Raphael.*

A Pietà; *after Annibale Carracci.*

St. Michael vanquishing the Devil; *after Guido.*

The Reconciliation of Jacob and Esau; *after Rubens.*

Christ praying in the Garden; *after the same.*

The Dying Magdalen; *after the same.*

The Combat of the Lapithæ; *after the same.*

The Holy Family; *after Theodoor Rombouts.*

The Crucifixion; *after Van Dyck.*

The Virgin in the Clouds; *after the same.*

Rinaldo and Armida; *after the same.*

Susanna and the Elders; *after Marten Pepyn.*

The Scourging of Christ; *after Diepenbeeck.*

Christ crowned with Thorns; *after the same.*

The Discovery of the true Cross by St. Helena; *after P. van Lint.*

Theodosius carrying the true Cross before St. Ambrose; *after the same.*

Christ bound to the Pillar, with Angels holding the Instruments of the Passion; *after J. Thomas.*

St. Anastasius reading; *after Rembrandt.*

DE BAST, DOMINICUS, a Belgian amateur marine painter, was born at Ghent in 1781, and died there in 1842. Although not an artist by profession, his works are highly appreciated by connoisseurs.

DEBAY, AUGUSTE HYACINTHE, a son of the eminent sculptor Jean Baptiste Joseph Debay, though really a sculptor, began life as an historical painter. He was born at Nantes in 1804, and in 1817, when only thirteen years of age, sent his first portraits to the Salon. After studying under Gros, he obtained the 'Prix de Rome' in 1823. Soon after this he gave up painting for sculpture, which he studied under his father, and in which he was very successful. His death occurred in Paris in 1865. Some of his historical paintings are at Versailles.

DE BEER, AART, a Flemish painter of historical subjects and portraits, was a son of Jan De Beer. He was born at Antwerp in 1490, and admitted into the Guild of St. Luke in 1529. Religious subjects and designs for glass-painting were his special pursuits. He died at Antwerp in 1542.

DE BEER, CORNELIS, was a Flemish painter, who went to Spain about 1630, and who painted easel pictures of considerable merit. In the Capuchin church at Murcia is preserved his 'Triumph of the Holy Sacrament,' a composition of many figures with a landscape background. His daughter, MARIA EUGENIA, practised the art of engraving at Madrid, in the middle of the 17th century, with considerable success. Besides an excellent frontispiece for Basilio Varen's 'Guerra de Flandes,' she executed a good portrait of Prince Baltasar Carlos, and the plates for the work of Don Gregorio de Tapia y Salcedo on 'Horsemanship.'

DE BEER, JOOST, was a native of Utrecht, who studied under Frans Floris. He painted historical pictures with some success, and was patronized by the Bishop of Tournai. He entered the Utrecht Guild in 1550, and died in 1596.

DE BEIJER, JAN, who was born at Aarau in Switzerland in 1705, went whilst young to Amsterdam and studied under C. Pronk and J. M. Quink-

hard. He painted many excellent pictures of Dutch towns, some of which have been engraved by H. Spilman, P. van Liender, and others. He was still living in 1768.

DE BIE, ADRIAEN, a Flemish painter, was born at Lierre, near Antwerp, in 1594. He received his first instruction in art from an obscure artist named Wouter Abts. At eighteen years of age he went to Paris, where he studied for some time under Rudolf Schoof, a Fleming, who was painter to Louis XIII. He afterwards visited Rome, where he remained eight years. In 1623, he returned to Flanders, and was much employed for the churches and in painting portraits. His most esteemed work was a picture of St. Eloy, in the collegiate church of St. Gomarus at Lierre. He died after 1661. He was the father of Cornelis De Bie, who has celebrated the works of the painters of his country in Flemish verse, under the title of 'Het Gulden Kabinet van de edele vrye Schilderkonst.' His works are usually marked with one or other of the accompanying monograms.

DE BIE, JACOB and MARCUS. See DE BYE.

DE BISSCHOP, JAN, a designer and engraver, who was born at the Hague, in 1646, was brought up to the law; and, according to Houbraken, practised in the courts in Holland. His favourite amusement was drawing, and his performances excited the admiration of the artists of his time. He excelled in copying the pictures of the most esteemed masters, in small coloured drawings, very well drawn and highly finished. As an engraver, he is more deserving of notice, and he has left a great number of plates, principally etched, and harmonized with the graver, in a free and pleasing manner. There is great relief and richness of effect in his prints. His most important work was a series of 157 engravings from celebrated antique statues and sketches by eminent painters, entitled, 'Paradigmata graphices variorum Artificum,' published at the Hague in 1671. This engraver Latinized his name into Episcopius, for which reason he marked his plates with the cipher

He died at Amsterdam, in 1686. Other good prints by him are:

A Bacchanalian subject.

Christ and the Samaritan Woman; *after Annibale Carracci.*

Joseph distributing Corn to the Egyptians; *after B. Breenbergh.*

The Martyrdom of St. Lawrence; *after the same.*

DE BLOIS, ABRAHAM, a Dutch engraver, who flourished from the year 1690 to 1720. He worked chiefly for the booksellers, by whom he was much employed. Among other portraits, he engraved that of Anthony van Leeuwenhoek, the celebrated physician, which was prefixed to his works published in 1695, and which is executed in a neat but formal style. He also executed part of the plates for the 'Figures de la Bible,' from the designs of Picart and others, published at Amsterdam in 1720.

DE BLOOT, PIETER, a native of Holland, flourished about 1650. He painted droll scenes, drunken frolics, and the quarrels of the peasantry, with much truth to nature. His works, which are somewhat rare, are much prized in Holland. De Bloot died at Antwerp in 1667.

DEBON, FRANÇOIS HIPPOLYTE, a French historical painter, was the son of Madame Sophie Debon, an artist upon porcelain, who was born in Paris in 1787, and died there in 1838. He was born in Paris in 1807, and studied first under Gros and afterwards under Abel de Pujol. One of his most important works was 'The Entrance of William the Conqueror into London,' which was exhibited at the Salon of 1855, and afterwards placed in the Luxembourg Gallery. His death occurred in Paris in 1872.

DE BRAEKELEER, FERDINANDUS, historical painter, was born at Antwerp in 1792. He was the son of Jean Ferdinand Joseph de Braekeleer and of Jeanne Bernardine Antoinette Seghers. He studied at the Antwerp Academy, and under M. J. van Bree. In 1819 he won the grand prize of the Academy, with the pension for Rome. He spent three years in Italy, painting historical pictures ('Healing of Tobias,' 'Esau and Isaac') in the manner of David. After his return to Antwerp he perfected a manner of his own, in which he painted genre subjects, scenes from Belgian history, &c. He died in 1883, at Antwerp. Among his pupils were Leys, Jacobs, De Block, and others. Pictures by him are in the Galleries of Antwerp, Berlin, and Munich.

DE BRAEKELEER, FERDINANDUS, son of the last named, was born at Antwerp in 1829, and had shown some promise as a genre painter when he died at the age of twenty-eight in 1857. Another brother, HENRI, born in 1840 at Antwerp, was a painter of genre, and died in 1888.

DE BRAUWERE, PASCHATIUS, was an engraver of whom little is known. Brulliot describes the only etching by him known; it is, he says, in the manner of Guido, and represents the executioner placing the head of John the Baptist in a dish held by the servant of Herodias; these two figures occupy the foreground, and Herodias is behind them. It bears the date 1631.

DE BRAY, DIRK, a painter and wood-engraver, was born at Haarlem in 1640, and specially depicted flowers, birds, and portraits. There is a small woodcut of the portrait of his father, Salomon De Bray, by this artist, dated 1664, which is very spiritedly executed. He also engraved 12 prints of fishes, poultry, hogs, &c., dated 1672, and 16 of birds, flowers, and figures, dated 1660. He was still living in 1675.

DE BRAY, JACOB, a Dutch painter, was born at Haarlem about the year 1625. He was the son of Salomon De Bray, an obscure portrait painter, by whom he was instructed. Van Mander mentions him as a reputable historical painter, and extols a picture by him at Amsterdam, representing 'David playing on the Harp, with a number of Priests and Levites.' He excelled in drawing on paper with black and red chalk, and his works of that description were much esteemed by collectors. They are often signed with this monogram, Jacob De Bray died in 1680. Writers, however, differ very much respecting the dates in the lives of this artist and of his son of the same names.

DE BRAY, JAN, an historical painter and etcher, was a brother of Dirk De Bray, and, like him, born at Haarlem. Two pictures by him, the 'Reception of the Orphans' and 'Prince Frederick Henry in the Town Hall,' are preserved at the Haarlem Orphanage, and others are in the Museums of that city and of Amsterdam. Of his etchings, mention is made of 'John the Baptist in the Wilderness.' He died in 1697.

DE BRAY, SALOMON, a poet and architect as well as a painter, was born at Haarlem in 1597, and died at the same place in 1664. He has left some paintings in the Orange Hall of the palace called the 'House in the Wood,' at the Hague.

DEBRET, JEAN BAPTISTE, was born in Paris in 1768, and was instructed by David. He painted historical subjects, and completed his studies at Rome. He then returned to France, where he lived some years, and afterwards went to Brazil and became professor at the Academy at Rio de Janeiro. His works chiefly represent scenes in the life of Napoleon. In 1836 he published a 'Voyage pittoresque et historique du Brésil.' He died in Paris in 1848.

DE BRIE. See DE BRY.

DE BROEN, GERRIT, a Dutch engraver, flourished about the year 1720. He was principally employed in engraving portraits for the booksellers. Among others, we have the portrait of Pieter Poicet, after Nicolaas Verkolje.

DE BRUIN, CORNELIS, called at Rome ADONIS, a Dutch portrait painter, was born at the Hague in 1652, and was instructed by Theodoor van der Schuur. His passion for travelling led him when he was young to Italy, where he passed some time at Rome with Robert Duval; he afterwards went to Venice, where he studied for some years under Johann Karl Loth. He painted portraits with success; but is more distinguished by the publication of his travels through Persia, India, and other countries, with plates from his own designs. He died at Zijde-Balen, near Utrecht, in 1726 or 1727.

DE BRUYN, ABRAHAM, a Flemish engraver, was born at Antwerp in 1538. He established himself at Cologne about the year 1577, and died there very old. He is ranked among the Little Masters, on account of his plates being usually very small. He engraved in the manner of Wierix, and worked entirely with the graver, in a neat and formal style, but his drawing is far from correct. It is believed that he worked also as a goldsmith. He usually marked his plates with one of these ciphers, $A\!\!\!\!\!\!\!-\!\!\!\!D\!B$. $D\!B$ or $A\!D\!B$. Among his portraits, and prints of small friezes of hunting, hawking, &c., which are esteemed for their neatness, may be mentioned :

Philip Louis, Elector Palatine. Anne, his consort. Albert Frederick, Duke of Prussia. Eleonora, his Duchess. William, Duke of Juliers. Mary, his Duchess. John Sambucus, physician; a woodcut. Charles IX., King of France. Anna, daughter of the Emperor Charles V. Moses and the Burning Bush. Four plates of the Evangelists, 1578. Christ and the Samaritan Woman. A Philosopher. The Seven Planets, 1569. The Five Senses. A set of one hundred plates, entitled 'Imperii ac Sacerdotii Ornatus. Diversarum item Gentium peculiaris Vestitus.' 1577-78. (*His best work.*) Reissued, with some additional plates, and entitled 'Omnium pene Europæ, Asiæ, Aphricæ atque Americæ Gentium Habitus,' 1581. Seventy-six plates of Horsemen, 1575. A set of small friezes of Hunting and Hawking, 1565. A set of twelve plates of Animals, 1583. A set of Arabesque Patterns. Pyramus and Thisbe; *after Frans Floris.* The Resurection of Lazarus; *after Crispen van den Broeck.*

DE BRUYN, NICOLAES, was the son of Abraham De Bruyn, and was born at Antwerp about 1570. Although he was instructed by his father in engraving, he did not follow his example, either in the style of his execution, or in the size of his plates. He appears to have studied and to have formed his manner from the works of Lucas van Leyden. His compositions are abundant, but he wanted taste in the selection of his forms. He finished his plates very neatly with the graver; but there is not much effect in his prints, from his ignorance of the management of the chiaroscuro. Notwithstanding this defect, which was very general at the time in which he lived, his works possess considerable merit. He died at Amsterdam in 1656. He signed his plates sometimes with his initials *N. de B.*, and sometimes with one of the following

monograms, **AB PINX. AB, AGB, NB, AB, RB**

The following are his principal works:

SUBJECTS FROM HIS OWN DESIGNS.

Adam and Eve in Paradise. 1600.
Adam and Eve standing under the Tree of the Forbidden Fruit. 1631.
The Israelites with the Daughters of Madian.
The great Festival of the Jews after six years' bondage. 1617.
King Balak speaking to the Prophet Balaam.
The Prophet Jeremiah, with a Lion. 1608.
The Vision of Ezekiel. 1600.
David and Goliath. 1609.
David meeting Abigail. 1608.
The Queen of Sheba before Solomon. 1621.
The Idolatry of Solomon. 1606.
Nebuchadnezzar's Dream.
Daniel in the Lions' Den.
Susannah accused by the Elders.
Susannah's Acquittal.
The Stoning of the Two Elders.
The Nativity of Christ. 1621.
The Adoration of the Magi. 1608.
The Repose in Egypt. 1621.
The Murder of the Innocents. 1644.
St. John preaching in the Wilderness.
Christ preaching on the Mount.
The Centurion imploring Christ.
Christ's Entrance into Jerusalem.
Christ bearing his Cross. 1617.
The Crucifixion. 1610.
The Resurrection. 1631.
St. Paul preaching. 1621.
St. Hubert. 1614.
Orpheus playing, surrounded by Animals.
A Family of Peasants.
A Landscape, with Lions, Tigers, and Stags.
A Spanish Assembly in a Forest.
A set of six Patterns for Goldsmiths.
A set of twelve of Quadrupeds. 1621.
A set of twelve of Birds.
A set of thirteen of Fishes.

SUBJECTS AFTER VARIOUS MASTERS.

St. John preaching in the Wilderness; *after Lucas van Leyden.*
A Miracle wrought at the Tomb of St. James; *after the same.* 1600.
The Golden Age; *after A. Bloemaert.*
Four Landscapes, with historical figures; *after G. van Coninxlo.*
Three Landscapes, with figures; *after D. Vinckebooms.*
A Landscape, with a Stag-hunt; *after Jan Brueghel.*
A Landscape, with Moses defending the Daughters of Jethro; *after J. Bol.*
Four of the Seasons; *after M. De Vos.*
St. Cecilia; *after Raphael.*
A Knight on Horseback, accompanied by Time, and followed by the Devil; *after A. Dürer.* 1618.

DE BRY, DIRK, or THEODORUS, a German engraver, was born at Liége in 1528. He resided chiefly at Frankfort, where he carried on the busi-ness of a print and bookseller. It is not known by whom he was instructed in the art of engraving, but from his style he appears to have paid particular attention to the works of Hans Sebald Beham. About the year 1587 he visited England, and at the suggestion of the great cosmographer Richard Hakluyt, who procured him many designs after nature, he published a large collection of voyages and travels in French, German, and Latin. He died at Frankfort in 1598. This laborious artist worked almost wholly with the graver, in a neat, free style, well adapted to the subjects of which he made choice, such as processions and ceremonials, containing a great number of figures, which he drew correctly, and to which he gave great spirit and expression. He usually marked his plates *T. B.*, or with the cipher **B**. He engraved the plates for the four first volumes of Boissard's 'Romanæ urbis Topographia et Antiquitates,' 1597-98; the two last volumes were completed by his sons, Johannes Theodorus and Johannes Israel De Bry. We have also the following prints by him:

St. John in the Wilderness; an etching; very scarce.
A Dance of Cavaliers and Ladies.
A Dance of Men and Women Peasants.
A Design for a Saucer, a Head representing Pride and Folly, surrounded with grotesque subjects; a circular plate; scarce.
Another Design for a Saucer, a Head of the Duke of Alva, with the Mask of Folly, with grotesque subjects; circular; scarce.
Another Design for a Saucer, the Head of William of Nassau, with grotesque figures, indicative of Prudence; circular; scarce.
A Medallion of Scanderbeg.
The companion; *Donice Scanderbegi Uxor.*
The Nine Muses.
'The Procession at the Obsequies of Sir Philip Sidney; drawn and invented by T[homas] L[ant], Gent., and engraven on copper by Derick Theodore de Brie, in the city of London,' 1587; thirty-four plates.
The Procession of the Knights of the Garter in 1576; twelve plates, dated 1578.
A set of Portraits, entitled 'Icones Virorum illustrium.' 1597-99.
The plates for Hariot's 'A briefe and true report of the new found land of Virginia,' published at Frankfort in 1590.
The plates for Las Casas' narrative of the cruelties of the Spaniards in America; entitled 'Narratio Regionum Indicarum per Hispanos quosdam devastatarum verissima.' 1598.
The plates for his great work, entitled, 'Collectiones Peregrinationum in Indiam Orientalem et Indiam Occidentalem,' in twenty-five parts, folio. 1590—1634.
Eighty-five plates of 'Emblemata.' 1592.

DE BRY, JOHANNES THEODORUS, the elder son and pupil of Dirk De Bry, was born at Liége in 1561. He greatly assisted his father in the important works in which he was engaged, as, for instance, the 'Florilegium novum,' which was published at Frankfort in 1612, and with the assistance of his brother Johannes Israel, he completed the two volumes of Boissard's 'Romanæ urbis Topographia et Antiquitates,' which were left unfinished at his father's death. He also published 'Emblemata secularia,' 1596, and added considerably to the collection of Portraits of Illustrious Persons, begun by his father. He died at Frankfort in 1623. His prints are signed with the initials *J. T. B.*, or with one of these monograms, **ITB, ITB, ITB.**

21

We have also the following prints by him:

Portrait of Gerard Mercator, geographer.
Portrait of Daniel Specklin.
Four plates of the Elements; *J. T. de Bry, inv. et fec.*
The Marriage of Rebekah; *after Baldassare Peruzzi.*
A March of Soldiers; a frieze; *after Titian.*
Another March of Soldiers, conducting Prisoners, with Death riding on a Horse; a frieze, called the Triumph of Death; *after the same.*
The Little Village Fair; *after H. S. Beham.*
The Fountain of Youth; *after the same.*
The Triumph of Bacchus; *after Giulio Romano.*
The Venetian Ball; *after Theodore Bernard;* a circular plate.
The Golden Age; from the print engraved by *N. De Bruyn; after A. Bloemaert.*

JOHANNES ISRAEL DE BRY, of whom mention is made in the two preceding articles, is recorded as having died in 1611.

DEBUCOURT, PHILIBERT LOUIS. See BUCOURT.

DE' BUONI. See DEI BUONI.

DE BUYTENWEG, WILLEM, (or BUYTEWECH,) a Dutch painter and engraver, was born at Rotterdam about the year 1600, but lived at Haarlem, and was instructed by H. Maartensz. He painted conversation-pieces and landscapes in a style which gained him much reputation. Houbraken designates him 'Geestige Willem' (William the Gay), and under this appellation he is to be found in the collection of Catalogues of Pictures by Hoet and Terwesten, as a painter of conversations and familiar scenes. He died in 1640. Some of his pictures have been engraved by G. H. Scheyndel and E. van de Velde. His principal work, as a painter, was 'The Triumph of William, Prince of Orange,' 1623, engraved by C. Kittenstein. He etched some plates from his own designs, in a pleasing style, among which are the following:

Two of Women going to Market, one with Vegetables, the other with Fowls.
Seven of Dresses of Noblemen.
Six of Dresses of Ladies.
Ten of Landscapes, with Ruins and Figures.

DE BYE, JACOB, (or DE BIE,) a Flemish engraver, was born in 1581 at Antwerp, where he followed the profession of a picture-dealer and antiquary. From the style of his plates, it is not improbable that he learned the art of engraving in the school of the Collaerts. He worked wholly with the graver; his execution is neat and firm, and his drawing tolerably correct. In conjunction with the Collaerts, he engraved some of the set of fifty plates of the 'Life, Passion, and Resurrection of Christ,' after the designs of Martin De Vos. Several of the plates in the 'Life of the Virgin,' from the designs of the same painter, were executed by this artist, together with Philip and Theodoor Galle. He died in Paris about 1650. The following are his principal prints:

The Medals of the Roman Emperors, in the collection of the Duke d'Arschot. 1617.
The Portraits of the Kings of France, for Mezeray's History; fifty-eight plates.
The Descendants of the House of De Croy; about sixty plates.
Portrait of Francis I.; *after M. De Vos.*
Christ healing Peter's Wife's Mother; fine; for Collaert's set.
The Resurrection of Lazarus; fine; for the same set.

DE BYE, MARCUS, (or DE BIE,) a Dutch painter and engraver, was born at the Hague in 1612. He was instructed in painting by J. van der Does, and produced some landscapes, with animals, in the style

22

of that master, which are not without merit; but he is chiefly deserving of notice for the excellent etchings he has left us of animals, after the designs of Paulus Potter and Markus Gerard. He died in 1670. We have by him:

The fat Spitzhund.
The Mule-driver.
Three sets, of eight each, of Cows and Oxen; *after Potter.*
A set of sixteen of Sheep; *after the same.*
A set of sixteen of Goats; *after the same.*
A set of sixteen of Lions, Leopards, Wolves, Bears, &c.; *after the same.*
A set of sixteen of the Natural History of the Bear; *after Markus Gerard.* 1664.

DECAGNY, VIRGINIE POLYXÈNE AUGUSTINE PHILIPPE. See DALLEMAGNE.

DE CAISNE, HENRI, a Belgian historical and portrait painter, was born at Brussels in 1799. As early as 1814 he began to study painting under François, and in 1818 upon the advice of David he went to Paris and entered the studio of Girodet, whence he removed to that of Gros. Several pictures by him are at Versailles; among them are the 'Entry of Charles VII. into Rouen' (1838), and the 'Institution of the Order of St. John of Jerusalem' (1842). In 1839 he completed his colossal work, 'Les Belges Illustres.' He died in Paris in 1852. Among his best works are:

PORTRAITS.

The Queen of the Belgians. 1835.
The Duke of Orleans. 1833.
The Princess Clementina of Orleans. 1833.
Madame Malibran as Desdemona. 1831.
Victor Schoelcher. 1833.
Alphonse de Lamartine. 1839.

HISTORICAL AND OTHER SUBJECTS.

An Indian Family in Exile. 1824.
Milton dictating 'Paradise Lost' to his Daughter. 1827.
Charles I. taking leave of his Children. 1827.
Cromwell and his Daughter. 1829.
Mater Dolorosa. 1835.
Hagar in the Desert. 1836.
The Guardian Angel. 1836. (*His best work.*)
Charity. 1839.
The Adoration of the Shepherds. 1841.

DECAMPS, ALEXANDRE GABRIEL, a French historical, landscape, animal, and genre painter, was born in Paris in 1803. When a child, he was sent into a retired part of Picardy, and for three years ran wild in the society of peasants. He thus acquired a distaste for serious study, which subsequently proved a great hindrance to his artistic development, and he contracted an aversion to discipline and to the ordinary habits of polite society. He subsequently studied desultorily in the studios of Bouchot, Abel de Pujol, David, and Ingres, and about this period produced many small genre works, pictures of dogs, horses, cattle, &c. To a man of his disposition, travel had a great charm, and he spent some years in the south of France, in Switzerland, in Italy, and in the Levant. It was in the East that he found the subjects most suited to his genius, and his oriental pictures were the first of a class in which there have been many followers. Decamps' constant aim, however, was to obtain fame by historical painting. In 1834 he produced a 'Defeat of the Cimbri by Marius,' and in 1845 a series of designs illustrating the life of Samson. But he met with no encouragement, and he complained bitterly of his disappointment. He was awarded medals at the Salon in 1831 and again in 1834; but his works were subse-

A. G. DECAMPS

Hanfstängl photo]   [Wallace Gallery, London

RELEASED FROM SCHOOL

A. G. DECAMPS

THE WATERING-PLACE

quently seldom exhibited, and they were generally sold without appearing in public. He died in 1860, through a fall from his horse while hunting at Fontainebleau. Decamps was a thorough member of the Romantic school. His rebellion against systematic training in his youth precluded him from obtaining success in historic art. The representation of wild scenery and objects was his *forte*, and in this he was aided in a marked degree by his great mastery of light and shade. Amongst his chief works are:

Soldier of the Vizier's Guard. 1827. (*Hertford House.*)
Turkish Patrol, Smyrna. 1831. (*Hertford House.*)
Turkish Children near a fountain. 1833. (*Duke d'Aumale.*)
Bertrand and Raton. (*Duke d'Aumale.*)
The Finding of Moses. 1837.
Joseph sold by his Brethren. 1839.
Turkish Execution. 1839. (*Hertford House.*)
Children with Turtles. 1839.
Village Street in the Papal States. 1839.
Joshua commanding the Sun.
The Guardians of the Sepulchre.
The Miraculous Draught of Fishes. (*Hertford House.*)
Turkish School. } 1846. (*Fodor Museum,*
The Shepherd's Return. } *Amsterdam.*)
Souvenir of Turkey in Asia. }
The Little Pastry-Cooks.
Avenue in a Park. (*Marseilles Museum.*)
Eliezer and Rebecca. 1851.
Towing-Horses. 1842. (*Louvre, Paris.*)
The Caravan, *a sketch.* (*Louvre, Paris.*)
Huntsman and Dogs at fault. (*Fodor Museum, Amsterdam.*)   O.J.D.

DE CAUWER, EMIL, was a painter of architectural subjects, born at Ghent in 1828. He was a pupil of his father, Joseph De Cauwer. His pictures are characterized by truth and very careful execution, but they are lacking in artistic effect. Amongst them may be noted the 'Church of St. Martin at Oudenarde,' the 'Town Hall at Oudenarde,' and the 'New Synagogue at Berlin.' He died at Berlin in 1873.

DE CAUWER, JOSEPH, a Belgian painter, was born at Beveren-Waes in 1779. He studied at the Academies of Antwerp and Ghent, at the latter of which he became eventually a professor. He painted portraits and historical subjects, and many of his pupils rose to eminence. His 'Prometheus,' dated 1832, is in the gallery at Ghent, his 'Death of Our Lord,' in the church of St. Bavon, and a 'Descent from the Cross,' in that of St. Nicolas. He died at Ghent in 1854.

DE CAYLUS, ANNE CLAUDE PHILIPPE, COMTE, (DE TUBIÈRES, DE GRIMOARD, DE PESTELS, DE LEVI,) engraver, painter, writer, and collector. He was born October 31, 1692. His mother was the celebrated beauty, the Marquise de Caylus, cousin of Madame de Maintenon. When a mere lad he was thrown into contact with artists, and learned to appreciate matters of art. His life-long intimacy with Watteau began in 1711, at M. De Crozat's. He was sent on foreign service, and was present at the siege of Freiburg in 1713. In 1714 he was in Rome. The following year he journeyed to the East, and did not return to Paris till 1717. His travels gave him the opportunity for studying the treasures of art in the great galleries and churches. He became an enthusiastic collector of antiquities, medals, curios of all kinds, and drawings. The latter he copied with great care, and was speedily distinguished as a draughtsman. He turned his attention next to engraving, and gained great facility and success in that art. Mariette speaks of his "vivacity of manner." He had, as was usual among the protectors of artists, his little côterie of good fellows, including Bouchardon, Duclos, Fagan, Collé, C. Coypel, and Watteau. He was elected Honorary Councillor-Amateur at the Academy on November 24, 1731. In 1732 he was at Florence with Gaburri, who spoke in the very highest terms of him and of his skill. He exercised a great influence upon the art of his time by his talent, his example, and his personality. His engravings are marked by truthfulness of design and fineness in the earlier stages of work. His coloured drawings and oil paintings were careful copies, or adaptations, of the work of the painters of the Fêtes Galantes. He had also great admiration for the style of Bouchardon. As a writer, in addition to the biography of Watteau (1748), he wrote the lives of C. Coypel, Mignard, Le Moyne, and other painters (1715–1757), and of Bouchardon (1762). He died in Paris September 5, 1765. Among his engravings were the following:

More than two hundred plates; *after the best pictures in the Royal Galleries.*
Collection of Heads; *after drawings by Rubens and Van Dyck, in the Crozat Gallery.*
Suite of Heads; *after drawings by Leonardo da Vinci, in M. Mariette's Cabinet.*
Six plates, History of Joseph; *after Rembrandt.*
Several plates, Life of Christ; *after Raphael.*
Twenty-four plates; *after 'Caricatures' by C. Gillot.*
Love the Teacher, and Goddess in Clouds; *after C. Coypel.*
Venus wounded by Love, Venus and Cupid, Acis and Galatea, Le Médecin, and others; *after Watteau.* (Sixty-eight plates.)
Fifty-eight plates; *after Boucher.*
Venus restraining Cupid, Five Senses, Fêtes Galantes, and others; *after Bouchardon.*
Plates after Baccio Bandinelli, Guercino, Titian, the three Carracci, Zuccari, J. Cesari, Lafage, and others.
More than three hundred heads from antique gems, and many reproductions of coloured drawings, ancient and modern, in the Royal Galleries.
(*Many examples are in the Louvre.*)

DECKER, C., was a German engraver, who, about the middle of the 17th century, went from Nuremberg to Amsterdam, and there learned the art from Romeyn De Hooghe. He appears to have been much employed by the booksellers, and his plates are often executed in a coarse, harsh style. They are principally executed from his own designs; and among his best are those engraved for Kircher's 'Turris Babel,' published at Amsterdam in 1679. He marked his plates with his name or with the cipher ⅅ.

DECKER, I. DE. See DE DECKER.

DECKER, JOHANN STEPHAN, a French painter, was born at Colmar in 1784. At the age of twenty he went to Paris, where he studied under David and Krapf, but at the end of seven years he returned to his native city. In 1821 he settled at Vienna, and was much employed at the court in teaching drawing and in the execution of miniatures and water-colour paintings. He died at Vienna in 1844.

DECKER, PAUL, an architect and engraver, who was born at Nuremberg in 1677, designed and engraved for Andreas Schlüter in Berlin, and was by him instructed in architecture. He died in 1713. His son, PAUL DECKER, excelled in painting history and portraits, and was for three years director of the Academy at Nuremberg. He died in 1742.

23

DE CLÉ, Cornelis, a Flemish historical painter, who was a native of Antwerp, was received into the guild of St. Luke in that city in 1660-1661. In 1690 he painted for the 'Sodalité des Hommes mariés,' a picture representing the 'Mount of Olives,' as well as the figures of Christ and Pilate. He died in 1724.

DE CLERCK, Hendrik, who was born at Brussels about 1570, was a pupil of Marten De Vos, and imitated that master. He painted historical subjects, of which there are several in the churches of the Netherlands; but his small pictures, in which he may be compared to Rottenhammer and Van Balen, are more esteemed. He died about 1629. Among his best works are:

Brussels.	*Museum.*	Holy Family (triptych).
"	"	Christ calling little Children to Him.
"	*St. James.*	Crucifixion.
"	*Notre-Dame.*	Holy Family.
"	"	Resurrection.
Vienna.	*Gallery.*	Cephalus and Procris (*in a Forest Landscape by Alsloot*). 1608.

DE COCK, Frans, a Flemish ecclesiastic, was born at Antwerp in 1643. His love for art led him to visit Rome, and after his return to Antwerp in 1662, all his leisure time was devoted to drawing and painting. Although but an amateur, his portraits were very successful. He died in 1709.

DE COCK, Jan Claus, a Flemish engraver, flourished about the year 1660. His name is affixed to an etching representing the 'Martyrdom of a Saint.' It is executed in a bold masterly style, and appears to be the production of a painter.

DE COCKQ, Paul Joseph, a Flemish historical painter, was born at Bruges in 1724. He was a pupil of Matthias De Visch, and became Director of the Academy at Bruges in 1775. He died in his native city in 1801. The following works by him are in the Bruges Academy:

The Holy Trinity.
Apollo crowning Poetry and Music.
Landscape with old Monuments; *after Canaletto.*

DE COENE, Jean Henri, a Belgian painter of genre and historical subjects, was born at Nederbrakel in 1798. He was a pupil of David and of Paelinck, and became professor in the Brussels Academy. He died in that city in 1866. His picture of the 'Incredulity of St. Thomas' gained him the prize in 1827.

DE CONINCK (or Coningh). See De Koninck.

DE' CONTI, Bernardino. See Dei Conti.

DE CORT, Hendrik, a Flemish landscape painter, was born in 1742 at Antwerp, where he studied. He settled in England, and, from 1790, exhibited many works at the Royal Academy. He died in London in 1810. His landscapes, previous to his settling in England, were embellished with figures and animals painted by Ommeganck and P. van Regemorter. They are much in the Italian taste, with views of cities and ancient ruins, pleasingly coloured and neatly finished. In the Belvedere at Vienna there is by him a 'View of the old Castle of Temsch on the Scheldt at Antwerp' (1774).

DE COSTER, Adam, was a native of Antwerp, and is supposed to have been a disciple of Theodoor Rombouts. He painted historical subjects and portraits with considerable skill; but he particularly excelled in depicting gallant assemblies and festivals, which are ingeniously composed, and coloured

with great force and vigour. We have a fine print of a 'Concert,' engraved by L. Vorsterman, after a painting by this artist.

DE COSTER, Dominicus, the son of the painter and poet Pieter Balten, was born at Antwerp in 1560. At an early period of his life he settled at Augsburg, where he assumed the name of De Coster or Custos, and formed a considerable establishment as a print-seller. He died in that city in 1612. He engraved several plates in a neat but somewhat formal style. Among them are:

A set of the effigies of the German Emperors. 1601.
Fourteen Plates, entitled 'Effigies piorum ac doctorum aliquot virorum.' 1594.
Twenty-eight Plates, entitled 'Tirolensium principum comitum genuinæ Icones.' 1599.
Sixty-four Portraits of the Fugger Family. 1593.
Edward VI.
Marco Bragadini; *after J. von Aachen.* 1591.
Charles III., Duke of Lorraine. 1597.
Dorothea, Duchess of Lorraine.
Pope Sixtus V.
Bust of Sigismund, Prince of Moldavia; *after J von Aachen.*
Maria Christina Carolina, his consort.
Cosmo de' Medici. 1609.
Rudolph II., Emperor of Germany.
Four Plates of the Prodigal Son; *D. Custodis inv. et fec.*
Judith with the Head of Holofernes; *after J. von Aachen.*
Christoph Fugger; *after the same.*
Georg Basta; *after the same.*

His three sons, Raphael, David, and Jakob, were also engravers; but the first only obtained any celebrity.

DE COSTER, Pieter, a painter and engraver of Antwerp, is usually known as Balthazar, or Balten, or Baltens (the shortened form of Baltenssone, *i.e.* the son of Balten, Balthazar). His father was Balten Janssone de Coster, a painter. Pieter entered the Guild of St. Luke at Antwerp in 1540, and became its Dean in 1569. He died about 1598. He painted landscapes, village festivals, and fairs, in the style of Pieter Brueghel. His small figures are correctly drawn and neatly touched, and his landscapes are painted with great precision. He engraved portraits, and also a sacred piece, 'Suffer Little Children to come unto Me,' after Ambrosius Francken.

DE CRAEYER, Gaspar, a Flemish painter, was born at Antwerp in 1582. He was first instructed in the art by Raphael van Coxie of Brussels, an artist of little repute, whom he soon surpassed. Taking for his guide the works of the able artists of his country, and indefatigable in his study of nature, he gave early proof of his ability in some public works, so that he was received a member of the Guild in 1607. His paintings also attracted the notice of the court of Brussels, and he was engaged to paint the portrait of the Cardinal-Infant Don Ferdinand, the Governor of the Low-Countries, to be sent to his brother, the King of Spain. This work gave so much satisfaction, that he was appointed painter to the court, with a considerable pension, and was also employed in the churches and public edifices. If De Craeyer had only looked for emolument, this flattering patronage, and the applause of the great, would have satisfied his ambition, and secured his fortune by fixing him at the court. But intent solely on excelling in his art, and desirous of that repose and tranquillity so essential to his work, he resigned his situation at Brussels, and sought the retirement he longed for, by removing to Ghent. This retreat did not diminish the reputation he had acquired, and he continued to receive commissions from every part of the country. It was at this time that he painted his fine picture for the refectory of the abbey of Affleghem, which is one of his most celebrated works. It represents the 'Centurion dismounting from his horse to prostrate himself before Christ.' It was this admirable picture that procured for him the flattering homage of Rubens, who, on beholding it, exclaimed aloud, "Craeyer, nobody will surpass you." The churches of the principal cities in Flanders and Brabant are decorated with a surprising number of the works of this master, who spent a long life in unremitting labour. The biographers of the Flemish painters have not hesitated to place De Craeyer on a level with Rubens and Van Dyck. Although this high compliment may be rather strained, he is undoubtedly entitled to rank next after them among the ablest artists of that school.

His compositions are learned and judicious; rejecting all superfluity and ostentation, he aimed at the higher qualities of correctness and simplicity. Less daring than Rubens, he is always correct; and, although he never soared to the height of that aspiring genius, his works possess both grandeur and dignity. His colouring is chaste and tender, resembling in its carnations the clear tinting of Van Dyck. He died at Ghent in 1669. The following are the principal among his numerous works, in which the landscapes are painted by De Vadder and L. Achtschellinck:

Amsterdam.	Museum.	The Taking down from the Cross.
Antwerp.	Museum.	Elijah in the Desert.
Berlin.	Gallery.	Christ at Emmaus.
Brussels.	Museum.	The Miraculous Draught of Fishes.
"	"	St. Paul and St. Anthony as Hermits.
"	"	The Blessed Virgin as Protectress of the 'Grand-Seorment de l'Arbalète.'
Ghent.	S. Michael.	Ascension of St. Catharine.
"	Museum.	Judgment of Solomon.
"	"	Martyrdom of St. Blaise.
Lille.	Museum.	Martyrdom of a Man by burying alive.
Madrid.	Gallery.	The Death of the Virgin. (His principal work.)
Munich.	Gallery.	Virgin and Child with Saints.
Nancy.	Museum.	The Plague at Milan.
Paris.	Louvre.	Virgin and Child adored by Saints.
"	"	St. Augustine.
"	"	Portrait of the Cardinal-Infant Don Ferdinand of Spain, on horseback.
Petersburg.	Hermitage.	Pan and Syrinx.
Rotterdam.	Museum.	The Descent from the Cross.
Valenciennes.	Gallery.	The Penitent Magdalen.
Vienna.	Gallery.	The Holy Family.

Some recent writers ascribe to him a woodcut representing St. Sebastian. Van Dyck painted his portrait, which Paulus Pontius engraved. His monogram is annexed: DC

DE CRITZ, JOHN, EMMANUEL, and THOMAS, were decorative painters in England in the first half of the 17th century. John, who had the greatest reputation of the three brothers, was serjeant-painter to James I. and Charles I., in which office he was succeeded by Emmanuel. They painted scenery, ceilings, &c. John bought many pictures at the sale of the collection of Charles I. He died after 1657.

DE CROOCK, HUBERT, a Flemish typographer and engraver on wood, was born at Bruges in 1490. His name is affixed to a large cut, representing the Trinity, which is neatly executed, but in a stiff, formal style. Albrecht Dürer engraved the same subject, but in so superior a manner, that the print by De Croock may be presumed to be a copy coeval with the original. Besides the name, it is marked with the monogram ⌘.

DE CUYPERE, ANDRIES. See STEVENS.

DE DECKER, I., is mentioned by Strutt as the engraver of a small copy of the print representing the 'Treaty of Münster,' engraved by Suyderhoef, after Terburg, in which he attempted to imitate the style of the original, but with no great success.

DE DEYSTER, LOUIS, born at Bruges in 1656, was a pupil of John Maes. He travelled in Italy during six years, chiefly spent at Venice and in Rome with Anthony Van den Eeckhout, whose sister he married. He was admitted as free master into the Guild of S. Luke on March 4, 1688. His pictures are well composed, the hands and feet well modelled; colour in the style of A. van Dyck. His etchings, which are rare, are remarkable. He died December 18, 1711. His younger daughter, ANNE, 1690–1747, was also a painter. Many of their paintings are preserved in the churches and convents of Bruges.

Bruges.	Museum.	Moses defending the Daughters of Jethro.

Bibliography: Weale, 'Catalogue du Musée de Bruges,' 1861; 'Bruges et ses Environs,' 1884.

DEDREUX, ALFRED, a French historical and portrait painter, was born in Paris in 1812. He was the son of the architect Pierre Anne Dedreux, and nephew of P. J. Dedreux-Dorcy. He studied under Léon Cogniet, and painted animals as well as portraits. He died in Paris in 1860.

DEDREUX-DORCY, PIERRE JOSEPH, a French genre painter, was born in Paris in 1789. He studied for some time under Guérin. His paintings, one of which, called 'Bajazet et le Berger,' is in the Museum of Bordeaux, are in the style of Greuze. He also painted, together with Géricault, a picture called 'La Baigneuse.' He died at Bellevue in 1874. His surname was Dedreux, but he was usually called Dorcy.

DEELEN, DIRK VAN, (or DELEN,) a Dutch painter, was born at Heusden in 1605. He afterwards settled at Arnemuiden in Zealand, of which town he became burgomaster. He possessed not only an extraordinary talent in representing Italian architecture, but was also thoroughly acquainted with linear and aërial perspective. He particularly devoted himself to the production of views of churches and other buildings, and the figures in his paintings are mostly by Van Herp, Palamedes, Stevens, and Wouverman. He died at Arnemuiden in 1671. The following are his most important works:

Berlin.	Gallery.	The Court of a Palace.
Hague.	Museum.	The Hall of the Binnenhof at the Hague.
Lille.	Museum.	The Interior of a Castle.
Paris.	Louvre.	Players at Ball.
Rotterdam.	Museum.	A Musical Party.
Vienna.	Gallery.	A building with columns.

DE' FASOLI, LORENZO. See FASOLO.

DE' FERRARI. See DEI FERRARI.

DE FOUR, PIETER, called DE SALZEA, a native of Liége, who flourished at the end of the 16th and beginning of the 17th centuries, was a scholar of Lambert Lombardus. There were by him in the cathedral at Liége two excellent altar-pieces dated 1578 and 1580, and in the church of St. Bartholomew, a 'St. Michael,' and a 'Descent from the Cross,' dated 1610.

DEFRANCE, LEONARD, born at Liége in 1735, was a scholar of J. B. Coclers. He painted historical pieces of large and small dimensions, also landscapes, game, fruit, flowers, and architecture. He was the first professor of design at the Academy of Liége, established by the Prince Velbruck, and afterwards filled the same post in the school of the central department of Ourthe. He died at Liége in 1805.

DE' FRANCESCHI. See DEI FRANCESCHI.

DE FREY, ANNA, a sister of Johannes De Frey, executed a large number of drawings from paintings by old masters, such as Jan Steen, Metsu, and Mieris. She was instructed by her brother-in-law, Jacobus Johannes Lauwers, and afterwards became herself a teacher of drawing at Mannheim, in which town she was married, and where she died in 1808. She also painted in oil.

DE FREY, JOHANNES, an engraver and etcher of distinction, was born at Amsterdam about 1760, and was instructed in the art by Jacobus Johannes Lauwers. Deprived by nature of the use of his right hand, he had the courage to pursue the art with his left, and by industrious application surmounted every difficulty. He became distinguished in his profession as an able designer, and for the boldness of his graver. He engraved many prints after Rembrandt, Flink, G. Dou, and other masters of that school, which are held in estimation. He settled in Paris in 1814, and died there in 1834. Among his best plates are:

The Anatomical Demonstration of Tulp; *after Rembrandt.* 1798.
The Magistrates; *after the same.* 1799.
The Ship-builder and his Wife; *after the same.*
The Family of Tobias; *after the same.*
Portrait of Rembrandt; *after the same.*
Portrait of Rembrandt's Mother; *after the same.*
The Presentation in the Temple; *after the same.*
Isaac blessing his son Jacob; *after G. Flink.* 1798.
The Family of G. Dou; *after G. Dou.* 1798.
The Philosopher; *after Brekelenkamp.* 1796.
The Hermit in a Cavern reading; *after the same.*
Portrait of Admiral Marten Harpertz Tromp; *after Lievens.* 1801.
Portrait of G. A. Brederode; *after Baillie.*

DE FROMANTIOU, HENDRIK, was a painter who excelled in flowers, birds, and objects of still-life. He was born at Nymegen in 1630, and was living in 1680. In the Gallery at Salzthalen is a beautiful flower-piece by him. It is also said that he painted in the manner of Rembrandt; and that Wouverman gave him his daughter in marriage, with a large dowry. This last circumstance, if authentic, would be confirmatory of his artistic talent; but the fact may be doubted, as Wouverman never became rich by his profession, and died of chagrin at finding his works so much neglected.

DE GAST, MICHEL, a Flemish landscape painter, was born at Antwerp in 1509, and became a member of the Guild of St. Luke in 1558. He appears to have passed the greater part of his life in Italy, and most of his pictures represent the ruins of ancient Rome and its environs. He died in 1564.

DE GEEST, WYBRAND, called 'De Friesche Adelaar' (The Frisian Eagle), was born, probably at Antwerp, about the year 1591. He travelled to Italy

when young, and resided there several years, chiefly at Rome, where he made drawings from the principal statues and pictures; and on his return to Holland painted historical subjects with considerable skill. He died at Antwerp in 1643. The plates in the book entitled 'Cabinet des Statues,' published at Amsterdam in 1702, are from the designs of his grandson, who bore the same names.

DE GELDER, ARENT, or AART, a Dutch painter, was born at Dordrecht in 1645. After studying for some time in his native town, under Samuel van Hoogstraeten, he went to Amsterdam, where he entered the school of Rembrandt, and became one of the ablest imitators of the style of that master. Like him he painted portraits and historical subjects, in which he exhibits the same uncouth choice of forms, with the same fascinating charm of colour; the same eccentricities and defects, with his admirable conduct of light and shade, and the richness and spirit of his brush. In his historical pictures, he also equally set at nought propriety of costume, and elevation of sentiment. His works still captivate by their surprising effects. He painted from nature all the accompanying objects in his pictures, and his painting-room, crowded with armour, old draperies, flags, and sabres, resembled rather the interior of a broker's shop than the studio of an artist. He was most successful in his portraits, some of which are not unworthy of Rembrandt, and have been frequently attributed to that master. He died at Amsterdam in 1727. Among his portraits is that of 'Peter the Great of Russia,' while his principal historical works are 'Simeon in the Temple,' 'Pilate binding Christ,' and 'Judah and Tamar.'

DE GEMPT, B., a Dutch animal painter, who died by his own hand in 1879. Amongst his works are 'A Congress of Dogs,' and 'The Miser's Death-bed.'

DE GHENDT, EMMANUEL JEAN NEPOMUCÈNE, a French engraver, was born at St. Nicholas in Flanders in 1738. He was a pupil of J. Aliamet, and has engraved several plates in a neat, pleasing style. He executed many of the prints and vignettes for the 'Voyage d'Italie' of the Abbé de Saint-Non. He died in Paris in 1815. We have also, among others, the following prints by him:

L'Amour Asiatique; *after Ch. Eisen.*
Les Moissonneurs dans les Champs; *after the same.*
La pleine Moisson; *after Isaac Moucheron.*
A View of the Fountain of Arethusa at Syracuse; *after Chatelet.*
The Four Times of the Day; *after Baudouin.*

DE GHEYN, JAKOB, (or DE GHEIN,) 'the elder,' a Flemish designer and engraver, was born at Antwerp in 1565. He was instructed in drawing by his father, who was a glass-painter, and learned engraving under Hendrik Goltzius. He imitated the style of that master, and his plates evince a great command of the graver. They are executed in a bold, free style, and his drawing is correct, and not without taste. He died at Antwerp, or elsewhere, about 1625. He engraved a great number of plates, both from his own designs and after other masters, and his prints are highly esteemed. He generally used the cipher ⟨DG⟩. The following are his principal works:

PORTRAITS.

Tycho Brahe, the Astronomer.
Abraham Gokevius, antiquary, of Amsterdam.
Hugo Grotius.
Philip de Marnix, the disciple of Calvin.

26

Cosmo de' Medici.
Sigismondo Malatesta ; circular.
Ivan IV. Vasilevich, Czar of Muscovy ; circular.

SUBJECTS AFTER HIS OWN DESIGNS.

Vanity ; represented as a Woman at her toilet.
The Penitent Magdalen ; a small oval.
Mars and Venus ; two small medallions.
A Gipsy telling a Girl her fortune.
The Statue of the Laocoon.
A Lion, in a landscape ; very scarce.
A set of ten plates, called the Masks ; very scarce.
The Twelve Roman Emperors ; circular ; fine.

SUBJECTS AFTER VARIOUS AUTHORS.

The Life and Passion of Christ ; fourteen plates ; engraved by *J. De Gheyn* and *Z. Dolendo, after C. van Mander.*
The Twelve Tribes of Israel ; twelve plates ; *after the same.*
The Four Evangelists ; *after Hendrik Goltzius.*
The Confusion of Tongues at the building of the Tower of Babel ; *after C. van Mander.*
The Adoration of the Trinity ; *after the same.*
The Judgment of Midas ; *after the same.*
The Prodigal Son ; in two sheets ; *after the same.*
The Crucifixion ; *after Crispin van den Broeck.*
The Assembly of the Gods ; *after the same.* 1589.
The Empire of Neptune ; *after W. Telrho.* 1587.
Twelve plates of Soldiers of the Guard of Rudolph II. ; *after H. Goltzius.*
The Annunciation ; *after A. Bloemaert.*
A Repose in Egypt ; *after the same.*
Christ preaching to the Jews ; *after the same.*
The Miracle of the Loaves ; *after the same.*
Daniel in the Lions' Den ; *after T. Bernard.*
Diana and Actæon ; *after the same.*
Polyphemus, with Acis and Galatea ; *after C. van Haarlem.*
A small Landscape ; an etching ; *after J. Brueghel.*

DE GHEYN, JAKOB, (or DE GHEIN,) 'the younger,' son of the elder Jakob De Gheyn, was born at Antwerp about the year 1595. He is supposed to have studied in Italy, under A. Tempesta, from the resemblance in their style. In conjunction with Cornelis Boel, he executed eight plates for 'Les Exploits de Charles-Quint pendant la Guerre d'Italie,' from designs by Tempesta.

DE GHEYN, WILLEM, (or DE GHEIN,) a Flemish engraver, probably related to Jakob De Gheyn, was born at Antwerp, and worked in the middle of the 17th century in Holland and in Paris. Jointly with Jeremiah Falck, he engraved the Four Seasons, represented by French ladies, attired in the costume of the time of Louis XII. We have also by him the following plates :

The Visitation ; *after Guido Reni.*
Louis XIV., when a boy, on horseback.
Bernard, Duke of Weimar, on horseback.

DEGL' AVANZI. See DEGLI AVANZI.

DE GLEN, JAN, was a printer and wood-engraver, who was born in the middle of the 16th century. He cut the blocks for the portraits of the Popes in the 'Vitæ Romanorum Pontificum' of his brother J. B. De Glen, which was printed in 1597 ; and also prepared, from his own designs, the cuts to a work published at Liége in 1601, entitled 'Des Habits, Mœurs, Cérémonies et Façons de faire anciennes et modernes,' and to 'Les Merveilles de la Ville de Rome' (Liége, 1631), and ' Europa, sive Primariarum Europæ Provinciarum Ritibus, Cæremoniis et Vestibus.' He was still living in 1631.

DEGLER, FRANZ, an Austrian historical and portrait painter, was born at Klausen in tne Tyrol in 1705. Among his works may be mentioned the portraits of the Emperor Charles VII. and his Empress, and of other high personages who were at Frankfort-on-the-Main at the time of their coronation, and the ten pictures of the Passion painted for the Capuchin church in that city, where he died in 1736.

DEGLER, JOHANN, an Austrian painter, was born at Lazfons in the Tyrol about the year 1800. He was a pupil of Denifle, and had already given evidence of the possession of great talent when he died at Brixen in 1829. In the Ferdinandeum at Innsbruck there are by him two pictures, and a chalk drawing of the ' Raising of Lazarus.'

DEGLI AFFLITTI, NUNZIO. See FERRAJUOLI.

DEGLI AMBROSI, MARCO, commonly called MELOZZO DA FORLI, was born at Forli in 1438. He is said to have been first instructed by Ansovino of Forli, who assisted Mantegna in several works, but he afterwards adopted much of the style of Piero della Francesca and Giovanni Santi of Urbino. Such was his desire of learning the best principles of the art, that, though of a noble and affluent family, he submitted to the menial duties of a domestic servant and colour-grinder to some of the principal painters of his time. To this venerable artist is attributed the first invention of foreshortening, which was afterwards carried to such perfection by Correggio. In the study of perspective, considerable progress had been made by Piero della Francesca, since its alleged invention by Paolo Uccello, the Florentine ; but the merit of first painting figures in perspective, on vaults and ceilings, by which the illusion is rendered completely effective, was reserved for Melozzo. He was patronized by the Count Girolamo Riario, with whom he visited Rome in 1472, and painted the tribune of SS. Apostoli with the 'Ascension' in fresco, the perspective of which was of surprising effect. In 1711, when the chapel was taken down and rebuilt, the greater part of this painting disappeared, but the figure of Christ is still preserved in the Quirinal. Melozzo was a member of the Academy of St. Luke at Rome. He died at Forli in 1494. Other paintings by him are :

London. *Nat. Gall.* Two Allegorical Figures : Rhetoric, and Music.
Paris. *Louvre.* Fourteen Portraits, painted for the Duke of Urbino. (*Ascribed also to Justus van Ghent.*)
Rome. *Barberini Palace.* Fourteen Portraits belonging to the same series as those in the Louvre.
„ *Vatican.* Sixtus IV. giving the custody of the Vatican Library to Platina.

DEGLI ANTONJ, ANTONELLO. See ANTONIO.

DEGLI AVANZI, JACOPO, a Bolognese painter of the later years of the 14th century, is chiefly known by a ' Crucifixion,' in the Colonna Gallery at Rome. There are three pictures in the Bologna Gallery also by this master. He painted, in conjunction with artists of no great importance, frescoes in the church of the Madonna di Mezzarata, near Bologna, which Malvasia says were praised by Michelangelo and the Carracci ; they have, however, been whitewashed and afterwards restored, and only fragments of them remain. Vasari says they were completed in 1404.

DEGLI AVANZI, SIMONE. See BOLOGNA.

DEGLI INNOCENTI, BATTISTA. See NALDINI.

DEGLI STEFANI, TOMMASO. Dominici, in his ' Lives of the Neapolitan Painters,' attempts to prove that the art was practised at Naples by this master before the time of Cimabue, and that it had, at that early period, reached a more improved

27

state at Naples than it had at Florence. Whatever may be allowed for the partiality with which the Italian writers speak of their particular country-men, Dominici appears to have established the authenticity of his statement. This venerable artist was born at Naples in 1231. He grounded himself upon the remains of Grecian art which had been preserved in the temples and public edifices at Naples, and had painted several pictures for the churches of San Francesco and Santa Maria delle Grazie previous to the year 1260, at which time he was employed by the Archbishop of Naples to ornament the chapel of his palace. Several other works by him are particularly described by Dominici. He died in 1310. He had a brother, PIETRO DEGLI STEFANI, who also was a painter, but was more celebrated as a sculptor.

DE GRAEF, TIMOTHEUS, was a Dutch landscape painter, who flourished at the close of the 17th century. The dates of his birth and death are not recorded; but Jacob Appel, of Amsterdam, was his pupil. The Sale Catalogues of Hoet and Terwesten mention many of his pictures, par-ticularly landscapes and views in the vicinity of Amsterdam.

DE GREBBER, FRANS PIETERSZ, was born at Haarlem in 1579; he was a scholar of Roland Savery, and obtained honourable mention as an artist. He also made copies of his master's works, and those of Velvet Brueghel. He died in 1649.

DE GREBBER, PIETER FRANSZ, a Dutch painter, was born at Haarlem in 1600. He was the son of Frans Pietersz De Grebber, who instructed him in the elements of design; but he afterwards became a scholar of Hendrik Goltzius. He died after 1665. He chiefly painted easel pictures, of which there are many in the collections in Holland. The Museum at Haarlem has, amongst others, 'The Emperor Barbarossa' and 'The Patriarch of Haar-lem,' which are quite in Rubens's style; also 'Jacob's Sons bringing to him Joseph's Coat.' The Dresden Gallery also contains examples of his art. He has also left several engravings, and an etching in Rembrandt's style of 'Christ and the Woman of Samaria.' He had a sister, MARIA DE GREBBER, who excelled in painting perspective and archi-tectural views.

DE GROOS, GERHARD and GEORG, probably two brothers, were working together as engravers at Prague about the year 1647. They produced a large number of portraits and pictures of Saints.

DE GROOT, JAN, a painter and engraver in mezzotint, was born at Flushing in 1650. He was first instructed by Adriaan Verdoel, and after 1666 by Adriaan van Ostade. The date of his death is not recorded. Some of his plates are marked *J. G. fec.* or *I. G. inc.* The best of those in mezzotint are:

Portrait of Desiderius Erasmus; *after Holbein.*
Portrait of Abraham van der Eyk; *after Van der Eyk.*
Boy singing, with a cup of wine; *after Van Dyck.*

DE HAAN, DAVID, was born at Rotterdam in 1602. He studied in Italy, and became a good historical painter, excelling especially in battle-pieces. He also painted game with great truth-fulness to nature. He died at Rome in 1659.

DE HAAS, WILLIAM FREDERICK, who was born at Rotterdam in 1830, studied in the Academy of his native city, and at the Hague under Johannes Bosboom. He went in 1854 to New York, where he became known as a painter of coast scenery. He

died at Fayal in 1880. The following are some of his best works:

Sunrise on the Susquehanna. 1867.
Fishing Boats off Mount Desert. 1874.
Midsummer Noon, Bideford Beach, Coast of Maine. 1875.
Narragansett Pier. 1877.

DE HAEN, ABRAHAM, a Dutch painter, born at Amsterdam in 1710, was a disciple of Cornelis Pronk. He painted portraits and architectural subjects, and a picture of 'Game' by him is in the Gallery at Christiania. He died in 1750.

DE HANGEST, EGBERT MARINUS FREDERIK, (or D'HANGEST,) an amateur painter, was born at Utrecht in 1746. While studying the law he took lessons in painting of Verstegh. After finishing his legal studies, he set out on his travels as an artist, painting landscapes in the manner of Zaft-leven; views on the Rhine, and rocky scenery; landscapes, with lakes and rivers; and sunsets and moonlights, in which he was very successful. His pencilling is vigorous and free, and his pictures would not discredit a professional artist. He died in 1810.

DE HEEM, CORNELIS, the son and scholar of Jan Davidsz De Heem, was born at Utrecht in 1630. Like his father he painted still-life, but his productions are inferior. He died at the Hague after 1692.

DE HEEM, DAVID, who was born at Utrecht in 1570, was an excellent painter of fruit, flowers, plate, crystal vessels, and other objects of still-life. There is a 'Group of Flowers' by him in the Museum at Brussels. He died at Utrecht in 1632.

DE HEEM, DAVID DAVIDSZ, a son and pupil of David De Heem, was a fruit painter of Utrecht in the 17th century. A picture by him, dated 1668, is in the gallery of that city, and one dated 1649 is at Amsterdam.

DE HEEM, JAN, a supposed nephew of David De Heem, is stated to have been born at Amsterdam in 1603. He studied under his uncle and followed his manner exactly. There is a picture of still-life ascribed to him in the Museum at Amsterdam. His death is set down in 1650. There is, however, some confusion between this artist and Jan Davidsz De Heem, to whom the catalogues of Berlin, Brunswick, Munich, and Vienna assign the pictures marked J. De Heem.

DE HEEM, JAN DAVIDSZ, was born at Utrecht after 1600. He was the son of David De Heem, the flower painter, by whom he was instructed. His pictures bear date from 1640 to 1669, and repre-sent fruit, flowers, vases and ornaments of gold and silver, musical instruments, and similar objects of still-life. He was a perfect master of chiaroscuro. He particularly excelled in imitating the transparent clearness of glass and crystal, which he was fond of introducing into his pictures. His paintings were so superior to those of every artist that had preceded him, in similar subjects, that they were anxiously sought after by the most distinguished persons of his time, and were purchased at large prices. They are still held in high estimation. Being obliged to leave Utrecht during the troubles which took place in Holland in 1671, he took refuge at Antwerp, where he died in 1674.

DE HEERE, LUCAS, a Flemish historical and portrait painter, who was born at Ghent in 1534, was the son of Jan De Heere, a sculptor and architect, and of Anna De Smytere, an excellent painter of miniatures. He studied for some time

MARY TUDOR

under his parents, and afterwards under Frans Floris at Antwerp. On leaving the studio of the latter he went to France, and was employed at Fontainebleau by the Queen-Mother, Catharine de' Medici, in making designs for tapestries for the royal residences. The time of his first visit to England is uncertain, but he must have been here in 1554, when he painted the fine portrait of Queen Mary which is in the collection of the Society of Antiquaries. On his return to Ghent he painted, among other portraits, that of a wealthy young Protestant lady, named Eleonora Carboniers, the daughter of the burgomaster of Vere, in Zealand. Her beauty and learning captivated the painter, but it was only after great perseverance that he won her as his wife. To her he addressed many amorous verses, for Lucas De Heere was a poet as well as a painter, and these he published in 1565, under the title, 'Den Hof en de Boomgaerd der Poësien.' His marriage led to a change in his religion, and when the Duke of Alva arrived in the Netherlands in 1567, and Ghent was occupied by a Spanish garrison, the adherents of the new faith had to flee from their homes. De Heere fled to England, and appears to have remained here until 1577, when the edict known as the Pacification of Ghent enabled him to return to his native city. During this second visit he painted, in 1569, the remarkable allegorical portrait of Queen Elizabeth, with Juno, Venus, and Pallas apparently fleeing before her, which is now at Hampton Court. Other fine examples of his art which exist in England are the portraits of Lord Darnley and his brother, Charles Stuart, dated 1563, also at Hampton Court, and the small full-length portrait of Queen Elizabeth, in the possession of the Duke of Portland, one of his most charming works. His abilities as an historical painter are best represented by a 'Crucifixion,' painted by him in 1565 for the church of the village of Saint-Paul, in the Pays de Waes. This altar-piece fully justifies the renown which his portraits have gained for him in England. Besides his paintings in oil, he completed, in 1576, a large collection of water-colour drawings of costumes, which he entitled 'Théâtre de tous les Peuples et Nations de la Terre.' This valuable work is now among the archives of Ghent. He also translated into Flemish verse the Psalms of David, and wrote, or at least began to write, the lives of the Flemish painters, in rhyme. Lucas De Heere died in 1584 in Paris, where he had taken refuge after the assassination of William the Taciturn.   R.E.G.

DE HEUR, CORNELIS JOSEPH, (or D'HEUR,) a Flemish painter of historical subjects and interiors, was born at Antwerp in 1707. He studied successively under Gaspard van Opstal the younger, J. J. Hormans the elder, and Peeter Snyers. In 1730, he went to Paris, and on his return to Antwerp became one of the directors of the Academy. He died in 1762 at Antwerp, where there are in the Museum several works by him in grisaille.

DE HEUSCH, ABRAHAM, was born at Utrecht in 1650, and was probably related to Jakob and Willem De Heusch. He excelled in painting plants, insects, and reptiles; which he designed and executed with surprising patience and labour. His pictures of that description are not inferior, in the delicate polish of their finishing, to the highly-wrought productions of Gerard Dou or Mieris. There are a few etchings of landscapes by Abraham De Heusch, from his own designs.

DE HEUSCH, JAKOB, called AFFDRUCK, the nephew of Willem De Heusch, was born at Utrecht in 1657. He was instructed in art by his uncle, and acquired his surname from his faithful imitation of his uncle's style. Having made considerable progress, he was recommended to visit Italy, where he passed several years. He met with very flattering encouragement at Rome, his pictures being much admired. He particularly attached himself to the study of the works of Salvator Rosa, whose picturesque style he imitated with considerable success. His pictures represent the most select views in the environs of Rome, enriched with groups of charming figures, correctly drawn and vigorously touched. We have a few etchings by him of landscapes, from his own designs, executed in a neat but slight style. He died at Amsterdam in 1701.

DE HEUSCH, WILLEM, was born at Utrecht in 1638. In 1656, or 1659, he was in Italy as a pupil of Jan Both, whose style he copied. He died at Utrecht in 1712. One of his landscapes in the Louvre is very finely executed, but a better specimen of his art is in the Belvedere at Vienna, a 'Landscape at Sunset.' Landscapes from his brush are in the galleries of Stockholm, Copenhagen, Frankfort, Brunswick, Amsterdam, Rotterdam, and the Hague. He also engraved several Landscapes, which have become very rare.

DEHNE, J. C., was a German engraver, who flourished in the first half of the 18th century. He engraved several portraits for the work entitled 'Icones Bibliopolarum et Typographorum,' published at Nuremberg in 1726-42. We have also by him a great number of plates, representing, in the most ludicrous manner, the gods and heroes of antiquity.

DEHODENCQ, EDME ALEXIS ALFRED, a French genre painter, was born in Paris in 1822. He was a pupil of Léon Cogniet, and first attracted notice by his picture of 'St. Cecilia' at the Salon of 1844. He travelled much in Spain and Northern Africa, and from these countries derived many of his subjects, which are painted with great truthfulness and richness of colour. He died in 1882. Among his best works are:

Virginia found dead on the sea-shore. 1849.
A Spanish Bull-Fight. 1850. (*Luxembourg Gallery.*)
The Arrest of Charlotte Corday. 1868.
Othello. 1873.
A Moorish Story-Teller. 1877.

DE HOEY, JAN, (or DE HOOY,) a Dutch painter, was born at Leyden in 1545. Van Mander says that he was a grandson of Lucas van Leyden and brother of Lucas Damissen, under whom he studied painting. He travelled in Italy and France, and made himself so acceptable at the court of Henry IV. that he was appointed keeper of the royal collections. He died at Fontainebleau in 1615. LUCAS DE HOEY, or DAMISSEN, his brother, who was born at Leyden in 1533, resided at Utrecht, and died there in 1604. CLAUDE DE HOEY, or DOUÉ, the son of Jan, who was also a painter, died in 1660. He had the care of the pictures at Fontainebleau from the time of his father's death until 1635, when he resigned in favour of his nephew, Jean Dubois.

DE HOND, (or DE HONDT). See HOND.

DE HONDECOETER, MELCHIOR, (or D'HONDECOETER, as he invariably signed his name,) a member of a noble family of Brabant, was born at Utrecht in 1636. He first studied under his father,

Gysbert D'Hondecoeter, and then with his uncle, Jan Baptista Weenix, and became famous for his pictures of birds of rare plumage, live fowl, game, and similar subjects. In this branch of art he stands unrivalled. He also painted a few marine pieces, and engraved a few prints.

From 1659 to 1663 he is mentioned in the 'Pictura' Society of the Hague. He then removed (in what year is not known) to Amsterdam, where he received the rights of citizenship in 1688, and where he died in 1695. His works are frequently met with in public galleries; the following are some of the principal:

Amsterdam.	*Museum.*	Dead Birds.
,,	,,	Animals and Plants.
,,	,,	The Philosophical Magpie.
,,	,,	The Menagerie.
,,	,,	The Floating Feather.
Berlin.	*Gallery.*	Foreign Water-fowl in a Park.
Brunswick.	*Gallery.*	Animals of the Ark.
Brussels.	*Museum.*	Peacock and Poultry in a Park. 1672.
,,	,,	Cock crowing.
Cassel.	*Gallery.*	Cocks fighting.
,,	,,	Poultry.
Dresden.	*Gallery.*	Hen and Chicken, and Bird of Prey.
,,	,,	A white Hen and Chicken.
,,	,,	A Concert of Birds.
,,	,,	Wild Fowl.
Florence.	*Pitti Pal.*	Poultry.
Frankfort.	*Städel.*	Poultry.
Hague.	*Museum.*	The Crow stripped of his borrowed feathers.
,,	,,	The Menagerie of William III. at the Château of Loo.
,,	,,	Geese and Ducks.
,,	,,	Fowl and Ducks.
Liverpool.	*Institution.*	Poultry.
London.	*Nat. Gall.*	Domestic Poultry.
,,	,,	Geese and Ducks.
Munich.	*Gallery.*	A Park with Poultry.
Paris.	*Louvre.*	Birds in a Park.
Petersburg.	*Hermitage.*	Fight between a Cock and a Turkey.
,,	,,	Trophies of the Chase.
Venice.	*Academy.*	Poultry.
Vienna.	*Gallery.*	A Cock and two Hens.
,,	*Liechtenstein Collection.*	Poultry.

DE HONT, H., (or DE HONDT,) is said to have been a scholar of David Teniers. His pictures represent similar scenes to those of that master, and sometimes approach very closely to his manner.

DE HOOCH, PIETER, was born at Rotterdam, probably in 1632. His style was formed from a study of the works of Karel Fabritius and of Rembrandt. He worked at Delft and at Haarlem, where he died, it is said, in 1681. He painted interiors and portraits; and his works are distinguished for their brilliant effects of light, and admirable colour. His name has been written in a variety of ways—De Hooche, Hoogh, Hooghe, and Hooge. Out of Holland, De Hooch's paintings are extremely scarce; and even in that country they are among the rarest art-treasures in the public and private galleries. The following are the principal:

Amsterdam.	*Museum.*	Portrait of Himself at the age of 19.
,,		The Buttery-hatch.
,,	*Van der Hoop Coll.*	Morning Toilet.
,,	*Six Coll.*	The Linen-Press.
Berlin.	*Gallery.*	A Dutch Interior.
Copenhagen.	*Gallery.*	Persons Playing and Dancing.
,,	,,	A Family Concert.
,,	,,	An Interior.

Frankfort.	*Städel.*	A Lady at her Writing-table.
Hague.	*Steengracht Coll.*	A Musical Party.
London.	*Nat. Gallery.*	The Courtyard of a Dutch House. 1665.
,,	,,	An Interior; two gentlemen conversing with a lady.
,,	,,	Courtyard of a Dutch House, paved with bricks. 1658.
,,	*Apsley House.*	A Lady at her Toilet.
,,	*Ashburton Coll.*	A Woman and a Child walking in a street of Utrecht.
,,	*Buckingham Pal.*	A Courtyard.
,,	,,	Three Gentleman and a Lady Playing Cards. 1658.
,,	*Northbrook Coll.*	An Interior.
Munich.	*Gallery.*	Dutch Interior; a Woman Reading.
Paris.	*Louvre.*	Dutch Interior; two Women and a Child, with a meal prepared on the table.
,,	,,	Dutch Interior; Card Players.
Petersburg.	*Hermitage.*	A Lady seated at a door.
,,	,,	Dutch Interior; a Lady playing the lute and singing, whilst a cavalier accompanies her in the song.
,,	,,	The Lace-maker.
Vienna.	*Czernin Coll.*	A Painter in his Studio.

DE HOOGHE, ROMEYN, a Dutch designer and engraver, born at the Hague about the year 1646, was a nephew of Pieter De Hooch. Several of his compositions show him to have been a man of great genius and readiness of invention. Few artists have handled the point with more spirit and facility than Romeyn De Hooghe, and his small figures and distances are executed with great delicacy and neatness. His foregrounds and principal figures are less happy, and there is a want of harmony in the effect, and in the management of the chiaroscuro. He founded a school of design at Haarlem, where he died in 1708. The number of his prints is very considerable, but the following are the principal:

The Portrait of Michael Adriaensz De Ruyter, Admiral-General of Holland; very fine.
An Allegorical Subject, in honour of Leopold II.
Another, in honour of William, Prince of Orange.
The Marriage of William, Prince of Orange, with the Princess Mary of England.
The Entry of the Prince of Orange into London.
The Coronation of William and Mary.
The Army of William III. in order of battle, on the banks of the Boyne; with medallions of King William and Queen Mary.
The Siege of Vienna by the Turks. 1683.
The Triumphal Entry of John III., King of Poland, into Warsaw, after raising the siege of Vienna.
Constantinople taken by the Turks.
A set of plates representing the Excesses committed by the French in Holland. 1672, 1673.
The Deluge of Coerverden.
The Massacre of the two De Witts. 1672.
The Defeat of the French at Hochstadt in 1704; with medallions of the Duke of Marlborough and Prince Eugene.
The Taking of Narva by Charles XII.
The Battle of St. Denys, near Mons; in two sheets.
The Jewish Synagogue at Amsterdam.
The Entry of Louis XIV. into Dunkirk; two sheets; *after Van der Meulen.*
Charles II. of Spain, descending from his carriage to pay homage to the Host.
Six Emblematical Subjects, relative to the abuses of the clergy of the Romish Church. 1679.
The Fair at Arnheim.
Twelve Figures habited in the mode of the end of the 17th century.

PIETER DE HOOCH

COURTYARD OF A DUTCH HOUSE

GERARD DOU

THE POULTERER'S SHOP

DE HULST, FRANS, a Dutch landscape painter, was admitted in 1631 into the Guild of St. Luke at Haarlem, where he died in 1661. There is by him in the Berlin Gallery a view of a town in Holland. He painted in the style of Ruisdael and Van Goyen, but his works are seldom met with.

DEI, MATTEO DI GIOVANNI, was one of the most celebrated of the goldsmiths and workers in niello who flourished at Florence in the middle of the 15th century. He executed in 1455 for the church of San Giovanni a pax which represented the 'Crucifixion of Our Lord.' He also engraved for a pax for the confraternity of St. Paul a silver plate, representing the 'Conversion of St. Paul,' which is preserved in the Florence Gallery. It has never been filled in with enamel, and modern impressions have been taken from it.

DEI BUONI, BUONO, was born at Naples, and, according to Dominici, flourished about the year 1430. He was a disciple of an old Neapolitan painter called Colantonio del Fiore, whom he assisted in several of his works, and after whose death he became one of the most reputable artists of his time. There are many of his works in the churches at Naples; one of the most esteemed is a painting in the church of the Restituta representing 'St. Francis receiving the Stigmata.' He died about the year 1465.

DEI BUONI, SILVESTRO, the son of Buono de' Buoni, was born at Naples about the year 1420. After studying for some time under his father, he had the advantage of being instructed by Antonio Solario. Under that master he became an eminent painter of historical subjects, and was employed in some considerable works for the churches and public edifices of Naples. He died about 1480. The following are his best works:

Naples.	S. Caterina.	Christ appearing after his Resurrection.
"	S. Restituta.	Virgin and Child, with SS. Restituta and Michael.
"	S. Pietro Martire.	Death of the Virgin.
"	"	Virgin and Child between two Saints.
"	Monte Oliveto.	Ascension.

DEI CONTI, BERNARDINO, an Italian painter, is said to have been born at Pavia in the latter part of the 15th century. He died in 1525. He was a follower of Zenale, but little is known of his life or works. The following paintings, however, are preserved:

| Bergamo. | Lochis-Carrara Gallery. | Madonna and Child (signed). 1501. |
| Berlin. | Gallery. | Profile of a Prelate. 1499. |

DEI CROCIFISSI, SIMONE. See BOLOGNA.

DEI FASOLI, LORENZO. See FASOLO.

DEI FERRARI, GIOVANNI ANDREA, was born at Genoa in 1598. He was first a scholar of Bernardo Castello, but he afterwards studied under Bernardo Strozzi. His principal historical works are his picture of 'Theodosius,' in the style of Castello, in the Jesuit church at Genoa; 'The Nativity,' in the cathedral of the same city; and in a church at Voltri, the 'Birth of the Virgin,' his most esteemed production, a composition of many figures; the two last pictures are in the style of Strozzi. He died at Genoa in 1669.

DEI FERRARI, GREGORIO, a Genoese painter, was born at Porto Maurizio in 1644. He was a disciple of Domenico Fiasella, called Il Sarzana, whose manner was not conformable to the genius of his scholar, which aimed at a style more grand

and free. He went to Parma, where he studied with attention the works of Correggio, and made a faithful copy of the great cupola. He was also much employed at Turin and Marseilles. He died at Genoa in 1726. Of his works the most esteemed are his 'St. Michael,' in the Madonna delle Vigne at Genoa, and his 'Apollo and the Muses' and 'Plato and Aristotle' in the University. The Palazzo Balbi, also in the same city, contains some pictures by him.

DEI FERRARI, LORENZO, the son of Gregorio de' Ferrari, was born at Genoa in 1680. He was instructed by his father, and, like him, he imitated the grace and suavity of Correggio. He assisted his father in some of his works, but surpassed him in foreshortening and correctness of drawing. He excelled in painting in fresco, but he also painted many pictures in oil for churches. In his works in the Doria Palace, he has emulated the vigour of the Carloni, and is little inferior to them. In the Carega Palace is a gallery of subjects from the Æneid, which were his last works. He died at Genoa in 1744.

DEI FERRARI, ORAZIO, was born at Voltri in 1606, and was a scholar of Andrea Ansaldo, under whom he became an able painter of historical subjects in oil and fresco. His merit recommended him to the patronage of the Prince of Monaco, who employed him for some years. His 'Last Supper,' in the Oratory of the church of San Siro at Genoa, is alone sufficient to establish his reputation. This artist was high in the public esteem when Genoa was visited in 1657 by the plague, which carried off a great number of the inhabitants, with this painter and all his family.

DEI FIORI, GASPARO. See LOPEZ.

DEI FIORI, MARIO. See NUZZI.

DEI FRANCESCHI, DOMENICO, who flourished at Venice in the latter half of the 16th century, was a type-cutter and printseller. The following two excellent prints are by him:

The Procession of Corpus Christi at Venice. 1565.
The Parade of the Emperor Solyman I. at Constantinople. 1565. A very rare plate.

DEI FRANCESCHI, PIETRO DI BENEDETTO, called PIERO DELLA FRANCESCA, and also PIERO BORGHESE, was born at Borgo San Sepolcro in Umbria about the year 1416. It is not known by whom he was instructed in the art of painting, but in 1438 he made the acquaintance of Domenico Veneziano, and was employed by him on the frescoes of Sant' Egidio at Florence, which were executed between the years 1439 and 1450. He was a complete master of linear perspective and thoroughly understood all its laws, as also the true art of projecting shadows, and thus giving an additional charm to his pictures. The majority of his pictures were painted in oil, then a comparatively new medium for colours, and he carried out many improvements in the usage of this vehicle. Between the years 1447 and 1452 it is thought that both Domenico and Piero were at Loretto, where the ceiling of the sacristy was commenced by them; and it was probably at about this period that Piero left Domenico and went to Rome, where, in conjunction with Bramantino, he painted two frescoes in the Vatican by order of Pope Nicholas V. These frescoes were afterwards removed by command of Julius II. in order to make room for Raphael's frescoes of the 'Deliverance of St. Peter from Prison,' and the 'Mass of Bolsena.' After 1451

31

Piero entered the service of Sigismondo Pandolfo Malatesta, Duke of Rimini, and adorned for him the chapel of the Relic in the church of San Francesco with a picture representing 'Malatesta kneeling before the enthroned St. Sigismund of Burgundy.' Soon afterwards he commenced the cycle of frescoes illustrating the Legend of the Cross in the church of San Francesco at Arezzo. This immense series commences with the Death and Burial of Adam, and follows the legend up to the Finding of the Cross by St. Helena. They are wonderful alike by the reality of their effects of light and shade, and their harmony of colour. They were finished about 1454. In 1445 he painted for the Compagnia della Misericordia the altar-piece of the 'Virgin of Mercy,' with Saints and scenes from the Passion, now in the Hospital at Borgo San Sepolcro. Whilst in his native city he executed many commissions for altar-pieces and banners, some of which still remain in its gallery and churches. From there he went to Urbino, where in 1469 he entered the service of the Duke Federigo, and also made the acquaintance of Giovanni Santi, the father of Raphael. He painted for the duke a 'Flagellation,' which is preserved in the sacristy of the cathedral, and an 'Apotheosis,' containing the portraits of Federigo da Montefeltro, and Batista Sforza, his wife. The last-mentioned picture is now in the Gallery of the Uffizi at Florence. He is also known to have gone to Ferrara, where he was employed by Duke Borso in the decorations of his palace called "Schifanoja," which means "Begone, dull care." The frescoes executed there by Piero have been destroyed, but the remains of others have been recovered, which clearly indicate the great influence possessed by this artist over other painters of his time. The statement that he became blind in 1458 is clearly incorrect, for he was still working in 1478, and it is probable that age alone at last incapacitated him from further work. Piero della Francesca died at Borgo San Sepolcro in 1492. Luca Signorelli, Melozzo da Forli, Bartolommeo della Gatta, and Perugino were among his pupils. He wrote a treatise on Perspective, of which there are copies in the Vatican Library and in the Ambrosian Library at Milan. Amongst his paintings may be mentioned:

Arezzo. *S. Francesco.* The Legend of the Holy Cross, with the Vision of Constantine.
Borgo S. Sepolcro. The Resurrection.
London. *Nat. Gall.* Portrait of a lady. (*Doubtful.*)
    "   " The Baptism of Christ.
    "   " Portrait, said to be that of the Contessa Palma. (*Doubtful.*)
    "   " The Nativity.
    "   " St. Michael.
Milan. *Brera.* Madonna with Saints, and Portrait of Federigo of Urbino.
Perugia. *Academy.* Virgin and Child enthroned, with Saints.
Rimini. *S. Francesco.* St. Sigismund (Sigismondo Pandolfo Malatesta).
Urbino. *Cathedral.* The Flagellation.
Venice. *Academy.* St. Jerome in the Desert.

DEI GIANNUZZI, Giulio, often called Giulio Pippi, but more commonly Giulio Romano, was born at Rome in 1492. He was apprenticed to Raphael when quite young, and assisted him in the Vatican; and he is generally considered Raphael's best pupil. He copied several of his master's Madonnas, and executed some few from his designs. While in Rome he painted mythical frescoes in the Villa Lanti, the Villa Madama, the Farnese Palace, and the church of Santa Trinità de' Monti. By his will, Raphael bequeathed his implements and works of art to his joint-executors, Giulio Romano and Gianfrancesco Penni, and entrusted to them the completion of his unfinished frescoes in the Sala di Costantino in the Vatican. In 1524 Giulio went to Mantua and entered the service of Duke Federigo Gonzaga. He was there architect for the Palazzo del Tè, and, assisted by numerous pupils (of whom the chief were Benedetto Pagni, Rinaldo Mantuano, and Primaticcio), decorated the interior with frescoes representing the 'Defeat of the Giants,' his greatest work, and with scenes from the 'History of Cupid and Psyche.' He also painted at Mantua, in the Ducal Palace, frescoes representing 'Diana hunting,' and the 'History of the Trojan War,' as well as frescoes in the cathedral and other churches. Those in the cathedral, however, he was not able to complete, for having accepted the post of architect to St. Peter's at Rome, in succession to San Gallo, he was about to set out for that city when he died at Mantua in 1546. Of his easel pictures the following are the most famous:

Dresden.	*Gallery.*	La Madonna del Catino.
Florence.	*Uffizi.*	His own Portrait.
"	"	Madonna and Child.
"	"	Portrait of Cardinal Accolti.
"	*Pitti Palace.*	Dance of Apollo and the Muses.
"	"	The Virgin with the Lizard.
Genoa.	*San Stefano.*	Martyrdom of St. Stephen (*one of his best works*).
London.	*Nat. Gallery.*	The Infancy of Jupiter.
Naples.	*Museum.*	La Madonna della Gatta (*a variation of Raphael's 'Perla'*).
Paris.	*Louvre.*	The Nativity.
"	"	The Holy Family.
"	"	Triumph of Titus and Vespasian.
"	"	Venus and Vulcan.
"	"	Portrait of a Man.
Rome.	*S. Peter's (Sacristy).*	Madonna.
"	*S. Prassede (Sacristy).*	The Flagellation.
"	*Borghese Pal.*	Madonna and Child.
"	*Colonna Pal.*	Madonna and Child.
Vienna.	*Gallery.*	Allegory.
"	"	St. Margaret and the Dragon.

His son and pupil, RAFFAELLO PIPPI DE' GIANNUZZI, died in 1562, at the age of thirty.

DEI INGANNATI, Piero. See BISSOLO.

DEI MEDICI, Maria. See MARY.

DEI MICHIELI, Andrea, known as Andrea Vicentino, or simply Vicentino, was born at Venice in 1539, and was a scholar of the elder Palma. He painted historical subjects in the style of his instructor, and was employed in several works, representing subjects from the history of the Republic, in the Sala del Gran Consiglio, in the Palace of St. Mark. He also painted easel pictures for private collections, of which there is one in the Florence Gallery, representing the 'Anointing of Solomon, King of Israel.' He died in 1614.

DEI MOTTI, Jacopo, was a Milanese painter in oil, in fresco, and on glass, who, between 1485 and 1490, painted several windows in the Certosa at Pavia, and in the succeeding years decorated with frescoes several of its chapels. He died at Milan in 1505.

Cristoforo de' Motti also practised as a painter in fresco and on glass at Genoa, Milan, and Pavia, between the years 1468 and 1514.

DEI PAESI, Girolamo. See Muziano.

CALLED

PIERO DELLA FRANCESCA

[Malatesta Temple (San Francesco), Rimini]

SIGISMONDO MALATESTA KNEELING BEFORE ST. SIGISMUND

PIETRO DEI FRANCHESCHI

CALLED

PIERO DELLA FRANCESCA

Alinari photo]   *[Brera Gallery, Milan*

THE MADONNA AND CHILD, WITH ANGELS AND SAINTS, AND
FEDERIGO, DUKE OF URBINO

DEI PICCINELLI, RAFFAELLO and ANDREA, known as the BRESCIANINI of Siena, were the sons of a dancing-master at Siena, where they flourished from 1507 to 1525. They were the pupils of a Sienese painter, named Giovan Battista Giusi, and they together painted an altar-piece, representing the 'Virgin and Child, with Saints,' which is in the Siena Academy, and in 1524 the 'Baptism of Christ,' for the baptistery of the cathedral of the same city. In 1525 they went to Florence, and in the same year Andrea, and probably Raffaello also, was registered in the Painters' Guild. A 'Holy Family' by Andrea, who was the better artist of the two, is in the Uffizi Gallery at Florence, and another 'Holy Family,' ascribed to him, is in the Berlin Gallery. The beautiful altar-piece, a 'Holy Family,' of the church of Torre di Bibiano, long attributed to Baldassare Peruzzi, is also supposed to be by him. The brothers appear to have worked under the influence of Fra Bartolommeo. Raffaello died at Florence in 1545.

DEI RITRATTI, FRANCESCO. See NEGRI.

DEI ROSSI, BERNARDINO, who worked at Pavia, was one of the artists called to Milan in 1490 to decorate the Porta Giovia Palace of Lodovico Sforza. In the church of Santa Maria della Pusterla, Pavia, is a picture of the 'Virgin, with Saints and Donors,' signed and dated by him in 1491. Between the years 1498 and 1508 he decorated the Certosa of Pavia with wall paintings, of which the frescoes of the 'Eternal,' the 'Prophets,' and the 'Virgin Annunciate' still remain. In 1511 he executed some frescoes for the church at Vigano, belonging to the Carthusians of Pavia, which have now disappeared. No certain dates can be given of his birth or death.

DEI ROSSI, FRANCESCO, called IL CECCHINO DEL SALVIATI, or IL SALVIATI, (which appellation he acquired from the favour and protection he experienced from the cardinal of that name,) and also FRÄNZCHEN, was the son of Michelangelo de' Rossi, a weaver of velvets, and was born at Florence in 1510. He was a fellow-student with Giorgio Vasari, first under Andrea del Sarto, and afterwards under Baccio Bandinelli. The two young friends pursued their studies at Rome with the same intimacy, and in the church of Santa Maria della Pace Salviati painted the 'Annunciation' and 'Christ speaking to St. Philip,' by which he gained considerable reputation. He also embellished the chapel of his patron, Cardinal Salviati, with a series of frescoes, representing the 'Life of St. John the Baptist.' He was employed by Pier Luigi Farnese to make designs for Flemish tapestries for his palace, in which he represented the 'History of Alexander.' In conjunction with Vasari he ornamented the apartments of the Cancellaria with several paintings in fresco. From Rome he went to Venice, where he painted several pictures for the public edifices and private collections, particularly the 'History of Psyche,' in a saloon of the Palazzo Grimaldi, which Vasari, with marked partiality for his fellow-countryman and co-disciple, calls the finest painting in all Venice. He afterwards visited Florence, and was employed by the Grand-Duke Cosmo to ornament one of the saloons of the Palazzo Vecchio, where he represented the 'Triumph and Exploits of Furius Camillus,' composed and painted with great genius and spirit, and with an accuracy in the delineation of the arms, habiliments, and costume of ancient Rome, which is worthy of the most learned antiquary.

The restless and unsettled disposition of Salviati did not permit him to reside long in one place, and he readily complied with the invitation of the Cardinal de Lorraine to accompany him to France, where Francis I. had engaged some of the ablest artists of Italy in the decoration of the palace of Fontainebleau. He was received with distinction, and was treated with great kindness by Primaticcio, the superintendent of the works; but the jealousy and turbulence of his nature returned these good offices with ingratitude and malevolence. During his stay in France he painted for the church of the Celestines at Paris a fine picture, representing the 'Taking down from the Cross.' The 'Incredulity of St. Thomas,' by him, is now in the Louvre. Dissatisfied with his situation in France, he returned to Rome, where he fell into new difficulties and disputes with Daniele da Volterra and Pietro Ligorio. The continual agitation of his mind brought on a fever, of which he died, at Florence, in 1563.

DEI ROSSI, GIOVAMBATTISTA, called IL ROSSO, and in France MAÎTRE ROUX, was born at Florence in 1494. Although he was not a disciple of Andrea del Sarto, he was at first an admirer of his manner, and afterwards improved his powers by studying the works of Michelangelo and Parmigiano. Endowed with a ready and inventive genius, he scorned to be the servile imitator even of Buonarroti, and at an early age he ventured to compete with the ablest of his contemporaries in the cloister of the Annunziata, where he painted a large fresco of the 'Assumption of the Virgin,' in which he displayed both originality and taste. After painting several other pictures for the churches at Florence, particularly the 'Marriage of the Virgin,' in San Lorenzo, he went to Rome, where his talents were already known. There, among other works, he painted an altar-piece for Santa Maria della Pace; and had acquired considerable celebrity when Rome was taken and plundered in 1527. Rosso was taken prisoner by the Germans, and very badly treated, but he at length escaped, and took refuge at Volterra, where he painted for the cathedral a fine picture of the 'Deposition from the Cross.' He afterwards went to Venice, but not meeting with the success he expected in Italy, he resolved, about 1530, on visiting the court of Francis I. of France, who was at that time the great encourager of art. He was very favourably received by that monarch, who immediately engaged him in his service, and appointed him superintendent of the great works upon which he was then engaged at the palace of Fontainebleau. As Rosso was not less eminent as an architect than as a painter, he undertook the building of the great gallery in that palace, which was executed from his design, and which he decorated with several paintings and with ornaments in stucco, some of which were afterwards destroyed by his rival and competitor, Primaticcio, to make way for his own works. Thirteen frescoes, allusive to the life of Francis I., still remain, but have been restored by MM. Couder and Alaux.

The style of Rosso, though singular, is grand. He displayed a dignity of character, a lively expression in his heads, a tasteful arrangement of his draperies, an effective management of his light and shadow, and a daring execution; though these excellences were accompanied by a wildness and extravagance, too frequently attached to a fertile and exuberant imagination. This able artist was well versed in literature, and had a taste for poetry and music. His conversation was agreeable, and his manners polished. The possession of such accomplishments secured him the regard and good graces of Francis I. He was in the full possession of royal favour, and of the public estimation, when he sacrificed these advantages to a mean and unfounded suspicion. He had contracted a friendship with Francesco Pellegrini, a Florentine painter, who was in the habit of visiting him frequently, when his house was robbed of a considerable sum. He rashly suspected Pellegrini to be the robber, and brought a formal accusation against him. Pellegrini was in consequence of the charge put to the torture, and, after suffering the most horrible torments, was declared innocent. The remorse of having so unjustly exposed an innocent person to so dreadful a trial, preyed upon his mind, and he put an end to his existence by poison, at Fontainebleau, in 1541. The principal works of Rosso which exist are as follow :

Berlin	*Gallery.*	The Four Seasons.
Città di Castello.	*Cathedral.*	The Transfiguration.
Florence.	*SS. Annunziata.*	The Assumption of the Virgin (*fresco*).
„	*S. Lorenzo.*	The Marriage of the Virgin.
„	*Pitti Palace.*	The Virgin enthroned, with St. Sebastian, St. Mary Magdalen, and other Saints.
„	*Uffizi.*	Moses driving away the Madianite Shepherds.
„	„	The Virgin enthroned, with the Infant Jesus, and SS. Jerome and Francis.
Fontainebleau.	*Palace.*	Francis I. crowned by Victory.
„	„	A Sacrifice and Thanksgiving for the King.
„	„	Jupiter and Europa.
„	„	Neptune and Amphitrite.
„	„	Alexander cutting the Gordian Knot.
„	„	Francis I. in Roman costume, holding a grenade.
„	„	The Burning of Troy.
„	„	A Hurricane, in allusion to the Battle of Pavia.
„	„	The Triumph of Venus.
„	„	Chiron and Achilles.
„	„	Æsculapius at Rome.
„	„	Cupid and Psyche.
„	„	The Battle of the Lapithæ and the Centaurs.
Paris.	*Louvre.*	A Pietà.
„	„	The Challenge of the Pierides.
„	„	Mars and Venus (*pen-and-ink drawing*).
„	„	Design for a Coffer (*pen-and-ink drawing*).
Petersburg.	*Hermitage.*	The Virgin and Child, with St. John the Baptist.
„	„	The Madonna in glory.

DEI ROTARI, Conte PIETRO, who was of a noble family of Verona, was born in 1707. For some time he merely practised painting as an amusement, but his progress was so flattering, that he at length resolved to adopt it as a profession, and he became a scholar of Antonio Balestra, under whom he studied until he was eighteen years of age. He afterwards visited Venice, where he passed two years in studying the works of the best masters of that distinguished school of colouring. In 1727 he went to Rome, where he entered the school of Francesco Trevisani, and spent four years in studying the great works of art in that city. By the advantages of travel, and an assiduous application to his pursuit, he became a correct and graceful designer, and joined

to the expressive airs of his heads an elegance of contour, and a tasteful disposition of his draperies, in which he was not surpassed by any artist of his time. His principal works in Italy are his picture of the 'Annunciation,' at Guastalla ; and the 'Birth of the Virgin,' in the church of San Giovanni, at Padua. He afterwards visited the courts of Vienna and Dresden, where he met with the most flattering encouragement ; and in 1756 was invited to St. Petersburg by the Empress of Russia, who appointed him her principal painter, in which capacity he died, in 1762. We have several slight but spirited etchings by this artist, some of which are from his own compositions, and others after the works of Balestra. Among them are the following :

The Portrait of Filippo Baldinucci. 1726.
St. Francis kneeling before a Crucifix ; *from his own design.*
The Education of the Virgin ; *the same.*
Abraham and the Angels ; *after A. Balestra.*
David with the Head of Goliath ; *after the same.*
St. Jerome ; half-length ; *after the same.*
Venus and Æneas ; *after the same.*

DEI SALVIATI, IL CECCHINO. See DEI ROSSI, FRANCESCO.

DEI SERAFINI, SERAFINO, who was living in Modena in the 14th century, is known by a 'Coronation of the Virgin' and other subjects in the cathedral of that city. It bears the inscription "*Seraphinus de Seraphinis pinxit* 1385 *die Jovis* X.X.I.I.I. *Marcii.*" Although there is but little recorded of this artist, we may conclude that he was probably of some importance in his time, from the following inscription in a chapel, not named, painted by him :

Mille trecento con septanta sei
Erano corso gli anni del Signore
E'l quarto entrava quando a so honore
Questa Capella al nobel fin minei.
Et io, che tutta in si la storiei
Fui Serafin da Mutina Pittore.

DEI SERVI, CONSTANTINO, was an architect and painter who was living at Florence at the beginning of the 17th century. After studying awhile under Santi di Tito, he went to Germany, where he painted in the manner of Pourbus. His Florentine mosaics earned him much renown, and he also worked as an architect and engineer for the Shah of Persia, the Prince of Wales, and the Emperor Rudolph II. He died in 1622.

DEI VECCHI, GIOVANNI, was born at Borgo San Sepolcro about the year 1536. He went to Rome when he was young, where he first became a disciple of Raffaellino dal Colle, but he afterwards studied under Taddeo Zuccheri, who was at that time employed by Cardinal Alessandro Farnese in the embellishment of his palace of Caprarola, where, in conjunction with his instructor, he executed several considerable works. There are many of his pictures in the churches at Rome, of which a particular description is given by Baglione. In San Lorenzo in Damaso is one of his most esteemed productions, representing the 'Martyrdom of St. Lawrence' ; in the cupola of the Chiesa del Gesù is a fresco of the 'Four Doctors of the Church' ; and in Santa Maria in Araceli are several pictures from the life of St. Jerome. He died at Rome in 1614.

DEI ZAGANELLI, FRANCESCO, called FRANCESCO DA COTIGNOLA, was born in the latter part of the 15th century at Cotignola, in the Duchy of

Ferrara. He afterwards lived at Ravenna, and learned his art under Rondinello. At the Brera, Milan, is a 'Virgin and Child, between SS. Francis and Nicholas, and a kneeling patron,' signed by him in 1505; another similar subject, in which his brother Bernardino is said to have assisted him, is in the same gallery. In 1509 he painted the 'Infant Christ,' now in the Dublin National Gallery. The Costabili Collection, in Ferrara, possesses a 'St. Sebastian,' painted in 1513; and of about that time is the altar-piece now in the gallery of Forli, representing the 'Eternal in Glory, adored by the Saints on earth.' His celebrated picture of the 'Resurrection,' at Classe, and his esteemed work of the 'Baptism of Christ,' at Faenza, are productions that do honour to his country. He also painted, in 1518, an admirable picture of the 'Madonna surrounded by Saints,' at the Osservanti at Parma, in which he was assisted by his brother Bernardino, who was an artist of considerable ability. Others of his most important works are the 'Virgin and Child, with SS. John the Baptist, John the Evangelist, and Bernardino'; and the two portraits of the Pallavicini family, painted in 1518, in the church of the Nunziata, outside the Porta Nuova of Parma. Signor Federico Mylius, of Genoa, possesses a bust of the Saviour executed by Francesco and his brother Bernardino. Of the latter's own work only a single example is known, viz., a 'St. Sebastian,' belonging to Signor Frizzoni, of Bellaggio. Many other paintings by Francesco are to be met with in the galleries and churches of Ravenna. The date of his death is uncertain, but after 1518 all traces of him are lost.

DE JAGER, GERARD, a native of Dordrecht, flourished about 1646. He painted marine subjects, and particularly excelled in the representation of still water. He was still living in 1663.

DE JODE, ARNOLD, the son of Pieter De Jode, the younger, was born at Antwerp in 1638. He was instructed in engraving by his father, but he never rose above mediocrity. He worked in the Netherlands and in Spain, and was in England in 1666, the year of the great fire in London, and in 1667. His best prints are portraits, though they are but indifferent. Among other plates, the following are by him:

PORTRAITS.

Cardinal Pallavicini; *after Titian.*
Catharine Howard, Duchess of Lennox; *after Van Dyck.*
Sir Peter Lely; *after Lely.*
Alexander Browne; prefixed to his 'Ars Pictoria'; *after Huysmans.*

VARIOUS SUBJECTS.

The Education of Cupid; *after Correggio.* 1667.
The Magdalen; oval; *after Van Dyck.*
The Infant Christ embracing St. John; *after the same;* inscribed *Arnoldus de Jode, sculp. Londini, tempore incendii maximi.*
A Landscape; *after L. De Vadder.* 1658.
Some other Landscapes; *after Jacques Fouquières.*

DE JODE, GERRIT, a Flemish engraver and printseller, appears to have been born at Antwerp in 1521. He was the head of a family greatly distinguished in the art of engraving. He executed several plates of historical and geographical subjects, in which his style appears to have been an imitation of that of Cornelis Cort. He died at Antwerp in 1591. The following are some of his principal prints:

A set of twenty-nine Portraits of the Popes. 1585.

A Roman Triumph, in twelve sheets; *after M. Heemckerk.*
The Crucifixion; a large print, in three sheets; *after Michelangelo Buonarroti,* but without the name of the painter.
St. Jerome in meditation; *after Titian.* 1565.

DE JODE, PIETER, 'the elder,' the son of Gerrit De Jode, was born at Antwerp in 1570. After being taught the rudiments of design by his father, he was instructed in engraving by Hendrik Goltzius. He afterwards went to Italy for improvement, particularly in drawing, and engraved several plates from the works of the great masters. About the year 1601 he returned to Antwerp, where he distinguished himself by producing various prints after the principal Flemish painters. He and his son were in 1631 in Paris, where they worked for some time. His drawing is very correct; and though his command of the graver is less daring and bold than that of his instructor, he is less mannered and extravagant. He died at Antwerp in 1634. He engraved about a hundred plates, of which the following are the principal:

PORTRAITS.

Erycius Puteanus, (Hendrik van der Putte,) a Dutch savant.
Giovanni Boccaccio; *after Titian.*
Ferdinand, Count Palatine of the Rhine; oval; *after Rubens.*
Philip III., King of Spain; oval; *after the same.*
Francisco de Mello, Count d'Azumar.
Ambrogio Spinola.

VARIOUS SUBJECTS.

The Five Senses; *apparently from his own designs.*
The Life and Miracles of St. Catharine; twelve plates; *after Francesco Vanni.* 1606.
The Life of Christ; thirty-six plates.
Costumes of the People of Europe; *after S. Francken.*
The Virgin and Child; *after Titian.*
The Marriage of St. Catharine; *after the same.*
The Holy Family; *after the same.*
The Adoration of the Shepherds; *after A. van Oort.*
Christ and Nicodemus; *after the same.*
The Beheading of St. John the Baptist; *after Rubens.*
Christ giving the Keys to St. Peter; *after the same.*
The Virgin fainting at the sight of Christ crowned with thorns; *after F. Vanni.*
The Coronation of St. Catharine; *after the same.*
The Last Judgment; *after Jean Cousin;* on twelve plates; one of the largest prints known.

DE JODE, PIETER, 'the younger,' the son of the elder artist of the same names, was born at Antwerp in 1606, and was instructed by his father, whom he surpassed in the taste and facility with which he handled the graver. He engraved upwards of three hundred plates, but they are very unequal. His best works are his portraits, several of which he engraved after Van Dyck. The date of his death is unknown. The following are his most esteemed prints:

PORTRAITS AFTER VAN DYCK.

Charles I.
Henrietta Maria, his Queen.
Thomas Wentworth, Earl of Strafford.
Prince Rupert.
Catharine, Countess of Newburgh.
Pieter De Jode, the younger.
Jacob Jordaens, painter, of Antwerp.
Cornelis van Poelenburg, painter, of Utrecht.
Jan Snellinck, painter, of Antwerp.
Daniel Mytens, painter.
Adam De Coster, painter, of Mechlin.
Andreas Colyns de Nole, sculptor, of Antwerp.
Hendrik Liberti, organist.
Albert, Duke of Friedland, Count of Wallenstein.

D 2

Geneviève d'Urfé, Duchess de Croy.
Jeanne de Blois.
Jean de Tserclaes, Count de Tilly.
Diodorus van Tulden, professor at Louvain.
Anthony Trieste, Bishop of Ghent.

PORTRAITS AFTER OTHER MASTERS.

Karl Heinrich, Baron von Metternich; *after A. van Hulle.*
August Adolph, Baron von Trautdorf; *after the same.*
Thomas Ricciardi; *after Simon Vouet.*
Ernest, Count d'Isembourg; *after J. Willeborts Bosch-aert.*
Petrus de Francavilla, sculptor and architect; *after Bunel.*

SUBJECTS AFTER VARIOUS MASTERS.

St. Augustine, crowned by Religion; *P. de Jode, fec.*
St. Francis kneeling before a Crucifix; *after Baroccio.*
The Holy Family; *after Titian.*
The Visitation of the Virgin to St. Elizabeth; *after Rubens.*
The Three Graces; *after the same.*
Venus rising from the Sea; *after the same.*
Cybele and Neptune; *after the same.*
St. Francis and St. Clara adoring the Infant Jesus; *after Gerard Segers.*
Christ with Nicodemus; *after the same.*
The Nativity; *after J. Jordaens.*
The Miracle of St. Martin of Tours; *after the same.*
Folly and Ignorance; *after the same.*
St. Augustine supported by Angels; *after Van Dyck.*
St. Augustine adoring the Mystery of the Holy Trinity; *after the same. (His best work.)*
Rinaldo and Armida; *after the same.*
The Holy Family, with St. Anne; *after A. van Diepenbeek.*
An Allegory of Peace; *after the same.*
St. John the Baptist in the Desert; *after P. van Mol.*

DE JONG, LUDOLF, (DE JONGH, or DE JONGE,) was born at Overschie, a village near Rotterdam, in 1616. He was the son of a shoemaker, who intended bringing him up to the same business, but from his aversion to the work and strong disposition for art, he was placed under Cornelis Sachtleven, with whom he passed two years. He afterwards studied successively under Anthony Palamedes of Delft, and Jan Bijlert of Utrecht. He subsequently went to France, and passed seven years at Paris, where he met with encouragement as a portrait painter, in which branch of art he chiefly excelled. He also painted easel pictures of hunting-parties and battles, which are ingeniously composed and touched with spirit and vigour. On his return to Holland he settled at Rotterdam, where he was much employed. His most considerable work is a large picture in the 'Salle des Princes' in that city, containing the portraits of the officers of the Company of Burghers. He died at Hillegersberg in 1697.

DE JONGHE, JEAN BAPTISTE, a Belgian landscape painter, was born at Courtrai in 1785. He studied under Ommeganck, and travelled in Holland, France, and England. He finally settled at Brussels, where he had many pupils and followers. He exhibited his works at Paris, Lyons, Brussels, Amsterdam, the Hague, Vienna, &c., and obtained various medals. He died at Antwerp in 1844. Amongst his best productions are:

Environs of Tournai (*Brussels Museum*).
Stream with Cattle (*Ghent Academy*).
View near Courtrai (*Ghent Academy*).
Interior of a Farm (*Haarlem Museum*).
Travellers Resting (*Haarlem Museum*).
Flock of Sheep; sandy road (*Tournai Museum*).

DEJUINNE, FRANÇOIS LOUIS, was born in Paris in 1786, and learned the art of painting under Girodet. He visited Rome, where he studied the works of Titian, Paolo Veronese, and other great masters. He died in Paris in 1844. His paintings were mostly historical; among them are the 'Ascension of the Virgin' and 'St. Geneviève' for Notre-Dame de Lorette, and 'The Four Seasons' for the Trianon Palace.

DE KEMPENEER, PIETER, better known by his Spanish name of PEDRO CAMPAÑA, which has been translated into French as CHAMPAIGNE, and into Flemish as VAN DE VELDE, was a painter born at Brussels in 1503, although from the character of his works and his subsequent life he should be classed with the Spanish school. He visited Italy early in life, and there studied the masterpieces of Raphael and Michelangelo. On his journey to Rome in 1530 he painted the triumphal arch which was erected at Bologna for the coronation of Charles V. He afterwards went to Spain, and subsequently to 1548 painted numerous devotional pictures for the churches of Seville. His masterpiece is the 'Descent from the Cross,' which he painted about 1548 for the church of Santa Cruz, and which, when that church fell into ruins, was removed to the cathedral of Seville. This work compares favourably with the productions of Albrecht Dürer. Such was at one time its lifelike awful character that Murillo used to stand watching, as he said, until these holy men should have finished taking down the Saviour. A 'Purification of the Virgin' and a 'Resurrection' by him, also in the cathedral, by the beauty of their design and the luminous character of their colouring are suggestive of the highest period of Italian art. The parish churches of Triana and of Santa Maria at Carmoña possess paintings by this master. De Kempeneer returned to Brussels not later than 1563, and died in that city in 1580. Besides the above-named works he has left the following:

Seville, *S. Isidoro*, St. Paul the Hermit; St. Anthony, Abbot. *S. Pedro*, Christ bound to the Pillar; St. Sebastian; St. Jerome enthroned. *S. Catalina*, St. Jerome enthroned, with Saints. *S. Juan de la Palma*, Crucifixion, with the Virgin and St. John. (*An early work.*)

DE KEYSER, NICAISE, a Flemish painter, was born at Santvliet, near Antwerp, in 1813. He was a pupil of J. Jacops and of Van Brée, and distinguished himself by his battle-pieces, &c., in the manner of Wappers and the reactionaries of 1830. In 1855 he became director of the Academy of Antwerp. He died in 1887.

DE KEYSER, THOMAS, (until recently, named in error Theodoor,) was born at Amsterdam about the year 1595. In the Gallery at the Hague is a fine picture by this Dutch painter, representing the Four Burgomasters of Amsterdam deliberating on the honours to be paid to Marie de Médicis, on her entrance into that city in 1638. The heads are admirably painted, and with a richness of colouring nearly approaching to Rembrandt. The portraits of Rombout Hoogerbeets, his wife, and family, and two other pictures, now in the Museum at Amsterdam, were also painted by him. There is also a picture by him in the National Gallery, representing 'A Merchant and his Clerk.' He died at Amsterdam in 1679. Some of his works are signed with the accompanying monogram:

DE KEYSER, WILLEM, (or DE KEYSAR,) was born at Antwerp about the year 1647. He was brought up as a jeweller, in which profession he became very eminent, but having been well educated, and taught to draw, he had a strong inclination for painting, and employed all his leisure hours in practising in miniature, enamel, and oil-colours. Having painted some altar-pieces at Antwerp, his business called him to Dunkirk, where he painted a picture for the chapel of the English nuns, who were so pleased with it, that they persuaded De Keyser to go to England, and gave him letters of recommendation to Lord Melfort, then in favour with James II. The enthusiastic painter could not resist the proposal; he embarked on board an English vessel, and, unknown to his wife or family, sailed for England. His reception was equal to his wishes. He was introduced to the king, who promised to countenance him, and several persons of rank, who had known him at Antwerp, encouraged him in his new vocation. Transported with this prospect he sent for his wife, ordering her to dismiss his workmen, and convert his effects into money. Within half a year the bubble burst; the Revolution happened, De Keyser's friends could no longer be his protectors, his business decreased, and the pursuit of the philosopher's stone, to which he had recourse in his despair, completed his ruin. He died at the age of forty-five, about the year 1692. He left a daughter, whom he had taken great pains to instruct, and with success. She painted small portraits in oil, and copied well.

DEKKER (or DECKER). There are several artists of this name, either German or Dutch, enumerated by different writers, with admirable confusion in apportioning their respective works. Some call Cornelis Gerrits, the landscape painter, Coenraet, others Karel, or Hendrik, each saying that his pictures resemble those of Ruisdael; Custos, like Frans, is said to have painted grotesque subjects; Adriaen, to have been a scholar of Everdingen; Jan, a painter of interiors, conversations, and landscapes in the manner of Murant; Hans was a sculptor; the others occur in the following articles. The Dekker whose works are best known in England is Frans, who painted views, similar to Ruisdael's, on a small scale, and also weavers' workshops. Brulliot, following Heinecken, says that Karel was an engraver, who flourished about the commencement of the 18th century.

DEKKER, CORNELIS GERRITS (often incorrectly called COENRAET DECKER), who was born in the earlier half of the 17th century, is supposed to have studied under Solomon Ruisdael. He died in poverty at Haarlem in 1678. A good example of his style is a 'Wooded Landscape,' in the Rotterdam Museum. There are likewise two Landscapes by him in the Louvre. He was of the same period and of the same school of landscape art as Ruisdael, to whom his works were for a long time attributed. Adriaan van Ostade and Adriaan van de Velde painted figures of men and animals in his pictures.

DEKKER, FRANS, is a painter of whom but little is known, although his pictures possess great merit, and are to be met with in almost every collection. He is stated to have been born at Haarlem in 1684, and to have died at the same place in 1751, having been a pupil of Romeyn De Hooghe and of Bartholomeus Engels. He painted landscapes in a very pleasing and natural style, resembling the charming productions of Ruisdael, but without the

servilty of an imitator. He also excelled in caricature.

DE KONINCK, DAVID, (DE KONING, DE KONINGH, or DE CONINCK,) called RAMMELAAR, was born at Antwerp in 1636. After studying for some time in his native country under Jan Fyt, he travelled in Germany, France, and subsequently in Italy. He settled at Rome, and eventually died there in 1687. His works, which are not numerous, represent chiefly landscapes ornamented with animals of all descriptions, and in every respect are nearly as good as those of his master, Jan Fyt. At Ghent there is a 'Garden with domestic animals' by De Koninck; and in the Museum of Amsterdam there are a 'Stag-hunt' and a 'Bear-hunt.'

DE KONINCK, PHILIP, (DE KONING, DE KONINGH, or DE CONINCK,) was born at Amsterdam in 1619, and was one of the ablest scholars of Rembrandt. He painted historical subjects and portraits, but was particularly eminent in the latter, in which he was one of the most distinguished artists of his time. His colouring, though rich and harmonious, is clearer than that of Rembrandt, and partakes of the chaste and tender tinting of Van Dyck. There is an uncommon appearance of truth and nature in his heads, with a more tasteful arrangement of the attitudes and habiliments than is usual in the portraiture of the artists of his country. There is a fine portrait of De Koninck, by himself, in the Uffizi at Florence. He died at Amsterdam in 1689. In the Museum of that city there is a 'Landscape with Animals' by him; another landscape is in the Museum at the Hague, a replica of which is in the National Gallery; another is in the Rotterdam Museum; and another, which is assigned to Rembrandt, is in the Uffizi at Florence. A 'View in the Environs of Scheveningen' is in the Brussels Gallery.

DE KONINGH, LEENDERT, a Dutch marine and landscape painter, was born at Dordrecht in 1777. He was instructed by A. Vermeulen and M. Versteeg, and in 1801 came to England, but was soon compelled to leave this country on account of the war. He then went to Paris, and studied under David. Thence he returned home by way of Germany, and afterwards paid a second visit to England, where he remained till after the fall of Napoleon. He died at Dordrecht in 1849.

DE LA BAER, JOHANNES, (or DE LA BARRE,) a Flemish painter upon glass, who has been often confounded with Jan Barra, a Dutch engraver, was a native of Bois-le-Duc, and was received as a master into the Guild of St. Luke at Antwerp in 1625. He was an artist of real merit, and belonged entirely to the school of Rubens. The windows of the chapel of the Virgin in the church of St. Gudule at Brussels, which were for a long time attributed to Rubens, are known now to have been executed from his designs. He also engraved a plate of the façade of the Jesuit church at Antwerp.

DE LA BERGE, CHARLES AUGUSTE, a French landscape painter, was born in Paris in 1805. In 1824 he entered the studio of Bertin, the landscape painter, and in 1827 that of Picot, the historical painter. He first exhibited at the Salon of 1831, and in the years 1837-39 painted entirely from nature, and at the time of day which it represents, a 'Landscape at sunset,' which is in the Louvre. He died in Paris in 1842.

DE LA BOISSIÈRE, SIMON, was a French engineer, who also distinguished himself as an engraver. He was born in Paris about 1637, and executed several plates from his own designs, and after Sébastien Le Clerc. There are by him:

The Death of a Prince, surrounded by his Court.
Several plates of Medals for Molinet's 'Historia Pontificum,' 1679.
A View of the Palais Royal; in two sheets.
Several plates for Desgodets' 'Traité des Edifices Antiques de Rome,' Paris, 1682.

DE LA CALLEJA, ANDREAS, a Spanish painter, was born at Rioja in 1705. He was a pupil of G. A. Ezquerra, and was so successful in his early efforts that he was soon appointed by King Philip V. to a post of honour. Philip VI. in 1752 made him first Director of the newly-founded Academy at Madrid, and he established a school of some repute. But we are told that the principal occupation of his latter years was that of restoring the ancient pictures belonging to the king! It would be unjust to visit on him all the iniquities that have been perpetrated on pictures in Spain by the process of restoring; for to such an extent has it been carried, that very few of them, really worth preserving, have escaped. His best works are in the churches of Santa Cruz and of San Felipe el Real at Madrid. He died in that city in 1785.

DELACAZETTE, SOPHIE CLÉMENCE, a French miniature painter, was born at Lyons in 1774. She was a pupil of Regnault and of Augustin, and exhibited annually at the Salon from 1806 to 1838. In 1808 she sent a portrait of Mlle. Barilli, which has been engraved by Masquelier. She died in Paris in 1854.

DE LA CHAPELLE, GEORGE, a painter born at Caen, visited the Levant in the early part of the 17th century. His work is known to us by a series of engravings executed probably by Nicolas Cochin.

DE LA CORTE, GABRIEL, the son of Juan de La Corte, was born at Madrid in 1648. Without the aid of a master he practised flower-painting by copying the works of Mario and Arellano. He arrived at such a degree of excellence that Antonio de Castrejon and Matias de Torres employed him to paint garlands of flowers to surround their mythological subjects. He died at Madrid in 1694.

DE LA CORTE, JUAN, a Spanish painter, was born at Madrid in 1597. He was instructed by Velazquez, and painted portraits and history, but chiefly excelled in battle-pieces and perspective views. He also painted small pictures of subjects from sacred history. He was painter to Philip III., and was continued in that situation by his successor, Philip IV. There are several of his pictures in the palace of Buen Retiro. He died at Madrid in 1660.

DE LA CROCE, JOHANN NEPOMUK, an Austrian painter, was born at Pressano, in the Tyrol, in 1736. He studied under Lorenzoni, and after travelling in Italy, Germany, Hungary, and France, he settled at Burghausen. The portraits which he painted are estimated by Lipowski at the immense number of 5000, and his historical pictures at 200. There are many altar-pieces by him in the churches of Bavaria. He died in 1819. His son, CLEMENS DE LA CROCE, who was also a painter, was born at Burghausen in 1783, and died in 1823.

DELACROIX, AUGUSTE, a French marine painter, was born at Boulogne in 1809, and died there in 1868. He produced some elegant sea-pieces taken on the French and North African coasts, and also painted some African genre pictures.

DELACROIX, FERDINAND VICTOR EUGÈNE, a French historical painter, was born at Charenton St. Maurice, near Paris, in 1798. His father held high office under the Republic and First Empire, being successively deputy in the Convention, minister under the Directory, and prefect of Marseilles, and subsequently of Bordeaux. Young Delacroix received his first instruction in the Lycée Impérial; but on the death of his father, he had to make his own way in life, almost unaided. In 1817 he entered the studio of Guérin, where amongst his fellow-pupils were Géricault, Ary Scheffer, Henriquel-Dupont, and Cogniet. His first exhibited work, 'Dante and Virgil,' appeared in 1822, and achieved a great success. Through it he spent some time in the studio of Baron Gros, and might have obtained great academic honours but for his divergence from the prevalent classicism. This breach widened, and Delacroix, Géricault, and others, became the recognized leaders of the Romantic School. The conflict between the rival schools was very bitter, and it was not till after the Revolution of 1830 that Delacroix and the Romanticists began to receive a share of the state patronage which exercises so great an influence on art in France. In 1831 he visited Spain, Morocco, and Algiers, and several important works were the result of this journey. In 1832, through the influence of Thiers, although not without great opposition, he received his first public commission. Between that year and 1855 he executed decorative works for the Chamber of Deputies, the Library of the Luxembourg, the Galerie d'Apollon in the Louvre, the Salon de la Paix in the Hôtel de Ville, and the Church of St. Sulpice. He was elected at the Academy in 1857. He last exhibited at the Salon in 1859, and died in Paris in 1863. Personally, Delacroix was a nervous man, objecting to visitors in his studio, although he was not deficient in those traits which render a man agreeable in society. His works show the attraction which the darker side of human nature had for him, and it was in the depiction of scenes of passion and of blood that he achieved his greatest successes, to which his excellence as a colourist no little contributed. Besides the decorative works already mentioned, the following are amongst his chief productions:

Arras.	*Museum.*	Martyrdom of St. Stephen. 1853.
Bordeaux.	*Museum.*	Greece expiring on the ruins of Missolonghi. 1827.
"	"	Lion Hunting. 1854. (*Destroyed by fire in 1870.*)
Chantilly.	*Duke d'Aumale.*	The Two Foscari. 1855.
"	"	A Moorish Guard.
Grenoble.	*Museum.*	St. George.
Lille.	*Museum.*	Medea. 1838.
London.	*Hertford House.*	Death of Marino Faliero. 1827.
"	"	Faust and Mephistopheles.
Lyons.	*Museum.*	The Last Words of Marcus Aurelius. 1845.
Melun.	*Museum.*	Head of Actæon.
Montpellier.	*Museum.*	A Mulatto Woman.
"	"	Charge of Arab Cavalry. 1832.
"	"	Algerian Women at home.
"	"	Daniel in the Lions' Den. 1853.
"	"	Michelangelo in his studio. 1853.
"	"	Portrait of Himself. 1829.
"	"	Portrait of M. Bruyas. 1853.
Nancy.	*Museum.*	Battle of Nancy. 1834.
Nantes.	*Museum.*	The Halt. 1837.
Paris.	*Louvre.*	Dante and Virgil. 1822.
"	"	The Massacre of Scio. 1824.
"	"	The 28th of July, 1830. 1830.
"	"	Algerian Women. 1834.
"	"	Portrait of Himself. 1837.
"	"	Jewish Wedding in Morocco. 1841.

Paris.	St. Paul.	Christ in the Garden of Gethsemane. 1827.
Rouen.	Museum.	The Justice of Trajan. 1840.
Toulouse.	Museum.	Muley-abd-el-Rahmann, Sultan of Morocco, leaving his palace at Mequinez. 1845.
Tours.	Museum.	Arab Musicians. 1848.
Versailles.	Museum.	Battle of Taillebourg. 1837.
"	"	Taking of Constantinople by the Crusaders. 1841.
"	"	Portrait of Marshal de Tourville. 1835.

O.J.D.

Delacroix also executed a considerable number of etchings, engravings, and lithographs, a list of which is to be found in Moreau's 'E. Delacroix et son œuvre,' Paris, 1873, 8vo. He likewise wrote some articles on painters and sculptors in the 'Revue des Deux-Mondes.' His 'Lettres' were published by M. Burty in 1878, and again, with additions, in 1880.

DE LA CRUZ, JUAN PANTOJA. See PANTOJA DE LA CRUZ.

DE LA CRUZ, MANUEL, a Spanish painter, was born at Madrid in 1750, and died in the same city in 1792. He distinguished himself by his pictures in the cathedral of Carthagena and in the monastery of San Francisco el Grande at Madrid. In the Gallery of the latter city there is a painting by him of 'The Annual Fair at Madrid.' He also etched a few plates of Heads of strongly-marked character.

DE LA CRUZ, MIGUEL, a Spanish painter of promise who died young, was employed in 1633 by Charles I. of England to make copies of the remarkable pictures in the Alcazar of Madrid.

DE LA FAGE, NICOLAS, a French painter and etcher of the first half of the 17th century, was a native of Arles in Provence. Robert-Dumesnil mentions nine plates by him, among which are:

The Virgin and Child; after Annibale Carracci.
Anne of Austria, Queen of France. 1648.
Louisa Mary Gonzaga, Queen of Poland.
François de Vendôme, Duke of Beaufort. 1649.

DE LA FAGE, RAYMOND, a French draughtsman, was born at L'Isle en Albigeois in 1656. He studied under Jean Pierre Rivalz at Toulouse, but soon left his master and went to Rome, where he resided three years. He afterwards went to Paris, where his wonderfully facile pen-and-ink sketches found many admirers. Crozat possessed no less than three hundred of them, and the Louvre has now about seventy. He died at Lyons in 1684. Robert-Dumesnil mentions twenty-five etchings by him.

DE LA FERTÉ, M., was a French amateur, who, according to Basan, etched several small plates of landscapes, from the designs of Boucher and other masters.

DE LA FLEUR, NICOLAS GUILLAUME, who was born in Lorraine about 1608, was a painter of flowers in miniature and an etcher. He was working at Rome in 1638, and in Paris in 1644. He died in Rome in 1670. His etchings, which are very rare, are executed with the point, and are very effective and tasteful. The principal of them are:

Thirteen plates of Flowers; copied by Danckerts. 1638.
Twelve plates of Flowers. 1639.

DE LA FOSSE, CHARLES, an eminent French painter, was born in Paris in 1636. He was educated under François Chauveau and afterwards under Charles Le Brun. At the age of twenty-two he went to Italy, where he made such satisfactory progress that Colbert obtained for him the pension of the King, in order that he might be able to continue his studies. He passed two years at Rome, and then went for three years to Venice to study the works of the great colourists. He appears to have been less sensible to the sublime beauties of the Roman School, than to the seductive colouring of the Venetian, and he returned to Paris one of the most accomplished colourists of the French School. He was immediately taken into the service of Louis XIV., and was first employed in painting four pictures for the apartments in the Tuileries. His next work was the marriage chapel in St. Eustache, where he painted in fresco 'Adam and Eve' and the 'Marriage of the Virgin.' He painted for Versailles the 'Sacrifice of Iphigenia' and 'Moses saved from the Waters'; in the chapel of the palace the 'Resurrection'; and at the Trianon, 'Apollo and Thetis.' At Marly, he painted a picture of 'Bacchus and Ariadne.' These works brought him into great repute; and he was received into the Academy in 1673, on which occasion he painted the 'Rape of Proserpine,' which is now in the Louvre. La Fosse visited England in 1689, and again in 1690, when he remained upwards of two years, during which time he was employed in decorating the mansion of the Duke of Montagu, afterwards the British Museum, in which he painted two ceilings, representing the 'Apotheosis of Isis' and an 'Assembly of the Gods.' His principal work at Paris is the fresco in the dome of the Invalides, which is fifty-six feet in diameter, and represents 'St. Louis placing his crown and sword in the hands of Christ, who is accompanied by the Virgin, and by Angels who bear the instruments of the Passion': in the angles are the Four Evangelists. This immense work was finished in 1705, and did great honour to the artist. In the choir of Notre-Dame he painted the 'Nativity' and the 'Adoration of the Magi.' Although the genius of La Fosse was equal to great and copious compositions, his drawing was neither elegant nor correct; and though he is considered to be one of the best colourists among his countrymen, he is very far distant from Titian or Paolo Veronese. He died in Paris in 1716. Besides the 'Rape of Proserpine,' the Louvre has by him 'Moses saved from the Waters,' the 'Annunciation of the Virgin,' the 'Marriage of the Virgin,' the 'Triumph of Bacchus,' and the 'Sacrifice of Iphigenia.'

DE LA FOSSE, JEAN BAPTISTE JOSEPH, a French engraver, was born in Paris in 1721. He was a pupil of Etienne Fessard, and engraved a large number of book-plates and vignettes after Eisen and Gravelot. He died in Paris about 1775. We have also several portraits by him after the drawings of Carmontelle, among which are the following:

The Duke of Orleans on horseback.
The same, with his Son, the Duke of Chartres.
M. Rameau.
The Abbé de Chauvelin.
The unfortunate Calas Family.

DE LA FOSSE, JEAN CHARLES, a French architect and draughtsman, was one of the best designers of ornaments, decorations, and furniture of the reign of Louis XVI. In 1768 was published his 'Iconologie Historique,' in which many of the plates were engraved by himself.

DE LA FUENTE, JUAN LEANDRO, was a Spanish painter, who flourished at Granada from 1630 to 1640. Although not mentioned by Palomino or by Pons, he was an artist of distinguished merit. He

39

followed the manner of Bassano both in subject and treatment, and his colouring is quite of the Venetian School. His pictures are to be found at Granada, Seville, and Madrid.

DE LA FUENTE DEL SAZ, JULIAN, was a Hieronymite monk, who painted miniatures at the Escorial. He is known to have been living from 1527 to 1598.

DE LA GOURDAINE, JEAN PIERRE NORBLIN. See NORBLIN DE LA GOURDAINE.

DE LA GUERTIÈRE, FRANÇOIS, a French historical painter, was born in 1624. He etched seventeen plates of the Grotesques by Raphael in the Vatican.

DEL AGUILA, FRANCISCO, was a Spanish fresco painter, who resided at Murcia in the latter part of the 16th century. In 1570 he painted and gilded the beautiful tomb of Alfonso the Wise, in the cathedral of that city.

DEL AGUILA, MIGUEL, a Spanish historical painter, was a native of Seville, where he died in 1736. His pictures are valued for their near approach to the style of Murillo.

DE LA HAYE, CHARLES, a French engraver, was born at Fontainebleau in 1641. He went to Italy, where he engraved, with C. Bloemaert, Spierre, Blondeau, and others, the paintings by Pietro da Cortona in the Palazzo Pitti at Florence. His style of engraving resembles that of Cornelis Bloemaert; and though his plates want harmony, they possess considerable merit. The following are among the best:

The Virgin and Child, with St. Catharine and other Saints; *after Ciro Ferri.*
St. Philip Neri kneeling before the Virgin; *after the same.*
Coriolanus refusing to see the Roman Ambassadors; *after the same.*
The Grecian Philosophers in the Gardens of Academus; *after Romanelli.*

DE LA HAYE, CLAUDE, was a French portrait painter, who flourished at Lyons in 1564, and was patronized by Charles IX. Catharine de' Medici visited his studio, and sat to him for her portrait.

DE LA HAYE, REYNIER, a Dutch painter, was a native of the Hague, and there entered the Guild named 'Pictura' in 1662. In 1669 he removed to Utrecht, and was admitted into the Guild of St. Luke. He painted scenes of private life, in the manner of Terborch and of Metsu; but his style is not so large or so light, his colouring is less vigorous, and his chiaroscuro defective.

DE LA HÈLE, ISAAK, a Flemish historical painter, was born at Antwerp about 1536. He was the younger son of Ysbrant de La Hèle, a sculptor, and left his native city early in life, but whether he went to Italy and studied under Michelangelo is uncertain. From 1562 to 1568 he was employed upon work for the cathedral of Toledo, and painted a capital picture of 'St. Nicasius,' which Pons mistook for the work of Berruguete, a certain proof of its merits. He returned to Antwerp probably in 1571, and was still living there in 1573. ABRAHAM DE LA HÈLE, his elder brother, was likewise a painter. He was born in 1534 at Antwerp, where he was still living in 1564, but in 1572 we lose sight of him in Augsburg.

DE LA HIRE, LAURENT, (or DE LA HYRE,) a French historical and portrait painter, was born in Paris in 1606. He was the son of Etienne de La Hire, an historical painter, who had acquired some reputation in Poland. He studied under him, and from the pictures at Fontainebleau, aiming especially at the style of Primaticcio. On his return to Paris he spent some time in the school of Lallemand, then in great reputation. His colouring was somewhat cloudy, but otherwise his execution was good, although he inclined to mannerism. One of his earliest and best pictures, 'The Martyrdom of St. Bartholomew,' is in the church of St. Jacques. In the Louvre are ten of his works, including 'St. Peter healing the Sick,' a 'mai' painted for the cathedral of Notre-Dame in 1635, and in the Belvedere is an 'Ascension of the Virgin.' In 1637 he painted another 'mai' for the cathedral of Notre-Dame, the 'Conversion of St. Paul.' He painted also a large number of portraits, but in the later years of his life he confined himself to landscapes and small easel pictures. La Hire was one of the twelve artists who in 1648 founded the Royal Academy of Painting and Sculpture. He died in Paris in 1656. He engraved forty-six religious and mythological subjects and landscapes, many of which were from pictures by himself which perished during the troubles of 1793 and 1794. Among them are the following:

The Holy Family, with St. John kissing the foot of the Infant Jesus.
The Holy Family reposing, surrounded by Angels.
The Holy Family, with the Palm-branch.
The Repose in Egypt.
The Crucifixion, with the Virgin, Magdalen, and St. John. 1639.
The Conversion of St. Paul.
The Judgment of Paris.
Venus and Adonis.

DE LA HIRE, PHILIPPE, the son of Laurent de La Hire, was born in Paris in 1640. He at first devoted himself to landscape painting, and painted several pictures in the style of Watteau, but afterwards studied astronomy, and attained some eminence in that branch of science. He died in 1719.

DE LA HUERTA, GASPAR, was born at Campillo de Altobuey in Cuenca in 1645. At an early age, seeking instruction in Valencia, he fell into the hands of Jesualda Sanchez, the bustling widow of Pedro Infant, a third-rate painter, who continued on her own account her husband's school for the manufacture of religious pictures. La Huerta, nevertheless, attained some skill as a draughtsman and colourist, and married the widow's well-dowered daughter. Working for moderate prices he found abundant employment in the neighbouring churches and convents. For the Franciscans he painted the 'Jubilee of the Porciuncula,' and for the Dominicans the picture which long served as a veil to the wondrous image of 'Our Lady of the Forsaken.' He died at Valencia in 1714. The Museum of Valencia possesses a pleasing picture of 'Christ and the Virgin enthroned,' the latter with the bright complexion peculiar to Valencian beauty.

DE LA HUERTA, MANUEL, a Spanish monk, who flourished at the beginning of the 18th century, produced some excellent miniature paintings in the monastery of La Merced Calzada at Valladolid.

DE LA HYRE. See DE LA HIRE.

DE LA IGLESIA, FRANCISCO IGNACIO RUIZ. See RUIZ DE LA IGLESIA.

DE LA JOUE, JACQUES, a French architectural painter, was born in 1687. He became a member of the Academy in 1721, and is noticed for a 'Perspective' which he executed in 1732 at the Library of St. Geneviève. He also designed the title-page to the works of Wouwerman. Etchings have been made after him by Cochin, Tardieu, and others. He died in Paris in 1761.

DE LA LIVE DE JULLY, Ange Laurent, Marquis de Rémoville, a French amateur engraver, etched several subjects after Boucher and Greuze; a set of caricatures, after Saly; and some portraits. He was born in Paris in 1725, and died in the same city in 1779. He formed a fine collection of works of art of the French School, but this was dispersed in 1770, in consequence of its owner having lost his reason.

DELAMAIN, Paul, a French painter of Algerian subjects, was born in Paris in 1821. He was a pupil of Leblanc and of Drolling, but, fascinated with a desire to visit the East, he left the studio of the latter to enlist in the cavalry for service in Algeria. In after years, when he could escape for a time from Paris, he went for a year or two to his favourite haunts, and lived on horseback and under canvas. Algeria has inspired many painters, but not one of them has represented the sentiment of Arab life more faithfully than Delamain. He died at Ornans in 1882.

DE LA MAISON, Nicolas. See Della Casa.

DE LA MARE-RICHART, Florent I., a French portrait painter and engraver, was born at Bayeux in 1638, became an academician in 1677, and died at Versailles in 1718. His prints have a resemblance to those of Lutma and Morin. Robert-Dumesnil has described twenty-one prints by him, including 'St. Jerome,' after L. de La Hire; and two, an 'Ecce Homo,' and the Virgin, after his own designs. The rest are fancy heads in the style of Livens, the scholar of Rembrandt.

DE LA MONCE, Raimond Ferdinand, an architect and designer, was born at Munich in 1678, and died at Lyons in 1753. He is chiefly known by his architectural works, but he also designed the plates for the beautiful French edition of Pope's 'Essay on Man.'

DELAMOTTE, William, a landscape painter in water-colours, was born in 1775. He studied for a time in the schools of the Academy, and under West. His works appeared at the Academy from 1796 to 1848, and also at the Water-Colour Society from 1806 to 1808. In 1803 he became drawing-master at the military school at Great Marlow. He died in 1863 at Oxford, where he spent the greater part of his life. His works are chiefly outlined with the pen and tinted. At the South Kensington Museum there are by him:

Bruges. 1819.
On the Scheldt, Antwerp in the distance. 1819.
Liége, the Bridge of Arches.
Christ Church, Oxford, from Hinksey Meadows.
Canterbury. 1844.

DE LANE, Solomon, a Scotch landscape painter, was born at Edinburgh in 1727. He was self-taught, and travelled much in France, Italy, and Germany. Several of his pictures appeared at the Royal Academy between 1771 and 1784, after which date there is no further trace of him.

DELANY, Mary. See Granville.

DE LA PEIGNE, Hyacinthe, (H. Pegna, or Peigna,) a painter of battles and an etcher, was born at Brussels about the year 1700. He was at first engaged in the French service as an engineer's artist and military painter, but subsequently he served the Sardinian, and lastly the Austrian Government. He was living at Rome when in advanced years, and died later than 1766. The Imperial Gallery at Vienna possesses two 'Views

of the Pont-Neuf at Paris' by him. He also engraved an 'Attack of the French upon Col d'Assiette in Piedmont;' and pictures of his have been engraved by C. François and A. Tischler.

DE LA PEÑA, Juan Fernandez. See Fernandez de La Peña.

DE LA PEÑA, Narcisse Virgile Diaz. See Diaz de La Peña.

DE LA POINTE, F., was a native of France, who flourished about the year 1678. He engraved a plan of the environs of Paris, in nine sheets, as well as some views of the palace of Versailles, the latter in conjunction with Israel Silvestre.

DE LA PORTE, Henri Horace Rolland. See Rolland de La Porte.

DE LA QUEWELLERIE, Guillaume, a native of France, was probably a goldsmith. He engraved a set of very small plates, representing ornamental crosses, and other designs for jewellery. They are neatly executed with dark backgrounds, and dated 1680.

DELARAM, Francis, an English engraver, was born in 1590, and died in 1627. He was contemporary with Elstracke and the Van de Passes, and engraved several plates in the neat but formal style which was prevalent at that time. His portraits are his best works, and among them are the following:

King Henry VIII.
Queen Mary.
Queen Elizabeth.
James I., on horseback, with a view of London.
Charles I., when Prince of Wales, with Richmond Palace in the background.
Henry, Prince of Wales.
Frances, Duchess of Richmond and Lennox.
Henry Percy, Earl of Northumberland.
James Montagu, Bishop of Winchester.
John Williams, Bishop of Lincoln (afterwards Archbishop of York), with Angels playing on Musical Instruments.
Sir Henry Montagu, Chief Justice of the King's Bench.
Sir Horatio Vere, with an armed Soldier on each side.
Robert Abbot, Bishop of Salisbury.
Sir William Segar, Garter King at Arms.
Sir Thomas Gresham, holding a Globe.
George Withers, poet. 1622.

DEL ARCO, Alonso, born at Madrid in 1625, was a disciple of Antonio Pereda. He was deaf and dumb from his birth, and was called 'El Sordillo de Pereda.' He was an eminent painter, both of history and portraits. Several of his pictures are mentioned by Palomino, particularly the 'Miraculous Conception,' and the 'Assumption of the Virgin,' in the cloister of the Trinitarios Descalzos at Madrid, and in the church of San Salvador is a fine picture of Santa Teresa. Cean Bermudez enumerates a great number of his works in the churches at Madrid, and in other public buildings throughout Spain. He died at Madrid in 1700.

DE LA RIVIÈRE, Charles Philippe Auguste. See Larivière.

DELAROCHE, Hippolyte, (or, as he usually called himself, Paul,) an eminent French painter, was born in Paris, on the 17th of July, 1797. He devoted himself first to landscape painting under Watelet, but afterwards took to history, and entered the studio of Gros, under whom for four years he applied himself to the human figure, and soon became distinguished by the rapid progress which he made. He soon began to evince the possession of original views, declaring his dissent from the hitherto prevalent "classicism"

41

of the French School, which was then yielding to the Renaissance, but taking up a position between the classic and the romantic, and labouring to create a style in harmony with the temper and habits of his time. It was in 1819 that Delaroche exhibited his first picture, 'Naphthali in the Desert,' which he painted at the age of twenty-two, but it attracted no attention; another, exhibited in 1822, the subject of which was 'Jehoash rescued by Jehoshabeath,' was more fortunate, and sufficiently indicated those powers which Delaroche subsequently developed and so judiciously tempered. In 1824 he produced three pictures, which won for him a gold medal. The first represented 'St. Vincent de Paul preaching in the presence of the Court of Louis XIII.'; the second, 'Joan of Arc examined in Prison by the Cardinal of Winchester'; the third, 'Saint Sebastian.' The first and second of these works have been engraved, the second being almost as well known in England as in France. In 1827 'The Capture of the Trocadero' appeared, in a work which had been commissioned by the Government, and for which he received the cross of the Legion of Honour. During some years after this period, Delaroche painted only what our neighbours call "moyenâge" subjects, although the term is scarcely suitable, as comprehending even those that come within a century or two of our own time. In 1830 he produced 'The Princes in the Tower,' which has been so often engraved and lithographed, and which induced M. Delavigne to compose his tragedy on the same subject. Another highly successful picture was 'Richelieu on the Rhone, with Cinq-Mars and De Thou;' as also was that representing 'Cardinal Mazarin presiding, while dying, at a game of lansquenet.' In 1831 he exhibited the most impressive, perhaps, of all his works, 'Cromwell contemplating the remains of Charles I.,' a subject well known by the engraving. In 1832 he became a member of the Institute. In 1833, under the ministry of M. Thiers, Delaroche was commissioned to decorate the church of the Madeleine, for which a vote of public money had been passed, but on hearing that the Administration had confided part of the work to another artist he, thinking that it should be by one hand only, returned the money advanced and resigned the task. In the same year he was appointed a professor at the Ecole des Beaux-Arts. In 1834, Delaroche proceeded to Italy, and at Rome, in 1835, he married Anne Elisabeth Louise, the only daughter of Horace Vernet, who was then director of the French Academy in that city. This lady died in 1843. Delaroche was amply compensated for his disappointment with respect to the Madeleine, by having confided to him the adornment of the Amphitheatre of the Ecole des Beaux-Arts, a task to which he devoted four years of assiduous labour, and completed in 1841. In this work he displayed great originality of conception, and obtained a great and imposing result by very simple means. Dramatic in his general tendencies, with a mind forming images the most vividly true of the stirring incidents of the past, and embodying them by his art with an utter independence of preconceived systems of painting, though with a practical perfection arising from earnest study of previous works, we are not surprised that, where others would have rushed into allegory, he seized upon the real. How has he accomplished his mission? By summoning, at his potent will, the chiefs of the arts in past ages, to witness the triumphs of the labourers in this. How engrossingly the artist's heart was in this work may be judged by some circumstances related of it. Delaroche, it is said, received the order from the Minister of the Interior to paint a work consisting of twenty-four figures, for which he was to receive the sum of £3000. He supplied the sketch, in conformity with this agreement: it was approved, and it was arranged that he should finish the picture in a year. Subsequently he so completely altered, or rather enlarged, his plan, that he introduced into the work no fewer than seventy-five figures: and in executing it he occupied no less than four years of his life. It would have been only just and reasonable that his pecuniary recompense should have been augmented in proportion; but upon a proposal to that effect being intimated to the painter, it was immediately declined. "No," said he, "of my own will I did what I have done; and I will receive nothing beyond the stipulated sum." He added, "and I shall be amply paid for my labour, inasmuch as I have learned more from the execution of this work, than by all my studies that preceded it." This was, indeed, true patriotism—the example of a great mind. This work may be divided into three portions. In the centre, elevated on a throne, are the three great artists of antiquity—Apelles, Ictinus, and Pheidias. Beneath and around them are the Genius of the Arts, and allegoric figures of Gothic Art (said to be a portrait of the painter's wife), Greek Art, Roman Art, and the Renaissanse. Upon their right are grouped the sculptors and the colourists,—Claude Lorrain, Ruisdael, Potter, Titian, Velazquez, Rubens, and Rembrandt, and further on, Paolo Veronese, Correggio, Murillo, and Antonello da Messina. Upon their left are the architects and the greatest masters of Italian and German Art,—Michelangelo, Raphael, Leonardo, Holbein, and Dürer, with Poussin at the extreme edge. All branches of art find representatives in this mighty work. It is a mass of picturesque groups and yet a uniform whole. It may not be uninteresting to give a complete list of all the figures which go to make up this work: they are named in order, beginning at the spectator's left.

Correggio	Jean Goujon
Paolo Veronese	Cellini
Antonello da Messina	Germain Pilon
Murillo	Puget
Van Eyck	Giovanni da Bologna
Titian	Allegoric figures of Gothic
Terborch	Art, Greek Art, Roman
Rembrandt	Art, and the Renaissance
Van der Helst	Ictinus
Rubens	Apelles
Velazquez	Pheidias
Van Dyck	Delorme
Michelangelo da Caravaggio	Peruzzi
Giovanni Bellini	Erwin von Steinbach
Giorgione	Sansovino
Ruisdael	Robert de Luzarches
Potter	Palladio
Claude Lorrain	Brunelleschi
Gaspard Poussin	Inigo Jones
Vischer	Arnolfo di Cambio
Pierre Bontems	Pierre Lescot
Luca della Robbia	Bramante
Benedetto da Majano	Mansart
Giovanni Pisano	Vignola
Baccio Bandinelli	Fra Angelicc
Donatello	Marc Antonio
Ghiberti	Edelinck
Palissy	Holbein

HIPPOLYTE (OR PAUL) DELAROCHE

THE DEATH OF QUEEN ELIZABETH

Le Sueur
Sebastiano del Piombo
Orcagna
Albrecht Dürer
Leonardo da Vinci
Domenichino
Fra Bartolommeo
Mantegna
Giulio Romano

Raphael
Perugino
Michelangelo
Masaccio
Nicolas Poussin
Andrea del Sarto
Cimabue
Giotto

The 'Hemicycle' has been finely engraved by Henriquel-Dupont. During its painting, Delaroche made a rapid journey to Rome, which he visited again for the last time in 1843, when he passed a twelvemonth there. After the Revolution of 1848, he declined, from generous scruples, to accept commissions on liberal terms for certain proposed works at Versailles, the Louvre, the Invalides, the Palais de Justice, and other public edifices, refusing alone to enjoy the emoluments of his profession, whilst his comrades in art were neglected and starving. On the 16th of December, 1855, a disaster occurred, which nearly obliterated for ever the greatest work of this noble painter. On the day appointed for the distribution of the medals in the Ecole des Beaux-Arts, the stage erected for the ceremony took fire, and the famous 'Hemicycle' was, it seemed at first, hopelessly destroyed. Delaroche contemplated restoring it himself, but he was prevented by his death, which occurred in Paris on the 4th of November, 1856. It was afterwards restored by Robert-Fleury. Besides historical subjects Delaroche executed many portraits of great merit. During his life-time two only (the Duke of Angoulême and Mdlle. Sontag) had been publicly shown. When, after his death, his collected works were exhibited, none excited more praise than his portraits. The most famous are those of M. de Rémusat, the Duke of Noailles, Prince Adam Czartoryski, M. de Salvandy, and M. Thiers. As the head of a school Delaroche exercised an important influence on art—not only in his own country, but likewise abroad. He numbered among his pupils several Englishmen, including Mr. Edward Armitage, R.A., and other foreigners.

Delaroche did not exhibit at the Salon after 1837. The following is a list of his principal works arranged in the chronological order of their execution:

1822. Jehoash saved by Jehoshabeath. (*Louvre, but not exhibited.*)
  „ Filippo Lippi.
1823. St. Vincent de Paul preaching before Louis XIII.
1824. Joan of Arc.
1825. Children surprised by a Storm.
1826. The Death of Agostino Carracci.
  „ The Massacre of St. Bartholomew: Young Caumont de La Force saved by Du Verdelet. (*Königsberg Museum.*)
  „ Flora Macdonald.
1827. The Death of President Duranti. (*Painted for the Conseil d'Etat.*)
  „ The Death of Queen Elizabeth. (*Louvre.*)
  „ The Capture of the Trocadero.
1829. Cardinal Richelieu on the Rhone, with Cinq-Mars and De Thou. (*Hertford House.*)
1830. Cardinal Mazarin on his death-bed. (*Hertford House.*)
  „ The Children of Edward IV. (*Louvre.*)
1831. Cromwell opening the coffin of Charles I. (*Nismes Museum.*)
1834. The Execution of Lady Jane Grey. (*Lord Cheylesmore.*)
  „ Galileo.
1835. The Assassination of the Duke of Guise. (*Duke d'Aumale.*)
  „ The Earl of Strafford on his way to execution. (*Duke of Sutherland.*)

1836. Charles I. insulted by the soldiers of Cromwell. (*Bridgewater Gallery.*)
1837. Napoleon in his Study. (*Countess of Sandwich.*)
1838. Portrait of Peter the Great.
1838–41. The Hemicycle. (*École des Beaux-Arts, Paris.*)
1839. The Conquerors of the Bastille in front of the Hôtel de Ville. (*Destroyed by fire at the Hôtel de Ville, Paris, in 1871.*)
1842. La Vierge à la vigne. (*Destroyed by fire at Mr. Thomas Baring's in 1853.*)
  „ The Childhood of Pico della Mirandola. (*Nantes Museum.*)
  „ Pilgrims at Rome.
1843. A Mother's Joys. (*Luxembourg Museum.*)
  „ Herodias.
1844. Portrait of Pope Gregory XVI. (*Versailles.*)
  „ The Little Beggar.
1845. Napoleon at Fontainebleau. (*Leipsic Museum.*)
  „ The Swing. (*Nantes Museum.*)
1847. Charlemagne crossing the Alps. (*Versailles.*)
1848. Bonaparte crossing the Alps.
1851. Marie Antoinette after her Condemnation.
1852. Napoleon at St. Helena. (*Edward VII.*)
  „ The Last Prayer of the Children of Edward IV.
  „ Mater Dolorosa. (*Liége Museum.*)
1853. Moses exposed on the Nile.
  „ The Entombment of Christ.
1854. The Last Communion of Mary Stuart.
1855. Beatrice Cenci going to Execution.
  „ Christ in the Garden of Gethsemane.
  „ A Martyr in the time of Diocletian.
1856. The Girondists.
  „ The Return from Golgotha.
  „ The Virgin in Contemplation.
1857. The Virgin with the Holy Women.

The 'Œuvre de Paul Delaroche,' published in folio in 1868, with a biographical notice by the Vicomte Henri Delaborde, consists of a series of eighty-six photographs from his chief paintings and drawings, with a descriptive account of them by Jules Goddé. An exhibition of his works was held in the Palais des Beaux-Arts in 1858.

DE LA ROSE, JEAN BAPTISTE, a native probably of Aix in Provence, was a marine painter who in his day enjoyed a considerable reputation. He was master-painter at the port of Toulon from about the year 1665 until his death, which appears to have taken place in 1687. He was succeeded as master-painter by his son, PASCAL DE LA ROSE, who died at Toulon in 1746, at about eighty years of age, after having resigned his office in 1731 to his son, JEAN BAPTISTE DE LA ROSE, who died before him at Toulon in 1740.

DE LA ROUSSIÈRE, FRANÇOIS, was a French engraver, who flourished about the middle of the 17th century. A portrait of Michel de Castelnau, Ambassador from France to England in the reign of Elizabeth, is attributed to him by Le Long.

DE LA RUE, PHILIBERT BENOÎT, a French painter and etcher, who was born in Paris in 1718, was a pupil of Charles Parrocel. His subjects were battles, landscapes, genre pictures, and portraits of the chief persons of his day. He also etched a large number of plates, principally of military scenes. His brother, LOUIS FÉLIX DE LA RUE, who was born in Paris in 1720, and died in the same city in 1765, was a sculptor, who also designed and etched six plates of Bacchanalian subjects. The two brothers are often confounded. Both signed their works *D. L.*

DE LA RUELLE, CLAUDE, was a painter and designer, who lived at Nancy about 1611, and was court-painter to the Dukes of Lorraine. He is best known by his drawings, with groups of figures, for the engravings illustrative of the funeral ceremonies of Charles III. and the accession of Henry II.

43

DE LAS CUEVAS, Eugenio, the son and scholar of Pedro de Las Cuevas, and the half-brother of Francisco Camilo, was born at Madrid in 1613. He was chiefly employed in painting small portraits, by which he gained great reputation at the Court of Spain, and was appointed by Philip IV. to instruct his son Don John of Austria in drawing. He died at Madrid in 1667. He was not only a painter, but also a poet and a musician.

DE LAS CUEVAS, Pedro, a Spanish painter, was born at Madrid in 1568. According to Palomino, he painted several pictures for private collections, for which he was more employed than for public edifices. He gained, however, more celebrity by his academy than by his own works. Some of the most distinguished painters of the time, such as Josef Leonardo, Antonio Pereda, Antonio Anias, and Juan Careño, were educated in his school, called the School of Madrid, which was distinguished for its extraordinary and masterly colouring. He died at Madrid in 1635.

DE LAS MARINAS, Henrique, a Spanish marine painter, whose family name is unknown, was born at Cadiz in 1620. He was celebrated for his representations of scenes of embarkation in the bay of his native city, which he executed with so much truth and beauty that he pleased both artists and seamen. He is praised for the transparency of his water and his aerial gradations. He realized a large fortune, and indulged himself in travelling; but having arrived at Rome he never quitted it, dying there in 1680. His pictures are still sought after by amateurs, but it is uncertain under what name they are sold in Italy.

DE LAS ROELAS, Juan, called El Clerigo Roelas and El Licenciado Juan, and by Palomino Doctor Pablo, was descended from a noble family, of Flemish origin. He was born at Seville between the years 1558 and 1560, and was brought up to the profession of physic, in which he had already taken a degree, when an inclination for the art of painting, which he had manifested in the early part of his life, induced him to devote himself to its study, and he travelled to Italy for the purpose of improvement. He went to Venice, where he studied for some years. Palomino says that he was a scholar of Titian, but as Titian died in 1576, when Roelas was only sixteen years of age, it is more probable that he received his instruction from a disciple of that great master. On his return to Seville, he was much employed in the churches of that city, where there are many pictures by him, which have been compared to the works of Palma and Tintoretto. To rich and harmonious colouring, which he had acquired in the Venetian School, he added correct drawing and perfect acquaintance with the anatomy of the human figure. One of his most admired works is the 'Martyrdom of St. Andrew,' in the College of St. Thomas. He went as a canon to Olivares in 1624, but whether he ever practised as a physician is not stated. His pictures are very numerous in Seville. His masterpiece is the 'Death of St. Isidore,' in the church of San Isidoro; another fine picture by him is the 'St. James,' in the chapel of that saint in the cathedral, in which the saint is represented riding over the Moors. Cean Bermudez says it is full of fire, majesty, and decorum. Ford, however, says that it is surpassed by the picture of the 'Conception,' in the Academy, and by three in the chapel of the University at Seville. Roelas has

been compared with Tintoretto and Carracci, and is certainly the best of the Andalusian painters. It is a subject of regret that none of his fine works have been engraved, as he excelled in design and composition, and displayed a grandeur of form and character which belong only to the greatest masters. He died at Olivares in 1625.

DELATOUCHE, Jacques Ignace, a French painter of miniatures and portraits, was born at Châlons-sur-Marne about the commencement of the 18th century. The beautifully executed canons for the altar of the church of Notre-Dame at Châlons are almost the only examples of his work which have not disappeared. The Chevalier Delatouche, who was also a poet, died at Châlons in 1781.

DE LA TOUR, Elisabeth M. (*née* Simons), was born at Brussels in 1780. She painted portraits and scenes from popular life, and in 1817 received the prize of the Antwerp Society for the Encouragement of the Fine Arts. She was still living in 1830.

DE LA TOUR, Maurice Quentin, the best of French artists in crayons, was born at St. Quentin in 1704. He became a pupil of Spoède, but he soon abandoned painting in oil for drawing in crayons. Early in his career he visited London, and upon his return to Paris he set up as an English portrait painter. The first works "en pastel" which he sent to the Salon were the portraits of Madame Boucher and of himself, in 1737. These created a great sensation, and the reputation of the artist increased with each succeeding Salon. Joseph Vernet alone shared with him the favour of the public. Diderot styled him a magician, and MM. de Goncourt call his work a magic mirror, in which is seen all the talent and all the glory, all the wit and all the grace, of the reign of Louis XV. But his genius shines more brilliantly in the Museum of his native town than in the Louvre. He acquired by the exercise of his profession a large fortune, which he employed chiefly in the advancement of art. La Tour became an academician in 1746, when he presented a portrait of Restout, and subsequently one of Dumont le Romain. That of Restout he afterwards retouched and ruined. Some of his best works shared a like fate when age had dimmed his sight and enfeebled his hand. He exhibited for the last time at the Salon of 1773. Towards the close of his life his reason left him, and he returned in 1784 to St. Quentin, where he died in 1788. La Tour executed several portraits of Louis XV. and of his Queen, Marie Leszczynska, of the Dauphin at different ages, and, at a later period, of the Dauphiness. His likenesses were considered to be so true that when Carle van Loo painted in 1747 the fine portrait of Marie Leszczynska, which is now in the Louvre, he consented to spare the Queen the trouble of sitting by painting the head from a drawing by La Tour. Some of his works were of large dimensions, but his masterpiece was the magnificent drawing of Madame de Pompadour, which adorned the Salon of 1755, and is now the chief ornament of the collection of crayon drawings in the Louvre. He received for it the large sum of 24,000 francs.

The Museum of St. Quentin possesses eighty-five of La Tour's works, among which are some of the highest quality. There are fifteen of his drawings in the Louvre, and others in the Dresden Gallery, and in the Museums of Dijon and Valenciennes. An excellent monograph on him is con-

44

tained in MM. de Goncourt's 'Art du xviiime siècle. A statue by Langlet has been erected in his honour at St. Quentin. R.E.G.

DE LA TRAVERSE, CHARLES FRANÇOIS, a French painter, born in Paris, was a scholar of Boucher. He was sent to Rome with a pension from the Crown to pursue his studies for six years, and afterwards went to Naples to explore the excavations at Herculaneum. From thence he went with the Marquis of Osuna to Madrid, and resided there for many years. He was not employed on any public work, but painted many small pictures for individuals. These consisted of landscapes and flowerpieces, which he painted more in accordance with the style of the Flemish than of the Spanish School, especially in colour. He painted an allegory in honour of the birth of an Infanta of Spain, which was engraved by Carmona, but it did not procure him any royal favour. He returned to Paris, where he died in 1778.

DELÂTRE, JEAN MARIE, a French engraver, was born at Abbeville in 1746. He came to England in 1770, and worked under Bartolozzi. He engraved in the chalk style after Angelica Kauffmann, Wheatley, Stothard, and Hamilton. He also furnished illustrations for Bell's 'British Poets,' and there is a good plate by him after Guercino's 'St. Cecilia.' He went to law with Copley in 1801, and gained a verdict for 600 guineas. He died in reduced circumstances at Fulham in 1845, within a few months of completing his hundredth year.

DELAUNAY, (or DE LAUNAY,) NICOLAS, "the engraver *par excellence* of the French School of the eighteenth century." Born in Paris 1739. His first master was L. Lempereur. He married in 1768; his wife died in giving birth to his only child, a daughter, in 1770. After her death he went to La Havre, and there worked under the name of De Valnay. He was received at the Academy on August 28, 1789, his reception works being portraits of Sébastien le Clerc, fils, and J. B. F. de Troy. He was also elected a member of the Royal Danish Academy. He had many pupils, one of them, F. Huot, has left a profile likeness of his master. He died March 22, 1792. It has been said of him, "None drew better, none interpreted better, no one prepared his plates with greater care, nor worked them up with greater brilliance, nor finished them with more perfect harmony." His larger plates and his elegant vignettes are equally admirable. He is chiefly remarkable as the interpreter of Fragonard, Badouin, and Lavreince. Bachaumont says, "His graver was as fertile as it was extended and gay." Among his works were:

March of Silenus ; *after Rubens.* 1777.
Le Cocu Imaginaire ; *after Moreau.* 1773.
Happiness of the Home (1779), and The Beloved Child (1785) ; *after Le Prince.*
Portraits engraved for the Cazin Collection : Boileau, La Fontaine, Voltaire, J. B. Rousseau, Rabelais, and others ; *after Marillier.* 1791.
The Pleasure Party ; *after Weenix.* 1783.
Les Soins tardifs
La Sentinelle en défaut } *after Badouin.* 1785–88.
L'Épouse indiscrète
Le Carquois épuisé
Le Billet doux
La Consolation de l'Absence
L'Heureux Moment } *after Lavreince.* 1785–88.
Qu'en dit l'Abbé
Le Séducteur
Le Petit Jour ; *after Freudenberg.* 1780.
Portrait of Louis XV. ; *after Moreau.*

Le Chiffre d'Amour
Le Serment d'Amour
La Bonne Mère
Les Hasards Heureux ('The Swing,' *Wallace Collection*) } *after Fragonard.* 1787–91.
L'Éducation fait tout
And five others.

His vignettes, which are most striking for delicacy and high finish, were :

For 'Chefs d'Œuvre d'Antiquité,' *Marmontel,* 1773.
Le Triomphe de Bacchus et d'Érigone ; *after Cochin.*
L'Abeille Justifiée
La Fausse Pudeur } *after C. D. J. Eisen.*
Les Jaloux Trompés

DELAUNAY, (or DE LAUNAY,) ROBERT, brother and pupil of Nicolas Delaunay. Born in Paris 1754. He was appointed engraver to the Galleries of the Palais Royal. His work lacks the brilliance and perfection of his brother's. He died in Paris April 20, 1814. Among his works are :

Les Adieux de la Nourrice, and four others ; *after Aubry.*
Les Soins Mérités (washing a pet dog !) ; *after Lavreince.*
Le Malheur imprévu ; *after Greuze.*
Les Adieux ; *after Moreau.* 1777.
J'y passerai ; *after Borel.* 1785.
Many portraits ; the best, J. J. Rousseau.
Many vignettes, including 'Ex Libris Duché' (1779), and 'Hero et Léandre' (1784).

DELAUNE, ÉTIENNE, (DELAULNE, or DE LAUNE,) a French engraver, was born in Paris, or more probably at Orleans, in 1518. He commenced his career as an engraver of medals, and is said to have been helped by Benvenuto Cellini, who was at that time living in Paris. He afterwards engraved many prints after Raphael, and the Italian masters of Fontainebleau, and still more after the designs of his son Jean, with whom he passed the greater part of his life at Strassburg. His style was formed upon that of the Little Masters of Germany. He died at Strassburg in 1595. Étienne Delaune was one of the most famous designers of goldsmith's work of his time. There are six of his designs in the Louvre ; two of them are for circular dishes representing the Histories of Moses and of Samson. His prints, which are generally small, are very numerous ; they are executed entirely with the graver, with great dexterity of handling, and are very highly finished. He copied some of the prints of Marc Antonio with success. He usually marked his prints with the initial of his Christian name, *S.,* or *S. F.,* or *S. fecit,* but sometimes *Stephanus, fecit.* His works are described in Robert-Dumesnil's 'Peintre-Graveur,' vol. ix. The following are the principal :

A set of thirty Subjects from the Old Testament.
A set of eighteen Mythological Subjects ; oval, very small.
The Twelve Months of the Year ; circular.
Jupiter, Neptune, Mercury, and Ceres ; four circular plates.
Four Subjects from Ancient History ; oval.
The Four Monarchies ; oval.
Four plates of Rural Occupations ; oval.
The Three Graces.
David and Goliath ; *after Marc Antonio.*
The Murder of the Innocents ; *after the same.*
The Martyrdom of St. Felicitas ; *after the same.*
The Rape of Helen ; *after the same.*
The Brazen Serpent ; *after Jean Cousin.* This is one of his largest prints.

DE LA VALLÉE, ÉTIENNE, a French historical painter, was born at Rouen in 1740, and became at Paris a pupil of Descamps and of Pierre. He went to Rome, where he assumed the name of LAVALLÉE-

POUSSIN, and produced landscapes in Poussin's style. He became a member of the Academy in 1789, and died in Paris in 1793. Some of his works are in the Museum of Alençon. Guyot engraved after him some plates of Arabesques for the decoration of rooms.

DE LA VILLA-AMIL, GERONIMO PEREZ. See PEREZ DE LA VILLA-AMIL.

DEL BARBIERE, ALESSANDRO. See FEI.

DEL BARBIERE, DOMENICO, called DOMENICO FIORENTINO, a painter, sculptor, and engraver, was born at Florence, about the year 1506. French documents mention him by the surname of Ricoveri. He was a disciple of Rosso, whom he followed to France, when that master was invited by Francis I. to decorate the palaces of Fontainebleau and Meudon, in which works Domenico gave him much assistance. Vasari says that he was the best of all the pupils of Rosso. He was also employed after the death of Primaticcio to execute some frescoes after the designs of that master. Subsequently to 1562 he retired to Troyes, where he painted works for the churches, and there he was buried in St. Pantaléon. Domenico del Barbiere has also left us some excellent engravings. He has sometimes been confounded with the French engraver Dominique Barrière, who lived about a century later; but the style of the latter is so different from that of Barbiere, that the mistake will easily be discovered. He sometimes signed his plates with his name, *Domenico del Barbiere;* sometimes with *Domenico Fiorentino;* and sometimes marked them with the initials *D. F.* We have the following prints by him:

'Gloria,' standing on a Globe, and holding two Trumpets; *after Rosso.*
The Holy Family.
The Penitent Magdalen ; *after Titian.*
Cleopatra.
The Martyrdom of St. Stephen.
Amphiaraus with his horses and chariot swallowed up in the earth ; *after Rosso.*
Venus, Mars, and Cupid ; *after the same.*
An ornamental Cartouche, in which is represented Soldiers leaving a camp ; an etching ; *after the same.*
Two Anatomical Figures, and two Skeletons ; *after the same.*
A Banquet ; *after Primaticcio.*
A Group of Saints ; from the 'Last Judgment' of *Michelangelo.*
A Group of Angels ; *from the same.*

DEL BARCO, ALONSO, a Spanish landscape painter, was born at Madrid in 1645. He was a scholar of Antolinez, and, according to Palomino, painted landscapes with great success. Many of his works were in the palaces and private collections at Madrid, in which city he died in 1685.

DEL BARCO, GARCIA, a Spanish painter of Avila, was employed in 1476, with Juan Rodriguez, by the Duke of Alva, to execute 'Obra Morisca,' or Moorish stucco-work, in his palace of Barco de Avila.

DEL BARRANCO, BERNARDO MARTINEZ. See MARTINEZ DEL BARRANCO.

DEL BASTARO, GIUSEPPE, was a native of Rome, who, according to Baglione, flourished during the pontificate of Urban VIII. (1623—1644). He painted for the church of Santa Maria Maggiore an 'Assumption of the Virgin,' and for San Girolamo, a 'Descent from the Cross,' and the 'Death of St. Jerome.'

DEL BRESCIANINO, RAFFAELLO and ANDREA. See DEI PICCINELLI.

46

DEL BRIZIO, MENICHINO. See AMBROGI.

DEL CAIRO, IL CAVALIERE. See CAIRO.

DEL CASTAGNO, ANDREA. See CASTAGNO.

DEL CASTILLO, AGUSTIN, a Spanish painter in oil and fresco, was born at Seville in 1565. He was instructed there by Luis Fernandez, but afterwards took up his residence at Cordova, where he died in 1626. In the cathedral at Cadiz is his 'Adoration of the Kings,' which is said to be his finest work.

DEL CASTILLO, FERNANDO, the younger brother of Josef del Castillo, was born at Madrid in 1740, and studied sculpture with Felipe de Castro. He afterwards studied painting in the school of Corrado Giacuinto, and gained a prize in the Academy in 1757. Subsequently he was appointed painter to the royal porcelain manufactory at Buenretiro. He died at Madrid in 1777.

DEL CASTILLO, JOSEF, a Spanish painter and engraver, was born at Madrid in 1737. His early promise of excellence in the art of painting, under Josef Romeo, induced the Minister of State, Josef Carvajal, to send him to Rome, at his own expense, to study the great masters there under Corrado Giacuinto, with whom he returned to Madrid in 1753. He visited Rome a second time in 1758, and became a disciple of Preciado. On his return to his native city in 1764, the king ordered his principal painter, Mengs, to give work to the young artist. Mengs did so, by employing him on designs for the royal tapestries, and in painting devotional pictures for the cells of the Royal Convent of Salesas, as well as two portraits of Charles III. Castillo made drawings for the edition of 'Don Quixote,' published by the Madrid Academy ; he etched the 'Supper at Emmaus,' after Cerezo, the 'Flight into Egypt,' and other works, after Luca Giordano, and made for the engravers small copies of the frescoes in the Retiro. His productions are to be met with in Madrid, at the Escorial, and in various churches, convents, and hospitals. He died at Madrid in 1793.

DEL CASTILLO, JUAN, the brother of Agustin del Castillo, was born at Seville in 1584. He had the advantage of being educated under Luis de Vargas, by whose instructions, joined to his own natural ability, he rose to be a distinguished historical painter. His principal works are at Seville and Granada. He enjoys the reputation of having been the instructor of Murillo, Alonso Cano, and Pedro de Moya. He died at Cadiz in 1640.

DEL CASTILLO Y SAAVEDRA, ANTONIO, a Spanish portrait painter, was born at Cordova in 1603. He was the son of Agustin del Castillo, from whom he received his first instruction in art. At his father's death he became the pupil of Francisco Zurbaran, who was at that time in high repute. The cathedral of Cordova possesses many paintings by him, which bear ample testimony to his merit ; and had his colouring been equal to his composition and design, few artists of his own country would have surpassed him, as may be judged from his paintings of the 'Assumption of the Virgin,' and 'SS. Peter and Paul.' The convent of St. Francis at Cordova possesses a painting taken from the life of that saint, which Castillo painted in competition with Juan de Alfaro, under whose name in this work will be found the story of the incident which led to its execution. In 1666 he revisited Seville at the time when Murillo was at the zenith of his fame. On seeing the pictures of that great master Castillo was so struck with their excellence and his own inferiority, that he cried "Ya murió Castillo!" and from that time sank into a state of despondency that hastened his death, which took place at Cordova in 1667.

DEL CERAJUOLO, ANTONIO, a painter of Florence, who flourished in the early part of the 16th century, was a pupil of Lorenzo di Credi, and subsequently an assistant of Ridolfo Ghirlandajo. He executed church pictures, amongst which was a 'Crucifixion, with St. Mary Magdalen and St. Francis,' now in the Pitti Palace; but he was especially celebrated for his portraits.

DELCLOCHE, PAUL JOSEPH, a Flemish painter of interiors and battle-pieces, was born at Namur in 1716. He was the son of Pierre Delcloche, an almost unknown painter, from whom he received his first lessons in art. Whilst still very young he went to Paris, but returned in 1747 to Liége, where he painted some pictures for the Salle des États and the churches. His small pictures are full of life and spirit, but his larger works are much less successful. He died about 1752.

DEL CONTE, JACOPO, a Florentine painter, was born in 1510. He was brought up in the school of Andrea del Sarto. Few of his works are to be met with in Florence, as he went to Rome when he was young, and resided there until his death. He was a respectable painter of history; but is more distinguished for his excellence in portraits, of which he painted a greater number, and of more distinguished personages, than any artist of his time. He visited Rome during the time of Paul III., and he painted his portrait, and that of each succeeding pontiff until Clement VIII., in whose pontificate he died. His principal historical works at Rome are, 'St. John preaching,' and the 'Deposition from the Cross,' in San Giovanni Decollato, the church of the Florentines; the 'Dead Christ,' with several figures, in the Madonna del Popolo; and at the Cappuccini on Monte Cavallo, a 'Pietà,' and 'St. Francis receiving the Stigmata.' He also painted a portrait of Michelangelo. He died at Rome in 1598.

DELCOUR, JAN GILLIS, a Flemish painter of religious subjects, was born at Hamoir, near Liége, in 1632. He was a scholar of Geraert Douffet, but went to Rome and there studied for a long time under Andrea Sacchi and Carlo Maratti. He made excellent copies of some of Raphael's most celebrated works, which still exist at Liége, where there are also some original pictures by him in the churches. He died at Liége in 1694.

DEL CROCIFISSAJO, GIROLAMO. See MACCHIETTI.

DE LEEUW, JAN, a Dutch engraver, was born at the Hague in 1660. In conjunction with Jan Lamsveld, he engraved the portraits for Le Vassor's 'Histoire du Règne de Louis XIII.,' published at Amsterdam in 1701. We have also by him the following portraits:

Carolus Niellius, D. Theol.
Jacob Wilhelm Imhof, Senator of Nuremberg.
Joseph Justus Scaliger.
John, Duke of Marlborough.
Abraham Cowley; for the edition of his works published in 1700.

DE LEEUW, THOMAS, (or DE LEU,) a native of Flanders, was in France from 1560 to 1612. He was a pupil of Jean Rabel, and afterwards of Antoine Caron, whose daughter he married. He engraved at first after Cornelis Cort, Sadeler, and Wierix, in a dry manner, but devoted himself afterwards to portraiture, in which he became one of the most distinguished artists of his time. He is supposed to have died about 1620. M. Duplessis has described the works of this engraver in vols. x. and xi. of Robert-Dumesnil's 'Peintre-Graveur.' They amount in number to 512, of which 213 are portraits, and are generally signed with his name. Among others are the following:

PORTRAITS.

Henry III., King of France and Poland.
Louise de Lorraine, his Queen.
Henri de Bourbon, Prince of Condé, at the age of nine years.
César, Duke of Vendôme, aged four years.
Bust of Henry IV.; *after Bunel.*
Henry IV.; *after Quesnel.*
Marie de Médicis; *after the same.*
Mary, Queen of Scotland and France.
Charles de Bourbon, Count of Soissons.
François de Bourbon, Prince of Conti.
Charles de Lorraine, Duke of Mayenne.
Henri de Savoie, Duke of Nemours.
Henri de Montmorency, Constable of France.
Anne, Duke de Joyeuse, Admiral of France.
Charles de Gontaut, Duke of Biron, Marshal of France.

SUBJECTS.

The Ecce Homo, with Angels bearing the Instruments of the Passion.
Eighteen plates of the Life of the Virgin.
The Twelve Sibyls; *from his own designs.*
Justice rewarding the Labours of the Husbandman; *after F. Zuccheri.*
The Coronation of Louis XIII.; *after Quesnel.*

DE LEEUW, WILLEM, a Flemish engraver, was born at Antwerp in 1610. He was a disciple of Pieter Soutman, but instead of following the neat, finished style of that artist, his etching is bold and free. There is a coarseness and want of harmony in his prints, except in those after Nieulant, where he handled the point with the greatest fineness; otherwise his manner is well adapted to some of the subjects he engraved, particularly his hunting pieces after Rubens. He died about 1665. The following are his most esteemed prints, which are sometimes signed with his name, and sometimes marked with the cipher W⅃.

Lot and his Daughters; *after Rubens.*
Daniel in the Lions' Den; *after the same.*
The Virgin, supported by Angels; called 'Mater Dolorosa'; *after the same.*
The Martyrdom of St. Catharine; *after the same;* fine and scarce.
Four large plates of Hunting scenes; *after the same.* The same subjects, viz. the Lion-hunt, the Boar-hunt, Hunting the Wolf, and the Crocodile and Hippopotamus, have been engraved by *P. Soutman.*
Tobit and his Wife; *after Rembrandt.*
David playing on the Harp before Saul; *after the same.*
Rembrandt's Wife; *after the same.*
A Female with a Veil; inscribed 'Marianne'; half-length; *after the same.*
St. Francis in Meditation; *after J. Lievens.*
A set of four large Landscapes; *after Adriaen Nieulant.* These prints are in a more finished style than is usual with De Leeuw, and are scarce.

DELEGORGUE-CORDIER, JOHN, a French line-engraver, was born at Abbeville in 1781. He engraved the 'Toilet of Venus' after Albano, 'Æneas and Anchises,' after Domenichino, and portraits of Napoleon and Joséphine after Lebel, and Madame de Sévigné after Nanteuil.

DELEIDI, LUIGI, an Italian painter, who was born in the Bergamese in 1774, painted landscapes and ornaments which are particularly happy in their grouping and colouring. He died at Bergamo in 1853.

DE LELIE, ADRIAAN, was born at Tilburg in 1755, and was a scholar of Peeters, a painter of tapestries and ornaments, and afterwards of Quertenmont at Antwerp. He made copies of many of the portraits by Rubens and Van Dyck at Düsseldorf, and also of historical pictures by Italian and Dutch masters. By the advice of Professor Camper, he established himself at Amsterdam, where he painted a great number of portraits and cabinet pictures; among the latter is one of the celebrated amateur Jan Gildemeester showing his collection to a party of ladies and gentlemen, in which the principal pictures are readily recognised. One of his best works is that representing the 'Drawing Academy' of the Felix Meritis Society at Amsterdam. His pictures are highly esteemed in Holland and Germany, where they are to be met with in the best collections. He died at Amsterdam in 1820.

DE LELIE, JAN ADRIAAN ANTONIE, who was born at Amsterdam in 1788, was instructed in art by his father, Adriaan De Lelie, and by Haan. He excelled in painting fruit-pieces and genre pictures; and also practised picture restoring. He died at Amsterdam in 1845.

DELEN. See DEELEN.

DE LE PASTURE, ROGIER. See VAN DER WEYDEN.

DELESTRE, JEAN BAPTISTE, a French artist and writer upon art, was born at Lyons in 1800. He was a pupil of Gros, and studied also water-colour painting and sculpture, but after a time he forsook the practice of art, and devoted himself to its history and criticism. He was a radical in politics, and took an active part in the revolution of 1848. He died in Paris in 1871. A 'Scene during the eruption of Vesuvius,' by him, is in the Museum of Nantes. His principal writings were 'Études progressives des têtes du Cénacle peint à Milan par Léonard de Vinci,' 1827, and 'Gros et ses ouvrages,' 1867.

DE LETH, HENDRIK, was a Dutch engraver, who lived at Amsterdam, where he published in 1729 a series of views of Kennemerland, which are very poorly executed.

DE LEU. See DE LEEUW.

DELF, COPPIN, a French historical painter, who flourished in the 15th century, and became painter in ordinary to King René and King Louis XI. He executed the mural paintings in the churches of St. Martin at Tours, St. Maurice at Angers, and St. Peter at Saumur, between 1456 and 1482.

DELFF, JACOB WILLEMSZOON, 'the elder,' a portrait painter of Delft, is known by a picture of an 'Archery-feast' in the Hôtel de Ville at Delft, dated 1592; and by a 'Reconciliation of Esau and Jacob,' in the Belvedere at Vienna, bearing the date 1584. He also painted 'The Sportsman's Dinner,' and a portrait group of his family. Delff died at Delft in 1611. His works display good conception and execution, but are somewhat heavy in colouring.

Jacob Delff had three sons, Cornelis, Rochus, and Willem. CORNELIS DELFF, born in 1571, was a pupil of Cornelis van Haarlem, and distinguished himself by very fine pictures of still life. He died in 1645. ROCHUS DELFF was a portrait painter, and a pupil of his father. WILLEM DELFF is noticed below.

DELFF, JACOB WILLEMSZOON, 'the younger,' the son of Willem Jacobszoon Delff, and grandson of the elder artist of the same names, was born in 1619 at Delft, where he afterwards resided. He was highly esteemed and much patronized by many celebrated personages of his country. He also held, with great credit to himself, several important civic posts, and at his death, which occurred at Delft in 1661, a marble monument was erected to his memory. He followed the style of Rembrandt. A Man's Portrait, by him, is in the Rotterdam Museum; a Female Portrait is in the Städel Institute at Frankfort; and the figure of a Boy is in the Liechtenstein Gallery at Vienna.

DELFF, WILLEM JACOBSZOON, was a Dutch portrait painter, but was more celebrated as an engraver. He was born at Delft in 1580, and received his instruction in design from his father, Jacob Willemszoon Delff. He practised for some time in the style of his father, but having attempted to engrave some plates after the portraits of Miereveld, whose daughter he married in 1618, his success was such as to induce him to abandon painting, and devote himself entirely to the graver, which he handled with uncommon freedom and precision. The plates he executed in the earlier part of his life are more neatly finished than those he afterwards produced, but the latter are engraved in a bold open style, producing a fine effect, and the heads are finely drawn. His plates are sometimes signed with his name, but at other times are marked with the cipher ⏀ or ᗺ.

Delff died at Delft in 1638. A full account of his works will be found in Franken's 'Œuvre de Willem Jacobszoon Delff,' published at Amsterdam in 1872. The following are his principal portraits:

Charles I. of England; *after D. Mytens.*
Henrietta Maria, his Queen; *after the same.*
Michiel Miereveld, painter; *after Van Dyck.*

PORTRAITS AFTER MIEREVELD.

George Villiers, Duke of Buckingham.
Jacob Cats, poet and philosopher.
Hugo Grotius, Syndic of Rotterdam; fine.
Three fine Heads of William, Maurice, and Henry, Princes of Orange.
Gustavus Adolphus, King of Sweden.
Frederick, King of Bohemia, Elector Palatine. 1632.
Elizabeth, Queen of Bohemia. 1630.
Wolfgang William, Duke of Bavaria.
Gaspar, Count de Coligni. 1631.
Louise, Countess de Coligni. 1627.
Florent, Count of Culenborch. 1627.
Catharine, Countess of Culenborch. 1636.
Philip William, Prince of Orange. 1628.
Marco Antonio de Dominis, Archbishop of Spalatro.
Sir Dudley Carleton, Ambassador at the Hague.
Jan Olden Barnevelt. 1617.
Abraham van der Meer.
Hans De Ries.
Jacobus Triglandus, Professor at Leyden. 1636.
Felix De Sambix, writing-master of Antwerp.

DELFINO, CARLO CLAUDIO. See DAUPHIN.

DEL FIORE, COLANTONIO. See TOMASI, NICCOLA.

DEL FIORE, JACOBELLO or JACOMELLO, flourished between 1385 and 1439. He was the son of Francesco del Fiore, the president of the Venetian Guild of Painters. His early paintings have disappeared from the churches of Pesaro. Jacobello was elected president of his Guild in 1415, and held that position until 1436. In 1415 he painted the 'Winged Lion of St. Mark,' now in the Ducal Palace; and in 1421 he was commissioned to paint for the Tribunal of the "Proprio" the subject of 'Justice, between SS. Michael and Gabriel.' The 'Coronation of the Virgin,' ordered in 1438 for the cathedral of Ceneda, is still there, and in the church of the Hospital of San Lorenzo, at Sarravalle, are frescoes representing scenes from the lives of SS. Lawrence and Stephen, though now much injured by time. The Venice Academy possesses a 'Virgin,' signed by Jacobello in 1436, and many other paintings by him exist in the private and public galleries of Venice.

DELFOS, ABRAHAM, a Dutch engraver, was born at Leyden in 1731. He engraved after Berchem, Teniers, and Brouwer, but his works are very scarce. We have by him:

A Landscape, with Figures and Animals; *after Berchem.*
A Sea-port, with Shipping; *after the same.*
Several Views in Flanders, with Boors; *after D. Teniers.*

DEL FRATE, CECCHINO, was a disciple of Fra Bartolommeo, but no painting can with certainty be attributed to him.

DELGADO, JUAN, a Spanish painter, was established at Madrid about the commencement of the 18th century. He painted a picture of 'St. Francis Xavier,' in the Hermitage of Our Lady, near the bridge of Segovia, which was well coloured, but somewhat mannered.

DELGADO, PEDRO, a Spanish painter, was born at Orgaz, where he painted in 1529 for the Hermitage of the Conception two large pictures, the one representing the 'Virgin surrounded by Saints,' and the other the 'Descent from the Cross': they are both in the style of the 15th century.

DEL GARBO, RAFFAELLINO. See CAPPONI.

DEL GESSI, ERCOLINO. See RUGGIERI.

DEL GOBBO, ANDREA. See SOLARIO.

DEL GRANO, GIORGIO. See GANDINI.

DEL GUASTA, BENVENUTO, called BENVENUTO DA SIENA, who was born at Siena in 1436, painted much in that city. His earliest known work is an 'Annunciation' signed 'Opus Benvenuti Joannis de Senis.' It was painted in 1466, and is in the church of St. Girolamo at Volterra. Frescoes by Benvenuto are in the Baptistery of Siena, and there are in the Gallery of that city three paintings by him. The National Gallery has a 'Madonna and Child enthroned,' with side panels. The date of his death is not recorded, but he was still living in 1517, for in that year he painted the baldacchino of the cathedral of Siena, on the occasion of a visit of Pope Leo X. to that city.

DEL GUASTA, GIROLAMO, the son of Benvenuto del Guasta, was born in 1470. He painted in 1508 a 'Virgin of the Snow,' which is now in the Oratory of St. Catharine in San Domenico at Siena, and in the Academy of that city are two or three other pictures by him. But little else remains of this artist, who died in 1524.

DEL HELE, ISAAK. See DE LA HÈLE.

DE LIEMAKER, NICOLAES, (or DE LIEMAECKERE,) surnamed ROOSE, and sometimes called NICOLAES ROOSE, a Flemish historical painter, was born at Ghent in 1601. He was the son of Jacob De Liemaker, a painter upon glass, and is said by Descamps to have been a pupil of Markus Geeraerts the younger, but as the latter joined his father in London in 1580, it is most likely that he studied under Otto van Veen at Antwerp. He attained a high rank in his profession, and in 1625 returned to Ghent, where he died in 1646. The Museum of Ghent and the churches of that city and of other towns of Flanders possess a great number of his works. His best picture is the 'Consecration of St. Nicholas, Bishop of Myra,' which is above the high altar of the church of St. Nicholas at Ghent.

DELIGNON, JEAN LOUIS, a French engraver, was born in 1755. He executed a considerable number of book-plates after Moreau and others, as well as some plates for the 'Galerie du Palais-Royal.' His best work, 'Le Seigneur chez son Fermier,' is to be found in the 'Monument du Costume.' He died in 1804.

DELIN, JOANNES JOSEPHUS, a Flemish historical and portrait painter, was born at Antwerp in 1774. He first visited the Academies of Brussels and Antwerp, and afterwards continued his studies under Vincent in Paris. In the old church of the Jesuits at Antwerp there is a picture by him representing the 'Purification of the Virgin,' and in the church of St. Charles Borromeo, 'Simeon in the Temple.' He died in Paris in 1811.

DELL' ABBATE FAMILY.

Giovanni (?—1559).
|
Niccolò (1512—1571). Pietro Paolo (?—1575?).

Giulio Camillo (fl. about 1560). Cristoforo (fl. about 1568). Camillo (fl. about 1570).
|
Ercole (1563?—1613).
|
Pietro Paolo (1592—1630).

DELL' ABBATE, ERCOLE, the eldest son of Giulio Camillo dell' Abbate, and grandson of Niccolò, was born at Modena about the year 1563. He possessed an extraordinary genius for the arts, which he disgraced by the depravity and intemperance of his conduct. Like most artists of that character, his works were the productions of negligence and haste. He painted, in concurrence with Bartolommeo Schedone, some pictures representing scenes in the Life of Hercules, in the Council-hall at Modena. He died at Modena in 1613. The Modena Gallery has three works by this artist—an 'Annunciation,' a 'Presentation in the Temple,' and a 'Birth of St. John the Baptist.' A 'Marriage of the Virgin,' in the same gallery, is by some attributed to Ercole dell' Abbate, and by others to his son, Pietro Paolo, the younger.

DELL' ABBATE, NICCOLÒ, was called by the Italians MESSER NICCOLÒ or NICCOLINO. He was born at Modena in 1512, and is said to have studied under his father, Giovanni dell' Abbate, who was a modeller in stucco, as well as a painter, and in the school of Antonio Begarelli, an able sculptor, but these statements are destitute of any proof; it is, however, supposed by many that he had the advantage of being instructed by Correggio, which supposition is supported by his superior knowledge of foreshortening, and the boldness of his relief. Certain it is that the works of Correggio and Parmigiano produced a great effect on his style. One of the first performances which brought him into notice was his picture of the 'Martyrdom of St. Peter and St. Paul,' painted in 1547 for San Pietro at Modena, of which celebrated work Vasari takes no further notice than to remark, that one of the executioners is taken from a picture of Correggio at Parma (the 'Martyrdom of SS. Placidus and Flavia,' now in the Gallery of that city). Dell' Abbate's 'Martyrdom' is now in the Dresden Gallery, and has been engraved by Folkema. He afterwards painted twelve pictures from the twelve books of the Æneid, formerly in the castle of Scandiano, nine of which are now in the Modena Gallery, three having perished by fire in 1815, and they are alone sufficient to establish his reputation. Lanzi, who was well acquainted with their merit, says "that in the correctness of the figures, the beauty of the landscapes, the architecture, and the animals, they merit every praise that can be bestowed on a distinguished follower of the style of Raphael." Whilst in the prime of life, Dell' Abbate went to Bologna, where he painted in a portico of the Leoni Palace, now the Marchesino, in fresco, an 'Adoration of the Shepherds,' and in the Poggi Palace, now the Instituto, a frieze, representing an 'Assembly of young Men and Women,' which was perhaps more suited to his genius. This was composed and drawn with admirable taste and elegance, and has been engraved by Crivellari. These works were the admiration, and became the models, of the Carracci; and Agostino wrote a sonnet in honour of the painter, in which, in the flowery language of poetry, he attributes to him "the symmetry of Raphael, the sublimity of Michelangelo, the truth of Titian, the greatness of Correggio, and the grace of Parmigiano." Such was the excellence of his work in fresco-painting, that he is said never to have had occasion to retouch it when dry; this gave an uncommon splendour and purity to his colouring. In 1552 Primaticcio prevailed on Dell' Abbate to accompany him to the court of France, as the most efficient coadjutor he could find to assist in the important works he was about to undertake. Dell' Abbate, in fact, painted most of the frescoes from the designs of Primaticcio in the magnificent gallery at Fontainebleau, of which more particular notice will be found in the account of that master. After the death of Primaticcio, he continued to be employed by the court of France, and died in Paris in 1571. Of his numerous fresco paintings, but few, comparatively, are extant. His oil pictures also are extremely rare. The 'Rape of Proserpine,' formerly in the Orleans Gallery, but now in the collection of the Duke of Sutherland, is a favourable specimen of his skill in landscape painting. A 'Holy Family' is in the possession of Lord Scarsdale at Kedleston Hall.

Niccolò dell' Abbate had three sons, GIULIO CAMILLO, CRISTOFORO, and CAMILLO, all of whom followed him to France, and assisted him in his work at Fontainebleau. The first-mentioned worked about 1560-61; the second from 1568 to 1570; and Camillo, who was the principal assistant of his father, about 1570.

DELL' ABBATE, PIETRO PAOLO, 'the elder,' the brother of Niccolò, was a native of Modena, where he lived all his life and died about 1575. He excelled in painting battle pieces, and was considered unequalled, in his time, for the spirit and animation with which he designed horses and the attacks of combatants. Some of the works of this painter are in the Gallery at Modena.

DELL' ABBATE, PIETRO PAOLO, 'the younger,' the son of Ercole, was born at Modena in 1592, and died there in 1630. He painted for the churches at Modena several pictures, which are spoken of with commendation. The Modena Gallery has a 'Christ in the Temple' by him.

DELLA BELLA, STEFANO, an Italian engraver, called in France ETIENNE DE LA BELLE, was born at Florence in 1610. He was the son of a goldsmith, and is said to have been intended for his father's profession, but having shown a genius for drawing, he was placed under Cesare Dandini to

50

learn painting. Subsequently, a decided inclination for the art of engraving induced his father to permit him to become a pupil of Canta Gallina, who was also the master of Callot. He at first imitated the manner of Callot, but soon abandoned it, and adopted a style of his own. No artist has handled the point with more facility and finesse than Della Bella. His execution is admirable, and his touch spirited and picturesque. He designed his subjects with infinite taste, and his plates produce a clear and brilliant effect. It is not surprising that some of his prints are but slightly etched, when we consider that the number of them exceeded one thousand four hundred. He visited Paris in 1640, where he engraved some plates for Henriet, the uncle of Israel Silvestre. Cardinal Richelieu employed him to make drawings of the siege and taking of the towns of Arras and La Rochelle, which he afterwards engraved. On his return to Florence, about 1650, he was appointed by the Grand-Duke instructor in drawing to his son Cosmo. He died at Florence in 1664. The following is a list of his principal works:

VARIOUS SUBJECTS.

Portrait of Stefano della Bella, in a Persian costume; *after his own design.*
Sigismondo Boldoni, of Milan.
Mont-Joie St. Denis, King at Arms; very scarce.
Horatius Gonzales; oval; very scarce.
Ferdinand II., Emperor of Germany.
Bernardo Ricci, Buffoon to Ferdinand II., on horseback. 1637.
St. Anthony, Archbishop of Florence. (*His first plate.*)
St. Anthony of Padua, mounted on a monster with two heads.
Jacob and Rachel leaving Laban.
Jacob's Journey to Egypt.
Battle of the Amalekites.
St. John the Baptist, with a lamb.
St. John the Baptist getting water with his cup.
The Virgin, with the Infant Jesus on her knee.
The Virgin, with the Infant Jesus standing on her knee.
The Virgin suckling the Infant Jesus.
The Virgin suckling the Infant Jesus, with St. Elizabeth and St. John.
The Virgin sitting, with the Infant standing on her knee; oval.
The Virgin suckling the Infant; *after Carracci.*
A small plate of the Flight into Egypt, St. Joseph leading the Ass.
A round plate of the Flight into Egypt, with the heads of Angels.
The Repose in Egypt; a round plate.
The Repose in Egypt, with St. Joseph reading, leaning against a tree.
The Holy Family, with St. John and St. Elizabeth, with a flowerpot.
The Infant Jesus explaining the Scriptures to the Virgin and St. Joseph; very rare.
Effigie del glorioso Martyre Sto. Benedetto; very scarce.
The finding of the miraculous Image of our Lady, near Florence. 1633.
The Triumph of the Church.
St. Prospero descending from Heaven; very scarce.
The Tyrant Phalaris ordering Perillus to be put into the Brazen Bull; *after Polidoro da Caravaggio.* 1634.
A basso-relievo, antique; *after the same.*
Lucretia; *after Parmigiano.*
Three Children carrying a plateau; *after Guido Reni.*
A basso-relievo, antique, a woman stopping a bull.
Clovis on horseback, carrying off Clotilda; scarce.
A Seaman, of whom a beggar is asking charity.
A Seaman, with his hand on the head of his dog, and other figures.
A Child teaching a dog to sit up.
Four Turks, half-length figures.
Three Turks, with a boy and a negro.
A Pole, with his battle-axe.
A Soldier, and a Woman on horseback, with a child.

A Florentine Sportsman, with his gun, and a Girl spinning.

A Lady holding a dog.

Mount Parnassus; very fine.

An Eagle devouring a fowl, with its wings extended, and below two horses, and a number of spectators.

The Rock of the Philosophers; fine and scarce.

The Fair, representing a Festival on the Arno; oval. This plate was long attributed to *Callot*.

Perspective View of the Catafalque of the Emperor Ferdinand II., with the Arms of the Medici.

A Thesis, on the Canonization of Francesco Solano. 1639.

Plan of the Siege of La Rochelle.

Plan of the Siege of Arras.

The Reposoir, or Fête Dieu.

View of the Pont-Neuf at Paris. (*His chef-d'œuvre.*) The first impressions of this plate are without the weathercock on the tower of St. Germain l'Auxerrois.

View of the Castle of Sant' Angelo.

SETS OF PRINTS.

Two Landscapes; in one, a peasant carrying a basket at the end of a stick; in the other, a peasant carrying a package on his head.

Two Landscapes; one with a man leading dogs; the other with a man leading a horse laden with sheep.

Six Views of the Port of Leghorn. 1655.

The Four Seasons; allegorical figures in ovals.

The Four Elements; Landscapes and Marines.

Eight Marine Subjects, in the style of Callot.

Six Plates of Vases.

Six Landscapes; circular. 1656.

Four charming Landscapes, with Figures.

Four Views of Roman Ruins.

Three Battle-pieces; large plates. 1622, 1627, 1641.

Eleven Plates of Moors, Hungarians, Asiatics, and Africans.

Sixteen small square plates: Soldiers, Hunters, Fishermen, Peasants, Children, &c. (attributed, by some, to *Callot*.)

Eighteen; entitled *Raccolta di varii Capricci*. 1646.

Twenty-four Views of Edifices; published by *Israel Silvestre*.

Twenty-two sketches, &c., by *Stefano della Bella*.

The Five Deaths; ovals. (*His last works.*)

The Sixth Death, plate begun by *Della Bella*, and finished after his death by *G. B. Galestrucci*, his scholar.

DELLA CASA, NICCOLÒ, (or NICOLAS DE LA MAISON,) was an engraver who flourished towards the end of the 16th century. From an inscription on one of his plates, he appears to have been a native of Lorraine. He worked entirely with the graver, his productions being after the style of the school of Marc Antonio, but they are not of a high class. We have by him:

Portrait of the Emperor Charles V.; oval, with a border copied from Enea Vico; inscribed *N. D. la Casa Lotaringus, fecit.*

Portrait of Baccio Bandinelli.

Portrait of Henry II. of France. 1547.

Portrait of Cosmo de' Medici.

A plate in eleven pieces of the 'Last Judgment' by Michelangelo. 1543. This plate is supposed to be copied from a work of *Beatrizet*, an artist of Lorraine, who was engraving at Rome at that time.

DELLA CASA, PIER ANTONIO. See BERNABEI.

DELLA CHIESE, GIOVANNI, who was living at Lodi in the 15th century, was one of the artists called by Lodovico Sforza in 1490 to decorate his palace of the Porta Giovia at Milan. No dates are known of his birth or death. He and his brother Matteo are the authors of the 'Coronation of the Virgin,' the organ screen, and other paintings in the church of the Incoronata, Lodi. The church of San Lorenzo, in the same town, also possesses some fragments of frescoes by Giovanni representing the 'Nativity,' &c.

DELLA CORNA, ANTONIO, who lived in the 15th and 16th centuries, was one of the artists called by Lodovico Sforza to decorate the Porta Giovia Palace at Milan in 1490. No dates are known of his birth or death. The Bignami Collection, near Cassal Maggiore, contains a picture representing a murder taken from the Legend of St. Julian, signed by Antonio in 1478.

DELL' ACQUA, BERNARDINO, commonly known as DEL AGUA, a painter of Venice, went in 1587 with Pellegrino Tibaldi to Spain, and executed under his direction frescoes in the Convent of the Escorial. Carducho mentions Dell' Acqua as an excellent designer and a clever fresco painter.

DELLA CROCE, TEODORO. See VERKRUYS.

DELLA FRANCESCA, PIERO. See DEI FRANCESCHI.

DELLA FRATTA, FLORI, who flourished about 1540, and died young, is said to have painted the 'Last Supper' in San Bernardino at Fratta, which is executed in the style of the best masters.

DELLA GATTA, BARTOLOMMEO, was probably born at Florence in 1408, and died in 1481. He was a friar of the Camaldolese Convent of the Angeli, at Florence, and afterwards became abbot at Arezzo, where he covered the walls of the monastery with frescoes, and also invented an organ of pasteboard, which yielded soft and perfect tones. He assisted Signorelli and Perugino in their paintings in the Sistine Chapel between 1479 and 1486. His miniatures on vellum are considered valuable, but his paintings show want of skill as a colourist, although clever in details and in landscape. The following paintings by him still exist:

Arezzo.	*Town Hall.*	Two panels representing scenes from the Life of St. Roch.
Castiglione Fiorentino.	*Collegiata.*	A Virgin and Child, with SS. Peter, Paul, Julian, and Michael.
Cortona.	*S. Domenico.*	The Assumption of the Virgin.

DELL' ALTISSIMO, CRISTOFANO. See PAPI.

DELLA MARCA, GIOVANNI BATTISTA, called also LOMBARDELLI and IL MONTANO, was born at Montenuovo in 1532. He was first a scholar of Marco da Faenza, and, according to Baglione, visited Rome in the Pontificate of Gregory XIII., and there devoted himself to an imitation of the works of Raffaellino da Reggio, whom he assisted in some fresco paintings in the Vatican. In the church of San Pietro Montorio he painted a series of pictures of the 'Life of St. Francis'; and in Santa Maria de' Monti, the 'Resurrection.' There are several of his works in the churches at Montenuovo. He died in 1587.

DELL' AMATRICE, COLA. See FILOTESIO.

DELLA PORTA, BARTOLOMMEO. See BARTOLOMMEO.

DELL' ARCA, LEONARDO, was an Italian engraver, who flourished about the year 1600. He engraved some plates of ornaments and grotesque figures.

DELL' ASTA, ANDREA, was born at Bagnuoli, near Naples, in 1673, and was brought up in the school of Francesco Solimena. After passing several years under that master he went to Rome, where he studied for some time, and introduced into the style of his country somewhat of an imitation of the works of Raphael. Amongst his best pictures, executed on his return to Naples, were the 'Nativity,' and the 'Adoration of the Magi,'

E 2

in the church of Sant' Agostino de' Scalzi. He died at Naples in 1721.

DELLA STRADA, GIOVANNI. See VAN DER STRAET.

DELLA VECCHIA, PIETRO, was born at Venice in 1605, and was brought up in the school of Alessandro Varotari, called Il Padovanino. He did not, however, adopt the style of that master, but applied himself to an imitation of the works of Giorgione and Pordenone, in which he was so successful, that some of his pictures have been mistaken for the productions of those masters. His powers were better adapted to familiar and fancy subjects than to the dignity of history, and his best pictures represent armed soldiers, banditti, and corps-de-garde, which he painted with great vigour and effect. His talent in imitating the works of the old masters induced the doge and senate of Venice to employ him to copy in oil the historical works in mosaic which are in the church of St. Mark, which he did with great ability. He also painted for the same church two altar-pieces of his own composition, representing the 'Crucifixion,' and 'Our Saviour driving the Money-Changers out of the Temple.' His colouring was warm and tender, and he was well versed in the principles of chiaroscuro. He died in 1678.

DELLA VIA, ALESSANDRO, was an Italian engraver, who resided at Venice about the year 1730. He engraved several portraits, which are very indifferently executed, and a plate, representing the 'Virgin and Infant Christ, with St. Sebastian and other Saints,' after Paolo Veronese.

DELLA VITE, GIOVANNI. See MIEL.

DELLA VITE, TIMOTEO, called by Vasari TIMOTEO DA URBINO, was the son of Bartolommeo della Vite and Calliope, the daughter of the painter Antonio Alberti of Ferrara, in which city he was born in 1469, and was brought up as a goldsmith. From 1490 to 1495 he was in Francia's workshop, where he also learned to paint, and then returned as master to Urbino, where he practised his art for fifteen years. In 1504, at the instance of Giampietro Arrivabene, Bishop of Urbino, he painted the altar-piece for the chapel of St. Martin in the cathedral of that city. It represents Bishop Arrivabene and Guidobaldo II., Duke of Urbino, kneeling at an altar, and above them St. Thomas à Becket and St. Martin. For the cathedral he also painted, about the year 1508, a 'Magdalen,' which is now in the Pinacoteca of Bologna; and for the church of Sant' Agata the 'Virgin Annunciate, between SS. John the Baptist and Sebastian,' now in the Brera, Milan. In 1518 he painted the 'Noli me tangere,' for the Brotherhood of Sant' Angelo Minore, at Cagli. About 1519 he went to Rome, where he worked by the side of Raphael, and is thought by Passavant to have executed the frescoes of the prophets Daniel, Jonah, and Hosea, above the Sybils, in the church of Santa Maria della Pace, and is said by Vasari to have assisted even with the Sybils. In the Academy of St. Luke at Rome is a panel representing 'St. Luke painting the Virgin and Child in the presence of a Youth,' that has been assigned by Messrs. Crowe and Cavalcaselle to Timoteo. The Berlin Gallery possesses a 'Madonna and Child, with Saints,' and a 'St. Jerome' by him. He died at Urbino in 1523, leaving a son, PIETRO DELLA VITE, who was a painter of some note.

DELLE BATTAGLIE, IL BRESCIANINO. See MONTI, FRANCESCO.

52

DELLE BATTAGLIE, L'ORACOLO. See FALCONE.

DELLE BATTAGLIE, MICHELANGELO. See CERQUOZZI.

DELLE GIRANDOLE, BERNARDO. See BUONTALENTI.

DELLE GRECCHE, DOMENICO. See THEOTOCOPULI.

DELLE LAME, BIAGIO. See PUPINI.

DELLE MADONNE, CARLUCCIO. See MARATTI.

DELLE MADONNE, VITALE. See CAVALLI.

DELLERA, GIOVANNI, an Italian historical painter, was born at Treviglio in 1765. He was the son of a brazier, but his predilection for art induced him to go to Bergamo and become a pupil of Francesco Dagiù, called Capella. In 1785 he went to Rome, and there became intimate with Angelica Kauffmann, with whom he painted several pictures. He died at Florence in 1798. His best work is the 'Fainting of Queen Esther,' in the church of Alzano Maggiore, near Bergamo.

DELLE VITI, GIOVANNI. See MIEL.

DELLE, DELLO, (an abbreviation of Daniello,) the son of Niccolò Delli, a doublet-maker, was born at Florence about 1404. In 1424 his father was condemned to death for high treason, and fled with his sons, from whence, about 1427, they went to Venice, where they remained for some time. Dello's name was registered at the Painters' Guild of Florence in 1433, in which year he went to Spain, where he acquired so great a reputation by the practice of sculpture and painting that he attained to great wealth and honour. In 1446 he returned to Florence, and obtained the recognition of his title of Cavaliere, and in the following year painted some of the stories from Genesis in the cloister of Santa Maria Novella. About 1448 he went back to Spain, and is known to have been still living between the years 1464 and 1466. He was a personal friend of Paolo Uccello, who painted his portrait as Shem in the fresco of the 'Inebriety of Noah,' in the cloister of Santa Maria Novella.

DELL' ORTOLANO, GIOVANNI. See BENVENUTO.

DEL LUPINO. See LUINI.

DEL MAGRO, GUGLIELMO. See GIRALDI.

DEL MAZO MARTINEZ, JUAN BAUTISTA, a Spanish painter, was born at Madrid about 1610. He was educated in the school of Velazquez, whose daughter he afterwards married, and whom he succeeded as court painter to Philip IV. He is said by Palomino to have excelled equally in history, portraits, and landscapes; he also painted sea pieces and views of towns, but hunting pieces and landscapes were his best works. He possessed extraordinary talent in copying the works of his master, as well as those of Raphael, Titian, Tintoretto, and Paolo Veronese: and was much employed by Philip IV. in copying the celebrated Venetian pictures in the royal collection, which task he so skilfully executed that his copies could with difficulty be distinguished from the originals. He died at Madrid in 1687. There are two portraits, a view of Saragossa, and several landscapes by him in the Madrid Gallery.

DEL MONTE, DEODATO. See VAN DER MONT.

DEL MORO, ANGOLO. See ANGOLO.

DEL MORO, GIOVANNI BATTISTA. See MORO.

DEL NERO, DURANTE. See ALBERTI.

DE LOOSE, JOANNES JOSEPHUS, a Belgian painter and writer on art, who was born at Zele in 1770, was a scholar at the Ghent Academy, where in 1794 he obtained the first prize for drawing from the model. He afterwards studied under Herreyns at Mechlin, and painted Scriptural scenes for the churches of Ghent and other places. He has also left a number of portraits. In 1812 the Literary Society at Ghent awarded him a prize for his writings, and in 1820 he received a medal from the Royal Society of the Fine Arts in the same city for his 'Treatise on the present Position of Painting.' He died at St. Nicolas in 1849.

DELORME, ANTOINE, a French designer and etcher of free subjects, was born in Paris in 1653, and died miserably in prison in 1723.

DE LORME, ANTON, who was born at Rotterdam in the 17th century, and was still living in 1660, was an architectural painter, who specially devoted himself to the interiors of churches and other public edifices, in some of which Terborch painted the figures. His works are very rare, and excel for the perspective and the illumination. A 'Church Interior by candlelight' (1645) is in Warwick Castle, and other 'Church Interiors' are in the Berlin, Munich, and Stuttgart Galleries, and in the New York Museum.

DELORME, PIERRE CLAUDE FRANÇOIS, who was born in Paris in 1783, studied in the school of Girodet, and afterwards at Rome. He distinguished himself as a painter of history, and finished the paintings in the chapel of the Virgin in St. Gervais, as well as those in Notre-Dame de Lorette, in Paris. He painted in the style of Girodet. He died in Paris in 1859.

DELORME DU RONCERAY, MARGUERITE LOUISE AMÉLIE, a French amateur engraver, was born in Paris in 1730. We have some neat and spirited etchings by her, after Bouchardon and other French painters; among them the following:

> Venus rising from the Sea; *after Bouchardon;* finished with the graver by *St. Aubin.*
> The Fountain of Grenelle, at Paris; six plates; *after the same.* These were afterwards finished with the graver by *Tilliard* and *St. Aubin.*
> Head of St. Paul; larger than life; after the cartoon by *Pierre,* for the church of St. Roch at Paris.
> View of the Tower of Palmeraux; *after Cochin.*
> A Sultan and Sultana; *after B. Picart.*

DEL PACCHIA, GIROLAMO, who was born at Siena in 1477, was the son of a Croatian cannon-founder, Giovanni 'delle Bombarde.' After studying in his native city and in Florence, he went about 1500 to Rome, and a few years afterwards painted an altar-piece, which has since perished, for the Pontignano Monastery. He returned to Siena about 1508, and executed a 'Coronation of the Virgin,' in the style of Raphael, for Santo Spirito, and a 'Virgin and Child, between SS. Paul and Bernard' in San Cristoforo. In 1518 he executed an 'Annunciation' in Santo Spirito, as well as frescoes in the manner of Bigi for the Brotherhood of San Bernardino, and three scenes from the 'Life of St. Catharine' in the Oratorio dell' Oca. He worked much in conjunction with Pacchiarotti, with whom he produced the 'Ascension' at the Academy of Siena; but he was induced by him to enter the dangerous club of the Bardotti, which in 1535 was dispersed, upon which the two artists betook themselves to France, and painted for Charles VIII. in the castle of Gaillon. The date of Del Pacchia's death is not known. Among his existing paintings are the following:

> London. *Nat. Gallery.* Virgin and Child (*assigned to Pacchiarotti*).

> London. *Duke of Westminster.* } Holy Family (*assigned to Fra Bartolommeo*).
> Munich. *Gallery.* St. Bernard.
> „ „ Virgin and Child (*assigned to Pacchiarotti*).
> Siena. *Academy.* Holy Family, with St. Anthony of Padua.

DEL PELLICCIAIO, GIACOMO, (or GIACOMO DI MINO,) a Sienese who lived in the 14th century, was the contemporary of Lippo Vanni and Luca Thomé, being in 1373 appointed to value one of the latter's pictures. His name appears in the Sienese records from 1362 to 1389. In 1367 he aided Bartolo di Maestro Fredi at Siena cathedral. He is known to have painted book-covers for the Biccherna, and was several times a member of the Grand Council of Siena. The dates of his birth and death are alike uncertain. There exist the following works by him:

> Siena. *Academy.* Coronation of St. Catharine. 1362.
> „ *Chiesa dei Servi.* Virgin and Child, known as the 'Madonna del Verde.' 1363.

DEL PIOMBO, SEBASTIANO. See LUCIANI.

DEL PO, GIACOMO, the son of Pietro del Po, was born in 1654, according to some accounts at Palermo, but according to others at Rome or at Naples, and was first instructed in art by his father, but afterwards by Nicolas Poussin. He was chiefly occupied in decorating the mansions of the Neapolitan nobility with emblematical and allegorical subjects, for which his inventive genius and extraordinary facility particularly qualified him. As is usual with the majority of mechanists, despatch and confidence led him into the negligence and incorrectness of a mannerist. Rome possesses only two of his pictures, one in the church of Sant' Angelo in Pescheria, and the other in Santa Marta; but his talents are seen to greater advantage in his frescoes in the gallery of the Marquis of Genzano, and particularly in the palace of the Prince of Avellino at Naples. He died at Naples in 1726.

DEL PO, PIETRO, was born at Palermo in 1610, and studied under Domenichino at Naples, during that celebrated painter's residence in that city. He painted some pictures for the churches at Palermo, and afterwards visited Rome, where, among other works, he painted a picture of St. Leo, for La Madonna di Costantinopoli. He was, however, more successful in easel pictures than in those of larger dimensions, and he was more distinguished as an engraver than as a painter. He died at Naples in 1692. There are several etchings by this artist, some of which are finished with the graver. They are not so correctly designed as might have been expected from the school in which he was educated. Among others are the following:

> St. John in the Wilderness; *after Annibale Carracci.*
> The Woman of Canaan before Christ; *after the same.*
> The Dead Christ on the Lap of the Virgin; *after the same.*
> The Virgin seated on a Throne with the Infant, and a choir of Angels; *after Domenichino.*
> The four Cardinal Virtues, with their attributes; *after the same.*
> St. Jerome kneeling, with an Angel; *after the same.*
> The Annunciation; *after N. Poussin.*
> The Flight into Egypt; *after the same.*

DEL PO, TERESA, was the daughter of Pietro del Po. She is said to have painted in oil and in miniature, and has etched a few plates in the style of her father; among which is 'Susannah and the Elders,' after Carracci. Bartsch says she engraved in the manner of her father so closely, that it is difficult to distinguish their works. He describes sixteen prints by her, and enumerates six more mentioned by Füssli. The date of her birth is not known; but she was a member of the Academy of St. Luke at Rome, and died at Naples in 1716.

DEL POGGIO, GIOVANNI. See GIOVANNI DI PAOLO.

DEL POLLAJUOLO, ANTONIO, an Italian goldsmith and painter, born at Florence in 1429, was the son of Jacopo d'Antonio de' Benci, a poulterer, for which reason Antonio and his brother Piero and their descendants took the name of 'Del Pollajuolo.' He was apprenticed to Bartoluccio Ghiberti, a goldsmith, whom he left in 1459 and opened a shop of his own as goldsmith, sculptor, and engraver. He was considered one of the most eminent goldsmiths of his time, and excelled in all the branches of that art. Soon after 1489 he went to Rome, where he cast and carved the Funeral Monuments of the Popes Sixtus IV. and Innocent VIII., and executed several commissions for the Cardinals Benevento and Ascanio. He next turned his attention to painting, and, in conjunction with his younger brother Piero, produced many paintings celebrated for their design, knowledge of anatomy, and power of colour. He also executed in niello several paxes for the church of San Giovanni at Florence. One only of these now remains: it represents the 'Deposition from the Cross,' and is in the Florence Gallery. Antonio died at Rome in 1498.

Vasari states that Antonio was the better artist of the two Pollajuoli; but, judging from their early education, Piero had gained the greater experience in painting, before they entered into partnership.

The following are their best works: Mr. Berensen is of opinion that the two 'Hercules' pictures in the Uffizi are by Antonio, and the others by Piero: other authorities differ.

Berlin.	*Museum.*	The Annunciation.
		David.
Florence.	*Uffizi.*	Hercules and Antæus.
„	„	Hercules and the Hydra.
„	„	Prudence (*one of the 'Virtues' painted for the Mercatanzia, Florence*).
„	„	Profile of a Lady.
„	„	St. James with SS. Eustace and Vincent (*formerly in San Miniato al Monte, Florence*).
London.	*Nat. Gall.*	The Martyrdom of St. Sebastian (*a masterpiece, 1475, formerly in San Sebastiano de' Servi, Florence*).
„	„	Apollo and Daphne.
S. Gemignano.	*Church.*	Coronation of the Virgin. 1483.
Turin.	*Gallery.*	The Archangel and Tobit.

Vasari states that this artist executed several engravings, but Bartsch mentions only three, and these are now very rare. They are as follow:

The Gladiators.
Hercules strangling Antæus.
Hercules fighting the Giants.

DEL POLLAJUOLO, PIERO, who was born at Florence in 1443, was a younger brother of Antonio del Pollajuolo. He studied painting for a short time under Andrea del Castagno, and then entered the workshop of his brother, in conjunction with whom he worked much. It is very difficult to assign to each his share in these jointly-executed

productions, but it is thought that those in which traces of the sculptor's art are plainly discernible are by the hand of Antonio, and that those of greater pictorial excellence owe their origin to Piero. Piero was dead when his elder brother made his will in 1496.

DEL PORTO, GIOVANNI BATTISTA, was an engraver who flourished about the year 1503, and was commonly known by the name of 'The Master of the Bird,' from his practice of marking his prints with a bird after the initials *J. B.* Amongst them there are:

St. Sebastian on the Tree.
Leda with the Swan.
The Rape of Europa.

He also executed the designs for the following woodcuts:

St. Jerome with the Lions.
Diana and Actæon.
The Three Graces.
The Rape of Ganymede.

DEL POZZO, MATTEO, was a pupil of Squarcione, who lived in the middle of the 15th century. He worked during the years 1469 to 1471 at the decorations of the Cappella Gattamelata in the Santo of Padua, where he painted a 'St. Francis.' He died in 1472.

DEL PRADO, BLAS, (or DE PRADO,) was a Spanish painter, who was born in the vicinity of Toledo, about 1540, and was a scholar of Alonso Berruguete. There are some of his works in the chapel of St. Blas at Toledo, but they are much injured by time and the dampness of the situation. At Madrid there are also some pictures by this artist, particularly an altar-piece in the church of San Pedro, representing the 'Descent from the Cross,' which is evidently the work of a great master. In the early part of his life Prado was invited to visit the court of the Emperor of Morocco, to paint a portrait of his daughter, and returned to Spain amply rewarded for his labour. Whilst at Fez he painted the portraits of the Princesses of the Harem. He died at Madrid about 1600.

DEL RICCIO, DOMENICO, called BRUSASORCI, was born at Verona in 1494, and was a disciple of Giulio Romano. His greatest improvement, however, was derived from an attentive study of the works of Giorgione and Titian, at Venice. His picture of 'St. Roch,' in the church of the Augustinians at Verona, is entirely in the style of the latter, as well as some pictures of fabulous subjects in private collections. His genius did not confine itself to the style of any individual master; and his works at Mantua partake of the depth of colouring of Giorgione, and of the graceful design of Parmigiano. His picture of 'Phaëton,' in the ducal palace, though somewhat damaged by time, still charms by the ingenuity of the composition, the harmony of the colour, and the admirable fore-shortening. Brusasorci's greatest merit was in fresco painting; and in the many admirable works with which he embellished the public edifices and palaces, he united the erudition of the poet to the skill of the painter. His best historical work was the 'Cavalcade of Clement VIII. and Charles V. on their entry into Bologna,' in the saloon of the Casa Ridolfi, a grand composition, which is spoken of by Lanzi in terms of the highest praise. He died in 1567. 'Brusasorci,' which signifies a 'burner of rats,' was a nickname given to his father because of his inflicting that

PORTRAIT OF A GENTLEMAN

ST. SEBASTIA

cruel punishment on all the rats caught in his house.

DEL RICCIO, FELICE, called BRUSASORCI 'the younger,' the son of Domenico del Riccio, was born at Verona about the year 1540, and was first instructed by his father, after whose death he continued his studies at Florence, under Jacopo Ligozzi. He painted for the private collections at Verona several pictures of Holy Families and Madonnas, with angels, which were admired for their grace and beauty of expression. His picture of the 'Forge of Vulcan, with the Cyclops,' in the collection of Count Gazzola, is designed in the best style of the Florentine school, and vigorously coloured. There are also some altar-pieces by him in the churches at Verona, of which the most admired is his picture of 'St. Helena,' in the church dedicated to that saint. He died in 1605.

DEL RINCON, ANTONIO, was born at Guadalaxara in 1446, and may be considered as the father of the Spanish School. He studied at Rome, and on his return to Spain was taken into the service of Ferdinand the Catholic, who appointed him his painter, bestowed on him the order of Santiago, and made him groom of his chamber. Among the few of his works that remain are the altar-piece in the church of Robledo de Chabela, a town in the archbishopric of Toledo, and two portraits of Ferdinand and Isabella, in the church of San Juan de los Reyes, at Toledo. Several of his works perished in the fire that destroyed the palace of the Pardo in 1608. He died in 1500.

DEL RINCON, FERNANDO, was the son and scholar of Antonio del Rincon. He assisted Juan de Borgoña in various works in Toledo Cathedral, about 1511-14, and his name appears in the archives of the College of St. Ildefonso at Alcala in 1518, when he received 500 maravedis for polishing the medallion of Cardinal Cisneros.

DEL SANTISIMO SACRAMENTO, JUAN. See GUZMAN.

DEL SARTO, ANDREA. See ANDREA D'AGNOLO.

DEL SAZ, JULIAN DE LA FUENTE. See DE LA FUENTE DEL SAZ.

DELSENBACH, JOHANN ADAM, a German engraver, was born at Nuremberg in 1687. He worked for some years in Vienna, but died in his native city in 1765. He engraved a series of forty-nine views in Nuremberg, between the years 1713 and 1716, and several portraits for Roth-Scholtz's 'Icones Bibliopolarum et Typographorum,' published at Nuremberg in 1726-42. He also engraved some plates for Scheuchzer's Bible, as well as twenty-eight views in Vienna.

DEL SERO, GUCCIO. See AGHINETTI.

DEL SIGNORACCIO, PAOLO, called FRA PAOLINO DA PISTOJA, and IL PISTOJESE, was born at Pistoja in 1490, and died there from the effects of a sunstroke in 1547. He received his first instructions from his father, Bernardino d'Antonio Detti, called Signoraccio, an inferior artist, by whom some works still remain at Pistoja. Fra Paolino entered the Dominican Order at an early age, and studied under Fra Bartolommeo, after whose death he finished many of his pictures. A 'Virgin and Child enthroned, with Saints,' by him, dated 1528, is in San Paolo at Pistoja; a 'Crucifixion,' dated 1516, is in Santo Spirito in Siena; and in the Belvedere in Vienna is a 'Virgin and Child enthroned, surrounded by six Saints,' dated 1510.

DEL SIGNOR GUIDO, PIETRO. See GALLINARI.

DEL VAGA, PERINO. See BUONACCORSI.

DELVAUX, EDOUARD, a Flemish landscape painter, was born at Brussels in 1806. He studied under Van Assche, and afterwards became director of the Academy at Spa, where he died in 1862. He loved to represent wooded scenery, and delighted particularly in enormous trees. Amongst his works are:

View on the Senne near Fozest.
Hilly Country; Windy Weather (*Brussels Museum*).
View near the Sambre (*Haarlem Museum*).

DELVAUX, FERDINAND MARIE, a Belgian historical and genre painter, was born at Brussels in 1782. He studied under Andries Lens, and twice visited Italy. On his way back to his native country he was seized with fever, and died at Bologna in 1815. Amongst his best works are:

Brussels.	*Franciscan Convent.*	Martyrdom of St. Stephen.
„	*Museum.*	Interior of the Cloisters of the Chartreuse, Rome.
„	„	Interior of a Nunnery at Rome.
Ghent.	*Academy.*	Saul and David.

DELVAUX, REMI HENRI JOSEPH, a French engraver, was born in Paris in 1748, according to some authorities, or at Lille in 1750, according to others. He engraved several plates for the 'Cabinet Choiseul' and the 'Galerie du Palais-Royal,' but the chief occupation of his life was to reproduce the designs of Moreau, whose illustrations to 'Les Amours de Psyché et de Cupidon' are Delvaux's most important work. He also engraved 'The Miraculous Draught of Fishes,' after Rubens; 'The Hunter,' after Metsu, and several portraits. He died in Paris in 1823. MARIE AUGUSTE DELVAUX, his daughter, born in 1786, learned the art of engraving from him.

DEL VERROCCHIO, ANDREA, was the son of Domenico di Michele de' Cioni, and was born at Florence in 1432. He is said to have been a pupil of Donatello, and like his contemporaries the Pollajuoli kept a goldsmith's shop. Vasari says of him, "He was a goldsmith, a master of perspective, a sculptor and carver, a painter, and a musician." He is chiefly celebrated for his works in bronze, and notably for the 'David' now in the Uffizi Gallery at Florence; for the 'St. Thomas examining the Wounds of Christ' in Or San Michele in the same city; and for the model for the equestrian statue of Colleoni, at Venice. He has left but one authentic example of his powers as a painter— namely, the 'Baptism of Christ,' now in the Florence Academy, in respect to which Vasari states that he received the aid of his pupil, Leonardo da Vinci. Verrocchio has also the credit of having taught Pietro Perugino. He died at Venice in 1488.

DEL VISO, CRISTOBAL, a painter, and a monk of the order of St. Francis, died at the end of the 17th century at Madrid, where he resided in quality of commissary-general of the Indies. All the Saints of his order which are to be seen in the chapter-house of the convent of San Francisco at Cordova, are by him, and show his talent.

DEL ZUCCA, JACOPO, (or JACOPO ZUCCHI,) was born at Florence about the year 1541. He was a disciple of Giorgio Vasari, and assisted that master in several of his works. According to Baglione, he visited Rome when young, in the pontificate of Gregory XIII., where he was favoured with the patronage of Cardinal Ferdinando de' Medici, who employed him in some considerable fresco works for his palace. There are also several altar-pieces by him in the public edifices at Rome, of which the most worthy of notice are the 'Nativity of St. John,' in the church of San Giovanni Decollato, and the 'Descent of the Holy Ghost,' in San Spirito in Borgo. He died about 1604.

DE MAN, CORNELIS, a Dutch painter, was born at Delft in 1621. He travelled through Lyons to Lombardy, and stayed two years at Florence and three in Rome. He afterwards went to Venice, where the works of Titian, particularly his portraits, were the chief objects of his attention. After an absence of nine years he returned to Holland, and established himself in his native city. One of the most admired paintings at Delft is a large picture by him, containing the portraits of the most eminent medical men of his time, painted for the hall of the surgeons, which has more of the attributes of the Venetian than of the Dutch school. De Man died at Delft in 1706. There is by him in the Rotterdam Museum a 'Village Interior'; in the Darmstadt Gallery an 'Interior of a Gothic Church'; and in the Cassel Gallery another 'Church Interior.' There exist also four portraits etched by him.

DE MAN, J., was a Dutch painter who flourished in the 17th century. The Hague Gallery has a 'Peasant Wedding' signed with his name.

DE MARE, PIETER, a Dutch engraver, was born at Leyden in 1757, and died in the same town in 1796. He was a pupil of Abraham Delfos. Besides the 'Great Fire of Rotterdam,' after Haasbroek, the 'Last Judgment,' after Lucas van Leyden, and some Heads after Teniers, he executed a large number of plates after the works of Berchem, Frans van Mieris, and Cornelis de Visscher.

DEMARNE, JEAN LOUIS DE MARNETTE, painter and etcher, born at Brussels in 1754, was the son of a Belgian officer, and of his wife, the Baroness Anschütz. When only twelve years old he was sent to Paris, and studied in the atelier of Gabriel Briard. He became a successful painter of landscapes with figures or cattle, in the manner of Berchem and Karel Dujardin. He also etched thirty-eight plates of similar subjects. In 1783 he became a member of the Académie des Beaux Arts. He was long employed as painter to the Sèvres porcelain factory. He died at Batignolles in 1829. In the Hermitage there are five of his pictures, and several were in the San Donato Collection at Florence.

DE' MEDICI, MARIA. See MARY.

DEMER, JACOB. See DOMER.

DE MEULEMEESTER, JOSEPH KAREL, a Belgian engraver, was born at Bruges in 1771. He was a pupil of Bervic in Paris, and afterwards studied in the French school of engraving at Rome. After twenty-two years' absence he returned to Belgium in 1820, and settled at Antwerp, where he died in 1836. His most important work was the series of drawings which he made from the fifty-two compositions which form the 'Bible of Raphael' in the Loggie of the Vatican. These copies of the frescoes occupied his whole time for twelve years, and after his return home he undertook their reproduction, both by means of engraving and of water-colour, on a scale of one-ninth of the originals. Thirty-six were completed in water-colours, but twelve plates only were engraved at the time of his death. All, however, existed in outline, and these were finished, and the entire work published with text by the Baron de Reiffenberg, between the years 1844 and

1853. He also engraved the 'Virgin and Child,' after Andrea Solario, 'Cupid triumphant,' after Domenichino, and the portraits of Rubens and Michelangelo.

DE MEYER, H., was a Dutch landscape painter, who flourished about the middle of the 17th century. There are by him in the Amsterdam Museum, the 'Surrender of the town of Hulst,' and the 'Departure of Charles II. of England from Scheveningen.'

DE' MICHIELI. See DEI MICHIELI.

DE MOMPER, FRANS, a Flemish landscape painter, who was a native of Antwerp, is inscribed in the 'Liggere' of the Guild of St. Luke in that city in 1629-30. He died at Antwerp in 1660-61. There are by him in the Augsburg Gallery, 'St. Philip baptizing the Eunuch,' and a 'Rocky Scene,' in which the figures are by F. Francken and the animals by J. Brueghel.

DE MOMPER, JODOCUS, called at Rome EERVRUGHT, a painter and etcher, was born at Antwerp about 1559. He was the son of Bartholomeus De Momper, a dealer in pictures, who is believed also to have painted landscapes, and to have instructed his son in the rudiments of the art. He entered the Guild of St. Luke in 1581, and became its dean in 1611. His pictures are frequently decorated with figures by the elder Teniers, Jan Brueghel, F. Francken, and H. van Balen. Van Dyck painted his portrait among the celebrated artists of his country, and etched a plate of it himself. De Momper etched a few plates of landscapes from his own designs, which are scarce. He died at Antwerp in 1634 or 1635. J. Visscher, E. van Panderen, and Th. Galle have engraved landscapes after him. His works are to be seen in the Galleries of Amsterdam, Bordeaux, Brunswick, Copenhagen, Darmstadt, Dresden, Madrid, and Venice, and as follow:

Antwerp.	*Gallery.*	The Archduke Maximilian of Austria hunting.
„	*Cathedral.*	The Repose in Egypt.
Berlin.	*Museum.*	Rocky Landscape.
„	„	Forest of Oaks.
„	„	Hermits.
„	„	A Flemish Village.
Bruges.	*Academy.*	Horsemen attacked by Brigands.
Brunswick.	*Gallery.*	The Four Seasons.
Cassel.	*Gallery.*	The Tower of Babel.
Dresden.	*Gallery.*	Rocky Landscape with Travellers on horseback.
Petersburg.	*Hermitage.*	Landscape.

DE MOMPER. See MOMPER.

DE MONI, LODOWYCK, who was born at Breda in 1698, was a scholar of Van Kessel, of J. B. Biset, and of Philip van Dyk at the Hague. He studied the works of Gerard Dou, and imitated the manner of Mieris. He accompanied Philip van Dyk to Cassel, and afterwards settled at Leyden, where he died in 1771. His paintings consist of portraits and genre pieces of a simple and pleasing character, though cold in colouring. There are by him:

Amsterdam.	*Museum.*	A Woman watering Flowers.
Hague.	*Gallery.*	The Lacemaker. 1742.
Paris.	*Louvre.*	A Family Scene.
Petersburg.	*Hermitage.*	A Fish-Woman.
„	„	The Bon Vivant. 1723.
Rotterdam.	*Museum.*	A Fish-Seller.

DE MOOR, KAREL, the elder, a Dutch painter and etcher, was born at Leyden in 1656. He was intended by his parents for one of the learned professions, but a decided inclination for art in-

THE BAPTISM OF CHRIST

duced his father to place him under the care of Gerard Dou. After a while he was sent to Amsterdam, where he became a scholar of Abraham van den Tempel. The death of that painter, when De Moor was only sixteen years of age, obliged him to attach himself to other artists, and it was by Frans van Mieris and Godfried Schalcken that he was chiefly influenced. He painted in the town-hall at Leyden the terrible subject of 'Brutus condemning his two Sons to Death,' which he represented in the most awful and impressive manner. The celebrity of Karel De Moor reached Italy, and the Grand Duke of Tuscany expressed a desire to place his portrait, painted by himself, among the illustrious artists in the Uffizi Gallery. It was accordingly sent to Florence in 1702, and the painter was honoured in return with a gold medal and chain. He was also commissioned by the Emperor of Germany to paint the portraits of Prince Eugene and the Duke of Marlborough, and these he executed so much to the satisfaction of that monarch, that he conferred on the artist the order of knighthood. One of his best works is in the hall of the magistrates at the Hague, representing the Burgomasters and Eschevins in the year 1719. The pictures of De Moor are cleverly composed, his figures are correctly drawn, and his colouring is clear and transparent. In some of his larger portraits he seems to have aimed at a style combining the chaste delicacy of Van Dyck with somewhat of the vigour of Rembrandt. Although his works are always very highly finished, his touch is firm and free. De Moor died at Warmond in 1738. He etched a few portraits, from his own designs, among which are those of Gerard Dou, Jan van Goyen, Frans van Mieris, and himself. The following are some of his principal works:

Antwerp.	*Gallery.*	A Lady with a Bouquet. (*This picture bears the forged signature of G. Metsu.*)
Dresden.	*Gallery.*	A Hermit praying.
Florence.	*Uffizi.*	His own Portrait.
Petersburg.	*Hermitage.*	Ecce Homo.
,,	,,	A Hermit. 1730.

DE' MOTTI, JACOPO. See DEI MOTTI.

DE MOUCHERON, FREDERIK. See MOUCHERON.

DENANTO, FRANCESCO, of Savoy, a painter and engraver on wood, worked at Venice from 1440 to 1450, and is said to have been a disciple of Titian. Among other wood-cuts by him, there is a large one representing 'Christ healing the Lame Man.' It is executed in a spirited, tasteful style, and, being inscribed, *Franciscus Denanto de Sabaudia, f.*, is probably from a design of his own. The annexed monogram is stated to be his:

DENBY, WILLIAM, an English painter, was born at Great Bookham, in Surrey, in 1819. He studied under Dyce in the School of Design at Somerset House, of which he became an assistant master in 1847. He subsequently superintended the Antique Department in the South Kensington School till his death in 1875, which was occasioned by illness contracted at Rome a few years previously. Amongst the few works which he exhibited at the Royal Academy may be mentioned: 'The Infant St. John,' 'A Girl reading,' and 'St. Peter and Rhoda.'

DEN DUYTS, GUSTAVE, a Belgian landscape painter of great skill, and not only well known and esteemed in his own country, but also abroad. He is represented at the Luxembourg in Paris, but he will be best remembered as a designer of

pageants. He had actually prepared a set of drawings for the cars and groups for the "cortège des cloches," one of the attractions of the International Exhibition at Brussels, when he died in 1895.

DE NECKER, JOBST, who also signed his name DE NEGKER and DIENECKER, a most skilful wood-engraver, was a native of Antwerp. He settled at Augsburg about 1510, and, in conjunction with several other artists, executed the wood-cuts of Burgkmair's and Schäuflein's designs. He engraved the designs which the latter made to illustrate the allegorical poem of 'Theuerdanck,' and also some of those which Burgkmair made for the 'Triumph' of the Emperor Maximilian. He was the inventor of chiaroscuro in three tints, of which the best example is the fine portrait of Hans Baumgartner, dated 1512, after the design of Burgkmair. His chief work is the 'Prodigal Son,' which appears to be likewise after Burgkmair. There is also by him an enlarged copy of Holbein's 'Dance of Death,' dated 1544. He died probably before 1561.

DAVID DE NECKER and SAMSON DE NECKER, who were wood-engravers and natives of Augsburg, were probably his sons, and HERCULES DE NECKER, another engraver on wood, is said to have been a son of David De Necker.

DE NEVE, FRANS, was born at Antwerp about the year 1627, and for some time studied the works of Rubens and Van Dyck. He afterwards visited Rome, where he resided for some years, and on his return to his native country gave proof of considerable ability as a painter of historical subjects; but he afterwards distinguished himself more as a painter of what are called heroic landscapes, with subjects from history or fable, in which he exhibited the fertility of his genius and the refinement of his taste. There are the following paintings by him:

Vienna.	*Gallery.*	The Archduke Leopold William of the Netherlands.
,,	,,	Charles II. of Spain.
,,	*Liechtenstein Gal.*	The Judgment of Solomon.
,,	,,	The Murder of the Innocents.

De Neve likewise executed several etchings in a slight but very masterly style. They are embellished with figures, correctly drawn and cleverly grouped. Among them are:

Narcissus.
A Shepherdess playing the Tambourine.

DE NEYN, PIETER, who was born at Leyden in 1597, studied for some time under Esajas van de Velde, and gave promise of becoming a good landscape painter, in the manner of his master; but he afterwards applied his talents to architecture, in which he succeeded so well that he was appointed architect to his native city, Leyden, where he died in 1639.

DENIS, SIMON ALEXANDRE CLÉMENT, called 'den Schelen,' was born at Antwerp in 1755. After studying for some time under Antonissen, he went, in 1786, to Italy, and there married a Roman lady. He afterwards settled at Naples, where he became painter to the king, and died in 1813. Denis's pictures, which are for the most part landscapes, are executed in an Italian manner, and, with the exception of colour, are good in every respect. The Antwerp Museum contains three specimens of his art, and the Louvre one.

DENNEL, ANTOINE FRANÇOIS, a French engraver, possibly a brother of Louis Dennel, was a pupil of Wille. He worked in Paris from 1760 to 1815, and engraved several plates for Filhol's 'Musée Français,' but his best works are the 'Essai du Corset,' and the 'Dédicace d'un Poëme épique,' after P. A. Wille.

DENNEL, LOUIS, a French engraver, was born at Abbeville in 1741, and died in Paris in 1806. He was a pupil of Beauvarlet, in whose style he engraved several plates, among which are the following:

The Triumph of Galatea; *after Luca Giordano.*
Pygmalion enamoured of his Statue; *after Lagrenée.*
The Triumph of Painting; *after the same.*
Painting cherished by the Graces; *after the same.*

DENNER, BALTHASAR, a German painter, whose works surprise by the toilsome servility of their finish, as much as they disgust by a total absence of all that is estimable in the art, was born at Hamburg in 1685. After being instructed in drawing by an obscure painter of that town, he went to Berlin in 1707, where his works were admired by Frederick II. The Duchess of Brunswick-Wolfenbüttel invited him to her court in 1720, where he painted her portrait; and from thence he went to Hanover, where he met with so much encouragement that he came to London in 1721, and remained here until 1728. The only productions of this mechanic in the art, that have any claim to notice, are his heads of old men and women, which still find collectors among the admirers of patient and persevering precision. There are examples of these at Hampton Court and in the Louvre, as well as in the Galleries of Berlin, Cassel, Copenhagen, Dresden, Florence, Munich, St. Petersburg, and Vienna. He died at Rostock in 1749.

Brulliot mentions a B. DENNER, an engraver, who executed some views on the Tiber after Cornelis Meyer for a work published in 1683, but he gives no particulars of the artist.

DENNING, STEPHEN POYNTZ, an English miniature and portrait painter, was born in 1795. He was a pupil of John Wright, and exhibited at the Royal Academy from 1814 to 1851, but he employed himself chiefly in copying the works of other artists. In 1821, he became curator of the Dulwich Gallery, and resided at the college until his death in 1864. There is in the National Portrait Gallery a vignette sketch in water-colours by him of James Hogg, the Ettrick Shepherd. He also painted portraits of Isaac D'Israeli and Sir Matthew Wood, Lord Mayor of London.

DENON, Baron DOMINIQUE VIVANT, (or DE NON,) born at Chalons on the Saône in 1747, was one of the train of artists and literary and scientific men who accompanied Napoleon Bonaparte to Egypt; where he wielded alternately the pen and the sword, it is said with equal dexterity. His great work on the Egyptian expedition, the 'Voyage de la Haute et Basse Égypte,' the numerous drawings for which were made by himself, is alone sufficient to immortalize his name. Napoleon was warmly attached to him, made him Director-General of the Museums, and consulted him on all matters connected with the fine arts. He took but little interest in politics, his thoughts being principally occupied by engraving, and by the fair sex, many of whose portraits he drew and etched during his diplomatic travels. He also etched the celebrated collection of painters' portraits in the Uffizi Gallery at Florence, but his most remarkable works were 58

his reproductions of Rembrandt's etchings, especially those of the 'Resurrection of Lazarus,' the 'Death of the Virgin,' and the painter's own portrait. His large etching of Luca Giordano's 'Adoration of the Shepherds' opened to him in 1787 the doors of the Academy. One of his best-known portraits is that of Benjamin de La Borde, which was engraved by Masquelier and published in his 'Chansons.' Denon died in Paris in 1825, universally beloved for his good qualities, and admired for his talents and the purity of his taste. He resembled Voltaire, as well in his wit as in his features.

DE NOTER, HERMANUS AUGUST, the son of Pieter François De Noter, was born at Ghent in 1806. He was instructed by his father, and gave early promise of success. He painted landscapes, winter scenes, marine views, and subjects in the manner of Wouwerman. He died at Ghent in 1837.

DE NOTER, PIETER FRANÇOIS, a Flemish painter of landscapes and interiors, was born at Waelhem, near Mechlin, in 1779. He became a professor in the Academy of Ghent and developed into an eminent painter of landscapes, marine subjects, winter scenes, views of the interiors of cities, and cathedrals. His most esteemed pictures are his views of cities and winter scenes; and during the latter part of his career he confined his talents almost exclusively to the representation of such subjects. His pencilling was delicate; and in this respect he may be considered as belonging to the Dutch school. His pictures are numerous and varied, and are to be found in the cabinets of Belgium, Holland, and the north of France. He also engraved a collection of landscapes, several of which are after Hobbema. He died at Ghent in 1842. Amongst his works, which show great minuteness of detail, are:

Brussels.	*Museum.*	View at Bruges.
"	"	View from Pont Neuf, Ghent.
Ghent.	*Academy.*	Abbey of St. Pierre, Ghent.
"	"	Winter view of Ghent.

DENTE, MARCO, called MARCO DA RAVENNA, an Italian engraver, born in the latter part of the 15th century, was one of the most eminent pupils of Marc-Antonio's school. His best works, remarkable for their purity and care of execution, are copies after Baccio Bandinelli, Giulio Romano, Raphael, and more especially Marc-Antonio, whom he imitated in a most deceptive manner. He generally used the accompanying monogram:

DENTONE, IL. See CURTI, GIROLAMO.

DEN TYN, LAMBERTUS, was born at Antwerp in 1770. He was a scholar of P. van Regemorter, and painted interiors by candle-light, and landscapes by moonlight. He died in 1816.

DENUELLE, ALEXANDRE DOMINIQUE, a French decorative painter and architect, was born in Paris in 1818. He studied under Delaroche, and afterwards served on the Commission for Historical Monuments. He died at Florence in 1879. He was largely engaged in mural paintings for churches, and specimens of his art will be found in the Abbey of St. Denis, in St. Paul at Nimes, St. Polycarp at Lyons, the Oratory at Birmingham, the Church of the Celestines at Avignon, and in Strassburg Cathedral.

DEN UYL, JAN (UIL, or VYL), is probably the artist by whom there are many drawings to be found in Holland, signed *I. den Uil,* or *I. den Uyl.* There are only five of his etchings described:

an Ox and a Sheep, a Bull, two Oxen, a Dog, and a Buffalo. In style they approach those of Nicolaes Moojaert, but do not equal them in merit. They appear to have been executed about the end of the 16th century.

DENY, JEANNE, was a French engraver of merit, who flourished in the last quarter of the 18th century. She executed some of Monnet's and Marillier's illustrations to the 'Romans et Contes' of Voltaire, of Desrais's designs for the 'Contes' of La Fontaine, and several of the plates for the 'Cabinet Choiseul' and the 'Costumes Français.'

MARTIAL DENY, her brother, likewise engraved subjects for the same works. The one or the other engraved also 'Le Restaurant' after Lavreince.

DENYS, FRANS, a Flemish painter of portraits, who may be ranked amongst the first artists of his time, is very often confounded with his son Jacob, a painter of less account. Frans was a native of Antwerp, and was received into the Guild of St. Luke in 1631, but the dates of his birth and death are not known.

DENYS, JACOB, a Flemish painter, the son of Frans Denys, was born at Antwerp in 1644, and received into the Guild of St. Luke in 1664. He was a scholar of Erasmus Quellinus, the elder, but at an early age he went to Italy, where he passed the greater part of his life. His merit recommended him to the patronage of the Duke of Mantua, in whose employment he passed several years. He afterwards was invited to Florence, where he painted for the Palazzo Pitti several historical pictures, and the portrait of the Grand-Duke, with those of the principal personages of the court. After fourteen years' absence, he returned to his native country, and died at Antwerp in 1708. The style of Denys, both in his historical works and in his portraits, resembles that of Van Dyck, with something more of the Italian taste, though with less purity of colouring. There are in the Antwerp Gallery two works by him, a portrait of Gregorius Martens, head-man of the corporation of St. Luke (dated 1694), and a 'Study from the Living Model.'

DENYS, SIMON ALEXANDRE CLÉMENT. See DENIS.

DEODATE, —. The name of this engraver is affixed to a portrait of Sir Theodore Mayerne, physician to James I. and Charles I.

DEODATO. See ORLANDI.

DE' PAESI, GIROLAMO. See MUZIANO.

DE PAPE, ABRAHAM, a Dutch painter, who lived probably at Leyden in the middle of the 17th century, is said to have been a scholar of Gerard Dou. Balkema, who is the only writer who notices him, says that in the sale of Cornelis van Dyck's collection of pictures in 1713, there was a picture by De Pape representing a 'Kitchen with a Woman paring Turnips'; and in Gerrit Muller's collection sold at Amsterdam in 1827, another of a 'Kitchen with a Woman plucking a Fowl.' The latter, he says, is more in the manner of Brekelenkam than of Gerard Dou. It is now in the Hague Gallery. He gives no particulars relative to his birth, place of residence, or death, though he says he was worthy of the school whence he proceeded. In the Marquis of Bute's collection is a picture signed by him of a 'Woman paring Apples,' and in the 'Exposition rétrospective' held at Brussels in 1873, was a painting by him, dated 1648, lent by the Comte G. Du Chastel.

DE PASSE. See VAN DE PASSE.

DE PATINIR, JOACHIM, (or DE PATENIER,) was born at Dinant about the year 1490. He resided chiefly at Antwerp, where he acquired considerable reputation as a landscape painter, and was admitted a master of the Guild of St. Luke in 1515. He was one of the earliest Flemish painters who painted landscapes independent of history. Many of his works exist, and, considering them as the earliest productions of their class, they fully justify the praise of Van Mander. In most of them is found a small clownish figure indecently exhibited. He also painted hunting scenes and battles, which, at that early period, were held in considerable estimation. Some historical pictures also are attributed to him. Those which are, perhaps, least liable to doubt are in the Gallery at Vienna. Albrecht Dürer found De Patinir to be the most agreeable of all the Flemish artists, and formed with him a close intimacy; he also painted his portrait. De Patinir died at Antwerp in 1524. The following paintings by him may be mentioned:

Antwerp.	Museum.	The Flight into Egypt.
	,,	The Adoration of the Magi.
Berlin	Gallery.	The Conversion of St. Hubert.
,,	,,	The Rest on the Flight into Egypt.
Brussels.	Museum.	Mater Dolorosa.
London.	Nat. Gall.	The Crucifixion.
	,,	St. Christopher.
Madrid.	Gallery.	The Temptation of St. Anthony.
Vienna.	Academy.	The Entombment.
,,	,,	Christ bewailed under the Cross.
,,	Gallery.	St. John the Baptist preaching.

DEPAULIS, ALEXIS JOSEPH, a French engraver, was born in Paris in 1792, and died there in 1867.

DE PAULIS, ANDREAS. See PAULI.

DE PAY, JOHANN, was born at Riedlingen in Swabia in 1609, and died at Munich in 1660. His own portrait, by himself, dated 1655, is in the Munich Gallery.

DE PETERS, ANTON, a painter and etcher, was born at Cologne in 1723, and studied in Paris under Greuze. He was raised to the rank of a noble by the king of France, and appointed court painter by the Danish king, Christian IV., as well as by Prince Charles of Lorraine. The Revolution drove him back to his native country, where he lived in poverty, and died at Cologne in 1795. There are by him:

PAINTINGS.

Death of Cleopatra (in miniature upon ivory).
A Girl leaving the Bath (Herr Merlo, Cologne).
The Girl with the Carp.

ETCHINGS.

Virgin and Child, in a landscape.
Holy Family on the Flight to Egypt (after Rembrandt).

DE POORTER, WILLEM, a native of Haarlem, who flourished from 1630 to 1645, was a pupil of Rembrandt, and his works, executed after that master, display considerable merit, and are somewhat rare. He usually painted historical subjects, but sometimes undertook interiors. His chef-d'œuvre is 'Solomon worshipping false Gods,' in the possession of M. Coster in Paris. Besides this, there are in public galleries the following works by him:

Berlin.	Gallery.	Samson and Delilah.
Brussels.	Arenberg Coll.	An Interior.
Cassel.	Gallery.	The Circumcision.
Copenhagen.	Gallery.	Mercury and Proserpine.
		Peace. 1643.
Dresden.	Gallery.	Ahasuerus and Esther. 1645.
,,	,,	The Woman taken in Adultery.

59

Dresden. *Gallery.* The Virgin and Child, with St. Joseph and St. Simeon; *after Rembrandt.*
Rotterdam. *Museum.* An Allegory of Human Instability. 1630.

DEQUEVAUVILLER, FRANÇOIS JACQUES, son of Nicolas Dequevauviller. Born in Paris in 1783; pupil of his father and of Desnoyers. Among his works are:

Episode in the Life of Fénelon; *after Hersent.*
Portraits of Cardinal de Beausset }
   "   Duc de Berry   } *after H. Rigaud.*
   "   M. de Daigrefeuille. }
Child playing a Flute, and Jason; *after antiques.*

DEQUEVAUVILLER, NICOLAS BARTHÉLEMI FRANÇOIS, a French engraver. Born at Abbeville in 1745, he became a pupil of J. Daullé. He made extensive travels in Italy, along the Mediterranean, and in Palestine, 1781–86. His chief plates are distinguished by good distribution of light. The figures and furniture are well executed. The *ensemble* is charming, full of youth and pleasure. His grading of the different parts of his compositions is admirable. He died in Paris in 1807. Among his works are:

The Assembly, The Concert, and Le Contretemps; *after Lavreince.* 1783.
Bed-time, Rising, and The Dancing School; *after the same.* 1784.
Plates for 'Paris Bridges,' and 'Travels in Syria and Palestine.'
Views at Auxerre, Nîmes, etc. 1780.
Temptation of St. Anthony; *after Salvator Rosa.*
Noon and Evening; *after C. Berghem.*
Illustrations for 'An Itinerary in France,' published by Reville et Lavallée, Paris, 1816.
The Travellers; *after Jan Both.* (*Uffizi, Florence.*)
The Flemish Nurse, and Flemish Girls bathing; *after C. Poelembourg.*

DE RAM, JAN, a Dutch engraver, was born about 1680. He was a scholar of Romeyn De Hooghe, but was more free and correct than his instructor. He worked for the booksellers, and also engraved in mezzotint, of which style there is a specimen in a portrait of Christian V., King of Denmark. The date of his death is not known.

DERBY, ALFRED THOMAS, a water-colour painter, was born in 1821. He was the eldest son of the miniature painter, William Derby. After having studied at the Royal Academy, his first attempts were in oil, but he afterwards painted in water-colour, assisting his father in his copies of pictures by well-known modern artists. After his father's death he still continued in the same line, painting many exact and carefully-finished copies, besides some original works. He frequently exhibited portraits at the Royal Academy. He died at Hammersmith in 1873.

DERBY, WILLIAM, an English miniature painter and copyist, was born in 1786, at Birmingham, where he received instruction from Joseph Barker. In 1808 he came to London and executed drawings for the 'Stafford Gallery,' and in 1825 for Lodge's 'Portraits.' He also made copies of ancestral portraits for Lord Derby. In 1838 he was struck with paralysis, but was able to pursue his avocations till his death in 1847. There are two water-colour drawings by him in the South Kensington Museum: 'A Fisherman,' and 'A Man holding a book.'

DE REYN, JAN, was born at Dunkirk about the year 1610, and went when he was young to Antwerp, where he became a scholar of Van Dyck. His principal works for the churches at Dunkirk were the 'Death of the four Royal Martyrs,' for the church of St. Eloi; and the 'Baptism of Totila,' for the church of the English convent. There are many of his portraits in private collections, which are little inferior to those of Van Dyck. The principal altar-piece in the parochial church of St. Martin, at Bergues St. Vinox, near Dunkirk, is by this master: it represents 'Herodias bringing the Head of St. John to Herod.' De Reyn died at Dunkirk in 1678. The Brussels Museum has a Female Portrait by him, dated 1637.

DE' RITRATTI, FRANCESCO. See NEGRI.

DEROCHE, VICTOR, a French landscape painter of some note, was born at Lyons in 1824 (?). He was a frequent exhibitor at the Salon of pictures illustrating the beauties of the Seine, and generally somewhat melancholy in sentiment. He lived for many years at Montigny, near Vernon-sur-Seine, and died in 1886.

DE ROORE, JACQUES, was born at Antwerp in 1686. He was the son of a goldsmith, who intended to bring him up to his own profession, but his father died when he was very young, and his mother permitted him to indulge the inclination he had shown for art. He was at first placed under the care of Louis van der Bosch, under whom he studied for two years, and then entered the school of Caspar Jacobus van Opstal. He painted historical subjects and conversations; in the former, he adopted the style of Richard van Orley, and in the latter imitated that of the younger Teniers. His works were held in the highest estimation, and he was loaded with commissions, not only for the collections of Brabant and Flanders, but also for those of Holland. When not more than twenty years of age he was received into the Academy at Antwerp, and was considered one of the ablest artists of his time. He was much employed in embellishing the saloons of the principal mansions, and in painting the ceilings of the public edifices. One of his most admired performances was a saloon and ceiling, representing the 'History of Pandora,' painted for the family of Hasselaer, in 1740. He died at Antwerp in 1747.

DE' ROSSI. See DEI ROSSI.

DE' ROTARI, PIETRO. See DEI ROTARI.

DERSON, N., a French engraver, appears from the inscription on one of his prints to have been of Reims in Champagne. We have by this artist a plate of the stately façade of the cathedral of Notre-Dame at Reims, neatly etched and finished with the graver, with several figures spiritedly touched in the style of Callot, and dated 1625.

DERTINGER, ERNST, who was born in 1816, engraved after Von der Embde, T. Schütz, W. Kaulbach, and other artists. He died at Stuttgart in 1865.

DE RUEL, JOHAN BAPTIST, was born at Antwerp in 1634. He was introduced as a singer to the court of the Elector of Mayence, and was there instructed in painting by Jan Thomas. He afterwards settled at Würzburg, where he executed altar-pieces and portraits. A portrait by him is in the Munich Gallery. He died in 1685, or, according to others, in 1715.

DERUET, CLAUDE, a painter and engraver, was born at Nancy, in Lorraine, in 1588, and died in the same town in 1660. He was a scholar of Claude Henriet, and living in habits of intimacy with his fellow-citizen Callot, he adopted the style of that master, and engraved in it a few plates, of which the best are:

Charles IV., Duke of Lorraine, on Horseback. 1628.
The Carrière, or Rue Neuve, at Nancy.
The Ducal Palace at Nancy.

DE RUYTER, JAN, was a Dutch painter of scenes from every-day life, who was still living in 1822. A 'Cook in a Kitchen' by him, in the Amsterdam Gallery, is dated 1820.

DE RUYTER, N., was a Flemish engraver, who flourished about the year 1688. He appears to have imitated the style of Paulus Pontius, but without much success. Among others, we have a plate by him representing 'Diana reposing after the Chase,' after Gerard Valck.

DE RY, DANCKERTS. See DANCKERTS DE RY.

DE RYCKE, DANIEL, a Flemish painter, was a native of Ghent, who flourished there and at Bruges between the years 1462 and 1469. His mural and decorative paintings and portraits caused him to be thought one of the most distinguished painters of his time, but his works have unfortunately perished by the hands of the Iconoclasts.

DE RYCKE, WILLEM, (DE REYCK, or DE RYKE,) a Flemish painter, was born at Antwerp in 1635. He was brought up a goldsmith, but quitted that business to study painting, and made some proficiency in history and portraits, though he never reached any eminence. He visited England in the reign of King William III., and died in London in 1697. He is also known as an engraver, and among his plates are the following:

Susanna surprised by the Elders.
St. Catharine before her Judges.
Mars and Venus. 1683.

His daughter, CATHARINA DE RYCKE, was a talented artist.

DE RYCKER, A., was a Flemish painter, who in 1591 executed for the church of St. Jacques at Antwerp a triptych, the centre panel of which, representing 'Christ on the Cross, between the two Thieves,' has since disappeared. The wings, however, which contain the portraits of the donor, Jan Doncker, and his wife, are sufficient to place the painter among the most distinguished masters of his time. There are in the Antwerp Gallery the two wings of another triptych which are ascribed to him, but the archives of the Guild of St. Luke fail to afford any information about this artist.

DE RYE, AEGIDIUS, was a painter who flourished in the Netherlands about 1597, which date is on a 'Burial of St. Catharine' by him in the Vienna Gallery.

DE RYNG, PIETER, a Flemish painter of subjects of still-life, flourished about the middle of the 17th century. In the Museum at Amsterdam there is a picture by him, representing a table covered with blue velvet, on which are various kinds of fruit, oysters, and other shell-fish. There is in the Antwerp Museum a fruit piece by him, dated 1651, and in the Dresden Gallery is a picture of shell-fish and fruit with his monogram—a ring with a diamond. Some twenty or thirty years ago several of his works were brought to England by dealers; but it is apprehended that they have changed their name, and assumed that of Jan Davidsz De Heem.

DESALLIER - D'ARGENVILLE, ANTOINE JOSEPH, a French amateur and writer on art, was born in Paris in 1680. He etched several plates of subjects and landscapes from his own designs,

and was the author of the well-known 'Abrégé de la Vie des plus fameux Peintres,' published first in 1745-52. He died in Paris in 1765.

DE SALZEA, PIETER. See DE FOUR.

DE SAN, GERARD, was born at Bruges in 1754, and studied under Légillon at the Academy of that city. In 1781 he travelled about France and to Rome, where he painted for four years, and received in 1782 a silver medal from the Papal Academy for drawing from the nude. He further received two gold medals from the Academy of Parma. On returning home he devoted himself to the painting of portraits, and in 1790 was made director of the Bruges Academy. After five years, however, the Revolution caused him to proceed to Gröningen, and in 1798 he became president of the newly-founded Academy in that town. He died at Gröningen in 1829.

DESANGIVES, NICOLAS, a French painter on glass, who acquired a great reputation early in the 16th century for his windows in the church of St. Geneviève, and in the charnel-house of the church of St. Paul, in Paris.

DESANI, PIETRO, was born at Bologna, according to Malvasia, in 1595, and was a disciple of Lionello Spada, under whom he became a very fair painter of history. He resided chiefly at Reggio, where there was scarcely a church or a public edifice that did not contain some of his works. Among the most esteemed were the 'Crucifixion,' with the Virgin Mary, the Magdalen, and St. John, in the Chiesa del Corpo di Christo, and 'St. Francis receiving the Stigmata,' in the church of the Padri Zoccolanti. The compositions of Desani are masterly, and his drawing correct; but there is a crudity and hardness in his colouring that give to his pictures a disagreeable effect. He died in 1657.

DESAUX, (HENRIETTE BROWNE,) SOPHIE, formerly BOUTEILLIER, was born in 1829 in Paris, where she studied under Chaplin. She received medals of the third class in 1855, 1857, and 1859, of the second class in 1861, and of the third class for engraving in 1863. Of her pictures, which frequently represent oriental and North African scenes, the most important are: 'The Poor School at Aix,' 'Sisters of Charity,' 'An Apothecary's' (1859), 'The Toilette,' 'A Woman of Eleusis' (1861), 'Oranges in Upper Egypt' (1870), and 'The Coptic Poet' (1874). She died in 1901.

DES BATAILLES, MARTIN. See MARTIN, JEAN BAPTISTE.

DESBOIS, MARTIAL, who was born in Paris in 1630, and died there in 1700, was an excellent engraver in mezzotint. He engraved 'Moses striking the Rock,' after Ciro Ferri, and other plates after Paolo Veronese, Guercino, N. Poussin, &c.

DESBOUTIN, MARCELLIN GILBERT, distinguished peintre-graveur, born at Cévilly in 1823. After preliminary study he became a pupil of Couture, whose studio he entered in his twenty-fourth year. After eighteen years spent in Italy he made his début in Paris as a portrait-painter, and the quality of his work at once attracted attention. Among the best known of his portraits we may mention: 'Leclerc, the painter' (1876), 'Dailly, the actor, in the rôle of Mes Bottes' (1878), 'M. Hyacinthe Loison and family en triptyque' (1880), 'Aristide Bruant' (1892), 'Miss Maud Gonne' (1894), 'Puvis de Chavannes' (1895), 'Portrait de l'Auteur,' now at the Luxembourg, and 'La Femme au Chapeau,' which was purchased in 1883 by the

State. The Luxembourg also possesses sixteen dry-paint engravings by him, in which manner he was particularly successful, as his etched portraits of Zola, Rochefort, Monet, Edmond de Goncourt and other celebrities attest. His various accomplishments included the writing of poetry and dramatic pieces. Desboutin obtained an Honourable Mention in 1883; he was made a Knight of the Legion of Honour in 1893, and his brilliant artistic career was fittingly crowned by the Grand Prix at the Universal Exhibition in 1900. After that date he retired to Nice, where his death occurred on the 23rd February, 1902.

DESCAMPS, GUILLAUME DÉSIRÉ JOSEPH, a painter and engraver, was born at Lille in 1779. He was a pupil of Vincent, but, obtaining the "prix de Rome," he improved himself by travelling in Italy, and became court-painter of Murat in Naples. He died in Paris in 1858. The following paintings were executed by him:

The Women of Sparta (*in the Lille Museum*). 1808.
The Martyrdom of St. Andrew (*in St. André, Lille*).
Murat on board the Ceres distributing Rewards (*engraved by himself*).
The Conversion of St. Augustine (*in St. Eustache, Paris*).
The Apotheosis of Cardinal Tommasi (*in San Martino di Monti, Rome*).
The Neapolitan Troops marching out against Capri.

As an engraver he also produced six plates from the 'Fable of Psyche.'

DESCAMPS, JEAN BAPTISTE, a French historical and subject painter, was born at Dunkirk in 1706. He studied under D'Ulin and Largillière, and painted several pictures for Louis XV., illustrating that monarch's coronation and visits to Havre. In 1764 he was received into the Academy, on which occasion he painted his best known work, 'A Mother in a Kitchen with her two Children,' which is now in the Louvre. His latter years were chiefly spent at Rouen, where he was director of a School of Design, which he had been instrumental in founding. In 1753-64 he published, 'La Vie des Peintres Flamands, Allemands, et Hollandois,' and in 1769 his 'Voyage pittoresque de la Flandre et du Brabant.' He died at Rouen in 1791.

DESCOMBES, Le Chevalier, a French painter, was a disciple of Largillière, of whom he painted a portrait, which has been engraved by Petit.

DES COUDRES, LUDWIG, an historical, portrait, and genre painter, was born at Cassel in 1820, and pursued his first studies under J. von Schnorr, at the Academy of Munich. He travelled in Italy in 1844-5, and placed himself in 1848-9 under Karl Sohn at Düsseldorf, where for a time he settled, but in 1855 was appointed professor in the School of Arts at Carlsruhe, in which city he died in 1878. Among his best pictures we find:

Francesca da Rimini. 1850.
The Weeping Magdalen. 1852.
The Lamentation before the Burial (*Carlsruhe Gallery*). 1855.
The Adoration of the Shepherds (*in possession of the Grand-Duke of Baden*). 1857.
The Holy Women before the Cross (*in St. Nicholas, Hamburg*). 1863.
Iphigeneia (*in possession of the Grand-Duke of Baden*). 1865.
Under the Red Cross. 1872.
Psyche and Pan.
Happy Existence—a child's picture.

DESCOURTIS, CHARLES MELCHIOR, a French engraver, was born in Paris in 1753, and died in the same city in 1820. He was a pupil of Janinet, and engraved in colour after his style. He executed

views in Paris and in Rome after De Machy, but his best works are a 'Village Fair,' a 'Village Wedding,' 'The Quarrel,' and 'The Tambourine,' after Taunay.

DE SEEUW, MARINUS. See ROYMERSWALEN.

DESENNE, ALEXANDRE JOSEPH, was born in Paris in 1785, and showed at an early age a taste for art. He was in his time the most celebrated designer of vignettes, and illustrated the works of no less than twenty-seven authors. He died in Paris in 1827.

DE' SERAFINI, SERAFINO. See DEI SERAFINI.

DES GODETS, ANTOINE, a French designer and engraver, as well as architect, was born in Paris in 1653, and died in the same city in 1728. He published in 1682 a folio volume of plates, entitled, 'Les Edifices antiques de Rome,' engraved from his own designs; and he etched the frontispiece himself.

DESGOFFE, ALEXANDRE, a French landscape painter, was born in Paris in 1805. He studied under Ingres, and travelled in Italy from 1837 to 1842. He usually introduced into his landscapes historical or mythological incidents, and he also painted some Biblical subjects. The Luxembourg Gallery has his 'Fury of Orestes,' and the Museum of Lyons his 'Cyclops.' He decorated the Salle des Études of the Bibliothèque Nationale in 1868, and died in Paris in 1882.

DES GRANGES, D., a miniature painter, said to have been the pupil of Peter Oliver. Of his history nothing is known, save that he is said to have fled to England on account of his holding the Catholic faith. Some of his best works are at Ham House, and there are others at Windsor Castle and Welbeck Abbey.

DESHAYS DE COLLEVILLE, JEAN BAPTISTE HENRI, a French historical painter, was born at Rouen in 1729. He was first instructed by his father, and afterwards became a pupil of Boucher, whose daughter he married. He also visited Italy, and was received into the Academy in 1759. He excelled particularly in painting altar-pieces, one of the best of which is a 'St. Jerome,' in the church of Le Plessis-Piquet (Seine). Deshays died in Paris in 1765. He had a younger brother, FRANÇOIS BRUNO DESHAYS DE COLLEVILLE, who painted portraits, but had not a spark of genius.

DESJOBERT, LOUIS REMY EUGÈNE, a French landscape painter, was born at Chateauroux in 1817, and died in Paris in 1863. As a specimen of his painting may be mentioned 'St. Ouen's Bay, Jersey.'

DESMAISONS, PIERRE ÉMILE, a French lithographer, died in 1880, aged 68, at Montlignon (Seine-et-Oise). Amongst his most successful works are his reproductions of paintings by Vidal and Édouard Frère.

DESMARAIS, JEAN BAPTISTE, a French historical painter, was born in Paris in the latter part of the 18th century. He studied at Rome from 1786 to 1790, and subsequently became professor and vice-president of the Academy at Carrara, where he died in 1814.

DESMARÉES, GEORG, (or DES MARÉES,) a portrait painter, was born in 1697 at Stockholm, where he was instructed in painting by Peter Martin van Meytens, whose assistant he afterwards became. In 1724 he made a stay in Amsterdam, and in the following year in Nuremberg and then in Venice, where he received further tuition from Piazzetta. In 1731 he settled in Munich, where he became court painter, and where he continued to reside till his death in 1776. A portrait of himself and one of his daughter are, with a third in the Munich Gallery, and other portraits by him are at Augsburg.

DESMARQUÊTS, Pauline. See Auzou.

DESMOLES, Arnaud, a French painter on glass, flourished about 1510. He executed some windows in the cathedral at Auch, between the years 1509 and 1513, by order of the Cardinal de Sourdis.

DESNOYERS, Auguste Gaspard Louis Boucher, Baron. See Boucher-Desnoyers.

DESPERRIÈRES, Madame, a French portrait painter, exhibited at the Salon from 1812 to 1819. A portrait of the Duchess of Angoulême by her is in the Bordeaux Museum.

DESPLACES, Louis, a French engraver, was born in Paris in 1682. He engraved a considerable number of plates, possessing great merit, some of which are in the style of Gérard Audran, and though he was unequal to that distinguished artist, his drawing is correct, and his works evince excellent taste. His best prints are those after Jouvenet. He worked with the point and the graver. He died in Paris in 1739. The following are his principal works:

SUBJECTS ENGRAVED FOR THE CROZAT COLLECTION.

Jupiter and Danaë; *after Titian.*
Paolo Veronese between Virtue and Vice; *after Paolo Veronese.*
Wisdom accompanying Hercules; *after the same.*
Christ washing the Disciples' Feet; *after G. Muziano.*
The Adoration of the Magi; *after Giulio Romano.*
The Triumph of Titus and Vespasian; *after the same.*
The Crucifixion; *after Annibale Carracci.*

SUBJECTS AFTER VARIOUS MASTERS.

The Martyrdom of St. Peter; *after Il Calabrese.*
The Purification; *after Tintoretto.*
Diana and Actæon; *after Carlo Maratti.*
The Rape of Helen; *after Guido.*
The Birth of Adonis; *after C. Cignani.*
The Gallery of the President Lambert; *after Le Sueur.*
The Roman Charity; *after Le Brun.*
Hercules combating the Centaurs; *after the same.*
Christ healing the Sick; *after Jouvenet.*
The Elevation of the Cross; *after the same.*
The Descent from the Cross; *after the same.*
St. Bruno praying; *after the same.*
Venus prevailing on Vulcan to forge Arms for Æneas; *after the same.*
The Triumph of Venus; *after Antoine Coypel.*
Cupid taking refuge with Anacreon; *after the same.*
Æneas saving his Family from the Burning of Troy; *after the same.*

PORTRAITS.

Mlle. Duclos as Ariana; *after Largillière.*
Evrard Titon du Tillet; *after the same.*
Marguerite Bécaille, veuve Titon; *after the same.*
The Abbé de Rancé; *after Rigaud.*
Charles François Silvestre; *after Hérault.*

DESPORTES, Alexandre François, a French painter of hunting scenes and animals, was born at Champigneul, in Champagne, in 1661. He was a scholar of Nicasius Bernaert, a Flemish painter then resident in Paris, who had studied under Snyders, but who died before his pupil had made any great progress in the art. Without further instruction, he applied himself with great assiduity to the study of nature, not only in animals and landscape, but in perfecting himself in the drawing of the figure after the Academy model. Desportes was not satisfied, as is frequently the case with artists in that branch, with painting the animals, and leaving to others the more important part of the picture. He painted the hunters, as well as their game, and his figures are well drawn and full of character. He was much employed by Louis XIV. in the palaces of Versailles, Fontainebleau, and Meudon, and was made painter to the king. In 1699 he became a member of the Academy in Paris. Walpole does not mention him in the 'Anecdotes,' but in 1713 he accompanied the Duke of Aumont in his embassy to England, and here painted several pictures. He died in Paris in 1743. There are twenty-seven of his works in the Louvre. Among them is his own portrait, painted for his reception at the Academy in 1699.

DESPORTES, Claude François, an animal painter, and the son of Alexandre François Desportes, was born in Paris in 1695, and died there in 1774. A large picture of 'Still Life' by him is in the Louvre; it constituted his reception painting on his entry into the Academy in 1723.

DESPORTES, Nicolas, a nephew and pupil of Alexandre François Desportes, was born in 1718. He at first painted animals, but afterwards, under the tuition of H. Rigaud, devoted himself to portrait painting. He was received into the Academy in 1757 with a picture of 'A Wild Boar pursued by a Dog.' He died in 1787.

DES PREZ, F., was a French engraver on wood, who resided in Paris about the year 1573. He executed a large plan of the town of Rochelle, with the additional fortifications made at the time it was besieged in the civil wars in 1573. It is inscribed, *A Paris, par F. des Prez, rue Montorgueil au bon pasteur.*

DESPREZ, Louis Jean, a French historical painter and architect, was born at Lyons in 1740. He produced some works in Paris, and then went to Rome, where he assisted in the production of the 'Voyage pittoresque de Naples.' He was patronized by Gustavus III., with whom he went to Sweden, and for whom he painted decorations, battle-pieces, &c. He died at Stockholm in 1804. His 'Costumes of Sweden' have been published.

DESROCHERS, Etienne Johandier, a French engraver, was born at Lyons about 1661. He engraved and published upwards of 600 portraits, which must have had in their day some popularity, for in 1723 he was elected a member of the Academy. He died in Paris in 1741.

DES RUINES, Robert. See Robert, Hubert.

DESSURNE, Mark, painter, born in 1825, was a student and frequent exhibitor at the Royal Academy. He also contributed to the Suffolk Street and British Institution Galleries between 1840 and 1870, and held an art mastership in connection with the Glasgow school of design for many years. He died May 4, 1885.

DESTOUCHES, Paul Émile. See Detouche.

DES TUILERIES, Bernard. See Palissy.

DE SUBLEO, Michele, (or De Sobleo,) was a native of Flanders, who went when young to Bologna. He was educated in the school of Guido Reni. He painted some pictures for the churches at Bologna, especially for that of Gesù e Maria, which partake of the style of his master, with something of the vigour of Guercino. He resided during a great part of his life at Venice, where there are several of his works, the most esteemed of which is an altar-piece in the church of the Carmelites, representing some Saints of that order. In the Bologna Gallery are four works by him: a 'St. Agnes,' a 'Virgin,' 'The Apparition of the Virgin to St. Augustine and others' (from the church of Gesù e Maria), and 'St. John the Baptist preaching.'

DETAILLE, Jean Baptiste Edouard, French painter born in Paris, October 5, 1848. In early childhood he showed great talent for drawing; and fortunately this was encouraged by his family. When his term of schooling came to an end he entered the studio of Meissonnier, whose favourite pupil he soon became. He sent in his first contribution to the Salon of 1867. It was entitled 'A Corner of the Studio' (Meissonnier's studio), which received but scant notice. But the following year the critics spoke in terms of high praise concerning his 'Halt of the Drums,' and their eulogy was confirmed in 1869 by the marked advance in his art made by the young painter, his 'Repose during the Manœuvres' being, in fact, the success of that year's Salon. On the other hand his 'Engagement between Cossacks and Guards, 1814,' exhibited at the Salon in 1870, did not meet with such favourable notice. Called to serve with the colours during the Franco-German war, Detaille acted as secretary to General Pajol, and later to General Appert, a post which gave him ample opportunity to study military life. The jury were obliged to reject his picture, 'Les Vainqueurs,' submitted to the Salon in 1872, but nevertheless they accorded it a recompense. His remarkable canvas, 'Charge of the 1st Hussars, 1807,' was acquired for the Musée du Luxembourg. M. Detaille, who, for military subjects, stands in the very first rank, gained two medals in 1869 and 1870; a second-class medal in 1872; a medal of honour in 1888, a Grand Prix at the Universal Exhibition of 1889. He was decorated with the Legion of Honour on November 3, 1873, being promoted to the rank of officer on July 13, 1881. He published an album for children, 'Les bonnes idées de Mlle. Lili'; and a number of his designs and sketches have been reproduced by different modern processes. Two large folio volumes, 'L'armée française: Types et Uniformes,' a sumptuous work, were illustrated by him in 1885–8. He painted with Alphonse de Neuville the 'Panorama de Champigny' and the 'Panorama de Rézonville.' He has been since 1892 a member of the Académie des Beaux Arts, President of the Society of French Artists, but has entirely given up painting.

P. P.

DETOUCHE, Paul Emile, called Destouches, a pupil of David, Guérin, Gros, and Girodet, was born at Dampierre in 1794, and was a painter of history and portraits, but distinguished himself more in genre pieces. His pleasing scenes of family life are spirited and carefully executed. 'The Orphan,' 'The Young Conscript,' and 'The Wounded Student' are considered his best paintings. He died in Paris in 1874.

DÉTREZ, Ambroise, who was born in Paris in 1811, studied at Lille, and subsequently became Director of the Painting School at Valenciennes, where he died in 1863. In the Lille Museum are a 'Presentation in the Temple' and two Landscapes by him.

DETROY. See Troy.

DEUERLEIN, Johann Hieronymus, was a painter of Würzburg, who in 1619 became a pupil of Büler, and was admitted in 1624 into the Brotherhood of St. Luke. He painted the 'Triumph of Death' in the choir of St. Peter's Church at Würzburg, and a votive picture in the cloister of the Cathedral.

64

DEUREN, O. van, is only known by his signature, and the date 1624, on a picture of a 'Hermit' now in the Dresden Gallery.

DEURER, Ludwig, a son of Peter F. Deurer, was born at Mannheim in 1806, and studied at Nuremberg, Munich, and Rome. He was an excellent painter of historical subjects, and painted 'The Knights of Malta before Jerusalem.' He died in 1847.

DEURER, Peter Ferdinand, a painter of history and portraits, who was born at Mannheim in 1779, studied art at Düsseldorf and Cassel. For saving the pictures of the gallery of his native town, during the siege by the French, he was made director of it and professor at the Academy. In 1826 he went to Rome and made a copy of Raphael's 'Burial of Christ,' which copy is now in the Art Hall at Carlsruhe. He died at Kissingen in 1844.

DEUTSCH, Manuel. See Manuel.

DE VADDER, Lodewijk, was born at Brussels about 1560. It is not known by whom he was instructed, but he may be ranked amongst the ablest landscape painters of his country. From the grandeur of his style, and the picturesque beauty of his scenery, it is probable that he resided some time in Italy, where he appears to have made the works of Titian the particular objects of his study, as his best productions bear a striking resemblance to the landscapes of that master. The forms of his rocks and trees are noble and select, and his distances are distinguished by a vapoury degradation. The pictures of De Vadder are deservedly esteemed in his native country, where they are found in the choicest collections. His merit would have been more generally known in England, had not his works been frequently imposed upon the public under borrowed names. He is said to have died at Brussels about 1623, but his death occurred probably earlier. A 'Landscape' by him is in the Darmstadt Gallery. There are a few spirited etchings of landscapes by this artist, executed in the style of Lucas van Uden.

DE VALCK. See Valck.

DE' VECCHI, Giovanni. See Dei Vecchi.

DEVEMY, Louis, who was born at Lille in 1808, first practised as an advocate. He adopted art as a profession in 1845, and established himself in Paris in 1852. He died there in 1874. A picture of 'Still Life' by him is in the Museum of his native city.

DEVERELL, Walter Howell. This artist was the son of the secretary of the Schools of Design (now enlarged into the Science and Art Department), and was an artist of the greatest promise, who died in 1854 at the very early age of twenty-six. He was associated with the Pre-Raphaelites; a great friend of Rossetti, and nominated for the place in the B.R.P. left vacant by the resignation of Collinson. It was Deverell who introduced Rossetti to Miss Siddal, who was at that time sitting to him for 'Viola,' and who afterwards became Mrs. Rossetti. His notable works were: 'A Scene from "Twelfth Night"'; 'A Lady with a Bird-cage,' at one time in the Leathart Collection; 'A Scene from "As you Like It,"' which Rossetti finished after the death of the artist; and 'The Doctor's Last Visit,' on which Deverell was working when he died, and which he was only just able to complete. He was a remarkably good-looking man, very genial, clever, and popular, and would have greatly distinguished himself had he lived.

DEVERIA, Eugène François Marie Joseph,

WALTER HOWELL DEVERELL

SCENE FROM 'TWELFTH NIGHT,' ACT II, SCENE IV.

who was born in Paris in 1805, was a brother of Achille Deveria; he frequented the school of Girodet. Besides several historical pieces, he painted for the Museum at Versailles, the ceilings in the Louvre, the Palais Royal, and Notre-Dame de Lorette. His portraits of Marshals Brissac and Crèvecœur are at Versailles. His own is in the Uffizi; and the Louvre possesses his 'Birth of Henri IV.' (1827). His 'Death of Joan of Arc' is in the Museum at Angers. He died at Pau in 1865.

DEVERIA, JACQUES JEAN MARIE ACHILLE, born in Paris in 1810, was a painter and lithographer. He was a pupil of Lafitte and of Girodet. His subjects were mostly of a religious character, and painted in a pleasing manner. He died in Paris in 1857. His best claim to notice, however, rests upon his successful administration of the department of engravings in the Bibliothèque Nationale, to the direction of which he was appointed in 1849. Before that date chaos had reigned supreme, and it was due to his patient labour, as well as to his refined taste and sound learning, that order by degrees took its place.

DEVIGNE. See VIGNE.

DEVIS, ANTONY T., an English landscape painter, the brother of Arthur Devis, was born in 1729. He exhibited a few times at the Society of Arts and at the Royal Academy. During the latter part of his life he lived at Albury, in Surrey, where he died in 1817. His works are in the early manner of water-colour drawings. There is a Landscape by him, dated 1772, in the South Kensington Museum.

DEVIS, ARTHUR, was born at Preston in Lancashire, about the year 1711, and was the pupil of Peter Tillemans. He painted in a variety of ways, sometimes portraits, but mostly small whole-lengths and conversation pieces. He was an exhibitor at the Society's Rooms, in the Strand, in 1761, but never joined either the Chartered Society or the Royal Academy. He died at Brighton in 1787.

DEVIS, ARTHUR WILLIAM, a portrait and historical painter, was born in London in 1763, and received his first instruction in art from his father, Arthur Devis. He made rapid progress, and obtained, at an earlier age than is usual, a silver medal from the Royal Academy, and, what was of more importance, the good opinion of Sir Joshua Reynolds. In his twentieth year he was appointed by the East India Company draughtsman to accompany Captain Wilson in the 'Antelope' in a voyage round the world. He afterwards went to Bengal, where he continued the exercise of his art, but returned to England in 1795, and painted for Mr. Alexander Davison some historical pictures. His life was one of vicissitudes and difficulties, and was terminated by a stroke of apoplexy in 1822. Devis, as an historical painter, was equal, if not superior, to any of his day, but circumstances did not conduce to bring his powers into action. His picture of the 'Detection of Babington's Conspiracy' was painted in competition with some of the most eminent members of the Royal Academy, West, Northcote, Copley, Smirke, Wilkie, and others; and, unquestionably, was the best in composition, delineation of character, truth of colour, and management of chiaroscuro. His own portrait is in the composition. The National Portrait Gallery possesses his portrait of Governor Herbert, painted at Calcutta in 1791.

DE VISCH, MATTHIAS, was born at the village of Reningen, in 1702. He studied under Joseph van den Kerkhove at Bruges, became a student of the Academy, and obtained the first prize in 1721. He went to Paris in 1723; thence to Italy, where he remained nine years. On his return to Bruges he painted the picture of 'Hagar and Ishmael in the Desert' for the church of St. James, and opened a school of design; and he is remembered more for his zeal in furthering the knowledge of painting among the youth of Bruges than for any superior talent shown by him in the practice of it. He painted the portrait of Maria Theresa for the city of Bruges, and several for other communities of Flanders. He collected materials for a history of painting in Belgium, which he gave to Descamps, who made use of them for his 'Lives of the Flemish Painters.' De Visch died in 1765, it is said from over-exertion in endeavouring to make the students of his own Academy rival those of that of Antwerp, upon the restoration of the former after its destruction by fire in 1755.

DE VLAMYNCK, PIERRE JEAN, a Belgian engraver, was born at Bruges in 1795. He received his first instruction in drawing in the studio of Odevaere, after whose 'Narcisse' he executed in 1820 his first plate. Having obtained from the King of the Netherlands a pension for four years, he went to Paris, and there, under the supervision of Dien, he engraved the 'Battle of Nieuport.' His chief work was the 'Ascension,' after Rubens, upon which he was engaged for many years. He also engraved portraits of Raphael, Rembrandt, Odevaere (after Diez), and Count Frédéric de Mérode. There are likewise many drawings in black chalk and several lithographic portraits by him. Besides these he executed in lithography some of the masterpieces of Flemish art which adorn his native city—Memlinc's 'Shrine of St. Ursula,' the triptych of the 'Mystic Marriage of St. Catharine,' the 'Adoration of the Magi,' and the 'Vierge à la pomme.' He died at Bruges in 1850.

DE VLIEGER, SIMON, was born at Rotterdam about 1600, and acquired a considerable reputation as a painter of sea-pieces and landscapes, although it is not known by whom he was instructed. He had the credit of being the master of Willem van de Velde, the younger, and, though his merit was eclipsed by the brilliant talents of his disciple, his pictures are deservedly placed in the choicest collections. In 1634 he entered the Guild at Delft, and in 1643 became a citizen of Amsterdam. He was still living in 1656, but died probably at Amsterdam shortly before 1660. This painter deserves more notice than has been bestowed on him. His selections are picturesque, his compositions are not crowded with unnecessary objects, his execution is remarkably free, and in the representation of the effects of a gale, or fresh breeze, he approaches the grandeur of Ruisdael. Unfortunately his colours, in many instances, have faded, or vanished altogether, particularly in the sky, so that his pictures appear cold or murky; still a master mind and hand may be discerned. He etched about twenty plates. The following are some of his principal works:

Amsterdam.	*Museum.*	The Regatta. 1655.
Antwerp.	*Museum.*	A Calm Sea.
Berlin.	*Gallery.*	A Sea-piece.
Dresden.	*Gallery.*	Storm at Sea.
Munich.	*Gallery.*	Storm at Sea.
Petersburg.	*Hermitage.*	The Arrival of the Prince of Orange at Flushing.
Vienna.	*Gallery.*	Calm Sea, with many Ships (*a masterpiece*).

DE VLIEGHER, SERAFYN, a Belgian painter, was born at Eecloo in 1806. He was at first a pupil of Antoon De Poorter, afterwards of Geirnaert, and finally a student of the Academy at Ghent. He painted genre subjects and portraits, and became director of the Academy at Alost, where he died in 1848.

DE VOIS, ADRIAAN, or ARY, was born at Leyden in 1641. His father was a celebrated organist, and was desirous of bringing his son up to the same profession; but the latter had so little taste for music, and so decided a disposition for painting, that he was induced to place him under the tuition of Nicolaes Knupfer, a painter of some repute at Utrecht, with whom he continued two years, when he returned to Leyden, and there became a disciple of Abraham van den Tempel. De Vois, however, did not adopt the manner of either of his instructors; he formed an intimacy with Pieter van Slingeland, who had been a disciple of Gerard Dou, whose highly-finished style he followed with the greatest success. Although he occasionally attempted history on a small scale, his best productions are portraits, conversations, and domestic subjects, which are little inferior to the works of Metsu or of Mieris. His drawing is very correct, and his colouring clear and transparent, with a perfect intelligence of the chiaroscuro. The pictures of this artist are extremely scarce, as they were very carefully finished, and therefore few; and he is said to have passed several years of his life in idleness and dissipation, in consequence of his having married a lady of considerable fortune. He died at Leyden; Balkema says in 1698. The following are some of his principal works:

Amsterdam.	Museum.	The Fish Merchant.
"	"	The Violin Player.
"	"	A Lady.
Antwerp.	Museum.	An Old Woman.
Berlin.	Gallery.	Venus and Adonis. 1678.
Cassel.	Gallery.	A Man smoking and drinking.
Dresden.	Gallery.	Landscape with Women bathing. 1666.
"	"	A Man in a grey hat.
"	"	A Shepherdess.
Frankfort.	Städel.	Head of an old Man.
Hague.	Gallery.	Portrait of a Huntsman.
Munich.	Gallery.	A Drinker.
"	"	A Smoker.
Paris.	Louvre.	Portrait of a Man seated at his bureau.

DE VOLLER, AERTGEN. See CLAESSOON.

DE VOS. There were several painters of this name, nearly contemporaries, but of different families. As most of them painted landscapes, portraits, and animals, their names and works have been confounded. Among them, in addition to those in the following articles, are, a second Pieter, a second Willem, a Hendrik, and other baptismal names, but there is very little information to enable the inquirer to distinguish their works. A race of painters of the name continues in Holland to this day.

DE VOS, CORNELIS, was born at Hulst about 1585, and became master in the Guild of St. Luke at Antwerp in 1608, having been mentioned in 1599 in the 'Liggeren' as a pupil of Remeeus; he was dean of the Guild in 1619-20. He painted historical pictures and portraits, the latter somewhat in the style of Rubens. He died in 1651. He was a friend of Van Dyck, who painted his portrait. The following are some of his principal works:

Antwerp.	Museum.	Portrait of Abraham Grapheus, Messenger of the Corporation of St. Luke. 1620.
"	"	Triptych—Adoration of the Magi. (From the Cathedral, Antwerp.)
Berlin.	Gallery.	Portrait of a Gentleman and his Wife. 1629.
"	"	Portrait of his Daughter.
Brussels.	Museum.	Portrait of the Artist and his Family.
Cassel.	Gallery.	Portrait of a Man.
"	"	Portrait of Salomon Cock.
Madrid.	Gallery.	Venus rising from the Sea.
"	"	Triumph of Bacchus.
"	"	Apollo and the Python.
Munich.	Gallery.	Family Picture.
Petersburg.	Hermitage.	Family Picture.
Rotterdam.	Museum.	An Allegory.
Vienna.	Gallery.	Baptism of Cloris.

DE VOS, CORNELIS, a painter of accessories in other artists' productions, was, in 1633-34, received into the Guild of St. Luke at Antwerp, as a master's son. He is no relation to the celebrated Cornelis De Vos.

DE VOS, JAN, lived at Antwerp in the middle of the 17th century. A portrait of a Man by him is in the Rotterdam Museum.

DE VOS, LAMBERTUS, a native of Mechlin, who entered the Guild of St. Luke in that city in 1563, went to Constantinople, and there executed in 1574 a volume of drawings of 'Oriental Costumes,' which is preserved in the Library at Bremen.

DE VOS, MARTEN, an eminent Flemish painter, was born at Antwerp in 1531. He was the son of Pieter De Vos, an artist of sufficient ability to be received into the Academy at Antwerp in 1519, and from whom he received his first instruction in painting. He had afterwards the advantage of frequenting the school of Frans Floris, under whom he studied until he was twenty-three years of age, when he determined to visit Italy, and passed some years at Rome, where he improved his style of design by studying with attention the works of the great painters of the Roman school. The charm of Venetian colouring led him to visit Venice, where he had the good fortune to win the esteem and friendship of Tintoretto, who not only instructed him in the best principles of colouring, but employed him as a coadjutor to paint the landscapes in his pictures. With the aid of such advice and assistance, De Vos became an admirable colourist, and gained such reputation, that he was employed in painting the portraits of several of the illustrious family of the Medici, as well as some historical subjects which added to his fame.

After an absence of eight years, De Vos returned to Flanders, where the celebrity he had acquired in Italy excited public curiosity, and he was commissioned to paint several altar-pieces for the churches at Antwerp and other cities of the Netherlands. He was also much employed as a portrait painter, and there is an appearance of nature in his heads which was unequalled at the period at which he lived. He was received into the Guild of St. Luke at Antwerp in 1559, and died in his native city in 1603. The following are some of his principal works:

Antwerp.	Mus.	Christ on the Cross.
"	"	A Triptych:—The Triumph of Christ. 1590.	Formerly in the Cathedral.
"	"	A Triptych:—Incredulity of St. Thomas. 1574.	

Antwerp. *Mus.* Birth of Christ. (*From the church of the Capuchins at Mechlin.*)

"   "   A Triptych:—The Tribute Money, &c. 1601. (*From the church of St. Andrew at Antwerp.*)

"   "   A Triptych:—St. Luke painting the portrait of the Virgin, &c. 1602. (*Parts of the wings are by Otho van Veen and Marten Pepyn. From the altar of the Guild of St. Luke in the cathedral.*)

"   "   Polyptych:—St. Francis of Assisi receiving the Stigmata, &c. (*From the church of the Récollets, Antwerp.*)

"   "   Temptation of St. Anthony. 1591. (*Formerly the centre-piece of a triptych over the altar of St. Anthony in the cathedral.*)

Brussels. *Mus.* The Wings of a Triptych. (*Portraits of the Donor and his Wife.*)

Florence. *Uffizi.* His own Portrait.

"   "   Crucifixion.

Madrid. *Gall.* Raising of Lazarus.

"   "   Samson and Delilah.

Seville. *Mus.* The Last Judgment.

The works of Marten De Vos had considerable influence on art in his time; but many of them were destroyed by the Iconoclasts.

His son, MARTEN DE VOS, who was also a painter, was born at Antwerp in 1576. He was admitted into the Guild of St. Luke at Antwerp in 1607, and died in 1613.

DE VOS, PAULUS, the brother of Cornelis De Vos, was born at Hulst, about the year 1600, and studied under Remeeus. From the subjects and style of his pictures, it is probable that he was a disciple of Frans Snyders. He painted animals and hunting scenes with great ability, and his works are little, if at all, inferior to those of that distinguished artist. His animals, particularly his dogs, are drawn with correctness and spirit, and his colouring is clear and harmonious. He died in 1654. There are in the Madrid Gallery no less than fifteen of his works, and in the Hermitage at St. Petersburg there are five.

DE VOS, PIETER, the elder, a Flemish painter, went to Antwerp from Holland, but whether from Gouda or Leyden is uncertain. His name occurs in the archives of the Guild of St. Luke in 1519, and he was dean of the Guild in 1536. He is believed to have died in 1566. He was the father of Marten De Vos.

DE VOS, PIETER, the younger, the brother of Marten De Vos, was a native of Antwerp. He entered the Guild of St. Luke in 1554, and is said to have been still living in 1590. He painted historical subjects, but his works are little known.

DE VOS, SIMON, was born at Antwerp in 1603, and entered the Guild of St. Luke in 1620. He had the advantage of studying in the school of Rubens, under whom he became a very eminent painter of history and portraits. There are some altar-pieces by him in the churches at Antwerp, which have been sometimes mistaken for the works of his illustrious instructor. Such are his picture of the 'Resurrection,' in the cathedral; the 'Descent from the Cross,' in the church of St. Andrew; and 'St. Norbert receiving the Sacrament,' in the abbey of St. Michael. Sir Joshua Reynolds commends this picture, and speaks of him as a portrait painter in the following terms: "De Vos was particularly excellent in portraits. There is at Antwerp his own portrait, painted by himself, in black, leaning on the back of a chair, with a scroll of blue paper in his hand, so highly finished, in the broad style of Correggio, that nothing can exceed it." He died in 1676. Besides the above works the following may be noticed:—

Berlin.   *Gallery.*   The Chastisement of Love.

Rotterdam. *Museum.*   Portrait of a Man. 1640.

"   "   Portrait of a Man. 1645.

DE VOS, WILLEM, the son of Pieter De Vos, the younger, and nephew and scholar of Marten De Vos, painted historical subjects in the style of his instructor, acquiring therein considerable reputation. He was born probably at Antwerp, and in 1593 entered the Guild of St. Luke, of which he became dean in 1600. His portrait was painted and etched by Van Dyck among those of the distinguished artists of his time.

DEVOSGE, ANATOLE, the son of François Devosge, was born at Dijon in 1770, and painted, after the manner of his master, David, several pictures, the subjects of which were taken from the Old Testament, and from mythology and Greek and Roman history. He succeeded his father as director of the School of Art at Dijon, where he died in 1850.

DEVOSGE, FRANÇOIS, was a French historical painter, founder of the School of Design, Painting, and Sculpture at Dijon. He was born at Gray in 1732, and taught by his father, Coustou, and Deshays, the painter; his principal works are, 'The Nativity,' 'St. Angela,' 'St. Peter, kneeling,' 'The Assumption of the Virgin,' 'The Martyrdom of St. Marcel,' &c. He died at Dijon in 1811.

DE VOUW, JOHANNES, was a Dutch landscape painter, of whom nothing more is known than that he lived in Rotterdam, and died not later than 1691. He painted landscapes with trees and buildings, and also drew maps and plans.

DE VREE, NICOLAAS, a flower painter, born at Utrecht about the year 1650, was celebrated in his day for the lightness of his pencil, and the fresh and natural brilliancy of his colours; his works, however, are but little known out of Holland. He died at Alkmaar in 1702. In the Hermitage at St. Petersburg is a 'Park,' by him, dated 1677.

DE VRIENT, FRANS, commonly known as FRANS FLORIS (the name of Floris having been borne by his great-grandfather, re-assumed by his father, and used by himself in signing his paintings), was born at Antwerp about 1517, and, until he was twenty years of age, studied sculpture under his uncle Claudius De Vrient. His love of painting induced him to change the chisel for the palette, and he became a scholar of Lambert Lombard, from whose instruction he derived great advantage. He afterwards visited Italy, where he studied attentively the works of Michelangelo and the antique. After passing some years at Rome, he returned to Flanders, with an ample collection of drawings he had made from the objects most worthy of admiration. His first productions exhibited a grander and more correct design, and a superior style of composition to what had before been witnessed by his countrymen, and he acquired the appellation of the 'Flemish Raphael.' He was patronized by the Counts of Hoorn and Egmont, and was received as a master into the Guild of St. Luke at Antwerp in 1540. When the Emperor Charles V. made his entry into Antwerp, in 1549, Floris was engaged to paint the triumphal arches; and he is said to have finished seven figures as large as life, with different attributes, in one day. On a similar occasion, when Philip II. visited the Low Countries, he painted in a few hours a large picture representing 'Victory,' with several figures of slaves, and the attributes of War and Peace.

Of this subject he etched a plate, dated 1552. His death occurred at Antwerp in 1570.

Frans Floris was the founder of a large school. He usually signed his paintings in full, or with a monogram composed of three Fs (Frans Floris Fecit). Among his extant works are the following:

Amsterdam.	Museum.	The Nine Muses.
,,	,,	Christ and the Little Children.
,,	,,	A Water Wedding at Middelburg.
Antwerp.	Museum.	The Fall of Lucifer (painted in 1554 for the altar of the Fencers in the cathedral of Antwerp; his best work).
,,	,,	The Adoration of the Shepherds.
,,	,,	Ryckaert Aertsz, the painter, as St. Luke.
Berlin.	Gallery.	Vulcan ensnaring Mars and Venus. 1547.
,,	,,	Venus and Cupid.
,,	,,	Lot and his Daughters.
Brussels.	Museum.	The Last Judgment (painted for Notre-Dame des Victoires au Sablon at Brussels). 1566.
,,	,,	The Adoration of the Magi. (A triptych, which was probably his last work, and was finished by Hieronymus Francken in 1571.)
Copenhagen.	Gallery.	Cain and Abel.
Dresden.	Gallery.	Adoration of the Shepherds.
,,	,,	The Emperor Vitellius.
,,	,,	The Laughing Maiden.
,,	,,	Lot and his Daughters.
,,	,,	Christ carrying his Cross.
Florence.	Uffizi.	Adam and Eve. 1560.
Hague.	Gallery.	Venus and Adonis.
Madrid.	Gallery.	The Deluge.
,,	,,	Two Portraits.
Petersburg.	Hermitage.	The Three Ages of Man.
Vienna.	Gallery.	Adam and Eve under the Tree of Knowledge.
,,	,,	Adam and Eve driven out of Paradise.
,,	,,	The Holy Family.

As an etcher Frans Floris executed, among other plates, 'Victory,' and 'Christ washing the Disciples' Feet': both from his own designs. His two sons, JAN BAPTISTA and FRANS DE VRIENT, were both painters. The first was assassinated at Brussels by the Spaniards; the second, who was born at Antwerp about 1545, settled at Rome, and became noted for his easel pictures. They were both living in 1579.

DE VRIES, ADRIAAN, a Flemish portrait painter, was admitted as a master into the Guild of St. Luke at Antwerp in 1634-35. His works possess considerable merit, and have been attributed to Ferdinand Bol, to Van Dyck, and to Rembrandt. He died subsequently to 1650. In the Dresden Gallery is a male portrait by him, dated 1639. In the Rotterdam Museum is his portrait of Adriaen Adriaensz Vroesen of Rotterdam, dated 1639, and in the Berlin Gallery is a Man's portrait ascribed to him.

Some confusion appears to exist between the works of this artist and those of ABRAHAM DE VRIES, who was admitted into the Guild of St. Luke at the Hague in 1644, and died before 1662.

DE VRIES, JAN (or HANS) VREDEMAN, was born at Leeuwarden, in East Friesland, in 1527. He was sent, when young, to Amsterdam, where he became a scholar of Reyer Gerritsz, under whom he continued five years, and applied himself with great assiduity to the study of perspective. In 1549 he went to Antwerp, where he was employed, with others, in painting the triumphal arches which were erected on the public entry of the Emperor Charles V. and his son Philip into that city; on which occasion he proved himself an artist of considerable ability. He was much employed in decorating the saloons of the principal mansions with perspective views, which he designed with such truth and effect that the illusion was complete. He travelled through Germany and Italy, and he everywhere met with encouragement and employment. After his return to Antwerp, the latter part of his life was principally occupied in making designs of architectural and other subjects for the print-sellers, particularly Hieronimus Cock, who published a great variety of prints from his designs. We have a book of monuments by him, entitled 'Cænotaphiorum, tumulorum et mortuorum monumentorum variæ formæ,' published at Antwerp in 1563. The plates are etched and finished with the graver, with considerable intelligence. In the Vienna Gallery is the 'Interior of a Church' by him; and the Bordeaux Museum has a Landscape.

DE VRIES, PAULUS, the eldest son of Jan Vredeman De Vries, was born at Antwerp in 1554, and died in 1598. He was specially employed at Prague in the service of the Emperor.

DE VRIES, ROELOF, was a Dutch landscape painter, who flourished at Haarlem from about 1643 to about 1669. Buildings are often seen in his works. There are by him:

Berlin.	Gallery.	Three Landscapes.
Frankfort.	Städel Inst.	Four Landscapes.
Vienna.	Liechtenstein Gall.	Landscape.
,,	Czernin Gall.	Landscape.

DE VRIES, SALOMON, born at Antwerp in 1556, was the second son of Jan Vredeman De Vries, by whom he was instructed. He painted landscapes ornamented with ruins, which are not badly composed, but their colouring has become dark, producing an unpleasant effect, and diminishing their value. He died at the Hague in 1604. His son, PIETER DE VRIES, who was born in 1587, was also a landscape painter.

DE VRIES, SIMON, (or SIMON FRISIUS,) a Dutch engraver, was apparently of the same family as Jan Vredeman De Vries. He was born at Leeuwarden, in 1580, and is regarded as one of the first who brought etching to perfection. Abraham Bosse, in his treatise on the art of engraving, observes, that the first artist to whom he was indebted for intelligence was Simon Frisius, whom he thinks entitled to great credit, as being one of the first that handled the point with freedom and facility. His etchings are bold and masterly; and in his hatchings he approaches the neatness and strength of the graver. The prints of De Vries are scarce, and are much esteemed. The small figures which he occasionally introduces into his landscapes are correctly drawn. He frequently marked his plates S. F. fecit, but sometimes with the word fecit only. The following are his principal works:

A set of twelve small heads of female Saints and Sibyls; after his own designs.
A set of Portraits; after Hendrik Hondius.
A set of twelve plates of Birds and Butterflies; after Marcus Geerarts.
Twenty-five Views and Landscapes; entitled, Typographia variarum Regionum; after Matthys Bril. 1611.
A mountainous Landscape on the Sea-coast, with figures; after Hendrik Goltzius.
A Landscape, with a Tower; after the same. 1608.
A Landscape, with the story of Tobit and the Angel; after P. Lastman.
A Landscape, with the Flight into Egypt; after H Hondius.

A Landscape, with two pastoral figures; highly finished, and very scarce.

DE WAAL. See DE WAEL.

DE WAARD, ANTONIE, born at the Hague in 1689, was a scholar of Simon van der Does; he afterwards studied in Paris. He is mentioned as a painter of historical subjects, portraits, landscapes, and animals, and also as a decorator of the interiors of apartments. Of his life nothing further is recorded, and his works are scarcely known out of Holland, but it is said that they are esteemed there, and obtain high prices. He died at the Hague in 1751.

DE WAEL, CORNELIS, (or DE WAAL,) a younger son of the elder Jan Baptist De Wael, was born at Antwerp in 1594. He received his first instruction in the art from his father; but he afterwards accompanied his brother, Lucas De Wael, to Italy, and resided some time at Genoa, where he painted some pictures for the churches, but he chiefly excelled in painting battles, marches, skirmishes of cavalry, and processions, in which he gained a distinguished reputation. He was much employed by the Duke of Arschot, and painted several of his best pictures for Philip III., King of Spain, by whom they were held in the highest estimation. He died at Genoa in 1662. In the Vienna Gallery is a 'Passage of the Red Sea' by him, and in the Cassel Gallery is a 'Venetian Market Crier.' We have by this artist several very spirited etchings from his own compositions, among which are the following:

> The Blind; 12 *plates.*
> The Market Sellers; 16 *plates.*
> Domestic Interiors; 20 *plates.*
> The Four Seasons.
> The Five Senses; 5 *plates.*
> The Slaves; 12 *plates.*

DE WAEL, JAN BAPTIST, (or DE WAAL,) was born at Antwerp in 1557, and was a disciple of Frans Francken the elder. He painted historical subjects in the style of his master, and acquired sufficient celebrity to be received a member of the Academy in his native city, where he died in 1633. Van Dyck painted his portrait. His pictures are very rare.

DE WAEL, JAN BAPTIST, (or DE WAAL,) a younger artist of the name, is stated to have been either the son or nephew of Cornelis De Wael. We have by him some slight etchings, among which is a set of eight prints, representing the 'History of the Prodigal Son,' from the designs of Cornelis De Wael, executed in 1658.

DE WAEL, LUCAS JANSZEN, (or DE WAAL,) the son of the elder Jan Baptist De Wael, was born at Antwerp in 1591, and first instructed in art by his father; but, as his genius led him to landscape, he was afterwards placed under the tuition of Jan Brueghel. He followed the style of his preceptor with great success, and, on leaving that master, he travelled to Italy, and passed some time at Genoa, where his works were highly esteemed, and he met with very flattering encouragement. Although his pictures occasionally represent battles and attacks of cavalry, which are well composed, and touched with great spirit and animation, his most esteemed works are his mountainous landscapes and waterfalls, in which the scenery is extremely picturesque. He died at Antwerp in 1676.

DE WEDIG, GOTTHARDT, a painter of still-life subjects, flourished at Cologne about 1630. An example of his art is in the Darmstadt Gallery.

DE WEERT, ADRIAEN, was born, according to Descamps, at Brussels about 1536, and studied at Antwerp under Christiaen van de Queborn, a landscape painter little known. He afterwards visited Italy, where he passed some years, and applied himself especially to the study of the works of Parmigiano. On his return to Flanders, he executed several pictures in the graceful style of that master, particularly a series of the 'Life of the Virgin,' and had acquired great reputation, when the troubles in the Low Countries obliged him, in 1566, to quit Brussels and take refuge at Cologne, where he died soon afterwards. All the notices of this artist are however unsatisfactory.

DE WEERT, JACOB, who flourished about the year 1605, was probably a native of the Low Countries, though he chiefly resided in Paris. He was principally employed by the booksellers, and engraved several frontispieces and other book ornaments in a neat, though tasteless style. We have also by him a set of prints from his own designs, representing the 'Life and Passion of Christ,' published by Jean Le Clerc, with French verses to each print.

DE WETT. See DÜWETT. See also DÜWETT.

DE WETT, JACOB, was a Dutch painter, who worked at Holyrood Palace between 1674 and 1686, and there painted the series of apocryphal portraits of the Scottish kings.

DE WETTE, FRANS, to whom are assigned, in Dr. Waagen's edition of Kugler, two pictures in the Schleissheim Gallery,—'The Three Young Men in the Fiery Furnace' and 'The Raising of Lazarus,' —may perhaps be identical with Jacob Willemsz De Wet, who was established at Haarlem in 1636, was master in the Guild at Alkmaar in 1637, and was living in that town as late as 1671. He executed Biblical and mythological scenes in the manner of Rembrandt, among which are:

> The Adulteress before Christ (*Augsburg Gallery*).
> Christ in the Temple. 1635. (*Brunswick Museum*).
> The Burning of Troy.

DE WILDE, FRANS, was a Dutch engraver, who was born about the year 1680. He resided at Amsterdam, where he etched a few very small plates, which are executed with great neatness and spirit, apparently from his own designs. Among others are the following:

> The Angel appearing to Abraham. 1705.
> Venus rising from the Sea.
> The Fable of the Wolf and the Dog; circular. 1704.
> A View of the City of Chalons.
> A View of a Sea-port.
> A Landscape, with figures.

DE WILDE, MARIA, was probably a relation of Frans De Wilde. She engraved a set of fifty plates from antique gems, which were published at Amsterdam in 1703.

DE WILDE, SAMUEL, an English portrait painter, was born in 1747. He painted both in oil and water-colour, and exhibited dramatic portraits at the Royal Academy between 1788 and 1821. He died in 1832. Several of his portraits are at the Garrick Club, and amongst his other works are:

> William Farren.
> John Emery.
> Harley as Kent in 'King Lear.' 1794. (*South Kensington Museum.*)

DE WINT, PETER, a water-colour painter, was born at Stone, in Staffordshire, in 1784. He was descended from a Dutch family which had settled in America. Although intended for his father's profession—that of a physician—he preferred to follow art, and studied under John Raphael Smith, the engraver, in whose studio he became friendly with Hilton, the historical painter, and brother of his future wife. In 1807 he entered the schools of the Royal Academy, where he occasionally exhibited up to 1828. He joined the Water-Colour Society as an Associate in 1810, becoming a full member in 1812, and it was here that most of his works appeared. He rarely quitted his native country, which furnished the subjects of the greater portion of his works, and the level country of Lincolnshire had a great charm for him. He occasionally painted in oils, and four specimens of his work in this medium, besides a large collection of his water-colour drawings, are in the South Kensington Museum. He died in London in 1849, and was buried at the Savoy Chapel.

Twenty-three drawings by De Wint were bequeathed to the National Gallery by Mr. Henderson in 1880, and among them are:

> Lincoln Cathedral.
> Bray on the Thames.
> Ruins of Lincoln Castle.
> Harvest Time, Lancashire.

The water-colour drawings in the South Kensington Museum include:

> Thornbury Castle.
> Gateway at Lincoln.
> The Cricketers.
> Nottingham.
> Walton-on-Thames.
> Hay Harvest.
> Mountain Tarn.
> Ferry on the Severn. 1840.
> Haddon Hall. 1839.
> Shap Fells, Westmoreland.
> Wilsford, Lincolnshire.
> Rick Making, near Lincoln.
> Tutbury Castle.
> View near Salt Hill, Bucks.
> Lincoln Cathedral.
> Torksey Castle.
> Cowes Castle.

DE WINTER, JILLIS, was born at Leeuwarden in 1650, and was a scholar of Richard Brakenburg, whose style he imitated with considerable success. He painted subjects similar to those of his master, representing Dutch boors regaling, and the recreations of the *cabaret*. His pictures are little known, except in Holland, and even there are not held in much estimation. He died at Amsterdam in 1720.

DE WIT, JAKOB, was born at Amsterdam in 1695, and when fourteen years of age was placed under the tuition of Albert van Spiers, an historical painter of some eminence, under whom he studied three years. The desire of contemplating the productions of Rubens and Van Dyck, and the other distinguished masters of the Flemish school, which embellished the public edifices at Antwerp, induced him to visit that city, where he became a scholar of Jacob van Hal, a painter of little celebrity, under whom he did not continue longer than two years, when he devoted himself entirely to the study of the works of Rubens and Van Dyck. In 1712 and 1713 he made drawings from the paintings by Rubens in the four ceilings of the Jesuits' church, in thirty-six compartments, which were destroyed by lightning in 1718, and we are indebted to De Wit for the preservation of these admirable compositions, which were afterwards engraved from his copies by Jan Punt. He was principally employed in painting ceilings, and the decorations of splendid apartments, consisting of

emblematical and allegorical subjects, which he composed with great ingenuity. He was particularly successful in the representation of children, whom he was fond of introducing into his pictures, generally at their play, and painted in chiaroscuro.

In 1736 he was employed by the magistrates of Amsterdam in the embellishment of their great Council-chamber with subjects from the Old Testament. He likewise painted several altar-pieces for the catholic churches in Holland, which are very creditable performances, and are held in considerable estimation. He died at Amsterdam in 1754. In the Cassel Gallery are four pictures of the 'Four Seasons' (represented by Children) signed and dated 1751 and 1752, and also two decorative subjects of children. In the Dresden Gallery is a painting (in imitation of bas-relief) of 'Children with the attributes of the chase,' dated 1753. The Rotterdam Museum possesses two pictures by him, 'Minerva and four Children' and 'Faith, Hope, and Charity,' in grisaille, dated 1743.

DE WITTE. There are several other artists of this name, in addition to those cited below, such as FRANS, and ANTHONIE, who were painters; and others who were engravers: but the accounts are much confused.

DE WITTE, CORNELIS, (or DE WIT,) a landscape painter of the 16th century, was a brother of Pieter De Witte, called Pietro Candido.

DE WITTE, EMANUEL, was born at Alkmaar in 1607, and was a scholar of Evert van Aelst, a painter of still-life. He did not, however, adopt the style of his instructor, but for some time applied himself to portrait painting. Not meeting with the encouragement he expected, he studied perspective and architecture, and became one of the most eminent artists of his country in painting interior views of churches and temples, which he embellished with figures correctly drawn, and touched with great spirit. His best pictures represent the interiors of churches at Amsterdam, with groups of figures, habited in the dresses of the time. He died at Amsterdam in 1692. The following works are by him:

Amsterdam.	*Museum.*	Interior of a Church.
Berlin.	*Museum.*	Interior of a Church. 1667.
”	”	Interior of the Nieuwekerk, Amsterdam.
”	”	Interior of the Synagogue, Amsterdam. 1680.
Brussels.	*Museum.*	Interior of the Church at Delft.
”	”	Interior of a Church. 1685.
Rotterdam.	*Museum.*	The Fish Merchant. 1672.

DE WITTE, GASPAR, was born at Antwerp in 1618. He visited Italy, where he remained several years, and on his return acquired considerable reputation in painting small landscapes very highly finished, in which he generally introduced architectural ruins, of which he had made sketches during his residence in Italy. He died at Antwerp in 1680 or 1681. In the Antwerp Museum are two Landscapes by him—one with a 'Fortune-telling' for subject, dated 1667, and another with 'Christ healing the Blind Man,' dated 1671. In the Vienna Gallery is a 'Landscape with Ruins of an Aqueduct.'

DE WITTE, LIEVEN, known also as LIVIENO DA ANVERSA, was a painter and architect, who practised at Ghent in the 15th century. He devoted himself to buildings and other perspective subjects, but also produced historical pictures. The windows of the cathedral of St. Bavon in Ghent were painted from his designs, and he is said to have worked at the miniatures in the Grimani Breviary now in the library of St. Mark at Venice.

DE WITTE, PIETER, called PIETER CANDID, or PIETRO CANDIDO, was born at Bruges in 1548. It is not known under whom he studied, but he travelled to Italy when he was young, and there formed an intimacy with Giorgio Vasari, whom he assisted in the works upon which he was employed in the Vatican. He painted with equal success in oil and in fresco, and was employed by the Grand-Duke of Tuscany in several considerable works in the palace at Florence, and designed some cartoons for tapestry. Maximilian, Elector of Bavaria, invited him to Munich, where he passed the remainder of his life. Jan Sadeler has engraved several prints from the works of this master, among which are the 'Annunciation,' 'Christ with the Disciples at Emmaus,' the 'Holy Women at the Tomb of the Saviour,' and the 'Last Supper.' He died at Munich in 1628. In the Vienna Gallery are the 'Death of St. Ursula,' and a 'Holy Family and St. Stephen,' by him.

DE WITTE, PIETER, who was well known in Rome as PETRUS ALBUS, was born at Antwerp in 1620, and died at Rome in 1669. He painted landscapes in the style of Claude Lorrain.

DEYNUM, J. B. VAN, a Flemish painter, was born at Antwerp in 1620, and died in 1669. He excelled in painting historical subjects and landscapes in distemper, and was an eminent miniature portrait painter.

DEYSTER, LODEWYK DE. See DE DEYSTER.

DE' ZAGANELLI, FRANCESCO. See DEI ZAGANELLI.

DEZALLIER D'ARGENVILLE, ANTOINE JOSEPH. See DESALLIER D'ARGENVILLE.

DE ZE, —, is the name affixed to a small print representing 'Christ dead in the Tomb, attended by an Angel.' It is executed entirely with the graver, in a style resembling that of Jan Sadeler, and is apparently from the artist's own design.

DE ZEEUW, MARINUS. See ROYMERSWALEN.

DE ZETTER, PAUL, was a native of Hanover, who flourished about the year 1630. He was chiefly employed in engraving portraits, from his own designs, which are executed with sufficient neatness, but in a stiff, tasteless style. He engraved several plates for Boissard's collection of portraits. His prints are sometimes marked *P. D. Z. fec.*, and sometimes with the accompanying monogram: **P.**

D' HANGEST, EGBERT MARINUS FREDERIK. See DE HANGEST.

D' HEUR, CORNELIS JOSEPH. See DE HEUR.

D' HONDECOETER, MELCHIOR. See DE HONDECOETER.

DIAMAER, HENDRIK FRANS, was a Flemish engraver, who flourished in the early part of the 18th century. There are by him a set of Biblical subjects etched in the manner of Sebastian Le Clerc, and also a few portraits, among which is that of Aubert Lemire, after Van Dyck.

DIAMANTE, Fra, was the pupil and assistant of Fra Filippo Lippi, and like him had been a novice in the Carmine of Florence. He survived his master, and became the guardian of Filippino Lippi. He seems to have been at Prato with Fra Filippo, and is said to have aided him in the decorations of the choir of its cathedral. In 1463 he was confined in his convent at Florence by order of his superior, and letters remain to prove that the 'comune' of Prato demanded his liberty. He afterwards went to Spoleto, and assisted Fra Filippo in the frescoes of the Duomo, and received two hundred ducats for their completion in 1470 after his master's death. From there he returned to Prato, where in 1470 he executed the portrait of the Podestà, Cesare Petrucci, in the portico of the palace. This work has now been destroyed, and it is very difficult to tell where Fra Diamante's work begins in any of the frescoes still remaining where the two friars worked together. The dates of his birth and death are unknown.

DIAMANTINI, GIUSEPPE, a painter who was more eminent as an engraver, was born at Fossombrone in 1660. He resided chiefly at Venice, where he distinguished himself both as a painter and as an engraver. In the church of San Moise is a picture by him of the 'Adoration of the Magi,' but he was more employed for private collections than for the churches, and must have devoted a great part of his time to engraving, as he has left a considerable number of plates, of which the greater part are etchings. They are executed in a free style, with considerable taste, and his design is graceful, and tolerably correct. He died at Venice in 1708. The following are his principal prints, which are frequently marked *Eques Diamantinus, in. f.*

The Holy Family, with St. John holding a Cross.
Hagar in the Desert ; oval.
The Marriage at Cana ; *after Paolo Veronese.*
The Dead Christ, supported by an Angel.
The Death of Dido ; octagon.
Venus, Ceres, and Apollo.
Mercury and Flora.
The Fall of Phaeton.
Mercury and Argus ; octagon.
Venus and Adonis.

DIANA. See GHISI, DIANA.

DIANA, BENEDETTO, was a companion of Carpaccio and Mansueti, who lived in the latter part of the 15th and early part of the 16th centuries. He was an inferior artist, and worked both in tempera and oils. He painted 'The Brethren distributing Alms,' in San Giovanni Evangelista, Venice ; and he assisted Lazzaro Bastiani in painting the standards on the Piazza of San Marco. Many galleries in Venice possess paintings by him. In the Academy, besides other paintings, are the 'Virgin and Child,' formerly in Santa Lucia at Padua, and a 'Transfiguration.' The church of Santa Maria della Croce, Crema, has an altar-piece representing the 'Gift of the Miraculous Girdle to St. Thomas.' No dates can be given of his birth or death.

DIAS, GASPAR, a Portuguese painter, studied at Rome under Raphael and Michelangelo, and on his return home devoted himself to the production of church pictures. He died at Lisbon in 1571.

DIAS, MANOEL, an historical painter, was born at San Sebastian in Brazil, and studied at Rome under Cavallucci towards the end of the 18th century. After his return to South America he became professor of drawing at Rio Janeiro.

DIAZ, DIEGO VALENTIN, a Spanish historical painter, and a familiar of the Holy Office, was a native of Valladolid. He painted many important pictures for churches and monasteries, especially for the church of San Benito, now a barrack, and the convents of St. Jerome and of St. Francis, of

71

which the 'Jubilee of the Porciuncula' in the latter house was one of the most esteemed. His 'Holy Family,' painted for San Benito, is now in the Museum at Valladolid; but his best work was the altar-piece representing the 'Annunciation of the Virgin,' painted for the Hospital for Orphan Girls which he founded at Valladolid. The architecture and perspective are in the finest style, and the statues introduced are admirably executed. Diaz died at Valladolid in 1660. He accumulated considerable wealth, the greater part of which he left for the support of this hospital, where he was buried, and where are preserved the portraits of the munificent artist and of his wife—"he a grey-haired sharp old man, she a dark-eyed dame."

DIAZ, GONZALO, a Spanish painter, was a scholar of Sanchez Castro. He executed in 1499 some small paintings for the altar of the Magdalen in the cathedral of Seville.

DIAZ DE LA PEÑA, NARCISSE VIRGILE, a French landscape painter, was born in 1809, at Bordeaux, where his parents, who were of Spanish extraction, had taken up their abode. Having been left an orphan at the age of ten, he was adopted by a Protestant clergyman at Bellevue, and from his earliest years he studied nature in the woods, the loss of his left leg being caused by sleeping on the grass. At the age of fifteen he was placed with a porcelain manufacturer, but left him in order to study under Sigalon. He then tried historical and genre subjects, but without success, and for several years endured great poverty. At length his landscapes won for him fame. He last exhibited at the Salon in 1859, and died at Mentone from the bite of a viper in 1876. Amongst his chief works are:

The Nymphs in the Grotto of Calypso. 1840.
The Dream. 1841.
Gipsies going to a Fête. 1844.
Interior of a Forest. 1846.
Dogs in a Forest. 1847.
The Promenade. 1848.
Diana setting out for the Chase. 1848.
A Bather tormented by Cupids. 1851.
The Last Tears. 1855.
The Close of a fine Day. 1855.
La Rivale. 1855.
Galatea. 1859.

The following works by him are in public galleries:
Girl with Dogs (South Kensington).
The Forest of Fontainebleau (Bordeaux Museum).
Four Studies (Luxembourg Gallery).

His eldest son, ÉMILE DIAZ, who was also a painter, died in 1860, at the early age of 25.

DIBDIN, CHARLES, the well-known song-writer, who was born at Southampton in 1745, and died in London in 1814, occasionally practised art as an amateur. John Hill engraved in aquatint some views of Lake Scenery after him. Dibdin also, it is said, executed some scene-painting.

DICEY, FRANK, an English painter of portraits, and of genre subjects of a somewhat ambitious class, exhibited at the Academy and with the British Artists between 1865 and 1880. A portrait by him of the Prince of Wales was engraved by Scott. Dicey died in May 1888.

DICHTL, MARTIN, (or DÜCHTL,) a German painter and engraver in mezzotint, practised at Nuremberg from 1623 to 1680. In the Gallery at Stockholm is a work by him called 'A Kitchen.'

DICKINSON, WILLIAM, an English engraver, was born in London in 1746. He obtained a premium from the Society of Arts in 1767. His works

were published by a firm of which he was a member. In his later years he lived in France, still pursuing his profession, and he died in Paris in 1823. Amongst his engravings are:

Sir Joseph Banks; after Sir Joshua Reynolds. 1774.
Dr. Percy, Dean of Carlisle; after the same. 1775.
Viscountess Crosbie; after the same. 1779.
Elizabeth Hamilton, Countess of Derby; after the same. 1780.
Lady Taylor; after the same. 1783.
Miss Ramus, afterwards Lady Day; after Romney. 1779.
Admiral Lord Keppel; after the same. 1779.
Sir Charles Hardy; after the same. 1781.
Lord Grantham; after the same. 1783.
John, Duke of Argyll; after Gainsborough.
Lord Auckland; after Sir T. Lawrence 1796.
Napoleon I.; after Gerard. 1815.
Sir R. Peel; after Northcote. 1818.

DICKSON, J., an English engraver, resided at Oxford about the year 1660. He engraved a portrait of Edward Parry, Bishop of Killaloe, prefixed to his 'Antidote against the Prosperity of the Wicked, and the Afflictions of the Just,' published in 1660.

DIDAY, FRANÇOIS, a Swiss landscape painter, was born at Geneva in 1812. He studied in Paris and travelled in Italy, but chiefly lived in his native country. He, however, frequently exhibited in the Paris Salon, where he obtained medals in 1840 and 1841. He died in 1877, at Geneva, to which city he bequeathed his property, valued at 400,000 francs. The following are among his best works:

Glacier of Rosenthal. (Lausanne Museum.)
The Oak and the Reed. (Geneva Museum.)
The Faulhorn in Switzerland. (Neue Pinakothek, Munich.)
Mont Salève. } (London International Exhibition,
Storm in a Forest. } 1862.)

DIEGO, —, a Spanish engraver, who in 1548 executed at Saragossa the frontispiece for Zurita's 'Anales de Aragon,' printed in 1562.

DIELAI, GIOVANNI FRANCESCO. See SURCHI.

DIEN, CLAUDE MARIE FRANÇOIS, a French engraver and painter, was born in Paris in 1787. He was instructed by Reboul and by Audouin, and died in Paris in 1865. The following works by him may be mentioned:

The Sibyls; after Raphael.
Raphael and Perugino; after the same.
The Holy Family; after the same.
The Madonna; after Murillo.
The Death of Demosthenes; after Boisselier.
St. Scolastica; after Lesueur.
The Battle of Austerlitz; after Gérard.

DIENECKER. See DE NECKER.

DIEPENBEECK, ABRAHAM VAN, was born at Bois-le-Duc in 1599, but most likely went to Antwerp about 1629. With the advantage of a classical education, and the tuition of Rubens, he was nurtured in a genial soil, and, like his great instructor, he treated with equal success subjects of history and fable. His first pursuit in art was painting on glass, and he produced some works in that branch which are highly esteemed, particularly the windows in a chapel in the cathedral of Antwerp, where he represented the 'Acts of Mercy,' and some others in the church of the Dominicans, in which he depicted the 'Life of St. Paul.' He abandoned glass painting soon after his return from Italy, whither he had been for improvement, and devoted himself to oil painting and designing. His inventive genius, and his rare facility of execution, caused him to be much employed in designs for the publications of his time, particularly for the Abbé de Marolles's 'Tableaux du Temple des Muses,' published at Paris in 1655, the plates for which were engraved by Cornelis Bloemaert. In the church of the Carmelites at Antwerp is a fine picture by this master, representing the 'Virgin in the Clouds, with St. Ely'; and at the Recollets there were some pictures by him which are said by Descamps to be equal to those of Van Dyck. This painter was in England in the reign of Charles I., and was much employed by the Duke of Newcastle, for whom he made the designs for his book on 'Horsemanship.' He died at Antwerp in 1675. The following are some of his best works:

Antwerp.	*Museum.*	The Ecstasy of St. Bonaventura.
„	*Cathedral.*	St. Norbert.
Berlin.	*Gallery.*	The Marriage of St. Catharine.
„	„	The Flight of Cloelia.
Bordeaux.	*Museum.*	The Rape of Ganymede.
Brussels.	*Museum.*	St. Francis adoring the Holy Sacrament.
Deurne.	*Church.*	St. Norbert and the first Abbot of St. Michel.
Dresden.	*Gallery.*	Neptune and Amphitrite.
Frankfort.	*Städel.*	Portrait of a Young Man. 1665.
	„	Portrait of a Young Woman.
Munich.	*Gallery.*	Abraham and the three Angels.
Paris.	*Louvre.*	The Flight of Cloelia.
	„	Portraits of a Man and Woman.
Vienna.	*Gallery.*	An Allegory of Mortality.
„	„	A Pietà.

There is an etching of a 'Peasant and his Ass,' by Van Diepenbeeck, which is very rare.

DIEPRAAM, ABRAHAM, a Dutch painter of the 17th century, painted drolleries and drunken frolics. He was a scholar of Hendrik Martin Rokes, called Sorgh, although he did not follow the style of that master, but imitated the works of Adriaan Brouwer, in which he was not very successful.

DIERIX, ADRIAEN, known as Broeder ADRIAEN RODRIGUEZ, of the Society of Jesus, was born at Antwerp in 1618, and died at Madrid in 1669. He went to Spain when he was about thirty, and entered the Imperial College at Madrid, where he entered the Society of Jesus, and changed his name from Dierix to Rodriguez, for the sake of euphony. He painted in the Flemish manner, for the refectory of the above-mentioned college, 'Abraham entertaining the three Angels,' the 'Marriage at Cana,' the 'Holy Family,' 'Christ at Emmaus,' and the 'Banquet at the house of the Pharisee, with the Magdalen anointing Christ.'

DIES, ALBERT CHRISTOPH, born at Hanover in 1755, acquired the rudiments of art under a painter in that town. He afterwards studied under Pigage at Mannheim and under Mechel at Basle, and then visited Rome and Naples. At Rome he executed some landscapes in water-colour for Volpato. Among his works may be mentioned the twenty-four etchings of Italy, contributed to the 'Collection de Vues pittoresques de l'Italie' (1799), of which those of Tivoli are very fine. In the Belvedere at Vienna there are by him two landscapes in oil, both views near Salzburg, dated 1796 and 1797; these, however, are of less importance than his water-colours. He died at Vienna in 1822.

DIEST, ADRIAAN VAN, was born at the Hague in 1655. He was the son of a painter of sea-pieces, by whom he was instructed in the art. When he was seventeen years of age he came to London, and was employed by Granville, Earl of Bath, for whom he painted several views and ruins in the west of England. He also painted portraits, but did not meet with much encouragement, although his pictures, particularly his landscapes, possess considerable merit; as a proof of which Horace Walpole states that there were seven pictures by Van Diest in Sir Peter Lely's collection. He etched several landscapes from his own designs, in a slight, masterly style. Van Diest died in London in 1704. Unfortunately for his reputation, he is generally known by his worst pictures, which are frequently found in old houses, on wainscots, or over doors, and are executed in a hasty manner, with much mountainous background. His better pictures have changed their name.

DIETEL, CHRISTOPH and FRANZ AMBROS. These artists, who were brothers, resided at Vienna in the early part of the 18th century. They engraved conjointly a set of plates, representing the principal fountains at Rome. Franz Ambros Dietel died at Vienna in 1730.

DIETERLEIN. See DIETTERLIN.

DIETISALVI. See DIOTISALVI.

DIETLER, JOHANN FRIEDRICH, was born at Solothurn, in Switzerland, in 1804, and was instructed in the rudiments of art by German, a drawing-master of that town. He distinguished himself as a portrait painter, and visited Paris and Italy, remaining also some time at Geneva; but he finally settled at Berne, where he died in 1874. He painted for the town of Solothurn 'The Burgomaster Wengi before the Cannon.'

DIETRICH, CHRISTIAN WILHELM ERNST, (afterwards called DIETRICI, or DIETRICY,) a German artist, was born at Weimar in 1712. He learnt the principles of art from his father, Johann Georg Dietrich, who was court-painter at Weimar, and was afterwards a scholar of Thiele, the landscape painter. He established himself at Dresden, where he was patronized by the court, and was in 1729 appointed court-painter to Augustus II., king of Poland; and in 1741 he received the same appointment with a yearly salary of 400 thalers, for which he was to produce yearly four cabinet pictures, for Augustus III., who sent him in 1742 to Italy, where he passed some time at Rome and Venice. His studies in Italy do not appear to have had much influence on his style, which remained entirely German. His chief talent consisted in a successful imitation of the works of Rembrandt, Ostade, Poelenborch, Salvator Rosa, &c., particularly as a colourist, in which he greatly excelled. In 1746 he became keeper of the Dresden Gallery, in which he is very fully represented. He was also Professor in the Academy of Arts at Dresden, and Director of the Painting School at the Meissen Porcelain Factory. Dietrich also executed, after his own compositions, a large number of etchings, in which he imitated successfully the manner of Rembrandt and of Ostade. He died at Dresden in 1774. The following are some of the best of his paintings:

Bordeaux.	*Museum.*	Holy Family.
„	„	Landscapes (*five*).
Brussels.	*Museum.*	His own Portrait.
Cassel.	*Gallery.*	Two Landscapes.
Darmstadt.	*Gallery.*	The Parable of the Woman and the Lost Penny.
„	„	The Parable of the Blind leading the Blind.
		Evening Landscape.
Dresden.	*Gallery.*	Fifty-four Pictures (bearing dates from 1739 to 1766).

73

Hampton Court.	*Pal.*	Nymphs in a landscape bathing.
"	" "	The Woman taken in Adultery.
"	" "	The Tribute Money.
London.	*Nat. Gallery.*	The Itinerant Musicians. 1745.
Milan.	*Brera.*	Landscape.
Paris.	*Louvre.*	The Woman taken in Adultery. 1753.
Petersburg.	*Hermitage.*	Repose in Egypt. 1757.
"	"	The Entombment. 1759.
"	"	The Squirrel.
"	"	A Camera Obscura.
"	"	Views in Italy (*two*).
Vienna.	*Gallery.*	Angel appearing to the Shepherds.
"	"	Adoration of the Shepherds. 1760.

Dietrich's etched work extends to nearly two hundred prints, several of which are very scarce, as he frequently destroyed the plate, after having taken off a certain number of impressions. His earlier works are marked with a monogram, composed of a *C.* and a *D.*, but he afterwards signed them with his name, or with his initials, *C. W. E. D.*, or with *D.* only. The following are his principal prints:

SACRED SUBJECTS.

Lot and his Daughters; scarce.
Abraham going to sacrifice Isaac; scarce. 1730.
The same subject differently composed; very scarce.
The Nativity. 1740.
St. Philip baptizing the Eunuch.
The Adoration of the Shepherds; in the style of *Rembrandt.*
The Circumcision.
The Flight into Egypt.
Another of the same subject, differently composed.
The Repose in Egypt; scarce. 1732.
Another Repose in Egypt. 1734.
The Return from Egypt.
Christ found disputing with the Doctors. 1731.
Our Saviour healing the Sick.
The Prodigal Son.
The Resurrection of Lazarus; in the style of *Rembrandt.*
The Descent from the Cross; in the same style; scarce. 1730.
Another of the same subject, differently treated; also in the style of *Rembrandt.* 1742.
The Disciples at Emmaus; extremely rare; the plate destroyed.
Christ appearing to the Magdalen; unfinished. 1760.
The Preaching of St. James. 1740.
St. Jerome writing. 1731.

VARIOUS SUBJECTS.

Famine and Pestilence; very scarce. 1731.
Nero on his Death-bed, tormented by Furies and the Shade of his Mother; scarce.
Jupiter and Antiope; one of his best etchings; scarce. 1735.
The Artist in his Painting Room. 1730.
The same subject with variations. 1732.
The Quack Doctor; in the style of *Teniers.* 1732.
The Hungarian Quack Doctor. 1757.
The Itinerant Musicians; in the style of *Ostade.* The picture by Dietrich is in the National Gallery.
The Alchemist in his Laboratory; in the style of *Rembrandt*; scarce. 1731.
Twenty plates of Busts and Heads; chiefly in the manner of *Rembrandt.*
About thirty-six plates of Landscapes, in the styles of *Berchem, Breenberg, Claude Lorrain, Ruisdael,* and *Salvator Rosa,* and in his own manner.

DIETRICH, JOHANN FRIEDRICH, a painter of historical subjects, was born at Biberach in 1789, and learned painting of Seele and Heideloff at Stuttgart. In 1820 he went to Rome, where he studied the works of the great masters, and executed several paintings, as well as copies, of considerable merit. After his return home, he was employed in the Hall of the Estates at Rosenstein, and painted in fresco for several churches. He was Professor

74

in the Academy at Stuttgart, where he died in 1846. His best works are:

The Resurrection of Christ (*in Stuttgart Cathedral*).
The Visitation, the Nativity, the Adoration of the Magi, Christ on the Mount of Olives, the Crucifixion, the Entombment, and the Resurrection (*in the Church at Bulach, near Carlsruhe*).
Abraham entering the Promised Land (*in the Royal Palace, Stuttgart*).
An Adoration of the Shepherds. } (*Stuttgart*
Christ with the Disciples at Emmaus. } *Gallery.*)
The Madonna di Foligno; *after Raphael* (*in the Church at Dotternhausen*).
Helios with the Hours. } (*in the Landhaus of Rosenstein.*)
Luna with Herse. }
Christ on the Mount of Olives (*in the Church of Ravensburg*). *His last and best work.*

DIETTERLIN, BARTHOLOMÄUS, (or DIETERLEIN,) a painter and engraver, who flourished in the early part of the 17th century, was the son of a painter named HILARIUS DIETTERLIN, of Strassburg. By him are known a very scarce plate—the 'Ascension of Christ'—and a Landscape.

DIETTERLIN, WENDEL, (DIETERLEIN, or DITTERLEIN,) who was born at Strassburg in 1550, was the grandfather of Bartholomäus Dietterlin. On the ceilings of the Lusthaus at Stuttgart there are paintings by him representing the 'Creation,' the 'Fall of Man,' and the 'Last Judgment,' and in the Belvedere at Vienna is the 'Calling of Matthew.' He also etched several portraits, and twelve spirited grotesques, and published a work on Architectural Design, with 209 engravings. There are 176 original designs by him in the Academy at Dresden. He died in 1599. Some of his works have the

monogram annexed :

DIETZ, FEODOR, a German historical painter, born at Neunstetten, near Krautheim, Baden, in 1813, was instructed in the principles of art by Kuntz at Carlsruhe. After studying in the Academy at Munich, and at Paris under Horace Vernet and Alaux, he returned to Germany and there commenced his career. In 1839 he became painter at the court of Baden, in 1862 professor at the Academy at Carlsruhe, and later on President of the German Artistic Society. He made several tours, and died in the course of one in 1870 at Gray, France. The following are some of his best paintings:

The Destruction of Heidelberg by Melac (*Carlsruhe Gallery*).
The Death of Piccolomini.
The Death of Pappenheim.
Gustavus Adolphus at Lützen.
The Night Review of Napoleon.
The Guard of Baden before Paris.
Napoleon at Wagram.
Blücher crossing the Rhine.
Blücher at La Rothière.
Blücher's March on Paris. 1814. (*Berlin Museum.*)
The Elector Max Emanuel of Bavaria storming Belgrade in 1688 (*Neue Pinakothek, Munich*).

DIETZSCH, JOHANN ALBERT, the younger brother of Johann Christoph Dietzsch, was born in 1720, and died in 1782. He engraved about twenty plates of views of Nuremberg and its vicinity, published in 1760. He also painted battle-pieces, landscapes, fruit, flowers, and portraits. Some of his landscapes have been engraved by Prestel.

DIETZSCH, JOHANN CHRISTOPH, a German painter in water-colours, especially of landscapes, flowers, and fruit, was born at Nuremberg in 1710. He has left some plates of landscapes etched in the style of Waterloo, which, though more finished, are very inferior to the works of that master in picturesque simplicity. He died in his native city in 1769. There are by him the following plates:

Portrait of Correggio.
Portrait of Raphael.
Sixteen Landscapes in the manner of *Ruisdael* and *Waterloo*.

DIEU, ANTOINE, a French painter, born in Paris about 1661, was a son of Édouard Dieu, an engraver, who died in Paris in 1703. He was instructed by Lebrun, and painted historical subjects and portraits in the style of his master, and not without merit. The ' Duke of Burgundy before the King,' and the ' Marriage of the Duke of Burgundy,' are in the Museum at Versailles, but his best work is the portrait of ' Louis XIV. on his Throne,' which was engraved by Nicolas Arnoult. He was received at the Academy in 1722, and died in Paris in 1727. His brothers, JEAN DIEU and JEAN BAPTISTE DIEU, were engravers; the former was born about 1658, and died in Paris in 1714.

DIEU, JEAN, called DIEU DE SAINT-JEAN, father and son, were French painters who flourished in the 17th century. Jean Dieu, the elder, was also an etcher. Jean Dieu, the younger, who was a portrait painter, was born about the year 1655, and died in Paris in 1695.

DIGHTON, DENIS, an English painter of battle scenes, the son of Dighton the caricaturist, was born in London in 1792. He studied in the Royal Academy, but obtained through the Prince of Wales a commission in the army. Resigning this, however, and marrying, he settled in London, and devoted himself to art, exhibiting at the Royal Academy from 1811 to 1825. Loss of the royal patronage, together with other causes, affected his reason, and he retired to Brittany, where he died at St. Servan in 1827. Amongst his works are:

Death of Nelson (*Bridgewater Collection*).
Defeat of the Turks at Klissura.
Cavalry skirmishing (*South Kensington*).
Battle of Waterloo (*Her Majesty's Collection*).

His wife was Fruit and Flower Painter to Queen Adelaide, and exhibited at the Royal Academy between 1824 and 1835.

DIGHTON, ROBERT, an English portrait painter and caricaturist, was born in 1752. He exhibited occasionally at the Free Society of Artists and at the Royal Academy. In 1799 he brought out a ' Book of Heads,' and thenceforth devoted himself chiefly to caricature. He died in London in 1814.

DIGHTON, WILLIAM EDWARD, a landscape painter, was a pupil of William Müller, and afterwards of Frederick Goodall. He exhibited English landscape scenery at the British Institution and Royal Academy from 1844 to 1851, after which he visited the East, and in 1853 sent to the Royal Academy two pictures, ' The Ruins of the Temple of Luxor' and ' Bethany.' Dighton died at Hampstead in 1853, aged 31. Had he lived, he would doubtless have made a name in the world of art. He left behind him many fine works, which are for the most part in private collections in Liverpool.

DILLENS, ADOLF, a Belgian genre-painter, was born at Ghent in 1821, and received instruction from his elder brother Hendrik Dillens. His first works were of an historical nature, but he afterwards devoted himself to pictures illustrating Zealand peasant life. He died in 1877. Amongst his best works are:

The Gossip at the Window.
Taking Toll at the Bridge (*of this picture he painted three versions*).
Asking in Marriage.
A Fair at West Capelle (*at Paris International Exhibition*, 1855).
A Ball at Goes (*at the same*).
The Juggler (*at London International Exhibition*, 1862).
Skaters (*in Brussels Museum*).
Recruiting: Austrian Soldiers halting at a Tavern (*in the same*).

DILLENS, HENDRIK, a Belgian genre painter, was born at Ghent in 1812, and died at Brussels in 1872. He executed several pleasing and spirited paintings, among the best of which are:

The French Trooper caressing his Child.
The Capture of the Maid of Orleans.
An Old Man giving Counsel to Two Youths.
Consecration of a Church (with over 200 figures).

DILLIS, IGNAZ, a brother and pupil of Johann Georg von Dillis, was born at Grüngiebing in 1772, and died at Munich in 1808. He etched some landscapes containing figures and animals, but abandoned art for the science of forestry.

DILLIS, JOHANN CANTIUS, a Bavarian landscape painter and etcher, was born at Grüngiebing in 1779. He was the youngest brother of Johann Georg von Dillis, by whom he was instructed, and with whom he went, in 1805, to Italy, where he stayed two years. His best pictures are a ' View in the Environs of Grotta Ferrata,' dated 1809, in the Schleissheim Gallery, and a ' View of the Alps near Reselau,' and ' Stone Bridges near the Mills at Audorf,' in the Leuchtenberg Gallery. He died at Munich in 1856. He etched twelve plates, among which may be mentioned, a ' View of the Castle of Harlaching,' ' A Rocky Country with Mills,' and ' A Farm Cottage hidden in Trees.'

DILLIS, JOHANN GEORG VON, a Bavarian painter, was born at Grüngiebing in 1759, and studied at the Academy of Munich and under Oefele. He afterwards paid frequent visits to Switzerland, Italy, Sicily, France, and Spain. He painted portraits and landscapes, but his engagements as director of several picture galleries in Germany occupied the greater part of his time, so that his works are not numerous. He died at Munich in 1841. In the Modern Gallery of that city there are by him a ' Landscape at Grotta Ferrata,' and a ' View of the Tegernsee,' and in the Schleissheim Gallery is an ' Autumnal Picnic.' He also etched 52 landscapes.

DINGLINGER, SOPHIE FRIEDERIKE, who was born in 1736 at Dresden, and died in the same city in 1791, practised as a miniature painter. The Dresden Gallery possesses seven portraits by her of members of the Dinglinger family—amongst them her own.

DIOLAI, GIOVANNI FRANCESCO. See SURCHI.

DIONISIO FIAMMINGO. See CALVAERT.

DIONYSIUS, of Colophon, who flourished about the middle of the 5th century B.C., was a contemporary of Polygnotus, whom he in part imitated and almost rivalled. The subjects which he chose to treat were less important; but, according to Ælian, "his works exhibited the same expressive character, the same choice of attitudes, a similar attention to propriety, and the same elegant arrangement of his draperies: but he represented the objects in a smaller proportion." By these expressions Ælian has been supposed to explain more clearly a passage in the 'Poetics' of Aristotle; and it has been thought to result from his suggestion, that Polygnotus designed his figures larger than life, Dionysius the size of life, and Pauson smaller than life. Winckelmann, however, interprets this in another manner. According to that writer, Polygnotus painted his figures better, that is to say, he stamped them with grandeur above the scale and conformation of man, and as he usually chose his subjects from mythology, or from heroic history, his figures resembled heroes, and represented nature in the most perfect form of ideal beauty. Pauson gave to his figures a more common and familiar air. In the opinion of Winckelmann, Aristotle meant to say that the pictures of Polygnotus were in painting what tragedy is in poetry, and that the figures of Pauson resembled the characters in a comedy, which are represented more than ordinarily ridiculous, to render the effect more ludicrous. Dionysius, whom Pliny places amongst the most famous painters, held a sober medium between Polygnotus and Pauson, and may be said to have been, with respect to Polygnotus, what Euripides was to Sophocles; the latter represented his heroines as they ought to be, the former as they were. This characteristic procured for Dionysius the appellation of ἀνθρωπογράφος, or the 'painter of mankind.'

DIOTISALVI, (or DIETISALVI,) was a contemporary of Duccio, who from 1259 painted miniatures at Siena, some of which are still preserved in the Academy of that city. He also produced some larger pictures, among which is a 'Madonna' in the church of the Servi, dated 1281.

DIOTTI, GIUSEPPE, who was born at Casal Maggiore in 1779, was instructed in the Academy at Parma, and later by Camuccini at Rome. He painted in fresco as well as in oil, distinguishing himself as a painter of historical subjects, and became a professor in the Academy at Carrara, and also in that at Bergamo, where he died in 1846. In the Belvedere at Vienna is a picture by him representing 'The Kiss of Judas,' and in the Milan Gallery is the 'Congress of Pontida.' Other noteworthy works by him are, 'Leonardo da Vinci and Lodovico Sforza,' and 'Tobias receiving his Sight.' His own portrait, dated 1821, is in the Uffizi.

DIRCKS, AUGUST, a German painter of genre pieces and a lithographer, was born at Emden in East Friesland in 1806, and studied at the Academy of Düsseldorf. 'The Decorated Schoolmaster,' a creditable work by him, is in the Gallery of that town. He died at Düsseldorf in 1871.

DIRICKSEN, DIRICK, a German engraver, worked at Hamburg in the earlier part of the 17th century, and was still living in 1647. He was principally employed by the booksellers, and engraved some portraits in a neat style, resembling that of the Van de Passes.

DISCEPOLI, GIOVANNI BATTISTA, was born at Lugano in 1590. He was usually called 'Lo Zoppo di Lugano,' from his being a cripple. Although he was for some time a scholar of Camillo Procaccini, he did not adopt the style of that master. Lanzi states that he was one of the best and most chaste colourists of his time. Several of his works are in the churches at Milan; his picture of 'Purgatory' in San Carlo is particularly esteemed. In the Brera is an 'Adoration of the Magi' from San Marcellino in Milan. Lugano and

Como also possess some of his works; in the church of Santa Teresa, in the latter place, is a picture of that Saint, which is much admired. He died in 1660.

DISTELI, MARTIN, was born at Olten, in Switzerland, in 1802. In early life he studied art, intending to become a painter, but afterwards gained some celebrity by drawing caricatures, which were published in the 'Distelikalender.' His Swiss battle-pieces indicate a strong patriotic feeling. He died at Solothurn in 1844.

DITMAR, HENRIK, (or DITTMARZ,) was a German portrait painter who flourished in Hamburg and in Denmark in the latter half of the seventeenth century. In the Copenhagen gallery there is by him a 'Hermit in his Cell,' dated 1665. He died in Denmark late in 1677 or early in 1678.

DITMAR, JAN, (or DITMER,) a Flemish engraver, was born in the Netherlands about 1538, and was admitted into the Guild of St. Luke at Antwerp in 1574. He engraved some plates after Martin De Vos, and other Flemish masters, among which is a print after Michiel Coxcie, representing 'Christ seated in the Clouds, surrounded by Angels holding the Instruments of the Passion and the Symbols of the Four Evangelists,' dated 1574.

DITTENBERGER, JOHANN GUSTAV, an historical and portrait painter, was born at Neuenweg, in Baden, in 1799. He was at first a pupil of Rottmann and Roux at Heidelberg, but in 1821 he entered the Munich Academy. After this he worked for a while in the studio of Baron Gros at Paris, and then removed to Rome. He returned to Vienna in 1831, and died in 1879. He executed a number of church pictures, among which we find 'The Annunciation,' 'St. Andrew converting the Russians,' 'St. Severinus blessing the Land of Austria,' 'The Angelic Salutation' (for Olmütz Cathedral), and two allegorical pictures of 'Germany' and 'Schleswig-Holstein' (1850). He also etched a number of illustrations to Schiller's poems. He frequently marked his works with the annexed

monogram: .

DITTERLEIN. See DIETTERLIN.
DITTMARZ, HENRIK. See DITMAR.
DIXON, JOHN, an English miniature, crayon, and water-colour painter, was a pupil of Lely. He excelled in nymphs, satyrs, cupids, &c. He was under William III. keeper of the King's picture closet, but in his later years he became impoverished, and retired to Bungay, where he died in 1715.

DIXON, JOHN, an engraver in mezzotint, was born at Dublin about 1740, and died in London in 1780. He studied under West in his native city, and became in 1766 a member of the Incorporated Society of Artists. There are several fine portraits engraved by him after Sir Joshua Reynolds and other masters.

DIXON, NATHANIEL. Nothing whatever is known as to this artist, although he has been called by some writers the brother of John Dixon. No one can identify the works of John Dixon, unless they are those signed with a D only, which are usually attributed to Nathaniel Dixon; but miniatures signed N. D. are frequently to be found, and two contemporary letters in the Welbeck Collection mention casually "Nathaniel Dixon the limner." Several of his portraits, one very large in size, are at Montagu House; there are also some at Ham, and a few very important ones in the Madresfield Collection, whilst one beauty is

THE DUKE OF GRAFTON AS A BOY *[Montagu House Collection*

WILLIAM DOBSON

PORTRAIT OF ENDYMION PORTER

to be found at Goodwood. His work is strong, well planned, and well coloured, and allied to the masterful portraits of Cooper. He flourished during the reigns of James II. and William III. G.C.W.

DIXON, ROBERT, a landscape painter, was born in 1780. He published, in 1810-11, thirty-six views of 'Norfolk Scenery.' Some of his works appeared at the Norwich Exhibitions. At the South Kensington Museum is a 'Farm Yard' by him in water-colours. He died in 1815.

DIZIANI, GASPARO, an Italian caricaturist, was a pupil of Bastiano Ricci. He died at Venice in 1767. In the Dresden Gallery is a 'Painter painting a portrait from life,' by him.

DOBIASCHOFSKY, FRANZ, was born at Vienna in 1818, and was instructed by Führich and Kuppel-wieser. He excelled in painting historical subjects and portraits, which have been praised for their good design and poetic feeling. He was a professor at the Academy at Vienna, where he died in 1867. Among his best works may be mentioned two in the Belvedere at Vienna, viz., 'A young Man and Woman in a Garden,' and 'Cimburgis saved from the bear by Duke Ernest Ironside' (1850).

DOBROVOLSKY, VASILY STEFANOVITCH, a Russian painter, was born in 1786. He was a member of the Academy of Arts, and one of the founders of the School for Painting and Sculpture at Moscow, in which city he died in 1855.

DOBSON, WILLIAM, a portrait painter, was born in London in 1610. He was placed as an apprentice to Robert Peake, a portrait painter and picture dealer, who was afterwards knighted by Charles I. From this master's instruction he was not likely to profit much, but he procured him the means of copying some pictures by Titian and Van Dyck, by which he acquired an excellent principle of colouring, and great freedom of hand. On leaving his master, Dobson appears to have lived in indigence and obscurity, until Van Dyck, passing a shop on Snow Hill, perceived a picture exposed in the window for sale, which had sufficient merit to excite his curiosity to discover the painter, whom he found at work in a miserable garret. The well-known liberality of Van Dyck soon released him from his wretched situation; he afterwards introduced him to the king, and zealously recommended him to his Majesty's protection. On the death of Van Dyck, Dobson was appointed serjeant-painter to the king, whom he accompanied to Oxford, where he painted his portrait, as well as those of Prince Rupert and several of the nobility. The melancholy fate of the king was followed by the overthrow of the arts and elegance, and Dobson, who was imprudent and extravagant, became involved in debt, and was thrown into prison. He was released by a patron, but not long afterwards he died in London in 1646. Of the painters of his time, Dobson appears to have approached nearest to the excellence of Van Dyck. His portraits are faithful transcripts of nature, and although he was not equally successful in his historical pictures, the few which he painted are not without considerable merit. One of his best works in history is 'The Decollation of St. John,' at Wilton. King Charles I. styled Dobson the 'English Tintoretto,' but very absurdly, as his manner of painting bears no resemblance to that of the Venetian master. There are in the National Portrait Gallery paintings by Dobson of Himself, Sir Harry Vane the younger, Francis Quarles the poet, and Endymion Porter; and at Hampton Court there are a picture of Himself and his Wife, and portraits of two Gentlemen.

DOBSON, WILLIAM CHARLES THOMAS, was born at Hamburg in 1817. His father was an English merchant in that city, and came to London in 1825. Dobson in 1836 entered the Royal Academy Schools, and in 1843 received an appointment at the Government School of Design, then at Somerset House. In 1843 he became headmaster of the School of Design at Birmingham, but resigned the post in 1845 and went to Italy. From there he went to Germany, where he remained several years. On his return he exhibited pictures on scriptural and other subjects, at first in oil, and afterwards in water-colour; the principal of which were: 'Tobias and the Angel' (1853), 'The Charity of Dorcas' (1854), 'The Almsdeeds of Dorcas' (1855), 'The Prosperous Days of Job' (1856), 'The Child Jesus going to Nazareth with His Parents,' and 'Reading the Psalms' (1857), 'The Holy Innocents' (1858), 'The Good Shepherd' (1865), and 'St. Paul at Philippi,' deposited in the Diploma Gallery (1873); and among secular subjects, 'The Picture Book' (International Exhibition, 1862), 'A Venetian Girl' (1879), 'Mignon' and 'Ione' (1880). His water-colour drawings included 'The Young Nurse,' 'The Camellia' (1873), and 'Nursery Tales' (1874). Dobson was elected Associate of the Royal Academy in 1867, and an Academician in 1872. In 1870 he was elected Associate of the Royal Water-Colour Society, of which, in 1875, he became a full member. He died at Ventnor in 1898.

DOCENO. See GHERARDI, CRISTOFANO.

DOCHARTY, JAMES, a Scotch landscape painter, was born at Bonhill, near Dumbarton, in 1829. He was at first engaged with his father in calico manufacture, and did not turn to art till 1862. His works appeared at the Edinburgh Academy, the Glasgow Institution, and the Royal Academy. In 1876 failing health caused him to visit the Continent and the East, but he died on his return to Glasgow in 1878. He was elected an Associate of the Royal Scottish Academy in 1877. Amongst his best works are:

The Haunt of the Red Deer. 1869.
The Head of Loch Lomond. 1873.
Glencoe. 1874.
The River Achray. 1876.
A Good Fishing Day. 1877.

DODD, DANIEL, was an English miniature and subject painter in the latter half of the 18th century. He was a member of the Free Society of Artists in 1763, where he exhibited. His chief works are:

The Royal Procession to St. Paul's.
Representation of the Royal Academy.

DODD, ROBERT, a marine painter, flourished in the latter part of the 18th century. His pictures are chiefly illustrative of the doings of the British navy. He also represented storms at sea very successfully. Redgrave has been unable to trace his name later than 1809 in the books of the Royal Academy. Among his works are:

Admiral Parker's Victory. 1781.
The Loss of the 'Centaur.' 1785.
Lord Rodney's Victory. 1785.
The British Fleet at Spithead escaping from the burning 'Boyle.' 1796.
Commencement of the Battle of Trafalgar. 1806.

DODGSON, GEORGE HAYDOCK, who was born at Liverpool in 1811, was at first apprenticed to

George Stephenson, the engineer. His duties in that capacity increased an innate love of art, and in 1836 was published a volume, illustrated by him, descriptive of the scenery of the Whitby and Pickering Railway. Giving up engineering, Dodgson went to London, where he was for some time employed by architects and several illustrated newspapers to make drawings. After a connection of some years with the New Society of Painters in Water-Colours, he was elected in 1848 an Associate-Exhibitor of the Society of Painters in Water-Colours, and became a full member four years later. His contributions to that society were usually landscapes. He was especially fond of painting beech trees. Dodgson died in London in 1880.

DOERBECK, FRANZ BURCHARD. See BURCHARD DOERBECK.

DOERR, OTTO ERICH FRIEDRICH AUGUST, was born at Ludwigslust in Mecklenburg-Schwerin in 1831, and died at Dresden in 1868. In the Dresden Gallery is the 'Interior of a Parisian Studio' by him.

DOES. See VAN DER DOES.

DOESBURGH, F., a Dutch engraver, flourished from about 1680 to 1714. He engraved a plate representing 'Admiral van Tromp engaging the English Fleet.' We have also by him several prints of the old Roman customs; they are etched and finished with the graver in a very indifferent style.

DOETECUM. See DUETECUM.

DOFIN. See DAUPHIN.

DOIX, FRANÇOIS JOSEPH ALOYSE, a French landscape painter, was born in Paris in 1777. The Museum of Tours possesses some works by this artist, the date of whose death is unknown.

DOLCE, LUZIO, (or DOLCI,) of Castel Durante in the state of Urbino, who flourished in 1589, is commended for his altar-pieces and other pictures in the churches there. It is said that he was employed by the Duke of Urbino to paint at the Imperiale. He executed many works at Rome, as well as at Castel Durante, and resided in the former city for some time. There are few particulars recorded of him, though he is often mentioned with high commendation.

DOLCI, AGNESE, was the daughter of Carlo Dolci, and arrived at some degree of excellence in copying the works of her father. She also painted some pictures of her own composition, but never approached the merit of Carlo. She died in 1686. Among her own works are:

Modena. *Gallery.* The Virgin adoring the Infant Jesus.
Paris. *Louvre.* The Consecration of the Bread and Wine.
Siena. *Institute.* Virgin and Child, with St. Joseph.

DOLCI, CARLO, or CARLINO, who was born at Florence in 1616, was a scholar of Jacopo Vignali. Without the possession of much genius or invention, he excited considerable interest by a number of pleasing and highly-finished pictures, chiefly confined to devout subjects, and most frequently representing heads of our Saviour, and of the Virgin. These are not so much admired for particular beauty of character, as for a soft and tranquil expression of devotion in the patient suffering of Christ, the plaintive sorrow of the Mater Dolorosa, or the compunction of a Saint in penitence. Subjects of that description he treated with great delicacy and tenderness. The general tone of his colouring is well appropriated to the character of his subjects, nothing is harsh or

obtrusive, all is modest, placid, and harmonious. He generally painted in a small size, though there are at Florence some pictures by him as large as life. His small pictures of heads of the Madonna are more numerous, and are highly valued by the admirers of polished and laborious finishing. He died at Florence in 1686. There are many repetitions of his small pictures by his pupils, Loma and Mancini, and his daughter Agnese. Many of his pictures are in England. The following are some of his best works:

Berlin.	*Gallery.*	St. John the Evangelist.
Burghley House.	*Marquis of Exeter.* }	Christ breaking the Bread.
Cassel.	*Gallery.*	St. Cecilia.
Copenhagen.	*Gallery.*	Christ.
,,	,,	The Madonna.
Darmstadt.	*Gallery.*	St. Dorothea and an Angel.
Dresden.	*Gallery.*	The Daughter of Herodias with the Head of St. John the Baptist.
,,	,,	St. Cecilia (*painted for the Grand-Duke Cosmo III.*).
,,	,,	Christ blessing the Bread and Wine.
Dulwich.	*College.*	St. Catharine of Siena.
,,	,,	St. Veronica.
Florence.	*Pitti Pal.*	His own Portrait when young.
,,	,,	Sleeping St. John.
,,	,,	Madonna and Child.
,,	,,	The Duchess Vittoria della Rovere.
,,	,,	Diogenes.
,,	,,	St. Peter weeping.
,,	,,	St. Rosa. 1668.
,,	,,	Moses.
,,	,,	St. John the Evangelist.
,,	,,	St. Margaret. 1664.
,,	,,	St. Andrew before the Cross. 1646.
,,	,,	St. Charles Borromeo.
,,	,,	St. Francis Xavier.
,,	,,	St. Nicholas of Tolentino.
,,	,,	Christ in the Garden.
,,	,,	Ecce Homo.
,,	,,	St. Casimir of Poland.
,,	,,	St. Dominic.
,,	,,	Vision of St. John the Evangelist.
,,	*Corsini Pal.*	St. Sebastian.
,,	*Uffizi.*	Madonna and Child, with St. Salome.
,,	,,	St. Mary Magdalen.
,,	,,	St. Galla Placidia. 1675.
,,	,,	His own Portrait. 1674.
,,	,,	St. Lucia.
,,	,,	The Saviour seated, with Saints.
,,	,,	St. Peter.
,,	,,	St. Simon.
Glasgow.	*Gallery.*	Adoration of the Magi.
,,	,,	Madonna and Child.
London.	*National Gall.*	Virgin and Child.
Munich.	*Gallery.*	Madonna & Child with Flowers.
,,	,,	Virgin with a Lamb.
,,	,,	Penitent Magdalen.
,,	,,	Infant Christ.
,,	,,	St. Agnes.
,,	,,	Ecce Homo.
Petersburg.	*Hermitage.*	Mater Dolorosa.
,,	,,	Magdalen.
,,	,,	St. Anthony.
,,	,,	St. Catharine.
,,	,,	St. Cecilia.
Rome.	*Corsini Pal.*	St. Apollonia.
Vienna.	*Gallery.*	Madonna and Child.
,,	,,	Sincerity.
,,	,,	Mater Dolorosa.

DOLENDO, BARTHOLOMEUS, a Dutch engraver, was born at Leyden about the year 1560, and is presumed to have been instructed in engraving by Hendrik Goltzius. He worked entirely with the

CARLO DOLCI

MADONNA AND CHILD

[Pitti Gallery, Florence

Brogi photo]

graver, in an open, clear style. There are by him several plates, some of which are from his own designs. He occasionally marked his prints with his name, but more frequently with one of these ciphers,

  Among other engravings by him are the following:

Jonah in the Sea, swallowed by the Whale; circular.
Jonah thrown back on the Sea-shore; the same.
A Dutch Merry-making; *after his own design.*
Adam and Eve taking the Forbidden Fruit; *after C. van Mander.*
Christ appearing to the Magdalen; *B. Dolendo, inv. et fec.*
The Holy Family; *after M. Coxcie.*
St. John preaching in the Wilderness.
Pyramus and Thisbe; *after Crispin van den Broeck.*
Jupiter and Ceres; an allegorical subject; *after B. Spranger.*
The Assumption of the Virgin.

DOLENDO, ZACHARIAS, was a brother of Bartholomeus Dolendo, whom he surpassed both in style and in correctness. He was born at Leyden in 1561, and is said by Huber to have been a disciple of Jacob De Ghein. There are some portraits by this master, which are not inferior in neatness to those by J. Wierix; his plates are frequently marked with this cipher. There are by him:

William, Prince of Orange; half-length, in armour. 1581.
Andromeda chained to the Rock; finely drawn; *after his own design.*
Adam and Eve embracing, whilst Eve receives the Apple from the Serpent; *after B. Spranger.*
St. Martin dividing his Cloak with two Beggars; *after the same.*
The Continence of Scipio; *after A. Bloemaert.*
The Virgin and Infant, with two Angels; *after J. De Ghein.*
The Crucifixion; *after the same.*
A Set of small Plates of the Gods and Goddesses; copied from the larger ones by *H. Goltzius.*

DOLIVAR, JUAN, is said by Huber to have been born at Saragossa in 1641. He studied engraving in Paris, and engraved some of the plates of ornamental and decorative subjects for Berain's 'Ornemens.' He was also employed in the set of the 'Little Conquests' of Louis XIV. His works are inferior to those of Le Pautre and Chauveau.

DOLLE, WILLIAM, an English engraver, was born in London about 1600. He was chiefly employed on portraits for the booksellers. These are sought after rather on account of their scarcity than their merit as engravings. Among them are the following:

Sir Henry Wotton, Provost of Eton.
Mark Frank, Master of Pembroke Hall, Cambridge.
John Cosin, Bishop of Durham.
George Villiers, Duke of Buckingham.
Robert Sanderson, Bishop of Lincoln.
John Milton.
Robert, Earl of Essex.
Samuel Botley, Short-hand Writer.

DOLOBELLA, TOMMASO, a native of Belluno, who was born about the year 1580, and flourished about 1630, was according to Ridolfi a scholar of Antonio Vassilacchi, called Aliense. He excelled in painting portraits, and was invited to the court of Poland by Sigismund III., where he painted the royal family and several of the nobility, and was favoured with the particular protection of that monarch. He painted a few historical subjects, but is more celebrated as a portrait painter. In

the Sala del Senato in the Ducal Palace, Venice, is a representation by him of 'The Doge and Procurators adoring the Host.'

DOMENCHIN DE CHAVANNE, PIERRE SALOMON, a French landscape painter, who was born in Paris, in 1672. He was received into the Academy in 1709, the picture which he painted upon the occasion, 'Les Pasteurs,' being now in the Louvre. He was an artist of moderate ability, and was employed in the Gobelins manufactory, where he died in 1744.

DOMENECH, ANTONIO, a painter of Valencia, who flourished in the latter half of the 16th century and devoted himself to Scriptural subjects, was a scholar of Nicolas Borras, whom he assisted in several of his works, and whose manner he so closely imitated, that even at Valencia, where the productions of Borras may be supposed to be well known, the works of Domenech are attributed to him.

DOMENICHINO. See ZAMPIERI.

DOMENICO, FRANCESCO, who was born at Treviso in 1488, studied under Giorgione. His own portrait, dated 1512, is in the Hermitage at St. Petersburg.

DOMENICO, SANO DI. See SANO DI PIETRO.

DOMENICO DI BARTOLO. See GHERZO.

DOMENICO DI MICHELINO, who lived in the 15th century, was the pupil of Fra Angelico. He painted the portrait of Dante from a design by Baldovinetti, in the Church of Santa Maria dei Fiore at Florence. The dates of his birth and death are alike unknown.

DOMENICO DI PACE. See BECCAFUMI.

DOMENICO FIORENTINO. See DEL BARBIERE.

DOMENICO VENEZIANO. See VENEZIANO.

DOMENIQUE, JEAN, was a native of France, who resided chiefly at Rome, where he died in 1684. He was a scholar of Claude Lorrain, and was a successful copyist and imitator of the works of that master.

DOMER, JAQUES, (DOOMER, or DEMER,) a Dutch artist, was born in 1647, and flourished about 1680. He is better known by his drawings than by his pictures in oil. His manner approximates to that of Rembrandt, and it may be believed that his dark landscapes have been ascribed to the latter. His compositions are simple, but strikingly true.

DOMINGO, LUIS, a Spanish painter and sculptor, born at Valencia in 1718, was a scholar of Hipolito Robira in painting, and of Bautista Balaguer in sculpture. The Dominican convent at Valencia possessed several pictures by him, among which was one of St. Louis Bertran. Domingo died at Valencia in 1767. His works in sculpture are to be seen in several churches of that city.

DOMINICI, BERNARDO, a Neapolitan painter and writer on art, flourished about the year 1740. He studied landscape painting under Joachim Franz Beisch, a German artist, who passed some time at Naples, and attached himself to the clear and finished style of that master. He also painted what are called 'bambocciate.' In 1742 and 1743, he published at Naples, in two volumes, 'Vite de' Pittori, Scultori, ed Architetti Napolitani.'

DOMINICI, FRANCESCO, a native of Treviso, was a pupil of Paris Bordone. Ridolfi commends a work by him in the dome of the Banca della Compagnia della Madonna at Treviso, representing a 'Procession of a Bishop and several Canons,' which is dated 1572. Dominici also excelled as a portrait painter, but did not survive his thirty-fifth year.

DONADO, ADRIANO, a Spanish monk of the

order of Barefooted Carmelites at Cordova, painted some excellent works for his convent. He died at a great age in 1630. The Lille Museum has a 'Flagellation of Christ' by him.

DONALD, JOHN MILNE, a Scotch artist born at Nairn in 1819. He began the study of art in Glasgow at a very early age, having from a child shown great desire to become an artist. In 1840 he went to Paris, and was there for some years, and then he settled down in London, where for four years he painted, and his works were very highly esteemed. Amongst his patrons and constant admirers was the poet-banker Rogers. Afterwards he returned to his native land, and is never known to have visited England again, whilst all his exhibits were confined to Scottish Galleries. He died in Scotland in 1866, and three of his finest works, 'A Highland Stream,' 'Bowling Bay,' and 'Loch Goil,' were exhibited at Glasgow in 1878.

DONALDSON, ANDREW, a Scotch landscape painter in water-colours, was born at Comber, near Belfast. Taken by his father, an operative weaver, to Glasgow, he met with an accident, which eventually led to his devoting himself entirely to art, in the pursuit of which he visited many parts of the United Kingdom. He died in 1846 at Glasgow, where he had obtained a large teaching connection. In the Glasgow Corporation Galleries there are by him the 'Old Theatre Royal, Glasgow, after the fire in 1829,' and a 'Scotch Highland Village.'

DONALDSON, JOHN, was born at Edinburgh in 1737, and distinguished himself as a miniature painter, both in enamel and water-colours. In the year 1764, and again in 1768, he obtained the premium given by the Society of Arts for the best picture in enamel. He occasionally amused himself with the point, and etched several plates of beggars, after Rembrandt, which possess considerable merit. He died in London in 1801.

DONATO, of Pavia, flourished at the close of the fifteenth century, and is the author of a 'Christ crucified, between the Virgin and St. John,' in the hospital of Savona; also of a 'Virgin in Glory with Saints' (signed in 1507), in the Louvre at Paris.

DONATO VENEZIANO. See VENEZIANO.

DONAUER, LORENZ, was an obscure German engraver, by whom there is only known a work representing 'St. Anthony,' after Albrecht Dürer, which he executed about the year 1539.

DONDUCCI, GIOVANNI ANDREA, called IL MASTELLETTA, was born at Bologna in 1575. He was at first a scholar of the Carracci, but did not long remain under their tuition. His impetuous disposition disdaining the control of academic precision, he attempted to establish a new style, founded on a spirited and graceful design, in imitation of the works of Parmigiano and Tiarini, which he particularly admired, and a promptness of execution which was natural to him. The novel manner of Donducci was not without its admirers; and he was employed in a great number of works for the public edifices at Bologna, where are his principal works. He also painted landscapes, which were entirely in the style of the Carracci, and were much esteemed, particularly at Rome. Annibale advised him to establish himself in that city, and to devote himself to those subjects; a counsel by no means agreeable to Donducci. His most admired performance is his 'St. Irene drawing the Arrow from the Breast of St. Sebastian,' at the church of the Celestines. He died at Bologna in 1655. The following of his works are also preserved:

80

Bologna.	S. Domenico.	St. Dominic restoring to life the Man killed by the furious Horse.
,,	,,	The Storm.
,,	S. Salvatore.	The Resurrection of Christ.
,,	S. Francesco.	The Last Supper.
,,	I Mendicanti.	The Flight into Egypt.
,,	S. Paolo.	Christ in the Garden.
,,	,,	Christ bearing the Cross.
,,	Pinacoteca.	Christ surrounded by Angels.
Florence.	Uffizi.	Charity.
Modena.	Museum.	Abraham and the Three Angels.
,,	,,	Elias sleeping.
,,	,,	Portrait of a Painter.
,,	,,	Finding of Moses.
,,	,,	St. John baptizing.
Paris.	Louvre.	Christ and the Virgin appearing to St. Francis of Assisi.

DONELLI, CARLO, called CARLO VIMERCATI, who was born at Milan in 1660, was a scholar of the Procaccini. He exhibited but few of his pictures at Milan; he painted more at Codogno, and in his best manner. He died in 1715.

DONGEN, DIONYS VAN, born at Dort in 1748, was a scholar of J. Xavery, at the Hague. He painted landscapes and cattle in the manner of his master for some time; but having removed with his parents to Rotterdam, he studied the works of Paul Potter, Cuyp, Wynants, and other masters, which, with a constant attention to nature, caused a sensible alteration in his style. His works found ready purchasers among the English, French, and Germans, as well as among his own countrymen. He died at Rotterdam in 1819. In the Städel Gallery at Frankfort is a 'Cattle-piece' by him.

DONI, ADONE, (or DONO DEI DONI,) who was born at Assisi, early in the 16th century, is said to have been a disciple of Pietro Perugino. His style retained but little of the Gothic manner of that master, and in his later years he abandoned the style of the school of Raphael, and adopted that of Michelangelo. He worked chiefly at Assisi, and after that city most at Fuligno, but all trace of his work at the latter place has disappeared. He also painted in Perugia, and throughout Umbria. In the church of San Francesco, at Perugia, is a picture by this master of the 'Last Judgment;' and one of the 'Adoration of the Kings' is in San Pietro in the same city. There are in the Lower Church of the Franciscan Convent at Assisi frescoes by him representing the 'Preaching and Martyrdom of St. Stephen,' and in the small refectory is the 'Last Supper,' painted in 1573, which was probably his last work. Doni died at Assisi in 1575. Vasari is wrong in stating that he was a nephew of Taddeo Bartoli. In the Berlin Gallery there is by him a 'Madonna with the Infant Jesus,' who is represented as reaching after a book which is in the Virgin's hand.

DONNE, W., a Dutch engraver, flourished about the year 1680. Among other prints, he engraved a plate representing 'Venus and Cupid,' in a landscape, with other figures in the distance, after A. Elsheimer. It is etched in a slight, poor style.

DONNEKER. See DE NECKER.

DONNET, S. This artist is mentioned by Strutt as the engraver of a very indifferent print representing a 'Man seated, reading a book.'

DONNINI, GIROLAMO, was born at Correggio in 1681, and studied first at Modena under Francesco Stringa, afterwards under Giovanni Giuseppe dal Sole at Bologna, and ultimately at Forli, under Carlo Cignani. He was chiefly employed in easel

PAOLO DI DONO
CALLED
PAOLO UCCELLO

Hanfstängl photo]

THE BATTLE

[*National Gallery, London*

pictures, although he occasionally painted larger works for churches. In the Madonna di Galiera, at Bologna, is an altar-piece representing 'St. Anthony of Padua.' There are some of his works in the churches of the Romagna, and at Turin, which are not unworthy of a scholar of Cignani. In the Modena Gallery are two pictures by him of the 'Birth of Christ.'

DONO, PAOLO DI, called PAOLO UCCELLO, from his love of painting birds, was born at Florence in 1397, and in early youth was apprenticed to Lorenzo Ghiberti, the founder of the famous bronze gates of the Baptistery of that city. It is doubtful from whom he learned to paint, or from whom he acquired the laws of perspective for which he became so famous, although it is known that Manetti taught him geometry. Vasari says that he wasted so much of his time over the study of perspective "that he became more needy than famous." Four paintings of battle-scenes executed by him for the Bartolini family, at Gualfonda, near Florence, are wonderful specimens of this artist's thorough knowledge of foreshortening and perspective. Of these designs one is in the National Gallery, another is in the Uffizi, a third is in the Louvre, and the fourth is still in private hands in Florence. The Louvre also possesses a panel by this artist which contains the portraits of Giotto, Donatello, Brunelleschi, Giovanni Manetti, and himself, as the representatives of painting, sculpture, architecture, mathematics, and perspective. It is certain that he lived in Florence nearly all his life, although during some short period in it he may have been at Padua, since Morelli states that the frescoes of the palace of the Vitaliani were executed by him. About the year 1436 he painted in the cathedral at Florence the colossal equestrian portrait of Sir John Hawkwood, the adventurer and soldier. This chiaroscuro painting, which is in terra verde, displays a wonderful power of foreshortening and proportion, and is intended to imitate a stone statue seen aloft standing out from the wall of the church. His masterpieces are the series of frescoes imitating bas-reliefs painted from about 1446 to 1448 in the cloisters of Santa Maria Novella. These paintings represent the 'Creation of Animals,' the 'Creation of Man,' the 'Temptation of Eve,' the 'Expulsion from Eden,' 'Adam and Eve labouring by the sweat of their brow,' the 'Sacrifice and Death of Abel,' the 'Building of the Ark,' the 'Entry of the Animals,' the 'Deluge,' 'Noah's Sacrifice,' and the 'Inebriety of Noah.' Genuine paintings by this master are very rare, although records prove that he executed several altar-pieces for churches in Florence and in Urbino. Paolo died at Florence in 1475. The Scolopi College, near the church of Sant' Agata, at Urbino, possesses a predella with six subjects relating to the theft of a pax, which Messrs. Crowe and Cavalcaselle consider to be a genuine production by Paolo Uccello. His principal paintings are:

Florence. *Cathedral.* Equestrian Statue of Sir John Hawkwood (Captain-General of the Florentines, known in Italy as Giovanni Acuto).—*Fresco executed in terra verde.*

„ *S. Maria Novella.* { Subjects from the Book of Genesis: the Creation, the Fall, the Deluge, Noah's Sacrifice, &c.—*Frescoes in terra verde in the cloister ; most of them in part destroyed.*

„ *Uffizi.* Battle-piece.

London.   *Nat. Gall.* The Battle.
Paris.   *Louvre.* Bust portraits of Giotto, Donatello, Brunelleschi, Giovanni Manetti, and himself.
„   „ Battle-piece.
Urbino. *Scolopi College.* Legend of the Theft of a Pax.

DONOSO, JOSEF XIMENEZ. See XIMENEZ DONOSO.

DONVÉ, JEAN FRANÇOIS, a French painter, was born at Saint-Amand in 1736. He was a pupil of Louis Watteau, and of Greuze, and so closely imitated the style of the latter that many of his pictures have been sold as those of his master. The Museum of Lille has three portraits by him, one being that of Sauvage, the enamel painter, and the other two portraits of himself. He died at Lille in 1799.

DONZELLO, PIERO and IPPOLITO, (or DEL DONZELLO,) were two brothers, the sons by different mothers of Francesco d'Antonio di Jacopo, bailiff ('donzello') of the Signoria of Florence, and were both born in that city—Piero in 1451, and Ippolito in 1455. The teacher of Piero is unknown. Ippolito was the pupil of Neri di Bicci from 1469 to 1471, and the brothers were companions in the 'Studio' at Florence up to 1480. In 1481, or soon after, they went to Naples to decorate the palace of Poggio Reale, which was then being built for Alfonso I., from the designs of Giuliano da Majano, and it is not unlikely that Ippolito died in that city. Piero died at Florence in 1509; but the death of Ippolito is not registered. They both assisted Antonio Solario, called Il Zingaro, in the frescoes in the cloisters of the monastery of San Severino at Naples, and in the Museum of that city may be seen two 'Crucifixions,' a 'Virgin and Child with Saints,' and other paintings assigned to them.

DOO, GEORGE THOMAS, an English engraver, was born in January 1800. He studied under Charles Heath, and published his first plate, a portrait of the Duke of York, after Lawrence, in 1824. In 1825 he visited Paris, and spent some time in the ateliers of the French engravers. On his return to London he opened a school in the Savoy, for study both from life and from the antique. He also lectured upon painting. In 1836 he was appointed engraver in ordinary to William IV., and in 1842 to Queen Victoria. In 1856 he was elected an Associate of the Royal Academy, and in 1857 a full member. In 1861 Doo became President of the Artists' Annuity Fund, and in 1863 he was a witness before the Royal Academy Commission at Westminster. He died at Sutton, Surrey, November 13, 1886. Among his best plates are :

The Infant Christ ; *after Raphael.* Ecce Homo ; *after Correggio.* The Combat ; *after Etty.* John Knox preaching ; *after Wilkie.* Pilgrims in sight of Rome ; *after Eastlake.* The Raising of Lazarus ; *after Seb. del Piombo.* St. Augustine and St. Monica ; *after Ary Scheffer.* Yorick and the Grisette ; *after Newton.* Gevartius (Cornelius van der Geest) ; *after Vandyck.* The Calmady Children ; *after Lawrence.* Six plates for the 'Elgin Marbles,' published by the trustees of the British Museum. Several plates in Jones's 'National Gallery.'

DOOMER, JAQUES. See DOMER.

DOOMS, CASPAR, an engraver in mezzotint, worked at Prague from 1644 to 1675, and afterwards at Vienna and Mayence. His best known plate is an 'Ecce Homo,' after Albrecht Dürer, now very rare.

DOORNIK, JAN VAN, a painter of Leyden, is said to have produced pictures in the manner of

Wouwerman. He also painted historical subjects and portraits. It is not known exactly at what period he lived.

DOORT, P. VAN, was a Dutch engraver, who worked entirely with the graver, and was a humble imitator of the style of Cornelis Cort. Among other prints by him, is one after Bernardino Passari, representing the 'Holy Family,' in which St. Elizabeth is presenting an apple to the Infant Christ.

DORBAY, —, a French engraver, flourished towards the end of the 17th century. He engraved, among other plates, some views of the Royal Palaces in France.

DORCY, PIERRE JOSEPH DEDREUX. See DEDREUX-DORCY.

DORÉ, LOUIS CHRISTOPHE GUSTAVE PAUL, a French historical painter and illustrator of books, was born at Strassburg in 1833. His name was originally DORER, a not unfrequent German name, which he modified into the French equivalent by which he became so widely known. In 1848, when but fifteen years of age, he began to exhibit at the Salon landscape sketches in pen and ink which showed considerable ability, and in the same year he became one of the regular contributors to the 'Journal pour rire.' He also contributed a large number of designs to the 'Journal pour tous.' His earliest exhibited works were the 'Battle of the Alma,' in the Salon of 1855, and the 'Battle of Inkermann,' in the Salon of 1857, but his best picture, and that which first brought him into notice as a painter, was 'Paolo and Francesca da Rimini,' exhibited in 1863. This was followed, among others, by 'The Titans,' a drawing heightened with white, in 1866, and 'The Neophyte' in 1868. Doré's ambition was to win fame as an historical painter, but in this he failed. Although gifted with marvellous fertility of imagination and wonderful facility of execution, he nevertheless possessed grave defects. Nowhere are his faults of composition and drawing more manifest than on the enormous canvases exhibited in the Doré Gallery in London. 'Christ leaving the Prætorium' (1867-72) and 'Christ's Entry into Jerusalem' (1876), each measuring twenty feet in height and thirty feet in length, are works to which he devoted his utmost energy, but which add nothing to his reputation. Besides these his most ambitious works were his 'Ecce Homo!' (1877), and 'Moses before Pharaoh' (1878-80). His 'Tobit and the Angel,' painted in 1865, is in the Luxembourg Gallery.

It is, however, as a designer of illustrations for books that the wonderful versatility of his genius becomes most apparent. The designs for the 'Contes drolatiques' of Balzac, published in 1856, are masterpieces of caricature, which breathe the true mediæval spirit. They were preceded by the illustrations to 'Rabelais,' issued in 1854, among which that of the 'Monks of Seville' is inimitable in its humour, and by those to the 'Legend of the Wandering Jew,' issued in 1856. The 'Contes drolatiques' and 'Rabelais' are unsurpassed even by the designs for Dante's 'Inferno,' terrible as are the latter in their weird imagination. These were published in 1861, accompanied by a blank-verse translation of the text by W. M. Rossetti, and were followed in the same year by the illustrations to the 'Contes' of Perrault, and in 1863 by a series of designs for 'Don Quixote,' which are careful studies of Spanish life. The 'Purgatorio' and 'Paradiso' of Dante, completing the 'Divina Commedia,' were not published until 1868. The designs

for the 'Bible' (1865-66), Milton's 'Paradise Lost' (1866), Tennyson's 'Idyls of the King' (1867-68), La Fontaine's 'Fables' (1867), Hood's 'Poems' (1870), Baron Davillier's 'Espagne' (1873), Coleridge's 'Ancient Mariner' (1876), Louis Enault's 'Londres' (1877), the 'Orlando Furioso' of Ariosto (1879), and Poe's 'Raven' (1883)—the last work on which he was engaged—marked the grades in a constantly descending scale of genius and of power.

Doré's reputation as an artist does not rest exclusively on his paintings and designs. He possessed also considerable ability as a sculptor, and was engaged upon the monument to the elder Dumas when death struck him down. A colossal vase decorated with groups of figures was sent by him to the Exposition Universelle at Paris in 1878. Gustave Doré died in Paris in 1883. He left unfinished a series of illustrations to Shakespeare, and unaccomplished the intention to execute a statue of the great dramatist. The following are his most important pictures:

The Battle of the Alma. (*Salon, 1855.*)
The Battle of Inkermann. (*Salon, 1857.*)
Paolo and Francesca da Rimini. (*Salon, 1863.*)
Tobit and the Angel. 1865. (*Luxembourg Gallery.*)
The Neophyte. (*Salon, 1868.*)
The Mountebank's Family. (*Salon, 1868.*)
Andromeda. 1868.
The Triumph of Christianity over Paganism. 1868.
Christian Martyrs. 1871.
Christ leaving the Prætorium. 1867-72.
The Massacre of the Innocents. 1869-72.
The Night of the Crucifixion. 1872-73.
The Dream of Pilate's Wife. 1873-74.
Christ's Entry into Jerusalem. 1876.
Ecce Homo! 1877.
The Ascension. 1879.
Moses before Pharaoh. 1878-80.
A Day Dream. 1882.
The Vale of Tears. 1882.   R.E.G.

DORFMEISTER, JOHANN EVANGELIST, an Austrian landscape painter, was born in 1741, and died in 1765. A 'Forest Party' by him is in the Vienna Gallery.

DORIGNY, LOUIS, a French historical painter and engraver, was a son of Michel Dorigny, and was born in Paris in 1654. His father died when he was only ten years of age, and he was placed under the tuition of Charles Le Brun. On leaving that master he studied for four years at Rome, visited Gubbio and Foligno, and from thence went to Venice, where he resided for ten years, and executed many decorative paintings. He then went to Verona, where he passed the rest of his life, and gave proof of his ability as a painter both in oil and in fresco. In 1704 he visited Paris and became a candidate for admission into the Academy, but was excluded through the influence of the architect Mansard. In 1711 he was summoned to Vienna by Prince Eugene, in whose palace he painted the ceilings of the grand staircase and of some other apartments. He died at Verona in 1742. His 'Susannah and the Elders' is in the Bordeaux Museum. He executed some etchings in a free, painter-like style, among which are the following:

A set of thirty-two vignettes, with the title, from his own designs, for an Italian edition of the 'Pensées Chrétiennes' of Père Bouhours.
Six subjects from Ovid's Metamorphoses.
Five Emblems of Horace; the designs for three of these are in the Louvre.
A View of the Amphitheatre at Verona.
The Descent of the Saracens at the Port of Ostia; *after Raphael.*

82

DORIGNY, MICHEL, a French painter and engraver, was born at St. Quentin in 1617, and was brought up under Simon Vouet, whose daughter he married. He painted historical subjects in the style of his master; and some of his pictures are in the château of Vincennes. His 'Flora and Zephyr' is now in the Louvre, and an 'Allegory' by him is in the Madrid Gallery. He is, however, better known as the engraver of several plates etched in a bold, spirited style, but with a considerable degree of harshness in the effect which is very disagreeable. Dorigny died in Paris in 1665. The following are his principal plates, all of which are after the pictures of Simon Vouet:

The Holy Family. 1649.
The Nativity.
The Adoration of the Magi; in four sheets, in the manner of a frieze.
Jupiter giving Apollo the conduct of the Chariot of the Sun.
Apollo killing the Python.
Peace descending on the Earth.
Venus at her Toilet.
Venus, Cupid, and Hope, plucking Feathers from the Wings of Time.
Mercury and the Graces.
Iris cutting the hair of Dido.
The Rape of Europa.

He also engraved from his own designs:

A set of Six Bacchanalian subjects.
A Caricature of the architect Mansard, entitled 'La Mansarde.'

DORIGNY, Sir NICOLAS, a French engraver, was the youngest son of Michel Dorigny, and was born in Paris in 1658. He was brought up to the bar, and followed that profession until he was thirty years of age, when, in consequence of deafness, he turned his thoughts to the arts, and visited Italy, where he remained twenty-eight years. His first plates were executed with the point; and if we were to judge of his talent by his early prints, his reputation would be very short of that which he acquired by a union of the point and the graver in his later productions. He took for his model the admirable works of Gérard Audran; and although he by no means equalled that celebrated artist, either in the style of his drawing, or in the picturesque effect of his light and shade, his prints will always be esteemed both for their merit as engravings and for the importance of the subjects of which he made choice. In 1711 he was invited to England by Queen Anne to engrave the Cartoons of Raphael at Hampton Court, which he finished in 1719, and in the following year he was knighted by King George I. Whilst he was in England he painted some portraits of the nobility, but with no great success. He returned to France in 1725, and was received into the Academy in the same year. He exhibited some pictures of sacred subjects at the Salon from 1739 to 1743, and died in Paris in 1746. The following are his principal prints:

Nine plates of the Seven Planets, and the Creation of the Sun and Moon; after the paintings by *Raphael* in the Chigi Chapel in La Madonna del Popolo.
The Cartoons at Hampton Court; *after the same;* eight plates, including the title.
The Transfiguration; *after the same.*
The History of Cupid and Psyche, and the Triumph of Galatea, twelve plates, including the title; after the paintings from the designs of *Raphael*, in the Farnesina.
The Descent from the Cross; *after Danielle da Volterra.*
St. Peter and St. John healing the Lame Man at the Gate of the Temple; *after L. Cigoli.*

The Martyrdom of St. Sebastian; *after Domenichino.*
The Martyrdom of St. Petronilla; *after Guercino.*
St. Francis kneeling before the Virgin and Child; *after A. Carracci.*
St. Catharine in Meditation; *after Carlo Cignani.*
St. Peter walking on the Sea; *after Lanfranco.*
The Virgin and Child, with St. Charles Borromeo and St. Liborius; *after B. Lamberti.*
The Trinity; *after Guido Reni.*
The Birth of the Virgin; *after Carlo Maratti.*
The Adoration of the Magi; *after the same.*
The Virgin and Child, with St. Charles Borromeo and St. Ignatius; *after the same.*
Eight plates of the paintings in the Cupola of St. Agnes; *after Ciro Ferri.*

DORN, JOSEPH, was born at Gratz-Sambach, near Pommersfelden in 1759, and studied in the galleries of Munich, Vienna, and Düsseldorf. He copied to deception the cabinet pictures of Frans van Mieris, Gerard Dou, Terborch, Van der Werff, and others, and was particularly celebrated for his skill in restoring old paintings. He died at Bamberg in 1841. His wife, ROSALIE DORN, excelled in portrait painting; she was the daughter of the historical painter Treu.

DORNER, JOHANN JAKOB, the elder, who was born at Ehrenstetten, near Freiburg in Breisgau, in 1741, was at first a pupil of Rösch at Freiburg and of Ignaz Bauer at Augsburg. He afterwards visited Italy, the Netherlands, and Paris; and excelled as a painter of historical and genre subjects. He was a professor and director of the Gallery at Munich in 1770, and died in that city in 1813. In the Darmstadt Gallery is a picture of 'Two Soldiers and a Maiden' by him; and in the Pinakothek at Munich, a 'Linen Draper,' which is a portrait of his wife, dated 1775.

DORNER, JOHANN JAKOB, a Bavarian landscape painter, the son of Johann Jakob Dorner the elder, was born at Munich in 1775. He was instructed in art by his father and by Mannlich, but he afterwards studied the works of Claude Lorrain and Karel Du Jardin. He travelled by himself through the picturesque regions of Bavaria, Switzerland, and France. His works are distinguished for spirited composition and taste in their execution. In 1803 he became Restorer, and in 1808 Inspector of the Royal Gallery at Munich, and was subsequently elected a member of the Academies of Hanau, Vienna, Berlin, and Munich. He died at Munich in 1852. The following works by him are in public collections:

Berlin.	*Gallery.*	A Forest Road. 1817.
Cassel.	*Gallery.*	Two Waterfalls.
Munich.	*Pinakothek.*	View of the Walchensee, in the Mountains of Upper Bavaria.
,,	,,	Waterfall, with a Huntsman.
,,	,,	Landscape and Mill near Pasing.
,,	,,	Landscape in the Tyrol during a Thunderstorm.

DORNER, JOHANN KONRAD, an Austrian painter, was born at Egg, near Bregenz, in 1810, and studied historical painting under Cornelius. In 1835 he went to St. Petersburg, and there painted many portraits and altarpieces. He afterwards returned to Munich, and in 1860 went to Rome, where he died in 1866. He executed his best works whilst in Rome; they are mostly of a religious character. A 'Madonna and Child, with St. John,' and the 'Infant Christ' are in the Pinakothek at Munich.

DORRELL, EDMUND, an English water-colour landscape painter, was born at Warwick in 1778.

He exhibited at the Royal Academy from 1807 to 1828, and at the Water-Colour Society from 1809 to 1818. He died in London in 1857. There are by him at the South Kensington Museum:

On the Thames.
Landscape, with cottage, church, figures, &c.
Fisherman and Boats, Mount Edgcumbe.
Crowhurst, near Hastings.
View from Box Hill.

DORSTE, I. V. This signature appears on a profile portrait of a Man, in the Dresden Gallery, which by Vosmaer is ascribed to Geraert Drost.

DOSSI, BATTISTA, was an Italian painter of landscapes and caricatures, who was a scholar of Lorenzo Costa, and worked mostly in conjunction with his brother Giovanni. In the Costabili Gallery at Ferrara are four landscapes by him; and in San Pietro at Modena are other works by him. He also executed two fantastic landscapes which are in the Palazzo Borghese at Rome, and assisted Raphael for a short time in 1520. He died in 1548. The Uffizi, Florence, has a 'Female Saint' by him.

DOSSI, GIOVANNI, commonly called DOSSO DOSSI, and sometimes GIOVANNI DI NICOLÒ DI LUTERO, appears to have been born about the year 1479 in the vicinity of Ferrara. His surname is supposed to have been derived from the village of Dosso, in the province of Ferrara. He was in 1512 a disciple of Lorenzo Costa in Mantua. He afterwards, with his brother Battista, visited Rome and Venice, and they there passed eleven years, studying the works of Giorgione and Titian, till they formed a style which may be called their own, and which, although not totally divested of the Gothic, is distinguished by originality of invention, and great harmony of colour. Giovanni excelled in painting figures, in which Battista was less successful; but Battista distinguished himself as a painter of landscape, in which Lomazzo considers him little inferior to Gaudenzio Ferrari, Pordenone, and even Titian. The brothers were much employed by Alfonso I., Duke of Ferrara, and by his successor, Ercole II. They painted the cartoons for the tapestries in the cathedral at Ferrara, and for those in the church of San Francesco, and in the ducal palace at Modena. Several of Dosso Dossi's frescoes are still to be seen in the ducal palace at Ferrara, but others were destroyed by fire in 1718. He excelled in portraits as well as historical subjects, and painted that of Ariosto, who employed him to make designs for his 'Orlando Furioso.' The poet has celebrated the names of the Dossi by enrolling them with those of Leonardo da Vinci, Michelangelo, Raphael, and Titian. Dosso Dossi died at Ferrara in 1542. The following paintings by him are known:

Berlin.	Gallery.	The Fathers of the Church in meditation on the Mystery of the Immaculate Conception of the Virgin.
Bergamo.	Museum.	Portrait of a Man.
Dresden.	Gallery.	The Virgin and God the Father in one Glory, with the Four Doctors of the Church below.
Ferrara.	Certosa.	The Virgin and Child, with St. John and two other Saints.
"	S. Agostino.	The Crucifixion, with the Virgin, St. John, and St. Augustine.
"	Museum.	The Virgin enthroned, crowned by Angels.
"	"	St. John at Patmos.
"	"	The Annunciation.

Ferrara.	Museum.	Madonna with Saints. (A very large picture in five compartments, from S. Andrea.)
"	Ducal Pal.	Decorative paintings with three Bacchanals.
		The Hours of the Day.
Florence.	Uffizi.	Massacre of the Innocents.
"	"	His own Portrait.
"	Pitti Pal.	Repose in Egypt.
London.	Nat. Gal.	Adoration of the Magi.
Milan.	Brera.	A Sainted Bishop with two Angels. 1536.
"	Ambrosiana.	Mary Magdalen washing Christ's feet.
Modena.	Cathedral.	Virgin in Glory adored by Saints. 1522.
"	Carmine.	A Dominican Saint and a Woman (allegorical).
"	S. Pietro.	Assumption of the Virgin.
"	Gallery.	The Nativity.
"	"	Virgin adored by SS. George and Michael.
"	"	Several Portraits, among them that of Alfonso I. of Ferrara (in the style of Titian).
Paris.	Louvre.	Holy Family.
"	"	St. Jerome.
Rome.	Borghese Pal.	Circe.
"	Doria Pal.	Vanossa.
Vienna.	Gallery.	St. Jerome.

DOSSIER, MICHEL, a French engraver, was born in Paris in 1684, and died in the same city in 1750. He was a pupil of Pierre Drevet, and engraved but a very few plates, the best known of which is 'Vertumnus and Pomona,' after Rigaud, the figure of Pomona being a portrait of Anne Varice de Vallière, wife of Jean Neyret de La Ravoye. The following may also be mentioned:

The Marriage of the Virgin; after Jouvenet
Christ healing the two Blind Men at Jericho; after Colombel.
Christ driving the Money-Changers out of the Temple; after the same.
The Supper at the house of Simon the Pharisee; after the same.
Jean Baptiste Colbert, Marquis of Torcy; after Rigaud.

DOU, GERARD, was born at Leyden in 1613, in the same year and the same city which had the glory of claiming Rembrandt as citizen. His father, Douwe Janszoon de Vries van Arentsvelt, who was a glazier, allowed his son to follow the path to which the boy's instincts led him, and apprenticed him, in 1622, to the studio of the engraver, Bartholomeus Dolendo. Here young Gerard spent some time in mastering the art of drawing. After quitting the engraver's desk he went, in 1624, into the workshop of Pieter Kouwenhoven, a painter on glass, and in 1628 he entered the studio of the great Rembrandt van Ryn, but he borrowed little of his master's style and manner. Dou's talent was all his own; his pictures, though small, are superb specimens of the art, finished with care, and true to nature.

After setting up for himself, Dou is reported to have worked at portrait painting; but his manner was too slow and laboured to please his sitters, and he then took as subjects for his paintings the scenes of humble industry that the neighbouring market-place afforded, and interiors graced by buxom maids.

No details have been handed down to us of Dou's life. It was probably passed happily and quietly at his work. He resided—with the exception of two gaps, from 1651 to 1657, and again from 1668 to 1672—in his native city. That he was a prosperous man is to be inferred from the

GIOVANNI DOSSI

CALLED

DOSSO DOSSI

THE ARCHANGEL MICHAEL

GERARD DOU

Hanfstängl photo]   [*National Gallery*

THE POULTERER'S SHOP

GERARD DOU

THE GROCER'S SHOP

large sums for which he sold his paintings. The wealthy connoisseur Van Spiring gave Dou an annual donation of a thousand florins merely to be allowed to have the first choice of the pictures that the artist had completed at the close of every year. Besides this annual grant, Van Spiring paid the ordinary price like any other purchaser for the pictures which he chose.

Gerard Dou died at Leyden in 1675, and was buried in the church of St. Peter. Among his pupils and followers were Frans van Mieris, Schalcken, Gabriel Metsu, and Van Slingeland. The following are his principal works:—

Amsterdam.	*Museum.*	Portrait of Himself.
„	„	The Night School.
„	„	The Hermit.
„	„	Curiosity.
„	„	Portraits of Pieter van der Werf, Burgomaster of Leyden, and his Wife. (*The portraits are by Dou, the landscape by Claes Pietersz Berchem.*)
„	*Six Coll.*	The Dentist.
„	„	A Girl at a Window. 1667.
„	„	A Candle-light Effect.
„	*Van der Hoop C.*	A Fish-woman.
Berlin.	*Gallery.*	The Penitent Magdalen. 1656.
„	„	Portrait of an Old Woman.
„	„	The Store-room.
Brussels.	*Gallery.*	Portrait of Himself.
„	*Arenberg Coll.*	An Old Woman sitting at a table covered with Gold.
Cassel.	*Gallery.*	Bust Portrait of an Old Man, with a blue feather in his hat.
Copenhagen.	*Gallery.*	A Doctor.
„	„	A Maid. 1658 ?
„	„	Bust Portrait of a Woman.
Dresden.	*Gallery.*	Portrait of Himself. 1647.
„	„	A Grey Cat on a Window-sill; in the back-ground, Dou before his easel. 1657.
„	„	A Girl plucking Grapes at a Window. 1658.
„	„	Gerard Dou playing the Violin. 1665.
„	„	A School-master mending his Pen. 1671.
„	„	The Dentist, with a Boy, whose tooth he has just extracted. 1672.
„	„	A Hermit praying. *And nine others.*
Dulwich.	*Gallery.*	A Lady playing on the Virginal.
Florence.	*Uffizi.*	Portrait of Himself. 1618.
„	„	The Pan-cake Seller.
Hague.	*Gallery.*	The Young Tailoress (or, The Young Mother). 1658.
„	„	A Young Woman holding a Lamp.
London.	*Nat. Gal.*	Portrait of Himself.
„	„	Portrait of his Wife.
„	„	The Poulterer's Shop.
„	*Buckingham Pal.*	An Old Man.
„	„	A Kitchen-Maid. 1646.
„	*Bridgewater Ho.*	The Violin Player. 1637.
„	„	Portrait of Himself.
„	*Northbrook Coll.*	A Lady playing the Spinet.
„	*Bute Collection.*	An Old Man reading.
Munich.	*Gallery.*	A Beggar asking Alms of an Old Woman selling Vegetables.
„	„	The Bakeress.
„	„	Portrait of Himself. 1663. *And eleven others.*
Paris.	*Louvre.*	The Dropsical Woman. 1663.
„	„	A Silver Ewer and Salver. (*Painted on the shutter of an ebony box which formerly contained the painting of 'The Dropsical Woman.'*)
„	„	The Village Grocer. 1647.
„	„	The Trumpeter.
„	„	The Dutch Cook.
Paris.	*Louvre.*	A Woman hanging up a Cock at a Window. 1650.
„	„	The Gold-weigher. 1664.
„	„	The Dentist.
„	„	Reading the Bible. (*The old man and woman represented are said to be portraits of Gerard Dou's father and mother.*)
„	„	Portrait of Himself, at a Window, holding his Palette and Brushes.
„	„	Portrait of an Old Woman reading at a Table.
Petersburg.	*Hermitage.*	A Doctor and an Old Woman.
„	„	The Herring-seller.
„	„	Portrait of Himself. 1665.
„	„	A Young Peasant Woman preparing to bathe.
„	„	A Young Soldier preparing to bathe.
„	„	A Young Woman combing her hair by the side of a river. *And six others.*
Vienna.	*Gallery.*	The Doctor and an Old Woman. 1653.
„	„	An Old Woman watering Flowers.
„	*Czernin Coll.*	Portrait of Himself.
„	„	A Party playing at Cards.
„	*Liechtenstein C.*	Portrait of Himself.

DOUDYNS, WILLEM, a Dutch painter, was born at the Hague in 1630. He was of a distinguished family, and followed the art rather as an amateur than a professor; but with a zeal that enabled him to reach a reputable rank among the painters of his country. After receiving some instruction from an obscure artist, named Alexander Petit, he travelled to Italy, where he passed twelve years studying the best productions of the art, and acquired a correctness of design and an elevation of taste, which distinguish his works. On his return to Holland, he executed several fresco paintings, particularly decorations for ceilings, in which, from his perfect knowledge of foreshortening, he excelled. Some of his works of that description are in the town-hall at the Hague. Two of his most admired easel pictures were in the possession of M. Van Heteren, representing 'Time discovering Truth,' and 'Wisdom triumphing over Vice and Intemperance.' Doudyns was one of the founders of the Academy at the Hague, of which he was appointed the director. He died in 1697.

DOUÉ, CLAUDE and JEAN. See DE HOEY.

DOUET, —, a French engraver on wood, flourished about the year 1530. Papillon notices a woodcut executed by him, representing the 'Virgin Mary and the Infant Christ,' after Andrea del Sarto.

DOUFFET, GERAERT, (DOUFEET, or DUFFEIT,) was born at Liége in 1594, and studied for some time at Antwerp in the school of Rubens, and afterwards in Italy. He composed and designed with good taste, and his historical pictures are much esteemed. 'Pope Nicholas V. at the Tomb of St. Francis of Assisi' (painted in 1627), 'St. Helena and the true Cross' (painted for the Abbey of St. Lawrence, Liége), and two male portraits (one dated 1624), are in the Munich Gallery. He died at Liége in 1660.

DOUGHTY, THOMAS. This clever landscape artist was born at Philadelphia in 1793, but did not adopt the artist's calling until he was nearly thirty years old, passing the earlier years of his life in mercantile pursuits. He worked for a long time in Paris, where he painted many of his most popular works, but for a short time he resided in London, finding in the suburbs of the great city scenes adapted to his pencil and brush. He then returned to America, and there he died in 1856. His pictures have steadily increased in value, and year by year their charm has been more readily recognized. Some of the more delightful scenes, which he depicted with silvery tone, grey light and soft harmonious colouring, were taken from the banks of the Susquehanna and amongst the Catskill Mountains. Doughty was one of the earliest American landscape artists who gained a European celebrity, and his pictures being few in number and executed with the utmost skill and great poetic feeling, will always be admired and valued.

DOUGHTY, WILLIAM, a painter and engraver, was a native of York. In 1775 he became a pupil of Sir Joshua Reynolds, and after an unsuccessful attempt as a portrait painter in Ireland, he in 1779 settled down in London; but in the following year he set sail for Bengal, having just married a servant girl from Reynolds's house. His ship, however, was captured by the French and Spaniards, by whom he was brought to Lisbon, where he died in 1782. Two paintings which he exhibited were a 'Circe' and a portrait of Sir Joshua Reynolds; but he was more successful with his etchings and mezzotint portraits, among which are the following:

Thomas Beckwith, the Antiquary of York.
Thomas Gray, the Poet.
Admiral Keppel; *after Sir Joshua Reynolds.*
William Mason, the Poet; *after the same.*
Mary Palmer, the niece of Sir Joshua Reynolds, afterwards Marchioness of Thomond; *after the same.*
Dr. Samuel Johnson; *after the same.*

DOUGLAS, Sir WILLIAM FETTES, was born at Edinburgh in 1822. After ten years of business life, whose leisure hours were devoted to art, his father, an accomplished amateur water-colour painter, consented to his following his bent and studying at the Academy. He had, however, only a few months' regular training. His pictures at the Royal Scottish Academy Exhibitions soon attracted attention, and he was elected an Associate of the Royal Scottish Academy in 1851, and Royal Scottish Academician in 1854. He visited Italy in 1857. He first sent to the Academy in London in 1862. In 1869 he was secretary to the Royal Scottish Academy for a short time, and in 1877 he was appointed curator of the Scottish National Gallery, succeeding Sir Daniel Macnee as President of the Royal Scottish Academy in 1882. In that year he was knighted, and in 1884 he received the honour of LL.D. from Edinburgh University. He died at Newburgh, Fife, in 1891. He was early attracted to romantic, antiquarian and occult subjects, as the titles of his works indicate. Of these perhaps the best are: 'The Astrologer,' 'The Bibliopolists' (now in South Kensington), 'In the Scriptorium,' 'Vesalius,' 'The Old Curiosity Shop, Rome,' 'The Alchemist on the Verge of a Discovery,' 'The Spell,' and 'The Summons to the Secret Tribunal.' He painted also genre and historical subjects, a few landscapes in oil, and, late in life, some charming landscapes in water-colour. He has been termed the greatest Scottish painter of still life; and the care and skill with which he painted old ivories, time-stained parchments, rich bindings, and old furniture, and harmonized their mellow colours, justify the title. His draughtsmanship was masterly, his colour at its best rich and glowing, and his composition varied and agreeable. He was, besides, a man of rare accomplishment, a learned antiquarian and historian. An illustrated monograph on him was

published by the Society for the Promotion of the Fine Arts in Scotland. J. H. W. L.

DOUVEN, JOHANNES FRANCISCUS VAN, was born at Roermond, in the Duchy of Guelders, in 1656. His father dying when he was young, he was placed under the care of a painter of Liége, named Gabriel Lambertin, who had studied in Italy, and had formed a collection of studies and drawings, which were of great utility to the progress of his pupil. On leaving that master he was taken into favour by a Spanish nobleman residing at Roermond, who possessed a valuable collection of the Italian school. He was permitted to copy and study these, and they were a mine of instruction to the young artist. His first essays were in historical painting; and he would probably have distinguished himself in that branch, had not the flattering invitation he received from the Elector induced him to visit Düsseldorf, where he painted the portraits of that prince and the principal personages of his court, and was appointed principal painter to the elector. This success seems to have inclined his future course chiefly to portrait painting; and his talents were employed at almost every court in Germany, where he received many honourable marks of favour and distinction. He was also patronized at the court of Tuscany, where the Grand Duke placed his portrait in the Florentine Gallery. He occasionally painted easel pictures of historical subjects, which were correctly drawn and well composed. Douven died at Düsseldorf in 1727. The following pictures are by him:

Cassel.	*Gallery.*	Susannah and the Elders. 1725.
"	"	Bathsheba bathing.
"	"	Clement Augustus, Elector of Cologne.
Florence.	*Uffizi.*	Portrait of Elizabeth Haurey.
"	"	Portrait of Himself.
"	"	St. Anne teaching the Virgin.
"	"	Portrait of Maria Luisa de' Medici.
Munich.	*Gallery.*	Portrait of the Elector Palatine, John William.
"	"	Portrait of a young Elector Palatine.

His son, BARTHOLOMEUS VAN DOUVEN, born at Düsseldorf in 1688, painted in the manner of A. van der Werff. He was employed at the court of the Elector of Cologne, and excelled in the execution of portraits. The Cassel Gallery has a picture of the 'Three Graces' by him, and in the palace at Cassel is a 'Holy Family,' known as 'La Vierge aux cérises,' which was taken to Paris by the French, but returned in 1815. There is by him in the Uffizi Gallery at Florence a picture containing medallion portraits of the Elector Palatine John William, and his wife Maria Luisa de' Medici, copied from the original by Van der Werff in the Munich Gallery.

DOUW, SIMON VAN, flourished at Antwerp, where he was free of the Guild of St. Luke in 1653-54. In the Lille Museum is a 'Landscape with figures' by him, signed and dated 1677.

DOVE, THOMAS, marine painter, began life as a house painter, but later entered the studio of George Chambers, with whom he worked for some time. His pictures were chiefly scenes from Liverpool or its neighbourhood, and he became well known in the north of England. Reduced to poverty in his old age, he died in the Whitby workhouse in January 1887.

DOW, GERARD. See DOU.

DOWNES, BERNARD, an English portrait painter, flourished in the latter half of the 18th century.

SIR W. FETTES DOUGLAS

THE CURIOSITY SHOP, ROME

[Collection of John Wordie, Esq.

He exhibited at the Royal Academy from 1770 to 1775, and at the Incorporated Society of Artists, of which he was a member. He died before 1780.

DOWNMAN, JOHN. It is not known for certain where this artist was born. His birthplace has usually been given as in Devonshire, but there is better reason for assuming him to have been a Welshman, and to have been born close to Wrexham, where he died. He was certainly born in 1750, and died at Wrexham on December 24, 1824, aged seventy-four years. He was a student of the Royal Academy Schools in 1769, and became an Associate in 1795. He studied under Benjamin West, P.R.A., and painted a clever portrait of his master which is still in existence. He practised portrait painting in Cambridge in 1777, visited Plymouth in 1806; and in 1807-8 was working in Exeter. He then returned to London and resided there for many years, afterwards removing to Chester, and finally taking up his abode as already stated at Wrexham, where his daughter had married, and where she also died in 1840. Downman married the daughter of William Jackson of Exeter, the musical composer, who was organist of Exeter Cathedral. He painted subject pictures in water-colour and oil, notable amongst which are:

A Lady at Work. 1770.
The Death of Lucretia. 1773.
Rosalind. (*Painted for the Shakespeare Gallery.*)
The Priestess of Bacchus.
The Return of Orestes.
Tobias.
Miss Farren and Mr. King in character.

His greatest works, however, were his portraits in pencil and colour, which he painted in the country houses of England, and in the towns where he worked for a time. They are extremely clever pieces of portraiture, lightly and gracefully sketched and tinged with very charming colour. Upon almost all of them the artist made some pencil notes which greatly added to their value. He generally gave the name of his sitter, the date when the picture was painted, and in many cases the name of the place where it was done, or some description of the person, his occupation, characteristics, position, dignity or style. In some cases he made comments upon the way in which the sitter behaved himself, or the number of times which he painted the same person, or alluded to some interesting circumstance as to himself or his sitter, and all these notes make his works of peculiar interest in the present day. Many of his portraits were engraved, and of this fact he also makes one aware by his notes. He painted in this sketchy manner all the great ladies of his day, the noblemen, actors, and notable personages as well as many members of the Royal families both of England and Prussia. Hardly any family of quality in England has not had some of its members painted by this hardworking and most popular artist, and his portraits are singularly attractive, full of character and expression, and those of ladies and children remarkable for their grace and charm. The largest collections of his portraits are to be found at the Manor House, Witley, and at Butleigh Court, Glastonbury. An important work on the artist is now in course of compilation, and will be issued by the publishers of this work. G. C. W.

DOYEN, GABRIEL FRANÇOIS, a French historical painter, was born in Paris in 1726. Before he had attained his twelfth year he entered the studio of Carle van Loo, and in 1746 obtained the 'grand prix de Rome.' On his return to Paris in 1755, he at once established his reputation by his 'Death of Virginia,' exhibited at the Salon of 1759, in which year he was received into the Academy upon his picture of 'Jupiter attended by Hebe.' He became a professor in 1776, and about this time he was employed to decorate the chapel of St. Grégoire at the Invalides. In 1791 he went to Russia, where he was greatly honoured by Catharine II. and Paul I., for whom he executed many ceilings and other works. He was also appointed director of the Academy at St. Petersburg, in which city he died in 1806. His best works are 'The Triumph of Amphitrite,' now in the Louvre, and 'The Descent of the Holy Spirit,' in the chapel of St. Geneviève in the church of St. Roch in Paris. The sketch for the latter is in the Louvre. The Darmstadt Gallery possesses his 'Adoration of the Kings.'

DOYEN, LE. See LE DOYEN.

DOYEN, PIERRE GABRIEL, a French painter, was born in Paris in 1723, and died there in 1799. He was a member of the Academy of St. Luke, and may therefore be presumed to have been not entirely devoid of talent.

DOYLE, JOHN, a caricaturist, well-known as 'H.B.,' was born in Dublin in 1797. At an early age he studied under an Italian landscape painter named Gabrielli, and also became a student in the Dublin Society's Drawing Academy and a pupil of Comerford. About 1822 he came to London, where, not succeeding very well as a portrait painter, he produced by lithography, and published, likenesses of the leading men of the day; among others the Duke of Wellington on a white charger, and the Duke of York. From this time he chiefly employed himself in producing caricatures of leading members of Parliament, under the initials 'H.B.' His death occurred in London in 1868. His political portraits, though caricatures, were always treated with a gentlemanly feeling, never descending to coarseness or vulgarity. The original sketches for 610 out of the 917 to which they amounted are in the British Museum. A portrait of Christopher Moore by Doyle is in the National Gallery of Ireland.

DOYLE, RICHARD, draughtsman and caricaturist, was born in London, September 1824. He was the second son of John Doyle (H.B.), who taught him from early childhood, and to such purpose that at the age of sixteen the boy was already an accomplished draughtsman. A remarkable specimen of his early powers is preserved in the British Museum. It is a MS. Journal, illustrated with a large number of humorous and fanciful sketches. (This work was published in facsimile by Smith, Elder and Co. in 1885.) Other productions of about the same date were, 'The Eglinton Tournament,' and 'A Grand Historical, Allegorical, and Classical Procession.' In 1843, two years after the establishment of 'Punch,' Doyle, then nineteen years old, was permanently engaged on the staff. He soon attracted attention by his cartoons of leading statesmen, and later by a series of humorous designs called 'Manners and Customs of ye Englyshe, drawn from ye Quick by Richard Doyle.' Akin to these were the 'Bird's-eye Views of Society,' contributed to the 'Cornhill Magazine.' One of his happiest contributions to 'Punch' was the now familiar cover. Besides work of this importance,

Doyle further contributed to 'Punch' innumerable small drawings, initials, and *culs de lampe*. His connection with the periodical came to an end in 1850, when conscientious scruples caused him to resign his post. A sincere Roman Catholic, he felt it unseemly to associate himself with attacks directed against Papal aggression. Henceforward he worked as an illustrator of books, and as a painter in water-colours. His original drawings were chiefly of Welsh and Devon scenery, into which he loved to introduce gracefully-fantastic figures of fairies, gnomes, and pixies. Among such the most important examples are:

The Triumphant Entry, a Fairy Pageant. (*Nat. Gal., Ireland.*)
The Witch's Home. (*Two Drawings.*)
The Manners and Customs of Monkeys. (*Both in the South Kensington Museum.*)

Doyle was seized with apoplexy at the Athenæum Club, December 10, 1883, and died on the next day. Among the books illustrated by him are:

Thackeray's 'Rebecca and Rowena.' 1850.
Ruskin's 'King of the Golden River.' 1851.
'The Foreign Tour of Brown, Jones, and Robinson.' 1854. (Begun in 'Punch.')
Thackeray's 'Newcomes.' 1853-5.
'In Fairy Land.' Elfin scenes, with verses by Mr. William Allingham. 1870.
Dickens' 'Battle of Life.'
Leigh Hunt's 'Jar of Honey from Mount Hybla.'

A number of his miscellaneous sketches are preserved in the British Museum, and in the Fitzwilliam Museum at Cambridge.

DRAEGER, JOSEPH ANTON, an historical painter, was born at Trèves in 1800, and died at Rome in 1833. He studied under Kügelgen in Dresden, but went in 1823 to Italy and took up his quarters in Rome, where he followed, as a nondescript in life and art, his own peculiar style of colouring. In his desire to attain the charm of the colours of the great Venetians, a very faded picture of that school led him to the conviction that they painted their pictures entirely in grey before putting on the bright colours. Working in this way he obtained an extraordinary clearness of colour, a good example of which is seen in his 'Moses protecting the Daughters of Jethro,' in the Berlin Gallery.

DRAGHI, GIOVANNI BATTISTA, was born at Genoa in 1657. He was a scholar of Domenico Piola, whose promptness and facility he imitated and acquired. He resided at Parma and Piacenza, where there are several of his works. They evince something of the design of the Bolognese school, with the taste of Parmigiano. In the church of San Francesco il Grande at Piacenza, is a picture by him of the 'Martyrdom of St. James.' The dome of Sant' Agnese, in the same city, is by this master; and in the church of San Lorenzo, a picture of the titular Saint. At Genoa there are some of his easel pictures in private collections. He died at Piacenza in 1712.

DRAKE, NATHAN, a portrait painter, flourished at York and Lincoln in the middle of the 18th century. He occasionally painted views, and was a member of the Society of Artists, with whom he exhibited from 1760 to 1780.

DRAPENTIÈRE, JOHN, an engraver, was probably from his name a native of France. He was in England about the year 1691, and was employed by the publishers in some plates of portraits and frontispieces, which are executed with the graver in a neat, but tasteless style. The following portraits are by him.

William and Mary, when Prince and Princess of Orange.
John Graham, Viscount Dundee.
Thomas White, Bishop of Peterborough.
Benjamin Calamy, Prebendary of St. Paul's.
Henry Cuttes, of the Middle Temple.
Sir James Dyer, Chief Justice of the Common Pleas.
Peter Perkins, Mathematician.
Daniel Burgess, Dissenting Minister. 1691.
Benjamin Keach, Anabaptist Minister.
Elias Keach.
John Todd, A.M.

He also engraved a satirical print of a lady shaving a gentleman; inscribed, 'Le Beau Service.'

DREBER, HEINRICH, (called FRANZ-DREBER,) a German landscape painter, was born at Dresden in 1822. Living in the house of a relation whose name Franz he adopted, he frequented the Academy of his native city, and afterwards the studio of Ludwig Richter. After he had gained the gold medal, he resided for some time in Munich, and in the spring of 1843 went as exhibitioner of the Dresden Academy to Rome, where he became a member of the Academy of St. Luke, and spent almost the entire remainder of his life. His study of Italian nature had the greatest influence on his works, and at the same time the impression made upon him by modern French landscape painters increased his desire to obtain a soft fusion of colours. He died in Anticoli di Campagna, near Rome, in 1875. His pictures, which were exhibited together in 1876 in the National Gallery at Berlin, are with few exceptions in the hands of private persons; there are two in the Berlin Gallery—a 'Landscape, with the Hunting of Diana,' and 'An Autumn Morning in the Sabine Mountains.'

DRECHSLER, JOHANN, a painter of flowers, was born at Vienna in 1756, and became a professor at the Academy of that city. He died at Vienna in 1811. He painted fruit and flower pieces in imitation of Van Huysum. There are examples of his work in the Hermitage at St. Petersburg, and in the Vienna Gallery.

DREUX, ALFRED DE, was born in Paris in 1808. He was a pupil of Léon Cogniet, and became a fashionable painter of race-horses and of equestrian portraits. Many of his pictures have been engraved. Among the best known are: 'The Postilion' (1836), 'The Imperial Guard' (1855), 'Equestrian Portrait of the Duc de Nemours' (1844), and several large hunting-pieces. He died in 1860.

DREVER, ADRIAAN VAN, a Dutch landscape and marine painter, flourished about 1673, and passed the greater part of his artistic life in England. In the Vienna Gallery there is a 'Winter Landscape' by him.

DREVET, CLAUDE, a French engraver, the nephew of Pierre Drevet, was born probably at Lyons about 1705. He was instructed by his uncle, and engraved some portraits in a highly finished style, which renders them of considerable merit. He died in Paris in 1781. The following portraits are by him:

Henri Oswald, Cardinal d'Auvergne; *after Rigaud.*
Charles Gaspard Guillaume de Vintimille, Archbishop of Paris; *after the same.*
Philippe Louis, Count de Zinzendorf; *after the same.*
Mme. Le Bret, in the character of Ceres; *after the same.*
Pierre Calvairac, Abbot of Pontignan; *after A. Le Prieur.*

DREVET, PIERRE, an eminent French engraver, was born at Loire in the Lyonnais in 1663. He was first a pupil of Germain Audran at Lyons, but

PIERRE IMBERT DREVET

JACOBUS BENIGNUS *BOSSUET EPISCOPUS*

BISHOP BOSSUET

afterwards finished his studies in Paris under Gérard Audran. In 1696 he became court engraver, and in 1707 was made an Academician, and for his reception he engraved, although not until 1722, the portrait of Robert de Cotte. He died in Paris in 1738. His works, which are chiefly portraits, are well drawn and very highly finished. The following prints are by him:

SACRED SUBJECTS.

Abraham's Sacrifice ; *after A. Coypel.*
The Annunciation ; *after the same.*
The same subject ; smaller.
The Crucifixion ; in two sheets ; *after the same.*
The Adoration of the Shepherds ; *after H. Rigaud.*

PORTRAITS.

Charles II., King of Great Britain.
James Francis Edward Stuart, called the Old Pretender.
James Fitzjames, Duke of Berwick.
Oliver Cromwell.
Louis XIV., full-length ; *after Rigaud.*
Louis XV., seated on his Throne ; *after the same.*
Philip V., King of Spain ; *after the same.*
Louis, Dauphin of France ; *after the same.*
Frederick Augustus, King of Poland ; *after F. de Troy.*
François Louis, Prince of Condé ; *after Rigaud.*
Louis Alexandre, Count of Toulouse, with the Glove.
The same Portrait, without the Glove.
René François de Beauveau, Archbishop of Narbonne ; *after Rigaud.*
André Hercule, Cardinal de Fleury ; *after the same.*
Marie de Neufchatel, Duchess de Nemours ; *after the same.*
Louis Antoine, Duke de Noailles ; *after the same.*
Louis Hector, Duke de Villars, Marshal of France ; *after the same.*
Ernest Augustus, Duke of Brunswick-Luneburg.
André Félibien ; *after Le Brun.*
Nicolas Boileau Despréaux ; *after De Piles.*
Hyacinthe Rigaud ; *from a picture by himself.*
Marie de Serre, mother of Rigaud ; *after Rigaud.*
Robert de Cotte, architect ; *after the same.*
Nicolas Pierre Camus de Pontcarré, first President of the Parliament of Rouen ; *after Jouvenet.*
Jean Forest, painter ; *after N. de Largillière.*

DREVET, PIERRE IMBERT, the son of Pierre Drevet, was born in Paris in 1697. He had the advantage of his father's instruction, and at a very early age was distinguished by the talent which he displayed. The works of this excellent artist may have been surpassed in boldness and freedom, but have hardly been equalled in the exquisite finish and clearness of his stroke. His celebrated portrait of Bossuet, engraved in 1723, is one of the finest line-engravings which has ever been executed, whilst that of Samuel Bernard is scarcely less admirable. About 1730 he became insane, but engraved until the year of his death, in which he executed the portrait of René Pucelle. He died in Paris in 1739. The following are his principal works:

SACRED SUBJECTS.

Adam and Eve after their Transgression ; *after A. Coypel.*
The same subject ; smaller ; very highly finished.
Rebekah receiving from Eliezer Abraham's presents ; *after the same.*
The Presentation of the Virgin in the Temple ; *after Le Brun.* The first work of the engraver.
The Holy Family ; *after Antoine Dieu.*
The Presentation in the Temple ; *after Louis de Boullongne.* The engraver's chef-d'œuvre.
Christ in the Garden of Olives, with Angels ; *after J. Restout.*
The Resurrection ; *after J. André.*
St. Theresa ; *after J. Lingre.*

PORTRAITS.

Louis XIV., when young, conducted by Minerva to the Temple of Glory ; *after A. Coypel.*

Louis, Duke of Orleans ; *after Charles Coypel.*
Mary Clementina Sobieska, wife of the Old Pretender ; *after Davids.*
François de La Mothe Fénelon, Archbishop of Cambrai ; *after Vivien.*
François Paul de Villory, Archbishop of Lyons ; *after Santerre.*
Claude Le Blanc, Minister of War ; *after Le Prieur.*
Cardinal Dubois, Archbishop of Cambrai ; *after Rigaud.*
J. B. Bossuet, Bishop of Meaux ; full-length ; *after the same.*
Samuel Bernard ; *after the same.*
Isaac Jacques de Vertamont, Bishop of Conferans ; *after De Troy.*
René Pucelle, Abbé and Counsellor of the Parliament ; *after Rigaud.* His last work. 1739.
Adrienne Lecouvreur, in the character of Cornelia ; *after Charles Coypel.*

Full particulars of the works of Pierre, Pierre Imbert, and Claude Drevet, are to be found in M. A. Firmin-Didot's work ' Les Drevet,' Paris, 1876, 8vo.

DREW, J. P., a portrait and figure painter, worked in London during the first half of the 19th century. He exhibited at the Royal Academy until 1852.

DREYER, DANKVART CHRISTIAN MAGNUS, a Danish landscape painter, was born in 1816 at Assens, where he died in 1852. The Copenhagen Gallery has a ' Landscape ' by him, dated 1839.

DRIELST, EGBERT VAN, born at Groningen in 1746, practised under several masters ; the last were H. Meyer of Haarlem, and J. Cats of Amsterdam. He particularly studied the works of Hobbema, Ruisdael, and Wynants, and compared them with nature. By this course his pictures approached nearer to the manner and taste of the great masters of the preceding century than to those of his own time. The subjects he represented were well-wooded landscapes, with farms and cottages, which he ornamented with figures and animals, correctly designed. He was fond of the picturesque effects of ruined hovels, old broken and uprooted trees, and barren heaths. These he depicted with a thorough knowledge of light and shade, and with a colour suited to the objects. Sometimes, however, there is a certain degree of negligence or inattention to be observed in his pictures ; and here and there he appears to be a mannerist. He died in 1818. His son, JAN VUURING VAN DRIELST, an artist of much promise, was born in 1790, and studied under his father, but died in 1813.

DRILLENBURG, WILLEM, a Dutch landscape painter, was born at Utrecht in 1625. He was for some time a scholar of Abraham Bloemaert, but abandoned the style of that painter in order to imitate the charming landscapes of Jan Both. Although he never approached the excellence of that master, his pictures are said by Houbraken, who was his scholar, to possess great merit.

DROECH SLOOT, JOOST CORNELISZ. See DROOCH SLOOT.

DROESHOUT, JAN, an engraver, was perhaps, from the date at which he flourished, a relation of Marten Droeshout. There are by him a few portraits, frontispieces, and other works for the booksellers, among which are :

The Portrait of Richard Elton ; prefixed to his ' Compleat Body of the Art Military,' 1650.
The Portrait of John Danes ; engraved for his ' Paralipomena Orthographiæ,' 1638.
Two plates for Heywood's ' Hierarchie of the blessed Angels,' 1635.

DROESHOUT, MARTEN, an engraver, who was probably a Dutchman, resided in England about the year 1623. He was chiefly employed by the book-sellers, and engraved some portraits, which, if they cannot be admired for the beauty of their execution, are valued for their scarcity. His best known portrait is that prefixed to the first folio edition of 'Mr. William Shakespeares Comedies, Histories, & Tragedies,' published in 1623. The excellence of this likeness of the great dramatist is attested by the following verses of Ben Jonson, which are printed opposite to it:

To the Reader.

This Figure, that thou here seest put,
    It was for gentle Shakespeare cut;
Wherein the Grauer had a strife
    With Nature, to out-doo the life:
O, could he but haue drawne his wit
    As well in brasse, as he hath hit
His face; the Print would then surpasse
    All, that was euer writ in brasse.
But, since he cannot, Reader, looke
    Not on his Picture, but his Booke.
                                    B. I.

Other portraits by Droeshout are:

James, Marquis of Hamilton.
Thomas, Lord Coventry.
John Donne, Dean of St. Paul's.
Helkiah Crooke, M.D.
John Fox, the Martyrologist.
John Howson, Bishop of Durham.
Lord Mountjoy Blount, afterwards Earl of Newport.

DROLLING, MARTIN, a native of Oberbergheim, near Colmar, was born in 1752. He received his first lessons in art from an obscure painter of Schlestadt, but afterwards went to Paris and entered the École des Beaux-Arts. He gained a momentary celebrity by his 'Interior of a Kitchen,' painted in 1815, exhibited at the Salon of 1817, and now in the Louvre. He usually painted interiors and familiar subjects of general interest. Although faulty in drawing and never above mediocrity, his works were popular during his lifetime, and many of them were engraved and lithographed. He died in Paris in 1827. The Louvre has by him a 'Woman at a window' and a 'Violin-Player.'

DROLLING, MICHEL MARTIN, a French historical and portrait painter, was born in Paris in 1786. He studied under his father, Martin Drolling, and under David, and obtained the 'grand prix de Rome' in 1810. In 1833 he was elected a member of the Institute, and in 1837 became a professor of the École des Beaux-Arts. He died in Paris in 1851. Amongst his best works, which are all conceived in the classical spirit in which he was brought up, are:

Orpheus and Eurydice. 1817.
Ulysses carrying off Polyxena. 1827.
The Good Samaritan. 1822. *In the Lyons Museum.*
The Death of Cardinal Richelieu. 1831.
Christ disputing with the Doctors: *in the church of Notre-Dame de Lorette, Paris.*
The Communion of Marie Antoinette: *in the chapel of the Conciergerie.*

DROOCH SLOOT, JOOST CORNELISZ, (DROOG-SLOOT or DROECH SLOOT,) a landscape and historical painter of Utrecht, flourished from 1616 to 1660. In 1616 he was admitted into the Guild of St. Luke at Utrecht, and in 1623-24 he became its dean. He gave to the hospital of St. Job, at Utrecht, in 1628, a picture of 'Job and his Friends,' the landscape part of which is said to be very beautiful: in 1638 he was named regent of the hospital. There is a portrait of him, painted by himself, in the manner of old Teniers; he is

90

seated at his easel, and his studio is furnished with pictures: it bears date 1630, and he appears about 50 years of age. Some of his works are signed with the annexed monogram: As he is classed with very respectable painters of the period, by writers on whose judgment reliance may be placed, he must not be confounded with Nicolaas Drooch Sloot, whose works of a like nature are known in England, and rank among the lowest of his country. The following pictures by Joost Drooch Sloot are in public galleries:

Cassel.	*Gallery.*	View of a Village.
Dresden.	*Gallery.*	View of a Village Street.
Hague.	*Museum.*	A Kermesse. 1652.
		A Dutch Village. 1652.
Madrid.	*Gallery.*	Skaters.
Modena.	*Gallery.*	Peasants.
Paris.	*Louvre.*	Troops passing through a Village. 1645.
Petersburg.	*Hermitage.*	A frozen Canal in Holland.
Rotterdam.	*Museum.*	A Village Fête. 1649.
Vienna.	*Gallery.*	Duel between the Dutch Gerhards and the French Briantès, 1600. (Painted in 1630.)

DROOCH SLOOT, NICOLAAS, was born at Dordrecht in 1650, and is supposed to have been a scholar of Hendrik Mommers. He painted village wakes and rural assemblies, which are distinguished by a disgusting vulgarity of character, which is not compensated by the agreeable tone of his colouring, or the spirit of his pencil. He died in 1702.

DROSSAART, ——, a Dutch painter of landscapes with ruins and stag-hunts, lived in the 17th century.

DROST, GERAERT, a Dutch painter, was born at Amsterdam about the year 1638. He was brought up in the school of Rembrandt, and afterwards visited Italy, where he improved his style of design, by studying the works of the great masters of the Roman school. He died in 1690. The Cassel Gallery possesses a 'Christ and the Magdalen after the Resurrection,' by him; and the Amsterdam Museum has a 'Daughter of Herodias receiving the Head of John the Baptist.' His works have occasionally been mistaken for those of Rembrandt. In the Dresden Gallery there is a profile portrait of a man in a large hat, signed 'I. V. DORSTE,' supposed to be by Drost; there are also in the same gallery, an 'Old Man teaching a Boy to read,' and 'Argus and Mercury'—both of which are ascribed to the same master.

DROUAIS, FRANÇOIS HUBERT, a French portrait painter, was born in Paris in 1727. He studied at first under his father, Hubert Drouais, and then became a pupil successively of Nonotte, Carle Van Loo, Natoire, and Boucher. He was received as an Academician in 1758 upon his portraits of the sculptors Coustou and Bouchardon, the former of which is now at Versailles, and the latter in the École des Beaux-Arts. These led to his introduction to the court, where he painted portraits of the whole of the Royal Family, and of most of the celebrities and beauties of the period. He exhibited at the Salon from 1755 to 1775, in which year he died in Paris. The Louvre has by him a picture containing the portraits of the Comte d'Artois, afterwards Charles X., and his sister, Madame Clotilde, afterwards Queen of Sardinia, when children. The Museum of Orleans possesses his charming portrait of Madame de Pompadour.

DROUAIS, HUBERT, a French portrait painter, was born at La Roque, near Pont-Audemer in Normandy, in 1699. He at first studied at Rouen,

FRANÇOIS HUBERT DROUAIS

[Collection of the Countess of Yarborough (Baroness Conyers)

AMELIA, NINTH BARONESS CONYERS

FRANÇOIS HUBERT DROUAIS

A LADY

but subsequently came to Paris, and entered the studio of De Troy, after whose death he was employed by J. B. Van Loo, A. S. Belle, Oudry, and Nattier. Besides painting portraits in oil, and in water-colours, he gained much celebrity by his miniatures. He was received into the Academy in 1730, and died in Paris in 1767.

DROUAIS, Jean Germain, the younger son of François Hubert Drouais, was born in Paris in 1763. He studied under his father and under Brenet, and then entered the school of David. In 1784 he astonished the Academy by his picture of 'Christ and the Woman of Canaan,' which gained the first prize, and is now in the Louvre. The next year he accompanied David to Rome, where he studied the works of Raphael and the antique, sending to Paris a study of a 'Wounded Gladiator,' 'Marius at Minturnae,' now in the Louvre, and 'Philoctetes breathing forth imprecations against the Gods,' which was his last work. He died of fever at Rome in 1788.

DRUEFKEN, —, a German engraver on wood, who usually marked his prints with a cluster of grapes, is mentioned by Evelyn in his 'Sculptura.' Among other cuts, he executed one representing the King of the Boors in Hungary eaten alive by the rebels whom he had duped.

DRUIVESTEYN, Aart Jansze, an amateur Dutch painter, was born at Haarlem in 1564. Van Mander speaks in very favourable terms of his talent as a painter of landscapes with figures, although, being of an opulent and distinguished family, he practised the art only for his amusement. He died in 1617.

DRUMMOND, James, a Scotch historical and genre painter, was born in Edinburgh in 1816. He studied under Sir William Allan, and first exhibited at the Scottish Academy in 1835, of which body he became an Associate in 1846, and an Academician in 1852. He became curator of the Edinburgh National Gallery in 1868, and died at Edinburgh in 1877. He studied archæology closely, and his works show great care for antiquarian details. Amongst the best are:

The Return of Mary, Queen of Scots, to Edinburgh after her surrender at Carberry Hill. *(In National Gallery of Scotland.)*
King James I. of Scotland seeing his future wife at Windsor.
The Porteous Mob.
Montrose on his way to execution.
Peace. *(Belonging to the Queen.)*
War.
Old Mortality.
Cromwell in Edinburgh.

DRUMMOND, Samuel, an English portrait and historical painter, was born in London in 1765. He studied in the Royal Academy, of which he became an Associate in 1808, and afterwards curator of the Painting School. He died in 1844. Amongst his works are:

Battle of Trafalgar.
Death of Nelson.
Admiral Duncan receiving the sword of Admiral De Winter (*Greenwich Hospital*).
Charles Mathews, the elder.
Richard Parker, leader of the Nore Mutiny.
Sir Isambard Brunel (*National Portrait Gallery*).
Mrs. Fry (*National Portrait Gallery*).

DUBBELS, Hendrik and Dirk, are mentioned by Balkema, as being found in the catalogues of Hoet and Terwesten, but without any information as to their family, or the time at which they lived. He speaks of a 'River-scene' painted in the manner of Willem van de Velde, of a 'Winter-piece with Skaters,' which was sold in 1773 under the name of Pieter Dubbels, and of another, sold in Van der Linden Slingelandt's sale, by Hendrik Dubbels. This is all he could collect among his countrymen, respecting artists who may claim rank with the best of their school as marine painters. In the incidental notices that occur of Hendrik Dubbels, he is by some called the master of Bakhuisen; by others, the scholar; the probability is in favour of the former. His works bear little or no resemblance to those of Bakhuisen or Van de Velde, except in their subjects; they are more analogous to those of Van de Capelle. In the Van der Hoop Collection at Amsterdam is one of great excellence, and many others are to be found in rich collections in this country, which fact proves that his merit has been appreciated, though, unfortunately for his reputation, it has been under a different name. There is by him in the Amsterdam Museum a 'River Scene,' and in the Copenhagen Gallery is a 'Sea-piece.'

DUBBELS, Jan, a scholar of Bakhuisen, painted marine subjects in the manner of his master; he was living in 1715. A 'Sea-piece' in the Pitti Palace, Florence, and a 'Calm Sea' in the Cassel Gallery are ascribed to him. It is not unlikely that he is identical with Hendrik Dubbels.

DUBOIS, Ambroise, was born at Antwerp in 1543. Going in 1568 to Paris, he was employed at Fontainebleau and in the Louvre, made painter in ordinary and 'varlet de chambre' to the king, and naturalized in 1601. Having been appointed painter to Mary de' Medici in 1606, he worked at the Luxembourg during her regency. Of his numerous works at Fontainebleau, only those in the chapel of St. Saturnin, the series of fifteen pictures of the 'Loves of Theagenes and Chariclea' (one of which is now in the Louvre), some of the eight subjects of 'Tancred and Clorinda,' painted for the bed-chamber of Mary de' Medici (one of which, the 'Baptism of Clorinda,' is now in the Louvre), and a few fragments on canvas, re-painted in the time of Louis Philippe, now remain. He died at Fontainebleau in 1614. Among his pupils were his two sons, Jean and Louis.

DUBOIS, B., (or Du Bois,) a French painter of landscapes and an etcher, was born about 1620, and from his etchings is supposed to have been a scholar of Claude Lorrain. Of his works, which are rare, may be mentioned, a 'Landscape with cattle,' another with a storm, and a third with a shepherd and a shepherdess.

DUBOIS, Charles, a French painter of historical landscapes, flourished in the early part of the 18th century. He was a native of Valenciennes, and executed some works for the church of St. Gery in that city. In 1734 he sent two landscapes to the 'Exposition de la Jeunesse' at Paris.

DUBOIS, Eduard, born at Antwerp in 1622, was a scholar of an obscure artist named Groenwegen. He afterwards went to Italy, and was for some time in the employment of Charles Emmanuel, Duke of Savoy. In the reign of William III. he came to England, and painted landscapes and portraits, with little success. He died in London in 1699.

DU BOIS, Elias, a native of France, was chiefly employed in engraving portraits. Among others, he engraved one of the Duke of Sully, which bears the date of 1614.

DUBOIS, ÉTIENNE JEAN, a French painter of historical subjects and portraits, was a native of Paris. He was a brother of François Dubois, and like him a pupil of Regnault. He died in Paris in 1854.

DUBOIS, FRANÇOIS, a French historical painter, was born in Paris in 1790. He studied under Regnault, and at the École des Beaux-Arts, and obtained in 1819 the 'grand prix de Rome.' Among his works may be noted the 'Annunciation' in the church of Notre-Dame de Lorette at Paris, and the 'Coronation of Pepin the Short,' and the 'Distribution of Colours to the National Guard, August 29th, 1830,' in the galleries of Versailles, the latter painted in conjunction with his brother, Étienne Dubois. There are also paintings by him in the Museums of Amiens and Angers. He died in Paris in 1871.

DUBOIS, GUILLAM, whose name has been erroneously given as CORNELIS, was born about 1622, and was registered in the Guild at Haarlem in 1646. In 1652-53 he visited Switzerland, accompanied by Cornelis Bega and others. He died at Haarlem in 1680. His pictures, which are landscapes, generally of the Rhine country, executed after the manner of Ruisdael, may be seen in several private galleries on the Continent. The Berlin Gallery and the Dulwich Gallery have each a 'View on the Rhine.'

DUBOIS, JEAN, born at Fontainebleau in 1604, a landscape painter and painter to the king, succeeded in 1635 to the office of keeper of the pictures at Fontainebleau before held by his uncle, Claude de Hoëy. This office he resigned to his son in 1674, and died at Fontainebleau in 1679. LOUIS DUBOIS, his brother, also was keeper of the pictures at Fontainebleau from 1644 to 1651, but resigned on receiving a grant of the pension of 2000 livres which had been enjoyed by Fréminet the younger, his half-brother. Jean Dubois had two sons, JEAN and LOUIS DUBOIS, born respectively in 1645 and 1646, the elder of whom succeeded to the office of keeper of the pictures which his father resigned in his favour in 1674. Jean died at Fontainebleau in 1694, and Louis at the same place in 1702.

DU BOIS, JULES CHARLES THÉODORE, a French marine painter, was born in Paris in 1804, and studied under Ary Scheffer and Eugène Isabey. There are three naval battle-pieces by him at Versailles. He was attached to the manufactory of Sèvres, and painted on porcelain and on glass. He executed nearly all the windows of the chapel at Dreux, and died in Paris in 1879.

DUBOIS, LOUIS, a Belgian painter, was born in 1830. He painted both landscapes and portraits, and occasionally genre and still-life subjects. In his style he was naturalistic in the extreme, his portraits having much of the vigorous life and colour of Frans Hals. His works are, however, very defective in drawing. He died at Brussels in 1880. The Brussels Museum possesses his picture of 'The Storks.'

DU BOIS, MARTIN, a French engraver, resided in Paris towards the close of the 17th century. He executed some of the plates for the collection of prints from the works of the Italian painters, published by C. Paten, in 1691. He also engraved frontispieces for books, after Dorigny and others.

DU BOIS, PIERRE, probably a relation of Martin Du Bois, engraved, according to Florent Le Comte, some plates of funeral processions, monuments, &c.

DUBOIS, SIMON, was the younger brother of

Eduard Dubois. After studying some time in Holland, under Philips Wouwerman, he came to England, where he painted a few pictures of battles and landscapes with cattle; but portrait painting being the only branch which was encouraged at that time, he was under the necessity of adopting it, though it was by no means suited to his genius or inclination. He painted the portrait of Lord Chancellor Somers, by whose recommendation he was employed by several of the nobility. He married the daughter of Van de Velde. His death occurred in 1708. A 'Corn-field' by him, with the forged signature of Ruisdael, is in the Lille Museum.

DUBOIS-D'AISSCHE, LOUIS, Count, was born at Edeghem near Antwerp in 1822. He was a pupil of Leys, and painted genre subjects, portraits, and landscapes. His chief works are, 'The Reader,' 'The Spinner,' and 'The Modern Eve.' He died in 1864.

DUBOIS DRAHONET, ALEXANDRE JEAN, a French portrait painter, was born in Paris in 1791. He also executed a great number of sketches of various national and military costumes, some of which are at Windsor. He died at Versailles in 1834. His portrait of the Duke of Bordeaux is in the Bordeaux Museum.

DUBOIS DUPERRAY, HONORÉ JEAN, a French historical painter, who also painted miniatures, was born at Chartres in 1770. He died at Grogneul (Eure-et-Loir) in 1857.

DUBORDIEU, PIERRE, who lived about 1650, painted portraits in the manner of Mireveldt, several of which have been engraved by Suyderhoef, Natalas, and Matham.

DUBOS, MARIE JEANNE, a French engraver, whose maiden name was Renard, was born in Paris in 1700. She was a pupil of C. Dupin, whose style she imitated, and she engraved several plates after Watteau, the younger Cochin, Robert de Séri, Rosalba, Mlle. Basseporte, and other artists. Her most popular work was 'A young Girl caressing a Rabbit,' after Mlle. Basseporte. There are several plates by her in 'Versailles immortalisé,' which appeared in 1720.

DU BOSC, CLAUDE, a French engraver, came to England about the year 1712, by the invitation of N. Dorigny, to assist him in engraving the cartoons of Raphael; but on account of some dispute, he left Dorigny, and engaged to engrave the cartoons for the printsellers. He also undertook the Duke of Marlborough's battles, and sent to Paris for Baron and Beauvais, to assist him in that undertaking, which occupied him two years. He published an English translation of Picart's 'Religious Ceremonies,' in which part of the plates were engraved by himself, and the others by Scotin and Gravelot. He engraved a plate of the 'Continence of Scipio,' after Nicolas Poussin, and others after some of the most eminent masters. His manner is coarse and heavy, and his drawing incorrect.

DU BOSC, J., was a native of France, and flourished about the year 1749. Among other prints, he engraved some plates of flowers, which are executed with the graver in a very neat style.

DUBOST, ANTOINE, a French historical painter and lithographer, who was born at Lyons in 1769, was killed in a duel in Paris in 1825.

DU BOUCHET, LOUIS FRANÇOIS. See SOURCHES.

DUBOULEAU, JEAN AUGUSTE, called DUBOULOZ, a French historical painter, born in Paris in 1800, was a pupil of Baron Gros. He also painted some portraits, and made designs for the illustration of

DUCCIO

Hanfstängl photo]

THE MADONNA AND CHILD, WITH ANGELS AND SAINTS

[National Gallery, London

the novels of Sir Walter Scott, and of several other works. He died in Paris in 1870.

DUBOURG, LODEWYK FABRICIUS, an historical painter, and an engraver, was born at Amsterdam in 1693, and died there in 1745. He was a scholar of De Lairesse and Jacob van Huysum. After producing several beautiful pictures, some of which may be seen at the Westerkerk, and the New Church at Amsterdam, he exchanged the brush for the graver, and executed some pretty vignettes and other small compositions, and also etched a number of plates from his own designs. His collection of pictures and drawings was sold at Amsterdam in 1776.

DU BOYS, HEINRICH, an historical painter of the school of Rubens, was working at Cologne up till his death in 1628. Several of the churches in that city possess pictures from his hand, as the 'Ascension of the Virgin,' 'St. Mary at the Capitol,' together with four smaller ones fixed to the pillars opposite the high altar; the 'Angel of the Annunciation,' and two small Saints, in the church of the Holy Virgin; and the 'Taking down from the Cross' (1623) in that of the Greater St. Martin.

DU BRÉUIL, TOUSSAINT, a French painter and pupil of Fréminet the elder, was born in Paris in 1561. He painted at Fontainebleau in the Pavillon des Poesles, 'Mars and Venus,' and fourteen pictures representing the 'History of Hercules,' and in the Galerie des Cerfs, thirteen bird's-eye views of royal residences. He likewise decorated the Galerie des Rois in the Louvre, but this was destroyed by fire in 1661. There are many drawings by Du Breuil in the Louvre, but all his pictures seem to have perished. He died in Paris in 1602.

DUBUFE, CLAUDE MARIE, a French historical and portrait painter, was born in Paris in 1790, and studied under David. His subjects were at first classical, and then scriptural, but his reputation rests chiefly on his portraits, of which he produced a large number. Dubufe, who was the last representative of the school of David, died at Selle-Saint-Cloud in 1864. Amongst his chief works are:

A Roman suffering starvation with his family rather than touch a sum of money entrusted to him. 1810.
Christ allaying the tempest. 1819.
Apollo and Cyparissa. 1822.
The Birth of the Duke of Bordeaux. 1824. (*Orleans Museum.*)
The Passage of the Bidassoa. 1824.
Four frescoes representing 'Egypt,' &c. (*Conseil d'État, Paris.*)
The Surprise. 1828. (*National Gallery, London.*)
Portrait of Louis Philippe.
    "   "   General Montesquiou-Fezenzac (*Versailles*).
    "   "   Nicholas Koechlin. 1841.
    "   "   the Queen of the Belgians.

DUBUFE, LOUIS ÉDOUARD, a French portrait painter, the son of Claude Marie Dubufe, was born in Paris in 1820. He was a pupil of his father and of Paul Delaroche, and made his début at the Salon of 1839, with an 'Annunciation,' and a 'Huntress.' His earlier works were mostly of a religious character, the chief of them being 'Christ's Entry into Jerusalem' (1845), and two scenes from 'Clarissa Harlowe' (1847), but from 1848 he devoted himself almost exclusively to portraiture, for which he possessed a talent like that of his father. Among his best known portraits are those of the Empress Eugénie, the Princess Mathilde, Madame Rouher, the Princess Ghika, General Fleury, the Count of Nieuwerkerke, M. Gounod, Jules Janin, Alexandre Dumas the younger, Émile Augier, and Philippe Rousseau, the painter. His large picture of the 'Congress of Paris in 1856,' now at Versailles, the 'Prodigal Son,' exhibited in the Salon of 1866, and the 'Death of Adonis,' in that of 1877, are the most important of his other works. He died at Versailles in 1883.

DUC, ANTON, who flourished in the middle of the 17th century, would, but for two or three works by him which are known, have remained in obscurity. One signed A. DUC is in the Vienna Gallery; it represents a 'Lady and Gentleman asking mercy of some infantry officers, who are plundering their house.' Another, of a similar character, is in the Dresden Gallery; it bears the monogram *L. D.* (interlaced), and represents a 'Peasant and his Wife begging for mercy of a soldier who threatens the life of the husband.' The Marquis of Bute possesses a third: a 'Guard-Room, with ladies and officers playing tric-trac.' These works are well executed in the style of Palamedes.

DUC, JACOB. See DUCK.

DUCCI, VIRGILIO, a scholar of Albani, flourished about 1660; he imitated the manner of his master, and painted in the cathedral of Città di Castello two pictures of Tobias, which are said to be executed in an elegant style.

DUCCIO, the son of Buoninsegna, was the first of the Sienese painters who abandoned the Byzantine manner. He is said to have been born about 1260, but the earliest mention of him is in 1282. He is also reported to have been a pupil of Segna di Buonaventura, but the works of the latter, and their dates, which are between 1305 and 1326, show him to have been, on the contrary, Duccio's scholar. In 1285 he made a contract with the Fraternity of Santa Maria in Florence to paint an altar-piece of the 'Virgin and Child, with Saints,' for their chapel in Santa Maria Novella, but this picture and the 'Annunciation,' which he painted for Santa Trinità in Florence, no longer exist. In 1302 he painted a 'Madonna' for the chapel of the Palazzo Pubblico of Siena, which is now lost. In 1308 he commenced his famous altar-piece for the high altar of the cathedral of Siena, which was finished and carried to its place with great ceremony in 1311. For this painting he had agreed to be paid at the daily rate of sixteen soldi, but, owing to the enormous amount of gold and ultramarine expended on it, the cost mounted up to 2000, or, as others say, 3000 gold florins. This picture was fourteen feet long, by seven feet high, and was painted on both sides—the front showing the 'Virgin and Child, surrounded by various Saints and Angels'; and the back twenty-seven subjects from the life of Christ. These latter designs were paid for by a separate contract, which is likewise preserved, at the rate of two and a half gold florins each. It has now been moved from its original position, and the two portions of which it consisted have been separated and hung "in the Gallery of the Opera del Duomo" of the cathedral. It is the only undoubted work by Duccio which remains. The date of Duccio's death is unknown, but it was probably soon after 1339. His pupils were Segna, Martini, the two Lorenzetti, and perhaps Ugolino. The following paintings are also ascribed to him:

Cologne. *Ramboux Coll.* St. John the Baptist preaching.
    "   "   Two panels: St. Peter and St. Paul.
London. *National Gall.* The Madonna and Child, with Angels; and David with six Prophets above; SS. Dominic

		and Catharine on the doors. (*A triptych*.)
Siena.	*Academy*.	Triptych—The Virgin, Child, and Saints.
„	„	Virgin and Child, with four Saints.
„	*Hospital of Santa Maria della Scala*.	Triptych—The Flagellation, The Crucifixion, The Entombment (*spoiled by restoration*).
Windsor.	*Castle*.	An Altar-piece: the Virgin and Child, the Crucifixion, and other subjects.

DUCERCEAU, JACQUES ANDROUET. See AN-DROUET-DUCERCEAU.

DUCHANGE, GASPARD, a French engraver, was born in Paris in 1662. He was a pupil first of Guillaume Vallet and afterwards of Jean Audran, and was received into the Academy in 1707. He died in Paris in 1757. Duchange may be ranked among the ablest artists of his country, particularly for the mellowness and harmony with which he has combined his etching with a tasteful management of the graver. His plates after Correggio are peculiarly expressive of the admirable style of that painter. The number of his works is considerable ; the following are the most esteemed :

PORTRAITS.

François Girardon ; *after Rigaud ;* presented for his reception into the Academy in 1707.
Charles de La Fosse, painter ; *after the same ;* presented upon the same occasion.
Antoine Coypel, with his Son ; *after a picture by himself.*

SUBJECTS AFTER VARIOUS MASTERS.

Jupiter and Io ; *after Correggio.*
Jupiter and Danaë ; *after the same.*
Jupiter and Leda ; *after the same.*
[The best impressions of the above fine prints are before the name of *Sornique*, who retouched the plates, and added draperies.]
The Entombment of Christ ; *after Paolo Veronese.*
Mary Magdalen washing the Feet of Christ *after Jouvenet.*
Christ driving the Buyers and Sellers from the Temple ; *after the same.*
The Sacrifice of Jephtha ; *after A. Coypel.*
Tobit recovering his Sight ; *after the same.*
Venus sleeping, with three Loves and a Satyr ; *after the same.*
The Death of Dido ; *after the same.*
The Bath of Diana ; *after the same.*
Solon explaining his Laws to the Athenians ; *after N. Coypel.*
Trajan dispensing Justice to the People ; *after the same.*
Diana disarming Cupid ; *after Désormeaux.*
The Birth of Mary de' Medici ; *after Rubens.*
The Landing of Mary de' Medici at Marseilles ; *after the same.*
The Marriage of Henry IV. and Mary de' Medici ; *after the same.*
The Apotheosis of Henry IV. and Regency of Mary de' Medici ; *after the same.*
The Interview of Mary de' Medici and her son, Louis XIII. ; *after the same.*

The five last plates were engraved for the Luxembourg Gallery.

DUCHATEL, FRANÇOIS, (or DU CHASTEL,) a Flemish painter, born at Brussels in 1616, is said to have been a pupil of David Teniers the younger, whose style he followed in some of his pictures, representing village festivals ; but he is more known for his small family portraits and conversations in the manner of Gonzales Coques, and his pictures are not unfrequently taken for those of that master. He is said to have worked also in

Paris in conjunction with Van der Meulen. His most considerable work is a large picture in the Museum at Ghent, representing 'The Inauguration of Charles II., King of Spain, as Count of Flanders, in 1666, in the Marché au Vendredi at Ghent ;' it is dated 1668, and has been engraved by Lucas Vorsterman. Duchatel's works are very rare : there is in the Louvre 'A Cavalier and two other persons ;' in the Museum at Avignon, 'The Interior of a Guard-House ;' in the Brussels Gallery, 'Portraits of two little Girls ;' and in the Copenhagen Gallery, 'Tric-Trac Players.' The 'Panorama of Valenciennes,' in the Antwerp Gallery, though ascribed to Teniers, is set down by some critics to Duchatel. He died in 1694.

DUCHEMIN, CATHERINE, a French flower and fruit painter, was born in Paris in 1630, and died there in 1698. She married, in 1657, the sculptor Girardon, and in 1663 was received into the Academy, being the first lady on whom this honour had been conferred.

DUCHESNE, JEAN BAPTISTE JOSEPH, known as DUCHESNE DE GISORS, a French painter of miniatures and enamels, was born at Gisors in 1770. He was the son of Jean Baptiste Duchesne, a sculptor, and a pupil of Vincent. He exhibited at first under the name of DUCHESNE, afterwards under that of DUCHESNE DES ARGILLERS, and finally, from 1833 until his death, under that of DUCHESNE DE GISORS. He died at Gisors in 1856.

DUCHESNE, NICOLAS, who was first painter to the Queen Mother, Mary de' Medici, was a mediocre painter in all but the direction of others. He was superintendent of the decorative works at Fontainebleau, where he maltreated all the artists in his charge. He died in 1627.

DUCHINO. See LANDRIANI.

DÜCHTL, MARTIN. See DICHTL.

DUCIS, LOUIS, born in Paris in 1773, was instructed by David, whom he partly imitated in his historical pieces, besides which he devoted himself also to genre and portrait painting. His 'Mary Stuart' and 'The Début of Talma' were formerly in the Luxembourg Gallery. He died in 1847.

DUCK, JACOB, a Dutch genre painter, entered the Guild of St. Luke at Utrecht in 1626. He gave a picture, representing a musical reunion, to the hospital of St. Job in that city. He painted military conversation pieces in the taste of Jan Le Ducq, but with less delicacy of touch and finish ; they are nevertheless of great beauty. His paintings are to be met with at Vienna, at Dresden, and at Christiania, where there is also an etching by him of the 'Adoration of the Kings.' Many writers state that this artist was the father of Jan Le Ducq, but this is extremely doubtful, as well by reason of the variation in the name, as by the fact that Jan Le Ducq is known to have been born at Haarlem in 1636, whereas Jacob Duck resided constantly at Utrecht from 1626 to 1646.

DUCORNET, LOUIS CÉSAR JOSEPH, a French historical painter, was born of poor parentage at Lille, in 1806. He was deformed from his birth, having neither arms nor thighs, and only four toes to his right foot. While still a child, he used to pick up pieces of charcoal from the floor with his toes, and made rough sketches on the wall, which evinced so much promise that he received some local instruction. By the help of the municipality of Lille, he was sent to Paris, studied under Lethière and Gérard, and for a time received a pension. He died in Paris in 1856. His chief pictures are :

Repentance. 1828.
The Parting of Hector and Andromache. (*Lille Museum.*)
St. Louis administering Justice. (*Lille Museum.*)
Death of Mary Magdalen. 1840. (*St. André, Lille.*)
The Repose in Egypt. 1841.
Christ in the Sepulchre. 1843.
Edith finding the body of Harold. 1855.

DUCORRON, JULES, a Belgian landscape painter, was born at Ath in 1770. At the age of thirty-two, he devoted himself to the art of painting under the direction of Ommeganck, and made marvellous progress as a landscape painter, obtaining several gold medals. He was afterwards director of the Academy at Ath, where he died in 1848. The Brussels Museum has by him a 'View in the neighbourhood of Irchonwelz, near Chièvres, Hainault,' and a 'Gale of Wind at Sunset.'

DUCQ, JAN LE. See LE DUCQ.

DUCQ, JOSEPHUS FRANCISCUS, a Flemish historical and portrait painter, was born at Ledeghem in 1763. He studied at Bruges, and then under Suvée in Paris, where he obtained the second grand prize in 1800, and a medal in 1810. He also spent a considerable time in Italy, but returned to Bruges in 1815, and became a professor in the Academy. He died at Bruges in 1829. Amongst his chief works are:

Meleager. 1804.
Devotion of a Scythian. 1810.
Marriage of Angelica and Medora. 1812.
Venus emerging from the Sea. (*Brussels Museum.*)
William I., King of the Netherlands. (*Bruges Academy.*)
Van Gierdergom. (*Bruges Academy.*)

DUCREUX, JOSEPH, a French portrait painter, was born at Nancy in 1737. He engraved his own portrait in three different characters, which were published in London in 1791, but he died in Paris in the same year.

DUCROS, PIERRE, a Swiss landscape painter in oil and water-colours, and an engraver, was born in 1748. He lived for a considerable time at Rome, and painted views of that city and its environs. He executed in a masterly manner twenty-four views of Sicily and Malta, besides numerous drawings made during his sojourn in Italy, some of which are of large dimensions. He died at Lausanne in 1810.

DUDERSTADT, HEINRICH VON, is said to have painted in the church of the Paulines at Göttingen, in 1424, the large altar-piece which is now in the library of that church. It represents scenes from the life of the Virgin and the Passion, and is signed, *frater Hs. Dudstadens.*

DUDLEY, THOMAS, an English engraver, was born about the year 1634. He was a pupil of Hollar, and though greatly inferior to that celebrated artist, his prints are not without considerable merit. He engraved a set of twenty-seven plates for Barlow's 'Life of Æsop,' published in 1687, as well as the following portraits:

Richard Russell, Bishop of Portalegre.
James Sharpe, Bishop of St. Andrew's.
Titus Oates.

DUETECUM, BAPTISTA, (or DOETECHUM,) who flourished from about 1614 to 1646, was probably a son of either Joannes or Lucas van Duetecum. He engraved a set of plates representing the various habits and manners of the Indians. They are executed entirely with the graver, in a stiff, indifferent style.

DUETECUM, JOANNES and LUCAS VAN, (or DOETECHUM,) who flourished respectively from about 1559 to 1585 and 1596, were natives of Holland, and are supposed to have been brothers. They etched conjointly, in a bold masterly manner, several large prints, representing the pompous funeral of the Emperor Charles V.

DU FAUR, CHRISTIAN WILHELM VON FABER. See FABER DU FAUR.

DUFFEIT, GERAERT. See DOUFFET.

DUFFIELD, WILLIAM, a painter of flowers, fruit, and still-life, was born at Bath in 1816. He studied under George Lance, and afterwards in the schools of the Royal Academy, and under Wappers at Antwerp. His early works were portraits, but in 1849 he sent to the Royal Academy a fruit-piece, his first exhibited work, and continued to exhibit there and at the Society of British Artists a number of pictures of a very high degree of excellence. He settled in London in 1857, and died there in 1863. He married, in 1850, MARY ELIZABETH ROSENBERG, of Bath, who is well known as a water-colour painter of flowers, birds' nests, and fish.

DUFLOS, CLAUDE, a French engraver, was born in Paris about 1662, and died in the same city in 1727. It is not known by whom he was instructed, but his style resembles that of François Poilly. We have by this artist a great number of plates, executed principally with the graver, and very neatly finished. The following are the most deserving of notice:

PORTRAITS.

Philip, Duke of Orleans; *after R. Tournières.*
Jean François Paul de Gondy, Cardinal de Retz.
Denis François de Chavigny, Bishop of Troyes.
Nicolas Lyon, Procureur du Roi; *after Herluyson.*
Jean Jacques Gaudart, Conseiller du Roi; *after Largillière.*
Marc René de Voyer; *after Hyacinthe Rigaud.*

SUBJECTS AFTER VARIOUS MASTERS.

The Entombment of Christ; *after P. Perugino;* for the Crozat Collection.
The same subject; *after Raphael.*
St. Michael discomfiting the Evil Spirit; *after the same;* for the Crozat Collection.
Christ with the Disciples at Emmaus; *after Paolo Veronese;* for the Crozat Collection.
The Adulteress before Christ; *after N. Colombel.*
Christ at table with the Disciples; *after Titian.*
Bust of the Virgin; *after Guido.*
The Annunciation; *after Albani.*
Christ appearing to Mary Magdalen; *after the same.*
St. Cecilia; *after P. Mignard.*
The Presentation in the Temple; *after Le Sueur.*
The Descent from the Cross; *after the same.*
The Murder of the Innocents; *after Le Brun.*
Christ on the Mount of Olives; *after the same.*
The Crucifixion; *after the same.*
The same subject; *after the same;* from the print by *Edelinck.*
The Dead Christ, with the Virgin and St. John; *after the same.*
The Descent of the Holy Ghost; *after the same.*
The Assumption of the Virgin; *after the same.*
The Penitent Magdalen; *after the same.*
The Annunciation; *after A. Coypel.*
The Crucifixion; *after the same.*
The Magdalen at the foot of the Cross; *after the same.*
A Concert; *after Domenichino.*
The Triumph of Galatea; *after the same.*
Cupid stung by a Bee; *after the same.*
The same subject; smaller and circular.
Bacchus and Ariadne; *after the same.*
The Triumph of Bacchus; *after C. Natoire.*
The Triumph of Amphitrite; *after the same.*

DUFLOS, CLAUDE AUGUSTIN, the son of Claude Duflos, and, like his father, an engraver, was born in 1700. He is supposed to have died in 1784 or 1785.

DUFLOS, FRANÇOIS PHILOTHÉE, a painter and engraver, was born in Paris about 1710. He studied under De Troy, gained the 'prix de Rome' in 1729, lived for some time in Italy, and in 1740 painted his own portrait for the Uffizi. He died at Lyons in 1746.

DU FOUR, N., was a native of France, who flourished about the year 1760. Among other prints, he engraved several small plates after Weirotter and other masters.

DU FRESNE, CHARLES, a French engraver, executed some copies of the works of Callot and Albrecht Dürer, besides a few other plates, among which was 'The Interview between St. Nilus and the Emperor Otho III.,' after Domenichino. He flourished from about 1791 to the early years of the 19th century.

DU FRESNOY, CHARLES ALPHONSE, is perhaps more celebrated for his poem on the art, than for his merit as a painter. Born in Paris in 1611, he was destined by his father, who was an apothecary, to the practice of physic, and, with that intention, he received the best education possible. His progress in his studies was more than usually promising; he soon became well versed in the classics, and at an early period of his life showed a marked genius for poetry. His love of painting was not less conspicuous; and when he was eighteen years of age he placed himself under the tuition of François Perrier, and afterwards entered the school of Simon Vouet. After studying under these masters for about three years, he formed the project of visiting Italy, although without any other resources than what he could derive from the exercise of his talent. On his arrival at Rome, his first attempts were views of the buildings and architectural ruins in the vicinity of that city, which, though not without merit, he had great difficulty in introducing to public notice. He languished at Rome for two years, in indigence and obscurity, when Pierre Mignard, who had been his fellow-student under Vouet, arrived there. The meeting of the young friends was most cordial, and from that moment an attachment sprang up which existed during the remainder of their lives. Mignard, who was the more successful, divided with his friend his earnings; and although he possessed greater facility than Du Fresnoy, he was frequently assisted by the counsels of his friend, and his perfect acquaintance with the theory of the art, of which he has given ample proof in his poem, 'De Arte Graphica.' The Cardinal of Lyons employed them in copying the works of Annibale Carracci, in the Farnese gallery; and they were most assiduous in their studies after Raphael and the antique. Félibien has given a particular account of his works at Rome, of which the following are the principal: 'The Ruins of Campo Vaccino;' 'A young Athenian visiting the Tomb of her Lover;' 'The filial Piety of Æneas;' 'Mars finding Lavinia sleeping on the Banks of the Tiber,' one of his best pictures; 'The Birth of Venus,' and 'The Birth of Cupid.' In 1653 he left Rome to return to France, by way of Venice, where he was so struck with the works of Titian, that he wrote to his friend to rejoin him in that city, and there he remained eighteen months, profiting greatly by his studies. In 1656 he returned to Paris, where he painted, among other works, a picture of 'St. Margaret,' for the church

96

dedicated to that saint, a saloon in the Château Raincy, and four landscapes in the Hôtel d'Hervart, afterwards the Hôtel des Postes, in which the figures were painted by Mignard. The remainder of his life was employed in preparing for publication his poem, which, however, did not appear until three years after his death. He died at Villiers-le-Bel, near Paris, in 1665. There are in public galleries the following paintings by him:

Paris. *Louvre.* St. Margaret.
   ,,   ,, Naïads.
Vienna. *Czernin Coll.* The Vision of Alcmene.

DUGGAN, PETER PAUL, a native of Ireland, went while quite young to America. He afterwards returned to England, and resided for some years near London, but died in Paris in 1861. He painted portraits in oil, but more often worked in crayons.

DUGHET, GASPARD, (commonly called GASPARD POUSSIN, or LE GUASPRE,) was born at Rome in 1613. His parents were French subjects, who had settled in the Eternal City. They appear to have been people of a kindly disposition, for about 1629 they received into their house their fellow-countryman, Nicolas Poussin, then a lonely and friendless student in Rome, and nursed him tenderly through a dangerous illness. This friendship brought about the great painter's marriage with a daughter of his hosts. Nay more, Poussin, seeing the inclination of the young Gaspard towards art, took him as his pupil, and for three years carefully superintended his instruction. Dughet owed much to the solid foundation thus laid by his brother-in-law, and he ever proved himself a most devoted disciple. He was fond of hunting, fishing, and out-door sports, and did not fail to profit by the opportunities thus afforded him of studying nature, and enriching his knowledge of her ever-changing aspects. After leaving Poussin's studio, his independent nature led him, though scarcely yet twenty, to set up for himself; and the progress he made in his art soon brought patronage.

He spent a year at Perugia and Castiglione with the Duke della Cornia, who treated him with great consideration, and escorted him back to Rome at the conclusion of his visit. With another patron he made a trip to Milan, and after a severe illness the Duke della Cornia took him away again for the recovery of his health, and procured him many commissions. This trip was followed by visits to Florence, where he painted some decorative works at the Pitti Palace, and to Naples, before he once more settled down in Rome.

This point may be said to mark the conclusion of the first period of Dughet's art, during which the works produced by him are to be distinguished by a coldness and certain want of freedom. He now came under the influence of Claude Lorrain, at this time in the zenith of his fame at Rome. The study of his works had a most beneficial effect on Dughet, and to it is due the warmth and mastery over light and air observable in the works of his maturer period. He never married, and with the exception of time given to sport and social pleasures—he was not a hermit-bachelor, but loved the society of genial spirits—his life was devoted to the pursuit of his art. The better to enable him to study the scenery of Rome and his loved Campagna, from which the subjects of the majority of his pictures were taken, he had four houses at which he spent his time: two in elevated situations in Rome itself, one at Tivoli, and another at Frascati. The facility of execution which he acquired was marvellous, and he is said to have required only one day to finish a large picture. Hence his works are almost innumerable, and specimens are found in nearly all the public and private collections of Europe. Besides easel works, he found time also to execute in fresco subjects from the life of the prophet Elias at the Carmelite Church of San Martino ai Monti at Rome. His finest works are in the Doria Palace, and others are in the Colonna and Borghese Palaces. It should not be forgotten that he received much assistance from his brother-in-law, from Pietro da Cortona, from Filippo Lauri, and from many others, in the figures introduced into his compositions; but this consideration is in no way sufficient to remove the feeling of surprise at his wonderful fertility. Amongst his pupils, the chief names are those of Crescenzio di Onofrio, Vincentio, and Jacques De Rooster of Mechlin. During his life he had saved 30,000 Roman crowns; but his generous habits, and an illness of two years before his death, which took place at Rome in 1675, did not leave more than sufficient to provide for his honourable burial.

In a brief summary of Dughet's characteristics, his partiality for quiet lights should first be mentioned. He excels in the representation of effects before sunrise, and in the reproduction of the peaceful tones of evening. But his great strength lies in the portrayal of tempests. D'Argenville observes that no painter before him had been able to reproduce the effects of wind and storm in his pictures: the leaves seem to move, and the trees cease to be inanimate objects under his brush. His works now convey an impression of great grandeur and solemnity, and this sombreness has probably increased in the course of years by his predilection for painting on a dark ground.

The drawings which he left are very finished in execution: some are outlined with the pen, and tinted with bistre or Indian ink: others are drawn with the pencil and touched up with white, or occasionally with black. There are also eight etchings by him, four of which are oval, inscribed with the Italian form of his name, *Gasparo Duche inv. sc. Romae*, or *G.D.s.*, or *Gasp. Dughet sculpsit.*

The following is a list of some of the pictures by which he is represented in the chief collections of Europe:

ENGLISH GALLERIES.

Belvoir Castle.	Christ and the Disciples going to Emmaus.
	Two other Landscapes.
" "	St. Jerome.
Brocklesby Park.	Five other Landscapes.
Cambridge. *Fitz-william Museum.*	Landscape.
Castle Howard.	Three Landscapes.
Chatsworth House.	Five Landscapes.
Clumber Park.	Three Landscapes.
Corsham House.	Landscape, Storm.
Dulwich. *Gallery.*	Destruction of Niobe.
" "	Conversion of St. Paul.
" "	Three other Landscapes.
Edinburgh. *Nat. Gal.*	Land Storm.
Hampton Court. *Palace.*	Christ's Agony in the Garden.
" "	The Angels appearing to the Shepherds.
Isleworth. *Sion House.*	Two Landscapes.
Knowsley Hall.	Two Landscapes.
London. *National Gal.*	Abraham and Isaac.
" "	Dido and Æneas.
" "	Four other Landscapes.

London.	*Bridgewater House.*	A Storm.
		Three other Landscapes.
"	*Buckingham Palace.*	Landscape.
"	*Grosvenor House.*	View of Tivoli and the Temple of the Sybil.
		Two other Landscapes.
"	*Dorchester House.*	Four Landscapes.
"	*Stafford House.*	Landscape.
"	*Hertford House.*	View of Tivoli.
"	*Bath House.*	Landscape.
Longford Castle.		Two Landscapes.
Osterley Park.		Four Landscapes.
Panshanger House.		Two Landscapes.
Petworth House.		One Landscape.
Wardour Castle.		Two Landscapes.
Welbeck Abbey.		Landscape.
Wilton House.		Landscape.
Windsor.	*Castle.*	Jonah (*figures by N. Poussin*).
"	"	Landscape, known as "Solitude."
"	"	Two other Landscapes.
Woburn Abbey.		Four Landscapes.

FOREIGN GALLERIES.

Ajaccio.	*Museum.*	Two Landscapes.
Avignon.	*Museum.*	Four Landscapes.
Basle.	*Museum.*	Three Landscapes.
Berlin.	*Gallery.*	Italian Landscape.
Bordeaux.	*Museum.*	Two Landscapes.
Cassel.	*Gallery.*	Three Landscapes.
Cherbourg.	*Museum.*	One Landscape.
Dijon.	*Museum.*	Alpheus and Arethusa.
		Apollo and the Cumæan Sybil.
Dresden.	*Gallery.*	View on a Lake.
		Three other Landscapes.
Florence.	*Uffizi.*	The Fishermen.
"	*Pitti Pal.*	Several Landscapes.
Gotha.	*Gallery.*	Landscape.
Hague.	*Museum.*	Landscape.
Lausanne.	*Arlaud Mus.*	Three Landscapes.
Lille.	*Museum.*	One Landscape.
Lyons.	*Museum.*	Hagar.
Madrid.	*Gallery.*	St. Jerome.
"	"	St. Mary Magdalen before the Cross.
		Five other Landscapes.
Milan.	*Pinacoteca.*	St. John the Baptist as a child.
Montpellier.	*Museum.*	Apollo and Daphne.
"	"	Temple of the Sybil at Tivoli.
		Nine other Landscapes.
Munich.	*Gallery.*	Temple of the Sybil at Tivoli.
"	"	Mountainous Landscape.
		One other Landscape.
Nantes.	*Museum.*	Three Landscapes.
Narbonne.	*Museum.*	Landscape.
Nismes.	*Museum.*	Landscape.
Oldenburg.	*Gallery.*	Landscape.
Paris.	*Louvre.*	A Landscape.
Petersburg.	*Hermitage.*	Five Landscapes.
Puy.	*Museum.*	Flight into Egypt.
		One other Landscape.
Quimper.	*Museum.*	Finding of Moses.
Rome.	*Barberini Palace.*	Three Landscapes.
"	*Borghese Pal.*	Several Landscapes.
"	*Colonna Pal.*	Several Landscapes.
"	*Corsini Pal.*	Several Landscapes.
"	*Doria Palace.*	St. Mary of Egypt.
"	"	Mercury.
"	"	A Forest.
"	"	The Flight into Egypt.
"	"	St. Augustine on the sea-shore with an Angel.
Stockholm.	*Gallery.*	Death of Adonis.
"	"	Temple of the Sybil at Tivoli.
"	"	View of Nemi.
		Seven other Landscapes.
Turin.	*Gallery.*	The Cascades of Tivoli.
Venice.	*Academy.*	Landscapes.
Vienna.	*Gallery.*	The Tomb of Cæcilia Metella.
"	"	A Landscape.
"	"	A Wooded Landscape.

Vienna.	Archduke Albrecht's Gal.	Landscape.
"	Liechtenstein Gallery.	Three Landscapes.
"	Harrach Gallery.	Landscape.
"	Czernin Gallery.	Two Landscapes. O. J. D.

DUGHET, JEAN, a brother of Gaspard Dughet, was born at Rome in 1614, and studied under Nicolas Poussin, after whose works he engraved. He died in 1676. Of his prints the following are the most worthy of notice:

The Seven Sacraments; from the pictures painted by *Nicolas Poussin* for the Cavaliere del Pozzo, differing from those formerly in the Orleans collection.
Mount Parnassus; *after the same.*
The Birth of Bacchus; *after the same.*
The Judgment of Solomon; *after the same.*

DU GUERNIER FAMILY.

Louis (1550—ab. 1620).
|
Alexandre (fl. ab. 1600).
|
Louis (1614—1659). Alexandre (d. 1655). Pierre (1624—1674).

DU GUERNIER, ALEXANDRE, the elder, son of Louis Du Guernier the elder, and like him a painter of portraits and miniatures, flourished about the year 1600. His portraits, equal to those of his father, are rare and much sought after. Being a Protestant, he went abroad in consequence of the revocation of the Edict of Nantes, and died in exile.

DU GUERNIER, ALEXANDRE, the younger, a landscape painter, was a younger son of Alexandre Du Guernier the elder. He died in Paris in 1655, being cut short in a career of great promise.

DU GUERNIER, LOUIS, the elder, a French miniature painter, born in 1550, executed numerous drawings for books of hours and breviaries, as well as portraits of many of the most noted persons of his time. He painted for the Duke of Guise a book of prayers, in which the ladies of the court were represented with the attributes usually given to the saints. He ordinarily worked on vellum, stippling without making use of white. He died about 1620.

DU GUERNIER, LOUIS, the younger, the eldest son of Alexandre Du Guernier the elder, was born in Paris in 1614. He was added to the foundation members of the Royal Academy of Painting in 1651, became professor in 1655, and died in Paris in 1659. His sister, Susanne, married the celebrated historical painter, Sébastien Bourdon.

DU GUERNIER, LOUIS, a French engraver, was born in Paris in 1677, and came to England in 1708. He assisted Du Bosc in engraving the battles of the Duke of Marlborough, and executed some illustrations to the works of Spenser and Gay. He died in 1716.

DU GUERNIER, PIERRE, who was considered the best enamel painter of his day, was a younger son of Alexandre Du Guernier the elder. He was born in Paris in 1624, became an academician in 1663, and died in Paris in 1674. His portraits are distinguished by a freshness and brilliancy of colour, afterwards surpassed by Petitot alone.

DUGY, ——, a French engraver, flourished about the year 1760. He engraved several slight prints, after the works of François Boucher and other masters.

DU HAMEEL, ALART, a goldsmith and engraver of the 15th century, is known by a plate of 'The Last Judgment,' after Jerom Bosch, and a 'Church Tabernacle.'

98

DU HAMEL, A. B., a French engraver, flourished about 1760. He resided in Paris, and was employed chiefly by the booksellers in engraving book-plates and portraits, among the latter being those of Jolyot de Crébillon and Jean Jacques Rousseau.

DUIVEN, JAN, born at Gouda in 1600, was a scholar of Wouter Crabeth, and had a great reputation as a portrait painter. He died in 1640.

DU JARDIN, KAREL, was born probably at Amsterdam about 1625. He was a pupil of Nicolaas Berchem, and was unquestionably the ablest scholar of that celebrated master. His progress was extraordinary, and to perfect himself he travelled to Italy when he was still very young. On his arrival at Rome he was received into the Bentevogel Society, where the title of 'Barbe de Bouc' was conferred on him. His studies were assiduous and constant, and his pictures acquired estimation in Rome, where they were admired beyond those of any artist of his country. After a residence of several years at Rome, where his pictures were not less admired than they had been in Italy, and he met with great success. Notwithstanding this flattering encouragement, his desire of revisiting Italy was so great that he left home for Venice, where he died in 1678. The pictures of Du Jardin are more conformable to the taste of Italy than to that of Holland, and they generally exhibit a warmth and brilliancy of atmosphere, with clear and sparkling skies. His landscapes are always pleasing in their scenery, and they are decorated with charming figures and animals, in which, to the truth and finish of Paul Potter, he unites a taste which is not found in the works of that celebrated cattle painter. As he died young, and his pictures are highly wrought up, they are scarce, and very valuable. The following are some of the best:

Berlin.	Museum.	Young man tasting wine. 1664.
"	"	Morning. } Italian Landscapes.
"	"	Evening. }
Bordeaux.	Museum.	Landscape and Animals.
Brussels.	Museum.	The Advance Guard. 1652.
"	"	The Return to the shed.
Cassel.	Gallery.	Charlatans.
Copenhagen.	Gallery.	Allegory. 1663.
Dresden.	Gallery.	Diogenes and the Boy who drinks with his hand.
"	"	Maid milking a Goat.
"	"	Ox and Goats in a Landscape.
Dulwich.	Gallery.	Smith shoeing an Ox.
"	"	Peasants in a Landscape.
Edinburgh.	Gallery.	Halt of Horsemen.
"	"	Farrier's Shop.
Hague.	Gallery.	Cascade in Italy. 1673.
"	"	The Spinner.
Lille.	Museum.	Pasturage.
London.	Bute Coll.	Fording a Stream.
"	"	Tobit and the Angel.
Paris.	Louvre.	Calvary. 1661.
"	"	Italian Charlatans. 1657.
"	"	The Ford.
"	"	The Pasturage.
"	"	The Grove. 1646.
"	"	Landscape and Animals. 1660.
"	"	Portrait of a Man. 1657.
Petersburg.	Hermitage.	Seven Landscapes.
Vienna.	Gallery.	Herdsman and Cattle.

He left about fifty-two admirable etchings of landscapes, figures, and animals, which are executed with uncommon taste and spirit. They are sometimes signed with his name at length, at other times with his initials or with a monogram.

KAREL DU JARDIN

LANDSCAPE WITH CATTLE REPOSING

KAREL DU JARDIN

Hanfstängl photo]

MOUNTAIN PASTURE SCENE, WITH CATTLE

[Buckingham Palace

DUJARDIN, LOUIS, a French engraver on wood, was born at Rouen in 1808, and died in Paris in 1859. He executed some of the illustrations to Charles Blanc's 'Histoire des Peintres.'

DULIN, PIERRE. See ULIN, PIERRE D'.

DULLAERT, HEINMAN, a Dutch painter, was born at Rotterdam in 1636. He was the son of a dealer in pictures, and having shown an early inclination for art, he was placed in the school of Rembrandt. Under that able instructor his progress was such, that in a few years some of his small pictures were painted so much in the style of his master as to be mistaken for Rembrandt's own. He generally painted cabinet pictures of historical subjects and portraits, which were deservedly admired for harmony of colour, a vigorous touch, and a masterly effect of light and shade. He died at Rotterdam in 1684.

DULONG, JEAN LOUIS, a French historical and portrait painter, was born at Astaffort (Lot-et-Garonne) in 1800. He was a pupil of Gros and of Abel de Pujol, and died in Paris in 1868.

DU MAURIER, GEORGE LOUIS PALMELLA BUSSON, humorous artist, was born in Paris in 1831. His mother was English, and his father, a son of French émigrés settled in London, was a naturalized British subject. Charming memories of his childhood and boyhood, spent chiefly at Passy with his parents, and at a Paris school, are to be found, charmingly illustrated, in the three novels, 'Peter Ibbetson,' 'Trilby,' and 'The Martian,' which won him an entirely new kind of fame in the closing years of his life. At the age of twenty he began the study of chemistry at University College, London, setting up shortly afterwards as an analytical chemist in Bucklersbury. But he had found his true vocation in 1856, and after some years of study in the Latin Quarter, and at Antwerp, in the studio of Van Lerius (where he gradually lost the use of his left eye, a lifelong misfortune), he returned to London, and in 1860 submitted a sketch to 'Punch,' which immediately won him the favour of its editor, Mark Lemon. Critics are agreed that Du Maurier's art was at its best during the next ten years. Excellent specimens of his work for 'Once a Week' and 'The Cornhill,' to both of which periodicals he was a regular contributor during this period, are given by Mr. Gleeson White in his 'English Illustrators of the Sixties.' Many of his most characteristic drawings were done for books, beginning with an edition of 'Fox's Book of Martyrs,' published in 1865. In 1866 he illustrated Mrs. Gaskell's 'Wives and Daughters'; in 1867, Jerrold's 'Story of a Feather'; in 1868, Owen Meredith's 'Lucile,' 'The Book of Drawing-Room Plays,' by H. Dalton, and 'Sooner or Later,' by C. A. G. Brooke; and in 1869, Thackeray's 'Esmond,' to which he added some additional vignettes ten years later, when he also illustrated Thackeray's 'Ballads.' He attained his highest level perhaps in some of his drawings for 'Esmond'; but whatever must be admitted in regard to his work for 'Punch,' there is little appreciable falling-off in his book illustrations in the seventies and eighties. In 1874 he illustrated Mr. C. W. Scott's 'Round about our Islands,' and Mr. G. E. Sargent's 'Hurlock Chase'; in 1876, 'Songs of many Seasons,' by J. Brown; in 1877, 'The Ingoldsby Legends' (in collaboration), and 'Pegasus Re-saddled,' by H. C. Pennell; in 1882, 'Prudence,' by L. C. Lillie; in 1889, 'As in a Looking-glass,' by F. C.

Phillips; and in 1891, 'Luke Ashleigh,' by A. Elwes. 'Peter Ibbetson,' 'Trilby,' and 'The Martian,' after appearing serially in 'Harper's,' were published in volume form, respectively, in 1892, 1894, 1897. In the same year, a collection of full-page drawings which he had contributed to 'Harper's' month by month, was republished under the title 'English Society,' with an appreciative introduction by Mr. W. H. Howells.

It was in 1865 that Du Maurier joined the staff of 'Punch' regularly as Leech's successor in the field of social satire, devoting himself chiefly, by Mark Lemon's advice, to the "light and graceful business," but with occasional excursions into the fields (outside Leech's province) of the *macabre* and the grotesque. In temperament, if not in technique, the two artists had much in common. While Charles Keene's mirth-provoking characters seldom arouse in one feelings either of love or hate—hardly even of like or dislike—Leech's pages, as Du Maurier himself remarked, "teem with winning, graceful, loveable types"; with "here and there a hateful one to give relief." This is equally true of Du Maurier's own work. There is feeling as well as fun in it; sympathy as well as satire. To a far greater degree than Leech, he is a critic, not merely a spectator, of life; the philosopher is as strong in him as the artist. It would be an injustice to him, therefore, to write only of his craftsmanship. Undoubtedly his 'Punch' drawings, in course of time, lost something of their first freshness and simplicity, and became mannered and machine-made, but, at his worst, one may fairly apply to him another of his own judgments upon Leech: "If he shines more by what he has to say than by his manner of saying it, perhaps that is the better thing of the two to shine by if you cannot shine by both." There may be too much cross-hatching in the representation of Sir Pompey Bedell's dress-clothes, but Sir Pompey himself, and Sir Gorgius Midas, and Mrs. Ponsonby de Tomkyns, will live for ever. The flaws in Du Maurier's craftsmanship are flaws, moreover, that are visible to experts alone. They are like the solecisms of construction and slips of grammar which for the too sensitive literary critic mar the masterpieces of Thackeray and Sir Walter Scott.

As a bachelor Du Maurier lived in lodgings in Bloomsbury with his friend Lionel Henley, afterwards A.R.A. In 1862 he married Miss Emma Wightwick, and settled down in a house near Hampstead Heath. His 'Punch' drawings reflect pleasantly the nature of his life—his active participation in all the functions of London Society, his own happy home and his holidays at Whitby and Scarborough, Boulogne and Dieppe. His faculty for hitting off the characteristics of racial types, one of his most distinctive gifts as an artist, is particularly noticeable in his various representations of life abroad; his Americans are almost his only failures. In 1881 he was elected a member of the Royal Society of Painters in Water-Colours, to whose exhibitions he had been contributing from time to time. In 1885 took place the first exhibition of his works at the Fine Arts Society. He died on October 8, 1896, and was buried in the Hampstead Cemetery. (See also under KEENE.)
F. W. W.

DU MESNIL, LOUIS MICHEL, a French historical painter, became in 1750 professor at the Academy of St. Luke at Rome. He painted the

'Visitation of the Virgin' for the church of St. Jean-en-Grève at Paris, and one of the 'Beatitudes' in the chapel of M. Turgot. A picture of his, 'Belle, quel est votre dessein?' was engraved by C. Dupuis. His son, PIERRE LOUIS DU MESNIL, who was born in 1698, and died in Paris in 1781, was also professor at the Academy of St. Luke, of which he became rector. He usually painted subjects of every-day life, some of which have been engraved.

DU MONSTIER, DANIEL, (DU MOUSTIER, or DU MOUTIER), the best known of his family, was born in Paris in 1574. He was the son of Cosme and grandson of Geoffroy Du Monstier, and worked in crayons and pastels at the courts of Francis I., Henry IV., and Louis XIII., executing portraits of all the most distinguished personages of his time. His master is unknown, but as his style resembles that of Primaticcio, he probably studied under one of the Italians at the court of Francis I. He died in Paris in 1646. NICOLAS DU MONSTIER, a son of Daniel, followed in his father's footsteps. He was born in Paris in 1612, was received into the Academy in 1665, and died in 1667.

DU MONSTIER, GEOFFROY, a French miniature painter, born early in the 16th century, and still living in 1547, was much employed at Fontainebleau by Il Rosso. He likewise painted upon glass, and etched several plates which are described in Robert-Dumesnil's 'Peintre-Graveur Français,' vol. v. He is supposed to have painted in grisaille the following miniatures in manuscripts: 'Francis I. conversing with Julius Cæsar,' in the British Museum, and 'The Triumph of Petrarch,' in the Library of the Arsenal at Paris.

DUMONT, JACQUES, called LE ROMAIN, on account of a long sojourn which he made at Rome, was born about 1700. He was an historical and genre painter, whose best work was his picture of 'Hercules and Omphale,' which he painted for his reception at the Academy in 1728, but he had more reputation than talent. Some of his works were engraved by his contemporaries. His drawing and composition are good, but his colour is mediocre. He died in Paris in 1781.

DU MOUSTIER. See DU MONSTIER.

DUNCAN, EDWARD, a water-colour painter, was born in London in 1803. He was articled to Robert Havell, the aquatint engraver, and was thus afforded frequent opportunities of studying, and occasionally of copying, the works of William Havell. These developed his taste for drawing and the use of colour, and in 1831 he became a member of the New Society of Painters in Water-Colours, but he afterwards withdrew, and in 1849 was elected an Associate of the Society of Painters in Water-Colours, and a full member in the following year. He died in London in 1882. His drawings comprise a wide range of subjects, treated with much grace and great truthfulness to nature, but his larger and more important works are chiefly coast scenery, with shipping and craft admirably characterized. Among the best of them are the following:

The Shipwreck. 1859.
The Life-Boat. 1860.
Blue Lights.
Oyster Dredgers—Swansea Bay.
Landing Fish on the Sands at Whitby.
Fishing Boats making for the Harbour of Boulogne— early morning.

DUNCAN, THOMAS, was born in 1807, at Kinclaven, in Perthshire, but was educated at Perth, whither his parents had removed shortly after his birth. He showed very early signs of a peculiar faculty by employing every moment in drawing such objects as struck his fancy, especially the portraits of his young companions; and while still at school he painted the whole of the scenery for a dramatic representation of 'Rob Roy,' which he and his schoolfellows performed in a stable-loft. His parents, however, considered this use of his pencil an unprofitable waste of time, and placed him in the office of a law-writer. Released in time from the drudgery of the desk, and more than ever desirous of accomplishing his favourite object, he at length procured the consent of his father to his visiting Edinburgh, where he was placed under the able instruction of Sir William Allan, then master of the Trustees' Academy for the study of art, an establishment endowed by Government. Duncan's talent, fostered and directed by such a master, speedily developed itself, and he made rapid progress in the drawing of the human figure. The first picture which brought him into general notice was his 'Milkmaid'; and shortly after he exhibited his 'Old Mortality' and 'The Bra' Wooer.' He was appointed, at an unusually early age, to one of the professorships—that of colour—at the newly-established Royal Scottish Academy, and subsequently, on the death of Allan, to the well-endowed mastership of the Trustees' Academy. In 1840 he sent to the Royal Academy his fine work, 'Prince Charles Edward and the Highlanders entering Edinburgh after the Battle of Preston Pans.' This picture brought the painter at once into most favourable notice. In 1841 Duncan exhibited a most touching picture from the ballad of 'Auld Robin Gray,' termed 'The Waefu' Heart' (now in the Sheepshanks Collection in the South Kensington Museum); in the following year, 'Deer-stalking'; and in 1843, 'Charles Edward asleep after the Battle of Culloden, protected by Flora MacDonald.' In 1844 Duncan exhibited 'Cupid,' and 'The Martyrdom of John Brown of Priesthill, in 1685.' This, which is now in the Corporation Galleries at Glasgow, was the last picture by the artist exhibited in London, excepting a portrait of himself, which, to the honour of his Scottish professional brethren, was purchased by subscription, and presented by them to the Royal Scottish Academy. Duncan was elected an Academician of the Royal Scottish Academy in 1830, and an Associate of the Royal Academy in 1843, but he did not long survive the latter honour, as he died at Edinburgh in 1845. Had his life been prolonged, there is no question but that he would have achieved a lofty position in historical painting; as a colourist, indeed, he had few superiors. His portraits deserve mention as being faithfully and skilfully rendered.

The following works by him are in the National Gallery of Scotland:

Thomas Duncan.
Anne Page inviting Slender to dinner.
Jeannie Deans and the Robbers.
Portrait of Lady Stuart of Allanbank.
John M'Neill of Colonsay.
Lord Colonsay.
Bran—a celebrated Scottish Deerhound.
The two Friends, Child and Dog.

DUNKARTON, ROBERT, a mezzotint engraver, was born in London in 1744. He was a pupil of Pether, and painted a few portraits, some of which, as also some portraits in crayons, were exhibited at the Royal Academy and at Spring Gardens until 1779. But his greatest success was gained as a mezzotint engraver. His plates are dated from 1770 to 1811, after which year there is no record of him. He engraved in a clear, finished style several portraits and historical subjects, of which the following are the principal:

PORTRAITS.

George, Lord Lyttelton; *after West.*
Jonas Hanway; *after E. Edwards.*
Dr. Arne; *after O. Humphrey.*
Miss Horneck; *after Sir Joshua Reynolds.*
John Elliot; *after N. Dance.*
Miss Bamfylde; *after W. Peters.*
James Brindley, engineer; *after Parsons.*
Miss Catley, in the character of Euphrosyne; *after Lawrenson.*

SUBJECTS AFTER VARIOUS MASTERS.

Lot and his Daughters; *after A. de Gelder.*
Christ and the Disciples at Emmaus; *after Guercino.*
Four subjects from the Life of Joseph; *after the same.*

DUNKER, BALTHASAR ANTON, a landscape painter and etcher, was born at Saal, near Stralsund, in 1746. He was a pupil of Jakob Philipp Hackert and of Vien, and was more distinguished as an etcher than as a painter. His works are after Roos, Van der Does, Hackert, and Schutz, and consist of costumes and manners of the French before the Revolution, illustrations of books, and other miscellaneous subjects. Among them were some excellent landscapes, as the 'Environs of Berne,' and views of Leghorn. He died at Berne in 1807.

DUNKER, PHILIP HEINRICH, son of Balthasar A. Dunker, was also an engraver, and a painter in water-colours. In both pursuits it seems that he was a copyist, as his drawings are after Kobell, Roos, Weenix, and others, and his engraving after a picture by Demarne is traced to one by Geisler. He died in 1836.

D'UNKER-HENNING-LÜTZOW, KARL HINDRICK, a genre-painter, was born at Stockholm in 1829. Up to 1851 he was an officer in the Swedish Guards; he afterwards studied at the Düsseldorf Academy under K. Sohn, and visited Paris and Amsterdam. Having by an accident lost the use of his right arm, he quickly learnt to paint with his left, but he soon after succumbed to a chest disease, and died at Düsseldorf in 1866. He was Swedish court painter, and a professor and honorary member of the Royal Academy at Stockholm. The Berlin National Gallery possesses an 'Announcement of Arrest' by him.

DUNLAP, WILLIAM, an American painter, was born at Perth Amboy, in New Jersey, in 1766. When only seventeen he painted a portrait of Washington. A group of himself and his parents, done in 1788, is in the collection of the New York Historical Society. He published in 1834 his 'History of the Arts of Design in the United States,' and died in New York in 1839.

DUNOUY, ALEXANDRE HYACINTHE, a landscape painter, born in Paris in 1757, was a pupil of Briard. He exhibited at the Musée Royal in 1800 'Plusieurs études d'après la nature prises à Villers-Paul et Hyères,' and during succeeding years many landscapes and views; in 1830 at the Luxembourg he exhibited 'Études d'après nature à Montmorency: Autres prises à Jouy.' He also engraved a series of thirty landscapes from his own compositions, and some views in Italy and in the environs of Paris. He died in 1843.

DUNSTALL, JOHN, who lived in London about the year 1660, engraved a few portraits and other plates, which are etched and finished with the graver in imitation of the style of Hollar. In 1662 he published a book of birds, beasts, flowers, fruit, &c., from his own designs. Among other portraits we have the following by him:

Mary, Queen of James II.
King William and Queen Mary.
Samuel Clarke, prefixed to his 'Puritan Divines.'
James Ussher, Archbishop of Armagh.

DUNTHORNE, JOHN, father and son, were two painters who practised at Colchester in the latter part of the 18th century. The father painted portraits, whilst the son painted genre subjects, several of which appeared at the Royal Academy between 1783 and 1794.

DÜNWEGE, VICTOR and HEINRICH, who were brothers, and painters of the school of Westphalia, executed conjointly a large altar-piece for the parish church of Dortmund. Though painted in the year 1523, it recalls the art of the 15th century, having a gold background, and being symmetrical in composition, but somewhat crude in colouring. It represents, in the centre, 'The Crucifixion'; on the interior of the wings, 'The Adoration of the Kings,' the 'Infant Jesus,' the 'Virgin and several of her kindred;' and on the exterior 'The Donor kneeling before Christ,' who is surrounded by Saints. Similar in character to this altar-piece are a 'Holy Family' in the Antwerp Gallery (formerly in the church of Calcar), and a 'Crucifixion' in the Berlin Gallery (not now exhibited), which are ascribed to the brothers Dünwege. The 'Adoration of the Kings,' dated 1512, in the Naples Museum, is by a Westphalian master, resembling these artists in style.

DUPÉRAC, ÉTIENNE, (or DU PÉRAC,) a French painter, architect, and engraver, was born at Bordeaux about 1525. He studied at Rome, and engraved the 'Last Judgment,' after Michelangelo, and the 'Judgment of Paris,' after Raphael. He etched in the manner of Fontana forty plates, entitled 'I Vestigj dell' Antichità di Roma,' and published in Rome in 1575. Henry IV. appointed Dupérac architect at Fontainebleau, where he painted the bath-room with 'Marine Deities' and the 'Loves of Jupiter and Calisto,' but these works were destroyed by fire in 1697. He died in Paris in 1604.

DUPERREUX, ALEXANDRE LOUIS ROBERT MILLIN. See MILLIN DUPERREUX.

DUPLESSI-BERTAUX, JEAN, a French draughtsman and engraver, was born in Paris in 1747. He engraved many plates for the 'Voyage à Naples et dans les Deux-Siciles' of the Abbé de Saint-Non, and for the 'Voyage en Grèce' of Choiseul-Gouffier, and etched some of the plates of the 'Galerie du Palais-Royal.' His best-known works, however, are those which he executed for the 'Tableaux historiques de la Révolution,' some of which are from his own designs, and the 'Campagnes d'Italie,' after the drawings of Carle Vernet. There are also plates by him in Denon's 'Voyage en Égypte,' the 'Musée Français,' and the 'Musée Filhol.' He died in 1818 or 1819.

DUPLESSIS, JOSEPH SIFRÈDE, a French portrait painter, was born at Carpentras, near Avignon, in 1725. He was destined for the priesthood, but at an early age he showed his inclination for the arts. He was taught by his father, Duplessis the elder, and afterwards by Frère Imbert. He visited Rome in 1745, and studied there under Subleyras; and on his return home, after a short stay at Lyons, he established himself in Paris, and was received into the Academy in 1774. Losing his fortune in the Revolution, he accepted the post of conservator of the Museum of Versailles, where he died in 1802. He possessed a high reputation for his portraits, among which are those of Gluck (now in the Vienna Gallery), Franklin, Marmontel, the Abbé Bossuet, and M. and Mme. Necker.

DUPLONICH, Vedastus, a Dutch engraver, flourished about the year 1660. Among other prints, we have a few plates by him representing views in Holland, which are neatly engraved.

DUPONCHEL, Charles Eugène, a French engraver, born at Abbeville in 1748, was a scholar of Jacques Tardieu. He resided in England about the year 1779, and among other prints engraved a view of Waterford, from a drawing by Paul Sandby, the 'Madonna della Seggiola' of Raphael, a 'Holy Family' after Andrea del Sarto, and several other historical subjects and portraits. He was living in 1804.

DUPONT, François Léonard, called Dupont Watteau, a French painter, was born at Moorsel in 1756, and studied at Lille under Louis Watteau, whose daughter he married in 1782. In 1798 he gave up art for mechanics, with the study of which he had begun life. He died at Lille in 1824. During the years devoted to art, Dupont painted in all mediums and all subjects—portraits, genre subjects, &c. In the Lille Museum is a picture by him, dated 1785, of the 'Attributes of the Fine Arts,' and in the Glasgow Corporation Galleries is 'The Vintage.'

DUPONT, Gainsborough, the nephew and pupil of Thomas Gainsborough, R.A., was born in 1767. He painted portraits and landscapes in imitation of the style of his uncle, and also landscapes with architectural ruins, in which he imitated Nicolas Poussin. His principal work is a large picture containing the portraits of the Trinity Masters, which is in their court-room on Tower Hill. He is, however, more distinguished as an engraver in mezzotinto, and his engravings of some of Gainsborough's portraits are imbued with the very spirit of the painter. He died in London in 1797. The following are his best plates:

George III., full length; *after Gainsborough.*
Queen Charlotte, full length; *after the same.*
The Princess Royal, and the Princesses Augusta and Elizabeth, full length; *after the same.*
George, Lord Rodney, full length; *after the same.*
General Conway, full length; *after the same.*
Colonel St. Leger, full length; *after the same.*
Rev. Sir Henry Bate Dudley, Bart., full length; *after the same.*
Rev. Richard Graves, half-length, oval; *after the same.*

DU PONT, Nicolas, who was born at Brussels in 1660, painted landscapes and architecture. The figures in his landscapes are attributed to Pieter Bout, the coadjutor of Bodewyns, in conjunction with whom he painted the perspective of a grand palace, now in the Museum at Ghent. He died at Brussels in 1712.

DU PONT, Paulus (better known as Paulus Pontius), an eminent Flemish engraver, was born at Antwerp in 1603, and was instructed in the art of engraving by Lucas Vorsterman; but he improved his designs by the advice and friendship of Rubens, from whose works he engraved many admirable plates. Few artists have equalled him

102

in the correct and faithful delineation of his model; and in the character and expression of his figures he appears to have possessed himself of the mind of Rubens. He was not less successful in the fine portraits he engraved after Van Dyck, in which he seems to have adapted his style to the particular character of the person represented. His plates are executed with the graver in a clear, bold style; and, though he did not possess the facility of Bolswert, or the delicacy of Vorsterman, his plates will ever be esteemed among the ablest productions of Flemish art. He died in 1658. The following are his principal works:

PORTRAITS AFTER VAN DYCK.

Paulus Du Pont, or Pontius, Engraver.
Peter Paul Rubens.
Jacob De Breuck, Architect.
Jan Wildens, Painter, of Antwerp.
Jan van Ravesteyn, Painter, of the Hague.
Palamedes Palamdesz, Dutch Painter.
Theodoor van Loo, Painter, of Louvain.
Theodoor Rombouts, Painter, of Antwerp.
Cornelis van der Geest, celebrated Connoisseur.
Gerard Honthorst, Painter, of the Hague.
Hendrik van Balen, Painter, of Antwerp.
Adriaen Stalbent, Painter, of Antwerp.
Daniel Mytens, Painter, of Holland.
Gerard Seghers, Painter, of Antwerp.
Simon De Vos, Painter, of Antwerp.
Gaspar De Craeyer, Painter, of Ghent.
Hendrik Steenwyck, Painter, of Antwerp.
Gaspar Gevartius, Jurisconsult, of Antwerp.
Nicolaas Rockox, Magistrate, of Antwerp.
Jan van den Wouwer, Counsellor of State.
Cæsar Alexander Scaglia, Abbot of Stophard.
Gustavus Adolphus, King of Sweden.
Mary de' Medici, Queen of France.
Francis Thomas, of Savoy, Prince of Carignan.
John, Count of Nassau.
Don Alvarez, Marquis of Santa Cruz.
Don Carlos de Colonna, Spanish General.
Don Diego Felipe de Guzman, Marquis de Leganez.
Mary, Princess of Aremberg.
Henry, Count de Berghe, in armour.
Sir Balthasar Gerbier.
Frederick Henry, Prince of Orange.

PORTRAITS AFTER RUBENS.

Philip IV., King of Spain. 1632.
Elizabeth of Bourbon, his Queen.
Isabella Clara Eugenia, Infanta of Spain.
Ferdinand, Infant of Spain, on horseback.
Gasparo Guzman, Duke of Olivarez.
Cristoval, Marquis of Castel Rodrigo.
Manuel de Moura Cortereal, Marquis of Castel Rodrigo.
The Mother of Manuel, Marquis of Castel Rodrigo.

VARIOUS SUBJECTS AFTER RUBENS.

Susannah and the Elders. 1624.
The Adoration of the Shepherds.
The Murder of the Innocents. In two sheets. 1643. Very fine.
The Presentation in the Temple.
Christ bearing His Cross.
The Crucifixion, with Angels, one of whom is overcoming Sin and Death.
The Dead Christ supported by the Virgin, with Mary Magdalen, St. Francis, and other figures; very fine.
The Descent of the Holy Ghost.
The Assumption of the Virgin.
The Virgin suckling the Infant Christ.
St. Roch interceding with Christ for the Plague-stricken; very fine.
Thomyris causing the Head of Cyrus to be put into a Vessel of Blood.

SUBJECTS AFTER VARIOUS MASTERS.

The Flight into Egypt; *after Jordaens.*
Twelfth-Night; *after the same.*

The Adoration of the Magi ; *after G. Seghers.*
The Virgin with the Infant Christ and St. Anne ; *after the same.*
St. Francis Xavier kneeling before the Virgin and Child ; *after the same.*
St. Sebastian, with an Angel drawing an Arrow from his breast ; *after the same.*
A Dead Christ, supported by the Virgin ; *after Van Dyck.*
St. Rosalia, receiving a Crown from the Infant Jesus ; *after the same.*
The Holy Family ; *after J. van Hoeck.*
The Entombment of Christ ; *after Titian.*

DUPONT, PIERRE, a French engraver, was born in Paris in 1730. He is often confounded with Gainsborough Dupont.

DUPPA, RICHARD, was an English copyist, who flourished in the latter half of the 18th and in the beginning of the 19th century. He studied for some time in Rome, and published two works containing copies of heads by Michelangelo and Raphael ; but he is chiefly known by his lives of these two painters, published in 1807 and 1816 respectively.

DUPRAT, ——, a French painter of the 18th century, is known by a portrait of the Princess of Asturias, Doña Maria Barbara, wife of Ferdinand VI., in the Madrid Gallery. No dates are known in connection with his life.

DUPRÉ, JULES, French painter, born at Nantes in the year 1811. He learnt the rudiments of his art whilst assisting his father, a manufacturer of porcelain (in the village of Parmain, facing L'Isle-Adam), in decorating his pottery. He practically taught himself, wandering through the neighbouring country, whence he brought home studies painted on the spot with simple fidelity. Untrammelled by any school traditions, young Dupré came to Paris, and at the age of twenty exhibited for the first time three pictures in the Salon of 1831. Two of these, both forest scenes, were painted direct from nature in La Creuse, where his father had undertaken the management of a china factory belonging to the Marquis de Bonneval. He exhibited up to 1837, and sent seven landscapes to the Salon of 1839. After this for thirteen years he did not contribute to the Salon, but reappeared for the last time, in 1852, with three pictures : 'Pastures,' 'The Outskirts of a Village in the Landes,' and 'A Sunset.' He sent a dozen works to the Universal Exhibition of 1867, which may be regarded as so many masterpieces, though he was only awarded a second-class medal. He had previously obtained one at the Salon of 1833. His 'View of the Fields near Southampton,' in 1835, had brought him congratulations from the most celebrated painters of the Romantic school. Eugène Delacroix was never tired of seeing and studying this picture. Dupré was passionately interested in the works of Constable, and assisted Theodore Rousseau to become known, even taking a studio for, and working with him. He endeavoured to paint on the system of etchers, merging the trees and background into the sky so as to represent the depth of air and space. At the Centenary Exhibition in the Champ de Mars, a fine collection of his works, with some of his most powerful sea-pieces were shown. These were mostly painted during the siege of Paris, when he was shut up in his house at Cayeux-sur-Mer. He was the last painter of the Romantic school of landscape, and died on October 6, 1889, at L'Isle-Adam.

DUPRÉ, LÉON VICTOR, a French landscape painter, was born at Limoges in 1816, and studied under his brother, Jules Dupré. He died in 1879, after a long and painful illness. Amongst his works are :

Meadows in Berry.
Environs of St. Junien.
Cows Drinking. 1855. (*South Kensington Museum.*)
View at Argentan. 1861.
Landscape in the Indre. 1864.

DUPRÉEL, ——, was a French engraver of whom no particulars are related, but whose works are to be found in the 'Musée Français,' the 'Galerie de Florence,' and other publications of the close of the 18th and commencement of the 19th centuries.

DUPRESSOIR, JOSEPH FRANÇOIS, a French landscape painter, was born in Paris in 1800. He painted chiefly views in the south of France, but sometimes ventured on historical subjects, as the 'Battle of Réthel' in the galleries at Versailles. He died in Paris in 1859.

DUPUIS, CHARLES, (or DU PUIS,) a French engraver, was born in Paris in 1685. He was a pupil of Gaspard Duchange, and engraved several plates of portraits and historical subjects. They are etched with taste, and finished with the graver in a free, masterly style. His drawing is correct, and his heads are full of expression and character. He was a member of the French Academy, and died in Paris in 1742. The following are his plates most worthy of notice.

PORTRAITS.

Louis XV. ; *after Ranc.*
Henry of Lorraine, Duke of Guise ; *after Du Monstier.*
Nicolas Coustou, sculptor ; *after Le Gros.*
Nicolas de Largillière, painter ; *after Gueulain.*

SUBJECTS AFTER VARIOUS MASTERS.

St. John preaching in the Wilderness ; *after C. Maratti.*
The Marriage of the Virgin ; *after Carle van Loo.*
Alexander Severus giving Corn to the Romans ; *after Noël Coypel.*
Ptolemy giving Liberty to the Jews ; *after the same.*
Two of the Elements, Earth and Air ; *after Louis de Boullongne.*
Cupid triumphing over Pan ; *after Antoine Coypel.*
Diana reposing, with her Nymphs ; *after the same.*
Rinaldo and Armida ; *after the same.*
The Passage of the Rhine ; *after Le Brun.*

DUPUIS, NICOLAS GABRIEL, the younger brother of Charles Dupuis, was born in Paris in 1696, and was instructed in the art of engraving by Gaspard Duchange. Although not equal to his brother, he possessed great merit, and was admitted a member of the Academy in 1754. He engraved several portraits and historical subjects, in the style of his brother. He died in Paris in 1771. There are by him the following prints :

PORTRAITS.

The Equestrian Statue of Louis XV. erected at Bordeaux ; *after Le Moine.*
The same, from that erected at Rennes ; *after the same.*
C. F. Paul de Normand de Tournehem, Director General of the Arts ; *after L. Tocqué.*
Philips Wouwerman, painter ; *after C. D. Visscher.*
Gaspard Duchange ; *after Van Loo.*
Jean de Betzkoy, Russian general ; *after Roslin.*

SUBJECTS AFTER VARIOUS MASTERS.

The Guardian Angel ; *after Domenico Feti ;* for the Crozat Collection.
The Adoration of the Magi ; *after Paolo Veronese ;* for the same.
The Holy Family ; *after Annibale Carracci ;* for the Dresden Gallery.

St. Sebastian; *after L. Carracci.*
St. Nicholas and St. Francis; *after Pierre.*
Amusement of a Pastoral Life; *after Giorgione;* for the Crozat Collection.
The Death of Lucretia; *after Guido.*
Æneas saving his Father Anchises; *after Carle van Loo.*
Nymph and Satyrs; *after L. Chéron.*

DUPUIS, Pierre François, an etcher and engraver in mezzotint, worked in Paris in the early part of the 18th century. His best plate is the portrait of his grandfather, Pierre Dupuis, the flower painter, who was born in 1610, and died in 1682.

DUQUE CORNEJO, Pedro, a Spanish sculptor and painter, was born at Seville in 1677. He was a pupil of Pedro Roldan for sculpture, but it is not known by whom he was instructed in painting. The pictures which he painted in oil for the Carthusian priory of Santa Maria de las Cuevas, representing St. Bruno and other monks of the order, and those which he painted in fresco for the monastery of San Geronimo de Buenavista, are not without merit. He had a ready invention, and produced numerous designs, which are much esteemed at Seville. He died at Cordova in 1757, and was buried with great pomp in the cathedral of that city. His works, as a sculptor and carver in wood, are to be seen in the cathedrals and churches of Seville, Cordova, Granada, and elsewhere.

DUQUEYLAR, Paul, a French historical painter, born at Digne in 1771, was a scholar of David. Most of the subjects painted by him are taken from the classic poets and ancient historians, and are of an elevated character. The 'Judgment of Minos,' and 'Belisarius,' both painted at Rome in 1804, are described by Kotzebue in his 'Souvenirs d'Italie.' He was still living in 1831.

DURAMEAU, Louis Jacques, a French historical painter, was born in Paris in 1733. He was painter to the king, and keeper of the pictures at Versailles, and was received into the Academy in 1774 upon his painting of 'Summer' on the ceiling of the Gallery of Apollo in the Louvre. He also painted the ceiling of the theatre in the palace of Versailles with the subject of 'Apollo.' There are pictures by him in the Museums of Alençon and Besançon, and some of his historical subjects have been engraved by Levasseur. He died at Versailles in 1796.

DURAND, Cyrile, a French genre painter, was born at Bordeaux in 1790, and died there in 1840. An 'Interior' by him is in the Museum of his native city.

DURAND-BRAGER, Jean Baptiste Henri, a French marine painter, was born at Dol in 1814. He studied under Gudin and Eugène Isabey, and in 1840 accompanied the fleet which brought Napoleon's remains from St. Helena, which island afforded him subjects for various pictures. He spent much of his time in travelling; he went to Buenos Ayres with the squadron, and explored Uruguay and Brazil; he accompanied the expeditions to Tangiers and Mogador, and to Madagascar, and he was in the Crimea during the war with Russia. He painted views of the places he visited, and also naval combats and sea-pieces. He died in 1879. There are several of his works in the galleries of Versailles.

DURANT, Jean Louis, a French portrait painter and engraver, was a native of Orleans. He worked at Geneva about 1670, but came to London about the year 1690. He was a very indifferent engraver, and was chiefly employed by the book-

sellers, for whom he engraved a variety of book ornaments and portraits. Among the latter is that of Queen Mary II., after Kneller.

DURANTE, Conte Giorgio, an Italian painter of flowers and birds, was born at Brescia in 1683, and died in 1755. His works were eagerly sought after, no less for their exact imitation than for their tasteful composition. They are rarely met with out of Brescia, though several noble Venetian families possess a few specimens, and the best are to be seen in the royal collection at Turin.

DURELLO, Simon, a German engraver, executed some of the portraits for the work entitled, 'Istoria di Leopoldo Cesare,' published at Vienna in 1674.

DÜRER, Albrecht, the great representative artist of Germany, was of Hungarian descent, and perhaps connected with a Hungarian family of the name of Ajtós, who had lived for many generations in a little village of the same name, (Eytas, as Dürer writes it,) near Gyula. This name of Ajtós, derived from "ajtó" (a door), signifies the same as the German Thürer or Dürer, which was probably a translation of it, and it is significant that Dürer bore the same arms—viz. the open door under a pent-house roof—that were borne by this family. Dürer's ancestors lived, as he himself tells us, "by tending oxen and horses." Albrecht Dürer the elder, however, deserted this patriarchal calling, and became a goldsmith, and after passing some time with the great masters of that craft in the Netherlands, he came to Nuremberg in 1455, where he engaged himself to a master goldsmith, named Hieronymus Holper (not Haller), whose young daughter Barbara he married in 1467, taking up about the same time his rights as burgher and master goldsmith in the city. Albrecht Dürer was the third of eighteen children, most of whom died in infancy. His birth took place on May 21st, 1471, and Anton Koberger, the celebrated printer, was his godfather. "When I had learnt to write and read," says Dürer, in a brief family chronicle of his own compiling, "my father took me from school and taught me the goldsmith's work." But he continues, "my inclination carried me more towards painting." Therefore, his father, giving in to his desire, bound him apprentice in 1486 to the best Nuremberg painter of his time—Michel Wolgemut—to serve with him for three years. "During this time," writes Dürer, "God gave me diligence so that I learnt well. And when I had served my time, my father sent me away, and I was absent four years, until my father required me back, as I set out in 1490 after Easter, so I returned in 1494 after Whitsuntide." This is all Dürer tells us concerning his "Lehr-und Wanderjahre," nor have we much other record concerning them. A portrait he drew of himself in the looking-glass in 1484 is, however, still preserved in the Albertina at Vienna, and a careful pen-drawing of the 'Virgin and two Angels,' dated 1485, is to be found in the Berlin Museum; but this may be a copy from some earlier master. Where Dürer went during his four "Wanderjahre" is not certain. Christoph Scheurl expressly states in one place that he made a tour through Germany, and both he and Neudörffer affirm that he was in Colmar in 1492, where he was entertained by Martin Schongauer's three brothers, as also by a fourth brother at Basle. The inscription on two portraits from which it has been argued that he was at Strassburg in 1494 is open to another inter-

Hieronymus Holzschuher (1526)

From the painting by Albrecht Dürer in the Berlin Gallery.

pretation. Many writers are of opinion that he crossed the Alps at this period, and passed some time in Italy, and this view has been supported by Thausing. Dr. D. Burckhardt, more recently, has endeavoured to prove that he resided from 1492 to 1494 at Basle, and was the author of a certain remarkable group of illustrations in books printed by Bergmann von Olpe. One woodcut, a 'St. Jerome,' in the edition of that Father's Epistles printed by N. Kesler in 1492, is certified as Dürer's work by his signature on the block, still preserved at Basle. All else is matter of inference. Wherever Dürer went during his "Wanderjahre," it is certain he returned to Nuremberg in May 1494. "And when I reached home," he writes in his usual laconic style, "Hans Frey treated with my father, and gave me his daughter Agnes, and he gave me with her two hundred florins, and the marriage was celebrated on the Monday before St. Margaret's Day (July 7th), in the year 1494." This is all Dürer tells us concerning his marriage, nor does he afterwards in any of his writings mention his wife except incidentally in the briefest manner. But he drew her portrait repeatedly, she accompanied him during his long visit to the Netherlands, and no word of Dürer's supports, though it must be admitted that no word contradicts, the old tradition that his marriage was unhappy. That tradition seems to rest entirely on a letter written by Pirkheimer in 1530 to Johann Tscherte of Vienna, architect to Charles V., which was merely the result of an overflow of spite on the part of the writer. He had never liked his friend's wife, and had recently been annoyed by her selling some stag-horns belonging to Dürer, which he especially desired. Hence his misrepresentations, which have blackened the character of Frau Agnes for centuries. A rough draft of the letter in Pirkheimer's own handwriting is preserved in the Stadtbibliothek at Nuremberg, and was published in full by Lochner in the 'Repertorium für Kunstwissenschaft,' vol. ii. 1879, p. 35.

The most probable date for Dürer's first visit to Venice is the winter of 1494–95, which agrees with the expression "eleven years ago" in his letter to Pirkheimer of February 7, 1506. Except during the time spent on this journey Dürer lived for some years after his marriage in his father's house, "Unter der Vesten," and his father dying in 1502, he appears from that time to have taken charge of his mother until her death in 1514, and of his young brother Hans, whom he educated as a painter. During this period, viz. from 1494 to 1505, he executed several of his larger copperplates, such as the magnificent 'Adam and Eve' (1504), 'The Nativity' (1504), 'The Great Horse' and 'The Little Horse' (1505). The beautiful conception of 'The Prodigal Son' is also referred to this period. But by far the greatest work that he executed at this time was the magnificent series of fifteen large woodcuts illustrating the 'Apocalypse,' of which editions in German and in Latin were published in Nuremberg in 1498, under the respective titles of 'Die heimlich Offenbarung Johannis,' and 'Apocalipsis cum Figuris.' The sixteenth cut, representing 'The Vision of the Virgin and Child beheld by St. John as he is writing his Revelation,' was added on the title-page to the second Latin edition published in 1511. These cuts mark an epoch in the history of wood-engraving. It is not only that in their conception and design they are grander than any that

had previously appeared, but also that they are far more skilfully executed. It was long a disputed point whether Dürer did not himself cut the blocks for these surprising works, but most authorities now agree that he could not have done so. A number of large single woodcuts of like dimensions were designed about the same time. Dürer's first painting of importance, 'The Adoration of the Magi,' now in the Uffizi at Florence, was likewise executed at this period. It is dated 1504.

In the autumn of 1505 Dürer undertook a journey to Venice, a city that had a large traffic with Nuremberg. It is stated by Vasari that he went there to defend his rights against Marcantonio, who was copying his plates and monogram. But that wholesale piracy of his works which was carried on to a great extent by Marcantonio and others at a later period had scarcely begun at this time, though it is possible that Dürer while in Venice suffered from it, and made some complaint to the Signory. The most probable reason that has been stated for his journey is, that he had already, before starting, received a commission from the German merchants in Venice for a picture to adorn their new Hall of Exchange—the Fondaco dei Tedeschi—upon the decoration of which Titian and Giorgione were also employed. He began, at any rate, soon after his arrival in Venice, to work on the magnificent picture known as 'The Feast of the Rosary' (or Rose-Garlands), now in the monastery of Strahow near Prague. During Dürer's sojourn in Venice, which lasted from the end of 1505 to the beginning of 1507, he wrote nine letters to his friend the learned counsellor of Nuremberg, Wilibald Pirkheimer.

On Dürer's return to Nuremberg in 1507 he painted several large altar-pieces : viz. in 1507, the two single figures of 'Adam' and 'Eve' on panels, of which the originals are in the Prado Gallery at Madrid, those in the Pitti Palace at Florence being copies ; in 1508, the 'Martyrdom of the ten thousand Christians,' now in the Vienna Gallery ; and a Madonna for the Bishop of Breslau, which is probably identical with the 'Virgin with the Iris' now in the collection of Sir Frederick Cook at Richmond ; in 1509, the 'Assumption of the Virgin,' painted for the merchant Jacob Heller of Frankfort as an altar-piece in the church of the Dominicans, but removed by the Elector Maximilian of Bavaria to Munich, where it was burnt in 1674 ; and in 1511 the splendid painting of the 'Adoration of the Trinity,' in the Imperial Gallery at Vienna. Besides painting these works, Dürer was busily engaged at this period upon various series of woodcuts. The year 1511, in which the great picture of the 'Trinity' was accomplished, was especially fruitful. In this year were published the first edition of the 'Life of the Virgin,' a series of twenty folio cuts, seventeen of which had been finished before the journey to Venice in 1505 ; the series known as the 'Great Passion,' consisting of twelve folio cuts, also in part of earlier date ; and the 'Little Passion,' containing thirty-seven small cuts. This is perhaps the best known of all the series of woodcuts. Thirty-five of the original blocks are preserved in the British Museum. Numerous other cuts of single subjects belong to the same period. But it is by his copper-plate engravings more than by his paintings or woodcuts that Dürer is now known to the world. The earliest copper-plates signed by

Dürer are the 'Holy Family with the Locust' (B. 44), and the 'Love Offer' (B. 93), about 1495. 'The Ravisher' (B. 92) may be some years earlier. His noblest conceptions belong to a later date. Among these may be named, 'The Prodigal Son'; 'The Arms of Death' (1503); 'Adam and Eve' (1504); 'The Nativity' (1504); 'The Knight, Death, and the Devil' (1513); 'Melancholia' (1514); 'St. Jerome in his Chamber' (1514); 'The Great Fortune,' and the 'St. Eustace' (or 'St. Hubert'). The two last are large plates of early date. The beautiful series known as the 'Passion in Copper' bears dates from 1508 to 1513.

Dürer produced six etchings during the years 1515–18, and four dry-point plates, one of which is dated 1510 and two 1512; all the rest were engraved with the burin.

Dürer's connection with the Emperor Maximilian I. began in 1512, and continued till his patron's death in 1519. The principal works which he executed for him are the marginal drawings in an incomplete copy (at Munich) of a printed prayer-book intended for the use of the Order of St. George (1515); the immense 'Triumphal Arch,' composed of ninety-two blocks, dated 1515, designed by Dürer but carried out in a large measure by his pupils; the small Triumphal Car with the Burgundian Marriage in the 'Triumphal Procession,' and the large 'Triumphal Car,' designed in 1518 but not published as a woodcut till 1522. Dürer drew the Emperor's portrait at the Diet of Augsburg in 1518, and made both a picture and a woodcut from the drawing.

In 1520–21 Dürer, accompanied by his wife, undertook a journey to the Netherlands, of which he has left us a detailed account in a journal he kept during his travels. This journal, with the letters written from Venice, and other correspondence and memoranda by Dürer, has been published in full in 'Dürer's Schriftlicher Nachlass,' edited by Lange and Fuhse, 1893. It is translated into English in the lives of Dürer by W. B. Scott and Mrs. Heaton. After his return from this journey, which appears to have been chiefly undertaken in order to get a ratification from the Emperor Charles V. of a pension that had been granted him by Maximilian, Dürer remained quietly working in Nuremberg until his death, which took place on April 6th, 1528. His last great work had been the painting of the 'Four Apostles,' grandly-conceived figures of SS. Peter, John, Paul and Mark, typifying the Four Temperaments, which he presented to his native city in 1526. They are now in the Munich Gallery.

Besides his artistic works Dürer wrote several treatises—the most important being, 'The Art of Mensuration' (1525); 'Instruction on the Fortification of Towns, Castles, and Places' (1527); and the 'Treatise on Proportion,' published after his death in 1528. The plastic works attributed to him are probably without exception apocryphal.

Dürer's art is essentially German in character, and those who only admire the Italian ideal find nothing in it to desire. It is the lament of many writers that he did not receive Italian training; but those who truly appreciate his art rejoice that, in spite of various influences that might have affected it, his style remained thoroughly individual and German. "In creative richness of fancy, in extensive power of thought, and in moral energy and earnest striving, Dürer," writes Lübke, "must be called the first of all German masters; and as

106

regards artistic gifts, need fear no comparison with any master in the world, not even with Raphael and Michelangelo. Notwithstanding, in all that concerns the true means of expression—the clothing of the idea in the garment of exquisite form— he lies so deeply fettered within the bonds of his own limited world that he rarely rises to the same height of thought or expression."

This is no doubt true to some extent. We do not find in Dürer's art the classic ideal of the perfection of man's physical nature, nor the spiritual ideal of the early religious painters, nor the calm dignity and rich sensuous beauty of the great masters of the Italian Renaissance, but in it we find a noble expression of the German mind, with its high intellectual powers, its daring speculative philosophy, its deep-seated reverence, its patient laboriousness, and its love for the weird and grotesque. Dürer was the companion of some of the most learned and thoughtful men of his day. Luther and Melanchthon were among the number of his friends, and there is no doubt but the reforming spirit of the age was powerfully at work within him, affecting his thought and art. Melanchthon bears testimony to his rare worth as a man by saying, "His least merit was his art."

BIBLIOGRAPHY.

Neudörffer, 'Nachrichten von den vornehmsten Künstlern und Werkleuten so innerhalb hundert Jahren in Nürnberg gelebt haben.' Nürnberg, 1547. (Edited by Lochner, 1875. The earliest account we have of Dürer.)

Vasari, 'Vite de' piu eccellenti Pittori,' &c. (Edited by Milanesi.) 1878–82.

Carel van Mander, 'Het Schilder-Boeck.' 1604.

Sandrart, 'Teutsche Academie.' 1675–79.

Friedrich Campe, 'Reliquien von Albrecht Dürer' (containing his letters and journal). 1828.

Joseph Heller, 'Das Leben und die Werke Albrecht Dürer's.' 1827. (Only the second vol. of this work, containing descriptive catalogues, was published.)

August von Eye, 'Leben und Wirken Albrecht Dürer's.' 1869.

W. B. Scott, 'Albert Dürer : his Life and Works.' 1869.

Mrs. Heaton, 'Life of Albrecht Dürer.' 1869. (Second edition, 1881.)

Lochner, 'Die Personen-Namen in Albrecht Dürer's Briefen aus Venedig.' 1870.

Moritz Thausing, 'Dürer's Briefe, Tagebücher, und Reime.' 1872.

Moritz Thausing, 'Dürer, Geschichte seines Lebens und seiner Kunst.' 1876. (Second edition, 1884.)

Moritz Thausing, 'Albert Dürer, his Life and Works.' Edited by F. A. Eaton.' 1882.

Charles Ephrussi, 'Albert Dürer et ses dessins.' 1882.

W. M. Conway, 'Literary Remains of A. Dürer.' 1889.

Anton Springer, 'Albrecht Dürer.' 1892.

Daniel Burckhardt, 'Albrecht Dürer's Aufenthalt in Basel.' 1892.

Gabriel von Térey, 'Albrecht Dürer's Venetianischer Aufenthalt.' 1892.

Lange und Fuhse, 'Dürer's Schriftlicher Nachlass.' 1893.

H. Knackfuss, 'Dürer.' (Editions 2–6, 1895–99, English Translation, 1900.)

Lionel Cust, 'A. Dürer. A study of his Life and Works.' 1897.

S. R. Koehler, 'Chronological Catalogue of the Engravings, etc., of Albert Dürer.' 1897.

M. Zucker, 'Albrecht Dürer.' 1900.

Ludwig Justi, 'Konstruirte Figuren und Köpfe unter den Werken A. Dürer's.' 1902.

'Studien zur Deutschen Kunstgeschichte,' nos. 6, 19, 23, 27, 38, 39, 41. No. 41, 'Versuch einer Dürer-Bibliographie,' by H. W. Singer, enumerates about 1300 books and articles relating to Dürer.

ALBRECHT DÜRER

THE DRESDEN ALTAR-PIECE

THE FLIGHT INTO EGYPT

PRINCIPAL PAINTINGS.

Virgin and Child with SS. Antony and Sebastian. (*Dresden.*)
Adoration of the Magi. 1504. (*Uffizi, Florence.*)
Feast of the Rose-Garlands. 1506. (*Monastery of Strahow, near Prague.*)
Virgin crowned by two Angels. 1506. (*Berlin*).
Crucifixion. 1506. (*Dresden*).
Martyrdom of the Ten Thousand. 1508. (*Vienna.*)
Adoration of the Trinity. 1511. (*Vienna.*)
Figures of the Four Apostles. 1526. (*Munich.*)
Madonnas at Augsburg, Berlin, and Vienna.

PORTRAITS.

Portrait of Himself. 1493. (*Late in the Felix Collection, Leipzig.*)
„ „ 1498. (*Madrid, copy at Florence.*)
„ „ 1508 ? (*Munich.*)
Albrecht Dürer the Elder. 1494. (*Uffizi.*)
„ 1497. (*Three replicas at Frankfort, Schleissheim, and Sion House.*)
A Young Man; probably Hans Dürer. 1500. (*Munich.*)
Oswald Krell. 1499. (*Munich.*)
Michel Wolgemut. 1516. (*Munich.*)
A man unknown (Hans Imhof ?). (*Madrid.*)
Bernard van Orley. 1521. (*Dresden.*)
Hieronymus Holzschuher. 1526. (*Berlin.*)
Jacob Muffel. 1526. (*Berlin.*)

DRAWINGS.

The richest collections are those of the Albertina, Vienna, the Royal Print Cabinet at Berlin, and the Print Room at the British Museum. Other important drawings are at Bremen, Hamburg, Florence, Milan, The Louvre, Windsor Castle, Chatsworth, the Blasius Collection at Brunswick, the Bonnat Collection at Paris, etc. Reproductions of nearly all the drawings have been published by Dr. Lippmann, ('Zeichnungen von A. D.,' Bd. i.–iv., 1883–96), with the exception of the Albertina drawings, which have appeared in Schönbrunner and Meder's 'Handzeichnungen aus der Albertina und anderen Sammlungen' (Vienna). M.M.H. (C.D.)

DÜRER, HANS, a younger brother of Albrecht Dürer, was born at Nuremberg in 1490. When, in 1502, they lost their father, Albrecht took the young Hans, a boy of twelve, under his protection, and gave him instruction in art. He afterwards became court painter to the King of Poland, at Cracow. His death is not recorded, though it is thought that he may have been dead in 1538, for in that year his brother Andreas went from Nuremberg to Cracow to collect debts. A few old German paintings with the initials *H. D.* and a drawing of the Crucifixion in the British Museum are attributed to Hans Dürer, but his most certain works are a part of the marginal drawings in that portion of the so-called Prayer-Book of Maximilian I. which is preserved at Besançon.

DURET, PIERRE, a French engraver, who was living in Paris in 1767. He engraved several plates of landscapes, principally after the Dutch masters, among which are the following :

A View in Holland ; *after Ruisdael.*
Two Moonlight subjects; *after Van der Neer.*
The Country Blacksmith ; *after Ph. Wouwerman.*
An Italian Sea-port ; *after Vernet.*

DÜRINGER, DANIEL, a Swiss painter, born at Steckborn, in Thurgau, in 1720, studied at Zurich, and distinguished himself as an excellent painter and etcher of animals. He died in 1786.

DURMER, FRANZ VALENTIN, an Austrian engraver and draughtsman, was born at Vienna in 1766. He studied at the Academy of that city, and executed after Guido Reni the 'Four Seasons,' and after Poelenborch the 'Nativity,' which are two of his best plates. He was still living in 1835.

DURNO, JAMES, an historical painter, was born about the year 1752. He studied first under Andrea Casali, and afterwards under West, and painted two pictures for Boydell's Shakespeare Gallery. The early productions of this artist gave promise of great ability, which was not, however, fulfilled. He went to Italy in 1774, and died there in 1795.

DU RONCERAY, MARGUERITE LOUISE AMÉLIE DELORME. See DELORME DU RONCERAY.

DURR, JOHN, a native of Germany, flourished about the year 1625. He was an engraver of little repute, and worked chiefly for the booksellers, for whom, among other book-plates, he engraved some portraits, particularly those of H. J. Ernest and his family, and J. Zimmer.

DUSART, CORNELIS, the elder, flourished in Holland in the 17th century. In the Amsterdam Museum is a 'Fish Market' by him, signed and dated 1653.

DUSART, CORNELIS, (or DU SART,) a Dutch painter and engraver, was born at Haarlem in 1660. He entered the guild of that city in 1679, and died there in 1704. He was a pupil of Adriaan van Ostade, whose style he imitated with considerable success. His works, like those of Ostade, represent Dutch peasants regaling and merry-making. Although not equal to his master in the richness of his tones and the harmony of his effect, his colouring is clear and agreeable, his compositions are ingenious, and his touch very spirited. There is great inequality in the works of Dusart; but some of his best pictures are in the following galleries :

Amsterdam.	*Museum.*	Fish Market. 1683.
„	„	The Ambulant Musicians.
„	„	A Village Fair.
„	„	A Village Inn.
Antwerp.	*Museum.*	Interior with Peasants.
Brussels.	*Museum.*	A Dutch Kermesse.
Dresden.	*Gallery.*	Woman and Child. 1679 (*his earliest known work*).
„	„	Peasants Fighting. 1697.
„	„	Nine-pins Players. 1688.
Dulwich.	*Gallery.*	A Peasant Family.
Frankfort.	*Städel Inst.*	A Dutch Inn. 1687.
Glasgow.	*Gallery.*	The Musicians.
Hague.	*Museum.*	Interior of an Inn.
London.	*Northbrook Coll.*	Family Scene.
„	*Bute Coll.*	Boors drinking.
Petersburg.	*Hermitage.*	A Donkey. 1681.
„	„	Interior of a Grocer's Shop.
„	„	A Peasant Family.
Vienna.	*Gallery.*	Peasants before an Inn.

Dusart executed some very spirited etchings, and a few plates in mezzotint, which are full of humorous character. The following are his best prints :

PLATES IN MEZZOTINT.

An old Man playing on the Violin.
A Girl confessing to a Monk.
A Dutch Boor reading a Paper, and holding a Bottle.
Monkeys regaling.
An Indian dancing with a Girl.
A Girl dancing with a Tea-Pot in her Hand.
Twelve plates of the Months of the Year.
The Five Senses.

ETCHINGS.

The Interior of an Alehouse, with Boors regaling.
The Great Fair. 1685.

The Little Fair. 1685.
The Amorous Cobbler.
The Village Surgeon. 1695.
The Village Physician. 1695.
The Inside of a Dutch Alehouse.
A Village Festival; *after himself.*

DUSCHER. See Tüscher.

DUSIGN, ——, a portrait painter, was a son of Colonel Dusign. He was a pupil of Sir Joshua Reynolds, and practised for a few years at Bath, where his family resided. He died at Rome in 1770.

DUTILLEUX, Henri Joseph Constant, a French landscape painter, who painted also a few portraits, was born at Douai in 1807. He studied under Hersent and at the École des Beaux-Arts, and worked at Arras from 1830 until 1860, in which year he removed to Paris, where he died in 1865. There are Landscapes by him in the Museums of Lille and of Douai.

DUTTENHOFER, Christian Friedrich, a German engraver, was born at Gronau in Wurtemberg in 1778. He studied under Klengel at Dresden, and is chiefly known by his landscapes after Claude, Poussin, Annibale Carracci, P. Bril, and various views in the Tyrol. He also copied Woollett's print of 'Solitude,' after Wilson, and was one of the artists employed on the 'Musée Napoléon.' He died at Heilbronn in 1846. His son, Anton Duttenhofer, who was likewise an engraver, and was a pupil of his father, died at Stuttgart in 1843, at the age of 31.

DUVAL, Amaury, painter, was born at Montrouge, Paris, in 1808. In 1826 he entered the atelier of Ingres, and afterwards travelled in Greece, where he made numerous studies and sketches. In 1834 he exhibited at the Salon his 'Greek Shepherd discovering a Bas-relief,' and soon became favourably known as an able exponent of his master's traditions. His portrait of 'Rachel as the Tragic Muse,' contributed to the Exhibition of 1855, attracted considerable attention. He painted various pictures for Parisian churches, and executed some decorations in St. Germain l'Auxerrois. He died in December 1885.

DU VAL, Charles Allen, a portrait and subject painter, was born in 1808. He practised at Manchester, and exhibited at the Royal Academy from 1836 till his death in 1872. Among his works are:

The Giaour. 1842.
Columbus in chains. 1855.
The Dedication of Samuel. 1858.
The Morning Walk. 1861.

DUVAL, Marc, called Bertin, after his brother-in-law, and also 'Le Sourd de Charles IX.,' a painter and wood-engraver, was born at Le Mans, and became court painter of Charles IX. of France. Among his engravings, which are very rare, may be mentioned the Brothers Coligni and Catharine de' Medici. He died in Paris in 1581.

DUVAL, Nicolaas. See Du Val, Robert.

DUVAL, Philippe, a French painter, flourished about the year 1672. He was first a scholar of Charles Le Brun, and afterwards studied at Venice. He came to England in the reign of Charles II., and painted some historical and mythological subjects, one of which, dated 1672, represented 'Venus receiving from Vulcan the Arms of Æneas.' He died in London in 1709.

DU VAL, Robert, a Dutch painter, who has often been called in error Nicolaas Duval, was born at the Hague in 1644. After studying

under Nicolaas Wieling he went to Italy, and became an imitator of Pietro da Cortona. On his return to Holland he was employed by William, Prince of Orange, afterwards king of England. It is said that he was sent to Hampton Court to put in order the Cartoons of Raphael; but whether to repaint, or, in modern phrase, to restore them, is not stated. He was appointed director of the Academy at the Hague, and died there in 1732.

DU VAL, S. This artist is mentioned by Papillon as an engraver on wood, who flourished about the year 1650, and was remarkable for the neatness and delicacy of his execution. There are twenty cuts by him for the 'Histoire miraculeuse de Notre-Dame de Liesse.' His other prints are chiefly from the designs of Jacques Stella and N. Cochin. S. Du Val is sometimes mentioned as Sebastiano, and sometimes as Stefano Du Val; but there is a degree of mystification about him which requires elucidation. He must not be confounded with Sebastiano D'Vl, or D'Val, who lived a century earlier.

DUVAL-LE-CAMUS, Jules Alexandre, a French historical and scriptural painter, the son of Pierre Duval-le-Camus, was born in Paris in 1817. He studied under his father, to whose style his own has considerable affinity, and under Drolling and Delaroche. He died in 1878. Amongst his chief works are:

Tobit and the Angel.
Petits Déjeuners de Marly.
Rousseau writing 'Héloïse.' 1846.
The Bear-Hunters. 1853.
Macbeth and the Witches. 1855.
The Flight into Egypt. 1857.
Jacques Clément. 1861. (*Luxembourg Gallery.*)
St. Elizabeth of Hungary. 1863.
Martyrdom of St. Laurence. 1867.

DUVAL-LE-CAMUS, Pierre, a French genre and portrait painter, was born at Lisieux in 1790. He studied under David, and became painter-in-ordinary to the Duchess of Berry. He died at St. Cloud in 1854. Amongst his works are:

The Baptism. 1819.
The Brothers of the Christian Doctrine. 1822.
Interior of a Kitchen. 1824.
Ennui. 1827.
Labourer's Family returning from school. 1827.
Halt of Huntsmen. 1837.
Wolf-Hunting. 1838.
The Blessing of Orphans. (*Louvre.*)
The First Gatherings of Harvest. (*Louvre.*)
Pifferaro teaching his Son. (*Louvre.*)
An Interior. (*Bordeaux Museum.*)

DUVAUX, Jules Antoine, painter and etcher, born at Bordeaux in 1818, was a pupil of Charlet, and a painter of battles and military subjects generally. Several of his pictures are in the Versailles Museum. He also worked much as an illustrative draughtsman and etcher for various publications. He died in 1884.

DUVEAU, Louis Jean Noël, a French painter, who was born at St. Malo in 1818, studied history and genre painting under Léon Cogniet in Paris, and afterwards visited Italy. He was successful in representing scenes of fisher-life in his native country. He died in Paris in 1867. In the Lille Museum is his 'Perseus and Andromeda,' painted in 1865.

DUVENEDE, Marcus van, a Flemish painter, was born at Bruges about 1674. He went to Rome when he was very young, and became a scholar of Carlo Maratti, in whose academy he studied four

Philip, Lord Wharton.
From the painting by Anthony Van Dyck.

years. There are several of his pictures in the churches and convents of his native city, of which the most esteemed is the 'Martyrdom of St. Laurence' in the chapel of St. Christopher. He died at Bruges in 1730.

DUVET, JEAN, (Master of the Unicorn,) a French engraver, was born in 1481 at Langres, and died after 1561. Goldsmith to Francis I. and Henry II. of France; engraved over sixty plates, among them the 'Apocalypse,' the 'Annunciation,' a series of animals, and several allegorical subjects, in which the unicorn is introduced.

DU VIVIER, G. See VIVIER, G. DE.

DU VIVIER, IGNAZ, a painter born at Rians in 1758, was instructed by Casanova, and executed battle-scenes in the style of his master. He afterwards removed to Vienna and turned his attention chiefly to landscapes; a 'Waterfall' by him is in the Vienna Gallery. He also etched a large number of landscapes and genre pictures. He died in Paris in 1832.

DUVIVIER, JEAN BERNARD, a native of Bruges, was a painter of historical subjects and professor at the Normal School in Paris. After having been instructed by Hubert, Paul de Kock, and Suvée, he studied for six years in Italy, and his style is distinguished for beautiful composition, correct drawing, and bright colouring. He died in Paris in 1837.

DU VIVIER, LOUISE. See under TARDIEU, JACQUES NICOLAS.

DÜWETT, GERRIT, (often called DE WETT, DE WET, DE WETH, or DE WEET,) was born at Amsterdam in 1616, and died there in 1679. He was a scholar of Rembrandt, whose manner he imitated; he also painted landscapes, and was accounted a good colourist. There is in the Copenhagen Gallery 'Jephthah's Daughter' by him.

DÜWETT, JACOB, (or DE WET,) was probably a son of Jan Düwett. In 1677 he entered the Guild of St. Luke at Cologne, where he flourished for many years.

DÜWETT, JAN, (DE WET, DE WETTE, or DE WETH,) is said to have been born at Hamburg in 1617, but the date of his birth was probably earlier. While quite young he entered the school of Rembrandt at Amsterdam, and his style partakes of that of his master and also of that of Gerard Dou. He produced a large number of biblical and mythological pictures, many of which have been sold as Rembrandt's. He afterwards settled in Hamburg, but the date of his death is not recorded. The 'Raising of Lazarus' by him, dated 1633, is in the Darmstadt Gallery, and 'Christ in the Temple' (1635) and the 'Burning of Troy' are at Brunswick: other pictures by him are at Kiel and Copenhagen. His brother, EMANUEL DÜWETT, (or DE WETT,) a native of Hamburg, who was likewise a pupil of Rembrandt, painted landscapes in the style of Uytenbrouck.

DUYNEN, ISAAC VAN, was a native of Antwerp, who went in 1664 to the Hague, where he became a pupil of Van Beyeren, and painted sea and river fish very successfully. He died at the Hague in 1688 or 1689. There is a picture of 'Cod-fish' by him in the Lille Museum.

DUYSTER, W. C., a Netherlandish painter, was the author of a painting representing 'Soldiers playing at Tric-trac' in the Hermitage at St. Petersburg.

DYCE, WILLIAM, a Scottish historical painter, was born at Aberdeen in 1806, and educated at Marischal College, where he graduated at the age of sixteen. He then studied art at the Royal Academies of Edinburgh and London. After two prolonged visits to Rome, which may be said to have formed his style, he settled at Edinburgh in 1830. Here, for the next few years, he painted portraits, and was elected an Associate of the Royal Scottish Academy in 1835. The year 1837 saw the publication of his pamphlet on art education, which led to his being placed at the head of the government Schools of Design throughout the country. He entered into the Westminster Hall competitions, and produced for the decoration of the Houses of Parliament 'The Baptism of Ethelbert,' and the series of frescoes illustrating the history of King Arthur. He also painted frescoes for the church of All Saints, Margaret Street, London, and executed decorative works for the Queen at Osborne and Buckingham Palace. He was elected an Associate of the Royal Academy in 1844, and an Academician in 1848. He died in London in 1864. The following are some of the chief works exhibited by him:

Bacchus nursed by the Nymphs. 1827.
The Infant Hercules. 1830.
The Judgment of Solomon. (A cartoon.) 1836. } *National Gallery of Scotland.*
Francesca da Rimini. 1837.
James Hamilton, M.D.
Piety and Faith. Sir Galahad and his Companions.
Mercy.
The Descent of Venus. 1836.
St. Dunstan separating Edwy and Elgiva. 1839.
The Christian Yoke. 1841.
Joash shooting the Arrow of Deliverance. 1844.
Jacob and Rachel. 1853.
Titian's First Essay in Colour. 1857.
St. John leading home the Virgin. 1860.
George Herbert at Bemerton. 1861.

DYCK, ANTHONIS VAN, the eminent portrait painter, was born of good family at Antwerp, on the 22nd of March, 1599. He was the seventh child of a family of twelve; his father, Frans van Dyck, was a silk merchant, and his mother, Maria Cuypers, was skilled in embroidery and other arts. Van Dyck was apprenticed to Hendrik van Balen when he was but ten years old, and in 1615 entered the academy of the great painter Rubens, with whom he remained till 1620 as his assistant. In 1618 Van Dyck was admitted into the Guild of St. Luke at Antwerp. In 1620 he paid a short visit to England, and worked in the service of James I., from whom he received £100 for special services. In 1621 he was back in Antwerp, and by the advice of Rubens, set out for Italy, where he arrived in November 1621, and executed many important works. He stayed chiefly at Genoa, but also visited Rome, Venice, and Palermo. On his return to Antwerp in 1626, Van Dyck at once became famous as a painter both of historical subjects and of portraits. Among the chief historical works which he then executed were a 'Crucifixion' for the church of St. Michael at Ghent, and a 'St. Augustine' for the church of the Augustines at Antwerp. He was now loaded with commissions, and became even a rival to Rubens.

In 1630 Van Dyck visited the Hague—whither he had been invited by the Prince of Orange—and is said to have gone to London, but, as he did not meet with the encouragement which he had been led to believe he should receive from the English monarch, to have returned to Antwerp. Charles I., on seeing a portrait of the musician, Nicholas Laniere, in 1632 invited the painter to return. Van Dyck was most graciously received by Charles, who gave him apartments at Blackfriars, where he was often honoured with a visit from the king, who frequently sat to him. He was styled "Principal Painter in Ordinary to their Majesties at St. James's,' and on the 5th of July, 1632, he received the honour of knighthood. In the same month he received £280 for "diverse pictures by him made for his Majestye," and in the following year he was granted an annual salary of £200. From this time Van Dyck became the favourite painter in England: not only the monarch, and his wife and children, but all the court sat to him. He was wont to receive, Walpole tells us, £60 for a full-length, and £40 for a half-length portrait. "He was indefatigable," adds that author, "and, keeping a great table, often detained the persons who sat to him, for an opportunity of studying their countenances, and of retouching their pictures again in the afternoon." In the State Paper Office there is preserved a document which shows that Van Dyck charged Charles I. on an average about £50 for a portrait. He lived in a grand and almost regal manner, in the summer at Eltham, and in the winter at Blackfriars. In 1634–5 Van Dyck visited Brussels and executed some of his finest paintings. After the death of Rubens in 1640 Van Dyck returned to Antwerp, but went to Paris in the hope of a royal commission there. Disappointed in this, and broken in health, he returned to England.

Van Dyck died in Blackfriars, London, December 9, 1641. Two days afterwards he was buried in the old cathedral of St. Paul, near the tomb of John of Gaunt. He bequeathed to his wife, Mary Ruthven, a grand-daughter of William, first Earl of Gowrie, and to his daughter Justiniana, all his goods, effects, and moneys due to him in England from King Charles, the nobility, and all other persons whatever, to be equally divided between them. He also left other legacies to his executors, to his trustees, to his daughter, to his sisters, to his natural daughter Maria Theresa, to his servants, and to the poor of St. Paul's and St. Anne's, Blackfriars. Lady Van Dyck married, as her second husband, Sir Richard Pryse, Bart.

In the Museum of Antwerp the precious tables are still preserved in which the names of the Deans of the Corporation of Painters were successively inscribed from its foundation in 1454 until its extinction in 1778. Two names only in this long list are inscribed in capital letters—that of Rubens, under the date 1631, and that of Van Dyck, under the date 1634.

It is, perhaps, without example in the history of the art, that a painter, cut off in the vigour of his life, should have left such a multiplicity of works, the number of which is perhaps not exceeded by those of Rubens. If we cannot, in a general view, place him on an equality with Rubens as an historical painter, it will be allowed that he surpassed him in the correctness of his design, in the delicate expression of his heads, in the truth and purity of his colouring, and in the tender blending of his tones. If he had less boldness of conception, and less fecundity of invention, his compositions are regulated by judgment and propriety, and it may be reasonably presumed, that if, like his illustrious instructor, he had devoted himself to that branch, and had not been chiefly engaged in portrait-painting, he possessed the genius, as well as every other

110

requisite, to have reached the highest rank among the painters of history.

In portraiture Van Dyck will not be denied the most honourable place after Titian, and it will even then be admitted that Titian is superior only in the heads of his portraits, but that in the hands and accessories he is inferior to Van Dyck, both in correctness and in elegance. Van Dyck's attitudes are easy and natural, and they captivate by an air of unaffected simplicity for which his portraits are singularly remarkable. His heads are full of life and expression, without anything of the coldness and insipidity which are frequently found in the productions of the portrait painter. The pictures which he painted in Italy have more of the Venetian colouring than those of a subsequent period. The influence of Titian is paramount, and at this period even stronger than that of Rubens. On his return to Antwerp he recurred to the Flemish mode, although he occasionally blended the two. The earlier portraits which he painted in England are brilliantly coloured and carefully finished in all their parts; but as business increased they were executed with more despatch, and much of the subordinate portion was left to be completed by his pupils or assistants, the head only being painted by the master. Besides the many admirable pictures which he painted of the king and the royal family, there are in England many fine portraits of distinguished personages, which are among the chief ornaments of the mansions of the nobility.

There were no less than seventy-two portraits of the English nobility attributed to Van Dyck exhibited in the National Portrait Exhibition of 1866, and Smith, in his 'Catalogue Raisonné,' gives a list of upwards of nine hundred and fifty works by this painter. There are many unnamed portraits in the public galleries of Europe as well as in private collections which are not mentioned in the following list. Many of these portraits, however, are only the work of his pupils and assistants.

PORTRAITS BY VAN DYCK.

Arundel, Thomas Howard, Earl of, and his grandson Thomas (afterwards 5th Duke of Norfolk) . .	Duke of Norfolk.
Balbi Children . . .	Earl Cowper.
Baltimore, Anne Arundell, Lady. *Bust*	Lord Arundell of Wardour.
Basset, Admiral Sir Francis. *Full length* . . .	Mr. J. F. Bassett.
Bedford, Ann Carr, Countess of	Duke of Bedford.
Bentivoglio, Cardinal .	Pitti Palace, Florence.
Berg, Count Henry de .	Madrid Gallery.
Bolingbroke, Family of the first Earl of. *Seven half-length portraits in a garden* .	Earl of Morley.
Brignole, La Marchesa de, and Child. *Full length* .	Earl of Warwick.
Brignole Family . .	Palazzo Brignoli, Genoa.
Bristol, George Digby, Earl of, and William Earl of Bedford. *Full length* .	Earl Spencer.
Brueghel, Jan . . .	Hermitage, St. Petersburg.
Buckingham, George Villiers, Duke of, and his Brother Francis, as boys. *Full length*	Windsor Castle.
Burlington, Richard Boyle, first Earl of . . .	Duke of Devonshire.
Cante Croix, Beatrice de Cusance, Princess de .	Windsor Castle.
Carew, Thomas, *the poet*, and Sir William Killigrew .	Windsor Castle.

[*The Louvre, Paris*

CHARLES I.

Carignan, Thomas François de, Prince of Savoy . . . Berlin Gallery.

Carignan, Prince Thomas of, on horseback . . . Pinacoteca, Turin.

Carlisle, Countess of . . Lord Leconfield.

Carlisle, James Hay, Earl of. Full length . . . . Lord Lyttelton.

Chaloner, Thomas . . Hermitage, St. Petersburg.

Charles I. Full length, with horse and attendants . . Louvre, Paris.

Charles I. Full length, wearing the collar and badge of the Order of the Garter. Dated 1636 . . . . The King.

Charles I. Full length . . Louisa Lady Ashburton.

Charles I. in armour, mounted on a dun-coloured horse, his equerry, Sir Thomas Morton, holding the king's helmet . National Gallery.

Charles I. in armour. For the picture at Blenheim . . Buckingham Palace.

Charles I. Equestrian portrait. M. St. Antoine, bearing the king's helmet, is on foot by his side . . . . Windsor Castle.

Charles I. Equestrian portrait. (A replica of the Windsor picture.) . . . . Hampton Court.

Charles I. Half length, full face, with baton, helmet, and crown . . . . Duke of Norfolk.

Charles I. Three heads in different positions, painted for Bernini's bust . . Windsor Castle.

Charles I., standing, in armour. Hermitage, St. Petersburg.

Charles I. . . . . Dresden Gallery.

Charles I. and Queen Henrietta Maria . . . . Duke of Grafton.

Charles I. and Queen Henrietta Maria, with their sons, Charles and James . . Windsor Castle.

Charles I. and Queen Henrietta Maria . . . Pitti Palace, Florence.

Queen Henrietta Maria. Full length . . . . Hermitage, St. Petersburg.

Charles I., Three Children of . Turin Gallery.

Charles, Prince of Wales, with the Princesses Elizabeth, Mary, and Anne, and James, Duke of York. Dated 1637 . Windsor Castle.

Charles, Prince of Wales, Princess Mary, and James, Duke of York, with two spaniels seated at their feet . Windsor Castle.

Charles II., when a boy . Windsor Castle.

The same, when a boy . Duke of Portland.

Charles V., on a white horse . Uffizi, Florence.

Charles Louis, Prince (elder brother of Prince Rupert) . Vienna Gallery.

Charles Louis, Prince, and his brother Prince Rupert . Louvre Palace.

Chesterfield, Catharine, Countess of. (Painted about 1636.) Earl of Radnor.

Clanbrazil, Countess of. (Painted in 1636.) . . . Earl of Denbigh.

Cleveland, Thomas Wentworth, first Earl of. Full length. Dated 1636 . . . Earl of Verulam.

Cleveland, Thomas Wentworth, first Earl of, with his wife and daughter . . . Earl of Strafford.

Cranfield, Lady Frances, wife of Richard, fifth Earl of Dorset . . . . Lord Sackville.

Craven, William, first Earl of. Full length . . . Earl of Craven.

Danby, Henry Danvers, Earl of. Full length . . . Mr. F. V. Wentworth.

Danby, Henry Danvers, Earl of. Hermitage, St. Petersburg.

Delawarr, Isabella Edmunds, Lady. Full length . . Earl Delawarr.

Dellafaille, Alexander, magistrate of Antwerp . . . Brussels Gallery.

Denbigh, William Fielding, first Earl of . . . . Duke of Hamilton.

Derby, James Stanley, seventh Earl of, his wife, Charlotte de la Trémouille, and daughter, Lady Katharine Stanley . Earl of Clarendon.

Derby, James Stanley (Lord Strange), seventh Earl of. Full length . . . . Earl of Derby.

Devonshire, Christian, Countess of . . . . . Duke of Northumberland.

De Wael, Jan and his wife . Munich Gallery.

De Wael, Lucas and Cornelis . Capitol Gallery, Rome.

Digby, Lady Venetia, wife of Sir Kenelm Digby . . Windsor College.

Digby, Lady Venetia, on her death-bed. Bust . . Dulwich Gallery.

Digby, Lady Venetia, on her death-bed. Bust . . Earl Spencer, Windsor Castle.

Digby, Sir Kenelm . . Windsor Castle.

Digby, Sir Kenelm. Half length . . . . National Portrait Gal.

Digby, Sir Kenelm, and Family. Half length, figures seated . Mr. Wingfield Digby.

Doria Family . . . Duke of Abercorn.

Dorset, Frances Cranfield, Countess of . . . Windsor Castle.

Dorset, Edward Sackville, fourth Earl of . . . Lord Sackville.

Dyck, Sir Anthon van. Bust . National Portrait Gal.

Dyck, Sir Anthon van . . Louvre, Paris.

Dyck, Sir Anthon van, and the Earl of Bristol . . Madrid Gallery.

Dyck, Sir Anthon van . . Windsor Castle.

Dyck, Sir Anthon van, when young . . . . Munich Gallery.

Elizabeth, The Princess, and Duke of Gloucester, children of Charles I. (A study of heads) . . . . Lord Chesham.

Ertvelt, Andries van, the marine painter . . . . Augsburg Gallery.

Fernando, Don, of Austria . Madrid Gallery.

Frederick Henry of Nassau, Prince of Orange . . . Madrid Gallery.

Grandison, William Villiers, Viscount. Full length . . Earl of Clarendon.

Hamilton, Mary, Duchess of, daughter of William, first Earl of Denbigh . . Earl of Denbigh.

Hamilton, James, first Duke of. Earl of Denbigh.

Hamilton, James, first Duke of. Duke of Hamilton.

Henrietta Maria, Queen . Ambrosian Library, Milan.

Henrietta Maria, Queen. Full face . . . . Windsor Castle.

Henrietta Maria, Queen. Three-quarter face . . . Windsor Castle.

Henrietta Maria, Queen. Profile . . . . Windsor Castle.

Henrietta Maria, Queen. Full length . . . . Earl of Clarendon.

Henrietta Maria, Queen. Full length . . . . Louisa, Lady Ashburton.

Henrietta, Maria, Queen. Standing by a table . . Hermitage, St. Petersburg.

Henrietta Maria, Queen . Dresden Gallery,

Henrietta Maria, Queen, with her dwarf, Sir Geoffrey Hudson . . . . Earl of Northbrook.

Henrietta Maria, Queen. Signed "M.R. 1632" . . . Earl of Radnor.

Hontsum Zeger van, canon of Antwerp Cathedral . . Buckingham Palace.

Huntly, George Gordon, second Marquis of. Full length . Duke of Buccleuch.

Isabella Clara Eugenia, Infanta of Spain . . . . Louvre, Paris.

Isabella Clara Eugenia, Infanta of Spain, in her widow's dress. Duke of Buccleuch.

Isabella Clara Eugenia, Infanta of Spain, in her widow's dress. Louvre, Paris.

Isabella Clara Eugenia, Infanta of Spain . . . . Marquis of Linlithgow.

Jones Inigo . . . . Hermitage, St. Petersburg.

Killigrew, Thomas, and Thomas Carew. *Signed, and dated* 1628 . . . . Windsor Castle.
(See Carew.)

Killigrew, Mrs. Cecilia Crofts. *Bust* . . . . Mr. R. H. Cheney.

Kirk, Madame . . . Earl Cowper.

Laud, William, Archbishop of Canterbury. *Half length.* Dated 1633 . . . . Lambeth Palace.

Laud, Archbishop. (*Replica.*). Hermitage, St. Petersburg.

Laud, Archbishop . . . Earl Fitzwilliam.

Leers, Burgomaster van, of Antwerp, his wife and their son . . . . . Cassel Gallery.

Leicester, Countess of, and Countess of Carlisle, daughters of Henry Percy, ninth Earl of Northumberland. *Half lengths, seated near a fountain* . . . . Mrs. Charles Morrison.

Leicester, Dorothy Percy, Countess of . . . Earl Spencer.

Lemon, Mrs. Margaret . . Hampton Court.

Lady Aubigny, Catharine Howard . . . Windsor Castle.

Le Roy, Philippe. *Inscribed* " Ætatis suæ 34. 1630" . . Wallace Collection.

Le Roy, the wife of Philippe. *Inscribed* " Et. sua 16. 1631 " Wallace Collection.

Liberti, Hendrik, *organist of Antwerp* . . . Madrid Gallery.

Liberti, Hendrik . . . Munich Gallery.

Lomellini Family . . . National Gallery of Scotland.

Malderus, Jan, Bishop of Antwerp . . . . Antwerp Gallery.

Mallery, Karel van, *the engraver* . . . . Munich Gallery.

Manchester, Lord Kimbolton, second Earl of. *Half length* Duke of Manchester.

Mary de' Medici, Queen of France . . . . Lille Museum.

Mary de' Medici . . . Munich Gallery.

Meerstraeten, Justus van. . Cassel Gallery.

Moncada, Francisco, Marquis de . . . . Vienna Gallery.

Moncada. Francisco de, *on horseback.* (*A study of this, a bust, is also in the Louvre.*) Louvre Palace.

Monmouth, the Countess of . Earl of Radnor.

Montfort, Johann van . . Uffizi, Florence.

Montfort, John . . . Vienna Gallery.

Morton, Anne, Countess of *Half length* . . . Earl Spencer.

Mowbray and Maltravers, Henry Frederick Howard, Lord . . . . Duke of Norfolk.

Nassau, John, Count of . . Munich Gallery.

Nassau, John, Count of . . Lord Ashburton.

Nassau, John, Count of, his wife, son, and three daughters. *Dated* 1634 . . Earl Cowper.

Naunton, Lady Penelope . . Dulwich Gallery.

Neuburg, Duke Wolfgang Wilhelm von . . . Munich Gallery.

Newcastle, William Cavendish, Duke of. *Full length* . Earl Spencer.

The same. *Full length* . Duke of Portland.

Newport, Mountjoy Blount, Earl of. *Full length* . Earl of Northcote.

Nole, Andreas Colyns de . Munich Gallery.

Nole, Andreas Colyns de, wife of . . . . . Munich Gallery.

Northumberland, Henry Percy, ninth Earl of. *Bust* . Earl of Denbigh.

Northumberland, Henry Percy, ninth Earl of. *Full length, seated* . . . . Lord Leconfield.

Northumberland, Algernon Percy, tenth Earl of. *Full length* . . . . Duke of Northumberland.

Northumberland, Algernon Percy, Earl of, his Countess, and their Child. *Half lengths* Marquis of Salisbury.

Odescalchi, Don Livio, nephew of Pope Innocent IX., *standing* . . . . Sir H. H. Campbell, Bart.

Orleans, Gaston, Duke of . Earl of Radnor.

Oxford, The Countess of . Madrid Gallery.

Parr, Thomas, in his 151st year Dresden Gallery.

Pembroke, Philip Herbert, fifth Earl of, with his family . Wilton House.

Pembroke, Philip Herbert, fifth Earl of. *Half length* . Dulwich Gallery.

Pembroke and Montgomery, Philip, fourth Earl of. *Half length* . . . . Earl of Carnarvon.

Peterborough, The first Countess of . . . Mrs. Elkington Bisset.

Peterborough, John, Earl of, *standing* . . . Mrs. Elkington Bisset.

Phalsburg, Henrietta of Lorraine, Princess of. *Full length* . . . . Lord Iveagh.

Portland, Countess of. *Full length* . . . . Lord Lyttelton.

Portland, Richard Weston, Earl of. *Full length* . Mr. Ralph Bankes.

Rich, Lady Isabella. *Life size, standing* . . . Lady Elizabeth Pringle.

Richardot, Jean Grusset, and his son . . . . Louvre, Paris.

Richmond, The Duchess of, *represented in the character of St. Agnes* . . . Windsor Castle.

Richmond and Lennox, Frances Howard, Duchess of. *Full length. Dated London,* 1633 Marquis of Bath.

Richmond, Mary, Duchess of, daughter of George Villiers, Duke of Buckingham, with the dwarf, Mrs. Gibson . Earl of Denbigh.

Richmond, The Duke of, *standing* . . . Louvre, Paris.

Richmond and Lennox, James Stuart, Duke of . . Duke of Buccleuch.

Richmond and Lennox, James Stuart, Duke of, with the dog which saved his life . Earl of Denbigh.

Richmond and Lennox, James Stuart, Duke of. *Full length, standing* . . . Earl of Leicester.

Richmond and Lennox, James Stuart, Duke of. *Life size, standing, with dog* . Marquand College, New York.

Rubens, Sir Peter Paul, *on a horse given him by Van Dyck* Earl of Radnor.

Rupert, Prince, *when twelve years old* . . . Vienna Gallery.

Rupert, Prince . . . Earl of Craven.

Ruthven, Mary (Van Dyck's wife), *as Herminia putting on Clorinda's armour* . Mr. J. E. Hartford.

Ryckaert, *the painter* . . Madrid Gallery.

Ryckaert, Martin, *the painter* . Dresden Gallery.

Scaglia, Cesare Alessandro . Captain Holford.

Simons, Quentyn . . . Hague Gallery,

Snayers, Pieter, *the painter* . Munich Gallery.

Snyders, Frans . . . Earl of Carlisle.

Snyders, Frans, and wife . Cassel Gallery.

Snyders, Frans, Wife of . . Earl of Warwick.

Scribani, Carolius . . . Vienna Gallery.

Solms, Amalia von (*wife of Prince Henry Frederick of Orange*) . . . . Vienna Gallery.

Solms, Emilie von . . . Madrid Gallery.

Southampton, Elizabeth, Countess of . . . Earl Cowper.

Southampton, Rachael, first Countess of . . . Earl Cowper.

Spinola, Andrea, Doge of Genoa. *Full length, seated* . Mr. Heywood-Lonsdale.

Thomas Wentworth Earl of Strafford and his Secretary, Sir Philip Mainwaring

From the painting by Anthony Van Dyck.

Spinola, The Marquis. *Full length* . . . . . Marquis of Linlithgow.
Spinola, Polixena, Marchioness of Leganes . . . . Madrid Gallery.
Strafford, Thomas Wentworth, first Earl of. *Full length, in half armour* . . . . Earl of Home.
Strafford, Thomas, first Earl of, and his secretary, Sir Philip Mainwaring. *Half length, seated.* . . . Earl Fitzwilliam.
Strafford, Thomas, Earl of . Earl Fitzwilliam.
Stuart, Lord John, and Lord Bernard, sons of the Duke of Lennox . . . . . Earl of Darnley.
Sunderland, Dorothy Sidney, Countess of. *Half length* . Lord De L'Isle and Dudley.
Sunderland, Dorothy Sidney, Countess of. *Half length* . Earl Spencer.
Triest, Anthonius, Bishop of Ghent . . . . . Hermitage, St. Petersburg.
Van den Wouver (Waverius), Jan . . . . . Hermitage, St. Petersburg.
Van der Borcht, *Burgomaster of Antwerp* . . . . Amsterdam Museum.
Van der Geest, Cornelis. *Formerly supposed to represent Gevartius* . . . . National Gallery.
Villiers, George and Francis, sons of the *Duke of Buckingham* . . . . . Windsor Castle.
Wandesford, Sir Rowland. . Hermitage, St. Petersburg.
Warwick, Earl of, *in armour* . Earl of Leicester.
Wemmel, Engelbert Taie, Baron of . . . . Dresden Gallery.
Wentworth, Lady Arabella . Earl Fitzwilliam.
Wharton Philip, Lord . . Hermitage, St. Petersburg.
Wharton, Lady . . . Hermitage, St. Petersburg.
Cary Family . . . . Hermitage, St. Petersburg.
Wharton, Sir Thomas . . Hermitage, St. Petersburg.
William, Prince of Orange, and his *fiancée*, the Princess Mary, Daughter of Charles I. Amsterdam Museum.
Worcester, Edward Somerset, second Marquis of. *Half length* . . . . Duke of Beaufort.

SACRED SUBJECTS.

Betrayal of Christ . . Madrid Gallery.
Betrayal of Christ . . Lord Methuen.
Christ Bound . . . Vienna Gallery.
Christ on the Cross . . Vienna Gallery.
Christ on the Cross . . Munich Gallery.
Christ on the Cross. 1629 . Antwerp Gallery.
Christ on the Cross . . Lille Museum.
Christ healing the Paralytic . Buckingham Palace.
Christ and the Pharisee . Palazzo Brignoli, Genoa.
Christ crowned with Thorns. (*An altered copy of Titian's picture at Munich.*) . . Madrid Gallery.
Crucifixion, The . . . St. Jacques, Antwerp.
Crucifixion, The . . . Notre-Dame, Courtray.
Crucifixion, The . . . Cathedral, Mechlin.
Crucifixion, The. (*Study.*) . Hermitage, St. Petersburg.
Dead Christ. (*Small.*) . . Louvre, Paris.
Descent of the Holy Ghost . Berlin Gallery.
Descent from the Cross . Antwerp Gallery.
Ecce Homo . . . . Marquis of Linlithgow.
Entombment, The . . . Antwerp Gallery.
Entombment, The. (*Study.*) . Hermitage, St. Petersburg.
Flight into Egypt . . . Munich Gallery.
Flight into Egypt . . . Pitti Palace, Florence.
Four Repentant Sinners before Christ . . . . Augsburg Gallery.

Incredulity of St. Thomas . Hermitage, St. Petersburg.
Infant Saviour embracing St. John . . . . . Windsor Castle.
Infant Christ and St. John . Mrs. Morrison.
Madonna and SS. Peter, Paul, and Rosalia. 1629 . Vienna Gallery.
Madonna and Child . . Bridgewater House.
Madonna and Child. (*A replica of the Bridgewater Gallery picture.*) . . . . Dulwich Gallery.
Madonna, The . . . . Brunswick Gallery.
Madonna, *as Queen of Heaven* . Dresden Gallery.
Madonna and Child, with Saints . . . . . Louvre, Paris.
Madonna and Child . . Buckingham Palace.
Madonna, The. *Life size.* . Buckingham Palace.
Madonna, The. *Life size.* . Uffizi, Florence.
Madonna and Donor . . Vienna Gallery.
Madonna and Donors . . Louvre, Paris.
Madonna and St. Anthony . Brera, Milan.
Madonna and Child . . Lord Ashburton.
Madonna and Child . . Munich Gallery.
Madonna and Child, with St. Catharine . . . . Duke of Westminster.
St. Mary Magdalen . . Vienna Gallery.
Magdalen, The Penitent . Amsterdam Museum.
Holy Family . . . Acad. of St. Luke, Rome.
Holy Family . . . Vienna Gallery.
Holy Family, with the partridges. (*Replicas are in the Pitti Palace and in the Museums of Nantes and Tours.*) Hermitage, St. Petersburg.
Holy Family . . . Munich Gallery.
Holy Family . . . Pinacoteca, Turin.
Holy Family . . . Miss de Rothschild.
Last Supper . . . Hermitage, St. Petersburg.
Marriage of St. Catharine . Buckingham Palace.
Miraculous Draught of Fishes. (*A study after Rubens.*) . National Gallery.
Mocking of Christ, The . Berlin Gallery.
Pietà . . . . . Berlin Gallery.
Pietà . . . . . Munich Gallery.
Pietà . . . . . Vienna Gallery.
Pietà . . . . . Louvre, Paris.
St. Anthony of Padua holding the Infant Saviour . . Brussels Gallery.
St. Augustine in Ecstasy . St. Augustine's, Antwerp.
St. Francis in Ecstasy . Brussels Gallery.
St. Francis in Ecstasy . Madrid Gallery.
St. Jerome . . . . Dresden Gallery.
St. Jerome . . . . Madrid Gallery.
St. John the Evangelist and St. John the Baptist . Berlin Gallery.
A Dying Saint. (*A sketch in grisaille.*) . . . Hampton Court.
St. Martin dividing his Cloak. Saventhem, Belgium.
St. Peter . . . . Berlin Gallery.
St. Peter, Martyrdom of . Brussels Gallery.
St. Sebastian . . . Louvre, Paris.
St. Sebastian . . . Munich Gallery.
St. Sebastian. (*A sketch.*) . Earl of Warwick.
St. Sebastian, Martyrdom of . National Gallery of Scotland.
St. Sebastian, Martyrdom of . Hermitage, St. Petersburg.
St. Stephen, Martyrdom of . Lord Egerton of Tatton.
Samson and Delilah . . Vienna Gallery.
Susannah and the Elders . Munich Gallery.

MISCELLANEOUS SUBJECTS.

Boys blowing Soap Bubbles . Hermitage, St. Petersburg.
Child's Head. (*Study in crayon.*) . . . . Academy of St. Luke, Rome.
Cupid and Psyche . . . Hampton Court.
Danäe and the Golden Shower. Dresden Gallery.
Dædalus and Icarus . . Earl Spencer.
Diana and Endymion . . Madrid Gallery.

Emperor Theodosius refused admission into the Church by St. Ambrose. (*Copy, with slight alterations, of Rubens's picture in the Vienna Gallery.*) . National Gallery.
Greenwich Palace, *with figures in the foreground, among which are portraits of Charles I., Henrietta Maria, Lord Arundell, and others* . . . Buckingham Palace.
Horses. (*A study.*) . . . National Gallery.
Rinaldo and Armida . . Louvre, Paris.
Rinaldo and Armida . . Duke of Newcastle.
Silenus . . . . Dresden Gallery.
Silenus . . . . Brussels Gallery.
Study of three Horses, with their Riders . . . Buckingham Palace.
Study of a Man on Horseback . Augsburg Gallery.
Venus and Vulcan . . Vienna Gallery.
Venus and Vulcan . . Louvre, Paris.

This distinguished painter occasionally occupied himself with the point, and has etched several plates, which are executed with a spirit and fire bordering on enthusiasm. They consist chiefly of portraits of the most eminent artists of his time, from his own designs, animated with a vigour and energy which are perhaps without example. The following are his principal works:

Christ crowned with Thorns; *A. Van Dyck, inv.*
A Holy Family.

PORTRAITS.

Adam van Oort, Painter.
Justus Suttermans, Painter, of Antwerp.
Pieter Brueghel, Painter.
Lucas Vorsterman, Engraver.
Jodocus De Momper, Painter.
Paulus Pontius, Engraver.
Jan Brueghel, Painter.
Frans Franck, Painter.
Jan De Wael, Painter.
Jan Snellinx, Painter.
Titian, with his Mistress, who is leaning on a casket, with a skull; *after Titian.*
Antonis Cornelissen, Amateur.
Desiderius Erasmus.
Sir Anthonius van Dyck.
Philippe Le Roy.
Frans Snyders, Painter.
Anthonius Triest, Bishop of Ghent.
William De Vos, Painter.
Paulus De Vos, Painter.
Jan van den Wouwer.

There are several other plates attributed to Van Dyck, but being doubtful they are here omitted.

These portraits form part of a series intended to represent the leading statesmen, warriors, and artists of the age. They appear to have been drawn originally in pencil by Van Dyck himself, then copied in grisaille, in some cases perhaps by Van Dyck, and then engraved by the best engravers. The first edition was published after Van Dyck's death by Martin van der Enden, the second in 1645 by G. Hending.

The works of Van Dyck are best studied in the great picture-galleries of Europe, such as the Louvre, Antwerp, Munich, Dresden, Cassel, Madrid, and St. Petersburg. In England Van Dyck is but scantily represented in the National collections, most of the finest specimens of his work being in the hands of private owners, or in the royal collections at Windsor Castle and Buckingham Palace. A fine set of his etchings and the other plates to the 'Iconographie' is in the Print-Room at the British Museum. Many of his finest paintings at Genoa

remain in their original positions in the palaces there, and in Belgium many of his altar-pieces remain in the churches at Mechlin, Ghent, and Antwerp, though in most cases seriously damaged by damp and neglect. Original sketches by Van Dyck, showing the variety of his ideas, are to be met with in all the great collections of drawings. The sketch-book used by him in Italy is in the possession of the Duke of Devonshire at Chatsworth.

BIBLIOGRAPHY.

Lionel Cust, 'Anthony van Dyck, an Historical Study.' London, Bell, 1900. (*The chief work on this artist.*)
Lionel Cust, 'The Chatsworth Sketch-Book,' with Notes. London, Bell, 1902.
Lionel Cust, 'Van Dyck.' London, Unicorn Press, 2 vols., 1903.
W. H. Carpenter, 'Pictorial Notices: consisting of a Memoir of Sir Anthony van Dyck, &c.' London, 1844, 4to.
Alfred Michiels, 'Rubens et l'École d'Anvers.' Paris, 1854, 8vo.
Georges Duplessis, 'Eaux-fortes de Antoine van Dyck, reproduites par Amand-Durand.' Paris, 1874, folio.
Carl Lemcke, 'Anton van Dyck.' Leipzig, 1875, 8vo.
Fr. Wibiral, 'Iconographie d'Antoine van Dyck, d'après les recherches de H. Weber.' Leipzig, 1877, 8vo.
Alfred Michiels, 'Van Dyck et ses élèves.' Paris, 1881, 8vo.
Jules Guiffrey, 'Antoine van Dyck, sa vie et son œuvre.' Paris, 1882, folio.:
L. C.

DYCK, DANIEL VAN DEN. See VAN DEN DYCK.

DYCK, HERMANN, a Bavarian painter, born at Würzburg in 1812, studied architectural and genre painting at Munich. His works are original and of great humour, and are neatly and carefully executed. The satirical designs for the 'Fliegende Blätter,' in reference to the rage for monuments, are incomparable. He was director of the Art Schools at Munich, where he died in 1874.

DYCKMANS, JOSEF LAURENS, a Flemish painter, was born at Lierre in 1811. He was a pupil of Tielemans and Wappers. He painted genre pictures, portraits in small, &c., in a style of the minutest finish. He was Professor in the Antwerp Academy, and died in 1888. Pictures:

The Blind Beggar. (*National Gallery.*)
Portrait Group. (*South Kensington Museum.*)

DYK, FLORIS VAN, (or DIJK,) a Dutch painter, was born probably in 1577. After residing some time in Italy, he entered the Guild at Haarlem in 1610, and became its dean in 1637. His death occurred probably in 1651. He executed historical pictures, but is better known as a painter of fruit and flowers, in which he excelled.

DYK, PHILIP VAN, (or DIJK,) called 'The Little Van Dyck,' a Dutch portrait painter, was born at Amsterdam in 1680. He was instructed by Arnold Boonen, and painted small portraits in the style of his master, but was more successfully employed in painting subjects similar to those of Mieris and Metsu, representing conversations, ladies at their toilets, and gallant assemblies. In 1710 he established himself at Middleburg, but was afterwards invited to the Hague, where he painted some of his best pictures. The reputation he had acquired recommended him to the notice of Prince William, afterwards Landgrave of Hesse, who not only engaged him to paint several pictures, but commissioned him to purchase the choicest works of art he could meet with in Holland and Flanders, for the rich collection he was then forming at

Cassel. On his return to the Hague he painted the portraits of the Stadtholder and his family, as well as several pictures for the cabinet of that prince. He died at the Hague in 1752. The following works by him are in public galleries :

Berlin.	Gallery.	The Lute-player.
„	„	The Drawing Lesson.
Brussels.	Gallery.	A Young Woman at her toilet. 1726.
Cassel.	Gallery.	The Landgrave Charles of Hesse and his Family.
„	„	The Penitent Magdalen.
Hague.	Gallery.	Judith. 1726.
„	„	A Young Woman playing the lute.
„	„	A Young Woman at her toilet.
„	„	The Book-keeper.
Paris.	Louvre.	Sarah presenting Hagar to Abraham.
„	„	Abraham sending away Hagar and Ishmael.

DYXHOORN, PIETER ARNOUT, a Dutch marine painter, was born at Rotterdam in 1810. He was a scholar of M. Schouman and of J. C. Schotel, and painted marine subjects and river scenes in an able manner. He died at Rotterdam in 1839.

E

EARLE, AUGUSTUS, a painter of historical and marine subjects, who, on account of his roving disposition, was known as "the wandering artist," was the son of Ralph Earle, the American portrait painter, who married when studying in London, and left his wife and children here when he returned home. Augustus Earle was the intimate friend of Leslie and of Morse, and their fellow-student at the Royal Academy in 1813. Many years afterwards, Morse inquired of Leslie for their old companion Earle. "He had visited every part of the Mediterranean," said Leslie, "roamed in Africa—rambled in the United States—sketched in South America—attempted to go to the Cape of Good Hope in a worn-out Margate hoy, and was shipwrecked on Tristan d'Acunha, where he passed six months with some old tars who hutted there —at length a vessel touched the desolate place —and released him. He then visited Van Diemen's Land, New South Wales, and New Zealand, where he drew from the naked figure, and saw the finest forms in the world addicted to cannibalism. Returning to Sydney, he, by way of variety, proceeded to the Caroline Islands—stopped at the Ladrones— looked in upon Manilla, and finally settled himself at Madras, and made money as a portrait painter. Not content, he went to Pondicherry, and there embarked for France, but stopped at the Mauritius, and after some few more calls at various places, found his way home." Besides a series of views in New South Wales, he published with illustrations in 1832, 'A Narrative of a nine months' residence in New Zealand, in 1827; together with a Journal of a residence in Tristan d'Acunha.' He exhibited at the Royal Academy between the years 1806 and 1815, and again in 1837 and 1838, after having accompanied Captain Fitzroy in the 'Beagle' to South America. The following were among his exhibited works:

The Judgment of Midas. 1806.
The Battle of Poictiers. 1808.
Banditti. 1811 and 1812.
A Man-of-war's Boats cutting out a French Barque. 1814
View of the Harbour and Town of Calais. 1815.

Life on the Ocean. 1837.
Divine Service on board a Man-of-war. 1837.
A Bivouac of Travellers in Australia. 1838.

EARLE, JAMES, an American portrait painter, was probably a brother of Ralph Earle. He was a native of Leicester, Massachusetts, and died of yellow fever at Charleston in 1796.

EARLE, RALPH, an American portrait and historical painter, was born at Leicester, Massachusetts, in 1751. He painted in 1775 four scenes in the battle of Lexington, which are believed to be the first historical paintings ever executed by an American artist. After the peace he came over to England and studied under West, but he returned to America in 1786, and died at Bolton, Connecticut, in 1801. He was of intemperate habits, and left his wife and children in London when he returned to his native country. Among his works are a large picture of the 'Falls of Niagara,' and portraits of King George III., Dr. Dwight, President of Yale College, and Governor Strong.

EARLOM, RICHARD, a mezzotint engraver, was born in London in 1743. He was a pupil of Cipriani, and was the first artist who made use of the point in mezzotint work. He first engraved for Boydell, who in 1777 brought out the 'Liber Veritatis,' comprising two hundred plates, executed by Earlom in the style of the original drawings by Claude Lorrain, which are for the most part in the possession of the Duke of Devonshire. He is especially known for his groups of flowers after Van Huysum and Van Os. He also executed some etchings, as well as some plates in the chalk style. Earlom died in London in 1822. The following are his principal plates :

ETCHINGS.

Portrait of Rembrandt; after Rembrandt.
Banditti and Travellers; after Salvator Rosa.
Jacob wrestling with the Angel; after the same.
David and Goliath; after the same.
Venus and Adonis; after N. Poussin.
The Death of Abel; after A. Sacchi.
Æneas saving Anchises from the Ruins of Troy; after Tintoretto.
The Holy Family; after Guercino.
Cupid bound; after Guido.

PORTRAITS IN MEZZOTINT.

William Henry, Duke of Gloucester; after Hamilton.
Thomas Newton, Bishop of Bristol; after West.
Sir Edward Astley, Bart.; after the same.
George Augustus Eliott, Lord Heathfield; after Sir J. Reynolds.
James Stuart, Duke of Richmond; after Van Dyck.
The Duke of Aremberg on horseback; after the same.
Rubens's Wife; after Rubens.
Portrait of Rembrandt; after Rembrandt.
Rembrandt's Wife; after the same.
Admiral Kempenfelt; after T. Kettle.
James Mac Ardell, engraver.

SUBJECTS AFTER VARIOUS MASTERS.

The Repose, called 'La Zingara;' after Correggio.
The Virgin and Infant; after Guercino.
The Virgin and Infant, with St. John; after Carlo Dolci.
Salvator Mundi; after the same.
The Virgin and Infant; after Cantarini.
The Infant Jesus sleeping; after Domenichino.
Simeon receiving the Infant Jesus; after Guido.
Christ curing the Blind; after Annibale Carracci.
Galatea; after Luca Giordano.
The Judgment of Paris; after the same.
The Misers; after Quentin Massys.
The Holy Family; after Rubens.
Mary Magdalen washing the Feet of Christ; after the same.

Nymphs and Satyrs ; *after the same.*
Meleager and Atalanta ; *after the same.*
The Death of Hippolytus ; *after the same.*
Rubens's Son and his Nurse ; *after the same.*
Elijah restoring to Life the Widow's Son ; *after Rembrandt.*
The Presentation in the Temple ; *after the same.*
Susannah and the Elders ; *after the same.*
A Boar attacked by a Lion ; *after Snyders.*
The Fruit-Market ; *after Snyders and Jan van Bockhorst.*
The Fish-Market ; *after the same.*
The Vegetable-Market ; *after the same.*
A Fruit-piece, and a Flower-piece ; *after Jan van Huysum ;* two plates ; extremely fine.
David and Bathsheba ; *after A. van der Werff ;* very fine.
The Enchantress ; *after D. Teniers.*
The Singing Master ; *after G. Schalken.*
The Interview between Augustus and Cleopatra ; *after R. Mengs.*
The Royal Family of England ; *after Zoffany.*
The Royal Academy ; *after the same.*
Angelica and Medora ; *after West.*
Cupid stung by a Bee ; *after the same.*
Meleager and Atalanta ; *after Richard Wilson.*
Apollo and the Nymphs ; *after the same.*
A Blacksmith's Shop ; *after Joseph Wright.*
An Iron Forge ; *after the same.*

WILLIAM EARLOM, his son, who was evincing decided talent as an artist, was cut off in 1789, when only seventeen years of age.

EASTLAKE, Sir CHARLES LOCK, the youngest son of George Eastlake, solicitor to the Admiralty and Judge-Advocate at Plymouth, was born in that town, November 17, 1793. He was educated at the Plympton Grammar School, where Sir Joshua Reynolds had previously studied, and he was one of the first pupils of Prout, also a native of Plymouth, whom he occasionally accompanied on his excursions into the country to study nature. When fourteen years of age, he was sent to the Charterhouse School, London, but he left in 1808 in order to study art under Haydon, his fellow-townsman. In 1809 he became a student in the Royal Academy Schools, and in 1814 visited Paris for a few months. In 1815, while Eastlake was employed painting portraits in his native town, Napoleon arrived there on board the 'Bellerophon,' and the young artist took advantage of every glimpse he could obtain of the ex-Emperor to make studies of him, by the aid of which he painted a life-size picture of Napoleon, standing at the gangway of the ship, attended by his officers. This work, which is now the property of the Marquis of Lansdowne, attracted great attention, and was so well sold as to enable the painter to visit Italy in 1817. He then, in 1819, proceeded to Greece, on a commission from Mr. Harman, his first patron, to make sketches of the architectural remains and the scenery of that classic soil. In some of these journeys he was accompanied by Brockedon, the painter, and Sir Charles Barry, the architect. On his return, after nearly a year's absence, and having visited Malta and Sicily in the course of his tour, Eastlake painted a life-size picture of 'Mercury bringing the Golden Apple to Paris.' Shortly after the death of his father, which had brought him back to England in 1820, he returned to Rome, and became much occupied in painting subjects illustrative of the local features, inhabitants, and customs of modern Italy. He resided in Italy altogether fourteen years, chiefly in Rome and in Ferrara. He first exhibited at the Royal Academy in 1823, his earliest contributions being scenes in which public buildings, such as the Castle of St. Angelo, St. Peter's, &c., were a

116

principal feature. These were followed by subjects taken from Italian life in the neighbourhood of Rome, subjects of banditti life, &c. Commissioned by the Duke of Devonshire, he painted, in 1827, a picture representing the story related by Plutarch of 'The Spartan Isidas,' who, appearing in battle naked, and armed with sword and spear, was mistaken for a god. This picture, consisting of numerous figures, and of medium gallery size, occupied the painter nearly two years, and produced considerable sensation amongst the artists and dilettanti at Rome. In England it was not so generally appreciated ; but its merit was acknowledged by the Royal Academy, of which body he was elected an Associate in 1827, the year of its exhibition. About this time, captivated by Venetian colouring, he painted some subjects of half-figures, life-size, sometimes of chivalrous character, sometimes taken from the picturesque peasantry of Italy. He was, in 1830, elected a Royal Academician. In the same year he returned to England, and established himself in London. The subjects now treated by him were undertaken chiefly in order to turn to account his materials from the costume and scenery of modern Greece. He varied his studies at this time by portrait-painting, and by his favourite half-figures in the Venetian style. He also occasionally treated small fancy subjects, and historic and modern Italian subjects. But henceforth his time was devoted to the service of art, by advice and by writing, rather than by any practical work. He exhibited but five pictures at the Royal Academy after his election as president.

In the year 1841 Eastlake was appointed secretary to the Royal Commission for decorating the new Houses of Parliament and for the promotion of the Fine Arts, and he conducted the business of that commission until its dissolution after the death of its president, the Prince Consort. In 1842 he was made librarian of the Royal Academy, and in the following year he became keeper of the National Gallery, which office, however, he resigned in 1847. On the death of Sir Martin Shee, in 1850, he was elected president of the Royal Academy and received the customary honour of knighthood. He also became a trustee of the National Gallery, of which he was, in 1855, made director for a period of five years. This appointment was renewed in 1860, and again in 1865, and during his tenure of office he was instrumental in obtaining for the nation many of its greatest treasures.

His literary productions were all connected with art ; he edited, in 1842, a translation of Kugler's 'Italian Schools of Painting' (subsequently re-edited by his widow) ; but his chief works were his 'Materials for a History of Oil-Painting' (1847), and 'Contributions to the Literature of the Fine Arts' (1848).

In August, 1865, Sir Charles Eastlake left England, exceedingly unwell, for his usual annual tour on the continent, taken with a view of acquiring further examples for the National Gallery. At Milan he became seriously ill, but rallying slightly, pushed on to Pisa, where he died December 24, 1865. He was buried first in the English cemetery at Florence, but was subsequently re-interred at Kensal Green. The following are some of his principal paintings :

The Raising of Jairus's Daughter. Brutus exhorting the Romans to revenge the Death of Lucretia. An Italian Contadina and her children. (*Now at South*

SIR CHARLES L. EASTLAKE

CHRIST LAMENTING OVER JERUSALEM

[Hanfstängl photo]

[National Gallery, London

Kensington.) Girl of Albano leading a Blind Man to Mass. 1825. Mercury bringing the Golden Apple to Paris. Lord Byron's Dream. (*Painted at Rome in 1827, now in the National Gallery.*) Pilgrims arriving in sight of Rome. (*Royal Academy,* 1828: *repeated in* 1835, *and again in* 1836.) Una delivering the Red Cross Knight. 1830. Haidee, a Greek Girl. (*Royal Academy,* 1831: *now in the National Gallery.*) A Peasant Woman fainting from the Bite of a Serpent. (*Royal Academy,* 1831: *now at South Kensington.*) Greek Fugitives. (*Royal Academy,* 1833.) Escape of the Carrara Family from the pursuit of the Duke of Milan, 1389. (*Royal Academy,* 1834: *a replica, of the year* 1850, *is in the National Gallery.*) An Arab selling his Captives, Monks endeavouring to ransom them. 1837. Gaston de Foix before the Battle of Ravenna. 1838. Christ blessing Little Children. (*Royal Academy,* 1840.) Christ lamenting over Jerusalem. (*Royal Academy,* 1841: *a replica is in the National Gallery.*) Hagar and Ishmael. (*Royal Academy,* 1843: *his diploma picture.*)

EATON, JOSEPH O., an American painter of portraits and figure subjects, both in oil and in water-colours, was born in 1829. He died at Yonkers on the Hudson in 1875. Among his exhibited works were:

Landscape: View on the Hudson. 1868.
Greek Water-Carrier. 1872.
Lady Godiva. 1874.
Looking through the Kaleidoscope. 1875.
His own Portrait. 1875. (*National Academy of Design.*)

EBERHARD, KONRAD, a German historical painter, better known as a sculptor, was one of the foremost artists of the so-called Nazarene School, which at one time gathered round Overbeck in Rome. He was born in 1768 at Hindelang in Algau, where his father and grandfather were sculptors and carvers. The Elector of Trèves and Bishop of Augsburg, Clement Wenceslas, often had occasion to go to Hindelang, where he made the acquaintance of Eberhard, and induced him to visit the Academy of Munich in 1798 to work under his fellow-countryman Boos. In 1816 he was appointed professor of sculpture at the Academy. Several pictures by him exist, one of which, 'The Adoration of the Magi,' is especially beautiful. He died at Munich in 1859. In most of his works he was assisted by his elder brother, FRANZ EBERHARD, an excellent sculptor, who was born at Hindelang in 1767, and died of cholera at Munich in 1836.

EBERLE, ADAM, one of the earliest and most gifted pupils of Cornelius, was born at Aix-la-Chapelle in 1805. He studied painting at the Düsseldorf Academy, and afterwards went with Cornelius to Munich. After commencing his career at Düsseldorf by painting 'The Entombment of Christ,' and 'St. Helena with two Angels,' he executed the large fresco-painting on the ceiling of the Odéon, representing ' Apollo among the Shepherds.' In 1829 he went to Rome, where he died in 1832.

EBERLE, ROBERT, a German animal painter, was born at Meersburg in 1815. He was first instructed by Bidermann at Constance, and afterwards went to Munich, where he studied from nature and the works of Van de Velde and Du Jardin. He especially excelled in painting sheep, and there is a 'Shepherdess' by him in the Modern Gallery at Munich. He died, through the discharge of a pistol, at Eberfing, near Munich, in 1859.

EBERLEIN, CHRISTIAN NICOLAUS, a German historical painter, was born at Rudolstadt in 1720. He worked in Göttingen, Wolfenbüttel, and Salzdahlum, and in 1775 became inspector of the gallery in the last-named town, and made good copies of many of the pictures therein. He died at Salzdahlum in 1788. His son, CHRISTIAN EBERHARD EBERLEIN, who was also a painter, was born at Wolfenbüttel in 1749, and died at Göttingen in 1804.

EBERLEIN, JOHANN CHRISTIAN, was born at Göttingen about 1770, and died there in 1815. An 'Italian Landscape' by him is in the Modern Gallery at Munich.

EBERMAYR, JOHANN EBERHARD, a German historical painter, was born at Nuremberg in 1659. He studied under Johann Murrer, and afterwards at Venice. He died in his native city in 1692.

EBERT, KARL, landscape painter, was born at Stuttgart in 1821, and studied there under Steinkopf, as well as at Munich. He died in 1885. In the Stuttgart Gallery there are two pictures by him.

ECCARDT, JOHANN ÆGIDIUS. See ECKHARDT.

ECHION. See AETION.

ECHTER, MICHAEL, a German historical and fresco painter, was born in 1810. He studied under Kaulbach, whom he assisted in decorating the staircase of the New Museum at Berlin. He died at Munich in 1879.

ECKARD, JOHANN CHRISTOPH, an engraver, was born in 1757 at Lauffen on the Neckar, and after studying architecture for a while, placed himself under Guibat and J. G. von Müller in the line which he afterwards adopted. He engraved portraits and historical pictures, and worked for some time at Düsseldorf in the illustration of various works; but in 1809 he obtained an engagement at Munich as an engraver upon lithographic stones of crests and ornamental writing. He died at Munich after 1832.

ECKEMANN-ALESSON, LORENZ. See EKEMANN-ALESSON.

ECKERSBERG, CHRISTOFFER VILHELM, a Danish painter of historical and genre subjects, sea-pieces, and portraits, was born at Blaakrog, Varnäs, in South Jutland, in 1783. He studied first in Aabenraa and in Flensburg; and in 1803 entered the Academy at Copenhagen, where he won the gold medal in 1809 with his 'Death of Jacob.' In the following year he went to Paris and entered David's studio, and in 1813 he visited Rome. Returning to Copenhagen, he was elected in 1817 a member of the Academy, to which he presented ' The Death of Balder.' In the following year he became one of its professors, and devoted much care, with great success, to the improvement of the talents of rising artists. In 1827 he was made Director of the Academy. Between the years 1818 and 1828 he executed a series of historical pictures relating to the House of Oldenburg in the palace of Christiansborg. He died at Copenhagen in 1853. Amongst his works are:

Loke and Sigyn. 1810. (*Copenhagen Gallery.*)
Portrait of Thorwaldsen. 1815.
The Israelites crossing the Red Sea. 1815. (*Copenhagen Gallery.*)
Axel and Walburg.
Christ in Gethsemane. 1824.
A Swedish Fishing Boat. 1833.
The Sermon on the Mount. 1834.
Portrait of the Princess Vilhelmine.
A Russian Ship. 1828.
A Danish Boat. 1835.
Vessels in the Sound. 1848.
Sea-piece. 1848.
} (*Copenhagen Gallery.*)

ECKERSBERG, JOHAN FREDERIK, a landscape

117

painter, was born at Drammen in Norway in 1822. He was placed in a mercantile office in Christiania at the age of eighteen, but having previously been in Holland for several years, and visited Amsterdam, he had there imbibed a taste for art, so that after two years, against his father's wish, he relinquished his post, and entered the technical drawing-school at Christiania. Rapidly developing his talent for painting, he in 1824 obtained one of the Government stipends for young artists, and went to Düsseldorf, where he studied landscape painting under Professor Schirmer. He returned to Christiania in 1848, where his works commanded a very fair sale. He married in 1850, but two years later he was obliged to visit Madeira for his health, where, having first devoted his time to portrait painting to increase his rather slender funds, he travelled over the island, making sketches, from which he afterwards painted his magnificent series of pictures of Madeira. He returned to Christiania in 1854, and in 1859 founded in that city an Academy of Painting, which was soon after taken under Government patronage. Every summer from the date of his return to Norway he visited the most grand and picturesque spots in his native country, making sketches from which he afterwards elaborated his pictures. Eckersberg died at Sandvigen, near Christiania, in 1870. His 'Grand Panoramic Scene from a Norwegian Plateau' was exhibited at the Paris Exhibition of 1867.

ECKERT, HEINRICH AMBROS, a German painter of battle-pieces, was born at Würzburg in 1807, and was at first instructed by Fessel. In 1825 he attended the Academy at Munich, and afterwards visited the Tyrol and France. Between 1835 and 1840, in conjunction with Monten and Schelver, he published a work upon the German federal army, with two hundred coloured lithographic plates; and another illustrating the return of the Russian troops to their homes. He died at Munich in 1840, while engaged upon a picture of the great review near that city before the Emperor of Russia. Besides genre subjects and battle-pieces he painted marine views.

ECKHARDT, GEORG LUDWIG, a German portrait painter, was born at Hamburg in 1770, and died in 1794. He was an artist of great promise, and wrote the 'Hamburgische Künstlernachrichten,' published in 1794.

ECKHARDT, JOHANN ÆGIDIUS, (or ECCARDT,) was a native of Germany, who visited England about the year 1740, and became a pupil of Jan Baptist van Loo. He was much employed as a portrait painter, about the time that Sir Joshua Reynolds returned from Italy. There is a print of Peg Woffington, the actress, engraved by Faber, and another of Dr. Conyers Middleton, engraved by the same artist, from pictures by this painter. He died at Chelsea in 1779.

ECKMAN, EDUARD, a Flemish wood-engraver, was born at Mechlin about the year 1610. He engraved some wood-cuts, which are admired for the neatness of their execution and the correct drawing of the small figures. He appears to have taken the prints of Callot for his model, and has copied some of them in wood-cuts with surprising delicacy and spirit, particularly the plate of the 'Fireworks on the River Arno.' He also engraved after Businck and Abraham Bosse. The work of Eckman consists of upwards of a hundred prints.

ECKSTEIN, JOHANN, a German modeller and painter, lived in the 18th century, and studied at the Royal Academy in London, where he spent the greater part of his life. He stayed some time at Potsdam, and was practising in Birmingham in 1792. In 1796 he painted 'The Soldier's Return,' and a 'Family Gathering.' The Berlin Museum has two beautiful reliefs, signed *J. E.*, which are said to be by this artist. He died in London in, or soon after, the year 1798.

ECKSTEYN, GEORG DAVID, a German engraver, resided at Nuremberg about the year 1721. He engraved some of the portraits for the 'Icones Bibliopolarum et Typographorum,' published by Roth-Scholtz at Nuremberg in 1726-42.

ECLECTICS. A name given to the Carracci Family.

ECMAN, JEAN, a French miniature painter, was born about 1641. He was received into the Academy in 1675, and died in Paris in 1677.

EDDELIEN, MATTHIAS HEINRICH ELIAS, was born at Greifswalde in 1803, and in 1819 went as a journeyman painter to Copenhagen, where he attended the Academy, and executed works in grisaille for Christiansborg. In 1837 he won the large gold medal for his picture of 'David amusing Saul by playing on the Harp,' and afterwards obtained a travelling allowance for a competitive painting of 'Christ making Himself known to His Disciples.' In 1839 he went to Rome, and while there painted for the church at Kronborg 'Christ blessing Little Children.' After his return he executed his *chef d'œuvre*, consisting of the frescoes in the chapel of Christian IV., in the cathedral of Röskilde; but becoming paralysed he was unable to complete them. He died in 1852. There is in the Copenhagen Gallery a 'Faun plucking Grapes,' dated 1830.

EDDIS, EDEN UPTON, was a portrait painter, a fellow-student and life-long companion of George Richmond, and divided, at one time, the world of fashion with his friend. He was a pupil of Sass, and afterwards at the Royal Academy Schools, and one of the medallists. At one time he was disposed to take up landscape work, but was persuaded to try portraiture, and so quickly obtained a success in that branch of art, that he relinquished all other work in its favour. His cleverest works were portraits of children, but amongst notable men whom he painted were Sydney Smith, Theodore Hook, and Macaulay. He was remarkable also for his pencil portraits, which were of great refinement and beauty. The last fifteen years of his life were passed at Shalford near Guildford, where he died in 1901 at the age of eighty-nine. He became very deaf as he grew old, and this deafness was one of the reasons for his retirement, but he was very popular as a raconteur down to the end of his life, as he had a wealth of anecdote, and a charming wit at his disposal, and was one of the kindest and most generous of men to children, and was always a great favourite with them.   G.C.W.

EDELINCK, GASPARD FRANÇOIS, the youngest brother of Gérard Edelinck, was born at Antwerp in 1652. He was instructed by his brothers, Gérard and Jean, but did not long pursue the art of engraving. He died in Paris in 1722, leaving behind him no work of note, except the plate of 'The Deluge,' after Alessandro Veronese, which had been commenced by his brother Jean, and was finished by him under the direction of Gérard Edelinck.

EDELINCK, GÉRARD, a French engraver, was born at Antwerp in 1640, and received his instruc-

After Kneller]

JOHN DRYDEN

tion from Cornelis Galle. In 1666 he went to Paris, where he entered the studio of François de Poilly, and was taken into the service of Louis XIV., who settled a pension on him, with apartments at the Gobelins. In 1675 he received letters of naturalization, and in 1677 he was received into the Academy, and was soon after knighted by the King. He worked entirely with the graver; and his execution is at the same time both bold and finished. His style is more delicate than that of Bolswert and Pontius, without being less picturesque. His plates, though exquisitely finished, display nothing of labour or littleness. The size and the number of his prints evince the most surprising facility. The pictures of Le Brun, under the graver of Edelinck and Gérard Audran, appear to have been the works of an accomplished colourist, and assume qualities in which they were really deficient. Edelinck died in Paris in 1707. Robert-Dumesnil, in his 'Peintre-Graveur Français,' vii. 169—336, describes 339 engravings by him, of which 200 are portraits: the following are his principal works.

PORTRAITS.

Louis XIV., bust on a pedestal; *after J. B. Corneille.*
Louis XIV., an equestrian statue, with a group of the eminent men of his reign; *after Bonet.*
Louis XIV. on horseback, with Providence hovering over him, and his Enemies overthrown at his feet; in two sheets; very fine; *after Le Brun.*
Louis XIV., bust on a shield borne by Religion seated in a triumphal car drawn by the Four Evangelists, called the 'Triumph of the Church,' or the 'Extirpation of Calvinism;' in two sheets; fine and scarce; *after Le Brun.*
Louis XIV. giving peace to Europe; in two sheets; *after Le Brun.*
Louis XIV., half-length; *after J. de La Haye.*
Louis, Duke of Burgundy; *after F. de Troy.*
Esprit Fléchier, Bishop of Nîmes; *after Rigaud.*
Charles Perrault; *after Tortebat.*
Paul Fontanier de Pellisson.
Jean de La Fontaine; *after Rigaud.*
Jean Racine.
Blaise Pascal; *after L. Q. V.*
Pieter van Bouc.
Nathanael Dilgerus. 1683.
Titian.
Abraham Teniers; *after a picture by himself.*
Albrecht Dürer.
Jean Cousin.
Gilles Sadeler, engraver.
Abraham Bloemaert.
Jacques Blanchard; *after a picture by himself.*
François Tortebat, Painter to the King; *after De Piles.*
Israel Silvestre, engraver; *after Le Brun.*
Pierre Simon, engraver; *after P. Ernou.*
François Chauveau, engraver; *after C. Le Fèvre.*
Marten van den Bogaert, sculptor; *after Rigaud.*
Hyacinthe Rigaud, painter; *after a picture by himself.*
Jules Hardouin Mansart, architect; *after Rigaud.*
Charles Le Brun; *after N. de Largillière.*
Philippe de Champaigne; *after a picture by himself;* very fine.
Charles d'Hozier, Genealogist of France; *after Rigaud.*
Frédéric Léonard, Printer to the King; *after the same.*
Jean Charles Parent; *after Tortebat.*
Madame Helyot, with a crucifix; *after Galliot.*
François Michel Le Tellier, Marquis de Louvois, bust, with Mars and Minerva as supporters; *after Le Brun.*
André Hameau, Doctor of the Sorbonne; *after Vivien.*
Nicolas de Blampignon, Doctor of the Sorbonne; *after the same.*
Jean Rouillé, Count of Meslay; *after Nanteuil.*
Charles Mouton, Musician to Louis XIV.; *after De Troy.*

SUBJECTS AFTER VARIOUS MASTERS.

The Holy Family, with St. Joseph, St. Elizabeth, St. John, and two Angels; after the picture by *Raphael* in the Louvre, presented to Francis I. by Pope Leo X.;

very fine. The first impressions are before the arms of Colbert, the second are with the arms, and the third have the arms effaced, while the frame in which they were inserted remains.
The Virgin Mary sewing, with the Infant sleeping in a Cradle, surrounded by Angels, called 'La Couseuse;' *after Guido;* fine.
The Holy Family, with St. Joseph presenting Flowers to the Infant Jesus; *after C. Maratti.*
The Holy Family, called the 'Benedicite;' *after Le Brun.*
A Female Saint, holding a Lily, and kneeling before the Virgin and Infant seated on a Throne, to whom she presents a Book; *after Pietro da Cortona.*
The Penitent Magdalen renouncing the Vanities of the World; after the picture by *Le Brun,* now in the Louvre at Paris. The portrait is that of Madame de La Vallière. The first impressions are without the inscription, and are very scarce; the next best are without the border.
St. Louis prostrating himself before a Crucifix; *after Le Brun.*
St. Charles Borromeo kneeling; *after the same.*
The Crucifixion, surrounded with Angels; on two sheets; *after the same.*
Moses holding the tables of the Law; *after Philippe de Champaigne;* commenced by Nanteuil, and finished after his death by Edelinck.
Christ and the Woman of Samaria; *after the same.*
The Virgin at the foot of the Cross; *after the same.*
St. Jerome; *after the same.*
St. Ambrose; half-length; *after J. B. de Champaigne.*
St. Basil and St. Gregory; half-length; *after the same.*
A Combat of Cavalry, four Horsemen fighting for a Standard, with three dead Figures on the ground; after the celebrated cartoon by *Leonardo da Vinci.*
Alexander, accompanied by Hephæstion, entering the Tent of Darius; on two sheets; *after Le Brun.* The first impressions have the name of Goyton at the bottom. This print completes the set of the 'Battles of Alexander' engraved by Gérard Audran after Le Brun.
Alexander entering the Tent of Darius; *after Mignard;* Edelinck's last work, finished after his death by *P. Drevet.*

EDELINCK, JEAN, a brother of Gérard Edelinck, and probably younger than the latter, was born at Antwerp, but in what year is not known. He preceded his brother to Paris, and there engraved several plates in imitation of his style. Although very unequal to the works of his brother, his prints are not without considerable merit. He died in Paris in 1680. He engraved several of the statues in the gardens at Versailles, and there are also by him:

The Portrait of Isbrandus de Diemerbroeck, a famous anatomist; *after Romeyn De Hooghe.*
The Deluge; *after Alessandro Turchi.* This plate was finished after his death by his youngest brother, Gaspard François Edelinck.

EDELINCK, NICOLAS, the son of Gérard Edelinck, was born in Paris about 1680. Although he had the advantage of his father's instruction, and of studying in Italy, he never rose above mediocrity. He engraved some portraits, and a few plates for the Crozat Collection. He died in Paris in 1730. Among other prints by him are the following:

Gérard Edelinck; *after Tortebat.*
Cardinal Giulio de' Medici; *after Raphael.*
Count Baldassare Castiglione; *after the same.*
Philip, Duke of Orleans, Regent of France, on horseback; *after J. Ranc.*
Adrien Baillet.
John Dryden; *after Kneller.*
The Virgin and Infant; *after Correggio.*
Vertumnus and Pomona; *after J. Ranc.*

EDEMA, GERARD, was born in Friesland (or according to others, at Amsterdam), in 1652. He was a scholar of Allart van Everdingen, and, like his master, painted landscapes with rocks and waterfalls, chiefly from views in Norway. At the

119

age of eighteen he came to England, where he met with encouragement, and made voyages to Norway and Newfoundland, to collect subjects for his pictures among those wild scenes of nature, for which he had a romantic predilection. The figures in his landscapes are generally painted by Th. Wyck. Although the pictures by Edema are painted with spirit, they possess little of the chaste and simple colouring, and the picturesque touch, which distinguish the landscapes of Van Everdingen. He died at Richmond in 1700. At Hampton Court are a 'River Scene' and a 'Landscape' by him.

EDEMA, NICOLAES, born in Friesland in 1666, went to Surinam to paint the landscapes, plants, and insects of that country. He became a good landscape painter, as his views are after nature, with a good tone of colour, and a spirited touch. He died in London in 1722.

EDENBERGER, J. N., a German miniature painter, was a native of Baden-Durlach. He possessed considerable talent, and was living in 1773 at the Hague, whence he came to England, but returned thither in 1776.

EDLINGER, JOHANN GEORG, a portrait painter, was born at Graz in 1741. He was a pupil of Desmarées, and became court painter at Munich, where he died in 1819. His portraits are well painted, and show a leaning towards the works of Rembrandt. Some of his portraits of eminent Bavarians, engraved by Friedrich John, appeared in 1821 under the title 'Sammlung von Bildnissen denkwürdiger Männer.'

EDLINGER, KARL FRANZ, a Saxon painter, was born at Dresden in 1785, and died there in 1823. He painted portraits, especially miniatures, but only one historical picture by him is known, 'Ariadne in Naxos.' His son, JOHANN MORITZ ELLINGER, who was born at Dresden in 1823, and died in 1847, was a portrait painter and etcher.

EDMONDS, JOHN W., an American painter of genre subjects, was born at Hudson, New York, in 1806. Engaged during the greater part of his life as a cashier in a bank, he devoted his mornings and evenings to painting; but this constant toil weakened his health so much that in 1840 he came to Europe for rest. He first exhibited at the New York Academy in 1836, under an assumed name, 'Sammy the Tailor.' This was followed, among other works, by 'Dominic Sampson' in 1837, the 'Penny Paper' in 1839, 'Sparking' in 1840, 'Stealing Milk' in 1843, 'Vesuvius' and 'Florence' in 1844, 'Bargaining' in 1858, and 'The New Bonnet' in 1859. In 1838 he was elected an Associate of the National Academy, and in 1840 an Academician. He died at his residence on the Bronx River in 1863.

EDMONSTONE, ROBERT, a Scottish subject painter, was born at Kelso in 1795. He pursued the study of art under many difficulties, but at last became a student in the Royal Academy, London, where he first exhibited in 1818. He then went to the continent, and studied for a few years in Italy. Returning, he practised portrait painting in London from about 1824 to 1831, when he paid a second visit to Italy. He died at his native place in 1834, from the effects of fever contracted at Rome. His forte lay in works in which he introduced children. Amongst the pictures he exhibited were:

Italian Boys playing at Cards. 1830.
Venetian Water-Carriers. 1833.
Kissing the chains of St. Peter
The White Mouse. (*His last work*.)

EDRIDGE, HENRY, a miniature painter, was born at Paddington in 1769. He was apprenticed to Pether, the mezzotint engraver and landscape painter, but his chief excellence lay in miniature portraits, which he executed in black lead and Indian ink, and subsequently in water-colours. In 1786 he exhibited at the Academy 'The Weary Traveller,' and in 1803 portraits of King George III. and Queen Charlotte. He was elected an Associate of the Royal Academy in 1820, and died in London in 1821. The following are among his works:

National Portrait Gallery:
  Marquis of Anglesey. 1808.
  Lord Auckland. 1809.
  Robert Southey. 1804.

National Gallery of Scotland:
  Coast Scene, with Figures.

South Kensington
  Chenies House, near Brambletye.
  Rick Yard, Ashford.
  Farm-House, Buckinghamshire. 1814.   } *Water-
  View near Bromley.   Colour.*
  Brighton Beach.
  Pont Neuf, Paris.
  Portrait of a Military Officer.

EDWARDS, EDWARD, an historical painter, born in London in 1738, was employed by Boydell to make drawings from the old masters for his publications, and by the Society of Antiquaries for the same purpose. He painted for Boydell's Shakespeare a subject from the 'Two Gentlemen of Verona;' he painted also arabesques, and published 52 etchings. He never arrived at distinction, except that he was appointed teacher of perspective in the Royal Academy in 1788, which situation he held until his death. He was elected an Associate of the Royal Academy in 1773, and sent pictures to its exhibitions pretty constantly from 1771 till the end of his life. He published in 1808 the 'Anecdotes of Painters,' intended as a supplement to Walpole; but in his facts he was too accurate to please his contemporaries, and consequently the work and its author were much decried. He died in 1806. A water-colour drawing by him, entitled 'North Dean, Castle Eden, Durham,' is at South Kensington.

EDWARDS, EDWIN, a landscape painter in water-colours and an etcher, was born at Framlingham in 1823. He was originally brought up for the law and practised as a proctor for many years. He commenced water-colour painting after a journey in the Tyrol, and through meeting the French artist Legros, in 1861, was induced to take up etching, on which his reputation chiefly rests. His works appeared at the Royal Academy, and at the Dudley Gallery. Amongst his best productions may be cited a series of etchings of English Inns. He died in London in 1879.

EDWARDS, GEORGE, a natural history draughtsman, was born at Stratford, in Essex, in 1694. From 1716 to 1731 he travelled much in Holland, Norway, Belgium, and France in pursuit of his art. In 1733 he was appointed librarian to the College of Physicians. In 1747-51 he published 'A Natural History of uncommon Birds and Animals,' and in 1758-64 'Gleanings of Natural History.' He retired to Plaistow, where he died in 1773.

EDWARDS, SYDENHAM, a draughtsman of animals and flowers, was born about 1768. He exhibited at the Royal Academy from 1792 to 1813. He published 'Cynographia Britannica,' 1800, the 'New Flora Britannica,' 1812, and founded the 'Botanical

AUGUSTUS L. EGG

BEATRIX KNIGHTING ESMOND

Hanfstängl photo]

[National Gallery, London

'Register' in 1815. He also made drawings for Rees's 'Cyclopædia,' the 'Flora Londinensis,' the 'Botanical Magazine,' and the 'Sportsman's Magazine.' He died at Brompton in 1819.

EDWIN, DAVID, an American engraver, was born at Bath, in England, in 1776. He was the son of John Edwin, a celebrated comic actor, and was apprenticed to an engraver, but he ran away to sea, and reached America in 1797. There he was employed by Edward Savage, the portrait painter, and soon gained much reputation by his portraits. After twenty years' work his sight failed, and he was compelled to resort to various means in order to obtain a livelihood. He died at Philadelphia in 1841.

EECKE, (alias EECKELE,) JAN VAN. He settled in Bruges in 1534, and was admitted as master painter into the Guild of Saint Luke in September of that year. He held the office of "vinder" in 1542-3, 1548-9, 1551-2 and 1557-8. He died in November 1561, and was buried in the church of Saint James. Only two paintings are known to be by him; both are signed with his cipher.

1. Mater dolorosa, a copy of a painting anterior to 1492, a woodcut after which adorns 'Ghedenckenisse van den VII. Weeden Onser Liever Vrouwen,' printed at Antwerp by Gerard Leeu in 1492. (Bruges: Cathedral.)
2. The Vision of Saint Bernard, and other episodes of his life. (Tournai: Museum.)

EECKHOUT, JACOB JOSEPH, was born at Antwerp in 1793, and studied first at the Academy of that city. He painted historical and genre subjects, and portraits, and in 1829 he was elected a member of the Academies of Amsterdam, Antwerp, Brussels, and Rotterdam. He settled at the Hague in 1831, and in 1839 became director of the Academy in that city, and after staying at Mechlin and Brussels he went to live in Paris in 1859. He imitated Rembrandt with some skill, and may be considered one of the most distinguished painters of the modern Dutch school. His compositions are expressive and lively, and the colouring vigorous. Eeckhout died in Paris in 1861. His best works are:

The Death of William the Silent.
Peter the Great at Zaandam.
The Departure of the Recruits of Scheveningen.
Collection de Portraits d'Artistes modernes, nés dans le royaume des Pays-Bas. 1822.

EECKHOUT, VAN DEN. See VAN DEN EECKHOUT.

EECKHOUT, VICTOR, a genre painter, the son of Jacob Joseph Eeckhout, was born at Antwerp in 1821. He studied under his father, and went to the East. He died in 1879.

EELKAMA, EELKE JELLES, a painter of landscapes, flowers, and fruit, was born at Leeuwarden in 1788. On account of his deafness, which was brought on by an illness at the age of seven, he was educated in the institution for the deaf and dumb at Gröningen, where he was instructed in the art of painting by G. De San. In 1804, he obtained the first prize of the Academy, and his works were highly praised. He visited Paris and London, travelled in France and Switzerland, and afterwards painted at Haarlem and Amsterdam. He afterwards lost his sight, and died at Leeuwarden in 1839.

EERVRUGHT. See DE MOMPER, JODOCUS.

EGAN, JAMES, an Irish mezzotint engraver, was born at Roscommon in 1799. He was employed in the lowest capacities by S. W. Reynolds, and, notwithstanding great difficulties and privations,

persevered in the pursuit of his art. He died in London in 1842. His last and best plate is after Cattermole's 'English Hospitality in the Olden Time.'

EGERTON, D. T., a landscape painter, was one of the original members of the Society of British Artists, where he exhibited in the years 1824 to 1829, and in 1838 to 1840. In the latter years of his life he travelled much in America, obtaining thus the subjects for several pictures, notably one of 'Niagara.' He was murdered in Mexico in 1842.

EGG, AUGUSTUS LEOPOLD, the son of the eminent gunmaker of Piccadilly, was born in London in 1816. Though he took to the pencil and brush whilst at school, he does not appear to have thought of adopting the arts as a profession till about the year 1834, when he went to Sass's Art School, and shortly afterwards, in 1835, he was admitted a student at the Royal Academy. Even thus early he had commenced painting pictures of Italian subjects, though a stranger to Italy, as well as scenes from the pages of Scott; but his first work of importance was 'The Victim,' from 'Le Diable Boiteux' of Le Sage, which was exhibited at the Liverpool Academy of Arts. To this he afterwards, in 1844, painted a companion picture. Egg then exhibited in London, and in 1836, and the following years, we find his works on the walls of the Society of British Artists, the British Institution, and the Royal Academy; but owing to his having inherited a considerable fortune from his father, he was independent of his art for support, and accordingly did not exhibit, as a rule, more than one work each year at the Royal Academy, to the exhibitions of which he sent, in all, twenty-eight pictures. Of these, seven are taken from Shakespeare, five are founded on scenes in well-known works of fiction, and of the remainder nine are from familiar incidents in history. He was elected an Associate of the Royal Academy in 1848, and an Academician in 1860. His pictures are comparatively few for one who had won the highest honours of his profession, but he was prevented from doing more in his art by delicate health, which compelled him to resort to the mild climate of Italy and the South of France, and latterly to Algiers, where he died and was buried in 1863.

Egg's talent was exercised in a rather peculiar field of study, comprising strictly historical incidents, and passages from classic fable. In the former class of subjects he stands quite alone; in the latter, he, in some sense, occupied the same ground as that in which Newton and Leslie frequently laboured; but his treatment of the latter class of subjects is more fanciful than that of either of those artists, whilst in subjects more properly considered as inventive, a philosophic spirit, somewhat melancholy in tinge, is observable, which they do not display. His principal works are:

A Spanish Girl. 1838.
Laugh when you can. 1839.
Scene from "Henry IV." 1840.
Scene from "Le Diable Boiteux." 1844. (National Gallery.)
Buckingham rebuffed. 1846.
The Wooing of Katharina. ("Taming of the Shrew.") 1847.
Lucentio and Bianca. ("Taming of the Shrew.") 1847.
Queen Elizabeth discovers she is no longer young. 1848.
Henrietta Maria in distress relieved by Cardinal de Retz. 1849.

Peter the Great sees Catharine, his future Empress, for the first time. 1850.
Pepys's Introduction to Nell Gwynne. 1851.
The Life and Death of Buckingham. (*Two pictures.*) 1855.
The Knighting of Esmond. 1858.
Past and Present. (*Three pictures.*) 1858.
The Night before Naseby. 1859.
Madame de Maintenon and Scarron. 1859.
The Taming of the Shrew: Dinner scene: Katharine and Petruchio. (*His last picture.*) 1860.

EGGERS, JOHANN KARL, a German historical painter, born at Neu Strelitz in 1790, was instructed by Matthäi at Dresden. He discovered the old mode of fresco-painting, and was employed in the Vatican at Rome, where he painted in the Braccio Nuovo. Subsequently he painted under the direction of Cornelius in the Museum at Berlin. Some of his oil-paintings are of considerable merit. He died in his native town in 1863.

EGGERT, FRANZ XAVER, a German painter upon glass, was born at Höchstädt on the Danube in 1802, and studied decorative painting at Augsburg and Munich; but he afterwards devoted himself entirely to glass-painting, in conjunction with Ainmüller, Hämmerl, and Kirchmair, and endeavoured to raise that art from its long decline. He especially distinguished himself by the magnificence of his ornamentation. His best works are in the new church of the suburb Au at Munich, in the cathedrals of Cologne and Ratisbon, and in several churches at Basle, Constance, &c. He died at Munich in 1876.

EGINTON, FRANCIS, an English painter upon glass, was born in 1737. He was brought up at Handsworth, near Birmingham, and from 1784 to 1805 he contributed greatly to the advancement of the art. Among his best works are to be noted the 'Resurrection' in Salisbury Cathedral and in Lichfield Cathedral; the 'Conversion of St. Paul' in St. Paul's, Birmingham; 'Christ bearing the Cross' in Wanstead Church; and 'Solomon and the Queen of Sheba' at Arundel Castle. Besides these there are windows by him in St. Asaph Cathedral, Fonthill Abbey, and Magdalen and All Souls' Colleges in Oxford. He died at Handsworth in 1805.

EGLEY, WILLIAM, a miniature painter, was born at Doncaster in 1798. His first employment was in a publisher's office in London, in the course of which occupation he found time to practise painting, of which he had been fond from an early age. After a short time he determined to follow portrait painting as a profession, and in 1824 two of his pictures were exhibited at the Royal Academy, one of them being the portrait of Yates, the actor. From this time he was a very constant exhibitor, painting a great many portraits of members of well-known English families, besides several foreigners of distinction. One of his latest works was a portrait of Foley the sculptor, which was exhibited at the Royal Academy in 1868. His death occurred in London in 1870. His miniatures were very carefully finished and pure in colour; and he was especially successful in his treatment of children.

EGLOFFSTEIN, JULIE VON, Countess, canoness of Hildesheim, born in 1792, was an amateur artist of much ability. She was one of the most beautiful and gifted women at the court of Weimar, and many of Goethe's poems bear witness to the lively interest which he took in her artistic development. She painted several portraits, including

those of the Grand-Duchess of Saxe-Weimar and of Queen Theresa of Bavaria. Among works of different character are 'Shepherds in the Roman Campagna,' painted in 1835, 'Hagar in the Wilderness,' 'The Exposure of Moses,' 'Italian Popular Life,' and others, some of which are in the possession of the Emperor of Russia and of Queen Victoria. She died in 1869.

EGMONT, JUSTUS VAN, was born at Leyden in 1602. He was in 1615 a pupil of Gaspar van den Hoeck, but was afterwards sent to Antwerp to be educated in the school of Rubens, whom he assisted in several of his works, particularly those relating to the life of Mary de' Medici, which he painted for the Luxembourg Palace. On leaving the academy of Rubens he went to Paris, where he was appointed painter to Louis XIII. and afterwards to Louis XIV., and executed several considerable works in conjunction with Simon Vouet. Van Egmont was one of the twelve elders at the establishment of the French Academy of Painting and Sculpture, in 1648. He died at Antwerp in 1674. In the Vienna Gallery there is a portrait by him of the Archduke Leopold Wilhelm, and two others of Philip IV. of Spain. The Hague Gallery has a portrait of Louis XIV. by him. Portraits of Algernon Sydney by him are in the National Portrait Gallery, and at Penshurst, the latter painted at Brussels in 1663.

EGOGNI, AMBROGIO. See STEFANI DA FOSSANO.

EGOROV, ALEKSYEI EGOROVICH, a Russian painter, was born in the steppes of the Kalmyks about 1776, and died at St. Petersburg in 1851. A 'Holy Family' and the 'Scourging of Christ' by him are in the Hermitage at St. Petersburg.

EHEMANT, FRIEDRICH JOSEPH, a German landscape painter, was born at Frankfort in 1804, and studied under Schirmer at the Düsseldorf Academy. He died at Munich in 1842.

EHNLE, ADRIAEN JAN, a Dutch painter of historical and genre subjects, was born at the Hague in 1819, and studied under C. Kruseman. He died in 1863. Among his works are 'Cornelis de Witt at Dordrecht' and 'The Reception of a Child at the Orphan House at Haarlem.'

EHRENBERG, WILLEM SCHUBERT VAN, a Flemish architectural painter, was born at Antwerp in 1630. He was received into the Guild of St. Luke in 1662, under the name of Van Aerdenberch. It has also been written Hardenberg, Eerdenborch, Aerdenborch, Aremberch, &c. He probably died about 1675. He painted the architecture in a picture by H. van Minderhout, representing 'Caricina before the King of Ethiopia,' which was presented by Van Ehrenberg in 1666 to the Guild of St. Luke, and is now in the Antwerp Museum, and in another by Biset, of 'William Tell,' formerly in the possession of the Guild of St. Sebastian at Antwerp, but now in the Brussels Gallery. The landscape part is by Hemelraet. In the Munich Gallery is an 'Interior of an Art-Collector's Gallery,' in which the architecture is by Van Ehrenberg, the figures by Gonzales Cocx and Jordaens, and in the Vienna Gallery is the 'Interior of a Church' by him, dated 1664. Van Ehrenberg added the architecture to the large picture in the Hague Gallery of the 'Interior of a Picture Gallery,' in which Gonzales Cocx put the figures and accessories, and the paintings are by the hands of various artists.

EHRENSTRAL, DAVID KLOECKER VON. See KLOECKER.

122

EHRET, Georg Dionysius, a German botanical draughtsman and engraver, was born at Baden in 1710. After working for Jussieu in France, he settled in England in 1740, and supplied the illustrations for Trew's 'Plantæ Selectæ,' and Brown's 'History of Jamaica.' He also painted a large botanical collection for the Duchess of Portland. He died in 1770.

EIBNER, Friedrich, a German painter of architectural subjects, was born at Hilpoltstein in 1826. He studied after the works of Heinrich Schönfeld, and travelled in Bavaria, and afterwards in Germany, France, Upper Italy, and Spain, making a large number of water-colour drawings of the places he visited. The Album for the Prince Metschersky, with whom he travelled in Spain in 1860-61, may be considered his best work. He died at Munich in 1877.

EICHENS, Friedrich Eduard, a German engraver, was born at Berlin in 1804. He studied engraving first under Buchhorn; and then went, in 1827, with a grant from the government, to Paris, where he received instruction from Forster, and later to Parma, where he studied for three years under Toschi. He subsequently visited Florence, Rome, Naples, Venice, and Milan. On his return in 1833 he became a drawing-master in a government school. He died at Berlin in 1877. Eichens engraved some of Kaulbach's frescoes in the Berlin Museum, and also his 'Shakespeare Gallery.' Among his prints are the following:

Madonna; *after Steinbrück.* 1833.
Adoration of the Kings; *after Raphael.* 1836.
The Magdalen; *after Domenichino.* 1837.
Madonna; *after Raffaellino del Garbo.* 1839.
Portrait of Mendelssohn; *after Hildebrandt.* 1840.
The Vision of Ezechiel; *after Raphael.* 1841.
Frederick the Great as Crown Prince; *after Pesne.* 1846.
'Come here'; *after Begas.* 1847.
The Woman taken in adultery; *after Pordenone.*

EICHHORN, Albert, an architectural and landscape painter, was born at Freienwalde-on-the-Oder in 1811, and studied under Tempeltei and Biermann at Berlin. In 1840 he visited Italy and Greece, where he made numerous sketches, which afterwards served him for the subjects of his paintings. Among his works, which are chiefly in the possession of the German Emperor, may be mentioned, 'Taygetus,' 'The Temple of Pheigalia,' 'St. Peter's at Rome,' 'The Temple of Corinth,' 'The Campagna,' &c. He died by suicide at Potsdam in 1851.

EICHHORN, Hans, a printer and wood-engraver of the 16th century, was employed by the Elector Joachim II. He died at Frankfort in 1583.

EICHLER, Gottfried, an historical and portrait painter, was born at Augsburg in 1677. He studied under Johann Heiss, but went afterwards to Rome to improve under Carlo Maratti. His 'Last Supper,' in the church of the Franciscans at Augsburg, gives ample proof of his talent. He died in 1759.

His son, Johann Gottfried Eichler, born at Augsburg in 1715, was a portrait painter and engraver in line and mezzotint. He died in 1770, leaving a son, Mathias Gottfried Eichler, also an engraver, who was born at Erlangen in 1748, and died at Augsburg in 1818.

EICK, Martin van, a Dutch painter, was a native of Remerswaal in Zealand. He flourished during the first half of the 16th century, and was a contemporary of Pieter Aartsen.

EIGNER, Andreas, who was born at Diedldorf, Upper Palatinate, in 1801, distinguished himself as a painter and a restorer of old pictures. He successfully employed alcoholic vapours, and a varnish of his own invention, to protect paintings against the destructive influence of the atmosphere. He was chiefly employed in the Galleries of Munich, Augsburg, Stuttgart, Carlsruhe, Basle, and Solothurn. He died at Augsburg in 1870.

EIMBECK, Johann Raphon von, was an early German painter, about whom we have no details. There is by him in the cathedral of Halberstadt a triptych, representing the 'Crucifixion,' dated 1508.

EIMMART, Georg Christoph, the elder, a German painter and engraver, born at Ratisbon in 1597, painted portraits, landscapes, still-life, and historical subjects. He died at Nuremberg in 1660.

EIMMART, Georg Christoph, the younger, a German draughtsman and engraver, was born at Ratisbon in 1638. He was instructed by his father, and resided at Nuremberg, where he died in 1705. He engraved some plates for Sandrart's 'Academia,' and some small etchings of ruins, buildings, and vases, ornamented with figures, which have considerable merit. He was also a mathematician and astronomer, and published in 1701 'Iconographia nova contemplationum de Sole.'

EIMMART, Maria Clara, a daughter of Georg Christoph Eimmart the younger, was a designer and engraver. She was born in 1676, and usually worked with her father. She married the astronomer, J. H. Muller, and died at Altdorf in 1707.

EINSLE, Anton, an Austrian portrait painter, was born at Vienna in 1801. He studied at the Academy of that city, and was largely patronized by the court and nobility. He died in 1871.

EISEN, Charles Domenique Joseph, French draughtsman, painter and engraver. He was born at Valenciennes on August 7, 1720. His father, Frans Eisen, and his mother, Marguerite Guisne, had eight children,—Charles was the third. The boy's first drawing-master was his father, who greatly developed his son's talent for designing and his taste for engraving. In 1741 he went to Paris, and in the following year entered the studio of Le Bas. His talent and his sparkling wit gained him admission to the court, where he became painter and draughtsman to the King, and drawing-master to Madame de Pompadour. The King appointed him Court painter. He worked assiduously, and with marked success, taking his inspirations direct from nature, but adding something of the ideal, after the manner of Watteau and Boucher. His work was as various in kind as it was attractive in quality. Large compositions, decorative panels, copies of statues and fountains, studies of the nude and portraits, exercised his brush, his pencil, and his graver; as well as lovely designs for furniture, costumes, and all sorts of pretty things *à la mode.* His vignettes were marked by unusual delicacy and grace. Almost all the more important books published in France in his time contain his exquisite plates; and their bindings testify to his good taste. Baudicour relates that "he engraved with a light point and with striking originality." He was never received at the Royal Academy, but the Academy of St. Luke opened wide its doors to him, and from 1751 to 1774 he passed through the various grades of member, Professor, Councillor and Rector. He

123

was also a member of the Academy of Fine Arts at Rouen. In 1777 he quitted Paris suddenly, having displeased Mme. de Pompadour, as some say, and settled at Brussels with his wife; and he died there on January 4, 1778. Among his pictures were:

Icarus and Daedalus; *Salon, 1751 (pièce de réception).* The Swing *(signed and dated* 1771); *Bourg Museum.* Shepherd and Shepherdess; The Bird's Nest; Villagers dancing; Villagers resting; *Bordeaux Museum.*

The last four are in Lancret's manner, and were in the La Caze Collection till 1829. The Museums at Alençon and Bourg also have pictures by Eisen. Of his etchings and designs the following were most remarkable:

Sixty-eight designs in black and red for 'Tales from La Fontaine.'
Illustrations for an edition de luxe for 'Les Fermiers Généraux,' in black chalk on vellum *(published at Amsterdam in 1762, originally in the collection of the Duc d'Aumale).*
Henri IV. et Gabrielle d'Estrées, black chalk and quill pen, engraved by Mouchy, and exhibited in 1779 at L'École des Beaux Arts in Paris; perhaps Eisen's *chef-d'œuvre.*
Bacchus arriving at Naxos, and other mythological subjects.
Saint Mary nourishing Christ, and St. Jerome.
St. Eloy preaching *(now in the church of St. Ésprit, Paris).*
Military Exercises. 1754.
Illustrations to Ovid's 'Métamorphoses.' 1767–70.
Illustrations to Voltaire's 'Henriade." 1771.
(These are exquisite vignettes in red chalk on cream paper.)
Diana and Endymion.
Aurora. } *Salon*, 1774.
Holy Family.

At the British Museum and at the Victoria and Albert Museum are many drawings, etchings by, and prints after, C. D. J. Eisen.

EISEN, FRANZ, Belgian-French painter and engraver. Born at Brussels 1695. His first art lessons were learned in the churches and galleries of his native city. He had a natural talent for historical and genre painting. In 1714 he settled at Valenciennes, where his talent was speedily recognized. He painted important pictures for the church of the Brigitines, for the high altar of the Béguinage, and for the refectory of the monastery of Vicoigne, and executed other similar commissions in that city. He married Marguerite Guisne, and had eight children—Charles Domenique Joseph being the third. In 1731 he married for a second time Marie Françoise Joseph Bulo, who also bore him a child. Professional jealousies arose which caused him to leave Valenciennes, and he bent his steps to Paris, where he arrived in 1745. At the age of eighty-two he and his wife were admitted into the Hospital for Incurables, where he died in 1777.

EISENHOUT, ANTONIE, a Dutch painter and engraver, flourished at Rome about 1590. He was a native of Varnbourg, and was still living in 1619. It appears that he has been miscalled 'Eisenhart' by Christ, and that some of his works have been ascribed to other masters. Brulliot refers to some attributed to Luca Ciamberlano by Bartsch, which he conjectures should be given to Eisenhout.

EISMANN, JOHANN ANTON, sometimes erroneously called LEISMANN, LISMANN, or LUISMON, a German painter of landscapes and battles, was born at Salzburg in 1634. Without the help of a master he had acquired some ability in drawing, by copying the prints and pictures to which he had access, when he resolved to visit Italy for improvement, and went to Venice, where his natural talent, assisted by the study of the works of the best masters of that school, soon asserted itself. Although he painted battle-pieces and portraits, he was more celebrated for his landscapes and seaports, which he embellished with architecture, somewhat in the style of Salvator Rosa. He died at Venice in 1698. There are in the Dresden Gallery two 'Landscapes with Ruins,' which are by him, and in the Vienna Gallery is a 'Landscape with a Combat of Cavalry.' He adopted his pupil, Carlo Briseghella, who took the name of Eismann, and painted the same class of subjects as his master. Hence there is some confusion in the accounts of both.

EISMANN BRISEGHELLA, CARLO, born at Venice in 1679, the pupil and adopted son of Johann Anton Eismann—who at Venice had formed a friendship with his father, Mattia Briseghella—painted landscapes, sea-pieces, and battles in the style of his master. The Dresden Gallery contains three cavalry fights and a battle-piece by him. After the death of Eismann he appears to have settled at Ferrara. He published in 1706 an account of the paintings in the churches of that city.

EISSNER, JOSEPH, an Austrian engraver, was born at Vienna in 1788. He studied under Schmutzer and afterwards under Leybold, and practised on his own account from 1814. From 1822 he was drawing-master at the Academy in the Neustadt at Vienna, where he died in 1861. He etched a number of plates, and engraved, along with other historical subjects and portraits, the following works:

La Madonna della Sedia; *after Raphael.*
The Praying Madonna; *after Sassoferrato.*
Rembrandt's Mother; *after Rembrandt.*
The Fall of the Angels; *after Luca Giordano.*

EKELS, JAN, the elder, born at Amsterdam in 1724, was a scholar of Dirk Dalens, the younger. He painted views of cities in the manner of Jan ten Compe. His pictures are generally of a small size, and are highly finished, with a good effect of light and shade. He died at Amsterdam in 1781.

EKELS, JAN, the younger, a Dutch painter of genre pieces and an imitator of the old masters, especially of J. Molenaer, was born at Amsterdam in 1759. Two pictures by him, one representing 'A young Man drawing,' and the other 'A Peasant lighting a Pipe,' are in the Städel Gallery at Frankfort. He died in 1793.

EKEMANN-ALESSON, LORENZ, (or ECKEMANN-ALESSON,) a lithographic artist, was born in Sweden in 1791. He studied and practised his art at Vienna, Munich, and Augsburg, but was afterwards appointed by the King of Würtemberg to be professor and director of the newly established Lithographic Institute at Stuttgart. He chiefly executed landscapes and architectural views after Adam, P. Hess, and Wagenbauer; but his best plates are 'A Forest Scene,' after Waterloo; a 'Landscape,' after Wynants; and 'Würtemberg Stallions,' after R. Kunz. He produced some other animal pieces, and also painted landscapes with animals. He died at Stuttgart in 1821.

EKMAN, ROBERT WILHELM, a genre painter, was born at Nystad in Finland in 1808, and died at Helsingfors in 1873. He was educated at the Stockholm Academy under Sandberg; and travelled much, especially in Italy. His pictures consist of scenes from northern life,—christenings, peasants' cottages, forest scenes, &c. Amongst them are:

An old Woman with a Bible.
A Dutch Sailor Family.
Robber Scene.

ELBURG, HANSJE VAN, (ELBURGH, ELBURCH, ELBURCHT, or ELBRUCHT,) called HÄNSKIN, or KLEYN HANSKEN ('Little John'), an historical painter, was born at Elburg, near Campen, in 1500. He represented the figures in the manner of Frans Floris, and also excelled in landscapes and storms at sea. In Antwerp cathedral is his picture of 'The Miraculous Draught of Fishes.' In 1536 he was admitted into the Guild of St. Luke at Antwerp. He died in that city in 1551.

ELDER, CHARLES, an historical painter, was born in 1821. He exhibited at the Royal Academy from 1845 till his death, which took place in London in 1851. Amongst his works are:

Sappho. 1845.
Florimel imprisoned. 1846.
The Death of Mark Anthony. 1847.
Ruth gleaning. 1848.
Rosalind. 1850.
Weary Travellers. 1851.

ELDER, WILLIAM, a Scottish engraver, resided in London about the year 1680. He was one of those who were employed by the booksellers; and we have a few portraits by him, among which are the following:

His own Portrait, with a fur cap.
The same, with a wig.
William Sancroft, Archbishop of Canterbury.
John Pearson, Bishop of Chester.
Ben Jonson, prefixed to his 'Works,' 1692.
Sir Theodore de Mayerne, Physician.
Admiral Russell.
Sir Henry Pollexfen, Chief Justice of the Common Pleas.
John Ray, Naturalist.
Richard Morton, M.D.
George Parker, Astrologer.
Charles Snell, Writing-master.

ELFORD, Sir WILLIAM, Bart., an amateur landscape painter, was born in Devonshire in 1747. From 1784 he occasionally exhibited at the Royal Academy, contributing landscapes, often with effects of sunset and of shower. He was made a baronet in 1800, and died at Totnes in 1837. There is a landscape by him at Windsor Castle.

ELIAERTS, JEAN FRANÇOIS, a Flemish painter of animals, flowers, and fruit, was born in 1761 at Deurne-Borgerhout, near Antwerp, in the Academy of which city he studied. He passed his life in France, but died at Antwerp in 1848. In the Antwerp Museum is a flower-piece by him.

ELIAS, MATHIEU, (ELYAS, or ELIE,) was born at Peena, near Cassel, in 1658. His parents were extremely poor, and he was employed when a boy in attending cattle, in which humble situation he was noticed by a painter of Dunkirk, named Philippe Decorbehem, tracing objects on the ground. The artist, struck with the singularity of the circumstance and the evident disposition of the boy, prevailed on his mother to intrust him to his care. After instructing him for some time he sent him to Paris for improvement, where he met with employment, and resided several years. On the death of Decorbehem, he settled at Dunkirk, and painted some altar-pieces for the churches in that town and its neighbourhood. He died at Dunkirk in 1741.

ELIZABETH, Princess, the third daughter of George III., was born in London in 1770. She married, in 1818, Frederick William Louis, Landgrave of Hesse-Homburg, and died at Frankfort in 1840. She was much attached to the arts of design, and several of the productions of her pencil were published, accompanied by the poetical effusions of the minor bards of the day, under the following titles:

The Birth and Triumph of Cupid; a poem, by Sir James Bland Burges, Bart. 1796.
Cupid turned Volunteer; with poetical illustrations by Thomas Park. 1804.
The Power and Progress of Genius. 1806.
Six Poems illustrative of engravings by H. R. H. the Princess Elizabeth. 1813.

ELKAN, DAVID LEVY, a lithographer and designer of arabesques, born at Cologne in 1808, studied at Düsseldorf, and became known by his imitations and compositions in the style of the middle ages. He died in his native city in 1866.

ELLENRIEDER, MARIE, the best German female painter of the first half of the 19th century, was born at Constance in 1791. She learned the rudiments of art from the miniature painter Einsle, and in 1813 went to Munich, and studied under Langer in the Academy there until 1820. After having twice visited Rome, she became acquainted with Overbeck, whose art-teaching she afterwards followed. Soon after her return from Rome she painted the 'Virgin and Child,' which is considered her best work. Subsequently she painted altarpieces and portraits, and etched twenty-four plates after Langer, Overbeck, Rembrandt, and Titian. She died at Constance in 1863. A 'St. Felicitas' by her is in the possession of the Queen.

ELLIGER, ANTHONIE, the son and pupil of the younger Ottomar Elliger, was born at Amsterdam in 1701, and died at Ede in 1781. He painted historical, mythological, and allegorical pictures upon ceilings and walls. His daughter, CHRISTINA MARIA ELLIGER, was a portrait painter.

ELLIGER, OTTOMAR, the elder, born at Gothenburg in 1633, was the son of a physician, who, finding in him a strong inclination for art, sent him to Antwerp, at that time the residence of so many able artists, where he became a scholar of Daniel Seghers. He painted flowers and fruit in the highly-finished style of his master, and attained sufficient ability to be invited to the court of Berlin, where he was appointed painter to William Frederick, Elector of Brandenburg. The pictures of this artist are almost entirely confined to Germany, where they are held in considerable estimation. Examples are in the Dresden Gallery and in the Städel Gallery at Frankfort. He died at Berlin in 1679.

ELLIGER, OTTOMAR, the younger, the son of Ottomar Elliger the elder, was born at Hamburg in 1666. After being instructed in the first elements of the art by his father, he was sent to Amsterdam, where he became a scholar of Michiel van Musscher, a painter of small portraits and conversations, under whom he studied a short time, but being ambitious of distinguishing himself in a higher walk of art, and the works of Gerard de Lairesse being then in high reputation, he entered the school of that eminent master, whose instruction enabled him in a few years to dispense with further assistance. Elliger painted historical subjects in the style of De Lairesse, which were judiciously composed and correctly drawn. Like his instructor, he was particularly attentive to propriety of costume, and

125

style of architecture. He was employed by the Elector of Mayence, for whom he painted the 'Death of Alexander,' and the 'Marriage of Peleus and Thetis.' His principal works are at Amsterdam, where he died in 1732. In the Vienna Gallery is a 'Woman with Fruit;' in the Cassel Gallery are 'The Feast of Cleopatra,' and 'The Daughter of Herodias dancing;' and in the Bordeaux Museum is an 'Allegory,' all of which are by him.

ELLINGER, Abbot of Tegernsee (1017—1048), is stated to have illustrated a manuscript of Pliny the Elder with figures of the animals described in the text; and in like manner the writings of other authors. In the Munich Library there is an Evangeliarium with paintings by him.

ELLIOT, WILLIAM, an engraver, was born at Hampton Court in 1727. He engraved several landscapes, which were admired for their taste and freedom, and of which the best are from the paintings of the brothers Smith, of Chichester. He died in London in 1766. We have by him the following plates:

A Landscape with Cattle; *after Rosa de Tivoli.*
A View near Maestricht, with Cattle; *after A. Cuyp.*
A Landscape with the Flight into Egypt; *after Poelenborch.*
A large Landscape; *after G. Smith.*
A set of four Landscapes; *after G. and T. Smith.*
A set of six plates of Horses; *after T. Smith.*
Two Landscapes, Spring and Summer; *after Van Goyen.*
Portrait of Helena Forman, the second wife of Rubens; *after Rubens.*

ELLIOT, WILLIAM, a marine painter, flourished in the latter part of the 18th century. Amongst his works are two pictures of the 'British Fleet' (one dated 1790) at Hampton Court, and 'The Loss of the Andromeda.'

ELLIOTT, CHARLES LORING, an American portrait painter, was born at Scipio, New York, in 1812. He began life as a clerk at Syracuse, but devoted all his leisure time to drawing and painting, and about 1834 went to New York, where he became a pupil of Trumbull. After practising for about ten years in the western parts of the State he settled in New York, and is said to have painted more than seven hundred portraits of eminent people. His likenesses are remarkable for their vigour and truth; indeed, that of Fletcher Harper was sent to the Paris International Exhibition of 1867 as a typical example of American portraiture. Among his best portraits are also those of Fitz-Halleck Greene, the poet, James Fenimore Cooper, Matthew Vassar, the painters Church and Durand, Governor Morgan, and Colonel Colt. There are among other works by him, 'Don Quixote,' 'Falstaff,' 'Andrew van Corlear the Trumpeter,' and 'The Head of Skaneateles Lake,' which is said to have been the only landscape he ever painted. Elliott died at Albany in 1868.

ELLIOTT, Captain ROBERT, R. N., an amateur marine painter, lived in the latter part of the 18th and the beginning of the 19th century. He made many sketches during his travels, from which Prout and Stanfield made drawings, and which were published in 1830. Amongst the works he exhibited at the Royal Academy between 1784 and 1789 were:

The Fleet in Port Royal Harbour. 1785.
View of the City of Quebec. 1786.
Breaking the French Line, Lord Rodney's Action. 1787.
Fire at Kingston, Jamaica. 1788.

126

ELLIS, EDWIN, a well-known landscape and marine painter. He was a native of Nottingham, where he was born in the year 1841. As a lad of fifteen he worked in a lace factory there for five years at lace-designing, but the occupation proved utterly uncongenial to him, and his life-efforts were subsequently devoted to art. He had the benefit of whatever instruction Henry Dawson could give him, and afterwards went to France to complete his artistic education. The principal part of his canvases were seascapes; and the power of his brush in depicting these was universally acknowledged. He became a member of the Society of Royal British Artists and exhibited the utmost industry; and his sudden death on April 19, 1895, cut short a career that had as yet never realized its full promise. One of his early watercolours, full of power, was the picture entitled 'Off Flamborough Head,' which showed the wreck of a schooner in an easterly gale. This canvas is now in the collection of Mr. Gilbert Moss, at Aigburth, near Liverpool; and some eighty-four of his pictures were exhibited at the Nottingham Art Museum in 1893; amongst them, 'After Three Days' Gale,' with its turbulent sea and flying clouds; and also his 'Full Summer,' showing the great white Yorkshire cliffs glistening in the sunlight.

ELLIS, JOSEPH F., a marine painter, born in Ireland about 1780, came to London about 1818, and exhibited a few pictures at the Royal Academy and the British Institution. He is, however, chiefly to be remembered by his clever imitations of Canaletto's works, which were palmed off on the public as originals by an unscrupulous picture-dealer, into whose hands, through misfortunes, he fell. He died at Richmond, in Surrey, in 1848.

ELLIS, WILLIAM, a landscape engraver, was born in London in 1747. He executed some plates in conjunction with William Woollett, whose pupil he had been; and there are several charming prints, mostly landscapes, by him from the designs of Paul Sandby and Thomas Hearne, as well as five views of the 'Battle of the Nile,' in aquatint, after William Anderson, published in 1800. The year of his death is unknown.

ELLYS, JOHN, a portrait painter, was born in 1701. He studied under Thornhill and Schmutz, and was a follower of Van der Banck, to whose house and connection he succeeded. Besides having a large practice, he held the two crown appointments of tapestry-weaver and keeper of the lions. In 1755 he was a member of the committee for the foundation of an Academy. Amongst his portraits are:

Lord Whitworth, the diplomatist. (*At Knole Park.*)
Figg, "the mighty combatant."

ELMER, STEPHEN, a painter of dead game and objects of still-life, was elected an Associate of the Royal Academy in 1772, the year of his first exhibition, and resided principally at Farnham in Surrey, where he died in 1796. He represented subjects of still-life with great fidelity, and with a very spirited pencil. His son practised in Ireland at the close of the century.

ELMORE, ALFRED, an historical and genre painter, was born at Clonakilty, in the county of Cork, on the day of the battle of Waterloo, June 18th, 1815. His father was a retired army surgeon, who when his son was about twelve years of age removed to London, where young Elmore began his career by drawing from the antique in the British Museum. In 1832 he entered the schools of the Royal Academy, and in 1834 exhibited there his first picture, a 'Subject from an Old Play.' After this he went abroad, visiting Paris, Munich, Venice, Bologna, Florence, and ultimately Rome, where he remained for two years. He returned home in 1844, and in that year exhibited his 'Rienzi in the Forum,' which attracted much notice, and with 'The Origin of the Guelph and Ghibeline Quarrel in Florence,' exhibited in 1845, secured his election as an Associate in the latter year. His next popular picture was 'The Invention of the Stocking Loom,' exhibited in 1847, and engraved for the Art Union of London. In 1857 Elmore was elected a Royal Academician, and painted as his diploma work a subject from the "Two Gentlemen of Verona." But the best picture which he ever painted was that which he exhibited in 1860 of 'The Tuileries, 20th June, 1792,' representing the terrible scene of Marie Antoinette assailed in her own palace by the revolutionary mob. One of the most impressive pictures which he exhibited after this was 'Within the Convent Walls,' in the Academy Exhibition of 1864. He painted chiefly pictures of romantic incident, the subjects of which were occasionally drawn from his own fancy, but oftener derived from fiction or poetry. His greatest successes, however, were won in historical painting. Elmore died at Kensington, January 24th, 1881, and was buried in Kensal Green Cemetery. Besides the pictures above mentioned, the following are his principal works:

The Martyrdom of St. Thomas à Becket. 1840. *Painted for Daniel O'Connell, and now in St. Andrew's Roman Catholic Church, Dublin.*
The Novice. 1843.
The Fainting of Hero. 1846.
The Deathbed of Robert, King of Naples. 1848.
Religious Controversy in the time of Louis XIV. 1849.
Griselda. 1850.
The Emperor Charles V. at Yuste. 1856.
An Incident in the life of Dante. 1858.
Marie Antoinette in the Temple. 1861.
The Invention of the Combing Machine. 1862.
Lucrezia Borgia. 1863.
On the Brink. 1865.
After the Expulsion. 1873.
Mary, Queen of Scots, and Darnley, at Jedburgh. 1877.
Lenore. 1871.

ELSASSER, FRIEDRICH AUGUST, a painter of landscapes and architectural views, was born at Berlin in 1810, and studied at the Academy of that city under Blechen, whose influence on art was at that time very great. In 1831 he went to Italy, and in 1834 and 1835 he visited Sicily. Among his choicest works are: 'The Forest of Calabria, 'The Interior of a Church at Palermo,' 'A View of the Ruins at Rome,' &c. The King of Prussia sent him the Order of the Red Eagle, and granted him a pension for life, which he did not long enjoy, as he died at Rome in 1845. His brothers, HEINRICH and JULIUS ELSASSER, were also landscape painters. The latter was born at Berlin in 1815, and died at Rome in 1859.

ELSEVIER, AERNOUT, a Dutch painter of landscapes and conflagrations, was born about 1575 at Douai, but his parents removed to Leyden in 1580. He died after 1629.

His son, LOUIS ELSEVIER, who was also a painter, was born at Leyden in 1615, and died at Delft in 1675.

ELSHEIMER, ADAM, (ELSHAIMER, or ELZHEIMER,) a German painter, was probably born at Frankfort in 1574, but the dates of his career are differently reported. He was the son of a tailor, and was placed at an early age under the care of Philipp Uffenbach, who, though a reputable artist, was soon surpassed by his disciple. Finding no further means of improvement in his own country, Elsheimer went to Rome, where he studied the works of the great masters, and in a short time his pictures, which were very distinct from the works of all of his contemporaries, were held in general estimation. He was fond of landscapes with figures of such importance that the landscape interest is subordinated to that of the incident represented. His pictures were small and finished with the greatest perfection and detail, a quality then entirely new in Italy, especially when studied with extreme fidelity to nature. His power over light and shade was nearly as great as that of Rembrandt, who, in the next generation, followed out the same characteristic of intense chiaro-scuro. Elsheimer delighted in torchlight, moonlight, and the dusk of evening, all of which effects he represented with greater excellence than had before been accomplished. He possessed so extraordinary a memory, that it was sufficient for him to have looked at an object or scene once to draw it with the most surprising precision. The extreme patience and labour with which he finished his pictures was such, that the prices he received for them never sufficiently repaid him for the time spent upon them. If the unfortunate painter had been paid for them a fourth part of what they have since produced, he might have lived in affluence instead of the state of indigence and distress in which he passed the greater part of his life. As it was, he was cast into prison, although a man of irreproachable habits, and this preyed upon his mind. His only benefactor was Count Goudt, who purchased some of his choicest pictures, and has engraved seven of them in a highly-finished manner, well adapted to their style. Elsheimer is perhaps better known by these engravings than by his own pictures. 'Ceres drinking from the Witch's Goblet,' 'Jupiter and Mercury in the home of Baucis,' 'The Flight into Egypt,' 'Tobit and the Angel going home,' are among the number. The copperplate of the last named fell into the hands of Rembrandt, and was partly erased and altered by him into another subject. The elder Teniers, as well as Rembrandt, studied carefully the works of Elsheimer. He died in Rome in 1620. The following works by him are in public galleries:

Cassel.	*Gallery.*	Meeting of Elias and Obadiah.
Dresden.	*Gallery.*	Flight into Egypt.
Dulwich.	*College.*	Susannah and the Elders.
Florence.	*Uffizi.*	His own Portrait.
„	„	Apostles.
„	„	Saints.
„	„	Two Landscapes.
Frankfort.	*Städel.*	Paul and Barnabas at Lystra.
„	„	Bacchus and the Nymphs of Nysa.
Hague.	*Museum.*	Two Italian Landscapes.
London.	*Nat. Gallery.*	Martyrdom of St. Lawrence.
Madrid.	*Gallery.*	Ceres in the house of Becubus.
Munich.	*Gallery.*	Martyrdom of St. Lawrence.
„	„	Triumph of Christianity.
„	„	Burning of Troy.
„	„	Flight into Egypt.
„	„	St. John the Baptist preaching.
Paris.	*Louvre.*	The Flight into Egypt.
„	„	The Good Samaritan.
Petersburg.	*Hermitage.*	St. John the Baptist in the Desert.
„	„	A Forest.
Rome.	*Sciarra Pal.*	Return of the Prodigal Son.
Vienna.	*Gallery.*	Rest on the Flight into Egypt.

ELSHEIMER, JOHANN, a brother of Adam Elsheimer, was born at Frankfort in 1593, and died previous to 1636. About 1632 he painted 'The Story of Virginia,' now on the Imperial Staircase in the Römer at Frankfort.

ELSHOLTZ, LUDWIG, a German painter of genre subjects and battles, born at Berlin in 1805, studied in the Academy of his native city, and afterwards in the studio of Franz Krüger, the painter of horses. His best work is 'The Battle of Leipsic,' painted in 1833, and now in the possession of the German Emperor. He died at Berlin in 1850. In the Berlin National Gallery is 'The Beginning of the Fight,' dated 1834.

ELST, PIETER VAN DER. See VAN DER ELST.

ELSTER, GOTTFRIED RUDOLF, an historical painter who worked for some time at Düsseldorf, executed a number of religious pictures, among which are a 'Holy Family,' in the possession of the Prince of Hohenzollern, and some cartoons for the Zionskirche at Berlin. He died in that city in 1872.

ELSTRACKE, REGINALD, an engraver who flourished in England about the year 1620, worked chiefly for the booksellers, and his plates are almost entirely confined to portraits. These are more sought after for their scarcity and their connection with English history, than for their merit as engravings. He also engraved the title-page and several of the portraits for Holland's 'Baziliωlogia. A Booke of Kings. Beeing the true and liuely Effigies of all our English Kings from the Conquest vntill this present.' The following portraits are by him:

James I.
Queen Elizabeth.
Mary, Queen of Scots. *One of his best prints.*
The same, with Lord Darnley.
Thomas Howard, Earl of Suffolk.
Robert Devereux, Earl of Essex.
Gervase Babington, Bishop of Worcester.
Sir Julius Cæsar, Master of the Rolls.
Sir Thomas More.
Sir Philip Sidney.
Thomas Sutton, founder of the Charter House.
Edmund, Lord Sheffield.
John, Lord Harrington.
William Knollys, Viscount Wallingford.
William Cecil, Lord Burghley.
Gustavus Adolphus, King of Sweden.
Richard Whittington.

ELTZ, JOHANN FRIEDRICH VON, born in 1632, was one of the first artists who worked in mezzotint. His works are now rare; examples of them are an 'Ecce Homo,' after Albrecht Dürer, and a portrait of Johann Philipp von Schönborn, Elector of Mayence, after Th. C. von Fürstenberg. He died at Mayence in 1686.

ELVEN, TETAR VAN. See TETAR VAN ELVEN.

ELYAS, MATHIEU. See ELIAS.

ELZHEIMER, ADAM. See ELSHEIMER.

EMBDE, VON DER. See VON DER EMBDE.

EMELRAET, PHILIPPUS AUGUSTUS. See HEMELRAET.

EMES, JOHN, a water-colour landscape painter, practised about the end of the 18th century, and exhibited at the Royal Academy in 1790 and 1791. He also engraved Jefferys' 'Destruction of the Spanish Batteries before Gibraltar.'

EMLER, BONAVENTURA, an Austrian artist, was born in 1831, and studied at the Academy of Vienna. He became celebrated by his illustrations to the 'Divina Commedia' of Dante, and died in 1862.

128

EMMANUEL, a Greek priest and painter, is the author of a picture in the Byzantine style in the National Gallery, London. It represents 'St. Cosmo and St. Damian receiving the Divine Blessing,' and is signed χείρ Ἐμμανουηλ ἱερεως τοῦ τζάνε ('the hand of Emmanuel, priest of Tzane'). It is suggested in the catalogue, that this Emmanuel may be identical with the Emmanuel mentioned by Lanzi, who lived at Venice in the 17th century, and executed a painting dated 1660.

EMMANUELLO DA COMO, Fra. See COMO.

EMMETT, WILLIAM, an engraver who flourished about the year 1710, among other prints engraved a large view of the interior of St. Paul's Cathedral, which is executed in a neat, clear style; as well as three exterior views of the same edifice.

EMPIS, CATHERINE EDMÉE SIMONIS. See SIMONIS-EMPIS.

EMPOLI, JACOPO DA. See CHIMENTI.

ENDER, JOHANN NEPOMUK, an Austrian historical and portrait painter, was born at Vienna in 1793. In 1829 he became a professor in the Academy of his native city, where he died in 1854. He is distinguished for his oil-paintings and water-colour drawings, and a 'Madonna and Child' by him is in the Vienna Gallery. His son, Eduard Ender, is a well-known Viennese painter of historical and genre subjects.

ENDER, THOMAS, an Austrian landscape painter, the twin brother of Johann Nepomuk Ender, was born at Vienna in 1793. From the age of twelve he studied in the Academy of Vienna, where, in 1816, he obtained the grand prize for painting. In 1836 he was appointed a tutor, and afterwards professor of landscape in the Academy. Through the patronage of the Archduke John and Prince Metternich, he accompanied, as draughtsman, the scientific expedition sent by Austria to Brazil in 1817, and made a collection of seven hundred drawings, which are now at Vienna. Three views by him are in the Vienna Gallery. He died in Vienna in 1875. In the Berlin National Gallery is his 'Italian Wood Chapel.'

ENDLICH, PHILIP, a Dutch engraver, was born at Amsterdam about the year 1700. He was a pupil of Bernard Picart, and was chiefly occupied on portraits, among which are the following:

Hendrik, Count of Moens.
John Taylor, a celebrated oculist. 1735.
Juan Felipe d'Almeria, Governor of the Isle of St. Martin.
Jan Gosewyn E. Alstein, ecclesiastic of Amsterdam. 1738.
Jan Noordbeck; the same.
Pieter Hollebeck; the same.
Leonard Beels; the same.

ENDRES, BERNHARD, was born at Owingen, in Baden, in 1805, and studied genre and historical painting at the Academy of Munich. Two of his works are in the Gallery at Carlsruhe, the portrait of Pope Julius II., after Raphael, and 'Christ bearing the Cross.' He died in 1874.

ENDTER, SUSANNA MARIA. See SANDRART.

ENGEL, KARL, a German painter, was born in 1817 at Londorf, and died in 1870 at Rödelsheim. The Darmstadt Gallery has a 'View of the Studio of the Sculptor Scholl,' by him.

ENGELBRECHT, CHRISTIAN and MARTIN, two printsellers and engravers, who resided at Augsburg, flourished about the year 1721. Christian Engelbrecht, conjointly with J. A. Pfeffel, engraved some ornamental works for goldsmiths, after A. Morrison; and some views for the 'History of

GEORGE ENGLEHEART

MISS BEDINGFELD

MISS ANN PRITCHARD

A GIRL
(NAME UNKNOWN)

MISS HESTER WOOLLEY

Architecture,' published in 1721 by J. Hernhard. Martin Engelbrecht engraved some plates after Rugendas and other masters, and some illustrations for Ovid's 'Metamorphoses.'

ENGELBRECHTSEN, CORNELIS, (or ENGELBERTS,) the son of a wood-engraver, was born at Leyden in 1468. The pictures of Jan van Eyck, the alleged inventor of oil-painting, being at that time the object of curiosity and admiration, Engelbrechtsen applied himself to study the works of that master, and is said by Van Mander to have been the first artist in his country that painted in oil. The paintings by this master which escaped the troubles of that country were preserved with great care in the church of Our Lady at Leyden. They represented the 'Crucifixion,' the 'Descent from the Cross,' 'Abraham sacrificing Isaac,' with some small pictures of the 'Life of the Virgin': these were well composed, and of a less Gothic style of design than was usual at the early period at which he lived. They sometimes bear the accompanying mark. His principal work was an altar-piece, painted for the Epitaph of the family of Lockhorst, in the church of St. Peter at Leyden, and composed of a great number of figures representing the 'Adoration of the Lamb.' The National Gallery has a 'Madonna and Child' by him. The Antwerp Museum has two double pictures by him: the one, 'St. Leonard delivering prisoners,' and 'St. George;' the other, scenes from the life of St. Hubert. A 'Crucifixion' by him is in the Munich Gallery. Engelbrechtsen died at Leyden in 1533. He is thought to be identical with the "Cornelis de Hollandere" who was free of the Guild of St. Luke at Antwerp in 1492.

ENGELMANN, GOTTFRIED, a German lithographer, who also painted in water-colours, was born at Mühlhausen in 1788, and died there in 1839. He was a pupil of Sennefelder, the inventor of lithography, and of C. von Mannlich, and he introduced the art into France.

ENGELRAMS, CORNELIS, (or ENGHELRAMS,) a Flemish painter, born at Mechlin in 1537, excelled in painting historical subjects in distemper. His best work, representing the 'Seven Works of Mercy,' is in the cathedral of St. Rombout at Mechlin. There are several of his pictures in Germany, where he passed some years. At Hamburg, in the church of St. Catharine, is a large altar-piece by him of the 'Conversion of St. Paul.' He died at Mechlin in 1583.

ENGERTH, ERASMUS, an Austrian artist, who was born at Vienna in 1796, studied at the Academy of his native city, and afterwards in Italy. On his return home he painted portraits and historical pictures, and also made successful copies from the great masters, but he subsequently devoted himself exclusively to the art of restoring paintings. He was keeper of the picture gallery of the Belvedere, and died at Vienna in 1871.

ENGHELSZEN, CORNELIS. See VERSPRONK.

ENGLEHEART, FRANCIS, a line-engraver, born in London in 1775, was a brother to George Engleheart, the miniature painter. He learned the art as an apprentice to Joseph Collyer, and as an assistant to James Heath. His first independent works were the illustrations to Akenside, after Stothard, whose 'Canterbury Pilgrims' he had a large share in engraving, and the illustrations to Homer after Cook. He also engraved some of Smirke's drawings for 'Don Quixote,' and several plates for the 'Literary Souvenir,' 'Amulet,' 'Gem,' and other Annuals, among which is the last portrait of Lord Byron, after W. E. West. He died in 1849. Besides the works already named, his best plates are:

Duncan Gray; *after Sir David Wilkie.*
The Only Daughter; *after the same.*
The Castle; *after Cook.*
Sir Calepine rescuing Serena; *after Hilton.*

ENGLEHEART, GEORGE, miniature painter to George III., and brother to Francis Engleheart, was born at Kew in 1750. As a lad he was sent first to the studio of George Barret, R.A., but did not long remain with him, and soon became a pupil to Sir Joshua Reynolds, many of whose works he copied in miniature. In 1775 he commenced to practise for himself, and from that time down to 1813 continued in constant work, painting 4853 portraits of the notable persons of his time, and exhibiting many at the Royal Academy. In 1813 he retired with a comfortable fortune, and left Hertford Street, Mayfair, where he had purchased considerable property, for his country home at Bedfont. Later on he resided with his son at Blackheath, and there he died in 1829. His miniatures were of great beauty and are very highly esteemed. He left behind him a Fee Book which mentions the names of every person whom he painted between 1775 and 1813.

See 'George Engleheart,' by G. C. Williamson, London, 1902.

ENGLEHEART, HENRY, son of George Engleheart, born 1801, died 1885, a clever artist in water-colour and in pencil. His architectural drawings, mainly of foreign cathedrals, are of great beauty and refinement, and resemble the work of Prout.

ENGLEHEART, JOHN COX DILLMAN, nephew of George Engleheart and his pupil, was born in 1783. He was a very popular artist, and exhibited 157 works at the Royal Academy, and many others at different exhibitions. His health failed when he was forty-four years of age, and he left England for Italy. On his return, being in possession of an ample fortune, he retired from his profession, and settled first at East Acton and then at Tunbridge Wells, where he died in 1862. His works are notable for their brilliant colouring and gorgeous effect, but some of his simpler portraits are of supreme beauty and full of character.

See 'George Engleheart,' by G. C. Williamson, London, 1902.

ENGLEHEART, THOMAS, was a brother of Francis Engleheart the engraver, and was chiefly known for his wonderful sculpture in wax, many examples of which he exhibited at the Royal Academy. He was also, however, an expert draughtsman, working with Flaxman for Josiah Wedgwood, and his pencil drawings are of great beauty and refinement. He was born in 1745, and had two sons, Timothy and Jonathan, both engravers. He died in 1786.

ENGLEHEART, TIMOTHY STANSFELD, a line-engraver, a son of Francis Engleheart, was born in London in 1803, and died there in 1879. He engraved several plates for the 'Literary Souvenir,' 'Forget me not,' and other Annuals.

ENGLISH, JOSIAS, was an amateur engraver, who resided at Mortlake, where he died in 1718. He executed an etching of 'Christ with the Two Disciples at Emmaus,' after Titian, and in 1654 a set of small upright plates of the 'Gods and Demi-gods.' His best work is a spirited etching of a half-length of a 'Man regaling,' after F. Cleyn.

ENGSTROM, WILHELM OSCAR, a Swedish animal painter, was born in 1831, and died at Düsseldorf in 1877.

ENHUBER, KARL VON, a genre painter, was born at Hof, in Voigtland, in 1811. He was the son of a civil officer, who when his son was eighteen months old removed to Nördlingen. After study-ing at the Munich Academy, he was at first an animal painter; he then worked at represent-ations of the Thirty Years' War; and only through the study of the works of Metsu and Terborch did he discover his true talent. He was admitted a member of the Munich Academy in 1858, and died at Munich in 1867. He excelled in characterizing middle-class home life, with its pleasures and troubles, and was gifted with natural humour, which was the foundation of his delicate deline-ation of character. To be mentioned amongst his works are :

Berlin.	Gallery.	Return of the Munich Guards-man. 1844.
Darmstadt.	Gallery.	Sessions Day in Bavaria.
Munich.	Gallery.	A Grandfather watching his Grandson at play with toy Soldiers.
„	„	A Carver in his Workshop.

ENNIS, W., an Irish historical and portrait painter, was born in the first half of the 18th cen-tury. He studied at Dublin under Robert West, and afterwards in Italy, and subsequently became a master in the Dublin Art School. He died, through a fall from his horse, in the county of Wicklow, in 1771.

ENS, GIOSEFFO. See HEINS.

ENSLEN, JOHANN KARL, a German landscape painter, who was born in 1759 and died in 1849, was well known in his time for his panoramas, which were the first introduced into Germany.

ENSLEN, KARL GEORG, an Austrian painter, born at Vienna in 1792, studied in the Academy of Berlin. He travelled in Italy, Sweden, Norway, and Denmark, and his panoramas give proof of a knowledge of excellent linear and aerial perspec-tive. He died at Lille in 1866. There is a view of the 'Bay of Naples' by him in water-colours in the Lille Museum.

ENSO, GIOSEFFO. See HEINS.

ENSOM, WILLIAM, a line-engraver, was born in 1796, and died at Wandsworth in 1832. He en-graved 'Christ blessing the Bread,' after Carlo Dolci, 'St. John in the Wilderness,' after Carlo Cignani, and several plates for the Annuals, of which the best are those in the 'Bijou' of George IV. and Lady Wallscourt, after Sir Thomas Lawrence.

EPINAT, FLEURY, a painter of historical sub-jects and landscapes, born at Montbrison in 1764, imitated his master David, with whom he went to Rome. He died at Pierre-Scise in 1830.

EPISCOPIUS, JOANNES. See DE BISSCHOP.

ERASMUS, DESIDERIUS, the eminent scholar, born at Rotterdam in 1467, painted in 1484 a picture representing 'Christ on the Cross, with Mary and St. John.' This work, which is little known, is in the style of the old Dutch masters, and is in the convent of Emaus, called Steyne, near Gouda. He died at Basle in 1536.

ERBETTE, FILIPPO DALL'. See MAZZUOLA.

ERCOLE DI GIULIO. See GRANDI.

ERCOLE DI ROBERTO. See GRANDI.

ERCOLINO DI GUIDO RENI, (or ERCOLE DI MARIA). See SAN GIOVANNI.

EREDI, BENEDETTO, an Italian engraver, was born at Florence in 1750. He engraved, in con-junction with J. B. Cecchi, nine plates of the Monument of Dante, with his portrait. There are also by him the following plates :

PORTRAITS.

Luca Cambiaso, Genoese painter; *after a picture by himself.*
Federigo Zucchero; *after himself.*
Angelo Bronzino; Florentine painter.
Annibale Carracci.

SUBJECTS.

The Transfiguration; *after Raphael.*
The Adulteress before Christ; *after Angelo Bronzino.*
The Death of Lucretia; *after Luca Giordano.*

EREMITA DI MONTE SENARIO. See STE-FANESCHI.

ERHARD, JOHANN CHRISTOPH, who was born at Nuremberg in 1795, was instructed by Zwinger and Gabler, and afterwards went to Vienna and Rome. Among the hundred and eighty-five plates which he etched are several landscapes and views of con-siderable merit. He committed suicide at Rome in 1822.

ERLINGER, GEORG, a printer and wood-engraver, was working at Augsburg in 1516, and at Bamberg from 1519 till his death in 1542. Among his wood-cuts, which are very scarce, is one of 'Christ on the Cross.'

ERMELS, JOHANN FRANZ, a German painter and engraver, a pupil of Holtzman, was born near Cologne in 1641. He resided at Nuremberg, and painted for the church of St. Sebald in that city a picture of the 'Resurrection'; he was more suc-cessful, however, as a painter of landscapes, in which he imitated the style of Jan Both. He died at Nuremberg in 1699. In the Städel Gallery at Frankfort is a 'Landscape' by him, with figures by J. H. Roos; and in the Vienna Gallery is a 'Landscape with Fishermen' by him. A 'Land-scape' is also in the Milan Gallery. There are by him a few etchings of landscapes, after Waterloo, Breenbergh, &c., executed with spirit and taste.

ERRANTE, GIUSEPPE, born at Trapani, in Sicily, in 1760, studied at Palermo and Rome, and was employed in the Caserta Palace, Naples. On account of his political opinions he was obliged to remove to Milan, and afterwards established him-self at Rome in 1810. Besides historical subjects, he painted portraits, in which he was especially successful. He died at Rome in 1821.

ERRAR, (or ERRARD,) JOHAN, an artist, who flourished at Liége about 1670, etched landscapes after Waterloo.

ERRARD, CHARLES, a French painter and archi-tect, was born at Nantes about 1601, and is better known as one of the chief founders and directors of the Academy at Paris than as a painter and engraver. He studied in Italy, where he also spent the greater part of his life. In 1635 he was admitted a member of the Academy of St. Luke, and in 1665 was made director of the French Academy at Rome, where he died in 1689.

ERRI, CAMMILLO, of Modena, is known only by a picture of 'St. John the Baptist Preaching,' with the date 1577, in the Modena Gallery.

ERSKINE, HENRY DAVID, EARL OF BUCHAN. See BUCHAN.

ERTINGER, FRANZ, a German engraver, is said by some to have been born at Colmar, by others at Wyl in Swabia, in the year 1640. He resided chiefly at Paris, where he engraved several plates, which are not without merit, and where he died in 1700. His best prints are the following:

PORTRAITS.

J. F. de Beughem, Bishop of Antwerp.
Niccolò Macchiavelli.
Gabriel du Pinau.

VARIOUS SUBJECTS.

The History of Achilles, in eight Plates; *after Rubens;* the same subjects have been since engraved by Baron.
Twelve Prints from the Metamorphoses of Ovid; *after the miniatures of Joseph Werner.*
Ten Plates of the History of the Counts of Toulouse; *after Raymond de La Fage.*
The Marriage at Cana in Galilee; *after the same.*
A set of Friezes of Bacchanalian subjects; *after the same.*
Several Views of Towns; *after Van der Meulen;* some of them in the manner of Callot.

ERVEST, JAKOB, a scholar of Adam Elsheimer painted marine subjects, and naval combats.

ES, JACOB VAN, (or ESSEN,) a Flemish painter, was born at Antwerp in 1606. He was very successful in the art of reproducing still-life, but more especially fish, which he painted with an almost deceptive similarity to nature. His masterpieces are two 'Fish Markets,' in the Vienna Gallery, with figures by Jordaens. The Madrid Gallery also has two pictures of fish and a fruit and flower piece by Van Es. The Städel Gallery at Frankfort has a fish-piece by him. In the Antwerp Museum is a good example of his still-life subjects, formerly in the Episcopal Palace, and in the Lille Museum is a picture of 'Oysters and Fruit,' which was formerly in the Abbey of Cysoing. He died at Antwerp in 1665-66.

ESBRAT, NOËL RAYMOND, a landscape and animal painter, was born in Paris in 1809, and died there in 1856. He was a pupil of Guillon-Lethière and of Watelet, and from 1844 sent pictures to various exhibitions.

ESCALANTE, JUAN ANTONIO, a Spanish painter, born at Cordova in 1630, was a scholar of Francisco Rizi, but he adopted the style of Tintoretto, as well in colouring as in composition. Several of his works in the churches of Madrid are highly commended by Palomino. In the church of San Miguel is a graceful picture of 'St. Catharine'; and in the church of the Espiritù Santo is an altar-piece of the 'Dead Christ,' with other figures, painted in the style of Titian. A similar picture in the Dresden Gallery is ascribed to him. The Hague Gallery has a 'Gipsy Woman telling an Officer's fortune.' In the Madrid Gallery are two works by him, 'A Holy Family,' and 'The Infant Christ and St. John;' and in the Hermitage, St. Petersburg, 'St. Joseph and the Infant Christ.' He died at Madrid in 1670.

ESCALANTE, JUAN DE SEVILLA ROMERO Y. See SEVILLA.

ESCHINI, ANGELO MARIA, a painter and engraver, flourished at Modena in the 17th century: by him more than one excellent plate representing the 'Virgin' is known.

ESCLAVO, EL. See PAREJA.

ESCOT, CHARLES, French painter and *pastelliste;* born 1836. Excelled as a portrait painter, and has left a large number of portraits that show breadth and vigour of draughtsmanship and vivid intensity of colouring. His house at Gaillac was a veritable museum, the main attraction in this being some thirty copies of 'La Tour.' Escot had

delayed his intention of bequeathing this interesting collection to the Museum of Albi, but his death occurred at Gaillac (Tarn) on May 5th, 1902, before he had been able to express his wish in proper legal form.

ESKILSSON, PETER, a Swedish genre painter, was born in 1820, in the Billeberga parish, Schonen. He was at first an under-officer in the Göta artillery regiment, and then a book-keeper at Göteborg; but by the assistance of a friend he was enabled in 1853 to go to Düsseldorf, where he studied under Tidemand. In 1859 he was compelled for a time to become a photographer at Stockholm, but he afterwards illustrated Bellman, depicting the Swedish popular life with great humour. He became an associate of the Academy in 1866, and died at Bremö, near Sigtuna, in 1872.

ESPAGNOLETTO. See RIBERA.

ESPAÑA, JUAN DE, or JUAN EL ESPAÑOL. See GIOVANNI DI PIETRO.

ESPINAL, JUAN DE, a Spanish historical painter, was a native of Seville. He was the son and pupil of Gregorio Espinal, who was also a painter, but he afterwards entered the school of Domingo Martinez, whose daughter he married. He was chosen director of the School of Design which Cean Bermudez and other lovers of art established at Seville. Cean Bermudez says that he possessed more genius than any of his contemporaries, and but for his bad training and indolence would have been the best painter whom Seville had produced since the time of Murillo. A visit to Madrid late in life made apparent his misspent time, and he returned saddened and abashed to Seville, where he died in 1783. His chief works were scenes from the life of St. Jerome, painted for the monastery of San Geronimo de Buenavista, and now in the Seville Museum, and some frescoes in the collegiate church of San Salvador.

ESPINÓS, BENITO, a Spanish flower painter, the son of Josef Espinós, was a native of Valencia. He was appointed director of the Royal Academy of San Carlos in Valencia in 1787, and died about 1817. Nine of his flower-pieces are in the Madrid Gallery, whilst others are in the Museum of Valencia, and in the Escorial.

ESPINÓS, JOSEF, a Spanish painter and engraver, born at Valencia in 1721, studied painting under Luis Martinez and Evaristo Muñoz. He painted for the convent of the Servites of the Foot of the Cross, in Valencia, pictures of 'Our Lady of Sorrows' and of the founders of that order. He engraved in line several prints of saints, and died at Valencia in 1784, leaving a choice collection of prints, drawings, and books.

ESPINOSA, ALONSO and ANDRES DE, Spanish historical painters, who dwelt at Burgos in the early part of the 16th century, were brothers, who usually worked together. In 1524, together with Cristobal de Herrera, they gilded and decorated with paintings the Lady chapel of the cathedral at Palencia.

ESPINOSA, GERONIMO RODRIGUEZ DE, a Spanish painter, born at Valladolid in 1562, was the father of Jacinto Geronimo de Espinosa. He married in 1596 Aldonza Lleó, at the Valencian town of Cocentayna, where he resided for many years. In 1600 he painted pictures of 'St. Lawrence' and 'St. Hippolitus,' and in the following year 'SS. Sebastian and Roch,' for the church of Cocentayna. These works were afterwards displaced, and passed into the hands of one Andreas Cister, a scrivener.

In 1604-7 he executed, in conjunction with a certain Jayme Terol, a scholar of Fray Nicolas Borras, the pictures for the high altar of St. John the Baptist's Church, at the town of Muro. Finally taking up his abode at Valencia, he died there about 1630.

ESPINOSA, JACINTO GERONIMO DE, a son and scholar of Geronimo Rodriguez de Espinosa, was born at Cocentayna, in Valencia, in 1600. He studied also under Francisco Ribalta, and went afterwards to Italy, where he acquired a boldness of design and a vigour of colouring that resemble the style of Guercino. His best pictures are in the churches at Valencia, particularly in San Esteban, and in the chapel of San Luis Bertran in Santo Domingo. The principal altar-piece in the church of the Carmelites is by this master, representing the 'Transfiguration.' He died at Valencia in 1680. Among his works are the following:

Dresden.	*Gallery.*	St. Francis of Assisi.
Madrid.	*Gallery.*	Mary Magdalen praying.
,,	,,	Christ at the column.
,,	,,	St. John the Baptist.
Valencia.	*Museum.*	Christ appearing to St. Ignatius Loyola.
,,	,,	The Communion of St. Mary Magdalen.
,,	,,	St. Louis Bertrand on his bier.

ESPINOSA, JUAN DE, born at Puente de la Reyna, in Navarre, was employed in 1653 to paint twenty-four scenes from the life of St. Millan, for the monastery of St. Millan de la Cogolla. He executed twelve with some skill, and after his death the work was completed by Fray Juan Rizi.

ESPINOSA, JUAN DE, a Spanish painter of fruit pieces, flourished towards the end of the 17th and the beginning of the 18th century. Nothing is known of his life. Two examples of his art are in the Madrid Gallery.

ESPINOSA, MIGUEL DE, of Saragossa, a painter of good repute, was invited in 1654 by the Benedictine fathers, to paint for their monastery of St. Millan de la Cogolla. Amongst his works executed at the expense of the brotherhood were pictures of the 'Miracle of the Water turned into Wine,' and the 'Miracle of the Loaves and Fishes.'

ESQUARTE, PABLO, a Spanish painter of the latter part of the 16th century, who studied at Valencia, but afterwards went to Venice and became a disciple of Titian. He had a great talent for portrait painting, and perhaps excelled in other departments, as the Duke of Villa Hermosa employed him to ornament his palace and country residence.

ESSELENS, JACOB, a painter of Amsterdam in the 17th century, is said to have been a pupil of Rembrandt, but his works do not corroborate the assertion. His pictures represent villages on the banks of rivers, woody landscapes, buildings with magnificent fountains, stag-hunts, and shipping pieces, painted in a clear tone of colour, and with figures spiritedly touched. The dates of his birth and death are not recorded. A picture of 'Figures by a River,' signed with his name, is in the Rotterdam Museum; a 'Fishing Piece' is in the Copenhagen Gallery; and in the Glasgow Corporation Galleries is a 'Rendezvous of a Hunting Party.'

ESSEN, HANS VON. See LADENSPELDER.

ESSEN, JACOB VAN. See ES.

ESSENBECK, J. VAN, was born at Rotterdam in 1627, and died in 1678; but no further details of his life are recorded. In the Glasgow Corporation Galleries is a 'Hawking Party' attributed to him.

ESSEX, RICHARD HAMILTON, an architectural water-colour painter, was born in 1802. He became in 1823 an associate of the Water-Colour Society, where he exhibited till 1836. His works also appeared at the Royal Academy. He died at Bow in 1855.

ESSEX, WILLIAM, a clever copyist in enamel of landscape and figure subjects, both by old and modern masters, first exhibited at the Royal Academy in 1818, and for the last time in 1862, having been appointed miniature painter to the Queen in 1839. Towards the end of his life he painted a few miniature enamels from the life. His death occurred at Brighton, in 1869, at the age of 85. His son, WILLIAM B. ESSEX, who was a portrait painter, died at Birmingham in 1852, aged 29.

ESTEBAN, RODRIGO, was painter to Sancho the Brave, King of Castile. No work of his is known to exist, but an account of a payment of one hundred maravedis from the privy purse in 1291-92 is to be found in a MS. book of accounts in the Royal Library at Madrid.

ESTENSE, BALDASSARE, of Reggio, who was born about 1443, has been supposed to have been an illegitimate scion of the house of Este, since no mention of his father's name ever occurs in contemporary records, whilst he was called 'Estensis,' and received unusual promotion and rewards from the Dukes of Ferrara. He was a pupil of Cosimo Tura, and was also a medallist. In 1469 he painted the likeness of Borso I., and was ordered to present it in person to the Duke of Milan. From 1471 to 1504 he was a salaried officer at the court of Ferrara, living first in Castel Nuovo, for which he painted a canvas that has perished, and afterwards in Castel Tedaldo, of which he was the governor. In 1483 he painted the portrait of Tito Strozzi, now in the Costabili Gallery at Ferrara. His will, dated 1500, is in the archives of Ferrara, but the exact date of his death is unknown.

ESTORGES, J., a French engraver of the 17th century, who etched a plate in the style of Pietro del Po representing 'Christ on the Mount of Olives.'

ESTRADA, JOSÉ MARIA, an historical and genre painter of Valencia, who died at Madrid in 1873. He has left, among other pictures, 'Diana observing the sleeping Endymion,' 'An Eating-house,' and the portrait of Count Villalobos.

ESTRADA, JUAN and IGNACIO, were two brothers, who worked together as painters, though Ignacio was also a sculptor. They were born at Badajoz, Juan in 1717, and Ignacio in 1724, and were instructed by their father, Manuel Estrada, but Juan received three years' further tuition from Pablo Pernicharo, at Madrid. Many of their pictures are still to be seen in the churches of Valencia, Ignacio having furnished the designs, and Juan carried out the execution. Juan died at Badajoz in 1792, and Ignacio in 1790.

ETHENARD Y ABARCA, FRANCISCO ANTONIO, a painter and engraver, the son of a German father, was born at Madrid. He served in the German body-guard under Charles II., and until it was disbanded in 1701 by Philip V., upon which he devoted himself entirely to the above branches of art, which he had already pursued as an amateur. He died at Madrid in 1710. He published a 'Philosophy of War' in 1675, and 'The Italian and

Hanfstängl photo]   [*National Gallery, London*

YOUTH ON THE PROW AND PLEASURE AT THE HELM

Spanish Fencing-Master' in 1697, and both of these he illustrated with engravings.

ETLINGER, GEORG, was a German engraver on wood, who resided at Bamberg. There is by him a wood-cut representing Bishop Blaize, enclosed in a border ornamented with symbols of the Gospel, and executed with great spirit.

ETTY, WILLIAM, the eminent painter, was born at York, March 10, 1787. "Like Rembrandt and Constable," writes Etty, in an autobiography published in the 'Art Journal' in 1849, "my father also was a miller." In 1798 he was apprenticed to Robert Peck, a letter-press printer at Hull, as a compositor, "to which business," he says, "I served seven full years faithfully and truly, and worked at it three weeks as journeyman; but I had such a busy desire to be a painter, that the last years of my servitude dragged on most heavily. I counted the years, days, weeks, and hours, till liberty should break my chains and set my struggling spirit free." In 1806 he was invited to London by his uncle, William Etty, of the firm of Bodley, Etty, and Bodley, of Lombard Street. William Etty was himself "a beautiful draughtsman in pen and ink," and saw promise in the crude performances of his young kinsman, and besides helping him during life, left him a sufficient sum after his death to enable him to pursue his studies. Arrived in town, he tells us:—"I drew from prints or from nature, or from anything I could; I was made at home at my uncle's, I was furnished with cash by my brother. My first academy was in a plaster-cast shop, kept by Gianelli, in that lane near to Smithfield, immortalised by Dr. Johnson's visit to see 'The Ghost' there." He soon received a letter of introduction to Opie, who introduced him to Fuseli, by whom he was admitted as a probationer in Somerset House. He entered the schools of the Royal Academy in the same week as Collins; and Hilton and Haydon were amongst his fellow-students. By his uncle's generosity, who paid one hundred guineas for him, Etty, in July, 1808, became an in-door pupil of Sir Thomas Lawrence, then residing in Greek Street, Soho. Lawrence frequently employed him to make copies of his portraits, but had little leisure to give substantial assistance to his pupil in his studies. When his year of study under Lawrence was expired, Etty painted from nature, and copied the old masters in the British Gallery: this, he says, he found easy, after copying Lawrence. He was also a constant student in the Life School of the Royal Academy, where his industry was indefatigable, yet he never gained a medal. He ventured at one time to send six pictures to the Academy exhibition, but all were rejected; this happened year after year at the Academy, and at the British Gallery, but by discovering his defects, and by great industry in endeavouring to correct them, he at last conquered his bad fortune. In 1811 he was comforted by finding one of his pictures, 'Telemachus rescuing Antiope,' hung at the Royal Academy, and from that time forward he always obtained an entrance for some of his works at the Academy or the British Institution. He painted portraits also at this time, but chiefly occupied himself on classical subjects. In 1816 he visited Paris and Florence, but returned home in less than three months. In 1822 he went to Italy, visiting Venice, Florence, Rome, and Naples, but it was in Venice that he found the greatest attractions:—"Venice, the birth-place and cradle of colour, the hope and idol of my professional life." He studied in the academy there, and was elected one of its honorary members. He returned to London early in 1824, and in the same year exhibited 'Pandora formed by Vulcan, and crowned by the Seasons,' which was bought by Lawrence, and secured his election as an Associate of the Royal Academy. He became an Academician in 1828, and it was then suggested to him that he should discontinue his practice in the Life School, where he had been accustomed for years to attend every evening during the session to paint studies in oil from the living models, as it was considered incompatible with the dignity of an Academician to continue to take his place amongst the students; but he said he would rather decline the honour of membership than give up his studies. He resided in London from 1826 till 1848, when, owing to failing health, he retired to his native city York, where he died November 13, 1849. An exhibition of Etty's works was held in the summer of 1849 at the Society of Arts, and his 'Life' by Alexander Gilchrist was published in 1855. In his autobiography Etty has himself pointed out what he considered his greatest works. "My aim in all my great pictures has been to paint some great moral on the heart: 'The Combat,' the beauty of mercy; the three 'Judith' pictures, patriotism, and self-devotion to her country, her people, and her God; 'Benaiah, David's chief captain,' valour; 'Ulysses and the Syrens,' the importance of resisting sensual delights, or an Homeric paraphrase on the 'Wages of Sin is Death'; the three pictures of 'Joan of Arc,' Religion, Valour, Loyalty and Patriotism, like the modern Judith; these, in all, make nine colossal pictures, as it was my desire to paint three times three." Besides the above-mentioned the following are his principal works:

Sappho. 1811.
The Coral Finders. 1820.
Cleopatra's Arrival at Cicilia. 1821.
The Judgment of Paris.
Venus attired by the Graces.
The Wise and Foolish Virgins.
Hylas and the Nymphs.
The Dance described in Homer's Shield.
The Prodigal Son.
The Bevy of Fair Women. (Milton.)
The Bridge of Sighs, Venice.
The Destruction of the Temple of Vice.
The Rape of Proserpine.
La Fleur de Lis.
Adam and Eve at their Morning Orisons.
The Prodigal in the depth of his Misery.
The Prodigal's return to his Father and Mother.
The Origin of Marriage. (Milton.) *Stafford House.*
Pandora.
The Parting of Hero and Leander.
The Death of Hero and Leander.
Diana and Endymion.
The Graces: Psyche and Cupid.
Amoret freed by Britomart from the power of the Enchantress.
Zephyr and Aurora.
Robinson Crusoe returning thanks to God for his deliverance.

In the National Gallery.

The Imprudence of Candaules, King of Lydia. 1830.
Window in Venice, during a Festa. 1831.
Youth on the Prow and Pleasure at the Helm. 1832.
The Lute-Player. 1833.
The Dangerous Playmate. 1833.
Study of a Man in Persian Costume. 1834.
Christ appearing to Mary Magdalen after His Resurrection. 1834.
Il Duetto. 1838.

Female Bathers surprised by a Swan. 1841.
The Magdalen. 1842.
The Bather 'at the doubtful breeze alarmed.' 1844.
Study for a Head of Christ.

At South Kensington.
Head of a Cardinal. 1844.
Cupid sheltering Psyche. 1823.
The Deluge (a nude female figure). 1815.

In the National Gallery of Scotland.
Series of three pictures illustrating the Deliverance of Bethulia by Judith. 1827-31.
Benaiah, one of David's Mighty Men.
The Combat—Woman pleading for the Vanquished. 1825. *Exhibited in* 1844.

In the Royal Institution, Manchester.
Ulysses and the Sirens.

ETZDORF, CHRISTIAN FRIEDRICH, a landscape painter, and the younger brother of Johann Christian Etzdorf, was born at Pösneck, in the duchy of Saxe-Meiningen, in 1807. He was educated in art at the Munich Academy, and at first practised porcelain painting, but afterwards devoted himself to landscapes, in which he followed much the same style as his brother, producing forest scenes, rocky valleys, and winter pieces. After his brother's death he returned for a while to Pösneck, but afterwards took to the business of tanning, and settled first in Kissingen and finally in Würzburg, where he died in 1858. Besides his paintings he has left eighteen etchings of landscapes, mostly after his brother, and one lithograph.

ETZDORF, JOHANN CHRISTIAN MICHEL, a German landscape painter, was born at Pösneck, in the duchy of Saxe-Meiningen, in 1801. He studied landscape painting in Munich and its environs, and displayed an especial talent in representing gloomy forests, taking as his models the works of Ruisdael and Van Everdingen. He visited Norway, the North Cape, Sweden, Iceland, and England. One of his best paintings is in the Modern Gallery at Munich; it represents a 'Forge by the side of a Waterfall.' He died at Munich in 1851.

EUMARUS, of Athens, the foremost of the early Greek painters, flourished about B.C. 540-500. He appears to have introduced a degree of chiaroscuro into his pictures, which would seem to have been not all monochrome. It is stated that he was also the first to distinguish the male from the female figure, and to denote age and disposition in the depicting of his characters.

EUPHRANOR, who was born on the Isthmus of Corinth, but resided at Athens, is stated to have lived from B.C. 375 to 335, and to have studied painting in the school of Aristeides. His chief works were in a porch in the Cerameicus at Athens. On the one side were the 'Twelve Gods,' and on the opposite side, 'Theseus, with Democracy and Demos,' in which picture Theseus was represented as the founder of the equal polity of Athens. In the same place was his picture of the 'Battle between the Athenian and Bœotian Cavalry at Mantineia,' containing portraits of Epaminondas and of Gryllus, the son of Xenophon. He also excelled as a statuary, both in marble and metals. He gave a peculiar dignity to his heroes, and Pliny extols him for an exact symmetry in his proportions. His picture of Theseus so satisfied him that in comparing it with one of the same hero painted by Parrhasius, he exultingly observed, that " the Theseus of Parrhasius appeared to have been fed on roses, and his with flesh."

EUPOMPUS, who flourished about B.C. 400-380,

founded the school of Sicyon upon his own principles as opposed to the softness of the Ionian school. The 'Victor in the Gymnastic Combat' is one of his best works. Pamphilus, the master of Apelles, was his pupil.

EUSEBIO DI SAN GIORGIO, a painter of Perugia in the early part of the 16th century, was a scholar of Perugino, and painted for churches. His works are imitations or copies after Raphael. A fresco of the Archangel Michael, formerly in the Palazzo Gualtieri at Orvieto, and now in the Leipsic Museum, and which has been ascribed to Signorelli, is probably by Eusebio.

EUXENIDAS, an ancient Theban painter, who flourished about B.C. 400 or 380, was the master of Aristeides, but little else is recorded respecting him.

EVANS, GEORGE, a portrait painter, who flourished about the middle of the 18th century, was a member of the Incorporated Society of Artists, where he exhibited. He died before 1770.

EVANS, RICHARD, a copyist, was employed for some time by Sir Thomas Lawrence to fill in the background and draperies of his pictures. He for many years resided in Rome, where he copied pictures by the old masters, besides painting some original portraits, and also attempting frescopainting. He died at Southampton in 1871, aged 87. The copies in the South Kensington Museum of the Raphael arabesques are by him; as are also the following portraits in the National Portrait Gallery:

Sir Thomas Lawrence; *after Lawrence.*
Lord Thurlow; *after the same.*
Thomas Taylor, the Platonist.

EVANS, WILLIAM, known as "Evans of Eton," a landscape painter in water-colours, was born at Eton in 1798, and succeeded his father as professor of drawing at Eton College in 1818. In 1828 he was elected an associate, and in 1830 a member, of the Water-Colour Society, where he continued to exhibit till 1875. In his later years he suffered much from a fractured jaw, and died at Eton in 1877. Amongst his best works are:

Llanberis. 1828.
Barmouth. 1828.
Ferry on the Tay.
Burnham Beeches.
Doune Castle.
The Gleam of Hope.
Mill at Droxford. (*South Kensington Museum.*)

EVANS, WILLIAM, an engraver and draughtsman, who flourished in the early years of the 19th century, assisted Benjamin Smith, and made drawings for Cadell's and Boydell's publications. He drew for Cadell's 'Gallery of Contemporary Portraits' (1822), and engraved some plates for the Dilettanti Society's 'Specimens of Antient Sculpture.' His portrait of James Barry, R.A. (drawn in chalk for the 'Gallery of Contemporary Portraits') is in the National Portrait Gallery.

EVANS, WILLIAM, a landscape painter in watercolours, known as " Evans of Bristol," was born in 1811. He lived for many years at an isolated spot in North Wales, where he had abundant opportunity of depicting the rough mountain scenery in which he excelled. He became in 1845 an Associate of the Water-Colour Society, and after 1852 he spent much time in Italy. He died in London in 1858.

EVELYN, JOHN, who was born at Wotton, in Surrey, in 1620, was an English gentleman who claims a place among the amateur artists of his country, as the engraver of five small plates of his journey from Rome to Naples, which were etched in Paris in the year 1649. They bear the annexed monogram. He etched likewise a view of his own seat at Wotton, and another of Putney. Evelyn was the author of one of the earliest English publications on the subject of engraving, entitled 'Sculptura,' published in 1662. He died in London in 1706.

EVENEPOEL, HENRI, a young Belgian artist, whose early death at Paris in his twenty-seventh year cut short a career of great promise. The son of a musician, Evenepoel studied at first in Brussels, and subsequently in Paris, his *début* being made at the Salon in 1895, with certain portraits which created a positive sensation in the Parisian art world by their vigour and their almost brutal sincerity of touch. The young artist's work, however, with each succeeding year lost those qualities of exaggeration and grossness which detracted from its merit, as his later portraits, exhibited at the Salon, amply proved. Passing from portraiture to the presentment of figures either in natural or artificial light, the artist produced several important works, such as his 'Moulin Rouge,' 'Folies Bergères,' 'Fête des Invalides,' &c. He died in Paris, December 30, 1899. P.P.

EVENOR, an eminent painter of Ephesus. who flourished about B.C. 420, was the father and instructor of Parrhasius.

EVERDINGEN, ALLART VAN, the younger brother of Cesar van Everdingen, was born at Alkmaar in 1612. He studied successively under Roeland Savery and Pieter Molyn, both of whom he greatly surpassed, and excelled in painting rocky landscapes. The talents of Van Everdingen were not, however, confined to subjects of that description ; he painted sea-pieces and storms with surprising effect, and represented the tempest-tossed waves with awful and terrific fidelity. In a voyage which he made to the Baltic, he was shipwrecked on the coast of Norway, where he was under the necessity of remaining some time, until the vessel was repaired. He employed this interval in making sketches of the romantic wilds of that uncultivated country, which furnished him with admirable subjects for his pictures, in which the grand forms of his rocks, and the picturesque effect of his waterfalls, are drawn with a taste, and painted with a spirit, that entitled him to the appellation of 'The Salvator Rosa of the North.' His colouring is simple and pure, his touch broad and facile, and it is evident that every object in his pictures was studied immediately from nature. The small figures with which he embellished his landscapes are correctly drawn, and very neatly touched. The admirers of etchings are indebted to this excellent artist for a number of plates executed in a free and masterly style. His prints of landscapes amount to about a hundred, of which eight of the largest and most finished are very fine. He also engraved a set of fifty-seven small prints for Gottsched's translation of 'Reynard the Fox,' published in 1752. He sometimes signed his plates with his name, sometimes with the initials *A. V. E.*, and at other times with the annexed monogram. He died at Amsterdam in 1675.

Amsterdam.	*Museum.*	Norwegian Landscape.
		Landscape.
Berlin.	*Gallery.*	Norwegian Waterfall.
	Gallery.	Norwegian Hilly Landscape.
		A Castle by a River.
Cassel.	*Gallery.*	Woody Landscape.
Copenhagen.	*Gallery.*	Rocky Landscape. 1648.
		River and Rocks. 1647.
		And three others.
Darmstadt.	*Gallery.*	Waterfall.
		A Rocky Valley.
Dresden.	*Gallery.*	Stag-hunt. 1643.
		Four Landscapes.
Frankfort.	*Städel Inst.*	Stormy Sea.
		Landscape with Mill.
		Northern Landscape.
Lille.	*Museum.*	Cascade. 1660.
London.	*Bute Coll.*	View in Norway.
Munich.	*Gallery.*	Landscape with Waterfall. 1656.
		Stormy Sea-coast.
Paris.	*Louvre.*	Landscape.
		Landscape.

EVERDINGEN, CESAR VAN, born at Alkmaar in 1606, was a scholar of Jan van Bronkhorst. He painted historical subjects and portraits, and was also an eminent architect. In 1632 he became a member of the Guild at his native place, and in 1651 of that at Haarlem. One of his most esteemed works was in the principal church of Alkmaar, representing the 'Triumph of David. He gained great reputation by a picture he painted of the Portraits of the Company of Archers, for their hall of assembly. He died in 1679. His works are signed with the initials *C. V. E.*, or with the monogram annexed. An important work by him (signed with his monogram and dated 1652) is in the Hague Gallery. It represents 'Diogenes in the market-place of Haarlem seeking an honest man,' and contains portraits of the Steyn family of Haarlem.

EVERDINGEN, JAN VAN, the youngest of the three brothers of the name, was born in 1625, and died in 1656. He was instructed by his brother Cesar, but painted only for amusement, being by profession an advocate.

EVERITT, ALLEN EDWARD, a clever archæologist, who executed water-colour drawings of mediæval remains both in England and on the Continent. He was Hon. Sec. of the Royal Society of Artists of Birmingham from 1858 to 1882, and died in that year, aged fifty-eight.

EVERSDYCK, CORNELIS WILLEMSZ, was a portrait painter of Goes, who died there in 1649. In the Rotterdam Museum are three pictures by him, representing Officers and Members of the Company of Archers, called "Edele Voetboog," at Goes; two of which are dated 1616 and 1624.

EVERSDYCK, WILLEM, the son of Cornelis Eversdyck, flourished at Goes about the year 1660. He was a portrait painter, and several of his portraits were engraved by Houbraken. A picture of Officers and Members of the Company of Archers, called "Edele Voetboog," at Goes, by him, is in the Rotterdam Museum.

EVRARD, PERPÈTE, a painter of portraits and miniatures, was born at Dinant about the middle of the 17th century, and was employed at several foreign courts. He died at the Hague in 1727.

EWBANK, JOHN WILSON, a landscape painter, was born at Darlington in 1799. Intended for the Roman Catholic priesthood, he was sent to Ushaw College, but, absconding, he apprenticed himself to a house-painter in Newcastle, whence he was taken to Edinburgh by Coulson, a decorator of considerable ability : he afterwards received instruction from Alexander Nasmyth. He became one of the foundation members of the Royal Scottish Academy in 1826, and about that time produced some works of a larger character, such as 'George IV. at Edinburgh Castle,' 'The Entry of Alexander the Great into Babylon,' 'Hannibal crossing the Alps,' 'View of Edinburgh from Inchkeith,' &c. He passed the last ten or twelve years of his life in Sunderland, where through intemperance he fell into great misery and want, and died in 1847. His sea and shore views were admirable in their simplicity, while their aerial effect has seldom been surpassed. A 'Canal Scene with Shipping' is in the National Gallery of Scotland.

EWOUTZOON, JAN, a Dutch wood-engraver, who flourished at Amsterdam in the first half of the 16th century, executed many of the designs of Cornelis Teunisse or Antoniszoon, of which 'Mucius Scævola,' a 'Woman mounted upon an Ass,' and an 'Allegory upon the Flight of Time,' bear his signature, and the two last the dates 1536 and 1537.

EXIMENO, JOAQUIN, a Spanish artist, born at Valencia in 1674, painted fruit, flowers, birds, fish, and objects of still-life, which he represented with great fidelity. He died in 1754. His works are classed by Cean Bermudez with those of his father, who bore the same Christian name, and in conjunction with whom he painted. Their pictures were much esteemed by amateurs of the time, and four of large size are in the church of Our Lady of the Pillar at Valencia.

EXSHAW, CHARLES, an historical painter and engraver, was born at Dublin in the early part of the 18th century. He studied at Rome, Amsterdam, and probably in Paris, and engraved portraits of the Van Loo family, but about 1758 he came to London and endeavoured to start a drawing academy. He died in 1771. His prints are chiefly imitations of the works of Rembrandt, and are not without merit. Among other plates the following are by him :

A Bust of an old Man, with a round hat ; *after Rembrandt*. 1758.
A Head of an old Man, with a beard ; *after the same*. 1758.
Joseph and Potiphar's Wife ; *after the same*.
St. Peter's Bark in the Storm ; *after the same*.
A Girl carrying a Basket of Cherries, with two Boys, each having a Gun ; *after Rubens*.

EYBEL, ADOLF, a German painter of historical and genre subjects and of portraits, was born at Berlin in 1808. He studied at the Berlin Academy, and under Professor Kolbe, as well as in Paris under Delaroche. One of his most noted pictures represents 'Richard Cœur-de-Lion with his Court listening to Blondel's Song.' He died at Berlin in 1882. The following works by him may also be mentioned :

A Gleaner.
The Battle of Fehrbellin.
Scene from Sir Walter Scott's 'Woodstock.'
Scene from 'Faust.'
A Wine Party.

EYBL, FRANZ, an Austrian portrait and genre painter, was born at Vienna in 1806, studied in the Academy of his native city, and became a member of it in 1843. He died in 1880. He was for some time custodian of the Belvedere Gallery, which possesses two characteristic works by him :

An old Austrian Peasant Woman leaving Church. 1847.
An old Beggar, in a mountainous landscape. 1856.

EYCK, GASPAR VAN, a Flemish painter of marine
136

subjects and sea-fights, was born at Antwerp about the commencement of the 17th century, and was received into the Guild of St. Luke in 1632. He died in 1673. Three pictures by him are in the Madrid Gallery.

EYCK, HUBERT VAN, if not the greatest, at least one of the greatest artists that ever lived, was the eldest of three brothers, born, according to Van Mander, at Maaseyck in the Duchy of Limburg, about the year 1366. Very little is known of his history. He probably learned his art at Maastricht ; having served his apprenticeship, he appears to have travelled and to have visited the borders of the Mediterranean and the north of Italy before settling in Ghent early in the 15th century. The treasurers of the municipality in 1424–5 paid him 6s. for a couple of sketches he made by order of the magistrates, who in the following year visited his works and tipped his apprentices. He died on September 18, 1426, and was buried in the church of St. John—now the cathedral. His brothers, who were not burghers of Ghent, had as strangers to pay duties to the town on his properties which they inherited. Bequests of paintings by Hubert occur in wills of the years 1413 and 1426. The following pictures are admitted by competent critics to be by him :

1. The three Marys at the Sepulchre. *Richmond, Sir F. Cook.*
2. Christ on the Cross, the Blessed Virgin and Saint John. *Berlin Museum.*
3. The Blessed Virgin and Child, Saint Anne and F. Herman Steenken, vicar of the Charterhouse of Saint Anne *ter Woestine*, near Bruges, from 1402 to 1404, and from 1406 until his death, April 23, 1428. *Paris, Baron G. Rothschild.*
4. The Blessed Virgin and Child standing before a hedge of roses ; lost. A fifteenth-century copy in the *Berlin Museum.*
5. The Fountain of living waters ; lost. A late fifteenth-century copy in the *Prado Museum, Madrid.*
6. Portrait of a young man. *Herrmannstadt.*
7. The Vision of Saint Francis of Assisi. *Pennsylvania, J. G. Johnson, Esq.* An enlarged copy in the *Turin Gallery.*
8. Robert Poortier protected by Saint Anthony ; the angel Gabriel on the outer side. Dexter shutter of an altar-piece. *Copenhagen Museum.*
9. The polyptych of the Adoration of the Lamb, painted for Jodoc Vyt, with the exception of the panels, on the face of which are the figures of Adam and Eve. *Ghent Cathedral, and Berlin Museum.*
The cypress, the stone pine, the great palm, the olive and the orange are all found in No. 9 ; the two first in No. 2 ; the cypress, the great palm and the orange in No. 4 ; the palmetto in 1, 2, 7 and 8. The landscapes in Nos. 1, 2, 3, 8 and 9 are artificially composed, not realistic renderings of nature. The architecture in 3, 5 and 1 is scenic, not constructive ; and in 1, 2 and 3 Southern, not Netherlandish. W. H. J. W.

EYCK, JAN VAN, born at Maaseyck after 1380, is said by Van Mander to have been about twenty years younger than his brother Hubert ; his statement to this effect, however, was probably only founded on their two portraits on one of the side-panels of the Ghent altar-piece. In these portraits Hubert looks almost an old man, and Jan quite young. The Duchy of Limburg seems to have had an early repute as a seat of art, and one Pol van Limburg, who was in the service of Jean de Berri from 1400 to 1416, is known to us as an excellent miniaturist. According to tradition the Van Eycks sprang from an artistic family, but nothing is known of their father. It is probable that it was while Jan was living with his brother that the new method of oil-painting was invented,

Hanfstaengl, photo.   Swan Electric Engraving Co.

Jean Arnolfini & his Wife (1434)

From the painting by Jan van Eyck in the National Gallery, London.

JAN VAN EYCK

MAN WITH A PINK

JAN VAN EYCK

[St. Bavon, Ghent

THE ADORATION OF THE LAMB

or rather, it should be said, that the unsatisfactory methods of oil-painting previously known were brought to perfection by them. It is difficult to determine exactly in what the Van Eyck discovery really consisted, for it is certain that a process of mixing oil with colour was known at a much earlier date. It was even described by the monk Theophilus in his treatise, 'tractatus Lombardicus qualiter temperantur colores,' written in the 11th century, and sculptured reliefs and statues were constantly painted with oil-colours in the Netherlands long before the 15th century. But the process invented by the Van Eycks must evidently have solved some difficulty that had hitherto prevented the successful application of oil-colour to panel-painting, for their discovery was at once eagerly welcomed by artists, and the greatest anxiety evinced by the painters of Italy, as well as by those of the Netherlands, to learn the secret of their success. Vasari gives a graphic account of the manner of the discovery, which in his first edition he attributes solely to Jan, the name of Hubert not being then known to him—he just mentions Hubert in the next edition; other early writers agree in ascribing the discovery to both brothers, Hubert being at the time about forty years of age, and Jan about twenty. With regard to the discovery itself, it seems to have consisted firstly in a varnish that was siccative without being dark, and secondly in a liquid and colourless medium that could be mixed with the colours, and so do away with the necessity of using the old coloured viscous varnish.

It is generally said that Van Eyck was in the service of John of Bavaria, prince bishop of Liége; if so, after 1390 and before 1418, when that prince resigned the bishopric, and seized the country of Holland; but of this there is no proof. The earliest mention of him is in the accounts of the treasurers of Holland, which show that he was engaged in painting at the palace of the Hague from October 25, 1422, until September 11, 1424. John of Bavaria died January 6, 1425, and on the 19th of May following Van Eyck entered the service of Philip duke of Burgundy at Bruges, by whom he was appointed court painter and "varlet de chambre," with a salary of one hundred pounds per annum, and all the "honours, prerogatives, franchises, liberties, rights, profits, and emoluments thereunto appertaining." In August he removed with his goods and chattels to Lille, where he was no doubt employed on work for the chapel of the duke's castle which had just been restored. He took up his abode in a house belonging to Michael Ravary, clerk of the works of the castle, where he resided until Midsummer 1428, except when absent on secret journeys undertaken at the duke's bidding. We are not told whither he went, but for the two first he was paid £91 5s., and £360. On October 19, 1428, he sailed for Lisbon with the embassy to the King of Portugal, his mission being to paint the Infanta Isabella; during his absence, besides stopping at Sandwich from October 20 to November 13, and at Falmouth from November 20 to December 2, he visited Lisbon, Arrayollos, Aviz, Compostella, Arjona and Cintra. It is probable that he was sent on other journeys, of which, owing to the destruction of the accounts of expenditure during several years, we have only mention of two: one, to Hesdin in 1431; the other, a secret journey to foreign parts, for the expenses of which he received £360. In addition

to his yearly salary he also received considerable sums as gratuities. One of these was probably connected with a transaction of a delicate nature relative to a lady who became the mother of one of the duke's many illegitimate children. In 1431 John bought a house and settled in Bruges. On July 17 in that year the two burgomasters and some other members of the town council went to see certain of his works, when they gave his servants a gratuity of 5s.g. About this time Van Eyck took to himself a wife; to their daughter Livina, born in 1434, the duke stood godfather, and gave her as a present six silver cups weighing 12 marks which cost £96 12s.g. In 1435 John polychromed six of the statues adorning the front of the Town-house, together with the tabernacles in which they stood; for this work he received £28 12s.g. He kept his office of Court painter until his death, which took place at Bruges on July 9, 1440. He was buried in the churchyard of Saint Donatian, but by request of his brother Lambert, on March 21, 1442, his body was removed into the church and reinterred in the baptistery. The following is a chronological list of paintings by Jan:

1421, October 30. Enthronement of S. Thomas of Canterbury; *entirely overpainted. Chatsworth.*
1432. Nicholas Albergati, Cardinal of Saint Cross. *Vienna.*
1432. The B. Virgin and Child. *Ince Hall.*
1432, October 10. Timotheus. *National Gallery.*
1432, October 21. Portrait of a man. *National Gallery.*
1434. John Arnolfini and wife. *National Gallery.*
1436. The B. Virgin and Child, S. Donatian and Canon G. de Pala, protected by S. George. *Bruges.*
1436. Jan De Leeuw, goldsmith. *Vienna.*
1437. S. Barbara. *Antwerp.*
1439, January 31. Head of Christ. *Berlin.*
1439, June 17. Portrait of his wife. *Bruges.*
1439. The Virgin and Child by a fountain. *Antwerp.*
1440. N. de Maelbeka, Provost of S. Martin's, Ipres, kneeling before the B. Virgin and Child; *unfinished. Kessel-Loo, near Louvain.*

The Annunciation (*Saint Petersburg*), the B. Virgin and Child enthroned (*Frankfort*), a portrait of Baldwin de Lannoy (*Berlin*), and the B. Virgin and Child, S. Katherine, the donor protected by S. Michael, and the Annunciation (*Dresden*), are also certainly by John.
Portraits of a man wearing a tau cross and holding pinks (*Berlin*), and of Chancellor Rolin kneeling before the Virgin and Child (*Paris*), are attributed by some to Jan, by others to Hubert.

Crowe and Cavalcaselle, 'The Early Flemish Painters,' 1872; O. Seeck, 'Kritische Betrachtungen über den Genter Altar,' 1889; L. Kaemmerer, 'Hubert und Jan van Eyck,' 1890; O. Seeck, 'Die charakteristischen Unterschiede der Brüder van Eyck,' 1899; Voll, 'Die Werke des Jan van Eyck,' 1900. The above are the latest volumes on the Van Eycks. There have been articles since in the 'Revue de l'Art Chrétien,' 'Zeitschrift für bildende Kunst,' 'Nineteenth Century,' 'Gazette des Beaux Arts,' and 'Athenæum.'

W. H. J. W.

EYCK, LAMBERT VAN. The name of Lambert van Eyck occurs in the accounts of the Duke of Burgundy; he was a brother of Hubert and Jan.
EYCK, MARGARET VAN. It is known that the Van Eyck brothers had a sister named Margaret, who is said by old writers to have been an excellent painter; but no works can with any certainty be assigned to her, though her name is often to be met with in catalogues. She died before Jan, and

was buried, like her brother Hubert, in St. Bavon at Ghent.

EYCK, NICOLAAS VAN, who was born at Antwerp in 1627, and died in 1677, painted cavalry encounters and camp scenes. In the Vienna Gallery is a picture by him of 'Troops quartered in a Village,' and in the Lille Museum is an equestrian portrait. He is presumed to have been a brother of Gaspar van Eyck.

EYCKEN, JEAN BAPTISTE VAN, a Belgian historical painter, was born at Brussels in 1809, and studied under Navez, obtaining the first prize at the Brussels Academy in 1835. He died at Schaerbeek, near Brussels, in 1853. Amongst his works are the following:

Abundance. (*In the possession of the Queen.*)
St. Sebastian.
The Crown of Thorns.
Parmegiano at the Sacking of Rome. (*Brussels Museum.*)
Descent from the Cross. (*Brussels Museum.*)
Tobit restoring his Father's Sight.
St. Cecilia.

EYCKENS. See YKENS.
EYDEN, JEREMIAS VAN DER. See VAN DER EYDEN.
EYK, ABRAHAM VAN DER. See VAN DER EYK.
EYNDEN, FRANS VAN, born at Nymegen in 1694, studied under Elias van Nymegen at Rotterdam. Aided by the counsels of Chevalier Van der Werf, he painted Arcadian scenes, which he executed in the manner of Jan van Huysum, but not with equal perfection. His skies and distances are serene and delicate, and the clouds illumined by the sun are pleasingly reflected in the waters. His scenes are skilfully varied, and the different kinds of trees characterized with a neat and masterly touch; his figures also are well painted, and disposed with judgment. He seldom signed his pictures, unless required to do so by the purchaser. He died at Nymegen in 1742.

EYNDEN, JACOBUS VAN, a nephew of Frans van Eynden, born at Nymegen in 1733, studied art under his father, and painted principally watercolour pictures of flowers, fruit, animals, and views of towns. He, however, devoted a large portion of his time to science. He died at Nymegen in 1824.

EYNDEN, ROELAND VAN, the younger brother of Jacobus van Eynden, was born at Nymegen in 1747, and died at Dordrecht in 1819. Like his brother he devoted but a portion of his time to painting, and is principally known by his works on art and artists, of which the most important is the 'Geschiedenis der Vaderlandsche Schilderkunst,' written in conjunction with Van der Willigen, and published in 1816-1842.

EYNHOUDTS, REMOLDUS, or ROMBOUT, a Flemish painter and engraver, was born at Antwerp in 1605, and died there in 1679. He was a pupil of Adam van Oort, and painted portraits; but he is better known as an engraver. He executed several plates after Rubens, Cornelis Schut, and other painters of the Flemish school; and some of the prints for the Teniers Gallery. They are engraved in a slight, dark style; and his drawing, though not very correct, is bold and masterly. Among other prints by him are the following:

SUBJECTS AFTER RUBENS.
The Adoration of the Magi.
The Resurrection.

138

The Virgin and Child, with St. Bonaventure and Rubens as St. George.
St. Gregory, surrounded with emblematical figures.
The Four Doctors of the Church, with St. Clara holding the Sacrament.
St. Christopher.
The Virgin with the Infant Christ, seated in a bower.
St. Peter and St. Paul.
The Judgment of Cambyses.
Peace and Prosperity.

SUBJECTS AFTER VARIOUS MASTERS.
The Assumption of the Virgin; *after Cornelis Schut.*
The Trinity; *after the same.*
The Martyrdom of St. George; *after the same.*
St. Anne; *after the same.*
The Risen Saviour; *after the elder Palma.*
St John the Baptist; *after the same.*
The Dead Christ; *after the younger Palma.*
The Ascension; *after the same.*

EYRE, JAMES, a landscape painter, was born at Derby in 1802, and received instruction from Creswick and De Wint. He died in 1829.

EZPELETA, —, a painter of Aragon, who excelled in miniatures and illumination, was born at Alagon, and died, aged 60, about the middle of the 16th century, at Saragossa, where he illuminated with great delicacy many choir-books for the cathedral.

EZQUERRA, GERONIMO ANTONIO DE, who was a scholar of Antonio Palomino, flourished in the early years of the 18th century. A specimen of his skill in landscape is in the Madrid Gallery; it represents 'Neptune with Tritons and Nereids,' on a wooded sea-shore. He produced a series of Saints for the church of San Felipe Neri at Madrid, and various works for the palace of Buenretiro.

F

FABER, FRÉDÉRIC THÉODORE, a Belgian landscape and genre painter, born at Brussels in 1782, was first instructed by his father, but in 1799 he went to Antwerp, and studied under Ommeganck. He afterwards established at Brussels a china manufactory, and abandoned painting on canvas for painting on porcelain. He also etched upwards of a hundred plates of landscapes and animals, some after his own designs, and others after Ommeganck, De Roy, and Van Assche. He died in 1844.

FABER, JOHAN, the elder, was one of the first artists who worked in mezzotint. He was born at the Hague about the year 1660, and came to London about 1687, where he executed a considerable number of plates after his own designs. He died at Bristol in 1721. The following are his best works:

The Portraits of the Founders of Colleges at Oxford and Cambridge.
The Heads of the Philosophers; *after Rubens.*
Dr. John Wallis, the mathematician; *after Kneller.*
Humphrey Lloyd, of Denbigh, antiquary. 1717.

FABER, JOHAN, the younger, who was born in Holland in 1684, was instructed by his father, Johan Faber the elder, and by J. van der Banck. He greatly surpassed his father as a mezzotint engraver, and was esteemed the ablest artist of his time in that branch of art, after John Smith. He died in London in 1756. Among his 165 plates, which are executed in a bold and free manner, there are.

In Indian ink and pencil]   [*De Pass Collection*

DRAWING OF JAMES I.

The Beauties of Hampton Court; *after Kneller.*
The Forty-eight Portraits of the Members of the Kit-Cat Club; *after the same.*
Charles II. in his robes, seated; *after Lely.* 1750.
Edmund Halley; *after Murray.* 1722.
A Man playing the Guitar; *after F. Hals.* 1754.
Ignatius Loyola; *after Titian.* 1756.
The Children of Frederick, Prince of Wales; *after Du Pan.*
Caroline, Queen of George II.; *after J. van der Banck.*
Sir Isaac Newton; *after the same.* 1726.
Michael Rysbrack, sculptor; *after the same.*
Enoch Seeman, painter; *after the same.*
George Lambert, landscape painter; *after the same.*

FABER, JOHANN, a landscape painter, was born at Hamburg in 1778, and died in the same city in 1846. He worked originally at historical subjects, and painted the altar-piece, 'Suffer Little Children to come unto Me,' for St. Catharine's Church at Hamburg. On his journey to Italy in company with J. A. Koch and Reinhardt, he was induced to adopt landscape painting, in which line he is best known. The Berlin Gallery contains a 'View of the Capuchin Monastery, near Naples,' by him (1830).

FABER, JOHANN THEODOR EUSEBIUS, a landscape painter, was born at Gottleube in 1772, and died at Dresden in 1852. There are two landscapes by him in the Dresden Gallery, one in the Harz mountains, and the other in the Tyrol.

FABER, PIERRE, a French engraver, who resided at Lyons about the year 1621. He was chiefly employed by the booksellers, for whom he engraved several plates, in a neat style, but without much taste.

FABER DU FAUR, CHRISTIAN WILHELM VON, a German painter, was born at Stuttgart in 1780. He first devoted himself to painting, but subsequently became a soldier, and as a lieutenant served in the Russian campaign, which he afterwards illustrated by his sketches in a work entitled, 'Blätter aus meinem Portefeuille im Laufe des Feldzugs 1812,' published in 1831-44. His most noteworthy paintings are, 'The Passage of the Beresina,' a work of great merit, and 'The Coffee-House at Wilna.' He died at Stuttgart in 1857.

FABER DU FAUR, OTTO, distinguished German painter of battle-scenes, was born at Ludwigsburg, in 1828, his father being a general in the Würtemberg army with considerable artistic talent. This the son inherited to the full, and after a brief term of service, resigned his commission in order to devote himself entirely to art. He studied at first with Max de Kotzebue in Munich, and subsequently in Paris with Yoon, completing his training with Piloty, the famous historical painter. He was soon destined to take a foremost place among German artists. At the outset he took Piloty as his pattern, and produced historical pictures such as the 'Departure of Frederick V. from Prague,' but soon felt the fascination of scenes from the career of the great Napoleon. The retreat from Russia provided him with numerous episodes for historical treatment; an interesting example in water-colour is now in the Luxembourg, representing 'The Passage of the Beresina.' The Franco-German war of 1870 also furnished him with subjects; and his 'Battle of Champigny,' 'Battle of Woerth' (at Hamburg), and above all his 'Ambulance behind a Barricade' may rank among his best and most representative work. The charm of the East was not lost upon Faber

du Faur, who, as the result of his travels in Spain and Morocco, brought back with him many vigorous sketches of Oriental life, a curious example of which was exhibited at the Salon in 1899, entitled 'La Razzia.' His death occurred at Munich on August 17, 1901. P. P.

FABIO, PIO, a painter of Udine, studied at Rome, and in 1678 became a member of the Academy of St. Luke. He afterwards returned to his native place, where he painted several altar-pieces.

FABIUS, called PICTOR, a Roman artist, descended from the celebrated family of the Fabii, painted principally at Rome, and in B.C. 304 decorated the Temple of Salus on the Quirinal Hill, with a representation probably of the battle gained by Bubulus over the Samnites. His paintings were preserved until the reign of the Emperor Claudius, when the above temple was destroyed by fire. They were probably held in little estimation, as Pliny, to whom they must have been known, neither acquaints us with the subjects, nor commends the execution. The art of painting in its rude and early forms was general in Italy, but was founded on the Etruscan style, which never advanced beyond a flat polychromatic treatment. In the fine arts Rome owes all to Greece, and in painting never acquired the individuality which she did in the other arts. That painting was then little respected by the Romans, and that the title of 'pictor' was not considered as an honourable distinction, but rather intended to stigmatize the illustrious character who had degraded his dignity by the practice of an art which was held in no consideration, may be inferred from a passage of Cicero, in the first book of his 'Tusculan Disputations': "An censemus si Fabio nobilissimo homini laudatum esset quod pingeret, non multos etiam apud nos Polycletos et Parrhasios fuisse." No tradition of Roman painting exists earlier than the time of Fabius, nor does his example appear to have been followed by any of his contemporaries; for an interval of nearly a hundred and fifty years occurs before any mention is made of another Roman painter.

FABRE, FRANÇOIS XAVIER, a French painter of historical subjects, portraits, and landscapes, was born at Montpellier in 1766. He studied under Jean Coustou and under David, and obtained the 'grand prix' in 1787. He was at Rome in 1793, and afterwards went to Naples and to Florence, where he resided for some years, becoming a professor in the academy, and marrying secretly (it is said) the Countess of Albany, after the death of Alfieri. He returned to Montpellier in 1826, and there founded the École des Beaux-Arts, of which he became director. He was created a baron in 1830. He died in 1837 at Montpellier, bequeathing to that city the collections of pictures, engravings, cameos, and books which form the Museum which bears his name. Amongst his chief works are :

Philoctetes at Lemnos.
Saul pursued by the Shade of Samuel.
The Judgment of Paris.
The Death of Milo.
Portrait of Alfieri. (*Uffizi, Florence.*)
Portrait of the Countess of Albany. (*Uffizi, Florence.*)
Neoptolemus and Ulysses taking from Philoctetes the arrows of Hercules. (*Louvre.*)
The Death of Abel. (*Musée Fabre, Montpellier.*)
The Holy Family. (*Musée Fabre, Montpellier.*)
The Death of Narcissus. (*Musée Fabre, Montpellier.*)

139

The Family of the Kings of Etruria, Dukes of Parma. 1804. (*Madrid Gallery.*)

FABRE, PIERRE, an engraver, was a native of Lyons, where he worked about 1620. He executed the engravings for some works published at Lyons, representing the decorations erected in that city for the reception of Louis XIII. in 1622.

FABRI, ALOISIO, an engraver, was born at Rome in 1778, and died there in 1835. Amongst his many works may be mentioned four plates after Raphael's frescoes in the Vatican, in continuation of a set of engravings commenced by Volpato and Morghen, ' Constantine presenting Rome to the Pope,' 'The Oath of Leo III.,' 'The Coronation of Charlemagne,' and 'Charlemagne's Victory over the Saracens'; and eleven plates after the paintings of Michelangelo in the Sistine Chapel, in continuation of a set of engravings commenced by Cunego: these represent 'David and Goliath,' the 'Brazen Serpent,' 'Judith and Holophernes,' the prophets Isaiah, Daniel, Jonah, and Zachariah, and the Cumæan, Delphic, Libyan, and Persian Sibyls. He also engraved 'The Magi,' after Andrea del Sarto.

FABRI, GIOVANNI, an Italian engraver, who worked at Bologna in the middle of the 18th century, and died probably about 1790, executed some plates in a neat but formal style, among which are:

St. Mary Magdalen; *after Pasinelli.*
Virgin and Child; *after Guido Reni.*
St. Jerome; *after Carracci.*

FABRIANO, ALLEGRETTO (or GRITTO) DA. See NUZI.

FABRIANO, ANTONIO DA, flourished in the 15th century, but the dates of his birth and death are alike uncertain. A 'Coronation of the Virgin' in the Casa Morichi is attributed to him; and also a 'St. Jerome,' with the date 1451, in the Fornari Gallery at Fabriano. He was a feeble assistant of Gentile da Fabriano.

FABRIANO, FRANCESCO DI GENTILE DA. It is uncertain whether this artist was the son or merely pupil of Gentile. He lived in the 15th century, and his paintings are of no very great merit. The following works by him may, however, be mentioned:

Fermo.   *S. Domenico.*   Ave Maria.
Rome.   *Vatican.*   The Virgin and Child.

FABRIANO, GENTILE DA. See MASSI, GENTILE.

FABRIQUE, NICOLAS LA. See LA FABRIQUE.

FABRITIUS, BERNHARD, a Dutch portrait painter, who flourished from about 1650 to 1672, was a disciple of Rembrandt, whose eminence he sometimes almost reached. His paintings, however, are not all executed with the same care, some of them being faulty in drawing and colouring, whilst others are bold and broad in style. The following works may be noted:

Brunswick.   *Gallery.*   St. Peter in the house of Cornelius. 1659.
Brussels.   *Camberlyn Collection.*   Goliath. 1658.
"   "   Joan of Arc. 1657.
Copenhagen. *Gallery.*   The Presentation in the Temple. 1668.
Frankfort.   *Städel Inst.*   Portrait of a Young Man. 1650.
"   "   The Birth of St. John the Baptist. 1669.
Vienna.   *Academy.*   Head of a Man.

FABRITIUS, KAREL, a Dutch painter, born at Delft about 1624, was a pupil of Rembrandt. He painted portraits and perspective views, and had

acquired considerable reputation, when he was killed by the blowing up of the powder magazine at Delft in 1654. A fine 'Head of a Man,' by him, in the Rotterdam Museum, was for a long time ascribed to Rembrandt. Fabritius was the instructor of Jan ver Meer of Delft. Besides the above work by him there are:

Amsterdam.   *Museum.*   Herodias with the Head of St. John the Baptist. (*Ascribed in the catalogue to Drost.*)
Berlin.   *Gallery.*   Head of a Man.
Cologne.   *Wallraf-Richartz Museum.*   } A Portrait.

FABRITIUS, KILIAN, was a German landscape painter, who from 1633 to 1680 worked at the court of the Elector John George II. of Saxony. Many of his paintings are to be met with at Darmstadt, where there is in the Museum a Landscape by him. At Stockholm there is 'The Expulsion of Hagar,' painted in 1650; and in the Vienna Gallery is a 'Pastoral Landscape.' The following etchings, which are very rare, are also by him:

Christ at the House of Nicodemus.
The Holy Family. 1633.
A Hunting Scene, with the Elector John George II.

FABRIZZI, ANTONIO MARIA, was born at Perugia in 1594. He went to Rome when he was very young; and is said by Pascoli to have commenced his studies under Annibale Carracci, of whose instruction he was deprived by the death of that great master, when he was only fifteen years of age; and it does not appear that he sought the aid of any other instructor. His works evince ingenuity in composition, and great freedom of hand. He died at Perugia in 1649.

FABULLUS. See AMULIUS.

FACCENDA, FRANCESCO, who worked at Perugia from 1760 to 1770, executed the plates of emblems for the edition of Cesare Ripa's 'Iconologia,' published at Perugia in 1764-67.

FACCHETTI, PIETRO, a painter and engraver, born at Mantua in 1535, was instructed by Girolamo and Ippolito Costa. He visited Rome in the pontificate of Gregory XIII., and died in that city in 1613. Although his first essays in historical painting were not without merit, he abandoned that line for the painting of portraits; and his portraits of some of the nobility were so much admired, that there was scarcely a person of distinction at Rome, of either sex, whose likeness he did not paint. His pictures had not only the merit of perfect resemblance, but were designed in a grand style, and admirably coloured. Facchetti was also an engraver, and there are two etchings by him, which are distinguished for their skilful and pure design; they represent a 'Holy Family' after Raphael, and 'Christ bearing the Cross.'

FACCHINETTI, GIUSEPPE, a native of Ferrara, flourished in the 18th century. He was instructed by A. F. Ferrari, and was one of the pupils who chiefly helped to build up the name of the school to which he belonged. He painted in a vigorous and yet tender style, and achieved most of his success in historical, architectural, and perspective paintings. His works are to be found in Santa Caterina da Siena at Ferrara, and in other churches in that neighbourhood.

FACCI, FRANCESCO, a painter of Verona, was a pupil of F. Ricci. He died in 1621.

FACCINI, BARTOLOMMEO, a native of Ferrara, painted portraits and architectural pieces in the

FAULTS ON BOTH SIDES

style of Girolamo da Carpi. He was killed by falling from a scaffold in 1577. There is a picture attributed to this artist in the Museum at Lille: it represents the 'Martyrdom of St. Agnes.' In many of his works he was assisted by his brother, GIROLAMO FACCINI.

FACCINI, PIETRO, (or FACINI,) was born at Bologna in 1560. He did not display any genius, or disposition for art, until he had arrived at the age of maturity; and it is told by Malvasia, that being in the habit of visiting the academy of the Carracci, though not for the purpose of study, one of the pupils drew a caricature of him, which excited the mirth and ridicule of his fellow-students. On the drawing being shown to Faccini, he took a piece of charcoal, and, without any previous instruction or practice, sketched a satirical likeness of the person who had ridiculed him, which astonished every one present, particularly Annibale Carracci, who persuaded him to study art, and took him under his particular tuition. His assiduity was so great that he practised drawing from the skeleton at night, and it is related that on one of these occasions Annibale, for a practical joke, slily pulled the cord and caused the skeleton to move, which so offended Faccini that he left their school. He met immediately with employment and applause from the public, and even established an academy in opposition to that of the Carracci, which for a short time was respectably frequented. The delusion did not, however, last long: it was soon discovered that Faccini's design was neither correct nor tasteful, that his figures were uncouth and disproportioned, and the character of his heads without expression or beauty. His colouring was admirable, resembling the freshness of Tintoretto, and this caused Annibale to declare, on seeing his picture of the 'Martyrdom of St. Lawrence,' in San Giovanni in Monte, that in his carnations he seemed to have worked human flesh into his colours. He died in 1602.

The principal works of Faccini are:

Bologna.	Pinacoteca.	The Marriage of St. Catharine.
"	"	The Guardian Saints of Bologna.
"	"	The Virgin and Child.
"	S. Giov. in Monte.	The Martyrdom of St. Lawrence.
"	S. Domenico.	The Virgin appearing to St. Francis.
"	S. Paolo.	The Crucifixion of St. Andrew.
"	S. Mattia.	The Adoration of the Magi.
Dresden.	Gallery.	The Marriage of St. Catharine.
"	"	The Virgin and Child with Saints.
Modena.	Estense Gall.	Study of a Man.

He etched also some plates, which are signed with the annexed monogram ⚏℟⚏

St. Francis of Assisi.
Two Blind Beggars; after Annibale Carracci.
A Boy in a Chimney Corner.
A Dog in a landscape.

FACHERIS, AGOSTINO, a painter of Bergamo, is noticed by Tassi in his 'Lives of the Bergamese Painters,' where he describes a picture by him in the Church of the Trinity at Borgo Sant' Antonio, representing 'St. Augustine with two Angels,' and dated 1528.

FACINI, PIETRO. See FACCINI.

FACIUS, GEORG SIGMUND and JOHANN GOTTLIEB, who were brothers and engravers, were born at Ratisbon, about 1750. Both studied at Brussels, where their father held the office of Russian consul. In the year 1776 they proceeded to London, in order to work for Alderman Boydell, and for whom they completed a great number of plates. They worked chiefly as etchers, and the impressions from their plates are either black or brown, or in colours. They were both living in 1802. Among their best works are:

Benjamin West and his Family; after West. 1777.
Apollo and the Muses; after C. Maratti. 1784.
Apollo with the Muses on Parnassus; after L. Guttenbrunn. 1794.
Hector and Paris; after Angelica Kaufmann.
Abraham entertaining the three Angels; after Murillo.
The Young Bull; after Paulus Potter.

FACKLER, JOSEPH, born at Salzburg in 1698, painted a picture of 'St. Rupert,' in the church of St. Peter in his native city. He died in 1745.

FACTOR, PEDRO NICOLAS, a Spanish painter, was born at Valencia in 1520. The early part of his life was devoted to study, and he is said to have distinguished himself as a poet as well as a painter. In 1537 he entered the Franciscan monastery of Santa Maria de Jesus, where he painted many of his pictures, the best of which is said to have been 'St. Michael triumphing over Lucifer.' None of his works are known to exist, but Cean Bermudez says that they displayed considerable skill in drawing, although somewhat poor in colouring. He also painted miniatures for the choir-books of his convent. Factor died at Valencia in 1583, and in 1786 was declared by Pope Pius VI. a "beato," or saint of the second order. Spain has produced many devout artists, but to Factor alone have the honours of canonization been accorded.

FADINO, IL. See ALENI.

FAED, JOHN, was born at Burley Mill, Kirkcudbright, in 1820. His bent was early shown, and the self-taught boy of twelve practised as a miniaturist until he went to Edinburgh in 1841. There he soon achieved great success in miniature painting. From 1841 he regularly exhibited at the Royal Scottish Academy, gradually abandoning miniature for genre subjects. In 1847 he was elected A.R.S.A., and in 1851 became full Academician. He removed to London in 1862, residing there for eighteen years, and exhibiting at the Royal Academy. Then he retired to his native place, and died at Gatehouse in 1902. Thomas Faed, the well-known Scottish Academician, and James Faed, the line-engraver, were his younger brothers. For subjects he went to the Bible and Shakespeare, and especially to Scottish history, poetry, and romance. Among his best pictures are 'The Cottar's Saturday Night,' 'Olivia and Viola,' 'Catherine Leyton,' 'John Anderson my Jo,' 'Auld Mare Maggie,' 'Annie's Tryst,' and 'The Poet's Dream.' These last two hang in the Scottish National Gallery. He was a good draughtsman, and had much command of pathos and humour, but was somewhat deficient in sense of colour, and his pictures often lack coherence and atmosphere. His careful and precise finish throughout showed the influence of miniature.

FAED, THOMAS, was born on June 8, 1826, at Gatehouse of Fleet, in Kirkcudbright, Scotland, and was the son of a millwright. The village where he lived was a very small one, Burley Mill, in which the lad was born, being the only important house in it, the rest being very small cottages. His parents were poor but very hardworking people, very fond of reading, and of a degree of culture above that of their neighbours.

An uncle of the lad had been an engraver, and many of his productions hung in the mill-house, and were very attractive to the boy from his earliest days. There was one elder brother who, like Thomas, was of an artistic temperament, and he left home early for Edinburgh to take lessons in the art which he loved. On the death of their father he recommended Thomas, who from the first days of boyhood had been devoted to sketching, and had neglected all other lessons and occupations for the practice of drawing, to come up to Edinburgh and join him in his humble lodgings, and thither Thomas Faed made his way. He got into the Art School at the age of fifteen, and amongst his fellow-students was Orchardson. He commenced very quickly in the special field of work which he so particularly made his own, that of representing scenes of pathos and character taken from the life of the Scotch peasant, but although he gained admission to the Scottish Academy as Associate at the age of twenty-three, he was not satisfied with the small measure of success which his labours realized, and determined to seek wider fields of action in London. He came up in 1852, and in 1855 exhibited at Trafalgar Square the first of his important pictures, called 'The Mitherless Bairn.' From that moment the artist never looked back, and, what was of peculiar interest, never rejected the class of subject which had brought him his first renown, and to the end of his life was faithful to the delineation of simple homely Scotch life with all its mingled pathos, dry humour, and with all the force of its somewhat melancholy characteristics represented with unbending truth and realism. Some of his notable works may be mentioned: 'Only Herself,' 'A Wee Bit Fractious,' 'From Hand to Mouth,' 'His Only Pair,' 'From Dawn to Sunset,' 'Evangeline,' 'Worn Out,' 'The First Break in the Family,' 'Lucy's Flittin',' 'The School Board in the Cottage,' 'In Time of War,' and most notable perhaps of all, the picture now in the Tate Gallery called 'Faults on Both Sides,' in which the artist has with rare sense for beauty painted the face of the woman full of delicate refinement and wonderful grace, and represented the touching scene with a mingling of pathos, reserve and humour which are most dexterously depicted. Faed's work was brilliant and harmonious, full of rich jewel-like colours marvellously combined. His technique was sure and definite, his handling was broad, and the quality of his work excellent throughout his long career. He outlived his popularity, as the scenes which he always adopted were no longer attractive to the public, but from an artist's point of view there is little that can be said against the pictures which he painted, so sound and wholesome are their subjects, so refreshing are their candour and truth, and so honestly are they painted that they seem able to last in their pristine excellence for ever. His work is, above all, virile, strong and direct. In 1893 the artist was compelled to resign his membership of the Royal Academy, into which he had been admitted as Royal Academician, by reason of failing sight, and soon afterwards the sight which he had so strained in the production of his many works with all their minute painting failed him altogether, and for the seven last years of his life he was a blind man. He died August 17, 1900.   G. C. W.

FAENZA, GIOVANNI BATTISTA DA, called BERTUCCI (the Monkey), who painted in the style of Perugino

142

and Pinturicchio, flourished in the early part of the 16th century at Faenza. In the Pinacoteca of that city there are various works ascribed to him, of which the most remarkable is a 'Majesty,' signed by him and bearing the date 1506. Crowe and Cavalcaselle also claim for Bertucci an 'Adoration of the Magi' in the Berlin Gallery, there ascribed to Pinturicchio, and a 'Glorification of the Virgin' in the National Gallery, given in the catalogue to Lo Spagna, who was a pupil of Perugino.

FAENZA, JACOPONE DA. See BERTUCCI.

FAENZA, MARCO DA. See MARCHETTI.

FAENZA, MARCO ANTONIO DA, called also MARCO ANTONIO ROCCHETTI, an Italian painter of the earlier part of the 17th century, is probably the artist mentioned by Vasari with the surname Figurino, who was one of the best disciples of Giulio Romano. His early paintings are of a small size, often representing scenes in the life of St. Sebastian. The following works are also by him:

Faenza. *Pinacoteca.* The Madonna of the Angels.
  „   *S. Rocco.* St. Roch. 1634.

FAENZA, OTTAVIANO DA, an Italian painter of the 14th century, who was instructed by Giotto, spent the greater part of his life at Faenza, where he died. There are several paintings attributed to him to be found in the neighbourhood of Faenza, and at Bologna.

FAENZA, PACE DA, an Italian painter, who flourished during the 14th century, was a pupil of Giotto, and is said to have executed some decorations in fresco on the exterior of San Giovanni at Bologna. He had a particular talent for representing small figures. About the year 1574 the following works by him existed at Forli:

The Holy Cross.
A small picture in tempera, representing the Passion.
Four Scenes from the Life of the Virgin.

FAENZONE, FERRAU. See FANZONE.

FAES, PIETER, a painter of flowers and fruit in the manner of Van Huysum, was born at Meir, near Hoogstraten, in the province of Antwerp, in 1750. His pictures are tastefully composed and delicately pencilled, but are somewhat deficient in vigour and chiaroscuro. Many of his works were transferred from Laeken to Vienna. He died at Antwerp in 1814.

FAES, PIETER VAN DER. See VAN DER FAES.

FAGAN, LOUIS, the late sub-director of the Print-room at the British Museum, and the man who certainly by merit ought to have been head of that department, merits a place in this work on account of his own excellent artistic work no less than for his literary work on Art subjects. He was born in 1846, the son of the British Minister at the Court of the Two Sicilies, and his birthplace was Naples. His sympathies were always very strongly with the Italian people, whose tongue he spoke with the most perfect accuracy, and much of his life was spent in Italy, and there it was that he died in January 1903, in his own house in Florence. He had travelled far and wide, as at one time when in the Foreign Office he was with his father in Venezuela, and his knowledge of Spanish and of Spanish manners rendered him a valuable assistant in the settlement, for the time, of the boundary questions. At another time he was in France, and yet again in Sweden, but eventually at the desire of his close friend Antony Panizzi he took office in the British Museum in

THOMAS FAED

Mansell photo]

[Liverpool Gallery

IN TIME OF WAR

order to be near his old companion and under his wing, and he then relinquished for good his duties in diplomacy. Few men took a greater interest in the work of his department than did Fagan, and few worked harder to render it available to students and useful to the public. His lectures on the treasures of his beloved museum were received with the greatest acclamation and were most popular, whilst his writings on prints and drawings, his valuable catalogues, and his history of the Reform Club and of the British Museum, and his excellent life of Panizzi proved the brilliance of his power and the ability with which he devoted himself to his work. He will be especially remembered by artists for his volumes on the works of Correggio, the art of Michael Angelo, the engravings of Faithorne, and the works of Wollett and Bartolozzi. He also wrote a 'History of Engraving,' and an important treatise on the Sonnets of Raffael. His water-colour drawings done to amuse himself during periods of ill-health were of much more than average excellence, whilst his drawings in pencil were of the utmost refinement and beauty. His love of Italy, his strong friendship for most of her greatest writers and skilful artists, and his passionate interest in her future, did not render him the more popular with certain persons who were narrow enough to resent any affection that was not devoted to British interests, and neither Panizzi nor Fagan were really appreciated at the Museum for this very reason. To those, however, who knew him, and who had sounded the vast depths of his knowledge and the intensity of his affection, he was a man greatly beloved, and a public demonstration of mourning took place on the occasion of his decease in Florence. A brilliant and profound scholar and one of the kindest-hearted of men, he was neglected by his own countrymen and ignored by his old colleagues in London, but his artistic and literary works will keep alive his memory for many a generation, and insure a remembrance of his life's work.

FAGAN, ROBERT, a portrait painter, who resided for some time in Rome, flourished towards the close of the 18th century.

FAGE, NICOLAS DE LA. See DE LA FAGE.

FAGE, RAYMOND DE LA. See DE LA FAGE.

FÄGERPLAN, AXEL JOHAN, a Swedish artist, born in West Gothland in 1788, was an historical and fruit painter of some renown. He died in 1865.

FAGIVOLI, GIROLAMO, an engraver who worked at Bologna about 1560, published several prints after Correggio, Cecchino de'Salviati, and Francesco Mazzuola.

FAHEY, JAMES, painter, was born at Paddington April 16, 1804. He was intended for an engraver, and studied for a time under Swaine, who was his uncle. He afterwards worked at Munich and Paris, where he was employed as a surgical draughtsman. He exhibited a portrait at the Academy in 1825, but shortly afterwards devoted himself to landscape in water-colours. In 1834 he joined the short-lived Associated Painters in Water-Colours, and in the following year he, with other leading members of that body, formed the New Society, now the Institute of Painters in Water-Colours. He was for more than forty years secretary to the society. In 1856 he was appointed drawing-master at Merchant Taylors' School, whence, after twenty-seven years, he retired on a pension. He died December 19, 1885.

FAHLCRANTZ, KARL JOHAN, a Swedish landscape painter, was born in Dalecarlia in 1774. He was instructed by P. Ljung, a sculptor and painter, and depicted Northern scenery with a masterly touch, his twilight and moonlight scenes being particularly effective. He died at Stockholm in 1861. Among his best known works are:

The Legend of Frithiof.
Several Views of Stockholm, Christiania, and Sparreholm, the Fortress of Bohns, the Hills of Smedjebakken, Cape Framnäs, the Balestrand, and the Waterfall of Donare.

FAIRAM, JOHN. See FAYRAM.

FAIRFIELD, CHARLES, a painter who died at Brompton in 1804, at the age of about forty-five, is chiefly known by his excellent copies of Dutch paintings.

FAIRHOLT, FREDERICK WILLIAM, a draughtsman, was born in 1818, in London, where his father, a native of Prussia, had settled as a tobacco manufacturer. His first attempts in art were as a drawing-master and scene-painter. He was next employed by Charles Knight in making designs for the 'Pictorial History of England,' 'Pictorial Shakespeare,' and other works. From the commencement of the 'Art Journal,' in 1839, he was a constant contributor, both as author and as artist, and about the same time he seems to have begun to take an interest in antiquities. He wrote several books on the pageants and costume of mediæval England, of which the best are 'Costume in England,' 1846, 'A Dictionary of Terms in Art,' 1854, and 'Rambles of an Archæologist,' 1871, and he left to the Society of Antiquaries a collection of works on these subjects. He died in London in 1866.

FAIRLAND, THOMAS, an engraver and lithographic artist, was born in 1804 After having studied under Fuseli in the Academy, where he gained a silver medal for drawing from the antique, he became a pupil of Charles Heath, but he afterwards gave up line-engraving for lithographic drawing, and eventually devoted himself to portraiture, in which he was very successful. His reproductions of the works of Landseer and Hunt, as well as 'The Recruit; or, Who'll serve the King?' and 'Left Leg foremost,' obtained great popularity. He executed many private portraits for the Queen, whose personal regard he enjoyed until his death in 1852. Among other lithographs by him may be mentioned:

The Poacher's Confederate; after Hancock.
The Rat-catcher; after A. Cooper.
The Deserter.
Mrs. Chisholm; after A. C. Hayter.

FAIRLESS, THOMAS KERR, a landscape painter, was born at Hexham in 1823. He first practised wood-engraving under Nicholson of Newcastle, and then came to London, exhibiting landscapes at the Royal Academy from 1848 to 1851. He died at Hexham in 1853.

FAIRMAN, RICHARD, DAVID, and GIDEON, were engravers of Philadelphia, who died respectively in the years 1821, 1815, and 1827.

FAISTENAUER, ANDREAS. See FEISTENAUER.

FAISTENBERGER. See FEISTENBERGER.

FAITHORNE, WILLIAM, the elder, an eminent engraver, was born in London in 1616. He was a pupil of Robert Peake, a painter and printseller, who was afterwards knighted by Charles I., and under him he worked three or four years, until the breaking out of the Civil War, when Peake took up arms for the king, and Faithorne was persuaded by his master to accompany him into the service. At the taking of Basing House, where Peake had the rank of lieutenant-colonel, Faithorne was made a prisoner, and was for some time confined in Aldersgate, during which period he resumed his profession, and, among other plates, engraved a small head of Villiers, Duke of Buckingham. With much difficulty the solicitation of his friends procured his release, on condition that he left the country. He retired to France, where he became acquainted with Robert Nanteuil, under whose instruction he made great improvement. After the year 1650, he was permitted to return to England, and he established himself as an engraver and printseller near Temple Bar, where he carried on a considerable trade in Italian, Dutch, and English prints. In 1680, however, he quitted his shop, and retired to a more private life in Printing-house Yard, Blackfriars, where he continued to engrave, and to draw portraits in crayons, an art which he had learned in Paris. He died in 1691.

The works of this excellent engraver consist chiefly of portraits, in which he specially excelled. Many of them are of an admirable execution, clear, brilliant, and full of colour. Previous to his journey to Paris, he had adopted the Flemish and Dutch mode of engraving; but on his return from France his style was greatly improved. In his historical prints he shows a deficiency and incorrectness of drawing; and it is not, certainly, from these that a just estimate can be formed of his great ability. His plates are extremely numerous, some of them exceedingly scarce, and very valuable. When he did not fix his name to them, he marked them with a cipher composed of two Fs. *F, F* The following are his best portraits; a more complete list will be found in Fagan's 'Descriptive Catalogue of the Engraved Works of William Faithorne,' 1888.

Sir William Paston, Bart.; 1659; extremely fine.
Lady Paston; *after Van Dyck;* 1649; very fine.
Margaret Smith, afterwards Lady Herbert; *after the same.*
Montagu Bertie, Earl of Lindsey; *after the same.*
William Sanderson; *after Zoust.* 1658.
Anne Bridges, Countess of Exeter; *after Van Dyck.*
Samuel Collins, M.D.; *W. Faithorne ad vivum del. et sculp.*
John Kersey, mathematician; *after Zoust.* 1672.
John La Motte, Citizen of London.
John, Viscount Mordaunt.
Thomas, Earl of Elgin. 1662.
Mary, Lady Langham.
Henry Cary, Earl of Monmouth.
Thomas Killigrew, with a Dog; *after W. Sheppard.*
Thomas Stanley; *after Lely.*
Robert Bayfield; æt. 25; with a large hat. 1654.
Robert Bayfield; æt. 27; without a hat.
Francis Rous, Provost of Eton. 1656.
Sir Henry Spelman.
Thomas Hobbes.
Samuel Leigh. 1661.
Queen Henrietta Maria, with a Veil; in the manner of *Mellan.*
Thomas Mace; *after Cooke;* prefixed to his 'Musicks Monument,' 1676.
Sir Orlando Bridgman.
Sir John Fortescue.
Robert Boyle; oval.
Elias Ashmole; bust, in a niche.
William Oughtred; *in the style of Hollar*
William Harvey.
Henry Lawes.
John Milton; drawn and engraved from life in 1670, as a frontispiece to Milton's 'History of Britain.'

John Wallis, D.D., prefixed to his 'Mechanica.'
Sir Francis Englefield, Bart.; oval; extremely scarce.
Oliver Cromwell, whole length, in armour, a large emblematical Print, with various devices and mottos; very scarce.

SUBJECTS AFTER MASTERS, &c.

The Holy Family; *after Laurent de La Hire.*
The Repose in Egypt; *after Simon Vouet.*
Landscape, with a waggon; *after Rubens.*
The Fall of Phaeton; *after Diepenbeeck.*
Title-page and ten plates for Bishop Jeremy Taylor's 'Great Exemplar,' or Life of Christ, 1653.
Æneas and the Golden Branch, and Æneas killing Turnus; *after F. Cleyn;* engraved for Ogilby's translation of Virgil, 1654.

FAITHORNE, WILLIAM, the younger, a son of William Faithorne the elder, was born in 1656. He was instructed in the elementary principles of design by his father, but practised a different branch of engraving, being chiefly engaged in scraping portraits in mezzotint. His merit in that line would have secured to him both profit and reputation; but neglecting his business, he fell into distress, which occasioned his father much sorrow. He died not earlier than 1701. The following are esteemed his best portraits:

Thomas Flatman, poet and painter.
Mary, Princess of Orange; *after Hanneman.*
Sir William Reade, oculist to Queen Mary.
Queen Anne, when Princess of Denmark.
George, Prince of Denmark.
Frederick, Duke of Schomberg; *after Dahl.*
John Dryden; *after Clostermann.*
Sir Richard Haddock; *after the same.*
John Moore, Bishop of Ely.
Sophia, Electress of Hanover.
Sophia Dorothea, Princess of Hanover.
Charles XII. of Sweden; *after Ehrenstrahl.*
Mrs. Plowden; *after Clostermann.*

FALBE, JOACHIM MARTIN, a portrait painter, born at Berlin in 1739, was instructed by Harper and A. Pesne. Several etchings after Rembrandt, or in the style of that master, which are attributed to him, and some of which are signed with Falbe's monogram, are in existence. In 1764 he was elected a member of the Academy at Berlin, in which city he died in 1782.

FALCH, JOHANN, an animal painter, was born at Augsburg in 1687, and died in 1727. In the Hermitage at St. Petersburg are two pictures by him of insects and reptiles.

FALCIERI, BIAGIO, was born at Brentonico in 1628, and studied at Verona under Locatelli, and at Venice under Cavaliere Pietro Liberi. Among his works there is in the church of the Dominicans at Verona, a large picture of 'The Council of Trent'; in the upper part of which he has represented 'St. Thomas vanquishing the heretics.' There exists also an etching by him, executed with great spirit, representing 'St. Jerome in the Wilderness.' He died in 1703.

FALCINI, DOMENICO, an Italian engraver, flourished at Siena in the latter part of the 16th century. There are by him some woodcuts after Raphael and other masters, which are executed on three separate blocks, one for the outline, another for the half-tint, and the third for the dark shadows. He also engraved on metal. He marked his prints with the annexed cipher, but he has left one plate with a monogram composed of the letters *D.F.F.*

FALCK, JEREMIAS, a designer and engraver, was born at Dantzic about 1619. He passed some time in Paris, and from the resemblance of his style

Large miniature after the picture by Lely]   [*Montagu House*

BARBARA VILLIERS, LADY CASTLEMAINE, DUCHESS OF CLEVELAND

WILLIAM FAITHORNE

After Van Dyck]

PRINCE RUPERT

to that of Cornelis Bloemaert, would appear to have studied the engravings of that master. On leaving France he went in succession to Copenhagen, Stockholm, and Amsterdam, where he executed several plates for the celebrated cabinet of Reynst. Subsequently he worked at Hamburg, and it is probable that he died there about 1663. His plates are distinguished for the splendour of their effect, and he engraved with equal success portraits and historical subjects, both of which have great merit. The following are among his best works:

PORTRAITS.

Louis XIII. of France; *after Justus van Egmont.* 1643. This is considered his best work.
Christina, Queen of Sweden; *after D. Beck.*
Peter Gembichi, Bishop of Croatia; *after the same.*
Leonard, Count of Torstenson; *after the same.* 1649.
Axel, Count of Oxenstjern; *after the same.* 1653.
Adolphus John, Prince Palatine; *after the same.*
Charles Gustavus, Prince of Sweden; *after the same.*
Nell Gwynne; *after Lely.*
Karl Gustav Wrangel; *after D. Klocker.*

SUBJECTS AFTER VARIOUS MASTERS.

The Large Crucifixion; *after Van Dyck.*
Christ with the Crown of Thorns; *after the same.*
The Concert; *after Giorgione.*
Esau selling his Birthright; *after Tintoretto.* 1663.
Hunters with Hares; *after the same.*
The House of Pleasure; *after Rubens.*
Pallas with the Shield and Lance; *after A. Bloemaert.* 1656.
St. John preaching in the Wilderness; *after the same.* 1661.
Satyr and Ceres; *after F. Snayers.*
The Virgin with the Infant uttering Blessings; *after Justus van Egmont.*
The Virgin with the Infant; *after J. Stella.*
Semiramis; *after Guercino.*
The Cyclops; *after Michelangelo da Caravaggio.*

FALCKEISEN, THEODOR, a Swiss designer and engraver, born at Basle in 1765, was instructed by Holzhall and Karl Guttenberg. Amongst his works is an excellent plate after Benjamin West's 'Death of General Wolfe.'

FALCKENBURG, FRIEDRICH VON, a German landscape and historical painter, etched a few portraits, and other subjects, in a slight, scratchy style; they are marked *F.V.F.* He lived at Nuremberg, and died in 1623.

FALCO, AGNOLO. The name of this artist is affixed to a rude, coarse etching, representing a landscape, into which is introduced the story of Apollo and Daphne. Though it is incorrectly drawn and very indifferently executed, it appears to have been the work of a painter, and is from his own design.

FALCO, JUAN CONCHILLOS. See CONCHILLOS FALCO.

FALCONE, ANIELLO, called L'ORACOLO DELLE BATTAGLIE, was born at Naples in 1600, and was a scholar of Giuseppe Ribera, called Spagnoletto. He spent some years in France, where may still be met with several of his paintings, which are rare and highly valued. He distinguished himself as a painter of battles and skirmishes of cavalry, which he composed and designed with great fire and animation. He was equally correct in the drawing of his figures and horses, and their various movements are expressed with the most characteristic propriety. His touch is bold and free, and his colouring vigorous and effective. He was not less successful in his easel pictures than in those of a larger size; and his best works were

esteemed little inferior to the admirable productions of Borgognone. Aniello Falcone was the founder of a large school in his native city, and was one of the masters of Salvator Rosa. He died at Naples in 1665. Among his paintings are the following:

Madrid.	Gallery.	A Fight between Romans and Barbarians.
"	"	A Fight between Turkish and Christian Cavalry. 1631.
Paris.	Louvre.	A Fight between Turks and Christians.

Falcone was also an etcher, and there are by him twenty prints, in which he shows lively imagination and bold and intelligent design; they somewhat resemble the works of Parmigiano, and are executed with a light and spirited point. Among his etchings may be mentioned:

A battle between naked Men on foot and on horseback. 1618.
Apollo and Marsyas; *after Parmeggiano.*
Four plates of Apostles: James the Less, James the Greater, John the Evangelist, and Matthew.
A young Woman sleeping and suckling a Child.
The Adoration of the Magi; *after Raphael.*

FALCONET, PIERRE ÉTIENNE, was the son of the eminent sculptor, Étienne Maurice Falconet, who executed the equestrian statue of Peter the Great at St. Petersburg. He was born in Paris in 1741, and about 1766 came to London, where he became a member of the Incorporated Society of Artists, and painted a great number of portraits until 1773, about which time he returned to Paris, where he died in 1791. Among his works may be mentioned the portraits of twelve of the foremost artists in London, the decorations in the Chinese Temple at the seat of the Baroness De Grey in Bedfordshire, and several extravagant historical pieces. Earlom and others have engraved some of his works.

FALCONETTO, GIOVANNI ANTONIO, was born at Verona in the 15th century. He was instructed by his father, Jacopo Falconetto, and excelled in painting animals and fruit. Many of his works are in Verona and its environs. He died at Roveredo.

FALCONETTO, GIOVANNI MARIA, the brother of Giovanni Antonio Falconetto, born in 1458 at Verona, was both a painter and an architect, and seems to have devoted himself more during his long life to the latter profession than to the former. He learned the elements of painting from his father, Jacopo Falconetto, and is said to have spent twelve years of his early life in Rome, measuring and studying the ancient edifices of that city. He was a follower of Liberale and an imitator of Melozzo da Forli, and he painted largely in the churches of Verona. In 1493 he decorated, in monochrome, the cupola of the chapel of San Biagio in SS. Nazzaro e Celso, and displayed a profound knowledge of perspective effect in his arrangement of its various subjects. His finest works are the religious allegories which he executed from 1509 to 1516, in the church of San Pietro Martire at Verona. Of his panel pictures there remain a 'Virgin and Child,' between SS. Augustine and Joseph,' painted in 1523, at San Giuseppe, Verona; an 'Annunciation,' above the altar of the Emilii Chapel in San Zeno, Verona; an 'Augustus and the Sibyl,' in the Museum of that city; and an 'Assumption of the Virgin,' in the Berlin Gallery. The latter years of his life were devoted to architecture, and his death occurred at Padua in 1534.

FALDA, GIOVANNI BATTISTA, an Italian architect and etcher, was born at Valduggia, in the Milanese, in 1648. It is not said by whom he was instructed; but his style bears a great resemblance to that of Israel Silvestre. He was at Rome from 1669 to 1691, and there are by him several designs and engravings of the churches, gardens, fountains, and public buildings of that city, distinguished for their good perspective, and embellished with figures neatly drawn. The date of his death is not known. The following are among his best works:

Two Views of the Piazza Navona.
Two Views in Rome; the Basilica of St. Peter's, and the Fountain of St. Peter's.
A large plate of St. Peter's, and the Buildings round it.
A View of the Interior of St. Peter's, on the occasion of the Canonization of St. Francis of Sales.
A View of the Castle of St. Angelo; _after Bernini._
The Fountains of Rome; 31 plates.
The Gardens of Rome; 19 plates.

FALDONI, ANTONIO, an Italian painter and engraver, born at Ascoli, in the Marca di Trevisano, about the year 1687, first studied landscape painting under Antonio Luciano; but his pictures are little known. He afterwards applied himself to engraving, and imitated first the style of Gilles Sadeler, and afterwards that of Mellan, in which he was very successful; and several of his prints are deservedly admired. He engraved a set of portraits of the Doges of Venice, and the Procurators of St. Mark; besides which, there are the following prints by him:

PORTRAITS.

Marco Ricci, painter; _after Rosalba Carriera._
Antonio Maria Zanetti, engraver; _after the same._
Luca Carlevariis, painter and engraver.
Sebastiano Ricci, painter.

SUBJECTS AFTER VARIOUS MASTERS.

A Holy Family, with Angels; _after Sebastiano Ricci._
The Conception; _after the same._
The Nativity; _after Pietro da Cortona._
David playing on the harp before Saul; _after G. Camerata._
David flying from the wrath of Saul; _after the same._
Part of the Drawings by _Parmigiano_ for the collection published by Zanetti.

FALENS, CHARLES VAN. See VALENS.

FALERI, DOMENICO, was a painter of the school of Siena, where he was born in 1595. In the church of the Hospital of Monagnese in Siena is a picture of the 'Nativity,' and other pictures are in a Benedictine priory in the neighbourhood. He died in 1640.

FALERO, LUIS, born in Toledo in 1851, was originally in the Spanish navy. He studied in Paris, and ultimately came over to London, where he died in 1896. He was well versed in astronomy, on which subject he executed several allegorical pictures, the most important being 'The Marriage of a Comet,' 'Double Stars,' 'Le Conchemar,' 'The Dream of Faust,' and 'Unto a Better World.'

FALGANI, GASPARE, an Italian landscape painter, was born at Florence in the beginning of the 17th century. He was a pupil of Valerio Marucelli, and devoted himself entirely to landscape painting, of which specimens are to be found in various Italian galleries.

FALIZE, LUCIEN, celebrated French artist and goldsmith. Born in 1838, he was sent to England to be educated, where, as a boy, his talent attracted the notice of Sir John Bennett. He subsequently became a partner of M. Bapst, the Crown Jeweller of the Empire, whom he succeeded as official goldsmith to the French government, and his work earned for him a world-wide reputation. His work is characterized by intense refinement, simplicity and purity of form. He exerted a genuine influence, both through his writings and through the artists with whom he collaborated, amongst whom we may mention Merson, Roty, Grandhomme, Gallé and Barrias. He was trained by his father, an accomplished chaser, and influenced by such masters as Moret-Ladessil and Désiré Attorge. He travelled much, studying antique art throughout Italy, and frequently visited England, where he knew the treasures of the South Kensington and British Museums by heart. His papers on 'Enamelling' in the 'Gazette des Beaux Arts' will remain admirable essays on the subject of the goldsmith's craft. As a member of the Central Union for Decorative Art he struggled energetically to reanimate it and infuse new ideas; and in 1879 succeeded in obtaining regular technological exhibitions, which were most successful. He attentively watched the development of modern English art, admiring the revival of decorative work here, and he never missed an exhibition of Arts and Crafts in London. Amongst his best-known creations is the magnificent toilet-set made for the Princess Letitia Bonaparte on the occasion of her marriage, where he has cleverly introduced certain features, such as the Imperial Eagle, in a design of Louis XV. style, which it would have seemed almost impossible to have assimilated successfully. His bust of 'Gallia' in ivory and gold, set with topazes, is in the Luxembourg. The 'Sassanide Vase,' the 'Urania Clock,' the bas-reliefs of Marguerite de Foix and Anne de Bretagne, and above all his gold cup, now in the Musée des Arts Decoratifs, adhere to the classical traditions of the early masters of the 17th century. The latter work, worthy of Benvenuto Cellini at his best, was one of his last creations, though the last official work his skilful hands accomplished was an olive branch in beaten gold, which was laid on the tomb of the Emperor Alexander III. of Russia, by the President of the French Republic. He left a large number of sketches for jewels, diadems and medallions, drawn with consummate knowledge, to his son and pupil, André Falize. He died from an attack of apoplexy in the latter part of 1897.

FALLARO, JACOPO, an Italian painter of the 16th century, was a contemporary with Titian. According to Vasari, there is in the church of the Jesuits at Venice, on the door of the organ, a painting by this artist of 'Giovanni Colombini receiving from the Pope the cloak of the Order.'

FALOCCO, NICCOLÒ, a painter and native of Ortina, who flourished about 1740, was instructed by Francesco Solimena, whose works he copied with great success.

FALOT, NICOLAS, a French historical painter, flourished between the years 1576 and 1627. The dates of his birth and death are unknown.

FALQUIÈRE, JEAN ALEXANDRE JOSEPH, famous French sculptor, was born at Toulouse on September 7, 1831. He was a pupil of Jouffroy, and won the "prix de Rome" in 1859. One of his earliest successes was 'Le Vainqueur au combat des Coqs,' now in the Luxembourg. Among his most notable works are, 'Tarcisius, the Martyr,' 'Ophelia,' 'Pierre Corneille' (a marble statue for the Théâtre-Français),

'Lamartine,' 'Diana,' 'Gambetta,' the 'Woman with a Peacock,' 'A Dancing Girl,' 'Balzac,' the artist being commissioned to execute this last-named work after the rejection by the Société des gens de Lettres of Rodin's statue. Falquière also completed an important statue (for Washington) of Lafayette; and it was his imprudence in determining to assist at the public unveiling at Nîmes of his statue of Alphonse Daudet, when already ailing, that brought his malady to a fatal conclusion. Falquière had also won some distinction as a painter, gaining a medal at the Salon in 1875, his 'Wrestlers' and 'Cain and Abel' receiving special regard. In 1870 he was decorated with the Legion of Honour, being promoted to the rank of officer in 1878, at the close of the Universal Exhibition, and Commander in 1889. He was appointed professor at the School of Fine Arts in 1882, being elected a member of the Academy of Fine Arts in the November of that year in succession to his master, Jouffroy. His death occurred, as the immediate result of a serious operation, on April 19, 1900.

FALZAGALLONI. See FERRARA, STEFANO DA.

FANCELLI, PIETRO, was born at Bologna in 1764, and painted in oil and tempera in the Venetian style for churches and castles, as well as scenes for theatres. He died in 1850.

FANO, BARTOLOMMEO and POMPEO DA, father and son, who were both painters, flourished at Fano about the year 1530. According to Lanzi, they painted in conjunction for the church of San Michele, in that city, a picture of the 'Raising of Lazarus,' dated 1534, on which he remarks that it is surprising to observe how little they had attended to the reformation and improvement which had almost generally been adopted by other artists of their time. It is painted in the Gothic style of the middle of the preceding century. Pompeo, however, after the death of his father, attempted the more modern taste, and painted some pictures which gained for him considerable reputation. Pompeo da Fano was the first instructor of Taddeo Zucchero.

FANOLI, MICHELE, an Italian lithographer and engraver, who was born at Cittadella about 1807, studied in the Venice Academy, and under Cicognara. He spent many years in Paris, whence in 1860 he was recalled by the Italian government to found a school of lithography at Milan, which he directed till his death in that city in 1876. He died poor, leaving a collection of sketches to the Venice Academy. Amongst his reproductions are:

Orpheus; *after Jalabert.* The Holy Women at the Tomb; Our Lord and SS. Peter and John; *after Landelle.*

FANSAGA, COSIMO, (or FANZAGA,) a painter, sculptor, and architect, was born at Bergamo in 1591, and was a scholar of Pietro Bernini at Rome. Most of his works were executed at Naples, where he erected a number of edifices, and in some instances decorated them with statues and pictures of his own production. He died in 1678.

FANSHAWE, CATHARINE MARIA, an amateur etcher, was born in London about 1775, and died about 1834. She etched a few historical and figure subjects with considerable ability.

FANTETTI, CESARE, a designer and etcher, was born at Florence about the year 1660. He resided chiefly at Rome, where he engraved several plates, after his own designs and those of other masters. Conjointly with Pietro Aquila, he engraved the plates from the paintings by Raphael in the Vatican, called Raphael's Bible, thirty-seven of the series being executed by Fantetti, and the remainder by Aquila. He also engraved the following prints:

Agrippina with the Ashes of her Husband; *after Franc. Rosa.*
Christ praying in the Garden; *after L. Carracci.*
A Charity, with three Children; *after Annibale Carracci.*
Latona insulted by Niobe; *after the same.*
Flora surrounded by Cupids; *after Ciro Ferri.*
The Death of St. Anne; *after Andrea Sacchi.*
Some Friezes, and other subjects, from various Italian masters.

FANTI, ERCOLE GAETANO, born at Bologna in 1687, was a pupil of M. A. Chiarini. He first painted in Italy stage decorations, but afterwards went to Vienna, where he was made Superintendent of the Liechtenstein Gallery. He died at Vienna in 1759.

FANTI, VINCENZO, the son of Ercole Gaetano Fanti, studied first under Altomonte, and then went to Rome and Turin, and eventually in 1744 to Vienna, where he succeeded his father as Superintendent of the Liechtenstein Gallery. The dates of his birth and death are not known. His portrait is in the Uffizi, Florence.

FANTONE, FRANCESCA, a painter of the Bolognese School, who flourished in 1760, was the niece and pupil of.Gian Gioseffo dal Sole, but she afterwards studied under Cavazzoni. She died about 1772.

FANTUZZI, ANTONIO. See TRENTO, ANTONIO DA.

FANZAGA, COSIMO. See FANSAGA.

FANZONE, FERRAU, (or FAENZONE,) was born at Faenza in 1562, and, according to the Abbate Titi, studied at Rome under the Cavaliere Vanni, where he painted several frescoes in San Giovanni in Laterano, the Scala Santa, and the church of Santa Maria Maggiore. There are, however, some pictures at Ravenna, particularly a 'Deposition from the Cross,' in the church of the Dominicans, and a 'Probatica,' at the Confraternità di San Giovanni, which partake so much of the fine style of Lodovico Carracci, that Fanzone has been supposed to have been educated in his academy. His design is grand and correct, with great amenity in his colouring, and a fine impasto. He died in 1645.

FA PRESTO. See GIORDANO, LUCA.

FARELLI, GIACOMO, a Neapolitan painter, was born in 1624, and brought up under Andrea Vaccaro, whose style he at first followed, but he afterwards imitated with more success that of Guido. He died in 1706. Of his productions there remain in Santa Maria Maggiore at Naples, 'The Fall of the Angels,' and 'The Ascension'; others are in SS. Apostoli and Redenzione dei Cattivi.

FARFUSOLA, BARTOLOMMEO, a painter born at Verona, flourished in the year 1640. He has left several pictures in the churches of Verona, among others a 'St. Ursula' in the church dedicated to that saint.

FARGUE. See LA FARGUE.

FARINA, PIER FRANCESCO, an Italian painter who lived in the latter half of the 17th century, and was employed in decorating the palace of Carlsruhe and several churches of Bologna.

FARINATI, GIOVANNI BATTISTA, called by Vasari BATTISTA DA VERONA, and by others in error BATTISTA ZELOTTI and BATTISTA FONTANA, was born at Verona in 1532, and is said to have been instructed by Paolo, his uncle, or, according to others, by Antonio Badile. He was the fellow-student and friend of Paolo Veronese, with whom he co-operated in several important works in the public edifices at Venice, as well as in the Villa Soranza at Castelfranco. He is numbered by Vasari among the disciples of Titian. His picture of the 'Holy Family,' in the Lochis-Carrara Gallery at Bergamo, is painted entirely in the style of that master, and it is to his studies in that school that he was indebted for the warmth and harmony of his colouring. His style is marked by its grandeur, though inferior in grace to that of Paolo Veronese. As a fresco-painter he possessed especial ability. He died in 1592. The following paintings are by him:

Venice.	*Palazzo Reale.*	The Virtues and Study.
Vicenza.	*Monte d. Pieta.*	The Decoration of the Façade.
„	*Cathedral.*	The Conversion of St. Paul.
„	„	The Miraculous Draught of Fishes.

FARINATI, ORAZIO, the son and disciple of Paolo Farinati, was an historical painter and etcher who was living at Verona in 1607. During his short career he gave proof of uncommon ability, and promised to reach an elevated rank among the artists of his country, when he died in the prime of life. He etched a few plates from the designs of his father, which are frequently confounded with those of the latter. There exist the following paintings by him:

Verona.	*S. Paolo.*	The Descent from the Cross (*a copy after his father*).
„	*S. Maria del Paradiso.*	St. James. 1607.
„	*S. Stefano.*	Pope Gregory. 1607.
		Descent of the Holy Ghost (*considered his best work*).

Both father and son signed their paintings with a snail, and their prints, in addition to the snail, with their initials or full names.

Orazio Farinati's best plates are :

The Descent from the Cross; *after Paolo Farinati.* 1593.
The Finding of the Cross, with St. Francis and other figures; *after the same.*
The Destruction of Pharaoh's Host; *after the same.* 1599.
The Holy Family, with St. John.

FARINATI, PAOLO, of the family of the Uberti, was born at Verona in 1522. He was a pupil of Niccolò Giolfino and A. Badile, but studied also the works of Parmigiano, and soon surpassed his instructors. To judge from the large style of his design, it would be thought that he had been brought up in the school of Giulio Romano; and it is certain that he studied for some time at Mantua the works of that master. His death occurred in 1606. Among his works there are:

Berlin.	*Gallery.*	A Presentation in the Temple.
Bordeaux.	*Museum.*	Venus seated, and two Loves.
Mantua.	*Cathedral.*	St. Martin.
Modena.	*Estense Gall.*	Angels playing a Trumpet (*water-colour*).
Petersburg.	*Hermitage.*	Adoration of the Magi.
„	„	Presentation in the Temple.
Venice.	*SS. Cosimo e Damiano.*	The Four Evangelists.
Verona.	*S. Giorgio.*	The Multiplication of the Loaves (*painted in his 79th year*).
„	*S. M. in Organo.*	The Murder of the Innocents.
„	„	The Emperor Constantine ordering a number of Children to be murdered.
„	„	Christ walking on the Sea.

Verona.	*S. M. in Organo.*	St. Gregory feeding the Poor.
„	*S. Giovanni in Fonte.*	The Baptism of Christ.
„	*Gallery.*	Christ before the People.
„	*SS. Nazzaro e Celso.*	Frescoes.
Vienna.	*Gallery.*	A Heathen Sacrifice.

There are several etchings by Paolo Farinati executed in a free, bold, and masterly style. Like his paintings he frequently marked them with the accompanying device of a snail; but he sometimes signed them with his name, or with the initials *P. F.* or *P. V. F.* The following are from his own designs:

St. John. 1567.
St. Jerome kneeling, leaning on a Bank.
Mary Magdalen seated, with a Book and a Crucifix.
The Virgin, with the Infant Jesus and St. John.
Angels holding the Instruments of the Passion.
Venus and Cupid. 1566.
A Charity, with three Children.
Venus and Cupid at the Forge of Vulcan.

FARINGTON, GEORGE, a painter of historical subjects, was born in 1754 at Warrington, of which place his father was rector. He was educated under West, and in 1780 obtained the gold medal at the Royal Academy for his 'Macbeth.' This promising artist afterwards went to the East Indies, where he would undoubtedly have acquired both fame and fortune, had he not died in the prime of life in 1788.

FARINGTON, JOSEPH, a landscape painter, the elder brother of George Farington, was born in 1747 at Leigh, in Lancashire. He was a scholar of Richard Wilson, and from 1778 to 1813 he exhibited constantly at the Royal Academy, where he was elected an Associate in 1783, and an Academician in 1785. He was also a member of the Incorporated Society of Artists. His works are chiefly views of the scenery of Westmoreland and Cumberland, which have been engraved by Byrne, Pouncey, Medland, and others. In 1794 he published seventy-six views of the river Thames. He died in 1821. The South Kensington Museum possesses two water-colour drawings by him.

FARJAT, BENOÎT, a French engraver, was born at Lyons in 1646. He was taught the elements of the art by Guillaume Chasteau, whose manner he at first adopted; but he afterwards went to Rome, and acquired a greater command of the graver, and a better style of design, though he is not always correct. He died in Rome about 1720. There are by him some portraits, and various subjects from the Italian masters; the following are the most esteemed:

PORTRAITS.

Cardinal Federigo Coccia; *after L. David.*
Cardinal Cornaro; *after the same.* 1697.
Cardinal Tommaso Ferrari; *after the same.* 1695.

SUBJECTS AFTER VARIOUS MASTERS.

The Holy Family, with St. John; *after Albani.*
The Holy Family, with St. John presenting a Cross; *after Pietro da Cortona.*
The Marriage, or, according to others, the Coronation, of St. Catharine; *after Agostino Carracci.*
The Virgin and Infant Jesus, with St. John presenting some fruit; *after Annibale Carracci.*
The Temptation of St. Anthony; *after the same.*
The Communion of St. Jerome; *after Domenichino.*
The Death of St. Francis Xavier; *after G. B. Gaulli.*
The Marriage of the Virgin; *after C. Maratti.*
The Nativity of Christ; *after the same.*
The Race of Atalanta; *after P. Locatelli.*

FARNBOROUGH, AMELIA LONG, Baroness, who was born in 1772, and died in 1837, was a very clever amateur water-colour painter. She exhibited as an honorary exhibitor many drawings at the Royal Academy. She was a daughter of Sir Abraham Hume, Bart., and in 1793 married Sir Charles Long, afterwards Lord Farnborough.

FARRER, NICHOLAS, a portrait painter, born at Sunderland in 1750, was a pupil of Pine, and a friend of Sir Joshua Reynolds and Northcote. His portraits, without being imitations, bear a strong resemblance to Sir Joshua's manner, and have sometimes been mistaken for that master's work. He painted the portraits of the Duke of Richmond and family. He died in 1805.

FARRIER, ROBERT, a little-known painter of miniature portraits, domestic subjects, and scenes from school-boy life. He was born in 1796, exhibited at the Academy after 1818, and died in 1879.

FARUFFINI, FEDERICO, a native of Sesto, who was distinguished as a painter and engraver, studied at Rome. His altar-pieces and other historical subjects are original in conception, but of especial merit is his 'Macchiavelli and Borgia,' which he both painted and engraved, and for which he obtained a medal in 1866. He died at Milan.

FASOLO, BERNARDINO, the son of Lorenzo Fasolo, was living in the 16th century at Pavia. He is known to have been a member of the council of the Guild of Genoa in 1520, but no dates can be given of his birth or death. The following pictures are by him:

Berlin.	*Gallery.*	A Holy Family.
Dresden.	*Gallery.*	Portrait of a Venetian Lady
Paris.	*Louvre.*	Virgin and Child. 1518.

FASOLO, GIOVANANTONIO, who was born at Vicenza in 1528, first studied under Battista Zelotti; but the brilliant reputation of Paolo Veronese induced him to enter the school of that distinguished master, under whom he became a good historical painter. In the church of San Rocco at Vicenza is a fine picture by Fasolo, representing the 'Pool of Bethesda,' a grand composition, executed in a style that would not have disgraced Paolo Veronese; in the church of the Padri Servi is another fine picture by this master, the 'Adoration of the Magi.' In the residence of the Prefect of that town there are also by him three pictures of subjects from Roman history, representing 'Mutius Scævola before Porsena,' 'Horatius defending the Bridge,' and 'Marcus Curtius leaping into the Gulf.' He died in 1572.

FASOLO, LORENZO, called LORENZO DI PAVIA, was a Lombard painter living in the early part of the 16th century, who went from Pavia to Genoa, and was one of the artists employed by Lodovico Sforza in 1490 in the decorations of the Porta Giovia Palace at Milan. His chief work is an altar-piece representing 'The Deposition from the Cross,' which he painted in 1508, for the nuns of Santa Chiara, at Chiavari, where it still remains. The Louvre has by him 'The Family of the Virgin,' dated 1513. His death occurred before 1520.

FASSETTI, GIOVANNI BATTISTA, born at Reggio in 1684 of poor parents, entered the studio of Giuseppe Dallamano as a colour mixer, and it was not till he was eighteen years of age that he made his first attempt at art. He entered the studio of Francesco da Bibiena, and became one of the best decorative painters of his day. He died after 1772.

FASSIN, NICOLAS HENRI JOSEPH DE, a Belgian landscape painter, was born at Liége in 1728. Early in life he served in the French army, and it was not until he was thirty-four years of age that he commenced the study of art in the Academy at Antwerp. He afterwards visited Italy and Switzerland, and resided for some time at Geneva. He painted a landscape for the Empress of Russia, for which he was handsomely rewarded, and many others are to be found at Liége, and in Germany and England. He died in his native city in 1811. His biography, with a list of his pictures, was published by Van Hust in 1837.

FATIO, ANTOINE LÉON MOREL. See MOREL-FATIO.

FATTORE, IL. See PENNI.

FAUCCI, CARLO, an Italian engraver, was born at Florence in 1729. He was a pupil of Carlo Gregori, and engraved portraits and historical pieces with ability. On leaving that artist, he engraved several plates for the collection of the gallery of the Marquis Gerini, and afterwards visited England, where he engraved some plates for Boydell. He died at Florence in 1784. Among others, the following prints are by him:

The Birth of the Virgin; *after Pietro da Cortona.*
The Adoration of the Shepherds; *after the same.*
The Martyrdom of St. Andrew; *after Carlo Dolci.*
The Coronation of the Virgin; *after Rubens.*
A Bacchanalian subject; *after the same.*
Cupid; *after Guido.*
Madonna and Child; *after the same.*

RAIMONDO FAUCCI, his nephew, assisted him in the execution of many of his plates.

FAUCHERY, AUGUSTIN, a French painter and engraver, was born in Paris in 1800, and was instructed by Guérin and Regnault. One of his best engravings is a plate of 'Mona Lisa,' after Leonardo da Vinci. He died in Paris in 1843.

FAUCHIER, LAURENT, a French portrait painter, was a pupil of Pierre Mignard. He flourished in the second half of the 17th century.

FAUCUS, GEORGE. See FOCUS.

FAULKNER, BENJAMIN RAWLINSON, a portrait painter, was born at Manchester in 1787, and until 1813 pursued a commercial life at Gibraltar. Then, returning to England on account of an attack of the plague, he devoted himself to art, receiving his first instruction from his brother. After some study in London, he began exhibiting at the Royal Academy in 1821; but his practice was chiefly in Manchester. He died at Fulham in 1849. Amongst his works are:

John Dalton, the chemist. 1841. (*Royal Society, London.*)
John McCulloch, the geologist. (*Royal Society, London.*)
Rev. Dr. Raffles. (*Lancashire Independent College.*)

FAULKNER, JOSHUA WILSON, a portrait painter, the brother of Benjamin Faulkner, was born in the latter part of the 18th century. He was a native of Manchester, where he spent the greater part of his life, but he exhibited at the Liverpool Institution, and occasionally at the Royal Academy. He died soon after 1820. There is a portrait of Sir John Ross, the Arctic discoverer, by him.

FAUR, CHRISTIAN WILHELM VON FABER DU. See FABER DU FAUR.

FAURAY, ANTOINE DE. See FAVRAY.

FAURE, EUGÈNE, a French painter of allegories, mythological subjects, and portraits, was born at Seyssinet, near Grenoble, in 1822. He studied under David d'Angers and Rude, and his first work, a landscape, now in the Grenoble Museum, appeared at the Salon in 1847. He died in Paris in 1879. The following are his chief works:

Dreams of Youth. 1857.
First Steps in Love. 1861.
Confidence. 1863.
Eve. 1864.
La Source. 1878.

FAURE, Léon, a French painter, and pupil of Eugène Delacroix, was a native of Toulouse. His first contribution to the Salon was a picture called 'L'Offrande,' exhibited in 1857. He was for many years Professor at the Art School of his native town, where he died in 1887.

FAVA, Giangiacomo, commonly known as Macrino d'Alba, was a painter of the old Lombard school, who worked from about 1496 to 1508. One of his best pictures, a 'Madonna and Child,' is in a chapel of the Certosa, near Pavia. The Städel Institute at Frankfort possesses a 'Madonna' by him, with side-pictures from the history of St. Joachim and St. Anne.

FAVA, Pietro da, Count, a Bolognese nobleman, who distinguished himself not only as a patron of art, but also as an amateur, was born at Bologna in 1667. He studied art under L Pasinelli, and was the protector and friend of Donato Creti and Ercole Graziani. He chiefly studied the works of the Carracci, whose style he preferred to every other. In the church of San Tommaso dal Mercato at Bologna is an altar-piece by him of the 'Virgin and Infant, with St. Albert, St. Paul, and other Saints'; and at Ancona, in the cathedral, are the 'Adoration of the Magi,' and the 'Resurrection.' He was a member of the Clementine Academy, and died in 1744.

FAVANNE, Henri de, (or Favannes,) a painter of historical subjects, was born in London in 1668, and was instructed by René Houasse. He travelled through England, and afterwards lived ten years in Spain. He then went to Paris, where he was elected rector of the Academy, and died in 1752.

FAVANNE, Jacques de, (or Favannes,) the son of Henri de Favanne, was at first an engraver, and was instructed by H. F. Thomassin, but he afterwards took to painting, and executed principally sea-pieces. He was residing in Paris about 1760. He is mentioned by Basan as the engraver of a plate after Watteau of 'The Pleasures of Summer.'

FAVRAY, Chevalier Antoine de, (or Fauray,) born in 1706, was a pupil of Jean François de Troy, the younger, whom he accompanied to Rome when the latter was appointed Director of the Academy in that city. At Malta, in the service of the Knights of the Order, he executed several representations of Maltese manners and customs, one of which in the Louvre served for his reception into the Academy in 1762. A picture of the 'Annual Thanksgiving of the Knights of St. John, in the church of their patron saint, for their deliverance from the Turks,' was sent with the above to Paris. In 1762 he went with the French ambassador, the Chevalier de Vergennes, to Constantinople, where he remained till 1771, when, on war breaking out between Turkey and Russia, he returned to Malta. From this time all further details of his life are unknown, though he seems to have been alive in 1789, and probably in 1791. In the La Caze collection in the Louvre is a picture of 'Maltese Ladies paying a visit.' His portrait is in the Uffizi, Florence.

FAVRETTO, Giacomo, painter, was born at Venice in 1849. He was one of the ablest of the little knot of Venetian painters whose practice is

150

founded more or less on the water-colours of Ludwig Passini. His pictures are generally market-scenes, and are notable for the skill with which positive greens are employed. Towards the end of his life his works became popular in London. The best perhaps is 'A Clothes Market in Venice.' He died at Venice in 1887.

FAXARDO, Juan Antonio, a Spanish painter, was a native of Seville, to whom Alonzo Miguel de Tobar was sent when a boy to learn painting.

FAY, Joseph, a German painter, born at Cologne in 1813, attended from 1833 to 1841 the Academy at Düsseldorf, and afterwards studied at Munich, and at Paris under Paul Delaroche. He first painted historical subjects, and had a happy talent in representing scenes from the life and manners of the old Germans, but not meeting with sufficient encouragement, he changed his style for genre painting, for which purpose he visited Italy. He died at Düsseldorf in 1875. The following are among his best works:

Samson and Delilah. 1839. (*Cologne Museum.*)
Cleopatra.
A large Frieze. (*Elberfeld Court-house.*) This has perished, but some cartoons of it still exist.
Thisbe listening.
Romeo and Juliet. 1846.
Gretchen in Prison. 1847.

FAYERMANN, Anne Charlotte. See Bartholomew.

FAYRAM, John, a portrait and landscape painter, practised in London about the year 1740. There are by him some slight, coarse etchings of views in the neighbourhood of Chelsea and Battersea, and also one of the Hermitage in Kew Gardens.

FEARNLEY, Thomas, a landscape painter of English parentage, was born at Fredrichshall in Norway in 1802. After spending a short time in his uncle's business, he entered the Copenhagen Academy, and was patronized by the Crown Prince Oscar, for whom he painted a 'View of Copenhagen.' In 1828 he set out on his travels through Europe, and did not return to Norway till 1836. He afterwards spent some time in England, and exhibited at the British Institution a 'Norwegian Cascade.' He died at Munich in 1842. Amongst his most noticeable works are:

The Blue Grotto of Capri.
The Glacier of the Grindelwald (*repeated several times*).
Labrofos Waterfall. (*Christiania National Gallery.*)

FEARY, John, a landscape painter, exhibited at the Royal Academy from 1772 to 1788. He obtained a premium at the Society of Arts in 1775.

FÈBRE, Valentin le. See Le Fèbre.

FEBURE, Claude le. See Lefebure.

FEBURE, François le. See Le Fèvre.

FECHHELM, Christian Gottlieb, a portrait and historical painter, born at Dresden in 1732, studied under Mengs, Manjocky, and Hutin, first portrait painting, and then miniature. In the Seven Years' War Maria Theresa commissioned him to paint the portraits of the generals engaged in that campaign for the Military School at Vienna. He died at Dresden in 1816. His son, Karl Christian, who was born at Dresden in 1770, and died in 1826, was likewise a painter.

FECHHELM, Karl Friedrich, who was born at Dresden about 1723, studied under Müller at Prague, and was engaged at Berlin, in the palace and other public places, in painting frescoes and architectural decorations. He died in 1785. There are some views of Berlin etched by him.

FECHNER, EDUARD CLEMENS, who was born at Gross-Särchen, near Moscow, in 1799, was a portrait painter and an etcher, who studied in 1814 at Dresden under Grassi and Retsch. In 1820 he went to Munich, where he improved his style under Stieler. He worked some time for the Duke of Leuchtenberg, and visited Paris in 1825. He excelled in painting portraits of ladies and children; he also executed eleven etchings in a spirited manner. He died in Paris in 1861.

FEDDES, PIETER, called PIETER VAN HARLINGEN, from the place of his birth, was born in 1588, and distinguished himself as a painter on glass. He also etched portraits, conversation and historical pieces, with a broad and spirited point. There are by him 119 plates, among which the most important are the following:

Johannes Bogerman, the President of the Synod at Dordrecht. 1620.
Martinus Hamconius.
Charity, or Love.
Fifty-two portraits of the Princes and Dukes of Friesland, for Hamconius's *Frisia* (Franeker, 1620).
The Portraits in Winsemius's *Cronycken van Vriesland* (Franeker, 1622).

His plates are signed *P. Harlingensis*, although not always in full. He died in 1634.

FEDERIGHETTO DI DALMATIA, Il. See BENCOVICH.

FEGATELLI, GIUSEPPE MARIA, a native of Bologna, and pupil of C. Gennari, flourished in the latter half of the 17th century, and painted pictures for the churches of his native city.

FEHLING, HEINRICH CHRISTOPH, a German painter, born at Sangerhausen, in Thuringia, in 1653, was instructed by Bottschildt, to whom he was related. After having lived several years in Italy, he was appointed court-painter to the Elector John George IV., and became director of the Academy and inspector of the Art Galleries at Dresden, where he died in 1725. In the Dresden Gallery is a portrait by him of Colonel Kaspar von Klengel, and a number of painted ceilings remain as specimens of his art in the palaces of that city.

FEI, ALESSANDRO DI VINCENZIO, called ALESSANDRO DEL BARBIERE, an historical painter, was born at Florence in 1543, and was a pupil first of Ghirlandajo, afterwards of Piero Francia, and lastly of Maso da San Frediano. His invention was fertile and prompt, adapted to the great works which he executed in fresco, and embellished with architecture in a grand style. He was fond of introducing buildings and grotesque figures into his paintings. His works are to be found in the churches and public edifices at Florence, Pistoja, and Messina. One of his most esteemed pictures is the 'Flagellation,' in the church of Santa Croce at Florence, in which city he died in 1592.

FEID, JOSEPH, an Austrian landscape painter, was born at Vienna in 1807. He possessed a great talent in depicting foliage and forest life, and died at Weidling, near Vienna, in 1870. The following works by him are in the Vienna Gallery:

A Scene in a Wood, with Nymphs bathing. 1828.
A Study of the Schneeberg.
A Forest Landscape, with a large Oak. 1841.
A Landscape with an approaching Storm.

FEIGL, JOHANN, an engraver, who flourished at Vienna in the last quarter of the 18th century, was a pupil of Schmutzer and of Wille. His best known work is, 'An old Woman washing the Head of a Boy,' after G. Dou, 1776.

FEISTENAUER, ANDREAS, (or FAISTENAUER,) a native of Rosenheim, in Bavaria, studied at Vienna under Stoll. He afterwards went to Munich, where he painted several pictures for the churches, and in 1658 was appointed court-painter to the Elector of Bavaria. The date of his death is not known.

FEISTENBERGER, ANTON, was born at Innsbruck, in the Tyrol, in 1678. He had no abler instructor than an obscure artist, named Bouritzsch, who lived at Salzburg, or Passau; but he had an opportunity of studying some of the works of Gaspard Poussin, by which he formed for himself so grand a style of painting landscape, that on seeing his pictures, it would be supposed that he had visited Rome. His landscapes are embellished with architectural ruins, and refreshed with waterfalls; the forms of his trees are grand and picturesque, and his foliage is light and spirited. He was invited to Vienna by the Emperor of Germany, by whom he was employed for several years, and many of his best works are in the Imperial and Liechtenstein Galleries in that city. Other landscapes by him are in the Dresden Gallery and at Weimar. He was not successful in drawing the figure, but was assisted in that branch by Hans Graf and Van Bredael. He died at Vienna in 1736.

FEISTENBERGER, JOSEPH, born at Innsbruck in 1684, was the brother of Anton Feistenberger, by whom he was instructed, and whom he assisted in some of his works. There are two landscapes by this artist in the Vienna Gallery. He died at Vienna in 1735.

FEKE, ROBERT, one of the earliest American colonial painters, was descended from a Dutch family, who settled at Oyster Bay, Long Island. It is said that having been taken prisoner and carried to Spain, he there learned to paint, and on his return home settled at Newport, Rhode Island, where, among other portraits, he painted that of the beautiful wife of Governor Wanton, now in the Redwood Library. He worked also at New York, and in 1746 at Philadelphia, where his portraits were considered the best after those of West. He subsequently went to Bermuda for his health, and died there at the age of about forty-four.

FELICE, SIMONE, was an Italian engraver of the 17th century, who, in conjunction with Giovanni Battista Falda, engraved a collection of prints, entitled 'Le Giardini di Roma.' Felice's plates are very neatly executed, with small figures, spiritedly designed, and are in no way inferior to the productions of Falda.

FELICIATI, LORENZO, an Italian painter, was born at Siena in 1732, and died in 1779. Several pictures by this artist are to be found in the churches of Siena and its neighbourhood.

FELIPE, Fray, was a Spanish miniature painter of the early part of the 16th century, who, in conjunction with Bernardino Canderron and Alonso Vazquez, between 1514 and 1518 decorated a missal for the cathedral of Toledo.

FELLINI, GIULIO CESARE, born about 1600, was a pupil of Gabriele Ferrantini and of Annibale Carracci. He excelled in painting horses and figures, and was assisted by his son Marcantonio Fellini.

FELLNER, FERDINAND, a designer and painter, was born at Frankfort in 1799. After receiving a high-class education he went to Munich to study art, and remained there from 1825 to 1831, but later on he established himself at Stuttgart and published a number of illustrations. As a painter his works are less meritorious. He died at Stuttgart in 1859. Some of the most remarkable of his designs for books are :

The Illustrations of the 'Seven Swabians.'
Sixteen Illustrations of 'Don Quixote.'
The Illustrations of 'Faust.'
Five Illustrations of 'Wilhelm Tell.'
Illustrations of 'Wallenstein,' 'The Maid of Orleans,' 'Macbeth,' 'Romeo and Juliet,' Bürger's 'Lenore,' 'Oberon,' 'Robert,' 'Gudrun,' &c.

His paintings bear the accompanying monogram, and among them are the following :

Burgberg.	*Church.*	The Holy Family (*partly painted by Pilgram*).
Frankfort.	*Emperor's Saloon.*	Conrad I.
„	„	Frederic the Beautiful.

FELLOWES, JAMES, a portrait painter, practised in the first half of the 18th century. He was reputed to be the painter of a picture, once well known, of 'The Last Supper,' at St. Mary's, Whitechapel.

FELOU, CHARLES FRANÇOIS, the Belgian armless painter. He first saw the light at Waermaede in the year 1830, being born without any arms. He did not follow an artistic career until comparatively late in life, for it was not until he had passed his twenty-fifth year that he seriously commenced work as an artist. He worked entirely with his feet, holding his palette with his left, and using his brushes with the other foot. He died at Brussels in the seventieth year of his age.

P. P.

FELSENTHAL, WOLFGANG, Edler von. See KÖPP.

FELSING, GEORG JAKOB, a German line-engraver, was born at Darmstadt in 1802. He was first instructed by his father, Johann Konrad Felsing, but he afterwards visited Italy and studied at Milan under Longhi, and at Florence the style of Raffaello Morghen. After residing some time at Naples he revisited Florence, and became a professor in the Academy of that city, and a member of the Academy of Milan. He returned to Darmstadt in 1832, when he was elected professor, and appointed engraver to the Court. During a stay in Paris he was influenced by the style of Desnoyers, and at Munich by the principles of the artists there. Felsing's plates show the talent of a great artist, and he worked with the graver in a clear and vigorous manner. He was also a member of the Academies of St. Petersburg, Berlin, and Vienna, and of the Institute of France. He died at Darmstadt in 1883. His most important works are :

Christ on the Mount of Olives; *after Carlo Dolci.* 1828.
The Madonna enthroned; *after Andrea del Sarto.* 1830.
The Marriage of St. Catharine; *after Correggio.* 1831.
The Violinist; *after Raphael.* 1833.
Girl at the Fountain; *after Bendemann.* 1835.
The Virgin with the Infant, St. Elizabeth, and St. John; *after Overbeck.* 1839.
St. Geneviève in the Forest; *after Steinbrück.*
The Saviour; *after Leonardo da Vinci.* 1844.
Christ with the Doctors; *after the same.* 1847.
Hagar and Ishmael; *after Köhler.* 1848.
Moses in the Bulrushes; *after the same.* 1849-52.
The Lorelei; *after Köhler the younger.* 1854.
The Betrayal of Christ; *after Hofmann.* 1861.
St. Cecilia; *after the same.*
Christ with the Cross; *after Crespi.*

FELSING, JOHANN KONRAD, a German engraver, was born at Giessen in 1766, and learned the

152

elements of his art in Darmstadt. He engraved many portraits in the dotted manner, but was more particularly distinguished by his topographical works, of which the last and best was the military plan of Mayence. He died at Darmstadt in 1819. He was the father of JOHANN HEINRICH FELSING, a celebrated copper-plate printer, who died in 1875, and of GEORG JAKOB FELSING, the eminent engraver.

FELTRE, MORTO DA. See LUZZI.

FELTRINI, ANDREA, called also ANDREA DI COSIMO, was a Florentine painter who excelled in grotesques. He was born about 1490, and died about 1554. His works are to be met with at Florence on the fronts of houses, on walls, and on ceilings. He is called by the first name, from his having been a scholar of Morto da Feltre, and by the second from his having studied art under Cosimo Roselli.

FEMINIA, GABRIEL, a Spanish painter, who flourished at the commencement of the 18th century. He had the reputation of being the best landscape painter of his time in Spain.

FENDI, PETER, a German genre and water-colour painter, engraver, lithographer, and designer, was born in 1796 at Vienna, in the academy of which city he studied. In 1818 he became draughtsman to the Cabinet of Antiquities, and in 1821 he went to Venice, and obtained a gold medal for his picture of 'The Grotto.' He produced pictures on various subjects of German history and poetry, and also designed illustrations for Dibdin's 'Bibliographical Tour in France and Germany,' and for Hormayr's 'History of Vienna.' He died in 1842. His 'Young Girl watching a Lottery' is in the Vienna Gallery, and his 'Bride' appeared at the London International Exhibition of 1862.

FENIS, BARTHELEMI, was an engraver who worked at Modena from 1653 to 1669, and etched several plates in the style of Callot.

FENNITZER, GEORG, who worked at Nuremberg towards the end of the 17th century, was an engraver in chiaroscuro, especially of portraits. His plates are signed *G. F.*, *G. Fenn.*, *G. Feni.*, or *G. Fenitz.* Among his portraits are :

Matthäus Müller.
Johann Conrad Götz. 1690.
Petrus Ihselburg.
Andreas Bergmann. 1693.

FENNITZER, MICHAEL, who was evidently a relation of Georg Fennitzer, was born at Nuremberg in 1641, and died there at the close of the century. He also was an engraver in mezzotint, and his best plates are 'The Last Supper,' after Adam Kraft's relief in the Church of St. Sebaldus at Nuremberg, and two or three portraits of local celebrities. He marked his productions with either his entire name or his initials.

FENOLLO, PAOLO, an Italian painter, is known by a 'Bacchic Scene' in the Madrid Gallery.

FENTZEL, GREGOR, an engraver, was a native of Nuremberg, who worked in that city about 1650. He engraved the 'Battle of King Alphonso and the Moors,' after Antonio Tempesta, and the portrait of General Don Balthasar Marradas, after F. Cleyn, as well as portraits and other illustrations in the style of Jan Sadeler, mostly for the books of Paulus Fürst of Nuremberg.

FERA, BERNARDINO, who flourished about 1700, was a pupil of Solimena, and was known for his frescoes and distempers.

FERABOSCO, GIROLAMO. See FERRABOSCO.

FERABOSCO, MARTINO, a native of Italy, who resided at Rome, engraved the plates for the work entitled 'Architettura della Basilica di San Pietro in Vaticano,' published at Rome in 1620.

FERABOSCO, PIETRO, an Italian painter, who flourished about 1616, spent the greater part of his life in Portugal, where his works are mostly to be found.

FERDINAND, LOUIS ELLE, the elder, a French painter of portraits, and an engraver, was born in Paris about 1612. He was the son and pupil of the painter Ferdinand Elle, a native of Mechlin, who settled in France, and was one of the instructors of Nicolas Poussin. Ferdinand Elle was known best by his baptismal name alone, and for this reason his sons, Louis and Pierre, appear to have adopted it as a surname. Independently of his talent as a painter, he etched several plates, in a spirited and tasteful style, and the prints for a book, entitled 'Le Livre original de la Portraiture,' printed at Paris in 1644. He was one of the foundation members of the Academy in 1648, and died in Paris in 1682. There are also by him the following plates :

Portrait of a Lady; *after Van Dyck.*
Nicolas Poussin; *V. E. pinxit.*
A set of six Friezes; *after L. Testelin.*
A set of six groups of Children; *after the same.*
Several allegorical and mythological subjects; *after Primaticcio.*

FERDINAND, LOUIS ELLE, the younger, the son and pupil of Louis Elle Ferdinand the elder, was born in Paris in 1648. He painted portraits with great reputation, and became a member of the French Academy, his reception pictures being a portrait of Samuel Bernard, the miniature painter, now in the Louvre, and a portrait of Regnaudin, now in the École des Beaux-Arts. In the National Portrait Gallery is a likeness by him of Dr. Thomas Burnet, dated 1675. He died at Reims in 1717. His brother, PIERRE ELLE FERDINAND, etched a few plates, including 'St. Potentiana,' after Correggio, and died in Paris in 1665.

FERDINANDI, FRANCESCO, (or FERNANDI,) called IMPERIALI, an Italian painter, worked at Rome in 1730. There are two works by him at Rome, one is the 'Martyrdom of St. Eustache,' in the church dedicated to that saint, and the other is the 'Death of St. Romuald.'

FERG, FRANZ DE PAULA, a painter and etcher, was born at Vienna in 1689. He was instructed first by his father, Pancrazius Ferg, and afterwards by J. Orient in landscape painting, and by Hans Graf in the drawing of figures. His reputation soon spread through Germany, and he was invited to the court of Dresden, where he passed some years. In 1718 he went from Brunswick to London, where he passed twenty years, and might have lived in affluence and respectability, had not an imprudent marriage involved him in difficulties, and kept him in continual indigence. He is reported to have been found dead in the street, near the door of his lodging, in 1740. The landscapes of Ferg are of very agreeable scenery, enriched with architectural ruins in a very picturesque style, and bear some resemblance to the works of Poelenborch: his scenes from common life resemble those of Ostade. His compositions, which are happily arranged, show great diligence in the execution, and bear the annexed monogram The following are among his paintings :

Brunswick.	*Gallery.*	The Four Seasons.
"	"	A Market Scene.
"	"	A Rural Feast.
Cassel.	*Gallery.*	Sea View.
Dresden.	*Gallery.*	Six Landscapes with ruins and figures.
Florence.	*Uffizi.*	Two small Landscapes.
Hampton Ct.	*Palace.*	Small Landscape.
Vienna.	*Gallery.*	A Fair.

There is a set of eight neat and spirited etchings by Ferg of ruins and figures, called 'Capricci fatti per F. P. F.'

FERGIONE, BERNARDINO, a painter of marine views and sea-ports, is stated by Lanzi to have flourished at Rome about the year 1718. Claude Joseph Vernet studied in Fergione's atelier on his arrival in Rome in 1732.

FERGUSON, JAMES, the Scottish astronomer, born near Keith, in Banffshire, in 1710, was a self-taught man. Though better known as an astronomer, he gained a living in Edinburgh and in England, for several years, by drawing miniature portraits in black lead. He died in 1776.

FERGUSON, WILLIAM GOW, was a native of Scotland, who after learning the first rudiments of art in his own country, passed some years on the continent. On his return to his native country, he acquired some reputation in painting dead game and still-life. He died in London about the year 1695. Some of his smaller pictures are so excellent that they are frequently attributed to Weenix, to whose works they bear strong resemblance. In the Berlin Gallery is a picture of still-life, a dead partridge, and in the National Gallery of Scotland is one of 'Sculptured Ruins and Figures.'

FERNANDEZ, ALEXEO, (or HERNANDEZ,) was a Spanish artist of considerable skill, who at the beginning of the 16th century painted for the convent of St. Jerome at Cordova several altar-pieces from the lives of Christ and the patron Saint, which were considered equal in execution to any contemporary productions. In 1508 he was employed to paint and gild the noble reredos of the high-altar of Seville Cathedral, designed at the close of the previous century by the Flemish architect Dancart. Fernandez remained at Seville until 1525. A 'Madonna with Angels,' in the church of Santa Ana in Seville, is by his hand.

FERNANDEZ, ANTONIO ARIAS. See ARIAS FERNANDEZ.

FERNANDEZ, FRANCISCO, who was born at Madrid in 1605, and brought up in the school of Vincenzo Carducho, was one of the most ingenious artists of his time, and his talent gained great reputation for him at an early age. He was employed by Philip IV. in the palaces at Madrid, and in the convent of La Victoria are pictures by him of the 'Death of St. Francis of Paola,' and 'St. Joachim and St. Anne.' He also etched five spirited plates of allegories for Carducho's 'Dialogos de la Pintura,' 1633. He was killed in a quarrel by Francisco de Baras in 1646.

FERNANDEZ, JUAN ANTONIO RIBERA Y. See RIBERA.

FERNANDEZ, LUIS, (the elder of the name,) was a painter in tempera of Seville, who about the year 1580 was the instructor of the elder Herrera, Juan and Augustin del Castillo, and Francisco Pacheco.

FERNANDEZ, LUIS, a Spanish historical painter, both in oil and in fresco, born at Madrid in 1594, was a pupil of Eugenio Caxes. There are by him in the cross-walk of the convent of La Merced

Calzada scenes from the life of St. Ramon, painted in 1625, and in Santa Cruz were several frescoes and oil paintings, which perished, however, by fire in the 17th century. His works, executed in the style of his master, are distinguished for correctness of design and beauty of colouring. He died at Madrid in 1654.

FERNANDEZ, Vasco, commonly known as Gran Vasco, or Grāo Vasco, ('Vasco the Great,') was a Portuguese painter, who has been variously cited as 'Ferdinand de Vizeu,' 'Gran Vasco de Vizeu,' 'Fernandez Vasco de Cazal,' or simply 'Vasco Pereira,' or 'Vasco Fernandez.' If reliance can be placed on Portuguese testimony, or rather assertion, he was the greatest painter that ever lived; not only are his pictures the most excellent, but the most numerous. All in Portugal that have not secured a name are by Gran Vasco. Zani notices Vasco Pereira, a Portuguese painter, who worked in 1594; and Cean Bermudez has given an account of him among the Spanish artists. Count Raczynski, who was desirous of identifying Vasco Pereira with Gran Vasco, and who examined a small picture by the former, with the date 1575, abandoned that idea, and left the elucidation of the subject to his friend M. J. Berardo. The conclusions at which the latter arrived in 1844, and which do not appear to have been subsequently shaken, were that Gran Vasco is identical with a certain Vasco Fernandez, whose baptismal register shows him to have been the son of a painter named Francisco Fernandez, and to have been born in 1552, and baptized in the church of Vizeu, though it is uncertain whether he was born within that town or in a mill in its vicinity. He flourished during the reign of Dom Sebastian. One of his paintings probably is the 'Christ on the Cross' in the Misericordia at Oporto, which is ascribed to Holbein.

FERNANDEZ DE CASTRO, Antonio, was a canon of Cordova, who painted two pictures of 'St. Ferdinand,' and the 'Virgin of the Immaculate Conception,' for the chapter-room of his cathedral. He died in 1739.

FERNANDEZ DE GUADALUPE, Pedro, a Spanish artist, painted in 1509-12 a number of wooden figures for Seville Cathedral, and in 1527 executed for the same edifice a 'Descent from the Cross,' with the body of the Saviour lying upon the knees of Mary, as well as some other pictures, one of which represented the 'Repentance of St. Peter.'

FERNANDEZ DE LAREDO, Juan, one of the best fresco painters of his time, was born at Madrid in 1632, and studied under Francisco Rizi, whom he assisted in his works at the Retiro. He painted many pictures for the churches at Madrid, where he was killed by a fall in his own studio in 1692.

FERNANDEZ NAVARRETE, Juan, commonly called El Mudo, from having been deaf and dumb, was born at Logroño about 1526. An acute malady at the age of three years deprived him of the sense of hearing, and consequently of the power of learning to speak. He received his first instruction in art from Fray Vicente de Santo Domingo, a monk of the order of St. Jerome, but subsequently went to Italy and studied at Venice under Titian. His sojourn in Italy lasted for at least twenty years, and whilst there he availed himself of the opportunity of visiting the studios of the most renowned masters. Although there is no account of any production of importance by him during his stay in that country,

yet it is certain that he obtained a great reputation among the artists, which no doubt was augmented by the circumstance of his infirmity. The fame of El Mudo, by which name he was known in Italy, reached Philip II., who was commencing the decorations of the Escorial, and he was commanded to attend at Madrid for the purpose of being employed on that work. He arrived there in 1568, and was appointed painter to the king, with an annual pension of 200 ducats, in addition to the price of his works. He had scarcely commenced his labours, when a serious malady compelled him to retire to the country for the benefit of air, and he remained for three years in his native place, Logroño, on leave of absence, but receiving his pension as painter to the king. In 1571 he returned to the Escorial, bringing with him four large pictures which had been commanded, and for which he received 500 ducats. These were an 'Assumption,' the 'Martyrdom of St. James the Great,' a 'St. Philip,' and a 'St. Jerome.' It is believed that in the first the face of the Virgin was the portrait of his mother, Catalina Ximenes, who in her youth had been very beautiful. In addition to these four pictures he painted for the Escorial 'The Nativity,' 'Christ at the Pillar,' a 'Holy Family,' and 'St. John writing the Apocalypse': these he finished in 1575, and for them he received 800 ducats. These eight pictures were Navarrete's principal works: unhappily three of them, the 'Assumption,' 'St. Philip,' and 'St. John,' were destroyed by fire; the other five were saved and placed in the principal cloister of the monastery. Besides their unquestionable merit, each picture is remarkable for some peculiar circumstance. Thus the 'Martyrdom of St. James' and the 'St. Jerome' are most minutely finished; a manner which he did not continue in his other compositions. The 'Christ at the Pillar,' seen in front, is an admirable head, which, by its meekness and beauty, contrasts marvellously with the ignoble features of the flagellators. In the 'Holy Family' the heads are equally beautiful and expressive; but, by a strange caprice, the painter has placed on one side of the fore-ground of the picture a partridge, and on the other, a dog and cat contending for a bone, with such comical contortions that it is impossible to regard them without laughing. In 'The Nativity,' El Mudo essayed to vanquish a formidable difficulty in painting. He has introduced three lights in the picture: the effluence from the holy Infant; that which proceeds from the glory above, and which extends over the whole composition; and that emitted from the torch which Joseph holds in his hand. The group of shepherds is the best part of the picture. It is related that Pellegrino Tibaldi, on seeing it, cried out in raptures, "Oh! gli belli pastori!" This exclamation gave its name to the picture, and it continues to be known as 'The Beautiful Shepherds.' In 1576 El Mudo painted his famous picture of 'Abraham and the three Angels,' for which he received 500 ducats, and about this time he entered into a contract with the prior, inspector, and treasurer of the Escorial, to paint thirty-two pictures, which he engaged to deliver within four years. Twenty-seven of these pictures were to be seven feet and a half in height and seven feet and a quarter in breadth, and the other five thirteen feet high and nine feet broad. In the contract, which is preserved in the archives of the monastery, all the details are specified: for example, the canvas of each is to be of one piece without seam; the work is to be entirely by the hand of Juan Fernandez Navarrete, and to be done either at the convent, at Madrid, or at Logroño; the figures are to be just six feet and a quarter in height; if the same Saint is repeated several times in the pictures he is always to have the same visage and the same vestments; the painter is not to put in the pictures either cat, or dog, or any immodest figure. He did not, however, live to complete this vast undertaking; he painted in 1577 and 1578 the eight which represent the Apostles, the Evangelists, St. Paul, and St. Barnabas; the rest were finished in the following years by Alonso Sanchez Coello and Luis de Caravajal. El Mudo's health had always been delicate, and he died at Toledo in 1579. In the Madrid Gallery there are by him a 'Baptism of Christ,' 'St. Peter,' and 'St. Paul.'

FERNANDI, FRANCESCO. See FERDINANDI.

FERNELEY, J. E., an English animal painter, was born in 1781, and died in 1860. He exhibited hunting pictures at the Royal Academy from 1818 to 1849.

FERON, FIRMIN ELOI, a pupil of Gros, born in Paris in 1802. He gained the grand prize in painting at l'École des Beaux Arts in 1825, and went on soon after that to Rome, where he studied with great earnestness for some considerable time. On his return he executed several pictures for the Gallery at Versailles, amongst which may specially be named, 'The Battles of Arsur,' 'Fornous,' 'Guntersdorff,' and 'Hollabrun.' He also painted 'The taking of Rhodes,' 'The entrance of Charles VIII. into Naples,' 'The arrival of the Duke of Orleans at the Hôtel de Ville, July, 1830,' and some fine portraits of the statesmen of his time. He died in 1876.

FERRABOSCO, GIROLAMO, (FERABOSCO, or FORABOSCO,) a native of Padua, painted at Venice from 1631 to 1659. He was a contemporary of Boschini, who gives to this master, and to the Cavaliere Liberi, the first rank among the Venetian painters of the time. He was more employed for private collections than for the churches, and was much engaged in portrait painting, in which he particularly excelled. Ferrabosco possessed a noble and penetrating genius, and united suavity with finish, and elegance with force; his works were studied in every part, particularly in the heads. He was still living in 1660. In the Dresden Gallery is a picture of 'A Young Woman snatched from the hand of Death.'

FERRACUTI, GIOVANNI DOMENICO, who, according to Lanzi, was a native of Macerata, flourished about the middle of the 17th century. He chiefly painted landscapes, particularly winter-pieces, which were much esteemed in his time.

FERRADO, CRISTOBAL, a Spanish painter, was born at Anieva, in the principality of the Asturias, in 1620. He had acquired some ability from the instruction of an unknown artist, and afterwards developed into an accomplished painter from his own unaided practice. In 1640 he became a monk of the order of Santa Maria de las Cuevas, near Seville. He continued, however, to exercise his art, and painted some pictures for the altars of his monastery. Several of his productions are in the cloister of San Miguel at Seville, and others have been removed to the Alcazar. Towards the end of his life he was made rector of the Carthusian Monastery of Cazaller. He died at Seville in 1673.

FERRAJUOLI, NUNZIO, called NUNZIO DEGLI AFFLITTI, was born at Nocera de' Pagani, in the Neapolitan territory, in 1660. After studying some time under Luca Giordano, he went to Bologna, where he became a scholar of Giuseppe dal Sole. His first efforts were in historical painting; but his genius decidedly led him to landscape in oil and fresco. He died at Bologna in 1735.

FERRAMOLA, FLORIANO, or FIORAVANTE, a native of Brescia, born before 1480, the son of a carpenter named Lorenzo Ferramola and the master of Alessandro Bonvicini (Moretto). Rossi relates of him that when Brescia was sacked by Gaston de Foix in 1512, he remained calmly working at his easel, and being there found by a gang of plunderers who demanded ransom, he, without discontinuing his labours, told them to help themselves, which they quickly did, and left his studio an empty wreck. Happily for the artist his talents gained for him the protection of Gaston de Foix, who ordered him to paint his portrait, and indemnified him for his losses. He was much employed as a fresco-painter in the churches and palaces of Brescia, though very little by him now remains there. In 1514 he painted half-lengths of Apostles on the spandrels of the arches in the nave of S. Maria at Lovere, and between 1516–1518 decorated the organ shutters in the old cathedral of Brescia, which were later removed to S. Faustino Maggiore and eventually to S. Maria at Lovere, where they are still preserved. His frescoes in St. Giulia at Brescia, executed in company with a painter named 'Paolo,' were finished in 1527, and in that year he was painting in the chapel of the Holy Cross in the cathedral at Brescia assisted by his pupil Moretto, but he died before the completion of the work, in 1528. Some critics attribute to him certain of the frescoes in S. Giulia, those in an oratory at the back of the choir in the church of the Carmine, an altar-piece in S. Maria delle Grazie, and other paintings at Brescia. The following may be ascribed to him with certainty:

Berlin.	*Gallery.*	Madonna and Saints, *dated* 1513.
Brescia.	*Carmine. Lunette fresco over W. door.*	The Annunciation.
Lovere.	*S. Maria.*	Frescoes, dated 1514.
"	"	The Annunciation (*outer shutters of the organ*), dated 1518. C. J. Ff.

FERRAND, JACQUES PHILIPPE, who was born at Joigny in Burgundy in 1653, was a miniaturist and painter in enamel. He was the son of a physician to Louis XIII., and studied under Mignard and Samuel Bernard. In 1690 he was received into the Academy, on which occasion he painted a portrait of Louis XIV. He excelled in his art, and published in 1721 a work entitled, 'L'Art du feu, ou manière de peindre en émail.' He travelled in Italy, England, and Germany, and died in Paris in 1732.

FERRANDINI, CLAUDIO, an engraver, worked in Paris and Toulon in the latter part of the 18th century. He engraved landscapes, sea-pieces, and views after Claude, Fontaine, J. Vernet, S. R. Vialy, Teniers, &c. He died about 1790.

FERRANTE, GIOVANNI FRANCESCO, who was born at Bologna about 1600 was a pupil of Gessi.

He executed several works in oil and fresco at Bologna and at Piacenza, where he died in 1652.

FERRANTI, DECIO and AGOSTO, father and son, were painters who flourished about 1500. Both of them painted miniatures exquisitely, and in the cathedral of Vigevano is an Evangeliarium and a Missal richly embellished by them.

FERRANTINI, GABRIELE, called GABRIELE DAGLI OCCHIALI, from his wearing spectacles, was born at Bologna about 1550, and was instructed in the school of Dionysius Calvaert. He painted historical subjects, both in oil and fresco, in a pleasing and tasteful manner. Several of his works are in the churches at Bologna, of which the following are the most esteemed: in San Benedetto, 'St. Francis of Paola'; in San Mattia, a fine picture of 'St. Jerome'; in La Carità, 'St. Francis receiving the Stigmata'; and in the church of the Servites, the 'Descent from the Cross' and the 'Birth of the Virgin.'

FERRANTINI, IPPOLITO, a brother of Gabriele Ferrantini, was instructed by the Carracci, whom he imitated with success. He was a member of the Accademia degli Incaminati. In the church of San Mattia in Bologna is a picture representing 'St. Michael.'

FERRARA, BONO DA, (or BONO FERRARESE,) lived in the 15th century, and seems to have been the pupil of both Pisano and Squarcione. He was employed by the Dukes of Ferrara to decorate their castles at Migliaro and Belfiore, in 1450 and 1452. He also painted a 'St. Christopher' in the chapel of the Eremitani at Padua, and he is said to have assisted in the decorations of the Cathedral of Siena in 1461. The National Gallery possesses a 'St. Jerome in the Desert,' by him, The 'Anonimo Morelliano' refers to his work at Padua, and says that he painted part of the chapel, and that the remaining parts were done by Mantegna and by Ansuino da Forlì. His style partakes of that of his master Squarcione, and also of that of his fellow-pupil Mantegna. Of his birth or death no dates can be given.

FERRARA, COSME DA. See TURA.

FERRARA, ERCOLE DA. See GRANDI.

FERRARESINO, IL. See BERLINGHIERI, CAMILLO.

FERRARI, ANTONIO FELICE, the son of Francesco Ferrari, was born at Ferrara in 1668. He was a painter of architecture, and distinguished himself by the grandeur of his style in the paintings for the palaces at Ferrara, Venice, Padua, and Ravenna. He died in 1720.

FERRARI, BERNARDINO, who was born at Vigevano about 1540, painted at that place the chapels of San Jacopo and San Filippo. He imitated the style of Gaudenzio Ferrari.

FERRARI, DIFENDENTE, a contemporary of Macrino, was a painter of numerous pictures, chief of which are a 'Pietà' in the cathedral of Chivasso, altar-pieces in the cathedral of Ivrea (1519-1521), and a 'Nativity, with Saints' (1531) in the church of Ranverso.

FERRARI, FRANCESCO, born at Castello della Fratta, near Rovigo, in 1634, was a painter of historical subjects, architecture, and landscapes. He was first employed in figure-painting, but afterwards studied decoration and scenery under Gabriele Rossi. He painted for the Marchese degli Obizzi, among other works, the theatre at San Lorenzo in 1650. Subsequently he was engaged upon theatre-decorations at Vienna, and painted in

156

San Francesco, the Gesù, San Giorgio, and the Bucci Mansion at Ferrara, and San Petronio at Bologna, where he executed 'The Martyrdom of St. Sebastian.' He died in 1708.

FERRARI, FRANCESCO BIANCHI, called IL FRARI, an excellent artist, born in 1447, executed many paintings at Modena, but a great number of his productions have perished. A fine picture by him in the Louvre at Paris, representing 'The Madonna enthroned, with Saints and Angels,' bears so striking a resemblance to Correggio's 'St. Francis' in the Dresden Gallery, that it has much strengthened the supposition that Correggio was Ferrari's pupil. He died in 1510.

FERRARI, GAUDENZIO, called by Vasari GAUDENZIO MILANESE, a painter and sculptor of the Lombard school, was born at Valduggia, near Novara, most probably in the year 1484. Nothing is known of his early years, or as to who was his first master, though he seems at one time to have been a pupil of Luini. That he was instructed in the principles of art by Girolamo Giovenone at Vercelli is a supposition devoid of foundation, but he studied under Stefano Scotto, a painter of arabesques, at Milan. His greatest advance was, however, derived from an attentive study of the works of Leonardo da Vinci. There is no proof that he was acquainted with Perugino or Raphael, or that he was at Rome, and painted in conjunction with the latter in the Farnesina and in the Vatican in 1519 and 1520. This devotion to the study of such models developed his great talent so rapidly as to cause him so early as in 1504 to be appointed for the execution of a considerable work in the Cappella del Sacro Monte at Varallo, representing the 'Sacrifice of Christ.' In 1508 he was at Vercelli. In 1510 he painted for the commune of Arona a picture in six compartments, the subject of the principal one being 'The Virgin adoring the Infant.' This, and others of his early works, was signed 'Gaudenzio di Vincio.' At Varallo he displayed great activity, and executed a considerable number of paintings and sculptures. He was also the instructor of many artists, as, Andrea Solario, Bernardino Lanini, Firmo Stello, Cesare Luini, and Antonio Zanotti. From 1527 until his death at Milan, where he left unfinished a 'Last Supper' in Santa Maria della Passione, he painted in oil and fresco in several churches in that city and its neighbourhood. There exists a great number of frescoes by Gaudenzio, which are scarcely inferior to those of his pupil Luini, with whom he painted from 1532 to 1535 in San Cristoforo at Vercelli. The latest mention of him is in 1545, and it is probable that he died at Milan in 1549 or 1550. The different styles of the great masters after whom he studied are very discernible in his works, while here and there he becomes fantastical and odd. He undoubtedly possessed an extraordinary fertility of invention, together with an elevation of style, and these characteristics have caused him to be considered one of the first painters of his time. His works are not so distinguishable for a correct delineation of muscular anatomy as for a choice of difficult and uncommon attitudes, which are bold and striking where the subject admits. The following is a list of several of his works:

Arona.	*Church.*	Madonna and Child.
Berlin.	*Gallery.*	The Annunciation.
Busto Arsizio, near Milan.	*Church.*	Several frescoes.

GAUDENZIO FERRARI

THE CHOIR OF ANGELS

Anderson photo

[*Saronno*

GAUDENZIO FERRARI

THE MARTYRDOM OF ST. CATHARINE

Cannobbio, Lago Maggiore.	Church.	Christ bearing the Cross.
Como.	Cathedral.	Marriage of Mary and Joseph.
,,	,,	The Flight into Egypt (in tempera).
London.	Mr. Holford.	The Virgin and Angels adoring the Infant.
Milan.	Brera.	Martyrdom of St. Catharine.
,,	,,	Scenes in the Life of the Virgin; in fresco. (Formerly in Santa Maria della Pace.)
,,	,,	Adoration of the Magi.
,,	,,	An Angel with a Harp.
,,	,,	An Angel with a Lute.
,,	,,	Presentation in the Temple.
,,	S. Ambrogio.	Virgin and Saints.
,,	S. M. delle Grazie.	The Flagellation of Christ. The Crucifixion. 1542.
,,	S. M. della Passione.	The Last Supper. Unfinished. 1543.
,,	S. M. presso S. Celso.	Baptism of Christ.
Novara.	Cathedral.	An Altar-piece. 1524.
,,	S. Gaudenzio.	The Virgin enthroned, surrounded by Saints.
Paris.	Louvre.	The Apostle Paul. 1543. (Formerly in Santa Maria delle Grazie, Milan.)
Saronno, near Milan.	Pilgrimage Church.	A Glory of Angels; in the cupola. 1535.
Turin.	Gallery.	Christ bewailed.
,,	,,	St. Peter.
,,	,,	St. Joachim driven from the Temple.
,,	,,	Meeting of the Virgin and St. Elizabeth.
Varallo.	Cappella del Sacro Monte.	The Sacrifice of Christ. 1504.
,,	Collegiata.	Marriage of St. Catharine.
,,	,,	The Procession of the Magi.
,,	S. M. delle Grazie.	Pietà. 1504.
,,	S. M. di Loretto.	Scenes in the Life of Christ. Adoration of the Infant.
Vercelli.	S. Cristoforo.	The Birth of Mary, The Annunciation, The Visitation, The Adoration of the Magi and the Shepherds, The Crucifixion, The Ascension of the Virgin, Madonna with Angels and Saints. 1532–1534.
,,	S. Paolo.	The Last Supper.

FERRARI, GIOVANNI ANDREA, GREGORIO, LORENZO, and ORAZIO DEI. See DEI FERRARI.

FERRARI, LEONARDO, called LONARDINO, was a native of Bologna, and a scholar of Lucio Massari. Although he is chiefly noticed by Malvasia as a painter of drolleries and carnival festivals, he acquired no little reputation by his historical works, of which there are several in the churches at Bologna. In SS. Gervasio e Protasio is a picture of the 'Virgin of the Rosary, with Mary Magdalen, and other Saints'; in San Francesco, the 'Death of St. Joseph'; and in La Madonna della Neve, 'St. Anthony of Padua.'

FERRARI, LUCA, called LUCA DA REGGIO, was born at Reggio in 1603. He had the advantage of studying under Guido Reni; and in the airs of his heads, and the elegant movement of his figures, he approaches the graceful style of his instructor. One of his most esteemed works is a 'Pietà,' in the church of Sant' Antonio at Padua; it is full of character and expression, and admirably coloured. In compositions which require a multiplicity of figures he is less successful, as appears in his

picture of 'The Plague,' at the Dominicans, painted in 1630. He was the instructor of Minorello and Cirello, the former of whom is often confounded with Luca, from the great resemblance of his works to those of his master. Luca da Reggio died at Padua in 1652. In the Estense Gallery at Modena are a 'Magdalen,' 'The Death of Cleopatra,' and 'Tomyris, Queen of the Massagetae, placing the head of Cyrus, King of the Persians, in a bottle filled with blood,' and in the Bordeaux Museum is 'Painting crowned by Fame.'

FERRARI, PIETRO, a native of Parma, was instructed by Giuseppe Baldrighi. He was a professor of the Academy of his native city, and imitated the old masters of that school rather than his instructor. He died in 1787.

FERRARO, FRANCESCO DEL BIANCHO. See BIANCHI.

FERRER, GARCIA, the Licentiate, an ecclesiastic and painter of some reputation at Valencia, executed some pictures for the altar of San Vicente Ferrer in the convent of San Domingo, and practised his art at Madrid. Cean Bermudez mentions a 'Crucifixion' by him, dated 1632, then in the possession of Don Mariano Ferrer, secretary of the Academy of San Carlos.

FERRERS, BENJAMIN, a portrait painter, flourished about the middle of the 18th century. He was deaf and dumb. Amongst his works are portraits of Bishop Hoadly and Bishop Beveridge; the latter is in the Bodleian Library, Oxford.

FERRETTI, GIOVANNI DOMENICO, called GIOVANNI DOMENICO DA IMOLA, was born at Florence in 1692. He was a scholar of Giovanni Gioseffo dal Sole, and painted historical subjects, both in oil and fresco, with considerable success. His works are principally in the palaces and churches of Imola, Leghorn, Siena, Florence, and Pisa. He also painted the cupola of the Filippini, at Pistoja. One of his best pictures is 'The Martyrdom of St. Bartholomew,' in the church dedicated to that apostle at Pisa.

FERRI, CIRO, an Italian historical painter, was born at Rome in 1634. He was the most distinguished scholar of Pietro da Cortona, with whom he executed many paintings, and whose style he imitated with a servility that renders it sometimes difficult to distinguish his works from those of his instructor, from which they only differ in their inferiority. He was patronized and employed by Prince Borghese and Pope Alexander VII., for whom he executed several works. The Grand-Duke Cosmo III. invited him to Florence to finish the great fresco works which were left imperfect by Pietro da Cortona, and in this he was so successful, that they appeared to be the production of one hand. Ferri died in 1689. The following are his most important paintings:

Amsterdam.	Museum.	Marriage of the Virgin.
Bergamo.	S. Maria Maggiore.	Scenes from the Bible. His largest work.
Copenhagen.	Gallery.	David refusing the Armour.
Darmstadt.	Gallery.	The Rape of Helen.
Dresden.	Gallery.	Dido and Æneas.
,,	,,	Dido dying on the funeral pile.
Florence.	Pitti Pal.	Frescoes (commenced by Pietro da Cortona).
,,	Uffizi.	Christ on the Cross.
,,	,,	Alexander on his couch reading Homer.
Hampton Court.	Pal.	Triumph of Bacchus.
Modena.	Estense Gall.	Coriolanus besought by his family not to besiege Rome.
,,	,,	A Roman Warrior.

157

Munich.	Gallery.	The Rest on the Flight to Egypt. Madonna and Child.
Nuremberg.	Landauer Brüderhaus.	The Holy Family.
"	"	Rebekah and Elieser at the Well.
Petersburg.	Hermitage.	Vision of St. Catharine of Siena.
Rome.	S. Ambrogio della Massima.	St. Ambrose healing a sick person. *His best work.*
"	S. Agnese.	The Cupola (*finished by Corbellini*).
"	Vatican.	Designs for the mosaics in the cupola of the right nave in St. Peter's.
Vienna.	Gallery.	Christ appearing to Mary Magdalen.

FERRI, GESUALDO, born at San Miniato in 1728, was still living in 1776. He was a pupil of Pompeo Batoni, and his works are to be found in Florence and other places. Among them is an 'Exaltation' in the Carmine Church in Florence.

FERRIÈRE, F. and L., father and son, of Swiss extraction, were miniature painters, who practised in London. The former exhibited at the Royal Academy from 1793 to 1822, and the latter from 1817 to 1828.

FERRONI, GIROLAMO, a painter and etcher, was born at Milan in 1687. It is not stated who was his first instructor in art; but at an early period of his life he painted the 'Death of St. Joseph,' for the church of Sant' Eustorgio, at Milan; and afterwards visited Rome, where he entered the school of Carlo Maratti. He died about 1730. There are some spirited and tasteful etchings by this artist, after C. Maratti, including the following:

Joshua stopping the course of the Sun.
Deborah celebrating the Victory over Sisera.
Jael slaying Sisera.
The Chastity of Joseph.
Judith with the Head of Holofernes.
St. Charles Borromeo; *after S. Cantarini.*

FERRUCCI, NICODEMO, was a native of Fiesole, and the favourite disciple and friend of Domenico Passignano, whose spirited style and facility of execution he emulated. He accompanied that master to Rome, and assisted him in his most important undertakings. He chiefly excelled as a fresco painter; and many of his works are in the public edifices at Florence and Fiesole, as well as in the neighbourhood of Rome. He died in 1650.

FERTÉ, M. DE LA. See DE LA FERTÉ.

FESEL, CHRISTOPH, born at Ochsenfurt in 1737, distinguished himself as a painter of historical subjects and portraits. After having studied some time under Mengs and Battoni at Rome, he returned to Germany, and painted a number of easel-pictures for churches, besides frescoes. All his works are of a bright colouring. He was professor at the Academy of St. Luke at Rome, and died at Würzburg, where he was court-painter and inspector of the Gallery, in 1805.

FESELEN, MELCHIOR, an historical painter, of Passau, lived at the same time as Altdorfer, whose works he imitated with assiduity. Though he was inferior to that artist, his paintings are rich in composition, with a great number of figures highly finished, and in a style quite peculiar to himself. He died at Ingolstadt in 1538. Among his paintings (marked with the annexed monogram) **MF.** there are:

Darmstadt.	Gallery.	The Crucifixion.
Munich.	Gallery.	The Siege of Rome by Porsena. 1529.
Munich.	Gallery.	Cæsar conquering the town Alesia in Gaul. 1533.
Nuremberg.	Museum.	The Adoration of the Magi. 1531.
Ratisbon.	Hist. Soc.	St. Mary of Egypt.

FESSARD, ETIENNE, a French engraver, was born in Paris in 1714. He was a pupil of Edme Jeaurat, and proved an artist of sufficient merit to be appointed one of the engravers to the king. He died in Paris in 1774. He executed a considerable number of plates, among which are the following:

PORTRAITS.

Hortensia Mancini, Duchess of Mazarin; *after Ferdinand.*
Marie Madeleine de Lavergne, Countess de La Fayette; *after the same.*
J. P. de Bougainville, of the French Academy; *after C. N. Cochin.*
The Marquis de Mirabeau; *after Van Loo.*
The Duke de Choiseul; *after the same.*

SUBJECTS AFTER VARIOUS MASTERS.

Diana and Actæon; *after Giacomo Bassano;* for the Crozat Collection.
The Virgin enthroned, with SS. Francis, John, and Catharine; *after Correggio.*
The Holy Family, with St. Charles Borromeo; *after Scarsellino.*
The Four Liberal Arts, personified by Children; four plates; *after C. van Loo.*
Jupiter and Antiope; *after the same.* 1758.
Herminia armed as Clorinda; *after J. B. Pierre.*
The Birth of Venus; *after F. de Troy.*
Jupiter and Leda; *after the same.*
The Triumph of Galatea; *after Bouchardon;* etched by *Count de Caylus,* and finished by *Fessard.*
The Triumph of Bacchus; *after the same;* etched by *Count de Caylus,* and finished by *Fessard.*
The Nativity; *after Boucher.*
A Flemish Festival; *after Rubens.* 1762.
Psyche abandoned by Cupid; *after Le Moine.*

FETI, DOMENICO, born at Rome in 1589, was a scholar of Lodovico Cardi, called Cigoli. While still very young he went to Mantua with Cardinal Ferdinando Gonzaga, afterwards Duke of Mantua, by whom he was much patronized, and who subsequently appointed him his principal painter. In this city he studied the works of Giulio Romano, and at Venice, to which city he went afterwards, the masters of the Venetian school. He represented scenes from the Bible and from mythology, as well as from life; but his oil paintings are superior to his frescoes. This able artist was unfortunately addicted to intemperance and excess, to which he fell a victim, at Venice, in 1624. The following are among his principal works:

Berlin.	Gallery.	Elijah in the Wilderness.
Brunswick.	Museum.	The Expulsion of Hagar.
"	"	The Return of the Prodigal.
Dresden.	Gallery.	The Martyrdom of St. Agnes.
"	"	David with the Head of Goliath.
"	"	The Return of the Prodigal.
"	"	Young Tobias pulling the Fish out of the Water.
"	"	Several Parables.
Edinburgh.	Nat. Gall.	The Beheading of St. John the Baptist.
Florence.	Corsini Pal.	Christ praying in the Garden.
"	"	Christ presented to the People by Pontius Pilate.
"	"	The Crowning with Thorns.
"	"	The Entombment.
"	Pitti Pal.	The Labourers in the Vineyard.
"	"	The Lost Coin.
"	Uffizi.	Artemisia.
Frankfort.	Städel.	The Visitation.
"	"	The Flight into Egypt.

Hampton Court. *Palace.* David with the Head of Goliath.
Mantua. *Academy.* The Miracle of the Loaves.
" *Cathedral.* Frescoes.
Modena. *Estense Gall.* The Virgin enthroned.
Munich. *Gallery.* Herminia.
" " St. Peter.
" " Tancred lying wounded in the arms of his Esquire.
Paris. *Louvre.* Nero.
" " Rural Life.
" " Melancholy.
" " The Guardian Angel.
Petersburg. *Hermitage.* The Adoration of the Shepherds.
" " Portrait of a Comedian.
" " David.
" " The Conception.
" " The Young Tobias healing his Father.
" " Dædalus and Icarus.
Venice. *Academy.* Melancholy.
Vienna. *Gallery.* A Market-place.
" " The Flight into Egypt.
" " The dead Leander.
" " Moses and the burning Bush.
" " The Marriage of St. Catharine.
" " The Triumph of Galatea.
" " St. Margaret.

FEUERBACH, ANSELM, a German historical painter, the son of a well-known archæologist, was born at Spires in 1829, and after his father's removal to Freiburg, he went, when seventeen years of age, to Düsseldorf, and there first studied art under the tuition of Schadow. But the religious sentiment of that school being little to his taste, he left Düsseldorf in 1848, and went to Munich, where, as a pupil of Genelli, he first disclosed that classical taste which afterwards gave him his high position in the ranks of art. In 1850 he betook himself to the Antwerp Academy, and in the following year to Paris, where he first worked under Couture, but afterwards quite independently. He did not, however, remain long in that city, for in 1853 we find him removing to Carlsruhe, in 1854 to Venice, and in 1855 to Rome.

The earliest of Feuerbach's productions of which we find mention is his 'Sea Nymph,' painted while studying under Genelli at Munich. Then in 1852, at Paris, he executed his graceful and natural 'Hafis at the Fountain'; at Carlsruhe, in 1853, his 'Death of Pietro Aretino,' which proved a most striking picture through the strong individualities of the characters, and the grandeur and comprehensiveness of the design. At Venice he copied Titian's 'Ascension,' and also painted poetical subjects, in which he developed a further advance in the direction of his previous picture. At Rome, in 1857, appeared his 'Dante with the noble Ladies of Ravenna,' now in the Carlsruhe Gallery, a production characterized by loftiness of conception together with depth of thought; in 1861, his 'Iphigenia in Tauris,' and 'Francesca da Rimini'; and in 1862, a magnificent and solemn 'Pietà.' At Vienna he painted upon the ceiling of the Museum of Modelling a powerful original design of 'The Titans.' His death occurred at Venice in 1880. Among his other works are the following:

Medea.
Orpheus and Eurydice.
Petrarch and Laura.
Ariosto in the Park of Ferrara.
The Boy Musicians. 1865.
The Banquet of Plato. 1869.
Medea going into Exile. 1870.
The Judgment of Paris. 1871.
The Battle of the Amazons. 1872.

Iphigenia. (*Stuttgart Gallery.*)
Romeo and Juliet.
Melancholy.
The Fall of the Titans.

FEURLEIN, JOHANN PETER, who was born at Boxberg in 1668, was instructed in painting by Oswald Onghers, and visited Vienna and Venice. He died at Anspach in 1728. He was an excellent painter of portraits and historical pieces, among which may be mentioned:

The portrait of the Emperor Joseph I.
The paintings in the Castles of the Duke of Saxe-Hildburghausen and the Margrave of Anspach.

FÈVRE, ROBERT LE. See LEFÈVRE.

FÈVRE, CLAUDE LE. See LEFEBURE.

FÈVRE, FRANÇOIS LE. See LE FÈVRE.

FÈVRE, ROLAND LE. See LEFÈVRE.

FÈVRE, VALENTIN LE. See LE FÈBRE.

FEYEN-PERRIN, FRANÇOIS NICOLAS AUGUSTIN, painter, was born in 1829 at Bey-sur-Seille (Meurthe et Moselle). As a child he displayed a precocious artistic gift, and after a short period of study at Nancy, he entered the École des Beaux Arts in Paris, and became the pupil of Cogniet and of Yvon. His first works were scenes for the Théâtre Italien; he then devoted himself to history, but his narrow means forced him to turn his attention to portraiture and studies of peasant life, in which he achieved great excellence. His best works are perhaps his 'Return from Oyster Fishing' (in the Luxembourg), 'La Vanneuse' (painted 1867), 'Les Cancalaises,' 'The Road to the Market,' a portrait of M. Alphonse Daudet, and a 'Death of Orpheus.' He was also an etcher of some ability. He died in 1888.

FEYERABEND, SIGMUND, born in 1527 or 1528, was a bookseller at Frankfort. To him are attributed the woodcuts from the designs of Virgil Solis in a German Bible printed at Frankfort in 1561, and the portraits of the Doges of Venice in Kellner's 'Chronica,' also printed at Frankfort in 1574. He died after the year 1585. He signed his cuts with *SF* or a monogram. Several of his relations also were wood-engravers, and one of them, M. FEYERABEND, who worked about 1578, executed several figures after Melchior Lorch.

FIACCO, ORLANDO, (or FLACCO,) a native of Verona, who flourished about 1560, was instructed by Francesco Torbido, called Il Moro. His style much resembles that of Badile. Vasari praises his portraits, and Lanzi says that his forms resemble those of Caravaggio. There are by him at Verona, in San Nazario, a 'Crucifixion' and an 'Ecce Homo.'

FIALETTI, ODOARDO, was born at Bologna in 1573. After studying for some time under Giovanni Battista Cremonini, at Bologna, he went to Rome, and afterwards to Venice, where he entered the school of Tintoretto. He died at Venice in 1638. His principal paintings are in San Marco and Sant' Andrea at Murano. Boschini mentions thirty-eight pictures by this painter, in the different churches at Venice. At Hampton Court Palace are 'Senators of Venice in the Senate House,' and 'Four Doges of Venice,' both of which were brought direct from Venice by Sir Henry Wotton, and by him bequeathed to Charles I. He also etched 243 plates from his own designs, and after other masters. These are usually marked with the cipher ⚷, and among them are the following:

A long frieze, with Tritons, Sirens, &c.

Venus and Cupid, Diana hunting, the god Pan, and a Man holding a Vase ; *after Pordenone.*

The Pastimes of Love, twenty plates, entitled 'Scherzi d'Amore.' 1617.

A set of plates of the Costumes of different Nations, and of the different Religious Orders. 1626.

The Marriage at Cana ; *after Tintoretto.*

St. Sebastian ; *after the same.*

Designs of all the parts of the Human Body.

Designs for Sieges

A Book on Fortification and Instructions for Fighting, in forty-three plates. 1628.

FIAMMINGHINO, GIAMBATTISTA, GIOVANNI MAURO, and MARCO. See ROVERE.

FIAMMINGO (FIAMINGO, FIAMMINGHO, or FLAMMINGO). This is a general name given by the Italians to Flemish artists, but they are so numerous that it is difficult to distinguish the Fiamminghi in the Italian writers. Zani names no less than sixty-four.

FIAMMINGO, ANSELMO, who flourished about 1680, was instructed by Luca Giordano. He was a most successful copyist of his master.

FIAMMINGO, ARRIGO, probably a native of Mechlin, was born about 1523. His family name is not known ; but he is called by the Italians Fiammingo (Fleming), on account of his nationality. He visited Rome in the time of Gregory XIII., and was employed by that pontiff in the Vatican. In the Sistine Chapel of the basilica of Santa Maria Maggiore there is a 'Resurrection of Christ' restored by him from the original of Domenico Ghirlandajo, but it has lost all trace of the style of that master. In La Madonna degli Angeli is a picture by this master of 'Christ and Mary Magdalen in the house of the Pharisee,' a grand composition, of many figures ; and in the same church is a fine picture of 'St. Michael discomfiting the rebel Angels,' designed in a grand and noble style. Many other works of this painter, in oil and fresco, are in the public edifices at Rome, where he died in 1601.

FIAMMINGO, CORNELIO. See CORT.

FIAMMINGO, DIONISIO. See CALVAERT.

FIAMMINGO, ENRICO, first studied under Giuseppe Ribera, called Spagnoletto, but was afterwards a scholar of Guido. There are some works by this artist, in the style of Guido, in the church of San Barbaziano, at Bologna.

FIAMMINGO, GIOVANNI MAURO. See ROVERE.

FIAMMINGO, GUALTIERI and GIORGIO. These two artists painted for the churches of Florence a great number of windows after the designs of Vasari. It is supposed that these glass-painters, mentioned by Vasari, are identical with Dirk and Wouter Crabeth of Gouda.

FIAMMINGO, GUGLIELMO, a scholar of Francesco Albani, painted in the style of that master at Bologna about 1660. His productions are remarkable for the landscapes.

FIAMMINGO, PAOLO. See FRANCESCHI.

FIAMMINGO, ROBERTO. See ROBERT LE LONGE.

FIASELLA, DOMENICO, called IL SARZANA (or SARAZANA), was born at Sarzana, in the Genoese state, about 1589. After passing some time in the school of Giovanni Battista Paggi, he went to Rome, where he studied attentively the works of Raphael. During a residence of ten years at Rome he was employed in several works conjointly with Passignano and the Cavaliere d'Arpino. On his return to Genoa he painted a great number of pictures for the churches in that city. His

160

powers were best adapted to the depicting of tragic scenes. As a colourist he is superior to the generality of the Genoese painters. He distinguished himself also as a portrait painter, and died in 1669. His principal works are :

Genoa.	*S. Sebastiano.*	St. Anthony finding the dead body of St. Paul the Hermit.
„	*S. Agostino.*	St. Thomas of Villanuova.
Piacenza.	*S. Vincenzo.*	St. Bernard (*in the manner of Raphael*).
Sarzana	*Cathedral.*	The Murder of the Innocents.

FICAROLO, IL MUTO DI. See SARTI.

FICATELLI, STEFANO, who was born at Cento about 1630, and died at the beginning of the 18th century, was a pupil of Guercino. He executed some pictures for the churches in Ferrara, but his chief works are his copies after Guercino.

FICHEL, EUGÈNE, French genre painter of distinction ; born 1826 ; as a lad entered the studio of Paul Delaroche ; began as a historical painter, but soon preferred to devote himself to genre, taking the famous leader of this school, Meisonnier, as his model. He obtained a medal at the Salon of 1857, and continued to exhibit up to the date of his death small canvases, executed with the utmost finesse, dealing with eighteenth-century life. Of his pictures the best known are, 'Le Cabaret de Pamponneau,' 'La Partie aux Cartes,' 'Soldats et Grisettes,' 'La Forge de Louis XVI.,' 'La Carte à Payer,' 'Diderot et le neveu de Rameau,' 'Buffon écrivant son Histoire Naturelle,' &c. Fichel was a Chevalier of the Legion of Honour. He died in Paris, aged 69, in February 1895.

FICHERELLI, FELICE, called FELICE RIPOSO, born at San Gimignano in 1605, was a pupil of Jacopo da Empoli. He acquired the name of Felice Riposo from his singular taciturnity, for which he was not more remarkable than for his uncommon indolence. This inertness is more to be regretted, as the few works he has left are distinguished by an elegance of design, a 'morbidezza,' a truth to nature, and a harmony of colour that charm. Such is his picture of 'Adam and Eve driven from Paradise,' in the Rinuccini Palace, and his 'St. Anthony,' in the church of Santa Maria Nuova, at Florence. His copies after Perugino, Andrea del Sarto, and others, have been mistaken for the works of those masters. He died in 1660. In the Dresden Gallery is a 'Lucretia and Tarquinius' by him.

FICQUET, ETIENNE, a French engraver, was born in Paris in 1719, and was instructed by G. F. Schmidt and Le Bas. He acquired great reputation by a set of small portraits which he engraved of distinguished literary characters of France. They are executed with extraordinary neatness and delicacy, and are very correctly drawn. One of his best plates is a portrait of Madame de Maintenon, after Mignard, now become very scarce. He engraved also several of the plates for Descamps' 'Vie des Peintres Flamands et Hollandais,' of which those of Rubens and Van Dyck are very highly finished. He died in Paris in 1794. The following are among his best prints :

Françoise d'Aubigné ; *after P. Mignard.*

J. de La Fontaine ; *after Rigaud.*

J. F. Regnard ; *after the same.*

J. J. Rousseau ; *after De La Tour.* 1763.

F. M. Arouet de Voltaire ; *after the same.* 1762

Pierre Corneille ; *after Le Brun.*

J. de Crébillon ; *after Aved.*

J. B. P. de Molière ; *after Coypel.*

René Descartes ; *after F. Hals.*

A. V. COPLEY FIELDING

VIEW IN SUSSEX

M. Montaigne; *after Dumonstier.* 1772.
De La Mothe Le Vayer; *after Nanteuil.*
F. de La Mothe Fénélon; *after Vivien.*
J. J. Vadé; *after Richard.*
P. P. Rubens; *after Van Dyck.*
Anton Van Dyck; *after the same.*

FICTOORS, JAN. See VICTOORS.

FIDANI, ORAZIO, a native of Florence, was born about 1610, and died shortly after 1642. He was a pupil of Giovanni Biliverti, whose style he imitated. Several of his pictures are to be found in Florence, among which may be named 'The Four Doctors' and 'The Four Evangelists' in the church of the Chartreuse. The Corsini Gallery possesses two portraits.

FIDANZA, FILIPPO, born at Sabina in 1720, was instructed in painting by Marco Benefial at Rome. Subsequently he studied and imitated the great masters, and many works by him of that description are still to be met with at Rome. He died in 1790.

FIDANZA, FRANCESCO, the son of Filippo Fidanza, was born at Milan in 1749. He studied under Vernet and Lacroix, and excelled in landscape painting. For Eugène Beauharnais he painted the Italian Harbours, two of which, Ancona and Malamocco, with a landscape, are in the Brera at Milan. He died at Milan in 1819.

FIDANZA, GREGORIO, brother of Francesco Fidanza, was a disciple of Claude Lorrain and Salvator Rosa, whom he imitated with success in his landscapes. He died in 1820.

FIDANZA, PAOLO, an Italian painter and engraver, of Rome, was born at Camerino in 1731, and studied after the great masters at Rome, from whose paintings he executed a series of heads. There are by him several plates after Raphael, Annibale Carracci, and Guido Reni, but very indifferently executed; among them are the following:

Mount Parnassus; *after Raphael.*
The Mass of Bolsena; *after the same.*
The Descent from the Cross; *after Annibale Carracci.*
St. Peter and St. Paul appearing to St. Francis; *after the same.*

FIEBIGER, JULIUS, a Saxon landscape painter, was born at Bautzen in 1813, and died at Dresden in 1883. There is a landscape by this painter in the Dresden Gallery.

FIEDLER, JOHANN CHRISTIAN, born at Pirna in 1697, was a painter of portraits, who studied in Paris under Rigaud and Largillière. As court-painter at Darmstadt, where he died in 1768, he executed the portraits of a number of distinguished personages. Among his productions in the Gallery of that town are 'The Burial of Christ,' 'The Seasons,' some portraits, among which is the artist himself, and some fruit and fish pieces.

FIELDING, ANTHONY VANDYKE COPLEY, an eminent water-colour landscape painter, was born in 1787. He was the second son of Theodore Nathan Fielding, and studied under John Varley. In 1810 he became an Associate of the Water-Colour Society, to the exhibitions of which he was a very large contributor. He became a full member of the Society in 1813, treasurer in 1817, secretary in 1818, and was president from 1831 until his death. He was awarded a gold medal at the Paris Salon of 1824. The public appreciation of his art, and a large teaching connection, enabled him to amass a considerable fortune, and in his later years he retired to Brighton. He died at Hove, and was buried in the parish churchyard there in

1855. His works are clever, although the rapidity with which they are executed—he frequently exhibited more than forty in one year at the Water-Colour Society—renders them slight. He is seen at his best in his sea-pieces and aërial effects. He occasionally painted in oil, and some of his works in this medium appeared at the Royal Academy. There is a large collection of his water-colour drawings in the South Kensington Museum.

FIELDING, JOHN, an engraver, was born about 1758. He studied under Bartolozzi and Ryland, for the latter of whom he worked much, so that few plates bear his own name; of these are 'Jacob and Rachael,' after Stothard, and 'Moses saved by Pharaoh's Daughter.'

FIELDING, NEWTON, a water-colour painter and an engraver, was the youngest son of Theodore Nathan Fielding. He painted animals, but he is chiefly known as an engraver and lithographer. His practice was large in France, where he had a considerable reputation. He died in 1856.

FIELDING, THALES, a water-colour painter, born in 1793, was a younger son of Theodore Nathan Fielding. He painted landscapes, with cattle and figures, and became drawing-master at the Woolwich Military Academy. He died in London in 1837. At the South Kensington Museum is a water-colour drawing, 'Greenwich Hill,' by him.

FIELDING, THEODORE HENRY ADOLPHUS, a water-colour painter, the eldest son of Theodore Nathan Fielding, was born in 1781. He exhibited occasionally at the Royal Academy, and became drawing master at Addiscombe Military College. He also wrote several works on the theory and practice of painting, engraving, and perspective. He died at Croydon in 1851. At the South Kensington Museum is a water-colour drawing of 'Manorbeer Castle' by him. His wife was a member of the Water-Colour Society, and from 1821 till 1835 exhibited drawings of flowers, birds, insects, &c. at its exhibitions.

FIELDING, THEODORE NATHAN, a portrait painter, had considerable practice in the latter half of the 18th century in Yorkshire and Lancashire. He was the father of the four water-colour painters, Theodore, Copley, Thales, and Newton Fielding.

FIELIUS, JAN. See FILICUS.

FIESOLE, Fra BENEDETTO DA, called also BENEDETTO DA MUGELLO, who was born at the village of Vicchio, in the province of Mugello, was a brother—probably younger—of the celebrated Fra Angelico, and with him entered the convent of San Domenico at Fiesole, in 1407, taking the name of 'Frater Benedictus,' by which he is usually known. For three years previous to his death, which occurred in 1448, he held the post of superior of that convent. Fra Benedetto was a miniaturist of talent. He illuminated the choral books of San Marco, Florence, and also books in the convent of San Domenico, Fiesole. He is supposed also to have assisted Fra Angelico in his frescoes in San Marco.

FIESOLE, Frate GIOVANNI DA, commonly, from the piety of his life and works, called FRA ANGELICO, was born at Vicchio, in the province of Mugello, in 1387. His father's Christian name was Pietro, his surname is unrecorded. He was christened Guido, and both he and his brother Benedetto entered the Dominican convent of Fiesole, near Florence, in 1407, when Guido took the name of Giovanni. His earliest works, it is believed, were illuminations for manuscripts. His novitiate was passed at Cortona, and at Cortona were spent the early years of his life as a religious, in consequence of the fact that the brotherhood were driven from Florence by the Archbishop for their allegiance to Gregory XII. He probably returned with the Dominicans to Fiesole in 1418, and remained there eighteen years, during which he executed many paintings and frescoes for the convent and churches. Amongst them may be mentioned 'The Madonna dei Linajuoli,' a triptych, painted in 1433, and now in the Uffizi Gallery. About 1436 he went to the monastery of San Marco, at Florence, which owed so much of its splendour to the liberality of Cosmo de' Medici ; and in 1439 he painted the altar-piece for the choir, which is now in the Academy of Arts. The numerous frescoes with which Fra Angelico has adorned the church and convent have rendered it for ever famous, and have so often been described and illustrated that it is unnecessary here to enlarge on them. He was engaged on the work about six years. In 1446 or early in 1447 he went, at the invitation of Pope Eugenius IV., to Rome, and shortly afterwards he was offered the Archbishopric of Florence, which through modesty he declined. In 1447 he visited Orvieto, where he painted 'The Last Judgment' in the Cappella Nuova of the cathedral. The subjects are 'The Saviour in the midst of a glory of Angels,' and sixteen figures of Saints and Prophets. He only painted a small portion of the vaulted roof of this chapel, which was subsequently adorned with frescoes by Signorelli in 1499. On his return to Rome he was employed by Nicholas V. to decorate with frescoes the chapel in the Vatican which bears his name ; these illustrate the lives of St. Stephen and St. Lawrence. Fra Angelico died at Rome in 1455, and was buried in the church of Santa Maria sopra Minerva in that city. The following are his principal works :

Berlin.	*Gallery.*	The Last Judgment (*a triptych*).
Boston.	*Mrs. J. L. Gardner's Collection.*	Assumption and Dormition of the Virgin (*a small panel, believed to be one of four reliquary pictures originally at S. Maria Novella*).
Cortona.	*San Domenico.*	The Virgin and Child, and the Four Evangelists (*fresco, much damaged*).
"	"	Virgin and Child, with Saints (*altar-piece: the predella is in the Baptistery, Cortona*).
"	*Baptistery (formerly the Oratorio del Jesu).*	Annunciation, with scenes from the Life of the Virgin.
"	"	Life of St. Dominic (*the predella of the altar-piece in San Domenico, Cortona*).
Dublin.	*National Gall.*	Martyrdom of St. Cosmo and St. Damian.
Florence.	*Academy.*	Descent from the Cross (*from Santa Trinità, Florence*).
"	"	The Virgin and Child, with Saints ; and, on the predella, a Pietà and Six Saints (*from the Convent of S. Buonaventura al Bosco in the Mugello*).
"	"	The Virgin and Child, with Saints (*from the Convent of San Marco*).
"	"	The Virgin and Child, with Saints (*from the Monastery of Annalena, Florence*).
"	"	Thirty-five scenes from the Life of Christ (*from the Convent of*

		the SS. Annunziata—*originally panels to ornament the plate cupboards*).
Florence.	*Academy.*	Two Scenes from the Lives of St. Cosmo and St. Damian.
"	"	Predella, with six scenes from the lives of St. Cosmo and St. Damian (*from the Chapel of St. Luke, in the cloister of the SS. Annunziata, Florence*).
"	"	The Coronation of the Virgin.
"	"	The Crucifixion.
"	"	The Entombment (*formerly in the Monastery of La Croce al Tempio*).
"	"	The Last Judgment (*formerly in the Monastery of S. Maria degli Angeli, Florence*).
"	*Uffizi.*	Virgin and Child, with Saints (*painted in 1433 for the Corporation of the Linajuoli*).
"	"	The Coronation of the Virgin (*from S. Maria Nuova, Florence*).
"	"	The Naming of John the Baptist.
"	"	The Preaching of St. Peter, the Adoration of the Magi, and the Martyrdom of St. Mark (*predella to the above 'Madonna dei Linajuoli'*).
"	"	The Assumption of the Virgin.
"	*Convent of San Marco. (Cloisters.)*	The Crucifixion, with St. Dominic.
"	"	St. Peter Martyr enjoining silence.
"	"	St. Dominic with the scourge of nine thongs.
"	"	A Pietà.
"	"	St. Thomas Aquinas.
"	"	Christ as a Pilgrim welcomed by two Dominican Monks.
"	" *(Chapter House.)*	The Crucifixion. Christ between the thieves, surrounded by a group of twenty Saints; with bust portraits of seventeen Dominicans below.
"	" *(Upper Floor.)*	The Annunciation.
"	"	Christ on the Cross, with St. Dominic.
"	"	Madonna enthroned, with Saints.
"	"	Noli Me Tangere.
"	"	The Entombment.
"	"	The Annunciation.
"	"	The Crucifixion.
"	"	The Nativity.
"	"	The Transfiguration.
"	"	Christ at the Praetorium.
"	"	The Resurrection.
"	"	The Coronation of the Virgin.
"	"	The Presentation in the Temple.
"	"	The Descent to Limbo.
"	"	The Agony in the Garden.
"	"	The Institution of the Eucharist.
"	"	The Nailing to the Cross.
"	"	The Crucifixion.
"	"	The Adoration of the Magi.
"	"	The Crucifixion.
"	"	Three Reliquaries. One Adorned with 'The Virgin and Child'; another with the 'Annunciation' and 'Adoration of the Magi'; and the third with a 'Coronation of the Virgin and Saints' (*from the Sacristy of Santa Maria Novella*).
Fiesole.	*S. Domenico.*	Madonna and Saints (*the predella is in the National Gallery*).
"	"	Crucifixion (*a fresco*).
"	*Sacristy.*	
London.	*National Gall.*	Christ, with the Banner of the Resurrection in His left hand, in the midst of a choir of Angels, and crowds of the Blessed. In five compartments

The Crucifixion.

From the painting by Fra Angelico, in the Convent of San Marco, Florence.

GIOVANNI DA FIESOLE

CALLED

FRA ANGELICO

THE ASSUMPTION AND DORMITION OF THE VIRGIN

GIOVANNI DA FIESOLE

CALLED

FRA ANGELICO

CHRIST AS A PILGRIM MET BY TWO DOMINICANS

(formerly the predella to the altar-piece in San Domenico at Fiesole).

Madrid.	*Gallery.*	The Annunciation.
Munich.	*Gallery.*	Three Scenes from the Lives of St. Cosmo and St. Damian (*part of a predella of the altar-piece, painted in 1438 for San Marco, Florence*).
Orvieto.	*Cathedral.*	Christ, in a glory of Angels, as Judge—with sixteen Saints and Prophets to the right (*all more or less damaged; finished by Signorelli in 1499*).
Paris.	*Louvre.*	Coronation of the Virgin: on the predella, seven subjects—six scenes from the Life of St. Dominic, and in the centre Christ risen from the Tomb (*formerly in San Domenico, Fiesole*).
„	„	The Crucifixion (*from the Convent of San Domenico, Fiesole*).
„	„	The Martyrdom of St. Cosmo and St. Damian (*one of the pictures of the predella of the 'Madonna' in the Florence Academy, formerly in the Convent of San Marco*).
Parma.	*Pinacoteca.*	Madonna and four Saints.
Perugia.	*Pinacoteca.*	The Annunciation (*from San Domenico, Perugia*).
„	„	Madonna and Saints.
„	„	Miracles of St. Nicholas of Bari.
St. Petersburg.	*Gall.*	Madonna and Saints (*a fresco, ruined*).
Pisa.	*Gallery.*	Salvator Mundi (*a banner*).
Rome.	*Vatican.* (*Cappella di Niccolò V.*)	Six scenes from the Life of St. Stephen.
„	„	Six scenes from the Life of St. Lawrence.
„	„	The Four Evangelists.
„	„	The Teachers of the Church.
„	„ (*Gallery.*)	St. Nicholas of Bari (*part of a predella*).
„	„	Madonna and Angels.
„	*Corsini Palace.*	The Last Judgment, The Ascension, and Pentecost.
Turin.	*Gallery.*	Two Angels kneeling on Clouds.

FIESSINGER, FRANZ GABRIEL, a Jesuit, born at Offenburg in Breisgau in 1752, studied without any master the art of engraving. He visited Munich, Vienna, Friburg (1786), Switzerland, France, and lastly London, where he died in 1807. Among his plates may be mentioned:

Prudence; *after M. A. Franceschini.* 1777.
Ecce Homo; *after Giuseppe Cesari.* 1781.
The portrait of Thaddäus Kosciuszko; *after J. Grassi.*

FIGINO, AMBROGIO, a native of Milan, was born about 1550, and was alive in the year 1595. He was a pupil of Giovanni Paolo Lomazzo, and not only distinguished himself in portrait painting sufficiently to be celebrated in the poetry of Marino, but was eminent for his historical works. He has left in his native city a 'St. Ambrose' in Sant' Eustorgio, a 'St. Matthew' in San Raffaello, an 'Assumption' in San Fedele, a 'Conception' in Sant' Antonio, and (in the Brera) the portrait of Lucio Foppa, and a 'Virgin and Child.'

FIGUEROA, JUAN FONSECA Y. See FONSECA.

FIL, JAN. See FILICUS.

FILHOL, ANTOINE MICHEL, a French engraver, born in Paris in 1759, was instructed by F. D. Née. He was very successful in depicting landscapes, and published several works on art, among which the most noted is the 'Musée Français,' 1804-15. He died in Paris in 1812.

FILICUS, JAN, (FILIUS, FIL, or FIELIUS,) a Dutch painter, was born at Bois-le-Duc in 1660. He was a scholar of Pieter van Slingelandt, and painted in the very highly-finished manner of his master. His pictures, like those of Slingelandt, represent conversations, or subjects taken from private life, and small portraits. His works, without possessing the extreme polish of those of his instructor, have great merit, and are found in the best collections in Holland. He died in 1719.

FILIPEPI, ALESSANDRO, better known as SANDRO BOTTICELLI, the youngest son of Mariano Filipepi, a Florentine tanner, was born at Florence in 1447, or somewhat earlier. He was apprenticed in his youth to a goldsmith; but he soon abandoned this art and devoted himself to painting, which he studied first under Fra Filippo Lippi and afterwards under the brothers Pollaiuoli. Amongst his earlier works are, an allegorical figure of 'Fortitude,' originally in the Mercatanzia, now in the Uffizi at Florence; a 'St. Sebastian' (now in the Berlin Gallery), which he painted to the order of Lorenzo dei Medici in 1473 for the church of Sta. Maria Maggiore at Florence; and a beautiful little picture of the 'Madonna and Child with an Angel,' formerly in the possession of Prince Chigi, but now in Mrs. Gardner's Collection at Boston. His first important work was an 'Adoration of the Magi,' painted about the year 1476, in which he seems to have emulated the style of Dom. Ghirlandajo. This picture, formerly in the church of Sta. Maria Novella, now in the Uffizi at Florence, contains several portraits of the Medici family, the first Mage representing Cosimo, *Pater Patriæ;* the second, Piero, Cosimo's elder son; and the third, Giovanni, his younger son. In 1478 Sandro was commissioned by Lorenzo dei Medici to paint the effigies of the Pazzi conspirators on the walls of the Bargello, or Public Palace, of Florence. In 1480 he executed a fresco of St. Augustine, in the church of Ognissanti, a work of great power and depth of thought; and in the same year he painted the political allegory of 'Pallas with a Centaur,' a very beautiful picture which for many years was completely lost sight of, and was discovered in the Pitti Palace in 1895. Botticelli was the favourite painter of Lorenzo the Magnificent, for whose sumptuous villas he painted the panel known as 'Mars and Venus' in the National Gallery, as well as his great masterpieces of the 'Allegory of Spring' (now in the Academy at Florence), and the 'Birth of Venus' (in the Uffizi). These pictures, decorative in character and poetical in subject, were to a great extent inspired by the classical imagery of the poems of Lorenzo the Magnificent and Agnolo Poliziano. Between the years 1481 and 1483, Botticelli, called to Rome by Pope Sixtus IV., collaborated with Ghirlandajo, Perugino, Pinturicchio, and Cosimo Rosselli, in the decoration of the Sistine Chapel. His work consisted of three frescoes representing (1) the 'Purification of a Leper,' with vignettes of the 'Temptation of Christ'; (2) 'Scenes from the Life of Moses'; (3) 'The Punishment of Core, Dathan, and Abiron'; and Vasari says that it brought him great renown "beyond any of his collaborators." On his return to Florence he executed commissions for some of the leading Florentine families; and, about the year 1480, he painted for his friend Antonio Segni his famous picture of 'Calumny,' in imitation of the lost masterpiece of the Greek painter Apelles, as described by Lucian. Amongst his religious pictures must be mentioned a large altar-piece of the 'Madonna and Child with Angels and Saints,' painted for the convent of St. Barnaba (now in the Academy at Florence), and a 'Coronation of the Virgin,' painted for the Guild of St. Marco (also in the Academy). Sandro was the originator of the *Tondi*, or circular pictures, of the 'Madonna and Child with Angels,' the most beautiful of which is the masterpiece of the 'Magnificat' (now in the Uffizi). These *Tondi* became very popular, and gave rise to a large number of imitative works by his scholars and followers, which, widely varying in merit, are now scattered through the Galleries of Europe, and in some cases have been mistakenly attributed to Sandro himself. Botticelli's pictures are generally distinguished by a quaint grace of form combined with a profound melancholy of sentiment. His most distinctive qualities as a painter lie in his unique power of conveying the sense of light, swift movement, and in his genius for lineal design. According to Vasari, he practised engraving to a limited extent; but none of the engravings attributed to him have as yet been identified as his work. There is no doubt that he furnished designs to some of the engravers of the period, especially to Baccio Baldini. The latter's copper-plate illustrations of the 'Inferno' (nineteen canti in all) in Landini's edition of Dante, published in 1481, were executed after Botticelli's designs. Later on Sandro himself illustrated (in silver-point gone over with pen and ink) a manuscript of the 'Divina Commedia' for Lorenzo di Piero Francesco dei Medici, a work to which Vasari says he devoted considerable time and labour. This MS., from which several drawings are missing, was formerly in the collection of the Duke of Hamilton, and is now in the Berlin Museum. Eight of the missing drawings have since been discovered in the Vatican Library. Towards the end of his career Botticelli fell under the influence of Savonarola; and the pictures of this period, though fewer in number and perhaps less masterly in execution, are far more devotional in feeling than the works of his youth and maturity. His last picture, and the only one he ever signed or dated, was the little 'Nativity' in the National Gallery, which is full of fervent, almost ecstatic, religious feeling. In his old age he became, Vasari says, infirm and incapacitated; and during the last ten years of his life he appears to have entirely abandoned painting. He died in May 1510, at about the age of sixty-five, and was buried in the church of Ognissanti, at Florence. The following works by Botticelli are in the public and private Galleries of Europe and America:—

Bergamo.	*Gallery.*	Story of Virginia.
Berlin.	*Museum.* 106.	Madonna and Child with SS. John Evangelist and John Baptist (from the Bardi Chapel in the Church of S. Spirito, Florence. 1485.
"	" 1128.	St. Sebastian.
"	*Gallery.*	Madonna and Child with Angels (*school-work*).
"	*Museum.*	Madonna and Child with Seven Angels (*school-work*).
"	"	Venus. Copied by a follower from a figure in the Birth of Venus.
Boston.	*Mrs. J. L. Gardner.*	Madonna and Child with an Angel (from Prince Chigi's Collection in Rome.)
"	"	Death of Lucretia (*late work*).

Dresden.	*Gallery.*	Scenes from the Life of St. Zenobius.
"	"	Madonna and Child (*school-work*).
Florence.	*Academy.* 73.	Coronation.
"	" 74.	*Predella* of above in five compartments.
"	" 80.	Primavera (Allegory of Spring). 1478.
"	" 85.	Madonna and Child with Angels and Saints (from the Convent of S. Barnaba).
"	" 157. 158. 161. 162.	Four panels which probably formed *predella* to above, and represent respectively: Christ rising from the Tomb; The Death of St. Ambrose; Salome with the Baptist's Head; and The Vision of St. Augustine.
"	*Uffizi.* 39.	The Birth of Venus.
"	" 1154.	Portrait of Giovanni di Cosimo dei Medici.
"	" 1156.	Return of Judith.
"	" 1158.	Holofernes' Dead Body in his Tent.
"	" 1179.	St. Augustine in his Study.
"	" 1182.	'Calumny.'
"	" 1267.	*bis.* Madonna of the Magnificat.
"	" 1286.	Adoration of the Magi (from the Maria Novella). About 1476.
"	" 1289.	Madonna and Child with Angels (known as the Madonna of the Melagrana).
"	" 1299.	Fortitude. 1470.
"	" 1303.	Madonna and Child (Rosebush Madonna).
"	" 1316.	Annunziation. 1490.
"	" 3436.	Adoration of the Magi (laid in by Botticelli).
"	*Palazzo Pitti.*	Pallas with a Centaur. 1480.
"	*Palazzo Capponi.*	Communion of St. Jerome.
"	*Church of the Ognissanti.*	St. Augustine (*fresco*). 1480.
Milan.	*Poldi-Pezzoli Collection.*	Madonna and Child.
"	*Ambrosiana.*	Madonna and Child with Angels.
Munich.	*Royal Gallery.* 1010.	Pietà.
London.	*National Gallery.* 592.	Adoration of the Magi (*early work*).
"	" 626.	Portrait of a Young Man.
"	" 915.	Mars and Venus.
"	" 1033.	Adoration of the Magi (*early work*).
	1034.	Nativity. 1500.
"	" 226.	Madonna and Child with St. John and an Angel (*school-work*).
"	" 275.	Madonna and Child with John and Angels (*school-work*).
"	*Mr. J. P. Heseltine.*	Madonna and Child with St. John.
"	*Mr. Ludwig Mond.*	Scenes from the Life of St. Zenobius (*late work*).
Paris.	*Louvre.*	Giovanni Tornabuoni with Venus and the Graces (*fresco* from Villa Lemmi). 1486.
"	"	Lorenzo Tornabuoni and the Liberal Arts (*fresco* from Villa Lemmi, Florence). 1486.
Rome.	*Sistine Chapel.*	Temptation of Christ.
"	"	Scenes from the Life of Moses.
"	"	Fall of Core, Dathan, and Abiron. 1481–1483.
"	"	Some Portraits of Popes. 1481.
"	*Prince Pallavicini.*	La Derelitta (the Outcast). (Doubtful.)
St. Petersburg.	*Hermitage.* 163.	Adoration of the Magi.

Walker & Cockerell Ph. Sc.

The Chigi Madonna
From the painting by Botticelli in the possession of Mrs Gardner. Boston.

FILIPPI, CAMILLO, was a native of Ferrara, who flourished about the middle of the 16th century. He was a disciple of Dosso Dossi, and painted historical works with some success. In the church of Santa Maria del Vado, at Ferrara, is a picture by this master representing the 'Annunciation'; and in that of Il Gesù is another of the 'Trinity.' His death took place in 1574.

FILIPPI, CESARE, the younger son and pupil of Camillo Filippi, was born at Ferrara in 1536. He assisted his father and brother Sebastiano in their works, and excelled in painting heads and grotesques in the ornamental style, although he sometimes attempted historical subjects, which are very feeble imitations of the style of his brother. Such is his picture of the 'Crucifixion' in the church of La Morte. He died after 1602.

FILIPPI, GIACOMO, a native of Ferrara, studied painting under Francesco Ferrari. His views and architectural paintings are deservedly esteemed. He died in 1743.

FILIPPI, SEBASTIANO, called BASTIANINO, and sometimes GRATELLA, born at Ferrara in 1532, was the son of Camillo Filippi. He was first instructed in art by his father, and when he was eighteen years of age he went to Rome, where he had the advantage of being admitted into the school of Michelangelo, but on account of the unhealthy climate of Rome he was obliged to leave that city and return to Ferrara. He was a fertile painter, but negligent in the execution of his works, which are very unequal in value and possess little originality. Though his drawing is correct, his figures are clumsy. His principal work is 'The Last Judgment' (1577-84), in the cathedral at Ferrara, a prodigious performance in which he imitated the style of Michelangelo. It has been spoiled by restoration. A 'Holy Family' and an 'Adoration of the Magi' are in the Costabili Gallery in the same city, in the churches of which there are no fewer than seven pictures of the 'Annunciation,' differing little from each other in composition. Among his best works may also be noticed his 'Martyrdom of St. Catharine,' in the church dedicated to that saint; in Santa Maria de' Servi, the 'Adoration of the Magi'; in the Certosa, a grand picture of St. Christopher, entirely in the lofty style of Michelangelo; in San Benedetto, a 'Dead Christ supported by Angels'; and at the Cappuccini, the 'Virgin and Infant, with St. John.' In the cathedral is a picture of the 'Circumcision,' which is supposed to have been painted before he went to Rome. Filippi died at Ferrara in 1602.

FILIPPINO (or FILIPPO DI FILIPPO). See LIPPI, FILIPPINO.

FILIPPO, Fra. See LIPPI, FILIPPO.

FILLEUL, GILBERT, was a French engraver, who is mentioned by Basan. He flourished about the end of the 17th century, and executed some plates after Le Brun, Simpol, &c.

FILLEUL, PIERRE, was the son of Gilbert Filleul. He engraved some plates for the 'Fables' of La Fontaine; as well as the 'Carriers,' after Wouwerman.

FILLIAN, JOHN, an engraver, flourished from about 1676 to 1680, in which year he died at an early age. He was a pupil of the elder Faithorne, and worked in the style of his instructor. The following are by him:

Thomas Cromwell, Earl of Essex.
William Faithorne; *after a print by Faithorne.*
The Head of Paracelsus.
The Frontispiece to Heylyn's 'Cosmography.'

FILOCAMO, ANTONIO and PAOLO, two brothers, were natives of Messina, and are noticed by Hackert in his 'Memorie de' Pittori Messinesi.' They were educated in the school of Carlo Maratti, at Rome; and on their return to Messina, established an academy, which was much frequented. They executed conjointly several works, both in oil and in fresco, in the former of which Antonio was very superior to Paolo. Their principal works are in the churches of Santa Caterina di Valverde and San Gregorio, at Messina, where they both died of the plague in 1743.

FILOTESIO, NICCOLA, (FILOTTESCHI, or FILATICHI,) usually called COLA DELL' AMATRICE, and sometimes COLA DALLA MATRICE, is mentioned by Vasari in his life of Calabrese. He painted from about 1513 to 1543, in Ascoli, Calavria, and Norcia, and was distinguished throughout all that province. His manner was hard in his earlier pictures, but in his subsequent works he exhibited a fulness of design, and an accomplished modern style. His 'Last Supper,' formerly in the oratory of the Corpus Domini, and now in the Foundling Hospital, is a work of merit. Ascoli possesses, in addition to this, several of his best works. A few are in Rome—an 'Ascension' is in the Museum of the Lateran, and a 'Madonna' in the Capitol. Cola died at Amatrice, but in what year is not known.

FINCH, FRANCIS OLIVER, a landscape painter in water-colours, was born in 1802. In early life he studied under John Varley, and painted portraits. He exhibited regularly at the Water-Colour Society, of which he was elected an associate in 1822, and a full member in 1827. His works were generally poetic compositions, and he excelled in twilight and moonlight scenes. He died in 1862. Several of his landscapes are at the South Kensington Museum. His 'Memorials' were printed in 1865.

FINCKE, HANS, a landscape and architectural engraver, was born at Berlin in 1800. He studied under Buchhorn, and in London under Finden, and died in 1859. His best plates are a view of the Cathedral at Meissen, after Schirmer, and a view of Salzburg, after Biermann. He commenced also a view of the Convent of San Miniato near Florence, after Biermann, which was finished after his death by Dröhmer.

FINDEN, EDWARD FRANCIS, a line-engraver, was the younger brother of William Finden, and like him a pupil of James Mitan. He was born in London in 1792, and died in the same city in 1857. He worked chiefly upon the various publications issued by himself and his brother, but executed also a few plates for the 'Literary Souvenir,' as well as the following:

The Princess Victoria; *after Westall.*
The Harvest Waggon; *after Gainsborough.*
Happy as a King; *after Collins.*
Othello telling his exploits to Brabantio and Desdemona; *after Douglas Cowper.*

FINDEN, WILLIAM, a line-engraver, was born in 1787. He was a pupil of James Mitan, and in conjunction with his brother Edward, and a number of assistants and pupils, he published several ably executed series of prints and book-illustrations. The principal of these were as follow:

Landscape Illustrations to the Life and Works of Lord Byron. 1831—1834.
The Gallery of the Graces; *after Chalon, Landseer, and others.* 1832—1834.

Landscape Illustrations of the Bible; *after Turner, Calcott, Stanfield, and others.* 1834.
Byron Beauties. 1834.
Landscape Illustrations to the Life and Poetical Works of George Crabbe. 1834.
Portraits of the Female Aristocracy of the Court of Queen Victoria; *after Chalon, Hayter, and others.* 1838-39.
The Royal Gallery of British Art.
The Beauties of Thomas Moore.

Besides these independent works, the Findens produced the illustrations to the 'Arctic Voyages,' published by Murray; to Brockedon's 'Illustrations of the Passes of the Alps,' 1827-29; to Campbell's 'Poetical Works,' 1828; and some of the plates for Lodge's 'Portraits of Illustrious Personages of Great Britain,' 1821-34. The 'Royal Gallery of British Art' and the 'Beauties of Thomas Moore' involved the Findens in a great loss from which they never recovered. William Finden died in London in 1852. The most important plates by his own hand are:

George IV., full-length, seated on a sofa; *after Sir Thomas Lawrence.*
The Highlander's Return; *after Sir Edwin Landseer.*
The Naughty Boy; *after the same.*
Deer-Stalkers; *after the same.*
The Interior of a Highlander's House; *after the same.*
The Fisherman's Daughter; *after the same.*
The Village Festival; *after Sir David Wilkie.*
The Crucifixion; *after Hilton.*
Returning from Market; *after Sir A. W. Calcott.*
Sickness and Health; *after Webster.*
Lord Byron at the age of nineteen; *after G. Saunders.*
The Rivals; *after Leslie.* ('Literary Souvenir,' 1826.)
The Blackberry Boy; *after Hamilton.* ('Anniversary,' 1829.)

FINI, TOMMASO DI CRISTOFORO, also called MA-SOLINO DA PANICALE, was the son of Cristoforo Fini, of the quarter of Santa Croce, at Florence, and was born at Panicale in 1383. He probably received his artistic education from Lorenzo Ghiberti, and afterwards from Gherardo Starnina, and was admitted into the Guild of the Medici and Speziale, at Florence, in 1423; shortly afterwards he entered the service of Philippo Scolari, Obergespann of Temeswar, in Hungary, who is better known as Pippo Spanno, and with whom he went to Hungary in 1427. At his death Masolino returned to Italy, and accepted from Cardinal Branda Castiglione the commission to paint the choir of the church, which that prelate had just finished in Castiglione di Olona, in 1428, and in which can still be seen the remains of a double course of frescoes representing scenes from the lives of the Virgin and SS. Stephen and Lawrence. He also decorated the whole of the Baptistery at Castiglione with scenes drawn from the life of St. John the Baptist, which still remain, and although much injured by time, are worthy of notice. Very little else that is really authentic remains of Masolino's work. The date of his death, though somewhat doubtful, is now set down as 1447. The famous Masaccio was one of his pupils.

FINIGUERRA, MASO or **TOMMASO,** born 1426; died 1464. Maso Finiguerra belonged to a family that had been long established in Florence, practising various crafts; his father was a goldsmith, named Antonio, living in 1427 in the quarter of Santa Lucia d'Ognissanti. In an official statement of his possessions for that year, he states that his son Tommaso is one year and five months old. The boy was brought up as a goldsmith, and appears to have joined the shop of the Pollaiuoli on the Ponte Vecchio. He was celebrated for his

works in niello, and received an order when in his twenty-fifth year from the Consuls of the Guild of Merchants or Calimala, for a silver pax in niello, to be presented to the Baptistery of San Giovanni; it was delivered and paid for in 1452. Tommaso married Piera di Domenica di Giovanni, before the year 1457. He was working as a goldsmith and jeweller in partnership with one Piero di Bartolommeo di Sali. Antonio Pollaiuolo was a partner in the same business. In this year the firm made a pair of silver candlesticks, probably decorated in niello, for the altar of the church of San Jacopo at Pistoja. In a manuscript *zibaldone* begun in 1459 by Giovanni Ruccellai, Maso Finiguerra is mentioned with Antonio Pollaiuolo, as a master in drawing, among the artists with whose work the Casa Ruccellai is enriched. In 1462 Finiguerra supplied open-work silver buckles decorated with niello to Cino di Filippo Rinuccini, and early in 1463 Alessio Baldovinetti notes that he is to receive, on February 21, payment from Giuliano da Majano, for work that he has done in colouring the heads of five figures designed by Tommaso Finiguerra for the inlaid wood panelling in the Sacristy of the Duomo, to be carried out by the said Giuliano. Finiguerra's cartoons are specified as consisting of a St. Zenobio between two deacons and a Virgin with an angel. These intarsias from the designs of Finiguerra are still to be seen in the Sacristy and the Opera del Duomo; they are perhaps the only undisputed works of the masters, left. In 1466 Rinuccini records that he revisited the same shop to buy another buckle, but this time he dealt with Tommaso's younger brother, for our artist was no longer living: he was buried on August 24, 1464.

Although Finiguerra has been deprived of late years of the glory given to him by Vasari of being the inventor of printing from engraved metal plates, yet he must be regarded as a great master in the art of niello engraving. A 'Crucifixion' in the Bargello is probably an example of his work in this beautiful art; the famous 'Coronation of the Virgin' in the same Museum often attributed to him is of another school. He was one of the pioneers of metal engraving in Italy, and Mr. Colvin in his monumental work on the master, almost proves that he is the author of certain very beautiful Florentine prints and drawings, all evidently by one hand and from the workshop of the Pollaiuoli. Several of these drawings are in the Uffizi, Florence, and were catalogued under his name in the eighteenth century. They consist of studies in pen and wash, of boys and workmen engaged in various crafts. Several of these were used in a modified form in the series of ninety-nine drawings, part of a Picture Chronicle by the same hand, in the Print Room of the British Museum; there are twenty-two other drawings in the collection of M. Bonnat, Paris. The following famous early Florentine engravings, in what is known as the fine manner, are by the same master:

The Series of the Planets.
      "   "   Prophets and Sibyls.
The Otto prints, including the Jason and Medea, the Judith and Holofernes, and several decorative designs.
The Battle of the Hose.
The March to Calvary.
Conversion of St. Paul; a unique proof at Hamburg.
Two subjects of Ships at Sea.
The Judgment Hall of Pilate; prints at Gotha and Chatsworth.
The Encounter of a Hunting party with a family of hairy wild men.

The Story of Theseus and Ariadne.
The Chariot of Ariadne and Bacchus; a unique proof in the British Museum.
Some Arabesques in the form of Candelabra.

There are other engravings from the same workshop, but as they were not published until after the death of the master, he cannot have had much to do with them. Such are the engravings for the Monte Santo di Dio, 1477, and those for the Lundini Dante, 1481. C. H.

FINK, FREDERICK, an American genre painter, was born at Little Falls, New York, in 1817. He commenced life as a student of medicine, but impelled by an irresistible love of art, he went to New York and studied under Morse. In 1840 he visited Europe, and made copies of the works of Titian and Murillo. Among his pictures are 'An Artist's Studio,' 'The Shipwrecked Mariner,' 'The Young Thieves,' and 'A Negro Wood-Sawyer.' He died in 1849.

FINKE, HEINRICH JONATHAN, was born at Nuremberg in 1816. He was instructed in the principles of art in that city, and afterwards visited Belgium and Holland, and settled in Altenburg, where he was mostly employed by the court. He excelled in portraiture, and his productions, which are entirely in the Dutch style, are executed in a clear and bold manner. He was professor at Altenburg, and died in 1868.

FINLAYSON, JOHN, an engraver, was born about the year 1730, and worked in London. In 1773 he received a premium from the Society of Arts, and about three years after this he died. He engraved in mezzotint several portraits, and a few plates of historical subjects, among which are the following:

PORTRAITS.

The Duchess of Gloucester; *after Sir Joshua Reynolds.*
Lady Charles Spencer; *after the same.*
Lady Elizabeth Melbourne; *after the same.*
The Earl of Buchan; *after the same.*
Miss Wynyard; *after the same.*
Lady Broughton; *after Cotes.*
The Duke of Northumberland; *after Hamilton.*
Miss Metcalfe; *after Hone.*
Signora Zamperini, in 'La Buona Figliuola'; *after the same.*
William Drummond, Scotch historian; *after C. Janssens.*
Shooter, Beard, and Dunstall, in 'Love in a Village'; *after Zoffany.*

SUBJECTS.

Candaules, King of Lydia, showing his Queen coming out of the Bath to his favourite Gyges; *after his own design.*

FINNEY, SAMUEL, a miniature painter, was born in Cheshire in 1721. He was a member of the Society of Artists, where he exhibited from 1761 to 1766. He became portrait painter to Queen Charlotte, and died in 1807.

FINOGLIA, PAOLO DOMENICO, a native of Orta, in the kingdom of Naples, flourished about the year 1640. He was brought up in the academy of Cavaliere Massimo Stanzioni, but painted more in the style of Spagnoletto. He was a correct and expressive designer, and possessed great fecundity of invention. His principal works were the vault in the convent of San Martino at Naples, with scenes from the life of St. Martin (his best work), and ten oil paintings in the Capitol. He died in 1656.

FINSON, LOUIS, or ALOIS, (or FINSONIUS,) was born at Bruges about 1580. He went to Rome about 1600, where he became a disciple of Caravaggio. He travelled in Germany and settled at Aix, but subsequently visited Naples, and returned to Aix, whence he removed in 1614 to Arles, where he was drowned in the Rhone about 1632. The following are among his works, which are excellent in colour but wanting in dignity:

Aix.	*Museum.*	The Incredulity of St. Thomas.
„	„	The Resurrection. 1613.
Andenne.	*Church.*	Massacre of the Innocents.
Arles.	*Museum.*	The Martyrdom of St. Stephen.
„	„	The Adoration of the Magi. 1614.
Marseilles.	*Museum.*	A dying Magdalen.
Naples.	*Museum.*	The Annunciation. 1612.
Rome.	*San Giovanni.*	The Resurrection. 1610.

FIORAVANTI, was an Italian painter of still-life and inanimate objects, who excelled in painting vases, fruit and flowers, and musical instruments, which he represented with great exactness and fidelity.

FIORE, COLANTONIO DEL. See TOMASI, NICCOLA.
FIORE, FEDERIGO. See BAROCCI.
FIORE, JACOBELLO DEL. See DEL FIORE.
FIORENTINO, DOMENICO. See DEL BARBIERE.
FIORENTINO, LUCA, a Florentine engraver, who flourished in the early part of the 16th century, followed the manner of Robetta. He used the annexed monogram: The following are some of his best works:

Herodias with the Head of St. John the Baptist.
A richly-dressed Woman seated on the Ground, with two Children.
A Man with a Bow.
The Virgin and Child, St. Anthony, and St. Francis.
St. Catharine and St. Lucia.

FIORENTINO, STEFANO, called STEFANO DA PONTE VECCHIO, and LO SCIMMIA (the ape), is questionably stated to have been the grandson and the disciple of Giotto. He was born at Florence in 1301, and, according to Vasari, greatly excelled his instructor in every department of the art. The rules of perspective were little known at the early period at which he lived, and he has the credit of establishing them on more regular principles. If he was less successful in his endeavours to overcome the difficulty of foreshortening, he has at least the credit of being the first artist who attempted it. He succeeded, better than any of his contemporaries, in giving expression to the airs of his heads, and a less Gothic turn to the attitudes of his figures. His works in the churches at Rome and Florence have perished, and the picture of the 'Virgin and Infant Christ,' in the Campo Santo at Pisa, which Lanzi mentions as the only vestige remaining of his productions, is clearly a work of the Sienese school. He died in 1350.

FIORENZO DI LORENZO. Little is known of this painter, excepting that a contract was made by him to paint a double altar-piece in the church of Santa Maria Nuova, now belonging to the Servites, in Perugia, in 1472; and that in 1521 he assisted Tiberio d'Assisi in the valuation of a picture by Giannicolo of Perugia. Parts of the above-mentioned altar-piece can be still seen at the Academy of Arts at Perugia, as also eight half-lengths of saints, a 'St. Sebastian,' and other paintings of less value. There are also by him:

Berlin.	*Gallery.*	Virgin and Child, on a gold ground. 1481.
Diruta.	*S. Francisco.*	An Eternal in a circular glory, between SS. Roman and Roch. 1475.
Madrid.	*Trinidad Mus.*	The Saviour, with four Saints.

Perugia.	*Palazzo Com-munale.*	Two panels, with half-lengths of Saints in prayer.
„	*S. Agostino.*	A half-length Virgin and Child.
„	*S. Giorgio.*	A Nativity. 1490.
„	*S. Maria Nuova.*	The Adoration of the Magi. (*This has been attributed to Perugino.*)
„	*S. Francesco.*	Eight paintings of the Life of St. Bernard (*probably by this artist, and not by Pisanello and Mantegna*). 1483.
„	„	St. Peter and St. Paul. 1487.

FIORI, GASPARO DEI. See LOPEZ.

FIORI, MARIO DEI. See NUZZI.

FIORILLO, JOHANN DOMINIK, born at Hamburg in 1748, was a painter and literary man. In 1759 he began to study at the Academy at Baireuth, and in 1761 went to Rome and became a scholar of P. Battoni. From 1765 to 1769 he studied at Bologna under Vittorio Bigari, but at the end of this term he returned to Hamburg, and was employed at the court at Brunswick, where he brought himself into notice. He became superintendent of the collections of engravings at Göttingen in 1784, and in 1799 professor at the University. He died at Göttingen in 1821.

FIORINI, GIOVANNI BATTISTA, was a native of Bologna. He flourished at the close of the 16th century, and died subsequently to 1595. He is chiefly known as a coadjutor of Cesare Aretusi, in conjunction with whom he painted several pictures at Bologna and Brescia, and distinguished himself especially as a good designer and a happy inventor. By him there are the following works:

Bologna.	*Cathedral.*	Christ giving the Keys to St. Peter.
„	*San Giovanni in Monte.*	Birth of the Virgin.
„	*San Benedetto.*	The Descent from the Cross.
„	*Padri Servi.*	The Mass of St. Gregory.
Brescia.	*S. Afra.*	The Birth of the Virgin.
Rome.	*Sala Regia, Vatican.*	A small painting by Fiorini alone.

FIORINO, JEREMIAS ALEXANDER, born at Cassel in 1793, painted several portraits now in the Dresden Gallery. He died at Dresden in 1847.

FIORONI, ADAMO, an Italian engraver, was born about 1800. He was a scholar of Longhi, and engraved several excellent plates at Milan, amongst which were:

The Virgin and Child, with St. John; *after Raphael.* 1829.
The Virgin and Child, called 'La Madonna del Adjuto'; *after B. Luini.* 1822.

FIRENS, PIERRE, was an indifferent French engraver, who, according to Basan, resided in Paris about the year 1640. He copied, in a stiff, clumsy manner, the 'Hermits,' after Sadeler, and engraved some portraits, among others that of Henry IV. of France.

FIRENZE, ANDREA DA (who is distinct from Andrea de Florentia), was an artist living in the 15th century, and known as the author of a large altar-piece, signed and dated 1437, in a chapel of the church of Santa Margareta, at Cortona, which represents the 'Virgin taken to Paradise by six Angels, with Saints.' There is also, in the Casa Kamelli, at Gubbio, a 'Conversion of Constantine,' signed by him. The dates of his birth and death are not known.

FISCHBACH, JOHANN, born at Gravenegg, in Lower Austria, in 1797, was a painter of landscapes and genre-pieces. He studied at the Academy at Vienna, and his twenty-eight crayon-designs, representing forest trees in Germany, brought him

168

into much notice. He died at Munich in 1871. The following are by him:

Munich.	*Gallery.*	A landscape in Salzburg.
Vienna.	*Gallery.*	A Farmer's Boy disputing with a Girl for a Bird.
„	„	A Widow in a Churchyard.

FISCHBACH, KARL. See VITTINGHOFF.

FISCHER, A., is the name of an engraver who executed a print of the 'Carriers,' after Wouwerman. The same subject is engraved by Filleul.

FISCHER, ANNA CATHARINA, a German lady, excelled in painting flowers in distemper and in oil. She was married to Benjamin Blok in 1664.

FISCHER, GEORG JOHANN PAUL, a miniature painter, was born in 1786 at Hanover, where he studied under Ramberg. He came to England in 1810, and exhibited at the Royal Academy from 1811 to 1871. He became miniature painter to George IV., and died in 1875.

FISCHER, HERMANN. See SWANEVELT.

FISCHER, ISAAC, a portrait and historical painter of Augsburg, died in 1705.

FISCHER, JOHANN, was an engraver on wood, to whom are attributed the cuts for the Bible printed at Strassburg in 1606.

FISCHER, JOHANN GEORG, an historical painter, was born at Augsburg in 1580. He travelled in Italy, but became an imitator of Albrecht Dürer. He died at Munich in 1643. The following are by him:

Munich.	*Gallery.*	Christ carrying the Cross.
„	„	The Apprehension of Christ.
Nuremberg.	*Landauer-Brüderhaus.*	The Apostles John, Peter, Mark, and Paul; *after Albrecht Dürer.*
„	*Moritz-Chapel.*	Ecce Homo (*supposed to be by him, but by some attributed to Albrecht Dürer*).
Pommersfelden.	*Gall.*	The Trinity; *after Albrecht Dürer.*

FISCHER, JOSEPH, who was born at Vienna in 1769, studied painting and engraving under Brand and Schmutzer at the Academy of that city. After having travelled some time he returned to Vienna, and became a professor in the Academy. He died at Vienna in 1822. Among his paintings in the Gallery of that city are a view of Vienna and a landscape. His best engraved works are the following:

The Entombment; *after Schidone.*
Christ in the Temple; *after Ribera.* 1793.
The Adulteress before Christ; *after Füger.*
The Emperor Francis, led by Minerva and Justice, receiving the homage of his people; in aquatint.
The Portrait of Correggio.

His sister, MARIA ANNA FISCHER, who was born at Vienna in 1785, was also an engraver, chiefly of landscapes and battle-pieces.

FISCHER, JOSEPH ANTON, born at Oberstorf, Algäu, in 1814, was at first a cow-herd, but being assisted by Ch. Schraudolf, he studied at the Academy at Munich under Schlotthauer, and visited Italy in 1832 and 1843. During this time he executed cartoons under H. Hess for the glass-paintings of the Auerkirche, representing 'The Flight into Egypt,' 'Death of the Virgin,' 'Burial of the Virgin,' 'Christ in the Temple,' 'The Three Kings,' 'The Angel's Salutation,' 'The Marriage of the Virgin,' and 'The Prophecy of Simeon in the Temple.' He was a follower of Fra Angelico, and painted from 1844 to 1848 the cartoons for eight glass-paintings for the cathedral at Cologne, representing 'St. John the Baptist preaching,' 'The Adoration of the Magi,' 'The Taking down from the Cross,' 'The Stoning of St. Stephen,' 'The

EDWARD FISHER

After Reynolds]

GARRICK BETWEEN TRAGEDY AND COMEDY

EDWARD FISHER

After Reynolds 1766]

LADY SARAH BUNBURY

Descent of the Holy Ghost,' 'The Four Great Prophets,' 'The Four Evangelists,' and 'The Four Western Fathers'; for these he obtained the gold medal of Prussia. Several beautiful pen-and-ink drawings by this artist are in different collections, especially in Munich, where he died in 1859. Among his oil paintings are the following:

Munich.	Gallery.	The Flight into Egypt. 1841.
"	"	The Adoration of the Magi. 1844.
"	"	The Visitation. 1845.
"	"	The Entombment. 1848.
"	Princess Narischkin's.	The Ascension of the Virgin.

FISCHER, VINCENZ, an historical painter and professor of architecture at the Academy of Vienna, was born at Schmidham, in Bavaria, in 1729, and died at Vienna in 1810. In addition to some pen-and-ink drawings, the following works by him are worthy of mention:

The Restoring of the Young Man of Nain to life. 1763.
The Raising of Lazarus. 1763.
Moses when a Boy treading on Pharaoh's Crown (*in the Academy at Vienna*).

FISEN, ENGELBERT, a Flemish painter, born at Liége in 1655, was a pupil of Bertholet Flemalle. When still very young he went to Italy, where he studied under Carlo Maratti, whose style he imitated. After eight years he returned to his native city, where his principal pictures are a 'Crucifixion,' painted for the chapel of the Hôtel-de-Ville; and a 'Martyrdom of St. Bartholomew,' and a 'Christ on the Cross,' painted for the church of St. Bartholomew. He died at Liége in 1733.

FISHER, ALVAN, an American portrait painter, who was a native of Needham, Connecticut, visited Europe in 1825, and studied for some time in Paris. He died at Dedham, Massachusetts, in 1863, having produced many satisfactory and refined likenesses, especially that of Spurzheim.

FISHER, EDWARD, a mezzotint engraver, was born in 1730 in Ireland, but resided in London during the time he was known as an artist, and died there about the year 1785. He engraved a number of portraits, chiefly after Sir Joshua Reynolds, which possess great merit. Among others are the following:

PORTRAITS AFTER SIR JOSHUA REYNOLDS.

John, Earl of Bute, when Lord Cardiff.
The Marchioness of Tavistock (Lady Elizabeth Keppel); full length.
Garrick between Tragedy and Comedy. 1769.
Kitty Fisher as Cleopatra.
Sir Thomas Harrison.
Lady Sarah Bunbury; whole length.
The Marquis of Rockingham.
Hugh, Earl of Northumberland.
Elizabeth, Countess of Northumberland.
Granville, Earl Gower. 1765.
George, Lord Edgcumbe, Vice-Admiral. 1773.
Viscount Downe.
Lady Elizabeth Lee; full length.
John, Viscount Ligonier, on horseback.
Augustus, Lord Keppel. 1759.
Augustus Hervey, afterwards Earl of Bristol.
Ladies Amabel and Jemima Yorke, daughters of the Earl of Hardwicke.
Hon. George Seymour Conway. 1771.
Lawrence Sterne, Prebendary of York.
John Armstrong, M.D.

PORTRAITS AFTER OTHER PAINTERS.

George III.; *after Benjamin West.*
Hon. Frederick Cornwallis, Archbishop of Canterbury; *after Sir N. Dance.*

Richard Terrick, Bishop of London; *after the same.*
William, Earl of Chatham; *after Brompton.*
Benjamin Franklin; *after Chamberlin.*
Paul Sandby, R.A.; *after F. Cotes.*
Mark Akenside; *after Pond.*
Eliza Farren, actress, afterwards Countess of Derby; whole length; *after Zoffany.*
Colley Cibber; *after Vanloo.*

FISHER, JONATHAN, an Irish landscape painter, was born at Dublin about the middle of the 18th century. He held a post in the Stamp Office, but his art was poor. He died in 1812.

FISHER, THOMAS, who was born at Rochester in 1782, was a clerk in the India Office. He practised art as an amateur, and made many drawings of antiquarian subjects, which he etched himself. He died at Stoke-Newington in 1836.

FISK, WILLIAM HENRY, a portrait and historical painter, was born in 1797 at Thorpe-le-Soken, Essex. He did not take up art as a profession till he was thirty-one years of age, having been for the ten previous years engaged in mercantile employment. His first picture exhibited at the Royal Academy was a portrait in 1831, and he continued painting in the same branch of art till 1835; from this date his pictures were chiefly historical. Among these we may mention 'Leonardo da Vinci dying in the arms of Francis I.,' exhibited at the Royal Academy in 1838; 'Attempted Assassination of Lorenzo de' Medici in Florence in 1478,' exhibited in 1839, and which was awarded the gold medal of the Manchester Institution in 1840; and 'The Trial of Charles I.,' exhibited in 1842, and afterwards engraved. His historical pictures are well composed, and accurate as to costume. He retired a few years later to a property he had purchased in the country, and from this time almost entirely relinquished painting. He died at Danbury, near Chelmsford, in 1872.

FISK, WILLIAM HENRY, painter, was the son and pupil of William Fisk, and was born about 1827. He studied at the Royal Academy schools, and was appointed anatomical draughtsman to the Royal College of Surgeons. He continued at the same time to practise painting, and many of his pictures were exhibited at the Academy, the British Institution, the Suffolk Street Gallery, and in Paris. He also contributed numerous essays and articles on art subjects to current literature, and lectured both in London and the provinces. His artistic powers were very considerable, but he was best known as a careful and able teacher, in which capacity he worked for forty years at University College School, London. He died at Hampstead, November 13, 1884.

FITTLER, JAMES, a line-engraver, was born in London in 1758. He entered the schools of the Royal Academy in 1778, and was elected an Associate Engraver in 1800. He distinguished himself by numerous works after English and foreign masters, of different subjects and character; and book illustrations by him abound. His best engravings are considered to be 'Lord Howe's Victory,' and 'The Battle of the Nile,' both after De Loutherbourg; the portrait of Benjamin West; the plates in Forster's 'British Gallery,' others in Bell's 'British Theatre,' and the portraits in Dibdin's 'Aedes Althorpianæ,' published in 1822, after which time he does not appear to have produced anything of importance. He died at Turnham Green in 1835.

FLACCO, ORLANDO. See FIACCO.

FLAMAEL, BERTHOLET. See FLEMALLE.

FLAMEN, AALBERT, (or FLAMAND,) a Flemish painter and etcher, resided in Paris from 1648 to 1664. He painted landscapes, birds, and fish, and particularly excelled in representing the last of these, to which he gave a surprising appearance of reality. He succeeded less in landscape painting, and the forms of the trees, as well as the modification in light and shadow, are defective. There are by this artist some neat etchings of the above-mentioned subjects, executed with the dry point and graver in the style of Hollar. He sometimes marked his plates with his name, and sometimes with the annexed cipher.

There are by him 601 plates, among which may be mentioned :

36 plates of Sea Fish.
24　,,　　Fresh-water Fish.
12　,,　　Livre d'Oyseaux.
13　,,　　Diuersæ Auium Species. 1659.
The Militia of Paris. 1660 and 1662.

There exist also several portraits by Aalbert Flamen, which have been engraved by Poilly and Boulanger.

FLAMEN, F., probably of the same family as Aalbert Flamen, was a native of Flanders, who resided in Paris about the year 1660. Among other prints, he etched a set of four plates of 'Views on the River Seine,' after the designs of Israel Silvestre.

FLAMENCO, JUAN, (that is, 'John the Fleming,') supposed to be identical with JUAN DE FLANDES, is mentioned under the former name by Cean Bermudez as a painter who resided in the Certosa di Mira-flores from 1496 to 1499, and painted the altar-pieces there, for which he was paid the sum of 53,545 maravedis, besides his maintenance. On the right-hand, or gospel side of the altar, he represented various passages in the life of St. John the Baptist, which were well treated, with good colouring and much expression, in the style of Lucas van Leyden ; the painting on the left, or epistle side, is much deteriorated, and it can only be seen that it represented 'The Adoration of the Kings.'

Under the name of Juan de Flandes, the same writer notices an artist who painted eleven pictures in the cathedral of Palencia, which he began in the year 1509, under an engagement to complete them in three years, for the sum of 500 gold ducats. Some have supposed that Hans Memlinc is the painter intended by these two appellations.

FLAMENGO, MIGUEL EL. See AMBÉRES.

FLAMMINGO. See FIAMMINGO.

FLANDES, JUAN DE. See FLAMENCO.

FLANDIN, EUGÈNE NAPOLÉON, a French land-scape painter, was born at Naples in 1809. After producing various pictures, which obtained considerable success, he was present in 1838 throughout the campaign in Algeria, and reproduced several of the scenes with his brush. In 1839 he was selected to pursue antiquarian investigations in Persia, and on the completion of this work he prosecuted further researches in the East, and published several works containing the fruits of his labours. The most important of these is his 'Voyage en Perse,' published in conjunction with Pascal Coste, the architect, in six folio volumes, Paris, 1843-54 ; and 'L'Orient,' published at Paris in folio, 1853-74. He did not return to painting till about 1850 ; and he died in 1876. Amongst his chief works are :

The Piazzetta and Ducal Palace at Venice. 1836.
The Bridge of Sighs. 1836.
A View of the Coast at Algiers. 1837.
The Breach at Constantine. 1839.
View of Stamboul. 1853.
View of the Royal Mosque at Ispahan. 1853.
General View of Constantinople. 1855.
The Entrance of the Bosphorus. 1855.
View of Bagdad. (*Marseilles Museum.*)

FLANDRIN, AUGUSTE RENÉ, a French painter, brother of Jean Hippolyte Flandrin, was born at Lyons in 1804. He was at first employed in book illustration, but in 1832 he went to Paris, where he worked for two years under Ingres. He painted several portraits, and after visiting Italy, became director of the Academy at Lyons, where he died in 1843. Amongst his works are :

Savonarola preaching at Florence.
Reposing after the Bath.
Interior of San Miniato, Florence.

FLANDRIN, JEAN HIPPOLYTE, a French historical and portrait painter, was born in 1809 at Lyons, where his father fought a hard battle against poverty as a miniature painter. He was the fourth son, and his mother, who had seen much of the cares and necessities which follow the pursuit of art, was resolutely opposed to his becoming a painter. She at length relented, and in 1821 he entered the studio of the sculptor Legendre, and afterwards studied under Revoil in the Lyons Academy. By dint of the strictest economy a little hoard was scraped together sufficient to enable him and his younger brother Paul to set out for Paris in 1829. To economize their slender means, the two brothers were obliged to travel thither from Lyons on foot. Arrived in the capital, they became pupils of Ingres, in preference to Hersent, to whom they had letters of introduction. The choice was most fortunate, for Ingres proved most kind to his pupils, and Flandrin to the end of his life ever showed himself loyal and devoted to his old master. The next three years was a period of great trial and privation. Besides suffering from cold and scanty food, he had what was no doubt a slight attack of cholera, then raging grievously in Paris. He was also laid low by rheumatism, from which he subsequently became a great sufferer. In 1832 he obtained the long-wished-for 'grand prix de Rome' with his 'Theseus recognizing his Father.' Early in the following year he arrived at Rome, and though not over-burdened with means, he now managed to send frequent remittances to help the home at Lyons. While studying here, he formed a friendship with Ambroise Thomas, the French musical composer, which lasted through life. He returned to Paris in 1838, and soon obtained ample employment in the mural decorations of churches. His first great work in the church of St. Séverin was completed in 1841, in which year he received the cross of the Legion of Honour. Two years later he married Aimée Ancelot, and their eldest son was born in 1845. The history of the remainder of Flandrin's life may be summarized in the decorative works which he executed. The chief of these were: St. Germain-des-Prés—sanctuary 1842-4, choir 1846-8, and nave 1855-61 ; St. Paul, Nîmes, 1847-9 ; St. Vincent-de-Paul, Paris, 1850-4 ; the Conservatoire des Arts et Metiers, 1854 ; and the church of Ainay, at Lyons, in 1855. He did not lack appreciation of his works, for he was promoted to the rank of officer of the Legion of Honour in 1853, and in the same year was elected to the Academy, becoming Pro-

THOMAS FLATMAN

[Collection of Dr. G. C. Williamson

JOHN, LORD SOMERS, LORD HIGH CHANCELLOR, 1683

[Victoria and Albert Museum

SIR THOMAS HENSHAW, AMBASSADOR
TO DENMARK AND NORWAY, 1677

THOMAS FLATMAN, 1662
(BY HIMSELF)

fessor of Painting in 1857. The popularity of his art drew to him a large connection as a portrait painter, and he had many eminent sitters. His health during the last few years had been anything but good; his sufferings from rheumatism, aggravated by his work in cold, damp churches, had been great; and in 1863 he undertook a long-looked-for journey to Italy, in hopes of a restoration of strength. But he was not destined to return, for he succumbed to an attack of small-pox at Rome, March 21st, 1864. Besides the decorative works already enumerated, the following are amongst the chief of his easel productions :

Dante and Virgil. 1835. (*Lyons Museum.*)
Euripides. 1835. (*Lyons Museum.*)
St. Clara healing the Blind. 1836. (*Nantes Cathedral.*)
Christ blessing little Children. 1837. (*Lisieux Museum.*)
The Reverie. (*Nantes Museum.*)
Mater Dolorosa. 1844.
The Tower of Babel. 1861. (*Lille Museum.*)
Portrait of Cherubini; *after Ingres.*
Marie Anne de Bourbon, Duchess of Bourbon.
Marie Françoise de Noailles, Marchioness of Lavardin. } *Versailles Museum.*
Cardinal de Tournon.
Diana of Poitiers.
Figure Study. 1855. } *Louvre, Paris.*
Portrait of a Young Girl. 1863.
Portrait of Napoleon III.
　　" 　　Prince Jerome Napoleon.
　　" 　　Comte Duchâtel.
　　" 　　Comtesse Duchâtel.
　　" 　　Comte Walewski.

Flandrin's 'Lettres et Pensées,' accompanied by a biographical notice and a catalogue of his works, were published by the Count Delaborde in 1865.

O. J. D.

FLANDRIN, JEAN PAUL, a well-known landscape painter, brother of the famous historical painter, Hippolyte Flandrin. He was born at Lyons on May 8, 1811. He received lessons in painting from Ingres, and exhibited constantly at the Salon since the year 1839; an achievement probably exceeded by few. His early landscapes, painted in the Campagna, were almost wholly based upon mythological and religious subjects; but about the year 1840 he turned his attention to portraiture. At Nantes are his pictures, 'La Solitude,' and the portraits of Hippolyte and Paul Flandrin, and the Duc de Feltre. Among his more famous landscapes we may cite: 'Au bord de l'Eau,' 'Ombrages,' 'La Vallée du Gardon,' 'Près d'Etretat,' 'Pornic,' 'Falaises du Tréport' and several scenes taken from Languedoc and Bearn. His work is also represented at Nismes, Lyons and Langres. The font and baptismal chapel at the church of St. Séverin, Paris, are also decorated by Flandrin; and he also executed several portraits and mural paintings at the Duc de Loynes' château at Dampierre. We must regard him as one of the legitimate representatives of classical landscape painting in France, and his industry and talent seemed to lose nothing of their vigour by the passing of the years, for even in the last Salon he was represented by two canvases. He obtained two medals of the Second Class in 1839; a First Class Medal in 1847; a bronze medal at the Universal Exhibition of 1889. He was also created Knight of the Legion of Honour in 1848. His death occurred in Paris on March 10, 1902.

P. P.

FLATMAN, THOMAS, was born in London in 1633, and was educated at Winchester school. From thence he went to New College, Oxford; but leaving the university without a degree, he removed to the Inner Temple, where, in due time, he became a barrister. It does not appear that he ever followed the profession of the law, but having a turn for the fine arts, he indulged his inclination, and gained some reputation as a poet and a painter in miniature. Horace Walpole mentions in his 'Anecdotes,' that Mr. Tooke, Master of the Charterhouse, had a head of his father by Flatman, which was so well painted that Vertue took it for Cooper's; and Lord Oxford had another portrait by him, which was so masterly that Vertue pronounced Flatman to be equal to Hoskins and next to Cooper. It is certain that he excelled more as a painter than a poet, and Granger asserts that one of his heads is worth a ream of his Pindarics. He died in 1688.

FLAVITSKY, KONSTANTIN DMITRIEVICH, a Russian historical painter, was born in 1829 or 1830, and studied at the Academy of St. Petersburg, of which he afterwards became a professor. He earned considerable praise in his country for his painting of 'The Death of the Princess Tarakanoff.' He died at St. Petersburg in 1866.

FLAXMAN, MARY ANN, a sister of John Flaxman, the celebrated sculptor, with whom she resided for some time, was an occasional exhibitor at the Royal Academy of portraits and subjects taken from poems, as well as domestic scenes, from 1786 till 1819. She died in 1833, in her 65th year. Blake engraved her designs for Hayley's 'Triumphs of Temper,' and her illustrations to 'Robin Goodfellow' were also engraved. Redgrave mentions the following, amongst others, of her works:

Turkish Ladies. 1786.
Ferdinand and Miranda playing Chess. 1789.
Portrait of Mrs. Billington. 1802.
Sappho. 1810.
Maternal Piety. 1819.

FLEGEL, GEORG, a painter of subjects of still-life, was born at Olmütz in Moravia in 1563, and resided at Frankfort, where he died in 1638. He painted fruit, flowers, fish, vases, glasses, and other inanimate objects. The flowers and fruit in the paintings of Martin van Valckenborch are by him. There are fruit-pieces by this artist in the Gallery at Cassel and the Museum at Darmstadt, and in the latter is a portrait of himself.

FLEISCHBERGER, JOHANN FRIEDRICH, was a German engraver, who worked for the booksellers. He engraved an ornamental frontispiece, and a portrait of the author, for Horst's 'Opera Medica,' printed at Nuremberg in 1660.

FLEISCHMANN, AUGUSTIN CHRISTIAN, was an obscure German engraver, who was employed by the booksellers at Nuremberg. He engraved some of the portraits for Roth-Scholtz's 'Icones Bibliopolarum et Typographorum,' published in 1726-42.

FLEISCHMANN, FRIEDRICH, a painter and engraver, was born at Nuremberg in 1791, and was instructed by Ambrosius Gabler. He executed many miniatures and portraits in oil, and engraved more than 1900 plates with the point. He died at Munich in 1834. His best works are:

His own Portrait.
The Four Apostles; *after Albrecht Dürer.*
Ecce Homo; *said to be after Leonardo da Vinci.*
The Portrait of Van Dyck.

FLEMALLE, BERTHOLET, (more commonly FLEMAEL, and sometimes FLAMAEL,) a son of Renier Flemalle, a glass painter, was born at Liége in

1614. He was first instructed in painting by Hendrik Trippez, but afterwards by Geraert Douffet, an historical painter, who had studied at Rome. Under this master he acquired sufficient ability to venture on visiting Italy. On his arrival at Rome in 1638, he was unremitting in his studies after the works of the best masters, and it was not long before he was noticed for the readiness of his invention and the freedom of his hand. The Grand-Duke of Tuscany invited him to Florence, and employed him in ornamenting one of the galleries of his palace. After passing some years in the service of that prince, he visited Paris, where he was patronized by the Chancellor Séguier, who employed him in some of the apartments at Versailles. In the sacristy of the Augustinian church in Paris he painted the 'Adoration of the Magi.' Notwithstanding this flattering encouragement, he quitted Paris and returned to his native country in 1647, after an absence of nine years. His first work after his return was a grand composition of the 'Crucifixion,' which he is said to have painted for one of the chapels of the collegiate church of St John, as well as for the King of Sweden. This performance gained him great reputation, and he was employed in several considerable works for the churches at Liége. In 1670 he was invited to return to Paris, where he painted the ceiling of the king's chamber of audience, in the palace of the Tuileries, representing an emblematical subject of religion. He was made a member, and afterwards a professor, of the Royal Academy in Paris, and was high in the estimation of Louis XIV. and the public. The love of his native country induced him, however, to return to Liége, where he was elected canon of the collegiate church of St. Paul, and continued to exercise his talents, under the protection of Henry Maximilian, Prince Bishop of Liége. A few years before his death, which took place at Liége in 1675, he fell into an extreme melancholy and gave up entirely all work. Bertholet Flemalle possessed an inventive genius, and had acquired by his studies in Italy a great style of composition, and a correctness of design that partake of the grandeur of the Roman school, but more especially the style of Nicolas Poussin. His forms are, however, too artificial, and his colouring is weak. The following is a list of his most important paintings:

Brussels.	*Museum.*	The Chastisement of Heliodorus.
Cassel.	*Gallery.*	The Death of Lucretia.
„	„	Alexander leaving for Asia.
Dresden.	*Gallery.*	Pelopidas.
„	„	Æneas leaving Troy with his wife Creusa, his father Anchises, and his son Ascanius.
Florence.	*Ducal Pal.*	Several paintings.
Liége.	*Dominican Church.*	The Elevation of the Cross.
„	*Cathedral.*	The Assumption of the Virgin.
		The Raising of Lazarus.
Liége.	*St. Paul.*	The Conversion of St. Paul.
„	*St. John.*	A Crucifixion.
Paris.	*Louvre.*	Mysteries of the Old and New Testament.

FLEMALLE, RENIER, (or FLEMAEL,) was a painter on glass, to whom is attributed 'The Adoration of the Magi,' in St. Paul's at Liége. He was the father of Bertholet and Willem Flemalle; and of a third son, Hendrik, who was a goldsmith.

FLEMALLE, WILLEM, (or FLEMAEL,) who was instructed by his father, painted several excellent glass-paintings for the Magdalen Church at Liége.

FLEMING, JOHN, a Scottish landscape painter, lived in the early part of the present century. He is best known from the series of views he painted for Swan's 'Lakes of Scotland,' published at Glasgow in 1834. In the Glasgow Corporation Galleries is a 'View of Greenock,' painted by him in 1827.

FLERS, CAMILLE, born in Paris in 1802, was a painter of landscapes and a scholar of Pâris. His 'Views of Normandy' and 'The Banks of the Marne and Eure' display a great amount of study and power or feeling in the colouring. He died at Annet (Seine-et-Marne) Paris in 1868. He was the instructor of Cabats. In the Louvre is a landscape by this artist of the 'Environs of Paris.'

FLESSHIER, B., is an artist mentioned by Walpole as a painter of sea-pieces, landscapes, and fruit. His pictures may be supposed to have possessed considerable merit, as some of them were thought worthy of being placed in the collection of King Charles the First, and in that of Sir Peter Lely.

FLETCHER, HENRY, was an English engraver who flourished about the year 1729. He engraved a print of 'Bathsheba and her Attendants at the Bath,' after Sebastiano Conca, and some portraits, among which is that of Ebenezer Pemberton, minister of Boston, prefixed to a volume of his sermons.

FLETCHER, NICOLAS, is mentioned by Basan as having engraved, about 1750, some views of Rome, after Canaletto.

FLEUNER, PETER. There is a woodcut executed in a very bold, spirited style, representing an emblematical subject, apparently 'The Procession of Gluttony,' with the name of this artist at length, and dated 1549.

FLEUR, NICOLAS GUILLAUME DE LA. See DE LA FLEUR.

FLEURY, ANTOINE CLAUDE, a French historical and portrait painter, was born about the middle of the 18th century. He studied under Regnault, and exhibited at the Salon from 1795 to 1822. Amongst his works are:

The Abduction of Helen from the Temple of Diana. 1800.
Theseus going to fight the Minotaur. 1804.
The Doom of Orestes. 1806.
Venus and Adonis.
The Origin of Painting. 1808.
Cornelia and her Sons. 1810.
The Flight into Egypt. 1819.
The Widow's Mite. 1819.
Portrait of Louis XVIII. 1819.

FLEURY, FRANÇOIS ANTOINE LÉON, a French landscape painter, was born in Paris in 1804. He was the son of Antoine Claude Fleury, under whom he at first studied, and then under Bertin and Hersent. Between 1827 and 1830 he made a sketching tour in France and the neighbouring countries. He occasionally painted figure subjects, such as 'The Baptism of Christ,' at the church of St. Marguerite, and 'St. Geneviève,' at St. Etienne-du-Mont, Paris. He died in 1858. Amongst his works are:

A View of the Ponte Ratto, Rome. 1831.
Wood in Normandy. (*Bar-le-Duc Museum.*)
View on the Road to Genoa, near Nice. (*Amiens Museum.*)
Pasturage in Normandy, near Trouville.
Water and Mill at Coutivert.
View on the Coast of Genoa. (*Orleans Museum.*)

FLICIUS, GERBARUS, is only known by his

portrait of Archbishop Cranmer, painted in 1546, now in the National Portrait Gallery. It has been engraved in Thoroton's 'Antiquities of Nottinghamshire,' and in Lodge's 'Portraits.'

FLINCH, ANDREAS CHRISTIAN FERDINAND, a wood-engraver, was born at Copenhagen in 1813, and studied at the Academy there from 1832 to 1838. He had previously worked as a goldsmith, but he afterwards took to wood-engraving from self-tuition, and introduced a special method of his own into Denmark, consisting in drawing the outline upon the block and working out the details with a free hand. In 1840 he settled down as a lithographer, and published the popular 'Flinchs Almanak' with woodcut illustrations. He died at Copenhagen in 1872.

FLINCK, GOVERT, was born at Cleves in 1615. It was the wish of his parents to bring him up to mercantile pursuits; but his desire of becoming a painter induced him to seek every opportunity of becoming acquainted with artists, and his father was at length persuaded to allow him to follow a profession for which he had shown so decided a propensity. He was first a scholar of Lambert Jacobsz, at Leeuwarden, and under him he remained some time; but he afterwards entered the school of Rembrandt, and made such progress that after a year his works were scarcely discernible from those of that master.

From 1640 to 1650 he executed his best productions of historical subjects and portraits, and in both he was one of the most successful and most employed artists of his country. The magistrates of Amsterdam engaged him in many considerable works for the town-hall, and he painted the portraits of some of the most illustrious personages of his time. In 1652 he became a burgher of Amsterdam. The Elector of Brandenburg and Prince Maurice of Nassau favoured him with their protection, and employed him in many important works. The burgomaster of Amsterdam had commissioned him to paint twelve pictures for the town-hall, of which he had finished the sketches when he died in 1660. In the latter part of his life he began to study after the works of the Italian masters. The following is a list of his best paintings :

Aix-la-Chapelle.	Hôtel de Ville.	The Regents. 1642.
Amsterdam.	Museum.	Fête of the Civic Guard of Amsterdam, in celebration of the Peace of Munster. 1648.
		Isaac blessing Jacob. 1638.
"	Palace.	Marcus Curius Dentatus as a Husbandman.
"	"	Solomon praying for the gift of Wisdom.
"	Town-hall.	The Archers of 1642.
"	Curios. Cab.	The Archers of 1645.
Antwerp.	Museum.	The Portraits of a Man and Woman.
Berlin.	Gallery.	A Female Portrait. 1641.
		The Expulsion of Hagar.
Bordeaux.	Museum.	A Landscape.
Brunswick.	Gallery.	A Female Portrait. 1636.
"	"	Pyrrhus and Fabricius.
		The Crowning of a Conqueror.
Brussels.	Museum.	Portrait of a Woman.
Cologne.	Museum.	Portrait of an old Man reading.
Copenhagen.	Gallery.	A Portrait.
		A Portrait Group.
Darmstadt.	Museum.	A Woman and Child.
Dresden.	Gallery.	David and Uriah.
		Three Portraits.
Dublin.	Nat. Gall.	Bathsheba's Appeal to David.
Frankfort.	Städel Inst.	A Female Portrait.

Lille.	Museum.	Solomon and the Queen of Sheba. (*A joint picture with Dirk van Deelen.*)
London.	Bute Coll.	Portrait of a Lady. 1648.
Munich.	Gallery.	Isaac blessing Jacob.
	"	A Dutch Guard-Room.
Paris.	Louvre.	An Angel announcing the Birth of Christ to the Shepherds.
		Portrait of a Girl. 1641.
Petersburg.	Hermitage.	Jacob Cats, the poet, and William of Orange.
"	"	Portrait of a Jewess.
"	"	Portrait of a Soldier.
Pommersfelden.	Gall.	A Polish Jew.
Rotterdam.	Museum.	A Landscape with Figures. 1646.
"	"	Portraits of Dirck Graswinckel and of his Sister. 1646.
Vienna.	Gallery.	Portrait of an old Man.

FLINDT, PAUL, born at Nuremberg about 1570, was a goldsmith and engraver on metals, and one of the first artists who worked with the stamp or swage. He died after 1644.

FLIPART, CHARLES JOSEPH, the brother of Jean Jacques Flipart, was born in Paris in 1721, and was instructed in the rudiments of art by his father. He visited Venice, and studied painting under Tiepolo and Amiconi, and engraving under Wagner. After staying some time at Rome he was appointed court painter and engraver by King Ferdinand VI. of Spain in 1770. His best plates are the portraits of the King and the Queen of Spain. Some of his paintings are in two of the churches at Madrid. He died in that city in 1797.

FLIPART, JACQUES NICOLAS, who was born in Paris in 1724, was a painter of no repute.

FLIPART, JEAN CHARLES, a French engraver, was born in Paris about the year 1683. He engraved some plates, which are executed entirely with the graver, in a neat, finished style, but without much effect. He died in Paris in 1751. Amongst his works are :

The Portrait of René Choppin ; *after Janet.*
The Virgin and Infant ; *after Raphael ;* for the Crozat Collection.
Christ praying on the Mount of Olives ; *after the same ;* for the Crozat Collection.
The Penitent Magdalen ; *after Le Brun.*
Apollo and Daphne ; *after R. Houasse.*

FLIPART, JEAN JACQUES, the son of Jean Charles Flipart, born in Paris in 1719, was instructed in the art of engraving by his father, whom he soon surpassed. He afterwards studied under L. Cars. His plates are partly etched, and finished with the graver, and possess great merit. He died in Paris in 1782, leaving a considerable number of plates, many of which were after the best masters of his time. They include the following :

Portrait of J. B. Greuze ; *after Greuze.*
A Sick Man surrounded by his Children ; *after the same.* 1767.
Twelfth Night ; *after the same.*
Portrait of Jacques Dumont le Romain ; *after De La Tour.*
The Holy Family ; *after Giulio Romano.*
Adam and Eve ; *after C. Natoire.*
Venus presenting the Arms to Æneas ; *after the same*
A Sea-storm at Night ; *after Vernet.*
A Sea-storm by Day ; *after the same.*
Christ curing the Paralytic ; *after Dietrich.*
A Bear-hunt ; *after C. van Loo.*
A Tiger-hunt ; *after F. Boucher.*
The Battle of the Centaurs and Lapithæ.

CHARLES FRANÇOIS FLIPART, the brother of Jean Jacques Flipart, who died in 1773, executed several plates after Fragonard.

173

FLODING, Pehr, a Swedish designer and engraver, was born at Stockholm in 1721. He was instructed by Charpentier, and resided chiefly in Paris, but finally returned to his native city, where he died in 1791. He engraved several plates, both in line and in aquatint, among which are the following:

The Portrait of Alexander Roslin, painter; *after Roslin.*
Apollo and Daphne; *after F. Boucher.*
Soldiers guarding a Prison; *after the same.*
A Girl sleeping, with a Dog by her; *after J. B. Deshais.*
Gustavus III., King of Sweden; *after L. Pasch.*
A Battle; *after Casanova.*

FLORENCE, William of, was a monk who, in the 13th century, painted in Westminster Abbey, in the old castle at Windsor, and in Guildford.

FLORENTIA, Andrea da, was an artist who lived in the 14th century, and painted the frescoes inside the east gate of the Campo Santo of Pisa, which represent incidents in the life of St. Ranieri. Records exist to prove that they were executed by order of Piero Gambacorta, and that Andrea received payment for them in 1377. These frescoes were afterwards completed by Antonio Veneziano in 1386. Crowe and Cavalcaselle have assigned to this artist an immense series of frescoes painted between 1339 and 1346 in the Cappellone dei Spagnuoli, in the convent of San Spiritù, Florence. These frescoes contain between three and four hundred life-size figures, and present an allegorical representation of 'The Triumph and Power of the Church Militant through the efforts of St. Dominic and the members of his Order.' On the north wall of this same chapel is a fresco representing 'Christ going to Calvary,' and 'The Crucifixion.' No dates are known as to this artist's birth or death.

FLORENTIA, Bernardus de, is a name found on a few pictures, as a triptych in the Academy, and a 'Virgin and Saints' in the convent of the Ognissanti at Florence. It was at one time thought that the author might possibly be identical with Leonardo di Cione, the brother of Orcagna.

FLORENTIA, Raffaellino di. See Capponi.

FLOREZ, Francisco, a painter of illuminations in the service of Isabella of Spain, whose missal embellished by this artist is now in the Cathedral of Granada.

FLORI della FRATTA. See Della Fratta.

FLORIANI, Francesco, a native of Udine, who flourished in the 16th century, was instructed by Pellegrino, and displayed a great talent for portraiture. Many of his paintings were in the possession of the Emperor Maximilian II., by whom he was employed. His 'Judith' has great merit.

FLORIANO, Flaminio, was a Venetian painter, who imitated the style and copied the works of Tintoretto with success, from which fact he is supposed to have been a disciple of that master. One of his best works is a picture of 'St. Lawrence,' in the church of that saint.

FLORIGERIO, Sebastiano, who lived in the 16th century, was probably born about the year 1500 at Udine. He was a pupil of Pellegrino, and is thought to have married his daughter Aurelia. His first altar-piece was painted in 1525 for the church of Santa Maria di Villanuova, and in 1529 he painted, by commission, the altar-piece of 'St. George and the Dragon' for the church of San Giorgio of Udine. Soon after this he went to Padua, where he painted the portal of the Palazzo del Capitaneo, and seems to have remained in that city until 1533. On his return to Udine he unhappily killed a man in a duel, and was obliged to flee for refuge to Cividale, which he was unable to leave until 1543. His death is believed to have occurred at Udine soon afterwards. The following are among his extant paintings:

Padua.	*S. Bovo.*	Deposition from the Cross, with Saints.
"	"	A Pietà.
Venice.	*Academy.*	The Conception, between SS. Roch and Sebastian.
"	"	Madonna and Child, with St. Augustine and St. Monica (*painted for the Shoemakers' Guild at Udine*).
"	"	St. Francis, St. Anthony, and St. John the Baptist (*painted for San Bovo at Padua*).
"	"	Madonna and Child enthroned, with St. John, St. Anthony, and St. Monica (*formerly in the Servi at Venice*).

FLORIMI, Giovanni, (or Florini,) an engraver, who was a pupil of Cornelis Galle, worked at Siena in 1630. His works consist principally of portraits, and among them is that of Francesco Piccolomini, after F. Vanni.

FLORIS, Frans. See De Vrient.

FLOS, Du. See Duflos.

FLÜGGEN, Gisbert, a German painter, was born at Cologne in 1811, and having there learned the rudiments of painting, visited in 1833 the Academy at Düsseldorf, but went soon afterwards to Munich, where he became known for his genre paintings. The characters, the expression of the faces, and the excellent arrangement of his pictures have a very pleasing effect. He was elected a member of the Academy at Munich in 1853, and died there in 1859. The following are some of his works:

Hanover.	*Museum.*	Jacob deceiving Isaac. 1848. (*His best work.*)
Leuchtenberg.	*Ducal Gall.*	The Chess-players.
Madrid.	*Gallery.*	The unlucky Player. 1841.
Munich.	*Gallery.*	The Ante-chamber of a Prince. (*His last unfinished work.*)

FO, G. R., was a native of Switzerland, who flourished about the year 1551. Papillon speaks of him as an excellent engraver on wood, and a contemporary of Hans Holbein. He executed the cuts for the 'History of Animals,' by Conrad Gesner, published at Zurich in 1551, and also engraved the coins and medals of the 'Roman Emperors,' for another work by the same author, published in 1559.

FOCK, Hermanus, who was born at Amsterdam in 1766, and died there in 1822, was a landscape painter as well as an etcher, of whose works there remain sixty-five plates of landscapes, caricatures of Napoleon, &c.

FOCOSI, Alessandro, who was born in 1839, painted historical subjects at Milan. His best works are 'Catharine de' Medici and Charles IX.' (1867), and 'Charles Emmanuel throwing the Insignia of the Golden Fleece to the Ambassador of Spain,' painted for the Government of Italy. He died in 1869.

FOCUS, George, born at Chateaudun about 1641, was a painter of landscapes and an etcher. His best plates are six 'Italian Views,' after Nicolas Poussin. He died in Paris in 1708. He is called Faucus by Félibien and Mariette.

FOGGO, George, who was born in 1793, worked

174

with his elder brother James Foggo. He lithographed the cartoons of Raphael, and he was the author of several essays written for the advancement of art. He died in 1869.

FOGGO, JAMES, was born in London in 1790. His father, who was a zealous friend of civil and religious liberty, having given offence to the Tory government at the time when they had suspended the Habeas Corpus Act, proceeded with his family to Paris, where his sons were educated in the Imperial Academy. In 1815, on the return of Napoleon from Elba, James Foggo hastened to England, full of hope and ambition; but after his long exile he sought in vain the friends of his childhood. Nevertheless, without the encouragement of patronage, he set to work in a humble second-floor room, and painted his 'Hagar and Ishmael,' which was exhibited at the British Institution, where it was favourably noticed by West and other artists, yet did not find a purchaser. In 1819 he was joined by his brother George, and during the next forty years the brothers, working together, produced various historical pictures, generally of a large size, which, however, were doomed to remain on their hands unsold, their slender means of living being chiefly derived from teaching. In 1821 and 1822 they painted their large picture representing the 'Christian Inhabitants of Parga preparing to emigrate in presence of the invading force of Ali Pasha.' This and subsequent works obtained the approbation of Sir Thomas Lawrence, Fuseli, Hilton, Flaxman, and other artists of eminence. An 'Entombment of the Saviour,' by them, forms the altar-piece of the French Protestant church in St. Martin's-le-Grand. Amongst their other works may be mentioned 'Napoleon signing the Death-warrant of the Duke d'Enghien, in spite of the entreaties of his mother,' 'General Williams amongst the inhabitants of Kars,' and 'Christ at the Pool of Bethesda' (1824). The Foggos contributed also to each of the cartoon and fresco exhibitions held in Westminster Hall in the years 1840 to 1843. James Foggo died in London in 1860.

FOGOLINO, MARCELLO, was probably born in the Friulan Provinces at the beginning of the 16th century. He learned his art in Vicenza, and one of his earliest paintings is a small 'Adoration of the Magi,' in tempera, formerly in San Bartolommeo, and now in the Public Gallery of that city. In 1523 he contracted with the Scuola di San Biagio, at Pordenone, for a 'Virgin and Child between SS. Blaise and Apollonia,' and a little later he executed the 'Glory of St. Francis between Daniel and St. John the Baptist,' both of which pictures are now in the cathedral of Pordenone. On his return to Vicenza he painted a 'Madonna surrounded by Angels,' now in Santa Corona; and a 'Nativity' that is in the possession of Signor Bernasconi of Verona. According to a letter in his own hand, still in existence, he was at Trent in 1536, having been appointed to aid in the decorations of that city for the visit of King Ferdinand. In the Santissima Trinità, Trent, is an altar-piece that may be assigned to him, as also other paintings and frescoes in the churches and cathedral of that city. The dates of his birth and death are uncertain. Among his extant paintings are the following:

Berlin. *Gallery.* Madonna and Child with Saints. (*Early work: formerly in San Francesco, Vicenza.*)

Pordenone. *S. Biagio.* Madonna with Saints.
    ,, *Cathedral.* St. Francis between Daniel and St. John the Baptist. (*Much in the style of Raphael.*)
Vicenza. *Council-house.* } The Adoration of the Magi.

His engravings, which are executed with the graver in a free and light manner, include:

A Virgin and Child, in a landscape with architectural ruins, and Joseph drawing water from a well.
A naked Woman and a Child.
A Statue of Marcus Aurelius on horseback.
The Fragment of a Female Statue.
A Nativity.
Mary going to the Temple.

FOHR, DANIEL, born at Heidelberg in 1801, first studied science, which he afterwards abandoned for the art of painting. After studying some time by himself, he went to Munich in 1829, and then to the Tyrol. He was court painter to the Grand-Duke of Baden, and died at Baden-Baden in 1862. There are by him in the Gallery at Carlsruhe:

Mazeppa. 1836.
A View of the Königsee, near Berchtesgaden. 1836.
The Steinberg, near Berchtesgaden. 1837.
The Four Seasons, representing four Epochs of German History.

FOHR, KARL PHILIPP, a brother of Daniel Fohr, was born at Heidelberg in 1795, and studied at Munich, chiefly by himself from nature and the great masters. His paintings, which are to be met with at Carlsruhe, Darmstadt, and Frankfort, display genius and grandeur of style. In the Städel Institute at Frankfort are views of Tivoli and Heidelberg. His death occurred in 1818 at Rome, from bathing in the Tiber.

FOKKE, SIMON, a Dutch designer, etcher, and engraver, was born at Amsterdam in 1712. He was a pupil of J. C. Philips, and was chiefly employed for the booksellers on small portraits and vignettes, which he executed with spirit, but for the most part superficially. The same must be said of the numerous drawings which he has left. He died at Amsterdam in 1784. There are by him, among others, the following plates:

His own Portrait; *after himself.*
A View of the Port of Leghorn; *after Vernet.*
A View near Narni, in Lombardy; *after the same.*
Six plates of Dutch Views, with Rivers, Ships, and Skaters; *after Avercamp.*
Several Portraits for Tycho Hofman's 'Portraits historiques des hommes illustres de Dannemark,' 1746.
Several plates of his own design for Wagenaar's 'Vaderlandsche Historie,' 1749-59.
The Treaty of Peace at Münster; *after Terborch.*
The Prodigal Son; *after Spagnoletto;* in the Dresden Gallery.
Jacob keeping the Flocks of Laban; *after the same;* in the Dresden Gallery.
The Death of Dido, a burlesque; *after C. Troost.*

FOLDSONE, JOHN, a portrait painter, was born about the middle of the 18th century. He exhibited at the Academy up to 1783, soon after which year he died. He was the father of Mrs. Mee, the miniature painter.

FOLER, ANTONIO, was born at Venice in 1528. He was a contemporary and friend of Paolo Veronese, whose splendid style he followed with some success in his colouring, though very deficient in his design, particularly in his large works. In his easel pictures this inferiority is less discernible, and they possess considerable merit. Among other works by this master, Ridolfi notices

175

the following: in the church of the Abbey of San Gregorio, three pictures of the 'Assumption of the Virgin,' 'The Scourging of Christ,' and 'The Crucifixion'; in Santa Barnaba, 'The Birth of the Virgin'; and in Santa Caterina, 'Christ praying in the Garden,' and 'The Resurrection.' He died in 1616.

FOLIGNO, PIETRO ANTONIO DA, a native of Foligno, studied under Benozzo Gozzoli. He lived in the 15th century, but the exact dates of his birth and death are unknown. Remains of frescoes by him may be seen in the convent of Sant' Anna, the monastery of Santa Lucia, the monastery of San Francesco, where is a 'Virgin and Child,' dated 1499, and in other churches in Foligno. At SS. Antonio e Jacopo at Assisi is a series of scenes from the life of St. James, probably painted by him about 1468.

FOLKEMA, JAKOB, a Dutch designer and engraver, was born at Dokkum, in Friesland, in 1692. He was first instructed by his father, Johann Jakob Folkema, a goldsmith, and studied afterwards under B. Picart at Amsterdam. During that time he worked for Royaumont's Bible, 1712, and Ruysch's Anatomy, 1737. Folkema was also an excellent engraver in mezzotint. He died at Dokkum in 1767. He had a sister, ANNA FOLKEMA, who painted miniatures, assisted her brother, and engraved some few plates. She was born in 1695, and died in 1768. By Jakob Folkema there are, among others, the following plates:

An Emblematical Print on the Death of the Prince of Orange.
Time discovering the Bust of F. Rabelais, with figures and satirical and emblematical attributes.
The Martyrdom of St. Peter and St. Paul; *after Niccolò dell' Abbate.*
Several plates for the Dresden Gallery; *after Le Brun and Niccolò dell' Abbate.*

PORTRAITS.

Miguel Cervantes de Saavedra; *after C. Kort.*
Johannes Ens, Professor of Theology at Utrecht; *after Colla.*
Petrus de Maestricht, Professor of Theology at Frankfort; *after the same.*
Humphrey Prideaux, Dean of Norwich; *after Seeman.*
Suethlagius, Pastor at Amsterdam; *after Anna Folkema.*

FOLLI, SEBASTIANO, who is stated by Baldinucci to have been a native of Siena, was born in 1568. He was a scholar of Alessandro Casolano, and distinguished himself by several frescoes in the churches at Siena, particularly the cupola of Santa Marta, and some subjects from the 'Life of St. Sebastian,' in the church of that saint, painted in competition with Rutilio Manetti, to whose pictures they are in no way inferior. He visited Rome, and was employed in some considerable works for the Cardinal de' Medici, afterwards Leo XI. He died in 1621.

FOLO, GIOVANNI, an Italian engraver, was born at Bassano in 1764. He was first instructed by Mengardi and Zanotti, two painters at Bassano, and studied next in Volpato's school at Rome, but subsequently he chose Raffaello Morghen as his model. In his earlier productions there appears something of hardness and dryness of style, from which even his beautiful engraving of the 'Madonna de' Candelabri,' after Raphael, is not altogether free; but this defect is wholly avoided in the 'Mater dolorosa,' after Sassoferrato. Here the engraver has succeeded in expressing the character of the original picture, and diffused over the copy the same harmony of light and shade, and delicate colouring, which are

176

the pleasing characteristics of the master. Folo merits the name of a great artist; he seeks rather to preserve grandeur of character than to produce a work that is merely pleasing to the eye by elaborate execution. His strokes throughout are powerful and firm; yet in subjects requiring amenity of treatment he varies his manner so as to give a corresponding delicacy, as may be instanced in his 'Adam and Eve,' after Titian. 'Christ raising the Widow's Son at Nain,' after Annibale Carracci, is considered his best work. Folo's style was not suitable for all subjects, as may be conjectured from the medallion of Pius VII.; his productions are for the most part of a large size. He was a member of the Academy of St. Luke at Rome, and received in 1807 the gold medal of the Academy at Milan for 'Time protecting Innocence against Evil and Envy,' after Nicolas Poussin. He died at Rome in 1836. Besides those abovementioned, his most important works are:

The Last Supper; *after Leonardo da Vinci.*
The Virgin and Child; *after Raphael.*
The Marriage of the Virgin; *after the same.*
Mater amabilis; *after Sassoferrato.*
Danaë; *after Titian.*
The Marriage of St. Catharine; *after Correggio.*
The Archangel Michael; *after Guido Reni.*
The Massacre of the Innocents; *after Nicolas Poussin.*
Diana, resting from hunting, found by the Nymphs *after B. Nocchi.*
The Death of Virginia; *after Camuccini.*
The Triumph of Scipio; *after Pierino del Vaga.*
St. Andrew; *after Domenichino.* 1799.
Christ on the Cross; *after Michelangelo.*
Hercules with Lichas; *after Canova.*

FOLTZ, PHILIPP, born at Bingen in 1805, was first instructed in art by his father, the architect, Ludwig Foltz. In 1825 he went to Munich, and became a scholar of Cornelius, under whose direction he executed several considerable works in the royal palace. 'The Founding of the Academy of Sciences by the Elector Maximilian III.,' in the arcades of the royal court garden at Munich, is one of his chief works. With Lindenschmit he decorated a saloon of the palace with scenes from Schiller's poems. After having finished his great work, 'Otho, King of Greece, taking leave of his paternal Castle,' containing forty-two portraits, and the nineteen scenes from Bürger's poems for the Queen's apartment in the new palace, he went in 1835 to Italy, where he considerably improved his style. In 1838 he returned to Munich, became in 1865 director of the Gallery, and died in that city in 1877. In many of his works he was assisted by Dietz and Wendling. Among his numerous paintings are:

Armansperg.	Castle Chapel.	The Madonna.
Cologne.	Museum.	The Singer's Curse; *from Uhland's ballad.*
Darmstadt.	Gallery.	A Scene on the Iser near Munich.
Frankfort.	Römersaal.	The Emperor Sigmund.

FONBONNE, QUIRIN, a Dutch engraver, worked at Paris from 1720 to 1734. Among other subjects he engraved some of the plates for De Monicart's 'Versailles immortalisé,' 1720-21.

FONSECA Y FIGUÉROA, JUAN, a Spaniard of high descent in the 17th century, who was canon and chancellor of the cathedral at Seville, and upper chamberlain to the court at Madrid, was known in art by the production of some excellent portraits, but more especially by his patronage of other artists, in particular Velazquez.

FONTAINE, E., a French engraver on wood, flourished about the year 1681. Among other cuts by him there is a print representing the figure of Christ, standing upon a pillar. It is a very indifferent performance.

FONTAINE, JACQUES FRANÇOIS JOSEPH SWEBACH DE. See SWEBACH.

FONTAINE, PIERRE JOSEPH LA. See LA FONTAINE.

FONTANA, ALBERTO, was born at Modena about the year 1537. He was a fellow-student with Niccolò dell' Abbate, under Antonio Begarelli, and in conjunction with his co-disciple, painted the panels of the Butchers' Hall at Modena; a work which is mostly executed in the style of Niccolò dell' Abbate. There is certainly a great similarity in their styles, but although Alberto Fontana resembles Niccolò in the airs of his heads, he is always unequal to him in his design, and there is something red and heavy in his colouring. He died in 1558. In the Estense Gallery at Modena are four figures in fresco representing Vigilance, Prudence, Hope, and Faith.

FONTANA, BATTISTA. See FARINATI.

FONTANA, CESARE, was a native of Italy, who flourished about the year 1620. He engraved several plates representing funeral processions and cavalcades. Zani says he was living in 1660.

FONTANA, DOMENICO MARIA, is stated to have been born at Parma about the year 1540, to have learned the art of engraving at Bologna, and to have engraved several plates from his own designs, as well as after other masters. The following plates have been attributed to him:

The Flight into Egypt, with a mountainous Landscape.
The Sabine Women making Peace between the Romans and the Sabines.
St. John preaching in the Wilderness.
Mount Calvary, with a Latin inscription.
Christ going to Calvary. 1584.

There appear to have been two artists at Parma of this name, the second of whom was living in 1644, and has left one plate, after Parmigiano, of 'Moses with the Tables of the Law.'

FONTANA, FRANCESCO, born in 1843, was a sculptor and painter. His water-colour drawings representing scenes from the Bible are highly valued. He died at Milan in 1876.

FONTANA, GIAMBATTISTA, born at Ala, in the Tyrol, in 1525, was a painter, etcher, and engraver. He learned under Giovanni Carotto, and subsequently became court painter of the Archduke Ferdinand at Vienna. He worked also at Venice and at Rome. Though the design of his figures is meagre, his extremities and expressions of the heads deficient, and his drapery mannered, he composed his productions in a rich and masterly style, and handled the point with lightness and carefulness, and the graver mostly with neatness. He died after 1584. Among his sixty-eight plates, partly of his own composition and partly after other masters, the most important are:

Christ bearing the Cross.
The Crucifixion.
St. Martin.
The Prophet Ezekiel. 1579.
The Martyrdom of St. Peter; after Titian.
St. Agatha in Prison; after Benedetto Caliari.

FONTANA, GIULIO, was a native of Verona. Only one plate by him is known; it represents 'The Fight of the Venetians with the Imperial Troops at Cadore,' 1569, after Titian.

FONTANA, LAVINIA, the daughter of Prospero Fontana, was born at Bologna in 1552, and was instructed in art by her father. She painted historical pieces, which are considerably esteemed. Her greatest merit was, however, in portrait painting, which she practised at Rome with much success. She first visited that capital during the pontificate of Gregory XIII., whose portrait she painted, as well as those of many persons of distinction; and she was considered one of the ablest artists of her time. She married Paolo Zappi of Imola, who painted the drapery of her works, and she died at Rome in 1602. Her most important paintings are the following:

Bologna.	S. Trinità.	The Birth of the Virgin.
,,	Madonna del Baraccano.	The Holy Family and St. Joachim.
,,	Mendicanti.	The Miracle of the Loaves.
,,	S. Lucia.	The Crucifixion.
,,	Pieve di Cento.	The Madonna, with SS. Cosmo and Damian.
,,	,,	The Ascension. 1593.
,,	Pinacoteca.	Louisa of France before St. Francis of Paola. 1590.
,,	Gall. Hercolani.	Virgin with Saints and Angels in glory.
,,	Gall. Zambeccari.	The Queen of Sheba.
Bordeaux.	Museum.	Portrait of the Senator Orsini.
Dresden.	Gallery.	The Holy Trinity.
Dublin.	Nat. Gall.	Visit of the Queen of Sheba to Solomon.
Florence.	Pitti Pal.	Her own Portrait.
,,	,,	A Female Portrait.
,,	Uffizi.	Portrait of Friar Panigarola.
,,	,,	Christ appearing to the Magdalen. 1581.
Imola.	Signor Zappi.	Her own and her Father's Portraits.
Madrid.	Escorial.	The Holy Family with St. John.
Milan.	Brera.	Seven Portraits.
Modena.	Estense Gall.	Portrait of a Franciscan.
Petersburg.	Hermitage.	Venus and Cupid.
Rome.	S. Paolo fuori le Mure.	The Stoning of St. Stephen.

FONTANA, PIETRO, an Italian engraver, born at Bassano in 1762, was first instructed in painting by Mingardi at Venice. He went in 1785 to Rome, where he devoted himself entirely to the art of engraving, and became a scholar of Volpato and Morghen. He engraved in a tender and clear manner, and his style is a mixture of the Italian and English principles. He was a member of the Academies of St. Luke at Rome and at Venice. He died at Rome in 1837. His best plates are the following:

The Sibyls; after Domenichino.
Judith, Jupiter, Semele, and the Entombment; all after Correggio.
Christ before Pilate; after Lodovico Carracci.
Christ healing the Blind; after the same.
The Four Evangelists; after Guercino.
Ecce Homo; after the same.
Christ and the Pharisee; after Guido Reni.
Herodias; after the same.
Aurora; after the same.
Portrait of De Marchi; after the same.
The Death of Cæsar; after Camuccini.
Lucretia; after the same.
Pompey; after the same.
The Feast of the Gods; after the same.
Hercules, Ajax, and the Wrestlers; after Canova.
The Apostles; after Thorvaldsen.

FONTANA, PROSPERO, was born at Bologna in 1512, and was a scholar of Innocenzio da Imola. He attached himself, however, more to the style of Giorgio Vasari, preferring his expedition and facility to the diligent and careful finishing of his master. Prospero went to Rome, and was employed by Pope Julius III. Being after this engaged by Primaticcio, who was painting at that time at Fontainebleau, he went there, but returned to Genoa, where he painted for the Doria Gallery. After his return to Bologna he became the instructor of Lodovico, Annibale, and Agostino Carracci, Dionysius Calvaert, Tiarini, and Achille Calici. He was several times administrator of the Guild at Bologna, where he died in 1597. The following is a list of his most important productions:

Bologna.	S. Silvestro.	The Adoration of the Magi. (His best work.)
"	S. Giacomo.	The Baptism of Christ.
"	"	The Beneficence of St. Alexius.
"	Pinacoteca.	The Entombment.
"	Gal. Hercolani.	Judith and Holofernes.
Città di Castello.	Pal. Vitelli.	The principal Achievements of the Vitelli Family.
Dresden.	Gallery.	The Holy Family with SS. Cecilia and Catharine.
Milan.	Brera.	The Annunciation.
Modena.	Estense Gall.	The Visit of St. Anne (in watercolour).

Fontana was also eminent as a portrait painter, doing better in this branch than in his historical productions, and distinguished himself at Rome in the pontificates of Julius III. and his three next successors. The most important of his portraits are:

Pope Julius III.
Ulisse Aldrovandi.
Achille Bocchi.

FONTANA, VERONICA, born in 1596, was the daughter of the elder Domenico Maria Fontana, and was instructed in design by her father and Elizabetta Sirani. She etched some plates, representing scenes in the life of Mary, and the portrait of Andreini, the poet, and executed some woodcuts for a Latin Bible, and the portraits for Malvasia's Felsina pittrice,' 1678. Some writers attribute also to her the 'Office of the Virgin,' published at Venice in 1661, and some neat woodcuts, principally small portraits.

FONTANIEU, M. DE, was a French amateur engraver, who etched for his amusement a few small plates of animals, &c., some of them dated 1760.

FONTANUS, E., a wood engraver, was a native of Flanders, who flourished about 1625. His name appears on some engravings in a book, published at Breda, entitled 'Kleynen gulden Gebedenboeck met de figuren des Levens Jesu Christi ende Gebeden toegevogt aen ceremonien der H. Misse,' published in 1678.

FONTEBASSO, FRANCESCO, was a painter and engraver who was born at Venice in 1709. He received his first instruction in art at Rome, but afterwards studied at Venice, under Sebastiano Ricci. He died in 1769. His works as a painter are little known, but as an engraver he has left the following:

The Virgin appearing to St. Gregory, who is praying for the Delivery of the Souls in Purgatory; after Sebastiano Ricci.
A set of seven fantastical subjects; from his own designs.

FONTEBUONI, ANASTASIO, a native of Florence, was educated in the school of Domenico Passignano. He visited Rome in the pontificate of Paul V. (1605-21), and there he painted some pictures for the churches. In San Giovanni de' Fiorentini are 'The Birth of the Virgin' and 'The Death of the

Virgin,' which are considered his best works; and in Santa Maria in Selci is 'The Annunciation.' The vault of San Giacomo de' Spagnuoli is painted by him, and there is a figure of 'St. John the Baptist' in the Uffizi. This promising artist died young in 1626.

FONTENAY, JEAN BAPTISTE BELIN DE. See BELIN.

FONTYN, PIETER, was born at Dordrecht in 1773, and was instructed in art by Pieter Hofman and Willem van Leen. He painted portraits, interiors with figures, and scenes of joviality and domestic enjoyment. He died at Dordrecht in 1839.

FOOTTIT, HARRISON, was a miniature painter, who practised in England towards the close of the 18th century.

FOPPA, VINCENZO, was a Brescian by birth, being the son, according to recent research in local archives, of a certain Giovanni of Bagnolo, a place eight miles from Brescia, and must have been born between 1425 and 1430, though the exact date has thus far not been discovered. It has been usually assumed that he was trained under Squarcione and became a disciple of Mantegna, but this view is scarcely in accordance with the evidence afforded by the painter's earliest known works. In the absence of all documentary proof they are the most important key we at present possess to the history of his training; from them it seems permissible to assume that Foppa was to some extent affected by the early painters of Verona, but that he must have been closely connected with Jacopo Bellini, who was probably his master either at Venice or Padua, and whose influence was certainly the most important factor in his development. Foppa's return to Brescia as a finished artist must have taken place soon after 1450, and here he married the daughter of a Brescian named Caylina. About 1456 he removed with his wife and family to Pavia, which became his settled home for over thirty years, and where, between 1467 and 1468, he bought a house and obtained the rights of citizenship. Of his first works at Pavia we have no record, but he was probably one of the painters employed by Francesco Sforza between 1459-60 to decorate the Palazzo dell'Arengo at Milan. In 1461 he was at Genoa executing for the Confraternity of St. John Baptist frescoes in their chapel in the cathedral of that city, the Duke of Milan having warmly recommended him to the Genoese as an excellent painter highly skilled in his art. Having completed the ceiling of the chapel he did not fulfil his contract to paint the walls also, but returned to Pavia, where a work (now lost) in the church of the Carmine bore his signature and the date, May 1462. In these years he executed many works in Milan and its neighbourhood: episodes from the history of Trajan and decorative paintings (c. ? 1463) in the Medici Bank, the palace given by Francesco Sforza to Cosimo de' Medici, and rebuilt and decorated on a scale of great magnificence under the direction of Pigello Portinari, the first Governor of the Bank; paintings in the principal colonnade of the great hospital at Milan (? after 1463), representing its foundation by Francesco Sforza, and other subjects; figures of prophets in one of the cloisters of the Certosa of Pavia (1465), and an altar-piece for the church of S. M. delle Grazie at Monza, (1466), all of which have perished. Foppa's name has also been connected with the frescoes in the

VINCENZO FOPPA

THE ADORATION OF THE MAGI

chapel of St. Peter Martyr (church of S. Eustorgio, Milan), probably commissioned by Pigello Portinari, and said to have been completed in 1468. With the exception of Padre Bugati's brief notice referring the execution of the paintings to Vincenzo Vecchio, no documents relating to the decoration of the chapel have been discovered, and the present aspect of the frescoes, which were covered with whitewash in the 17th century, from which they were only freed in 1873, does not justify their attribution to Foppa with any certainty. In 1469 Vincenzo endeavoured to obtain employment in the Campo Santo at Pisa, but failing in this, probably returned to Genoa, where we find him in 1471 receiving payment for further work in the chapel of St. John Baptist. After 1474 he was actively employed at Pavia with other painters upon the great altar-piece for the chapel in the Castello, and at this period of his career must have executed many paintings for Milan and other cities, some few of which still survive. During his frequent visits to Genoa he produced among other works an altar-piece for the Spinola family in the church of S. Domenico, and another for the chapel of Lazzaro Doria in the Certosa of Rivarolo for which he received payment in 1489; but of all his works in Liguria only two have been preserved: the large altar-piece commissioned by Giuliano della Rovere for the cathedral of Savona (now in the oratory of S. M. di Castello), and a much injured picture in the Gallery at Savona ordered by Manfredo Fornari for the Certosa of Loreto. In December 1489 a petition was brought before the Council of Brescia by two of its members in which Vincenzo Foppa prayed to be allowed to repatriate and to settle at Brescia and teach painting and architecture there for the remainder of his life. The members of the Council, while unanimously agreeing to engage Foppa at a yearly salary of £100 planet, reserved to themselves the right to cancel the appointment whenever they should deem it desirable. Foppa's engagement lasted until May 1495, when for some reason at present unknown to us it was cancelled and never again renewed. The painter continued to live at Brescia for many years, having taken the lease of a house there in 1502, though he appears to have been frequently absent at Milan and Pavia. He must have died between May 1515 and October 1516, when he is spoken of as deceased. The date 1492, hitherto accepted as that of Foppa's death, was based on a mistaken interpretation of the inscription on his tombstone (now lost), and is disproved by the testimony of recently discovered documents; the character of some of the painter's works, obviously later than 1492, shows that he must still have been actively employed in the first decade of the sixteenth century. In spite of his long sojourn at Brescia no paintings have been preserved there which can be ascribed to him with any degree of certainty. The 'Anonimo' and other writers speak of Foppa as Vincenzo Vecchio, a name doubtless bestowed upon him on account of his great age, and not, as has been assumed, in order to distinguish him from a younger Vincenzo Foppa, of whom no trace has so far been discovered in Brescian archives. The following is a list of the principal works by Foppa at present known:

Arcore (near Monza). Signor G. B. Vittadini.		The Annunciation.

Arcore (near Monza). Signor G. B. Vittadini.		The Annunciation, Visitation, Nativity, and Flight into Egypt; two Angels with instruments of the Passion. (Part of the predella of an altar-piece from S. M. delle Grazie at Bergamo (now Brera. The central panel, the Ecce Homo, is missing.)
Bergamo.	Gallery. Carrara Collection.	Christ on the Cross between the two thieves. Signed: Vincencius Brixiensis 1456.
„	Lochis Collection.	St. Jerome kneeling in a landscape before a crucifix. Inscribed: Opus Vincentii Foppa.
Berlin.	Gallery.	Madonna and Child.
„	„	Lament over the Dead Body of Christ.
Florence.	Mr. Bernhard Berenson.	Madonna and Child.
London.	Nat. Gall.	Adoration of the Magi.
„	Sir M. Conway.	Madonna and Child.
Milan.	S. Eustorgio. Portinari Chapel.	Frescoes. (Ascribed to Foppa and other painters.)
„	Brera Gall.	Madonna and Child with Angels, eight figures of Saints, and St. Francis in a landscape receiving the stigmata. (Altar-piece from S. M. delle Grazie at Bergamo.)
„	„	St. Sebastian. Fresco.
„	„	Madonna and Child between St. John and a (?) Prophet. Dated Oct. 1485. Fresco.
„	Castello.	Madonna and Child.
„	„	St. Sebastian.
„	„	St. John Baptist. Fresco.
„	„	St. Francis receiving the stigmata. Fresco.
„	Poldi Pezzoli Museum.	Madonna and Child. (Ascribed to Foppa.)
„	Private Collections: Signor Crespi.	Madonna and Child. (Ascribed to Foppa.)
„	Dr. Frizzoni.	Madonna and Child with an Angel.
„	Cav. Aldo Noseda.	St. Paul.
„	Prince Trivulzio.	Madonna and Child with Angels.
„	„	Madonna and Child.
„	„	Two Bishops.
Savona.	Oratory of S. M. di Castello.	Altar-piece (in part). Inscribed: Vincencius, Aug. 5, 1490.
„	Gallery.	Madonna and Child with Saints. Inscribed: April 9, 1489.

C. J. Ff.

FOPPA, VINCENZO the Younger (see Caylina, Paolo the Younger).

FORABOSCO, GIROLAMO. See FERRABOSCO.

FORBICINI, ELIODORO, who flourished from 1550 to 1570, was a native of Verona, who excelled in grotesques. He decorated two rooms in the Palazzo Canova, which have been much admired.

FORBIN, LOUIS NICOLAS PHILIPPE AUGUSTE, Comte de, born at La Roque d'Antheron (Bouches-du-Rhône) in 1777, was instructed in the rudiments of the art by De Boissieu. Whilst a soldier in the Garde Nationale at Nice and Toulon, he became acquainted with the painter Granet, who exercised great influence over him. After quitting the service he studied at Paris under David, but in 1799 was again obliged to change the artist's for the soldier's life, and went through the campaigns in Portugal and Germany. In 1809 Forbin, who was then a lieutenant-colonel, took leave of the army and went to Italy to study. He stayed there five years, and then returned to Paris, where he was elected a member of the Institute, and appointed director of the Royal Museums, and subsequently superintendent of the collections in the Louvre, the Luxembourg, and at Versailles. In 1817 he visited Syria, Greece, and Egypt, and published in

1819 his 'Voyage dans le Levant,' an excellent work, with eighty lithographic plates. Later on he went to Sicily, from whence he brought back a great number of sketches. He wrote also several other works. He died in Paris in 1841. Among his best paintings are:

The Death of Pliny at the Eruption of Vesuvius.
The Death of King Andrew of Hungary.
A Nun in the Vaults of the Inquisition.
A Monk accused of having helped a Nun to escape.
Interior of the Peristyle of a Monastery. 1830. (*Louvre, Paris.*)
A Chapel in the Colosseum at Rome. 1834. (*Louvre.*)

FORD, MICHAEL, an Irish engraver in mezzotint, was probably a pupil of John Brooks, to whose business as a printseller in Dublin he succeeded about 1747. He is supposed to have been lost at sea in 1758. There are several portraits by him, some of which are after his own paintings. They include the following:

William III.; *after Kneller.*
George II.; *after Hudson.*
William, Duke of Cumberland; *after the same.*
William Stanhope, Earl of Harrington; *after Du Pin.*
Henry Singleton, Chief Justice of the Common Pleas in Ireland; *after himself.*

FORD, RICHARD, the author of the 'Handbook for Travellers in Spain,' who was born in London in 1796, practised art as an amateur. He illustrated Lockhart's 'Spanish Ballads,' and etched several plates. He died at Heavitree, near Exeter, in 1858.

FORD, SAMUEL, an Irish historical painter, was born at Cork in 1805. Although brought up in great poverty, he managed to study at the Cork School, and in 1828 became master of the Cork Mechanics' Institute, but he died of consumption in the same year. Amongst his works were:

The Genius of Tragedy 1827.
The Fall of the Angels.

FORE, LE. See LE FORE.

FOREST, JEAN BAPTISTE, a French landscape painter, was born in Paris in 1636. He was instructed in the first rudiments of art by his father, Pierre Forest, an artist little known. He went afterwards to Italy, and at Rome became the scholar of Pietro Francesco Mola. After studying the works of that master for some time, he applied himself to an imitation of the grand landscapes of Titian and Giorgione. On his return to France he was esteemed one of the ablest landscape painters of his country, and was received into the Academy in Paris in 1674. From an unfortunate process he made use of in the preparation of his colours, some of his pictures have since become dark. He died in Paris in 1712.

FORESTIER, HENRI JOSEPH DE, born at San Domingo in 1790, was a pupil of Vincent and David, and obtained in 1813 the first prize, which enabled him to go to Rome. There he became very favourably known through his paintings of 'Anacreon' and 'Cupid.' He died in 1872. Among his historical and genre paintings may be mentioned:

Christ healing the Demoniac. 1817. (*Louvre, Paris.*)
The Funeral of William the Conqueror.

FORGUE, APOLLONIE DE. See SEYDELMANN.

FORLI, ANSUINO DA, was the painter of the 'Adoration of St. Christopher' in the Eremitani Chapel, Padua. In the Correr Gallery at Venice is a tempera profile 'Portrait of a Man,' which is

assigned to Ansuino. No dates of his birth or death can be given.

FORLI, FRANCESCO DA. See MINZOCCHI, and MODIGLIANI.

FORLI, GUGLIELMO DA, called GUGLIELMO DEGLI ORGANI, who was the earliest painter of Forli, flourished in the 14th century. He was a pupil of Giotto, and painted frescoes in the churches of San Domenico and the Franciscans in his native city, but none of his works are extant.

FORLI, MARCO DA. See PALMEZZANO.

FORLI, MELOZZO DA. See DEGLI AMBROSI.

FORMELLO, DONATO DA, was a native of Formello, in the duchy of Bracciano. He was a disciple of Giorgio Vasari, and, according to Baglione, visited Rome early in the pontificate of Gregory XIII. He greatly surpassed the style of his instructor, as is evident in his fresco works on a staircase in the Vatican, representing subjects from the life of St. Peter. He died about 1580.

FORNARO, IL. See CIVERCHIO.

FORNAVERT, J. P., was an obscure engraver, chiefly employed by the booksellers. Strutt mentions a frontispiece to a book of devotion by this artist, representing 'Moses and Aaron, with the Four Evangelists.' It is neatly executed with the graver, but in a stiff, formal style.

FORNAZERIS, JACQUES DE, (probably the same as FORNAZORI,) was a French engraver, who flourished from 1594 to 1622. He resided at Lyons, and appears to have been principally employed for the booksellers, though his plates are executed in a style very superior to that of the generality of artists of that class. He engraved portraits of historical personages, and also several frontispieces, which he generally embellished with small historical figures, correctly drawn. His plates are executed with the graver. Among his fifty-six engravings may be noticed:

PORTRAITS.

Henry IV. (*Five plates.*)
Mary de' Medici. (*Two plates.*)
Pope Leo XI.
Pope Paul V.
Charles Emmanuel, Duke of Savoy.
James I., King of Great Britain.
Gabrielle d'Estrées.
Louis XI.

FRONTISPIECES.

To the 'Biblia Sacra,' Lyons. 1606; in quarto.
To the 'Biblia Sacra,' Lyons. 1618; in folio.
To the 'Tabula Chronographica,' Lyons. 1616.
To the 'Praxis Fori Pœnitentialis,' Lyons. 1616.
To the 'Commentaries of J. Fernandus.' 1622.

FORRESTER, ALFRED HENRY, a caricaturist, known by the pseudonym of 'Alfred Crowquill,' was born in London in 1805. His family was connected with the Stock Exchange, on which he was himself more or less engaged till 1839. His works were generally in illustration of his own letterpress. He also contributed to 'Bentley's Miscellany,' 'The Illustrated London News,' 'The Humourist,' &c. He died in 1872. Amongst his productions were:

Leaves from my Memorandum Book.
Eccentric Tales.
The Wanderings of a Pen and Pencil.
The Comic English Grammar.
Comic Arithmetic.
A Bundle of Crowquills.

FORRESTER, JAMES, an engraver, flourished about the year 1760. He resided some years in

MARIANO FORTUNY Y CARBÓ

PORTRAIT OF A BOY

Italy, where he etched several plates of landscapes, which are executed in a neat, pleasing style.

FORSELL, CHRISTIAN, born in 1777, studied first at the Academy at Copenhagen, and afterwards improved his talent for art by travelling. He was court engraver and professor at the Academy at Stockholm. The following are some of his best works:

The Coronation of the Virgin; *engraved after a design by Ternite.*
The Poet Camoëns; *after Gérard.*
Charles John, King of Sweden; *after the same.*
Louis XVIII; *after Augustin.*
'Une Année en Suède,' in forty-eight plates; *partly from his own drawing, partly after those of Sandberg.* 1837.

FÖRSTER, ERNST JOACHIM, painter and writer upon art, was born in 1800, at Munchergosserstädt, on the Saale. After a stay at the Universities of Jena and Berlin he took up art as his career, and studied under Schadow at Berlin, and under Cornelius at Munich. In 1824–5 he was working under Hermann on the frescoes in the Aula at Bonn, and was afterwards employed on those in the arcades of the Munich Hofgarten. He married a daughter of Jean Paul Richter, and this connection led him again in the direction of literature. After the death of his father-in-law he published several biographical notices of him, and edited his literary remains. He was employed in 1832 by the then Crown Prince Max of Bavaria to visit Italy, and make a series of drawings from the antique, and his archæological researches in connection with this work were afterwards embodied in his 'Material for a new History of Art' (1835). He also carried out various decorative works in the new palace at Munich. Of his numerous literary productions in connection with art the most important are: 'A History of German Art' (1851–60); 'Monuments of German Architecture, Sculpture and Painting' (1853–69); 'Life of Raphael' (1867–69); 'History of Italian Art' (1869–75). He published the continuation of Schorn's German version of Vasari, and was joint editor with Kugler of the 'Kunstblatt' from 1842–49. He died in 1885.

FORSTER, FRANÇOIS, a Swiss engraver, born at Locle in 1790, was instructed by P. G. Langlois in Paris. In 1814 he obtained the first prize, by which he was sent to Rome, and after his return he soon gained a reputation, his numerous plates being remarkable for the skill with which he represented the original. He handled the graver with great ability, and his faculty of imparting both vigour and tenderness in the execution gives the whole a beautiful and harmonious effect. In 1844 Forster was elected a member of the Institute of France and the Academies of Brussels and Berlin. He died in Paris in 1872. The following were his most important plates:

The Disciples at Emmaus; *after Paolo Veronese.* 1812.
The Portrait of a Woman; *after the same.* 1818.
Aurora and Cephalus; *after Guérin.* 1821.
Dido and Æneas; *after the same.* 1828.
The Portrait of Albrecht Dürer; *after Dürer.* 1823.
Arthur, Duke of Wellington; *after Gérard.*
La Vierge au Basrelief; *after Leonardo da Vinci.* 1835.
Titian's Mistress; *after Titian.*
La Vierge de la Maison d'Orléans; *after Raphael.* 1838.
La Vierge à la Légende; *after the same.* 1846.
The Holy Family; *after the same.* 1854.
The Three Graces; *after the same.*
The Portrait of Raphael; *after the same.* 1835.

Christ on the Cross; *after Sebastiano del Piombo.* 1850.
Louis I. of Bavaria; *after Stieler.*
Alexander von Humboldt; *after Steuben.*
St. Cecilia; *after Delaroche.*

FORSTER, THOMAS, an artist who lived in the early years of the 18th century, drew miniature portraits on vellum with lead pencil.

FORSTMAN, GREGORIO. See FOSMAN.

FORTI, GIACOMO, a painter of the Bolognese school, who flourished in 1483, was a pupil of Zoppo. He assisted his master in his frescoes, but in the church of San Tommaso al Mercato in Bologna, is a fresco of the Virgin, which is attributed to him.

FORTIER, CLAUDE FRANÇOIS, a French engraver, was born in Paris in 1775, and died in the same city in 1835. His best plates are 'The Entry of the French into Milan,' after Gérard; 'A Virgin Forest in Brazil,' after Clarac; and 'Morning,' after Moucheron.

FORTIN, AUGUSTIN FÉLIX, a French painter of landscapes, and of genre and historical subjects, was born in Paris in 1763, and studied under his uncle, the sculptor Lecomte. He was, however, chiefly noted for his sculpture, for which he obtained the grand prize in 1783. He became a member of the Academy in 1789, and died in Paris in 1832. Amongst his paintings are:

Invocation to Nature.
A Satyr.
Lesbia.

FORTIN, CHARLES, a French genre and landscape painter, the son of Augustin Félix Fortin, was born in Paris in 1815. He studied under Beaume and Roqueplan, and first exhibited in 1835. He died in Paris in 1865. Amongst his works are:

The Rag-seller.
The Return to the Cottage.
The Chimney Corner.
The Butcher's Shop.
The Village Barber.
Chouans. 1853. (*Lille Museum.*)
The Blessing. (*Luxembourg Gallery.*)
The Music Lesson.
The Smoker. 1855.
During Vespers, Morbihan. (*Paris Exhibition,* 1855.)
Rustic Interior. 1859.
The Country Tailor. 1861.
Between two Halts. 1864.

FORTNER, GEORG, who was born at Munich in 1814, studied under Schlotthauer and Heinrich Hess. He executed frescoes for the Bavarian National Museum; but he is better known for his designs for church windows. He died at Munich in 1879.

FORTUNY Y CARBÓ, MARIANO, a Spanish painter in oil and water-colours, was born of humble parentage at Reuss, near Barcelona, in 1841. Showing great artistic promise in his childhood, he was enabled by a local magnate to study at Barcelona and Madrid, and he further pursued his studies at Rome and Paris. He soon became known, and worked with great assiduity on the commissions he received, many of which were from Goupil of Paris. With the exception of the time during which he was on the staff of General Prim in Morocco, the rest of his life was passed chiefly at Rome and Paris. His death, which occurred at Rome in 1874, was occasioned by an attack of fever, contracted while sketching in damp weather in the vicinity of Naples. The pictures remaining in his studio were sold in Paris, and realized 800,000 francs. He married the daughter of Señor Madrazo, the director of the Madrid Academy. The following are amongst his chief works :

A Marriage in the Cathedral of Madrid.
Rehearsal at the Opera Buffa.
Snake-charmers.
Fantasy of Morocco. 1866.
A Book-lover in the Library of Richelieu. 1869.
The Fencing Lesson.
The Tribunal of a Cadi.
The Academy of the Arcadians. 1874.

Baron Davillier published at Paris in 1875, with illustrations, 'Fortuny, sa vie, son œuvre, sa correspondance.'

FOSCHI, FERDINANDO, was a landscape painter who flourished at Bologna in the 18th century. There is a landscape by him in the Lille Museum, and a winter scene in the Darmstadt Museum.

FOSCHI, SIGISMONDO, a son of Antonio Foschi, was born at Faenza, and flourished about 1530. There is a 'Madonna and Child' by this artist in the Brera at Milan, which came from the church of San Bartolommeo in Faenza.

FOSMAN, GREGORIO, (or FORSTMAN,) is considered the best of the Spanish engravers of title-pages during the reign of Charles II. Among his works are the following :

Title-page to a 'Life of St Domingo de Silos.' 1653.
Title-page to Ximena's 'Catalogue of the Bishops of Jaen.' 1654.
Title-page to Gandara's 'Glory of the Church in Galicia.' 1677.
The Auto-da-fè held in the Plaza-Mayor of Madrid, 30th June, 1680.
One of the plates of Vera Tassis's 'Obsequies of Queen Maria Louisa.' 1690.
St. Francis Xavier.
Portrait of Cardinal Errico Noris.

FOSSANO, AMBROGIO DA. See STEFANI.

FOSSATI, DAVIDE ANTONIO, a painter and etcher, was born at Morco, near Lugano, in 1708, and studied drawing under Mariotti at Venice, and painting under Daniel Gran, with whom in 1723 he went to Vienna. In 1728 he painted the dining-hall in the monastery of St. Martinsberg at Pressburg ; but in 1730 he returned to Venice, and in the next year executed the wall-paintings in the villa at Torre, near Este, as also in the nunnery of Santa Margaretta, near Lauis. He afterwards took to etching, but did not succeed at first. His death occurred at Vienna about 1780. His works as a painter are little known, but he has left among his later and happier efforts several etchings of landscapes and historical subjects after various masters. The following are his plates most worthy of notice : they are sometimes marked with the cipher AD

Diana and Calisto ; after Solimena.
The Family of Darius before Alexander ; after Paolo Veronese.
Jupiter destroying the Vices ; after the same.
Rebekah and the Servant of Abraham ; after A. Bellucci.
The Calling of St. Peter to the Apostleship ; after the same.
A set of twenty-four Views of Venice, and Landscapes ; after Marco Ricci.

FOSSATI, DOMENICO, was born at Venice in 1743, and studied painting at the Academy of that city. He distinguished himself as a painter of architecture and a decorator, and his works are to be met with in the theatres and palaces of Venice, Padua, Vicenza, Verona, Udine, Monza, and Gratz, and in the Scala at Milan. He died at Venice in 1784.

182

FOSSATI, GIORGIO, an engraver and architect, who was born at the commencement of the 18th century, and died about 1770, executed the plates to the 'Raccolta di varie Favole' (Venice, 1744), and also made the designs for the carving in the Scuola di San Rocco at Venice.

FOSSE, DE LA. See DE LA FOSSE.

FOSSEYEUX, JEAN BAPTISTE, who was born in Paris in 1782, and died there in 1824, studied under Delaunay and Moreau the younger. He engraved after Velazquez, Domenichino, &c.

FOSTER, MYLES BIRKET, was a member of an old north-country Quaker family. He was born at North Shields on February 4, 1825, the youngest but one of seven children. His father removed to London when he was but five years of age, so that his early youth was spent away from the district of his birth. His grandfather was a naval officer of renown who was acquainted with Thomas Bewick the engraver, but Birket seems to have been the only member of the family who had inclinations towards art. Birket is said to have been able to draw before he could speak, but whether this was true or not it is certain that at very tender years he was able to make quite a creditable sketch, and the local renown of Bewick, and the traditions as to his friendship with the grandfather of young Foster helped to enkindle in the lad the strongest desire that he too might become a great artist. At the first schools to which he went, those kept by Quakers at Tottenham and at Hitchin, he was taught drawing, and then later on he had special lessons from an intelligent master named Parry ; but his education terminated before he was sixteen, and the question of a profession was before him. It was at first decided that he should be sent to a steel engraver named Stone, but as the man committed suicide on the day that the articles were signed that could not be accomplished, and eventually Foster was sent to the studio of Ebenezer Landells the wood engraver, a man who had known Bewick, and was therefore of the greatest importance to Foster. Here he worked for a good many years doing drawings for 'Punch,' 'Punch's Almanack,' the 'Illustrated London News,' and its 'Annual Almanack,' and many of the illustrated books of the day, notably one by S. C. Hall on Ireland. It was very little actual engraving that Foster did, as his work in drawing on the blocks was so acceptable that his time was fully occupied with it, and he himself was always ready to add to his knowledge by steady work out-of-doors, or by sketching events which took place with a view of using them for illustrations. He left Landells in 1846, starting on his own account, and worked as a book illustrator for Vizetelly. His first great success was in illustrating 'Evangeline,' and after that he was sent up the Rhine that he might make drawings for 'Hyperion,' and for a book on the famous river itself. From that time to 1859 he illustrated many of the most notable works of the day, especially of poetry, but at length he determined to give up black and white work and take to more congenial labour in colour. His first work in the Royal Academy represented a farm near Arundel, and was hung in 1859 ; in the following year he was an Associate of the Old Water-Colour Society, and attained full rank as a member two years afterwards. The death of his father in 1861 was not altogether a loss to Foster, for a confusion having arisen between his name and that of his parent an obituary account of the

MARIANO FORTUNY Y CARBÓ

THE SPANISH MARRIAGE (LA VICARIA)

artist was issued praising him in no measured terms, and lamenting the loss caused to British art by so untimely a decease. This was at once, of course, contradicted, but the critics had already spoken, and the reputation of Foster gained in strength by this strange occurrence. In 1862 Foster settled down in Surrey, eventually building a house at Witley, which became a most popular resort for his artist friends, and in which he resided for many years. His work was always worthy of respect, conscientious and pleasing, and although it ever bore traces of his earlier practice of black and white drawing, and was as elaborate sometimes in its stippling as though it was intended for a block, yet this fault gradually became less and less, and his work assumed a stronger and broader character. He had a great love for the rustic cottage scenes of Surrey, and painted them with a daintiness and loving skill which few have excelled. His greatest triumphs in water-colour were obtained in the country side, in the winding lane, the hedgerow, with its flowers ; the cottage, the hamlet, or the village, and he painted all these over and over again with a careful attention to details, a graceful daintiness and a freshness of colour which invariably caused the pictures to be popular and attractive. There was a sweetness and a gentleness as has been well said about his work which redeemed it, and although it was monotonous it never failed to be pleasant and thoroughly English. His home at Witley was adorned by the work of all his friends. Burne Jones painted on the staircase, Rossetti adorned the dining-room, Keene devised some of the stained glass, Morris and Hunt, Linnell, Walker, Pinwell, Houghton and Lewis, all had their share in the decoration, and the result was very remarkable and of great beauty. Towards the close of his life Foster had to leave this place, and settled in failing health, and with his mental powers at times over-clouded, at Weybridge. There he died March 27, 1899, at the age of seventy-three, having made a very important name in English water-colour art. He was in earlier days fond of etching, and produced some notable plates. He also worked in lithography, and whatever he did was marked by the same restful charm, daintiness and grace which are the main characteristics of his well-known work in colour. An 'Art Annual' respecting him was written by Mr. Huish, and issued by the 'Art Journal' in 1890.　　　　　　　　　　G. C. W.

FOSTER, THOMAS, an Irish portrait painter, was born in 1798. He came to England early, and entered the schools of the Royal Academy, where he exhibited from 1819 to 1825. He died by his own hand in 1826. Amongst his portraits are:

Miss Tree.
Right Hon. John Wilson Croker.
Sir Henry Bishop, the composer.

FOUACE, GUILLAUME, a French painter of still life, born at Réville (Manche); a pupil of Yvon; exhibited regularly with success at the Salon des Champs Elysées, where in 1884 he obtained an honourable mention, in 1891 a medal of the third class, and in 1893 a medal of the first class. He also showed much talent as a sculptor, and made his mark in this branch of art in the Salon of 1890. His death occurred January 12, 1895.

FOUCEEL, ——, a Dutch landscape painter and engraver, flourished in the early part of the 17th century. Three very tenderly executed plates, now very rare, are known by him : 'The Group of Trees,' 'The Avenue,' and 'The Terrace.'

FOUCHER, NICOLAS, born in Paris in 1650, was instructed by Mignard, and painted portraits and historical subjects. He also etched in a spirited manner the portrait of 'Jaque Roland, sieur de Belebat, maistre chirurgien.' Foucher died about 1700.

FOUCHIER, BARTRAM DE, a Dutch painter, was born at Bergen-op-Zoom in 1609. He was sent to Antwerp when very young, and there became a scholar of Van Dyck, but when that master left Antwerp to visit England, Fouchier returned to Holland, where he studied under Jan Bylert, at Utrecht. He afterwards went to Rome, where he remained three years, and would probably have acquired a distinguished reputation if he had not been implicated in a quarrel, which obliged him to quit the city. The fame of the Venetian painters drew him to Venice, where he particularly devoted himself to studying the works of Tintoretto. After an absence of eight years he returned to Holland, where he soon found that neither the style he had acquired in Italy, nor the subjects of his pictures, were agreeable to the taste of his countrymen. He therefore abandoned historical painting, and applied himself to paint similar subjects to those of Ostade and Brouwer, representing assemblies of peasants and drunken frolics, which were admired in his time, and are still to be found in the collections in Holland. He died at Bergen-op-Zoom in 1674.

FOULLON, BENJAMIN, the son of Pierre Foullon, a native of Antwerp, who received letters of naturalization from Francis I. of France, flourished in 1583. By him there are forty-eight crayon drawings in the National Library in Paris, which resemble in style those of François Clouet. He was painter at the court of Henry IV. of France.

FOUNTAIN. See LA FONTAINE.

FOUQUET, JEAN, (or FOUCQUET,) a French miniature painter, was born at Tours about 1415. At that time there were two different schools in France: the one adopted the principles of Van Eyck, the other united the manner of that artist with the Italian style, and of the latter Fouquet was a great adherent. His first-known work is dated 1461 ; his last, 1475. He was court painter to Louis XI., and died in 1483. Among his miniatures and oil paintings are the following :

Antwerp.	Gallery.	The Virgin and Child. (The half of an altar-piece in oil.)
Frankfort.	Brentano-Laroche Collection.	Forty Miniatures, painted in 1461 for Étienne Chevalier, Treasurer of Charles VII. (Three more are in other private collections.)
„	„	Étienne Chevalier, the donor, and St. Stephen. (The other half of the Antwerp altar-piece.)
Munich.	Royal Library.	The Miniatures in a French translation of Boccaccio, by Pierre Faure, curé of St. Denis. 1458.
Paris.	National Library.	Eleven Miniatures in a French translation of Josephus's 'History of the Jews,' representing scenes in the life of Joseph.
Versailles.	Gallery.	The Portrait of Guillaume Juvenal des Ursins (in oil).

FOUQUIÈRES, JACQUES, was born at Antwerp in 1580, where he received some instruction from Jodocus De Momper, and afterwards studied under Jan Brueghel, though he adopted a style of landscape painting very superior to that of either of those masters, and in this branch of art arrived at an excellence that induced Rubens occasionally to employ him to paint the backgrounds of his pictures. Under this master he gained so high a reputation that the Elector Palatine employed him at his court when still young. He afterwards visited Rome and Venice, where he greatly improved his style by studying the works of Titian, whose fine landscapes were the particular objects of his admiration. In 1621 he went to Paris, and was employed by Louis XIII. in the great gallery of the Louvre. His pictures were so much admired by that monarch that he conferred on him the honour of knighthood, which mark of distinction is said by D'Argenville to have rendered him so vain and ridiculous, that he afterwards never painted without his sword by his side. He became so proud and overbearing that his insolent conduct to Nicolas Poussin, who was employed by the king at the same time in the Louvre, was the means of depriving France of the talents of that admirable painter, who left Paris in disgust, and resided at Rome for the remainder of his life. Fouquières was, notwithstanding these foibles, a distinguished painter of landscapes; his pencil is free and firm, and his colour, both in oil and in fresco, is clear and fresh, though occasionally cold, and too green. The figures with which he embellished his landscapes are correctly drawn, and touched with great spirit. He fell into disgrace, and died in Paris, in poverty, in 1659. There is a small landscape by this artist in the Darmstadt Gallery, and another in the Bordeaux Museum.

FOUR, N. DU. See DU FOUR.

FOURDRINIER, PIERRE, was a French engraver, who flourished for upwards of thirty years in London. He engraved many plates for the embellishment of books, plays, and pamphlets, and also executed some large plates of architectural views, which are his best performances. Some of these were for a large folio volume of the 'Villas of the Ancients,' published by Robert Castell in 1728. He also engraved some of the plans and elevations of Houghton Hall. He died in London in 1758.

FOURMOIS, THÉODORE, a Belgian artist, who was born at Presles in 1814, first devoted himself to pencil drawing, afterwards to water-colour, and lastly to oil painting. He was a diligent and tasteful artist, and painted with a bold brush. His subjects are mostly views of Brussels and the Ardennes. He died at Brussels in 1871.

FOURNIER, ——, a French engraver, executed part of the plates for a small folio volume, entitled 'Les Tableaux de la Pénitence.'

FOURNIER, DANIEL, an à-la-mode beefseller, shoemaker and engraver, was born early in the 18th century. He published in 1764 a work on Perspective, and died about 1766. There is a mezzotint by him of Cuthbert Mayne, a Catholic priest.

FOURNIER, JACQUES. See FORNAZERIS.

FOURNIER, JEAN, a native of France, was a scholar of F. de Troy, and gained the first prize at the Royal Academy of Painting in 1737 for a picture of 'Samson and Delilah.' He passed the greater part of his artistic life at the Hague, and painted the portraits of many distinguished persons of his time; among others, those of the Duke of Cumberland and Admiral Anson. He died at the Hague in 1765.

FOURNIER, JEAN BAPTISTE FORTUNÉ DE, born

at Ajaccio, Corsica, in 1798, studied at the Polytechnic School at Naples, and was distinguished for his water-colour views of interiors, as 'The Saloon of Louis XIV. in the Tuileries.' He died in Paris in 1864.

FOUTIN, J., an engraver of Chateaudun, was probably a goldsmith, as the only prints known by him are some plates of ornamental foliage, with grotesque heads, figures, &c., dated 1619.

FOWLER, WILLIAM, a draughtsman and engraver, was brought up as a carpenter at Winterton in Lincolnshire, where he died in 1832.

FOWLER, WILLIAM, a portrait painter, was born in 1796. His best known work is a portrait of Queen Victoria, which was engraved in mezzotint by J. R. Jackson. He died in London about 1880.

FOX, CHARLES, who was born at Falmouth in 1749, and who began life as a bookseller, later turned his attention to art, practising both landscape and portraiture. He likewise published some translations from the Persian, and died at Bath in 1809.

FOX, CHARLES, was born in 1794, at Cossey, near Norwich, where his father was steward to Lord Stafford, of Cossey Hall. After a period of studying engraving under Edwards at Bungay, he came up to London, became an inmate in the studio of John Burnet, who was at that time engaged in engraving some of Wilkie's principal works, and assisted Burnet in their completion. The engravings executed entirely with his own burin are several small plates after Wilkie for Cadell's edition of Sir Walter Scott's novels, and various illustrations to the Annuals of the day. His large engravings are a whole-length portrait of Sir George Murray, after Pickersgill; 'The First Council of the Queen,' and 'Village Recruits,' after Wilkie. His early habits and love of flowers never left him; and on Dr. Lindley, his fellow-townsman, being appointed secretary of the Horticultural Society, Fox was chosen as a judge and arbitrator for the various prizes; and during the whole time gave the greatest satisfaction, both on account of his scientific skill and his strict impartiality. He also executed all the engravings for a periodical called 'The Florist.' At the time of his decease, which took place at Leyton in 1849, he was engaged upon a large print after Mulready's picture of 'The Fight interrupted.'

FRACANZANO, CESARE, a Neapolitan painter, who flourished in the 17th century, was a pupil of Spagnoletto. He died in France some years after 1657. His son, MICHELAGNOLO FRACANZANO, who was also a painter, died in France about 1685. There is in the Madrid Gallery a picture by the latter, representing 'Two Wrestlers.'

FRACANZANO, FRANCESCO, the brother of Cesare Fracanzano, was a pupil of Spagnoletto and the master of Salvator Rosa, whose sister he had married. His married life was an unhappy one, as by the instigation of his wife he committed crimes for which he suffered death at Naples in 1657.

FRACASSI, CESARE, (or FRACASSINI,) was born in 1838. He studied painting in Rome, where he executed several frescoes for San Lorenzo. He died in 1868. One of his most important pictures is 'The Martyrs of Gorinchum.'

FRADELLE, HENRI JOSEPH, an historical painter, was born at Lille in 1778, but passed his life in England. From 1816 to 1855 he occasionally exhibited at the Royal Academy, but his works chiefly appeared at the British Institution. He

JEAN HONORÉ FRAGONARD

LA FOIRE DE ST. CLOUD

died in 1865. Amongst his works (several of which were engraved) are :

Milton dictating 'Paradise Lost.' 1817.
Mary, Queen of Scots, and her Secretary.
Rebecca and Ivanhoe.
Belinda at her Toilet.
The Earl of Leicester and Amy Robsart.
Queen Elizabeth and Lady Paget.
Lady Jane Grey.

FRAGONARD, ALEXANDRE EVARISTE, a French historical painter, was born at Grasse in 1780. He was a son of Jean Honoré Fragonard, and studied under David. Besides painting, he devoted himself to sculpture, and to designs for lithography. He died in Paris in 1850. His chief paintings are :

Maria Theresa and her Son.
Francis I. knighted. 1819. (*Versailles.*)
The Triumphal Entry of Joan of Arc into Orleans. (*Orleans Museum.*)
The Burgesses of Calais in the Tent of Edward I.
Francis I. receiving Works of Art brought from Italy by Primaticcio.
Henry IV. and Gabrielle d'Estrées.
Siege of Ptolemaïs. (*Versailles.*)
Battle of Marignan. 1836. (*Versailles.*)

FRAGONARD, HIPPOLYTE EVARISTE ETIENNE, a French historical and genre painter and lithographer, was born in Paris in 1806. He was the grandson of Jean Honoré Fragonard, and was for many years connected with the porcelain manufactory at Sèvres. He died in Paris in 1876. There is at Versailles a copy by him of Bronzino's 'Isabella of Aragon supplicating Charles VIII. of France.'

FRAGONARD, JEAN HONORÉ, was the pupil and legitimate successor of Boucher, and the last of the great French decorative painters of the 18th century. Born at Grasse in 1732, after a short probation as a notary's clerk he quitted that profession, and attended the atelier of Boucher, who placed him under the influence and teaching of Chardin, by whom he was well instructed and where he made rapid progress. He is said to have handled the brush before he could draw a line, and obtained the Grand Prix de Peinture in 1752, though he had not yet been admitted to the Academy course. The picture by which he gained the prize was entitled 'Jeroboam sacrificing to Idols.' He studied at Rome, afterwards visiting Naples and Sicily, and many of the drawings made by him while on this trip were engraved by the Abbé de St. Non, who accompanied him and his fellow-traveller, Hubert Robert. He returned to Paris in 1763, and exhibited his 'Coresus and Callirrhoë' two years later. This picture was given by the King to the Gobelins to be reproduced in tapestry, but the artist applied for payment of his work in vain. He exhibited once more at the Salon of 1767, but soon deserted the classical style of painting for that in which he came to excel, exactly hitting off the corrupt taste of the time. His famous life-sized portrait of the celebrated dancer La Guimard, with whom it is alleged he had tender passages, the preludes to a violent quarrel, reminds one of his master Boucher, and is in the collection of M. Groult. Fragonard's work shows great variety of method, sometimes painting very rapidly, with a broad free brush, at other times finishing like a miniature or enamel. His crayons and water-colour drawings are characterized by a most graceful and light touch. The beautiful 'Foire de St. Cloud' which hangs in the dining-room of the Banque de France shows

genuine feeling for the charm and colour of open air, whilst his 'Gardens at Fontainebleau' in the Hertford House collection, which also contains 'The Fountain of Pleasure' and 'Chances of the Swing' (this latter painted for the Baron St. Julien, and afterwards in the possession of M. de Morny), is much to be admired. He again visited Italy in 1773 on the invitation of M. de Bergeret, and the sketches he then executed are preserved at Besançon. The year 1789 brought Fragonard's brilliant career in Paris suddenly to a close, and after a brief period of activity, under the protection of his quondam fellow-pupil, the all-powerful David, during which he was nominated one of the Conservateurs du Musée by the Assemblée Nationale, he retired to Grasse, his birthplace, repeating in an old house, the Maison Malvilan, his familiar themes. When he fled from Paris he is said to have borne with him four works which he had begun in 1772 for Madame Dubarry's Pavillon of Louveciennes, and these he adapted to the walls of the principal salon on the ground floor of the house he inhabited, completing the series by the addition of a fifth subject. These five paintings were sold on February 8, 1898, for £50,000, and passing into the possession of Mr. Pierpoint Morgan, were exhibited by him at the Guildhall in London in 1902. They represent 'The Lovers' Progress.' The large canvas, 'Love and the Maiden,' begins the series. The maiden, weary of wandering alone, rests and dreams at the foot of a column in the shadow of a little wood, while Love, hovering above, seems to beckon from afar the lover pictured by the girl's fancies. In 'The Surprise of Love' the lover appears and finds her seated in her garden, but she turns from him in fear. 'The Offering of the Rose' forms the third of the series. In this the maiden, thinking herself alone with her little sister, is suddenly disturbed by the advent of her lover, who propitiates her anger with a rose. In 'The Love Letter' the girl and boy read the letter together whilst he holds her closely embraced. Overhead the leafy branches cut the blue sky and luxuriant creepers wind round the feet of a marble statue. The fifth panel shows 'The Crown of Love' bestowed on the lover by his mistress. She holds it above his head, he kneels to receive it, whilst in the shadow a third figure sits, a youth, ready with sketch-book and pencil to immortalize the happiness of his friend. These pictures were engraved by Desboutins and reproduced in De Pourtale's 'Fragonard.' They were his last important work, and breathe the air of amorous gaiety which rendered his talent so delightful to the Paris of his youth. He returned thither but found no place in the new order, dying poor and obscure at his lodging at the Louvre on August 22, 1806. His wife, MARIE ANNE GÉRARD, to whom he was married in 1769, was distinguished as a miniature painter. She was born at Grasse in 1745, and died in Paris in 1823. An account of Fragonard and of his works will be found in Lady Dilke's 'French Painters of the Eighteenth Century.' Among his chief paintings are the following :

Besançon.		The Triumph of Bacchus.
Lille.	*Museum.*	Adoration of the Shepherds.
London.	*Wallace Gall.*	The Chances of the Swing.
"	"	The Fountain of Pleasure.
"	"	Garden of the Château of Fontainebleau.
"	*J. P. Morgan's Collection.*	The entire decoration of a room, painted at Grasse, and once belonging to M. de Malvilan.

Paris.	*Louvre.*	Coresus and Callirrhoë.
"	"	The Music-Lesson.
"	"	A Landscape.
"	"	The Shepherd's Hour.
"	"	The Bathers.
"	"	A Sleeping Bacchante.
"	"	Music.
"	"	The Storm.
"	"	The Inspiration.
"	*M. Groult.*	L'amour folie.
"	"	Le coucher des ouvriers.
", *Baron G.de Rothschild.*		The Sermon of Love.
Vienna.	*Baron A. de Rothschild.*	The Premeditated Flight.

There are by this artist several etchings from his own designs, and after various masters, among which are the following :

The Circumcision ; *after Tiepolo.*
The Circumcision ; *after Sebastiano Ricci.*
Christ with the Disciples at Emmaus ; *after the same.*
The Last Supper ; *after the same.*
St. Roch ; *after Tintoretto.*
The Conception ; *after the same.*
The Presentation ; *after the same.*
Four Bacchanalian subjects ; *after his own designs.*
L'Armoire. 1778.

FRAISINGER, KASPAR, a painter and etcher of Ingoldstadt, in Bavaria, died at that town in 1600. The following etchings are by him :

The Virgin. 1595.
The suffering Redeemer attended by two Angels. 1598.
The suffering Redeemer seated on a Stone. 1599.
The Virgin lamenting over the Dead Body of Christ. 1599.

FRANÇAIS, FRANÇOIS LOUIS, French painter born at Plombières (Vosges), November 17, 1814. Commenced mathematical studies which he could not continue, but at fifteen years of age went to Paris, where he became office boy to a librarian. After five years of hard struggle he was able to live by his designs, executing wood-cuts for éditions de luxe, and made himself a name as a lithographer. He then studied under Gigoux and Corot, and produced his first landscape at the Salon of 1837, entitled ' A Song under the Willows,' painted with H. Baron. He afterwards exhibited ' Antique Garden, Park of St. Cloud,' with figures by Meissonier. His picture of 'An Italian Sunset' is in the Luxembourg. Prince Napoleon purchased his ' View at Basmeudon' in 1863. An occasional portrait, such as that of M. Ildefonse Rousset in 1874; and a decorative panel, ' L'hiver,' for the Beauvais Manufactory in 1888, varied his long series of landscapes. He gained a third class medal in 1841, and a first class in 1848. He also obtained first class medals at the Universal Exhibitions of 1855 and 1867, also a medal of honour at that of 1878, and the medal of honour at the Salon of 1890. Chevalier of the Legion of honour in July 1853, he was promoted officer June 29, 1867. Elected a member of the Academy des Beaux-Arts, replacing Robert Fleury, July 5, 1890, he also became a member of the Institute of France. He died in Paris in 1897.

FRANCART, GILBERT, a French painter, whose only known work is a picture of 'St. Sebastian' in the church of Bazoches-du-Morvand. It is well drawn and coloured in the style of Le Brun, and dated 1661. He was still living in 1692.

FRANCESCA, PIERO DELLA. See DEI FRANCESCHI.

FRANCESCHI, PAOLO, called PAOLO FIAMMINGO, was born at Antwerp in 1540, but went when

186

young to Venice, where he became a scholar of Tintoretto, and resided during the remainder of his life. He principally excelled in painting landscapes, although he sometimes produced historical subjects. In the church of San Niccolò de' Frari, at Venice, are two pictures by this master, of 'The Descent from the Cross,' and 'St. John preaching in the Wilderness,' and in the Munich Gallery is 'The Dead Christ in the lap of the Virgin.' He was employed by the Emperor Rudolph II., for whom he painted several landscapes and other subjects. He died at Venice in 1596.

FRANCESCHIELLO. See LA MURA.

FRANCESCHINI, BALDASSARE, called IL VOLTERRANO, the son of Gasparo Franceschini, a sculptor, was born at Volterra in 1611. He was called ' Il Volterrano giuniore,' to distinguish him from Daniele Ricciarelli da Volterra, and first studied under Matteo Rosselli, but he afterwards became a scholar of Giovanni da San Giovanni. He is said to have excited the jealousy of that master, who, having engaged him as his coadjutor in some works in the Palazzo Pitti, after witnessing his capacity, thought it prudent to dismiss him. He was one of the most distinguished fresco painters of his time, and was more employed in that line than in easel pictures. He died at Florence in 1689. His most important productions are as under:

Bordeaux.	*Museum.*	Moses before Pharaoh.
"	"	Apollo and Marsyas.
"	"	The Apotheosis of Ovid.
Florence.	*S. Annunziata.*	The Coronation of the Virgin. (*His best work.*)
"	*Ducal Palace.*	Four large paintings, representing the Deeds of the Medici.
"	*Pitti Palace.*	Venus.
"	"	Sleeping Cupid.
"	*Uffizi.*	St. Peter.
"	"	St. Catharine of Siena.
"	"	An Augustinian Friar.
"	*S. M. Maggiore.*	The Ascension of Elijah.
"	*S. M. Nuova.*	St. Louis.
"	*S. Felicità.*	The Ascension of the Virgin.
Volterra.	*Convent of Badia di S. Giusto.*	Several large frescoes, representing Elijah.
"	*S. Agostino.*	St. Roch.
"	"	The Purification of the Virgin.

FRANCESCHINI, DOMENICO, was an indifferent Italian engraver, by whom we have a slight etching of the 'Amphitheatre of Flavius,' dated 1725.

FRANCESCHINI, GIACOMO, the son and scholar of Marc Antonio Franceschini, was born at Bologna in 1672. He painted historical pictures in the style of his father, and there are some of his works in the churches at Bologna. In Santa Maria Incoronata is a picture of 'St. Usualdo, St. Margaret, St. Lucy, and St. Cecilia'; in San Simone, 'The Crucifixion'; and in San Martino, 'St. Anne.' Franceschini died at Bologna in 1745.

FRANCESCHINI, Cavaliere MARC ANTONIO, who was the founder of the Upper Italian school, and whose first performances are to be met with at Imola, Ozzano, and Piacenza, was born at Bologna in 1648. From the Academy of Giovanni Maria Galli he passed into that of Carlo Cignani, of whom he became the most assiduous assistant. Together with that master he completed the works in the Palazzo del Giardino of the Duke Ranuccio II. at Parma, which were begun by Agostino Carracci. Franceschini also painted under Cignani at Bologna, Piacenza, Modena, Reggio, and other places, in fresco, tempera, and oil. Endowed with such capacities, Franceschini met with great encouragement. In 1702 he painted scenes from the history of the Republic in the Council-palace at Genoa, and in 1711 designed at Rome for Pope Clement XI. several cartoons for the mosaics in St. Peter's, for which he was honoured with the Order of Christ. On returning to Genoa in 1714, he executed several frescoes and paintings in the church of the Padri Filippini, and in the Pallavicini and Durazzo palaces. After having adorned the chapel of the Madonna del Carmine at Crema, in 1716, he returned to Bologna, and did not let his brush rest until he was nearly eighty years of age. He died there in 1729. His principal works at Bologna are a ceiling in the Palazzo Ranuzzi; a fine picture of the 'Annunciation' at the Pinacoteca; the 'Death of St. Joseph,' in the church of Corpus Domini; 'St. John in the Isle of Patmos,' in La Carità; and 'St. Francis of Sales kneeling before the Virgin and Infant,' in La Madonna di Galeria. At Rimini, in the church of the Augustines, is a fine picture of 'St. Thomas of Villanova giving Alms to the Poor.' His picture of the 'Founders of the Order,' at the Padri Servi at Bologna; and his 'Pietà,' at the Agostini at Imola, painted when he was near eighty, have no appearance of feebleness or senility. Other paintings by him are:

Bologna.	*Pinacoteca.*	Holy Family.
Brunswick.	*Gallery.*	Joseph and Potiphar's Wife.
Copenhagen.	*Gallery.*	Diana as a Huntress.
Dresden.	*Gallery.*	A Magdalen.
"	"	Birth of Adonis.
Edinburgh.	*Nat. Gall.*	St. Jerome.
Florence.	*Uffizi.*	Cupid.
Modena.	*Estense Gall.*	Genii bearing flowers.
Petersburg.	*Hermitage.*	The Judgment of Paris.
Vienna.	*Gallery.*	The penitent Magdalen.
"	"	Charity.
"	"	St. Charles Borromeo during the Plague at Milan. 1576.
"	"	Venus and Cupid.
"	"	Jacob and Rachel.

FRANCESCHINI, Vincenzo, was probably a relation of Domenico Franceschini. He executed part of the plates for the 'Museo Fiorentino,' published in 1748.

FRANCESCHINO. See Carracci, Francesco.

FRANCESCHITTO, (or Francisquito,) is stated to have been a native of Spain, born at Valladolid in 1681, and a scholar of Luca Giordano, who was accustomed to assert that the disciple would surpass his master. He accompanied that painter to Italy, on his leaving Madrid, and at Naples gave proof of the prediction of Luca, in a picture which he painted for the church of Santa Maria del Monte, representing 'St. Pasquale,' with a beautiful choir of angels, and a grand landscape. This promising artist died at Naples in 1705.

FRANCESCO. See Liechtenreiter, Franz.

FRANCESCO D' ALBERTINO. See Ubertini.

FRANCESCO DA COTIGNOLA. See Dei Zaganelli.

FRANCESCO DI CRISTOFANO. See Bigi.

FRANCESCO DI GENTILE DA FABRIANO. See Fabriano.

FRANCESCO DI GIORGIO, who was born at Siena in 1439, was more famous as an architect and an engineer than as a painter. His paintings are cold and unrelieved, and the strange conceits in his composition are both surprising and unpleasant. Six or eight panels by him are still in the Academy of Siena, and there is an altar-piece by him with scenes from the life of 'St. Benedict' in the Uffizi at Florence. His brilliant successes in the laying

out of fortresses, and in the invention of means for their attack and reduction, were only surpassed by Leonardo da Vinci, whom he met in 1490 at Pavia. He died in 1502.

FRANCESCO DI GIOVANNI, who lived at Florence in the 15th century, is the author of a 'Dead Christ,' painted in 1491, and now in one of the chapels of the Pieve of that city. He had a son named Raffaello, who finished an altar-piece ordered of his father in 1504 by the church of Empoli. It represents the 'Deposition from the Cross,' and is now in the Uffizi Gallery at Florence.

FRANCESCO DI MARCO. See Raibolini.

FRANCESCO DI SIMONE. See Santa Croce.

FRANCESCO DI STEFANO, commonly called Pesellino, to distinguish him from his grandfather Pesello, was born at Florence in 1422. His father, Stefano, who was a painter, died before 1427, and left his widow, the daughter of Pesello, in poor circumstances. It thus happened that the young Francesco was brought up by his grandfather, with whom he remained till the old man died, in 1446, when he continued to carry on the business in the atelier till he himself died young, in 1457, at Florence. In his works he, to some extent, copied the style of Filippo Lippi, and the predella of an altar-piece by that artist in the Florence Academy is said to be by him:

The following are the works usually ascribed to **Pesellino:**

Florence.	*Academy.*	The Nativity; Miracle of St. Anthony of Padua; Martyrdom of St. Cosmo and St. Damian. (*Part of the predella of the 'Virgin and Saints' by Filippo Lippi, also in the Academy.*)
"	*Buonarroti Coll.*	Three scenes from the Life of St. Nicholas. (*Predella from the Cappella Cavalcanti, in Santa Croce, Florence.*)
"	*Palazzo Torrigiani.*	Meeting of David and Goliath (*cassone*).
"		David Triumphant (*cassone*).
"	*Santo Spirito (formerly the sisterhood of S. Giorgio).*	Annunciation.
Frankfort.	*Städel.*	Virgin and Child.
Liverpool.	*Gallery.*	St. Bernardino preaching in the Cathedral at Florence.
London.	*Nat. Gall.*	A Trinità (*from the church of the Trinità, Pistoja*).
Paris.	*Louvre.*	St. Francis receiving the Stigmata; St. Cosmo and St. Damian healing a sick man. (*Part of the predella of the 'Virgin and Saints' by Filippo Lippi, in the Academy, Florence.*)
"	"	The Nativity. (*Ascribed in the catalogue to Filippo Lippi, but Crowe and Cavalcaselle attribute it to Pesellino.*)
Rome.	*Doria Palace.*	Two Scenes from the Life of St. Sylvester.

FRANCESCO DI TOLENTINO. See Tolentino.

FRANCESE, Claudio. See Claude.

FRANCHI, Antonio, an Italian historical painter, was born at Lucca in 1634, and settled at Florence. He was a scholar of Baldassare Franceschini, called Il Volterrano, though he rather followed the style of Pietro da Cortona. His picture of 'St. Joseph of Calasanzio,' in the church of the Padri Scolopi, is admired for the correctness of its design and the vigour of its effect. His best work,

'Christ giving the Keys to St. Peter,' is in the parochial church of Caporgnano near Lucca. He was employed by the Grand-Duke of Tuscany, for whom, as well as for private collections, he painted several easel pictures. He wrote a book on art, entitled 'La Teorica della Pittura,' printed at Lucca thirty years after his death. He died in 1709. His son and daughter, GIUSEPPE and MARGHERITA, also became artists.

FRANCHI, CESARE, who gained repute by painting figures of a small size, was a native of Perugia, and was instructed by Giulio Cesare Angeli. Franchi died in 1615.

FRANCHI, LORENZO, was born at Bologna about 1563, and was instructed by Camillo Procaccini; but after leaving that master he attached himself to the manner of the Carracci, whose works he copied, or imitated in small. He became eminent in this way; but the masters he chose for his models have the credit of the performance, and the name of Lorenzo Franchi is scarcely recognized out of his own country. He died about 1630.

FRANCHINI, NICCOLÒ, who was born at Siena in 1704, and died in 1783, was a son of the sculptor Giacomo Franchini. Among his pictures in Siena are 'St. Francis of Sales,' in the Baptistery (now San Giovanni); 'St. Christopher,' in Sant' Agostino; and the 'Death of the Virgin,' in San Giorgio.

FRANCHOYS, LUCAS. See FRANÇOIS.

FRANCI, FRANCESCO, who was born at Siena in 1658, and died there in 1721, has left in that city a number of pictures, among which may be named 'St. Jerome,' at the church of Fonte Giusta, and a 'Last Supper' in the refectory of the Osservanti.

FRANCIA, DOMENICO, a painter and architect, born at Bologna in 1702, was a son of the engraver Francesco Maria Domenico Francia, and studied under Ferdinando Galli (called Bibiena), whom he assisted in his paintings at Vienna. He was afterwards appointed builder to the King of Sweden, and on the expiration of this service painted at other European courts. He died in 1758.

FRANCIA, FRANCESCO GIACOMO. See RAIBOLINI.

FRANCIA, FRANÇOIS LOUIS THOMAS, a water-colour landscape painter, was born at Calais in 1772. In early life he settled in London, and exhibited at the Royal Academy from 1795 to 1822. He attained considerable reputation, and was appointed water-colour painter to the Duchess of York. He was an unsuccessful candidate for the associateship of the Academy in 1816, and shortly afterwards returned to his native place, where he died in 1839. There are nine of his works in the South Kensington Museum.

FRANCIA, GIULIO. See RAIBOLINI.

FRANCIA, PIETRO, was a native of Florence who painted for the catafalque of Michelangelo a work representing that artist standing before Pope Pius IV., holding in his hands the model of the cupola of St. Peter's at Rome, 1563. Alessandro del Barbiere was his pupil.

FRANCIABIGIO. See BIGI.

FRANCIONE, PEDRO, was a Spanish artist who flourished about the year 1521, and whose works are to be found at Naples.

FRANCIOSO. See JAQUET.

FRANCIS. See CONSCIENCE, FRANÇOIS ANTOINE.

FRANCISCO, DON. See FRANCKEN, FRANS, the younger.

FRANCISQUE. See MILLET.

FRANCISQUITO. See FRANCESCHITTO.

188

FRANCK, FRANÇOIS. See also FRANCKEN.

FRANCK, FRANZ FRIEDRICH, born at Augsburg in 1627, was instructed by his father, Hans Ulrich Franck. He died at Augsburg in 1687. The following productions are by him:

Augsburg.	St. Anna.	The History of Jacob and Esau.
Carlsruhe.	Ducal Pal.	The Passage of the Red Sea.
Mannheim.	Gallery.	The Israelites after the Passage through the Red Sea.
„	„	A Saloon of Pictures and Antiquities.
Ratisbon.	Cathedral.	St. Francis dying.
Vienna.	Gallery.	Portrait of a Man.

FRANCK, HANS. See LÜTZELBURGER.

FRANCK, HANS ULRICH, a German historical painter and etcher, was born at Kaufbeuren, in Swabia, in 1603. He resided chiefly at Augsburg, where he died in 1680. Among other engravings the following are by him:

Twenty-five plates of scenes in Military Life. 1656.
The Meeting of David and Abigail.
Alexander and the dying Darius. 1644.

FRANCK, JAN WILLEM, a Dutch painter of flowers, birds, and fruit, was born at the Hague in 1720. He copied after Berchem, Potter, Wynants, Van de Velde, Van Huysum, &c., and died at the Hague in 1761.

FRANCK, JOHANN, an engraver, was the son of Hans Ulrich Franck. He engraved several portraits for the booksellers, of which are some of those in Priorato's 'Historia di Leopoldo Cesare,' 1670; and in conjunction with Susanna Sandrart and J. Meyer, he engraved a set of plates of the gardens and fountains in the vicinity of Rome.

FRANCK, JOSEPH, a Belgian line-engraver, was born at Brussels in 1825. He was a pupil of Calamatta, and engraved many portraits and other plates after ancient and modern masters, besides which he completed the engraving of Rubens's 'Descent from the Cross,' which had been left unfinished by Erin Corr. He died in 1883. His principal works are:

The Virgin with the Lily; after Leonardo da Vinci.
The Entombment of Christ; after Quentin Massys.
A Pietà; after Van Dyck.
The Prisoner; after Gérôme.
Paul and Virginia; after Van Lerius.
La Glycine; after Portaels.
Meditation; after A. Robert.

FRANCKALLS, BAPTIST, an obscure engraver, is mentioned by Florent Le Comte, who says he excelled in engraving tournaments, theatrical scenes, and magnificent decorations.

FRANCKEN (or, as it is sometimes written, FRANCK,) is the name of a numerous family of Flemish painters, whose works are found in many of the public galleries of Europe. Owing to the fact that they all painted much in the same style as Frans Francken the elder, who was a pupil of Frans Floris, and the chief of the family, their works have doubtless been ascribed in some cases wrongly.

Nicolaes Francken
(1520?—1596)

Hieronymus I. (1540—1610)	Frans I. (1542—1616)	Ambrosius I. (1544—1618)
Hieronymus II. (1578—1629)	Frans II. (1581—1642)	Ambrosius II. (?—1632)
Frans III. (1607—1667)		Hieronymus III. (1611—?)
		Constantinus (1611—1717)

FRANCKEN, Ambrosius, the elder, a younger son of Nicolaes Francken, was born at Herenthals, in 1544. He was instructed in the art of painting by Marten De Vos, or, according to other writers, by Frans Floris. About the year 1570 he visited France, and in 1573 became a master, and in 1581-82 the dean of the Guild of St. Luke at Antwerp. Though his productions are too overcharged in every respect, Ambrosius possessed a fecundity and warmth of invention which was superior to that of his brothers. He died at Antwerp in 1618. His most important works are the following:

Antwerp.	Gallery.	Martyrdom of St. Crispin and St. Crispinian.
"	"	Scenes from the Lives and Martyrdom of St. Cosmo and St. Damian. (The wings of a triptych.)
"	"	Scenes from the Life of St. Sebastian.
"	"	The Miracle of the Loaves and Fishes. 1598.
"	"	The Last Supper. (A triptych.)
"	"	The Disciples at Emmaus. (The left wing of the above triptych.)
"	"	Melchizedek sacrificing. (The reverse of the same.)
"	"	The Ordination of St. Paul and St. Barnabas. (The right wing of the above triptych.)
"	"	Visit of the Angel to Elijah. (The reverse of the same.)
"	"	Scenes from the Life of St. George. (The wings of a triptych.)
"	"	St. George and St. Margaret. (The reverses of the above.)
"	"	The Martyrdom of St. Catharine.
"	St. Jacques.	Christ raising the Daughter of Jairus.
"	St. Jacques.	Christ and the Adulteress. (The two laterals of an altar-piece painted in 1600.)
"	"	Christ on the Mount of Olives with the Disciples. (The reverse of both wings.)
Dresden.	Gallery.	Mary, the Queen of Heaven.

FRANCKEN, Ambrosius, called the younger, to distinguish him from his uncle of the same name, was born at Antwerp in the latter part of the 16th century. He studied under his father, Frans Francken the elder, whose style he imitated. In 1624 he was registered as a master in the Guild of St. Luke at Antwerp, and he is said to have painted some time in Louvain. He died in 1632. Little else is known of him.

FRANCKEN, Constantinus, a skilful painter of siege and battle scenes, born at Antwerp in 1661, was the son of Hieronymus Francken the third, and grandson of Frans Francken the younger. In 1694 he became dean of the Guild of St. Luke. 'The Siege of Namur,' with William III. and his generals, is by some considered his best work. He died at Antwerp in 1717.

FRANCKEN, Frans, the elder, the second son of Nicolaes Francken, was born at Herenthals in 1542, and learned painting in the school of Frans Floris. In 1567 he received the freedom of the city of Antwerp, and became a master in the Guild of St. Luke, of which he was dean in 1588-89. He possessed great ability in design and in colouring, but his pictures are wanting in depth and spirit. After 1597 he signed his paintings D o F. (den ouden Frans), 'the elder Francis.' He died at Antwerp in 1616. His portrait has been etched by Van Dyck. Among his pupils were his sons.

Hieronymus, Frans, and Ambrosius Francken, G. Goltzius, Jan De Waal, and Herman van der Maest. The following are among his principal works:

Amsterdam.	Museum.	The Holy Family.
Antwerp.	Gallery.	Eteocles and Polynices.
Berlin.	Gallery.	Christ on the Cross.
Brunswick.	Gallery.	Overthrow of Pharaoh in the Red Sea.
"	"	Neptune and Galatea.
"	"	King Midas.
"	"	The Opening of Joseph's Coffin.
"	"	The Adoration of the Magi.
"	"	The King's Marriage Feast.
Darmstadt.	Gallery.	Christ stripped of His Garments.
"	"	Esther before Ahasuerus.
Dresden.	Gallery.	Christ going to Calvary. 1597.
"	"	The Flight into Egypt.
"	"	Innocence and Slander.
"	"	The Creation of Eve.
"	"	The Creation of Animals.
Dublin.	Nat. Gall.	St. Christopher and the Infant Christ.
Glasgow	Gallery.	The Procession to Calvary.
Lille.	Museum.	Christ on the Mount of Olives.
Munich.	Gallery.	A Banquet, with Musicians.
Paris.	Louvre.	Esther appearing before Ahasuerus.
Pommersfelden.	Gallery.	The Seven Works of Mercy.
"	"	The Annunciation to the Shepherds.
"	"	The Sacrifice at Lystra.
Stockholm.	Museum.	Lazarus and Dives.
Stuttgart.	Gallery.	The Wise Men presenting their Gifts.
Vienna.	Gallery.	A Saloon with Pictures.
"	"	A Cavalier leading a Lady out to Dance.
"	"	The Scourging of Jesus.

FRANCKEN, Frans, the younger, called Don Francisco, was a younger son of Frans Francken the elder, and was born at Antwerp in 1581. He was instructed in the art by his father, whose style he followed for some time. He afterwards visited Italy, and resided chiefly at Venice, where he studied the works of the great colourists of that school. After an absence of three years he returned to Antwerp, and in 1605 was received into the Guild of St. Luke, of which he was dean in 1614-15. He died at Antwerp in 1642. His paintings represent scenes from the Bible and mythology, allegories, balls, masquerades, festivals, and landscapes, with figures of a small size. The figures in the works of the younger De Momper, the elder Neeffs, and Bartelmees van Bassen were inserted by him. He was undoubtedly superior in design, colouring, and expression to his brothers Ambrosius and Hieronymus, and even to his father. Before his father's death he signed D. j. F. (den jongen Frans), but afterwards D. o. F. (den ouden Frans), to distinguish himself from his nephew. Among his works are the following:

Amsterdam.	Museum.	The Adoration of the Virgin and Child. 1616.
Antwerp.	Gallery.	The Miracles at the Tomb of St. Bruno.
"	"	The Martyrdom of the Four with the Crowns. 1624.
"	"	The Works of Mercy. 1608.
Augsburg.	Gallery.	Seven paintings: Christ with Martha and Mary; Christ bearing the Cross, &c.
"	"	The Continence of Scipio.
Berlin.	Gallery.	The Temptation of St. Anthony.
"	"	Christ washing the Apostles' Feet.
"	"	Christ on the Mount of Olives.

189

Berlin.	*Gallery.*	Solon and Crœsus.
Bordeaux.	*Museum.*	Christ at Calvary.
"	"	Different ways of gaining Immortality.
Brussels.	*Gallery.*	Crœsus, King of Lydia, showing his treasures to Solon.
Cassel.	*Gallery.*	A Holy Family.
"	"	The Adoration of the Virgin.
"	"	The Kiss of Judas.
"	"	The Painter Apelles.
Dresden.	*Gallery.*	The Adulteress before Christ.
Florence.	*Uffizi.*	Flight into Egypt.
"	*Pitti Pal.*	Christ on the way to Calvary.
Hague.	*Museum.*	Ball at the Court of Albert and Isabella in 1611. (*Seven figures are by the younger Pourbus.*)
Lille.	*Museum.*	Jesus going to Calvary.
Munich.	*Gallery.*	A Skirmish of Cavalry. 1631.
"	"	The Works of Mercy. 1630.
"	"	Allegorical Picture.
Paris.	*Louvre.*	Christ on the Cross.
"	"	A Prince visiting a Church. 1633.
"	"	The Prodigal Son. 1633.
Petersburg.	*Hermitage.*	Seven Works of Mercy.
Vienna.	*Gallery.*	The Witches' Sabbath. 1607.
"	"	Christ crucified. 1606.
"	"	Meeting of Christ and Nicodemus.
"	"	Crœsus and Solon.

FRANCKEN, FRANS, the third, called 'den rubenschen Francken' (Rubens's Francken), but for what reason is not known, was a son of Frans Francken the younger. He was born at Antwerp in 1607, and became dean of the Guild of St. Luke in 1655 He usually painted small figures, with which he often decorated the interiors of churches by the younger Pieter Neeffs. Before the death of his uncle he signed his paintings *den jonge*, and after 1642, *F. F.* He died in 1667. The following works by him are known :

Antwerp.	*Gallery.*	Family Group in a Picture Gallery.
Augsburg.	*Gallery.*	St. John preaching.
"	"	Moses striking the Rock. 1654.
Dresden.	*Gallery.*	Interior of Antwerp Cathedral. 1648.
Hague.	*Gallery.*	Interior of a Cathedral. (*Signed by him and Pieter Neeffs.*)

FRANCKEN, GABRIEL, a son of Sebastiaen Francken, of whom it is only known that he was a pupil of one Gerard Schoofs in 1605, and a member of the Guild of St. Luke at Antwerp in 1634.

FRANCKEN, HIERONYMUS, the elder, the eldest son of Nicolaes Francken, was born at Herenthals, near Antwerp, in 1540, and was a disciple of Frans Floris. He afterwards visited France on his way to Italy, and passed some time in Paris ; he painted in 1565 at Fontainebleau, and about the same time, in the church of the Augustinians in Paris, a 'Crucifixion.' He afterwards went to Rome, where he studied for some time, and then returned to Paris. He was employed by Henry III., and was appointed portrait painter to the king. In Flanders he established an academy, and after the death of Frans Floris, the scholars of that master placed themselves under his tuition, and even Abraham Bloemaert attended his school. When Henry III. was murdered in 1589, he returned to Antwerp, but being patronized by Henry IV. and Louis XIII., he again took up his residence in Paris in 1595, and died there in 1610. His best productions are his portraits, which may be compared with those of Pourbus. Among his paintings may be noted :

Amsterdam.	*Museum.*	Allegory of the Abdication of Charles V. at Brussels.
Antwerp.	*Cathedral.*	The Miracles of St. Gomer. 1607.

190

Dresden.	*Gallery.*	The Beheading of St. John the Baptist.
Fontainebleau.	*Palace.*	Several paintings.
Lille.	*Museum.*	Charles V. taking the Religious Dress.
Paris.	*Augustinian Church.*	The Crucifixion.
"	*Franciscan Church.*	The Nativity of Christ. 1585.
Stockholm.	*Museum.*	Assembly of Sea Gods.

FRANCKEN, HIERONYMUS, called the younger to distinguish him from his uncle, was born at Antwerp in 1578. He studied under his father, Frans Francken the elder, and under his uncle Ambrosius. He was free of the Guild of St. Luke in 1607, and died at Antwerp in 1629. He was especially successful in his portraits. In the Antwerp Gallery is a picture by this artist of 'Horatius Cocles at the Sublician Bridge,' painted in 1620.

FRANCKEN, JAN BAPTIST, the son of Sebastiaen Francken, was born at Antwerp in 1599. He received his first instruction from his father, and for some time followed his style, which he afterwards improved by an attentive study of the works of Rubens and Van Dyck. His first efforts were historical subjects ; but he adopted a mode of representing the interiors of saloons and galleries, embellished with pictures and statues, &c., with gallant assemblies of figures and conversations. His works of that description were painted with great beauty of colouring, and a very spirited touch. They were greatly sought after, and were placed in the choicest collections. He possessed a talent of imitating so exactly the peculiar touch and style of each master in the small pictures he introduced into his galleries, that it was easy to point out the original painter. It was the possession of this talent that induced so many contemporary artists to solicit his assistance to decorate their pictures with small figures, both in landscapes and interiors. Many of Pieter Neeffs's are so ornamented. He died in 1653. Pictures by him of the 'Beheading of St. John the Baptist' are at Augsburg and Brussels, and at Bruges there is a picture of 'Christ among the Doctors.'

FRANCKEN, JOHANNES, called by the Italians GIOVANNI FRANCO, entered the school of Jacob van Utrecht in 1512, and afterwards went to Italy, and established himself at Naples in 1550. In San Francesco, at Naples, the painting of the 'Adoration of the Magi,' dated 1556, is by this artist.

FRANCKEN, LAURENS, was instructed in painting by his uncle, Gabriel Francken, in 1623. He chiefly excelled in historical and landscape subjects. About 1660 he established himself in Paris.

FRANCKEN, NICOLAES, born at Herenthals about 1520, is said to have been instructed by Frans Floris, and was the father of Hieronymus, Frans, and Ambrosius Francken. He died at Antwerp in 1596.

FRANCKEN, P. H., who flourished about the middle of the 17th century, painted for the Carmelite Church at Antwerp a picture of 'Elijah on Mount Carmel,' which has disappeared, and for the church of the Recollets, pictures of 'St. Francis of Assisi,' 'St. Anthony of Padua,' 'St. Louis,' and one called 'The Poisoned Blow,' in reference to the attempt made on the life of St. James, Archbishop of Milan. These pictures are now in the Antwerp Gallery.

FRANCKEN, SEBASTIAEN, (or VRANCX,) was born at Antwerp in 1578. He was a disciple of Adam van Noort, and distinguished himself in painting battles and cavalry skirmishes, also conversation pieces, hunting parties, and landscapes with figures and animals. He likewise executed several paintings in conjunction with his son, Jan Baptist, and adorned the works of Pieter Neeffs, De Momper, and other artists, with figures. Several etchings were also made by him of European costumes. He died at Antwerp in 1647. His portrait, painted by Van Dyck, has been engraved by Hondius. Among his works, which are sometimes signed with the accompanying monogram, are the following:

Dresden.	Gallery.	Temptation of St. Anthony.
Lille.	Museum.	A Virgin. (*Painted in conjunction with Jan Brueghel.*)
Petersburg.	Hermitage.	Passage of the Red Sea.
Rotterdam.	Museum.	A Pillaged Village.
Stockholm.	Museum.	Arrival of Mary de' Medici at Antwerp.
Vienna.	Gallery.	Interior of the Church of the Jesuits at Antwerp.

FRANCO, AGNOLO, or ANGIOLO, was a Neapolitan artist whose death occurred about 1455. The frescoes in the Cappella Brancaccio at San Domenico Maggiore, Naples, representing the 'Crucifixion,' and scenes taken from the lives of the saints and martyrs, are assigned to him.

FRANCO, ALFONSO, was born at Messina in 1466, and died there in 1524. He is the author of a 'Pietà,' dated 1520, in the church of San Francesco di Paola, Messina.

FRANCO, GIACOMO, an Italian designer and engraver, was a relation of Giovanni Battista Franco. He was born at Venice in 1566, and instructed by Agostino Carracci. He generally signed his plates with his name, but sometimes with a monogram. The following prints are the most worthy of notice:

Part of the plates for an edition of Tasso's 'Gerusalemme liberata,' published at Genoa in 1590; *after the designs of Bernardo Castelli;* the rest were engraved by *Agostino Carracci.*
Habiti delle Donne Venetiane; published in 1626.
A collection of portraits of Great Men; dated 1596.
St. Jerome; *J. Franco Romæ, sc.*
The Crucifixion; signed *Giacomo Franco, fec.*
Hercules between Virtue and Pleasure; from an antique basso-relievo.

FRANCO, GIOVANNI. See FRANCKEN, JOHANNES.

FRANCO, GIOVANNI BATTISTA, called IL SEMOLEI, was born at Udine in 1510, and distinguished himself as an historical painter and an etcher. He went to Rome when he was young, devoted himself to an attentive study of the works of Michelangelo, and became one of the ablest designers of his time. He excelled especially in representing mythological and allegorical decorations of small size, but was less successful in larger works. He was engaged by several masters to assist in the execution of their designs. In 1536 he painted at the triumphal arch for the entry of Charles V. into Rome, and went afterwards to Florence with Raffaello da Montelupo for a similar purpose, and executed with Vasari several works in a palace for Ottaviano de' Medici, where there were also some of his own compositions. He executed for the Dukes Alexander and Cosmo I. several portraits of the Medici after Sebastiano del Piombo, Titian, and Pontormo. He was subsequently employed by the Duke of Urbino in the majolica manufactory at Castel Durante, and several times at Rome. The latter part of his life he spent at Venice, where he

died in 1580, leaving unfinished his works in the chapel of San Francesco della Vigna. Among his paintings may be mentioned:

Florence.	*Pitti Palace.*	The Battle of Montemurlo.
Rome.	*Frat. d. Misericordia.*	Imprisonment of St. John the Baptist (*fresco*).
„	*S. Maria sopra Minerva.*	Scenes from the Bible (*fresco*).
Venice.	*S. Francesco della Vigna.*	The Baptism of Christ.
„	*S. Giobbo.*	Madonna with Saints.

There are by him 108 etchings, which are very different in value and in manner of execution. It is said that only those are by him which are etched in a broad style and finished off with a light and spirited point. He handled the graver most mechanically. It is not known with certainty from whom he learned this branch of art, but it has been supposed that he was instructed by Marc Antonio; and this conjecture is strengthened by a near resemblance between his style and that of Giulio Bonasone, who was unquestionably a disciple of Marc Antonio. He generally marked his plates *B. F. V. F.*, (*Battista Franco Venetus fecit*). The following are his principal etchings:

Moses striking the Rock.
Abraham meeting Melchizedek.
Abraham sacrificing Isaac.
The Israelites gathering Manna in the Desert.
The Captive Kings brought before Solomon.
The Adoration of the Shepherds, with Angels in the Clouds.
The Virgin and Infant, with St. John.
St. John the Baptist.
St. Jerome holding a skull.
Christ disputing with the Doctors.
The Entombment of Christ.
Simon the Magician before the Apostles.
The Cyclops at their Forge.
Hercules and Deianira.
The Flagellation; *after Titian.*
The Raising of Lazarus; *after Raphael.*
The Donation made to the Church by the Emperor Constantine; *after the same.*
The Last Judgment; *after M. Rotta.*
Christ on the Cross, with two Angels; *after Michelangelo.*
Cupid and Psyche in the Bath; *after Giulio Romano.*
The Clemency of Scipio; *after the same.*
The Deluge; *after Pietro da Caravaggio.*

FRANCO BOLOGNESE. See BOLOGNESE.

FRANCOFORTO, ADAMO DA. See ELSHEIMER.

FRANÇOIS, ALPHONSE, one of the most famous of modern French engravers, was born in Paris in 1811. Left an orphan in his childhood, he was early thrown on his own resources, and began life as a goldsmith's engraver. His skill and industry soon insured him a modest livelihood in Paris, but, oppressed by the mechanical drudgery of his craft, he turned his thoughts to music, and was even engaged for a time in the orchestra of the Conservatoire concerts. He next tried the stage, and was fond, in after life, of describing a memorable occasion on which he played with Rachel. Through his elder brother, Jules, he was introduced at the mature age of twenty-six to Henriquel-Dupont, the engraver. Henriquel received him kindly, and agreed to let him work in his atelier. Though absolutely ignorant even of the elements of drawing, François set to work, confident of success. It happened during the first year of his apprenticeship that he saw a portrait of Titian at the house of the well-known collector, M. Chaix d'Est-Ange, and asked leave to make a drawing of it. To the amazement of Henriquel, he then announced his intention of engraving it. The result was extraordinarily successful for a first effort. With each fresh undertaking his powers developed. His plates began to attract attention at the Salon, where he first exhibited in 1842, and Paul Delaroche persuaded Messrs. Goupil to intrust one of his own pictures to the *débutant*, the 'Napoleon crossing the Alps.' This was followed by numerous commissions from the same firm, and by plates after Fra Angelico's 'Coronation of the Virgin,' and Cabanel's 'Birth of Venus,' for the Chalcographie du Louvre. Henceforth commissions poured in on him, and the story of his later years is one of uneventful prosperity, up to the time of his loss of sight. Debarred by this calamity from the work in which he delighted, his health and spirits alike gave way, and he died in Paris July 6, 1888. Among his later undertakings was a commission from the directors of the Doré Gallery, in London, to reproduce the pictures in their exhibition. This long and laborious work was carried out with the help of pupils and assistants, the plates being finally worked over by François himself. Of his finer plates after other masters we may also name :

The Mystic Marriage of St. Catherine; *after Memlinc.*
The Virgin on the Steps; *after Titian.*
Marie Antoinette leaving the Revolutionary Tribunal; *after Delaroche.*
The Youth of Pico de la Mirandola; *after the same.*
Psyche; *after Jules Lefèbvre.*

FRANÇOIS, CHARLES REMY JULES, a French engraver, was born in Paris in 1809. He was a scholar of Henriquel-Dupont, and died in 1861. Some of his plates are :

Hebe; *after Ary Scheffer.*
Napoleon at Fontainebleau; *after Delaroche.* 1830.
Pilgrims in the Square of St. Peter's at Rome; *after the same.* 1847.
The Happy Mother; *after the same.* 1853.
Le galant Militaire; *after Terborch.*

FRANÇOIS, JEAN CHARLES, a French engraver, was born at Nancy in 1717. He is said to have been the first who engraved in Paris in the style representing drawings made in crayons, and for this he received a pension of 600 francs from the king, and was entitled 'Graveur des dessins du Cabinet du Roi.' He also executed some portraits, the most important of which are those for the quarto edition of Saverien's 'Histoire des Philosophes modernes,' 1761–69. He died in Paris in 1769. Among other plates by him are the following :

A Body Guard; *after Vanloo.*
The Virgin; *after Vien.*
Benedetto Spinosa; *after Deshays.*
Louis XV., King of France.
Marie Leszczinska, Queen of France.
Pierre Bayle; *after Carle Vanloo.*
Desiderius Erasmus; *after Holbein.*
Thomas Hobbes; *after Pierre.*
John Locke; *after Vien.*
Nicolas Malebranche; *after Bachelier.*
The Dancers; *after F. Boucher.*
A March of Cavalry; *after Parrocel.*

FRANÇOIS, LUCAS, (or FRANCHOYS,) the elder, a painter and engraver, was born at Mechlin in 1547. It is not mentioned by whom he was instructed in art, but he painted historical subjects with considerable skill, and was also much employed as a portrait painter. He passed the early part of his life at the courts of France and Spain, but after an absence of six years he returned to Flanders, where he painted several altar-pieces for the churches, which are deservedly admired. He died

192

at Mechlin in 1643. Among the productions of Lucas François are :

Antwerp.	*Gallery.*	Education of the Virgin.
"	"	Apparition of the Virgin to St. Simon Stock.
Mechlin.	*St. Catharine.*	Martyrdom of St. Lawrence.
"	*Museum.*	Portrait of Philippus Snoy. 1619.
"	*St. John.*	St. Agatha.
Tournai.	*Abbey of St.* } *Martin.* }	St. Placidus and St. Maurice.

Among his engravings may be mentioned :

The Adoration of the Magi; *after Van Dyck.*
The portrait of an old Man; *after the same.*

His two sons, Pieter and Lucas, were also successful painters.

FRANÇOIS, LUCAS, the younger, a son of Lucas François the elder, born at Mechlin in 1616, was a pupil of his father, whom he assisted in his works. He afterwards entered the studio of Rubens, where he imitated the style of Bockhorst. Following his father and brother, he went to France, but after some years he returned to his native city, in the churches and Museum of which may be found several of his works. He died at Mechlin in 1681.

FRANÇOIS, PIERRE JOSEPH CÉLESTIN, a Flemish historical, genre, and miniature painter, as well as an etcher, was born at Namur in 1759. He was a pupil of Lens, and travelled in France, Italy, and Germany, but finally established himself at Brussels, where he became a professor in the Academy. His pupils were very numerous, including Navez, Decaisne, Madou, and others. He died in 1851. Amongst his works are :

Marius sitting on the Ruins of Carthage. (*Brussels Gallery.*)
A Physician consulted by two old Women. (*Haarlem Museum.*)
The Assumption. (*Ghent Academy.*)

FRANÇOIS, PIETER, the son of Lucas François the elder, was born at Mechlin in 1606. For some time he studied under his father, and followed his style in his larger historical works; but he afterwards entered the school of Gerard Seghers, whose academy was then in great repute, and adopted a mode of painting history and portraits of a size smaller than life. The Archduke Leopold invited him to his court, where he was favoured with the esteem and patronage of that prince. He was also solicited to visit Paris, where he met with the most flattering encouragement, and rendered himself extremely acceptable to the Parisians by his accomplishments as a man of the world, and his knowledge of music. After passing four years in France he returned to Flanders, where he continued to exercise his talents with great success. He died at Mechlin in 1654. Pieter François was ingenious in his compositions, firm and correct in his drawing, and clear and seductive in his colouring. The Museum at Lille possesses a portrait by him of Gisbert Mutzarts, Abbot of Tongerloo, dated 1645, and in the Dresden Gallery is a picture of a 'Man in Armour.' There exists also an etching by him, which is very rare and of great spirit; it represents 'Christ and St. John as children, seated under a tree and kissing each other.'

FRANÇOIS, SIMON, a French painter, was born at Tours in 1606. Without the help of a master, he had made some progress in the art, when he went to Italy, where he studied some years. At Bologna he became acquainted with Guido Reni, who made him a present of his portrait, painted by himself. On his return to France he settled in

Paris, where he painted the portrait of Louis XIV. as Dauphin, and many other distinguished personages, so much to the satisfaction of the court, that he looked forward with confidence to the acquisition of fortune and fame. In these flattering expectations he was, however, disappointed, for he fell into disgrace, and died in obscurity in Paris in 1671. He painted for several churches, and is said to have etched a 'Magdalen in a Cavern,' and a 'St. Sebastian,' two plates of a good design and a noble expression.

FRANCQUART, Jaques, a Flemish painter, was born at Brussels in 1577. He received a liberal education from his parents, who were of good position, and having shown an early inclination for art, he was sent to Italy to study painting and architecture, and remained there some years. On his return to Flanders he was appointed principal painter and architect to Albert and Isabella, then governors of the Low Countries. He was greatly esteemed by those illustrious personages, who employed him in several public works, both in painting and architecture. The church of the Jesuits, at Brussels, was built from his designs, and ornamented with some of his pictures. He died at Brussels in 1651.

FRANCUCCI, Innocenzo, called Innocenzo da Imola, was born in 1494 at Imola, but principally resided at Bologna. In 1508 he entered the school of Francesco Francia, but, according to Malvasia, he afterwards passed some years at Florence, under Mariotto Albertinelli. His style partakes of that of Fra Bartolommeo and Andrea del Sarto, whose works he appears to have studied attentively. His pictures are numerous in the churches at Bologna; and in some of them he approaches so near to the beauty and simplicity of Raphael, that they appear to have been painted from his designs. Some of his altar-pieces have small pictures under them, which are extremely beautiful. In the church of San Giacomo, under his large painting of the 'Marriage of St. Catharine,' there is an exquisite little picture of the 'Nativity'; and in San Matteo is an altar-piece of 'The Virgin and Infant, with several Saints,' and below five small pictures, representing 'Christ appearing to the Magdalen in the Garden,' 'The Presentation in the Temple,' 'St. Peter Martyr,' 'The Nativity,' and 'Christ disputing with the Doctors.' That he was well skilled in architecture Francucci has shown in his immense fresco in the cathedral at Faenza, and in the Osservanti at Pesaro, in which his landscape and perspective are compared by Lanzi to those of Leonardo da Vinci. He died in 1550, according to Vasari, of a pestilential fever. Of his paintings, in addition to the above, may be mentioned:

Berlin.	Gallery.	Virgin and Child with Saints.
Bologna.	Servi.	Annunciation.
„	„	Marriage of the Virgin.
„	Pinacoteca.	Madonna glorified, with Saints (painted for San Michele in Bosco). 1517.
„	„	Madonna with SS. Francis and Clara.
„	„	The Virgin coming forth from a Church.
„	„	Madonna and Child with Saints.
„	S. Michele in Bosco.	Annunciation.
„	„	Death and Assumption of the Virgin.
„	„	The Four Evangelists.
„	„	The Virgin and Child in the

Clouds, and below SS. Michael, Peter, and Benedict (in the style of Raphael).

Bologna.	S. Salvatore.	Christ on the Cross, with Saints. 1549.
Frankfort.	Städel.	The Virgin Mary with St. John the Baptist and St. Sebastian.
London.	Solly Coll.	Virgin enthroned (chef-d'œuvre formerly at Faenza). 1527.
Modena.	Estense Gall.	A Virgin (in the style of Raphael).
Munich.	Gallery.	Virgin and Child with Saints.
Petersburg.	Hermitage.	Virgin and Saints.

FRANGIPANE, Niccolò, is believed by some to have been a native of Padua, by others of Udine. He flourished from the year 1565 till 1597, and executed a number of church pictures, but was more successful in mythological scenes, particularly the legends of Bacchus. At Padua, in the church of San Bartolommeo, is a fine picture by him of 'St. Francis,' painted in 1588; and at Pesaro, an altar-piece in San Stefano. But his most admired work is an 'Assumption,' in the church of the Conventuali, at Rimini.

FRANK, Michael Sigismund, born at Nuremberg in 1769, was instructed there in the art of painting on porcelain by Trost. He afterwards painted on glass, in which he was very successful, and helped to raise the almost forgotten art from its long decline, by discovering in 1804 the method which was formerly in use. He executed for the chapel of the Castle of Stauffenberg in Franconia several devices of coats of arms, and in 1808 those for the court of Bavaria, for which he was highly praised. King Maximilian I. gave him a building in which to paint on glass. Among the works of that period executed on a large scale are a 'Circumcision' after Goltzius, and a 'Nativity of Christ' after Bolswert. From 1814 to 1818 he was employed by the Prince of Wallerstein; he afterwards returned to Munich, where he was made royal glass-painter for his 'Treatise on Glass-Painting.' In 1827 he was appointed director of the Institute founded by King Louis, and executed the large windows for the cathedral at Ratisbon, which constituted his chief production. He died at Munich in 1847.

FRANK, Pauline. See Steinhäuser.

FRANKEN, Theodor, a genre painter, was born at Geilenkirchen, near Aix-la-Chapelle, in 1811. He studied under Schadow at Düsseldorf, and produced spirited scenes of popular and home life. He died at Düsseldorf in 1876.

FRANKENBERGER, Johann, an Austrian portrait painter, was born at Hadamar in Nassau in 1807, and died at Vienna in 1874.

FRANKENDORFFER, Conrad, a native of Nuremberg, flourished about 1498, and was an excellent miniature painter.

FRANKFORT, Hieronymus von. See Greff.

FRANQUE, Jean Pierre, a French painter, was born at Le Buis in 1774. He studied under David, and excelled in historical subjects and portraiture, imitating the style of his master. He married Lucile Messageot, also an artist, who died in 1802, at the age of twenty-two years. Franque died in 1860, leaving among others the following works:

Versailles.	Gallery.	The Passage of the Rhine; after Le Brun. 1835.
„	„	The Siege of Lille; after Van der Meulen and Le Brun. 1836.
„	„	The Battle of Lens. 1841.

FRANQUE, Joseph, the twin brother of Jean Pierre Franque, was born at Le Buis in 1774, and died in 1812. He also was a painter, and there is by him at Versailles a picture of the Empress Maria Louisa and the King of Rome.

FRANQUELIN, JEAN AUGUSTIN, born in Paris in 1798, was instructed by Regnault, and became known through his works, representing scenes in public life, conversation-pieces, &c., which have often been copied. He died in Paris in 1839. The painting of 'The Occupation of Brissac,' by this artist, is at Versailles.

FRANQUINET, WILLEM HENDRIK, born at Maestricht in 1785, was instructed by Herreyns at Antwerp. He afterwards visited Germany, and was a drawing-master at his native town from 1804 to 1815. In 1816 he settled in Paris, and in 1821 painted the 'Bacchanal,' and in 1822-34 published a 'Galerie des Peintres,' for which J. Chabert wrote the text. He died at New York in 1854.

FRANS, NICOLAES, was born at Mechlin in 1539. It is not said under whom he studied; it is only known that at an early age he entered the order of the Franciscans, in which he continued to exercise his art, and became a fair historical painter. In the collegiate church of Our Lady at Mechlin is an altar-piece by this master, representing the 'Flight into Egypt'; and in the church of Hanswyck, near Mechlin, are two pictures by him of the 'Visitation' and the 'Annunciation.' His drawing is correct, and he was an excellent colourist.

FRANSSIÈRES, J. DE, was a French engraver of little celebrity. He engraved part of the plates for a set of Turkish costumes, published in Paris in 1714, by M. de Ferriol.

FRANZ, C., who studied under Schwind, practised first as an historical painter, but afterwards turned his attention towards genre subjects. He died at Munich in 1876.

FRANZ-DREBER, HEINRICH. See DREBER.

FRÄNZSCHEN. See DEI ROSSI, FRANCESCO.

FRASER, ALEXANDER, a Scottish painter, was born at Edinburgh in 1786, and commenced his artistic career by studying at the Trustees' Academy in that city, where he had David Wilkie and Watson Gordon for fellow-students. He first exhibited at the Royal Academy in 1810, settling in London three years later. Soon after this Wilkie employed him to fill in the minor details and still-life of his pictures, a practice which he continued for a good many years. Among the works exhibited by him at the Royal Academy may be mentioned 'The Village Sign-Painter,' 'The Blackbird and his Tutor,' and 'Tapping the Ale-barrel.' He does not appear to have exhibited after 1859, and during the latter years of his life seems to have been quite an invalid. His death occurred at Wood Green, near London, in 1865. A great part of his earlier works consisted of coast scenes, and at a later date he painted pictures in illustration of the 'Waverley Novels,' some of which have been engraved. He became an Associate of the Royal Scottish Academy in 1842. In the National Gallery is the 'Interior of a Highland Cottage' by him, and in the National Gallery of Scotland is a view 'At Barncleuth.'

FRASER, ALEXANDER, was born in 1828 at Woodcockdale, near Linlithgow. Even as a boy he was employed in stippling in backgrounds for portraits. His father, an able amateur artist, sent him to study in Edinburgh. He was first represented in the Royal Scottish Academy Exhibition by a figure subject, but his true forte was landscape. He was early appreciated, and was elected an Associate of the Royal Scottish Academy in 1858. In 1862 he

194

became Royal Scottish Academician, and his diploma work 'At Barncleuth' hangs in the gallery. Some of his best landscapes were painted in Surrey and in Cadzow Forest. He died in Musselburgh in 1899. His principal works comprise 'Among the Surrey Hills,' 'Sunshine in Spring-time,' 'Glenfalloch,' 'The Margin of the Forest,' and 'A Trout Stream in the Highlands.' He depicted especially the brighter moods of Nature, delighting in the changing lights on hill and moor and the rich colour of summer woodland and autumn fields; and the fine composition, sound technique, and fresh atmospheric quality of the pictures of his best period entitle him to an honourable place among our landscape painters.

J. H. W. L.

FRASER, CHARLES, an artist born at Charleston in 1782, studied law, but afterwards devoted himself to art. In 1825 he painted the portrait of Lafayette. His talent was very diversified, and in 1857, at an exhibition of his works at Charleston, there were shown 313 miniatures and 139 landscapes and other pieces by him. He died at Charleston in 1860.

FRASSI, PIETRO, born at Cremona in 1706, was a pupil of Angiolo Massarotti. He went to Florence, but afterwards to Rome, where he died in 1778. His best work was a picture of 'The Miracle of St. Vincent Ferrer,' painted for the Dominicans in Cremona, which caused him to be made a member of the Academy of St. Luke.

FRATACCI, ANTONIO, born at Parma in the beginning of the 18th century, received his first lessons in art from Ilario Spolverini. He afterwards entered, at Bologna, the school of Carlo Cignani, whose style he imitated. There is a picture in the church of San Giorgio at Bologna of 'Christ healing St. Pellegrini Laziozi,' and at Sant' Eustorgio, at Milan, a 'St. John' and an 'Adoration of the Magi.'

FRATELLINI, GIOVANNA, was born at Florence in 1666. The early disposition she showed for art recommended her to the notice of the Grand-Duchess Victoria, who took her under her protection, and had her instructed by the best masters in drawing and music. She was afterwards taught miniature painting by Ippolito Galantini, and finished her studies under Antonio Domenico Gabbiani. She painted historical subjects and portraits in oil, pastel, enamel, miniature, and crayons, but chiefly excelled in the last, in which she is no way inferior to the celebrated Rosalba. Her reputation spread throughout Italy, and she painted the portraits of Cosmo III. and his wife, her patroness, the principal nobility of the court, and the most illustrious personages of the country. One of her best works is in the Ducal Gallery at Florence; it represents her painting the portrait of her son. This distinguished lady died at Florence in 1731.

FRATELLINI, LORENZO MARIA, the son of Giovanna Fratellini, by whom he was instructed in the elementary principles of design, was born at Florence in 1690. He afterwards studied under Antonio Domenico Gabbiani, who had been the instructor of his mother. Under that master he acquired a ready and correct manner of designing, and became a promising painter, both of history and of portraits, but he died in the prime of life, in 1729.

FRATREL, JOSEPH, born at Epinal in 1730, was a scholar of Baudouin in Paris, and distinguished himself as a painter and etcher. He was court painter of King Stanislaus and the Elector-Palatine Charles Theodore : in the Darmstadt Museum is a portrait of the Electress. He died at Mannheim in 1783. The following are his best-known works :

Joseph's Dream; *after L. Krahe.*
The Miller's Son.
St. Nicholas.

FRATTA, DOMENICO MARIA, born at Bologna in 1696, studied under Giovanni Viviani, Carlo Rambaldi, and Donato Creti. He abandoned the art of painting, and devoted himself entirely to drawing with the pen, in which he acquired such perfection as to give to his productions a European fame. He died in 1763.

FREDEAU, AMBROISE, called FRÈRE FREDEAU, who flourished about the middle of the 17th century, was a monk of the Augustinian order. He imitated Vouet in his paintings.

FREDERICH, EDUARD, born at Hanover in 1813, attended the Academy at Düsseldorf from 1836 to 1843, and studied in particular landscape and genre painting, which he, however, changed afterwards for scenes of encampments and manœuvres. He was court painter, and died at Hanover in 1864.

FREDI, BARTOLO DI. See BARTOLO.

FREEBAIRN, ALFRED ROBERT, an engraver, is chiefly known by his engraving of Flaxman's 'Shield of Achilles.' He died in 1846, in his 53rd year.

FREEBAIRN, ROBERT, a landscape painter, was born in 1765. He was for a short time with Richard Wilson, who died before Freebairn's education was completed, and afterwards went to Italy, where he remained about ten years, but never rose above mediocrity. His pictures are simply pleasing, never striking. On his return to England, Freebairn met with several patrons, and as he was slow in performance, it is probable they were the chief purchasers of his works. He died in 1808. There are about forty prints of Italian and English scenery published by him.

FREEMAN, JAMES EDWARD, painter, was a native of Nova Scotia, but was educated in the National Academy in New York. He settled in Rome, where he painted genre pictures, mostly of Italian subjects. He is known also by his publication, 'A Portfolio of Italian Sketches.' He died in 1884.

FREEMAN, JOHN, an historical painter, flourished in the latter half of the 17th century. He was also scene painter to Covent Garden Theatre. There are five works attributed to him in the Louvre.

FREEMAN, SAMUEL, an engraver, was born in 1773, and died in 1857. Amongst his plates are :

A Holy Family ; *after Correggio.*
A Madonna ; *after Raphael.*
The Infant Christ and St. John ; *after the same.*
St. Ambrose refusing admission to the Church to Theodosius ; *after Van Dyck.*

FREESE, JOHANN OSKAR HERMANN, a painter of animals and hunting scenes, was born in Pommerania in 1813. He was destined by his father to be a farmer, in spite of his early inclination to art, but in his 34th year he devoted himself, after many heavy misfortunes, to painting as his vocation. He visited for a short time the atelier of Brücke, then that of Steffeck in Berlin. In 1857 his first work, 'Stags Fighting,' appeared. His subjects of study were field and wood, and principally hunting, which he loved passionately.

He died at Hessenfelde, near Fürstenwald, in 1871, of brain fever, which he contracted whilst out shooting in trying to cross a river when in a heated state. He is very happy in his bolder designs, but less so in his idyllic representations. Among his works are especially to be mentioned, 'Deer Fleeing,' 'Stags attacked by Wolves,' and a 'Boar Hunt,' all in the Berlin National Gallery.

FREESE, N., a miniature painter, exhibited at the Royal Academy from 1794 to 1814.

FREESEN, JOHANN GEORG, (or FREEZEN,) a portrait painter, was born at Palts, near Heidelberg, in 1701. He first studied under Jan van Nikkelen, and afterwards under Philip van Dyk, of whom he became one of the best scholars, and with whom he stayed seven years at the Hague. He was patronized by the Duke of Hesse, and was appointed historical and portrait painter to the court of Cassel. He possessed a great knowledge of paintings, which he acquired in Germany, Italy, France, and in the school of Philip van Dyk—an acquisition which was of the greatest use in the establishment of the Cassel Gallery. He died at Cassel in 1775.

FREGEVIZE, FRIEDRICH, a Swiss landscape painter, was born in Geneva in 1770, and died there in 1849. He lived for a long time in Berlin, where he was elected in 1820 a member of the Academy; he returned to Geneva in 1829, and went to Dessau in 1839. The Berlin National Gallery contains views painted by him of 'The Lake of Geneva,' and 'The Valley of the Rhone, near Geneva.'

FREIDHOFF, JOHANN JOSEPH, a German mezzotint engraver, born at Heggen, in Westphalia, in 1768, studied under J. G. Huck. He visited Holland and France for his improvement, and died at Berlin in 1818. There are by him :

Night ; *after Correggio.* 1800.
The Death of Germanicus ; *after Poussin.* 1798.
Joseph and Potiphar's Wife ; *after Cignani.* 1796.
Alexander von Humboldt ; *after Weitsch.*
A Waterfall ; *after Ruisdael.* 1797.

FRÉMIET, SOPHIE. See RUDE.

FRÉMIET, VICTORINE. See VAN DER HAERT.

FRÉMINET, MARTIN, a French historical painter, born in Paris in 1567, received his first instruction from his father, a tapestry designer. He soon made some progress in his career in Paris, and executed several commissions, including a picture of 'St. Sebastian' for the church of St. Joseph. But it was to Italy that his thoughts turned, and about 1592 he set out thither. At this time the controversies raised by the Naturalisti were at their height, and into them Fréminet entered with ardour. His time was chiefly passed at Rome, Parma, and Venice, and he directed his most serious attention to the works of Parmigiano and Michelangelo, the study of the latter having a great influence on him. After an absence of about sixteen years he returned to his native country by way of Lombardy and Savoy, and in the latter he painted some important works for the ducal palace. His fame had preceded him, for on the death of Toussaint Du-Breuil in 1602 he was appointed by Henry IV. his principal painter, obtaining at the same time by purchase a sinecure post about the court. In 1608 he commenced for the king the decoration of the chapel at Fontainebleau, which was executed in oil on plaster. In the five compartments of the ceiling he depicted 'Noah entering the Ark,' the 'Fall of the Angels,' 'Our Lord in Glory,' the

O 2

'Angel Gabriel,' and the 'Creation.' Behind the altar he painted the 'Annunciation,' and he also executed other frescoes representing kings, prophets, &c., and scenes from the life of Christ. This masterpiece was not finished until the succeeding reign, and on its completion, in 1615, he received the cross of the Order of St. Michael. Fréminet died in Paris in 1619, and was buried, in accordance with his desire, in the Abbey of Barbeaux, near Fontainebleau, for which he had painted several pictures, which were destroyed when that Abbey was burnt in 1793. He left a son Louis, who followed in his father's footsteps as a painter. The poet Regnier was his friend, and dedicated to him his tenth Satire. Fréminet had a good knowledge of architectural perspective and of anatomy, though his aspirations after the grandeur of Michelangelo frequently led him into exaggerations, and have caused him to be much decried. To do him justice, however, it must be owned that he marks a great advance in the history of the French school. The works of his predecessor, Cousin, are no doubt the earliest which show the impress of Italian art, but it was Fréminet who first fully felt and evidenced the influence of the great Italian masters. He is seen at his best in those works in which the spirit of Parmigiano is most apparent. His style of working was singular: he painted a picture in separate portions, without sketching or designing the rest of the composition. The following are some of his existing works:

Liverpool.	*Institution.*	The Birth of Venus. (*A sepia drawing.*)
Orleans.	*Museum.*	St. Matthew.
"	"	St. Mark.
"	"	St. Luke.
"	"	St. John.
"	"	St. Augustine.
"	"	St. Ambrose.
"	"	St. Gregory.
"	"	St. Jerome.
Paris.	*Louvre.*	Mercury ordering Æneas to abandon Dido.
Tours.	*Museum.*	The Last Judgment (*doubtful*).

A 'Virgin and Child' is the only etching by Fréminet which is known.   O.J.D.

FRENCH, HENRY, an Irish historical painter, was born about the end of the 17th century. He studied at Rome, and gained a medal in the Academy of St. Luke. He came to England, but did not meet with success. His death took place in 1726.

FRENZEL, JOHANN GOTTLIEB ABRAHAM, born at Dresden in 1782, was instructed by Darnstedt, and excelled in engraving landscapes. He was director of the Royal Collection of engravings at Dresden, and wrote several works on his art. He died at Dresden in 1855. Among his best plates are:

Ruins; *after Ruisdael.*
Evening; *after the same.*
A Landscape with Cattle in the Water; *after Poelenborch.*

FRÈRE, CHARLES THÉODORE, (BEY,) painter, was born in Paris in 1815. He was a pupil of Roqueplan and Léon Cogniet, and made his *début* at the Salon in 1834 with landscapes from Northern France. Two years later he went to Algiers, and afterwards spent some time in Africa, whence he drew his subjects for the rest of his life. He died in Paris March 24, 1888.

FRÈRE, PIERRE EDOUARD, a French genre painter, was born in Paris January 10, 1819. He studied under Delaroche, and made his *début* at the Salon of

1843. His early pictures were chiefly interiors of cottages, workshops, &c., with cobblers, coopers, cooks, and other industrious members of the lower classes at work. They were warm and transparent in colour, and often forcible in chiaroscuro. In later years he almost entirely confined himself to painting incidents of child life, and became cold in colour and feeble in his light and shade. He produced a great number of drawings in which coloured figures are set against monochrome backgrounds, generally sketched in black chalk. His works are well known in England, where he frequently exhibited, first at the French Gallery in 1854. His first picture in the Royal Academy was one of his most characteristic works, the 'Girls leaving School.' Frère lived at Écouen, and died there May 23, 1886.

FRERES, DIRK, or THEODORUS, a Dutch painter, was born at Enkhuizen in 1643. He was of an ancient and opulent family, who gave him an education suited to his birth; and, among other accomplishments, he was taught drawing, for which he showed so strong a predilection, that his parents acceded to his desire of visiting Italy, and he passed several years at Rome, studying after the antique, and the best productions of modern art. He returned to Holland with a large collection of drawings which he had made in Italy, and distinguished himself by several historical works; among which were the ceiling of a public hall at Amsterdam, and some pictures in one of the palaces of the Prince of Orange. In his studies in Italy he appears to have been more attentive to purity and correctness of design than to the blandishments of colouring, in which he is less successful. He is said to have been invited to England by Sir Peter Lely, but finding on his arrival that the situation he expected was filled by Antonio Verrio, he returned to Holland. He died at Enkhuizen in 1693.

FRESNE, DU. See DU FRESNE.

FRESNOY, DU. See DU FRESNOY.

FREUDENBERGER, SIGMUND, born at Berne in 1745, was a painter and engraver, who was instructed in the rudiments of art by Em. Handmann. He afterwards went to Paris, and improved himself under Wille, Boucher, Greuze, and Röslin. His scenes of Swiss life in the Bernese Oberland were first engraved and afterwards painted. In the town-library at Berne there is a portrait of Haller by this artist. He died in 1801.

FREUDWEILER, HEINRICH, a Swiss portrait and genre painter, was born at Zürich in 1755, and was first instructed by H. Wüst; he afterwards studied at the Academies at Düsseldorf and Mannheim, and visited Dresden and Berlin, where he became acquainted with Graf and Chodowiecky. In 1785 he returned to Zürich, and died in 1795. He painted several historical scenes relating to his country.

FREY, JAKOB, a grandson of Johann Jakob Frey, is known by a plate of Leonardo da Vinci's 'Last Supper,' which, however, is taken from the old copy by Marco d'Oggione.

FREY, JOHANN JAKOB, a Swiss engraver, was born at Lucerne, in 1681. After learning the principles of design he went, when he was twenty-two years of age, to Rome, where he received some instruction from Arnold van Westerhout, and had afterwards the advantage of studying in the school of Carlo Maratti, at the same time with Robert van Auden-Aerd. His progress was rapid, and he was soon regarded as one of the ablest artists at Rome. His drawing is correct and tasteful, and he was a perfect master of harmony and effect. He etched his plates with spirit, and worked over the etching with a firm and masterly hand. Few artists have approached nearer to the style of the painters from whom they engraved than Frey. He died at Rome in 1770. His prints, which exceed the number of one hundred, are generally of a very large size. The following are the principal:

PORTRAITS.

Carlo Maratti; *after a picture by himself.*
Pope Innocent XIII.; *after A. Masucci.*
Pope Benedict XIII.; *after the same.*
Pope Gregory XIII.; *after the marble by Camillo Rusconi.*
Girolamo Pico della Mirandola; *after P. Nelly.*
Mary Clementina Sobieska, wife of the Old Pretender.

SUBJECTS AFTER VARIOUS MASTERS.

The Holy Family; copied from Edelinck's print *after Raphael.*
Charity, with three children; *after Albani.*
The Death of St. Petronilla; *after Guercino.* 1731.
The Coronation of the Virgin; *after Annibale Carracci.*
The Virgin giving the Scapular to St. Simon Stock; *after Seb. Conca.*
The Adoration of the Shepherds; *after the same.*
St. Francis of Paola restoring a Child to life; *after B. Lambertini.*
The Archangel Michael; *after Guido.*
The Four Fathers of the Church; *after the same.*
Aurora, with the Hours dancing before the Chariot of the Sun; *after the same;* in two sheets.
Bacchus consoling Ariadne after the Departure of Theseus; *after the same;* in two sheets.
The Death of St. Anne; *after A. Sacchi.*
St. Romualdus; *after the same.*
The Martyrdom of St. Sebastian; *after Domenichino.* 1737.
The Communion of St. Jerome; *after the same.* 1729.
The Four Angels of St. Carlo a Catenari at Rome, representing Justice, Temperance, Fortitude, and Prudence; *after the same.*
The Rape of Europa; *after Albani.*
St. Charles Borromeo interceding for the Plague-stricken; *after Pietro da Cortona.* 1744.
An allegorical picture of Clemency; *after Carlo Maratti.*
A Reposo, with St. Joseph presenting cherries to the Infant Christ; *after the same.*
Augustus shutting the Temple of Janus; *after the same.* 1738.
St. Andrew kneeling before the Cross; *after the same.*
St. Bernard; *after the same.*

FREY, JOHANN MICHAEL, who was born at Biberach in 1750, painted at Augsburg, and excelled in landscapes, and also as an engraver. His plates are executed in the manner of Bega; the best is a large landscape, after Ruisdael. He died at Augsburg in 1813.

FREY, JOHANNES, a Swiss landscape painter, a native of Basle, studied principally in Italy, and his views of that country are much valued. From Egypt, whither he accompanied Professor Lepsius, he brought many excellent sketches of the Pyramids, Labyrinths, &c. It is to be regretted that he was obliged to make but a short stay on account of his health. His painting of 'Chamsyn in the Desert,' in the possession of the Emperor of Germany, was produced in 1845, and is greatly admired. He died at Frascati, near Rome, in 1865. The Modern Gallery at Munich has his 'Two Memnons near Thebes.'

FREY, JOHANNES PIETER DE. See DE FREY.

FREY, MARTIN, born at Wurzach in 1769, was a scholar of Johann Gottlieb von Müller at Stuttgart, and subsequently resided at Vienna, where he was still living in 1821. Among his best etchings are:

The Temptation of St. Jerome; *after Domenichino.*
The Virgin with Jesus and John; *after the painting in the Esterhazy collection at Pesth, attributed to Raphael.*
The Infant Christ on a bed, and holding the Cross; *after Albani.*
St. Justina; *after Pordenone.*
An Old Man; *after G. Maes.*

FREY, SAMUEL, a Swiss painter of landscapes, the father of Johannes Frey, was born at Sissach in 1785. He devoted himself first to engraving under Von Mechel, but at Antwerp he studied oil-painting. In 1810 he returned to Basle, where he died in 1836.

FREYBECHKE, JOHANN, a monk of the convent of Königsbrück, in Alsace, who flourished about the year 1428, mentions himself at the end of a Bible containing some good miniatures, as its author. Whether he executed the miniatures is considered by Dr. Waagen to be an open question. The Bible is in the Royal Library at Munich.

FREYBERG, ELEKTRINE, born at Strassburg in 1797, was the daughter and pupil of Johann Stuntz, a painter of landscapes, under whose tuition she gave proof of great ability. She visited France and Italy, and stayed at Rome some time. Her paintings of historical scenes are distinguished for a tender touch, and she was not less successful in portraiture and landscape painting. One of her best works is a 'Holy Family.' 'The Birth of St. John,' and two landscapes, in the album of King Louis of Bavaria, are by this artist; in the Leuchtenberg Gallery 'The Virgin and Child,' and 'The Three Maries at the Tomb'; and in the Munich Gallery a 'Holy Family,' 'The Naming of St. John the Baptist,' and 'A Boy playing the flute.' She died at Munich in 1847.

FREZZA, GIOVANNI GIROLAMO, an Italian engraver, was born at Canemorto, near Tivoli, in 1659, and died at Rome in 1730. He was instructed in engraving at Rome by Arnold van Westerhout. His plates are etched with care, and very neatly finished with the graver, but without much force or effect. The following, among others, are by him:

The Gallery of the Verospi Palace; seventeen plates *after the frescoes by F. Albani.*
A set of ten plates, including the title, after the nine pictures by *Niccolò Berrettoni*, in the church of Santa Maria in Monte Santo, at Rome.
The Virgin suckling the Infant; *after Lodovico Carracci.*
The Holy Family; *after Carlo Maratti.*
The Assumption of the Virgin; *after the same.*
The Twelve Months; *after the same.*
The Judgment of Paris; *after the same.*
The Riposo, called the Zingarella; *after Correggio.*
The Descent of the Holy Ghost; *after Guido.*
Polyphemus on a Rock, and Galatea and her Nymphs on the Sea; *after Sisto Badalocchio.*
Polyphemus hurling a Rock at Acis and Galatea; *after the same.*
Venus; *after an antique painting;* for the Crozat Collection.
Pallas; *after an antique painting;* for the Crozat Collection.

FREZZA, ORAZIO, a native of Naples, lived in the 17th century, and was instructed by G. B. Benaschi. He afterwards studied the works of Lanfranco and Domenichino, whom he imitated with some success.

FRICK, J. F., born in 1774, was an engraver and a professor at the Academy of Berlin, who gained much repute for his aquatints. His best work is the series of illustrations of 'The Castle of Marienburg in Prussia,' in nineteen plates, 1799. He died in 1850.

FRIDERICH, Jacob Andreas, a German engraver, was born in 1683. He engraved some plates of Hussars and other horsemen, after Rugendas. He died in 1751.

FRIED, Heinrich Jakob, born at Queichheim, near Landau, in 1802, studied at Stuttgart and Augsburg, and from 1822 under Langer and Cornelius at the Academy of Munich. In 1834 he went to Rome, and afterwards to Naples, and from thence returned to his native country in 1837. Being patronized by Prince Karl von Wrede, he settled at Munich in 1842, and became conservator of the Artistic Society in 1845. He died at Munich in 1870. Fried was a great lover of legends, often taking these and similar sources for the subjects of his best pictures. He also executed a great number of landscapes, as well as genre and historical pieces and portraits, the best of which are:

A Hunting Party before the Castle of Trifels.
The Blue Grotto at Capri. (*Munich Gallery.*)
A View of Hohenschwangau.
The Wounded Knight.
Italian Flute-Players.
The Cloister of San Scolastica.
Views of the Palaces of Italy.

FRIEDERICI, Julius, a painter of Trèves, who was educated at the Düsseldorf Academy, has left two paintings of merit, 'Adam and Eve,' and a 'Flight into Egypt.' He died quite young in 1833.

FRIEDLÆNDER, Julius, a genre painter, was born at Copenhagen in 1810, and entered the Academy there in 1824, afterwards studying under Lund. In 1843-44 he visited Paris and Italy, whence he derived additional subjects for his art. Still later he took to depicting military and naval life. He died in 1861. Among his pictures are:

Polish Exiles.
A Doctor by a Sick Bed.
Rope-Dancers about to perform. (*Copenhagen Gallery.*)
The Spanish Staircase at Rome. (*Copenhagen Gallery.*)
Boys at Play at Capri.
Scene in a Children's Bedroom.

FRIEDRICH, Caroline Friederike, a flower painter, was born at Friedrichsstadt in 1740, and died at Dresden in 1812. She was court painter and a member of the Dresden Academy, and produced a number of admired bouquets in oil and water-colours.

FRIEDRICH, Caspar David, born at Greifswald in 1774, studied first at the Academy at Copenhagen under Quisdorf, and went to Dresden in 1795, where he painted landscapes. Subsequently he visited Rügen, the Giant and the Harz Mountains, and Italy. He also etched several plates of landscapes and trees. In 1817 he became professor at the Academy of Dresden, and in 1840 a member of that at Berlin. He died at Dresden in 1842. His best landscapes are:

Berlin.	Castle.	An Abbey in an Oak Forest, on a Winter Evening.
"	"	A Traveller on the Seashore.
"	Nat. Gall.	Evening View in the Harz Forest.
"	"	The Moon rising over the Sea.
Dresden.	Gallery.	Two Men looking at the Moon.
"	"	A Giant's Grave.
"	"	Rest after Haymaking.

FRIEDRICH, Franz, (or Friederich,) a designer, engraver, and carver, worked at Frankfort-on-the-Oder about the year 1550. He was employed by the printer Eichhorn, and was considered the first engraver of his district at that time. His

woodcuts are signed with two monograms, with the addition of 'Peter Hille'; this is supposed to mean that the design only is by him. He died after 1583. Some of his copper-plates are marked with a different monogram, and are very rare. The following are perhaps the best:

Portrait of the Elector Joachim II.
Portrait of Ludolph Schrader. 1581.
Portrait of the Archbishop Heinrich Julius of Brunswick.
Portrait of Heinrich Paxmann. 1580.

FRIES, Bernhard, a German landscape painter, was born at Heidelberg in 1820. He studied successively at Carlsruhe, Düsseldorf, and Munich, and for many years resided in Italy, where he produced his most important work—a series of forty Italian landscapes. He died at Munich in 1879.

FRIES, Ernst, a landscape painter, and brother of Bernhard Fries, was born at Heidelberg in 1801, and died at Carlsruhe in 1833. He was taught first by the elder Rottmann, and then by K. Kuntz at Carlsruhe. The English painter Wallis, who was then residing in Heidelberg, made a great impression upon him. Afterwards he went to Darmstadt, where he studied architecture and perspective under Moller. In 1821 he removed to Munich, where he visited the Academy. From 1823 to 1827 he lived in Italy, and returned to Munich and Carlsruhe in 1831, but died in the prime of his activity in 1833. Among his paintings are:

A View of Tivoli.
Sorrento and the House of Tasso.
Pozzuoli and the Gulf of Baiae.
Capo Misene.
The Waterfall of Liris at Isola di Sora. 1833. (*Munich Gallery.*)
The Castle of Massa.
A View of Heidelberg.
Valmontone. (*Berlin National Gallery.*)

He lithographed six plates, representing views of Heidelberg Castle, 1820-21, and the 'Death of Siegfried,' from the Nibelungen Lied, after C. Ganglof. With Thürmer he executed an etching of the Roman Forum.

FRIES, Hans, a Swiss painter, was born at Freiburg in the middle of the 15th century. It is probable that he studied in Germany. He was a member of the Guild at Basle in 1487-88, and at Freiburg in 1501. He died subsequently to 1518. The following paintings are by him:

Basle.	Museum.	Scenes from the Life of the Virgin (*painted for the Johanniter-Comthurei*). 1514.
"	"	Six Scenes from the Life of the Virgin (*painted for Berne*).
Freiburg.	Council Chamber.	The Last Judgment (*now removed*). 1501-6.
"	Franciscan Convent.	The Legend of St. Anthony.
"	Arsenal.	Coats of Arms and seventeen Flags. 1506.
Vienna.	Gallery.	A young Man, with Death behind him. 1524.

FRIES, Karl Friedrich, born at Winnweiler, in the Palatinate, in 1831, studied first at the Academy at Munich, and afterwards under Berdellé. He visited Vienna, and painted there under Rahl; then went to Venice, Florence, and Calabria, where he studied the old masters. He died at St. Gall, Switzerland, in 1871. His style much resembles that of the Venetian painters. The following are some of his works:

Wine, Woman, and Song; in the style of *Paolo Veronese.* 1862.
The Mineral Bath in the Abruzzi.

FRIES, WILHELM, a brother of Bernhard and Ernst Fries, was a landscape painter, and the conservator of the Wessenberg Museum. He was born in 1819, and died at Constance in 1878.

FRIPP, ALFRED DOWNING, younger brother of George A. Fripp (q.v.), was born in Bristol in 1822. In his early years he was chiefly influenced by W. J. Müller, and he soon (1840) followed his brother to London where he studied in the sculpture-galleries of the British Museum and at the Royal Academy. Choosing water-colour as a medium he began his career in 1842 by sending three drawings to the British Artists' Gallery. In 1844 he was elected an Associate of the Royal Society of Painters in Water-colour, and thenceforward his reputation steadily grew. In 1846 he became a full member of the Society. He went to Rome in 1850 and remained in Italy till 1859. In 1870 he was appointed Secretary to the Old Society. He visited Ireland thrice, and found there the subjects of some of his most charming works, e.g. 'Irish Reapers meeting their Friends after harvesting in England.' He painted many pictures of Italian life and scenery, of which 'Pompeii—the City of the Dead' (1853), is the most important. This is one of the few pictures where figures are not the leading motive. On his return he reverted to Welsh and English scenes; figure-subjects with a subordinate but often highly-finished landscape setting. He died in 1895. He contributed to the Gallery about 270 works. Two of his pictures—'Young England' and 'The Irish Mother'—are widely known through engravings. He had a delicate and tender touch, painting rather in low tints, and his drawings show a poetic refinement, a grace and an idyllic simplicity that never fail to charm.

J.H.W.L.

FRIPP, GEORGE ARTHUR, the son of a clergyman and grandson of Nicholas Pocock, one of the founders of the old Water-colour Society, was born in Bristol in 1813. Bristol was then the headquarters of a notable group of painters; and from two of these he received his art-training, learning oil-painting from J. B. Pyne, but owing most to Samuel Jackson, his master in water-colour. He painted portraits in oil in his native town for some years, maintaining a close friendship with W. J. Müller with whom he travelled in Italy. In 1841 he migrated to London, and in the same year was elected an Associate of the Royal Society of Painters in Water-colour. A large landscape in oils, 'Mont Blanc from near Cormayeur, Val d'Aosta,' which was exhibited at the Academy in 1848, elicited the praise of Turner, and was bought and presented to the Corporation of Liverpool, in whose gallery it now hangs. He painted but little in oil, and soon devoted himself entirely to water-colour. In 1845 he became full member of the Society, and in 1848 was appointed Secretary, a post he retained till his resignation in 1854. He was elected a member of the Belgian Society of Painters in Water-colour in 1872 or 1873. He was a regular contributor to the Exhibitions of his Society (sending in fifty years nearly 600 drawings), and was always active and zealous in its service. He died in Hampstead in 1896 after a period of failing health. He was an accomplished landscape-painter. Early in his career he painted some Swiss and Italian scenes, but most of his work was done at home. He particularly excelled in river-scenery, and his numerous views on the Thames are of high merit. Picturesque ruins, Scottish and Welsh mountain scenery, rustic subjects and rocky coast-pieces (Dorset, Cornwall and Sark), were treated by him with firm draughtsmanship, close fidelity to natural truth, and much feeling for pure colour and tender atmospheric effect. He painted in transparent colours, avoiding the use of body-colour.

His son, C. E. FRIPP, is an Associate of the Royal Society of Painters in Water-colour.

J.H.W.L.

FRIQUET, JACQUES CLAUDE, called FRIQUET DE VAUX-ROSE, or VAUROZE, was born in 1648. Little is known of this artist except that he was a scholar of Bourdon, and painted, after the drawings of his master, the gallery of the hotel of M. de Bretonvilliers, president of the Chambre des Comptes. He also painted, in 1667, an allegorical picture of the campaign in Flanders, and another of the conquest of Franche Comté in the following year. He was elected a member and professor of anatomy in the Academy of Paris in 1670: his reception work, 'The Peace of Aix-la-Chapelle,' is in the Louvre. He also engraved some of the works of Bourdon. He died in Paris in 1716.

FRISCH, JOHANN CHRISTOPH, an historical painter, was the son of the designer and engraver, Ferdinand Helfreich Frisch, and was born at Berlin in 1737. He was a pupil of B. Rode, but afterwards studied further at Rome. He died at Berlin in 1815, while holding the posts of court painter and director of the Academy. He painted numerous ceilings in the palaces at Berlin, Potsdam, and Sans Souci, with portraits, mythological representations, and scenes from the life of Frederick the Great.

FRISCH, JOHN DIDRIK, a Norwegian landscape painter, was born at Charlottedal, near Slagelse, in 1835, and studied in the Academy at Sorö under Harder, and afterwards in that at Copenhagen. In 1867 he went to Italy for further improvement, but died at Florence in that year. He was fond of introducing animals into his landscapes. One of his pictures is entitled 'Two old Neighbours procuring a Night's Lodging.'

FRISIUS. See DE VRIES.

FRISIUS, JAN EILLART, was very likely one of the De Vries family. He was chiefly employed by the booksellers, for whom he engraved some plates of portraits; among others:

Henry IV., King of France.
Henry of Nassau, Prince of Orange.

FRISTER, KARL, an Austrian painter, was born at Vienna in 1742, and died in the same city in 1783.

FRITS, PIETER, a Dutch painter, was born probably at Delft about 1627. He spent some time in Italy, and was employed at several European courts. In 1683 he established himself at Delft. He painted incantations, spectres, and other eccentric absurdities, in the style of Jerom Bosch; but not meeting with sufficient encouragement in this line, he abandoned it for that of a printseller, in which he amassed a large fortune. He was still living in 1702.

FRITSCH, DANIEL, a German painter, lived in the latter part of the 16th century. He copied, or imitated, the works of Lucas Cranach, as appears by a picture in the church at Tempelhof, near Berlin, mentioned by Kugler, and supposed to be by Lucas Cranach, but which, on cleaning, was discovered to be the work of Fritsch, and painted in the year 1596. Kugler observes that in power of colouring it is inferior to the later works of Cranach, but is distinguished by the excellence and individual truth of the heads.

FRITZSCH, CHRISTIAN, an engraver, was a native of Hamburg. He was chiefly employed in engraving portraits, among which are:

Pope Benedict XIV.
John Churchill, Duke of Marlborough.

FRITZSCH, CLAUDIUS DITLEV, a Danish flower painter, was born at Kiel in 1765, and died at Copenhagen in 1841. There are some specimens of his art in the Gallery of the latter city.

FRÖHLICHER, OTTO, was born in Solothurn, Switzerland, in 1840. He studied in Munich, and was influenced by Schleich and Lier. In 1868–69 he lived a year in Paris, and painted in the forest of Fontainebleau, receiving a powerful stimulus from Theodôre Rousseau and the Barbizon painters. The wide plains of Peissenberg, seen under brooding rain-clouds, Alpine and Bavarian landscapes are the subjects of his best pictures. His studies of forest scenery are fresh and powerful, but the finished pictures less successful. He died in Munich in 1891. J. H. W. L.

FROMANTIOU, HENDRIK DE. See DE FRO-MANTIOU.

FROMENTIN, EUGÈNE, a French painter of Algerian subjects, and an art writer, was born at La Rochelle in 1820. He studied under Cabat, and travelled in the East from 1842 to 1846. He died at St. Maurice, near his birthplace, in 1876. Amongst the books he wrote are 'Les Maîtres d'autrefois,' 'Un Été dans le Sahara,' 'Une Année dans le Sahel,' and a romance called 'Dominique.' His chief paintings are:

The Gorge of the Chiffa.
Hawking in Algeria. (*Luxembourg Gallery.*)
Arab Encampment (*unfinished*). (*Luxembourg Gallery.*)
The Simoom. 1859.
Arabs attacked by a Lioness. 1868.
The Halt of Muleteers. 1869.
Rendezvous of Arab Chiefs.
A Souvenir of Esneh. 1876.
The Nile. 1876.

A memoir of Fromentin by M. Louis Gonse was published in 1881, and has since been translated into English.

FROMMEL, KARL LUDWIG, born at Birkenfeld in 1789, was instructed in painting by Philipp Jakob Becker, and in engraving by Haldenwang. He afterwards went to Paris and Italy for improvement, returned to Germany in 1817, and became professor of painting and engraving at Carlsruhe. He visited England in 1824, and founded, with H. Winkles, an atelier for engravers on steel. In 1829 he was made director of the Gallery at Carlsruhe. He died at Ispringen, near Pforzheim, in 1863. Frommel's landscapes are very spirited and tasteful compositions. Among them are:

Sorrento.
The Eruption of Vesuvius.
The Blue Grotto at Capri.
Scylla in Calabria.
The Convent Garden at Sorrento.
The Churchyard at Salzburg.
The Castle of Hohenstaufen.
A View of Rome.
Ætna and Taormina.
Bellaggio on Lake Como.
The House of Tasso at Sorrento.
The Villa Serbelloni on Lake Como.

200

Among his engravings are:

Ariccia, near Rome.
View of the Villa d'Este at Tivoli.
A Landscape with Goats and Shepherds.
A View of Vesuvius.
A View of Mount Ætna.
La Grotta delle Sirene.

FRONTIER, JEAN CHARLES, was born in Paris in 1701. He was a pupil of Claude Guy Hallé, and took the first prize at the Academy in 1728, with a picture of 'Ezekiel abolishing Idolatry and establishing the Worship of the true God.' He was received as an academician in 1744, with the picture 'Prometheus bound on Caucasus,' now in the Louvre. He exhibited at the Salon from 1743 to 1751, and became director of the Academy of Lyons, where he died in 1763.

FROSNE, JEAN, a French engraver, was born in Paris about the year 1630, and was still living in 1676. He was principally employed in engraving portraits, of which the Abbé de Marolles collected forty-three. He also engraved part of the large ornamental plates for the collection of views, &c., by S. de Beaulieu. Among others, the following portraits are by him:

Claude Baudry, Abbé de La Croix; *after Le Bon.* 1657.
Louis de Lorraine, Duc de Joyeuse.
Henri d'Orléans, Duc de Longueville.
Nicolas Dauvet, Comte de Desmarez; *after Stresor.*
Nicolas Potier, President of the Parliament.
M. Dreux d'Aubray.

FROST, GEORGE, an English landscape painter, son of a builder, was born at Barrow, in Suffolk, in 1744. He was employed in connection with the Ipswich coach, and only pursued art as a pleasure. He was a follower of Gainsborough, and on friendly terms with Constable. He died at Ipswich in 1821. In the Glasgow Gallery is a sketch by this artist entitled 'Courtship.'

FROST, WILLIAM EDWARD, an English mythological and allegorical painter, was born at Wandsworth in 1810. He received his first instruction in art from an amateur, then at Sass's academy, and finally at the schools of the Royal Academy, which he entered in 1829, and where, in 1839, he won the gold medal with his 'Prometheus bound.' For the first fourteen years of his career he painted portraits, and then relinquished that branch of art to follow in the footsteps of Etty, to whom he had been introduced at the age of fifteen, and who had given him much advice. At the Westminster Hall competition in 1843 he obtained a prize of £100 for his 'Una surprised by Fauns.' He was elected an Associate of the Royal Academy in 1846, but did not become an Academician until 1871, when he deposited as his diploma picture 'A Nymph and Cupid.' He died in London in 1877. His chief works are:

Sabrina. 1845.
Diana surprised by Actæon. 1846.
Una and the Wood Nymphs. 1847.
The Disarming of Cupid. 1850.
Chastity. 1854.
Narcissus. 1857. (*International Exhibition*, 1862.)
The Syrens. 1860.
A Dance. 1861.
The Graces and Loves. 1863.
Hylas and the Nymphs. 1867.
Puck. 1869.

FROYEN, —, the name of an obscure and very indifferent engraver, is affixed to a print representing the head of our Saviour. It is executed entirely with the graver.

FRUMENTI, Niccolò, who flourished about 1460, was the painter of a triptych in the Uffizi at Florence, representing the 'Raising of Lazarus,' dated 1461.

FRUTET, Francisco. This name appeared first in the pages of Cean Bermudez, whence it has been copied again and again during the present century. Cean Bermudez appears to have been misled by certain documents in the archives of the convent of La Merced Calzada at Seville, and so to have ascribed to an artist who never existed the triptych of the 'Adoration of the Magi,' now in the Brussels Gallery, which was probably the last work of Frans Floris. The question has been discussed by M. Fétis in the 'Bulletin des Commissions royales d'Art et d'Archéologie' for 1880.

FRUTTI, Il Gobbo da'. See Bonzi.

FRUYTIERS, Philippus, a Flemish painter and etcher, was born at Antwerp about the year 1610. He first painted historical subjects in oil, and had given proof of considerable ability in an altar-piece representing the 'Virgin and Infant seated on a Globe, with a Choir of Angels,' painted for the cathedral, when he quitted oil-painting for distemper and miniature, and became the most celebrated artist of his time in those branches. His colouring is excellent, and his compositions evince a ready invention. His works were greatly esteemed by Rubens, and it is no slender proof of his merit that he was employed to paint the portraits of that great master and his family, which he executed entirely to his satisfaction. There is at Windsor Castle a miniature by him of the wife and family of Rubens. He died at Antwerp in 1665. Fruytiers etched some plates in a very masterly style ; they are principally portraits. The most important are :

Jacob Edelheer, the Ambassador.
M. Ambrosius van Capelle, Bishop of Antwerp.
Gottfroy Wendelinus. 1648.
Hedwiga Eleonora, Queen of Sweden.
Don Laur. Ramires de Prado, Eques. 1649.
Innocens a Calatayerone, head of the Capuchins in Belgium.
Benj. Sardagna. 1650.
St. Joachim and St. Anna presenting the Child Mary to the Trinity.

FRY, William Thomas, who was born in 1789, and died in 1843, practised engraving with some success.

FRYE, Thomas, a portrait painter and engraver in mezzotint, was born in the vicinity of Dublin in 1710, but afterwards resided in London, and in 1749 established a porcelain manufactory at Bow, which did not prove a successful venture. He painted portraits with success, both in oil and in miniature. His portrait of Jeremy Bentham at the age of thirteen is in the National Portrait Gallery. He also scraped in mezzotint several plates of portraits, most of which are as large as life. He died in 1762. Among his engravings are the following heads :

George III.
Queen Charlotte.
His own Portrait.
Portrait of his Wife.
Miss Pond.

FUCHS, Adam, an engraver on copper and wood, flourished in Germany in 1550-80. Among his plates, which are marked with his name or initials, or with one or other of the accompanying monograms, are :

The Elector Frederick the Wise.
Martin Luther kneeling before a Crucifix. 1568.
A Hare mounted as General.
Twelve Plates of Love-pieces of Sea-horses and Monsters.

FUCHS, Maximilian Heinrich, who was born in 1767, became deservedly known for his architectural design for the cathedral at Cologne. He restored with ability the 'Crucifixion of Peter,' in St. Peter's church in that city, and Stephan's painting in the cathedral. He died at Cologne in 1848.

FUCKERAD, Bernard, a Jesuit, born in Thuringia in 1601, executed a number of paintings for the Jesuits' Church and that of St. Andrew at Cologne. He is said to have been so skilful in copying the works of other artists, that an imitation by him of a picture by Johann Hulsman deceived that painter into the belief that it was his own production. He died at Cologne in 1662.

FUENTE. See De La Fuente.

FUENTES, Giorgio, born at Milan in 1756, studied under Gonzaga, and distinguished himself as a painter of decorations in the Scala at Milan, at Frankfort (1796—1805), and in the Grand Opera in Paris. He died at Milan in 1821.

FUERSTENBERG, Theodor Caspar von, one of the first artists who worked in mezzotint, is said to have been instructed by Ludwig von Siegen. All that is now known of this artist is that he was a prebendary at Mayence in 1624, and provost in 1673. He died at that town in 1675. His very rare and beautiful plates are :

The Portrait of the Archduke Leopold William of Austria. 1656.
Christ with the Crown of Thorns ; after Albrecht Dürer.
The Bust of a Prince. 1658.
The Head of St. John.
Herodias with the Head of St. John.
The Portrait of the Margrave Frederick of Baden.

FUES, Friedrich Christian, an historical, genre, and portrait painter, was born at Tübingen in 1772, and was educated at Stuttgart under Harper and Hetsch. He then found employment in Stobwasser's varnish factory at Brunswick, and after that with J. D. von Mayr at Nuremberg, in the preparation of pictures for snuff-boxes and ornaments, until he was appointed professor of painting in the art school of the latter city. He died in 1836. He etched thirteen plates of landscapes, and lithographed four. Among his paintings are :

The Minnesingers.
The Family of an old Knight in the Castle Hall.
A Peasant laughing.
Summer and Winter. 1835.
Consecration of a Swabian Church. 1839.
Nine Portraits of distinguished Nurembergers. (Town Hall, Nuremberg.)

FUESSLY is the name borne by a numerous family of artists, who flourished at Zurich in the 18th and 19th centuries. The most important member was Heinrich Fuessly, better known as Henry Fuseli, R.A. The others painted portraits, flowers, miniatures, &c., and some of them wrote on art.

FUESSLY, Heinrich, or, as he is commonly known in England, Henry Fuseli, second son of Johann Kaspar Fuessly, was born at Zurich in 1741. He was originally intended for the Church, and actually entered it, but compelled by the enmity of a magistrate, whose dishonesty he had exposed, to leave his native town, he went to

Berlin, and for some time devoted himself to literature, in which he was engaged at intervals throughout his life. In 1765, at the instigation of the British ambassador at the court of Berlin, he visited England, and in 1767 an introduction to Reynolds, who praised his drawings, induced him to become a painter, and in the following year he went to Italy, where he stayed for nearly nine years, studying the works of Michelangelo; but he never fairly mastered the principles of drawing or colouring, and his works are esteemed more for the powerful imagination they display than for any artistic merit. He was of most eccentric habits and extravagant ideas, and these ideas are everywhere apparent in his pictures. Leaving Italy in 1778, and passing through Zurich, he reached England in the following year, and in 1782 produced his famous picture of 'The Nightmare.' In 1786 he became a zealous worker in Boydell's Shakespeare Gallery, for which he executed nine paintings. In 1788 he was elected an Associate of the Royal Academy, and an Academician two years later, and in 1790, too, he married one of his models. In 1799 he opened his Milton Gallery, comprising forty-seven paintings, the result of several years of labour. In the same year he was elected Lecturer on Painting at the Royal Academy, and in 1804 he was made keeper, the bye-laws being altered to allow him to retain the lectureship. He died at Putney in 1825. Fuseli was an artist in mind, but devoid of technical knowledge. His most famous productions are, perhaps, his illustrations to Shakespeare.

FÜGER, FRIEDRICH HEINRICH, was born at Heilbronn in 1751. Some of his works exhibit elegance of form and an agreeable colour; but he is very unequal, as may be seen from those in the Vienna Gallery, which are not his best. He first learned painting under Guibal at Stuttgart, but finding himself not yet apt enough for the art, he studied jurisprudence at Halle in 1768. In 1770 he took up the brush again, and painted under Oeser at Leipsic. He then went to Dresden, where he executed several portraits. In 1772 he returned to Stuttgart in order to study composition under Guibal. At Vienna, to which city he went in 1774, he was patronized by Maria Theresa, who assisted him to visit Rome, in which city he studied after the antique and the great masters, especially after Mengs and Battoni. After having finished several frescoes in the Caserta Palace, near Naples, in 1782, which represent 'Allegories upon the Origin of the Sciences,' he was appointed vice-director of the Academy at Vienna in 1783. He died at Vienna in 1818. His most important paintings are:

Brunswick.	*Gallery.*	The Portrait of Count Ludolff.
London.	*Nat. Port. Gallery.*	Portrait of Nelson (*painted at Vienna in 1800*).
Munich.	*Gallery.*	The Magdalen.
Vienna.	*Gallery.*	St. John the Baptist.
,,	,,	The Magdalen.
,,	,,	Ariadne at Naxos.
,,	,,	Orpheus in the Lower World.
,,	,,	Dido on the Funereal Pile.
,,	,,	Adam and Eve lamenting over the body of Abel.
,,	,,	The Judgment of Brutus.
,,	,,	Semiramis.
,,	,,	Virginia.
,,	,,	The Farewell of Coriolanus.
,,	*Academy.*	The Death of Germanicus.
,,	Count Zinzendorf.	Prometheus.

Other portraits by him are:

The Emperor Joseph.
The Elector of Mentz.
General Loudon.
The Princess of France.
The Countess Rzewuska with her Children.

He illustrated Klopstock's 'Messiah' with twenty designs which were engraved by Leybold, and likewise executed fifteen etchings of portraits and mythological subjects.

FÜHRICH, JOSEPH, was born at Kratzau, in Bohemia, in 1800, and studied first at Prague under Bergler, and in 1827 at Vienna, where he designed and painted several romantic scenes. In 1829 he went to Rome, and executed three frescoes in the Villa Massimi, representing scenes from Tasso's 'Gerusalemme liberata.' He afterwards became a follower of Overbeck. In 1854 he began his great works in the Altlerchenfelder Church at Vienna, representing the 'Raising of Lazarus' and the 'Last Judgment.' He died at Vienna in 1876. Though his religious subjects are not free from fault, they are well conceived, the figures being natural and the draperies simple. Among his numerous paintings and drawings may be mentioned:

Fifteen drawings for Tieck's 'Genovefa.'
Illustrations to Goethe's 'Erlkönig.'
Twelve drawings for Goethe's 'Hermann and Dorothea.'
Jesus entering the Garden.
Joshua and his army giving thanks on the Fall of the Walls of Jericho.
The Nativity of Christ.
The Creator in the Clouds giving Moses the Commandments. (*Vienna Gallery.*)
The Appearance of fighting Horsemen in the Clouds, terrifying the inhabitants of Jerusalem, before the occupation by Antiochus. (*Vienna Gallery.*)
The Virgin going over the Mountain. (*Vienna Gallery.*)
Fourteen scenes from the Crucifixion. (*St. John Nepomuk, Vienna.*)
Eight scenes in the life of the Prodigal Son.
Sixteen scenes of the Spiritual Rose.
Fifteen scenes of the Resurrection.

FULCARUS, SEBASTIANUS. See FURCK.

FULCO, GIOVANNI, was born at Messina in 1615. After having learned the first principles of design in his native city, he went to Naples, where he entered the school of Cavaliere Massimo Stanzione. He is said by Hakert, in his 'Memorie de' Pittori Messinese,' to have been a firm and correct designer, and to have excelled particularly in the representation of children. Many of his pictures have been destroyed by the earthquakes, to which his country is subject. Of those that remain are his fresco works, and a picture in oil of the 'Birth of the Virgin,' in the chapel of the Crucifixion, at the Nunziata de' Teatini, at Messina. He died about the year 1680.

FULIGNO, NICCOLÒ DA. See LIBERATORE.

FULIGNO, PIER ANTONIO DI, flourished about the middle of the 15th century, and executed the frescoes in Santa Cattarina at Assisi.

FULLER, ISAAC, an English painter, was born in 1606. Nothing is known of his family, or of his instructor in his own country, but he studied some years under François Perrier, in Paris. He was principally employed in England, and especially at Oxford, in wall pieces. In the chapel at Wadham College he painted the 'Children of Israel gathering Manna,' and at Magdalen College an altar-piece which was praised by Addison. He also painted five pictures of the 'Escape of Charles II. after the battle of Worcester,' which were presented to the

Irish Parliament. His own portrait, which is at Queen's College, Oxford, though eccentric, is touched with great force, and full of character. Fuller etched some plates for a drawing-book, called 'Libro da disegnare'; and in conjunction with Tempesta and Henry Cooke, etched the plates for the 'Moral Emblems,' by Cesare Ripa; they are very indifferently executed. He died in London in 1672.

FULLER, RICHARD, an American landscape painter, was born at Bradford, in New Hampshire, in 1822. In 1840 he was apprenticed to a cigar manufacturer at Boston, and later on he was made street inspector and night watchman. From 1852 to 1866, however, he made attempts at the pursuit of art in his leisure hours, deriving his instruction from the pictures which he saw in shop-windows. From 1867 until his death he was able to devote himself entirely to painting, and depicted American landscapes with much poetical feeling. He died at Chelsea, near Boston, in 1871, and bequeathed to the art club of that city ninety of his paintings, which entitle him to rank among the best landscape painters of his country.

FUMACCINI, ORAZIO. See SAMACCHINI.

FUMIANI, GIOVANNI ANTONIO, was born at Venice in 1643, and was educated at Bologna. After acquiring an excellent style of design and composition in that school, he returned to Venice, where he studied for some time the works of Paolo Veronese. Lanzi considers his picture of 'Christ disputing with the Doctors,' in the church of La Carità, as his best performance. Among other things the immense ceiling painting in San Pantaleone, representing the 'Glorification of St. Pantaleon,' is remarkable. He died in 1710.

FUMICELLI, LODOVICO, was a native of Trevigi, who flourished about the year 1536. It is not known with certainty whether he was a scholar of Titian or not; but Lanzi regards him as one of the ablest and most memorable of his imitators. In 1536 he painted the principal altar-piece of the church of the Padri Eremitani at Padua, representing the 'Virgin and Infant seated in the clouds, with St. Augustine, St. James, and St. Marina below'; which, according to Ridolfi, is designed and coloured in a style worthy of the greatest masters. In the church of the Padri Serviti, at Trevigi, he painted a picture of 'St. Liberale and St. Catharine,' with two laterals, representing 'St. Sebastian and St. Philip,' the latter the founder of their order. It is to be regretted that the offer of an advantageous situation in the engineers tempted him to abandon painting.

FUNGAI, BERNARDINO, was a native of Siena, who was born about 1460, and died in 1516. He was instructed in the art of painting by Benvenuto del Guasta. His style retains something of the dry, stiff manner which preceded him, though not more so than that of many of his contemporaries. Among the works of this artist, in which he was partly assisted by Pacchiarotti, the following are the most important:

Chiusi.	Cathedral.	The Nativity of Christ. (Assisted by Pacchiarotti.)
London.	South Kensington Museum.	The Virgin with the Child. (Falsely ascribed to Vivarini.)
Siena.	S. M. de' Servi.	Coronation of the Virgin.
„	„	Madonna di Fontegiusta. 1500.
„	Carmine.	The Virgin and Child, with Saints. 1512.

Siena.	Academy.	The Ascension.
„	„	Christ between St. Francis and St. Jerome.
„	„	A Madonna. (Assisted by Pacchiarotti.)

FUNK, HEINRICH, born at Herford, in Westphalia, in 1809, learned the rudiments of art from his father, and studied in 1829 under Schirmer at the Academy at Düsseldorf. He soon became known as an excellent painter of landscapes, and was employed at Frankfort from 1836 to 1854. Subsequently he settled at Stuttgart, where he became professor of the art school, and died in 1877. Funk was a student of nature, who possessed a fine taste for the beautiful, and painted in a simple manner. The following of his paintings are noteworthy:

Berlin.	Gallery.	A Summer's Day on the Rhine.
„	„	A Ruin in the Evening Light.
Frankfort.	Städel Inst.	The Lower Valley of the Inn. Landscape.
Stuttgart.	Gallery.	An approaching Thunderstorm in the Eifel Mountains.

FURCK, SEBASTIAN, (or FULCARUS,) a German engraver, was born at Alterkülz, Hundsrück, about 1589. In the early part of his life he resided at Rome, where he engraved some plates as early as 1612. From 1620 to 1630 he was established at Frankfort-on-the-Main. He engraved many portraits and historical pieces, chiefly for the booksellers, among which are those of the Colonna family; also some plates after Titian, and other masters. He died at Frankfort in 1666. He worked principally with the graver, though there are a few etchings by him. When he did not sign his plates with his name, he marked them with the cipher 𝔉. The following prints are by him:

The Last Judgment; after Michelangelo.
St. Sebastian; a half-length figure.
An ornamental Frontispiece to the works of Gul. Fabricius, dated 1646. It is etched in a very spirited style, and is signed S. Furck, f.

FURICH, JOHANN PHILIPP, born at Strassburg in 1655, studied under Johann Heinrich Roos at Frankfort, and became so successful an imitator of that master, that his works are often mistaken for those of Roos. He died after 1735.

FURINI, FRANCESCO, who is styled by Lanzi the Guido and Albani of the Florentine school, was the son of Filippo Furini, a respectable portrait painter, and was born at Florence in 1604. He was first instructed by his father, and afterwards studied under Passignano and Roselli; and on leaving their schools, visited Rome and Venice. In 1644 he was appointed curate at Mugello, near Borgo San Lorenzo, where he painted some of his best pictures. But he acquired the high reputation in which he is held by his admirable easel pictures, which are found in the first collections in Florence. He had a preference for imitating the style of Albani, in which he was very successful. He drew with elegance and correctness, particularly the delicate forms of women and children, and he generally made choice of those subjects in which they could be introduced with the happiest effect. Such are his pictures of the 'Three Graces,' in the Palazzo Strozzi, and of 'Nymphs carried off by Satyrs,' in the Casa Galli. Furini died at Florence in 1649. Among his paintings are the following:

Borgo San Lorenzo.	*Church.*	St. Francis receiving the Stigmata.
"	"	The Ascension of the Virgin.
Copenhagen.	*Gallery.*	The Penitent Magdalen.
Darmstadt.	*Museum.*	A Female Saint.
Dresden.	*Gallery.*	St. Cecilia.
Edinburgh.	*Nat. Gall.*	A Head of St. Sebastian.
		A Poetess.
Florence.	*Pitti Pal.*	Adam and Eve in Eden.
	"	An Allegorical Figure.
Madrid.	*Gallery.*	Lot and his Daughters.
Rome.	*Pal. Capponi.*	David and Abigail.
"	*Pal. Corsini.*	Mythological Subjects.
Vienna.	*Gallery.*	The Magdalen.

FURNIUS, Pieter Jalhea, a Flemish designer and engraver, was born in Flanders about 1540, and was residing at Antwerp about the year 1570. He was a contemporary of the Galles and the Sadelers, who engraved some plates from his designs. His style of engraving bears a near resemblance to that of those artists. Though he drew the figure correctly, in attempting to imitate the lofty style of Michelangelo he fell into affectation and extravagance. He worked entirely with the graver in a slight, feeble manner. The many plates which he engraved after M. Heemskerk, J. Stradanus, M. De Vos, P. Brueghel, M. van Coxie, and others, are signed with the accompanying monogram The date of his death is not mentioned. Among other prints the following are by him:

The Parable of the Good Samaritan : a set of six plates.
The Martyrdom of St. Felicia ; *P. Furnius in. et fec.*
The Escape of Cloelia ; *P. Furnius fecit.*

FÜRST, Rosine Helene, was an embroiderer and engraver of Nuremberg in the 17th century. Her sister, Magdalene Fürst, painted flowers.

FÜRSTENBERG, Theodor Caspar von. See Fuerstenberg.

FURTMAYR, Perchthold, a miniature painter of the Upper German School, flourished between 1470 and 1501. There are by him in the castle of Wallerstein, Maihingen, near Nördlingen, a Chronicle in two folio volumes, with a great number of miniatures, and a Bible, with vignettes ; and at Munich, in the Royal Library, a Missal in five folio volumes, with miniatures, beautiful monograms, and flowers, executed for the Archbishop Bernhard of Salzburg in 1481.

FUSELI, Henry. See Fuessly, Heinrich.

FUSS, Hans. See Suess, Hans.

FÜTERER, Ulrich, who was born at Landshut, and flourished at Munich, is the author of a 'Crucifixion,' painted in imitation of sculpture, in the Gallery at Schleissheim. It was painted about 1480, and is a specimen of very undeveloped art. Füterer is better known as a poet than as a painter.

FYFE, William Baxter Collier, a Scottish genre and portrait painter, was born at Dundee about 1836. He became a student of the Royal Scottish Academy, and exhibited his first picture of importance, 'Queen Mary resigning her Crown at Loch Leven Castle,' in the Exhibition of 1861 ; but this was surpassed in later years by 'The Raid of Ruthven.' In 1863 he settled in London, and from that time onward was busily engaged with portraiture, which he varied with landscapes and genre subjects of interest and merit. Some of his most important portraits are those of the Earl and Countess of Dufferin, Admiral Grenfell, Alderman Sir William McArthur, Dr. Lorimer and John Faed, R.S.A. He died suddenly in London in 1882. His best-known genre pictures are :

204

On Household Cares intent.
What can a Young Lassie dae wi' an Auld Man ?

FYOLL, Conrad, who flourished at Frankfort-on-the-Main from the year 1464 to 1476,—the only space of time of which record concerning him has been handed down to us,—is a painter whose works display graceful drawing and subdued colouring. The chief picture ascribed to him is an altar-piece in the Städel Institute at Frankfort. It represents, in the centre, 'Christ on the Cross,' with the donor and his sons on the right wing, and his wife and daughters on the left wing. There is also a picture of the 'Family of St. Anne.' Mention may also be made of a triptych in the Berlin Gallery formerly assigned to him, but now thought to be of rather later date, representing the 'Virgin and Child with St. Anna,' and ' SS. Barbara and Catharine ' and the 'Annunciation' on the wings ; and of another in the Antwerp Museum, with the 'Adoration of the Magi ' in the centre, and the 'Nativity ' and 'Circumcision ' on the wings.

FYT, Jan, a Flemish painter and etcher, was born at Antwerp in 1609. He studied in the atelier of Jan van Berch in that city in 1621, became a master in the Guild of St. Luke in 1629, and afterwards visited Rome. When he returned to Antwerp he joined the Guild of the Romanists in 1650, and became its dean in 1652. He excelled in the representation of every species of animal, but in dogs he is perhaps without a rival. It is impossible for art to approach nearer to nature than in the pictures of Fyt of that description. His touch is without manner, or the formality of practice ; it is loose, spirited, and playful, but peculiarly characteristic, and full of energy. Such was his extraordinary merit, that he was courted by the greatest painters of his time to embellish their works with the additional attraction of his admirable animals. Rubens, Janssens, De Craeyer, and Jordaens employed him in that way, which was the more flattering to his talent as Rubens himself excelled in painting animals of every description. His works are to be met with at Antwerp (the 'Meal of the Eagle' and the 'Sleeping Hound '), Augsburg, Berlin, Brunswick, Dresden, Cassel, Munich, Madrid, Paris, Venice, and Vienna. A group of 'Dead Birds ' is in the National Gallery. He died at Antwerp in 1661. There are by Fyt some admirable etchings, executed in the bold and spirited style of his pictures ; they are as follow :

A set of eight of Dogs and other Animals. 1640.
A set of seven of Dogs, of different species, with backgrounds of landscapes ; dated 1642, and inscribed *Johannes Fyt, pinx. et fecit.*
A set of eight small plates of a Cart, a Horse, a Dog, Foxes, Goats, and three of Cows. These are very scarce.

Lanzi mentions a *Gio. Fayt di Anversa*, who resided for some time at Venice, and was employed in the Casa Sagredo and Casa Contarini: this statement, if correct, cannot apply to Jan Fyt.

G

GAAL, Barent, (or Gael,) a Dutch painter, was born at Haarlem in 1650. He was a scholar of Philip Wouwerman, until the death of that master in 1668, when he found himself capable of dispensing with further instruction. He painted hunting parties, battles, horse-fairs, and other subjects similar to those of his instructor, and he frequently painted figures in the landscapes of

Isaac Koene, a scholar of Jacob Ruisdael. He died in 1703. The Rotterdam Museum has paintings by him of 'A Woman making Cakes,' and 'The Village Inn'; and the Brunswick Gallery one of 'Soldiers playing Cards.' In the Hermitage at St. Petersburg are a 'Coast Scene' and a landscape, and in the Augsburg Gallery is 'A Pig Market.

GAAL, PIETER, was oorn at Middelburg in 1769, and received his first instructions from his father, Thomas Gaal, under whom he made some progress; he afterwards became a pupil of Schweickhardt, at the Hague. After visiting London, Paris, and several places in Germany, he settled in his native city, where he painted portraits, landscapes, animals, live and dead game, and subjects of ordinary life, some of which were of large dimensions. He died at Middelburg in 1819.

GAAL, THOMAS, a painter of portraits, birds, and flowers, was born at Dendermonde in 1739. He fixed his residence at Middelburg, and was one of the founders and directors of the Academy in that town. J. Perkois, J. H. Koekkoek, and S. De Koster were his pupils. He died at Middelburg in 1817.

GABBIANI, ANTONIO DOMENICO, an Italian painter, was born at Florence in 1652. After he had studied some time under Justus Sustermans and Vincenzo Dandini, the Grand-Duke Cosmo III., having been made acquainted with his promising talent, took him under his protection, and sent him to the Florentine Academy at Rome, where he frequented the school of Ciro Ferri. After passing three years at Rome he visited Venice, and improved his style of colouring by the study of the great painters of that school. He was invited to the court of Vienna, where he painted the portrait of the Emperor and some historical subjects for the Imperial Gallery. On his return to Florence he painted several altarpieces for the churches, particularly a fine picture of the 'Assumption,' and a 'Repose in Egypt'; also his celebrated picture of 'St. Philip,' in the church of the Padri dell' Oratorio. For his easel pictures he generally selected subjects into which he could introduce children, in which he excelled. He continued to paint until he was killed by a fall from a scaffold at Florence, in 1726. His principal works in public galleries are:

Cambridge.	*Fitzwilliam Museum.*	Portrait.
Dresden.	*Gallery.*	Christ at the house of Simon the Pharisee.
Florence.	*Uffizi.*	His own Portrait.
"	"	Rape of Ganymede.
"	"	Madonna.
Munich.	*Gallery.*	St. Francis of Assisi performing Miracles.
"	"	St. Peter of Alcantara.

Four engravings by him are known:

The Madonna; *after Parmigiano.*
Portrait of an old Man.
Portrait of a young Woman.
A Landscape.

GABBIANI, GAETANO, the nephew of Antonio Gabbiani, studied under his uncle, and became a meritorious portrait painter in pastel. He worked at Florence, and died about 1750.

GABBUGIANI, BALDASSARE, an Italian engraver, executed some of the plates for the 'Museo Fiorentino,' published at Florence between the years 1747 and 1766.

GABET, CHARLES HENRY JOSEPH, a French painter of miniatures and of portraits in watercolours, was born at Courbevoie in 1793. He is also known as the author of a 'Dictionnaire des Artistes de l'École Française au XIXᵉ siècle,' published in 1831. He died in Paris in 1860.

GABET, FRANZ, an Austrian etcher, was born at Vienna in 1762, and died in the same city in 1847. He executed several landscapes after M. Molitor, as well as some from his own designs, and six plates of Ruins, &c., after F. E. Weirotter (1791).

GABIOU, JEANNE ELIZABETH. See CHAUDET.

GABLER, AMBROSIUS, a German painter and engraver, born at Nuremberg in 1764, painted beautiful miniatures. His father, Nikolaus Gabler, painted in oils and etched.

GABLER, JOHANN JAKOB, an engraver, was a native of Augsburg. He worked at Leipsic, and engraved the 'Battle of Lutzen' in 1632.

GABRIEL, GEORGES FRANÇOIS MARIE, a French miniature painter and designer, born in Paris in 1775, was a pupil of Naigeon and Regnault. Among his designs are those ordered by the French Government for the great work of the Institute on Egypt; and among his portraits is one of Madame de Maintenon, engraved by Mécou, which forms the frontispiece to her memoirs by Lafont d'Ausonne. The date of his death is unknown.

GABRIEL, PAULUS JOSEPH, a painter and sculptor, was born at Amsterdam in 1785. He learned sculpture from his father and Canova, and devoted himself principally to that branch of art; but he at first practised miniature painting, and in his twentieth year proceeded to Paris specially to improve himself therein. In 1820 he was made a member of the Institute at Amsterdam, and director of the Royal Academy there. He died at Amsterdam in 1833.

GABRIELLI, CAMILLO, a native of Pisa, was a scholar of Ciro Ferri. Lanzi states that he was the first who introduced the style of Pietro da Cortona among his countrymen. He painted some oil pictures at the Carmelites, and for private collections; but he was more distinguished for his fresco paintings, which were much esteemed. His principal work was the decorations of the great saloon in the Palazzo Allicata. He died in 1730.

GABRIELLO, ONOFRIO, was born at Messina in 1617. After studying six years in his native city, under Antonio Ricci, called Barbalonga, he went to Rome, and entered the school of Pietro da Cortona. He afterwards visited Venice, and on his return to Messina he was much employed in the churches, for private collections, and in portrait painting. He was in great repute when the Revolution, which took place in 1674, obliged him to quit Sicily, and he settled at Padua, where he resided several years, and was usually called Onofrio da Messina. Some of his best works are in the church of San Francesco di Paola at Messina, and in the 'Guida di Padova' are mentioned several of his pictures in the public edifices and private collections of that city, particularly in the Palazzo Borromeo. He died in 1706.

GABRON, WILLEM, born at Antwerp in 1625, was a good painter of fruit and flowers, and excelled in the representation of gold and silver vases, porcelain, and ornaments of a like kind. He spent several years in Italy, but died at

Antwerp in 1679. The Munich, Brunswick, and Darmstadt Galleries have works by him.

GADDI, Agnolo, the son of Taddeo Gaddi, was born at Florence apparently after 1333, and at his father's death was left under the joint tutorship of Giovanni da Milano and Jacopo del Casentino. In the early portion of his career he painted the 'Resurrection of Lazarus,' in the church of San Jacopo tra Fosse, at Florence. The frescoes in the Pieve of Prato, representing the two legends of the Virgin and the Sacred Girdle, that were painted in his prime, and show evident traces of Giotto's principles, are still to be seen there. Unfortunately they are much damaged both by time and by repairs, but they still show considerable power and ability. Many other productions from his brush exist in Prato. In the choir of Santa Croce, at Florence, are eight frescoes illustrating the Legend of the Cross. Altar-pieces by him may also be found in many of the churches in and around Florence. He is said to have lived for some time at Venice, engaged in mercantile pursuits. He died at Florence in 1396, and was buried in the church of Santa Croce. Among his paintings are the following:

Florence.	Academy.	Virgin and Child in Glory, surrounded by Saints.
„	„	Evangelists and Doctors of the Church.
„	„	Scenes from the Lives of St. John the Evangelist, St. John the Baptist, St. Nicholas, and St. Anthony.
„	S. Croce.	Eight subjects from the Legend of the Cross—frescoes.
„	„	Figures of Saints.
„	Uffizi.	The Annunciation.
Paris.	Louvre.	The Annunciation.
Prato.	Cathedral.	Thirteen subjects from the Life of the Virgin, and the Legend of Dagomari (who carried the Holy Girdle from Palestine to Prato).
„	Museum.	Virgin and Saints.

GADDI, Gaddo, the intimate friend and contemporary of Cimabue, was born at Florence about 1260. From Tafi, Gaddo learned the art of mosaic, and one of his earliest works was the figures of the prophets beneath the windows in the baptistery of San Giovanni at Florence. The influence of Cimabue is chiefly shown in his mosaic inside and above the portal of Santa Maria del Fiore at Florence, representing a 'Coronation of the Virgin, with Saints and Angels.' This artist seems to have visited Rome, and to have been employed in mosaic work in Santa Maria Maggiore, and in the choir of St. Peter's. He also painted in the upper church of St. Francis at Assisi, and executed the mosaics of the old Duomo outside Arezzo. His portrait, as well as that of Tafi, was painted by his son Taddeo Gaddi in the 'Sposalizio' in the Baroncelli Chapel at Santa Croce. Gaddo Gaddi was still living in 1333, but probably died about that year, and was buried in the cloisters of Santa Croce.

GADDI, Giovanni, an inferior artist, was a son of Taddeo Gaddi, and a pupil of his brother Agnolo. He painted in San Spirito at Florence a 'Dispute of Christ with the Scribes in the Temple,' and some similar works, but they were all destroyed on the rebuilding of the church. He died in 1383.

GADDI, Taddeo, the son of Gaddo Gaddi, was born at Florence about 1300, and was first instructed by his father, but afterwards by his godfather Giotto, whose assistant he became for twenty-four years. When Giotto left Florence to visit Naples, the Baroncelli Chapel in Santa Croce was completed, and Taddeo, after painting the 'Virgin and Child between four Prophets' on the funeral monument at the entrance, executed on the walls of the chapel itself scenes from the life of the Virgin, and in the diagonals of the double ceiling the Eight Virtues. One of these works was an altar-piece now in the Berlin Gallery, and inscribed "Anno Dñi MCCCXXXIIII mensis septembris Tadeus me fecit." The centre panel represents the 'Virgin and Child,' with the patrons kneeling at the foot of the throne. On the right wing is the 'Birth of the Saviour,' and a scene from the life of St. Nicholas of Bari, and on the left wing, beneath two prophets, is the 'Crucified Saviour,' with the Magdalen grasping the foot of the cross, and the Virgin and St. John on either side. Another is an altar-piece in the sacristy of San Pietro at Megognano, near Poggibonsi, inscribed "Taddeus Gaddi d Florētia me pīxit MCCCLV.," representing the 'Virgin and Child enthroned among angels.' Taddeo's activity may well be compared with that of his master, though but few of his works survive. His frescoes in San Spirito, the altar-pieces in San Stefano del Ponte Vecchio, the frescoes in the church of the Serviti, the allegories in the tribunal of the Mercanzia, have all disappeared. He laboured also at Pisa, where a portion of his work executed in San Francesco in 1342 still remains. He afterwards worked in Arezzo and Casentino. Taddeo Gaddi died at Florence in 1366, and was buried in the cloisters of Santa Croce.

Giovanni da Milano and Jacopo del Casentino were his pupils. He was also celebrated as an architect. The following are among his works:

Berlin.	Gallery.	Virgin adored by Saints and Donators. 1334.
„	Academy.	History of St. Francis.
„	„	Scenes from the Life of Christ.
Florence.	S. Croce.	Subjects from the History of the Virgin—frescoes.
„	„	The Last Supper—fresco.
„	S. Maria Novella.	Scenes from the Life of Christ—frescoes.
„	„	The Triumph of St. Thomas Aquinas. (A grand composition, attributed to Gaddi, but bearing all the marks of the Sienese school.)
„	S. Felicità.	Virgin surrounded by Saints—altar-piece.
Gotha.	Gallery.	Christ.
Paris.	Louvre.	Scenes from the Beheading of St. John the Baptist; Calvary; Christ and Judas Iscariot; Martyrdom of a Saint. (Predella in three compartments.)
Pisa.	S. Francesco.	The Apostles; St. Francis; several Saints; Allegorical Figures of the Virtues. Frescoes. 1342.
Poggibonsi.	S. Pietro, Megognano.	Virgin enthroned, surrounded by Saints. 1355.
Prato.	Gallery.	History of the Girdle of the Virgin. (A predella.)

GAEL, Barent. See Gaal.

GAELEN, Alexander van, who was born at Amsterdam in 1670, was the scholar of Jan van Huchtenburgh. He went to Germany, and he passed some time at Cologne, in the employment of the Elector. After a few years he returned to Holland, where he did not long remain, but

TADDEO GADDI

Alinari photo]　　　　　　　　　　　　　　　　　　[*Accademia, Florence*

CHRIST DEPOSITED IN THE SEPULCHRE

TADDEO GADDI

ST. PETER WALKING ON THE SEA

determined to visit England. He accordingly came to this country, and is said to have painted a picture of Queen Anne in a coach drawn by eight horses. He also painted pictures of the principal battles between the Royal Army and that of the Commonwealth, and the 'Battle of the Boyne.' He died in 1728.

GAESBEECK, A. VAN, a Dutch painter of genre subjects and portraits, flourished from about 1670 to about 1700, but no particulars of his life are known. His works, which are rare, are in the manner of Gerard Dou and Pieter van Slingeland. The Berlin Gallery possesses 'The Seamstress,' and the Amsterdam Museum a portrait of a young Man.

GAETA, SCIPIONE DA. See PULZONE.

GAGLIARDI, BARTOLOMMEO, born at Genoa in 1555, is said to have been a painter of some reputation. He executed works after the manner of Michelangelo. There are also several plates by him, both etched and finished with the graver, among which is a large print representing an emblematical subject, executed in a style resembling that of Cherubino Alberti, though very inferior. He died in 1620.

GAGLIARDI, BERNARDINO, was born at Città di Castello in 1609. He was a scholar of Avanzino Nucci. In the cathedral at Città di Castello, he painted the 'Martyrdom of St. Crescentianus,' but his best performance is his picture of 'St. Pellegrino,' in the church of San Marcello at Rome. He died in 1660.

GAGLIARDI, FILIPPO, is mentioned as having executed architectural paintings about the year 1640. The Madrid Gallery possesses an 'Interior of St. Peter's at Rome,' by him.

GAGNERAUX, BÉNIGNE, born at Dijon in 1756, was first instructed in the school at Dijon under François Devosge, from whence he proceeded to Rome, where he acquired a reputation by his picture of the 'Meeting of Gustavus III. of Sweden with Pope Pius VI.,' which is now at Stockholm. In Dijon are several of his pictures. Owing to the disturbances in Rome he quitted that city, and retired to Florence, where he died in 1795. In the Uffizi at Florence are his own portrait, a 'Battle Scene,' and a 'Lion Hunt.'

GAGNIÈRES, JEAN. See GANIÈRES.

GAILLARD, CLAUDE FERDINAND, engraver and painter, was born in Paris, January 7, 1834. He entered the École des Beaux Arts in 1850, and worked under Léon Cogniet. He won the Prix de Rome as an engraver in 1856, and from 1863 onwards was a constant contributor to the Salon, of portraits, classical and sacred subjects, both painted and engraved. He executed several important commissions for the Chalcographie du Louvre, among them the reproduction of Leonardo's 'Mona Lisa' and 'Last Supper,' and engraved a number of plates for the 'Gazette des Beaux Arts.' His plates were principally after the old masters, but he also engraved occasionally from his own pictures, and those of other modern painters. His style, both with paint-brush and burin, was a marvel of accurate minuteness. Several of his works are in the Luxembourg. He died in January, 1887.

GAILLARD, ROBERT, a French engraver, born in Paris in 1722, executed a considerable number of plates and portraits, historical and other subjects, and landscapes. He died in Paris in 1785. The following are his best prints :

Cardinal Étienne René Potier de Gesvres ; *after P. Batoni.* Christophe de Beaumont, Archbishop of Paris ; Jean Joseph Languet, Archbishop of Sens ; *after Chevalier.* The Queen of Sweden ; *after Lantinville.* Venus and Cupid ; Jupiter and Calisto ; Bacchantes sleeping ; Sylvia delivered by Amyntas ; Villagers fishing ; *after Boucher.* The Cabaret ; The Russian Concert ; *after Le Prince.* The Father's Malediction ; The Son's Punishment ; *after Greuze.* The Lace-maker ; A Girl spinning ; *after Schenau.*

GAILLARD DE LONJUMEAU, PIERRE JOSEPH, a French amateur engraver, etched several small plates for his amusement ; among others, a set of views of the 'Antiquities of Aix,' dated 1750.

GAILLOT, BERNARD, a French historical painter, born at Versailles in 1780, was a pupil of David. He died in Paris in 1847. His principal pictures are :

Cornelia, 1817 ; St. Martin ; Conversion of St. Augustine, 1819 ; Dream of St. Monica, 1822 ; St. Louis visiting the Holy Sepulchre ; St. Louis bearing the Crown of Thorns, 1824 ; Holy Angels, 1824 ; Dream of St. Joseph, 1824 ; The Assumption, 1827 ; Christ blessing little Children, 1831.

GAINSBOROUGH, THOMAS, who was born at Sudbury in 1727, was the youngest son of John Gainsborough, a clothier. He very early discovered a propensity for art, which was nursed, as he loved to acknowledge in after years, by the Suffolk scenery with which he was surrounded. Before he was ten years old he was sent to the Grammar School, of which his uncle, the Rev. Humphrey Burroughs, was master ; but he does not seem to have made much progress, as he employed himself chiefly in making sketches. At last, when he was in his fifteenth year, it was decided to send him to London, and so in 1741 he was intrusted to the care of a silversmith, who introduced him to Gravelot, an engraver and teacher of drawing, from whom he learned the art of etching. Gravelot, recognizing his talent, obtained for him admission to the Martin's Lane Academy, where he worked for three years with Francis Hayman, the historical painter, and then set up for himself in Hatton Garden, where he did a little modelling and produced a few landscapes. After a year's experience of Hatton Garden, he returned, in 1745, to Sudbury, where he set up as a portrait painter, and in the same year married a young lady named Margaret Burr, whose brother was a traveller in his father's employ. After a brief residence at Sudbury, he removed to Ipswich in 1746, and there made the acquaintance of Joshua Kirby, which ripened into a warm friendship, and lasted till the death of the latter in 1771. When Kirby left Ipswich for London, it was Gainsborough's destiny to become acquainted with Philip Thicknesse, who had just been appointed Governor of Landguard Fort, Ipswich, and who afterwards influenced the painter's career, and became his first biographer ; for it was at his suggestion that in the year 1760 he removed to Bath. There he took apartments in the newly-erected Circus at the rent of £50 a year, and business came in so fast that the price of a portrait was raised from five to eight guineas, and eventually settled at forty guineas for a half-length, and a hundred guineas for a whole-length. On the foundation of the Royal Academy in 1768, Gainsborough was one of the thirty-six original members, though he does not seem to have taken any part in the work, for which in 1775 the Council moved that "the name of Mr. Gainsborough be omitted from their lists," which was, however, rescinded at the next general meeting. On his original election to the Academy he contributed 'A Romantic Landscape, with Sheep at a Fountain.' In 1774, owing to a quarrel with the Thicknesses, Gainsborough left Bath, and for a second time set up in London, taking up his residence at Schomberg House, a noble mansion in Pall Mall, where commissions came in so fast that he was unable to keep up with the demand made on his services. In 1779 he was at the very height of his fame; all the eminent men of the day sat to him, and he was the favourite painter of the King and Royal Family. From 1769 to 1783 (excepting in the years 1773 to 1776) he was a constant contributor of portraits and landscapes to the exhibitions of the Royal Academy; but in the year 1783, owing to a disagreement with the Council about hanging the picture of the three Princesses, he withdrew his pictures, and never again contributed to the exhibitions. In 1787 a lump in his neck, which he first felt when present at the trial of Warren Hastings in Westminster Hall, developed into a cancer, of which he died in the next year. He was buried at his own desire in Kew churchyard, where a simple flat stone records his name, age, and date of death. Gainsborough will always occupy the highest place in the English school, whether as a portrait painter or a landscape painter. In his early landscapes he showed traces of the influence of the Flemish school, but as time went on Nature alone became his mistress. As a colourist he ranks with Rubens, and in technical work Ruskin says that "Turner is a child to him." In his life and character Northcote says that "he was a natural gentleman, and with all his simplicity had wit too." The principal features in his character were his kindness and his passionate love of music. His failings seem to have been his capriciousness and infirmity of temper.

Gainsborough designed and etched with much spirit at least eighteen plates, among which are:

A plate for Kirby's 'Perspective.'
An Oak Tree, with Gipsies.
A Man ploughing.
The Watering Place.
Evening.
Repose.

Besides these he executed three plates in aquatint, one of which is most carefully finished. His life work consisted of upwards of 300 paintings, of which over 220 were portraits. George III. was painted eight times, Pitt seven times, Garrick five times. Among other names are those of Lord Camden, Sir William Blackstone, Dr. Johnson, Laurence Sterne, Richardson, Clive, Burke, Sheridan, Windham, Franklin, Canning, Mrs. Graham, Lady Mary Wortley Montagu, Lady Vernon, Lady Maynard, Quin, and Mrs. Siddons. Lists of his works are to be found in Fulcher's 'Life of Thomas Gainsborough, R.A.,' London, 1856. The following are some of his most famous pictures in public galleries and well-known private collections ·

London, National Gallery.
The Market Cart.
The Watering-Place.
Musidora bathing her Feet.
Woody Landscape, Sunset.
Landscape:—'Gainsborough's Forest.'
Rustic Children.
Study for a Portrait of Abel Moysey.
Portrait of Mrs. Siddons.

208

Portrait of Ralph Schomberg, M.D.
Portrait of Orpin, Parish Clerk of Bradford, Wilts.
Portraits of Mr. J. Baillie, Wife, and Four Children.
Portrait of Rev. Sir Henry Bate Dudley, Bart.
And many others.

Dulwich Gallery.
Portrait of Mrs. Sheridan and Mrs. Tickell.
Portrait of P. J. de Loutherbourg, R.A.
Portrait of Thomas Linley.
Portrait of Samuel Linley, R.N.
Portraits of Mrs. Moody and her Children.

National Portrait Gallery.
Portrait of Jeffery, first Lord Amherst.
Portrait of Charles, first Marquis Cornwallis.
Portrait of George Colman.

Hampton Court.
Portrait of Fischer, the Musician.
Portrait of Colonel St. Leger.

Grosvenor House.
The Blue Boy (Master Buttall).
The Cottage Door.

Buckingham Palace.
Duke and Duchess of Cumberland.

Cambridge.	*Fitzwilliam Museum.*	Hon. W. Fitzwilliam.
Dublin.	*Nat. Gall.*	Duke of Northumberland.
Edinburgh.	*Nat. Gall.*	Hon. Mrs. Graham.
Glasgow.	*Gallery.*	Donkeys in a Storm.
Greenwich.	*Hospital.*	Lord Sandwich.
„	„	Portraits of the Royal Family.
London.	*Royal Academy.*	His own Portrait.
Stratford-on-Avon.	*Mus.*	David Garrick.
Windsor.	*Castle.*	George III.; full-length.
„	„	Portraits of the Royal Family.

GALANINO, IL. See ALOISI.

GALANTINI, IPPOLITO, called IL CAPPUCINO, and sometimes IL PRETE GENOVESE, was born at Florence in 1627, and was for some time a scholar of Padre Stefaneschi, through whose influence he became a monk of the order of the Capuchins, whence the two names by which he is frequently known. He was sent as a missionary to India, where he passed several years, and on his return to Europe painted several pictures for the churches of his order. In the Uffizi is his own portrait. He died in 1706, in the monastery of Montughi, near Florence.

GALARD, GUSTAVE DE, Count, a French painter and designer, was born at the château of Lille, near Lectoure, about 1777, and died at Bordeaux in 1840. In the Bordeaux Museum there is by him a 'View at La Teste.' His son, GEORGES DE GALARD, was born at Bordeaux, and died there in 1834, and there is in the Museum of that city a 'Study of a Sweep,' by him.

GALASSI, GALASSO, (sometimes called GALASSO ALGHISI,) the son of a shoemaker of Ferrara, was born about 1423. From the account-books of the House of Este, it appears that he was called Maestro Galasso de Mattheo Calegaro, and was employed in the decorations of the palace of Belreguardo between the years 1450 and 1453. In 1455 he composed the 'Assumption,' and finished the portrait of Cardinal Bessarion, at Santa Maria in Monte, Bologna. Amongst his early paintings were the 'Trinity,' in the Museum of Ferrara; and the 'Entombment,' and a 'Virgin and Child, with donor and patron Saint,' in the Costabili Gallery in the same city. Professor Saroli possesses a 'Christ on the Mount of Olives,' and the Marquis Strozzi a 'Crucifixion,' both in Ferrara. Galassi died in 1473.

Master Buttall
(The Blue Boy)
From the painting by Thos. Gainsborough. R.A. in the possession of the Duke of Westminster.

THOMAS GAINSBOROUGH

THE PARISH CLERK

GALCERAN, Antonio, who was a pupil of Esquarte, was brought from Italy to Zaragoza in 1580. He painted in the palace of the Bishop of Barbastro, and enriched the cathedral there with historical pictures.

GALCERAN, Vicente, a Spanish engraver, was born in 1726, and studied under Ravanals and Rovira, executing a print of St. Vincent Ferrer, when only eleven years old. Leaving Valencia for Madrid in 1750, he was soon after employed by the Chapter of Toledo to retouch some plates sent from Rome by Cardinal Portocarrero. He executed plates for works on natural history and horsemanship, and the portraits of the kings of Spain for Berni's 'Titulos de la Castilla,' printed at Valencia in 1769, the last but little to his credit. He returned to Valencia in 1768, where he engraved portraits of Bishop Cervera of Cadiz, and others. He died at Valencia in 1788, leaving, it is said, no less than 700 plates, great and small.

GALEAS, Fray Francisco de, an excellent Spanish illuminator and miniaturist, was born at Seville in 1567. He studied law until 1590, when he entered the convent of Santa Maria de las Cuevas. He was afterwards promoted to the priory of Cazalla, but he resigned this dignity after two years, and returned to his Sevillian convent, to die of vexation in 1614. The convent possesses two of his miniatures, 'The Saviour dead' and 'The Saviour rising'; also some illuminations in books, which display great clearness and beauty.

GALEN, Thyman van, a native of Utrecht, who flourished early in the 17th century, is chiefly known by a picture of the 'Ruins of a Temple' placed in the Hospital of St. Job in Utrecht.

GALEOTTI, Sebastiano, born at Florence in 1676, first studied under Alessandro Gherardini, but afterwards went to Bologna, where he became a scholar of Giovanni Gioseffo dal Sole. He possessed a ready invention, and was a good designer; and his powers were well adapted to fresco painting, in which, according to Ratti, he executed some considerable works in the church of La Maddalena at Genoa. Few of his works are to be found in his native city, from which it would seem that he was not held in so much reputation there as in Upper Italy; but there are several at Piacenza and Parma, and particularly at Turin, where he was made director of the Academy. He died at Turin in 1746, leaving two sons, Giuseppe and Giovanni Battista, who were also painters.

GALESTRUZZI, Giovanni Battista, a painter and engraver, was born at Florence in 1618. He studied painting under Francesco Furini, and afterwards went to Rome, where he was received into the Academy of St. Luke in 1652. The date of his death is uncertain, but he was still living in 1661. He was the friend of Stefano della Bella, whose style he imitated, and, according to Huber, finished some of the plates left imperfect at his death. He etched a great number of plates, of which there is a catalogue by Giacomo Rossi.

GALIMARD, Claude. See Gallimard.

GALIMARD, Nicolas Auguste, a French historical, portrait, and landscape painter, was born in Paris in 1813. He studied under his uncle, Auguste Hesse, and with Ingres, and soon became known for his pictures, chiefly of Biblical subjects. He painted the 'Disciples at Emmaus' for St. Germain-l'Auxerrois, and mural decorations in St. Germain-des-Prés, Paris. His picture of 'The Ode,' exhibited at the Salon in 1846, is now in the Luxembourg Gallery. Many of Galimard's works have been engraved by Aubry-Lecomte and others. He made several designs for stained-glass windows, and wrote treatises on the subject. He died at Montigny-les-Cormeilles (Seine-et-Oise) in 1880.

GALINDEZ, Martin, a Spanish painter, was born at Haro in Old Castile, in 1547. In 1584 he entered the Chartreuse of Paular, where he devoted his leisure to the arts and to mechanical pursuits, and where he died in 1627, after executing a number of tolerable devotional pictures, and a variety of wood-carvings, sundials, and alarums.

GALIZIA, Fede, (or Gallizi,) was a native of Trento, in the Milanese, who flourished about the year 1616. She was the daughter of Annunzio Galizia, a miniature painter, who resided at Milan, from whom she received her instruction in art. She painted historical subjects and landscapes, in a pleasing and finished style, resembling that of the Bolognese school anterior to the Carracci; but she excelled in small portraits. One of her best historical pictures is 'Christ appearing to Mary Magdalen,' in the Brera at Milan, from the church of La Maddalena.

GALLAIT, Louis, painter, was born at Tournay in 1810, and was educated in his native town. He showed his artistic talent at a very early age, and gained a prize from the Ghent Academy while still a boy. The municipal authorities of Tournay bought one of his early performances, a 'Christ restoring sight to the Blind Man,' and presented it to the cathedral. The city further granted him a sum of money in 1835, which enabled him to study in Paris under Hennequin. Henceforth his career was one of assured success. His ambitious and melodramatic pictures were received with great favour by the public, though condemned by artists and connoisseurs. His art had much in common with that of his contemporary, Scheffer, with whom he was often compared, though Gallait was a very much more accomplished craftsman. He was a member of the Institute of France, and an honorary foreign Royal Academician. Several of his pictures were at the International Exhibition of 1862. He died November 20, 1887.

GALLAND, Pierre Victor, distinguished decorative artist, born at Geneva July 15, 1822. His first artistic efforts were devoted to metal work, but he subsequently studied architecture and painting in the studios of Labrouste and Drölling, while earning a livelihood as a decorative artist. His work may be admired in many of the public and private buildings not only of Paris, but also of Madrid, St. Petersburg, New York and London. He filled the post of Professor of Decorative Art at the École des Beaux Arts in Paris, and was Director of Works of Art at the Gobelins. In 1883 he was appointed officer of the Legion of Honour. He died suddenly in Paris on November 30, 1892.

GALLARDO, Mateo, was a Spanish painter, who resided at Madrid in 1657. There is a figure of Christ, signed with his name, and several of the Virgin, of the size of life.

GALLE Family, The.

PHILIPP GALLE.
1537—1612.

Theodore (1571—1633).	Cornelis I. (1576—1659).
Jan or Joannes (1600—1676).	Cornelis II. (1615—1678).
	Cornelis III. (1642—1701).

GALLE, CORNELIS, the elder, a younger son of Philipp Galle, was born at Antwerp in 1576, and was taught engraving by his father. He followed the example of his brother Theodoor in visiting Italy, where he fell under the influence of Titian and Palma Vecchio. He resided several years in Rome, and acquired a correctness of design, and a freedom of execution, in which he greatly surpassed both his father and his brother. After engraving several plates at Rome from the Italian masters, he returned in 1601 to Antwerp, passing through Siena and Florence. He set up in business as a printseller and collector, with so much success, that he came to be regarded as the chief authority on the subject in the Netherlands. He worked also assiduously at his proper calling, and engraved many plates after the works of his countrymen and his own designs. "He equalled," say Huber and Rost, "the most famous engravers, and surpassed all the Galles." He had two styles, one, somewhat stiff and hard; the other, much more easy and attractive. The first is seen in his early Antwerp work after M. de Vos and J. Stradanus; the second, with his Italian inspirations, after G. Paggi, F. Vanni, A. Carracci, Salimbeni, and Villamena. Towards the end of his life Rubens affected him greatly, and his work is marked by a delightful freedom. His naked figures are beautifully finished, and his landscapes are done with perfection. His work was signed *Cornelis Galle* simply; and consequently there is some confusion between him and the two others of his family bearing the same name. He died in 1656. Previous to going to Italy he engraved these plates:

> A part of the plates of the Life of Christ; *after Martin de Vos.* A set of plates of the Life of the Virgin Mary; A set of plates of the Life of St. John the Baptist; *after Stradanus.*

The following are some of his best prints:

> St. Charles Borromeo, Cardinal Archbishop of Milan. Philipp Rubens, the brother of Peter Paul Rubens. Ferdinand III.; *after Van Dyck.* Jan van Havre; *after Rubens.* Charles I., King of England; in an allegorical border; Henrietta Maria, Queen of Charles I.; with a border of flowers and figures; *after Van der Horst.* Artus Wolfart, painter; *after Van Dyck.* Jan Wiggers; *after H. de Smet.* Isabella of Arenberg; *after Ch. Wautier.* Abraham Ortelius; *after H. Goltzius.* Henri IV. and Marie de Medici, done at Siena in 1600. Adam and Eve; The Holy Family returning from Egypt, with a Choir of Angels; Venus caressing Cupid; St. Peter baptizing St. Priscia; *after Giov. Batt. Paggi.* The Virgin and Infant, to whom St. Bernard is offering a Book; The Crucifixion, with the Virgin, St. Francis, and St. Theresa; *after Francesco Vanni.* Venus bound to a Tree, and Minerva chastising Cupid; Procne showing the Head of her son Itys to her husband Tereus; Seneca in the Bath; *after Agostino Carracci.* The Virgin caressing the Infant Jesus; The Entombment of Christ; *after Raphael.* The Virgin Mary, under an arch, ornamented with flowers by Angels; Judith cutting off the Head of Holofernes; The Four Fathers of the Church. A Banquet, with Musicians. Commentaria Acta Apostolorum, 1647. Ten Plates, 'Missale Romanum,' 1650. Ecce Homo; Christ and St. John the Baptist; many Frontispieces to religious works; Judith; *after Rubens.* St. Martin and the Beggar; *after Van Dyck.* Five scenes from the Life of Christ; *after A. Carracci.* Plates for the Life of St. Ignatius Loyola. Legend of St. Cecilia; *after Vanni.* Magdalene at Simon's Feast; *after Cigoli.*

GALLE, CORNELIS, the younger, the son of
210

Cornelis Galle the elder, was born at Antwerp in 1615, and was instructed in the art of engraving by his father. It does not appear that he had the advantage of studying in Italy, which may account for his drawing being less correct than that of his father or his uncle. His elegance and his facility have gained him much renown. He sometimes signed his name *Cornelis Galle, junior;* but very many plates undoubtedly by him pass muster as the work of his father. His portraits are more meritorious than his larger pieces. These are of great interest and value, and form almost an unique gallery of literary and commercial worthies of the period. The features, in each case, are done with the greatest care, and the accessories are characteristic. Several of this series are now in the celebrated Plantin Museum at Antwerp. He died at Antwerp in 1678. The following are his most esteemed prints.

> The Emperor Ferdinand III., 1649; Mary of Austria, his Empress, 1649; Henrietta of Lorraine; Jan Meyssens, painter and engraver; *after Van Dyck.* Jodocus Christophorus Kress de Kressenstein, Senator of Hamburg; Ottavio Piccolomini; in a border of fruit and flowers; *after Anselmus van Hulle.* Job and his wife; St. Dominic receiving the Rosary from the Virgin; Descent from the Cross; The Crucifixion; Jupiter and Mercury, with Baucis and Philemon; *after J. van den Hoeck.* The Nativity, with the Angels appearing to the Shepherds; *after David Teniers the elder.* The Resurrection; *after Gaspar de Craeyer.* Venus suckling the Loves; Flight into Egypt; Christ in the Tomb; *after Rubens.* Christ at the Pharisee's Table; *after L. Cigoli.* Frontispiece, 'De Hierarchia Mariana,' 1640; Frontispiece, 'Opera Lintripandi,' 1640; Three plates, 'Legatus Frederici Marselere,' 1666; *after Rubens.* Frontispieces, 1647, 1648; *after A. Diepenbeeck.*

GALLE, CORNELIS, the third, son of Cornelis Galle, the younger, was born at Antwerp in 1642. He learned his art at the atelier of the family. Not much is known about him, and the accident of his name makes identification of his work difficult. There is, however, a class of engravings, mostly humorous, bearing the signature *C. Galle.* This may differentiate him from the other Cornelises, who usually signed their first names in full. An example exists at the British Museum, 'A Feathered Parliament.' His work is marked by correctness of composition, but there is an absence of that fine finish which is such a convincing attribute of his family. He married a wealthy wife, by whom he had three sons, but none of them followed the family profession. He died at Antwerp in 1701.

GALLE, HIERONYMUS. In the Uffizi Gallery at Florence is a picture of a 'Festoon of Flowers,' signed *Hieronymus Galle. f. A.* 1655.

GALLE, JAN, a son and pupil of Theodoor Galle, was born at Antwerp in 1600. Little is known of his early training. He worked with his father and his uncle, and also with the Wierixes. Many plates have his name along with theirs. Some of the most beautiful examples of his art are to be found in a series called a 'Rosary,' and these bear the following signature, *Anton Wierix fecit Joan Galle excudit.* His work is marked by fine composition and freedom in execution. To him belongs one of the most lovely volumes at the British Museum, 'Vita St. Joseph B.V. Sponsi.' It bears no date, but its miniature plates are perfect specimens of what the graver can do. He engraved many subjects after Goltzius. He was enrolled in the Guild of St. Luke under the designation of "Wynmeester," because, as was usual with the sons of Masters of the Guild, he had to pay his entrance fee with a present of wine! Ultimately he became Master, and died, a wealthy man, in 1676. Among his plates are:

The Wise and Foolish Virgins; *after Marten de Vos.* Christ surrounded by the Instruments of His Passion. The fat Cook and the thin Cook; Lubricitas Vitæ Humanæ, 1553; *after P. Brueghel the elder.*

GALLE, Philipp, a Dutch engraver, was born at Haarlem in 1537. He studied at Amsterdam under Dirk V. Cuerenherdt, the celebrated engraver and controversialist. He travelled through Italy, France and Germany, and settled at Antwerp in 1570, where he established a studio of engraving. Among his better-known pupils, in addition to his son, were his celebrated son-in-law Adrien Collaert, and Jan B. Barbé. He was a writer and historian, as well as a skilful draughtsman. He became a member of the Guild of St. Luke, under the title of Free Master Engraver. He took as his model the style of Lucas de Leyden. He drew very correctly, and excelled in *clair obscur*; but his manner was somewhat dry and hard. His subjects were chiefly scriptural. He engraved plates for many books issued by Christopher Plantin, the first being dated 1573. He worked with great rapidity; M. Mariette says, "Il maniait le burin avec facilité." He did a lucrative business as a printseller. He was the founder of the famous Galle family of engravers. He died at Antwerp in 1612. The number of his prints is considerable, and they are generally marked with one of the annexed ciphers: 𝕯𝕲 or 𝕯𝕲. The following are his principal plates:

Calvin. Luther. Zwingli. Pirkheimer. Sir Thomas More. Dante. Marten van Heemskerk. Willem Philander; Duke of Alva, 1571. The Seasons; The Three Young Men in the Furnace; Memorabiliores Judaicæ Gentis Clades; Acta Apostolorum; Histories of St. John, the Prodigal Son, Samson, Esther, and Ahasuerus; *after Marten van Heemskerk.* The Passion, Death, and Resurrection; The Battles of the Tuscans; The Victories and Triumphs of the Medici Family, 1583; *after Stradanus.* A set of thirty-four plates of the Life and Miracles of St. Catharine of Siena, 1603. Ten plates of the Sibyls; *after A. van Blocklandt.* The Trinity, 1584; *after Marten de Vos.* The Seven Wonders of the World; The Triumph of Death, Fame, and Honour; *after Marten van Heemskerk.* Plates; entitled 'Divinarum Nuptiarum conventus et acta'; dated 1580. The Death of St. Anne; The Good Shepherd; *after Brueghel.* The Trinity; large plate; *after M. de Vos;* his best print. Solomon directing the building of the Temple; Abraham sacrificing Isaac; Lot and his Daughters; Mutius Scævola in the Tent of Porsena, 1563; Massacre of the Innocents; large plate; *after F. Floris.* Funeral Ceremonies; large plate, 1562. Frontispiece, 'Sapientia Hominum,' 1572. Les Niobides, 1557; *after Jules Romain.* Christ at Emmaus, 1574. The Heavenly Choir, 1574. Sea Gods and Nymphs and Naiads, 1587.

GALLE, Theodoor, the elder son of Philipp Galle, was born at Antwerp in 1571, and was instructed in the use of the graver by his father. He afterwards went to Rome to study the antique, and whilst there he engraved several plates after the great masters, more especially Raphael. His style was less conventional than his father's. His touch

was remarkable for delicacy; he was a patient elaborator of detail. His work exhibits a distinct breaking away from the bald fashion of the period. He collaborated much with Jean Collaert, his nephew. Their manner approached very nearly that of the Wierixes—a more polished style than that of his father. He held a commanding position in his city, and was Master of his Guild. He died at Antwerp in 1633 or 1634. The following are his principal works:

Justus Lipsius. St. Jerome. St. John. St. Hildrude and St. Hildegonde. Emblematical subjects, entitled 'Litis abusus, &c.' The Life of St. Norbert. The Life of the Virgin and St. Joseph (twenty-eight). Thirteen figures, each with a title and explication; entitled 'Typus occasionis, &c.'; 1600. The Infant Jesus regarding the Instruments of the Passion. St. John. St. Jerome. Count Ugolino and his Children; Coriolanus entreated by the Roman Women; Cornelia, the Mother of Gracchi; Phaethon guiding the Chariot of the Sun; Susannah; *after Stradanus.* A Frontispiece to Mascard's 'Silvarum libri'; a Frontispiece to 'Las Obras en Verso' of Francisco de Boria, 1624; Frontispiece to 'Opera Senecæ,' 2nd edition, 1615; Frontispiece to 'Opera Senecæ,' 4th edition, 1652; Frontispiece to 'Annales Sacri'; *after Rubens.* Eleven plates for 'Studiosæ Juventuti.' Suite: New Discoveries; *after J. Stradanus.* Seven Deadly Sins. Seven Conspicuous Virtues.

GALLEGOS, Fernando, a Spanish painter, was born at Salamanca in 1475. It is said that he studied under Albrecht Dürer, but it is more likely that Berruguete was his master; and he only followed the taste which then prevailed in Europe. Some of his pictures bear so strong a resemblance to those of Dürer, that acknowledged connoisseurs have mistaken them. His best work is an altarpiece in the chapel of St. Clement at Salamanca. Count Raczynski, in his work 'Les Arts en Portugal,' says there are many of Gallegos's pictures there, but neither Palomino nor Cean Bermudez mentions the circumstance of his having painted in Portugal. He died in 1550. There are six scriptural subjects by him in the Madrid Gallery.

GALLETTI, Fra Filippo Maria, a Florentine painter, was born in 1664, and died in 1742. His portrait is in the Uffizi.

GALLI, Alessandro, called Alessandro da Bibiena, a painter and architect, was a son of Ferdinando Galli. He was skilful in both oil and fresco painting, and was employed at the court of the Elector Palatine, in whose service he died about the year 1760.

GALLI, Antonio, was a brother of Alessandro Galli, and, like him, a painter and architect. He was born at Bologna in 1700, and died at Milan in 1774. He painted theatrical decorations.

GALLI, Carlo, a son of Giuseppe Galli, was, like his father, a painter and architect. He visited the various courts of Germany, as well as those of England, France, and Italy, and is known to have been still living in 1769.

GALLI, Ferdinando, called Ferdinando da Bibiena, the son of Giovanni Maria Galli, was born at Bologna in 1657. His father dying when he was only eight years of age, he was placed in the school of Carlo Cignani, who, finding the genius of his pupil led him to architecture and perspective, rather than the design of the figure, recommended him to devote himself to that particular department, which he thereupon studied

P 2

under Aldrovandini, Trogli, and Manni, and with such success that he became the most distinguished master of his time in the ornamental and decorative branches of the art. There was scarcely a sovereign in Europe who did not invite him to his court. He was much engaged for the Dukes of Parma and Milan, and was invited to Vienna by the Emperor Charles VI. The public festivals on all occasions of victories, the triumphal entries of princes, &c., were celebrated under the direction of Bibiena, and were more sumptuous and magnificent than any before witnessed in Europe. He became blind, and died at Bologna in 1743. A painting by him is in the National Gallery. It is entitled the 'Teatro Farnese, Parma,' and represents the pit and stage of a theatre, in which 'Othello' is being played. To him the theatre is indebted for very great improvements in its scenery, and the illusive enchantment of its decorations. But his talents were not confined to scene-painting; he painted also many admirable architectural and perspective views, which are placed in the principal galleries in Italy. In these, the figures are usually painted by his brother Francesco. He likewise published several works on civil architecture.

GALLI, FRANCESCO, called FRANCESCO DA BIBIENA, the younger brother of Ferdinando Galli, was born at Bologna in 1659. He first studied under Lorenzo Pasinelli; but he was afterwards instructed in the school of Carlo Cignani. His knowledge of architecture and perspective was considerable; but he excelled in figures. He worked successively for the Emperors Leopold I. and Joseph I., and was invited to Madrid by Philip V., who appointed him his principal architect. He died in 1739.

GALLI, GIOVANNI MARIA, called GIOVANNI MARIA DA BIBIENA, was born at Bibiena, in the Bolognese state, in 1625. He studied under Albani, and his productions have often been mistaken for those of his master. He died in 1665. Of his larger works in the churches at Bologna the following are the most esteemed: 'The Ascension,' in the Certosa; 'St. Anne,' in La Carità; 'St. Andrew,' in San Biagio; and 'St. Francis of Sales,' at the Padri Servi. This artist was the founder of a family of whom no fewer than nine are known to fame, all of whom bore the surname of Bibiena.

GALLI, GIUSEPPE, a painter and architect, was a son of Ferdinando Galli, and was born in 1696. After studying under his father, he worked in conjunction with him at Barcelona and Vienna, and afterwards by himself at several German courts. He died at Berlin in 1756.

GALLI, MARIA ORIANA, was a daughter of Giovanni Maria Galli, who studied painting under Carlo Cignani and Franceschini.

GALLIARI, BERNARDINO, an Italian painter, was born at Andorno about 1707, and died about 1794. There is an 'Adoration of the Shepherds' by him in the Brera at Milan.

GALLIARI, GASPARE, an Italian painter, was born at Treviglio about 1760, and died at Milan in 1818. In the Brera at Milan is a view of Venice by him.

GALLIMARD, CLAUDE, a French engraver, was born at Troyes, in Champagne, in 1720. He passed some time at Rome, and on his return to France became a member of the Academy at Paris. We have by him several plates after De

Troy, Subleyras, and Sébastien Bourdon. He also engraved a number of ornaments for books, among which are fourteen frontispieces and vignettes after Cochin the younger. The following also are by this artist:

The Bust of Nicolas Vleughels; *after M. A. Slodtz.* 1744.

The Queen of Sheba before Solomon; *after J. F. de Troy.*

GALLINA, REMIGIO CANTA. See CANTA-GALLINA.

GALLINARI, JACOPO, who was probably born at Bologna, worked there in 1676, and at Padua in 1685. He is known by two etchings, 'A Lady,' and 'Venus and Cupid.'

GALLINARI, PIETRO, called PIETRO DEL SIGNOR GUIDO, was a native of Bologna, and a favourite scholar of Guido Reni. He painted a few historical pictures, which are said to have been retouched by Guido. He died young in 1664.

GALLIS, PIETER, an amateur painter of flowers, fruit, and objects of still-life, was born in 1633, and lived at Enkhuysen, where he died in 1697.

GALLIZI, FEDE. See GALIZIA.

GALLO, IL PRETE. See GUILLAUME, Le Frère.

GALLO, BERNARDO and GIOVANNI. See SALOMON.

GALLO, SAN. See SANGALLO.

GALLOCHE, LOUIS, a French painter, born in Paris in 1670, was a scholar of Louis de Boullongne, but afterwards studied in Italy. Upon his return to France he founded a school, and one of his first pupils was François Le Moine. His picture of 'Hercules restoring Alcestis to her Husband' gained him his election to the Academy in 1711, of which he became successively professor in 1720, rector in 1746, and chancellor in 1754. He died in Paris in 1761. The above painting is now in the Louvre, while in the cathedral of Notre-Dame in Paris is a picture by him of the 'Departure of St. Paul for Jerusalem.' His chief work was the 'Removal of the Remains of St. Augustine to Pavia,' a picture which has disappeared.

GALLUS, BERNARDUS and JOANNES. See SALOMON.

GALLUS, RICARDUS. See TAURINI.

GALOFRÉ, BALDOMERO, a distinguished Catalonian painter, was born in 1848. After years of academical training he visited Italy, where his strong individuality soon asserted itself. On his return to Spain, Galofré travelled through the country, ever in search of the picturesque and the characteristic. In his feeling for colour and light and joyous movement, Galofré greatly resembled Fortuny, and he delighted to depict country fairs, processions, and popular assemblies, scenes to which he could give infinite colour and life. As a master of technique and a brilliant colourist the latter-day art of Spain can produce no rival to him, as his famous canvases 'Feria Andaluza' and 'Lechera Asturiana' will show us. He also produced numerous water-colours and *gouaches* having great breadth and freedom of style. He was an indefatigable worker, and he had long planned a monumental work to be entitled 'España,' and to this end had made an infinite variety of studies and sketches whilst travelling through his native country. His death occurred at Barcelona on July 26, 1902.

GALOFRÉ Y COMA, JOSÉ, a Spanish historical painter, was born at Barcelona, and died in the same city in 1877. He studied in Rome, where he became an associate of Overbeck. In 1854 he painted for the Queen of Spain 'An Episode from the Conquest of Granada in 1494.' He also published a book on 'Art in Italy and other Countries of Europe.'

GALVAN, JUAN, a Spanish painter, was born at Lucena, in the kingdom of Aragon, in 1598. According to Palomino, he went to Rome for improvement, where he remained some time, and on his return to Spain in 1624 resided chiefly at Zaragoza, where he was named painter by the Corporation, and executed various pictures for the cathedral and Carmelite convent. For the cathedral of Zaragoza he executed pictures of the 'Nativity,' 'Santa Justa,' and 'Santa Rufina,' as well as other large works, which Cean Bermudez praises for their colouring. He painted the cupola of Santa Justa y Rufina, and a picture of the 'Trinity' for the Barefooted Carmelites; but his principal work was the 'Birth of the Virgin.' He died at Zaragoza in 1658.

GAMARRA, JUAN CIRILO MAGADAN Y. See MAGADAN.

GAMBARA, LATTANZIO, born at Brescia in 1541 or 1542, was the son of a tailor, who, driven by necessity from his native city, took refuge at Cremona, and supported himself and his son by the exercise of his trade, which he destined the latter to follow. The disposition of the boy inclined to a different pursuit, and he employed all his leisure moments in sketching, for which he was often severely chastised by his father. These quarrels, and their cause, came to the knowledge of Antonio Campi, a painter of Cremona, who interested himself in favour of the youth; and, on examining his drawings, found in them evidence of genius, and prevailed on his father to entrust him to his care. He studied in the school of the Campi for six years; and when he was eighteen years of age, he was placed under the tuition of Girolamo Romanino, who entertained a high opinion of his talents, and ultimately gave him his daughter in marriage. He surpassed his father-in-law both in the correctness of his design, and in the grandeur of his compositions. To the principles he had acquired under the Campi, he added the charm of Venetian colouring, in which he approached the rich tones of Pordenone. In the Strada del Gambaro at Brescia are several fine fresco paintings by him of mythological and classical subjects; but these are less surprising than his admirable works in the cloisters of the Benedictine Fathers of Sant' Eufemia at Brescia. They represent 'Moses and the Brazen Serpent,' 'Cain slaying Abel,' 'Samson and Delilah,' 'Judith with the Head of Holofernes,' 'Jael and Sisera,' and a 'Deposition from the Cross.' In the Castello at Brescia are frescoes of the 'Triumphs of Bacchus.' The most studied of his works are his twelve frescoes in the cathedral at Parma, representing subjects from the Life of our Saviour, which captivate even in their close proximity to Correggio's masterpieces. Of his oil pictures, the most admired are the 'Birth of the Virgin,' in the church of San Faustino Maggiore at Brescia; and a 'Pietà,' in San Pietro at Cremona. In the Glasgow Gallery is the Head of a Female. He died in 1574, in consequence of a fall from a ladder.

GAMBARINI, GIUSEPPE, born at Bologna in 1680, was a scholar of Lorenzo Pasinelli, until the death of that master, when he entered the school of Cesare Gennari, whose style he followed in his colouring, and some of whose works he copied. Finding himself unequal to

the dignity of historical painting, he abandoned it, and applied himself to subjects taken from ordinary life, in which he was more successful. He died in 1725. There are some of his works in the churches at Bologna: in Santa Maria Egiziaca, is a picture of that Saint; and at the Osservanti, 'St. Catharine Vigri's Entrance into Bologna.'

GAMBERUCCI, COSIMO, a Florentine painter, flourished about the year 1610, and was a scholar of Battista Naldini. He did not attain to great celebrity in the art, although some of his works in the churches at Florence, particularly his picture of 'St. Peter curing the lame Man,' in San Pietro Maggiore, just amount to respectability. He also painted easel pictures, which are found in the collections at Florence.

GAMELIN, JACQUES, a French painter, was born at Carcassone in 1739, and died at Narbonne in 1803. There are by him in the Bordeaux Museum, 'Socrates drinking Hemlock,' 'The Departure of Abradates for the Fight,' and 'The Death of Abradates.'

GAMMON, JAMES, was an English engraver of no great reputation, by whom there are a few portraits, executed in a stiff, formal style. He was working in London about 1660. Among others, the following are by him:

Queen Catharine of Braganza.
Henry, Duke of Gloucester.
George, Duke of Albemarle.
Richard Cromwell.
Sir Toby Matthews.
Edward Mascall, the painter.

GAMPERLIN. See GRAF, URS.

GANDIA, JUAN DE, was a Spanish painter, celebrated for his pictures of architecture and perspective views. He lived about 1720.

GANDINI, ANTONIO, was a native of Brescia, who had the advantage of being educated under Paolo Veronese, whose style he followed, together with something of that of Palma. He possessed a fertile invention, and was a correct designer, as is apparent in his principal work, the 'Crucifixion,' in the old cathedral at Brescia. He died in 1630. He left a son, BERNARDINO GANDINI, who was also a painter, and who died in 1651.

GANDINI, GIORGIO, sometimes called GIORGIO DEL GRANO, from the family name of his mother, was a native of Parma, who died in 1538. Orlandi not only states that he was a disciple of Correggio, but also asserts that his pictures were occasionally retouched by that master. The Padre Zapata, in his description of the churches of Parma, ascribes to this painter the great altarpiece of San Michele, which had erroneously been attributed by Ruta, in his 'Guida di Parma,' to Lelio Orsi. Correggio had been engaged to paint the tribune of the dome of that church, but died before it was commenced; and the commission was offered to Gandini, who also was prevented by death from executing it. In the Oldenburg Gallery are pictures of a 'Penitent Magdalen' and a 'Holy Family.'

GANDOLFI, GAETANO, an Italian painter and etcher, was born at San Matteo della Decima, in the Bolognese, in 1734. He first studied under his elder brother, Ubaldo, then he went to Venice, and from thence to Bologna. He painted several pictures for the churches at Bologna, and other cities in Italy, of which the most esteemed are, 'The Assumption,' in the ceiling of Santa Maria della Vita, and 'The Marriage at Cana,' in the church

213

of the Santissimo Salvatore, at Bologna; 'The Martyrdom of St. Pantaleone,' in the church of the Girolimini at Naples, and his own portrait, in the Pinacoteca. There are likewise by this artist an etching of the 'Adoration of the Shepherds,' after the picture by Niccolò dell' Abbate, in the Palazzo Leoni at Bologna; also 'St. Peter and St. Paul' after Guido Reni. He died at Bologna in 1802.

GANDOLFI, MAURO, an engraver, was born at Bologna in 1764, and studied under his father, Gaetano Gandolfi. Early in life he entered the army, and came with his regiment to Paris, where he devoted himself to engraving. He afterwards visited England, and there studied under Sharp and Bartolozzi, returning by way of Rome to Bologna, where he for a while pursued oil painting. His first large engraving was 'Diogenes before Alexander' (1802), after his father. An unpleasant critique of one of his productions affected him so much that he left Europe, and travelled in America, and afterwards in Africa. In 1821 he returned to Bologna, engraved several plates after Correggio, and Raphael's 'St. Cecilia,' of which he also made a beautiful copy in watercolours. He also engraved 'The Child Jesus sleeping on the Cross,' 'Judith with the Head of Holofernes,' and various other subjects. In the Bologna Gallery is his portrait painted by himself. He died in 1834.

GANDOLFI, UBALDO, the elder brother of Gaetano Gandolfi, was born in 1728. He was both a painter and sculptor, and studied under Torelli and Graziani. His principal works are 'The Prophets' in San Giuliano at Bologna, his anatomical preparations for pupils, and in the Pinacoteca a 'Head of a Girl,' the 'Resurrection of Christ,' and a 'Holy Bishop.' He died at Bologna in 1781.

GANDY, JAMES, a portrait painter, born at Exeter in 1619, is said to have been instructed by Van Dyck. He went to Ireland under the protection of the Duke of Ormond, and painted many portraits of the nobility and gentry. He died in Ireland in 1689.

GANDY, WILLIAM, a portrait painter, was born in the second half of the 17th century. He was the son of James Gandy, and is supposed to have studied under Gaspar Smitz. He chiefly lived at Exeter, and many of his works are to be found in Devon and Cornwall. He died after 1715.

GANGLOFF, KARL WILHELM, a designer, born at Leutkirch in 1790, was one of those artists by nature who produce works of great promise in their youth before they have received any instruction. He was originally employed as a clerk, but on his artistic productions becoming in some degree known, he was induced in 1813 to go to Stuttgart and study under De Necker. Unhappily he died in 1814, at Merklingen in Würtemberg, but he has left several compositions from the Old and New Testament and the 'Nibelungen Lied' which show much originality and depth of feeling. Uhland has dedicated three sonnets to his memory.

GANIÈRES, JEAN, (or GAGNIÈRES,) a French engraver, flourished in Paris about the year 1650. He engraved a few plates after Blanchard, Valentine, &c., but was more employed on portraits. His plates are executed with the graver in a stiff and tasteless style. Among others, the following are by him:

The Penitent Magdalen; *after J. Blanchard*.
A Boy sleeping, with a skull near him. 1640.
Louis XIII. of France; an oval, with ornaments. 1640.
Cardinal Flavio Chigi.
M. de La Melleraye. 1679.

GANSES, PAUL, was a Neapolitan painter of sea pieces and moon-light effects, who lived in the 17th century.

GANTREL, ETIENNE, a French engraver, was born in Paris about the year 1646, and died there in 1706. There are by this artist several plates of portraits and historical subjects, executed in a neat style, of which the following are the best:

PORTRAITS.

Louis XIV. of France; life-size.
Sebastiano Pisani, Bishop of Verona.
Antoine Bruneau, President of La Tournelle; *after La Dame*.
J. L. de La Bourdonnaye, Bishop of Lyons; *after Fontanne*.
M. Poncet de La Rivière. 1682.
Louis Berrier, Counsellor to the King. 1674.

SUBJECTS AFTER VARIOUS MASTERS.

The Rod of Moses, changed into a Serpent, devouring the Rods of the Magicians of Pharaoh; *after N. Poussin*.
The Israelites passing the Red Sea; *after the same*.
The Israelites dancing round the Golden Calf; *after the same*.
The Descent from the Cross; *after the same*.
St. Francis Xavier restoring an Indian to life; *after the same*.
St. Gervais and St. Protais before the Proconsul; *after Le Sueur*.
St. Benedict kneeling; *after Philippe de Champagne*.
St. Francis in ecstasy; *after Carracci*.
The Head of Christ; *after Le Brun*.

GANZ, JOHANN PHILIPP, a German engraver, born at Eisenach in 1746, was appointed engraver to the Court of Hanover.

GARAVAGLIA, GIOVITA, an Italian engraver, was born at Pavia in 1790, and studied under Anderloni. In 1803 he entered the Academy of Milan, where in 1813 his 'Herodias,' after Luini, gained a prize, and in 1817 another was adjudged to him for his 'Holy Family in a Landscape,' after Raphael. In 1833 he was elected Professor of Engraving at Florence, where he died in 1835. His principal works are:

The Madonna and Infant St. John; *after Gimignani*.
Hagar and Ishmael; *after Barocci*.
Jacob and Rachel; *after Appiani*.
The Magdalen; *after C. Dolci*.
The Ascension; *after Guido Reni*.
Charles V.; *after the same*.

GARBIERI, CARLO, the son and scholar of Lorenzo Garbieri, painted historical subjects in the style of his father. In the church of San Giovanni in Monte, at Bologna, is a picture by him of the 'Death of St. Mary of Egypt'; and in San Paolo is one of 'St. Paul taken up into Heaven.'

GARBIERI, LORENZO, called IL NIPOTE, was born at Bologna in 1580, and was brought up in the school of Lodovico Carracci, of whose style he was one of the most successful imitators. Naturally of a dark and gloomy turn of mind, he selected the most austere and melancholy subjects; and his pictures generally represent the most tragical and terrible events, as massacres, martyrdoms, and pestilence. To the style of the Carracci, he added something of the vigorous light and shadow of Caravaggio. Such are his pictures in the church of Sant' Antonio at Milan, which Sant' Agostino, in his 'Catalogo,' has attributed to the Carracci. In San Paolo de' Barnabiti at Bologna he painted the 'Plague of Milan,' with St. Charles Borromeo communicating the diseased; and a 'Penitential Procession.' At the Filippini at Fano is an admirable picture of 'St. Paul raising Eutychus,' painted with such power and expression that it excites both terror and devotion. In San Maurizio at Mantua is his celebrated 'Martyrdom of St. Felicità and the seven Virgins.' At Bologna, in the church of San Lodovico, is a fine picture of the 'Death of St. Joseph'; at the Cappuccini, the 'Crucifixion'; in S. Michele in Bosco, scenes from the life of St. Benedict and St. Cecilia; and at the Pinacoteca, 'The Magician Circe.' In consequence of his marriage with a rich lady, he abandoned his profession many years before his death, which took place in 1654.

GARBO, RAFFAELLINO DEL. See CAPPONI.

GARCIA, BERNABÉ, a Spanish painter, was born at Madrid in 1679, and died in the same city in 1731. He was a scholar of Juan Delgado, and painted 'The Four Doctors of the Church' for a church at Alcalá de Henares.

GARCIA, FERRER, ('the Licentiate Don Pedro',) though an ecclesiastic, exercised the profession of a painter at Valencia and Madrid, about the middle of the 17th century, and obtained a great reputation, especially in perspective. He painted Crucifixions, one of which bears date 1632, and the usual religious subjects. His collection of pictures by the great masters, as well as his own performances, was sold at his death for a large sum.

GARCIA, FRANCISCO, was a Spanish painter at Murcia, at the commencement of the 17th century, as is shown by the inscription on an altar-piece in the chapel of Los Velez, in the cathedral of that city; it represents 'St. Luke writing.' The artist was in the employ of the Marquis de los Velez.

GARCIA, MIGUEL and GERONIMO, were twin brothers, and canons of the Collegiate Church of San Salvador at Granada, one being a painter and the other a sculptor; the first coloured the images which the second carved. They followed the style, and perhaps profited by the instruction, of Alonso Cano.

GARCIA DE MIRANDA, JUAN, was born of Asturian parents at Madrid in 1677, and studied painting under Juan Delgado, producing chiefly devotional pictures, particularly 'Immaculate Conceptions,' for private patrons. Born without a right hand, he made use of the stump of the arm to hold pencils, maulstick, &c. He was appointed to clean and restore the pictures injured in the fire at the Alcazar, and acquitted himself so well as to be appointed, in 1735, painter-in-ordinary to Philip V. He also held, with Palomino, from 1724, the post of public valuer of pictures. He died in 1749, leaving a son JUAN, of great promise as a painter, who, however, died at the age of twenty-one. His brother and disciple, NICOLAS GARCIA DE MIRANDA, who was born in 1698, and died in 1738, painted landscapes with religious figures.

GARCIA HIDALGO, JOSEF, was a Spanish painter, who wrote notes of his life, but omitted to state where and when he was born. From circumstances narrated by him it is conjectured that he was a native of Murviedro, in Murcia, and born about 1656. He was named by the artists of the day 'El Castellano.' He studied in the city of Murcia

under Mateo Gilarte and Nicolas de Villacis. After passing some years under those masters he went to Italy, and at Rome became a scholar of Giacinto Brandi, under whose tuition he made considerable progress. Pietro da Cortona, Salvator Rosa, and Carlo Maratti assisted him with their counsels; but the climate of Italy proving detrimental to his health, he returned to Spain, where he attached himself to Carreño, and, though far advanced in the art, worked as a young pupil. In 1674 he went to Madrid, and was employed by Charles II. in a series of twenty-four pictures on the life of St. Augustine, for the cloisters of San Felipe el Real, which occupied him, with other commissions from the king, till 1711. He was also much employed by Philip V., who made him his principal painter in 1703, and shortly after a chevalier of the order of St. Michael. In the latter part of his life he retired to the convent of San Felipe, and died there probably soon after 1711, but in what year is not known. He published 'Principios para estudiar la nobilissima arte de la Pintura,' 1691, and several other works on anatomy and painting for the benefit of students. His productions are at Madrid, Valencia, Siguenza, San Jago, and Guadalaxara.

GARCIA REYNOSO, ANTONIO, a Spanish painter, was born at Cabra, in Andalucia, in 1623, and studied under Sebastian Martinez, an artist of some eminence, at Jaen. He painted landscapes and historical subjects; and there are several of his works noticed by Palomino, particularly an altar-piece in the church of the Capuchins at Andujar, representing the 'Trinity,' with several Saints. There are also some of his pictures in the churches and private collections at Cordova, in which city he died in 1677.

GARCIA SALMERON, CRISTOBAL, a Spanish painter, born at Cuenca in 1603, was a disciple of Pedro Orrente. He was a good painter of historical subjects and of animals, one of his most esteemed works being a picture of the 'Nativity,' in the church of San Francisco at Cuenca. He was employed by Philip IV. to paint a bull-fight in honour of the birthday of Charles II. of Spain, and he executed several works for the cathedral at Cuenca and for the convent of Barefooted Carmelites. He died at Madrid in 1666.

GARDELLE, ROBERT, born at Geneva in 1682, studied under Largillière in Paris, where he distinguished himself as a portrait painter, producing also etchings of portraits and of views of Geneva. He died in 1766.

GARDELLE, THÉODORE, a Swiss miniature painter, was born in 1722 at Geneva, where he was apprenticed to an engraver. He was of dissipated habits, and wandered about from Geneva to Paris, Brussels, and finally to London, where he was executed for murder in 1761.

GARDINER, WILLIAM NELSON, an Irish engraver, was born at Dublin in 1766. He studied at the Dublin Academy, and then came to London, where, after various vicissitudes, he became an assistant to Bartolozzi, with whom he prepared plates for Harding's Shakespeare, De Grammont's 'Memoirs,' and Lady Diana Beauclerk's illustrations to Dryden's 'Fables.' He subsequently studied at Cambridge, with a view of taking orders, but afterwards took to copying portraits, and finally became a bookseller. He died by suicide in London in 1814.

GARDNER, DANIEL, an English portrait painter,

215

born at Kendal in 1750, studied at the Royal Academy, and was patronized by Reynolds. His portraits, which were in oil and crayons, were successful, and he was enabled to retire early from practice. He died in London in 1805.

GARDNER, THOMAS, was an English engraver, who lived in the first half of the 18th century. He chiefly worked for the booksellers, and engraved a set of plates for the 'Book of Common Prayer,' paraphrased by James Harris in 1735.

GARDNOR, Rev. JOHN, an English landscape painter, was born in 1729. In 1767 he received a premium at the Society of Arts, and his works, both in oil and water-colours, appeared at the Royal Academy from 1782 to 1796. He furnished illustrations for Williams's 'History of Monmouthshire,' and published 'Views on the Rhine' in 1788. He was Vicar of Battersea, where he died in 1808.

GARDNOR, RICHARD, nephew of above, exhibited with the Free Society and at the Academy, 1786–93.

GAREIS, FRANZ, a painter, born at Marienthal in 1776, studied at Dresden under Casanova. He afterwards went to Rome, where by his picture of 'Orpheus in the Lower World,' he gained a considerable reputation, but unfortunately he died at Rome in 1803, at the early age of twenty-seven.

GAREMYN, JAN, a Flemish painter and engraver, was born at Bruges in 1712, and studied under Louis Roons and Matthias De Visch. He painted numerous altar-pieces for the churches at Bruges and Courtrai; and others for private persons at Brussels and Ghent. His pictures are highly esteemed by his countrymen for their warmth of colouring. He painted several pictures in imitation of Rembrandt and Teniers, and designed and executed several of the plates for the 'Chronicles of Flanders,' published in 1736. He became professor in the Academy of Bruges, and died in that city in 1799.

GARGIUOLI, DOMENICO, called MICCO SPADARO, an historical and landscape painter, born at Naples in 1612, was a fellow-student with Salvator Rosa, in the school of Aniello Falcone. He was employed in decorating the architectural views of his friend Viviani Codagora with a number of small figures in the style of Callot and Della Bella. He died in 1679. The following paintings by him are known:

Gotha.	Gallery.	Two Men playing at Cards.
"	"	Two Ship Boys.
Naples.	Museum.	Revolution of 1647.
Paris.	Louvre.	A Combat in the Crusades.

GARIBALDO, MARC ANTONIO, a Flemish painter, was born at Antwerp in 1620, and in 1651-2 became a member of the Guild of St. Luke. He painted for the Jesuits' College at Antwerp a picture of 'The Virgin, as the Queen of Martyrs.' The date of his death is unknown, but he was living in 1690. There are by him:

Flight into Egypt. (Antwerp Gallery.)
St. Bernard reproving William of Aquitaine. (St. Gilles, Bruges.)

GARIGUE, —, was a French painter of the 18th century, by whom there is a portrait of Charles de Siffredy de Mornas in the Avignon Museum.

GARNER, THOMAS, a line-engraver, was born at Birmingham in 1789, where he was apprenticed to a Mr. Lines. In the early part of this century he contributed many engravings to the various Annuals that flourished at that period; he also

executed several plates for the 'Art Journal,' of which that of 'L'Allegro,' after W. E. Frost, R.A., is considered one of his best works. He passed nearly all his life in Birmingham, where he executed many portraits of local celebrities, and died in 1868.

GARNERAY, AMBROISE LOUIS, a French marine painter, born in Paris in 1783, received his first instruction from his father, Jean François Garneray. At the age of thirteen he went to sea, and after various adventures (of which he subsequently published an illustrated history) was taken prisoner by the English in 1806. He remained in England till 1814, and on his return to France was patronized by Louis XVIII. A 'View of the Port of London' was his first exhibited work in 1816, and he received a gold medal in 1819. In 1833 he was appointed director of the Rouen Museum, and he subsequently designed for the Sèvres manufactory for six years. He studied aquatint, and designed and engraved sixty-four views of the principal ports of France, and forty views of foreign ports, which were published with text by Jouy in 1821–32. At the Paris Exhibition of 1855 he received a medal for his invention of a new kind of artists' canvas. He died in Paris in 1857. Amongst his works are:

Boulogne.	Museum.	View of Sidon: sun setting.
Marseilles.	Museum.	The Canal at Furnes.
Nantes.	Museum.	An Incident of the Battle of Navarino. 1853.
Rochefort.	Museum.	The Frigate 'Virginie' attacking an English Squadron.
Rochelle.	Museum.	The Capture of the 'Kent.'
Rouen.	Museum.	Cod Fishing off Newfoundland. 1839.
Versailles.	Gallery.	Battle of Augusta. 1836.
"	"	Battle of Navarino.
"	"	The Return from Elba.

GARNERAY, AUGUSTE, the second son of Jean François Garneray, was born in Paris in 1785, and died there in 1824. He studied under Isabey, and painted chiefly in water-colours. Besides numerous portraits, he has produced several pictures from tales of interest, as also designs for vignettes, and for a work on Egypt.

GARNERAY, JEAN FRANÇOIS, a French painter of portraits, architectural views, and fanciful subjects, was born in Paris in 1755, and died at Auteuil in 1837. He was a pupil of David, and his earlier portraits are said to be in the Flemish style.

GARNIER, ANTOINE, was a French engraver, who flourished in Paris from about 1625 to 1646. He etched his plates in a bold style, and finished them with the graver. He engraved some of the paintings by Primaticcio at Fontainebleau, and a set of twelve plates after the pictures by the same painter in the chapel of Fleury. He also engraved some plates after Nicolas Poussin and Michelangelo da Caravaggio, and the following after J. Blanchard:

The Holy Family.
Charity.
St. John the Baptist.
St. Sebastian.

He usually marked his plates with the cipher AG.

GARNIER, ETIENNE BARTHÉLEMY, a French portrait and historical painter, was born in Paris in 1759. He was a pupil successively of Durameau, Doyen, and Vien, and obtained the "grand prix" in 1788. His subjects are chiefly from the ancient poets, or relating to the popular monarchs of France, such as Dagobert, Henry IV., and Napoleon.

In 1828 he was an unsuccessful competitor with Horace Vernet for the directorship of the School of Rome. At Avignon is a portrait of Cardinal Maury. He died in Paris in 1849.

GARNIER, Louis Hippolyte, a painter and lithographer, excelled in miniature portrait painting. He was born in Paris in 1802, and died there in 1855. Among his lithographs are 'Rebekah,' and 'Ruth and Boaz,' after Chopin; 'On the road to Market,' after Eugène Devéria; and others after Ary Scheffer, Schlesinger, &c.

GARNIER, Noël (Master of the Knot), a French engraver, flourished 1520–1540. He engraved two Gothic alphabets and other pieces, mostly copies after German engravings.

GAROFALO, Benvenuto da. See Tisi.

GARRARD, George, an animal painter, was born in 1760. He studied under Sawrey Gilpin, and in 1778 entered the schools of the Royal Academy, at which he first exhibited in 1781. He practised largely in modelling, and in 1800 was elected an Associate of the Academy. He died at Brompton in 1826. Amongst his works are:

View of a Brewhouse Yard. 1784.
Sheep Shearing. 1793.
A Peasant attacked by Wolves in the Snow. 1802.
An Agricultural Show. (*Woburn Abbey.*)

GARRARD, Marc. See Geerarts.

GARRET, William, a wood-engraver, practised at Newcastle in the 18th century. He published a series of thirteen small designs, the last of which is 'Death leading a Female to the Grave.'

GÄRTNER, Georg, the elder and the younger, were painters who lived at Nuremberg in the 17th century, the former dying in 1640, and the latter in 1654. The elder painter executed portraits in water-colours, whilst the younger was an imitator and copyist of Dürer.

GÄRTNER, Johann Philipp Eduard, an architectural painter, was born at Berlin in 1801. He was taught painting when a child by Müller at Cassel, and returned to Berlin when but twelve years of age to paint in a porcelain factory. In 1821 he made a student's tour to the North Sea, and then engaged himself to Gropius. Three years' study in Paris followed, and he then devoted himself to architectural painting. In 1837-39 he worked in Russia for the Emperor Nicholas. He died at Berlin in 1877. Many of his architectural pictures are in the royal palaces, and one is in the National Gallery of that city. In the Leipsic Gallery is an Italian landscape.

GARVEY, Edmund, a landscape painter in both oil and water-colours, is supposed, from his connection, to have been of an Irish family. In 1770 he was elected an Associate of the Royal Academy, and an Academician in 1783. He lived at Bath from 1769 to 1777, and died in 1813. He imitated Richard Wilson, to a certain extent, in his manner of painting.

GARZI, Luigi, was born at Pistoja in 1638, and studied under S. Boccali, in his native city, until he was fifteen years of age. In 1653 he went to Rome, to Andrea Sacchi, and was the contemporary and rival of Carlo Maratta. After having painted several pictures for the public edifices at Rome, he was invited to Naples to paint in the church of Santa Caterina a Formello, and in the royal palace. In the cathedral at Pescia he painted an immense picture of the 'Assumption,' which is considered his best performance. Of his works at Rome, the principal are the cupola of the Cibo chapel, in Santa Maria del Popolo; 'The Maries at the Tomb of our Saviour,' in Santa Marta; and 'The Prophet Joel,' in San Giovanni in Laterano. In the Liverpool Institution is a landscape by Salvator Rosa, with the figures by Luigi Garzi, and in the Munich Gallery is a 'Flight into Egypt.' He died in 1721.

GARZI, Mario, was the son of Luigi Garzi, by whom he was instructed in art. He was an artist of very promising talent, but died quite young. Two of his pictures are noticed in Pascoli's 'Guida di Roma.'

GARZON, Juan, a Spanish painter, for a short time the pupil of Murillo, was associated with Meneses Osorio in many of his works, but none of his own are known to survive. He died at Madrid in 1729.

GARZONI, Giovanna, was a native of Ascoli, who flourished about the year 1630, and resided chiefly at Rome, where she distinguished herself as a painter of flowers, and of portraits in miniature. At Florence she painted the portraits of some of the Medici and other nobility. She died at Rome in 1673, and bequeathed all her property, which was considerable, to the Academy of St. Luke, where a marble monument is erected to her memory.

GASCAR, Henri, a French portrait painter, was born in Paris in 1635, and visited England in the reign of Charles II. He was greatly patronized by the Duchess of Portsmouth, and met with so much encouragement, that he is said to have realized above ten thousand pounds during a residence of a few years. He left England about 1680, and died at Rome in 1701. His best portrait was that of Philip, Earl of Pembroke. He scraped a few miserable mezzotints, after his own pictures.

GASPARI, Giovanni Pietro, born at Venice in 1735, painted the decorations for the Court Theatre at Munich, and etched fourteen architectural plates.

GASPARINI, Gaspare, was a native of Macerata, who flourished about the year 1585. He was a disciple of Girolamo da Sermoneta, whose style he followed, though in a less finished manner; as appears in his two pictures in the church of San Venanzio at Fabriano, representing 'The Baptism of Christ' and 'The Last Supper.' He is seen to more advantage in his picture of 'St. Peter and St. John curing the Lame Man,' in the same church, a grand composition, in which he seems to have imitated the style of Raphael. In the church of the Conventuali, in his native place, there is a fine picture of 'St. Francis receiving the Stigmata.'

GASPARINI, Sebastiano. In the 'Descrizione delle Pitture d'Ascoli,' by Orsini, a painter of this name is noticed, who painted several pictures in fresco, in a chapel in the church of San Biagio, in that city.

GASPARRI di Spinello. See Spinelli.

GASPERS, Jan Baptist (or Jaspers), a native of Antwerp, was a scholar of Thomas Willeborts. He visited England during the civil war, and was much employed by General Lambert. After the Restoration he became an assistant to Sir Peter Lely, and afterwards to Sir Godfrey Kneller. He drew well, and excelled in making designs for tapestry. The portrait of Charles II. in Painter-

Stainers' Hall, and another of the same king, in the hall of St. Bartholomew's Hospital, were painted by him. He died in London in 1691.

GASSEL, LUCAS VAN, called also, from his birthplace, LUCAS VAN HELMONT, was a landscape painter, who was born about 1480. It is supposed that he resided chiefly at Brussels, where he died about 1555, but certainly not later than 1560. His landscapes are very rare: they are painted sometimes in oil, and sometimes in water-colours. There is a picture by him in the Vienna Gallery bearing his monogram and the date 1548, and there is another in the Lille Museum. His portrait by Jacob Bink is in the collection of "persons who died before 1572," engraved by Jan Wierix.

GASSEN, FRANCISCO, a painter of Barcelona, was born in 1598. He executed, in conjunction with Pedro Cuquet, a series of pictures on the Life of St. Francis of Paola, for the Minimite convent in his native city. He died at Barcelona in 1658.

GASSIES, JEAN BRUNO, a French historical and genre painter, was born at Bordeaux in 1786. He studied under Vincent and Lacroix, and died in Paris in 1832. He chiefly executed historical subjects from the Old and New Testaments, or from French history; but the pictures exhibited by him embrace a great variety of subjects—historical, poetical, and allegorical—landscapes, marine views, interiors of churches, and striking scenes on the coasts of England and France. Amongst his works are:

Hagar and Ishmael. 1811. (*Brussels.*)
Horace at the Tomb of Virgil. 1817.
Portrait of Louis XVIII. 1819. (*Bordeaux.*)
The Communion of St. Louis. 1819.
The Clemency of Louis XII. 1824. (*Versailles.*)
View of the Church of Boulogne. 1826.
A Bivouac of the National Guard. 1831.

GASSNER, SIMON, a painter and engraver, was born at Steinberg in the Tyrol, in 1755. He studied in Munich under Gallrap and Demel, and excelled in historical and landscape painting. He was engaged by the Margrave of Baden to decorate a room at Carlsruhe, but returned to Munich in 1790, and was still living in 1825. He also engraved with the needle and in the aquatint manner, and produced an etching of the 'Temple in the English Garden in Munich,' which bears his monogram.

GAST, MICHEL DE. See DE GAST.

GASTALDI, ANDREA, Italian historical painter, born at Turin in 1810. He studied in Paris, where he became deservedly popular, his wife being Mlle. Leonie Lescuyer, herself an artist of considerable talent. One of his most dramatic pictures is 'Frederic Barbarossa,' who is depicted escaping after his rout at Legnano and stumbling over the corpses of his followers. Gastaldi was created a chevalier of the Legion of Honour, and received other decorations of a like nature. He had made a special study of the processes used by the ancients in wax-painting, but his researches into this subject were never destined to reach completion. In his later years he filled the post of director of the Turin School of Art, and it was here that he died in January, 1889.

GASTINEAU, HENRY, a landscape painter in water-colours, was born in 1797. After studying in the schools of the Royal Academy, he commenced work as an engraver. He then took to oil-painting, but finally joined the Water-Colour Society as an

Associate in 1818, being elected a full member in 1824. He was intimately connected with Turner, David Cox, Copley Fielding, and others of the English water-colour school. He died at Camberwell in 1876. Amongst his works are:

Penrhyn Castle. (*South Kensington Museum.*)
Netley Abbey. (*The same.*)
The Pass of Klamme, Styria. (*Paris Exhibition, 1855.*)
Glenarm, Antrim. (*London International Exhibition, 1862.*)
Hospice and Pass of St. Gothard. (*The same.*)
The Pass of Killiecrankie. (*Paris Exhibition, 1867.*)

GASULL, AGUSTIN, an historical painter of Valencia, studied at Rome under Carlo Maratti. His 'St. Andrew,' 'St. Stephen,' 'La Vierge de l'Espérance,' and 'St. Joseph,' which he painted for the church of San Juan del Mercado at Valencia, are much admired; and there are many pictures by him in other churches of the same city. He died at Valencia at the commencement of the 18th century.

GATTA, BARTOLOMMEO DELLA. See DELLA GATTA.

GATTI, BERNARDINO, called IL SOJARO, or SO-GLIARO, was born at Pavia in 1495. He was one of the ablest disciples of Correggio, and approached nearer to the style of his instructor than any other of his pupils. Parma, Piacenza, and Cremona are rich in his works, among which are a 'Riposo,' in the church of San Sigismondo, and a 'Nativity,' in San Pietro, at Cremona; and a 'Pietà,' in the church of La Maddalena at Parma. He succeeded Pordenone in the work left unfinished by that master in the tribune of Santa Maria di Campagna at Piacenza; where, according to Vasari, the whole appears to be by the same hand. One of his most considerable works is the 'Assumption,' in the cupola of the Madonna della Steccata, at Parma, painted in 1560, in which the Madonna is of the most captivating beauty. In the refectory of the church of San Pietro at Cremona is his great work of the 'Miracle of the Multiplication of the Loaves,' painted in 1552, a composition of many figures, larger than life, admirably varied in the heads and attitudes, and conducted with a beauty of colour, and a harmony of effect, which atone for some slight defects in the aerial perspective. An 'Ecce Homo' and a 'Crucifixion' by him are in the Museum at Naples. He died at Parma in 1575.

GATTI, GERVASIO, called IL SOJARO, was a native of Cremona, who flourished from the year 1571 to 1631. He was the nephew of Bernardino Gatti, under whom he studied, and from whom he learned to copy Correggio, as his early works testify, whilst his later ones are more in the manner of the Carracci. In the church of San Pietro at Cremona is a fine picture of the 'Death of St. Cecilia,' with a glory of angels, truly Correggiesque. He was also an excellent painter of portraits, upon which he was much employed.

GATTI, GIROLAMO, was born at Bologna in 1662, and was a scholar of Marc Antonio Franceschini, whilst his colouring is after the style of Cignani. Several of his works are in the churches and palaces at Bologna. In Santa Maria Incoronata is a picture of 'St. Augustine, St. Petronius, and St. Gregory, interceding for the Souls in Purgatory'; in the church of La Natività, the 'Presentation in the Temple'; and in the Palazzo Pubblico, 'Charles V. crowned by Pope Clement VII.' He, however, painted more works of a smaller class. He died in 1726.

GATTI, OLIVIERO, an Italian painter and engraver, was a native of Parma. He was a scholar of Giovanni Lodovico Valesio, and, from the resemblance of his style, although greatly inferior, to that of Agostino Carracci, was probably instructed in engraving by that master. His works as a painter are little known; but he engraved several plates, some of which are after his own designs, which possess considerable merit. He was received into the Academy at Bologna in 1626, and was working in that city up to 1648. The following prints are by him:

St. Francis Xavier kneeling on the sea-shore, and taking up a Crucifix, which is floating on the water; *after his own design.*
The Virgin caressing the Infant Christ; *after Lorenzo Garbieri.*
St. Jerome; *after Agostino Carracci.* 1602.
St. Roch. 1605.
An emblematical subject, representing an Armorial Bearing, supported by two River Gods, with an armed figure, standing alone, surrounded by Jupiter, Hercules, Neptune, Apollo, and Minerva; *after L. Carracci.*
A set of four small plates, representing the Deity forming the World, the Creation of Adam, the Sacrifice of Abraham, and Judith with the Head of Holofernes; *after Pordenone.*
A Drawing-book; *after the designs of Guercino.*

GATTI, TOMMASO, born at Pavia in 1642, was a scholar of Carlo Sacchi. He afterwards went to Venice, where he studied the works of the great masters of that celebrated school; and on his return to Pavia he painted several pictures for the churches.

GATTI, URIELE, called IL SOJARO, flourished about the year 1601, as appears from the date inscribed on a picture by him of the 'Crucifixion,' in the church of San Sepolcro at Piacenza. Lanzi conjectures that this painter was a brother of Gervasio Gatti.

GATTY, MARGARET, an amateur etcher, was born at Burnham in Norfolk in 1809. She was the daughter of Dr. Scott, Lord Nelson's chaplain, and married the Rev. Alfred Gatty, D.D., vicar of Ecclesfield, near Sheffield, in 1839. Between 1837 and 1843 she etched several landscapes, but she is best known as an authoress of books for children. She died at Ecclesfield in 1873.

GAUBERT, PIERRE, a French portrait painter who was working in 1701, was a member of the Academy. There is a portrait of a lady by him in the Dresden Gallery.

GAUCHER, CHARLES ÉTIENNE, a French engraver, born in Paris in 1740, was first a pupil of Basan, and afterwards of J. P. Le Bas. He died in Paris in 1804. He engraved several portraits and other subjects, of which the following are the principal:

PORTRAITS.

Maria Cecilia, Ottoman Princess, daughter of Achmet III.; *after his own design.*
M. du Paty, celebrated Advocate; *after Notte.*
Louis Gillet.
Louis Augustus, Dauphin of France; *after Gautier.*
J. P. Timoléon de Cossé, Duke of Brissac; *after St. Aubin.*
Louis de Grimaldi, Bishop of Le Mans. 1767.

VARIOUS SUBJECTS.

An allegorical subject, to the memory of J. P. Le Bas; *after Cochin.*
The Crowning of Voltaire; *after Moreau.*
The Card-players; *after Tilborch.*
Repose; *after Gaspar Netscher.*

GAUCHEREL, LÉON, engraver, etcher, and painter in water-colours, was born in Paris in 1816. He was a pupil of Viollet le Duc, with whom he travelled in Italy and Sicily. He was a constant exhibitor at the Salon, where he gained numerous official honours from 1853 onwards. He etched many plates for the 'Gazette des Beaux Arts,' for 'L'Art,' the 'Portfolio,' and other publications. He died in Paris in 1885.

GAUDENZIO MILANESE. See FERRARI.

GAUDIN, LUIS PASCUAL, a Spanish painter, was born at Villafranca in Catalonia in 1556. He entered in 1595 the Carthusian monastery of Scala Dei, where he painted the 'Saviour washing the Disciples' Feet,' the 'Prayer in the Garden,' and two series of Evangelists and Apostles. For the Carthusian monastery at Seville he executed a series of pictures from the life of the Virgin, and a 'Last Supper' for Portacœli, near Valencia. He died in the monastery of Scala Dei in 1621.

GAUERMANN, FRIEDRICH, a landscape and animal painter, was born at Miesenbach on the Schneeberg in 1807. He was the son of Jakob Gauermann, and, in spite of his weak state of health, he showed talent very early, delighting in the study of animals. From 1825 to 1846 he made numerous excursions in various parts of Germany, and in 1836 became a member of the Academy at Munich. He died at Vienna in 1862. Amongst his works are:

A Peasant digging. The End of the Chase. Halt on the Mountain. A Bear Hunt. Wolves and Deer. Wild Boar and Wolf. The Harvest Waggon. The Approach of a Storm. Styrian Charcoal Burners. Watering-Place in Tyrol; Tyrolese Village Smithy. (*Berlin.*) The Labourer; Peasants reposing. (*Vienna.*) Wolves and a Dead Horse. (*Städel Institute, Frankfort.*)

GAUERMANN, JAKOB, a German landscape and genre painter and engraver, was born at Oeffingen, near Canstatt, in 1773. He at first worked as a stone-mason at Hohenheim, but his strong inclination for drawing brought him to the knowledge of Duke Charles of Würtemberg, who enabled him to receive an education in art. He travelled for six years in Switzerland, went to Vienna, and visited in succession the Tyrol and Styria, making sketches, which he worked up into water-colour drawings and oil pictures. He died at Vienna in 1843. He also executed several etchings of landscapes.

GAUFFIER, LOUIS, was born at La Rochelle in 1761. He was a pupil of Hugues Taraval, and he won the first prize for painting in 1784. He exhibited as an Associate of the Academy in 1789, but his health necessitated a residence at Florence, where he died in 1801. 'The Three Angels with Abraham at Mamre,' and 'Cornelia, the mother of the Gracchi,' represent Gauffier in the Louvre. Among other works are 'Cleopatra,' 'Jacob and Laban's Daughter.' His wife, PAULINE CHATILLON, to whom he was married at Rome, was a painter of genre subjects, and a pupil of Drouais. Many of her works were engraved by Bartolozzi, and she was herself an exhibitor at the Salon of 1798.

GAUGAIN, THOMAS, an engraver, born at Abbeville in 1748, came to England whilst young, and studied under Houston. He engraved many plates after Reynolds, Morland, Cosway, Northcote, and others, and died in London about 1805. The following are his principal works:

The Snow Man; *after J. Barney.*
The Young Pedlar; *after the same.*
Maria; *after Müller.*
The Death of Prince Leopold of Brunswick; *after Northcote.*
Mary Stuart hearing her death-warrant; *after the same.*

GAUJEAN, Eugène, an eminent etcher, born at Pau in 1850. He was a pupil of Pilo, Vernet-Lecomte, Martinet and Waltner. He made his *début* at the Salon in 1877 with an engraving of Henner's 'La Chaste Suzanne.' At the Salon of 1880 he was awarded a third-class medal, seven years later a second-class, and at the Universal Exhibition of 1889 a gold medal. Amongst his most important etchings are 'The Blessed Bread' by Dagnan-Bouveret; 'The Virgin' by Memling; Gustave Moreau's 'Apparition'; 'St. Cecilia' by Van Dyck; Botticelli's 'Spring'; and 'The Virgin of the Rocks' by Leonardo da Vinci. Perhaps his masterpiece was 'Flamma Vestalis' by Sir E. Burne-Jones. He died at the age of fifty.
P. P.

GAULLI, Giovanni Battista, called Il Baciccio, was born at Genoa in 1639. After acquiring the first principles of art in his native city under Borzone, he went to Rome, where, by studying the works of the best masters, aided by the counsel of Bernini, he soon rose into repute, and established a style of his own. The great vault of the church of the Gesù, at Rome, representing 'St. Francis Xavier taken up into Heaven,' is one of his most considerable works. In his picture of 'St. Anne kneeling before the Virgin and Infant,' with a beautiful group of angels, in the church of San Francesco a Ripa, he exhibits everything that is cheerful, pleasing and graceful. Contrasted with this is his 'Death of St. Francis Xavier,' in Sant' Andrea al Quirinale, which he has treated in an austere style, with all the solemnity and pathos which the subject requires. In the church of Sant' Agnese he painted the 'Four Cardinal Virtues,' and such is their force and brilliancy, that the neighbouring works of Ciro Ferri are nearly eclipsed by them. His best efforts were intended for fresco designs, and he excelled more particularly in his figures of children. He is stated by Pascoli to have painted seven different pontiffs. His own portrait is in the Uffizi at Florence, and 'St. John the Baptist preaching' is in the Dijon Museum. He died in 1709.

GAULT de SAINT GERMAIN, Pierre Marie, was born in Paris in 1754. He studied under Dumoreau, and died in 1822, leaving a very large number of historical, landscape, and fancy pictures, besides portraits. Among his portraits are those of Voltaire, Mademoiselle Clairon, Crébillon, and Stanislaus, King of Poland. He wrote accounts of the lives and works of Leonardo da Vinci and Nicolas Poussin; a 'Guide des Amateurs de Tableaux pour les Écoles allemande, flamande et hollandaise,' 1818; and other works relative to painting, in which he displayed much knowledge and judgment.

GAULTIER, J., a French engraver little known, was probably from his style a relation of Leonard Gaultier. Among others, he engraved some small plates of emblematical subjects.

GAULTIER, Leonard, (or, as he sometimes signs himself, Galter,) a French engraver, was born at Mayence about 1561, and died in Paris in 1641. His style of work resembles that of Wierix and Crispyn van de Passe. His prints are executed entirely with the graver, with great precision, but in a stiff, formal manner. He must have been very

laborious, as the Abbé de Marolles possessed upwards of eight hundred prints by him, many of which were after his own designs. They consist of portraits, and various subjects, of which the following are the most worthy of notice. They are sometimes signed with his name, and sometimes with the cipher **Ⅽ.**

PORTRAITS.

Henry IV. of France.
Henry, Duke of Montpensier.
J. Amyot, Bishop of Auxerre.
Alexandre Bouchart, Viscount de Blosseville.
Philip de Mornay, Seigneur du Plessis. 1611.
Charles de Gontaut de Biron, Marshal of France.
Etienne Pasquier.
Jean Caron.

VARIOUS SUBJECTS.

A set of small plates of subjects from the Old and New Testament.
A set of the Prophets, Apostles, and Evangelists.
Thirty-two plates of the History of Cupid and Psyche; *after Raphael.*
The Procession of the League; a satirical print.
The Family of Henry IV.; nine figures.
The Assassination of Henry IV.
The Coronation of Mary de' Medici. 1610.
The Cyclops forging the Thunderbolts; *after J. Cousin.* 1581.
A Sacrifice; *after M. Fréminet.*
The Last Judgment; copied from Martin Rota's engraving *after Michelangelo.*

GAULTIER, Pierre, a French painter and engraver, flourished from about 1730 to 1762, or later, and resided chiefly at Naples. He etched the following plates, after Francesco Solimena:

David and Bathsheba.
Ecce Homo!
The Visitation of the Virgin to St. Elizabeth.
St. Michael discomfiting the Evil Spirit.
The Defeat of Darius.
The Battle of the Centaurs.
The Four Quarters of the World; small ovals.

GAUTHEROT, Claude, who was born in Paris in 1769, and died there in 1825, was a pupil of David, whose friendship involved him in the troubles of the Revolution. He opened a school of design where the most noted artists studied under his direction. His principal work, 'Napoleon haranguing his troops on the Bridge of the Lech at Augsburg,' is at Versailles.

GAUTHIER DAGOTY, Édouard, an engraver, the son and pupil of Jacques Fabien Gauthier Dagoty, was born in Paris in 1745, and died at Florence in 1785. In 1780 he issued a series of twelve plates, printed in colours, chiefly from the pictures in the gallery of the Duke of Orleans. He has also left plates after Correggio, Raphael, Titian, Van Dyck, and others.

GAUTHIER DAGOTY, Jacques Fabien, who was at the same time a painter, engraver, author, anatomist, and physical scientist, was born at Marseilles in 1717, but came to Paris in 1737, and there engaged in the business of printing in colours from several mezzotint plates. He was for a time an assistant to J. C. Le Blond, the inventor of this art, and after his death, in 1741, succeeded to the privilege of his patent. He died in Paris in 1786. He published a number of coloured illustrations of anatomy and natural history, as also some portraits, including those of Louis XV. and Cardinal Fleury.

GAUW, G., is mentioned by Strutt as the engraver of a singular plate of the 'Head of Mercury,' after J. Mathan, engraved in imitation of a pen-drawing.

GAVARNI. See CHEVALIER.

GAVASETTI, CAMILLO, was a native of Modena, who flourished about the year 1625. He studied under his father, Stefano Gavasetti, a miniature painter and gilder, but he rather followed the Carracci. His principal works are at Piacenza, where he is better known than at Parma or Modena. He was engaged with Piarini in painting Scriptural subjects, and at the Presbiterio, or parsonage of Sant' Antonio at Piacenza, is a fresco representing a subject from the Apocalypse, which was esteemed by Guercino the finest work of art in that city. He died young in 1628.

GAVASIO, AGOSTINO, was probably the son of Giovanni Giacomo Gavasio. There is by him in the parish church of Nembro, near Bergamo, an altar-piece of wood called "di Tutti Santi"; in San Niccolò, a repainted altar-piece with 'St. Augustine enthroned between St. Stephen and St. Lawrence'; in San Sebastiano, an altar-piece with the 'Virgin and Child;' and in the court of the Casa Longhi, a fresco of the 'Virgin and Child, with Saints.' Tassi notices a picture by this master in the parochial church of San Giacomo at Piazzatore, in the valley of Brembana, of the 'Virgin and Infant,' dated 1527.

GAVASIO, GIOVANNI GIACOMO, a native of Poscante, in the valley of Brembana, was a Bergamese artist who flourished early in the 16th century, but of whom no records exist. He is the author of five arched panels with figures of the Apostles, and of three paintings in tempera of half-length figures of Saints and Bishops in couples, on a gold ground, in the Lochis-Carrara Gallery in Bergamo. There is also a painting by him of 'The Virgin crowned by Angels,' dated 1512, in Sant' Alessandro at Colonna.

GAVAZZI. See GAVASIO.

GAVIN, ROBERT, a Scottish landscape and genre painter, was born at Leith in 1827. He early manifested a taste for art, and when about twenty-one years of age he entered the Edinburgh School of Design. His earlier works partook much of the style of Sir George Harvey, and a few of them, as, for instance, his 'Reaping Girl' and 'Phœbe Mayflower,' were reproduced in chromo-lithography, and became very popular. Soon after 1870 he made a tour in America, and afterwards went to the continent; he then settled for a time at Tangier, where he painted numerous Moorish subjects. He was elected an Associate of the Royal Scottish Academy in 1855, and an Academician in 1879, when he painted as his diploma picture 'A Moorish Maiden's First Love.' He died at Newhaven, near Edinburgh, in 1883.

GAWDIE, Sir JOHN, Bart., a portrait painter, was born at West Harling in Norfolk in 1639. He was deaf and dumb, and studied under Lely. Succeeding to the baronetcy on the death of his father in 1666, he pursued art only as an amusement, but Evelyn speaks of him in commendatory terms. He died in 1699.

GAYWOOD, RICHARD, an engraver, was born about 1630, and died about 1711. He was a pupil of Hollar, whose style he imitated. The most interesting of his works are his portraits, among which are the following:

Mary, Queen of Scots, with a Crucifix in her hand.
Charles I.; oval, with a hat and cloak.
Henrietta Maria, his Queen, in mourning.
Elizabeth, daughter of Charles I., with an Angel drawing a veil from her face.

Charles II.; after Hanneman.
Charles II., on horseback. 1661.
The same, with a hat and feather.
Catharine, Queen of Charles II.
Oliver Cromwell.
Richard Cromwell.
George Monck, Duke of Albemarle.
Jerome Weston, Earl of Portland.
The Countess of Portland.
Sir Bulstrode Whitelocke.
Sir Peter Temple, Bart.
Sir George Croke, Chief Justice of the King's Bench.
Sir Kenelm Digby.
Sir Peter Paul Rubens.
Hans Holbein.
William Camden, historian and antiquary.
William Fairfax, General in the Palatinate. 1656.
Inigo Jones, architect.
Margaret Lemon; after Van Dyck.
James Shirley, poet.
William Drummond, the Scottish historian.
John Playford, musician.
Matthew Stevenson, poet.
John Evelyn, antiquary.
Sir Anthony Van Dyck.
Lady Van Dyck.
Countess of Arundel.
Countess of Carlisle.
Dr. Sibbes.
Archy, the King's Jester.

He also engraved the picture of 'Venus reclining, with a Man playing on the Organ,' after Titian, as well as:

A set of eight plates of Birds; after F. Barlow.
A set of Animals; after the same.
A set of Lions and Leopards; after Rubens.
A Hare; after B. Poel.

GAZAN, FRANCISCO, was a Spanish engraver of the 18th century, who engraved, about 1713, a portrait of Quevedo, after a drawing of Salva Jordan.

GEBAUER, CHRISTIAN DAVID, an animal painter and an etcher, was born in 1777 at Neusalz in Silesia, and educated at the Copenhagen Academy from 1800 under Lorentzen. He devoted himself to landscapes as well as animals, executing the latter at first in Indian ink, but afterwards in oil. In 1813 he proceeded to Dresden, where he took to drawing, painting, and etching military scenes, and in 1815 was received into the Academy there. Later in his life he established a school of design at Aarhus, where he died in 1831. His pictures of horses and dogs, several of which are in the Copenhagen Gallery, are among his best works.

GEBHARD, W. M., a German landscape painter and engraver, flourished at Nuremberg from 1730 to 1750. There are by him 'The Sacrifice of Iphigeneia,' and two sets of landscapes with ruins and waterfalls.

GEDDES, ANDREW, a Scottish portrait painter, was born at Edinburgh about the year 1789. He was the son of David Geddes, an auditor of excise, and was educated at the High School and University of Edinburgh. He showed an early predilection for the fine arts, but did not commence his career as a professed artist until after the death of his father. He entered the schools of the Royal Academy in 1807, about the same time that Haydon, Jackson, and Wilkie were students there, and after some years' study he settled down to practise in Edinburgh. In 1814 he took a residence in London for his artistic pursuits, and continued annually to spend some months there. About this time he painted the portraits of Sir David Wilkie, Henry Mackenzie (the author of 'The Man of Feeling'), Dr. Chalmers, and other persons of note. The approbation which these portraits elicited induced him to put down his name as a candidate for the honours of the Royal Academy; but he was unsuccessful, and the Associateship was not awarded him till 1832. In 1818 he painted a picture of 'The Discovery of the Regalia in Scotland,' in which he introduced the portraits of several of the most distinguished men of his native city, among them Sir Walter Scott. In 1828 he visited the continent, and passed some time in Italy, Germany, and France. On his return in 1831 he painted an altar-piece for the church of St. James, Garlick Hill, and a picture of 'Christ and the Woman of Samaria.' He visited Holland in 1839, and he was skilful as an etcher in the manner of Rembrandt. He died in London in 1844. His principal works are:

Edinburgh.	*Nat. Gallery.*	Summer.
„	„	His own Portrait.
„	„	Hagar.
„	„	Portrait of the Artist's Mother.
„	„	Portrait of George Sanders.
London.	*Nat. Gallery.*	Dull Reading (Portraits of Terry and his Wife).
„	*South Kensington Museum.*	A Man Smoking.
„	„	A Study from Giorgione.

GEDDES, Margaret Sarah. See Carpenter.

GEEDTS, Pierre Joseph, a Belgian historical painter, born at Louvain in 1770, studied at the Antwerp Academy under Herreyns. In 1800 he was appointed one of the professors of the new Academy of Louvain, which post he held till 1833, when he was, as he always considered, unjustly dismissed. He died at Louvain in 1834. His best works are a 'Calvary,' and 'The Archbishop of Cologne delivering a miraculous host to an Augustine Monk;' the latter is in the church of St. Jacques at Louvain.

GEEDTS, Pierre Paul, the son of Pierre Joseph Geedts, was born at Louvain in 1793, and studied under his father and at the Louvain Academy, where he carried off the principal prizes. He was appointed professor of modelling, but resigned on his father being dismissed. He was a good portrait painter, but there is only known by him one historical picture, painted in 1824 for the church of St. Jacques. He died at Louvain in 1856.

GEEFS, Aloys, a Belgian historical painter and sculptor, was born at Antwerp in 1817, and died at Auteuil near Paris in 1841. 'The Scourging of Christ' was one of his best paintings.

GEEL, Joost van, a Dutch painter, was born at Rotterdam in 1631, where he died in 1698. He was a scholar of Gabriel Metsu, whose polished style he imitated so exactly, that it is not always easy to distinguish their works. He also painted marines and sea-ports, which are highly finished, and very agreeably coloured. In the Amsterdam Museum is a portrait of Van Geel, by himself, and in the Hermitage, St. Petersburg, 'A Concert.'

GEELEN, Christiaan van, a painter born at Utrecht in 1755, was a pupil of Jakob Maurer. He painted portraits, family pieces, and landscapes, and died in 1826. His son, also named Christiaan, born in 1794, showed great talent, but died in 1825 at the early age of thirty-one years.

GEELKERKEN, Nicolaas van, (or Geilkerk,) was a native of Holland, who flourished at Leyden from about 1624 to 1654. He was chiefly employed in engraving maps, but executed also some portraits, among which is that of Maurice, Prince of Nassau.

GEERAERTS, Martin Joseph, a Flemish historical painter, born at Antwerp in 1707, was intended for the law, and studied in the Jesuits' College. Preferring art, however, he became a pupil of Abraham Godyn, and was made free of the Guild of St. Luke in 1731. In 1741 he became one of the six directors of the Academy of Antwerp, who filled that office gratuitously. He died at Antwerp in 1791. He excelled in grisaille painting in imitation of bas-reliefs, of which there are the following examples:

Antwerp.	*Gallery.*	The Fine Arts. 1760.
Brussels.	*Gallery.*	Christ and the Disciples at Emmaus.
„	„	The Saviour at the House of Simon the Pharisee.
„	„	The Sons of Aaron punished by Fire from Heaven.
„	„	The Woman taken in Adultery.
„	„	Abraham and Melchisedeck.
„	„	The Sacrifice of Abraham.
„	„	The Sacrifice of Eli.
Hague.	*Museum.*	Autumn.
Lille.	*Museum.*	Children with Goat.
Vienna.	*Gallery.*	Cupid and Psyche.

GEERARTS, Marc, (whose name is found variously written Gerard, Geraats, Gheeraerts, Guerards, &c.,) the elder, a Flemish painter and engraver, born at Bruges in the 16th century, was a pupil of Marten De Vos. During the religious wars he came to England, and became painter to Queen Elizabeth. He died in this country before 1604, as Van Mander, in his book published in that year, complains of not being able to gain any authentic date about his death from his son. He was the author of a remarkable plan of Bruges made before 1566, of which the original is in the possession of the Corporation of that city. In the Vienna Gallery are two portraits, and in the church of Notre-Dame in Bruges is a 'Descent from the Cross,' by some assigned to Frans Pourbus. Geerarts painted the procession of Queen Elizabeth to a marriage that took place at Blackfriars about 1600, which he himself engraved, and which was reproduced by Vertue, who, in defiance of an earlier and well-grounded tradition, conjectured that it represented a royal visit to Hunsdon House, Hertfordshire, in 1571. He also engraved some plates for an edition of Æsop's 'Fables' published at Bruges in 1567. In the Burghley House collection are portraits by him of Queen Elizabeth, Lord Burghley, and the Earl of Essex. There are in the National Portrait Gallery portraits by him of Mary, Countess of Pembroke, Lord Burghley, and William Camden.

GEERARTS, Marc, the younger, a son of Marc Geerarts the elder, was born at Bruges, and was a pupil of Lucas De Heere. The dates of his birth and death are alike unknown. He is supposed to have come to England, but some confusion exists between the works of the father and son. The most important of all the works attributed to this artist is the 'Assembly of English, Spanish, and Austrian Plenipotentiaries held at Somerset House in 1604,' recently acquired for the National Portrait Gallery at the Hamilton sale, which formerly bore the forged signature of Pantoja de La Cruz. There is a picture of Elizabeth, signed *M. G.*, belonging to the Duke of Portland, a head of Camden in the Bodleian, a full-length portrait of Thomas Cecil, first Earl of Exeter, painted in 1612, at Woburn Abbey, and other signed specimens at Barrow Green and Penshurst.

GEERTGEN VAN SINT JANS. See HAARLEM, GERRIT VAN.

GEEST, CORNELIS VAN, was a Dutch engraver, by whom there is a half-sheet print of Gilbert Burnet, Bishop of Salisbury.

GEEST, WYBRAND DE. See DE GEEST.

GEFFELS, FRANZ, was a painter, etcher, and builder from the Netherlands, who was working at Mantua from about 1651 to 1671. He has left seven plates of buildings and ruins.

GEGENBAUER, JOSEPH ANTON VON, a German historical painter, was born in 1800 at Wangen in Würtemberg. He studied under Langer at Munich, and during his stay there from 1815 to 1823 produced a 'St. Sebastian,' an altar-piece for his native town, and two idyllic pieces which attracted great notice. In 1823 he went to Rome. Here he produced 'Adam and Eve after their Expulsion from Eden,' and 'Moses striking the Rock,' now in the palace at Stuttgart. Upon his return home in 1826 he was employed to decorate the palace of Rosenstein. He went again to Rome in 1829, and was employed in fresco painting, and afterwards up to the end of his life was occupied in the same way in Stuttgart. He died at Rome in 1876. In addition to the pictures mentioned above, the following are among his works in oil:

A sleeping Venus and two Satyrs. Leda and the Swan. Madonna and Child (*an altar-piece at Wangen*). Several portraits. While in fresco are:

Scene from the Story of Cupid and Psyche. The four Seasons and Aurora. Hercules and Omphale. Ascension of the Virgin. The Crucifixion. Scenes from the Life of Count Eberhard II. of Würtemberg.

GEHRTS, KARL, German historical and genre painter; born 1853 at Hamburg. Studied at the Art School of Weimar; Professor at the Düsseldorf Academy of Fine Arts. His most important work is the series of frescoes that decorate the staircase of the Düsseldorf Museum, in which the artist makes a *résumé* of the history of art. He also achieved considerable notoriety by his book illustrations and drawings for 'Fliegende Blätter.' His quaint, weird figures of gnomes (Kobold and Heinzelmännchen) have made his name familiar throughout Germany. He died at Endenich, near Bonn, in July 1898.

GEIGER, ANDREAS, a mezzotint engraver, was born at Vienna in 1773, and died there in 1856. Among his best plates are 'Antiochus and his Physician Erasistratus,' after Füger, 'The Death of Cato,' after Caravaggio, 'Helen and Paris,' after David, and 'The Burial of Christ,' after Van der Werff.

GEIKIE, WALTER, a Scottish subject painter, was born at Edinburgh in 1795. He became deaf and dumb, and studied in the Trustees' Academy. His works first appeared in 1815, and he was elected an Associate of the Royal Scottish Academy in 1831, and an Academician in 1834. He died in 1837. He published a volume of etchings: and there is in the National Gallery of Scotland a 'Cottage Scene' by him.

GEILKERK, NICOLAAS VAN. See GEELKERKEN.

GEIRNAERT, JOSEPH, a Flemish genre painter, born at Eecloo in Flanders, in 1791, was a pupil of Herreyns and of Paelinck. From 1830 to 1836 he practised at the Hague, but died at Ghent in 1859. Amongst his works are:

The Schoolmaster. (*Mechlin Museum.*)
A Consultation at the Doctor's. (*Brussels Gallery.*)
Leonardo da Vinci painting the Gioconda.

Moses saved from the Waters.
Joseph and Potiphar.
Asking in Marriage.
The Card Players.
The Little Marauders.
The Return of the Fishermen.
An Election.
Albrecht Dürer at the tomb of Van Eyck.
The Arrest of Count Egmont. 1823.
The Lesson on the Harp. (*Ghent Museum.*)
Giving a Pledge. (*Ghent Museum.*)
The Visit of the Doctor. (*Haarlem Museum.*)

GEISSLER, JOHANN MARTIN FRIEDRICH, an engraver, born at Nuremberg in 1778, was first instructed by Heinrich Guttenberg, but spent from 1803 to 1814 in further study in Paris, devoting himself especially to architecture and landscapes. He died at Nuremberg in 1853. The best of his plates are from his own designs, but he also executed views of churches, &c., after Ainmiller and others, and 'The Return of the Herd,' after Berchem, 'The Road through the Beech-wood,' after Ruisdael, and 'A Landscape with an Oak and a fallen Beech-tree,' after Wynants.

GEIST, AUGUST CHRISTIAN, a landscape painter, born at Würzburg in 1835, was at first a pupil of his father, Andreas Geist (who died in 1860), under whom he executed many landscapes, architectural and marine views, and heads, both in oil and water-colours. In 1853 he proceeded to Munich, and improved himself in landscape work by study under Friedrich Bamberger. In 1854 he travelled in the Rhone mountains, and produced therefrom twenty-four Indian ink drawings. He then established a studio of his own; but in 1859 he made a tour around Carlsruhe with Schirmer; in 1860 visited the Rhine and Antwerp; in 1862 the Highlands of Bavaria; in 1863 Franconian Switzerland; and in 1864 the Allgau. The years 1865 to 1867 he spent in Rome on account of his health; and he died at Munich in 1868. The following are some of his best works:

Achach Castle. 1853.
Pleasure Party at Carlstadt. 1853.
Winter Landscape at Schäftlarn. 1853.
Landscape near Polling. 1856.
Festal Morning on a Mountain Lake. 1863.
The Idyll. 1864.
Thunderstorm in the Campagna.
Fountain near Ariccia.
Theatre of Tusculum.

He also etched thirteen 'Ruins of Franconian Fortresses' for the Polytechnic Association at Würzburg, for which also the above Indian ink drawings were executed.

GELASIO DI NICCOLÒ, a Ferrarese painter of the 13th century, is said to have studied in Venice under the Greek Theophanes, and on his return to Ferrara, in 1240, to have executed various works there for the bishop, Filippo Fontana. The paintings usually ascribed to him belong to a later date.

GELDER, ARENT DE. See DE GELDER.

GELDER, N. VAN, was an animal painter of the Netherlands, who flourished about 1660. The Vienna Gallery contains one or two pictures of game by him, and in the Fitzwilliam Museum at Cambridge is a picture of 'Boors playing at cards.'

GELDER, PIETER, was a Dutch painter, supposed to have been a scholar of Rembrandt, whose manner he imitated. He was living in 1655.

GELDERBLOEM, LAURENT, born at Dordrecht about 1748, was a pupil of Joris Ponsen. This artist gave promise of considerable talent, but died before reaching the age of thirty.

GELDERSMAN, VINCENTIUS, a Flemish painter, was born at Mechlin about 1539. It is not known under whom he studied, but he painted historical subjects with some success. Among his most esteemed works may be noticed a picture of 'Susannah and the Elders,' and a 'Descent from the Cross,' in the cathedral at Mechlin ; also a 'Leda' and 'Cleopatra with the Asp.'

GELDORP, GEORG, a portrait painter, was born at the end of the 16th century, probably at Cologne, though Walpole calls him a native of Antwerp. He certainly studied at Antwerp, and then went to London, where he was appointed keeper of the pictures to Charles I. Rubens and Van Dyck were successively his guests on their arrival in England. He died in London about 1658. Among his portraits may be named those of the Duke of Lennox and the Earl of Lindsay, both of which have been engraved, and one of George Carew, Earl of Totness, in the National Portrait Gallery.

GELDORP, GORTZIUS, (or GUALDORP,)—sometimes known by his Christian name alone—was a Flemish painter, born at Louvain in 1553. After learning the rudiments of art in his native city, he went, at seventeen years of age, to Antwerp, where he became a disciple of Frans Francken the elder. On the death of that master he passed into the school of Frans Pourbus, under whom he became one of the best artists of his time, particularly in portraits, in which he was greatly employed. His talents were not, however, confined to portraits : he painted likewise several historical subjects for the Duke of Terra Nova at Cologne. Among his best pictures are :

Cologne.	*Wallraf-Richartz Museum.*	The Four Evangelists.
Darmstadt.	*Gallery.*	Two portraits.
Gotha.	*Gallery.*	Four portraits.
Milan.	*Brera.*	Portrait of a Lady.
Munich.	*Gallery.*	Portrait of a Man.
Petersburg.	*Hermitage.*	Lucretia.
”	”	Portrait of a Man.

He died at Cologne in 1616 or 1618.

GELDORP, MELCHIOR, a portrait and historical painter, was a son and scholar of Gortzius Geldorp. He was working at Cologne from 1620 to 1640, and some works of his are there preserved, among which may be named :

Portrait of an Ecclesiastic. 1615.
Portrait of a Lady. 1618.
Portrait of a Child. 1624.
Portrait of Wolfgang William, Count Palatine of the Rhine and Duke of Bavaria.

GELÉE, FRANÇOIS ANTOINE, a French engraver and lithographer, was born in Paris in 1796, and studied under Girodet and Pauquet. He died in Paris in 1860. Amongst his plates are :

Daphnis and Chloe ; *after Hersent.*
Justice and Divine Vengeance pursuing Crime ; *after Prud'hon.*
Venus and her Doves ; *after Lambert.*
The Shepherd of Virgil ; *after Boisselier.*

GELENIUS, SIGISMUND, was a German engraver, who flourished about the year 1576. Professor Christ attributes to him a set of twelve small woodcuts of the 'Labours of Hercules,' which are executed with considerable spirit.

GELIBERT, JEAN PIERRE PAUL, a French animal painter, was born in 1802, and died at Barthe-le-Neste, Hautes Pyrenées, in 1883.

224

GELISSEN, MAXIMILIEN LAMBERT, a landscape painter, was born at Brussels in 1786. In 1820 he won the first prize medal for a 'View of Ruysbroeck,' now in the Ghent Museum, and later in life he travelled in England and Scotland. He died at Brussels in 1867.

GELL, Sir WILLIAM, an English topographical draughtsman, was born in 1774. He studied in the schools of the Academy, and practised as an architect, but is best known by the illustrated books he published on the topography and antiquities of Greece and Italy. In 1820 he settled in Italy, where he acted as Chamberlain to Caroline, Princess of Wales. He died at Naples in 1836. Amongst the works he published are :

Topography of Troy. 1804.
Geography and Antiquities of Ithaca. 1807.
Itinerary of Greece. 1810.
Attica. 1817.
Itinerary of the Morea. 1818.
Pompeiana. 1817–19.
The Walls of Rome. 1820.
Narrative of a Journey to the Morea. 1823.
Topography of Rome and its Vicinity. 1834.

GELLE, JOHANN, a German engraver, flourished about the year 1628, and resided chiefly at Cologne. He engraved some of the plates for the 'Académie de l'Espée,' published at Antwerp, by Gerard Thibault, in 1628, as well as a portrait of the Emperor Ferdinand II. in a border of medals, dated 1619. They are worked entirely with the graver, in a stiff, formal style.

GELLÉE, CLAUDE, commonly called CLAUDE DE LORRAIN, a French landscape painter and etcher, was born in 1600 at Chamagne, a village on the Moselle in the Vosges country, then in the ancient province of Lorraine. His parents, Jean Gellée and Anne Pedose, were in humble circumstances, and had five sons, of whom Claude was the third. Concerning his early life, his biographers differ considerably ; their information coming from two sources. The first is Joachim von Sandrart, a German painter, who resided for some years at Rome, where he became intimate with Claude, and whose reminiscences are included in his 'Academia Artis Pictoriæ.' The other authority is Filippo Baldinucci, a Florentine artist, whose account was derived from the two grandnephews of the painter.

According to Sandrart, Claude showed so little aptitude for study when at school that his parents apprenticed him to a pastry-cook. He afterwards found his way to Rome, in company with some other young Lorrainers practising the same vocation. Here he lived for some time in the house of Agostino Tassi, a Perugian landscape and marine painter, who had studied under Paulus Bril. He acted as the painter's factotum : looked after the kitchen and household affairs, groomed the horse, ground the colours, and cleaned the palettes and brushes. While engaged on these duties he applied himself, with the help of his master, to a diligent study of perspective and the ground-work of art.

According to Baldinucci, when Claude was twelve years old he became an orphan, and had to seek the shelter of his eldest brother's home. Jean had settled at Freiburg, on the opposite bank of the Rhine, where he pursued the arts of wood engraving and carving. From him Claude, who had already shown a taste for art, received his first instruction in drawing. His stay in the Swabian country was not long, for about a year after, a

CLAUDE GELLÉE

CALLED

CLAUDE DE LORRAIN

Hanfstängl photo]

Art. Repro. Co

EMBARKATION OF THE QUEEN OF SHEBA

[National Gallery

CLAUDE GELLÉE

CALLED

CLAUDE DE LORRAIN

CEPHALUS AND PROCRIS

kinsman, passing through Freiburg on his way to Rome in pursuit of trade as a lace merchant, took him with him to the Eternal City. His relative was soon compelled to leave him, and Claude, a boy of fourteen years, was left alone in a foreign land. For some time he remained at Rome in lodgings near the Pantheon, eking out a scanty subsistence, and endeavouring to improve his knowledge of art by such humble means as lay within his reach. Owing to the wars which then ravaged Europe, the slender remittances he received from his friends at length entirely ceased, and he had to trust to his own unaided efforts to maintain himself. Nothing daunted, he set out for Naples to obtain some instruction from Gottfried Wals, a painter of Cologne. With this master he remained about two years, devoting his attention to perspective and architecture. He then returned to Rome, and gained admission to the studio of Tassi. Baldinucci states that he lived in the painter's house, and significantly admits that he looked after the household accounts.

Comparing these two accounts, it will be seen that they are in entire agreement on one point only: the fact of Claude having passed some time with Tassi, from whom he received instruction. As to the precise character of the relationship in which they stood to each other, it is evident from the admission of Baldinucci that Claude did not enter Tassi's house simply as a pupil, but as some sort of a dependent. As to the time of this sojourn, it appears that it must have commenced before 1619. A deposition by Tassi has lately been discovered, in which he speaks of Claude as one of his assistants in some decorations which he was executing for Cardinal Montalto in that year. Thus far there is certainty. Less certain is the account of the pupilage at Naples under Wals. Still it does not absolutely conflict with Sandrart, and may be accepted as supplying a link in the history. As regards the pastry-cook incident, and the manner in which Claude originally reached Rome, the two accounts are entirely at variance, and they must be left thus, until, perchance, further research shall have thrown more light on the subject.

In the spring of 1625 Claude left Rome, and set out on a series of wanderings. The first point aimed at was Venice. On his way thither, he spent a few days in devotion at the well-known shrine of the Virgin at Loretto. At Venice he stayed some time and executed several works. He had then intended to return to Rome, but, altering his plans, he determined to visit his native country. Passing through Trent and Innsbrück, he made a short sojourn in Bavaria at the village of Harlaching. During the journey he was laid low by sickness, when he had the misfortune to be robbed of all his worldly possessions. In this forlorn condition he returned to his native place, and after a short stay there proceeded to Nancy. Here he again took up the brush as assistant to De Ruet, the court-painter to the Duke of Lorraine. With him he continued till the summer of 1627, employed on various works, and more especially on the decoration of the Carmelite church at Nancy. His desire to return to Italy was quickened by an accident to the scaffolding used in the latter work, in which he had a narrow escape, and he set out on his return journey, making a halt of a few days at Lyons. On his arrival at Marseilles he was seized by illness, and again had the misfortune to be robbed of his little store of money. Before he

could proceed further he was obliged to raise the means to continue his journey by painting some pictures for a local patron of the arts. His troubles were not even yet ended, for the voyage to Cività Vecchia was so stormy that there were grave doubts whether the vessel would reach land.

Claude arrived at Rome on the 18th October, 1627. The years which immediately succeeded his settlement there appear to have been devoted to a close and direct study of nature. During this period he became acquainted with Sandrart, his future biographer, to whose account we are chiefly indebted for what is known of his mode of working. He sketched indefatigably in the open air, from the earliest dawn to nightfall, so that he might be thoroughly imbued with the ever-changing aspects of nature under the varying conditions of light. He mixed his colours while the effects were still before him, and then, returning home, applied them to the work which he had in hand. The German mentions Claude's weakness in drawing men and animals. He says that though he bestowed great attention on this branch of art, and for many years studied diligently from statues and living models in the Academy, yet he was never able to remedy this failing. That he was well aware of it is testified to by Baldinucci, who relates that he was accustomed to observe jocularly that he sold his landscapes but gave the figures. Following the example of many other painters, he frequently had recourse to other hands for the groups which serve to animate and give titles to his works. His chief assistant in this way was Filippo Lauri, the son of a Flemish painter who had settled at Rome, and he is also said, though perhaps doubtfully, to have been assisted by J. Miel, F. Allegrini, and the two Courtois.

Sandrart and Claude became very friendly; made sketching excursions together, and exchanged specimens of each other's art. This acquaintance is really the only trace of the Lorrainer having been intimate with his brother artists. He is mentioned casually, very casually, in connection with other painters, but he does not seem to have formed any other close intimacy. This isolation, combined with the small amount of information which has come down to us concerning Claude's life subsequent to his settlement at Rome, leads to the conclusion that his whole time and energies were devoted to art. Whether in his studio or in the short excursions he made into the surrounding country, his devotion to art never flagged. He remained a bachelor, and, to secure himself against the distractions caused by the care of a house, he induced a relative to migrate from Lorraine about 1636, and to take charge of his household. He carried his isolation so far that his name only occurs once in connection with Nicolas Poussin, the chief figure amongst the French artists then resident in Rome, and it is likewise absent from the biographies of the many great painters who were his contemporaries. There is no trace of his name in the records of the Academy of St. Luke, neither was he included amongst the members of the French Academy at Paris, which was founded while he was in the heyday of his reputation.

Claude does not appear to have at once sprung into fame after settling down at Rome. Some ten years probably elapsed before he attracted the attention of Cardinal Bentivoglio, one of the leading men in the Papal Court. A commission which he executed for this patron was so much appreciated that he was introduced by him to the reigning Pope, Urban VIII. This Pontiff ordered four works from him, two of which are now in the Louvre, and bear the date 1639. Henceforth his position was assured, and but few events occurred to disturb the even tenor of his career. The chief facts of his subsequent life might be included in a list of the works he painted, and of the patrons for whom they were executed. It must suffice within the limits of this notice to mention among the latter: M. de Bethune, French Ambassador at Rome; Cardinal Giorio; Innocent X. and his nephew, Prince Pamfili; the Duc de Bouillon; the King of Spain; Cardinal Giovanni de' Medici; Pope Alexander VII.; the Bishops of Montpellier and of Ypres; Cardinal Rospigliosi, afterwards Pope Clement IX.; M. de Bourlemont; the Constable Colonna; Cardinal Massimi; Prince Altieri, and the Elector of Bavaria.

There is an incident recorded by Baldinucci of the latter part of Claude's life which must not be omitted. In a spirit of compassion he had, about the middle of his career, taken into his studio a deformed and friendless boy, named Giovanni Domenico. The lad grew up in the master's house, and remained with him as pupil and assistant for twenty-five years. Then the enemies of Claude spread a report that the works which issued from his studio were really executed by Domenico. The ungrateful assistant joined the cabal, left his benefactor, and brought an action against him for the payment of a salary during all the years he had spent with him. Without waiting for the decision of the court, Claude at once paid the claim, and thenceforth closed the door of his studio to all assistants.

It now remains to speak of what is known as the "Liber Veritatis." This is a collection of 200 drawings of Claude's pictures, executed in bistre, and occasionally touched up with white. Nearly all bear inscriptions giving details as to when and for whom the pictures they represent were painted. The volume which contains them was bequeathed by the painter to his nephews as an heirloom, but their successors in the trust sold it. After various vicissitudes it at length found a resting-place in England in the collection of the Duke of Devonshire. Until of late years it was considered, following the account of Baldinucci, that the drawings were done by Claude as a means of identifying his works, and of protecting himself against the spurious productions which his fame caused unscrupulous contemporary artists to palm off as his. It is not necessary to enter into the details of the controversy, as the painter's will, which has recently been discovered, no longer leaves it open to doubt that the "Liber Veritatis" was intended by him as a record, whether complete or not, of his pictures and their destination.

During the latter part of his life Claude suffered much from ill-health, his chief foe being the gout. A severe illness in the early part of 1663 caused him to make the will which has just been mentioned. From it we learn that, besides his relative and housekeeper, Jean, there was also living with him an adopted daughter named Agnès, then 11 years old, whom he affectionately calls "mia zitella." To her he leaves for life the precious "Liber Veritatis," and makes minute and careful provision as to the property bequeathed for her maintenance. After his recovery from this

226

attack, the painter resumed the brush. The state of his health in the remaining years of his career probably precluded his working in the open air as formerly, but the record of pictures executed during this period shows that he manfully persevered, and produced many important works. The inscriptions on two designs in the "Liber Veritatis" attest that he painted pictures from them as late as 1681. The end came in the November of the following year, probably on the 23rd, and not on the 21st, as stated in the inscription placed on his grave by his nephews. He was buried, according to his desire, in the church of the Trinità dei Monti. In 1840, however, his remains were removed to the French church of San Luigi, where a memorial was erected to him by his country. The property which he left, estimated by Baldinucci at 10,000 scudi, chiefly consisted of obligations in the Papal "monti." There were twenty-two of these "luoghi," of which fourteen were left, either absolutely or for life, to his adopted daughter, and eight to his nephew Jean. A codicil made in 1670 somewhat altered the disposition of his possessions, but Agnès and Jean still remained the chief legatees.

Claude devoted considerable attention to etching, and many of his works in this medium show no less than his pictures his peculiar excellences. Meaume gives a list of thirty-two plates executed by him, which date from 1630 to 1663. Besides these, there is a series of etchings of the fireworks exhibited at Rome on the election of Ferdinand III. as King of the Romans in 1637.

The pictures painted by Claude number about 400. Of these the majority are in England, where the private collections are very rich in specimens of his art. For many years there was a great rage amongst English amateurs for his works. The galleries of the Dukes of Devonshire, Rutland, and Westminster, Earls of Ellesmere, Leicester, Northbrook, and Yarborough alone contain nearly half a hundred.

It will be noticed that many of his pictures bear as a title some scriptural or classical incident. But it must not be inferred that the incident occupies any important part in the composition. The figures introduced are quite subordinate, and frequently only serve to give a title to the work. The interest centres in the landscape. This is seldom an exact reproduction of any particular view. It is frequently a scene, more or less idealized, from the neighbourhood of Rome. In other cases it is a composition pure and simple, in which, however, can often be traced many existing features, such as the Colosseum, the temple of the Sibyl, and other remains of classic buildings, the heights of Tivoli, &c.

The following is a list of Claude's pictures in the public galleries of Europe:

Augsburg.	Gallery.	Roman Ruins.
Berlin.	Gallery.	Landscape; the Arcadian Shepherds. 1642.
Bordeaux.	Museum.	Landscape.
Brussels.	Gallery.	Æneas hunting the stag on the coast of Lybia.
Copenhagen.	Gallery.	Sunset.
Dresden.	Gallery.	Flight into Egypt.
"	"	Polyphemus and Acis and Galatea.
Dulwich.	Gallery.	The Flight into Egypt.
"	"	Jacob and Laban.
"	"	Embarkation of St. Paula.
"	"	Seaport.
"	"	Two Landscapes.

Florence.	*Uffizi.*	Seaport.
„	„	Landscape. 1672.
Gotha.	*Gallery.*	Marine View.
Grenoble.	*Museum.*	Seaport.
„	„	Landscape.
Hague.	*Museum.*	Landscape.
Innsbrück.	*Museum.*	Two Landscapes.
London.	*National Gal.*	Cephalus and Procris. 1645.
„	„	Seaport. 1644.
„	„	David at the Cave of Adullam. 1658.
„	„	Marriage of Isaac and Rebecca. 1648.
„	„	Embarkation of the Queen of Sheba. 1648.
„	„	Narcissus and Echo.
„	„	Embarkation of St. Ursula.
„	„	Death of Procris.
„	„	The Annunciation.
„	„	Anchises and Æneas at Delos.
„	„	Landscape.
„	*South Kensington.*	Landscape. 1670.
„	*Buckingham Pal.*	Rape of Europa. 1667.
Madrid.	*Gallery.*	Burial of St. Sabina.
„	„	The Finding of Moses.
„	„	Embarkation of St. Paula.
„	„	Tobit and the Angel.
„	„	Temptation of St. Anthony.
„	„	The Magdalen before the Cross.
„	„	Landscape with Hermit.
„	„	The Ford.
„	„	Two Landscapes with Shepherds and Cattle.
Munich.	*Gallery.*	The Expulsion of Hagar and Ishmael.
„	„	Hagar in the Desert.
„	„	Seaport.
„	„	Three Landscapes.
Naples.	*Museum.*	Marine View.
„	„	Diana reposing after the Chase.
Paris.	*Louvre.*	The Campo Vaccino.
„	„	The Village Dance. 1639.
„	„	Samuel anointing David. 1647.
„	„	The Ford.
„	„	Siege of La Rochelle.
„	„	Forcing the Pass of Susa. 1651.
„	„	Disembarkation of Cleopatra at Tarsus.
„	„	Ulysses restoring Chryseis.
„	„	Six Marine Views.
„	„	Two Landscapes.
Pesth.	*Gallery.*	Landscape.
Petersburg.	*Hermitage.*	Meeting of Jacob and Rachel.
„	„	Flight into Egypt.
„	„	Tobit and the Angel.
„	„	Jacob wrestling with the Angel.
„	„	Apollo and the Cumæan Sibyl.
„	„	The Journey to Emmaus.
„	„	Apollo and Marsyas.
„	„	Ulysses and Diomede received by Lycomedes.
„	„	Landscape.
„	„	Three Seaports.
Rennes.	*Museum.*	Landscape.
Stockholm.	*Museum.*	Landscape.
„	„	Arch of Constantine and Colosseum.
Strassburg.	*Museum.*	Landscape.
Stuttgart.	*Gallery.*	Two Landscapes.
Tarbes.	*Museum.*	Village Fête.
Turin.	*Gallery.*	Two Landscapes.
Vienna.	*Academy.*	Two Landscapes.
Windsor.	*Castle.*	Landscape near Tivoli.
„	„	Landscape: Claude sketching.
„	„	Landscape.
„	„	Seaport. 1643.
„	„	Marine View.

BIBLIOGRAPHY.

J. *von Sandrart*, 'Academia Artis Pictoriæ.' 1683.

F. *Baldinucci*, 'Notizie dei professori del disegno.' 1681—1728.

Comte Guillaume de L[eppel], 'Œuvre de Claude Gellée.' 1806.

J. P. *Voiart*, 'Éloge historique de Claude Gellée.' 1839.

Victor *Cousin*, 'Sur Claude Gellée.' 1853. ('Journal du Musée Lorrain.')

C. *Héquet*, 'Essai biographique sur Claude Gellée.' 1863. ('Journal de la Société d'Archéologie Lorraine.')

Robert-Dumesnil, 'Le Peintre-Graveur français,' vol. xi. 1871. (Claude Gellée, par E. Meaume.)

F. *del Tal*, 'Le Livre des Feux d'artifice de Claude Lorrain.' 1861. ('Gazette des Beaux Arts,' vol. xi.)

M. F. *Sweetser*, 'Claude Lorrain.' 1878.

Mrs. *Mark Pattison* (now Lady Dilke), 'Claude Lorrain.' 1884.

O. J. D.

GELLIG. See GILLIG.

GEMIGNANI. See GIMIGNANI.

GEMIGNANO, VINCENZO DA SAN. See TA-MAGNI.

GEMINUS, THOMAS, (or GEMINIE,) who was an engraver, as well as a printer, executed several plates to ornament his publications. In the year 1545, he published a translation of Vesalius's 'Anatomy,' which was first printed at Padua in 1542, with woodcuts. Geminus copied them on copper, and the book was dedicated to Henry VIII., with the title 'Compendiosa totius Anatomie Delineatio, ære exarata,' and published in folio in 1545. These plates, according to Ames, were some of the first rolling-press printing in England. He afterwards published an English translation of the same work by Nicholas Udal, in 1552, dedicated to Edward VI. Geminus lived in Blackfriars, where he published a 'Prognostication,' relating to the weather, the phenomena of the Heavens, &c., with a number of plates, engraved by himself. Vertue states, that he published another small work on Midwifery, with copper cuts by himself.

GEMMEL, HERMANN, an architectural painter, was born in 1813 at Barten in Eastern Prussia. He was instructed by E. Biermann and W. Schirmer, and afterwards travelled in Italy. In 1855 he was made professor of perspective and architecture at the Academy of Painting in Königsberg, where he died in 1868. Mention is made of the following works by him :

Family Room in a mediæval Castle. 1855.
Chapel of Cardinal Zeno in San Marco.
Baptistry in San Marco.

GENAELS, ABRAHAM. See GENOELS.

GENDALL, JOHN, an English landscape painter, was born about the year 1789. He assisted in the production of many illustrated books of scenery, notably with Pugin in 'Picturesque Views of the Seine,' 1821, and with Westall and Shepherd in 'Views of Country Seats,' 1823-28. Between 1846 and 1863 he exhibited at the Royal Academy many oil and water-colour views in Devonshire, where he lived. He died at Exeter in 1865.

GENDRON, ERNEST AUGUSTIN, a French historical painter, was born in Paris in 1817. He studied under Paul Delaroche, and afterwards spent six years in Italy, whence he sent to the Salon of 1844 his first exhibited picture—'Dante commented on by Boccaccio.' There also he painted 'The Willis,' which has been often lithographed, and 'The Nereids.' Among his later works may be mentioned 'Sunday: a Florentine Scene in the Fifteenth Century' (1855); 'The Funeral of a young

Girl at Venice (1859); 'Nymphs at the grave of Adonis' (1864); and 'Lucretia' (1869). He likewise decorated the chapel of St. Catharine in the church of St. Gervais in Paris. He died in 1881.

GENELLI, CAMILLO, who was born at Munich in 1840, was a son of Buonaventura Genelli, and while a boy drew landscapes under his father's tuition. From 1856 to 1859 he attended the Munich Academy, and went, in 1864, to Vienna, where, under Rahl, he executed oil and sepia compositions from Grecian mythology, among which is 'Ulysses slaying the Suitors.' In 1865 he removed to Weimar, where he died in 1867.

GENELLI, JANUS, the father of Buonaventura Genelli, was born at Copenhagen in 1771, and died at Berlin in 1813. He was instructed in Rome, and painted warmly-coloured landscapes, particularly from the Harz mountains.

GENELLI, BUONAVENTURA, a German historical painter, was born at Berlin in 1798. He was the son of the landscape painter, Janus Genelli, and received his first tuition from Bury and Hummel, and from his uncle, Hans Christian Genelli, the architect, who obtained for his pupil the assistance of the Queen of the Netherlands, who enabled him to go to Italy in 1820. In 1832 he was recalled to paint some wall-pictures for Dr. Härtel, and in 1836 he went to Munich, where he remained until 1859. He then settled at Weimar, where he died in 1868. A 'Rape of Europa' by him is in the Berlin National Gallery.

GENGA, BARTOLOMMEO, the son of Girolamo Genga, was born at Cesena in 1518. According to Vasari, he painted some historical pictures in the style of his father, but he is more known as a sculptor and an architect, than as a painter. He died at Malta in 1558.

GENGA, GIROLAMO, was born at Urbino in 1476, and was first a disciple of Luca Signorelli, whom he assisted in several of his works, particularly at Orvieto. After some years he entered the school of Pietro Perugino, at the time when Raphael was a student under that master, and there he remained three years and became an intimate friend of his greater fellow-pupil. He then lived for a time at Florence and Siena, but returned to Urbino to execute a commission for Duke Guidobaldo II. He, however, worked as a coadjutor with Signorelli, and with Timoteo Viti, and afterwards with Raffaello dal Colle in the Imperiale at Pesaro. His services to the Duke of Urbino were more in the capacity of an architect than a painter, though he made many designs for the decorations of the theatre. He afterwards resided at Rome, where he painted a fine picture of 'The Resurrection' for the church of Santa Cattarina di Siena. About 1512 he returned to Urbino at the bidding of the Duke Francesco Maria, whom he afterwards followed into banishment to Cesena, and there painted an altar-piece representing 'God the Father, with the Virgin and Four Fathers of the Church,' which is now in the Brera at Milan. In the Pitti Palace at Florence is a 'Holy Family' by him. He died at Urbino in 1551. He was also a sculptor and modeller. Among his pupils were Francesco Menzocchi, and Baldassare Lancia.

GÉNILLON, JEAN BAPTISTE FRANÇOIS, a marine painter of the school of Joseph Vernet, was born about 1749. His subjects are naval combats, shipwrecks, sea-ports, eruptions of Vesuvius by moonlight, and conflagrations at sea under a similar aspect. He died in Paris in 1829.

GÉNISSON, VICTOR JULES, a Flemish painter, was born at St. Omer in 1805. He studied at Antwerp under the brothers Van Bree, and died at Bruges in 1860. He excelled in painting the interiors of churches, and amongst his works are:

The Archduke Albert and Archduchess Isabella visiting Tournai Cathedral in 1600. (*Brussels Gallery.*)
Interior of the Chapel of the Holy Sacrament, St. Gudule, Brussels. 1835.
Interior of St. Jacques, Antwerp. 1836 (*Dublin National Gallery.*)
Interior of Antwerp Cathedral. 1837.
Confessional in St. Paul, Antwerp.
Interior of Strassburg Cathedral.
Interior of Amiens Cathedral.

GENNARI, BARTOLOMMEO, son of Benedetto Gennari the elder, was born at Cento in 1594. He was nearly of the same age with Guercino, and rather emulated his style than copied him. In the church of Santa Maria del Carobio, at Bologna, is a fine picture of the 'Assumption' by this master. He died in 1661.

GENNARI, BENEDETTO, the elder, who was born at Cento in 1570, and died there in 1610, was the instructor of Guercino, and has left a painting of 'Christ at Emmaus,' now in the Capuchin monastery at Cento, which has passed for a work of that master. He also produced a number of portraits.

GENNARI, BENEDETTO, the younger, born at Cento in 1633, was the nephew and the scholar of Guercino, with whom he soon became associated in his work. Finding that his uncle's productions were highly valued by Louis XIV. of France, he proceeded to Paris in 1672, where he was well received. Lanzi states, that he saw in the Palazzo Ercolani, a picture of 'Bathsheba' by Guercino, together with a copy of the same by Gennari, and remarks that the former appeared to be freshly painted, and the copy to be the older picture. He also painted some pictures of his own composition for the churches at Bologna and Cento. He came to England in 1674, and was for some time in the service of Charles II. and of James II. When the latter was dethroned he returned to France, and in 1690 went to Bologna, where he died in 1715. His principal works are:

Bologna.	*S. Domenico.*	St. Rosa.
„	*S. Giovanni in Monte.*	St. Anianus baptizing a Pagan King.
„	*Pinacoteca.*	Head of St. Peter.
„	*Cappuccini.*	St. Anthony of Padua.
Dresden.	*Gallery.*	Painting and Drawing.
Florence.	*Pitti Palace.*	David.
Forli.	*Filippini.*	St. Zacharias.
Madrid.	*Gallery.*	St. Jerome.
Modena.	*Estense Gallery.*	St. Justin.
„	„	St. Peter.
„	„	Head of an Apostle.
„	„	Philip II.
Osimo.	*Cathedral.*	St. Leonard.
Vienna.	*Gallery.*	St. Jerome.

GENNARI, CESARE, the younger brother of Benedetto Gennari, was born at Cento in 1637, and was also instructed by his uncle Guercino, whose style he followed with success. He painted several pictures, from designs of his own, for the churches at Bologna. In San Martino Maggiore is a picture of 'St. Mary Magdalen of Pazzi,' painted entirely in the style of Guercino; in San Niccolò, 'St. Nicholas kneeling before the Virgin;' at the Padri Servi, 'St. Apollonia;' in San Bartolommeo, 'Christ praying in the Garden,' and in the Pinacoteca the

'Vision of the Virgin and Child to St. Nicholas.' In the Pitti Palace at Florence is a 'Madonna and Child.' He died at Bologna in 1688.

GENNARI, ERCOLE, a son of the elder Benedetto Gennari, was born at Cento in 1597, and died there in 1658. He was instructed by his brother-in-law Guercino, whom he closely imitated in his works.

GENNARI, GIOVANNI BATTISTA, was a native of Cento, who flourished about the year 1606. He is stated by Lanzi to have been one of the masters of Guercino, and to have been a successful historical painter. In the 'Guida di Bologna' is noticed a picture by this master in the church of the Trinità representing the 'Madonna in glory, with Saints,' painted in the style of Procaccini. It is dated 1606.

GENNARI, LORENZO, was probably related to Benedetto Gennari. He was a scholar of Guercino, and flourished about the year 1650. One of his best pictures is at the Cappuccini at Rimini.

GENNARO DI COLA. See COLA.

GENOD, MICHEL PHILIBERT, a French genre and historical painter, was born at Lyons in 1796, and died there in 1862. He was instructed by Révoil, and became one of the most noted artists of his native city. 'The Family Festival' (1855) is one of his best paintings.

GENOELS, ABRAHAM, sometimes called ARCHIMEDES, was born at Antwerp in 1640. When he was twelve years of age, he became a pupil of Jacob Backereel, with whom he remained until he was fifteen. His ambition confined itself at first to portrait painting; but having made some successful attempts at landscapes, he attached himself to that branch of the art, to which his genius was more adapted. To perfect himself in perspective, he studied for some time under Fierlants, a native of Bois-le-Duc, who resided at Antwerp, and who was esteemed the most correct professor of that science of his time. His desire for improvement prompted him to travel; and he visited Paris at the time when Poussin, Mignard, and Le Brun were in the zenith of their fame. It was not long before his talent distinguished itself in that metropolis; and he was employed to paint the cartoons for eight large landscapes to be executed in tapestry for M. de Louvois, in which the figures were painted by De Sève. He was engaged by Le Brun to paint the backgrounds of his 'Battles of Alexander;' and in 1665 was made a member of the Academy at Paris, under the auspices of Le Brun. These flattering distinctions could not, however, detain him at Paris; and after having in 1672 been made a member of the Guild of St. Luke in his native city, he proceeded to Rome, where he arrived in 1674, and was received into the Bentevogel Society, who conferred on him the name of 'Archimedes,' on account of his knowledge of mathematics, and with this title he sometimes signed his etchings. He painted several large pictures of views in the vicinity of Rome, for Cardinal Rospigliosi; and after a residence of eight years in Italy, he returned to Flanders in 1682 with an ample collection of drawings which he had made of the environs of Rome. He died at Antwerp in 1723. Genoels may be ranked among the ablest landscape painters of his country. His colouring is natural and vigorous; he possessed a commanding facility, and a touch which he could appropriate to the particular objects he had to represent. A painting by him of 'Minerva and the Muses' is in the Antwerp Museum, and two of his landscapes are at Brunswick.

We have by this painter some masterly etchings of landscapes, from his own designs, executed in a bold, free style, and ornamented with figures and cattle. He sometimes marked his plates with the cipher ℭ⅍. among them are the following:

A set of four mountainous Landscapes, with ruins and figures. 1684.
Two rocky Landscapes, with figures. 1675.
Two grand Landscapes, with ruins and figures.
Four mountainous Landscapes, with ruins and waterfalls.
Four views of Gardens, with figures and statues.
Two large Landscapes, with waterfalls.

GENOVA, LUCHETTO DA. See CAMBIASO, LUCA.

GENOVESE, EL. See CASTELLO, GIOVANNI BATTISTA.

GENOVESE, IL PRETE. See GALANTINI.

GENOVESE, IL PRETE. See STROZZI.

GENOVESINO, IL. See CALCIA, GIUSEPPE.

GENOVESINO, IL. See MIRADORI.

GENSLER, JAKOB, a genre painter, was born at Hamburg in 1808, and received his first instruction in that city under Gerold Hardorf the elder. In 1824 he was placed under J. H. W. Tischbein at Eutin, and remained with him for two years, after which, in 1828, he attended the Academy at Munich. After a short stay in the Tyrol and Salzburg, he proceeded in 1830 to Vienna for further study, and returned in the following year to Hamburg, where he settled down. He visited Holland and Belgium in 1841, and died at Hamburg in 1845.

GENTIL. See ALAUX, JEAN PAUL.

GENTILE, LUIGI. See PRIMO.

GENTILE DA FABRIANO. See MASSI.

GENTILESCA, SOFONISBA, a French lady, illustrious in art, is mentioned by Palomino as coming from France in the train of Queen Isabella of Valois, third wife to Philip II. of Spain. She painted with great skill miniature portraits of their Majesties, the Infant Don Carlos, and many of the court ladies. She died at Madrid in 1587.

GENTILESCHI, ARTEMISIA, the daughter and the disciple of Orazio Gentileschi, was born at Rome in 1590. She accompanied her father to England, where she painted some portraits of the nobility, and some historical pictures for the king, the best of which was 'David with the Head of Goliath.' Her portrait by herself is at Hampton Court. But she passed the chief part of her life at Naples and Bologna, where she was much admired for her accomplishments and her talents as a painter. She was favoured with the friendship and advice of Guido, and studied attentively the works of Domenichino. In the Pitti Gallery at Florence are her best performances, representing 'Judith with the Head of Holofernes,' and 'Mary Magdalen;' and in the Madrid Gallery the 'Birth of St. John the Baptist,' and a Portrait. She married Antonio Schiatessi. She died in 1642.

GENTILESCHI, FRANCESCO, who flourished in the first half of the 17th century, was the son of Orazio Gentileschi, with whom he came to England. He studied under Domenico Fiasella, called Sarzana, but his pictures, which are said to have been historical, are little known.

GENTILESCHI, ORAZIO, called LOMI, after his step-father, was born at Pisa in 1562. He studied under his half-brother, Aurelio Lomi, and his uncle Bacci Lomi, and then went to Rome, where he improved his style by studying the works of the best masters, and by the advice and assistance of

Agostino Tassi, with whom he formed an intimate friendship, and whose landscapes he frequently decorated with figures. Several of their joint works are in the Quirinal and Rospigliosi Palaces, and in other places in Rome. He also painted historical subjects for the churches and public edifices, particularly for La Pace, and a fine picture of 'St. Cecilia and St. Valerian,' in the Palazzo Borghese. Some of his best works are in the royal palace at Turin, and at Genoa. He afterwards visited France, from whence his repute travelled to England, and caused Van Dyck to send for him to London, where he was employed by Charles I. Nine pictures by Gentileschi in the royal collection were sold after the king's death for six hundred pounds, and are now the ornaments of the hall at Marlborough House. He also painted two pictures for the Duke of Buckingham—a 'Magdalen,' and the 'Holy Family.' Van Dyck painted an admirable portrait of him, which has been engraved by Vorsterman. He resided in England twelve years, and died in London in 1647. The following are some of his paintings:

Compiègne, Meditation. *Hampton Court*, A Sibyl; Joseph and Potiphar's Wife. *Madrid*, Assumption; Moses rescued by Pharaoh's Daughter. *Milan*, SS. Cecilia, Valerian, and Tiburtius, crowned by an Angel. *Paris*, Repose of the Holy Family. *Vienna*, The Penitent Magdalen.

GENTSCH, ANDREAS, was a German engraver, who resided at Augsburg, and flourished early in the 17th century. He engraved several small copper-plates of grotesque ornaments, some of which are dated in 1616. He usually marked his plates with the same cipher as Heinrich Aldegrever

; but they are inferior to the works of that artist, and the date also furnishes a distinction.

GENTZ, WILHELM, eminent German painter of Oriental subjects; born at Neu-Ruppin, December 9, 1822. He received his early training at the Berlin Academy, which was supplemented by a long course of study abroad, particularly in the East. He chose Antwerp as a place in which to work, and subsequently studied in Paris with Gleyre and Couture. His pictures represent life and scenery in Spain, Egypt, Nubia, Palestine, and Turkey, and his very rich colouring was well suited to the vivid scenes which he portrays. His 'Entrance of the Crown Prince of Prussia into Jerusalem in 1869' is in the National Gallery of Berlin, and other notable works are 'The Flamingoes,' 'Evening on the Nile,' 'Arab Storytellers at Cairo,' and 'Prayer in the Desert.' He died at Berlin on August 23, 1890.

GEOFFROY, CHARLES MICHEL, a French engraver, was born at Joinville in 1819, and died at Passy in 1883. He engraved the 'Médée' of Delacroix, the 'Harem' of Diaz, the 'Watermill' of Ruisdael, and several portraits of theatrical celebrities.

GEORGI, FRIEDRICH OTTO, a German painter, was born at Leipsic in 1819, and died at Dresden in 1874. There is by him in the Dresden Gallery a picture of 'Jerusalem and Mount Moriah.'

GERA. See JACOPO DI MICHELE.

GERAATS, MARC. See GEERARTS.

GÉRARD. See GRANDVILLE.

GERARD, FRANÇOIS PASCAL SIMON, Baron, a French historical and portrait painter, was born in 1770 at Rome, where his father was in the service of the ambassador of France. About 1782, he came to Paris, and studied for eighteen months in an aristocratic academy. He then became a pupil of the sculptor Pajou, then of Brenet, and finally, in 1786, of David, by whom his style was chiefly influenced. In 1789 he competed for the 'prix de Rome,' but only succeeded in obtaining the second place. The following year saw the death of his father, which caused him to accompany his mother, who was a native of Italy, back to Rome. On his return to Paris, he managed with some difficulty to escape the whirlpool of revolutionary politics, and to devote himself to art. One of his best works, 'Belisarius,' appeared in 1795, and was bought by the Dutch minister. His chief support, however, for some years was in working for the publishers, for whom he produced drawings illustrating editions of Virgil and Racine. He at length won a position by means of his portraits, and was patronized successively by Napoleon I., Talleyrand, Louis XVIII., the Emperor of Russia, the King of Prussia, Charles X., Louis Philippe, and others. With such patrons he did not lack honours: he was one of the original knights of the Legion of Honour, he was elected a member of the Institute, and in 1819 he was created a Baron. In his latter years his house was the resort of many celebrities, and he attracted a large circle of friends. During this period he was much occupied in the completion of some large decorative works at the Panthéon, representing 'Death,' 'Patriotism,' 'Justice,' and 'Glory.' Gérard did not keep an atelier for students as is customary with French painters, but he was assisted in his numerous works by Paulin Guérin, Steuben, and his only pupil, Mademoiselle Godefroid. He died in Paris, after a short illness, January 11th, 1837. It is computed that Gérard produced 28 historical pictures, 87 full-length, and about 200 half-length portraits, besides a great number of subject pictures. The judgment of his contemporaries has been ratified: Gérard's historical and subject pictures lack that greatness of idea and power of execution which would have entitled him to a place in the front rank of painters. It is by his portraits that he is to be judged, and, thanks to the opportunities he enjoyed, few portrait painters have had a greater chance by the distinction of their sitters, of transmitting their names to posterity. He may be considered as one of the last of the direct followers of David: he did not seek for any new or striking inspirations which might form a starting-point for a new departure in art, but adhered closely to the canons of classicism as enunciated by his master.

Baron Gérard's 'Œuvre' was published with descriptive text by his nephew in 1852-57, in three folio volumes, and his 'Correspondance' with artists and distinguished persons of his time in 1867. The following is a list of the works by him to be found in some of the chief European collections:

HISTORICAL AND SUBJECT PICTURES.

Angers.	*Museum.*	Joseph recognized by his brethren. 1789.
Caen.	*Museum.*	Achilles and Patroclus.
Frankfort.	*Städel Inst.*	Sappho. 1810.
London.	*Lansdowne House.*	Hope. 1829.
Lyons.	*Museum.*	Corinna at Misenum. 1819.
Marseilles.	*Santé.*	The Plague at Marseilles. 1835
Munich.	*Gallery.*	Belisarius. 1795.
Naples.	*Museum.*	The Three Ages. 1806.
Orleans.	*Museum.*	Christ descending on earth and dispelling darkness.

Paris. *Infirmerie de Marie Thérèse.*		St. Theresa.
„	*Louvre.*	Cupid and Psyche. 1798.
„	„	History and Poetry.
„	„	Daphnis and Chloe. 1825.
„	„	Victory and Renown.
Tarbes.	*Museum.*	Achilles finding the body of Patroclus.
Versailles.	*Gallery.*	Battle of Austerlitz. 1810.
„	„	Entry of Henry IV. into Paris. 1817.
„	„	Philip V. called to the throne of Spain. 1824.
„	„	Coronation of Charles X. 1829.
„	„	Louis Philippe at the Hôtel de Ville. 1836.

PORTRAITS.

Ajaccio.	*Hôtel-de-Ville.*	Louis Bonaparte.
„	„	Napoleon I.
„	*Museum.*	Louis XVIII.
Angers.	*Museum.*	Lareveillere-Lepeaux.
	„	Madame de St. Jean d'Angely.
Arras.	*Museum.*	His own Portrait.
Avignon.	*Museum.*	Queen Hortense as a child.
Dijon.	*Museum.*	Duc de Bassano.
Dresden.	*Gallery.*	Napoleon I.
Hatfield.	*House.*	Louis XVIII.
Marseilles.	*Museum.*	Louis XVIII.
Montpellier.	*Museum.*	Madame Pasta.
Nancy.	*Museum.*	Napoleon I.
Paris.	*Louvre.*	Isabey and his Daughter. 1796.
„	„	Antonio Canova.
„	„	Charles X.
„	*Préfecture de la Seine.*	Madame Récamier.
Toulouse.	*Museum.*	Louis XVIII.
Versailles.	*Gallery.*	Madame Bonaparte.
„	„	Empress Joséphine.
„	„	Empress Marie Louise, and the King of Rome.
„	„	Joachim Murat, King of Naples.
„	„	Charles X.
„	„	Duke of Berry.
„	„	Duchess of Berry and children.

O.J.D.

GÉRARD, Louis Auguste, a French landscape painter, was born at Versailles in 1782, and studied under Bertin. He died in Paris in 1862. Amongst his works are:

View of the Porte d'Auteuil. 1819.
View of Rouen. 1822.
View of the Chapel of Betharam. 1827.
The Bridge of Neuilly.
View at Senlis.
View of Château de Polignac. (*Narbonne Museum.*)

GERARD, Marc. See Geerarts.

GÉRARD, Marguerite, born at Grasse in 1761, was a pupil of Fragonard. There are by her in the Bordeaux Museum full-length portraits of M. Tallien and M. Récamier, and at Fontainebleau a picture entitled 'Les Torterelles.'

GERARD of ST. JOHN. See Haarlem, Gerrit van.

GERARDI, Antonio, is mentioned by Le Comte as an engraver of funeral pomps, monuments, &c.

GERARDIN, Jean, a French engraver, flourished about the year 1680. He worked entirely with the graver, in a neat style, but without taste. He engraved a set of plates after the pictures by Pietro da Cortona, in the palace at Florence.

GERARDINI, Melchiorre, (Gherardini, Giraldini, or Gilardino,) a painter and engraver, was, according to Orlandi, a native of Milan, and was a scholar of Giovanni Battista Crespi, called Cerano. After the death of that master, Gerardini was employed to finish the pictures he left imperfect;

and he also painted for the churches several altar-pieces of his own composition. At San Celso, a small town near Milan, is a picture by him of St. Catharine of Siena, of which Lanzi speaks in favourable terms. He etched some plates after Pietro da Cortona, Guido, and others, as well as several from his own designs in the style of Callot, representing battles and other subjects, executed with neatness and spirit. He died in 1675.

GERARDS. See Zyll, Geraerd P. van.

GERBIER, Sir Balthasar, Baron d'Ouvilly, was born at Middleburg in 1592, and distinguished himself as a miniature painter, at a period when the ablest artists of his country were in their greatest celebrity. He came to England as a retainer of the Duke of Buckingham in 1613, and painted the portraits of the principal nobility of the time. He accompanied the Duke of Buckingham to Spain, where he was sent to bring about the treaty of marriage. Among the Harleian manuscripts is a letter from the Duchess of Buckingham to her lord, when in Spain, in which she says, "I pray you, if you have an idle time, sit to Gerbier for your picture, that I may have it well done in little." The Earl of Denbigh possesses a portrait of Donna Maria, Infanta of Spain, by Gerbier. On it is inscribed: "This is the picture of the Infanta of Spain that was brought over by the Duke of Bucks. She was to have married King Charles the First." In the collection of the Duke of Northumberland is a large oval miniature of the Duke of Buckingham on horseback, by him, dated 1618. The head is well painted, and it is finished with great labour. The head of the horse is spirited. In a letter dated 1628, it is said, "That the King and Queen were entertained at supper at Gerbier's, the Duke's painter's house, which could not stand him in less than one thousand pounds." In 1641 he was appointed master of the ceremonies, and the same year was naturalized as an English subject, and also made successor to Inigo Jones as surveyor of the royal palaces. But falling into disfavour soon after, he left England and went to Surinam, where he was seized as a Dutch subject and sent back to Holland. He returned to this country during Cromwell's Protectorate, and founded an academy, which, however, had but very slight success. He was employed on the decorations for Charles II.'s triumphal entry into London, and met with considerable occupation as an architect. He died in London in 1667, while engaged upon the building of Lord Craven's residence, Hempstead Marshall, and there he was buried. He published several works, including an 'Encyclopædia of Art.' Van Dyck painted a fine picture of Sir Balthasar Gerbier and his family, which is now at Windsor Castle.

GERBO, Louis, a Flemish painter, was born at Bruges in 1761, but went to Paris, where he was engaged as a decorative painter. In the church of St. Jacques in Ghent is a 'Holy Family,' and several pictures are at the château of St. André near Bruges. He died in 1818

GERCO, B., a Dutch engraver, executed some plates in imitation of the charming prints of Waterloo. After etching the plates he scratched upon them with the graver, and from not having afterwards cleared away the barb, has left a clumsy effect.

GERHARD, Otto, a painter of Regensburg, flourished about the year 1720. His historical pictures and other works, which are in the style of Bourguignon, show considerable talent.

GERHARD van HAARLEM. See Haarlem.

231

GÉRICAULT, Jean Louis André Théodore, a French animal and historical painter, was born at Rouen, September 26th, 1791. He was the son of an advocate in good circumstances, and was sent to Paris to complete his education at the Lycée Impériale. While still at school, the bent of his inclinations was plainly to be seen. His holidays were spent at the circus, and in the streets there was no greater attraction to him than the horses in a well-appointed equipage. In 1808 he became for a short time the pupil of Carle Vernet. He then studied under Guérin, with whose academic traditions he had but little sympathy. His art-training was really due to his study of the old masters in the Louvre, and the works of Rubens exercised a very powerful influence on him. His family was much opposed to his becoming a painter, and his ardent spirits, checked in one direction, sought other pursuits. He became a member of the Jockey Club, and plunged into all the dissipations of the 'jeunesse dorée.' At length, in 1812, he was enabled to have a studio of his own, and the first-fruits of his work in it was the 'Chasseur de la Garde,' now in the Louvre. On the Restoration in 1814, he served for three months in the Royal Musketeers, and for the next two years he did but little painting. In 1816 he set out for Italy, where he occupied himself in making copies from the old masters. Hitherto he had devoted his attention chiefly to animal painting, but on his return to Paris he produced what is really his only great historical work, 'The Raft of the Medusa.' It was exhibited at the Salon of 1819, where it evoked a great storm of criticism, and its appearance may be said to mark the commencement of the struggle between the Classic and Romantic schools in France. Géricault shortly after visited England, in company with his friend Charlet, and by the exhibition of this work in London realized the sum of £800. During his stay in this country, he practised the then new art of lithography with much ardour. Many of his works in this medium represent English scenes, amongst which mention should be made of 'The Coal Waggon.' On his return to France, his health, sorely tried by dissipation, began to give way, and his condition was aggravated by a fall from his horse. He, nevertheless, produced at this time a great number of sketches, studies, &c., and also made some progress in sculpture. His death took place in Paris on January 18th, 1824. The following is a list of Géricault's works in public galleries :

Chalons-sur-Saone.	Museum.	A Negro.
Grenoble.	Museum.	Two Horses in a stable.
Montpellier.	Museum.	Portrait of Lord Byron.
”	”	Two Horses in a stable.
”	”	Sketches.
Nantes.	Museum.	Officer of Chasseurs of the Guard. (A study for the Louvre picture.)
Paris.	Louvre.	The Derby at Epsom. 1821.
”	”	Wounded Cuirassier quitting the field. 1814.
”	”	Head of a Bull-dog.
”	”	Turkish horse in a stable.
”	”	Spanish horse in a stable.
”	”	A Carabineer.
”	”	Stable with five horses.
”	”	The Lime-kiln.
”	”	Officer of the Chasseurs of the Guard. 1812.
”	”	The Raft of the Medusa. 1819.
Rouen.	Museum.	Study of a horse.
”	”	Study of heads of goats.

O.J.D

GERIKE, Samuel Theodor, an historical painter, was born at Spandau in 1665, and studied under Romandon. He was court-painter in Berlin, and is also known by two etchings, 'The Virgin kissing her Son's Body at the Tomb,' and 'John the Baptist in the Wilderness.' He died at Berlin in 1730.

GERINI, Lorenzo di Niccolò, the son of Niccolò di Pietro Gerini, flourished in the 15th century. In the passage leading to the chapel of the Medici in Santa Croce at Florence is a 'Coronation of the Virgin, with attendant Saints,' painted by him in 1410; but his principal work is an altarpiece in San Domenico, Cortona, representing the 'Coronation of the Virgin,' with a predella containing the 'Adoration of the Magi,' signed by Lorenzo in 1440. Little is known about his life or death, but the following works by him are preserved :

Florence.	Academy.	Coronation of the Virgin. 1401. (The central panel of an altar-piece.)
San Gimignano.	Gallery.	Glorification of St. Bartholomew. 1401.
”	”	Virgin and Child.
”	”	Four scenes from the lives of SS. Fina and Gregory.

GERINI, Niccolò di Pietro, who flourished in the closing years of the 14th century, probably received his early instruction from Taddeo Gaddi, but afterwards became the pupil and assistant of Spinello d'Arezzo. His earliest existing work is a series of frescoes representing scenes from the 'Passion,' with the 'Resurrection,' the 'Noli me tangere,' the 'Ascension,' and the 'Descent of the Holy Ghost,' in the convent of San Francesco, Pisa, which are signed by him and dated 1392. At Prato, in the convent of San Francesco, is likewise a series of frescoes by Niccolò, representing scenes from the life of St. Matthew, and other subjects from the New Testament. At San Bonaventura he painted scenes from the Passion, of which but fragments remain. The sacristy of the church of Santa Croce, Florence, contains frescoes that are assigned to this artist. His latest known work is dated 1401. It is the right side of an altar-piece in three compartments, preserved in the Academy at Florence, and contains the figures of 'St. Peter, St. John the Evangelist, St. James, and St. Benedict.' The central panel contains the 'Coronation of the Virgin,' by his son Lorenzo, whilst the left side consists of figures of Saints by Spinello Aretino. An 'Entombment,' likewise in the Florence Academy, assigned to Taddeo Gaddi, is by Crowe and Cavalcaselle ascribed to Niccolò di Pietro Gerini.

GERINO da PISTOJA, a native of Pistoja, was, according to Vasari, a friend of Pinturicchio and a follower of Vannucci. His earliest recorded work was the 'Virgin of Succour' at Sant' Agostino in Borgo San Sepolcro, where also are some frescoes by the same artist. In 1505 he was employed in the cathedral of his native city, and in 1509 he furnished for the church of San Pietro Maggiore an altar-piece of the 'Virgin and Child, with Saints.' About 1513 he was labouring in the Convent of San Luchese, near Poggibonsi, and two scenes from the life of Christ, signed and dated, are preserved in a refectory. His later works, a fresco of 'St. Agatha and St. Eulalia' in San Paolo, a 'Coronation of the Virgin' in the Palazzo della Communità, Pistoja, and the 'Virgin with Saints,' of 1529, originally in the Convento di Sala at Pistoja, and now in the

Uffizi Gallery at Florence, are decidedly inferior to his earlier works.

GERMAIN, Louis, a French engraver, was born in Paris in 1733. There are by him some spirited etchings of the 'Ruins of Pæstum,' published in 1769, from the designs of Dumont.

GERMAN LLORENTE, Bernardo, a Spanish portrait painter, the son of an obscure artist, was born at Seville in 1685. He studied under Cristobal Lopez, whom he soon surpassed; and upon Philip V. visiting Seville, he was made choice of to paint the portrait of the Infant, Don Philip, in the execution of which he gave such satisfaction, that he became the favourite painter of the court. He, however, refused the offer of the post of court painter, and preferred, though in the prime of life, to betake himself to the seclusion of a hermitage, in which he pursued his art in accordance with his own simple taste. He was called 'Pintor de las Pastoras,' because he painted many of his Virgins in the attire of shepherdesses, one of the best specimens of which adorned the chapel of St. John Nepomuk in the church of San Ildefonso. He gave to his heads so much grace, sweetness, and relief, that many were sold as the work of Murillo, and pass for such out of Spain. At the latter part of his life, for the purpose of increasing the force of his chiaroscuro, he darkened his pictures with a kind of brown varnish, which was very detrimental, as it made them almost unintelligible. He died at Seville in 1757. The following works by him may be mentioned:

| Madrid. | Gallery. | The Virgin as a Shepherdess. |
| „ | Merced Calzada. | The Virgin with the dead Body of Christ. |

GERMYN, Simon, a native of Dordrecht, born in 1650, was a scholar of G. Schalcken, whose manner he for some time followed; he afterwards studied under Ludowyk Smits, called Hartcamp, who instructed him in his peculiar manner of painting fruit; but his productions in that way are not much esteemed. He next turned his attention to landscape painting, which he practised till his death, in 1719.

GEROLA, Antonio. See Giarola.

GERON, Matthias, a painter and wood-engraver of Lauingen in Bavaria, is known by a picture of the 'Siege of Lauingen by Charles V.,' dated 1551, and also by the large tapestry in Neuburg, representing the 'Expedition of the Count Palatine Otto,' and the paintings of the 'History of Paris' and the 'Destruction of Troy,' executed in 1540, in the gallery of Duke Litta. Some woodcuts in a Missal for the use of the diocese of Augsburg, printed in 1555, are also attributed to him, and it is judged from them that he was a pupil of Hans Burgkmair. His best wood-cuts are 'Christ on the Cross,' and the 'Deposition from the Cross.'

GERRIT van HAARLEM. See Haarlem.

GERRIT van SINT JANS. See David, Gheerardt.

GERST, Johann Karl Jakob, a painter of landscapes and of theatrical scenes, was born at Berlin in 1792, and was in 1818 appointed royal decorative painter in that city, where he died in 1854. He executed several of the grand designs of Schinkel, as scenes for the 'Zauberflöte,' 'Nurmahal,' 'Fernando Cortez,' &c., as well as a host of splendid original decorations for operas, ballets, and plays.

GERTNER, Johan Vilhelm, a Danish portrait painter, etcher, and lithographer, was born at Nyboder in 1818. He studied at Copenhagen, but afterwards travelled a great deal. Among his portraits, which are much esteemed, are those of King Frederick VII., Count von Frysenberg, Thorvaldsen, Dahl, Eckersberg, and Count Moltke. At first Gertner painted also landscapes and interiors, and his earliest important work was 'A Shepherd driving a Flock of Sheep,' painted in 1839, and now in the Copenhagen Gallery. He died at Copenhagen in 1819.

GESELSCHAP, Eduard, a genre and historical painter, was born in 1814 at Amsterdam, where his parents had taken refuge from the storming of Wesel, their native place. Upon their return to Wesel, Eduard obtained his first lessons in drawing from a painter named Welsch. In 1831 he settled in Düsseldorf, and attended the Academy there from 1834 to 1841, receiving the instructions of Schadow. He died after many years' illness at Düsseldorf in 1878. Many of his pictures have been engraved by Martinet, Fritz Verner, and others. Among them may be named:

Faust in his Study.
The Bride at the Grave of her Lover.
Götz von Berlichingen before the Council.
Valentine's Death.
Romeo and Juliet in the Vault.
The Burial of Christ.
The Discovery of the dead body of Gustavus Adolphus. 1848.
The Eve of St. Nicholas. 1852.
The Eve of St. Martin.
The Grandmother's Picture Bible.
Old Woman at the Spinning Wheel.

GESSI, Ercole and Giovanni Battista del. See Ruggieri.

GESSI, Francesco, was born at Bologna in 1588. He studied under D. Calvaert and Cremonini, and was afterwards one of the ablest scholars of Guido Reni, so that he obtained the name of a second Guido, and was employed by that master to finish many of his pictures. He possessed a vivacity of genius, and a facility of execution, which are said by Lanzi to have excited the jealousy of his master. His 'Assumption' in the church of La Morte at Bologna; his 'Martyrdom of St. Catharine,' in the church of that Saint; and, above all, his 'St. Francis,' at the Nunziata, have frequently been mistaken for the works of Guido. In later years he left Guido, and founded a school of his own, but his want of application impaired his genius, so that his works of this period are very indifferent. There are, however, several early pictures by him in the churches at Bologna, which are greatly admired, such as his picture of 'St. Charles Borromeo interceding for the Plague-stricken,' in the church of La Compagnia de' Poveri; 'St. Anthony of Padua,' in Santa Maria delle Muratelle; and the 'Descent of the Holy Ghost,' at the Cappuccini. He died at Bologna in 1649. The following pictures by him are in public galleries:

Bologna.	Pinacoteca.	St. Francis of Assisi receiving the Stigmata.
„	„	The Madonna and Child.
„	„	Christ praying to the East.
„	„	The Holy Family with two Angels.
„	„	St. Bonaventura.
„	„	Madonna and Child, with Angels.
Dresden.	Gallery.	A Magdalen.
Madrid.	Gallery.	Cupid.
Milan.	Brera.	Madonna and Child, with Saints.
Modena.	Estense Gal.	St. Francis.
Stockholm.	Gallery.	Christ as a Child.
		Christ with the Crown of Thorns.
Stuttgart.	Gallery.	Diana and Actæon.
Vienna.	Gallery.	Morpheus appearing to Halcyon.

233

GESSNER, KONRAD, a painter and etcher of horses and battle-pieces, born at Zurich in 1764, was the elder son of Salomon Gessner. After studying first at home, and then under Landolt and J. H. Wüst, he went in 1784 to the Dresden Academy, where he received the instructions of Graff and Zingg, and where he exhibited his first large battle-piece in 1785. After a brief term at home, he proceeded in 1787 to Italy, but on his father's death in the following year he once more returned to Zurich, where he remained till 1796, when he proceeded to England, and continued successfully working here till 1804. He again returned home, and prosecuted his experiments in etching upon stone, which he had commenced in England with Senefelder. He died in 1826. Among his best etchings are those of 'A Riding Horse at the Water-trough,' 'Horses at a Manger,' and 'A Dragoon leading a Horse.' In the South Kensington Museum are two water-colour drawings by him, 'Horses at a Pool,' and 'Soldiers playing at Cards in a Stable.'

GESSNER, SALOMON, was born at Zurich in 1730, and died in 1788. He is well known to the literary world by his 'Death of Abel,' and other poetical works. His paintings, which are mostly in water-colours, are in various European countries. He etched several plates of ornaments for his 'Death of Abel' and his 'Pastorals,' and over three hundred by him are known. He practised art as an amateur till he was thirty, when he took to it as a profession, studying nature, and engravings from the works of Claude and Poussin. He also executed several landscapes in a very pleasing and finished style.

GESTELE, MARCUS VAN, a native of the Netherlands, flourished in the first half of the 15th century. In conjunction with Van Coudenberghe he painted for the church of Roselede, and in 1485 an altar-piece for the church of St. Martin at Courtrai.

GEUZENDAM, G. J., a native of Pekel-A, a village in the province of Gröningen, received his education from G. de San in Gröningen, where he established himself from 1801 to 1811 as a miniature portrait painter. After that time he travelled in Russia for a short time, and died shortly after his return to his own country, either at Deventer or at Zutphen, after 1815.

GEYER, ALEXIUS, landscape painter, was born at Berlin in 1826, and studied in the academies of Berlin, Munich, and Dresden. He worked for some years in Rome and Paris, and was patronized by King Otho of Greece. He painted a number of large water-colours for the Archæological Museum at Berlin, and also worked for King Frederick William IV. of Prussia. He died in 1883.

GEYER, JOHANN, a genre and historical painter, was born at Augsburg in 1807, and originally brought up as a cartwright. He, however, attended the school of the higher arts in that city, and in 1826 went to the Munich Academy, where he studied under Clemens Zimmermann. He then travelled in Belgium and France, and in 1833 was appointed professor of figure drawing at the Augsburg Polytechnic School. He died at Augsburg in 1875. Among the best of his works, in which he was fond of introducing the costume of the reign of Louis XIV., the following may be mentioned :

The Night Watchman.
The Emperor Louis committing himself to the Protection of Augsburg. (*Augsburg Town-hall.*) 1844.
Capture of a Patrician. (*Bremen Art Coll.*) 1863.

234

Opening the Will. (*Bremen Art Coll.*) 1857.
Reception of a Prince. (*Hanover Gallery.*)
Götz von Berlichingen in Heilbronn. (*Erfurt Art Coll.*) 1859.
Rehearsal for a Concert. (*Leipsic Museum.*)
Interior of a Menagerie. (*The same.*)
Concilium Medicum. (*Munich Gallery.*)
End of a Bal Masqué. (*The same.*)
Christening Feast.
Betrothal.

GEYN, G. D., (or GEIJN,) an obscure Flemish engraver, who flourished from 1640 to 1650, was principally employed in engraving book ornaments for the booksellers, in which he attempted a humble imitation of the style of Paul Pontius. Among other prints by him is the portrait of Carolus Aleaspinæus.

GEYSER, CHRISTIAN GOTTLIEB, an engraver, was born at Görlitz in 1740. He executed several plates for different works, among which are the vignettes in Heyne's edition of Virgil, after Fiorillo, and in Hinchfeld's 'Theory of Gardening.' He died at Leipsic in 1803. His son, CHRISTIAN GOTTLIEB, born at Leipsic in 1772, was also an engraver.

GFALL, ANTON, was born at Kaunserthal in the Tyrol, in 1725, and educated first at the Imperial Academy of Vienna, and afterwards under Antonio Galli and Servandoni. He executed historical pictures in oil and fresco, but was especially successful in architectural and decorative painting. He died at Vienna in 1770.

GHANDINI, ALESSANDRO, was a wood-engraver, who worked for Andrea Andreani at Rome about 1610. One of his productions (marked *A. G.*) is a chiaroscuro of two blocks, representing 'St. Catharine.'

GHEDINI, GIUSEPPE, was born at Ficarolo in 1707, and was a scholar of Giacomo Parolini. There are several of his works in the churches at Ferrara. In Santa Cattarina da Siena is a picture by him of 'St. Lucy;' in San Leonardo, 'The Martyrdom of St. Catharine;' in Corpus Domini, 'The Annunciation,' and 'The Death of St. Joseph;' and in the refectory of the monastery of Santa Maria degli Angeli, his principal work, representing 'The Multiplication of the Loaves,' painted in 1755. He died in 1791.

GHEERAERTS, MARC. See GEERARTS.

GHEIN, DE. See DE GHEYN.

GHENDT, EMANUEL JEAN NEPOMUCÈNE DE. See DE GHENDT.

GHENT, GERHARD OF, a pupil of Hans Memlinc, was engaged in 1479 in assisting his instructor upon the miniatures for a large prayer-book now in the Library of St. Mark at Venice.

GHENT, JOSSE, or JUSTUS OF, who was born at Ghent in 1410, and flourished up to the last quarter of the century, was probably a scholar of the Van Eycks. He is supposed to have assisted those masters in some of their most celebrated pictures ; and Waagen is of opinion that 'The Last Judgment' in the church of St. Mary at Dantzic is by him, though long held by connoisseurs to be the work of Jan van Eyck. This picture is ranked by Kugler, who has given a very full description of it, among the greatest masterpieces of art. Kugler, however, does not say that it is by Justus of Ghent; he speaks only of 'The Communion' in the church of Sant' Agata at Urbino, and a small picture in the collection of M. van Huyvetter at Ghent, of 'The Finding of the Cross, and its Verification by the raising of a dead woman to life.' The picture at Urbino was probably finished in 1475, as Justus was paid in that year the sum of 300 florins, by the brotherhood of the 'Corpo di Cristo,' for whom it was originally painted. The series of 'Poets,' 'Philosophers,' and 'Doctors' in the library of the Duke Federigo of Urbino are probably his, but there is much uncertainty about the painters of this era. The late Sir Charles Eastlake possessed a picture by this artist of 'The Burial of Bishop Hubertus;' and a 'Last Supper' is in the church of the Lion at St. Petersburg.

GHERARDI, ANTONIO, who was born at Rieti in 1664, and died at Rome in 1702, was a pupil of P. F. Mola, and afterwards of Pietro da Cortona. He painted for various churches in Rome, and has also left six etchings of 'The Torture of St. Martina.'

GHERARDI, CRISTOFANO, called DOCENO, born at Borgo San Sepolcro in 1500, was a disciple of Raffaellino dal Colle. He went to Florence, where he became acquainted with Giorgio Vasari, with whom he remained on friendly terms until his death. He excelled particularly in fresco, and assisted Vasari in many of his most considerable works. There are several grotesque subjects by him in the Casa Vitelli. Of his oil paintings the principal are, 'The Visitation of the Virgin to St. Elizabeth,' in the church of San Domenico at Città di Castello; and his picture of 'Santa Maria del Popolo,' at Perugia, painted in conjunction with Lattanzio della Marca. In 1539 Vasari induced him to go to Bologna, where he assisted in painting three altar-pieces for San Michele in Bosco. He also assisted Vasari in his fresco paintings for the brotherhood of the Scalza at Venice. He died at Borgo San Sepolcro in 1556, whilst in the course of an engagement for assisting Vasari with the frescoes for the ducal palace at Florence.

GHERARDI, FILIPPO, born at Lucca in 1643, studied under Pietro da Cortona, and worked with Giovanni Coli at several large paintings. His work is so similar to that of Coli, that it is hard to distinguish one from the other. Pietro da Cortona invited him back to Rome, to assist him in painting the cupola of Santa Maria in Campitelli. In the Colonna Gallery are two fine pictures by him of 'The Battle of Lepanto,' and 'The Triumph of Marc Antonio Colonna.' There are several pictures by him in the churches at Lucca, where he died in 1704.

GHERARDINI, ALESSANDRO, born at Florence in 1655, was a scholar of Alessandro Rosi. He proved a distinguished painter of history, both in oil and in fresco. In the Monastery of the Augustines at Florence, is a fine picture by this painter of 'The Crucifixion;' and in the Casa Orlandini, a subject from the life of Alexander the Great. He died in 1723.

GHERARDINI, MELCHIORRE. See GERARDINI.

GHERARDINI, STEFANO, was a bamboccia painter of Bologna, who studied under Giuseppe Gambarini, and died in 1775.

GHERARDINI, TOMMASO, born at Florence in 1715, was a pupil of Vincenzo Meucci. Three masterpieces by him are in the Vienna Gallery —'An Offering in Honour of Pan,' 'Victory and Fame upon a Triumphal Car,' and a 'Triumphal Procession of Ariadne.' He died at Florence in 1797.

GHERARDO, one of the best Florentine miniature painters, was employed by Lorenzo the Magnificent, for whom he worked in mosaic in conjunction with Ghirlandaio in the cathedral of Florence, and by Matthias Corvinus, King of Hungary, whose Bible, illuminated by him, is in the library of the Vatican, and is a lasting memorial of the excellence of Gherardo's art. A Missal of the year 1494, in the Laurentian Library at Florence, and a Breviary in the National Library in Paris, are also ascribed to him. In the Bologna Gallery is a picture of the 'Marriage of St. Catharine.'

GHERINGH, ANTONIUS, was a Flemish painter of the 17th century. He decorated churches in the Renaissance style, and pictures of his may be seen in the Dresden and Vienna Galleries. He was made free of the Guild of St. Luke in 1662, and died at Antwerp in 1667 or 1668. In the Munich Gallery is a picture of the 'Interior of the Jesuit Church at Antwerp,' with the date 1663.

GHERWETT, —— VAN, a pupil of Rembrandt, lived in the middle of the 17th century. In the Munich Gallery is a picture by this artist of 'Abraham on the point of sacrificing Isaac.'

GHERZO, DOMENICO, commonly known as DOMENICO DI BARTOLO, was born at Asciano in the early part of the 15th century. He belongs to the decline of Sienese art. The frescoes which he executed, in 1435-40, in the sacristy of the cathedral of Siena, have perished; but a weak production, illustrating various works of mercy in connection with the institution, in the hospital of Santa Maria della Scala, Siena, still exists, with the exception of the Angel of Mercy. This work was painted between 1440 and 1444, and after that date nothing further is recorded of him. His death appears to have occurred in 1449. The galleries of Berlin, Bruges, Perugia, Rouen, and Siena have works ascribed to Domenico di Bartolo.

GHEYN, DE. See DE GHEYN.

GHEYSELS, PEETER. See GYSELS.

GHEZZI, GIUSEPPE, son of Sebastiano Ghezzi, was born in 1634 in the Comunanza, near Ascoli, and was for some time instructed by his father; but he afterwards went to Rome, where he studied the works of Pietro da Cortona, whose style he adopted. He was employed and highly esteemed by Pope Clement XI., and at the time of his death, in 1721, was secretary to the Academy of St. Luke at Rome.

GHEZZI, PIER LEONE, who was born at Rome in 1674, was the son of Giuseppe Ghezzi, and studied under his father, whom he surpassed. In conjunction with L. Garzi, F. Trevisani, and B. Luti, he was employed by Benedict XIV. to paint 'The Prophets' in San Giovanni in Laterano, and in other works. He was also employed in several considerable works by the Duke of Parma, who conferred on him the order of the Golden Spur. But he was most celebrated for his talent in caricature, and his works of that description are frequently found in the collections at Rome, where he died in 1755. There are by him a few etchings, executed in a clear, neat style, from his own designs, and after the works of his father. Among them are:

The Virgin and Infant Jesus; *after Giuseppe Ghezzi* 1700.

Portrait of the Abbate Pietro Palatio.

Portrait of Nicola Zabaglia, engineer of St. Peter's.

GHEZZI, SEBASTIANO, was born in the Comunanza, near Ascoli, and flourished about the year 1634. He was a scholar of Guercino, and painted historical subjects with some success. At the Barefooted Augustines at Monsammartino, there is a fine picture by him of 'St. Francis receiving the Stigmata.'

GHEZZO, GUIDONE DA. See SIENA.

GHIRLANDAIO. See BIGORDI.

GHISI, ADAMO. See SCULPTORE.

GHISI, DIANA. See SCULPTORE.

GHISI, GIORGIO, called GIORGIO MANTOVANO, was born at Mantua in 1520, and died in the same city in 1582. He was the elder brother of Teodoro Ghisi, and like him a pupil of Giulio Romano. He became one of the chief artists in damascene work. He drew the nude very correctly, and excelled more particularly in the depicting of hands and feet, but his representations are all very much alike, and his style is very monotonous. This defect is particularly discernible in his immense print of the 'Last Judgment,' after Michelangelo. His engravings, especially those after the works of Raphael and Michelangelo, approach in the excellence of their drawing and execution those of Marc-Antonio. They are generally signed with his name, or marked with the cipher **GAF. NAT**. The following are his principal plates:

Portrait of Pope Julius II.; *after Raphael.*
The Holy Family, half-lengths; *after the same.*
The School of Athens; *after the same.* Two sheets.
The Dispute of the Sacrament; *after the same.*
An emblematical subject; sometimes called 'Raphael's Dream,' and sometimes 'The Melancholy of Michelangelo.' It represents an old man looking at a shipwrecked vessel, whilst a nymph appears approaching him; in the background are seen several horrible and fantastical figures. It is inscribed *Raphelis Vrbinatis inventum, &c.,* and on a tablet, *Georgius Ghisi Mant. F.* 1561.
The Prophets and Sibyls; after the paintings by *Michelangelo,* in the Sistine Chapel. Six large plates.
The Last Judgment; *after the same.* Ten large plates.
An allegorical subject, representing the Birth of a Prince of the House of Gonzaga; *after Giulio Romano.* 1568.
Cupid and Psyche crowned by Hymen; *after the same.*
The Birth of Memnon; *after the same;* very fine.
Cephalus and Procris; *after the same.*
The Interview between Hannibal and Scipio; *after the same.*
Regulus led to death by the Carthaginians; *after the same.*
Regulus shut up in the Tun; *after the same.*
Venus in the Forge of Vulcan, sharpening the Arrows of Cupid; *after Perino del Vaga.*
Venus and Mars; *after Raffaello Motta.*
An allegorical subject, representing a Judge on his Tribunal, with an Ass's Ears; *after Luca Penni.*
Endymion carrying Diana to the Chase on his shoulders; *after the same.*
Hercules conquering the Hydra; *after Giovanni Battista Sculptore.*
The Judgment of Paris; *after the same.*
The Siege of Troy; *after the same.*
The Taking of Troy; *after the same.*
A print representing tombs, skeletons, &c., called 'The Resurrection of the Dry Bones;' *after the same.* 1554.
Venus and Adonis; *after Teodoro Ghisi.*
Angelica and Medora; *after the same.*
The Birth of the Virgin; *after B. Spranger.*
The Trinity; *after his own design.* 1576.
The Adoration of the Shepherds; *after Angelo Bronzino;* in two sheets. 1554.
The Last Supper; *after Lambert Lombard.*
The Visitation of the Virgin to St. Elizabeth; *after his own design.*
The Crucifixion; *after the same.*

GHISI, GIOVANNI BATTISTA. See SCULPTORE.

236

GHISI, TEODORO, called TEODORO MANTOVANO, was born at Mantua in 1536. He was the younger brother of Giorgio Ghisi, and had the advantage of being educated under Giulio Romano, one of the ablest of whose scholars he was. After the death of Giulio, he was selected by the Duke of Mantua to complete the works which were left unfinished by that great master. He died at Mantua in 1601.

GHISLANDI, DOMENICO, was a native of Bergamo, who flourished about the year 1662. He excelled in painting architectural and perspective views in fresco; though he occasionally painted historical subjects. Tassi mentions some pictures of the life and miracles of St. Francis of Paola by him, in the cloisters of the Padri Minimi at Bergamo; and in the Palazzo Terzi is a saloon ornamented with architecture, in which the figures are painted by Giacomo Barbella.

GHISLANDI, Fra VITTORE, called 'Il Frate PAOLOTTO,' the son of Domenico Ghislandi, was born at San Leonardo, in the Bergamese state, in 1655. He was a scholar of Sebastiano Bombelli, but he soon went to Venice, where he in 1675 entered the convent of St. Francis of Paola, and became a most accomplished portrait painter. He died at Venice in 1743. In the Rothan Gallery there is by him a lifelike picture of a young Bergamese.

GHISOLFI, GIOVANNI, (or GRISOLFI,) born at Milan in 1632, was a pupil of Salvator Rosa. There are two architectural compositions of 'Ruins' by him in the National Gallery of Scotland. His 'Marius among the Ruins of Carthage,' and several of his decorative pictures are in the Dresden Gallery. He died at Milan in 1683.

GHISONI, FERMO. See GUISONI.

GHISSI, FRANCESCUCCIO, was living at Fabriano in the 14th century, and is the author of an altarpiece of the 'Virgin and Child,' with rays issuing from the person of the Virgin, which illuminate the darkness, symbolised by a crescent moon and stars on a dark blue background; it is dated 1374, and is now in the Augustine church of San Salvatore at Monte Giorgio. The Fornari collection at Fabriano possesses a 'Virgin and Child, between two kneeling Angels,' which is signed by him in 1395. Other examples by this artist may be seen in the church of San Domenico at Fermo; at Ascoli; and in the Museo Cristiano at Rome.

GHISSONI, OTTAVIO, was a native of Siena, who at an early age went to Rome, where he studied several years, chiefly under Cherubino Alberti. In 1610 he visited Genoa, and was for some time a scholar of Ventura Salimbeni. He painted some pictures in fresco for the public edifices.

GHITTI, POMPEO, was born at Marone, a small town near Brescia, in 1631. He was first a scholar of Ottavio Amigoni, but afterwards went to Milan, where he studied five years under Giovanni Battista Discepoli, called 'Lo Zoppo di Lugano,' to whom he subsequently became assistant. His death is assigned to the year 1703, though it is stated that one of his works bears the date 1704. Four etchings by him are known; they are, 'The Holy Family;' 'The Rest in Egypt,' after Discepoli; 'The Crowning with Thorns,' after Titian; and 'St. Maurus healing the Sick.'

GHUENS, BOUDEWYN, (GHEENS, or GEENS,) a Flemish painter, born at Mechlin in 1599, was a son of Jan Ghuens, called 'Prins.' He was still living in 1672.

GHUENS, Jacob, a native of Mechlin, was a painter who flourished about 1558.

GHUENS, Jan, a native of Mechlin, painted in 1528 a picture of 'Christ on the Cross,' surrounded by different figures.

GHUENS, Jan, called 'Prins,' or 'Prinske' (the 'Little Prince'), flourished at the end of the 16th and beginning of the 17th century. The Museum at Mechlin has a picture by this artist of the 'Siege of Lierre' in 1595. In 1596 he executed a strategical plan of Mechlin and its surroundings. He died at Mechlin after 1617.

GIACCHINETTI GONZALEZ, Juan, called Il Borgognone dalle Teste, a Spanish portrait painter, was born at Madrid about 1630. It is not known by whom he was instructed, but his best studies were from the works of Titian. He excelled in portrait painting, and from his extraordinary talent in that branch, acquired the name of 'Il Borgognone dalle Teste.' About the middle of his life he went to Italy, and painted many portraits at Brescia and Bergamo. He died at the latter city in 1696.

GIACHETTO. See Jaquet.

GIALDISI, Francesco, or Giovanni. According to Zaist, in his 'Notizie de' Pittori Cremonesi,' this painter was of Parma, but flourished at Cremona about the year 1720. He excelled in painting flowers and fruit, and particularly in his pictures of still-life, such as carpets, with musical instruments, books, &c., which he represented with a fidelity of form and a truth of colour which are admirable.

GIAMBONO. See Boni, Michele Giovanni.

GIAMPICCOLI, Giuliano, an Italian engraver, was born at Venice in 1698. He was the nephew of Marco Ricci, and his style renders it probable that he was brought up in the school of Wagner. He was still living in 1765. He engraved several plates after Marco Ricci and others, among which are the following:

A set of twelve Landscapes, with a frontispiece; *after Marco Ricci.*
A set of four pretty Pastoral Subjects.
A set of four Landscapes; *after M. Ricci and F. Zuccarelli.*

GIANCARLI, Polifilo. See Zancarli.

GIANNETTI, Filippo, was a landscape painter of Messina, who studied under the Dutch painter Casembroodt. He excelled his master in the greatness of his designs, but was not his equal in execution. He painted so quickly that he was called 'The "Fa presto" of Landscape Painters.' He died at Naples in 1702.

GIANNICOLA DI PAOLO MANNI. See Manni.

GIANNUZZI, Giulio dei. See Dei Giannuzzi.

GIANOLI, Pietro Francesco, born at Campertogno about 1620, was a pupil of Antonio Rossi. His portrait is in the Brera at Milan, where he died about 1690.

GIAQUINTO, Corrado. See Corrado.

GIAROLA, Antonio, (or Gerola,) called 'Il Cavaliere Coppa,' was born at Verona in 1595, and studied at Bologna under Guido and Albani. In the church of San Bernardo at Bologna is a picture by him of 'St. Maurus kneeling before the Virgin and Infant;' but he is seen to more advantage in his 'Magdalen in the Desert,' in the church of the Padri Servi. In the refectory of the seminary at Verona is a fine picture by Giarola of 'Christ with the Disciples at Emmaus.' His pictures are crowded with figures. He died in 1665.

GIAROLA, Giovanni, a painter of Reggio, who died in 1557, is said to have been a pupil of Correggio. Wall-pictures of his are still to be seen in the Donelli Palace at Reggio.

GIBB, Robert, a Scottish landscape painter, was born at Dundee about the beginning of the 19th century, and on the formation of the Royal Scottish Academy in 1830, was elected one of its first members. He died in 1837. The following works by him are in the National Gallery of Scotland:

Craigmillar Castle.   Borthwick Castle.

GIBBON, Benjamin Phelps, a line-engraver, was born in 1802. He was the son of the vicar of Penally, Pembrokeshire, and after having been educated at the Clergy Orphan School, learned engraving under Scriven and J. H. Robinson. He died in London in 1851. Amongst his plates after Sir Edwin Landseer are:

The Twa Dogs.   Suspense.   Jack in Office.   A Fireside Party.   The Highland Shepherd's Home.   The Shepherd's Chief Mourner.   The Shepherd's Grave. There's no Place like Home.   Roebuck and Hounds.

GIBELIN, Esprit Antoine, a French historical painter, was born at Aix in 1739. He studied under Arnulfi at Florence, and resided for a long time in Italy, receiving in 1768 a prize from the Academy of Parma. He returned to France in 1771, and revived fresco painting in monochrome. The frescoes decorating the School of Medicine in Paris are by him. He died at Aix in 1813. There is in the Museum of Aix a picture by him entitled, 'Post equitem sedet atra cura.'

GIBERTONI, Paolo, was a native of Modena, who flourished about the year 1760. He resided chiefly at Lucca, and excelled in grotesque subjects in fresco, in which he introduced little animals of every description. He also painted landscapes.

GIBOY, ——, a French engraver, who flourished from 1810 to 1824, executed vignettes for Tasso's 'Gerusalemme liberata,' after Perrenot, as well as plates for the work of De Clarac on the Louvre. The following may also be mentioned:

Gaspard l'Avisé; *after Horace Vernet.*
The Year, drawn by the twelve months; *after Perrenot.*

GIBSON, David Cooke, a Scottish genre painter, was born at Edinburgh in 1827. He was at first taught by his father, who died early. He then, by his own exertions, was enabled to enter the schools of the Royal Scottish Academy, and afterwards to study in London, Belgium, and Paris. His works first appeared at the Royal Academy in 1855, and he was showing much promise, when, after a visit to Spain, he died in London in 1856. His exhibited pictures were:

The Little Stranger, 1855.   Rustic Education, 1855.
Un Corrillo Andaluz, 1856.   Gipsies of Seville, 1857.

GIBSON, Edward, an English portrait painter of the 17th century, was the son, or near relative, of Richard Gibson the Dwarf, and was also his pupil. He died in his 33rd year.

GIBSON, John, a Scottish portrait painter, who died in 1852 from the effects of a fatal accident. He exhibited largely at the West of Scotland Academy.

GIBSON, Patrick, a Scottish landscape painter, was born at Edinburgh in 1782. He received a good general education, and then studied under Nasmyth, and in the Trustees' Academy. He did much literary work, contributing to the 'Encyclopædia Edinensis,' the 'Edinburgh Encyclopædia,' the 'Edinburgh Annual Register,' and the 'New Edinburgh Review.' In 1818 he published a volume of etchings of Edinburgh. He left Edinburgh in

1824, and settled as a teacher at Dollar, where he died in 1829. His works are in the classic style, and there is a characteristic Landscape composition by him in the National Gallery of Scotland.

GIBSON, RICHARD, usually called "The Dwarf," from his diminutive size, being only three feet ten inches in height, was born in 1615, probably in Cumberland. He was, when a boy, page to a lady at Mortlake, who, perceiving in him a disposition for art, placed him under the care of Franz Cleyn, under whom he made considerable progress. His talent attracted the notice of King Charles I., who made him one of his pages. He was married to a little lady of his own height, named Anne Shepherd, and their marriage was celebrated in the presence of Charles I. and his Queen, who ordered a diamond ring for the bride. The union of this diminutive couple was commemorated by Waller in one of his prettiest poems. After the death of the king Gibson was taken under the protection of Philip, Earl of Pembroke, and is said to have painted the portrait of Oliver Cromwell several times. When Sir Peter Lely visited England, Gibson improved himself greatly by copying the portraits of that master; and he rose into such repute that he was sent to Holland to teach the Princess Mary to draw, and had also the honour of instructing Queen Anne. He lived to the age of 75, and died in 1690. His widow died in 1709, at the age of 89. They had nine children, five of whom lived to grow up to the ordinary stature of mankind.

GIBSON, SUSAN PENELOPE, a miniature painter, the daughter of Richard Gibson the Dwarf, was born in 1653, and died in 1700. There is a portrait of Bishop Burnet by her.

GIBSON, THOMAS, a portrait painter, was born about 1680. His art was good, and he had a large practice. Highmore said that Thornhill was much indebted to him. He retired to Oxford in 1730, but returned again to London, where he died in 1751. Amongst his works are:

Flamstead, the astronomer. (*Royal Society, London.*)
Vertue, the engraver. (*Society of Antiquaries, London.*)
Archbishop Wake. (*National Portrait Gallery.*)

GIBSON, WILLIAM, a miniature painter, born in 1644, was a nephew of Richard Gibson the Dwarf, under whom and Lely he studied. He made many copies of the latter's works, and purchased part of his collection. He died in 1702.

GIDE, THÉOPHILE, French painter; born in Paris, August 15, 1822; pupil of Delaroche and Cogniet; devoted himself to historical and genre painting. He excelled in the portrayal of Italian convent life, as such pictures as 'Le Réfectoire,' 'Les Adieux au Couvent,' 'Visite du Pape au Couvent de Femmes,' 'Couvent St. Barthélemy à Nice,' and others attest. Of his more famous historical canvases we may mention 'Sully quittant la Cour de Louis XIII.,' 'Coligny sortant du Louvre,' 'Othello raconte ses Combats,' 'Louis XI. en prière,' &c. In 1861 M. Gide obtained a medal of the third class; also medals in 1865 and 1866; and in the last-named year he received the decoration of the Legion of Honour. He died in Paris, November 29, 1890.

GIERYMSKI, MAX, a Polish genre painter, was born at Warsaw in 1846. His father, a military administrative officer, sent him to the Polytechnic School in Pulawy to learn mechanics. In 1863 he took part in the Polish Revolution, and remained till January 1864 an officer of the national troops. He visited the University of Warsaw after peace

238

had been signed, and showed a great inclination for music; but the Governor, General Berg, persuaded him to devote himself to painting, and helped him with an allowance, by which he was enabled to visit the University of Munich, where his great talent was developed under Alexander Wagner and Franz Adam. In 1870 he established a studio of his own. In 1872 he revisited his native land, but had to go to Meran in 1873 on account of his health, which his life as a soldier had greatly impaired; he spent the summer at Reichenhall, and the winter at Rome, but returned to Reichenhall in a worse condition, and died there in 1874. His first picture was 'An Attack by Cossacks.' He afterwards devoted his time to winter scenes, rainy landscapes, moonlight nights, and so forth, all more or less of a melancholy cast. Other well-known pictures by him are:

A Polish Spinning-room.
Duel with Pistols on Horseback.
Jews at the Evening Prayer.
A Visit by Moonlight.
The Meet for the Hunt.
Cossacks in a Country Street.
Hunting in the reign of Louis XIV. (*Berlin National Gallery.*)

GIESMANN, FRIEDRICH, an historical painter, born at Leipsic in 1810, was the son of a sculptor and wood-engraver, and devoted himself to the study of sculpture for a while, but afterwards abandoned it for painting. He took to the depicting of scenes from nature, and in particular of wild beasts from a menagerie; further on he produced portraits. He received the patronage of the King of Saxony during a two years' stay at Dresden, but in 1832 he left that city for Munich, with the intention of devoting himself exclusively to historical painting. He died there in 1847. He executed numerous wall paintings, as well as decorative and encaustic work, and he assisted Schnorr von Karolsfeld in adorning the halls of the new royal residence at Hohenschwangau, where he painted from Schnorr's cartoons five large wall pictures from the lives of Charlemagne, Rudolf of Hapsburg, and Frederick Barbarossa, as well as four friezes from his own designs. Of his easel paintings, 'The Parable of the Prodigal Son' is specially praised.

GIETLEUGEN, JOSSE, a painter and engraver, was a native of Courtrai, who was living in 1545. His original name was Van Gulleghem, but he changed it for some unknown reason. He engraved the wood-cuts for Hadrianus Junius's 'Emblemata,' printed at Antwerp in 1585.

GIFFART, PIERRE, was born in Paris in 1638. He engraved a considerable number of portraits and book ornaments, which are neatly executed with the graver, but without much taste, though his merit was sufficient to procure him admission into the Academy in 1682, and the distinction of engraver to the king. He died in Paris in 1723. The following prints are by him:

PORTRAITS.

Marie Anne Victoire of Bavaria, Dauphiness of France.
Françoise d'Aubigné, Marchioness de Maintenon.
Philip, son of Thomas XIII., Count of Savoy.
Edward, son of Amadeus XV., Count of Savoy.

VARIOUS SUBJECTS.

A set of Medals from the French King's Cabinet.
A set of designs for Chimney-pieces; twenty plates, engraved in conjunction with *Scotin; after Berain.*

GIFFORD, GEORGE, an engraver of portraits, flourished about the year 1640. He was chiefly employed by the booksellers, and his plates are very indifferently executed. Among others, he engraved the following:

Hugh Latimer, Bishop of Worcester.
Sir Edward Marmion.
John Bate; prefixed to his 'Mysteries of Nature,' 1635.

GIFFORD, SANDFORD ROBINSON, an American landscape painter, was born at Greenfield, in Saratoga county, New York, in 1823. He studied art at Hudson, New York, where he was influenced by the works of Thomas Cole, and in the National Academy of Design, New York. In 1850 he visited England and the Continent, and on his return, in 1851, he was elected an Associate of the National Academy, and became a full member three years later. He subsequently, in 1860, started on a journey through parts of Europe, Asia, and Africa, and in 1870 he visited the Rocky Mountains. His works bear ample proof of the results of his travels. He died in New York in 1880. The following are some of his best paintings:

Mount Mansfield. 1869.
Twilight on Mount Hunter. (*Exhibited at Paris in* 1867.)
Morning in the Adirondacks. 1867.
San Giorgio, Venice. 1870. (*Exhibited at Paris in* 1878.)
Fishing Boats on the Adriatic. 1871.
Near Palermo. 1876.
The Ruins of the Parthenon. 1880.
Sunrise on the Matterhorn. 1880.

GIGANTE, GIACINTO, an Italian painter, lithographer, and etcher, born at Naples in 1806, was descended from a family of artists. He was at first a geographer, but studied painting under Pitloo, and then executed water-colour drawings for H. Wolfensberger, etchings of the 'Bay of Naples,' along with Vianelli, and landscape studies in lithography. In 1846 he accompanied the Emperor and Empress of Russia to Sicily, and composed an album of the island, after which he was appointed drawing-master in the family of King Ferdinand II. He died at Naples in 1876. He chiefly produced landscapes and architectural pictures in water-colours, for which he received the principal prize at Brussels. Two of his best works are: 'The Interior of the Treasury of St. Januarius on the Miracle Day' (Gallery of Capodimonte), and 'The Tomb of Giovanni Caracciolo at Carbonara.'

GIGOLA, GIOVANNI BATTISTA, was born at Brescia in 1796, and after studying five years in Rome, where he painted numerous portraits, and further in Paris, became first a miniature, and afterwards an enamel painter. He died at Milan in 1841. He executed miniatures on vellum for 'Gli Amori di Dafne e Cloe,' and Da Porto's 'Giulietta e Romeo,' as well as for Byron's 'Corsair.' The Ambrosian Library at Milan also contains several admired miniatures by him.

GIGOUX, JEAN, French painter; born at Besançon in January 1806; studied in Paris, and exhibited his first pictures at the Salon in 1833. Historical painting was then in vogue, and it was to this that Gigoux accordingly devoted himself. Among his most notable works of this period were, 'La Mort de Léonard da Vinci,' 'Henri IV. et Gabrielle d'Estrées,' 'Antoine et Cléopatre,' 'Héloïse et Abélard,' 'Manon Lescaut,' 'La Veillée d'Austerlitz,' &c. Gigoux was a regular contributor to leading French art exhibitions, and at the close of his career took up portrait-painting again, some studies of girls, charming in their freshness and grace, coming as a veritable surprise from the brush of the veteran, as well as sundry vigorous portraits of Jules Simon, Henner and Bonnat. Gigoux left a valuable collection of pictures, and embodied his art experiences in a volume of souvenirs ('Causeries sur les Artistes de mon Temps, 1885'). He ranks as the last of the romantic school. He died December 10, 1894.

GIL, GERONIMO ANTONIO, a Spanish painter and engraver, born at Zamora in 1732, was a pupil of Tomas Prieto. His works show correct drawing and attention to technical detail. He died at Madrid in 1798.

GILARDI, PIETRO, was born at Milan in 1679, and was instructed in art by Federigo Bianchi, but he afterwards went to Bologna, where he became a scholar of Marc Antonio Franceschini and Giovanni Gioseffo dal Sole. He was successful in historical painting, and especially excelled in large fresco works, his talents being particularly adapted to the embellishment of cupolas, ceilings, and other extensive operations. Such are his frescoes in the refectory of San Vittore at Milan. The year of his death is not recorded, but he was in his best repute from 1700 to 1718. Sassi completed such of his works as were left unfinished at his death.

GILARDINO, MELCHIORRE. See GERARDINI.

GILARTE, MATEO, a Spanish painter, was born at Valencia about 1648. He was a scholar of Francisco Ribalta, and proved an eminent painter of history, both in oil and in fresco, working principally in Murcia, where he formed a great friendship with Juan de Toledo, the battle painter, with whom he worked. In the Madrid Gallery is a picture of the 'Birth of the Virgin.' In the church of Nuestra Señora del Rosario are three large pictures in fresco, representing 'Esther before Ahasuerus,' 'Jacob wrestling with the Angel,' and 'St. Dominic with other Saints.' For the convent of that church he painted the 'Miracle of the Loaves and Fishes.' He died at Murcia in 1700. His daughter, MAGDALENA GILARTE, painted much in his style for the cloisters of Murcia, Toledo, and Madrid.

GILBERT, ARTHUR. See WILLIAMS.

GILBERT, JOHN GRAHAM. See GRAHAM-GILBERT.

GILBERT, JOSEPH FRANCIS, a landscape painter, was born in 1792. He resided at Chichester, and exhibited at the Royal Academy and the British Institution. He contributed to the Westminster Hall competition a picture of 'Edwin and Emma.' He died in 1855. Amongst his works are:

View of East Street, Chichester.
Goodwood Race-course: Priam winning the Gold Cup.
View of the Ruins of Cowdray.

GILBERT, Sir JOHN; this eminent artist was born at Blackheath in 1817. His father was a captain in the Royal East London Militia, who, after the disbanding of his regiment, adopted the calling of an estate agent, and young Gilbert was brought up to the same business. Early in his life, after a very scanty education, he was placed with a firm in Charlotte Row, City of London, as a clerk; but the work was such a drudgery to him, and his interests were so completely on the side of art, that after two years his parents were convinced of their error, and allowed him to select his profession and devote himself to art. From the very earliest years he had sketched with more than ordinary ability, and had taken off prizes repeatedly for his drawings, but he needed education, and on release from the work of the office he set about obtaining it. He failed in his attempt to enter the Academy schools, greatly to his father's disappointment; but he placed himself under George Lance, who had been a pupil of Haydon, and worked for a while in his studio. He also attended evening classes, and filled up every scrap of his time by sketching and by learning from others wherever he could. At the age of nineteen he sent in his first picture for exhibition, a water-colour of the 'Arrest of Lord Hastings,' which was hung at the Society of British Artists in 1836. Two years after that, he was exhibiting at the Royal Academy, and there he exhibited till 1851, when a picture of his, having been badly hung, he declined to send in on the following year, and continued, with the exception of a single exhibit in 1863, his refusal to have anything to do with the Academy. In 1867, however, he was persuaded to return to the Gallery, and from that time to the date of his death he was a constant exhibitor. He became A.R.A. in 1872, and R.A. in 1876, and his works were always great attractions to the annual show at Burlington House. He was elected an Associate of the Old Water-Colour Society as far back in his career as 1852, and in the following year became a full member. In 1871 he was President, and at that time the honour of knight-hood was conferred upon him by Queen Victoria. Many of his works he had kept in his own hands, refusing to part with them on any consideration, and his purpose in such action was revealed in 1893, when, having gathered together a large collection of his pictures, he presented them to the various important art galleries of the country, giving them to the Guildhall Gallery in London, and to the Galleries of Birmingham, Blackburn, Liverpool, and Manchester. His large collection of sketch-books he presented to the Royal Academy. His gifts were received with much acclamation, and the City of London gave him its freedom, he being the first artist upon whom such a signal honour had been conferred. His most popular work was that of an illustrator, and it is in this department of his labours that he has earned undying fame. In 'Punch' and the 'Illustrated London News' his best work can be seen, whilst such books as Mackey's 'Thames,' Knight's 'Shakespeare,' 'Wordsworth,' 'Scott,' 'Cowper,' 'Longfellow,' 'Percy Tales,' 'English Ballads,' and the 'Proverbs of Solomon,' owe much of their interest and delight to the charming and always suitable illustrations which Gilbert drew for them. The extraordinary feature of the whole of his work is that it was not drawn from models. He had so stocked his mind with figures, with ornaments, and with scenes, from his constant habit of sketching upon every occasion, that he could sit down wherever he was and prepare a drawing, which was wonderful in its accuracy and in its dramatic force. All his armour according to one credible account was drawn from a dish-cover which he kept in his studio, most of his vestments from some scraps of velvet and brocade which he had by him, and yet the truth of the work was quite wonderful, and his memory was so extraordinary that his results were seldom at fault. He is said to have painted nearly 450 pictures, but in addition to those, to have executed nearly 40,000 drawings, so that his total output must have been a tremendous one, and can only be accounted for by the fact that he was never idle, and always hard at work, even up to the last few days of his life. His facility, as has been well said, was prodigious, and his work was original, brilliant and full of verve. He was supreme in composition, in depicting movement and in a sense of dignity, and was fond of incident and of historical scenes. His colouring was rich and robust, his drawing sensitive and charming, with a wonderful quality of beauty about it, but there was no repose, no poetry, and but little grandeur in any of his works, and they were to the last strangely sketch-like and curiously lacking in finish. Their vigour is, however, unmistakable, and the characteristics of breadth, robust colour, spirited incident, and buoyant life are never lacking; and although he ignored questions of "tone" and "value," and the deeper problems of atmosphere, and was frankly pictorial and gloried in opulent colour, yet his pictures will ever be popular and noteworthy, and so sound was his craftsmanship that they are likely to perpetuate his fame for many a long year to come. He lived beloved by all who knew him, and died in 1897.

See 'Sir John Gilbert,' by M. H. Spielman, in 'Magazine of Art,' and other articles which appeared soon after his death.　　　　　　　　　　G. C. W.

GILES, JAMES WILLIAM, a Scottish landscape painter, the son of an artist of local reputation in Aberdeen, was born at Glasgow in 1801. After having studied painting under his father, he passed a short time in Italy. In 1830 he was elected a member of the Royal Scottish Academy, and about this time sent several works to the Royal Academy. His pictures chiefly depict Highland scenery, especially fishing, to which sport he was much addicted. A picture by him, 'The Weird Wife,' is in the National Gallery of Scotland. He died at Aberdeen in 1870.

GILFILLAN, JOHN A., a Scottish painter, was in his early life in the Royal Navy. He afterwards devoted himself to art, and from 1830 to 1840 held the appointment of professor of painting in the Andersonian University at Glasgow. He afterwards emigrated to New Zealand, where he died. In the Glasgow Corporation Galleries is a picture of 'Robinson Crusoe landing stores from the Wreck;' and in the South Kensington Museum is a picture of a 'Scotch Loch.'

GILIO, a native of Siena, painted a book-cover, preserved in the Academy of Arts, representing a monk of St. Galgano in a white dress, seated in profile on a chair, dated 1257.

GILIOLI, GIACINTO, a Bolognese painter, born in 1584, was brought up in the school of the Carracci. Of his works at Bologna, the most esteemed are his picture of the 'Death of St. Joseph' in Santa Mattia, and 'David with the Head of Goliath' in San Salvatore. He died in 1665.

GILL, ANDRÉ, a French painter and political caricaturist, was born in October 1840. He studied under Leloir, and at the Académie des Beaux Arts. He exhibited a few portraits, &c., at the Salon, but was best known by his caricatures of notabilities under the Second Empire. He became insane about five years before his death, which took place in 1885.

GILL, CHARLES, a portrait painter, was the son of a pastry-cook at Bath. He became a pupil of Sir Joshua Reynolds, and exhibited a few portraits at the Royal Academy between 1772 and 1819.

GILL, EDMUND, born in Clerkenwell, November 29, 1820. The son of a japanner, he was at first destined to follow his father's trade, but, owing to

SIR JOHN GILBERT

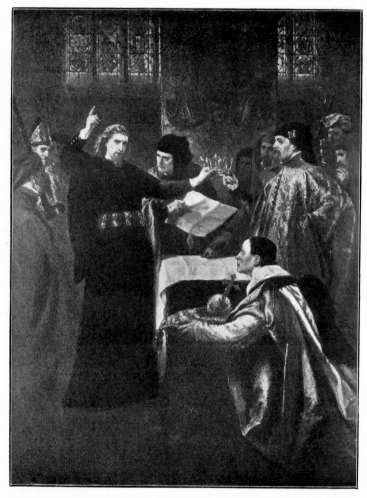

RICHARD II. RESIGNING THE CROWN TO BOLINGBROKE

his marked liking for art, he became a portrait painter, in which capacity he at first established himself with limited success at Ludlow. It would not appear that he received any regular training at the Academy or elsewhere, but great industry served to help his natural sympathies, and he very soon obtained considerable skill in the branches of art he had chosen. At Hereford he found so much favour that a local subscription helped him to undertake landscape-painting in Wales, and afterwards to go to London. His first picture, 'View in Croft Park,' was shown at the British Institution in 1842, and four years later he sent a 'Storm Scene' to the Royal Academy, and was also represented at the Suffolk Street Galleries. To these last-named he was indeed a very frequent contributor, sending in over a hundred and fifty works. His taste led him to paint cascades (hence his nickname "Waterfall Gill") and breaking seas, especially as viewed from lofty cliffs. After a brief illness he died at Hackbridge, Carshalton, on May 14, 1894.

GILLARDINI, MELCHIORRE. See GERARDINI.

GILLBERG, JACOB, a Swedish engraver, was born in Wermland in 1724. He engraved several portraits of distinguished personages of Sweden; and afterwards went to Paris, where he executed several plates in imitation of chalk drawings; among which were some heads after Raphael, and some landscapes engraved jointly with Demarteau. He died in 1793.

GILLBERG, JACOB AXEL, a Swedish miniature painter, the elder son of Jacob Gillberg, was born in Westmanland in 1769. He is known by his equestrian portrait of Charles XIII., and his portraits of Charles XIV. (Bernadotte) and his Queen, after Gérard. The date of his death is not known.

GILLE, JEAN BAPTISTE. See COLSON.

GILLEMANS, JAN PAULO, a fruit and flower painter, born at Antwerp in 1650, was the pupil of Georgius van Son. In 1673, along with his brother, Pieter Matthias, he was made free of the Guild of St. Luke. He then went to Paris, and from there in 1713 to Amsterdam. He is said to have fallen into a canal and been drowned about 1742. There are by him a signed picture in the Museum at Lille, and another in the South Kensington Museum.

GILLEMANS, PIETER MATTHIAS, brother of Jan Paulo, was born at Antwerp, where he also died in 1692. He had a high reputation as a fruit and flower painter.

GILLES OF ANTWERP. See CONGNET.

GILLIES, Miss MARGARET, the daughter of a Scotch merchant settled in London, and niece of Lord Gillies the judge, was born in Throgmorton Street in 1803. Her father having lost his fortune, she lived as a girl under the care of her uncle in Edinburgh, where she enjoyed the society of some of the most notable men of the day, among them Scott, Erskine, and Jeffrey. Determined, however, to earn an honourable livelihood for herself, she resolved to become an artist, and went to Paris to study, where she made the acquaintance of the Scheffers, and worked more or less under their direction. She made her *debut* as a painter of miniatures, and afterwards devoted herself to water-colour drawings of domestic or romantic subjects. In 1852 she was elected an associate of the Water-Colour Society, of which she was the first lady member. With that body she was a constant exhibitor, contributing down to the year before her death, which took place at her house at Hampstead in the spring of 1888.

GILLIG, JAKOB, (or GELLIG,) a Dutch painter, was born at Utrecht about the year 1636, and is stated by Balkema to have died there in 1688. He excelled in painting fish, which he represented with great fidelity. He also painted portraits, and it is said landscapes. Several of his works are in the Berlin and Cassel Galleries, and the Kunsthalle at Carlsruhe. He married a daughter of Adam Willaarts, the landscape painter.

GILLIG, MICHIEL, a Dutch painter, flourished in the latter part of the 17th century, and executed a portrait of Gerard De Vries in 1685.

GILLIS, F., a painter, born at Besançon at the commencement of the 18th century, was a professor of the Academy at Tournai. In the Museum of that town are a 'Group of dead Birds,' a portrait of Jean Baptiste Fauquez, a 'Head of an old Man,' and 'St. Nicholas.' He died at Froidmont, near Tournai, in 1790.

GILLIS, HERMAN, born at Antwerp in 1733, was a pupil of Geeraerts, and painted portraits and historical subjects. In 1768 he became a member of the Guild of St. Luke, and afterwards travelled in Germany and Austria. At Vienna he painted a portrait of the famous General Laudon. He executed some pictures for the church of Hoogstraeten on the legend of the Holy Blood, and in 1773 was appointed Director of the School of Design at Louvain. The date of his death is not known.

GILLOT, CLAUDE, a French painter and engraver, was born at Langres in 1673. He was sent to Paris when young, and became a scholar of J. B. Corneille. He chiefly excelled in designing fauns, satyrs, and grotesques, in which he acquired some reputation, and was received into the Academy in Paris in 1715. Antoine Watteau was his scholar, and greatly surpassed him. He died in Paris in 1722. His works as a painter are little regarded; but he has left us a considerable number of etchings, from his own designs, which are executed in a bold, free style. Including the plates he engraved for the 'Fables' of La Mothe-Houdard, Gersaint makes his prints amount to one hundred and eighty. Among others, the following are by him:

The Feast of Diana disturbed by Satyrs; *Cl. Gillot fec.*
The Feast of Bacchus celebrated by Satyrs and Bacchantes.
The Triumph of Pan celebrated by Nymphs and Sylvans.
The Triumph of Faunus, the God of the Forests.
The Milk-jug and the Upset Pot.

GILLRAY, JAMES, the most eminent of English caricaturists, was born in 1757, and is supposed to have been of Irish descent. Scarcely any particulars of his early years are known. It is said that he was the son of a Chelsea pensioner, and a person of the same name, who was probably his father, filled the office of sexton to the Moravian cemetery at Chelsea for forty years, and was buried there in 1799. Like the illustrious Hogarth, and the celebrated engraver Sharp, he began his career as a letter engraver, though we have been unable to find any specimens of his works of that description. Being disgusted with this monotonous occupation, he ran away from his employer, joined a company of strolling players, and after undergoing the various hardships which this course of life invariably entails, he returned to London, and became a student of the Royal Academy, where he pursued most energetically his studies in the art of design. That he must have attained remarkable proficiency is very evident from several plates which he engraved after his own designs, particularly two subjects from Goldsmith's 'Deserted Village,' inscribed 'The Village Train' and 'The Deserted Village,' published in 1784. These are designed in a remarkably free and picturesque manner, and have some resemblance to the earlier works of Stothard. They are exceedingly well engraved in the dotted manner, and though the name of his instructor in this art is not known, they so much resemble the works of the unfortunate Ryland, that one can have but little hesitation in assigning the credit of the tuition to him. Among other works of this class, and executed about the same time, are, a capital portrait of Dr. Arne, after Bartolozzi; 'Colonel Gardiner's last Interview with his Children;' 'The Burning of the Duke of Athole East Indiaman, 1785;' 'The Wreck of the Nancy Packet off Scilly, 1784;' and two portraits of William Pitt, all after his own designs. The two last, though admirable representations of the man, are nevertheless somewhat approaching to caricature. He also engraved a few plates after Lady Spencer's drawings. Either for the purpose of amusement or of mystification, he occasionally adopted fictitious names. Thus the following plates, which are known to be by him, have other names attached to them: 'The Nativity,' after Copley, *J. Hurd fecit*, 1785; 'The Return,' a child with a dog in a landscape, *J. Kent fecit*, 1781; 'A Storm,' *J. Penn fecit*, 1786; and, were it necessary, many others of his works might be quoted bearing these names. He also, on many of his earlier caricatures, made use of a monogram composed of the letters *J. S.*, interlaced in such a manner as to resemble that used by Sayer the caricaturist, which he probably adopted to mislead the public as to the real author of the publications.

In 1792 he engraved a droll representation of 'John Bull and his family landing at Boulogne' for his friend Banbury, and in the same year he accompanied De Loutherbourg in his travels in France and Flanders to collect materials for the latter's great picture of the 'Siege of Valenciennes.' The memorial of this tour is preserved in two groups known as 'Flemish Characters.'

Gillray appears to have worked as an engraver long after his career as a caricaturist had commenced, for he engraved in 1792 a large plate after Northcote, representing the delivery of the prisoners from the Bastille, inscribed, 'Le Triomphe de la Liberté, ou, L'Élargissement de la Bastille;' and in 1794, 'Marquis Cornwallis receiving the royal Hostages at Seringapatam,' after the same painter: probably the last of his productions of this description.

Admirable as many of these works are, it is as a caricaturist that Gillray is best known, and upon which his fame entirely rests. In this art he has no rival; and the exquisite tact with which he seized upon points, both in politics and manners, most open to ridicule, is only equalled by the consummate skill and wit with which he satirized them. His earlier works are more carefully than spiritedly executed, and look like the productions of an engraver only. The earliest of his undoubted caricatures, though many others antecedent have been with great reason attributed to him, is dated 1779; it is probably a satire on the Irish Fortunehunter, and is called 'Paddy on Horseback,' the so-called horse being a bull, on which he is riding with his face to the tail. But his improvement was rapid and extraordinary, and he soon attained

242

a marvellous freedom both of design and in the management of the etching needle. It is said that he etched his ideas at once upon the copper without making a previous drawing, his only guides being sketches of the distinguished characters he intended to introduce made on small pieces of card, which he always carried about with him. His caricatures amount to more than twelve hundred, of which the following are a few of the more important, arranged according to the dates at which they appeared.

A New Way to pay the National Debt. George III. and his Queen are coming out of the Treasury loaded with money, which is overflowing their pockets; on the right is the Prince of Wales in a very shabby condition, gratefully receiving money from the Duke of Orleans. April 21, 1786.

Ancient Music. A caricature of the King and Queen in ecstasy at a concert performed by the ministers. May 10, 1787.

Monstrous Craws. A satire on the grasping avarice of George III. and Queen Charlotte. May 29, 1787.

March to the Bank. An etching, executed in the most masterly style. August 22, 1787.

Market Day. Lord Thurlow, as a grazier, is attending Smithfield Market, and examining the beasts, the heads of which represent the leading political characters of the day. May 2, 1788.

Election Troops bringing in their Accounts to the Pay Table. A satire on the means employed by ministers, unsuccessfully, however, to frustrate the election of Fox for Westminster. This is the first caricature on which the name of Gillray appears. 1788.

Frying Sprats, and *Toasting Muffins.* Two small but very clever caricatures on the parsimonious habits of George III. and Queen Charlotte. 1791.

Anti-Saccharites, or John Bull and his Family leaving off the use of Sugar. The King and Queen, from economical motives, are enjoying and praising their tea without sugar, while the Princesses are evidently very much disgusted. The Royal Family, it is said, were highly delighted with this caricature. 1792.

A Connoisseur examining a Cooper. A very bold and happy idea, capitally carried out. George III. is represented almost purblind, looking with great attention at a miniature of Oliver Cromwell, by Samuel Cooper, which he holds in one hand, while he has a candle in the other. The bitterness of this satire was occasioned by the disparaging observations the King made on the portraits Gillray had sketched during his tour in Flanders with De Loutherbourg. The King had said, "I don't understand these caricatures." The exasperated artist made this drawing, and said, "I wonder if the royal connoisseur will understand this?" 1792.

Temperance enjoying a frugal Meal, and *A Voluptuary under the Horrors of Digestion.* Two most admirable productions, unsurpassed in humour, design, or execution. The temperate habits of George III. in the former, and the Epicurean manners of the Prince of Wales in the latter, are portrayed with the most consummate ability. 1792.

Bengal Levée, from an original drawing made on the spot by an amateur. A very large and skilfully-executed plate. 1792.

The Dagger Scene, or the Plot discovered. A capital representation of a well-known scene in the House of Commons, in which Edmund Burke was the chief performer. 1792.

Fatigues of the Campaign in Flanders. The Duke of York luxuriating in the company of Flemish women, attended by his soldiers, who are bringing in large bowls of punch. 1793.

The Loyal Toast. The Duke of Norfolk giving his celebrated toast, "The majesty of the people," at the Crown and Anchor Tavern, for which he was dismissed from his offices. 1798.

The Consequences of a successful French Invasion. A set of four plates, in which the horrors to be expected are given with extraordinary spirit.

The Cow-pock, or the wonderful effects of the new Inoculation. A very humorous burlesque on the popular opinions respecting Jenner's invaluable discovery.

L'Assemblée Nationale, or a grand co-operative Meeting at St. Anne's Hill (the residence of Charles James Fox), *respectfully dedicated to the admirers of a Broad-bottom'd Administration.* This is undoubtedly the most talented caricature that has ever appeared. The King is supposed to have been executed, the Republic proclaimed, and Fox, as first consul, is holding his levée at his house at St. Anne's Hill. All the leading Whigs are present, of whom the likenesses are most admirable, and in the right corner is seen a portion of the figure of the Prince of Wales, to whom this caricature gave so much offence that he offered a large sum of money for its suppression, which being accepted, he ordered the plate to be destroyed. The plate, however, was not destroyed, but secreted, and it still exists. 1804.

The King of Brobdingnag and Gulliver (George III. and Bonaparte); two plates. 1803 and 1804.

The Middlesex Election. Sir Francis Burdett dragged in his carriage to the poll by the Duke of Norfolk, Charles James Fox, and other leading Whigs. 1804.

The Reconciliation (between George III. and the Prince of Wales). Admirably treated. 1804.

The Life of William Cobbett, written by himself. Eight satirical plates. 1809.

Installation of the Chancellor of Oxford (*Lord Grenville*), *August 8*, 1810. A large plate, and the last political engraving bearing Gillray's name.

Other pieces not of a political nature, but full of humour, and sometimes severely satirical on the fashionable frivolities of the time, wherein he did not spare the persons of the prime leaders of society, may be added:

A Pic Nic Orchestra. This plate contains the portraits of the Marchionesses of Buckingham and Salisbury, Lady Mary Cholmondeley, Lord Edgcumbe, and Charles Greville.

Dilettanti Theatricals. The same characters are introduced as in the preceding plate.

Blowing up Pic Nics. The same parties assailed by Sheridan in the character of Harlequin, assisted by Mrs. Siddons and John Kemble.

The Bulstrode Siren. Mrs. Billington and the Duke of Portland.

Push-pin. Duke of Queensberry and Miss Vanneck.

Twopenny Whist. The party consists of Betty Marshall, the assistant to Mrs. Humphreys, Mrs. Turner, Mr. Mortimer, and a German of the name of Schotter. Betty Marshall is showing the trump card.

Cockney Sportsmen; four plates. 1800.

Elements of Skating; four plates. 1805.

Rake's Progress at the University; five plates. 1806.

Gillray executed a series of twenty stippled plates, usually printed in a red colour, bearing the title 'Hollandia Regenerata.' They have Dutch inscriptions, were published in Holland, and were intended principally to ridicule the republican costumes and appointments. The last plate published during his life was 'A Barber's Shop in Assize time,' from a drawing by Bunbury. It is dated January 9th, 1811, but was engraved much earlier.

Gillray was unfortunately another example of the imprudence that so frequently accompanies genius and great talent. His habits were in the highest degree intemperate, and for many years he resided in the houses of his publisher, Mrs. Humphreys, in New and Old Bond Streets, and lastly in St. James's Street. By her he was most liberally supplied with every indulgence, and during his residence with her he produced nearly all his most celebrated works, which were bought up with unparalleled eagerness, and circulated not only throughout England, but all over Europe. Though under an engagement not to work for any other publisher, yet, to satisfy his insatiable desire for strong drink, he now and then etched plates for

Mr. Fores of Piccadilly, disguising, and occasionally very successfully, both his style and handling.

It has been before observed, that the last of his works is dated in 1811; soon after this he sank into a state of mingled imbecility and delirium, and died in London in 1815.

There exists a specimen of his practice of the art of lithography. It represents a 'Domestic Musical Party;' the mother is playing on the pianoforte, the husband stands behind her playing the flute, the children are singing. It exhibits considerable ability, and is excessively rare. He engraved on wood a medallion portrait of William Pitt, placed against a rustic monument overshadowed by the branches of an oak, and a few small woodcuts, among which are 'A Woman crying Fish,' 'A Boy near a Cottage drinking,' and 'A Beggar at a Door.'

GILPIN, SAWREY, an animal painter, was born at Carlisle in 1733. He was the son of a captain in the army, from whom he received some instruction in drawing. On his arrival in London, he was for some time under a ship painter. His genius, however, led him to drawing animals; and some of his sketches having been shown to the Duke of Cumberland, he took Gilpin under his patronage, and employed him in painting the portraits of his favourite racers, and other subjects, at Newmarket. He became one of the most correct and spirited drawers of horses that the art has produced; and that he possessed powers of a superior cast, which would have enabled him to distinguish himself in the more elevated walk of historical painting, is evident in his pictures of the 'Election of Darius' and the 'Triumph of Camillus.' Gilpin was elected an Associate of the Royal Academy in 1795, and an Academician in 1797. He died at Brompton in 1807. The animals, particularly the horses, in Barret's pictures, are generally by Gilpin; and the landscape part of Gilpin's pictures is by Barret. In the South Kensington Museum is a picture of 'Cows in a Landscape;' and in water-colours, 'Sketch of a Lion and Lioness,' and 'A Mansion in process of construction.' There are a few very spirited etchings by this estimable artist; among others, the following:

A set of Oxen, Cows, &c.
A small Book of Horses.
Some Heads for his brother's, Rev. William Gilpin's, 'Lives of the Reformers.' 1809.

GILPIN, WILLIAM, a landscape draughtsman, born in 1724, near Carlisle, was the brother of Sawrey Gilpin. He graduated at Oxford, and was afterwards master of Cheam School, and finally vicar of Boldre, Hants, where he died in 1804. He published a large number of topographical works, for which he drew and engraved the illustrations. There are four landscapes in Indian ink by him in the South Kensington Museum.

GILPIN, WILLIAM SAWREY, born 1762, a water-colour painter, was the son of Sawrey Gilpin. He was the first president of the Water-Colour Society (1804—1806), exhibiting there till 1814; and he held the appointment of drawing-master at the Royal Military College at Great Marlow. He died in 1843.

GILSON, JEAN HENRI, called "Frère ABRAHAM D'ORVAL," was born at Habay la Vieille in 1741. He established himself in the Ardennes as a hermit, till on the suppression of the hermits by Joseph II. he entered the Abbey of Orval. The Prior, struck by his talent, made him travel to Rome,

R 2

Antwerp, Brussels, and Paris, and then sent him to the Academy at Düsseldorf. There he carried off the first prize with a picture of 'Adam and Eve lamenting the Death of Abel.' On his return to the Abbey he set to work to fill the refectory, halls, and church of the Abbey with pictures. In 1793 the Abbey with all its pictures was destroyed by the French, and Gilson retired to Florenville, where he opened a studio, and died in 1809. He executed a large number of portraits and religious pictures.

GILTLINGER, JOHANNES GUMPOLT. See GÜLTLINGER.

GIMIGNANI, GIACINTO, (or GEMIGNANI,) was born at Pistoja in 1611, but studied at Rome, first under Nicolas Poussin, and afterwards in the school of Pietro da Cortona. In his composition and design he followed the classic style of his first instructor, but in his colouring, and the taste of his architecture, that of the second. He worked in competition with Andrea Camassei and Carlo Maratti, in the Baptistery of San Giovanni in Laterano, where he painted in fresco some subjects from the life of Constantine. Several of his works are in the Palazzo Niccolini at Florence; and a fine picture of 'Leander,' in the Uffizi, is so much in the style of Guercino, that Lanzi says it was for some time attributed to that master. In the church of San Giovanni at Pistoja are two pictures of subjects from the life of St. John; in the cathedral, 'St. Roch;' and in the Pitti Palace at Florence, 'Rebecca at the Well.' He died in 1681. There are a few etchings by this master, executed with great spirit, and marked with the annexed monogram: Among them are:

The Rape of the Sabines. 1649.
The Siege and Capitulation of Tournai in 1581.
A set of twelve small plates of the Sports of Children.
Anthony and Cleopatra.
Queen Semiramis quelling a Revolt.

GIMIGNANI, LODOVICO, (or GEMIGNANI,) was the son of Giacinto Gimignani, and was born at Rome in 1644. He chiefly excelled in fresco; and there are several of his works in the churches at Rome, as well as others executed in conjunction with his father. The vault of Santa Maria delle Vergini is one of his most admired performances; the principal altar-piece of the same church is by him. He died in 1697.

GINDERICK, THEODORICH VON, painted in 1475 'Two Angels,' and a baldacchino, for the chapel of St. Michael in the Victor's church at Xanten.

GINDTER, MATHÄ. See GÜNTHER.

GINNASI, CATTARINA, the niece of Cardinal Domenico Ginnasi, was born at Rome in 1590. She was taught painting by Giovanni Lanfranco, after whose designs she painted the whole of the pictures in the church of the convent of Santa Lucia at Rome. She died in 1660.

GIOCCHIO, ULISSE, a painter of the Florentine school, born at Monte San Savino, flourished in the early part of the 17th century. In 1616 he painted a lunette, representing 'St. Dominick and a procession of Corpus Domini,' over the principal entrance of the church of Santa Maria Novella in Florence, and in the following year decorated with frescoes the cloisters of San Lorenzo in Pistoja.

GIOJA, GAETANO, a painter of Rimini, who lived in the last quarter of the 18th century, studied at Florence and Rome, and executed historical and mythological pictures. He was still living in 1824.

GIOLFINO, NICCOLÒ called by Vasari NICOLA

244

URSINO, was a contemporary of Falconetto, and born at Verona about 1465. His paintings are chiefly to be seen in the churches of his native city. The Museum of Verona possesses two of the 'Madonna and Saints;' and the Berlin Gallery has a 'Virgin and Child between four Saints.' The church of Santa Maria in Organo, Verona, is especially rich in frescoes by him. The National Gallery, London, possesses two panels, originally in one, containing portraits of the Giusti family. He was a friend of Mantegna, and the master of Paolo Farinati, a celebrated fresco painter of Verona. The exact date of his death is unknown, but he was alive in 1518.

GIOLFINO, PAOLO, a painter of Verona in the 16th century, was a brother and pupil of Niccolò Giolfino. The Verona Gallery contains a 'Madonna enthroned,' and a 'Resurrection,' by him.

GIOLITO, GABRIELE, was a native of Ferrara, who resided in Venice, where from 1542 to 1567 he carried on the business of a printer, and also engraved on wood the illustrations for his edition of the 'Orlando Furioso' of Ariosto, first issued in 1542. He died before 1577.

GIONCOY, MICHEL, (or GIONCQUOY,) a painter, was a native of Tournai, who studied at Rome. In conjunction with B. Spranger he produced several works, but died in the year 1600, in the prime of life.

GIONIMO, ANTONIO, born at Padua in 1697, was first instructed by his father, Simone Gionimo, and afterwards studied under Aureliano Milani and Crespi. His principal residence was at Bologna, where he painted some pictures for the churches. Among his best works are the 'Finding of Moses,' in the church of Santa Cristina; and the 'Martyrdom of St. Floriano,' in Sant' Agata. He died at Bologna in 1732.

GIONIMO, SIMONE, the father of Antonio Gionimo, was born in Dalmatia in 1655, but afterwards removed to Vienna. He painted somewhat after the manner of Guercino.

GIORDANO, LUCA, called 'FA PRESTO,' was born at Naples in 1632. He was the son of Antonio Giordano, an obscure artist, whom he had surpassed when he was only eight years old, and the astonishment which he created caused the Viceroy of Naples to place him under the care of Giuseppe Ribera, called Lo Spagnoletto. Before he was thirteen years of age he had acquired a fertility of invention, and a readiness of hand, that are perhaps without example. Animated by the report he had heard of the wonders of Rome, he withdrew himself from his father's house, and made the best of his way to that city. He there habitually copied the works of Raphael, Michelangelo, and Caravaggio. His talents recommended him to the notice of Pietro da Cortona, who employed him to assist him in the many considerable works in which he was at that time engaged. The brilliant style of this master was particularly congenial to the taste of Luca Giordano; and he appears to have aimed at excelling him in the facility and splendour of his execution. His father, who had lived in a state of indigence and obscurity, followed him to Rome; and from the produce of the talent of his son, whose designs after the works of the great masters were esteemed and sought after, he received a considerable emolument. Such was the demand for his drawings and sketches, that his father continually urged him to despatch, by repeating to him, 'Luca, fa presto,' ('Luke, make haste,') and hence he came to be designated by this phrase.

LUCA GIORDANO

THE JUDGMENT OF PARIS

Hanfstängl photo]

[*Berlin Gallery*

In the last edition of Bellori's 'Vite de' Pittori,' in which is introduced the life of Luca Giordano, he is said to have made twelve different copies of the paintings by Raphael in the Loggie of the Vatican, and twenty drawings after the 'Battle of Constantine,' by Giulio Romano; besides those from Michelangelo, Caravaggio, and others. The fruits of his industry enabled him in company with his father to make a journey through Lombardy to Venice, where he studied the works of Titian and Paolo Veronese. He then returned by way of Florence and Leghorn to Naples. His first public works in his native city were a picture of the 'Holy Rosary' for the church of San Potito, three small frescoes from the life of St. John the Baptist for the chapel of San Giacomo della Marca, and some oil paintings for the church of Santa Teresa. In 1655 he painted in competition with Giacomo Farelli, for the church of Santa Brigida, a picture of 'St. Nicholas borne away by Angels,' which was a work of such power as to establish his reputation at the early age of twenty-three. In 1678, on peace being established between France, Spain, and Holland, he painted an immense picture to commemorate the event. In 1679 he was invited to Florence to paint the chapel of Sant' Andrea Corsini, and was overwhelmed with kindness by the Grand-Duke Cosmo III. On his way to Florence he was received by the Marquess of Heliche, the Spanish Ambassador to Rome, who afterwards became viceroy of Naples, by whom, as also by his successor, the Count of Santistevan, he was largely patronized. By imitating the style of every distinguished painter, he formed one which partook of the manner of each. He is compared by Bellori to the bee, that collects honey from the sweets of every flower. It would have been better for his fame if he had established a character of his own, and if imitation were not so apparent in all his productions. Some of his pictures having reached Spain, he was invited to Madrid by Charles II., in 1692, where he was appointed painter to the king. He has nowhere left greater proofs of that despatch for which he is so celebrated. In the space of two years he painted in fresco the immense ceiling of the church, and the staircase of the Escorial; the latter, representing the famous 'Battle of St. Quentin,' and the 'Taking of Montmorency,' is considered as one of his finest works. His next productions included the great saloon in the Buen Retiro, the sacristy of the cathedral at Toledo, the chapel of Our Lady of Atocha, and the vault of the Royal Chapel at Madrid. After the death of Charles II. he was retained in the service of Philip V., and during a residence of ten years in Spain he completed a prodigious number of pictures, which might reasonably have been supposed to have occupied a long life of the most industrious painter. In 1702 he accompanied Philip V. to Naples, where the high reputation he had acquired in Spain rendered his reception enthusiastic. It was with difficulty that even he could keep pace with the eagerness of his fellow-citizens to possess his works. It is reported of him, that the Jesuits, having engaged him to paint a picture of 'St. Francis Xavier,' complained to the viceroy that they could not prevail on him to finish the picture, though it was to be placed at their principal altar on the day of the festival of that saint. Luca Giordano, finding himself pressed on all sides, painted the picture in a day and a half. Perhaps no painter has left so many pictures, without even excepting Tintoretto. To such un-common powers it would not be reasonable to refuse the claim to genius; but it was certainly that species of mechanical skill which produced little that was marked with depth and originality. He died at Naples in 1705. His pupils were his son, Paolo de' Matteis, Aniello and Niccolò Rossi, Pavelli, Tommaso Fasano, Simonelli, Francisquito, and some others. The following paintings by him are preserved in the galleries of Europe:

Berlin.	Gallery.	The Judgment of Paris.
Bordeaux.	Museum.	Sleeping Venus.
"	"	Hercules and Omphale.
"	"	Head of an old Woman.
Brunswick.	Museum.	Jacob's Dream.
"	"	Moses and the Burning Bush.
"	"	The Sorceress Circe.
"	"	Roman Envoys to Æsculapius.
Cassel.	Gallery.	The Presentation in the Temple.
		The Birth of the Virgin.
Copenhagen.	Gallery.	The Judgment of Paris.
"	"	Roman and Sabine Women.
"	"	The Death of Abel.
"	"	Adam and Eve weeping over Abel.
Darmstadt.	Gallery.	The Rape of Europa.
Dresden.	Gallery.	Hercules and Omphale.
"	"	Perseus with the head of Medusa.
"	"	Lucretia and Tarquinius.
"	"	The Rape of the Sabine Women.
"	"	The Death of Seneca.
"	"	Bacchus and Ariadne.
"	"	Abraham expelling Hagar.
"	"	David with the head of Goliath.
"	"	Jacob and Rachel at the Well.
"	"	The Slaughter of the Amalekites.
"	"	Lot and his Daughters.
"	"	Susanna.
"	"	Virgin and Child.
"	"	The Penitent Magdalen.
"	"	Gideon's slaughter of the Midianites.
"	"	Burial of St. Sebastian.
"	"	Eliezer giving presents to Rebecca.
"	"	Two Portraits.
Florence.	Uffizi.	His own Portrait.
"	Pitti Pal.	The Conception.
"	Riccardi Pal.	Olympus (frescoes).
Genoa.	Spinola Pal.	St. Anne and the Virgin.
Hague.	Museum.	The Musicians.
Hampton Court.	Palace.	The Wise Men's Offering.
"	"	Cupid and Psyche (12 pictures).
Lille.	Museum.	Combat of Turnus and Æneas.
		Æneas healed by Venus.
Liverpool.	Royal Inst.	Dionysius, the Tyrant of Syracuse, as a Schoolmaster.
Madrid.	Gallery.	Twenty Scenes from the Old Testament.
"	"	Ten Scenes from the New Testament.
"	"	St. Jerome.
"	"	St. Anthony.
"	"	The Assumption.
"	"	Battle of St. Quentin.
"	"	Five Allegorical pictures.
"	"	Flight of Æneas from Troy.
"	"	Scenes in the lives of Hercules, Andromeda, Ixion, Tantalus, and Prometheus.
"	"	Tancred and Clorinda.
"	"	Portrait of Charles II.
		Portrait of a Cardinal.
Milan.	Brera.	Virgin and Child, with Saints and Angels.
Munich.	Gallery.	The Massacre of the Innocents.
"	"	Christ raised on the Cross.
"	"	Portrait of the Artist's Father.
"	"	Portrait of the Artist.

245

Munich.	Gallery.	Death of Lucretia.
,,	,,	Christ blessing the Loaves and Fishes.
,,	,,	A Cynical Philosopher.
,,	,,	Archimedes.
,,	,,	An old Man.
,,	,,	Christ in the Wilderness.
,,	,,	Christ at the Well.
,,	,,	Two Scholars.
Naples.	S. Restituta.	St. Restituta carried by the Angels.
,,	S. Maria degli Angeli.	Birth of the Virgin.
,,	,,	The Presentation in the Temple.
,,	,,	The Annunciation.
,,	,,	The Nativity.
,,	Gesù Nuovo.	Virgin and Saints.
,,	,,	St. Charles Borromeo.
,,	S. Martino.	The Triumph of Judith.
,,	S. Filippo Neri.	Christ driving the Dealers from the Temple (fresco).
,,	Museum.	The Virgin with the Rosary.
,,	,,	A Pietà.
,,	,,	St. Francis Xavier baptizing the Indians.
,,	,,	Consecration of Monte Cassino.
,,	,,	Herodias.
,,	,,	Semiramis.
,,	,,	Marsyas.
,,	,,	Venus asleep.
Paris.	Louvre.	Diana's Hunt.
,,	,,	Marriage of the Virgin.
,,	,,	Adoration of the Shepherds.
,,	,,	Tarquinius and Lucretia.
,,	,,	Death of Seneca.
,,	,,	Circle of the Loves.
,,	,,	Mars and Venus.
Petersburg.	Hermitage.	Sleep of Bacchus.
,,	,,	Mater Dolorosa.
,,	,,	The Judgment of Paris.
,,	,,	The Entombment.
Rome.	Capitol.	The Golden Fleece.
,,	Corsini Pal.	Jesus with the Doctors.
,,	Borghese Pal.	Death of St. Ignatius.
Venice.	Academy.	Descent from the Cross.
Vienna.	Gallery.	The Expulsion of Hagar.
,,	,,	The Massacre of the Innocents.
,,	,,	The Martyrdom of St. Bartholomew.
,,	,,	The Promise to St. Joachim.
,,	,,	The Birth of the Virgin.
,,	,,	The Presentation in the Temple.
,,	,,	The Marriage of the Virgin.
,,	,,	The Visitation.
,,	,,	The Adoration of the Shepherds.
,,	,,	The Dream of St. Joseph.
,,	,,	The Death of St. Joseph.
,,	,,	The Death of the Virgin.
,,	,,	The Archangel Michael. 1666.

There are some very spirited etchings by Luca Giordano, executed in a free, masterly style; among them are:

Elijah calling Fire from Heaven to destroy the Priests of Baal.
The Virgin and Infant Jesus.
St. Joseph and St. John.
The penitent Magdalen.
The Adulteress before Christ.
Christ disputing with the Doctors.
St. Anne received into Heaven by the Virgin.

GIORDANO, SOFIA, was born of poor parents at Turin in 1779. She was placed under the tuition of M. de Maron, the sister of Raphael Mengs, at Rome, but she returned to Turin in 1801, and married a surgeon named Giordano. Her chief works were in miniature and pastel. She died at Turin in 1829.

GIORDANO, STEFANO, was born at Messina, and is known by a splendid picture of 'The Last

Supper,' produced in 1541, in the cloister of San Gregorio at Messina.

GIORGETTI, GIACOMO, born at Assisi about the year 1610, was a scholar of Giovanni Lanfranco. He excelled in historical paintings and frescoes, and several of his works are in the churches of his native city, the most considerable being the dome of the principal church. In the sacristy of the Conventuali he painted some pictures of the 'Life of the Virgin.'

GIORGIO, a miniature painter of the 15th century, was a son of Alberto of Germany. In 1441 he was employed by the Marquis Leonello of Ferrara in the preparation of breviaries and other ecclesiastical work, which occupied him till 1462. He left a son, who is known in art as Martino da Modena.

GIORGIO, GIOVANNI, was an Italian engraver, who was employed chiefly by the booksellers. He resided at Padua, where he engraved the plates for a work on antique lamps, published in 1653, entitled 'De Lucernis Antiquorum reconditis.' He also engraved a frontispiece with figures to Vesling's 'Anatomy,' published at Padua in 1647. There is also by him a ludicrous print, called 'The Bath of the Anabaptists,' after Raphael. He died at the age of 77.

GIORGIO DE FLORENTIA, flourished from 1314 to 1325, and was probably a pupil of Giotto. He is supposed to have painted at Borghetto and at the castle of Chambéry.

GIORGIONE, BIG GEORGE, or ZORZO DA CASTELFRANCO, as he is called by his contemporaries, was born about the year 1477 or 1478, in this picturesque old city of the Trevisan March. He was of humble origin, being the son of a peasant of Vedeago, who settled at Castelfranco in 1460, and the fable of his supposed connection with the Barbarelli family was not invented for more than a hundred years after his death. As a boy Giorgione came to Venice and studied painting in the shop of Giovanni Bellini, where he had Titian and Palma for his companions. Like Leonardo, whom he resembled in many ways, the young artist was noted for his personal beauty and musical tastes. He sang and played the lute with rare charm, and became a welcome guest in the most distinguished circles. "But he was none the less ardent in his studies," Vasari tells us, "and was so enamoured of beauty in nature, that he only cared to draw from life, and represent all that was fairest in the world around him." The originality of his genius soon made itself felt. The earliest works that we have from his hand are the 'Trial of Moses,' and the 'Judgment of Solomon' in the Uffizi, probably painted when he was seventeen or eighteen. These small panels were evidently executed as companion pieces for Giovanni Bellini's 'Allegory,' and, like that curious little picture, once adorned the Medici villa at Poggio Imperiale, but the romantic treatment of the Bible stories, the brilliant colour and slender grace of the forms already reveal Giorgione's strong individuality. The same bold conception and lyrical fancy meet us in another early work, the 'Christ bearing the Cross' formerly at Casa Loschi in Vicenza, now in Mr. Gardner's collection at Boston. This Christ with the delicately-modelled features and dreamy air is quite unlike the common traditional representations of the subject, and haunts us with the power of its strange and mysterious pathos. Another version of the theme, a sadly-injured, but deeply impressive figure of Christ

GIORGIONE

THE JUDGMENT OF SOLOMON

(UNFINISHED)

dragged along by a Jew on his way to Calvary, which Vandyck copied in his Chatsworth Sketch-book, may still be seen in the church of San Rocco, where it was an object of the highest veneration and brought more gold crowns to the confraternity, Vasari tells us, than Giorgione or Titian earned during their whole lifetime! The great altar-piece which Giorgione painted in the first years of the new century for the Costanzi chapel in the church of Castelfranco, marks a new stage in his artistic development. Here we see the Madonna raised high above the altar, with Persian hangings draping her throne, and the gallant soldier-saint Liberale, with his banner in his hand, standing by the side of St. Francis, at her feet. The whole conception is marked by a freedom and novelty which could only have been inspired by a genius of the most daring type, and in spite of its damaged state, this famous work remains a typical example of the "modern manner" which was first introduced by Giorgione. The lovely oval of the Virgin's face and the embroidered patterns of the dossal behind her throne are repeated in the Madrid altar-piece, while the boldness and realism of the conception is carried still further in the dimpled Babe, and in the vigorous forms and characteristic attitudes of the attendant saints. Venice soon awoke to a sense of the young master of Castel-franco's genius, and his contemporaries hailed his works with a sudden burst of applause. In their enthusiasm for the wealth of his fancy and the impassioned beauty of his creations, they felt the old terms to be inadequate and coined a new phrase—"*il fuoco Giorgionesco*." Early in his career Giorgione attained great reputation as a portrait painter, and Vasari, who saw his portraits of the Doge Leonard Loredano, of Caterina Cornaro and other noble personages, pronounces him to be unrivalled in this kind of art. Unfortunately few of these "admirably life-like paintings" have come down to us. One early work—a youth with refined features and wavy locks, is in the Museum of Berlin; another portrait of a lady in a quaint frilled head-dress, standing at a window, is at the Villa Borghese, while the little Gallery of Buda-Pesth contains the likeness of the sad-faced poet, Antonio Brocardo, laying his hand with a speaking gesture on his heart, and the noble figure of the Knight of Malta clad in the gleaming armour which Giorgione loved, is the pride of the Uffizi. To these we may add the splendid portrait of the great Venetian lady in the Crespi collection at Milan, which, whether it is an original work, or as Mr. Berenson thinks, only an old copy, evidently represents the Queen of Cyprus, Caterina Cornaro, that illustrious lady whose villa at Asolo lay close to Giorgione's native city, and who was one of his first patrons. Fresco-painting was another branch of art in which this master, we are told, took great pleasure and attained rare excellence. He decorated the house of Andrea Loredano, the Soranzo Palazzo and his own house in the Campo di Si Silvestro with friezes of musicians and children, and was employed by the Signoria to adorn the façade of the new Fondaco dei Tédeschi, or Exchange of Foreign Merchants, with a colossal figure of Justice and a stately procession of horse-men. Unfortunately these frescoes, which were finished in 1507, have suffered grievously from exposure to sun and sea-air, and at the present time have almost completely disappeared. The admiration which they excited led the Signoria to give the painter a commission for a large picture which was to hang in the Audience-hall of the Council, but this work was left unfinished if, indeed, it was ever begun. During the last year of his short life Giorgione devoted his attention chiefly to those classical myths and *fantasie* in which the scholars and great ladies of the day took so much delight, and which were especially suited to his genius. The twelve panels of the story of Psyche and the numerous subjects from Ovid's 'Metamorphoses' which Ridolfi describes, have vanished, but among the masterpieces of his ripest art we have the 'Sleeping Venus' which Morelli discovered in the Dresden Gallery, the wonderful storm-landscape of the Giovanelli Palazzo, in which Professor Wickhoff recognized the poet Statius's fable of Adrastus and Hypsipyle, the charming panel of Apollo and Daphne in the Seminary of Venice, and the scene from the 'Æneid,' in the Vienna Gallery, in which Evander and Pallas meet Æneas at the feet of the Tarpeian rock and show him the future site of Rome. In all of these we find the same romantic invention and love of natural beauty, the same delight in the magical effects of light and shade, of setting sun and passing storm-cloud, in feathery grasses and moss-grown rocks, in green meadows and running waters. To the same period we may ascribe the beautiful head of the Shepherd with his flute, perhaps the identical boy with the curling hair which Giorgione painted for his friend, the Patriarch Grimani, the graceful little idyll of the Golden Age in the National Gallery, and the lovely pastoral of the Louvre which is the latest and most perfect expression of the master's art. In these later works Giorgione displays a perfection of form and beauty of line in which he comes nearer to the Greeks than any other master of the Renaissance, while at the same time he reveals a sense of high romance, a note of yearning which the Greeks never knew. This mysterious feeling of passionate longing and infinite regret which meets us in the eyes of Giorgione's fairest faces and divinest forms, was prophetic of the coming end. For his brilliant career was brought to a premature close, and in the flower of his age and the fulness of his powers, Giorgione died of the plague which carried off 20,000 citizens in one fatal year. The exact date of his death is proved by a letter of the merchant Taddeo Albano, who, writing to Isabella d'Este, Marchioness of Mantua, on the 8th of November, 1510, informs her that Zorzo da Castelfranco has lately died, "more of exhaustion than of plague." Among the works that remained unfinished in his shop were the matchless 'Venus' of the Dresden Gallery, which was completed by Giorgione's friend Titian, the 'Evander and Æneas' which received the last touches from the hand of Sebastiano del Piombo, and the magnificent landscape of 'St. Mark stilling the Tempest,' the most dramatic of all the master's conceptions, which is said to have been finished by Paris Bordone. The extraordinary popularity which Giorgione enjoyed in his lifetime, and the immense demand that sprung up for Giorgionesque subjects after his death, proves how completely he had succeeded in expressing the spirit of his age. Idyllic scenes and Arcadian groups, piping shepherds and sleeping nymphs became the rage. There was hardly a painter in Venice who did not imitate his style or try to reproduce his compositions. Catena, Palma, Lotto, Sebastiano del Piombo, and Bonifazio each in turn fell under the spell. Above all, Titian caught the fire from the dead master's lips, and followed Giorgione's style so closely that, in Vasari's words, his pictures were often taken for those of the master himself. One result of this widespread fashion was that a countless number of inferior works were ascribed to Giorgione's hand and passed under his name. The more scientific spirit of modern criticism has reduced the amount of the painter's genuine works to a very limited number. Morelli's list includes nineteen, that of Mr. Berenson only seventeen. On the other hand, Mr. Herbert Cook, the painter's latest biographer, extends the number to upwards of forty, and accepts several others with reserve. The following list includes the chief paintings that are now generally recognized to be Giorgione's work:

Berlin.	*Museum.*	Portrait of a Young Man.
Boston, U.S.A. *Mrs. Gardner.*		Christ bearing the Cross.
Buda-Pesth.	*Gallery.*	Portrait of Antonio Brocardo.
Castelfranco.	*Duomo.*	Madonna with St. Francis and S. Liberale.
Dresden.	*Gallery.*	Sleeping Venus.
Florence.	*Uffizi.*	The Trial of Moses.
,,	,,	The Judgment of Solomon.
,,	,,	Portrait of a Knight of Malta.
Hampton Court.		Shepherd.
Madrid.	*Prado Gall.*	Madonna with St. Roch and St. Anthony of Padua.
Milan.	*Signor Crespi.*	Portrait of Caterina Cornaro.
Venice.	*St. Rocco.*	Christ bearing the Cross.
,,	*Palazzo Giovanelli.*	Adrastus and Hypsipyle.
,,	*Seminario.*	Apollo and Daphne.
,,	*Accademia.*	Storm at sea calmed by St. Mark.
Vienna.	*Gallery.*	Evander and Pallas.
Paris.	*Louvre.*	Fête Champêtre.
London.	*Nat. Gall.*	Golden Age.
Rome.	*Villa Borghese.*	Portrait of a Lady.
St. Petersburg. *Hermitage Gall.*		Judith.

This last-named picture was formerly ascribed to Moretto, but is now pronounced to be the work of Giorgione by Mr. Claude Phillips and several German critics who have seen the original. Morelli and Mr. Berenson, however, consider it to be an old copy.

The chief authorities for the Life and Works of Giorgione are the following :

G. Vasari. 'Le Vite de' piu eccellenti Pittori, con nuove annotazioni di Gaetano Milanesi,' 1879.
C. Ridolfi. 'Le Maravigliè dell'arte della pittura,' 1648.
Anonimo. 'Notizia d'opere di disegno,' 1525, ed. by G. Frizzoni, 1884, and by Dr. Williamson in English, 1903.
G. Morelli. 'Italian Painters.' Translated by C. J. Ffoulkes, 1892.
A. Conti. 'Giorgione,' 1894.
B. Berenson. 'The Venetian Painters of the Renaissance.' Third edition, 1897.
Crowe and Cavalcaselle. 'History of Painting in North Italy,' vol. ii., 1871.
G. Gronau. 'Zorzon da Castelfranco,' 1894.
F. Wickhoff. 'Gazette des Beaux-Arts,' 1893. 'Jahrbuch der preussischen Kunstsammlungen,' 1895.
A. Venturi. 'L'Arte,' 1900.
H. Cook. 'Giorgione' ('The Great Masters in Painting and Sculpture'). G. Bell & Sons, 1900. J. C.

GIOTTINO, whose real name is not known with certainty, is supposed, from late researches, to have been Giotto di Maestro Stefano, who lived in the 14th century, and was evidently a careful and conscientious pupil of Giotto ; another account has given his name as Tommaso di Stefano. There are still in the chapel of San Silvestro in Santa Croce, at Florence, a series of frescoes, attributed to Giottino, illustrating 'The Miracles of St. Sylvester.' The drawing and general composition of these frescoes is admirable, the colouring warm

and clear, and plainly show that the maxims and spirit of Giotto aided and animated this artist. The frescoes in the crypt chapel of the Strozzi in Santa Maria Novella, which represent scenes from the life of Christ, and a 'Pietà,' formerly in San Romeo, but now in the Uffizi Gallery, are also to be attributed to him. All the above-mentioned works are of the latter half of the 14th century. The frescoes in the chapel of the Holy Sacrament at Assisi, representing scenes from the life of St. Nicholas, and now much damaged by damp and partly obliterated, are considered by many to be by Giottino. Nothing authentic is known concerning the birth or death of this artist.

GIOTTO. See BONDONE.

GIOVANI, FRANCESCO, (or JUVANIS,) an engraver, is stated to have been born in 1635, and to have studied under Carlo Maratti. Plates by him are known of 'The Child Jesus upon a Cloud beside the Manger,' 'The Adoration of the Shepherds,' after Maratti, and 'Saturn enthroned.'

GIOVANNARIA, a monk of the Carmelite order, born at Brescia about 1460, excelled in perspective. His brother, GIOVANNI ANTONIO, was also a painter.

GIOVANNI, Maestro. See BOCCARDI.

GIOVANNI BATTISTA DI FRANCIA. See MOLA.

GIOVANNI BATTISTA DI RAFFAELLO. See GRASSI.

GIOVANNI DI FRANCESCO. See TOSSICANI.

GIOVANNI DI MARTINI. See MARTINI.

GIOVANNI DI PAOLO, called GIOVANNI DEL POGGIO, was a contemporary and occasional assistant of Sano di Pietro ; he was already known in 1423, and was on the roll of the Guild at Siena in 1428. He died about 1481. The Academy at Siena possesses a 'Last Judgment' by him, dated 1453, and several panels of his production are in the collection of M. Ramboux of Cologne. Giovanni del Poggio has also some repute as a miniature painter.

GIOVANNI DI PIERO, who was born at Naples, lived in the 14th century at Pisa, where he kept a shop, and had as partner Martino Bartolommei, with whom he painted an altar-piece for the hospital of Santa Chiara, Pisa, in 1402, for the sum of ninety-five golden florins. This painting represents the 'Virgin and Child enthroned between four Saints,' with a Trinity, and SS. Mark and Luke in its pinnacles. In 1403 and 1404 he also furnished a canvas, and did other work in the hospital ; and in 1405 he executed the 'Crucifixion' on canvas that is now hanging in the inner choir of the church of San Domenico, Pisa, with his signature and date. No dates can be given of this artist's birth or death.

GIOVANNI DI PIETRO, who flourished in the 15th century, was an occasional assistant of Sano di Pietro, and is of little note. In the choir of Santa Maria dei Servi, at Siena, is a 'Virgin of Mercy' by him. No further details concerning him are known.

GIOVANNI DI PIETRO, called, from his nationality, LO SPAGNA, (or GIOVANNI SPAGNUOLO, also JUAN DE ESPAÑA and JUAN EL ESPAÑOL,) first appears as his own master at Todi in 1507. His instructors in the art seem to have been Perugino and Pinturicchio ; he was the companion of Raphael at Perugia, and his style shows a mixture of Peruginesque and Raphaelesque, without the higher qualities of either school. His death took place at Spoleto between 1528 and 1530. Amongst

GIORGIONE

THE CONCERT

other paintings by him, the following may be cited:

Assisi.	*S. Francesco.*	Virgin enthroned, with Saints. 1516.
Berlin.	*Gallery.*	Adoration of the Magi. (*Formerly ascribed to Raphael.*)
London.	*National Gall.*	Virgin in Glory.
„	*Stafford House.*	Christ crowned with Thorns.
„	*Mr. Fuller* } *Maitland.* }	Christ on the Mount of Olives.
„	*Earl Dudley.*	Six Saints (*in two frames*).
„	„	St. Catharine.
Paris.	*Louvre.*	The Nativity.
„	„	The Virgin and Child.
Perugia.	*Gallery.*	Virgin and Child, with four Saints.
Petersburg.	*Hermitage*	Adoration of the Infant Christ.
Rome.	*Vatican.*	The Nativity.
„	*Colonna Pal.*	St. Jerome.
Spoleto.	*Palazzo* } *Comunale.* }	Virgin and Child, with Saints. (*Fresco.*)
Todi.	*Riformati.*	Coronation of the Virgin. 1507.
Trevi.	*Madonna delle* } *Lagrime.* }	Deposition from the Cross. (*Fresco.*)
„	„	St. Catharine.
„	„	St. Cecilia.

GIOVANNINI, CARLO CESARE, a son of Jacopo Maria Giovannini, was born at Parma in 1695, and died at Bologna in 1758, having resided in the latter city from 1723. It is not said by whom he was instructed, but he was a good historical painter. He, however, devoted himself rather to the restoration of pictures. Several of his works are in the public edifices at Bologna, the following being the most esteemed: 'St. Anne teaching the Virgin to read,' in the church of La Morte; 'Adam and Eve driven from Paradise,' in La Madonna del Piombo; and 'Christ giving the Keys to St. Peter,' in San Giovanni in Monte. He had a sister, BIANCA GIOVANNINI, a portrait painter, who died in 1744.

GIOVANNINI, JACOPO MARIA, (JOVANNINUS, or JOANNINUS,) was born at Bologna in 1667, and died at Parma in 1717. He was a scholar of Antonio Roli. He painted some pictures for the churches at Bologna; one of the most esteemed being that of 'The Magdalen worshipping the Cross,' in the church of San Niccolò degli Alberi. He is more known as an engraver than a painter. There are by him several plates after the great masters, particularly after Correggio and the Carracci, of which the following are the principal:

A set of twenty large plates; *after the paintings by Lodovico Carracci, and others, in the cloister of San Michele in Bosco, at Bologna.*
Twelve prints from the frescoes by *Correggio, in the cupola of San Giovanni at Parma.*
St. Jerome; *after Correggio.*
The Virgin and Infant, with St. George; *after Correggio.*
St. Sebastian; *after Lodovico Carracci.*
The Communion of the Apostles; *after Marc Antonio Franceschini.*

GIOVANNINO DEL PIO. See BONATTI.

GIOVENONE, GIROLAMO, (or GIUVENONE,) was a native of Vercelli, who flourished at the beginning of the 16th century, as appears from two of his pictures in the church of San Paolo in that city, dated 1514 and 1516. At Vercelli, in the church of the Augustines, there is a fine picture by him of the 'Resurrection,' with two laterals representing St. Margaret and St. Cecilia. Other works of his are in the same town and in Bergamo.

GIOVENONE, GIUSEPPE, a painter of Vercelli, appears to have flourished at the end of the 15th century. His pictures are peculiar from the contrasts they exhibit. One of them, a representation of 'Christ's Resurrection,' is in the Turin Gallery.

GIRALDI, GUGLIELMO, (called MAGRI, or DEL MAGRO,) was a painter of Ferrara, who, between 1450 and 1477, painted miniatures for various books, including a Missal, Breviary, and Psalter, and the works of Tibullus, Appian, and Petrarch.

GIRALDINI, MELCHIORRE. See GERARDINI.

GIRAN, ÉMILE GEORGES, French painter and lithographer; born at Montpellier in 1870; exhibited at the Société Nationale des Beaux Arts ever since 1895; achieved considerable success as a painter of popular scenes and landscapes, and he also did good work as a lithographer, some of his more striking posters attracting much notice. He was a brother of the landscape painter, Max Giran; his death occurred, at the age of 32, at Beauvoisin in March 1902.

GIRANDOLE, BERNARDO DELLE. See BUONTALENTI.

GIRARD, ALEXIS FRANÇOIS, a French engraver, was born at Vincennes in 1789. He studied painting under Regnault, but later on turned his attention to engraving, in which he achieved much success. He succeeded in uniting together in his works the mezzotint, roulette, and Indian ink styles. He died in Paris in 1870. The following are among his best plates:

The Virgin with the Fish; *after Raphael.*
The Virgin with the Pearl; *after the same.*
Portrait of Talma; *after Gérard.*
Corinna; *after the same.*
Louis XVIII. in his Cabinet; *after the same.*
Cardinal Mazarin on his Death-bed; *after Delaroche.*
Cardinal Richelieu on the Rhone; *after the same.*
The Archangel Gabriel; *after the same.*
The Last Day of Pompeii; *after C. Bruloff.* 1839.
Mary Stuart; *after Decaisne.*
The Happy Mother; *after Prud'hon.*
Dolce far niente; *after Winterhalter.*
Vintage at Naples; *after the same.* 1842.
Daniel in the Lions' Den; *after Ziegler.* 1839.
Bonaparte crossing the St. Bernard; *after Steuben.*
Abduction of Rebecca; *after Coignet.*

GIRARD, JEAN GEORGES, a French painter, born at Epinal in 1635, was a pupil of Legrand. He died at Nancy in 1690.

GIRARD, ROMAIN, a French engraver, was born in Paris in 1751. He engraved after Cipriani 'The Sacrifice of Love,' and 'Love caressing Beauty;' and after Greuze, 'The Broken Pitcher;' he also copied 'The Death of Dido,' from Bartolozzi.

GIRARDET, ABRAHAM, an engraver and etcher, was born at Locle, in the canton of Neufchâtel, in 1764, and when but thirteen years of age engraved 466 plates to a Biblical work. He then became a pupil of B. A. Nicolet in Paris, and in 1794 sought further improvement in Rome. The vignettes which he engraved for editions of Horace and La Fontaine are his best works. He died in Paris in 1823. The best of his larger plates are:

The Transfiguration; *after Raphael.* 1806.
The Triumph of Titus and Vespasian; *after Giulio Romano.* 1810.
The Rape of the Sabine Women; *after Poussin.*
The Dead Saviour; *after Andrea del Sarto.*
The Supper; *after Philippe de Champaigne.*
The Death of Arnold Winkelried.

GIRARDET, CHARLES SAMUEL, an engraver and lithographer, was born at Locle in 1780. He received his first instruction from his brothers Abraham and Alexander Girardet, and completed his studies in Paris. At first he engraved views of Swiss scenery, but executed 'The Resurrection of Christ,' after Le Brun, in 1804. In 1811 he

249

turned his attention to lithography, and in that medium depicted the 'Biblical Narratives,' after Hübner; 'The Transfiguration,' after Raphael; 'The Battles of Alexander,' after Le Brun; and 'The Death of Eudamidas,' after Poussin. From 1833 to 1840 he made designs for the 'Magasin Universel.' He died in Paris in 1863.

GIRARDET, ÉDOUARD HENRI, a Swiss painter and engraver, was born at Neufchâtel in 1819. He studied art under his father, Charles Samuel Girardet, and with his brother Karl, and became famous as a painter of genre subjects and landscapes. Journeys in Egypt and Algiers resulted in several good pictures representing those countries and their people. Among his most successful paintings of Swiss peasant-life are the following:

A Sale by Auction in a village.
A Dying Peasant blessing his family.
A Young Mother dying in the snows of the Great St. Bernard.
The Doctor's Visit.
The Little Apple Thieves.

Girardet, in the midst of work such as this, suddenly gave it up in favour of engraving, and worked in aquatint, mezzotint, and a mixed style, with as much success as he had done in painting. The following are his best prints:

Divicon; *after Gleyre.*
The Banquet of the Girondins; *after Delaroche.*
The Fainting of the Virgin; *after the same.*
The Return from Golgotha; *after the same.*
The Virgin in contemplation before the Crown of Thorns; *after the same.*
The Cenci; *after the same.*
Molière at the table of Louis XIV.; *after Gérôme.*
The Education of a Prince; *after Zamacoïs.*
A Spanish Wedding; *after Fortuny.*
Raphael in his Studio; *after Jalabert.*
The Marriage of Henry IV.; *after Lechevalier-Chevignard.*

He died at Versailles in 1880.

GIRARDET, JEAN, an historical painter, was born at Nancy in 1709. He studied first in his native city, but more especially in Italy, and painted for churches and palaces in oil and fresco. He died at Nancy in 1778. Some of his work, of a classical character, may be seen in the town-hall of that city.

GIRARDET, KARL, a genre and landscape painter, was born at Locle in 1810. He was a son of Charles Samuel Girardet, and after being instructed under Léon Cogniet he travelled in Switzerland, Germany, Italy, Spain, Egypt, &c., and from 1836 brought out landscapes and representations of the manners of those countries. In 1842 he excited much attention by a picture of 'A secret Protestant Meeting in a cave attacked by Troops and Monks.' He succeeded especially with views of Swiss lakes, North Italian landscapes, scenes from popular and military life, children's games, and so forth. He also illustrated Ariosto, and Thiers's Histories of the Consulate and Empire. His death occurred in Paris in 1871.

GIRARDET, PAUL, famous French engraver, the son and grandson of engravers of note; born at Neuchâtel, March 8, 1821. A pupil of his father, whose talent and fame he was soon to inherit. In the Salon of 1842 he exhibited certain landscapes engraved from works by his elder brother, Karl. He subsequently published plates which have become famous, as, for instance, his engravings of Delaroche's 'Marie Antoinette au Tribunal révolutionnaire,' Knauss' 'Escamoteur and Cinquantaine,'

Brion's 'Noce en Alsace,' Müller's 'Appel des Condamnés,' and Dubufe's 'Enfant Prodigue.' He was a chevalier of the Legion of Honour, and in 1883 was appointed member of the Académie des Beaux Arts. Died in Paris, February 26, 1893.

GIRARDIN, ALEXANDRE FRANÇOIS LOUIS DE, Count, a French historical and landscape painter, was born in Paris in 1767, and became a pupil of Bidault. He exhibited at the Salon of 1822 a 'View of Ermenonville,' and various other landscapes at the subsequent exhibitions until 1835, after which year there is no further record of him.

GIRARDON, CATHERINE. See DUCHEMIN.

GIRAUD, ANTOINE COSME, a French engraver, born in Paris in 1760, was a pupil of Lingée, and executed vignettes and plates for booksellers. His best works are two plates after Borel, the one representing 'Two Young Women lying on a bed,' the other 'A Young Woman bathing her feet.' He died after the commencement of the 19th century.

GIRAUD, VICTOR, a French genre painter, born in Paris in 1840, was a pupil of Picot and Eugène Giraud. His best known picture, 'The Slave-Market,' was formerly in the Luxembourg Gallery; he also painted 'The Bird-Charmer.' He died in 1871, from disease brought on by exposure on the fortifications of Paris during the siege.

GIRLING, EDMUND, an amateur etcher, who flourished in the early part of the 19th century, was a clerk in a bank at Yarmouth. He etched after Rembrandt, Crome, and the Dutch masters, and his works were exhibited at the Norwich Society.

GIRODET-DE-ROUSSY-TRIOSON, ANNE LOUIS, a French historical painter and writer, was born at Montargis in 1767. Having lost his parents when very young, he was adopted by an army surgeon, M. Trioson, whose name he subsequently added to his own. After some elementary instruction from a painter named Luquet, he entered the studio of David in 1785. In 1787 and 1788 he unsuccessfully competed for the 'prix de Rome,' but at length, in 1789, obtained the coveted distinction with a picture of 'Joseph making himself known to his brethren.' He spent some time in Rome, and there painted the 'Endymion,' which first brought his name into notice. The political troubles of the time obliged him to fly to Naples, and thence to Venice, but on his way home he fell ill at Genoa, and was carefully tended by Gros. Once more settled in Paris, he devoted himself assiduously to historical painting, and he met with such success that at the decennial competition in 1810, he was awarded the 'grand prix' for his 'Scene from the Deluge,' in preference to David's 'Sabines.' In 1812 Girodet's adopted father died, and with the property bequeathed to him he was enabled to indulge a taste for architecture. This amateur house-building, and his literary pursuits—for he wrote a poem on painting, and contributed freely to the art literature of the day—did not leave him much leisure during the next few years for the production of any large works. In fact, throughout his career, he painted but few pictures. His time was greatly occupied with studies and sketches, and he executed an immense number of designs for the illustration of the classic authors, notably for editions of Anacreon, Virgil, and Racine. In his latter years Girodet suffered much in health, and he owed much to the attention of his friend, the great physician Larrey. He died in Paris in 1824, and previous to his burial at Père-la-Chaise, Louis XVIII. ordered the cross of officer of the Legion of Honour to be affixed to his breast. Like David himself, and most of his disciples, Girodet lacked a mastery over colour. His power of drawing was his forte, and to this is due the charm of many of his works. He is seen at his best in his less ambitious subjects, such as the 'Atala' and the 'Endymion;' whilst in such works as the 'Insurrection at Cairo' and the 'Deluge,' he is strained, not to say theatrical. The following is a list of some of his works :

Ajaccio.	Hôtel de Ville.	Portrait of Charles Bonaparte.
Amiens.	Museum.	The Burial of Atala. (A replica of the Louvre picture.)
Angers.	Museum.	Romulus and Tatius. 1788.
Avignon.	Museum.	Head of a Turk.
Cherbourg.	Museum.	Portrait of a Man.
Compiègne.	Palace.	The Four Seasons.
,,	,,	Apollo.
,,	,,	Flora.
,,	,,	Aurora.
Leipsic.	Museum.	Venus.
Le Puy.	Museum.	Head of a young Man.
Lyons.	Museum.	Head of a young Woman.
Orleans.	Museum.	Erigone.
Paris.	École de Médecine.	Hippocrates refusing the presents of Artaxerxes. 1792.
,,	Louvre.	Scene from the Deluge. 1810.
,,	,,	The Sleep of Endymion. 1792.
,,	,,	The Burial of Atala. 1808.
Quimper.	Museum.	Head of a young Girl.
Tarbes.	Museum.	Head of a Child.
Versailles.	Gallery	Napoleon receiving the Keys of Vienna. 1808.
,,	,,	The Insurrection at Cairo. 1810.
,,	,,	Portrait of Charles Bonaparte.
,,	,,	Portrait of J. B. Belley.

O.J.D.

GIROLAMO DA TREVIGI. See PENNACCHI.

GIROLAMO DAI LIBRI. See DAI LIBRI.

GIROLAMO DI TIZIANO. See DANTE.

GIROLAMO PADOVANO. See SORDO.

GIROUST, A. L. C., an historical and portrait painter, born at Versailles about 1780, was a pupil of David. He was still living in 1835.

GIROUST, JEAN ANTOINE THÉODORE, a French historical painter, was born at Bussy-Saint-Georges (Seine and Marne) in 1753. He was a pupil of Lépicié, obtained the 'grand prix' in 1778, and was received into the Academy in 1788 upon his 'Œdipus at Colonus.' He died at Mitry-Mory (Seine and Marne) in 1817. He executed a great number of works, among which were 'St. Theresa,' in the cathedral of Boulogne-sur-Mer, 'The Tortures of the Maccabees,' 'Eponine and Sabinus,' and 'St. Godeliva.'

GIRSCHER, BERNHARD, a landscape painter, was born at Rothenburg, near Görlitz, in 1822. He at first studied medicine, but in 1848 turned his attention to art, and worked under the portrait and landscape painter Resch at Breslau. In 1849 he proceeded to Munich, where he remained four years, passing the summer months in walking through the Bavarian highlands and the Tyrol. He spent some time at Liegnitz, and then in 1854 removed to Berlin, travelling, however, after this in the Tyrolese and Styrian Alps. He died in 1870. Among his best paintings are 'Moonlight Night in the Tyrolese Highlands,' 'Water-Mill in Silesia,' and those in which glaciers are represented.

GIRTIN, THOMAS, water-colour painter, was born in Southwark, Feb. 18, 1775. His family was of French Huguenot origin, the name being Englished from "Guertin." He was apprenticed to Edward Dayes, and afterwards coloured prints for John Raphael Smith. As a boy he was a close comrade of Turner, the two sketching together Thames-side scenes, and copying old masters at Dr. Monro's. He exhibited at the Royal Academy from 1794 to 1801. In the latter year he sent an oil picture, 'Bolton Bridge,' which seems to have disappeared ; his other exhibited works were all in water-colour. Beginning with the topographical drawing then so much in demand with publishers, Girtin soon developed a powerful, free, and masterly style which was the admiration of his contemporaries. His practice was founded less on his predecessors in water-colour art, Sandby, Hearne, and Dayes, than on the paintings of Canaletto, Rubens, and Wilson. Many copies, chiefly of Canaletto, made by him in boyhood for John Henderson, who, like Dr. Monro, was an early patron and friend, are now in the British Museum. Girtin drew in many parts of England, his favourite subjects being the ruined castles and abbeys, moorlands and mountains of Yorkshire, Northumberland, and Wales. About 1798 he painted a semicircular panorama of the Thames from Lambeth and Westminster to the City ; and in 1802 he made a number of views of Paris, twenty of which were etched by him in outline and afterwards aquatinted by other artists. He had gone to Paris in search of health ; but the visit failed to improve his rapidly-declining condition, and he died on November 9 of the same year. He was only twenty-seven. At the time of his death Girtin had admittedly gone farther and shown more original power in art than Turner, who once said, "If Tom Girtin had lived, I should have starved." Many of Girtin's finest works, such as the beautiful 'White House at Chelsea,' or 'Battersea Reach,' are in private hands ; but there are more than a hundred of his drawings in the British Museum, including some of his best, a few in the Victoria and Albert Museum, and some fine examples in the Whitworth Institute, Manchester. S. W. Reynolds engraved in mezzotint on a small scale a set of Girtin's drawings, which was published under the title of 'Liber Naturæ' ; and David Lucas made a larger mezzotint from his 'Ouse Bridge, York,' with greater sympathy and skill. Roget's 'History of the Old Water-Colour Society' contains a full and careful account of Girtin's life and times.

PRINCIPAL DRAWINGS IN THE BRITISH MUSEUM.

Bridgenorth. 1802.
Cayne Waterfall, Wales.
Denbigh.
Near Beddgelert.
Knaresborough Castle.
Set of studies for the London Panorama.
Kirkstall.
Great Hall, Conway.
Durham Cathedral.
Lindisfarne Abbey.

L. B.

GISBRANT, JOHN, was an English historical painter of the 17th century. He spent many years at Lisbon, where he painted an altar-piece for the church of St. Mary Magdalen.

GISELAER, N. B. In the Fitzwilliam Museum at Cambridge is a picture of the 'Interior of a Hall,' signed N. B. Giselaer, fecit Anno Dni. 1631. The colouring and perspective are good, but the figures are too large, and the animals bad.

GISMONDI, PAOLO, called PAOLO PERUGINO, was a native of Perugia, but was educated at Rome under Pietro da Cortona, and was received into the Academy in that city in 1668. Some of his best fresco works, which are historical, are those in the church of Sant' Agnese and in the tribune of Sant' Agata at Rome.

GIUDICI, CARLO MARIA, a painter, sculptor, and architect, was born at Viggiù, in the Milanese, in 1723. From his thirtieth year he studied the great masters in Rome, and afterwards settled down in Milan, where he in 1760 started a school, by means of which he sought to develope a purer style, and inculcate closer study of the antique and of nature. He died at Milan in 1804. His works as a sculptor were considerable ; as a painter he executed a few frescoes in San Francesco di Paola at Milan, and some easel pictures from both sacred and profane history, which in the heads recall the style of Guido Reni.

GIUGNI, FRANCESCO. See ZUGNI.

GIULIANO DI ARRIGO. See GIUOCHI.

GIUNTA PISANO. See PISANO.

GIUNTALODI, DOMENICO, (*i. e.* GIUNTA DI LODO,) was a painter and architect, who was born at Prato in 1505, and learned painting under Niccolò Soggi, and afterwards at Rome. He died at Guastalla in 1560. He executed several important works as an architect, and was made engineer to Charles V. As a painter, in addition to the portraits of some notable persons of his time, he is known to have produced a picture of 'The Coliseum,' which was engraved by Girolamo Fagivoli, and of 'An Old Man in his Drawing Chair,' engraved by Agostino Veneziano.

GIUOCHI, GIULIANO, called PESELLO, the son of Arrigo di Giuocolo Giuochi, was born at Florence in 1367. He was more of a sculptor and architect than a painter, and in 1390 was commissioned to design a monument to Pietro Farnese in Santa Maria del Fiore. In 1414-16 he painted flags for the interior of San Giovanni, and in 1419 he unsuccessfully competed for the erection of the cupola of Santa Maria del Fiore, but was made Brunellesco's substitute in the following year. In 1424 occurs the only record of his name in the Guild of St. Luke. He died in 1446 at Florence, and was buried in the church of the Carmine. Owing to a confusion on the part of Vasari, much doubt exists as to the authorship of various works attributed indiscriminately to Giuliano and his grandson Francesco, who resided for many years in his grandfather's atelier in the Corso degli Adimari. In the Uffizi Gallery at Florence is an 'Annunciation,' painted for the church of San Giorgio sulla Costa by Giuliano, who is said to have excelled in the representation of animals. Both grandfather and grandson were employed in painting 'cassoni.'

GIUSTI, ANTONIO, was born at Florence in 1624, and first studied under Cesare Dandini, but afterwards under Mario Balassi. He painted with equal success historical subjects, landscapes, animals, and hunting-pieces ; and continued to exercise his profession with unabated vigour until he reached his eighty-first year. He died in 1705.

GIUSTI, FELICE, who was born at Pistoja, and died at Bologna, flourished about the middle of the 18th century. He studied under Crespi, and painted sea-pieces and landscapes with figures. He was surpassed by his brother, GIACOMO GIUSTI, who also was born at Pistoja, and died at Bologna.

GIUSTI, GREGORIO, who was born at Pistoja in 1732, studied at Rome under Seblonca, and after-

wards under Battoni. In 1756 he executed several pictures for the church of San Vitale, but he was principally employed by the Directors of the Kircher Museum in painting art objects.

GIUSTO DI ANDREA. See MANZINI.

GIUSTO DI GIOVANNI (or GIUSTO PADOVANO). See MENABUOI.

GIUVENONE, GIROLAMO. See GIOVENONE.

GIXON, JUAN CARLOS RUIZ. See RUIZ GIXON.

GLADIATOR. See DE BAEN, JACOBUS.

GLAESER, GEORG, a portrait and historical painter, was born at Altorf, near Nuremberg, in 1719. After receiving tuition from his own friends he underwent a ten years' apprenticeship, and was then appointed court painter to the Margrave Friedrich at Baireuth, who sent him first to Vienna, where he twice obtained the prize, and then to Italy, from whence he only returned after seven years, and died at Baireuth in 1748. The following paintings by him are in the gallery of the Landauer Brüderhaus at Nuremberg :

Lucretia stabbing herself.
Cleopatra applying the Asp to her Breast.
Alexander on entering India received by the High Priest.
The Baptism of Christ.
Portrait of a Rabbi. 1735.

GLANTSCHNIGG, ULRICH, was born at Hall, in the valley of the Inn, in 1661, and after studying at Venice, settled in 1686 at Botzen, where he died in 1722. He chiefly painted altar-pieces, but also genre scenes. The following are among his works :

Botzen.	*Franciscan Ch.*	St. Francis receiving the Stigmata. 1712. (*Restored by Sies in 1856.*)
"	*Parish Ch.*	The Three Wise Men from the East.
Brixen.	*Chapter House.*	The Marriage at Cana.

His son and pupil, JOSEPH ANTON GLANTSCHNIGG, who was born at Botzen in 1695, and died there in 1750, but who lived chiefly at Würzburg, was a painter of historical, genre, and landscape subjects.

GLASER, HANS, a wood-engraver and card-painter, lived at Nuremberg about the middle of the 16th century. His works, which are very rare and have chiefly an historical interest, are for the most part views of old castles and fortresses ; one of them represents 'An Owl surrounded by other Birds.'

GLASER, JOHANN HEINRICH, was a Swiss wood-engraver, who flourished at Basle about 1630.

GLASS, JAMES W., an American artist, born about 1825. He was in his early days a pupil of Huntingdon, but travelled to London in 1847, and studied there for many years. It was there that he painted his equestrian portrait of the Duke of Wellington, which attracted some attention and was purchased by Lord Ellesmere, but a replica of it was commissioned at once by Queen Victoria, and the picture was engraved by Faed, and was deservedly popular. Glass excelled in drawing and painting horses. Some of his best-known works are the 'Battle of Naseby,' 'Edge Hill,' 'The Royal Standard,' 'Puritan and Cavalier,' and 'Free Companions.' It may be noted as a curious fact, that although greatly attached to his native land, there are not any of the works of Glass which represent scenes in America, nor are his historical pictures derived from the history of the United States, but always from that of England. He returned to America in 1856 and died in the following year. The best of his works are in English Galleries.

GLASS, JOHANN KILIAN, (not KLASS, as given by Nagler,) was born at Dornsied in the province of Hanau in 1701, and afterwards settled down at Frankfort-on-the-Main. He worked variously at the painting of portraits, house façades, ornaments, snuff-boxes, &c. He was much employed by Oppenheimer, the Finance Minister of Würtemberg, and at Lausanne (in 1742) for the Margrave of Baden and some English noblemen. He afterwards went to Paris, where he was lost sight of.

GLAUBER, DIANA, the sister of Johannes and Jan Godlieb Glauber, was born at Utrecht in 1650, and was instructed in design by her elder brother. She painted historical subjects and portraits, in which she distinguished herself at Hamburg, where she chiefly resided. In the latter part of her life she became blind.

GLAUBER, JAN GODLIEB, called MYRTILL, the younger brother and scholar of Johan Glauber, was born at Utrecht in 1656. At the age of fifteen he accompanied Johannes Glauber in his journey through France to Italy. Whilst at Paris, he studied under Jacob Knyf, who was in some repute as a painter of architectural views and seaports. After this he rejoined his brother at Lyons, and went with him to Rome, where he studied two years. In 1684 he went to Hamburg, and met with great encouragement, but was afterwards invited to the court of Vienna, where he passed a great part of his life. Jan Godlieb Glauber painted landscapes in the style of his brother,—hence his nickname,—though with a less masterly handling; but he excelled in seaports, which he embellished with small figures, correctly drawn and neatly touched. He died at Breslau in 1703. Some good landscapes by him are in the Augsburg, Munich, Pommersfelden, and Vienna Galleries. In the Glasgow Gallery is a picture of 'The Snake in the Grass.'

GLAUBER, JOHANNES, surnamed POLYDOR, was the son of German parents, but was born at Utrecht in 1646. He studied for some time under Nicolaas Berchem, but having seen some Italian landscapes he was seized with a desire to go to Italy, and in 1671 left Holland upon a journey to Rome, travelling through France in company with his brother and sister and the brothers Van Dooren. He remained a year at Paris and two at Lyons, studying under various masters. Arriving at length in Rome he received the name of 'Polydor,' upon joining the Artists' Guild. He passed two years in that city, sketching the most remarkable scenery in the vicinity; and afterwards visited Padua, Venice, Hamburg, and Copenhagen. On his return to Holland in 1684, he settled at Amsterdam; and formed an intimacy with Gerard de Lairesse, who was then in the height of his reputation, and joined him in his studio. The landscapes of Glauber, decorated with the classic figures of the 'Poussin of Holland,' obtained such reputation, that it was with difficulty they could execute the commissions which they received. It was at this time that Glauber painted the fine landscapes in the château of Soestdijk, for the Prince of Orange, in which the figures are painted by De Lairesse. He died at Schoonhoven in 1726. His works exhibit nothing of the taste of his country, his forms and scenery being entirely Italian. Among his principal pictures are the following:

Amsterdam.　　*Museum.*　Diana at the Bath.

Amsterdam.	*Museum.*	Mercury carrying off Io.
Berlin.	*Gallery.*	Italian Landscape.
Brunswick.	*Museum.*	Five Landscapes.
Cassel.	*Gallery.*	Landscape.
Copenhagen.	*Gallery.*	Landscapes.
Dresden.	*Gallery.*	Idyllic Landscape.
Hague.	*Gallery.*	Departure of Adonis for the chase.
Madrid.	*Gallery.*	Four Landscapes.
Munich.	*Gallery.*	Two Landscapes.
Paris.	*Louvre.*	Landscape.
Petersburg.	*Hermitage.*	Mountain Landscape.

There are by him several etchings, executed in a slight, spirited style, some of them after his own designs, and others after Berchem and Gaspard Poussin. He also etched some plates from the designs of Gerard de Lairesse. The following are his principal prints:

> Various Landscapes and Cattle; *after Berchem.*
> Two Landscapes; *after Gaspard Poussin.*
> A set of six oblong Landscapes; *from his own designs.*
> A set of six upright Landscapes; *from the same.*
> A set of circular plates of allegorical subjects, from the histories of the four great Monarchies of Assyria, Persia, Greece, and Rome; *after De Lairesse.*

GLAUCION, a painter of Corinth, is only known through being recorded by Pliny as the instructor of Athenion.

GLEDITSCH, PAUL, an engraver and etcher, was born at Vienna in 1794. He was instructed by J. F. Leybold, and in 1819 obtained the first prize, whilst in 1848 the King of Prussia awarded him a gold medal for his plate of 'St. Catharine,' after Carlo Dolci. He died at Vienna in 1872. Other engravings by him are:

> Mary observing the sleeping Child; *after Guido Reni.*
> Madonna and Child, with St. Jerome; *after Raphael.*
> Madonna and Child, with the Magdalen and St. Catharine; *after Perugino.*
> Madonna Velata; *after Sasso Ferrato.*
> Cupid the Bow-Cutter; *after Parmigiano.*
> Portrait of the Emperor Joseph I.; *after Pompeo Battoni.*

GLEICHAUF, RUDOLF, German historical painter; born at Hüfingen in Baden, June 29, 1826. Completed several important mural paintings; and was prominently associated with Moritz von Schwind in decorating the Treppenhaus of the Art Gallery at Carlsruhe. It was in this town that he died on October 18, 1896.

GLEN, JAN DE. See DE GLEN.

GLEYRE, MARC CHARLES GABRIEL, an historical painter belonging to the French School, but Swiss by birth, was born at Chevilly, a small village near La Sarraz, in the Canton of Vaud, in 1806. His father, who was a farmer, encouraged his son's predilection for art. He first studied at Lyons, but in 1824 he migrated to Paris, and became a pupil of Hersent. This master did not exercise any marked influence on him, and he owed more to his study of the old masters in Italy, where he went in 1828. He stayed chiefly at Padua, Florence, and Rome, and whilst in the latter city, he sent some water-colour portraits to the Salon of 1833—his first appearance at the annual exhibition. He then made a long tour in the Levant, visiting Egypt, Greece, and Asia Minor. The fruits of his travels were seen in two decorative works, a 'Nubian Girl,' and 'Diana,' typifying Egypt and Greece, which he painted in 1838 for M. Lenoir of Paris. Two years later he made his *début* at the Salon with an important picture called 'St. John inspired by the Apocalyptic Vision.' Soon afterwards he suffered from a dangerous attack of ophthalmia, which at one time threatened him with loss of sight. On his

253

recovery, he painted the well-known 'Evening,' which established his position, and henceforth the history of his life is almost contained in the list of the works he executed. It should be mentioned that from some cause not clearly ascertained, he did not exhibit his pictures at the Salon after the year 1849. Paul Delaroche had a high appreciation of Gleyre's art, and on giving up his atelier, recommended his pupils to him. Amongst those who passed through his studio were the English painters, Poynter, Marks, and Calderon. Gleyre died on the 4th May, 1874, from the rupture of a blood-vessel while visiting the exhibition at Paris on behalf of the expatriated inhabitants of Alsace. The chief characteristics of his works are the softness and poetic feeling with which they are imbued, although in some of his productions, as the 'Pentheus' and the 'Battle of Leman,' he exhibits considerable strength and vigour. The following are some of his principal pictures :

St. John in the Island of Patmos. 1840.
Evening, or Lost Illusions. 1843.
The Departure of the Apostles. 1845.
Dance of Bacchantes. 1849.
The Pentecost. 1851. (*St. Marguerite, Paris.*)
Execution of Major Duval. 1852. (*Lausanne Museum.*)
Battle of Leman. (*Lausanne Museum.*)
Venus on a Goat.
Hercules at the feet of Omphale. 1863.
Pentheus pursued by the Maenades. (*Basle Museum.*)
The Charmer. (*Basle Museum.*)
The Bath. 1868.
Joan of Arc in the Forest.
The Deluge.
Ruth and Boaz.
Minerva and the Graces.
Portrait of General Jomini. ⎫
    „   M. W. Haldimand. ⎬ (*Lausanne Museum.*)
    „   Thomas Carlyle. ⎭   O.J.D.

GLIEMANN, PHILIPP ALBERT, a German portrait painter, was born at Wolfenbüttel in 1822. He had from his youth to struggle for his subsistence, so that it was not until 1844 that he was able to resort to the Dresden Academy for instruction. After this he entered Julius Hübner's atelier, and then, with the exception of brief trips to Paris and Antwerp, he remained settled in Dresden, where he died in 1872. There is a 'Head of a bearded Jew' by him in the Dresden Gallery.

GLINK, FRANZ XAVIER, a German historical painter, was born at Burgau in 1795. He was the son of a carpenter, and learned his father's trade ; he went with his parents in 1809 to Munich, where his talent for art induced him to attend the Academy. In 1824 he went to Italy, and upon his return painted the altar-piece for the chapel of the Military Hospital at Munich as a token of gratitude for his travelling allowance. He painted several church pictures, amongst them some for the Frauenkirche. He died at Munich in 1873. His finest pictures are :

The Flight into Egypt.
The Virgin's Visit to Elizabeth.
The Virgin and Child.
Christ in Gethsemane.
Christ in Glory.

GLINZER, KARL, (or GLINTZER,) an historical and landscape painter, was born at Breitenau, near Cassel, in 1802. He was first instructed by J. Krausskopf, a pupil of David, next passed two years at the Munich Academy, and in 1825 made a brief stay with Schadow at Düsseldorf; he then proceeded by way of Belgium to Paris, where he entered the atelier of Baron Gros. In 1833 he made a journey to

254

Rome and Naples, which had much influence on the character of his subsequent productions. Later in life he partially abandoned the practice of art in order to pursue the theoretical department, and in 1865 he published a treatise entitled 'Art and School.' On the reopening of the Cassel Gallery, however, he furnished chalk drawings from Rembrandt, of the size of the originals, for the publication of the Rembrandt Album. He died at Cassel in 1878. Among his paintings, in addition to numerous portraits, are the following :

Joseph's bloody Coat. 1838.
Susannah.
The Good Samaritan.
The Slave Dealer. 1840.
Pan and Syrinx. 1852.

GLOCKENDON, ALBERT, (or GLOCKENTON,) the elder, a German engraver and miniature painter, was born at Nuremberg about the year 1432. He was educated in the school of the elder Rogier van der Weyde, and was working at Würzburg in 1481-85. His plates are wrought entirely with the graver, in a neat but stiff style ; and he appears to have imitated the manner of Martin Schongauer, some of whose plates he copied. He usually marked his prints with his initials in Gothic letters, thus : **AG** The following plates are by him :

Twelve plates of the Passion of Christ ; *after Martin Schongauer.*
Ten plates of the Wise and Foolish Virgins ; *after the same.*
Christ bearing His Cross ; *after the same.*
The Death of the Virgin ; *after the same.*
The Virgin and Infant seated on an altar.

GLOCKENDON, ALBERT, the younger, a glass painter, illuminator, and wood-engraver, lived at Nuremberg, where he is known to have been working from 1531 to 1543. He is probably identical with an Albert Glockendon of whom Neudörffer speaks as a brother of Nikolaus, and as a diligent illuminator and "half a poet." The Berlin Library possesses a Calendar, dated 1526, under this latter name, adorned with cuts and verses to each month. By the former (if they are really to be regarded as two distinct men) are a fine engraving of 'Two Honourable Women' (1531), and thirty-two plates of various Saints.

GLOCKENDON, GEORG, the elder, a woodengraver and illuminator of Nuremberg, was working as early as 1480, and died in 1520. Two of his plates are, 'Mary surrounded by five holy Women,' and 'The Ascension of Christ' (1520).

GLOCKENDON, GEORG, the younger, who was born at Nuremberg in the year 1492, executed miniatures in the manner of Albrecht Dürer. He was also an engraver on wood. He died in 1553.

GLOCKENDON, NIKOLAUS, of Nuremberg, the son of Georg Glockendon the younger, studied under his father, and became a miniaturist of great merit. His works display much feeling and sentiment in addition to great technical knowledge ; they are, however, often incorrect in drawing. In the Royal Library at Aschaffenberg there is a Missal, painted by Glockendon for Albrecht of Brandenburg, Archbishop of Mayence, for which he received 500 gulden. It contains twelve illuminated borders to a calendar, with pictures representing the twelve months, and numerous miniatures after Schongauer, Albrecht Dürer, and Cranach. On the last page of the missal is written the following inscription, "Ich Niklas Glokendon zu

Nurenberg hab disses Bhuch illuminiert und vollent im jahr 1524." The Aschaffenberg Library contains also a prayer-book with designs by Glockendon. This artist died in 1560; the date of his birth has not been recorded. He had twelve sons, all of whom he brought up to his own profession.

GLOVACHEVSKY, KIRIL, a Russian painter, born at Korop in 1735, studied at Kiew, but afterwards went to St. Petersburg, where he became a Professor of the Academy of Fine Arts, and died in 1823.

GLOVER, GEORGE, an engraver, was born about the year 1618. He worked chiefly for the booksellers, and engraved several portraits of persons distinguished in English history. They are executed in a bold, open style, though without much taste. He also engraved some frontispieces and emblematical subjects; but his portraits are his best works. The following are by him:

James I.
Charles I.
Henrietta Maria, Queen of Charles I.
Mary, Daughter of Charles I.
Charles II.
Catharine, Queen of Charles II.
James II.
Mary Beatrice, Queen of James II.
Oliver Cromwell.
Francis Russell, Earl of Bedford.
William Russell, Duke of Bedford.
Algernon Percy, Earl of Northumberland.
Robert Devereux, Earl of Essex.
Henry Rich, Earl of Holland.
Thomas Wentworth, Earl of Strafford.
James Ussher, Archbishop of Armagh.
Sir Thomas Urquhart.
Sir Edward Dering. 1640.
Sir James Campbell.
Sir Henry Oxenden of Barham.
Sir Anthony van Dyck.
John Pym, M.P. for Tavistock.
John Fox, the Martyrologist.
Lewis Roberts, merchant. 1637.
John Goodwin, presbyter. 1642.
William Bariff. 1643.
John Lilburne. 1641.
Henry Burton, Rector of St. Matthew's, Friday Street. 1648.
Natt. Witt, an idiot.

GLOVER, JOHN, a landscape painter in water-colours, was born at Houghton-on-the-Hill, Leicestershire, in 1767. He received no instruction in art, and in 1786 became writing-master at Appleby Free School. He, however, employed all his spare time in drawing, and in 1794 removed to Lichfield, where he devoted himself to practising and teaching art. In 1805 he came to London, and joined the newly-formed Water-Colour Society, of which he was President in 1815. He resigned his membership in 1818, and having been an unsuccessful candidate for Academy honours, he, in 1824, assisted in founding the Society of British Artists, where he exhibited till 1830. In the following year he emigrated to Australia, occasionally sending home works until his death in 1849 at Launceston, Tasmania. Glover's art was fashionable, and his works commanded high prices during his lifetime. He occasionally painted in oils, but his fame rests on his work in water-colours. Amongst his best drawings are:

Durham Cathedral. (*Earl of Durham.*)
Loch Lomond.
Tivoli. (*South Kensington Museum.*)
Windsor Castle. (*The same.*)
Landscape: Windsor Castle in the distance. (*The same.*)
River Scene. (*The same.*)

Matlock Bath—Mist clearing off
Chepstow Castle.
Landscape near Cività Vecchia.
Elter Water.
Wingfield Manor, Antrim.

GLUME, JOHANN GOTTLIEB, who was born at Berlin in 1711, and died in 1798, was a pupil of Pesne and Harper. He painted historical and genre subjects and landscapes, and also etched several portraits, &c.

GMELIN, WILHELM FRIEDRICH, an engraver, was born at Badenweiler in 1745, and studied under Christian von Mechel in Basle. He went to Rome in 1788, and died there in 1821. His engravings after Claude Lorrain and Poussin are of a high order of merit. His best plates are:

The Temple of Venus; *after Claude Lorrain.*
The Mill; *after the same.*
Landscape with the Flight into Egypt; *after the same.*
Acis and Galatea; *after the same.*
The Waterfalls of Tivoli; two plates.
The Villa of Mæcenas at Tivoli; two plates.
The Grotto of Neptune at Tivoli; two plates.
Waterfall of Velino. 1795.
The Lake of Albano near Rome.' 1796.
Rinaldo and Armida; *after G. Poussin.*
View of Pozzuoli; *after Hackert.*

GNOCCHI, PIETRO, was a native of Milan, who was born about 1550, and, according to Morigia, flourished about the year 1595. He was a scholar of Aurelio Luini, and surpassed his instructor in the elegance and taste of his figures. Lanzi conjectures that this artist may be the painter called Pietro Luini, as it was not unusual at that time for the disciple to adopt the name of his master. His best performance is his picture of 'Christ giving the Keys to St. Peter,' in the church of San Vittore at Milan.

GOBAU. See GOUBAU.

GOBBO, ANDREA. See SOLARIO.

GOBBO DA CORTONA, IL (or IL GOBBO DE' CARRACCI, or DALLE FRUTTA). See BONZI.

GÖBELL, GERRIT HENDERIK, a Dutch landscape painter, was born at Raalte in 1786, and died at Deventer in 1833. The Amsterdam Museum has a 'Winter Landscape' by this artist.

GÖBEL, KARL PETER, an Austrian portrait and historical painter, born at Würzburg in 1791, was educated at the Academy at Vienna, where he died in 1823. The Vienna Gallery has a picture by him of 'Jacob blessing the Sons of Joseph.' Besides this may be mentioned his 'Moses,' and 'Death of Dido.'

GOBERT, PIERRE, a French portrait painter, was born at Fontainebleau in 1666. He became an academician in 1701, and died in Paris in 1744. There is by him in the Madrid Gallery a portrait of Louis XV. when Dauphin.

GODBY, JAMES, an English engraver, lived at the beginning of the 19th century. He prepared the illustrations for 'The Fine Arts of the English School,' 1812, and engraved also Raphael's 'Miraculous Draught of Fishes.'

GODDARD, BOUVERIE, an English animal painter, was born in Wiltshire in 1834. He came to London in 1849, and studied for two years in the Zoological Gardens. In 1851 he settled in Salisbury, but six years later returned to London. He was a constant exhibitor at the Royal Academy. He died at Brook Green in 1888. His 'Struggle for Existence' is in the Walker Art Gallery, Liverpool.

GODDARD, JOHN, was an English engraver, of the 17th century. He engraved some frontispieces, maps, and other subjects, for the booksellers. One of his best prints is the portrait of Martin Billingsley, a writing-master, dated 1651, which is prefixed to his copy-book. Strutt mentions a small upright print of a woman standing, under which is inscribed *Vetura*, and another its companion.

GODDYN, PIETER, a Flemish painter, was born at Bruges in 1752. He was educated at the Bruges Academy, and afterwards in Rome, and in 1782 won the first prize at Parma, for the best picture from a scene in Virgil's 'Æneid.' In 1784 he returned to his native city, where he died in 1811.

GODEFROID, MARIE ELÉONORE, a daughter and pupil of the painter Ferdinand Joseph Godefroid, was born in Paris in 1778. In 1795 she became a teacher of art and music in the Institute of St. Germain; but in order to devote herself more entirely to painting she renounced this position and entered the atelier of Gérard, whom she assisted in his works, while she also independently painted portraits in oil, water-colour, and pastel. She had an elder brother a painter, who completed her education after their father's death. She died in Paris in 1849.

GODEFROY, ——, was a French miniaturist, who worked at Fontainebleau early in the 16th century, and rivalled Fouquet, Beauneveu, the Pascals, and other celebrated artists of that time. In 1519-20 he executed for Francis I. the miniatures in the fine manuscript of Cæsar's 'Commentaries,' of which the first volume is now in the British Museum, the second in the National Library at Paris, and the third in the collection of the Duke d'Aumale. He also painted those in the beautiful manuscript of the French translation of the 'Triumphs' of Petrarch, which is in the library of the Arsenal in Paris.

GODEFROY, FRANÇOIS, a French designer and engraver, was born at Rouen in 1748, and died in Paris in 1819. He was the father of Jean Godefroy, and one of the best scholars of Le Bas, under whose tuition he engraved landscapes after Casanova and Claude Lorrain, genre pieces after Fragonard, and historical subjects from the Revolution in North America. Among his best plates are:

Landscape with a Herd of Cattle; *after Villemont.*
A pair of Landscapes, called 'Le Temple des Amours,' and 'La Tour des deux Amans;' *after Lantara.*
A View of the Village of Moutiers Travers; *after Chatelet.*
Amusement of Brabant; *after Teniers.*
The Georgian Bath; *after L. de La Hire.*
A pastoral Landscape; *after Casanova.*
A Landscape, with a Waterfall; *after Le Prince.*
A Landscape; *after Claude Lorrain.*

GODEFROY, JEAN, a French engraver, the son of François Godefroy, was born in London in 1771, and was a scholar of J. P. Simon. He engraved the works of the most eminent French painters of his time; particularly those of Gérard, Prud'hon, Carle Vernet, Isabey, and Chaudet. There are also by him engravings after Raphael, Correggio, Poussin, and the Carracci. He died in Paris in 1839. He is said to have been also a painter. The following are among his best plates:

Cupid and Psyche; *after Gérard.*
The Battle of Austerlitz; *after the same.* 1813.
Ossian with his Harp charming up Pictures of Phantasy; *after the same.*

The Congress of Vienna; *after Isabey.* 1819.
Bonaparte at Malmaison; *after the same.*
The Death of Hippolytus; *after Carle Vernet.*

GODEFROY, PETER LUDWIG DE LARIVE. See LARIVE-GODEFROY.

GÖDELER, ELIAS, (JOHANN,) an Austrian historical and landscape painter, as well as an architect, was born in 1620. He painted in oil and in fresco principally at Nuremberg, Baireuth, and Hildburghausen, and died in the last-named town in 1693.

GODEMAN, an English monk of the latter half of the 10th century, was a miniature painter, who executed thirty designs in gouache and gold in a Benedictional of Bishop Athelwold of Winchester, now in the possession of the Duke of Devonshire, and in a Benedictional and a Missal now in the Library at Rouen.

GODETS, ANTOINE DES. See DES GODETS.

GODEWYCK, MARGARITA, born at Dordrecht in 1627, was a pupil of Nicolaas Maes, and painted landscapes and flower-pieces. She possessed a remarkable talent of executing similar subjects in needle-work. She died at Dordrecht in 1677.

GODFREY, G., an English artist, engraved, among other things, some of the plates for Grose's 'Antiquities' in 1785.

GODFREY, RICHARD B., an engraver, was born in London in 1728. He engraved several views and antiquities, and some English portraits for Bell's 'British Theatre' and the 'Antiquarian Repository;' among them the following:

Edward, the Black Prince.
Thomas, Duke of Gloucester.
Margaret, Countess of Salisbury.
Sir Henry Upton, British Minister in France.
Simon Forman, astrologer.
Sir Anthony Weldon, historian.
John Evans, astrologer.
Abraham Cowley, poet.
Richard Cromwell, son of the Protector.

GODWIN, JAMES, an English designer for illustrated books, was born early in the 19th century. He studied in the schools of the Royal Academy, and exhibited there and at the Society of British Artists between the years 1846 and 1851 some works, among which was his 'Hamlet and Ophelia.' He died in London in 1876.

GOEBOUW, ANTOON. See GOUBAU.

GOEDAARD, JOHANNES, born at the beginning of the 17th century in Middelburg, where he died in 1668, painted insects and other objects of natural history.

GOEDIG, HEINRICH, (or GOEDIGEN,) a painter and engraver, was a native of Brunswick, who in 1558 went to Dresden, and entered the service of the Elector of Saxony. In the Ducal Art Cabinet at Gotha is a little book containing thirteen miniature pictures by him representing scenes from the life of Christ. His most important work as an engraver is a series of subjects taken from the History of Saxony and published in 1597-98, but these plates are surpassed by seven historical landscapes which he executed about the same time. After 1598 every trace of the artist disappears.

GOEIMARE, JAN, a landscape painter, was a native of Flanders, who flourished at the beginning of the 17th century.

GOEKINDT, PIETER, (or GOETKINT,) an amateur painter, was a native of Antwerp, who flourished about 1581, and was the first master of Jan Brueghel.

GOENEUTTE (NORBERT), French painter-engraver, born in Paris in 1854; became a pupil of Pils at the École des Beaux Arts, exhibiting his first two pictures in the Salon of 1876, which provoked much comment. One of these was the 'Boulevard de Clichy.' Parisian to the core, Goeneutte at once devoted himself to reproducing certain characteristic types and aspects of the French capital with signal success. Their qualities of keen observation and subtle humour should serve to prevent many of his pictures from being forgotten. Of these we may mention 'L'Appel des Balayeurs,' 'La Soupe du matin à la porte de chez Brébant,' 'Les Bonnes de chez Duval,' &c. Goeneutte ranks with Desboutin and Somm as one of the most remarkable draughtsmen and drypoint engravers of modern times. His work deeply influenced latter-day engraving, and in this perhaps his originality and talent are best displayed. He died at Anvers-sur-Oise, October 9, 1894.

GOEREE, J., was a Dutch engraver, who resided at Amsterdam about the middle of the 17th century. He engraved a variety of frontispieces and other book plates, which are chiefly, if not entirely, from his own designs.

GOES, HUGO VAN DER. See VAN DER GOES.

GOESIN, PIERRE ANTOINE FRANÇOIS DE, a Flemish historical painter, was born at Ghent in 1753. He was Professor at the Academy, and Director of the Institute at Ghent, but he abandoned art in order to take the management of the printing office which had been carried on by his family for upwards of a century. He died in 1831.

GOESTELINE, WILLEM, a native of Brussels, painted in 1463 an altar picture in the church of St. Nicholas at Ghent.

GOETHE-MEYER, JOHANN HEINRICH. See MEYER.

GOETZ, GOTTFRIED BERNARD, a German painter and mezzotint engraver, was born at Kloster-Welchrod, in Moravia, in 1708. He was instructed in painting by Eckstein, and afterwards was a scholar of Johann Georg Bergmüller, at Augsburg, where he died in 1768. His works as a painter are little known out of his own country; but he has scraped some plates in mezzotint, among which are the following:

The Emperor Charles VII.; *after a picture by himself.*
Bust of Louis XV.
St. Amandus; *after J. G. Bergmüller.*
St. Walburg; *after the same.*

GOIEN, JAN VAN. See GOYEN.

GOLCHI, PETER, is mentioned by Walpole as having painted in England in the reign of Queen Elizabeth.

GOLD, CHARLES, a colonel of the Royal Artillery, was an English amateur draughtsman. He entered the army in 1790, and after having served in India and the Netherlands, and at Waterloo, retired from the service in 1825, and died at Leamington in 1842. He published in 1806 'Oriental Drawings,' representing Indian costumes, &c.

GOLDAR, JOHN, an engraver, was born at Oxford in 1729, and died of apoplexy in Hyde Park, London, in 1795. He engraved several humorous subjects, among which is a set of four plates, after John Collet, called 'Modern Love.' He also engraved a print of 'Ships after an Engagement,' after Wright.

GOLDING, RICHARD, a line-engraver, was born in London of humble parentage in 1785. He was apprenticed in 1799 to an engraver named Pass, for seven years, but left him after five, when his indentures were transferred to James Parker, who, however, died shortly after; Golding completing some of the plates he had left unfinished. Rapidly improving in his profession, Golding soon after obtained through a Mr. Fuller, an American artist, for whom he had engraved a plate, an introduction to West, for whom he executed a plate of the 'Death of Nelson.' He also became known to Smirke, from whose paintings he executed many beautiful engravings for book illustration; among the best are those for editions of 'Don Quixote' and 'Gil Blas.' In 1818 he engraved for Sir Thomas Lawrence his portrait of the 'Princess Charlotte of Wales,' a very fine plate, for which he received much praise, so that he now became famous, and obtained many commissions. Some years after, however, he seems to have become apathetic, and discontinued work almost entirely. He died at Lambeth in 1865 in comparative poverty. The chief of his larger works are:

St. Ambrose refusing the Emperor Theodosius admission to the Church; *after Paolo Veronese.*
A Peep into Futurity; *after Maclise.*
The Princess Charlotte of Wales; *after Sir Thomas Lawrence.*
The Princess Victoria (the Queen) in her ninth year; *after Westall.*
The Princess Victoria (the Queen); *after Fowler.* 1830.
Henry Calvert, Esq.; *after T. Phillips.*
Thomas Hammersley, Esq.; *after Hamilton.*

GOLDSCHMIDT, HERMANN, a painter, but more distinguished as an astronomer, was born at Frankfort-on-the-Main in 1802. A visit to Holland in 1832 decided him to devote himself to art, and he then studied under Schnorr and Cornelius at Munich. In 1834 he took up his residence in Paris, where his 'Romeo and Juliet' was purchased by the state. He became an astronomer in 1847, and has left a name in that science by his discovery of thirteen of the asteroidal planets. He died at Fontainebleau in 1866.

GOLE, JACOBUS, a Dutch engraver, was born at Amsterdam in 1660, and died in the same city in 1737. There are by him several prints, some of which are executed with the graver, and others in mezzotint; the former are the better. Among them are the following:

LINE-ENGRAVINGS.

Charles XI., King of Sweden. 1685.
Duchess de La Vallière. 1685.
Mahomet IV., Sultan of Turkey.
Kara Mustapha, Grand Vizier.
Abraham Hellenbroek, Minister of the Gospel.
Nicolas Colvius, Pastor of the Walloon Church; *after B. Vaillant.*

MEZZOTINT PORTRAITS.

Charles III., King of Spain.
Frederick, King of Poland.
George Augustus, Elector of Brunswick-Luneburg.
Charles, Landgrave of Hesse-Cassel.
Cornelis Tromp, Admiral of Holland.
Balthasar Becker.

SUBJECTS IN MEZZOTINT.

Peasants smoking; *after Adriaan van Ostade.*
Dutch Boors regaling; *after Adriaen Brouwer.*
The Tooth-drawer; *after Teniers.*
The Schoolmaster; *after E. Heemskerk.*
Heraclitus; *after Cornelis Dusart.*

GOLS, CONRAD (or GOLTZIUS), an engraver, was working at Cologne at the end of the 16th century. There are known of his works:

St. Bernard with the Instruments of the Passion.
The History of Susannah; seven plates.
The Annunciation.
The Seven Sacraments.

GOLTZIUS, HENDRIK, a painter and an engraver both on metal and on wood, was born at Mülbrecht, in the duchy of Jülich, in 1558. His father, Johann Goltzius, was an eminent glass-painter, who instructed him in the first principles of art; and he was taught engraving by Dirk Cuerenhert. His progress was such, that he soon surpassed his master, who employed him to engrave some plates, and he also executed several for Philipp Galle. In his twenty-first year he married a wealthy widow, the mother of Jakob Matham, which enabled him to establish a printing office of his own, but did not advance his happiness, and in fact the continued domestic discord so preyed upon his health that it led to his travelling to southern lands. He passed through Germany to Italy, where his studies were particularly directed to the works of Michelangelo, Raphael, and Polidoro da Caravaggio. A too vehement desire to imitate the style of Michelangelo led him frequently into outrageous and extravagant designs, which are not always compensated by the extraordinary excellence of his graver. During his residence at Rome, he engraved several plates after Raphael, Polidoro, and others; and on his return to Holland he settled at Haarlem, where he engraved several plates from the Flemish and Dutch masters. He imitated with the greatest success the styles of Albrecht Dürer, Lucas van Leyden, and other admired old masters, and produced a set of six large plates, called the 'Masterpieces of Goltzius,' not because they are his best productions, but as showing how perfectly he could copy the particular manner of those artists whose works were held in higher estimation than his own. He had reached his forty-second year when he commenced painting. His first picture represented the 'Crucifixion,' with the Virgin Mary and St. John, and it is commended by Van Mander for the excellence of the colouring, and the boldness of the design. He died at Haarlem in 1617. His principal pictures are:

Petersburg.	*Hermitage.*	Adam and Eve.
„	„	The Circumcision of Christ.
„	„	The Adoration of the Magi.
„	„	The Baptism of Christ.
Rotterdam.	*Museum.*	Juno receiving the eyes of Argus. 1615.

Goltzius is more famous as an engraver than a painter, and his prints amount to more than five hundred in number; they are frequently marked with the cipher **HG** The following are his principal plates:

PORTRAITS.

Henndrik Goltzius.
Henry IV., King of France; oval. 1592.
Frederick II., King of Denmark; oval. 1588.
William, Prince of Orange, in armour, with an emblematical border.
Charlotte de Bourbon, Princess of Orange.
Dirk Cuerenhert; *after his own design.*
Gerbrand Adriaansz Brederods; with an oval border of laurels.
Hans Bol, painter of Mechlin; in an ornamental border.
Jan Stradan, painter.
Philipp Galle, engraver.
Pieter Forest, or Forestus, physician. 1586.
Justus Lipsius. 1587.
Johannes Zurenus; *after M. van Heemskerk.*

258

M. de La Faille; very highly finished.
Madame de La Faille, with a Skull; the companion. 1589.
Christopher Plantin, the printer.
Françoise d'Egmont, with her hand on a Skull; oval.
Robert Dudley, Earl of Leicester; oval. 1586.
S. Sovius, without his name; inscribed, *Bene agere et nil timere.* 1583.

VARIOUS SUBJECTS FROM HIS OWN DESIGNS.

Judah and Tamar; circular; supposed to be one of his earliest plates.
The Life and Passion of our Saviour; twelve plates, executed in the style of Albrecht Dürer; *H. Goltz fec.* 1597. There is a set of copies after these, in a stiff, formal style.
Christ and the Apostles; fourteen plates. 1598.
Six large plates, known by the name of the 'Masterpieces of Goltzius.' They are executed in the style of each of the masters he wished to imitate, and are as follow:
    The Annunciation; in the style of *Raphael.*
    The Visitation; in imitation of *Parmigiano.*
    The Annunciation; in the manner of *Bassano.*
    The Circumcision; in the style of *Albrecht Dürer.*
    The Adoration of the Magi; in imitation of *Lucas van Leyden.*
    The Holy Family; in the manner of *F. Barocci.*
The Nativity; unfinished and extremely scarce. 1615.
The Adoration of the Magi.
The Murder of the Innocents; very scarce; the plate was not finished.
The Repose in Egypt; *H. Goltzius fec.* 1589.
The Woman of Samaria. 1589.
The Wise Men's Offering; a curious composition.
The Infant Jesus holding a globe, with a glory of Angels; *H. Goltz fec.* 1597.
The Temptation of St. Anthony.
A Female Saint, holding a book; very scarce. Some parts of the plate are merely traced.
A set of fifty-two plates for the 'Metamorphoses' of Ovid. It is supposed that Goltzius was largely assisted by his scholars in these plates.
A set of ten plates of Eight of the Heroes of ancient Rome, with the introduction and conclusion. 1586. Engraved in a free, bold style, with fine backgrounds.
Venus reclining against a Tree, holding a bunch of grapes, whilst Cupid presents to her a handful of corn; a circular plate, of highly finished and beautiful execution.
Three plates; Bacchus, Venus, and Ceres; dedicated to Cornelis van Haarlem.
Three plates; Juno, Minerva, and Venus; ovals. 1596.
Mars and Venus. 1585.
Three plates; Jupiter and Juno, Neptune and Amphitrite, and Pluto and Proserpine.
Pygmalion and his Statue. 1593.
Mercury and Argus; a small plate, very scarce.
Nine plates of the Muses; each with four verses. 1592.
Three plates of the Graces.
The Three Fates; in circular plates.
The Apollo Belvedere, with the Portrait of the Designer, in half-length.
The Hercules Commodus.
The Farnese Hercules.
The three prints last mentioned, after the famous antique statues, are executed with surprising beauty and energy.
Hercules holding his Club; in the back-ground are represented his labours. 1589. In this plate Goltzius has overcharged the outline of the figure in the most barbarous manner, the parts are scattered, and the whole is without effect.
The Judgment of Midas. 1590.
The seven Cardinal Virtues; Faith, Hope, Charity, Justice, Prudence, Fortitude, and Temperance; in seven plates.
Three fine plates, of Diligence, Patience, and Wisdom; personified by female figures.
Labour and Diligence; represented by a male and female figure. 1580.
An emblematical subject of Christian Prudence, in a

female figure, richly clothed; small circular, highly finished.

The Blind leading the Blind; circular.

The Chariot of War; an immense composition; *Henricus Goltzius fecit*; very scarce.

The Boy and Dog. The boy is supposed to be the portrait of the son of Theodoor Frisius, a painter of Venice, to whom Goltzius dedicated the print. It is considered one of his finest plates.

Corydon and Sylvia; a pastoral.

A Mountainous Landscape, with the story of Dædalus and Icarus; an etching.

WOODCUTS AFTER HIS OWN DESIGNS.

A Landscape, with a Cottage, and a Woman drawing Water from a Well.

A Landscape on the sea-coast, with a large Rock, and a Hermit kneeling.

A pastoral Landscape, with a Shepherd and Shepherdess.

A Warrior, with a Helmet and a Spear; half-length.

Hercules slaying Cacus.

A set of seven plates of the Heathen Divinities; fine.

SUBJECTS AFTER VARIOUS ITALIAN MASTERS.

St. Joachim; *after Raphael.*

The Triumph of Galatea; *after the same.*

Eight plates of the Heathen Divinities; in niches; after the paintings by *Polidoro da Caravaggio*, in the Quirinal.

Two Sibyls; *after the same.*

The Last Supper; *after Paolo Veronese.* 1585.

The Marriage at Cana; *after G. Salviati;* in two sheets.

St. Jerome in the Desert, in meditation; *after Palma;* fine.

SUBJECTS AFTER VARIOUS FLEMISH AND GERMAN MASTERS.

The Fall of Adam and Eve; *after B. Spranger.* 1585.

The dead Christ supported by an Angel; *after the same.*

The Banquet of the Gods on the Marriage of Cupid and Psyche; in three sheets; *after the same.*

The Venetian Ball; *after Theodore Bernard;* in two sheets.

The Dragon devouring the Companions of Cadmus; *after Cornelis van Haarlem.* 1588.

The dead Christ, with the Four Evangelists at the Tomb; *after A. van Blocklandt.*

GOLTZIUS, HUBRECHT, (or GOLTZ,) an eminent artist and learned antiquary, born at Venloo in 1526, was the son of an obscure painter of Würzburg, named Rüdiger, who taught him the rudiments of design, and placed him under the tuition of Lambert Lombard of Liége. He assumed his mother's name of Goltz, which he Latinized into Goltzius. Lambert Lombard had, during a long residence in Italy, made drawings from the most celebrated remains of antiquity : these were given to Goltzius to copy, and they inspired him with a wish to visit Italy himself. He therefore went to Rome, and resided there several years. On his return he settled at Bruges, where he published several antiquarian works embellished with prints, in which he was assisted by Josse Gietleugen of Courtrai, who executed the woodcuts. Little is known of his works as a painter, but Van Mander commends a set of pictures by him, representing the history of the Golden Fleece, painted for the House of Austria. All he did must have been executed before 1557. In 1563 he published at Bruges his work entitled 'C. Julius Cæsar,' with forty-six copper-plates of ancient coins, &c. In 1566 he issued at Bruges another work entitled 'Fasti Magistratuum et Triumphorum Romanorum,' with two hundred and thirty-four plates and woodcuts. His collected works appeared at Antwerp in 1644-45, in five volumes, as 'Romanæ et Græcæ Antiquitatis Monumenta ex priscis numismatibus eruta.' Goltzius died at Bruges in 1583.

GOLTZIUS, JAKOB, an engraver, who was working at the close of the 16th century, was probably a relative of Hendrik Goltzius. Two plates, engraved after the latter, are known of his work: 'Pallas in the midst of a number of Warriors,' and 'A young Man endeavouring to bribe an old Woman into Love.'

GOLTZIUS, JULIUS, a son of Hendrik Goltzius, flourished about the year 1580. The following engravings are by him :

The Good and Bad Shepherd; a set of middle-sized plates; *after Marten De Vos.*

Christ appearing to the Magdalen; *after F. Zucchero.*

Part of the plates for Boissard's 'Habitus Variorum Orbis Gentium.' 1581.

The Virgin suckling her Child; *after M. De Vos.*

The Good Samaritan; *after H. Bol.*

The Evangelist Matthew; *after A. van Blocklandt* (one of a series of four).

GOMEZ, FRANCISCO, was the son and pupil of Martin Gomez. He executed six pictures for the Carmelite Friars in Granada, but in 1750 he went to America, and died in Mexico about 1755.

GOMEZ, JACINTO, born at San Ildefonso in 1746, was a pupil of Francisco Bayeu. He was appointed chamber painter to Charles IV., and died in 1812. In the Madrid Gallery is a picture by him of 'The Angelic Hierarchy adoring the Holy Spirit.'

GOMEZ, JUAN, was a Spanish historical painter in the service of Philip II. in 1593. He painted the large picture of 'The Martyrdom of St. Ursula and her Companions,' which was designed and traced by Pellegrino Tibaldi to supply the place of the same subject by Luca Cambiaso, which had been removed to the old church of the Escorial. He painted also several subjects from the Life of St. Jerome. He restored the 'Annunciation,' and the 'St. Jerome penitent,' by Federigo Zucchero, which Philip had rejected, and ordered to be retouched. He died in 1597.

GOMEZ, JUAN DE ALFARO Y. See ALFARO.

GOMEZ, LUCIANO SALVADOR. See SALVADOR GOMEZ.

GOMEZ, MARTIN, a Spanish painter, was a brother of Sebastian Gomez, and flourished in the latter part of the 16th century. He lived at Cuenca, for the cathedral of which city he painted several pictures.

GOMEZ, SEBASTIAN, called EL MULATO DE MURILLO, born in 1646, was a mulatto servant of the celebrated Murillo. From witnessing the exercise of his master's talents he conceived a liking for art, and passed his leisure time in efforts to follow it, which were successful. After the death of Murillo, in 1685, he painted some pictures for the churches and convents at Seville. In the portico of the convent of the Mercenarios Descalzos, there is a painting by him of 'The Virgin and Infant Christ'; and at the Capuchins, 'Christ bound to the Pillar.' There are several other works by him at Seville, where he died in 1682. In the Hermitage at St. Petersburg is a picture of 'St. Francis.'

GOMEZ, SEBASTIAN, a painter of Granada, who flourished about the middle of the 16th century, was instructed in the school of Alonso Cano, but by no means approached him in his workmanship. A

S 2

259

picture by him of 'The Virgin with Angels and St. Dominick' is at the monastery of San Pablo at Seville, and one of 'St. Rosa of Viterbo preaching' is in the Franciscan convent at Ecija.

GOMEZ, VICENTE SALVADOR. See SALVADOR GOMEZ.

GONDOLACH, MATTHÄUS, (or GUNDELACH,) a portrait and historical painter of Hesse-Cassel, was for some considerable time in the service of the Emperor Rudolph II. at Prague, and died at Augsburg in 1653. The Vienna Gallery contains a 'Madonna and Child with Saints,' dated 1614.

GONSALVEZ, NUNO, who was court painter to King Alfonso of Portugal (1438—1481), painted the altar of St. Vincent in the Cathedral of Lisbon, and 'Christ at the Pillar' in the convent of the Trinity in the same city. He apparently studied in Italy, as he was a good imitator of the great masters of that country.

GONZAGA, ——, (or GONSAGO,) a scene-painter, who also executed landscapes and perspective pictures, worked for theatres in Italy, and from 1794 to 1804 in St. Petersburg. He is known to have been living in 1827.

GONZALEZ, BARTOLOMÉ, was born at Valladolid in 1564, but he visited Madrid when young, and became a pupil of Patricio Caxes. He was employed by Philip III. to paint the portraits of different branches of the Austrian royal family, for the palace of Pardo, and on the death of Castello he was made painter to the king. There are many of his works in the Escorial, at Valladolid, and at Burgos. Of his historical works, the principal are the angels in the church of the Augustines at Madrid; and an allegory of the Arts, in the royal collection. In the Madrid Gallery are portraits of Queen Margaret of Austria, wife of Philip III., and the Infanta Clara Isabella Eugenia, daughter of Philip II. He died at Madrid in 1627.

GONZALEZ, CRISTOBAL, a Spanish painter, lived at Madrid about 1590, and executed several pictures for the convent of the Barefooted Carmelites.

GONZALEZ, FERRAN, was a painter and sculptor of Toledo, who died in 1399.

GONZALEZ, FRANCISCO MIGUEL, was an engraver, and one of the founders of the school of design at Seville about the year 1660.

GONZALEZ, JUAN GIACCHINETTI. See GIACCHINETTI GONZALEZ.

GONZALEZ, PEDRO RUIZ. See RUIZ GONZALEZ.

GONZALEZ BECERRIL, JUAN, a Spanish painter, who lived at Toledo in the 15th century, was the pupil of Pedro Berraguette, whose daughter he married. He assisted his father-in-law in decorating the cloisters of Toledo cathedral in 1498.

GONZALEZ DE CEDILLO, ANTONIO, a Spanish painter, born at Toledo about 1635, studied at Madrid under Rizi. He then went to Rome, where he occupied his time in copying the best masters, and on his return to Spain painted several pictures rich in colouring and pure in design. He died about 1680.

GONZALEZ DE LA VEGA, DIEGO, was born at Madrid in 1622, and was a scholar of Francisco Rizi, whose style he followed. After marrying early and soon becoming a widower, he entered the convent of the Fathers of the Saviour. There are many of his works in the public edifices at Madrid, and some of his easel pictures in the private collections. In the cloister of the Franciscans are several pictures by him of the Life and Passion of our Saviour; and in the convent of the

Religiosas Mercenarias, are some subjects from the Life of the Virgin. He died at Madrid in 1697.

GONZALEZ RUIZ, ANTONIO, a Spanish painter, was instructed first under Hovasse at Madrid, and afterwards successively in Paris, Rome, and other Italian towns. In 1752 he was made director of the Academy of San Fernando, and in 1757 court painter. He died in 1785. He was a member of the Academies of Valencia and St. Petersburg. His pictures are to be seen in Madrid and Salamanca.

GONZALEZ VELAZQUEZ, ALEXANDRO, was the second of three brothers, all painters, the sons of Pablo Velazquez Gonzalez, a native of Andujar, who practised carving at Madrid. He was born at Madrid in 1719, and assisted his brother Luis in the coronation decorations in 1746, and in many subsequent works. He painted some frescoes in the Bernardine and other nunneries at Madrid, and in conjunction with one Guillermo l'Anglois (probably a Frenchman), he painted a ceiling in the palace from the designs of Mengs. He was also an architect. He had just completed some scenery for the theatre in the Calle del Principe, when he died at Madrid in 1772.

GONZALEZ VELAZQUEZ, ANTONIO, the youngest of the three sons of Pablo Velazquez Gonzalez, and the most famous, was born at Madrid in 1729. He was sent with a pension from the crown to study at Rome, where he became the pupil of Giaquinto Corrado, and acquired some reputation by a fresco which he painted in the church of the Trinitarian friars of Castile, and a picture of the 'Anointing of King David,' which he sent to the new Royal Academy at Madrid. In 1753 he returned to Spain to adorn with frescoes the chapel of Our Lady of the Pillar in the cathedral of Zaragoza. From there he went to Madrid, and assisted his brothers in painting the domes of the church of the Incarnation and of the Royal Salesian Nunnery. He likewise executed a picture of the 'Assumption' for the cathedral at Cuenca. In 1754 he was made deputy-director in the Academy, and in 1765 full director, and in 1757 he was appointed court-painter. In the New Palace he executed an allegorical fresco on the ceiling of the Queen's ante-chamber, and in another saloon a fresco of 'Ferdinand and Isabella receiving the New World from the hands of Columbus.' He executed many other paintings in oil and fresco in various churches and convents, and as court-painter executed several portraits, including that of Charles III. He died at Madrid in 1793, leaving three sons, of whom the eldest and youngest were painters, and the second an architect.

GONZALEZ VELAZQUEZ, LUIS, the eldest of the three sons of Pablo Velazquez Gonzalez, was born at Madrid in 1715. He was one of the earliest students in the School of Art, established in 1744, and in 1746 he furnished the decorations for the streets and the theatre of Buenretiro at the coronation of Ferdinand VI., who appointed him his painter in ordinary. He was a member and director of the Academy of San Fernando, and died at Madrid in 1764. The frescoes on the dome of the church of San Marcos were esteemed his best work, but are pronounced to be very feeble.

GONZALEZ y TAVE, FEDERICO, was born at Cadiz in 1823, and showed so much talent when young that the municipality paid his expenses to Madrid and Paris. Upon his return he became a successful painter of portraits, made many copies of the works of Van Dyck, Velazquez, and Murillo, and obtained great praise for his picture of 'Pedro I. consulting his Horoscope,' now in the Cadiz Museum. He died at Cadiz in 1867.

GOOCH, T., was an English animal painter, who exhibited pictures of horses and dogs at the Royal Academy from 1777 to 1802, when he retired to Lyndhurst in Hampshire.

GOOD, THOMAS SWORD, an English genre painter, born at Berwick in 1789, was brought up as a house-painter, but subsequently devoted himself to art, and produced works in the style of Wilkie. He came to London, and exhibited at the Royal Academy from 1820 to 1833, when having inherited some property he retired to Berwick, where he died in 1872. Amongst his works are:

A Scotch Shepherd. 1820.
Practice. 1823.
Music.
Fishermen.
The Industrious Mother.
Idlers. 1829.
The Truant. 1830.
Medicine. 1831.
The Newspaper.
No News.
Fisherman with a Gun.
Study of a Boy.
} *(National Gallery, London.)*

GOODALL, EDWARD, a line-engraver, was born at Leeds in 1795. Entirely self-taught, he at an early age practised both engraving and painting, but having attracted the attention of Turner, he received from that master a commission to engrave from his pictures as many plates as he would undertake, and by these engravings Edward Goodall is chiefly known. Among the best may be mentioned those after the great landscape painter's 'Tivoli,' 'Cologne,' 'Caligula's Bridge,' 'Old London Bridge,' and 'Richmond Hill,' and others in the 'England and Wales' and 'Southern Coast' series, besides some of the exquisite little vignettes illustrating Rogers's 'Italy' and 'Poems.' He also engraved many plates for the 'Art Journal,' and several after the works of his son, Frederick Goodall, R. A. He died in London in 1870, leaving behind a family of artists, three of his sons being well-known painters, and one of his daughters having exhibited several pictures at the Royal Academy. Besides his plates after Turner, the following are his most important works:

Raising the Maypole; *after Frederick Goodall.*
The Swing; *after the same.*
The Angel's Whisper; *after the same.*
The Soldier's Dream; *after the same.*
The Piper; *after the same. (Art Union of London.)*
A Summer Holiday; *after the same.*
Cranmer at the Traitor's Gate; *after the same.*
The Happy Days of Charles the First; *after the same.*
The Castle of Ischia; *after Stanfield. (Art Union of London.)*
The Bridge of Toledo; *after David Roberts.*
Amalfi; *after G. E. Herring.*
The Chalk Waggoner; *after Rosa Bonheur.*
Evening; a composition; *after Cuyp. (Pye's National Gallery.)*
An Italian Sea-Port; *after Claude Lorrain. (The same.)*
The Marriage Festival of Isaac and Rebecca; *after the same. (The same.)*
The Market Cart; *after Gainsborough. (The same.)*
The Ferry; *after F. R. Lee. (Finden's Royal Gallery of British Art.)*

GOODALL, FREDERICK TREVELYAN, the eldest son of Frederick Goodall, R.A., born in 1848, was a student of the Royal Academy, where he gained, in 1870, the gold medal for his painting of 'The

Return of Ulysses.' He soon after went to Italy, but unhappily lost his life by an accident at Capri in 1871.

GOODALL, HOWARD, the second son of Frederick Goodall, R.A., was born in 1849. He exhibited at the Royal Academy in 1870, 'Nydia in the House of Glaucus,' and in 1873, 'Capri Girls winnowing.' This promising young artist died at Cairo in 1874.

GOODALL, WALTER, youngest son of Edward Goodall, the engraver, and brother of Frederick Goodall, R.A., and Edward A. Goodall, R.S.W., was born in 1830. He studied at the Government School of Design and the Royal Academy, and restricted himself to water-colour painting. In 1853 he was elected an Associate of the Royal Society of Painters in Water-Colours, and in 1861 became a full member of the Society, in which he took an active interest, and in whose Gallery he almost exclusively exhibited. In 1875, after an attack of paralysis, his health gave way, and he painted but little afterwards, retiring in 1887 from the Society, and dying in 1889 at Clapham, near Bedford. His subjects were chosen for the most part from rural life, and he treated them in a refined and somewhat idealized way; delicacy rather than vigour being the characteristic of his figure-drawing. He drew many of the pictures in the Vernon Gallery for engraving for the 'Art Journal.'

GOODRICKE, MATTHEW, (or GOTHERICKE,) is mentioned as a painter in the reign of Charles I. of England.

GOODWIN, EDWARD, a landscape painter in water-colours, exhibited at the Royal Academy from 1802 to 1808. In 1806, he was an unsuccessful candidate for admission to the Water-Colour Society, but exhibited at its open exhibitions from 1814 to 1816.

GOODYEAR, JOSEPH, a line-engraver, was born at Birmingham in 1799. He came to London, and studied under Charles Heath, and was subsequently employed on Finden's 'Royal Gallery of British Art,' for which he engraved the 'Greek Fugitives,' after Eastlake. He also executed several plates for the 'Keepsake.' He died in London in 1839.

GOOL, JAN VAN, a Dutch painter and writer on art, born at the Hague in 1685, studied under Terwesten and Simon van der Does. His cattle pieces are praiseworthy, but not to be considered as masterpieces. He is better known by his 'Lives of the Artists of the Netherlands,' published in 1718, in continuation of the work of Houbraken. He died at the Hague in 1763. In the Rotterdam Museum is a picture of a 'Girl milking a Cow.'

GOOVAERTS, HENDRIK, a Flemish painter, was born at Mechlin in 1669, but on his father's death he went to reside in Antwerp, where he commenced his artistic studies. In his twentieth year he travelled through Germany, exercising his art in Frankfort and other cities. He then went to Prague and Vienna, at each of which cities he resided about three years, and then travelled through Hungary and Slavonia. After an absence of nearly ten years he returned to Antwerp in 1699, when he was made free of the Corporation of St. Luke. He died at Antwerp in 1720. In the Antwerp Gallery is a picture of the 'Junior Archers' Guild inaugurating the portrait of their chief, Jean Charles de Cordes,' dated 1713.

GORDON, Sir JOHN WATSON, a Scotch portrait painter, the eldest son of Captain James Watson, R. N., was born at Edinburgh in 1790. He was originally intended for the army, but having studied in the Trustees' Academy, he preferred an artistic career, and at first turned his attention to historical painting. It was not long, however, before the exigencies of life compelled him to devote himself to portraiture, and on the death of Raeburn in 1823, he became the chief portrait painter in Scotland, when he assumed the name of Gordon. He had a considerable share in the foundation of the Royal Scottish Academy, of which he was one of the earliest members, and he became its president in 1850, at the same time being knighted and appointed Queen's 'Limner.' His works were also exhibited in London, where he was elected an Associate of the Royal Academy in 1841, and an Academician in 1850. He died at Edinburgh in 1864. Amongst his portraits are the following:

Earl of Hopetoun. } Archers' Hall, Edinburgh.
Earl of Dalhousie. }
Principal Lee. (Edinburgh University.)
Sir James Hall. (Royal Society, Edinburgh.)
Lord Murray.
Lord Cockburn.
Sir William Gibson Craig, Bart.
Sir John George Shaw Lefevre.
Sir William Johnston, Lord Provost of Edinburgh.
Lord Rutherfurd. } (National Gallery of Scotland.)
Sir Walter Scott, Bart. (unfinished).
A Grandfather's Lesson.
Roderick Gray, Provost of Peterhead.
Fancy Portrait of a Lady in White Satin.
Professor Ferrier. (United College, St. Andrews.)
Sir David Brewster. (National Gallery.)
David Cox. (Birmingham and Midland Institute.)
Thomas De Quincey. (National Portrait Gallery.)

GORDOT, CLAUDE MARIE, was a French painter of the 18th century, by whom there is in the Musée Calvet, at Avignon, a picture of the Pope's Palace at Avignon, dated 1774.

GORE, CHARLES, an English marine draughtsman, flourished about the end of the 18th century. There are several of his drawings in the Cracherode Collection in the British Museum.

GORGASUS, an ancient Greek modeller and painter, was engaged along with Damophilus, about B.C. 490, in adorning the Temple of Ceres at the Circus Maximus in Rome in both branches of his art. It is stated that he worked upon the left and Damophilus upon the right side of the edifice.

GORI, ANGIOLO, a Florentine painter of the 17th century, painted genre subjects, and fruit and flower pictures. He was a pupil of Chiavistelli, and in 1658 was engaged with others in decorating the corridor of the Public Gallery at Florence.

GÖRIZ, CHRISTIAN, was a native of Vienna, who flourished in the 17th century, and painted Italian views.

GORTZIUS. See GELDORP.

GOSLING, WILLIAM, landscape and figure painter, was born in 1824. He took to painting somewhat late in life, but in 1852 he was elected a member of the Society of British Artists; he exhibited frequently with that body, and with the Royal Academy. He died at Wargrave, Henley-on-Thames, December 6, 1883.

GOSSART, JEAN, son of Simon, a bookbinder, was born about 1472 at Maubeuge, a small town in Hainault. It is not known where he learnt his art, but in 1503 he was admitted as free master into the Guild of St. Luke at Antwerp, his name in the

register being entered as Jennyn van Henegouwe (John of Hainault). He signed his early pictures Jennyn Gossart, but later on he adopted the Latin form Ioannes Malbodius (John of Maubeuge). Once in the register of the Guild of Our Lady at Middelburg he is entered as Jan de Waele (John the Walloon). At Antwerp he fell under the influence of Quentin Metsys. In 1508 he went to Rome with his patron Philip of Burgundy, Admiral of Flanders; starting from Mechlin on October 26, 1508, they visited Verona and Florence on their way to the Eternal City, where, after the return of Philip, Gossart remained copying works of art for him until July 1509, when he set out for the Netherlands, arriving at Middleburg in November. There, at Philip's castle of Zuytburg, he and Jacques de Barbary were employed painting for Philip. In 1515 he was at Mechlin, and again in 1516, when he painted the portrait of Leonora of Austria, sister of Charles V. When Philip became Bishop of Utrecht, Gossart was employed in painting for him at his palace of Duerstede. After Philip's death on April 7, 1524, he entered the service of Adolphus of Burgundy, Marquis of Veere, at Ter Veere; there he was in close relations with Christian II., who had been driven out of Denmark, as also with Lambert Lombard of Liége, and Luke of Leyden, with the latter of whom he travelled through the Low Countries. In 1526 he designed the tomb of Isabella of Austria, Christian's Queen, in the abbey church of St. Peter at Ghent. Gossart died in August 1533, and his widow, Margaret De Molenaere, in 1536; their son, Peter, was still a minor in 1537.

Gossart varied his style at different periods of his life. The best specimen of his earlier purely Netherlandish manner is the 'Adoration of the Magi' in the possession of Lord Carlisle, at Naworth, a work remarkable for its warm and brilliant colouring, and for the elaborate finish of every detail of the costumes, but lacking depth of feeling. The 'St. Luke painting the Blessed Virgin and Child,' formerly in the cathedral of Mechlin, now in that of Prague, is a fine specimen of his composite style of Italianized Netherlandish art. One of his most celebrated pictures was a large triptych representing the 'Descent from the Cross' painted for Maximilian of Burgundy, Abbot of the Premonstratensian monastery of Our Lady and St. Nicholas at Middelburg, which Dürer saw and admired in December 1520, the composition of which, he says, was not as good as the execution; it perished in the flames when the church was burnt on January 24, 1568. Gossart's portraits are remarkable. Other paintings:

Amsterdam.	Museum.	Portrait of a Knight of the Order of the Golden Fleece. (A replica in the possession of Percy Macquoid, Esq.)
Berlin.	Gallery.	Adam and Eve in Paradise.
”	”	Neptune and Amphitrite. 1516.
”	”	The Blessed Virgin and Child with cherries; under influence of Andrea Solario. (A replica at Oldenburg.)
”	”	The Blessed Virgin offering grapes to the Child.
”	”	A maiden weighing a gold piece.
Dresden.	Gallery.	Adoration of the Magi; SS. Dominic and Luke. (Formerly in the church of St. Luke outside Genoa).

Hampton Court.	*Palace.*	The three children of Christian II., King of Denmark (*of which the Duke of Leeds has a replica*).
"	"	Adam and Eve in Paradise. (*A replica at Berlin.*)
London.	*National Gallery.*	Portrait of a man holding a rosary.
"	"	Portrait of a man holding his gloves.
Madrid.	*Prado Gallery.*	The Blessed Virgin and Child enthroned; presented to Philip II. in 1888 by the municipality of Louvain. (*A replica in the possession of the Earl of Northbrook.*)
"	"	Christ, the Blessed Virgin, and St. John.
Munich.	*Pinakothek.*	A donor protected by St. Michael.
"	"	Danaë receiving the shower of gold. 1527.
"	"	The Blessed Virgin and Child enthroned. 1527.
Munster.	*Museum.*	The Blessed Virgin and Child.
Oldenburg.	*Gallery.*	The Blessed Virgin and Child, with cherries.
Palermo.	*Museum.*	The Blessed Virgin and Child enthroned, with Angels.
Paris.	*Louvre.*	The Blessed Virgin and Child, with portrait of John Carondelet, Dean of Besançon. (*Diptych.*)
Prague.	*Cathedral.*	St. Luke painting the Blessed Virgin and Child. 1515.
Richmond.	*Sir F. Cook.*	Hercules and Omphale. 1516.
Tournai.	*Museum.*	St. Donatian; painted for Canon John de Carondelet, Chancellor of Flanders.
Vienna.	*Mr. O. Miethke.*	Hercules throwing Anteus; *after Pollaiuolo.* 1523.
"	*Gallery.*	St. Luke painting the Blessed Virgin and Child.
"	"	The Circumcision.
"	"	The Blessed Virgin and Child enthroned.

GOSSE, NICOLAS LOUIS FRANÇOIS, a French historical and portrait painter, was born in Paris in 1787. He studied under Vincent in the École des Beaux-Arts, and died at Soncourt in 1878. His best pictures are:

The Adoration of the Magi.
The Birth of Christ.
St. Vincent of Paola.
The Death of St. Vincent Ferrer. (*Vannes Cathedral.*)
Napoleon receiving the Queen of Prussia at Tilsit.
The Meeting of Napoleon and the Emperor Alexander at Erfurt.

GOSSELIN, CHARLES, French landscape painter; born in Paris, January 26, 1834. He was a pupil of Gleyre, and subsequently of Charles Busson. He exhibited his first pictures in 1863, and from that date onward he was a constant contributor to the Salon. It was from the Jura, La Somme, and L'Ile-Adam, where he had long resided, that he was able to find subjects for his brush; and later on, in 1882, when appointed keeper of the Versailles Museum, the park furnished him with a variety of landscapes which he treated in a masterful, if somewhat frigid, fashion. He obtained medals in 1865 and 1870; a medal of the second class in 1874. He was appointed Chevalier de la Legion d'Honneur in 1878, receiving awards at the Paris Universal Exhibition. He died in Paris, November 5, 1892.

GOSSWYN, GERHARD, a Flemish flower and fruit painter, born at Liége in 1616, was a pupil of Gerhard Douffet. Whilst still very young he went to Italy, and worked for a lengthened period in Rome and Paris, and became the first art instructor of the Dauphin, afterwards Louis XV. He died at Liége in 1691.

GOTHERICKE, MATTHEW. See GOODRICKE.

GOTTI, BARTOLOMMEO, a Florentine painter, who flourished in the 17th century, was a pupil of Ghirlandaio. He went to France and worked for Francis I.

GOTTI, VINCENZO, a native of Bologna, was born about 1580, and became a scholar of Dionysius Calvaert at the time that Guido Reni studied under that master. At twenty years of age he went to Rome, in company with Guido, and there painted some pictures. He was then invited to the court of Naples, where he passed the remainder of his life. This painter possessed so ready an invention, and such surprising facility, that Orlandi states, from a list of his works, found after his death, that he had painted no fewer than two hundred and eighteen pictures for public positions in the different towns of the kingdom of Naples. He died at Reggio in 1636.

GÖTTING, ANDREAS, a painter who flourished at the close of the 16th and beginning of the 17th century, is the author of a picture in the Rotterdam Museum, representing 'Diana surprised by Actæon;' signed and dated 1607.

GOTTLANDT, PETER, called also PETER VON RODDELSTET, was a painter and engraver from the town of Roddelstet (Rudestedt?), who was working at Weimar from 1548 to 1572, where he was made court painter in 1553. He both painted and engraved on metal and on wood the portraits of the three Electors Johann Friedrich. Besides these and other portraits, there are among his engravings:

The Victory over Death and Hell. 1552.
The Fall of Man; *after L. Cranach.* 1552.
The Prophet Jonah. 1552.
Madonna in a Landscape. 1555.
The Redemption; *after L. Cranach.* 1556.

GÖTZENBERGER, JACOB, an historical painter, was born at Heidelberg in 1800, and educated after 1820 in Düsseldorf under Cornelius, and after 1824 in Munich. It is stated that so early as 1823 Cornelius could pass off as his own a painting by this artist. He was employed, together with Hermann and E. Förster, to decorate with frescoes the hall of Bonn University, and in 1828 he visited Rome and Naples to gain ideas for this work. He returned in 1832, and executed his undertaking, painting alone the designs for Jurisprudence, Medicine, and Philosophy, and that for Theology in conjunction with his two collaborators. After this he obtained the two appointments of court painter at Baden and inspector of the gallery at Mannheim. He visited Paris and London in company with Cornelius, and on his return executed a new cycle of frescoes in the chapel at Nierstein in Rhenish Hesse, as well as in the drinking hall at Baden-Baden, the latter of which, painted in 1844, represented legends from the Black Forest. An offence led to his dismissal from his offices, upon which he proceeded to England, where he painted both portraits and frescoes, and especially distinguished himself by his performances in Bridgewater and Northumberland Houses. The last of these works was accomplished in 1863-5. His death occurred at Darmstadt in 1866.

GÖTZLOFF, KARL WILHELM, a landscape painter, was born at Dresden in 1803, and became a member of the Academy there in 1835. He, however, went to Italy in 1823, and remained there painting principally the scenery of the country. He died at Naples in 1866.

GOUBAU, ANTOON, (GOBAU, or GOEBOUW,) who was born at Antwerp in 1616, is said to have studied under one Jan de Farius. He was admitted into the Guild of St. Luke in 1636-37. He visited Italy in later life, and was there much impressed by the works of Jan Asselyn, whose style he afterwards copied. In 1668, he received as a pupil the young Nicolas de Largillière, and afterwards Petrus Cornelis Hessels. Goubau died at Antwerp in 1698. His works, which are rather scarce, are noteworthy for good drawing and colouring, but more especially for excellence of composition. The Antwerp Gallery possesses two good examples of this master, 'Artists studying from Ruins near Rome,' signed and dated 1650, and a 'Market-scene in the Piazza Navona in Rome,' dated 1680 ; and in the church of St. Jacques is a 'Last Supper.' In the Brunswick Museum is a 'Landscape with old ruins ;' at the Hague is an 'Italian Landscape ;' and in the Museum at Lille is an 'Italian Market-place.' Specimens of his early style, which are camp scenes, are in the galleries at Meiningen and Prague.

GOUBAU, FRANS, born at Antwerp in 1622, is supposed to have studied under Gerard Zegers, and was free of the Corporation in 1649. He painted for the Carmelite Church a picture of 'St. Agabus building the first Chapel to the Virgin ;' and for the church of St. Willebrod, a portrait of Pieter Luycx, both of which pictures have disappeared. In the Antwerp Gallery is the 'Adoration of the Sacrament,' dated 1650, and in the church of St. Jacques a 'Dead Saviour,' and a portrait of Frans van den Bossche, Dean of St. Jacques. Goubau died about 1678.

GOUDA, CORNELIS VAN, a Dutch painter, was born at Gouda in 1510, and was the best known scholar of Marten van Heemskerk. He died in 1550.

GOUDT, HENDRIK, a distinguished amateur artist of a noble family of Holland, and a Count of the Palatinate, was born at Utrecht in 1585. A passionate admiration for art led him to an early application to drawing, and when he was young he went to Rome in search of improvement. Arrived in that capital, he was one of the most assiduous students of his time, and daily frequented the Academy to draw from the model. He contracted an intimacy with Adam Elsheimer ; and purchased some of his most finished works, which he has engraved in a style peculiar to himself, and perhaps better adapted to express the polished finish and the admirable effect of chiaro-scuro of the originals, than any other that could have been adopted. His plates are wrought entirely with the graver, and their extraordinary effect is produced not by the usual mode of deepening and strengthening the stroke, but by delicately crossing and recrossing them several times in the shadows. The following are the seven prints by him, after Adam Elsheimer, as described by Strutt :

Ceres drinking from a Pitcher. An old woman appears holding a candle at the door of a cottage, and a boy naked standing by her, is laughing and pointing at the goddess, for which contempt he was metamorphosed into a frog. This print was well copied by Hollar. It is distinguished by the name of 'The Sorcery.'

The Flight into Egypt ; a night scene.

The Angel with Tobit ; who is drawing a fish by his side.

The Angel with Tobit crossing a stream of water ; Tobit holds the fish under his arm. Hollar has copied this print with much success.

Baucis and Philemon entertaining Jupiter and Mercury ; a small plate, nearly square.

Aurora, representing the Dawn of Day ; a small landscape. The effect is very beautiful.

The Beheading of St. John the Baptist in Prison ; a very small oval print, very scarce.

GOUGE, —. This little-known portrait painter was a pupil of Riley, and many of his best portraits have been ascribed in error to Kneller, Lely, Dahl, and Richardson. He painted the portraits of many of the nobility of his time in England, notable among which are the full-lengths of Sir Roger and Lady Hudson at Shottesbrook, Berks, and the full-length of Sir Robert Vansittart, and the three-quarter-length of Sir John Stonehouse, comptroller to the household of Queen Anne, which are at North Cray Place, Kent. Very little is known of the history of this talented artist, whose works are sound in drawing and opulent in colour, albeit a little dull in conception, and the dates either of his birth or death are uncertain.

GOULD, THOMAS R., an American sculptor who deserves mention in these pages on account of the beauty of his drawings, and on his wonderful ability to sketch a portrait in pencil prior to the execution of the work in marble. He was born at Boston in 1818, studied for some time in Italy, and settled down for some ten years or more in Florence, where he executed many of his most notable works. In 1878 he returned to Boston, and there he died in 1881. Many of his busts may be seen in the chief libraries of the United States, in exhibitions and in town halls in that country, but his sketches remain mostly in the possession of his descendants. He was a profound student of the imaginative works of Blake, and much influenced by the mystic ideas of that great artist and poet. His work was very original, free from anything approaching the commonplace, and always distinguished by force, character, and living actuality, combined with a quality of mystic imagination and poetic feeling very rare in sculpture or pencil-drawing.

GOULDSMITH, HARRIET. See ARNOLD.

GOUPIL, JULES ADOLPHE, born in Paris in 1839, was a pupil of Henri and Ary Scheffer, and a popular painter of portraits and genre. He first exhibited at the Salon in 1878. He died in Paris of consumption, April 28, 1883.

GOUPY, BERNHARD, a French miniature painter, was the brother of Joseph Goupy, and like him he practised in London about the middle of the 18th century.

GOUPY, JOSEPH, a French painter and engraver, was born at Nevers in the beginning of the 18th century. He came to England when he was young, and about 1725 was engaged together with Tillemans in painting scenes for the Italian Opera. He taught drawing to Frederick, Prince of Wales, and to Prince George, afterwards King George III., who on his accession allowed him a small pension. He resided here the remainder of his life, and died in London at an advanced age in 1763. He excelled in painting landscapes in water-colours, which he treated with great spirit and intelligence. His pictures in the style of Salvator Rosa have considerable merit. He etched several plates in a very spirited and masterly style, some of which are from his own designs. Among others, the following are by him :

F. JOSÉ DE GOYA Y LUCIENTES

A LADY

Mutius Scævola burning his hand before Porsena; *from his own design.*

Zeuxis painting Helen; *after Solimena.*

Diana hunting with her Nymphs; *after Rubens.*

St. Philip baptizing the Eunuch; *after Salvator Rosa.*

St. John preaching in the Wilderness; *after the same.*

The Calling of St. Andrew to the Apostleship, in a landscape; *after Pietro da Cortona.*

A grand Landscape, with the story of Pyramus and Thisbe; *after N. Poussin.*

A View of Castel Gandolfo, and of the Campagna near Rome; *after Bolognese.*

A set of eight Landscapes; *after Salvator Rosa.*

GOUPY, LOUIS, was a miniature painter and copyist, who practised in London early in the 18th century. He was the nephew, and, probably, the pupil of Bernard Lens.

GOURAND, CLAUDE. See GOYRAND.

GOURDEL, PIERRE, a native of Paris, who lived in the 16th century, was painter to Henry III. He drew all the birds in a work by Pierre Belon entitled 'Histoire de la Nature des Oyseaux,' Paris, 1555.

GOURMONT, JEAN DE, a French painter and engraver, was living in 1557, and is supposed to have worked chiefly for the illustration of books. There is a picture in the Louvre assigned to this artist, entitled 'The Nativity,' and there is a portrait engraved by him of Charles, Duke of Bourbon.

GOUSBLOOM, C., (GOUSBLOM, GOUTSBLOEM, or GOUDTSBLOEM,) was an obscure Dutch engraver, by whom there are portraits of the naval heroes Jan van Galen and M. H. Tromp, after Jan Lievens, and others.

GOUT, JOHANN FRANZ, a landscape and architectural painter, and an etcher, was born at Berlin about the middle of the 18th century. He travelled through Germany and Switzerland, and became theatrical painter at Darmstadt; he also painted Swiss landscapes in fresco. In 1782 he designed sixty plates of Ruins near Spires for Counsellor Merk at Darmstadt. He died after 1812.

GOUWEN, WILLEM VAN DER. See VAN DER GOUWEN.

GOVAERTS, A., was a landscape painter of the 17th century, who adopted the style of Savery, on what has been called a mixture of those of Jan Brueghel and Paulus Bril. Mention may be made of the following works:

Augsburg. *Gallery.* Landscape with Peasant's Cottage.
Brunswick. *Gallery.* Landscape with the Four Elements as Nymphs. 1624.
Hague. *Museum.* Oak Forest. 1612.
Milan. *Brera.* A Wood, with Abraham and Isaac.

GOVERT, —, a painter of landscapes with humorous figures, is stated by Van Mander to have been a pupil of Gerrit Pietersz at Amsterdam at the commencement of the 17th century.

GOVERTZ, THEODORUS, was a portrait painter of Utrecht, and the master of H. Verschuuring and T. Camphuysen, who lived about the middle of the 17th century.

GOWER, GEORGE, was an English portrait painter, who was appointed in 1584 Queen Elizabeth's sergeant-painter in oils for life.

GOWI, I. P., appears to have been a painter of the Antwerp school, who flourished in the 17th century, but the dates of his birth and death are unknown. The Madrid Gallery has two pictures by him of the story of 'Hippomenes and Atalanta,' and 'The Battle of the Titans.'

GOYA Y LUCIENTES, FRANCISCO JOSÉ DE. This peculiar genius and imaginative painter was born at Fuendetodos in Aragon, March 30th, 1746. His parents were humble, living on the produce of a small piece of land surrounding their cottage. Here Francisco lived to the age of sixteen without any knowledge of art, when his passion for painting was awakened by a monk of Santa Fé near Zaragoza, after which he got admitted into the studio of José Luxan Martinez, who had been educated in Italy. Here he distinguished himself not so much in the studio as in the streets, in the quarrels of painters and confraternities, sometimes ending in bloodshed. After one of these fights he saw the emissaries of the Inquisition approaching, and having some reason to fear them, he there and then took to his heels and escaped to Madrid. Even at that late time the different provinces of Spain resembled distinct countries, so he lived in safety till similar exploits exposed him to new dangers. He was struck down by the blow of a poniard in the back, and had to secrete himself till he recovered, when he made his way to Italy. He settled down in Rome, where he met Louis David, with whom he fraternized, exchanging ideas not only on art, but also on religion and politics. In 1774 he returned to Spain, married, and began industriously to follow his profession.

This sketch of Goya's youth indicates the character of his painting: bizarre and wild, with a gleam, so to say, of infernal splendour in his choice of beauty. In his execution, he is the only Spaniard of extraordinary quality during the latter half of the 18th century and the beginning of the 19th. His works are numerous—church pictures in fresco and in oil; incidents in life of a highly fantastic kind; about 200 portraits; and many miscellaneous works, came from his hand. Etchings and engravings in aquatint also, now much prized, were executed by him. Of these 'The Caprices' are the most surprising, showing humanity in all the stages of brutality and ugliness, with a *mélange* of beauty and demonology quite unexampled. All through the occupation of Spain by the French, and during their expulsion by Wellington, he lived quietly without taking any part in public affairs. He had been made 'pintor de camera' by Charles IV. in 1789, and in 1814, on the return of Ferdinand VII., he published 'The Disasters of War,' in seventeen designs, as repulsive and fascinating as it is possible to imagine. He also engraved thirty-three plates of scenes in the Bull-ring. Not the least valuable productions of his graver are his etchings of the five great equestrian portraits, the 'borrachos,' 'meninas,' dwarfs, and single figures, executed by Velazquez. The British Museum possesses an exceedingly fine collection of Goya's etchings and aquatints. He died at Bordeaux, April 16th, 1828. His principal paintings are:

Lille. *Museum.* Young Girls.
„ „ Old Women.
„ „ A Criminal garotted.
Madrid. *Gallery.* Equestrian Portrait of Charles IV.
„ „ Equestrian Portrait of Maria Louisa, Queen of Charles IV.
„ „ Charles IV. and his Family.
„ „ Charles IV.; full-length.
„ „ Queen Maria Louisa; full-length.
„ „ A Mounted Picador.
„ „ Episodes of the French Invasion. 1808.
„ „ Portrait of the Infanta Maria Josefa.

Madrid.	Gallery.	Portraits of the Infants Don Francisco and Don Antonio.
„	„	Portrait of the Prince of Parma.
„	„	Portrait of the Artist's Wife.
„	„	His own Portrait.
„	„	Portrait of Ferdinand VII.
„	„	The Crucifixion.
„	Academy of San Fernando.	La Maja clothed.
„	„	La Maja nude.
„	„	Portrait of Juan de Villa-Nueva.
„	„	Portrait of La Tirana.
„	„	Equestrian Portrait of Ferdinand VII.
„	St. Francisco.	St. Francis preaching.
„	„	Equestrian Portrait of the Prince of Peace.
„	„	The Mad-House.
„	„	A Bull Fight.
„	„	Portrait of Bayeu.
„	Museo de Fomento.	The Crucifixion.
Paris.	Louvre.	Portrait of F. Guillemardet, French Ambassador to Spain in 1798.
„	„	A young Spanish Woman.
Seville.	Cathedral.	St. Justina and St. Rufina.
Toledo.	Cathedral.	The Treason of Judas.
Valencia.	Cathedral.	Two subjects from the Life of St. Francis of Borja.
„	Museum.	Portrait of Bayeu.
„	„	Portrait of Doña Jacquina.
Zaragoza.	Madonna del Pilar.	The Virgin in Glory. (Fresco.)

W.B.S.

GOYEN, JAN VAN, who was born at Leyden in 1596, studied under Jan Nicolaï, Schilderpoort, Jan De Man, Hendrik Klok, and Willem Gerritsz, all unimportant masters. While still young, he made a journey through France, and on his return received some final instruction from Esaias van de Velde. After a short stay at Haarlem he settled at Leyden, where in 1618 he married Annetje Willems van Raelst. About 1631 he went to the Hague, and in 1640 was elected a member of the Painters' Guild. He died at the Hague in 1666. Van Goyen was one of the earliest of the Dutch landscape painters, and has etched a few landscapes. He was father-in-law to Jan Steen. The following are some of his principal works :

Amsterdam.	Museum.	A River. 1645.
„	„	View on the Meuse.
„	„	The Castle of Valkenhof, near Nymwegen.
		Landscape. 1641.
Antwerp.	Gallery.	Landscape.
Augsburg.	Gallery.	Landscapes (seven).
Berlin.	Gallery.	Hilly Landscape. 1629.
„	„	Summer.
„	„	Winter. 1621.
„	„	Winter Landscape. 1650.
„	„	View of the Town of Arnheim. 1646.
„	„	View of Nymwegen. 1649.
„	„	Bank of a River.
Brunswick.	Museum.	A Village Scene.
Brussels.	Gallery.	View of Dordrecht. 1644.
Cambridge.	Fitzwilliam Museum.	Two River Views.
„	„	View near Dort.
„	„	Landscape.
„	„	Sea-piece.
„	„	Winter Scene.
Cassel.	Gallery.	Three Landscapes.
Copenhagen.	Gallery.	Dutch Village in a Flood.
Darmstadt.	Gallery.	Sea-piece.
Dresden.	Gallery.	Landscape. 1633.
„	„	Skating Scene. 1647.

Dresden.	Gallery.	River Bank. 1643.
Frankfort	Städel Inst.	Canal with boats.
Gotha.	Gallery.	Four Views in Holland.
Lille.	Museum.	River Scene in Holland.
London.	Grosvenor House.	View of Nymwegen.
„	Bute Coll.	Scene at Scheveningen. 1649.
„	Kensington Palace.	River Scene.
Paris.	Louvre.	Banks of a Dutch River. 1653
„	„	River Scene.
„	„	Sea-piece.
„	„	Banks of a Canal.
Petersburg.	Hermitage.	The Meuse near Dordrecht.
„	„	The Meuse.
„	„	Winter Landscape.
„	„	The Dunes near Scheveningen.
„	„	Three Landscapes.
Rotterdam.	Museum.	River Scene.
Vienna.	Gallery.	Landscape.

GOYET, EUGÈNE, a French historical and genre painter, was born at Chalon-sur-Saône in 1798, and died in Paris in 1857. His best pictures are 'The Death of St. Paul,' 'St. Francisca,' and a portrait of Pope Pius IX.

GOYET, JEAN BAPTISTE, an historical and genre painter, the father of Eugène Goyet, was born at Chalon-sur-Saône in 1779, and died in Paris in 1854. He was self-instructed. A 'Virgin and St. Anne' by him was exhibited at Paris in 1855.

GOYRAND, CLAUDE, (or GOURAND,) a French engraver, was born at Sens about 1620, and died in 1662. He resided some time at Rome, as appears from the inscription on one of his plates. There are by this artist a variety of neat and spirited etchings of landscapes and views after Callot, Della Bella, and others, of which the following are the principal :

A set of twenty Landscapes, &c. ; after Callot.
A set of four Views ; the Castle of Bicêtre, the Invalides, the Ruins of an old Tower, and the Fountain in the Garden of Tivoli.
Four Landscapes ; after Della Bella.
Eight Views in Paris and its environs ; after the same. 1645.
The Chapel of Santa Maria Maggiore at Rome ; after the same.
A small Head with an ornamental border ; worked with the graver.

GÖZ, JOSEPH FRANZ FRIEDRICH, a painter and etcher, was born at Hermannstadt in 1754, and after studying jurisprudence, was for some time in the state service, but went in 1779 to Munich, then to Augsburg, and in 1791 to Ratisbon, where he died in 1815. He brought out a series of character pictures in 160 etchings from his own designs, entitled 'Impassioned Outlines for Friends of Art and the Drama' (Augsburg, 1784). He is also known by his scenes from 'Bavarian Popular Life,' in gouache, and by various portraits of notables, some etched and some painted in oil.

GOZZI, MARCO, an Italian landscape painter, was born about 1759, and died about 1839. There are nine landscapes by him in the Brera at Milan.

GOZZOLI, BENOZZO, the son of a doublet maker, was born at Florence in 1420. He followed Fra Angelico to Rome, and having acted in 1447 as his assistant at Orvieto, he in 1449 applied, but unsuccessfully, for permission to finish Fra Angelico's frescoes in the cathedral of that city. In the same year he went to Montefalco, and there painted in the church of San Fortunato a 'Virgin and Child,' and a 'St. Thomas receiving the Girdle'; the last-named is now in the Museum of St. John Lateran at Rome. By 1452 he had completed the

JAN VAN GOYEN

A RIVER SCENE

JAN VAN GOYEN

SCENE NEAR AMSTERDAM

BENOZZO GOZZOLI

THE ARRIVAL OF THE THREE KINGS

[*Fresco in the Palazzo Riccardi, Florence*

PARADISE

frescoes in the hexagonal choir of the monastery of San Francesco at Montefalco. These decorations consist of a triple course of twelve scenes from the life of St. Francis, five medallions of illustrious Dominicans, and portraits of Petrarch, Dante, and Giotto, besides numerous figures of saints and angels. Benozzo also decorated the chapel of St. Jerome, in the same church, with a fresco of the 'Madonna and Child' that simulated an altar-piece, the 'Crucifixion,' the four Evangelists, scenes from the life of St. Sebastian, and various figures of saints and angels. In the year 1453, and for at least a part of 1454, he was at Viterbo, where in the church of Sta. Rosa he painted a series of frescoes, now perished, illustrating the life of that saint. After finishing this work he probably returned to Umbria ; at any rate he executed, in 1456, for a church at Perugia, a 'Virgin and Child, between SS. Peter, John the Baptist, Jerome, and Paul,' with a predella representing the 'Resurrection,' with SS. Thomas, Laurence, Sebastian, and Bernard, which is now in the Academy at Perugia. Soon afterwards he returned to Florence, where he was employed to decorate the walls of the chapel in the palace of the Medici, now the Riccardi Palace. He there painted an immense fresco which covers the walls of the body of the chapel ; it represents the Magi, with a long train of attendant knights, pages, servants, hunters, and followers of every description, wending their way through a splendid landscape towards Bethlehem. The sanctuary of the chapel is decorated with various groups of angels, who are represented as being in a beautiful garden typifying the heavenly Eden. The altar-piece is lost, but the predella, containing the 'Resurrection,' and the 'Marriage of St. Catharine,' is in the Uffizi Gallery at Florence. About 1464 Benozzo went to San Gimignano, where he executed a large series of frescoes in the church of Sant' Agostino, under the patronage of Fra Domenico Strambi, called Parasinus. His first production there was a painting of 'St. Sebastian,' represented standing erect on a pillar, with a long mantle held by angels so as apparently to shield a crowd of people from the thunder-bolts cast by the Eternal, whilst the Virgin baring her breast, and the Saviour showing His wounds, seem likewise to implore the Divine pity. This subject was probably intended to commemorate the delivery of the city from the plague in 1464. Beneath the above design is a 'Crucifixion,' and four adoring saints, with twelve medallions and a miniature likeness of Parasinus, the donor of the frescoes. Gozzoli next decorated the choir of the same church with a triple course of seventeen scenes from the life of St. Augustine, and other designs from the lives of Tobit, St. Sebastian, and St. Bartolus, as well as figures of various saints and martyrs. His assistant in this immense work was Giusto d'Andrea. Having finished his commissions for Sant' Agostino, he in 1465 decorated the space between the portals of the Collegiata with the 'Martyrdom of St. Sebastian,' and figures of Christ and the Virgin, in a glory of Seraphim and Cherubim, with figures of different saints and martyrs. In 1466 he painted two Madonnas, one of which is in the Collegiata at San Gimignano, and the other at Sant' Andrea near that town. In the same year he painted a 'Marriage of St. Catharine' for the church of San Francesco at Terni. By him too is a fresco of the 'Crucifixion' in the cloister of the suppressed monastery of Monte Oliveto. He

remained at San Gimignano until 1467, when he restored the frescoes of Lippo Memmi, in the Palazzo del Podestà. Early in 1469 Benozzo commenced his largest and most important work, the frescoes in the Campo Santo at Pisa. These consisted of a series of twenty-four designs, three of which are now obliterated, drawn from Bible history, commencing with the curse of Ham, and including the lives of Abraham, Isaac, Jacob, Esau, Joseph, Moses, the fall of Jericho, the story of David and Goliath, and the visit of the Queen of Sheba to King Solomon. This enormous work took Benozzo and his assistants, among whom was Zanobi Macchiavelli, sixteen years to complete, the last payment being made in May 1485. During the execution of this work, the authorities of the Campo Santo, in testimony of their appreciation of Gozzoli's talents, presented him in 1478 with a tomb therein, in order that he might rest in the midst of the glorious achievements of his life. Notwithstanding this immense undertaking, he yet found time to decorate a chapel on the road to Meleto, near Castelfiorentino, in 1484, with frescoes of the 'Virgin and Child, with Saints,' over the altar, and also the 'Death, Burial, and Ascension of the Virgin,' and the 'Gift of the Miraculous Girdle to St. Thomas.' In 1497 he valued the frescoes of Alesso Baldovinetti in the Gianfigliazzi Chapel in Santa Trinità at Florence. Benozzo Gozzoli died in 1498. The following are some of his extant paintings :

Berlin.		Virgin and Child, Saints and Angels.
Castelfiorentino.	*Tabernacolo della Visatazione.*	Scenes from the Life of the Virgin (*frescoes*).
Castelfiorentino (near).	*Madonna della Torre.*	Madonna and Saints, Death of the Virgin, and Assumption of the Virgin (*frescoes*).
Florence.	*Riccardi Pal.*	Procession of the Magi (*fresco*). 1459.
,,	*Uffizi.*	A Predella.
London.	*National Gallery.*	Virgin and Child enthroned, with Angels and Saints.
Montefalco.	*S. Francesco.*	Scenes from the Life of St. Francis (*fresco*). 1452.
Paris.	*Louvre.*	Apotheosis of St. Thomas Aquinas.
Perugia.	*Pinacoteca.*	Altar-piece and Predella. 1456.
Pisa.	*Campo Santo.*	Subjects from the Old Testament (*frescoes*). 1469-1485.
,,	*Academy.*	Virgin and Child, with Saints.
,,	,,	The Conception.
,,	,,	Study for the fresco in the Campo Santo of the Queen of Sheba.
Rome.	*Lateran Museum.*	The Virgin giving her girdle to St. Thomas.
San Gimignano.	*S. Agostino.*	Life of St. Augustine (*frescoes*). 1465 and 1467.
,,	,,	St. Sebastian preserving the town of San Gimignano from the Plague in 1464.
,,	*Collegiata.*	Virgin surrounded by Saints. 1466.
,,	,,	Martyrdom of St. Sebastian. 1465.
Vienna.	*Gallery.*	Virgin and Child, with Saints.

GRAAF, HANS, (or GRAF,) born at Vienna in 1680, was a scholar of Van Alen, and painted fairs and market-places, horses, and other animals. He was also a good landscape painter. He died at Vienna in 1734. A 'Tower of Babel' by him is in the Landauer Brüderhaus at Nuremberg.

GRAAF, JOSUA, (or GRAVE,) a painter of landscapes and views of cities, fortified places, &c.,

lived at the end of the 17th century, and was an officer in the service of Holland. In the Cassel Gallery are two landscapes by this artist.

GRAASBEEK, JOOST VAN. See CRAESBEECK.

GRAAT, BAREND, (or GRAET,) a Dutch painter, was born at Amsterdam in 1628. Whilst very young he was placed under the care of his uncle, a reputable painter of landscapes and animals, under whom he made rapid progress. The pictures of Pieter De Laer, called Bamboccio, were then in the highest estimation, and he applied himself to study and imitate the style of that master, in which he was so successful, that some of his pictures were mistaken for those of Bamboccio. The success he met with in that branch of the art disposed him to attempt historical painting, in which he was not unsuccessful. To perfect himself in the design of the figure, he established a kind of school or academy in his house, where his contemporary artists and himself occupied themselves in drawing from life. The Dutch biographers speak highly of his talents in historical painting, and particularly commend a picture he painted for the Council-chamber at Amsterdam, representing 'Time discovering Truth.' Another admired picture by him was 'David and Bathsheba.' A 'Home Scene,' in the Queen's collection at Buckingham Palace, is also much praised. He also painted portraits with great success, and produced some admired pen-and-ink and pencil drawings, as well as etchings upon copper. He died at Amsterdam in 1709.

GRAAUW, HENDRIK, a Dutch historical painter, was born at Hoorn, in North Holland, in 1627. He was successively the scholar of Pieter De Grebber and of Jacob van Kampen the younger, and on leaving those masters, he was employed by Prince Maurice of Nassau to paint four frescoes in the cupola of the Palace in the Wood, which established his reputation as one of the most promising artists of his time. Ambitious of improvement, and elated with the description he had heard of the wonders of Italy, he resolved to visit that country, and in 1648 he embarked for Leghorn, and made the best of his way to Rome. For three years he was assiduously employed in designing; and he returned to Holland with an ample store of materials for his future studies. On establishing himself at Amsterdam, he was loaded with commissions. He painted for the family of Bronckhorst a series of historical and fabulous subjects, of which two, the 'Triumph of Julius Cæsar,' and the 'Education of Bacchus,' were particularly admired. He resided chiefly at Amsterdam and Utrecht, and died at Alkmaar in 1682.

GRACE, Mrs., a portrait painter and copyist, whose maiden name was Hodgkiss, was born early in the 18th century. She was self-taught, and exhibited at the Society of Artists from 1762 to 1769, but in the latter year she retired with a competence to Homerton, where she died about 1786.

GRACHT, JACOB VAN DER. See VAN DER GRACHT.

GRADILLA, JUAN MARTINEZ DE. See MARTINEZ DE GRADILLA.

GRADO, FRANCESCO DE, an engraver, who resided chiefly at Naples, flourished about 1690. He engraved the plates of the 'Illustrious Personages' published at Naples in 1693, and executed part of the portraits for Bellori's 'Vite de' Pittori, Scultori, et Architetti moderni,' 1672.

GRAEF, TIMOTHEUS DE. See DE GRAEF.

GRAET, BAREND. See GRAAT.

268

GRAF, HANS. See GRAAF.

GRAF, HANS, (or GRAVE,) was a wood-engraver from Amsterdam, who worked at Frankfort-on-the-Main, where in 1553 he executed a view of that city for the widow of the painter Konrad Faber, and also engraved on wood a plan of the same, which Faber himself had designed. He likewise worked on Sebastian Münster's 'Cosmographia.'

GRAF, URS, who has also been known by the names of URS GAMPERLIN or GEMBERLIN, and VAN GOAR, was a wood-engraver, who at early periods in his life was a goldsmith, painter, and engraver on copper. He was born at Solothurn between 1485 and 1490, and after working with a goldsmith at Zurich, he in 1515 took part in the Swiss war in Lombardy, and again in 1522, being taken prisoner in the following year. He died at Basle between 1529 and 1535. He appears to have been a wild and reckless character, but he managed to execute 327 woodcuts, chiefly book illustrations, many of which are marked with one or other of the annexed

monograms: V G, ♉ The earliest of these was a set of twenty-five woodcuts for the 'Passion of our Saviour,' printed at Strassburg by Johann Knoblauch in 1506. They are neatly cut, but very incorrectly drawn. He has written the names of the different figures over their heads, as was not unusual at the time. Single plates of his are, 'The Monk crowned by two Bishops,' 'Death lying in wait,' 'The Satyr Family,' and 'The Raising of Lazarus.' He also produced a few copper-plates and etchings, as well as nielli. The Basle Art Collection, and the Albertina at Vienna, possess many of his pencil-drawings.

GRAFF, ANTON, a portrait-painter, was born at Winterthur in Switzerland in 1736, and died at Dresden in 1813. He studied under Johann Ulrich Schellenberg in his native town, but soon went to Augsburg, and thence, on the invitation of the court, to Dresden, where he was appointed court-painter in 1766. He was often summoned to Berlin, Leipsic, and other places, where he painted many of his more celebrated contemporaries, as Lessing, Herder, Moses Mendelssohn, Schiller, Gluck, Weisse, and Frederick William II. The following also are by him:

Berlin.	*Gallery.*	Two Portraits of Johann Joachim Spalding.
Brunswick.	*Museum.*	Portrait of Friedrich Albrecht, Prince of Anhalt-Bernburg.
Dresden.	*Gallery.*	His own Portrait.
”	”	Portrait of Frederick Augustus, King of Saxony.
”	”	Portraits of Karl Hommeyer and his wife.
”	”	Portraits of Christian Voight and his daughter.
”	”	Portrait of Johann Jakob Mesmer.
Gotha.	*Gallery.*	Portrait of Eckhoff.
Leipsic.	*Museum.*	Portrait of Frau Gabain.
Munich.	*Gallery.*	His own Portrait.

GRAFF, JOHANN ANDREAS, a painter and engraver, born at Nuremberg in 1637, was instructed in art under Häberlin and the flower painter Marrel, in Frankfort, after which he studied for two years in Vienna and four years in Rome. In 1664 he returned to Nuremberg, where he married the artist Maria Sibylla Merian. Twenty years later he removed to Frankfort, but returned to Nuremberg, where he died in 1701. He designed and engraved numerous landscapes, plans, and figure subjects, among which are:

Interiors of the churches of St. Lawrence and St. Sebald at Nuremberg.
The Römerberg at Frankfort.
John Maurice, Prince of Nassau-Orange. 1658.
The Emperor Leopold and the Seven Electors; *after Marrel.*

GRAFF, JOHANNA HELENA. See HEROLD.

GRAFF, KARL ANTON, a landscape painter, the son of Anton Graff, was born at Dresden in 1774, and was first instructed there under Professor Zingg, but he afterwards devoted six years to travelling in Switzerland and Italy. He died in 1832. His best works were mountain landscapes from Bavaria and Switzerland.

GRAFF, MARIA DOROTHEA HENRICA. See GSELL.

GRAFF, MARIA SIBYLLA. See MERIAN.

GRAFFICO, CAMILLO, was a native of Friuli, who flourished about the year 1588. He engraved several plates of devotional subjects, among which is one representing the 'Holy Family,' after Bernardino Passari. He worked entirely with the graver, in a style resembling that of Cornelis Cort, but very inferior to it.

GRAFFIONE, GIOVANNI, a Florentine painter; born 1455; pupil of Baldovinetti. He painted a 'God in Glory' over the door of the hospital of Santa Maria degli Innocenti in Florence. Died 1527.

GRAHAM, G., an English engraver, worked in the latter half of the 18th century. He produced some of the illustrations for Campbell's 'Pleasures of Hope' in 1799, and also some of Rowlandson's works. He engraved chiefly in the dotted manner, but the following mezzotint plates are also by him :

John, Earl of Bute; *after Ramsay.*
Mrs. Collier; *after Sir Joshua Reynolds.*
Van Tromp; *after Rembrandt.*
Poverty; *after Rising.*

GRAHAM, JOHN, an English historical painter, was born about 1706. He studied in Paris, London, and Italy, and finally settled at the Hague, where he was still living in 1776.

GRAHAM, JOHN, a Scottish historical painter, born in 1754, was at first apprenticed to a coach-painter in Edinburgh, but coming to London he entered the schools of the Royal Academy, where he exhibited from 1780 to 1797. In 1798 he was appointed master of the Trustees' Academy in Edinburgh, where he had amongst his pupils Wilkie, Allan, Burnett, and Watson Gordon. He died at Edinburgh in 1817. His chief works are :

Daniel in the Lions' Den. 1780.
Una. 1783.
Ceres in search of Proserpine. 1786.
The Escape of Mary, Queen of Scots, from Lochleven. 1788. (*Stationers' Hall, London.*)
Portrait of Alderman Boydell. (*Stationers' Hall, London.*)
The Funeral of General Fraser at Saratoga.
Queen Mary, the morning before her Execution. 1792.
King David instructing Solomon. 1797.
The Disobedient Prophet. (*National Gallery of Scotland.*)

GRAHAM-GILBERT, JOHN, a Scottish portrait painter, the son of a West India merchant named Graham, was born at Glasgow in 1794. When about twenty-four years of age he came to London, and having entered the schools of the Royal Academy, he gained in 1821 the gold medal for painting, afterwards proceeding to Italy to study the old masters, especially those of the Venetian school. The collection of pictures which he formed was bequeathed by his widow, who died in 1877, to the city of Glasgow, and forms a most valuable feature of the Corporation Galleries.

After having been in Italy two years he returned to London, but in 1827 he went to Edinburgh, and was elected a member of the Royal Scottish Academy in 1830. Soon after this he married and settled in Glasgow, at the same time adding his wife's name, Gilbert, to his own. He was an occasional contributor to the Royal Academy in London from 1844 to 1864, having also exhibited a few pictures there after his return from Italy. He died at Yorkhill, near Glasgow, in 1866. He executed many fancy studies of young girls, especially Italian, and other subjects, besides many portraits; his drawing was good and natural, and his colouring rich in tone, his portraits especially recalling the Venetian richness of painting. Among his subject pictures may be mentioned 'Females at a Fountain' (Royal Academy, 1846), 'A Roman Girl' (Royal Academy, 1864), and a portrait of Charles Lawson, Provost of Edinburgh, exhibited at the Royal Scottish Academy in 1866, the year of his death. In the National Portrait Gallery is a portrait of Sir Walter Scott by him, and in the National Gallery of Scotland are:

Sir John Watson Gordon, P.R.S.A.
John Gibson, R.A., sculptor.
An Italian Nobleman.
The Bandit's Bride.

GRAHL, KONRAD, (GRAHLEN, or GRAHLEIN,) was an engraver on metal and wood, who lived at Leipsic about 1620, working chiefly for booksellers.

GRAMBS, JOHANN VALENTIN, a portrait painter, born at Frankfort-on-the-Main in 1630, was a follower of the style of Van Dyck. His works were much admired, and amongst them was the portrait of the Empress Eleonora Magdalena, third consort of Leopold I., which was engraved by Kilian.

GRAMMARSEO, PIETRO, a native of Montferrat, in Piedmont, flourished about 1523, in which year he painted an altar-piece, which is in the conventual church of Casale.

GRAMMATICA, ANTIVEDUTO, born at Siena in 1571, was a disciple of Domenico Perugino. Several of his works are in the public edifices at Rome. In the church of Santa Maria in Trastevere there is a picture of the 'Virgin and Infant in the clouds, with Angels, and St. Hyacinth below;' and in San Giacomo degl' Incurabili is a fine picture of the 'Nativity,' with the 'Adoration of the Shepherds.' His talents raised him to the presidency of the Academy of St. Luke, but of this distinction he was deprived, on account of a nefarious attempt to dispose of a picture by Raphael belonging to the Academy, and to substitute for it a copy which he had made. He did not long survive this disgrace, and died at Rome in 1626.

GRAN, DANIEL, an historical painter, born at Vienna, or Mähren, in 1694, studied under Ferg and Wernle at Vienna, and afterwards under Ricci at Venice, and Solimena at Naples. Upon his return from Italy he executed a great number of large ceiling frescoes, mostly of an allegorical character, in the imperial palace, and in various castles, churches, and cloisters. He also produced several oil paintings, of which the Vienna Gallery possesses a 'Holy Family,' and the Karlskirche a 'St. Elizabeth,' and left some good pen-and-ink drawings. He died at St. Pölten in 1757.

GRANACCI, FRANCESCO, a Florentine painter, was born at Florence in 1477. He was a fellow-pupil with Michelangelo in the studio of Ghirlandajo, and was much attached to the former, whose style he at first greatly imitated. Granacci was one of the artists who went to Rome to assist Michelangelo in the Sistine Chapel, but when the master, finding he could not manage to get on with his assistants, shut both the door of the chapel and that of his own house against them, Granacci was justly incensed. He is said to have evinced his acquirement of the principles of Michelangelo in his picture of 'St. Zenobius and St. Francis, with the Virgin and Infant in the Clouds;' but still more in his 'Assumption,' formerly in San Pier Maggiore, and now in the Rucellai palace, in which the figure of St. Thomas is entirely in the style of that master. He died at Florence in 1543. Not many pictures by this artist remain, but his principal works are:

Berlin.	Gallery.	Portrait of a Girl.
„	„	Virgin and Child enthroned.
„	„	The Trinity.
Florence.	Academy.	Virgin and Saints.
„	„	Three pictures, representing the Life and Martyrdom of St. Apollonius.
„	Pitti Pal.	Holy Family.
Munich.	Gallery.	St. Jerome.
„	„	St. Apollonia.
„	„	St. John the Baptist.
„	„	The Magdalen.
Petersburg.	Hermitage.	The Nativity.

GRANDE, Francisco Agustin y. See Agustin.

GRANDHOMME, Jacques. See Granthomme.

GRANDI, Ercole di Giulio, commonly called Ercole da Ferrara, whose works have been confused with those of Ercole di Roberto, was a native of Ferrara. He was in the service of the Duke of Ferrara from 1492 till 1499, and died in 1531. He was a disciple of Lorenzo Costa, and was the author of 'St. Sebastian, with other Saints and Patrons,' in San Paolo, Ferrara; of an 'Adoration of the Kings,' in the Ferrara Gallery; of a 'St. George and the Dragon,' in the Corsini Gallery, Rome; and also of 'The Conversion of St. Paul,' and a 'Madonna and Child with Saints,' in the National Gallery, London. Other pictures by him are in private collections in Italy.

GRANDI, Ercole di Roberti, was a partner with his brother as a painter and gold-beater in Ferrara in 1479. He was in the paid service of the Duke of Ferrara, and was frequently employed in painting chests. He built a triumphal car; decorated the garden lodge of the Duchess; and in 1494 painted the likeness of Hercules I. for Isabella of Mantua. He was a disciple and imitator of Mantegna, and executed, amongst other works, the decorations (since destroyed) of the Garganelli chapel in San Pietro, Bologna, finished about 1483, and much admired by Michelangelo. He also, it is said, finished a view of Naples in 1490–93. He died in 1495. The following works also are ascribed to him:

Bergamo.	Gallery.	St. John the Evangelist.
Dresden.	Gallery.	Betrayal of Christ.	*Parts of the predella of an altar-piece by Lorenzo Costa, formerly in San Giovanni in Monte, Bologna.*
„	„	Procession to Golgotha.
Liverpool.	Royal Inst.	Pietà. (*Part of the predella of the same altar-piece.*)
London.	Nat. Gall.	The Last Supper.
		The Israelites gathering Manna.
Milan.	Brera Gall.	An altar-piece (*ascribed to Stefano*).
Rome.	Vatican.	Miracles of St. Hyacinth.

A full account of the Grandis is given in Crowe

270

and Cavalcaselle's 'History of Painting in North Italy,' 1871 ; i. 530-534.

GRANDIN, Jacques Louis Michel, a French historical painter, born at Elbeuf in 1780, was a pupil of David, but he adopted a style differing considerably from that of his master. He mostly painted idylls and mythological scenes. The date of his death is not known.

GRANDJEAN, Jean, was born at Amsterdam in 1752, and after instruction under Jacobus Verstegen and Jurriaan Andriessen, as well as at the Academy of his native city, where he obtained three prizes, proceeded first to Düsseldorf, and then in 1779 to Italy. He painted landscapes, portraits, and historical subjects, and has also left one etching of a 'Bacchanal.' He died at Rome in 1781.

GRANDVILLE, Jean Ignace Isidore, whose real name was Gérard, a French designer and lithographer, was born at Nancy in 1803. He first studied miniature painting under his father, and then under Mansion and Hippolyte Lecomte, but abandoning this branch of art, he devoted himself to the then newly-discovered invention of lithography. He soon obtained a large practice, and illustrated a great number of periodicals and books. His later years were clouded with domestic misfortune, and he died in a lunatic asylum at Vanves, near Paris, in 1847. Besides the journals and books which he illustrated, the following are a few of the works he published on his own account:

Le Dimanche d'un bon Bourgeois.
Les Métamorphoses du Jour. 1828.
Les Animaux peints par eux-mêmes. 1841.
Les petites Misères de la Vie humaine. 1842.
Un autre Monde. 1843.
Cent Proverbes. 1844.
Les Fleurs animées. 1846.

GRANELLO, Niccolò, who was probably the step-son of Giovanni Battista Castello, called Il Bergamasco, flourished in the 16th century. He especially excelled in battle-pieces, which he executed in conjunction with other artists, as Tabaron and Cambiaso, and among which are the 'Battle of St. Quentin,' in the Escorial, and the 'Battle of Higueruela,' after a painting by Dello, in the Alcazar at Segovia. He was the half-brother and instructor of Fabrizio Castello, and died at Madrid in 1593.

GRANET, François Marius, a French architectural and historical painter, was born at Aix in 1775. His father, who was a mason, apprenticed him to an Italian painter who chanced to stop at Aix while upon a tour, and after having learnt the rudiments of art from him, he entered the school of the landscape painter Constantin, and afterwards the atelier of David at Paris. He there won a prize with the picture of 'The Court of a Monastery,' and then proceeded in 1802 to Rome, where he passed many years of his life. On returning to Paris for the first time in 1819, he brought with him a copy of his 'Choir of the Capuchin Monastery,' which met with such extraordinary admiration that he was compelled to execute fifteen or sixteen variations of it. Louis XVIII. gave him the decoration of the Legion of Honour in the same year, and afterwards the order of St. Michael; while in 1826 he became conservator of the paintings in the Louvre, in 1830 a member of the Institute, and in 1833 an officer of the Legion of Honour. After the revolution of 1848 he returned to Aix, where he died in 1849. He bequeathed to the town his property, and presented his pictures as the foundation of a museum; at the same time setting apart a yearly allowance of 1500 francs for the education in art of a youth of that town, and a further sum of money for establishing in the hospital for incurables two beds for masons as a memorial of his father. His paintings consist chiefly of the interiors of churches and other buildings, set out with historical scenes, and in this line he is considered to have been wholly unrivalled. The following are among his best works:

Poussin uncovering the painting of the 'Communion of St. Jerome.'

Jacques Stella painting the Madonna on the wall of his Prison Cell. 1810. (*Leuchtenberg Gallery.*)

The Choir of the Capuchin Monastery in the Piazza Barbarini at Rome. (*Buckingham Palace.*)

Inner Court of the Carthusian Monastery at Rome.

Communion of the first Christians in the Roman Catacombs.

The Alchymist. (*Stafford House.*)

Beatrice Cenci on her way to Execution.

View of the Choir of St. Scolastica at Subiaco. (*Avignon.*)

The Painter Sodoma brought into the Hospital. 1815. (*Louvre.*)

Interior of the Lower Basilica of St. Francis at Assisi. 1823. (*The same.*)

Ransoming of Christian Slaves in Algiers. 1831. (*The same.*)

GRANGER, DAVID, an engraver, practised in London in the early part of the 17th century. There is by him a 'St. George,' after Raphael.

GRANGER, JEAN PERRIN, a French historical painter, was born in Paris in 1779, and died in the same city in 1840. He was educated under Allais and Regnault, and in David's school, and he executed pictures from ancient mythology and from Greek and Roman history, as well as several of a sacred character. His 'Adoration of the Kings,' in Notre-Dame de Lorette at Paris, partakes of the style of Paolo Veronese. In the Bordeaux Museum is a picture of 'Ganymede'; in the Dijon Museum one of 'Homer and Glaucus'; and in the Leipsic Museum, 'Apollo and Cyparissus.'

GRANGES, D. DES. Hardly anything is known of this artist, save the facts that he was a Catholic and fled to this country, and was acquainted with Inigo Jones. He was probably a pupil of Peter Oliver, and copied more than one of his works. He painted a great many miniatures, which are generally signed *D. D. G.*, and dated. Some of his finest works are at Welbeck and in Montagu House, and there is a portrait by him set in a famous jewel in the Waddesdon Collection at the British Museum. Most writers, including the Keeper of the Waddesdon Collection, spell the name of this artist incorrectly as De Grange; but on a miniature at Ham House his full signature spelt as we give it can be seen. Des Granges also painted in oil, and one portrait by him is at Mottisfont Abbey. It represents a lady, and is signed and dated 1661.　　　　G. C. W.

GRANO, GIORGIO DEL. See GANDINI.

GRANT, Sir FRANCIS, a portrait painter, was born at Kilgraston in Perthshire in 1810. He was the fourth son of Francis Grant of Kilgraston, and was educated at Harrow, with the intention that he should study for the bar, but he preferred the pursuit of art, and adopted it as a profession. He first exhibited at the Royal Academy in 1834, and among his early works were hunting meets, of which his liking for field sports rendered him a faithful delineator. He subsequently devoted himself to full-length portraits, and became the fashionable portrait painter of the day, most of the celebrities of his time sitting to him. He was elected an Associate of the Royal Academy in 1842, and an Academician in 1851. On the death of Sir Charles Eastlake in 1866, and after the refusal of the office by Maclise and Sir Edwin Landseer, he was chosen President of the Academy, and knighted, honours which he owed more to his urbanity and social position than to his art. He died, after several years' suffering, in 1878, at Melton Mowbray, where he was buried, his family declining the honour of a grave in St. Paul's Cathedral. The following is a list of some of his chief works:

The Breakfast at Melton. 1834.

Count D'Orsay. 1836.

The Meeting of H.M. Staghounds at Ascot Heath. 1837. (*Earl of Chesterfield.*)

The Melton Hunt. 1839. (*Duke of Wellington.*)

Equestrian Portrait of Queen Victoria. 1840. (*Army and Navy Club.*)

Shooting Party at Ranton Abbey. 1841. (*Earl of Lichfield.*)

Marchioness of Waterford. 1844.

Queen Victoria. 1846. (*Christ's Hospital, London.*)

Albert, Prince Consort. 1846. (*The same.*)

Sidney Herbert, afterwards Lord Herbert of Lea. 1847.

Sir Richard Sutton's Hounds. 1848.

Viscount Hardinge. 1849. (*National Portrait Gallery.*)

Lord John Russell. 1854.

Lord Macaulay. 1854. (*National Portrait Gallery.*)

Sir Edwin Landseer. 1855. (*The same.*)

Benjamin Disraeli, Earl of Beaconsfield. 1852.

General Sir Hope Grant. 1862.

A Jewish Rabbi. (*National Gallery of Scotland.*)

Edward, fourteenth Earl of Derby.

Viscount Palmerston.

John Gibson Lockhart.

Lord Chancellor Truro.

Lord Chancellor Campbell. (*National Portrait Gallery.*)

George Moberley, Bishop of Salisbury.

GRANT, WILLIAM JAMES, an historical painter, was born at Hackney in 1829. At about the age of sixteen he entered the schools of the Royal Academy, and within two or three years exhibited his first work, 'Rabbits,' and was from that time a frequent exhibitor, sending in 1852 'Samson and Delilah;' in 1858, 'The Last Trial of Madame Palissy;' in 1860, 'The Morning of the Duel;' and in 1861, 'The Last Relics of Lady Jane Grey.' He was a promising artist, but died in 1866, at the early age of thirty-seven.

GRANTHOMME, JACQUES, a German engraver, born at Heidelberg, flourished about the year 1600. Little is known of him than that he was educated in France in the school of Thomas De Leeuw and Rabel, and that being expelled as a Huguenot, he settled at Frankfort, where, as well as at Heidelberg, he worked as an engraver, in the style of Sadeler and Cornelis Cort. Some writers speak of three artists of this name, and attribute to them the plates of Jean de Gourmont and Jan Georg van Vliet. Granthomme is known to have executed eighty-two plates, of which the best are his portraits. He worked entirely with the graver, and usually marked his plates with one of these ciphers: The following are his principal prints: 　　*J* or *GHE.*

Portrait of Henry III.

Louis XIII.

Charles IX.

James I., King of Great Britain.

Pope Sixtus V.

Frederick IV., Count Palatine of the Rhine.

Henry of Bourbon, Prince of Condé.

Thirteen Portraits of the Doctors and Reformers of the Church; or, as they are often styled, the Heresiarchs; *after a painter whose initials are P. M.*

The Narrative of the Good Samaritan; four plates.

271

The Marriage of Henry IV. and Catharine de' Medici.
The Infant Dauphin strangling a Serpent. 1601.
Adam and Eve.
Venus and Adonis; four plates.
Laocoön.
The Murder of the Innocents.
The Apostles; twelve small prints; *after his own designs.*
The Rape of Helen; copied from the print by *Marc-Antonio, after Raphael.*

GRANVILLE, —, was an English engraver, who flourished about the year 1760. He executed landscapes, among which are some plates from the pictures of Thomas Smith of Derby.

GRANVILLE, MARY, (Mrs. DELANY,) an English portrait painter and copyist, who was a great favourite with George III., was born in 1700. She was first married to a Mr. Pendarves, and secondly to Dr. Delany, Dean of Down. She died in 1788. There is a very good portrait of the Duchess of Queensberry by her.

GRASDORP, WILLEM, a painter of fruit and flowers, who resided at Amsterdam, was a scholar of Ernst Stuven in 1710. His pictures are held in great estimation, and are to be found in some of the finest private collections in Holland. There is a picture by him in the Brunswick Gallery, and another in the Hermitage at St. Petersburg.

GRASHOF, OTTO, an historical, genre, portrait, and animal painter, was born at Prenzlau in 1812. He was educated at Düsseldorf under Schadow, and afterwards resided some years in Russia, Mexico, and La Plata, but finally settled in 1845 at Cologne, where he died in 1876. He had been blind from 1861. Some of his best known works are:

The Battle of Schumla. 1848.
Russian Bears in a Forest.
The Guardian Angel. 1845.
Russian Pilgrims.
Portrait of Franz Liszt.
Christ and the Samaritan Woman. 1846.
Wolves by a dead Horse. 1847.
St. Wapitz of Novgorod.
Fight of a Tscherkessan and a Russian.
Till Eulenspiegel.
Scene from 'Nathan the Wise.'

GRASSI, GIOVANNI BATTISTA, lived at Udine in the 16th century, and practised there both as an architect and painter. His first known painting there was the altar-piece of the church of San Cristoforo, executed in 1547. In 1554 he painted on the front of the Casa Sabbatini frescoes representing the Medusa, and Jove and Vulcan. In 1556 he painted the organ in the cathedral with designs representing the 'Annunciation,' the 'Nativity,' the 'Marriage at Cana,' and 'Christ healing the Sick;' and in 1569 he executed the decorations of the castle of Udine, which are now nearly ruined. He died after 1578. Two paintings of his are:

Buia.   *Church.*   Martyrdom of St. Lawrence. 1558.
Gemona.   *Church.*   Organ Shutters. 1577.

GRASSI, JOSEPH, an historical and portrait painter, born at Udine in 1756, was made professor at the Dresden Academy in 1800, and in 1817 director of the Royal Saxon Pensioners at Rome. He died at Dresden in 1838. His portraits are much esteemed, and he was particularly successful with those of females. The Dresden Gallery possesses two of his paintings, 'St. John the Baptist,' and 'St. Peter.'

GRATELLA. See FILIPPI, SEBASTIANO.

GRATELOUP, JEAN BAPTISTE, a French engraver, was born at Dax in Gascony in 1735, and

died in the same town in 1817. He executed portraits in the manner of Savart and Ficquet, among which are:

Rousseau; *after J. Aved.*
Adrienne Lecouvreur; *after C. A. Coypel.*
Montesquieu; *after Dassier.*
Descartes; *after F. Hals.*
Dryden; *after Kneller.*
Bossuet (two portraits); *after Rigaud.*
Fénélon; *after Vivien.*

GRATI, GIOVANNI BATTISTA, was born at Bologna in 1681, and was a scholar of Giovanni Gioseffo dal Sole. There are several of his pictures in the churches at Bolonga, of which the most esteemed are 'The Virgin and Child, with St. Francis, St. Joseph, and St. Gaetano, with a glory of Angels,' in Santa Maria Incoronata; and 'St. Anne teaching the Virgin to read,' in San Giacomo Maggiore. He died in 1758.

GRATIANI, BARTOLOMMEO, the son of Guido Gratiani, settled in Perugia in 1319, and painted for the church of Montelebate.

GRATIANI, GUIDO, superseded Diotisalvi in 1287, 1290, and 1298 as painter of the books of the Biccherna. He is mentioned as the painter of a banner, and he executed in 1295 a 'Majesty, between St. Peter and St. Paul,' in the Public Palace of Siena, and gilded three hundred letters for an image of the Virgin. In 1302 he executed the portraits of twelve forgers for the front of the Tribunal of Justice.

GRATIANI, MINO, a brother of Bartolommeo, painted in 1289 a 'Virgin and Saints' for the Hall of the Great Council in the old Public Palace of Siena, and in 1303 a 'St. Christopher.' In 1298 he produced the portraits of several false witnesses. His name is not found in the public records after 1329.

GRATTON, GEORGE, an Irish genre painter, flourished at the beginning of the 19th century, and in 1807 was awarded 100 guineas by the Dublin Society for his 'Beggar Woman and Child.' He afterwards removed to London, and exhibited at the Royal Academy in 1812, 'The Guard Room,' 'The Gathering,' and 'Noon Tide.' No trace of him exists after this date. There is a water-colour view of 'Christ Church, Dublin,' by him, in the South Kensington Museum.

GRAVE, ALDE. See ALDEGREVER.

GRAVE, HANS. See GRAF.

GRAVE, JAN EVERT, a designer and engraver, was born at Amsterdam in 1759, and died there in 1805. He was a scholar of Jakob Cats and Jan Punts, and chiefly executed landscapes and views of towns.

GRAVE, JOSUA. See GRAAF.

GRAVELOT, HENRI, whose original name was D'ANVILLE, a French designer and engraver, was born in Paris in 1699. He was the brother of the geographer D'Anville, but he assumed the name of Gravelot on coming to England, whither he was invited in 1733, by Claude Du Bosc, to assist him in the plates for the 'Religious Ceremonies,' which he published in English, copied from Picart. Gravelot returned to France in 1745, but was soon in England again, and after a highly successful course here, he finally settled in Paris in 1754, where he died in 1773. He was an excellent draughtsman, and made designs for ornaments, and drawings of ancient buildings, monuments, &c., with great taste. He etched several plates for books; among which were those for Sir Thomas

Hanmer's edition of Shakespeare, some of which were from his own designs, and others after Francis Hayman. He also engraved the plates for Theobald's Shakespeare, from his own designs. He is also well known as one of the earliest caricaturists. His best plate is a view of Kirkstall Abbey.

GRAVELOT, HUBERT FRANÇOIS BOURGUIGNON. See BOURGUIGNON-GRAVELOT.

GRAVES, ROBERT, a line-engraver, was born in London in 1798. At an early age he manifested a strong predilection for art, and studied in the life-school held in Ship Yard, Temple Bar, until 1812, in which year he became a pupil of John Romney, the engraver. Afterwards he made for collectors many copies in pen-and-ink of rare portraits by Hollar, Van de Passe, and others; but at length he devoted himself entirely to engraving. In 1836 he was by an unanimous vote elected an Associate Engraver of the Royal Academy, on which occasion he presented as his diploma work the portrait of Lord Byron, after Thomas Phillips. This and the 'Highland Whiskey-Still,' after Sir Edwin Landseer, are his two most successful engravings. Besides a great number of portraits and book-illustrations, he engraved several plates after Wilkie, Landseer, and Mulready, for the Author's Edition of the 'Waverley Novels,' and others for the 'Literary Souvenir,' 'Iris,' 'Amulet,' 'Keepsake Français,' and 'Forget-Me-Not.' He died in London in 1873. His plates generally are characterised more by their refinement and delicacy, and in these qualities they can scarcely be surpassed, than by any remarkable vigour of line. The following are his most important works:

The Enthusiast; *after T. Lane.* 1831.
Mathematical Abstraction; *after the same.* 1833.
The Musical Bore; *after R. W. Buss.* 1834.
The Romance; *after the same.*
The Venetian Girl; *after J. Wood.* 1836.
Lord Byron; *after Thomas Phillips.* 1836.
The Abbotsford Family; *after Sir David Wilkie.* 1837.
The Examination of Shakespeare before Sir Thomas Lucy on a charge of deer-stealing; *after Sir George Harvey.* 1839.
A Castaway; *after the same.* 1841.
The Highland Whiskey-Still *after Sir Edwin Landseer.* 1842.
The First Reading of the Bible in the crypt of Old St. Paul's; *after Sir George Harvey.* 1846.
Lord Nelson; half-length; *after Abbott.* 1847.
The Baron's Charger; *after J. F. Herring.* 1850.
The Highland Cradle; *after Sir Edwin Landseer.* 1850.
Haidee, a Greek Girl; *after Sir Charles Eastlake.* 1850.
The Princess Amelia; *after Sir Thomas Lawrence.* 1855.
The Princess Victoria Gouramma of Coorg; *after Winterhalter.* 1857.
Cromwell resolving to refuse the Crown; *after C. Lucy.* 1858.
The Sisters; *after Sir Charles Eastlake.* 1859.
The Princesses Mary, Sophia, and Amelia, daughters of George III.; *after J. S. Copley.* 1860.
The Slide; *after Webster.* 1861.
The Origin of the Harp; *after Maclise.* 1862.
The Good Shepherd; *after Murillo.* 1863.
The Immaculate Conception; *after the same.* 1865.
Paolo and Francesca da Rimini; *after Sir John Noel Paton.* 1866.
Hon. Mrs. Graham; full-length; *after Gainsborough.* 1866.
The Blue Boy (Master Burrell); *after the same.* 1868.
Mrs. Lloyd, afterwards Mrs. Peter Beckford; full-length; *after Sir Joshua Reynolds.* 1868.
Mrs. Siddons; half-length; *after Gainsborough.* 1869.
Via Dolorosa; *after Raphael (?).* 1869.
Georgiana, Duchess of Devonshire; full-length; *after Gainsborough.* 1870.
Lady Bowater; full-length; *after the same.* 1872.
(*Left unfinished: completed by James Stephenson.*)

GRAY, —, an English engraver of little celebrity, executed a set of views for a work published about 1727, entitled 'Thirty different Drafts of Guinea,' by William Smith, Surveyor to the Royal African Company of England. There is a frontispiece to the work, representing an Elephant, which is etched in the style of Hollar, very superior to the plates by Gray.

GRAY, HENRY PETERS, an American artist, a pupil of the renowned Huntingdon, and born in New York in 1819. After learning the elements of his profession in his native city he set out for Italy, and studied in Venice and Rome for two years. He then returned to the United States, remaining in New York till 1846, and producing there some of his best-known works, especially 'Cupid begging his Arrow.' Again he went to Europe and again he returned to his native city, and there he became a member of the National Academy, rising in 1869 to the office of President, in which he succeeded his old master Huntingdon. He continued to hold this position till 1871, when once again the attractions of Europe were too strong to be overcome, and he left for Florence, where he passed the remainder of his life, dying in 1877. Amongst his better-known works are: 'The Pride of the Village,' 'The Apple of Discord,' 'Wages of War,' which is in the Metropolitan Museum in New York, 'Just Fifteen' and 'The Flower of Fiesole,' which belong to Mr. M. O. Roberts, 'The Model from Cadore,' and 'The Pride of the Rialto.' Most of his works are the result of his long sojourn in Italy, but on one occasion certainly, in 'The Birth of our Flag,' he treats of events in the history of the United States.

GRAY, PAUL, an Irish draughtsman on wood, was born at Dublin in 1842, and there passed his earlier years; but when about twenty-one years of age he came to London. He showed some skill as a painter, but having to support his mother he was driven to become a wood-engraver. He designed the illustrations to Charles Kingsley's 'Hereward,' and he also contributed many of the cartoons to 'Fun.' He, however, suffered from bad health, and died at the early age of twenty-four, in 1866.

GRAZIA, LEONARDO, known as LEONARDO DA PISTOJA, was a native of Pistoja, and a scholar of Giovanni Francesco Penni, a distinguished disciple of Raphael. His family name appears to have been Grazia, from an inscription on a picture of the 'Annunciation,' by him, in the chapel of the sacristy of the cathedral of Lucca. He painted historical subjects and portraits, but particularly excelled in the latter. His works are to be found chiefly at Rome, Naples, and Lucca. According to Zani he flourished from 1516 to 1540; but there is a doubt whether there were not two painters of the same name who lived about the same time.

GRAZIADEI. See PESCIA.

GRAZIANI, ERCOLE, a Bolognese painter, was born at Bologna in 1688. He was brought up in the school of Donato Creti, whose style he improved by a grander character of design, a more harmonious colouring, and a greater freedom of hand. His powers approximate to those of Marc Antonio Franceschini and others that issued from the school of Cignani. He was an artist of unusual assiduity, and painted a prodigious number of pictures for the public edifices at Bologna and Piacenza. The churches at Bologna abound with his works, of which the most esteemed is his celebrated picture of 'St. Peter consecrating St. Apollinaris amidst an assemblage of the primitive Christians.' Cardinal Lambertini, Archbishop of Bologna, on becoming Pope, as Benedict XIV., commissioned Graziani to paint a replica of this picture for the church of Sant' Apollinare at Rome, where is also his 'Baptism of Christ.' In San Bartolommeo di Reno, at Bologna, are two admired pictures by him of the 'Marriage of St. Catharine,' and 'St. Anne teaching the Virgin to read.' In the church of La Purità is the 'Ascension;' and in the Madonna delle Rondini is the 'Annunciation,' one of his most celebrated works. He died in 1765.

GRAZIANI, PIETRO, was a painter of battles, who flourished at Naples in the 18th century.

GRAZZINI, GIOVANNI PAOLO, born at Ferrara about the year 1570, passed the first and greater part of his life as a goldsmith. He learned the rudiments of design, as was at that time usual with those of his profession, and being intimate with Carlo Bononi, he was prompted by the celebrity of his friend to make an essay of his own powers in painting, though he had already passed the prime of life. His first public performance, which occupied him eight years, was a picture of 'St. Eloy,' which Lanzi says was painted for the Scuola degli Orefici. Barotti, in his description of the works of art in Ferrara, places it in the church of San Giuliano, and adds, that Carlo Bononi embellished it with four angels at the corners, in chiaroscuro, and that Scarzellino environed it with nine small pictures of the principal actions of the saint. Grazzini also painted several easel pictures, which were much esteemed by his fellow-citizens. He died in 1632.

GREBBER. See DE GREBBER.

GRECCHI, MARC ANTONIO, was a native of Siena, whose works are dated from 1590 to 1634. There is a picture by him, mentioned by Lanzi, in a church at Foligno, representing the 'Holy Family.' It is painted in a style resembling rather the Bolognese taste of Tiarini, than that of any of the Sienese painters.

GRECHE, DOMENICO DELLE. See THEOTOCOPULI.

GRECHETTO, IL. See CASTIGLIONE, GIOVANNI BENEDETTO.

GRECO, IL. See THEOTOCOPULI.

GRÉE, PIETER JAN BALTHASAR DE, a Flemish painter, born at Antwerp in 1751, was a pupil of Geeraerts, from whom he acquired the taste for painting bas-reliefs, and in this line he gained a reputation. About 1786 he went to Ireland, and settled in Dublin, where he died in 1789.

GREEN, AMOS, a flower and landscape painter, who flourished in the latter half of the 18th century, was the brother of Benjamin Green. He was born at Hales Owen, and died at York in 1807.

GREEN, BENJAMIN, a mezzotint engraver, born at Hales Owen about 1736, was probably the elder brother of Valentine Green. He was a member of the Incorporated Society of Artists, with whom he exhibited from 1765 to 1774, and he taught drawing at Christ's Hospital. He died in London about 1800. He engraved the plates in Morant's 'History and Antiquities of the County of Essex,' 1768, as well as the following prints:

The Horse before the Lion's Den; after *Stubbs*. 1768.
The Lion and the Stag; after *the same*. 1770.
The Horse and the Lioness; after *the same*. 1774.
Portrait of Lord Pigot; after *the same*.
Portrait of Miss Baldwin; after *Kettle*.

GREEN, BENJAMIN ROBERT, a water-colour painter, born in London in 1808, was the son of James Green, the portrait painter. After having been educated in the schools of the Royal Academy, he became a member of the Institute of Painters in Water-Colours. He taught much, and was for many years Secretary of the Artists' Annuity Fund. He died in London in 1876. There is a water-colour drawing by him of the 'Interior of Stratford-on-Avon Church' in the South Kensington Museum.

GREEN, CHARLES, was born in 1840. He studied at the Newman Street studios, and under Mr. J. W. Whymper. His earliest work was in black and white, many of his illustrations appearing in 'Once a Week,' 'London Society,' 'The Churchman's Family Magazine,' 'Cassell's Magazine' and other periodicals, including the 'Illustrated London News' and the 'Graphic,' to the latter of which he was among the first contributors. In 1864 he became an Associate of the Royal Institute of Painters in Water-Colours, and a full member in 1868. He took great interest in the affairs of the society and was a regular contributor to its exhibitions. His water-colour drawings, which he exhibited for the first time in 1862, were remarkable for their finished execution. In early life he illustrated many books, including Cumming's 'Life of Our Lord,' Watts' 'Divine and Moral Songs,' and Thornbury's 'Legendary Ballads.' His illustrations to Dickens are among his best work. For the Household edition of the 'Old Curiosity Shop' he executed thirty-two drawings. His best known illustrations, however, were produced in the last few years of his life; they are —twenty-seven drawings for 'A Christmas Carol' (1892), twenty-nine for 'A Battle of Life' (1893), thirty for 'The Chimes' (1894), and thirty for 'The Haunted Man' (1895); his last work being ten designs for the Gadshill edition of 'Great Expectations.' Scenes from Dickens' novels figured largely as subjects for his water-colour drawings: these include 'Nell and her Grandfather at the Races,' 'Captain Cuttle and Florence Dombey,' 'Barnaby Rudge and the Rioters,' 'Mr. Mantalini and the Brokers,' and 'The Pickwick Club.' He also painted in oil-colours, and exhibited several pictures at the Royal Academy. He died at Hampstead in 1898.

H. C. S.

GREEN, JAMES, a portrait painter, was born at Leytonstone in 1771. He at first practised in water-colours, and belonged to the Associated Society of Water-Colour Artists, but afterwards exhibited at the British Institution, where he obtained a prize of £60 in 1808. His later works appeared at the Royal Academy. He died at Bath in 1834. There are portraits by him in the National Portrait Gallery of Thomas Stothard, the painter, and Sir John Ross, the Arctic navigator.

GREEN, JOHN, an engraver who worked in the 18th century, was a native of Hales Owen. He was brother to Benjamin Green, and a pupil of James Basire. Some of the plates in Borlase's 'Natural History of Cornwall,' and on the Oxford Almanacks are by him. He died about 1757. Among other portraits, the following are by him:

Thomas Rowney, M.P.
Thomas Shaw, D.D., Master of St. Edmund Hall, Oxford.
William Derham, D.D., Canon of Windsor.

GREEN, JOSHUA, was a water-colour painter, by whom there is a drawing of 'Ullswater Head' in the South Kensington Museum. The dates of his birth and death are unknown.

GREEN, MARY, a miniature painter, born in

VALENTINE GREEN

After Reynolds, 1780]

MARY ISABELLA, DUCHESS OF RUTLAND

After Reynolds, 1779]

LADY BETTY DELMÉ AND HER CHILDREN

1776, was the second daughter of William Byrne, the landscape engraver, and wife of James Green, the portrait painter, whom she married in 1805. She studied under Arlaud, and exhibited at the Royal Academy from 1795 to 1834. She died in 1845. There are good portraits by her of Queen Adelaide and Lady Alicia Peel.

GREEN, NATHANIEL EVERETT, landscape and subject painter, received his early training at the Royal Academy. He was a Fellow of the Royal Astronomical Society, and well known for the excellence of his planetary observations and drawings, particularly those of Mars, made at Madeira in 1877. He was the second president of the British Astronomical Association. Since 1854 he was a frequent exhibitor in Trafalgar Square, Suffolk Street, and with the New Water-Colour Society. His death occurred at St. Albans, November 11, 1899.

GREEN, VALENTINE, a mezzotint engraver, was born at Hales Owen, near Birmingham, in 1739. He was intended by his father for the profession of the law, for which purpose he was placed under a respectable practitioner at Evesham, in Worcestershire, with whom he passed two years; but having a taste for drawing, he abandoned his office, and, without his father's concurrence, became a pupil to an obscure line-engraver at Worcester. His progress in that branch of engraving not succeeding to his wishes, he came to London in 1765, and turned his attention to scraping in mezzotint, in which, without the aid of an instructor, he arrived at a perfection which has seldom been equalled. Green participates with MacArdell and Earlom in the merit of having been the first artists who gave consequence and variety to the particular mode of engraving to which they devoted themselves; and it is worthy of remark, that Green's celebrated prints of 'Hannibal' and 'Regulus,' after the pictures by West in the Royal Collection, were the first plates of equal magnitude and importance that had appeared. These were succeeded by several others of similar consideration, which will ever rank among the ablest and most energetic efforts of mezzotint. This indefatigable artist, by his unremitting exertions during a period of upwards of forty years, produced nearly four hundred plates, engraved from the works of the most celebrated painters, ancient and modern. In 1789 he obtained a patent from the Duke of Bavaria, giving him the exclusive privilege of engraving and publishing prints from the pictures in the Düsseldorf Gallery; and in the year 1795, he had published twenty-two prints from that collection. The enterprise promised to remunerate him amply for so spirited an undertaking, but unfortunately, during the siege of that city by the French in 1798, the castle and gallery were laid in ruins, and a very valuable property belonging to him was destroyed. Other speculations, flattering in their outset, were lost to him by the overwhelming eruption of the French Revolution, of which Green thus became one of the innumerable victims. In 1767 he was elected a member of the Incorporated Society of Artists of Great Britain; and in 1775 one of the six Associate Engravers of the Royal Academy. On the foundation of the British Institution he was appointed keeper; and his zealous exertions to promote the purposes of that institution contributed greatly to its success. Valentine Green died in London in 1813. The following are among his most important works:

T 2

PORTRAITS AFTER SIR JOSHUA REYNOLDS.

Sir Joshua Reynolds; *after the picture by himself at the Royal Academy.* 1780.
The Duke of Bedford, Lords Henry and William Russell, and Miss Vernon. 1778.
Lord Dalkeith, afterwards Duke of Buccleuch. 1778.
Maria Isabella, Duchess of Rutland.
Emily Mary, Countess of Salisbury. 1787.
Anne, Viscountess Townshend. 1780.
The Ladies Waldegrave. 1784.
Lady Louisa Manners. 1769.
Lady Elizabeth Cavendish. 1781.
Louisa, Countess of Aylesford. 1783.
Lady Elizabeth Delme. 1779.
Lady Talbot. 1782.
Lady Caroline Howard. 1782
Georgiana, Duchess of Devonshire. 1780.
Lady Jane Halliday. 1779.
Jane, Countess of Harrington, with her two Sons. 1780.

PORTRAITS AFTER OTHER MASTERS.

Charles Theodore, Elector of Bavaria; *after P. Batoni.*
Sir Thomas Wharton; *after Van Dyck;* for the Houghton Gallery.
Henry, Earl of Danby; *after the same;* for the same.
George, Marquis of Huntly; *after the same;* for the same.
Richard Cumberland; *after Romney.* 1771.
Mrs. Yates, as the Tragic Muse; *after the same.* 1772.
William Powell and Robert Bensley in the characters of King John and Hubert; *after Mortimer.*
John Hamilton Mortimer, painter; *after the same.*
Garrick and Mrs. Pritchard, in Macbeth; *after Zoffany.*

HISTORICAL SUBJECTS AFTER WEST.

The Stoning of Stephen. 1776.
The Raising of Lazarus.
Christ calling to him the little Children.
Peter denying Christ.
Jacob blessing the Sons of Joseph. 1768.
Daniel interpreting Belshazzar's Dream. 1777.
Nathan and David. 1784.
St. Peter and St. John going to the Sepulchre.
The Three Maries at the Sepulchre.
Alexander and his Physician.
Regulus leaving Rome to return to Carthage.
Hannibal vowing eternal hatred to the Romans.
Mark Antony's Oration on the Death of Cæsar.
Agrippina weeping over the Urn of Germanicus.
The Death of Epaminondas.
The Death of the Chevalier Bayard.

SUBJECTS AFTER VARIOUS MASTERS.

The Annunciation; *after F. Barocci.*
The Nativity; *after the same.*
The Virgin and Infant; *after Domenichino.*
St. John with the Lamb; *after Murillo.*
The Assumption of the Virgin; *after the same.*
The Entombment of Christ; *after L. Carracci.*
Time clipping the Wings of Love; *after Van Dyck.*
Venus and Cupid; *after Agostino Carracci.*
The Descent from the Cross; *after Rubens.*
The Visitation; *after the same.*
The Presentation in the Temple; *after the same.*
The Sulky Boy; *after R. Morton Paye.*
The Disaster of the Milk-pail; *after the same.*
The Child of Sorrow; *after the same.*

GREEN, WILLIAM, an engraver, was born at Manchester in 1761. He originally practised as a surveyor, and then came to London to study engraving; but he afterwards settled in the Lake district, and drew and engraved many views of its scenery. He died at Ambleside in 1823. There is by him in the South Kensington Museum a water-colour drawing of 'Raven Crag, Thirlmere.'

GREENAWAY, KATE, artist, was born at 1, Cavendish Street, Hoxton, March 17, 1846. She was daughter of John Greenaway, woodengraver and draughtsman, whose chief work is to be found in the 'Illustrated London News.' At twelve she was a prize-winner at the South Kensington Art School (Islington branch), and later won several medals, including the "National." She attended life classes at "Heatherley's" and the newly-opened Slade School. Amongst her fellow-students and friends were Elizabeth Thompson (Lady Butler) and Helen Paterson (Mrs. Allingham). Beyond designing Christmas cards and valentines she did not appear before the public until 1868, when she first exhibited at the Dudley Gallery. Here six little drawings on wood attracted the attention of Rev. W. J. Loftie, who had them written up to and published in the 'People's Magazine.' She was now beginning to recognize the possibilities which lay in a revival of our grandmothers' gowns. These she made up with her own hands, and with them costumed her little models and lay figures. It was largely due to this thoroughness in the beginning that she achieved her ultimate success. In 1870 she exhibited for the first time in Suffolk Street. In 1871 she illustrated Madame d'Aulnoy's 'Fairy Tales' for Messrs. Cronheim. In 1872 she designed some covers for yellow-back novels. In 1873 she began work on 'Little Folks' (Cassell), and was employed by Marcus Ward to design Christmas cards, which proved an immense success. The same year she exhibited and sold her picture 'A Fern Gatherer' at the Royal Manchester Institution. In 1874 she illustrated 'Topo,' a youthful performance of Miss Blood's (Lady Colin Campbell), for Marcus Ward, and the same year published with that firm 'The Quiver of Love,' a volume of Valentine's. In 1877 she sold her first Academy picture, 'Missing,' and was working for the 'Graphic' and 'Illustrated London News.' Of greatest importance, however, at this time was the beginning of her long business connection with Mr. Edmund Evans, the well-known colour-printer, and the turning-point in her career was his production of 'Under the Window,' of which both illustrations and letterpress were hers. Of this 70,000 copies were sold. This was followed, amongst others, by the 'Birthday Book,' 'Mother Goose,' 'A Day in a Child's Life' (1881), 'Little Ann' (1883), 'The Language of Flowers,' the 'Painting Book' and 'Mavor's Spelling Book' (1884–5), 'Marigold Garden' and 'An Apple Pie' (1886), 'The Queen of the Pirate Isle' and 'The Pied Piper of Hamelin' (1887), the 'Book of Games' (1888), 'King Pepito' (1889), the 'April Baby's Book of Tunes' (1901), and a series of 'Almanacks.' An idea of the success of the Greenaway-Evans partnership may be gathered from the fact that in this space of ten years the number of copies of her works printed reached a grand total of 714,000. She early attracted the attention of Frederick Locker (afterwards Locker-Lampson), Stacy Marks and Ruskin. For the latter's opinion of her works reference should be made to 'Fors Clavigera' and 'The Art of England.' With him she carried on a voluminous correspondence for over seventeen years. In 1880 she was invited to exhibit at the Grosvenor Gallery. Up to this year she had sold her drawings out and out, but from henceforth she retained the copyrights as a protection against imitators and pirates. In 1881 the Crown Princess of Germany (the Empress Frederick) and Princess Christian sought her acquaintanceship and received her at Buckingham Palace and Cumberland Lodge. In 1883 she had made enough money (four of her books alone having brought her in £8000), to build

herself a fine house and studio at 39, Frognal, Hampstead. This, which was designed by Mr. Norman Shaw and finished in 1885, she inhabited till her death. In 1883 she began the series of Almanacks (mentioned above), which were continued (1896 excepted) until 1897. Her designs were now being freely copied on glass, crockery, linen fabrics, wall-papers, stationery, tiles, chocolate-boxes and pottery, both at home and abroad. In 1885 she did some extra illustrations for the old ballad, 'Dame Wiggins of Lea,' which was published with extra verses and an introduction by Ruskin. In 1889 she was elected a member of the Royal Institute of Painters in Water-Colours, to the exhibitions of which body she became a frequent contributor of genre subjects and portraits. In 1891, 1894 and 1898 she held exhibitions of her pictures at the Fine Art Society (Bond Street), and sold several thousand pounds' worth of pictures. It was, too, in the early nineties that she made the acquaintance of Mr. M. H. Spielmann, her future biographer. During her later years she designed several charming bookplates, and finally in 1899, at the age of fifty-three, she set herself to master the technicalities of portrait-painting in oils. But her health was now failing, and, after two years of suffering, she died on November 7, 1901.

Technically Kate Greenaway was not a great artist, but she influenced greatly the art of the nineteenth century. In a limited sense she was the founder of a school, but she will be chiefly remembered for the revolution which she accomplished in the dress of the children of two continents. Her name has passed not only into the English language but into the French, where "greenawisme" has gone to stay.　G. S. L.

GREENBURY, —, a portrait painter, employed by Charles I. as a copyist, is mentioned by Sir Theodore de Mayerne, and by Walpole. He died about 1670. There is in New College, Oxford, a portrait of Arthur Lake, Bishop of Bath and Wells, by him, dated 1626.

GREENHILL, JOHN, a portrait painter, was born at Salisbury in 1649. He was one of the ablest scholars of Sir Peter Lely, and before he was twenty copied Van Dyck's picture of 'Thomas Killigrew and his Dog,' now in the collection of the Duke of Devonshire, so well that it was mistaken for the original. His heads in crayons were much admired; and he appears to have been more employed in that way than in oil. He would probably have reached a high position in the art, had he not fallen a victim, in the prime of life, to an intemperate and dissolute course of life. He died in London in 1676. There are in the National Portrait Gallery portraits by him of Charles II., and of Anthony, first Earl of Shaftesbury. He also etched a portrait of his brother, Henry Greenhill, the mathematician.

GREENWOOD, JOHN, a painter and mezzotint engraver, was born at Boston, in Massachusetts, in 1729. In 1752 he migrated to Surinam, and thence to Holland, arriving in England in 1763. Here he exhibited engravings at the Incorporated Society of Artists from 1764 to 1776, when he became an auctioneer. He died at Margate in 1792. Amongst the plates he engraved are:

The Curious Maid; *after a picture by himself.*
Amelia Hone; *after Hone.*
John Wesley; *after the same.*
George Whitefield; *after the same.*
An Old Man; *after Eeckhout.*

GREENWOOD, Thomas, the son of John Greenwood, the painter and engraver, was for many years at the close of the 18th century, chief scene-painter at Drury Lane Theatre. He died in 1797.

GREFF, Hieronymus, a German engraver, was a native of Frankfort, who flourished early in the 16th century. He is supposed to have been a pupil of Albrecht Dürer; but this conjecture probably arose from his having copied some of the designs of that artist with great exactness; among which are the woodcuts of the 'Apocalypse,' copied in 1502 in the same size as the originals. He is sometimes called 'Hieronymus of Frankfort,' and he usually

marked his prints with the monogram 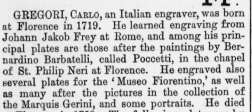.

GREGORI, Carlo, an Italian engraver, was born at Florence in 1719. He learned engraving from Johann Jakob Frey at Rome, and among his principal plates are those after the paintings by Bernardino Barbatelli, called Poccetti, in the chapel of St. Philip Neri at Florence. He engraved also several plates for the 'Museo Fiorentino,' as well as many after the pictures in the collection of the Marquis Gerini, and some portraits. He died at Florence in 1759. The following plates are by him:

PORTRAITS.

Francesco Maria, Grand-Duke of Tuscany; *after Campiglia.*
Eleonora Vincentina of Gonzaga, his consort; *after the same.*
Sebastiano Bombelli; *after a picture by himself.*

SUBJECTS AFTER VARIOUS MASTERS.

The Image of the Virgin; *after a design by Fratta.*
Saint Catharine; *after Bartolozzi.*
Fourteen plates of the Life of St. Philip Neri; *after Bernardino Barbatelli.*
The Three Maries at the Sepulchre; *after Raphael.*

GREGORI, Ferdinando, the son of Carlo Gregori, was born at Florence in 1743. After receiving some instruction in engraving from his father, he went to Paris, where he became a pupil of J. G. Wille, and afterwards returned to Florence, where he died about 1804. He engraved several plates, of which the following are the principal:

Portrait of Carlo Gregori; *after his own design.*
La Madonna della Sedia; *after Raphael.*
The Holy Family under a Palm Tree, surrounded by Angels; *after C. Maratti.*
Venus sleeping; *after Guido.*
St. Sebastian bound to a Tree; *after the same.*
Venus, with Cupid mounted on a Dolphin; *after Casanova.*
Two Groups of Sculpture; *after Cellini.*
The Holy Family; *after Andrea del Sarto.*
The Stoning of Stephen; *after L. Cardi.*
The Death of St. Louis Gonzaga; *after Cipriani.*

GREGORIO, Fra, a Polish miniature painter of the 17th century, worked in Rome for the house of Barberini, and afterwards in London for Charles I. and his Queen in 1640. He was also a carver in ivory.

GREGORIO, Marco di, who was born at Resina in 1829, studied in the Art School at Naples. In 1868 he went to Egypt, where he remained for three years, made several studies, and painted a drop scene for the theatre at Cairo. He died at Resina in 1876.

GREGORIO DI CECCO. See Cecco.

GREGORIUS, Albertus Jakob Frans, a portrait painter, and director of the Academy at Bruges, was born in that city in 1774, and after 1802 was a scholar of David at Paris. He painted, amongst others, the portraits of Napoleon, Louis XVIII., Charles X., and Louis Philippe. He returned to Bruges in 1835, and died there in 1853.

GREIG, George M., a water-colour painter, was an artist better known in Scotland than in England, who confined himself almost entirely to painting picturesque interiors and old buildings. He exhibited some sketches of the interior of Holyrood Palace at the Royal Academy in 1865, and died at Edinburgh in 1867.

GREIN, Kaspar Arnold, was born at Brühl, near Cologne, in 1764. He was instructed under J. M. Metz, in Cologne, where from 1794 he lived as a teacher of drawing, and died in 1835. He was especially successful as a flower-painter, but was clever also in portraits, landscapes, still-life, and historical subjects. The Wallraf-Richartz Museum at Cologne contains one of his pictures.

GREISCHER, M., a German engraver mentioned by Basan, is said to have engraved several plates after various masters, which are signed with the

annexed monogram: *NG*. One of them is a

print of 'The Virgin and Infant Christ, with St. John,' after F. Barocci.

GRENIER de SAINT-MARTIN, François, who was born in Paris in 1793, studied in David's school, and devoted himself to historical subjects. Later in life he painted genre and fancy subjects, many of which are well known from engravings and lithographs. He died in Paris in 1867. Amongst his pictures may be mentioned:

The Marriage Project.
The Sailor with his Boy.
The Strolling Players with the Stolen Child.
The Recovered Child.
The Old Vagabond; (from Béranger).
The Poacher fallen asleep on the Watch.
The Little Wood Thieves.
Prudence. (*Compiègne.*)

GRENVILLE, Jones, an Irish engraver, was born at Dublin in 1723. He chiefly executed landscapes, among which are two after Poussin.

GRESLY, Gabriel, a French genre painter, was born at L'Isle-sur-les-Doubs about 1710, and died at Besançon in 1756. There are examples of his art in the Museums of Dijon and Besançon.

GRESSE, John Alexander, born in London of Swiss parentage in 1741, was first instructed by Gérard Scotin, the engraver, but afterwards studied for some years under Cipriani, as well as under Zuccarelli. He was one of the first students who attended the Duke of Richmond's gallery, and in a short time afterwards he entered the Academy in St. Martin's Lane. Though possessed of considerable talents, he was not sufficiently assiduous to distinguish himself in the higher branches of painting; and as he inherited a small fortune at the death of his father, he relinquished the more arduous exercise of the profession, and became a drawing-master, in which pursuit he acquired great reputation and extensive employment, and in 1777 was appointed drawing-master to the princesses. In the early part of his life he etched the figures, &c., for Kennedy's 'Description of the Antiquities and Curiosities in Wilton House,' 1769, in which he had the advantage of being assisted by Bartolozzi. There are also four other etchings by this artist, a 'View of Framlingham Castle, Suffolk;' a 'Cottage;' a 'St. Jerome;' and a 'Satyr sleeping,' after Nicolas Poussin. Gresse died in London in 1794.

On account of his corpulency he was known among his comrades by the name of 'Jack Grease.' In the South Kensington Museum is a water-colour drawing by him of 'Llangollen Bridge.'

GREUT, JOSEPH, noticed by Strutt as the engraver of a portrait of Hieronymus Bartholomeus, is supposed to have been a German, and to have worked chiefly for booksellers.

GREUTER, JOHANN FRIEDRICH, the son of Matthäus Greuter, was born at Rome about the year 1600, and was instructed by his father, whom he surpassed. He died in 1660. He engraved the plates for the 'Flora' of P. Ferrari, as well as the following prints:

Portrait of Giovanni Battista Marino; *after S. Vouet.*
Hercules in the Garden of the Hesperides; *after Pietro da Cortona.*
Marc' Antonio Colonna carried in triumph by Sea Gods; *after the same.*
The Forge of Vulcan; *after Lanfranco.*
The Hesperides arriving in the Port of Naples, with their Fruit borne by Tritons; *after the same.*
Apollo and the Muses; *after A. Camassei.*
The Virgin and Infant, with St. Francis kneeling; *after his own design.*
The Death of St. Cecilia; *after Domenichino.*
The Growth of Christianity; *after Romanelli.*
Battle-piece; *after A. Tempesta.*

GREUTER, MATTHÄUS, a German engraver, was born at Strassburg about the year 1564. After receiving some instruction in his native city, he travelled to Italy, by way of Lyons and Avignon, in both of which cities he was for some time employed. He resided chiefly at Rome, where he engraved several plates, executed in a neat style, though his design is generally incorrect. He died in 1638. Some of his plates are wrought entirely with the graver; others are etched, and finished with the graver, in a slighter style. He signed his prints sometimes with his name at length, and sometimes with the monogram MG. The following are his principal works:

Pope Sixtus V.
Cardinal Serafino Olivaro Razalio.
The Virgin seated, with the Infant Jesus and St. John; *after F. Barocci.*
St. Mary Magdalen seated, holding a Book, and leaning her hand on a Skull; *after Luigi Gaetano.* 1584.
Venus standing on a Globe, with Figures emblematical of Virtue and Vice; *after his own design.* 1587.
The Fall of Phaeton; *after W. Dietterlin.* 1588.
The Burning of Troy: *after Lanfranco.*
The grand Cavalcade of the Emperor Charles V.; engraved conjointly with *Lucas Vorsterman.*
A set of small plates of Insects; etched in a style like that of *Gaywood.*
View of Strassburg in 1587; *after D. Speckle.*

GREUZE, JEAN BAPTISTE, a French genre and portrait painter, was born at Tournus, near Macon, in Burgundy, on the 21st August, 1725, and from his eighth year amused himself with drawing, although his father at first opposed his inclinations. His earliest regular instruction in art was due to a Lyonnese painter, Grandon—his maternal grandfather—who took him to Lyons, and eventually to Paris, where he studied in the Academy. His first picture, 'A Father explaining the Bible to his Children,' obtained a great success, and it was for some time doubted whether he was really the painter. His subsequent productions dispelled these doubts, and in 1755, his picture of 'L'Aveugle trompé' procured his acceptance by the Academy, on the nomination of Pigalle, the sculptor.

He then passed a short time in Italy, and his sojourn there affected his style for a time, but did not leave any permanent traces. On his return he continued to exhibit at the Academy, without fulfilling the required academic conditions, and he was at length, after repeated warning, excluded from the Salon of 1767. It was not till after he had produced his 'Severus reproaching Caracalla' (now in the Louvre) in 1769, that he was admitted into the Academy, and then not in the highest class as a painter of history, but in the ranks of the genre painters. At this rebuff Greuze withdrew in dudgeon, and did not exhibit again until after the Revolution. But it was then too late: the classic school reigned supreme, and, moreover, age had begun to tell on his art. Troubles fell thickly upon him in his latter years: the competence he had saved was dissipated by failures, and his nature was not such as to attract friends. He died in indigence in Paris on the 21st of March, 1805. Greuze has with justice been styled the painter of the bourgeoisie: his happiest efforts are taken from the daily life of the middle classes, *e.g.* 'The Father's Curse,' 'The Broken Pitcher,' 'The Village Bride,' 'The Sleeping Girl,' &c. Charming as his works are, they often suggest doubts as to his sincerity, and give rise to an impression that he, equally with his contemporaries, was influenced by the pursuit of mere prettiness. Still, however, to give him his due, Greuze merits some recognition of his efforts after a more natural style than the false and sickly sentiment of the sham pastorals with which the Bouchers and the Fragonards were inundating French art.

An account of Greuze and of his works is to be found in MM. de Goncourt's 'Art du XVIIIme siècle.' The following paintings by him are to be found in the chief European collections:

Aix.	Museum.	Triumph of Galatea.
,,	,,	Study of a Child.
Berlin.	Gallery.	Little Girl with music-book.
Cambridge.	Fitzwilliam Museum. }	Beggar Boy.
		Beggar Girl.
Dresden.	Gallery.	A Father explaining the Bible to his Children.
Edinburgh.	Nat. Gall.	Interior of Cottage with Peasant's family.
,,	,,	Girl with dead canary.
,,	,,	Boy with lesson-book.
,,	,,	Two studies of Girls.
Glasgow.	Gallery.	A Child's Head.
,,	,,	The Sulky Boy.
Gotha.	Gallery.	The Emperor Caracalla.
London.	National Gall.	Girl's head draped with a scarf.
,,	,,	Head of a Girl.
,,	,,	Girl with an apple.
,,	,,	Girl with a lamb.
,,	Wallace Collection.	Girl with doves.
,,	,,	The Listening Girl.
,,	,,	Portrait of Sophie Arnould.
,,	,,	Votive offering to Cupid.
,,	,,	The Broken Mirror.
,,	,,	Innocence.
,,	,,	Espièglerie.
,,	,,	Girl with a gauze scarf.
Leipsic.	Museum.	Study of a Woman.
Lille.	Museum.	Psyche crowning Love.
Madrid.	Gallery.	Old Woman with crutch.
Montpellier.	Museum.	The Morning Prayer.
,,	,,	Twelfth Cake. 1774
,,	,,	The young Mathematician.
,,	,,	The Paralytic.
,,	,,	The Idle Child. 1755.
,,	,,	Six studies of Girls.
Munich.	Gallery.	Portrait of a young Girl.
Narbonne.	Museum.	Study of a young Girl's head.

JEAN BAPTISTE GREUZE

L'ACCORDÉE DE VILLAGE

J. B. GREUZE

Mansell, photo]   [*Wallace Gallery*

INNOCENCE

Nimes.	*Museum.*	Study of an old Woman's head.
Paris.	*Louvre.*	Severus reproaching Caracalla. 1769.
„	„	The Village Marriage. 1761.
„	„	The Father's Curse.
„	„	The Son punished.
„	„	The Broken Pitcher.
„	„	Two studies of young Girls.
Rome.	*Academy of St. Luke.* }	Contemplation.
Petersburg.	*Hermitage.*	The Paralytic.
„	„	Study of a young Girl.
Rotterdam.	*Museum.*	Young Woman and Child.
Vienna.	*Academy.*	Five studies of heads.

PORTRAITS.

Angers.	*Museum.*	Madame de Porcin.
Besançon.	*Museum.*	Count Alexandre Strogonof.
„	„	Paul Strogonof.
„	„	Head of a Girl.
Cherbourg.	*Museum.*	Baron Denon.
Hampton Court.	*Palace.*	Madame de Pompadour.
„	„	Louis XVI.
London.	*South Kensington.*	The Artist's Mother.
Lyons.	*Museum.*	His own Portrait.
Marseilles.	*Museum.*	Unknown Man.
Nantes.	*Museum.*	M. de St. Morys.
„	„	Count de St. Morys as a Child.
Paris.	*Louvre.*	His own Portrait.
„	„	His own Portrait. (*Sketch.*)
„	„	Étienne Jeaurat, the painter.
„	„	Armand Gensonné.
„	„	Fabre d'Eglantine.
Troyes.	*Museum.*	Eugène de Baculard d'Arnaud. 1776.
Versailles.	*Gallery.*	Napoleon I. as Consul.
„	„	Fontenelle. 1793.

See 'Greuze,' Bell's Miniature Series, 1902.

GRÉVEDON, PIERRE LOUIS, known as HENRI, a portrait painter and lithographer, was born in Paris in 1782, and died there in 1860. He was instructed under Regnault, and at first painted historical pieces and scenes from popular life, but before long he devoted himself wholly to lithography, in which he produced portraits and fancy heads.

GREVEN, ANTON, a portrait and genre painter, was born at Cologne in 1810, and after studying at Düsseldorf betook himself to Munich, where he was exciting high hopes of future distinction, when he died at Cologne in 1838. Among his best paintings are:

Monks drinking.
The Coffee Quaffers.
The Knight and his Lady Love ; (from Uhland).

GREVILLE, Lady LOUISA AUGUSTA, the eldest daughter of Francis, first Earl of Warwick, was born in 1743, and married in 1770 to William Churchill, Esq. She etched after Salvator Rosa, Annibale Carracci, and others, and the Society of Arts awarded her gold medals in 1758, 1759, and 1760, for various drawings.

GRIBELIN, SIMON, a French engraver, was born at Blois in 1661. He was instructed in engraving in Paris, and came to England in 1680 ; but it was above twenty years before he was noticed. The first work that raised his reputation was a plate he copied from Gérard Edelinck's fine print of 'Alexander entering the Tent of Darius,' after Le Brun. This was followed in 1707 by a set of the Cartoons of Raphael at Hampton Court, which had some success, being the first complete set that had appeared ; but the plates were on too small a scale for the grandeur of the subjects, and the contracted powers of Gribelin, both in execution and drawing, were wholly inadequate to express

the sublimity of Raphael. He afterwards published several plates after pictures in the Royal Collection ; but his prints give no idea of the style of the masters after whom they are engraved. He also produced some portraits, and a variety of other subjects. He died in London in 1733. The following are his principal prints :

PORTRAITS.

William III. ; *after Fowler.*
Queen Mary II. ; *after the same.*
William, Duke of Gloucester ; *after Kneller.*
Queen Anne.
Frederick, Prince of Wales.
George Granville, Lord Lansdowne.
James Butler, Duke of Ormonde ; *after Dahl.* 1713.
Thomas Herbert, Earl of Pembroke.
The Duke of Schomberg.
The Earl of Shaftesbury ; *after Clostermann ;* prefixed to the 'Characteristics.'
Sir William Dawes, Archbishop of York ; *after the same.*

SUBJECTS AFTER VARIOUS MASTERS.

The Cartoons ; seven small plates ; *after Raphael.* On the title is the portrait of Queen Anne, and the representation of the room at Hampton Court in which the paintings then hung.
The Apotheosis of James I. ; *after the ceiling at Whitehall by Rubens ;* in three plates.
Hercules between Virtue and Vice ; *after P. Matheis.*
The Adoration of the Shepherds ; *after Palma.*
Esther before Ahasuerus ; *after Tintoretto.*
Apollo and the Muses ; *after the same.*
The Birth of Jupiter ; *after Giulio Romano.*

GRIDEL, JOSEPH ÉMILE, French painter ; member of the Society of French Artists ; born Oct. 16, 1839 ; a frequent exhibitor at the Salon ; a pupil of Feyen-Perrin. Gridel excelled in depicting hunting scenes in Lorraine, his canvases showing rare energy of treatment and conception. He first exhibited at the Salon in 1865, where his work was always welcome. He was quite an authority on sport, and wrote several books which had hunting as their theme. His death occurred in Paris on Jan. 15, 1902.

GRIEF, ANTON, (GRIF, GRIFIR, or GRYEF,) a Flemish painter of wooded landscapes with dead game, dogs, and accessories of the chase, was born at Antwerp in 1670. His pictures are small, but painted with spirit and well coloured, though somewhat too sombre. He lived at Brussels, and died there in 1715, but there are no particulars of him recorded, though from his style it is conjectured that he was a pupil of Frans Snyders. There seem to have been two painters of the same name, but whether father and son is unknown. Among his works are :

Dijon.	*Museum.*	Game.
Lille.	*Museum.*	Vegetables and Fruit.
Paris.	*Louvre.*	Landscape, with dead Game.
Petersburg.	*Hermitage.*	Trophies of the Chase.
„	„	Poultry-yard.

GRIEGO, EL. See SERAFIN ; and THEOTOCOPULI.

GRIENINGER. See REINHART, HANS.

GRIEVE, JOHN HENDERSON, a scene-painter, was born in 1770, and died in 1845.

GRIEVE, WILLIAM, a scene-painter, was born in London in 1800. He was the son of J. H. Grieve, and as a boy began scene-painting at Drury Lane Theatre, where, and at Covent Garden, he made his reputation, notably by the scenery for 'Masaniello' and 'Robert le Diable.' He died in London in 1844.

GRIF, ANTON. See GRIEF.

GRIFFIER, JAN, called OLD GRIFFIER ; was born

at Amsterdam in 1645, and first placed under a flower-painter; but his taste leading him to landscape, he became a scholar of Roeland Roghman, whose works were then highly esteemed. He preferred, however, the brighter and more agreeable style of Ruisdael and Lingelbach, and he studied their pictures more than those of his master. In a short time he became a very pleasing painter of landscapes and views of the Rhine, in which he particularly excelled.

Jan Griffier came to England soon after the fire of London, and his pictures being much admired, he met with great encouragement. His favourite subjects were views of the Thames; and in order that he might study nature more intimately, he purchased a yacht, embarked his family and his pencils, and passed his whole time on the river between Windsor and Gravesend. After staying here many years, he sailed in his own yacht for Rotterdam, but was shipwrecked, and lost the produce of his industry in England. Nothing daunted, he built a new yacht, and sailed from port to port, studying with earnestness. He returned to England in 1687, found a liberal patron in the Duke of Beaufort, and died in London in 1718. His best known works are:

Amsterdam.	*Museum.*	A River Scene.
Augsburg.	*Gallery.*	River and Mountain Views.
Bordeaux.	*Museum.*	Two Rhine Views.
Brunswick.	*Gallery.*	Two Winter Scenes.
Cambridge.	*Fitzwilliam Museum.*	Landscape.
„		Dogs and Game.
Dresden.	*Gallery.*	Fifteen Landscapes.
Gotha.	*Gallery.*	Winter Landscape.
Hampton Court.	*Palace.*	Ruins.
„	„	View of Windsor Castle.
Paris.	*Louvre.*	Two Views on the Rhine.
Petersburg.	*Hermitage.*	Landscape.

GRIFFIER, John, a landscape painter, the son of 'Old Griffier,' was born in the latter part of the 17th century. He practised in London, and excelled in his copies of Claude's works. He died in London about 1750. The only two pictures of this artist, at present known to be extant, are in the Marquis of Bute's Collection. They are both imaginary river scenes, and one is dated 1743.

GRIFFIER, Robert, the son of Jan Griffier, was born in London in 1688, and instructed by his father. His pictures, like the early works of the latter, represent views on the Rhine, with boats and figures, very neatly painted, and agreeably coloured. He resided for many years in Amsterdam, but late in life he returned to England, and died here in 1750. There is a 'Landscape' by him in the Hermitage at St. Petersburg.

GRIFFITH, Moses, a draughtsman, born in Carmarthenshire in 1749, was the servant of Pennant, the antiquary, for whom he drew and engraved illustrations for some of his works. In 1801 he published on his own account some etchings of Welsh scenery. He was living in 1809. There is a 'Landscape' by him, in water-colours, in the South Kensington Museum.

GRIFIR, Anton. See Grief.

GRIFOL, Francisco, was a Valencian painter of religious daubs for the people. In the course of his practice he learned to paint landscapes, marine views, and fruit pieces of some merit, but in spite of this success, he came to poverty, and died in the public hospital at Valencia in 1766.

GRIGNION, Charles, an English portrait and historical painter, was born in London in 1754.

He studied under Cipriani, and in the schools of the Royal Academy, where he obtained the gold medal in 1776 for his 'Judgment of Hercules.' In 1782 he went to Rome with the Academy studentship, and thenceforth chiefly resided in Italy. There he painted 'The Death of Captain Cook,' and a portrait of Lord Nelson. He purchased several fine pictures in Italy, notably the Altieri Claudes, which were sent to London. He exhibited at the Royal Academy between 1770 and 1784, and died at Leghorn in 1804.

GRIGNION, Reynolds, an English engraver of the 18th century, executed the plates for Baskerville's edition of Addison, Pennant's 'Scotch Tour,' &c. He died at Chelsea in 1787.

GRIGNON, Charles, probably a relative of Jacques Grignon, was born in London, of foreign parentage, in 1716. He was one of the committee appointed in 1755 to arrange for the establishment of the Royal Academy. He engraved several plates in a masterly style; some of which were executed in conjunction with his contemporaries. Among his earliest works were several of the plates for the celebrated anatomical work of Albinus, published by Knapton in 1757. He engraved also some of the plates of the 'Antique Statues,' after the designs of Dalton, as well as the tapestries of the Vatican, published in 1753. There are some good examples of his art in the illustrations to 'Bell's British Poets,' especially those after Stothard. He died at Kentish Town, near London, in 1810. The following prints are also by him:

A View taken from the Star and Garter at Richmond; *after Heckel.*
Two perspective Views of the Foundling Hospital; *after Valée.*
The Election; four plates; *after Hogarth;* engraved conjointly with *Le Cave* and *Aveline.*
Garrick, in the character of Richard III.; engraved in conjunction with *Hogarth.* 1745.
Phryne and the Philosopher Zenocrates; *after Salvator Rosa.*

GRIGNON, Jacques, a French engraver, flourished about the year 1680. The best of his works are portraits, some of which possess great merit. They are executed entirely with the graver, in a neat, clear style. In his plates of historical subjects he is less successful, as his drawing is very incorrect, and his management of the lights and shadows heavy and without effect, particularly in his plates after Poussin and the Carracci. He engraved some of the plates for a work entitled 'Les Tableaux de la Pénitence,' after the designs of Chauveau. The following portraits are also by him:

Francesco Maria Rhima; an ecclesiastic.
Pierre Barbereau, Doctor in Theology; *after Ph. de Champaigne.*
Jacques Cœur, Seigneur de St. Fargeau.
Jean Bureau, Mayor of Bordeaux.

GRIGOLETTI, Michelangelo, was born at Rorai Grande di Pordenone in 1801, and was educated at the Academy at Venice, of which he, in 1839, became a professor. In 1824 he first came out with historical paintings of his own, and a church picture by him in Sant' Antonio at Trieste excited much attention. In 1837 he executed a like work for the new cathedral at Erlau, and in 1846 an altar-piece for that at Gran in Hungary. He died at Vienna in 1870. Among his works, in addition to some portraits, may be mentioned:

Erlau.	*Cathedral.*	The Archangel Michael.
„	„	Holy Family.

Gran.	*Cathedral.*	Ascension of the Virgin.
Treviso.	*Sig. Sugana.*	An Odalisque.
Trieste.	*S. Antonio.*	St. Anne with the Virgin and Child.
,,	*Herr Caal.*	The Prodigal Son.
,,	*Sig. Sartorio.*	Francesca da Rimini.
Vienna.	*Gallery.*	Francesco Foscari committing his Son to Prison.

GRILLANDAIO. See BIGORDI.

GRIMALDI, ALESSANDRO, the son and scholar of Giovanni Francesco Grimaldi, flourished in the latter half of the 17th century, and painted landscapes in the style of his father, but did not equal him in execution. He appears to have etched a good many of his father's figures. There is an etching by him entitled 'An Allegory upon Religion,' which is in the style of Pietro Santi Bartoli; and another of the 'Brazen Serpent,' after his own design.

GRIMALDI, GIOVANNI FRANCESCO, called IL BOLOGNESE, was born at Bologna in 1606, and studied under the Carracci, in whose academy he became a skilful designer of the figure; though his inclination led him later on to landscape painting, in which he endeavoured to rival Annibale Carracci and Titian. He next went to Rome, where he soon rose to distinction, and was taken under the protection of Innocent X., who employed him in the Vatican, and in his gallery at Monte Cavallo. These commissions were executed so satisfactorily, that Prince Pamfili, nephew to the Pope, engaged him to decorate his villa of Bel Respiro, which he embellished with some admirable landscapes with figures, in the style of the Carracci. His reputation reached Paris, whither in 1648 he was invited by Cardinal Mazarin, and where Louis XIV. employed him in the palace of the Louvre, and rewarded him with his accustomed munificence. On his return to Rome, after the death of his protector, Innocent X., he was equally patronized by his successors, Alexander VII. and Clement IX., and was one of the most successful artists of his time. He was twice appointed president of the Academy of St. Luke. His death occurred at Rome in 1680. Many of his pictures are in the Colonna Palace at Rome and the Vienna Gallery, and the following also are preserved:

Darmstadt.	*Gallery.*	Baptism of Christ.
Edinburgh.	*Nat. Gall.*	Landscape.
Paris.	*Bibl. Nat.*	Landscapes.
,,	*Louvre.*	Landscapes.
,,		The Washerwomen.
Rome.	*Quirinal.*	Scenes from the Old Testament.
,,	*Borghese Pal.*	Series of Landscapes.

Grimaldi also left a number of etchings, among which the following may be named:

A set of-four small Landscapes.
A grand Landscape, with Buildings, and in the foreground Figures at play; *Gio. Fran. Grimaldi Bolognese inv. et fec.*
A grand Landscape, with Buildings and Fishermen; *signed as above.*
A Landscape, with the Baptism of Christ.
A Landscape, with Ruins and Figures.
A mountainous Landscape, with Figures.
Two upright Landscapes; *after Annibale Carracci.*
A set of four Landscapes; *after the same.*

GRIMALDI, WILLIAM, an English miniature painter, born in Middlesex in 1751, studied under Worlidge, and afterwards at Paris. He first exhibited at the Free Society of Artists, and then at the Royal Academy. He practised successively at several country towns, and in Paris from 1777 to 1785. He then settled in London, and became miniature painter to several members of the Royal Family. He died in London in 1830.

GRIMANI. See JACOBSZ, HUBERT.

GRIMBALDSON, WALTER, a landscape painter of no repute, practised early in the 18th century.

GRIMM, LUDWIG EMIL, a painter and etcher, was born at Hanau in 1790. He was the younger brother of Jacob and Wilhelm Grimm, and was educated under Karl Hess at Munich, as well as at the Academy in that city. In 1840 he published a hundred of his own etchings, comprising landscapes, historical and genre subjects, portraits, and heads, under the title of 'The Story-teller' ('Die Mährchenzählerin'), and in 1854 another thirty as a supplement. He died in 1863 at Cassel. Among his other etchings are:

Portraits of Luther and Melanchthon; *after L. Cranach.*
The Brothers Grimm. 1823.
Gipsy Life.
Children's Games in Electoral Hesse.
Entertainment of Artists at Munich. 1812.

GRIMM, SAMUEL HIERONYMUS, a water-colour painter and draughtsman, born at Burgdorf, in the canton of Berne, in 1734, was taught by his father, a miniature painter. He settled in London about 1778, and was much employed in topographical work, such as Burrell's 'Sussex,' the Society of Antiquaries' 'Vetusta Monumenta,' &c. He made a large number of pen-and-ink sketches, shaded with indian-ink or bistre, or tinted with water-colours, in the counties of Northumberland and Durham, Derbyshire, Nottinghamshire, and the environs of London, which are correct, although somewhat stiff and weak. He occasionally exhibited at the Royal Academy some subject pictures, and also published caricatures. He died in London in 1794. There are at the South Kensington Museum the following water-colour drawings by him:

The North Foreland Lighthouse.
Mother Ludlam's Hole, near Farnham. 1781.

GRIMMER, ABEL, perhaps a son of Jakob Grimmer, is known by two pictures: a 'Christ at the house of Martha and Mary,' dated 1614, in the Brussels Gallery, and a picture dated 1604 in possession of Herr Van Lerius, Antwerp. Grimmer entered the Guild of St. Luke in the latter city in 1592.

GRIMMER, HANS, who studied under Matthäus Grünewald, flourished at Mayence towards the close of the 16th century. The portraits by him which remain testify to his excellence as an artist. The Vienna Gallery has one of Adam von Puechhaim, painted in 1570, and in the chapel of St. Maurice at Nuremberg there are two—one of a man, and the other of a woman. In the Städel Institute at Frankfort are two wings of a picture, of which the centre is missing.

GRIMMER, JAKOB, was born at Antwerp in 1510, and was for some time a disciple of Matthys Cock, but afterwards studied under Christian Queborn. He was a reputable landscape painter, and was received into the Academy at Antwerp in 1546. He died in the same city in 1560. His pictures are generally embellished with buildings and ruins, in which he excelled. A 'Legend of St. Eustace,' in the Brussels Gallery, is attributed to him, and in the Ghent Museum there is an 'Adulteress before Christ.'

GRIMOU, ALEXIS, (GRIMOUX, or GRIMOUD,) born at Romont, in the canton of Fribourg, Switzerland, about 1680, was the son of one of the

Swiss guards at Versailles. He had no master, but acquired his art by copying the works of Van Dyck and Rembrandt in a broker's shop. His portraits and genre pictures were very popular; but the irregularity of his life and his eccentricities prevented his attaining the eminence which he might otherwise have done. He painted many pictures of women playing and singing, and was admitted to the Academy at Paris in 1705, but he left it in disgust at the mediocre pictures of the other associates, and took his picture to the Academy of St. Luke, where he was admitted on payment in 1709. He died in Paris in 1740. The Louvre contains a portrait of himself, a 'Toper,' a 'Female Pilgrim,' and two portraits of young soldiers. In the Kunsthalle in Carlsruhe there are two half-length portraits of women; in the Städel Institute at Frankfort, the portrait of a young man; in the Avignon Museum, three portraits of ladies; in the Dulwich Gallery, a portrait of a lady; in the Dresden Gallery, a 'Boy blowing a whistle;' and in the Bordeaux Museum, a 'Monk,' a 'Young Pilgrim,' and an 'Instrument Player.'

GRINGONNEUR, JACQUEMIN, a French miniature painter, is known to have flourished from 1392 to 1420, and to have executed various games of cards for Charles VI. The National Library at Paris possesses seventeen cards belonging to one of these games. The picture at Versailles of the family of Jean Juvenal des Ursins, who died in 1431, is attributed to him.

GRISOLFI, GIOVANNI. See GHISOLFI.

GRISONI, GIUSEPPE, was born at Florence about the year 1700, and was a scholar of Tommaso Redi. The rising merit of the disciple is said to have occasioned so much jealousy and uneasiness in the master, that it shortened his life. He painted historical subjects and portraits; but particularly excelled in the latter, of which his own portrait, in the Gallery at Florence, is a fine specimen. He died in 1769.

GROBON, MICHEL, a French genre and landscape painter and engraver, was born at Lyons in 1770, and studied painting under Prud'hon, and engraving under J. J. de Boissieu. His works are much in the style of the old painters of the Netherlands, and he also etched, in the manner of his master, a plate of 'The Interior of a Forest.' He died at Lyons in 1853.

GROEGER, FRIEDRICH CARL, a portrait painter and lithographer, was born at Ploen, in Holstein, in 1766. He was a self-taught artist, and settled down to work in Hamburg, where he died in 1838. In the Dresden Gallery is his own portrait.

GROENENDAEL, CAMILLE, a Belgian historical and portrait painter, was born at Lierre in 1785, and after studying at the Antwerp Academy and in Paris he returned to his own country in 1814 an accomplished artist, and died at Antwerp in 1834. His portraits are considered his best works. Those of M. and Mme. van Donick are in the Antwerp Gallery.

GROENEWEGEN, GERRIT, a painter and etcher, was born at Rotterdam in 1754, and studied under Muys. He became noted for his pictures of ships and marine views, and died at Rotterdam in 1826. His works are rare, but eighteen plates of Dutch marine views, etched in Bakhuisen's manner, are known to be by him, as also twelve of Dutch costumes.

GROENSVELD, JOHAN. See GRONSVELT.

GROGAN, NATHANIEL, an Irish landscape painter, born at Cork about the middle of the 18th century, was originally a wood turner, and also served in the army during the American war. On his return to Cork he taught drawing, and endeavoured to gain a living by art. He engraved a set of views in the south of Ireland, and died at Cork about 1807. His best known works are, 'An Irish Fair,' and 'An Irish Wake.'

GROGNARD, ALEXIS, a French portrait painter, was born at Lyons in 1765, and died in the same city in 1840. He was a pupil of Vien, and director of the school of Fine-Arts at Lyons.

GROISEILLIEZ, MARCELIN DE, a French landscape painter and etcher, born in Paris in 1837, studied under Boyer and Pasini, and became skilful in the delineation of southern landscapes. He died in Paris in 1880. Among his paintings are:

A Morning on the Banks of the Sédelle.
The Banks of the Gardon.
The Beach at St. Malo.
The Plain of Samois, near Fontainebleau.

He also etched 'Recollections of Beuzeval.'

GROLLERON, PAUL LOUIS NARCISSE, a French military painter, born at Seignelay (Yonne), June 11, 1848. At first devoted his talent to decorative art, but subsequently entered the studio of Bonnat and exhibited in the Salons sundry genre pictures, including 'La Partie de Picquet' (1875), 'Valet qui Prend' (1877), and others. It was only in 1882 that Grolleron took up military painting with such remarkable success that he remained true to it all his life. The picture by which he first attracted attention was the 'Combat dans une usine sous les murs de Paris,' 1870, and this gained him a Mention Honorable. We may also note his 'Episode de la Bataille de Loigny,' exhibited in 1886, which obtained for the artist a medal of the third class. Another of his pictures, and one of the best of them, was 'Janville,' 1870, exhibited in 1888; his 'Sergent Tanvireau,' exhibited in 1891, won a medal of the second class. His death occurred in Paris on October 28, 1901.

GRONIGIUS, GERHARD, was a Dutch engraver of the middle of the 16th century, whom Strutt mentions as having etched ten plates, emblematical of the 'Life of Man,' from ten to a hundred years. The drawing is incorrect, and the outline hard; but they are not devoid of merit.

GRÖNINGEN, GIOVANNI DI. See SCHWARTZ, HANS.

GRÖNLAND, THEUDE, a painter of landscapes and still-life, was born at Altona in 1817. He went to the Academy in Copenhagen in 1833, and then resided three years in Italy, three years in England, and twenty-five years in Paris. From 1868 he lived at Berlin, where he collected many students around him, and died in 1876.

GRONSVELT, JOHAN, a Dutch engraver, was born at the Hague about the year 1650. He etched several views and landscapes, after Berchem, Van Goyen, Lingelbach, and others; and engraved some historical subjects and portraits. The following are his principal prints:

Dorothy, Countess of Sunderland; *after Van Dyck.*
A Girl with a Cat; *after Abraham Bloemaert.*
A Man sleeping on a Barrel; *after Brouwer.*
The Adoration of the Magi; *after Paolo Veronese.*
Christ before Pilate; *after A. Schiavone.*
A set of six Landscapes; *after Berchem.*
A set of four Landscapes; *after the same.*
A set of twelve Oriental and Italian Harbours; *after J. Lingelbach.*

Six Dutch Landscapes ; *after Verboom.*
Cows ; *after A. van de Velde.*

GROOMBRIDGE, WILLIAM, a water-colour painter, practised in the latter part of the 18th century. He painted landscapes and moonlight scenes with cattle and figures.

GROOS, GERHARD and GEORG DE. See DE GROOS.

GROOT, JAN DE. See DE GROOT.

GROPIUS, KARL WILHELM, a decorative painter, was born at Brunswick in 1793, but went when young to Berlin and painted for the exhibitions of his father, after which he travelled through Germany and Switzerland, and made himself acquainted in Paris with the arrangement of Daguerre's diorama. Next he travelled in Italy and Greece, and made numerous landscape and architectural sketches. After his return he opened, in 1827, a diorama in Berlin in connection with a permanent exhibition of paintings. He was at the same period appointed court theatrical painter, in which office he produced some superior decorations from the designs of Schinkel. He was considered the first wit in Berlin, where he died in 1870.

GROS, ANTOINE JEAN, Baron, a French historical and portrait painter, was born in Paris, March 16th, 1771. His early surroundings were artistic, for his father, Jean Antoine Gros, was a miniature painter, and his mother drew in crayons. In such an atmosphere, it is not surprising that his inclination to art was soon developed. In 1785 he commenced to study seriously by becoming a pupil of David, and in 1792 he competed unsuccessfully for the 'prix de Rome.' His desire to visit Italy was not, however, to be frustrated. Notwithstanding the death of his father, and the want of means, he resolutely overcame all obstacles, and, having obtained a passport through David, arrived at Geneva in 1793. He devoted himself assiduously to study, and was fortunate in obtaining good introductions. He at length, in 1801, attracted the notice of Bonaparte, then in command of the French army in Italy, by his picture of 'Bonaparte at the Battle of Arcola.' From him he received an honorary staff appointment, and he was also employed in the collection of works of art for the adornment of the French galleries. Compelled to quit Milan by the reverses of the French arms, he took refuge in Genoa, and in the siege of that city he underwent severe hardships. On his return to Paris in 1801, he commenced the series of works on which his fame rests :—'Bonaparte visiting the Plague-stricken at Jaffa' (1804); 'The Battle of Aboukir' (1806); 'Napoleon at Eylau' (1808); 'The Battle of the Pyramids' (1810) ; 'Francis I. and Charles V. at St. Denis' (1812). On the Restoration, Gros—ever faithful to the traditions of the Classic School, and to his master David—took over the atelier of the latter, and was much occupied in instruction : more than four hundred pupils passed through his studio. He also endeavoured to obtain the recall of his master from banishment, and had a medal struck in his honour, which he took to Brussels and presented to him. Gros did not, however, lack under the Bourbons the patronage he had received under the Empire. For several years he was much occupied with the pictures in the dome of the Panthéon, and honours and offices were freely bestowed on him, culminating in the title of Baron. But, though official approval of his works was not wanting, his art was violently and incessantly criticized by partisans of the Romantic School. These criticisms reached such a point on the appearance of his 'Hercules and Diomedes' in 1835, and, aggravated by the state of his health, had such an effect on him, that he committed suicide on June 26th in that year. His body was found in the Seine, near Meudon, and was buried in Père-la-Chaise, Paul Delaroche and others pronouncing funeral orations over his grave. Although Gros was in one sense always a strict adherent to the canons of classicism, yet he was one of the first of David's pupils to abandon classic and mythologic scenes. It has been aptly remarked that he painted classic forms underneath modern costume. His style is bold and full of movement, and his colouring, though not unfrequently exaggerated, is a great improvement on the coldness of the founders of the Classic School. The following are some of Gros's principal works :

Besançon.	*Museum.*	Girl bathing. 1791.
Bordeaux.	*Museum.*	Embarkation of the Duchess of Angoulême. 1816.
Nantes.	*Museum.*	Combat of Nazareth. 1801.
Paris.	*Louvre.*	Bonaparte visiting the Plague-stricken at Jaffa. 1804.
"	"	Napoleon at Eylau. 1808.
"	"	Francis I. and Charles V. at St. Denis. 1812.
Toulouse.	*Museum.*	Hercules and Diomedes. 1835.
		Venus and Cupid. 1832.
Versailles.	*Gallery.*	The Battle of the Pyramids. 1810.
"	"	Interview of Napoleon and Francis II. after Austerlitz. 1812.
"	"	The Capitulation of Madrid. 1810.
"	"	Louis XVIII. quitting the Tuileries in 1815. 1816.
"	"	The Battle of Aboukir. 1806.
"	*Trianon.*	Apotheosis of St. Germain. 1824.

PORTRAITS.

Besançon.	*Museum.*	Madame Dufresne.
Grenoble.	*Museum.*	Dr. Clot-Bey.
Marseilles.	*Museum.*	Madame Favréga. 1798.
Montpellier.	*Museum.*	Eleven Miniatures.
Nancy.	*Museum.*	Marshal Duroc.
Paris.	*Vicomte de Peyronnet.*	Louis XVIII. (*This head was copied for all the official portraits.*)
Toulouse.	*Museum.*	Madame Gros.
		His own Portrait.
Versailles	*Gallery.*	Duke de Bellune.
"	"	Eugène Beauharnais.
"	"	Equestrian Portrait of Jerome Bonaparte, King of Westphalia. 1808.
"	"	Marshal Duroc.
"	"	Count Daru.
"	"	General Count Fournier-Sarlovèse. 1812.
"	"	His own Portrait.
"	"	Equestrian Portrait of Charles X. 1826. O.J.D.

GROSE, FRANCIS, a topographical draughtsman, was born in 1731 at Richmond, in Surrey, where his father was a jeweller. He was of independent means, and devoted to antiquarian pursuits, on which he published several learned works. He occasionally exhibited tinted drawings of ruins, &c., at the Royal Academy. In one of his visits to Scotland, he became 'The chiel amang ye taking notes' of Burns. He died at Dublin in 1791.

GROSNIER, Mlle., a French lady, is mentioned by Basan as the engraver of several plates ; but they are wholly unknown.

GROTEFEND, ADOLPH, a miniature painter,

was born at Klausthal in Hanover, in 1812. He for a time studied law at Göttingen University, but his love for art caused him in 1836 to proceed to Munich to fit himself for a portrait painter. In this line he was becoming conspicuously successful, when ill-health drove him in 1846 to Italy, and he died at Florence in the following year.

GROTH, —, a German painter, flourished in England in the reign of George II. He painted in water-colours and enamel, but was not very proficient.

GROUX, CHARLES CORNEILLE AUGUSTE DE, (or DEGROUX,) a Belgian genre and historical painter, was born at Commines in France in 1826, and studied at the Brussels Academy under Navez. He at first produced pictures from popular life, but afterwards took to historical subjects, in which he was less successful, and he finally returned to his former department. He decorated the market-place of Ypres. His death occurred at Brussels in 1870. Among his paintings are:

Ash Wednesday.
Grace before Meals. (*Brussels Gallery*.)
The Doctor's Visit.
The Death of Charles V.
The Citizens of Calais before Edward III.

GROZER, JOSEPH, a mezzotint engraver, was born about 1755, and probably died before 1799. He practised in London, and amongst his works are:

Shepherds with a Lamb; *after Sir J. Reynolds*. 1784.
Master Braddyll; *after the same*. 1786.
Mrs. Mackenzie of Seaforth; *after the same*. 1787.
Innocence; *after the same*. 1788.
William, Earl Fitzwilliam; *after the same*. 1786.
Lady St. Asaph and Child; *after the same*. 1792.
Miss Johnson, dancing; *after the same*. 1792.
James, Earl of Cardigan; *after Romney*. 1792.
Lady Charlotte Legge; *after the same*. 1799.
The Duke and Duchess of York; *after Singleton*. 1797.
Robert, Lord Hobart; *after Sir Thomas Lawrence*. 1796.

GRUND, JOHANN JAKOB NORBERT, a German painter and author, was born at Gunzenhausen, in Anspach, in 1755. He originally intended to become a Jesuit, but afterwards devoted himself to miniature painting. He subsequently went to Italy, and was appointed a professor in the Academy at Florence. He published in 1789, 'An Artistic Tour to Rome,' and in 1810, 'The Painting of the Greeks.' He died about 1815.

GRUND, NORBERT, a German painter of landscapes, cattle, fairs, battles, &c., born at Prague in 1714, was the son of a painter, and studied at the Vienna Academy under Ferg. He was of a vagrant nature, and in his latter years his carelessness and improvidence reduced him to want. He died at Prague in 1767. In the Dresden Gallery are two pictures, 'Country Dances,' and 'A Gathering at a Table in a Garden.'

GRUNDY, THOMAS LEEMING, a line-engraver, was born at Bolton in 1808. He was at first apprenticed to a writing engraver, and then came to London, where he was employed on the Annuals then in fashion. He afterwards worked for Doo and Goodall, and died in London in 1841.

GRUNER, WILHELM HEINRICH LUDWIG, a clever engraver, born at Dresden in 1801, and a pupil of Klinger and Führich. He commenced life as a scene-painter, but afterwards studied engraving under Ephraim Gottlieb Krüger in Dresden, and from 1826 to 1836 in Milan, under Longhi and Anderloni. He resided in Rome from 1837 to 1841, when he came to England, and remained here until 1856, in which year he was made

director of the Cabinet of Engravings at Dresden. He spent considerable time in Spain, and engraved the works of Velazquez in the Prado, and also those of Raphael in the same Gallery. Later on he produced a fine set of plates from the celebrated cartoons of Raphael which belong to the English Crown; but being troubled for a while with a serious affection of the eyes, was compelled to relinquish engraving, and devoted himself to fresco work and decorative painting. He was commissioned in 1846 to decorate the garden pavilion in Buckingham Palace, and of his work there a clever account was written by Mrs. Jameson, who highly praised his productions. Later on he was enabled by an operation to recover the use of his eyes, and again took up with engraving, and was at work upon the paintings of Raphael till his death at Dresden in 1882. He engraved many separate plates, especially after the works of Raphael and Overbeck, by which he gained much reputation. Among his chief works are:

Portrait of Giulio de' Medici (?); *after Raphael*. 1835.
The Vision of a Knight; *after the same*.
La Fornarina; *after the same*.
Christ's Agony in the Garden; *after the same*. 1849.
The Ansidei Madonna; *after the same*. 1856.
The Conversion of Saul; *after the same*. 1864. (Arundel Society.)
Christ, the Good Shepherd; *after Overbeck*.
Hagar in the Wilderness; *after the same*.
Moses defending the Daughters of Jethro; *after the same*.

GRÜNEWALD, E., was an engraver of Darmstadt, who studied under Frommel, and produced some praiseworthy landscape plates about 1825.

GRÜNEWALD, HANS, was the brother of Matthäus Grünewald, but nothing authentic is known of him. A portrait of Maximilian I., in the Vienna Gallery, is ascribed to him.

GRÜNEWALD, MATTHÄUS, who was born probably in Frankfort, settled in Aschaffenburg, where he was employed by the Archbishop Albrecht of Mayence. He seems to have died about the year 1530, and to have been, after Dürer and Holbein, the greatest German painter of the period, though but little of his life is known. His most important work is an altar-piece of six panels, which was executed for the church of SS. Maurice and Mary Magdalene at Halle, but afterwards transferred to the church of SS. Peter and Alexander at Aschaffenburg. It is now in the Munich Gallery. The centre picture represents the 'Conversion of St. Maurice by St. Erasmus,' and the wings contain the figures of St. Lazarus, St. Mary Magdalene, St. Martha, St. Chrysostom, and St. Valentinian. There is another work in the church of Our Lady at Halle, of which the centre picture, representing the 'Virgin in Glory,' the inner sides, and perhaps the outer sides, are assigned to Grünewald. A 'Rosary' in the chapel of St. Anthony in the cathedral of Bamberg, and the wings of altar-pieces at Heilsbronn in Franconia, and at Annaberg in Saxony, are also assigned to this master.

GRUSS, JOHANN, an historical painter, born early in the 19th century, was a native of Bohemia. Among his works are a 'Virgin and Child,' a 'Sleeping Jesus,' and 'St. Aloysius.' He died at Vienna in 1872.

GRÜTZNER, EDUARD, born at Great Carlowitz in Silesia in 1846, was the son of a peasant. He was destined for the church, but Hirschberg, an architect of Munich, induced him in 1864 to repair to that city, where his first work was a ceiling

FRANCESCO GUARDI

SAN GIORGIO MAGGIORE, VENICE

in a private house. He showed great humour in his pictures, 'The Cloister Cellar,' 'Wine Tasting,' 'Sleepless Nights,' and especially in his representation of Falstaff and other characters in the 'Merry Wives of Windsor.' He died in 1878.

GRYEF, ANTON. See GRIEF.

GRYPMOED, GEERLIG, born at Zwolle in 1760, learned the art of drawing from A. D. Prudhomme. He afterwards went to Amsterdam, where he studied under H. Meyer and Troost van Groenendoele, who employed him largely in painting curtains. He also painted landscapes. He died in 1788.

GSELL, MARIA DOROTHEA HENRICA, the daughter of Johann Andreas Graff and Maria Sibylla Merian, was born at Nuremberg in 1678. She painted flowers and insects, and was acquainted with Hebrew. She married the portrait and still-life painter Gsell, and accompanied him to St. Petersburg, where they both worked for the Academy of Sciences, and where she died in 1745.

GUADALUPE, PEDRO FERNANDEZ DE. See FERNANDEZ.

GUALDO, MATTEO DA, a painter of the Umbrian school, was born at Gualdo Tadini, but the dates of his birth and death are alike unknown. A genuine fresco by him is at Santa Maria della Circa, near Sigillo; it represents a 'Madonna and Child,' with a dog in the arms of the latter, also a 'Lady of Mercy.' In SS. Antonio e Jacopo of Assisi, are some frescoes by him, although now very much damaged; they include a 'Madonna,' dated 1468. These works are executed somewhat in the style of Benozzo Gozzoli.

GUALDORP, GORTZIUS. See GELDORP.

GUARANA, JACOPO, (or incorrectly VARANA,) was a painter of the Venetian school, who was born at Verona in 1727, and became a pupil of Sebastiano Ricci, G. B. Tiepolo, and especially of Carlo Cignani. The Academy of Copenhagen offered him the position of first painter, and the Empress of Russia also invited him to her court from her admiration of the work he painted for her; but he could not be induced to leave his own country. He died at Venice in 1808, having been a member of the Academies of Venice, Florence, and Bologna. The following are among his paintings, the first two being in oil, the others in fresco:

The Sacrifice of Iphigenia. (*Painted for the Empress of Russia.*)
The Heart of Jesus. (*San Paolo, Venice.*)
The Virtues. (*Patriarch's Palace, Venice.*)
St. Mark. (*Doge's Palace, Venice.*)
Apotheosis of St. Martin. (*San Martino, Venice.*)
The Dome of San Vitale, Ravenna.

He also etched several plates, and supplied the designs for the engravings in the work entitled 'Oracoli della Religione pagana,' published at Venice in 1792. His son, VINCENZO GUARANA, who was born at Venice in 1750, and died there in 1815, painted in the style of his father, but did not equal him.

GUARDI, FRANCESCO, a Venetian painter, was born at Venice in 1712, and died there in 1793. He was a scholar of Canaletto, and excelled in architectural views of Venice, but his works are less accurate in perspective and details than are those of his master. The following pictures by him are in the chief European galleries:

Bergamo.	*Academy.*	Three Views in Venice.
Berlin.	*Gallery.*	View on the Grand Canal, Venice.
Berlin.	*Gallery.*	Two Views of San Michele, Venice.
"	"	View on the Lagoons.
Brussels.	*Gallery.*	Interior of San Marco at Venice.
Cambridge.	*Fitzwilliam Museum.*	Views in Venice.
"	"	The Island of Anconetta.
Dublin.	*Nat. Gallery.*	The Doge's State Barge.
Glasgow.	*Gallery.*	Grand Canal and Church of San Giorgio, Venice.
"	"	Piazzetta of San Marco.
London.	*Nat. Gallery.*	View of the Church, Campanile, and Piazza of San Marco, at Venice.
"	"	View in Venice.
" *Bridgewater House.*	"	View on the Grand Canal.
"	"	Seven Views of Venice.
" *South Kensington Museum.*		Church on the Grand Canal, Venice.
Modena.	*Gallery.*	The Grand Canal, Venice.
"	"	The Fondaco dei Tedeschi.
Nantes.	*Museum.*	Two Views of Venice.
Paris.	*Louvre.*	View of Venice.
"	"	Church of La Salute.
"	"	The Fête of Shrove Tuesday.
"	"	The Fête of Corpus Domini.
"	"	Procession of the Doge to the Church of San Zaccaria.
"	"	The Hall of the Ducal Palace.
"	"	View of Venice.
Venice.	*Correr Mus.*	The Island of San Giorgio.
Verona.	*Museum.*	Two Views of Venice.

GUARDOLINO, IL. See NATALI.

GUARIENTI, PIETRO, a painter of Verona, was born before 1700. He was a pupil of Crespi, but followed the study of the great masters of the various countries in which he travelled, seeking to acquire the faculty of painting in every style. He settled in Dresden, and died there before 1769.

GUARIENTO, a painter of Padua, was living in the 14th century, and is known to have been amongst the first artists employed to decorate the Great Hall of Council at Venice in 1365. His work there was a 'Paradise,' and incidents from the war of Spoleto. These paintings were effaced to make room for the successive designs of Gentile Bellini and of Titian. In the Eremitani at Padua may still be seen many frescoes by this artist representing the Life and Passion of Christ, the life of St. Augustine, and several subjects from the Old Testament. According to Brandolese, Guariento flourished about 1360 at Padua, and was buried there in the church of San Bernardino. He died before 1378. There are preserved of his works:

Bassano.	*Pinacoteca.*	A Crucifixion, with the Virgin and Saints.
Padua.	*Academy.*	Six portions of frescoes, with subjects from the Old Testament.

GUARINO, FRANCESCO, who was born at Solofra, near Naples, in 1612, was a pupil of Massimo Stanzioni. He painted in the church of his native town, and died at Gravina in 1651. In the Naples Museum there is by him a picture of 'Susanna.'

GUASTA, BENVENUTO and GIROLAMO DEL. See DEL GUASTA.

GUBBIO, ODERIGI DA, was a miniature painter, who is said to have been born at Gubbio, near Perugia, in 1240. No undoubted work by him is now in existence, although some miniatures contained in two Missals of the Virgin and of St. George, in the Archivio de' Canonici di San Pietro, at Rome, are strongly supposed to be by him. He painted at Gubbio in 1264, at Bologna in 1268, and in Rome in 1295. According to Vasari, he made the acquaintance of Giotto in Rome, and died there in

285

1299. He has been mentioned with much praise by Dante, who calls him the 'Glory of Agobbio,' and represents him as expiating in Purgatory the pride with which his skill had inspired him.

GUBITZ, FRIEDRICH WILHELM, a wood engraver, was born at Leipsic in 1786, and was a member of the Academy of Berlin, where he died in 1870. The cuts in his 'Volkskalender,' issued from 1835 to 1869, are much admired, as is also his portrait of the Saviour, after Lucas Cranach. He also published some 'Plays and Poems,' a newspaper called 'Der Gesellschafter,' and a volume entitled 'Occurrences.'

GUCCIO DEL SERO. See AGHINETTI.

GUCHT, VAN DER. See VAN DER GUCHT.

GUDIN, JEAN ANTOINE THÉODORE, a French marine painter, was born in Paris in 1802. He attended for some time the atelier of Girodet-Trioson, but left it and enrolled himself in the Romantic School, in company with Géricault and Delacroix. He restricted himself entirely to landscapes and marine subjects. His first success dated from about the year 1822, and in 1827 he produced 'The Burning of the "Kent," East Indiaman,' and 'The Return of the Fishermen,' two of his best pictures. Gudin's works are remarkable for vigorous, but, too generally, exaggerated, treatment. He painted between the years 1838 and 1848 a series of ninety marine subjects for the Galleries at Versailles, where many of them still are. They record the achievements of the French navy in Algeria, whither Gudin was sent by Louis Philippe. Early in life he travelled in the East, in Russia, and in Germany, but he spent much of the latter part of his life in Scotland. He also practised the arts of etching and lithography. He died at Boulogne near Paris, in 1880. Among his best works are:

The Hurricane of the 7th of January, 1831, in the Roadstead of Algiers. 1835.
Coast Scene. (*Brussels Gallery.*)
Breton Coast. 1845. (*Berlin National Gallery.*)
A Smuggler's Felucca. 1845. (*The same.*)
The Ship in Distress.
Shipwreck on the Coast of Genoa. (*Leipsic Museum.*)
View of Havre. (*Avignon Museum.*)
Explosion of the Emperor's Fort at Algiers.
View of Constantinople, taken from Pera.
The Boarding of the English galeot 'Hazard' by the 'Courier.'
Devotion of Captain Desse. (*Bordeaux Museum.*)

GUDMUNDSSON, SIGURD, an Icelandic painter, born at the farm of Helluland in 1833, entered the Copenhagen Academy in 1849, and on his return to Iceland in 1858, produced almost a revolution in the manners and costumes of the island. He died at Reykiavik in 1874.

GUE, JULIEN MICHEL, a French landscape and historical painter, born in St. Domingo in 1789, was a pupil of David and of Lacour. The Bordeaux Museum possesses the 'Death of Patroclus,' and there are other works by this artist at Versailles, Compiègne, and Rheims. He died in Paris in 1843.

GUÉLARD, B., a French painter and etcher, is mentioned by Basan as the engraver of several plates after Oudry, J. F. van Bloemen, &c. He lived in Paris about 1730.

GUÉRARD, EUGÈNE CHARLES FRANÇOIS, a French landscape painter and lithographer, was born at Nancy in 1821. He was a pupil of Paul Delaroche and of Dieudonné Pierre of Nancy, in which city he died in 1866.

GUÉRARD, HENRI CHARLES, a French painter

and engraver. In early life he made a great number of experiments in colour-printing from engravings, with more or less success. He threw in his lot with the Société Nationale des Beaux Arts at its formation in 1891, and exhibited annually at the New Salon. He became an officer of the Academy, and was a Chevalier of the Legion of Honour. He died towards the middle of 1897, in the fifty-second year of his age.

GUÉRARDS, MARC. See GEERARTS.

GUERARDS, N., a French engraver, who flourished about the year 1700, executed the plates for a work entitled 'Les Edifices antiques de Rome,' published at Paris in 1682, after the designs of A. Des Godets, who engraved the frontispiece. He also engraved the frontispiece to a book of ornaments, published by Pierre Bourdon in 1703; and a small plate of 'Soldiers marching,' in imitation of Callot.

GUERCINO. See BARBIERI, GIOVANNI FRANCESCO.

GUÉRIN, CHRISTOPHE, a draughtsman and engraver, born at Strassburg in 1758, was a pupil of Jeulain and P. Müller. He became conservator of the Museum, and a Professor of the School of Design at Strassburg. He died in 1831. His chief works are:

Cupid disarmed ; *after Correggio.*
The Dance of the Muses ; *after Giulio Romano.*
The Angel leading Tobit ; *after Raphael.*
Two Landscapes ; *after De Loutherbourg.*

GUÉRIN, FRANÇOIS, a French historical and genre painter, was a native of Paris. He exhibited first at the Academy of St. Luke in 1751, and became an Academician in 1761, his reception work being 'A Market.' He continued to exhibit at the Salon until 1783, but in 1791 he was residing in Strassburg, where he died, but in what year is not known.

GUÉRIN, GABRIEL CHRISTOPHE, a son of Christophe Guérin, was born at Kehl in 1790. He was a pupil of Regnault, and in 1817 received the gold medal for his 'Death of Polynices.' He painted a 'Burial of Christ' for the church of St. Francis of Assisi in Paris, and he succeeded his father as conservator of the Museum, and Professor of the School of Design at Strassburg. He died at Hornbach in Bavaria in 1846.

GUÉRIN, JEAN, a miniature and water-colour painter, born at Strassburg in 1760, was a brother of Christophe Guérin. He went to Paris, where he became a pupil of Regnault, and soon gained a reputation, as well as the protection of Queen Marie Antoinette, whose cause he espoused so warmly as to cause him to be banished from Paris. He returned to that city at the beginning of the Consulate, and devoted himself to miniature painting. He died at Obernay in 1836.

GUÉRIN, JEAN BAPTISTE, the second son of Christophe Guérin, was born at Strassburg in 1798. He was a pupil of his father and of Regnault, and practised in his native city, but the year of his death is not recorded.

GUÉRIN, PAULIN JEAN BAPTISTE, a French portrait and historical painter, born at Toulon in 1783, was the son of a blacksmith, which trade he at first followed, but showing a disposition for art he went to Paris, where he entered the studio of Vincent, and supported himself with the greatest difficulty, till he gained a reputation by his picture of 'Cain after the death of Abel.' He died in Paris in 1855. Among his other works are:

The Dead Christ in the Lap of the Virgin. 1817.
Anchises and Venus. 1822.
Adam and Eve driven out of Paradise. 1827.
Christ crucified. 1834.
Ulysses fighting with Neptune. 1824.
Anne of Austria, Regent of France, with her two sons, Louis XIV. and the Duke of Orleans.
Portrait of Louis XVIII., full-length.
Portrait of Charles X., full-length.

His son and pupil, FÉLIX PIERRE ANTOINE GUÉRIN, who was born in Paris in 1825, painted portraits, and died in Paris in 1865.

GUÉRIN, PHILIBERT JEAN PIERRE, a French landscape painter, born at Marseilles in 1805, was a pupil of Paulin Guérin. He exhibited at the Salon from 1824 to 1844, and died in Paris in 1846.

GUÉRIN, PIERRE NARCISSE, Baron, a French historical painter, was born in Paris on the 13th March, 1774. In his early years he showed but little inclination to art, and it was owing to his parents that he entered the studio of Brenet. His progress, however, was small, until he became the pupil of Regnault. With this master he found his vocation, and at the competition of 1797 he obtained one of the three prizes. The disturbed state of Europe did not at once permit of his pursuing his studies at Rome, and while waiting at Paris he produced his ' Return of Marcus Sextus,' which, on being exhibited in 1799, was crowned by his brother artists. On arriving at Rome, his weak health soon compelled him to remove to Naples, where he remained about a year. On his return to Paris, he resumed his studies with such success that in 1803, while still a pupil, he received the cross of the Legion of Honour. He was received into the Institute on the return of the Bourbons in 1815, and in 1816 was appointed director of the French School at Rome, but his health did not allow him to accept the appointment. At the next vacancy he was again offered the post, which he accepted, though the state of his health allowed him only to attend to the duties of his office, and prevented his applying himself to any of his own works during his stay in Rome. On his return to Paris in 1829, he was created a Baron, and he devoted himself for the next two or three years to his own art. Contrary to the advice of his physicians and friends, he accompanied Horace Vernet to Rome, where he died on the 16th July, 1833, and was buried in the church of the Trinità dei Monti. Guérin's art reached its highest point in the 'Marcus Sextus.' In his later works he lost the vigour which characterized his earlier productions, and affected a spurious energy, which has—not without reason—been called theatrical. This may in some degree have arisen from his custom of sketching the actors at the Théâtre Français. The following is a list of Guérin's chief works:

Angers.	Museum.	Death of Priam. (Sketch.)
,,	,,	St. Louis. (Sketch.)
Avignon.	Museum.	Portrait of Charles X.
Bordeaux.	Museum.	Pyrrhus and Andromache. (A small replica of the Louvre picture.)
Compiègne.	Palace.	St. Geneviève.
Hampton Court.	Pal.	Portrait of Louis XVIII.
Paris.	Louvre.	The Return of Marcus Sextus. 1799.
,,	,,	Offering to Æsculapius. 1802.
,,	,,	Hippolytus and Phædra. 1802.
,,	,,	Pyrrhus and Andromache. 1810.
,,	,,	Æneas and Dido. 1813.
,,	,,	Clytemnestra. 1817.
Rennes.	Museum.	Ulysses.
Valenciennes.	Mus.	Death of Marshal Lannes.
Versailles.	Gallery.	The Revolt of Cairo. O.J.D.

GUERINI, GIOVANNI FRANCESCO, (or GUERRIERI,) a native of Fossombrone, in the Roman state, flourished about the year 1650. It is not said under whom he studied, but he painted historical pictures in the style of Caravaggio and Guercino. Lanzi mentions several of his works in very favourable terms, particularly a picture in the Filippini at Fano, of 'St. Charles contemplating the Mysteries of the Passion,' with two laterals, representing subjects from the life of that saint. There are many of his paintings in his native town, and a 'St. Sebastian cured by St. Irene' particularly is attributed to him. He had the peculiar taste to introduce into each of his pictures the portrait of one of his lady-loves.

GUERNIER, DU. See DU GUERNIER.

GUERNIER, RENÉ, was probably a native of France. According to Florent Le Comte he excelled in engraving ornaments and grotesque figures.

GUEROULT, GUILLAUME, is mentioned by Strutt as the engraver of a set of woodcuts for a Bible, published at Paris in 1564, and dedicated to Catharine de' Medici.

GUERRA, CRISTOFORO. See CHRIEGER.

GUERRA, GIOSEFFO, (or QUERRA,) a painter of Venice, was one of the best scholars of Solimena. He painted numerous large historical pictures for churches and monasteries in the kingdom of Naples, but having resorted to the trick of copying paintings disentombed at Herculaneum, and selling them as originals, he was detected and compelled to flee to Rome, where he died in 1761.

GUERRA, GIOVANNI, a painter, engraver, and architect, was born at Modena in 1544, and went in his eighteenth year to Rome, where he painted, in conjunction with Cesare Nebbia, a large part of the pictures commissioned by Pope Sixtus V. He then for some time devoted himself to trade, and when he had thereby lost all his means he returned to art, and brought out a series of forty-eight plates entitled 'Varie Acconciature di Teste usate da nobilissime Dame in diverse Città di Italia.' He also prepared the model for the Scala Santa in Rome, and the designs for several churches in Modena, as well as a great number of drawings from subjects in the Old and New Testaments, and from Greek and Roman history, in readiness for engraving. He died at Rome in 1618.

GUERRIERI, GIOVANNI FRANCESCO. See GUERINI.

GUERRINI, GIACOMO, was born at Cremona in 1718, and while quite young painted 'The Beheading of St. John the Baptist' for the Oratory of St. Jerome in his native city. He afterwards executed for the church of Sant' Agostino, 'The Meeting of St. Joachim and St. Anna' and 'The Presentation in the Temple.' Some of the churches in Milan also possess paintings by him. He died in 1793.

GUERTIÈRE, FRANÇOIS DE LA. See DE LA GUERTIÈRE.

GUEST, DOUGLAS, an English historical and portrait painter, practised in the early part of the 19th century. He studied in the schools of the Royal Academy, and in 1805 gained the gold medal for his ' Bearing the dead body of Patroclus to the Camp, Achilles's Grief.' He occasionally exhibited at the Academy from 1803 to 1817, and again in 1834 and 1838. He painted the 'Transfiguration,' an altar-piece for the church of St. Thomas, Salisbury, and in 1829 published a work on the decline of historical painting.

GUEVARA, FELIPE DE, was an amateur painter, who acquired the friendship of Titian when he accompanied the Emperor Charles V. to Bologna to receive the imperial crown from Clement VII. He distinguished himself as a cavalry officer in the expedition to Tunis in 1535, and was the author of 'Commentaries on Painting,' published in 1788. He died at Madrid in 1563.

GUEVARA, JUAN NIÑO DE, born at Madrid in 1632, was the son of a captain of the guards of the Viceroy of Aragon, under whose patronage he was placed as a disciple of Miguel Manrique, a Fleming, who had been educated in the school of Rubens. He afterwards studied at Madrid, under Alonso Cano, and became a very reputable artist, adopting a style that partook of the character of both his masters, uniting with the grandeur and correctness of Alonso Cano the splendid and brilliant colouring of the head of the Flemish School. His principal works are at Malaga, Granada, and Cordova. In the church of La Caridad at Malaga, is a fine picture of 'The Triumph of the Cross'; and in the cathedral, 'The Ascension of Christ,' and 'The Assumption of the Virgin.' At Cordova, in the cloister of the Augustines, there are some pictures of the life of the founder of the order, and several portraits, which are compared by Palomino to those of Van Dyck. He died at Malaga in 1698.

GUGLIELMI, GREGORIO, a painter born at Rome in 1714, was a pupil of Conca; but he was little known in his native city on account of his having gone when young to Vienna, Dresden, and St. Petersburg. He executed a few frescoes in the hospital of Santo Spirito at Rome, but others that gained more attention in the cities named above, as well as at Augsburg and in the castle of Schönbrunn. His works in oil were feebler. He died at St. Petersburg in 1773.

GUIBAL, NICOLAS, a painter and architect, born at Lunéville in 1725, was the son of Barthélemy Guibal, a sculptor. He worked at first at sculpture under his father, but afterwards abandoned it for painting, and studied under Claude Charles at Nancy, but came in 1741 to Paris, and then studied under Natoire. In 1745 he was made a pensioner of the Academy, and won the second prize. In 1749 he proceeded to Stuttgart, and in 1752 Duke Charles Eugene sent him to Rome with a commission to execute for him four paintings. He there improved himself under Rafael Mengs, so that on his return in 1755 he was appointed by the duke first court painter and architect, professor of painting, and director of the picture gallery. He was made an Academician in 1784, on the completion of his 'Aurora' on the ceiling of the gallery of Apollo in the Louvre, and died at Stuttgart in the same year. His best work is the ceiling above the marble staircase in the Palace at Stuttgart. Other paintings by him are in the bathhouse at Schwetzingen, in the former dining-hall of the Academy (now the king's private library), in the halls at Hohenheim and Monrepos, in the Ordenskapelle of Ludwigsburg Castle, and in the churches of Gmund, Zwiefalten, and Solothurn. Guibal wrote the 'Éloge de Mengs' (1780), and 'Éloge de Nicolas Poussin' (1783).

GUICHARD, JOSEPH ALEXANDRE, a French marine painter, born at Marseilles about 1830, was a pupil of Isabey and Durand-Brager. He died

in his native city in 1877. Amongst his works are:

Souvenir of Villafranca. 1866.
The Fisherman's Return. 1869.
Sunrise at the Martigues. 1870.
The Marriage of Camacho.

GUIDI, RAFFAELLO, an Italian engraver, was born at Florence in 1540, and died probably about 1613. His plates are executed entirely with the graver, which he handled in a masterly manner, and from his style it would appear that he was instructed by Cornelis Cort or Agostino Carracci. The following are his principal prints:

David playing on the Harp; after Giuseppe Cesari.
Dædalus and Icarus; after the same.
The Crucifixion; after Christoph Schwartz.
The Entombment of Christ; after F. Barocci.
Æneas carrying his father Anchises; after the same.
Jupiter; after Polidoro da Caravaggio.
Vulcan; after the same.
The Madonna seated, distributing Rose Garlands to various Ecclesiastical Orders.

GUIDI, TOMMASO, commonly called MASACCIO, the son of the notary Ser Giovanni di Simone Guidi, was born at Castel San Giovanni di Valdarno, in 1401, and is thought by some to have studied under Masolino. That he was precocious in the display of his talent, is shown by the fact that about 1417 he went to Rome, where he received a commission from Cardinal San Clemente to decorate a chapel that still bears his name. Masaccio painted there a 'Crucifixion,' and different scenes drawn from the lives of St. Catharine and St. Clement. When at Rome he painted several pictures, amongst others one which represented 'Pope Martin V. with the Emperor Sigismund and the Virgin, between four Saints,' which was, in after years, much admired by Michelangelo. In 1421 he was received into the Guild of the Speziali at Florence, and twice painted the portrait of Giovanni di Bicci de' Medici, who returned to power in Florence in 1420. In the interval extending from 1423 to 1428, he adorned the Brancacci Chapel in the Carmine with frescoes, twelve in number, which represent scenes drawn from the Bible, and from the life of St. Peter; these prove his great skill as an artist, and also that he had really studied the sister arts of architecture and sculpture. He died at Rome about 1428, at the early age of twenty-six. Masaccio's paintings are all far in advance of his time, and foreshadow the rules which afterwards guided art in the 16th century. Of his other paintings and frescoes, not previously mentioned, there remain at the Carmine a portion of a design in the cloisters, representing part of a procession, that has recently been recovered from beneath the whitewash. The galleries of Berlin, Munich, and Modena possess paintings attributed to him, and the National Gallery has a portrait considered to be that of Masaccio himself.

GUIDO, ASCANIO, an Italian engraver, flourished about the year 1567. There is a print by him of the 'Last Judgment,' after Michelangelo, rather smaller than the plate engraved by Martino Rota, and not much inferior to it in merit. It is dated 1567, two years previous to that by Rota.

GUIDO, PIETRO DEL SIGNOR. See GALLINARI.
GUIDO DA SIENA. See SIENA.
GUIDO RENI. See RENI.
GUIDO RENI, ERCOOLIN DI. See SAN GIOVANNI.
GUIDOBONO, BARTOLOMMEO, called 'Il Prete di Savona,' was born at Savona in 1654. His

TOMMASO GUIDI

CALLED

MASACCIO

ADAM AND EVE DRIVEN FROM PARADISE

TOMMASO GUIDI

CALLED

MASACCIO

AN OLD MAN

father, Giovanni Antonio Guidobono, who was majolica painter to the court of Savoy, taught him his own art. He then became a priest, (whence his sobriquet,) but his love of art caused him to relinquish that office. Having seen some pictures by Benedetto Castiglione, he copied them with so much exactness, that it was difficult to distinguish the reproductions from the originals. He afterwards visited Parma and Venice, studying the works of the best masters, and on settling at Genoa, he was much employed in that city. He particularly excelled in painting animals, flowers, and fruit; and he was no despicable designer of the figure, as he has shown in some fabulous subjects in the Palazzo Centurioni. Some of his best pictures are in the Palazzo Brignole Sale; among them that of 'Lot and his Daughters.' He died at Turin in 1709.

GUIDOLINO. See FIESOLE, GIOVANNI DA.

GUIDONE DA GHEZZO. See SIENA, GUIDO DA.

GUIDOTTI, PAOLO, called 'IL CAVALIERE BORGHESE,' was born at Lucca in 1569, and went when young, in the pontificate of Gregory XIII., to Rome, where he improved the instruction already received by studying the great works of art in that city. He was employed by Sixtus V. in several fresco works in the library of the Vatican, in the Scala Santa, and in the Palace of San Giovanni in Laterano. He distinguished himself as a sculptor as well as a painter; and for some productions in that art was honoured by Paul V. with the permission to take the name of 'Borghese,' and was made a knight of the order of Christ. He was also an architect, and in fact he boasted of the knowledge of fourteen arts; but in spite of all these he was reduced to great misery, and died in 1629 from a fall while attempting the additional art of flying. There are several of his works in the public edifices at Rome. In San Girolamo degli Schiavoni, is a picture of 'St. Matthew'; and in the cupola of Santa Maria de' Monti, the 'Assumption of the Virgin.'

GUIDUCCI, ANGELO, a landscape painter and etcher, lived at Rome about 1750. He engraved two portraits of Joseph II. of Austria, and others after Van Dyck, as well as two plates representing peasants.

GUIGNET, JEAN ADRIEN, a French historical and landscape painter, was born of French parentage, at Annecy in Savoy in 1816. Against his father's wishes he went to Paris, and studied under his brother, Jean Baptiste Guignet, and under Blondel; but it was not until after some years of uphill work that he succeeded in achieving a position. In style he inclined considerably to that of Decamps. He died in Paris in 1854. Amongst his works are:

Moses exposed on the Nile. 1840.
St. John the Baptist preaching. 1842.
Salvator Rosa amongst the Brigands. 1844.
Joseph explaining Pharaoh's Dream. 1845. (*Rouen Museum.*)
Xerxes bewailing his Army. 1846.
Don Quixote playing the Fool. 1848.
Travellers surprised by a Bear.
Hagar in the Desert.
Episode in the Retreat of the Ten Thousand.
The Defeat of Attila by Aetius.
Belshazzar's Feast.

GUIGNET, JEAN BAPTISTE, a French historical and portrait painter, born at Autun in 1810, was the brother of Jean Adrien Guignet, and studied under Regnault. He died at Viriville in 1857. Amongst his portraits are.

General Pajol.
Gilbert Louis Duprez, the tenor.
James Pradier, the sculptor.

GUIGOU, V., a French engraver, flourished about the year 1676. He engraved some bird's-eye views of châteaux and other buildings in France, which are executed in a neat but stiff style. He also engraved several portraits for books.

GUILLAIN, SIMON, a French sculptor, who for amusement practised etching, was born in Paris in 1581, and died in the same city in 1658. There are the following prints by him:

A set of twenty plates of the Life of St. James; *after Annibale Carracci.*
Eighty plates of the Cries of Bologna; *after Annibale Carracci*, engraved in conjunction with *Alessandro Algardi.*

GUILLAUME, Le Frère, known as 'Le Prieur,' and 'Il Prete Gallo,' was a French painter, who was born at Marseilles in 1475, and died at Arezzo in 1537. Being implicated in some criminal affair, he entered holy orders, and accompanied Frère Claude to Rome, and there assisted him in his works for Pope Julius II. He was afterwards employed and protected by Cardinal Silvio Passerini at Cortona, and he visited Florence, Castiglione, Perugia, and Arezzo, establishing himself in the last-mentioned town. He was one of the best glass painters in his time, and worked equally well in oil and fresco. Vasari was his pupil.

GUILLEBAULT, SIMON, a French historical painter, was born at Le Mans in 1636. He chiefly executed Scriptural subjects, among which was 'The Triumph of the Church,' painted for his reception at the Academy in 1687. He died at Le Mans in 1708.

GUILLEMARD, SOPHIE, a pupil of Regnault, was born in Paris in 1780, and from 1801 to 1819 exhibited at the Salon historical pictures, as well as some portraits and genre subjects; amongst them were 'Alcibiades and Glycerion,' and 'Joseph and Potiphar's Wife.' The date of her death is not recorded.

GUILLEMART, —, was an obscure French engraver, who was chiefly employed in engraving portraits for the booksellers. Among others is that of Setani, Abbé of St. Geneviève.

GUILLEMIN, ALEXANDRE MARIE, who was born in Paris in 1815, studied under Gros, and became a painter of genre subjects. He died at Bois-le-Roi, near Fontainebleau, in 1880. The following are a few of his works:

Huntsman and Milk-woman. 1844.
The old Sailor. 1845.
Sunday Morning. 1864.
La Trilla; souvenir of Upper Aragon. 1869.
Los Pordioseros; souvenir of Upper Navarre. 1877.
Sunday Morning in Brittany.
Women of the Pyrenees.

GUILLEMOT, ALEXANDRE CHARLES, a French historical painter, was born in Paris in 1786. He was a pupil of Allais and of David, and in 1808 obtained the 'prix de Rome' for his picture of 'Philip, the physician, discovering the cause of Antiochus's illness in his love for Stratonice.' In 1819, after his return from Rome, a first-class medal was awarded to Guillemot for his picture of 'Christ raising the Widow's Son at Nain.' His last important work was the 'Stoning of St. Stephen.' In the Palace at Compiègne is a picture of 'Mars surprising Rhea Sylvia.' He died in Paris in 1831.

GUILLEROT —, a French landscape painter,

who flourished in the 17th century, was a pupil of Fouquières, and worked with considerable success under Sébastien Bourdon at the Tuileries.

GUILLO, VICENTE, a painter of the Valencian school, was born at Alcalá de Gilbert, about 1660, and at one time lived at Barcelona. The hospital of Santa Tecla at Tarragona possessed a good 'Adoration of the Kings,' dated 1690. He executed some frescoes in the Sagrario of his native town, in the hermitage of San Pablo at Albocacer, and in the church of San Juan del Mercado at Valencia, where he is said to have died in 1701 of disappointment at having been superseded by Palomino. AGUSTIN GUILLO, who does not appear to have been related to Vicente, contributed about the same time some indifferent frescoes to the same church, and to the Dominican convent at Valencia. The latter left a son, FLORENCIO GUILLO, a painter even feebler than himself.

GUINACCIA, DEODATO, born at Messina about the year 1510, became the best and most renowned pupil of Polidoro da Caravaggio, when he visited that city, after the sacking of Rome. After the death of Polidoro he was engaged to complete the fine picture of the 'Nativity,' in the church of Alto Basso, which was left unfinished by that master. In the church of the Pellegrini is a picture of Guinaccia's own composition, representing the 'Trinity,' and another of the 'Transfiguration' is in San Salvatore de' Greci. He founded a school which flourished for a long time in Messina, and many of its scholars attained celebrity.

GUIRRI, VICENTE, a native of Valencia, became a friar in the Augustine convent of that city in 1608, and devoted his time to prayer and penitence, and to the execution of devotional pictures within its walls, till 1640, when he died.

GUIRRO, FRANCISCO, a Spanish historical painter, was born at Barcelona in 1630, and died there in 1700. His principal work was a 'St. Monica,' in the convent of the Recollets, which places him in the first rank of the better Spanish artists.

GUISONI, FERMO, a native of Mantua, who worked between the years 1540 and 1568, was educated in the school of Giulio Romano. He became one of the favourite disciples of that great master, from whose cartoons he painted in the dome of the cathedral the 'Calling of St. Peter and St. Andrew to the Apostleship,' esteemed one of the finest compositions of Giulio. In the church of Sant' Andrea, there is a fine picture of his own composition, representing the 'Crucifixion.'

GUISONI, RINALDO, who was possibly a brother of Fermo Guisoni, and was a pupil of Giulio Romano, flourished at Mantua in the 16th century.

GUITARD, PEDRO, a Spanish painter, was born in Catalonia about 1540. In 1576—79, he executed six pictures in oil from the life of St. Peter, for the high altar of the church of San Pedro, at Reus.

GUIZZARDI, GIUSEPPE, an Italian painter, born at Bologna in 1779, made himself famous by a picture of 'Æsculapius,' which is now in the Museum of that city. He died at Bologna in 1867.

GULDENMUND, HANS, an old German engraver on wood, flourished at Nuremberg from about 1520 to 1540. His works are extremely numerous, more than 200 being known, of which the best are, 'The Triumphal Procession of Charles V. in 1537,' and a bust portrait of Hans Sachs. The first work which brought him into notice, and which appeared in 1526, was an emblematical print

290

of 'The Course of the World,' in which Greed, as the companion of Tyranny, is flaying an Ass, which throws out its legs, and brings Dissimulation to the ground.

GÜLICH, JOHN PERCIVAL, a well-known black-and-white artist. Born at Wimbledon in 1865, he was educated at the Charterhouse and then entered his father's office in Mincing Lane, where he spent most of his time drawing caricatures on his blotting-paper, and eventually had one of his sketches accepted by a comic journal. After four years he gave up his office stool and came rapidly to the front as an illustrator, though he had but a slight training at the evening classes at Heatherley's. He worked for the 'Graphic' and 'Harper's Magazine,' whilst his charming drawing of 'A Violin Obbligato,' exhibited at the Royal Institute, brought about his election to membership of that Society. He was also a gifted musician, and his untimely death from typhoid fever, contracted whilst on a holiday tour in 1899, was much deplored.   P. P.

GULIELMUS, a painter, who flourished about 1138, worked in the cathedral of Sarzana, and also, it is believed, executed the figures upon the façade of that at Modena.

GULSTON, ELIZABETH, was an English amateur etcher in the beginning of the 19th century, who copied several of her father's collection of portraits at Ealing Grove, and exhibited at the Royal Academy from 1795 to 1801. She died before 1840.

GÜLTLINGER, JOHANNES GUMPOLT, (GÜT-LINGER, or GILTLINGER,) a painter of the 15th century, was probably born at Augsburg. Several altar-pieces by him are still in St. Ulrich's Church in that city. He was paid 400 florins for his work upon St. Michael's altar, which is a sufficient evidence of the value set upon his productions.

GUNDELACH, MATTHÄUS. See GONDOLACH.

GUNKEL, FRIEDRICH, a native of Cassel, painted historical subjects in the style of Cornelius, among which may be named the 'Battle of the Granicus.' He died by suicide at Rome in 1876.

GUNST, PIETER VAN, a Dutch line-engraver, was born at Amsterdam about the year 1667, and died in 1724. He worked entirely with the graver, and from the style of his prints, it is probable that he formed it upon that of the Drevets. His best plates are his portraits, and they form the larger part of his productions. His greatest work was a set of ten full-length portraits, after Van Dyck, of Charles I., his Queen, and some of the English nobility. Arnold Houbraken, the father of the celebrated engraver of that name, came to England to make the drawings from the pictures. Van Gunst also engraved a set of portraits for Larrey's 'History of England.' The following are his principal plates:

PORTRAITS AFTER VAN DYCK.

Charles I.
Queen Henrietta Maria.
William Villiers, Viscount Grandison.
Lucy Percy, Countess of Carlisle.
Viscount Chaworth.
Margaret Smith, Lady Herbert.
Ann, Countess of Chesterfield.
Lady Wharton.
Elizabeth, Countess of Lindsey.
Arthur Goodwin, of Winchendon, Bucks.

VARIOUS PORTRAITS.

King William III.; *after Brandon.*
Queen Mary II.; *after the same.*

Queen Anne; *after Kneller.*
George, Prince of Denmark; *after Wissing.*
John Churchill, Duke of Marlborough; *after A. van der Werff.*
George I.; *after Kneller.*
Earl of Peterborough; *after the same.*
John Locke; *after Greenhill.*
John Dryden; *after Riley.*

He also engraved nine plates of the 'Loves of the Gods,' after Titian, the same subjects that Smith has scraped in mezzotint.

GÜNTHER, CHRISTIAN AUGUST, a designer and etcher on copper, was born at Pirna in 1760, and died at Dresden in 1824. He first drew from nature, but Professor Zingg observed his talent and took him into his school. His coloured drawings won much admiration at the Dresden Academical exhibitions. He also painted portraits in pastel. His etchings were mostly landscapes—among them are 'The Baggage Waggon,' after Zingg, and two after Wouwerman and Dietrich for the third volume of the Dresden Gallery.

GÜNTHER, MATTHÄUS, (or MATHÄ GINDTER,) was born at Bisenberg in Bavaria in 1705, and after studying under Cosmas Damian Asam in Munich, took to imitating the style of Johann Holzer, with whom also he passed some time. He was director of the old Academy at Augsburg, where he died in 1791. His best known productions were ceiling pictures in churches and halls.

GUNTHER, OTTO EDMUND, a German decorative painter, born at Halle in 1838, and a pupil of Preller and Von Ramberg. He was educated at the Düsseldorf Academy, and at the Art School of Weimar, gained a gold medal at Berlin, and eventually became a Professor at Königsberg. The Franco-German war gave him many opportunities for indulging his passion for painting war and military scenes, and he went with the troops to Versailles, where he was constantly at work painting the events of the campaign. On his return to Berlin he devoted himself more to genre paintings, and exhibited 'A Thuringian Family Scene,' 'A Wedding Procession in Thuringia,' 'Grandpapa, a Kiss,' and 'Disputing Theologians.' He executed some fine decorative work in Cologne and Leipsic, and died in 1884.

GURK, EDUARD, an Austrian painter, born at Vienna in 1802, accompanied the Archduke Friedrich on the expedition to Syria, and on remaining there for the sketching of memorable spots, he died of the plague in 1841. His chief works are architectural views in water-colours, which are in the possession of the Emperor of Austria.

GURLITT, LUDWIG, Danish landscape painter, born at Altona, March 8, 1812, had for masters his father, then Gensler of Hamburg, and Bendixen. He visited Denmark, Sweden and Norway, but in 1837 went to Munich and then into Italy. On his return to Copenhagen he was elected member of the Danish Academy. After fresh travels through Mid-Europe, he settled in Vienna, where the sister of the novelist, Fanny Lewald, became his third wife in 1847. He again visited Italy in 1855, Greece in 1858, and then settled near Gotha, making sketching tours to Holstein, Portugal and Spain. In 1873 he passed to Dresden, and resided near that town. The best of his landscapes, which mostly have Italian scenery for their subjects, belonged to King Christian VIII., or to the Museum of Copenhagen, and others were owned by the King of Hanover and Empress

Dowager of Russia. He died in 1898, in the eighty-fifth year of his age.

GUTEKUNST, JOHANN GOTTLOB, a painter and photographer, was born at Tübingen in 1801. He manifested an early taste for art, and received assistance from King William of Würtemberg, which enabled him to study for three years in Italy, and at the end of that term he adorned his patron's pleasure-palace at Rosenstein with frescoes representing the story of 'Cupid and Psyche.' After 1849 he associated photography with water-colour painting. He died at Stuttgart in 1858.

GÜTERBOCK, LEOPOLD, was a German genre painter, who died at Berlin in 1881. His mediæval subjects are often very humorous.

GUTIERREZ, ESTACIO, was a native of Valladolid, who was appointed painter to Philip III. in 1605. He died at Madrid in 1609.

GUTIERREZ, GENNARO, engraved some plates for the 'Museo Fiorentino,' and a large upright plate of the 'Virgin and Infant in the Clouds,' after Carlo Maratti, executed in a neat style, in the manner of Johann Jakob Frey, though inferior. He flourished about the year 1760.

GUTIERREZ, JUAN SIMON, was born in Seville about 1644, and succeeded in copying Murillo's style of colouring so exactly that it is sometimes difficult to distinguish their productions. The drawing of his pictures, however, is very inferior. In the Liverpool Institution is a picture of 'St. Francis in ecstacy,' and in the Seville Gallery one of 'Christ surrounded by the Virgin and Angels.'

GUTIERREZ, El Licenciado PEDRO, was a Spanish engraver who lived at Granada about the middle of the 17th century. Engravings by him are contained in the 'Life of St. Eufrasio,' by Antonio Torrones de Robres, published in 1657.

GÜTLINGER, JOHANNES GUMPOLT. See GÜLTLINGER.

GUTTENBERG, HEINRICH, a German engraver, the brother and pupil of Karl Gottlieb Guttenberg, was born at Wöhrd, near Nuremberg, in 1749. Through his pupils Geissler and Reindel he founded a new school of engraving at Nuremberg. He lived many years in Paris, returning home, however, on the outbreak of the Revolution, but again repairing to the French capital after order was restored. He died at Nuremberg in 1818. He engraved several plates in the style of his brother; among them are the following:

St. Francis; *after Rembrandt.*
The Burgomaster; *after the same.*
Charles V.; *after Van Dyck.*
The Deposition from the Cross; *after Rubens.*
The Women below the Gateway; *after Bega.*
A Dutch Family; *after the same.*
A Repose in Egypt; *after Barocci.*
A Mountainous Landscape; *after Dietrich.*

GUTTENBERG, KARL GOTTLIEB, a German engraver, was born at Wöhrd, near Nuremberg, in 1743. He was the elder brother of Heinrich Guttenberg, and a pupil of J. G. Wille, at Paris, and has engraved several plates, in the neat style of that artist. From 1780 till the Revolution he lived in Paris, but afterwards returned to Nuremberg, where he died in 1790. His principal works were the plates he executed for the 'Voyage pittoresque du Royaume de Naples,' by the Abbé de St. Non. There are also by him:

Portrait of Catharine II., Empress of Russia; *after Rotari.*
Wilhelm Tell; *after Füssli.*

Le petit Boudeur; *after Greuze.*
L'Invocation à l'Amour; *after Théolon.*
The Chemist; *after Mieris.*
The Dance; *after P. Bol.*
The Evening Party; *after Rembrandt.*
The Death of General Wolfe; neatly copied from the
print by *Woollett.*
Two Views in Switzerland; *after Schutz.*
The Eruption of Monte Novo; *after Fragonard.*
The Harbour of Ostend.

GUTTENBRUNN, L., was a native of Dresden, who came to England about the year 1789. He painted portraits and small historical subjects, and exhibited at the Royal Academy from 1790 to 1795, when he went to St. Petersburg, by the recommendation of the Russian Ambassador. He was a member of the Academy of Florence, whence it may be presumed that he had studied in Italy.

GUYARD, ADÉLAIDE. See VINCENT.

GUYOT, LAURENT, a French engraver, born in Paris in 1756, was a pupil of Le Grand and Tillard. He died in 1806.

GUZMAN, JOSEF COBO Y. See COBO.

GUZMAN, JUAN DE, known as FRAY JUAN DEL SANTISIMO SACRAMENTO, was born at La Puente de Don Gonzalo, near Cordova, in 1611. After studying some time at Cordova he went to Rome, but did not devote much attention to the antique, or the works of Raphael; colouring, and mathematics as applicable to architecture and perspective, being his chief objects. He returned to Spain in 1634, and went to reside in Seville; where he signalized himself more by turbulence, and dexterity in the management of arms, than in the skilful use of the pencil. The consequence was, that having taken part in a revolt, and having been unsuccessful, he was obliged to seek refuge in the convent of the Carmelitas Calzados, or Shod Carmelites, and assume the habit as a lay brother. His restless character caused him soon to be sent from that establishment to the Carmelitas Descalzos, or Barefooted Carmelites, and he received orders to reside in the convent of Aguilar, where a severer discipline effected a change in his behaviour, and he now appeared in the character of a humble and pious monk. He took the name of Fray Juan del Santisimo Sacramento, and had permission to exercise his talent as a painter in decorating the walls of the convent, and other establishments appertaining to the order. At intervals he employed himself in translating Pietro Accolti's 'Practical Perspective' from Italian into Spanish, to which he added notes correcting the errors of the author; and it is said that he even engraved plates illustrative of the work, which, however, was never published. In 1666 he went to Cordova to paint pictures for the monastery of his order in that city, which he accomplished so much to the satisfaction of the bishop, that he retained him to decorate his episcopal palace, and other places in his diocese. He remained at Cordova till 1676, when he returned to his convent at Aguilar, where he died in 1680. His merit as a painter is but small.

GUZMAN, PEDRO DE, called GUZMAN EL COXO ('the lame'), was a Spanish painter of the beginning of the 17th century, a pupil of Patricio Caxes, who was also court-painter to Philip III., and helped to decorate for him the Palace of El Pardo.

GWINN, JAMES, born in the county of Kildare, was originally a coach painter. He came to London in 1755, and gained his livelihood by decorating the lids of snuff-boxes in enamel. He fell into great want, and was found dead in his room in 1769.

GYLES, HENRY, a glass painter, who also painted historical subjects and landscapes, worked chiefly at York, where he resided from 1640 to 1700, and established a school of glass painting. His own portrait in crayons, by himself, is in the British Museum.

GYSBRECHTS, CORNELIUS N., was a painter of Hamburg at the beginning of the 17th century. In Schleissheim Palace is a painting by him of 'Transiency, with her Attributes,' by the side of his own portrait; whilst in Augsburg there is a 'Vanitas' by him. He succeeded well with subjects of still-life, of which specimens are to be seen in the Cassel Gallery.

GYSELS, PEETER, (GYSENS, GYZELS, or GYZENS,) a Flemish painter, born at Antwerp in 1621, was a pupil of J. Boots. He entered the Guild of St. Luke in 1642, becoming a master therein in 1649, and was most successful in painting flowers, fruit, still-life, and small landscapes. He died at Antwerp in 1690 or 1691. Among his best works are:

Amsterdam.	*Museum.*	A Town.
Antwerp.	*Gallery.*	Still Life (known as 'Le Cercueil de Pierre Gysels').
Berlin.	*Gallery.*	View of a Village Street.
Brussels.	*Gallery.*	Dead Game in a Landscape.
Dresden.	*Gallery.*	Five Rustic Scenes, two Landscapes, and one still-life piece.
Hague.	*Museum.*	Game, with Hunting Implements.
London.	*Bute Coll.*	Dead Game.
Petersburg.	*Hermitage.*	A Garden.

END OF VOL. II.